Readings on
Social Movements

Readings on Social Movements

Origins, Dynamics and Outcomes

SECOND EDITION

Doug McAdam
Stanford University

David A. Snow
University of California – Irvine

New York   Oxford
OXFORD UNIVERSITY PRESS
2010

Oxford University Press, Inc., publishes works that further Oxford University's
objective of excellence in research, scholarship, and education.

Oxford   New York
Auckland   Cape Town   Dar es Salaam   Hong Kong   Karachi
Kuala Lumpur   Madrid   Melbourne   Mexico City   Nairobi
New Delhi   Shanghai   Taipei   Toronto

With offices in
Argentina   Austria   Brazil   Chile   Czech Republic   France   Greece
Guatemala   Hungary   Italy   Japan   Poland   Portugal   Singapore
South Korea   Switzerland   Thailand   Turkey   Ukraine   Vietnam

Published by Oxford University Press, Inc.
198 Madison Avenue, New York, New York 10016
http://www.oup.com

Oxford is a registered trademark of Oxford University Press

Library of Congress Cataloging-in-Publication Data

Readings on social movements : origins, dynamics and outcomes / [edited
by] Doug McAdam, David A. Snow.—2nd ed.
    p. cm.
Rev. ed. of: Social movement. c1997.
Includes bibliographical references.
ISBN 978-0-19-538455-0 (alk. paper)
1. Social movements. 2. Social movements—United States. I. McAdam,
Doug. II. Snow, David A. III. McAdam, Doug. Social movement.
HN28.M33 2010
303.48'4—dc22   2009019329

Printed in the United States of America
on acid-free paper

Contents

Between 1980 and 1995 the study of social movements emerged as one of the largest, most intellectually vibrant subfields in American sociology. Having taught courses in the area for years, we recognized the need for a reader that would pull together a good many of the articles that had helped to shape this emerging area of study. With that in mind, we compiled and edited the 37 articles that made up the original edition of the reader, first published by Roxbury Press in 1997.

The volume sold consistently well over its 12-year life span, but the rate of publication of high-quality work in the field has only increased since 1997, motivating us to bring out this second edition of the reader substantially oriented to the most recent, cutting-edge work in the field. The number of original versus wholly new selections underscores our commitment to make this a very different volume from the first edition. Of the 39 selections in the new edition, only nine are holdovers from the 1997 volume. And of the 30 new selections, 24 have been published since 2000.

Besides the heavy reliance on new selections, the new edition highlights some of the most exciting new lines of work in the study of social movements. These include the role of emotions in social movements, work at the intersection of the sociology of law and social movements, transnational social movements, the policing of social movements, and the role of narrative and "identity work" in social movements.

Finally, besides the incorporation of these specific new lines of inquiry, the volume also reflects the more general geographic expansion of the field that has occurred in recent years. So while the field was largely born out of a careful empirical study of recent reform movements (U.S. civil rights, women's, environmental) in the Democratic West, more and more work is now being devoted to contention in other times and places. A comparison of the selections in the first and second editions underscores this welcome shift. The 1997 edition included only 11 selections on movements or contention outside the U.S. The new volume features 17.

But while highlighting new directions and more recent work in the field, we have elected to preserve the conceptual organization of the first edition. That organization is intended to mirror the temporal unfolding of social movements from initial "facilitating conditions" (Unit One), through "processes of micromobilization" (Unit Two) and "movement dynamics" (Unit Three) to a consideration of movement outcomes (Unit Four). We adopted this structure originally because it dovetailed with the organization of our own courses on social movements. But since it first came out, this conceptual structure has been the feature of the book most often praised by others using it in their courses. For this reason, we agreed to preserve the structure in the new edition. But for those who organize their courses differently, we encourage you to look at the grid provided on page xi–xii, which groups the selections according to alternative topics or conceptual themes. However you choose to use the book, we hope you will find the selections a useful supplement to your course design.

We close, as last time, by acknowledging and thanking a number of people who assisted in the preparation of the volume. The "first among equals" in this regard is our editor at Oxford, Sherith Pankratz, who not only catalyzed the project by urging us to consider developing a second edition of the reader, but provided timely assistance throughout preparation of the reader. We also owe special thanks to Laurie Andress for helping assemble clean copies of the selections; to Kendra Bischoff for her assistance in compiling the biographies of the contributors; and finally to Dana L. Cloud (University of Texas), Colleen Eren (Queens College), Agnieszka Paczynska (George Mason University), and a host of anonymous reviewers for their helpful suggestions on the structure and content of the new volume. We close with the most important thanks of all: to all those instructors who have used the reader in the past and helped us improve it by passing along their praise and criticism of the first edition.

Doug McAdam
David A. Snow

Alternative Uses Course Grid

	Culture	Gender & Sexualities	Identity	Inequality/Poverty	Law & Policy	Non-U.S. or U.S. Comparison	Organization	Politics	Race/Ethnicity	Right-Wing	Religion	Social Psychology	Social/Demo. Change	Transnational
Part 1														
1 Snow et al.	X			X								X	X	
2 Goldstone						X							X	
3 Van Dyke/Soule										X			X	
Part 2														
4 Jenkins et al.								X	X				X	
5 Kriesi et al.						X		X						
6 Kay					X	X		X					X	X
7 Almeida						X	X	X					X	
Part 3														
8 Cress/Snow					X			X	X					
9 Armstrong		X						X					X	
10 Smith								X						X
Part 4														
11 Zhao						X	X	X						
12 Morris								X	X					
13 Futrell/Simi			X					X		X		X		
Part 5														
14 Dixon/Roscigno				X				X				X		
15 McAdam/Paulsen	X			X				X	X			X		
16 Smilde	X			X			X				X	X		
Part 6														
17 Snow/Byrd	X						X	X				X	X	X
18 Diani	X						X	X						
19 Ferree	X	X					X	X						
20 Pedriana	X	X			X								X	
Part 7														
21 Klandermans et al.					X		X					X	X	
22 Polletta	X							X				X		
23 Einwohner			X				X		X			X		
24 Nepstad			X								X	X		

Jon Agnone is a Ph.D. candidate in the department of Sociology at the University of Washington. His publications in the *American Journal of sociology*, *Social Forces*, *Social Problems*, and *Politics & Society* have focused on how collective action on the part of social movements can affect individual and group outcomes. His dissertation research extends his interest in the effects of social movements and related institutions to how involvement in U.S. labor unions affect racial and ethnic differences in individually held wealth.

Paul D. Almeida's research centers on collective mobilization in response to political and economic transitions in the developing world. Almeida's articles have appeared in the *American Journal of Sociology*, *Mobilization, Research in Political Sociology, Revista Centroamericana de Ciencias Sociales, Social Problems*, and other scholarly outlets. He is author of *Waves of Protest: Popular Struggle in El Salvador, 1925–2005* (University of Minnesota Press, 2008) and co-editor with Hank Johnston of *Latin American Social Movements: Globalization, Democratization and Transnational Networks* (Rowman & Littlefield, 2006). He is currently engaged in field work under the sponsorship of a Fulbright Faculty Fellowship entitled "Globalization, Democratization, and Civil Society in Central America."

Edwin Amenta is Professor of Sociology and History at the University of California, Irvine. He is the author, most recently, of *When Movements Matter: The Townsend Plan and the Rise of Social Security* (Princeton, 2006) and *Professor Baseball: Searching for Redemption on the Softball Diamonds of Central Park* (Chicago, 2007).

Joel Andreas, Assistant Professor of Sociology at Johns Hopkins University, studies political contention and social change in contemporary China. A forthcoming book, *Rise of the Red Engineers: The Cultural Revolution and the Origins of China's New Class* (Stanford University Press, 2009), analyzes the contentious process through which old and new elites coalesced during the decades following the 1949 Communist Revolution. He is currently investigating changing relations between managers and workers in Chinese factories between 1949 and the present.

Kenneth (Andy) T. Andrews is Associate Professor of Sociology at the University of North Carolina at Chapel Hill. His research focuses on social movements, political institutions, and social change. His book, *Freedom Is a Constant Struggle* (2004), examined the influence of the civil rights movement on electoral politics, school desegregation, and social policies. He is completing projects on leadership, strategy, and organization in the North Carolina environmental sector and in a study of local Sierra Club organizations. Currently, Andrews is investigating the dynamics and impact of local desegregation campaigns from the 1960 sit-ins to the 1964 Civil Rights Act.

Elizabeth A. Armstrong is Associate Professor of Sociology at Indiana University. Her research interests include sexuality, gender, social movements, sociology of culture, and higher education. She is the author of *Forging Gay Identities: Organizing Sexuality in San Francisco, 1950–1994* (Chicago, 2002). With Suzanna Crage, she investigated how the Stonewall riots came to be viewed as the starting point of the contemporary gay movement. This paper, "Meaning and Memory: The Making of the Stonewall Myth," was published in the *American Sociological Review*. She is working with Laura Hamilton on a book exploring college peer culture and social inequality based on longitudinal ethnographic study of a women's floor in a residence hall.

Mary Bernstein is Associate Professor of Sociology at the University of Connecticut. Her scholarship seeks to understand the role of identity in social movements and how movement actors interact with the state and the law. Her recent publications include "Identity Politics" (*Annual Review of Sociology*), "Paths to Homophobia" (*Sexuality Research and Social Policy*), and "Nothing Ventured, Nothing Gained? Conceptualizing Social Movement 'Success' in the Lesbian and Gay Movement" (*Sociological Perspectives*). She is also co-editor of *Queer Families, Queer Politics* (Columbia University Press 2001) and *The Challenge of Law: Sexual Orientation, Gender Identity and Social Movements* (New York University Press, forthcoming).

Scott C. Byrd is a doctoral candidate in sociology at the University of California, Irvine. His dissertation explores transnational coalition building and collaboration among social movements. He has held appointments as a Visiting Fellow at the Kroc Institute for International Peace Studies and the Center for the Study of Social Movements and Social Change at the University of Notre Dame. Scott's research and writing has appeared in *Mobilization, An International Journal* and *Globalizations*. He, along with Elizabeth Smythe, has also co-edited a special issue on the World Social Forums for the *Journal of World System Research*.

Neal Caren is Assistant Professor of Sociology at the University of North Carolina, Chapel Hill. His research interests center on the quantitative analysis of protest and social movements, the intersection of place and political action, and the environmental justice movement and pollution disparities. His work has been published in the *American Sociological Review*, the *Annual Review of Sociology*, *Sociological Methods & Research,* and the *Journal of Urban Affairs*.

Catherine Corrigall-Brown received her Ph.D. from the University of California, Irvine, and is currently a Post-Doctoral Fellow at the University of British Columbia. Her research is focused in the areas of social movements, political sociology, and social psychology. Among her publications, she has

written on framing (*Social Forces*) and coalition formation (*Mobilization*). She is currently working on a book project on individual participation in social movements examining the multiple trajectories individual engagement can take over the life course.

Daniel M. Cress is Professor of Sociology at Western State College of Colorado in Gunnison, Colorado. His teaching and research interests encompass the areas of social movements, religion, family, the environment, and ethnographic research methods. His published research focuses primarily on protest activity by homeless people, homelessness, and dynamics of voluntary associations. He is currently working on a research project that examines sexual assaults on college campuses in the United States When not working, he can be found roaming the central Colorado mountains on cross country skis or a mountain bike and playing in his band, Rock Bottom.

Mario Diani is Professor of Sociology at the University of Trento. He has worked extensively on social movements, collective action, and social networks. His publications include *Social Movements* (with Donatella della Porta, Blackwell, 2006), *Social Movements and Networks* (co-edited with Doug McAdam, Oxford University Press, 2003), *Beyond Tocqueville* (co-edited with Bob Edwards and Michael Foley, University Press of New England, 2001), *Green Networks* (Edinburgh University Press, 1995), and *Studying Collective Action* (co-edited with Ron Eyerman, Sage, 1992), as well as articles in *American Sociological Review, American Journal of Sociology, Theory & Society, Sociological Review, Environmental Politics, Mobilization*, and *Acta Sociologica*.

Marc Dixon is Assistant Professor of Sociology at Dartmouth College. His research interests include political sociology, social movements, and historical and contemporary labor mobilization. He has written numerous articles on protest, strikes, and labor policy in the United States and is currently conducting research on the timing of state labor legislation following the New Deal as well as more recent healthcare reform policies and coverage outcomes in the American states.

Liam Downey is Assistant Professor of Sociology at the University of Colorado at Boulder and faculty research associate in the Population Program at the University's Institute of Behavioral Science. His primary research interests revolve around race and class inequality in the environmental, political, and economic realms. He is currently studying environmental inequality in metropolitan America, racial and ethnic differences in residential mobility into and out of neighborhoods with varying levels of environmental hazard, and the role that undemocratic and elite-controlled institutions play in fostering environmental degradation.

Jan Willem Duyvendak studied both sociology and philosophy and obtained his Ph.D. in 1991 at the University of Amsterdam on the basis of his research, *The Power of Politics. New Social Movements in an Old Polity. France 1965–1989* (Westview Press, 1994). His recent topics of interest are disadvantaged neighborhoods in large cities, community development, multiculturalism, social cohesion, urban renewal, and "feeling at home." After having being the Director of the Verwey-Jonker Instituut, Research Institute for Social Issues, he was appointed Professor of Sociology at the University of Amsterdam in 2003.

Jennifer Earl is Associate Professor of Sociology at the University of California, Santa Barbara. Her research focuses on social movements and the sociology of law, with research emphases on social movement repression, the Internet and social movements, and legal change. She has published widely, including in *The American Sociological Review* and *The Annual Review of Sociology*, as well as in respected specialty journals such as *Sociological Theory* and *Mobilization*. Current projects include a five-year study of Internet activism funded by a National Science Foundation CAREER Award and a study of arrests made at the 2004 Republican National Convention.

Rachel L. Einwohner is Associate Professor of Sociology at Purdue University, where she is also

affiliated with the Jewish Studies Program. Her research interests focus on questions related to protest success, identity in social movements, and the emergence of collective action in highly repressive settings. She has explored these topics in studies of a variety of cases of protest and resistance, including the U.S. animal rights movement, the college-based anti-sweatshop movement, and the Warsaw Ghetto Uprising. She is also the co-editor (along with Jo Reger and Daniel J. Myers) of *Identity Work in Social Movements* (University of Minnesota Press, 2008).

Myra Marx Ferree is Martindale-Bascom Professor of Sociology at the University of Wisconsin-Madison. Her most recent book is *Global Feminisms* (NYU Press 2006, edited with Aili Mari Tripp) and she is also engaged with her students in several other studies of political discourses—over the Iraq war in the United States, the headscarf debates in Germany, and about teenage homosexuality in South Korea.

Robert Futrell is Associate Professor of Sociology at the University of Nevada, Las Vegas. His research addresses issues in social movements, environmental sustainability, and science and technological disputes. Most recently, he has collaborated with Pete Simi on a series of ethnographic articles and a book that analyze the persistence of U.S. white power activism. He is also writing on the political and scientific controversy surrounding the U.S. Army's Chemical Weapons Disposal Program and the limits to sustainable development in the southwestern United States.

William A. Gamson is Professor of Sociology and co-directs, with Charlotte Ryan, the Media Research and Action Project (MRAP) at Boston College. He co-authored *Shaping Abortion Discourse: Democracy and the Public Sphere in Germany and the United States* (Cambridge University Press, 2002) and is the author of *Talking Politics* (Cambridge University Press, 1992) and *The Strategy of Social Protest* (2nd edition, Wadsworth, 1990), among other books and articles on political discourse, the mass media, and social movements. He is a past president of the

American Sociological Association and a Fellow of the American Academy of Arts and Sciences. His current work involves the development of a game simulation on global justice issues available at the following website: www.globaljusticegame.mrap. info

Jack A. Goldstone is Hazel Professor of Public Policy at George Mason University. He is the author of *Revolution and Rebellion in the Early Modern World* (University of California Press, 1991), and editor of *The Encyclopedia of Political Revolutions* (Congressional Quarterly, 1998). He has received the Distinguished Contribution to Scholarship award of the American Sociological Association, the Arnoldo Momigliano Prize of the Historical Society, and fellowships from the ACLS and the MacArthur Foundation. Professor Goldstone has written or edited 10 books and over 100 academic articles or essays on topics ranging from demography and conflict to long-term social and economic change.

Marco G. Giugni is a researcher at the Laboratoire de recherches sociales et politiques appliquées (resop) and teaches at the department of political science at the University of Geneva. He has authored or co-authored several books and articles on social movements and contentious politics. His research interests include social movements and collective action, immigration and ethnic relations, unemployment, and social exclusion.

Frances Hasso is Associate Professor in the Sociology Department at Oberlin College. She is also affiliated with the Oberlin College Institute for Gender, Sexuality and Feminist Studies (GSFS). She has received numerous research grants and fellowships, including from the Rockefeller Foundation, Woodrow Wilson Foundation, American Sociological Association/National Science Foundation, the Social Science Research Council, the American Council of Learned Societies, and the International Institute for the Study of Islam in the Modern World (the Netherlands). Dr. Hasso has published widely. Her research interests focus on the intersections of transnational processes, states, social movements,

and identities, especially in the Middle East and North Africa.

David Jacobs is Professor of Sociology and (by courtesy) Political Science at Ohio State. He uses a political economy approach to study the politics of outcomes in the criminal justice system and other issues in political sociology and stratification. Current and future projects include investigations of racial politics, the social determinants of rape law reforms, the politics of labor and unionization, the social determinants of the percentage of women with seats in the state legislatures, and the social determinants of hate groups.

J. Craig Jenkins is Professor and Chair, Department of Sociology and Research Fellow, Mershon Center for International Security, Ohio State University. He specializes in the study of contentious politics and political change and is the author of *The Politics of Insurgency* (Columbia University, 1985), *The Politics of Social Protest* (University of Minnesota, 1995), and *Identity Conflicts* (Transaction 2007) and the co-editor of *The Handbook of Politics* (Springer, 2009). His current research focuses on contentious politics globally and in the Middle East, high technology development, and the U.S. environmental movement.

Andrew W. Jones is Assistant Professor of Sociology at St. Lawrence University. He is interested in organic integrity in social and ecological systems and the way that social inequality (class, race, and gender) disrupts that integrity. He is currently researching the cultural and structural roots of the ecological crisis and is interested in environmental movements. His article, "Caring Labor and Class Consciousness," won both the Szymanski and the Braverman Awards. He has published in *American Sociological Review, Social Forces, Sociological Forum*, and *Mobilization*.

Tamara Kay is Assistant Professor of Sociology at Harvard University and co-director of the Transnational Studies Initiative, which is based at Harvard's Weatherhead Center for International Affairs. Her work centers on the political and legal implications of regional economic integration, transnationalism, and global governance. She recently completed a book titled *NAFTA and the Politics of Labor Transnationalism* that examines NAFTA's effects on labor transnationalism in North America. Her new project focuses on transnational relationships between economic development organizations in the United States and developing countries—particularly how they negotiate cultural issues—and the effects of different organizational structures and strategies on development outcomes.

Bert Klandermans is Professor in Applied Social Psychology at the VU-University, Amsterdam, the Netherlands. He has published extensively on the social psychology of participation in social movements. He is the editor of "Social Movements, Protest, and Contention," the prestigous book series of the University of Minnesota Press. His *Social Psychology of Protest* appeared with Blackwell in 1997. He is the editor and co-author (with Suzanne Staggenborg) of *Methods of Social Movement Research* (University of Minnesota Press, 2002), (with Nonna Mayer) of *Extreme Right Activists in Europe* (Routledge, 2006), and (with Conny Roggeband) of *Handbook of Social Movements Across Disciplines* (Springer, 2007).

Ruud Koopmans is Director of the Department of "Migration, Integration, Transnationalization" at the Science Center for Social Research (WZB) in Berlin and Professor of Sociology at the Vrije Universiteit in Amsterdam. His research interests are social movements, immigration politics, European integration, and evolutionary sociology. He is the co-author of several books, including *Democracy from Below* (Westview, 1995), *New Social Movements in Western Europe* (University of Minnesota Press, 1995), and *Contested Citizenship* (University of Minnesota Press, 2005). His articles have appeared in major social science journals such as *American Sociological Review, American Journal of Sociology, European Journal of Political Research,* and *Theory and Society.*

Hanspeter Kriesi holds the Chair in Comparative Politics at the department of political science of the University of Zurich. Previously, he taught at the Universities of Amsterdam and Geneva. He is a specialist of social movements, but his wide-ranging research interests also include the study of direct democracy, political parties and interest groups, public opinion, the public sphere, and the media. He has co-edited (together with David Snow and Sarah Soule) *The Blackwell Companion to Social Movements* (Blackwell 2004). His most recent book, written with colleagues, is *West European Politics in the Age of Globalization* (Cambridge University Press, 2008). He is now the director of a Swiss national research program on the "challenges to democracy in the 21st century."

Doug McAdam is Professor of Sociology at Stanford University and former Director of the Center for Advanced Study in the Behavioral Sciences (2001–2005). He has authored or co-authored 13 books and some 80 articles in the area of political sociology, with a special emphasis on the study of social movements and other forms of "contentious politics." His best known works include *Political Process and the Development of Black Insurgency, 1930–1970,* (University of Chicago Press, 1999), *Freedom Summer* (Oxford University Press 1988), and *Dynamics of Contention* (with Sidney Tarrow and Charles Tilly). (Cambridge University Press, 2001). He was elected to membership in the American Academy of Arts and Sciences in 2003.

Holly McCammon is Professor of Sociology at Vanderbilt University. Her research focuses on U.S. women's activism in the late nineteenth and early twentieth centuries. Her work has appeared in the *American Sociological Review, American Journal of Sociology, Mobilization,* and *The Sociological Quarterly.* She is currently writing a book on strategic adaptation in the women's jury movements. She is also investigating the economic and political circumstances in which state-level Married Women's Property Acts were passed in the United States.

John D. McCarthy is Professor and Head of the Department of Sociology at Pennsylvania State University. His work on social movements, protest, and collective action is widely published. He is currently at work on projects that focus on 1) the dynamics of U.S. protest, 2) campus public order disturbances, and 3) the growth of U.S. advocacy organizations. In 2007 he received a Lifetime Scholarly Achievement Award, named in his honor, from the Center for the Study of Social Movements and Change at Notre Dame University.

David S. Meyer is Professor of Sociology, Political Science, and Planning, Policy and Design at the University of California, Irvine. He has published numerous articles on social movements and social change and is author or co-editor of six books, most recently, *The Politics of Protest: Social Movements in America* (Oxford University Press 2006). He is most interested in the connections among institutional politics, public policy, and social movements, particularly in regard to issues of war and peace.

Aldon Morris is the Leon Forrest Professor of Sociology at Northwestern University. His interests include race, social inequality, religion, politics, theory and social movements. Morris is the author of *The Origins of the Civil Rights Movement*. He is co-editor of the volumes, Frontiers in Social Movement Theory and *Opposition Consciousness*. He has published widely on a variety of topics. His recent articles include "Naked Power and The Civic Sphere," *The Sociological Quarterly*, 2007 and "Sociology of Race and W.E.B Du Bois: The Path Not Taken," *Sociology in America*, (University of Chicago Press, 2007). He is currently working on a book that examines the sociology of W. E. B. Du Bois.

Courtney Sanders Muse is Lecturer in Sociology at Vanderbilt University. Her doctoral dissertation research involved an examination of identity conflicts that social movement participants experience when their personal identities do not align with the collective identity of a social movement organization. In this work she focuses specifically on the Log Cabin Republicans. Her results indicate that different characteristics of movement participants influence the types of organizational frames these individuals are able to use to overcome identity conflicts that arise during the course of movement participation, thus emphasizing the importance of social movement framing to identity conflict resolution.

Harmony D. Newman is completing her Ph.D. in the department of sociology at Vanderbilt University. Her research interests include the sociology of social movements, health, gender, motherhood, and qualitative methods. Harmony is currently working on her dissertation, for which she conducted a cross-cultural comparison of strategic framing in breastfeeding activism and mothers' interpretations of these strategies. She has previously co-authored publications in the *American Journal of Sociology*, *American Sociological Review*, and *Gender Issues*.

Sharon Erickson Nepstad is Professor of Sociology and Director of Religious Studies at the University of New Mexico. She has also been a Visiting Fellow at Princeton University's Center for the Study of Religion and at the Kroc Institute for International Peace Studies at Notre Dame University. Her research has focused on the role of religion in peace movements. She is the author of *Convictions of the Soul: Religion, Culture, and Agency in the Central America Solidarity Movement* (Oxford University Press, 2004) and *Religion and War Resistance in the Plowshares Movement* (Cambridge University Press, 2008).

Sheera Joy Olasky is a graduate student in the department of sociology at New York University. Her research interests include political sociology, social movements, and urban sociology. She is currently studying environmental justice and social policy.

Johan Olivier holds B.A. and B.A. (Hons) degrees from the University of Pretoria. He pursued his graduate studies at the University of South Africa (M.A.) and Cornell University (Ph.D.). He was in the employment of the Human Sciences Research Council in Pretoria, South Africa, up to 2000. He is currently a management/research consultant, in which capacity he is involved in assignments for the South African government, government agencies, and donors. He taught by invitation at the

University of Cape Town, University of Pretoria, and Stanford University in the United States. He has authored/co-authored more than 60 publications in the areas of social change, democratization, and political stability.

Susan Olzak is Professor of Sociology at Stanford University, where she teaches and does research on ethnic/racial conflict and social movements. She has published *The Dynamics of Ethnic Competition and Conflict* (Stanford University Press 1992) and *The Global Dynamics of Race and Ethnic Mobilization* (Stanford University Press 2006), and a number of articles on U.S. race riots, the Equal Rights Amendment, the West German women's movement, and anti-partheid protest in South Africa. Current research includes analysis of the impact of globalization on ethnic conflict, anti-immigrant violence in contemporary Western Europe, and the impact of environmental movement protest on relevant environmental legislation in the U.S. Congress.

Nicholas Pedriana is a sociologist and currently a visiting lecturer in the department of legal studies at Northwestern University. His primary research interests are law, organizations, culture, and collective action/social movements for progressive change. His past work includes articles on the early legal development of equal employment law, and in particular the dynamic relationship between legal institutions and the civil rights and women's movements. He is currently working on a historical-comparative analysis of the divergent trajectories of U.S. equal employment, equal housing, and voting rights policy from their origins in the 1960s to the present.

Francesca Polletta is Professor of Sociology at the University of California, Irvine. She studies social movements, experiments in radical democracy, and culture in politics. She is the author of *It Was Like a Fever: Storytelling in Protest and Politics* (University Chicago, 2006) and *Freedom Is an Endless Meeting: Democracy in American Social Movements* (University of Chicago, 2002) and editor, with Jeff Goodwin and James M. Jasper, of *Passionate Politics: Emotions and Social Movements* (University of Chicago, 2001).

Marlene Roefs holds a Ph.D. in Social Psychology from the Free University in Amsterdam. Her Ph.D. thesis, for which she received the annual award for the best thesis in or related to the field of political science from the Dutch Political Science Association, and other academic publications focus on perception of and reactions to social, economic, and political change. Marlene has moved from the academic to the applied fields of change and development and heads Social Dimensions, a consultancy in South Africa that focuses on planning, monitoring, and evaluation of development programmes.

Vincent J. Roscigno is Professor of Sociology at Ohio State University and currently Editor of *American Sociological Review*. His research centers on social stratification, work and labor, collective action and insurgency, educational inequality, and the sociology of culture. Along with many articles on these topics, he is author of *The Face of Discrimination: How Race and Gender Impact Work and Home Lives* (Rowman & Littlefield, 2007) and, with William Danaher, *The Voice of Southern Labor: Radio, Music, and Textile Strikes, 1929–1934* (University of Minnesota Press, 2004). Currently he is writing on the linkages between power and bureaucracy relative to workplace bullying and race, gender, and age discrimination and is also involved in a project analyzing culture and resistance among Native Americans between 1880 and 1900.

Pete Simi is Assistant Professor in the School of Criminology & Criminal Justice at the University of Nebraska, Omaha. His research interests include the cultural aspects of political activism, the intersection between social movements and street gangs, and the emotional dimensions of violent political conflict. Most recently he has collaborated with Robert Futrell on a series of articles and forthcoming book manuscript that rely on ethnographic data to analyze the persistence of white power activism within the United States.

David Smilde, who received his Ph.D. from the University of Chicago, is Associate Professor of Sociology at the University of Georgia. His work focuses on the way marginalized populations use culture to gain agency over the social processes that affect them. His project on conversion to Evangelicalism in the barrios of Caracas culminated in the book *Reason to Believe: Cultural Agency in Latin American Evangelicalism* (California, 2007). He has also done ethnographic research on street protest in Venezuela and is author of "Popular Publics: Street Protest and Plaza Preachers in Caracas" in the *International Review of Social History*. His current research looks at the three-way conflict between the Evangelical movement, the Catholic Church, and the government of Hugo Chávez. He is co-editor of *Participation and Public Sphere in Venezuela's Bolivarian Democracy* (forthcoming with Duke University Press).

Jackie Smith is Associate Professor of Sociology and Peace Studies at the University of Notre Dame, where she also directs the Center for the Study of Social Movements and Social Change. Her research focuses on relationships between global political processes and social movements. In particular, she has examined how global economic and political changes affect transnational organization and political participation. Her most recent book is *Social Movements for Global Democracy* (Johns Hopkins University Press, 2008). Smith is a co-author of *The World Social Forums and the Challenge of Global Democracy* (Paradigm Publishers, 2008). She has co-edited three books and more than 30 articles on transnational activism, including *Coalitions Across Borders: Transnational Protest in a Neoliberal Era* (with Joe Bandy Rowman & Littlefield, 2004), which explores transnational alliances among people of widely varying cultural, political, and economic backgrounds.

David A. Snow is a Chancellor's Professor of Sociology at the University of California, Irvine. He has written numerous articles and chapters on homelessness, collective action and social movements, religious conversion, self and identity, framing processes, symbolic interactionism, and qualitative field methods. He has co-authored or co-edited *Down on Their Luck* (with L. Anderson) (University of California Press, 1993), *The Blackwell Companion to Social Movements* (with S. Soule and H. Kriesi), (Blackwell, 2004), *Together Alone* (with C. Morrill and C. White), (University of California Press, 2005), *Analyzing Social Settings* (with John Lofland, Leon Anderson, and Lyn Lofland) (Wadworth/Thomson, 2006), and A Primer on Social Movements (with Sarah Soule) (W.W. Norton Publishing Co.).

Sarah A. Soule's research has long focused on how social movements affect organizational processes and how organizational theory and models can shed light on social movement processes. Recent publications (both co-authored with Brayden King) related to these two themes include "Competition and Resource Partitioning in Three Social Movement Industries" *(American Journal of Sociology*, May 2008) and "Social Movements as Extra-Institutional Entrepreneurs: The Effect of Protest on Stock Price Returns" (*Administrative Science Quarterly,* September 2007). She is currently completing a book on how protest affected U.S. corporations between 1960 and 1990, which is tentatively entitled *Private and Contentious Politics and Corporate Social Responsibility*. She has also recently completed a book, co-authored with David Snow, entitled *A Primer on Social Movements* (W.W. Norton and Company). She received her Ph.D. in Sociology from Cornell University.

Suzanne Staggenborg is Professor of Sociology at the University of Pittsburgh. She received her Ph.D. from Northwestern University and previously taught at Indiana University and McGill University. Her work includes *Social Movements* (Oxford University Press, 2008), *Methods of Social Movement Research* (co-edited with Bert Klandermans; University of Minnesota Press, 2002), *Gender, Family and Social Movements* (Pine Forge Press, 1998), *The Pro-Choice Movement* (Oxford University Press, 1991), and a number of articles about abortion politics and social movements. Her current projects include studies of the women's movements in the United States and Canada and of local environmental groups.

Sidney Tarrow, who earned a Ph.D. at Berkeley, is Maxwell M. Upson Professor of Government and Professor of Sociology at Cornell University. Tarrow's first book was *Peasant Communism in Southern Italy* (Yale, 1967). In the 1980s, after a foray into comparative local politics (*Between Center and Periphery;* Yale, 1978), he turned to a reconstruction of Italian protest cycle of the late 1960s and early 1970s, *Democracy and Disorder* (Oxford, 1989). His recent books are *Power in Movement* (Cambridge, 1994, 1998), *Dynamics of Contention* (with Doug McAdam and Charles Tilly; Cambridge, 2001), *Contentious Europeans* (with Doug Imig; Rowman and Littlefield, 2001), *Transnational Protest and Global Activism* (ed., with Donatella della Porta; Rowman and Littlefield, 2004), *The New Transnational* Activism (Cambridge, 2005) and, with the late Charles Tilly, *Contentious Politics* (Paradigm, 2006). He is a fellow of the American Academy of Arts and Sciences, has served as Program Co-Chair of the American Political Science Association Annual Convention, President of the Conference Group on Italian Politics, and President of the APSA Section on Comparative Politics. He is currently working on warmaking, state building, and human rights.

Verta Taylor is Professor and Chair of Sociology at the University of California, Santa Barbara. She is co-author of *Drag Queens at the 801 Cabaret* and *Survival in the Doldrums: The American Women's Rights Movement, 1945 to the 1960s,* author of *Rock-a-by Baby: Feminism, Self-Help and Postpartum Depression,* and co-editor of eight editions of *Feminist Frontiers.* Her articles on women's movements, the gay and lesbian movement, and social movement theory have appeared in *American Sociological Review, Signs, Social Problems, Mobilization, Gender & Society, Contexts, Qualitative Sociology, Journal of Women's History, Journal of Homosexuality,* and *Journal of Lesbian Studies.*

Teresa M. Terrell received her Ph.D. in Sociology from Vanderbilt University in 2007. Her dissertation was entitled "Community Participation in Birmingham, Alabama: How Leadership, Social Networks, Framing and Participatory Democracy Shape Inner-City Civic Participation." Her research compares urban neighborhoods that have high levels of political participation to those that do not. Rather than dismissing all low-income neighborhoods as deficient in social capital, Terrell studies black women's activism and their work as community leaders. She is currently a Post-Doctoral Fellow in Race, Gender and Public Policy at the Hubert H. Humphrey Institute of Public Affairs at the University of Minnesota.

The late **Charles Tilly** must be counted as one of the preeminent social scientists of his generation. Through his published work he made seminal contributions to the study of social movements and revolutions (*From Mobilization to Revolution, Dynamics of Contention, European Revolutions*), collective violence (*The Politics of Collective Violence*), democratization (*Democracy*), and inequality *(Durable Inequality),* among other topics. The recipient of many awards and honorary degrees during his lifetime, he was awarded the 2008 Albert O. Hirschman Prize just prior to his death in 2008.

Nella Van Dyke is Associate Professor of Sociology at the University of California, Merced. Her research focuses on social movements and hate crime, with an emphasis on how characteristics of the social context influence levels of collective action. Her work has been published in journals including *Social Forces, Social Problems,* and *Mobilization.* Recent projects include studies of the AFL-CIO's Union Summer student internship program and how it has inspired student anti-sweatshop protests, the factors that influence variation in the incidence of hate crimes on college campuses, and a meta-analysis of the research on coalition formation.

Dingxin Zhao is Associate Professor of Sociology at the University of Chicago. He is interested in political sociology broadly defined. His research covers the areas of social movements, nationalism, historical sociology, and economic development. His interests also extend to sociological theory and methodology. Zhao's publications have appeared in journals such as *American Journal of Sociology, American Sociological Review, Social Forces,*

Sociology, and *Problems of Post-Communism.* He has published an award-winning book entitled *Power of Tiananmen* (University of Chicago Press 2001), and is working on a project which, based on a comparison with the European experience, seeks to explain China's precocious rise of bureaucracy around the 7th BCE, unification in 221 BCE, the emergence of the Confucian state around 140 BCE, and the patterns of the Chinese past in the last two millenniums.

Readings on
Social Movements

Social Movements: Conceptual and Theoretical Issues

Social movement and kindred collective action, such as protest crowds, riots, and revolutions, are conspicuous and significant social phenomena. They are conspicuous in that they occur frequently and are striking features of the social landscape. Any daily newspaper or weekly news magazine is likely to refer to movement and protest activity in relation to one of the hotly contested issues of our time: abortion, the death penalty, immigration, same-sex marriage, global warming, terrorism, globalization, and layoffs at work. Indeed, it is difficult to think of a major social issue in which social movements are not involved on one or both sides.

The movements associated with such issues are important social phenomena as well, capturing our attention because they bring into bold relief sizable numbers of people attempting to promote or resist change as they act on behalf of common interests or values. To understand the politics and conflicts associated with important or contemporary and historical social issues, it is crucial to acquire an understanding of the character and dynamics of the social movements associated with these issues. The central objective of this book is to provide such an understanding by presenting readings that illuminate the dynamics of social movements from their emergence through the trials and tribulations of mobilization, development, decline, as well as their long-term consequences.

In this introduction we provide a working conceptualization of social movements, explain the various components of that conception, identify the various sets of social actors relevant to social movements, discuss the relationship between social movements and other forms of collective action, and elaborate the logic for the substantive issues addressed and the way in which we have organized the book.

CONCEPTUALIZING SOCIAL MOVEMENTS

Although many definitions of social movements have been proposed, most of them include the following elements: (1) some degree of organization; (2) some degree of temporal continuity; (3) change-oriented goals; and (3) at least some use of extrainstitutional forms of action (e.g. street protests, vigils) to supplement more institutional forms of claims making (e.g., voting, letter writing). Blending these elements together, we define a social movement as a loose collectivity acting with some degree of organization, temporal continuity, and reliance on noninstitutional forms of action to promote or resist change in the group, society, or world order of which it is a part.[1] To elaborate on this definition, we turn to a discussion of each of its major components.

MOVEMENTS AND SOCIAL CHANGE

Since the promotion or resistance of change is the raison d'être of all social movements, we begin with this defining feature. Caution must be exercised, however, lest we generalize to all movements as if they are cut from the same cloth. Even though most social movements are carriers of change, they vary dramatically in the kinds and degree of change sought. Virtually all typologies of social movements acknowledge this point, at least with respect to the degree or amount of change pursued. The most common distinction in this regard is

1

		LOCUS OF CHANGE	
		Individual	Social structure
Amount of Change	**Partial**	alterative	reformative
	Total	redemptive	transformative

between *reform* and *revolution*. Neil Smelser (1962) provides a more subtle distinction, differentiating between *norm-oriented* and *value-oriented* movements. Norm-oriented movements are concerned with producing more limited but specific changes within a social system, often with respect to rules of access to, and operation within, the various institutional arenas of society. Thus, movements that have sought to introduce or change labor laws, decriminalize or legalize drugs such as marijuana, or restrict or expand immigrant rights would be considered reform movements. Value-oriented movements, on the other hand, are concerned with more fundamental change, and thus seek to alter basic values and the institutional bedrock on which they rest. The most obvious examples would be revolutionary movements, such as those that birthed the French, American, and Russian revolutions, or broad-based struggles, such as the African American civil rights movement or contemporary gay and lesbian movement, which seek to redefine the fundamental rights and privileges of citizenship.

A similar scheme is provided by Roy Wallis's distinction between *world-rejecting* and *world-affirming* movements (1984). Although this dichotomy was developed with religious movements in mind, its application parallels that of the value-oriented/norm-oriented distinction. Thus, world-rejecting movements, like value-oriented movements, condemn the prevailing social order as a whole, including both its underlying values and institutional arrangements. Like the norm-oriented movement, the world-affirming movement is less contemptuous of and hostile toward the prevailing social order and thus only seeks relatively modest modifications in the status quo.

One of the problems with the above typology is that it are based only on one dimension: the extent of change sought. The fact that change can have a

different locus, or occur at different levels, is not addressed. Long ago, the anthropologist David Aberle addressed this oversight in his 1966 book on *The Peyote Religion Among the Navaho*. Aberle differentiates social movements based both on the amount of change and the locus or level of change sought. The locus dimension directs attention to the target of change, which can vary from the individual to some aspect of the broader social structure. Although any movement can be situated along continua of both dimensions, the crossclassification of these two dimensions yields four generic types of movements, as diagrammed in the following table:

Alterative movements seek partial change in individuals. Presumed or actual character and psychological tendencies and habits are regarded as troublesome and in need of change or repair. Examples of such tendencies or habits targeted for change by social movements include the use of alcohol, sexual practices, level of personal assertiveness, abusive interpersonal behavior, and low self-esteem. In each case, the object of change is some individual shortcoming, deficit, or patterned tendency. The therapeutic and self-help movements that have flourished in the United States since the 1970s and 1980s are examples of movements that seek to do something about such shortcomings or tendencies.

It is reasonable to wonder whether such self-improvement efforts are really social movements inasmuch as the individual is the primary focus of change. Yet it is difficult to argue with the contention that the alteration of thousands of individuals may be one avenue to social change. Insofar as self-help themes are mixed with the idea of social change through personal transformation, as is the case with the rhetoric of many such groups, they do constitute a type of social movement.

The link between individual transformation and social change is even more transparent in the case of what Aberle calls *redemptive* movements. These movements also focus on individuals as the object of change or control, but they seek total rather than partial change. From the vantage point of these movements, social ills and problems of all varieties are seen as rooted in individuals and their misguided behavior or ill-informed ideas and beliefs. If individuals are transformed or redeemed, then the larger problem is resolved. Personal transformation is thus seen as the key to thoroughgoing social change. Religious movements and cults are among the best known examples of this highly individualistic approach to broader social issues. A large number of such movements surfaced and flowered in much of the Western world in the 1970s: few were as well known as the Hare Krishna movement, the Unification Church (or "Moonies" as they were known more colloquially), and the Nichiren Shoshu Buddhist movement. All of these movements are still active in varying degrees, and all still claim to be interested in transforming the world by affecting personal transformation of the masses.

The third category of movement in Aberle's typology is termed *reformative*. Movements of this ilk seek limited change in the social system in which they are embedded. There is no blanket rejection of the present order, but an attempt instead to rectify or neutralize specific perceived wrongs. The objective may be to reduce or remove some actual or perceived threat to the interests of a specific group or population segment. Or it may involve a category of threatened species or a specific locale earmarked for a type of project (nuclear plant) or facility (homeless shelter) opposed by the movement. Perhaps even more common are movements that seek to improve or preserve the lifestyle or treatment of a particular category of individuals, such as women, gays and lesbians, illegal immigrants, and unborn babies.

The final generic category of movement seeks total change in the broader social structure and its associated ideational bedrock. Aberle termed such movements *transformative*, though we might just as easily call them revolutions. Because the amount of change sought tends to be all-embracing, these movements are typically the most dramatic and

historically consequential. Some of the more notable examples of transformative movements include the so-called "great revolutions" (e.g., French, Chinese, Russian) as well as such sweeping religious movements as the Protestant Reformation and the rise and spread of Islam.

Although movements seldom fit neatly into one of the four types, they are typically skewed more in one direction than another along the two-change dimensions. Thus, a typology such as Aberle's is useful in helping to illuminate the diversity among movements, especially in their social change goals. But, as we will see, the course and character of social movements are influenced not only by their objectives, but also by the context in which they arise, the external relations with the communities they are a part of, as well as their own internal dynamics.

However movements are categorized, the fact that there are different kinds raises questions about the sociohistorical conditions that account for their emergence and why some individuals take part in them while others do not. But these and other questions pertaining to the origins, operation, and dynamics of social movements will have to wait until we clarify the other fundamental elements of our conceptualization.

Movements as Collectivities Acting Outside of Institutional Channels

In thinking of movements as vehicles of change, it is important to keep in mind that the unit of analysis is a collectivity—that is, a group of interrelated persons engaged in joint action—rather than an aggregate of persons acting in a parallel but disconnected manner. This understanding helps to distinguish social movements from other social phenomena that are sometimes related to, but different from, movements. *Social trends* are one such phenomenon. Trends are large-scale, far-reaching changes in patterns of social organization and behavior over an extended period of time. Prominent examples of such trends include industrialization, urbanization, and bureaucratization, as well as long-term changes in employment, family formation, and education. By disrupting or changing longstanding social routines, such trends may provide the grievance or organizational bases for social movements, but in and of themselves they are not social movements.

Nor, in our view, are *changes in public opinion* the same as social movements. McCarthy and Zald, for example, have defined social movements in this fashion by referring to them as "a set of opinions and beliefs in a population which represents preferences for changing some elements of the social structure or reward distribution of a society" (1977: 1217–1218). Sets of change-oriented opinions and beliefs do not, however, constitute collective *action*. They may be a necessary condition for such action, but again, they are not movements in themselves.

Also sometimes confused with social movements are *mass migrations* of individuals, as in the case of a gold rush, a land rush, or a large-scale migration of large numbers of citizens from one region of a country to another or across national borders. Such mass migrations share some characteristics of social movements, but not the most essential one, namely the pursuit or resistance of social change through engagement in nonroutine forms of collective action. Additionally, the behaviors that comprise a mass migration tend to be more individualistic than collective.

Interest groups comprise one final collective phenomenon that is often seen as synonymous with social movements. Clearly, interest groups, such as the American Medical Association or the National Rifle Association, bear a striking resemblance to social movements insofar as both seek to promote or resist change in some aspect of social/political life. Yet there are differences, the most important of which is that interest groups stand in a different relationship to the system of institutionalized policy making. Interest groups are embedded in that system and are typically regarded as legitimate actors within the political arena. Social movements, on the other hand, typically stand at some remove from the mainstream political system or overlap with it only precariously. Another important difference follows from this: interest groups pursue their collective objectives almost always through institutionalized means, such as lobbying or by contributing to electoral campaigns, whereas social movements tend to rely on a mix of routine and nonroutine tactics. Thus, to paraphrase William

Gamson (1990), interest groups and social movements are not so much different species as members of the same species positioned differently in relation to the polity. But that differential positioning is sufficiently important to produce different sets of strategic and tactical behaviors, and thus different kinds of collectivities.

Movements as Organizations and Organized Activity

Dating back to the work of some of the earliest movement theorists, such as Lenin (1929) and Michels (1949), the organizational dimension of social movements has been featured in most treatments of the subject. But it was not until McCarthy and Zald's (1973, 1977) articulation of the resource mobilization perspective that this dimension took center stage and social movement organizations (SMOs) became the focal unit of analysis. Since then, there has been ongoing debate about the centrality of SMOs to the operation of social movements and whether formal organization makes movements more or less effective as vehicles of significant social/political change (Gamson 1990; Melucci 1989; Piven and Cloward 1977).

In attempting to clarify this debate, Tarrow (1998) has distinguished between social movements as formal organizations and the organization of collective action. We think this is an important distinction, but we also think it is difficult to understand the operation and dynamics of social movements, including most movement-related collective actions, without reference to the organizations that tend to serve as the movement's organized public face. It is hard, for example, to think of the AfricanAmerican civil rights movement of the 1960s without recalling groups such as the National Association for the Advancement of Colored People (NAACP), the Congress of Racial Equality (CORE), the Southern Christian Leadership Conference (SCLC), and the Student Non-Violent Coordinating Committee (SNCC), who were responsible for the major campaigns that shaped the struggle. The same is true for just about any enduring social movement.

Virtually all such movements are associated with one or more formal SMOs. Local movements may spawn only one such organization, but enduring national struggles are often represented by many more. No matter how many SMOs comprise a movement, these groups tend to carry and dramatize the concerns and grievances of their respective constituencies, thus making social movements and social movement organizations opposite sides of the same coin. It is for this reason that a semblance of organization needs to be included as a component of the conceptualization of social movements, but without specifying the character of the organization of any specific movement. We add this qualification because the character of a movement's organization—formal or informal, centralized or decentralized—and the impact of that structure on the nature and success of the movement are themselves important topics for investigation.[2]

Movements Existing with Some Temporal Continuity

The final element of our conceptualization requiring brief elaboration is the observation that social movements exist or operate with some degree of temporal continuity. This characteristic helps to distinguish movements from more ephemeral kinds of collective gatherings, such as unconventional crowds or gatherings. The point is that social movements are rarely, if ever, fly-by-night phenomena that are here today and gone tomorrow. The word movement itself implies some degree of development and continuity. Moreover, the kinds of changes movements pursue typically require sustained, organized activity. Indeed, it is difficult to imagine any movement making progress in pursuing its objectives without persistent, almost nagging, collective action. Continuity, like organization, is a matter of degree, of course. But some degree of sustained collective is an essential characteristic of social movements.

Categories of Actors Relevant to Social Movements

We have conceptualized social movements as collectivities working with some degree of organization and continuity to promote or resist change through a mixture of extrainstitutional and institutional means. But what kind of collectivity is a social movement? What is the relationship between the various actors relevant to social movements? How do we conceptualize movement participants? How do they differ from other pertinent actors?

Borrowing on the work of Hunt, Benford, and Snow (1994), we suggest that the various sets of actors relevant to the course and character of a social movement fall into three categories: protagonists, antagonists, and bystanders.[3]

Protagonists

The protagonists include all groups and collectivities that are supporters of the movement or whose interests are represented by it. They include a movement's adherents, constituency, and beneficiaries. At the core of a movement's protagonists are its *adherents*. The adherents include those individuals who engage in movement activities conducted in pursuit of its objectives. At a minimum, such engagement typically involves participating in one or more movement activities, be it a protest rally, a sit-in, or a more formal organizational meeting. Presumably these individuals share certain key values and objectives and identify themselves with the movement. It is useful to keep in mind, however, that most adherents are not equally involved. Some may devote considerable time and energy to movement activities and campaigns, while others may do little more than write a check or attend an occasional meeting or activity. It is therefore "useful to distinguish *activists* from the bulk of the adherents by the level of effort and sacrifice they give to the cause" (Turner and Killian 1987: 225).

Most movement adherents are drawn from its *constituency*, the second set of actors that comprise the movement's protagonist base. Although the term is borrowed from politics, it refers in the context of social movements to the aggregation of individuals the movement or organization claims to represent and which typically is a major source of resources and support. In actuality, not all individuals who comprise a movement's constituency are wildly enthusiastic about it; some may be indifferent, others sympathetic but uninterested or unable to provide direct support, while still others may constitute the movement's primary resource base. As suggested above, it is from this latter group of constituents that adherents are likely to be drawn.

Turning to the third category of protagonists it is often assumed that a movement's constituents are the direct *beneficiaries* of the change it is trying to effect. Although this is often the case, the relationship between a movement's constituency and its beneficiaries is not so simple. If the good or change sought is a public one, such as clean air or clean water, then clearly it is not something that can be secured and/or preserved for a specific group or aggregation.[4] Instead, the larger public benefits. In such cases, most of the beneficiaries can be thoughts of as free riders inasmuch as they have contributed neither sympathetic support nor more tangible resources to the movement.[5] In other cases, when the objective of a movement is to expand the rights and opportunities of a particular disadvantaged group, such as Native Americans and the disabled, all of the direct beneficiaries may be constituents, but not all of the constituents will necessarily be beneficiaries. Consider, for example, "straights" marching in support of gay and lesbian rights, men linking arms with women in support of the Equal Rights Amendment, and over 1,000 northern college students, most of them white, volunteering to go to Mississippi in June 1964 to register black voters and staff "freedom schools" as part of the Freedom Summer campaign organized by the Student Non-Violent Coordinating Committee.[6] In each of these examples, individuals are supporting a movement without standing to benefit directly if movement objectives are attained. Such individuals can be thought of as either *conscience adherents* or *conscience constituents*, depending on the nature of support they provide (McCarthy and Zald 1977).

Antagonists

Standing in opposition to a movement's adherents and constituents are the set of actors we refer to as antagonists. Included among a movement's antagonists are the *targets* of its actions, such as a city, state, or national government, sometimes a corporation like ExxonMobil, or perhaps a university where research or admissions practices are targeted. Any set of individuals, groups, or institutions can be the target of the change a movement is attempting

to effect. Since many individuals and groupings within a movement's field of action may not only be unsympathetic to the movement's objectives and activities, but also perceive the movement's interests as antithetical to their own, it is not uncommon for *countermovements* to emerge. The objective of these countermovements is to halt or neutralize the goal attainment activities of the movement in question. Thus, the antiabortion or pro-life movement emerged in response to the success of the pro-choice movement, as manifested in the 1973 *Roe v. Wade* Supreme Court decision.

Bystanders

The third category of actors relevant to the operation of social movements are bystanders, which include community members who are initially uninterested in the issue at hand. Bystanders have no perceptible stake in the objectives and outcomes of a movement, and thus remain somewhat aloof and indifferent. But interest in a movement and its activities can be activated. In some instances, a change in orientation may result from disruption of bystanders' taken-for-granted daily routines. When this occurs, bystanders are more likely to call for cessation of the activity than to choose a side. In other instances, bystander interest is piqued by movement activities and appeals, often through the media, and some bystander groups are transformed into constituents or even adherents. And in still other cases, the actions of movement antagonists, be they the police or countermovements, may engender opposition to the movement. Just as likely, however, is the possibility that police are perceived as overreacting and unwittingly generate sympathy for the movement. In light of these possibilities, it is clear that the relationship between a movement's protagonists, antagonists, and bystanders, including the media, is a dynamic, ongoing process that is central to a movement's career.

SOCIAL MOVEMENTS AS A FORM OF COLLECTIVE ACTION

At several points throughout this introduction we have suggested that social movements are a form of collective action. Since the term "collective action" is used broadly and sometimes interchangeably with the term "social movement," it is useful to clarify the relationship between these concepts and such related constructs as collective behavior and crowds.

Although the term collective action is widely used, there is not a clear, consensual definition of the term. Broadly conceived, collective action encompasses any goaldirected activity jointly pursued by two or more individuals. The action is pursued jointly because an individual is unlikely to attain the objective alone. Thus, at a rudimentary level, collective action is joint action in pursuit of a common objective.

Since this basic conception encompasses a significant proportion of human behavior, it is useful to distinguish between the collective actions that are institutionalized or normatively sanctioned and those that fall outside of institutional channels. Since social movements are defined in part by their operation outside of institutional channels, introducing this distinction reduces the number of joint actions that bear a resemblance to movements. As Sidney Tarrow notes (1998: 3), collective action not only "takes many forms—brief or sustained, institutionalized or disruptive, humdrum or dramatic," but "most of it occurs within institutions on the part of constituted groups acting in the name of goals that would hardly raise an eyebrow."

Still, many collective actions fall into the noninstitutional category. Traditionally, most of these noninstitutionalized collective actions, including those associated with social movements, have been discussed and analyzed as varieties of collective behavior. Broadly conceived, collective behavior refers to "extrainstitutional, group problem-solving behavior that encompasses an array of collective actions, ranging from protest demonstrations, to behavior in disasters, to mass or diffuse phenomena, such as fads and crazes, to social movements and even revolution" (Snow and Oliver 1995: 571). Thus, just as social movements are a form of collective action, so they also constitute a species of collective behavior. But they also differ from most other variants of collective behavior because of their change-oriented goals, semblance of organization, and temporal continuity.

To note the distinction between social movements and other species of collective behavior is not to say that they do not overlap or comingle at times. The relationship between nonconventional crowd behavior activity and social movements is illustrative. Although some crowds arise spontaneously and dissipate just as quickly, such as those that spring up around fires and accidents, others are the result of prior planning, organization, and negotiation. In such cases, they are typically orchestrated by a social movement and constitute part of its tactical repertoire for dramatizing its grievances and pressing its claims. When this occurs, which is probably the dominant pattern for most protest gatherings, neither the crowd phenomenon nor the movement can be thoroughly understood without understanding the relationship between them. Thus, while social movements can be distinguished conceptually from other varieties of collective action and collective behavior, social movements and some crowd phenomena are often closely linked, especially when movements dramatize their concerns and press their claims in public settings.

ORGANIZATION OF THE BOOK AND UNDERLYING LOGIC

We have organized this reader around four central issues: the emergence of social movements, micro-mobilization processes, the dynamics of movements, and the outcomes or impacts of social movements. We use these issues as the book's "linchpins" because together they focus attention on the character and operation of social movements over their life course, from the conditions giving rise to them to their impact and consequences. Although we do not claim to have covered these focal issues exhaustively, we do believe that our coverage provides the basis for understanding the central issues in the life histories of social movements as well as some of the factors associated with movement participation.

The issue of emergence focuses attention on the various contextual conditions that nurture the soil for social movements and thus facilitate their development. The first section explores this issue, with Part 1 considering conditions of disruption or breakdown or threat, Part 2 taking up political opportunity as a condition of conduciveness, Part 3 examining facilitative resources and organizational contexts, and Part 4 considering the importance of facilitative spaces and contexts.

The second section explores processes of micro-mobilization as they pertain to differential recruitment and participation—that is, why do some people participate rather than others? The role of social networks in relation to this issue is examined in Part 5. Part 6 examines interpretive framing processes in relation to micromobilization and participation. And Part 7 considers various social psychological dimensions of participation, with a focus on grievances, identity, and emotion.

The third section focuses on the dynamics or actual operation and functioning of social movements. Part 8 considers movements in action by exploring strategic and tactical considerations. Part 9 examines the relationship between movements and various categories of actors in their environment of operation. And Part 10 looks at internal movement processes and dynamics and their implications for the ongoing functioning of movements.

In the book's fourth and last section, we address the question of whether movements make any difference by considering their outcomes or consequences.

It is our hope that the chapter introductions and corresponding selections will increase the reader's understanding of the factors that influence the course and character of social movements. We also hope that this book stimulates further interest in collective action and social movements.

NOTES

1. This conceptualization of social movements borrows from and is similar to those provided by Snow and Oliver (1995: 571), Turner and Killian (1987: 223), and Wilson (1973: 9). See McAdam et al. (2001) for a more political, state-based conception, and Snow (2004a) for a more institutionally and culturally based conceptualization.

2. See Clemens and Minkoff (2004) for further discussion of the organizational dimension of social movements.

3. See Rucht (2004) for an elaborated and more nuanced discussion of the various sets of actors relevant to the operation of social movements.

4. Public goods are typically conceptualized as goods that are indivisible and nonexcludable. This means that public goods are shared by all within a community whether or not everyone contributed to their attainment or production. See Olson (1965).

5. "Free riders" are individuals who benefit from a public good without having contributed toward attaining it. For discussion of the concept of free rider, see Olson (1965).

6. See McAdam (1988) for discussion and analysis of the Freedom Summer campaign.

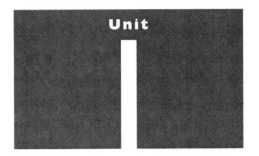

Unit

Emergence: Facilitating Conditions

Part I

Disruptions and Threats

Under what conditions do social movements emerge? What factors give rise to or facilitate the emergence and operation of social movements? Such questions are among the most frequently asked and researched in the study of social movements. Of the various factors posited as necessary conditions for the emergence of social movements, none have received more scholarly attention historically than a cluster of unsettling social conditions that have been conceptualized metaphorically as "strains."

The traditional strain argument—dating back to at least the writings of Emile Durkeim ([1893] 1964) and extending through William Kornhauser's (1959) treatise on the dangers of "mass society" (1959) and Neil Smelser's (1962) attempt to develop an integrative theory of crowd behavior, social movements, and revolutions—is that social movements are the by-products of the clamor for change that is triggered by disintegrative events like wars and economic downturns or by exclusionary social arrangements that render the victims vulnerable to the appeals of social movements. Because of its emphasis on social disintegration, this argument was dubbed "breakdown theory" in the mid-1970s (Tilly, Tilly, and Tilly 1975).

From that point on for the next 20 to 25 years, strain/breakdown arguments, whether structurally or social psychologically oriented, not only fell out of fashion but were relegated by many social movement scholars to the dustbin of tried but failed hypotheses and theories. The reasons for the demise of strain/breakdown theory have been chronicled in Steven Buechler's essay (2004), aptly titled "The Strange Career of Strain and Breakdown Theories of Collective Action" and are discussed in abbreviated fashion by the first selection included in this section. But the reasons for the apparent demise

of strain/breakdown theory were not sufficient to bury it, in large part because of the obdurate fact that social movements do not arise in an issueless, trouble-free vacuum. Rather, they arise in response to events, trends, or social practices that some number of people find or experience as troublesome and about which they have considerable concern and often strong passions. So it is not surprising that remnants of strain/breakdown theorizing have been salvaged and resuscitated (see Buechler 2004; Goldstone and Tilly 2001; Useem 1998). But the form of theorizing has shifted from a presumption of a determinant relationship between certain unsettling conditions to a realization that the relationship between such conditions and movement emergence is generally likely to be indeterminant because of the affect of other sets of facilitative conditions discussed in subsequent parts of this section. Additionally, the conceptual nomenclature for theorizing and discussing these conditions is changing as well, grounded in large part in the realization that certain social conditions can be experienced and/or seen as disruptive or threatening without generating social breakdown or chaos. The title of this section and the three included selections reflect these changes.

Before summarizing these selections, several cautionary considerations should be kept in mind. First, we do not assume that people respond automatically, in a stimulus/response-like fashion, to disrupting and threatening trends and events. Rather, as highlighted in Part 6, any response or action that evolves depends in part on interpretive, framing processes. At the same time, collective actors rarely, if ever, manufacture events entirely apart from the social context in which they find themselves. In other words, their framing of events is anchored in part in some set of experienced or perceived empirical conditions. Here we highlight a number of facilitative unsettling conditions that have been associated empirically with movement emergence.

In the first selection, Snow, Cress, Downey, and Jones provide an alternative conceptualization of traditional breakdown theory by contending that it is not associational ties and bonds of solidarity that are disrupted or broken in the face of unsettling social conditions or events, but rather patterns of everyday functioning and routinized expectancies associated with those patterns. The core argument is that actual or threatened disruption of taken-for-granted routines and attitudes of everyday life, referred to as "the quotidian," is especially generative of mobilizing grievances because it renders problematic and uncertain previously habituated ways of doing daily life. Snow and his colleagues also argue that some types of conditions or events are more unsettling and disruptive of the quotidian than others. One such category of disruptive events includes accidents and disasters. A second category includes intrusions into or violations of culturally defined areas of privacy and control, such as community or neighborhood spaces, by strangers or outsiders. A third set of events conducive to quotidian disruption involves dramatic alterations to subsistence routines because of changes in the ratio of resources to claimants or demand. The fourth set of disruptive events involves dramatic changes in structures of social organization and control, as when tightly regimented systems of control are displaced and routinized patterns of hierarchy and patronage are disrupted, or when there are significant changes in policing practices resulting in the monitoring, harassment, and arrest of individuals engaging in patterns of behavior not previous criminalized. These four types of quotidian-disrupting events or conditions are elaborated upon and illustrated with the research findings of numerous studies of a variety of movements across time and place.

The second selection provides an elaborated example of how changes in the ratio of resources to demand can alter quotidian subsistence patterns by focusing on the sometimes disruptive effects of population change. At least since the time of Thomas Malthus, the late eighteenth- and early nineteenth-century British economist who proposed a causal link between population growth and hunger and poverty, some observers of social movements have assumed that significant population increases will increase the scale of poverty to such a degree that social movement activity will escalate as well. Today, it is generally agreed that there is little direct connection between human suffering and the rise of social movements to alleviate that suffering. However, the absence of a direct link between population growth and social movement activity does not rule out the possibility of a more indirect association. Jack Goldstone takes this position in the second selection, arguing that state breakdown and revolution in early modern agrarian-bureaucratic states in both Europe and Asia were stimulated by dramatic population growth. In his examination of state breakdown in England between 1640 and 1642, for example, he found that the English population grew from just over 2 million to more than 5 million between 1500 and 1650 and that London alone grew from 50,000 to 400,000 inhabitants during the same period. Goldstone does not advocate a simple demographic approach, however. Instead, he sees the association between demographic change and state breakdown and revolutionary social movement activity as more nuanced, as reflected in his linkage of population change in England and elsewhere to declining state revenues and fiscal crisis, elite competition and turnover, and an increase in the mobilization potential of the masses. The selection included from his book, *Revolution and Rebellion in the Early Modern World*, clarifies his position, which he calls a structural-demographic model of state breakdown and revolution.

Even though Goldstone's model incorporates a number of interconnected factors, demographic change remains the starting point of the process and the unifying theme of the analysis. Moreover, he establishes population growth as the pivotal factor. However, it is important to note that demographic change associated with social movement emergence may sometimes entail population decline rather than growth, as revealed by research on the relationship between population change among Native Americans and the Ghost Dance Movement of 1890 (Thornton 1981).

In the final selection of Part 1, Nella Van Dyke and Sarah Soule examine the mobilizing effect of various types of threat triggered by structural changes in relation to patriot/militia movement organizing in the UnitedStates in the 1990s. In particular, they seek to account for variation in state-level counts of patriot/militia groups and find that economic restructuring, measured by a decrease in manufacturing jobs and the decline of the family farm, affected the mobilization of these movement groups in the 1990s. This finding was also reaffirmed by an analysis of the patriot/militia groups across 300 U.S. counties. Together, these findings not only help to illuminate the reasons for the emergence of the patriot/militia movement in the 1990s, but also underscore empirically the importance of including measures of disruptive events and threats in our theorization of social movement emergence.

Considered together, the three selections that make up this section provide compelling theoretical and empirical justification for retaining remnants of strain theory refashioned in terms of unsettling quotidian disruptions and threats.

I.

Disrupting the "Quotidian": Reconceptualizing the Relationship Between Breakdown and the Emergence of Collective Action

DAVID A. SNOW, DANIEL M. CRESS, LIAM DOWNEY, AND ANDREW W. JONES

One of the older and more persistent ideas in the study of social movements is that movements have their origins in troublesome, unsettling social conditions, traditionally conceptualized as "strains." Over twenty years ago, in a review essay on strands of theory and research in collective behavior. Marx and Wood not only used the strain concept as one of their organizing themes, but concluded that the "term strain should be retained as [a] basic analytic category," and that "greater specification of the strain-movement link...is needed" (1975: 380, 382). In the same year, somewhat ironically, the Tillys (1975) made their now widely cited distinction between "breakdown" and "solidaristic" theories of collective action. Since then, the breakdown metaphor has supplanted the strain metaphor as a way of thinking about one set of conditions underlying the origins of collective action. Today, neither strain theory nor the various strains that were once posited to be associated with movement emergence receive much attention. The breakdown alternative, although bandied about in some of the literature, has not fared much better. Indeed, it appears as if it is a candidate for the dustbin of failed social science theories. Not only was its death knell apparently sounded when Tilly announced that the relevant ideas of Durkheim, the perspective's founding father, were "useless" (1981: chapter 4), but since then the bulk of social movement research has been animated by other theoretical and empirical concerns, namely those having to

do with resource mobilization, political opportunity, framing processes, and collective identity.[1] In each instance, the traditional concern with the link between strains or breakdown and movement emergence is either secondary or sidestepped altogether.

Both the tendency to treat strains and breakdown as different metaphors for the same phenomena and the now popular assumption that the link between breakdown and movement emergence is misguided are unfortunate in several respects. For one thing, strain and breakdown are not isomorphic. The strain concept is broader and more inclusive. Breakdown, as used in the literature, is clearly a variant of strain, but not all strains can be subsumed under the rubric of breakdown. For example, conflict based on class, ethnic, and racial divisions could be construed as a variant of strain, but the underlying dynamic of intergroup tension is different from that associated with breakdown, as will be discussed shortly. Likewise, Smelser's (1962) concept of "structural strain"—one of the six necessary conditions purportedly underlying any instance of collective behavior—is broader than breakdown in that it covers all levels of social action. Secondly, the tendency to assume that breakdown bears no relationship to movement emergence is questionable because of the narrow way in which breakdown has been conceptualized. Additionally, a number of scholars have argued that the abandonment of breakdown theory is empirically premature (Piven and Cloward 1992: Useem 1980, 1985; Walsh 1981). Thus, Marx and Wood's (1975: 382) call for "greater specification of the strain-movement link" still remains current.

We attend to this call by conceiving of breakdown as a variant of strain broadly construed and by providing an alternative formulation of the

Snow, David A., Daniel Cress, Liam Downey, and Andrew Jones. 1998. Disrupting the Quotidian: Reconceptualizing the Relationship between Breakdown and the Emergence of Collective Action." *Mobilization: An International Journal* 3: 1–22. Reprinted by permission.

breakdown concept. We do this by reconceptualizing the linkage between social breakdown and movement emergence in a fashion that fits better with the realities of the empirical world, and then illuminate and ground this theoretical recasting with qualitative empirical materials drawn from our research as well as that of others. Our objective is neither to test existing theory nor elucidate a body of data with that theory, but to elaborate and illustrate the cornerstones of a different understanding of breakdown as it relates to movement emergence.

Our argument is that the key to the relationship between breakdown and movement emergence resides in the "quotidian" and its actual or threatened disruption. The term quotidian derives from Latin and refers to the routines of daily life or what in sociology today is called "everyday life." We contend that the kind of breakdown most likely to be associated with movement emergence is that which penetrates and disrupts, or threatens to disrupt, taken-for-granted, everyday routines and expectancies.

In order to better understand this hypothesized link between quotidian disruption and movement emergence, we draw on prospect theory in cognitive psychology (Kahneman and Tversky 1979: Tversky and Kahneman 1981). Prospect theory argues that individuals are especially averse to loss and therefore will endure considerably more risk in order to preserve what they already have than they will in order to gain something new. In the more formal language of prospect theory, individuals are said to be especially risk-seeking in the contexts of loss because losses are felt more keenly as disutility than gains are felt as utility. Since quotidian disruptions constitute contexts of loss, we contend that they are especially likely to be generative of social movement activity.

In postulating this linkage, we do not assume that quotidian disruption covers all underlying conditions that people seek to redress through social movements. Rather, we see quotidian disruption as encompassing only one set of underlying conditions that is associated with the emergence of only one category of movements. Thus, the argument we propound should be construed as but one step in a broader project that seeks to specify the relationship between different strain-like conditions and movement emergence.

Critical Overview of Breakdown Theory

The traditional orienting premise of breakdown theory holds that all varieties of collective action—including riots, civil disorder, social movements, and revolution—are by-products of rapid social change and disintegration. The formula advanced to account for disintegration and change varies somewhat from writer to writer, but the core argument is much the same: the sources of social cohesion and integration are weakened or destroyed by war, economic crisis, disaster, and other large-scale structural rearrangements. These cause ruptures or strains in the sociopolitical order and give rise to tensions and frustrations which incite collective action. Embedded within this orienting premise are two assumptions often associated with alternative theoretical perspectives. One focuses on the structural manifestation of breakdown at the mesolevel, as reflected in mass society theory with its emphasis on the loosening of social ties and constraints that presumably bind citizens to the larger system (Coleman 1971; Kornhauser 1959). The central idea is that individuals become more available for movement participation as their ties and commitments to community are weakened or severed. The second perspective is more individually-oriented, focusing on the social psychological consequences of disaffiliation and disintegration, which often are conceptualized as variants of alienation, deprivation, or status inconsistency. While these two perspectives are often treated as if they are disconnected, they are linked logically and theoretically inasmuch as the latter is a function or consequence of the former (Seeman 1972). Thus, the classical breakdown hypothesis is that individuals are rendered susceptible to participation in various forms of collective action by processes of social disintegration.

Although this perspective was the dominant account of movement emergence throughout the first two thirds of the twentieth century, it fell out of favor during the latter third of the century. Disenchantment was based on a number of vexing observations and issues. The first is that societies are seldom, if ever, in a state of harmonious equilibrium. Conflicts, uncertainties, and other perturbations are constant features of social life and, therefore, cannot account for the waxing and waning of social movement activity (McCarthy and Zald 1977: 1214–1215). The second vexing issue is that there is no determinant relationship between breakdown conceptualized as disintegration and disaffiliation and social movement activity (Marx and Wood 1975: 380).

Equally troubling, the breakdown model has not fared well when subjected to empirical scrutiny. At the macrolevel, Tilly and his associates (Tilly, Tilly, and Tilly 1975; Tilly 1986) have found little support for the breakdown thesis in several European countries. Their research suggests that while large-scale changes associated with industrialization altered patterns of social organization, it was new forms of organization, with new bonds of solidarity, that were carriers of collective action. Tilly and his associates thus proffered a solidarity model of collective action in lieu of the breakdown model. Relatedly, analyses at the meso- and microlevel have been equally unsupportive of the breakdown model. Collective action participants, rather than being disconnected and socially isolated, are typically integrated into the community in terms of both primary and secondary associations. Indeed, one of the most firmly established findings among social movement scholars is that preexisting network linkages, both interpersonal and organizational, function to channel recruitment to and participation in social movement activity (Gould 1991: McAdam 1986: Snow, Zurcher, Ekland-Olson 1980).

Finally, breakdown theory has been a victim of various fads and fashions that have been operative within the study of collective behavior and social movements as well as sociology more generally (Lofland 1990; Lofland 1993). Two outcomes of these processes are particularly relevant to the fate of breakdown theory. One Ignores the questions raised by the perspective even if its answers may be empirically off track: the other scraps the perspective in its entirety because it is not in accord with more fashionable currents of work, such as those associated with the resource mobilization and political opportunity perspectives.

These various observations and currents have resulted in generalized disinterest in the hypothesized linkage between breakdown and movement emergence. Not everyone has jumped on the bandwagon, however, as there are a few voices of discontent. Some argue that critics have prematurely dismissed breakdown approaches because they have misspecified the dependent variable—norm-violating collective action (Piven and Cloward 1992). Others have empirically demonstrated the relevance of breakdown concepts for understanding nuclear accidents, antibusing movements, and prison riots (Walsh 1981; Useem 1980, 1985). Both of these cases suggest that it is premature to jettison the breakdown perspective.

Based on our reading of this literature and our research on the emergence of social movements among the homeless across the country, we agree that the baby has been thrown out with the bath water and that the breakdown metaphor continues to have analytic utility. Our aim is to reconsider the issue of breakdown, not by reassessing empirically the classical breakdown argument, but by reconceptualizing the breakdown concept so that it is directly relevant to everyday lives and routines. This reconceptualization is empirically consistent with an array of research on the emergence of collective action, and is compatible with the idea of solidarity.

The Quotidian and Its Disruption

The term quotidian derives from Latin and refers to the routines of daily life. It is our contention, as well as that of a number of other students of collective action (Flacks 1988: Johnston 1991; Lefebyre 1971: Roberts and Kloss 1979), that the kinds of dislocations most likely to be associated with collective action mobilization are those that disrupt or threaten to disrupt the quotidian—that is, the taken-for-granted substrate of everyday life. As Johnston observed in his analysis of the development of broad-based opposition to the Franco regime in the Catalonia region of Spain from 1939 to 1979: "no grievances" were "more pressing or meaningful than the ones grounded in everyday experience, especially the ones that render(ed) the routine accomplishments of daily business problematic" (Johnston 1991:54). Likewise, Flacks contends that "the most likely circumstance in which collective mobilization occurs is a situation of perceived threat to accustomed patterns of everyday life" (1988: 71).[2]

Although these discussions highlight the link between mobilization and quotidian disruption, they do not extend the theoretical implications of their observations. Furthermore, they tend to gloss everyday life inasmuch as they do not clearly specify the key constituent parts that are disrupted. Borrowing on strands of cultural theory, phenomenology, and symbolic interactionism, we conceptualize everyday life in terms of two constituent dimensions: daily practices or routines, and the natural attitude. The empirical referent for daily practices are the routinized patterns of making do, such as daily subsistence routines and chores, that are often performed in an almost habituated, unthinking fashion (Bourdieu 1977; Foucault 1983; Williams 1973). They will vary for people situated differently in the social structure, of course. The habituated routines of middle- and upper-middle class homeowners, for example, will be strikingly different from those of lower-class folks. Even groups on the margins, such as the homeless, may develop daily subsistence routines. These routines may be economically, politically, or morally aberrant and demeaning, but they may be pursued in a predictable and habituated fashion suggestive of a taken-for-granted moral order (Snow and Anderson 1993).

The natural attitude (Schutz 1962, 1964)—also referred to as the attitude of everyday life (Berger and Luckmann 1966)—is the cognitive component of the quotidian. It refers to the customary orientation of people in the course of everyday life, to their routinized expectancies. It is characterized by what Schutz (1962, 1964) called the "suspension of doubt." This means that things are taken-for-granted; they are not seen as problematic; they are approached and accomplished in an almost unreflective and mechanical manner. Schutz contrasts this natural attitude to a scientific attitude, which is characterized by the "suspension of belief." such that what-

ever one was doing, or had grown accustomed to, is now problematic. Whereas the natural attitude is associated with a sense that "nothing unusual is happening" (Emerson 1970), the scientific attitude is associated with the sense that something out of the ordinary is occurring or is about to occur. When this happens outside of the organizational context of routine science, it is because the natural attitude is disrupted and things can no longer be taken-for-granted.

The quotidian thus refers to the state of being in which things are done in a taken-for-granted way; it involves the routinization of everyday life both behaviorally and cognitively. It is analogous to what Mead referred to as the "specious present" (1938: 220–223) and can be contrasted to what might be thought of us the problematic present. In the specious present doubts, uncertainties, and inhibitions are not at the forefront of consciousness, and action is largely habituated and routinized (see Miller 1973: 38–41): in the problematic present action is inhibited, routine is stymied, and uncertainties emerge. The problematic present thus arises when the specious present, or the quotidian, is disrupted.

When the quotidian is disrupted, then, routinized patterns of action are rendered problematic and the natural attitude is fractured. Routines and understandings associated with everyday patterns of making do are now matters of doubt, uncertainty, and sometimes even confusion. Since this disruption can occur at a purely individual level, as when one gets into a traffic accident and becomes excessively anxious about driving, it is necessary, if collective action is to occur, that the disruption be experienced collectively and its repair through institutional channels be seen as unlikely.

The question arises as to whether there are some kinds of events that are more likely than others to lead to the disruption of the quotidian in a fashion conducive to the emergence of social movement activity. We have identified four such categories of events: community disrupting accidents and disasters; actual or threatened intrusion into or violation of culturally defined zones of privacy and control; alteration of taken-for-granted subsistence routines as a result of an emergent disparity between available resources and resource demand; and dramatic changes in structures of social control. Drawing on literature on the emergence of collective action in a variety of contexts and on the findings of our study of homeless mobilization in eight U.S. cities during the 1980s and early 1990s we elaborate and ground empirically these four categories of disrupting events and specify their linkage to movement emergence.[3]

Events Conducive to Quotidian Disruption
Quotidian Disrupting Accidents

One category of disrupting events includes accidents that throw a community's routines into doubt and/or that threaten a community's existence. One widely researched accident that had this effect was the 1979 partial meltdown of a nuclear reactor in the Three Mile Island area of eastern Pennsylvania. Walsh (1981, 1988) did extensive research on the communities in the area and described citizens' responses, both individual and collective. Among his findings, three are particularly pertinent to our thesis. First, a number of antinuclear organizations were operative in the area prior to the accident, but they "had little success mobilizing the local population against the twin reactors of the island" until after the accident (Walsh 1981: 18). The near-meltdown shattered, albeit temporarily, the daily routines of many residents. Not only were "more than 200,000 people within a twenty-five mile radius of TMI evacuated during the first few days of the accident" (Walsh 1988: 37), but the accident and evacuation left many residents with a sense that their personal lifeworlds were crumbling before their very eyes. As one resident put it: "On Friday, all hell broke loose" (Walsh 1988: 39). And another added that "Friday stands out in my mind as a day of chaos I could never again live through" (Walsh 1988: 41). As a result of this chaos, Walsh noted: "Evacuees left large portions of themselves behind—not only their homes and all the memories associated with them, but also their jobs, neighbors, and many other personal symbols of meaningful existence" (1988: 42). Even social support personnel, who were charged with encouraging their clients trust in public officials, could not withstand the thoroughly disruptive character of the accident. As one mental health therapist recalled:

I reassured a patient in my Thursday evening group who was very upset about events at the island, suggesting that his fears were exaggerated. As it turned out, his fear was quite legitimate and I was wrong for trying to eliminate it. I've lost so much with that accident! I've much less trust in public officials at all levels. I just don't know what to believe any more... (Walsh 1988: 43).

As noted above, prior to the TMI accident, local antinuclear organizations had trouble recruiting volunteers. After the accident, however, many residents attended public meetings concerning TMI and became active in anti-TMI and antinuclear organizations. Thus, "the accident and evacuation were central to the transformation of conservative TMI communities into hotbeds of antinuclear activism" (Walsh 1988: 61).

The second observation of Walsh's pertinent to our thesis concerns his phrase "suddenly imposed grievances" to capture the sense of immediate threat that the accident posed to the surrounding communities (1981: 18) Walsh argues that insofar as grievances are sudden, they are more likely to trigger collection action, and that accidents are particularly likely to generate sudden grievances. However, we contend that the emphasis on "suddenness" glosses what is critical about such accidents: it is not their suddenness that generates collective action but rather the disruption of the daily order of things. This was clearly indicated by the finding that those who evacuated during the emergency period were more likely to become anti-TMI activists than those "who remained home during the emergency period" (1988: 158). Thus, those whose lives were most disrupted during the emergency period, and whose cognitive templates were most likely to be fractured, were the ones most likely to become activists.

Lastly, we agree with Walsh's contention that any number of technical accidents attributable to human negligence and error, such as oil spills, could generate grievances associated with collective action (Walsh 1981: 18), but only insofar as the accidents are disruptive of the quotidian. Those that are not, no matter how sudden their materialization, are not likely to generate grievances associated with collective action. The other proviso, that

Walsh acknowledges, is that responsibility for the accident be attributable to human agency rather than forces of nature or "acts of God." This is partly an issue of social construction and framing, but not fully. Previous research on collective blaming has found repeatedly that it is most likely to occur when the incident in question can be clearly attributed to human negligence or error (Bucher 1957; Drabek and Quarantelli 1967).

In light of these observations, we suggest the following proposition regarding the relationship among accidents, quotidian disruption, and collective action:

> 1. Accidents are especially likely to generate collective action insofar as they (a) disrupt the quotidian, and (b) can be attributed in human negligence and/ or error rather than to natural forces or "acts of God."

Intrusion into or Violation of the Protective Surround or *Umwelt*

A second category of disruptive events is constituted by actual or threatened intrusions into or violations of what Goffman (1971) referred to as the immediate protective surround or *Umwelt.* The concept of *Umwelt* is borrowed from ethologists to refer the area around animals within which there is a sense of ease and safety unless signals of alarm indicate otherwise (Goffman 1971: 248–256). Extended to humans, the *Umwelt* can be thought of as a culturally elastic zone of privacy and control regarded as out of bounds to the uninvited, strangers, and corporate and governmental agents. It is a kind of culturally protective bubble that defines a set of choices and actions as the sacred province of those within this bubble or zone. Words such as "family," "home," and "neighborhood" insinuate the existence of such culturally inviolable zones, as evidenced by the tendency within moral philosophy, literature and poetry, and law to regard their actual or threatened violation as taboo and almost sacrilege.[4] Thus, assuming citizens' family, home, and neighborhood are regarded in a similar fashion, their intrusion and/or violation constitute quotidian disruption and the stuff of which social movements are born.

Examples of this phenomenon are abundant. Mothers Against Drunk Driving, emerged after a grieving and outraged mother whose teenage daughter was killed by a drunken driver began to organize against this kind of slaughter of innocent loved ones and bystanders. The movement was not just against drunk driving, but extended the reach of parents to protect their unsuspecting children (McCarthy 1994). Similarly, antibusing movements surfaced in many cities across the country in the 1970s in an attempt of parents to regain control of what they saw as fundamental to both parenthood and family: the decision of where one's children should and can go to school (Rubin 1972; Useem 1980). The point in both cases is that there is a kind of parental *Umwelt* that expands and contracts with the coming and going of children, and when that is threatened or violated, parents are likely to act to regain control and reconstitute that protective bubble or zone.

Further illustration is provided by community and neighborhood movements that cluster together under the acronym NIMBY, which stands for "not in my backyard." Across the country, proposed halfway houses, group homes, restitution centers, soup kitchens and shelters, and toxic waste dumps have all prompted NIMBY mobilization. Why? Because such facilities and/or the people they serve are perceived, rightly or wrongly, as direct threats to the community or neighborhood *Umwelt,* and thus to the quotidian. This is clearly illustrated in Snow and Anderson's discussion of the relocation efforts of Austin's Salvation Army (Sally) in the mid-1980s.

> The path to a new site was thorny, engendering rancorous community opposition as it wound its way through one prospective neighborhood after another.... Underlying citizen opposition to the "frightening possibility" of the Sally relocating nearby was the repeatedly voiced fear that "thousands of womenless, homeless men" would inundate their neighborhoods and "rob their homes" and "rape the women." Thus, in one prospective neighborhood, signs were hung on the door asking, "Do you want your women raped and your children mauled." In another, residents appeared before the city council carrying placards that rend "Vagrance (sic) and kids don't mix," and gave testimony,

Table 1. The Relationship Between Resources, Demand, and Collective Action

	CLAIMANTS/DEMAND	
RESOURCES	Constant	Increase
Constant	(1) No Disruption CA Unlikely	(3) Disruption CA Likely
Decrease	(2) Disruption CA Likely	(4) Disruption CA Likely

highlighting the threat to women and children posed by the homeless (1993: 97).

The result of the successive surges of neighborhood protest was that the Salvation Army was neither relocated in or nearby residential neighborhoods. Residents could therefore resume their daily routines in the manner to which they had grown accustomed.

In the case of NIMBY mobilization, busing boycotts, and citizens' movements against drunk driving, collective action participants perceived themselves, their families, and their neighborhoods as being violated and victimized by intrusive citizens, or by corporate or governmental initiatives, in a fashion that threatens citizens' control of their own lives and thus disruption of the quotidian. Hence, the following proposition:

> 2. Actual or threatened intrusion into culturally defined zones of privacy and control by strangers, uninvited persons, corporate and/or governmental agents is likely, all else being equal, to generate collective action to reestablish the zone of privacy and control.

Changes in Taken-For-Granted Subsistence Routines

Other events that are equally disruptive of the quotidian involve dramatic alterations in subsistence routines because of a decrease in available resources relative to resources demand. Demand may change due to variations in routinized expectations or as a result of increases or decreases in the number of resource claimants.[5] Taking these sources of demand fluctuation into account, there are at least three major ways in which the taken-for-granted ratio of resources to demand varies. As shown in table 1: resources decline while demand remains

relatively constant (cell 2); demand increases while resources remain relatively constant (cell 3); or resources decline while demand increases (cell 4). In each of the situations, the quotidian is disrupted inasmuch as people find that they can no longer make do in the fashion to which they have grown accustomed. Below we clarify the disjunction between resources and demand by illustrating Cells 2 and 3. *Resources Decline But Claimants Remain Constant,* Much of the literature on peasant rebellions and movements highlights the centrality of a declining resource base, and resultant alteration in subsistence routines and expectancies, in relation to collective action (Paige 1975; Scott 1976; Wolf 1969). A case in point is Scott's (1976) examination of events leading up to peasant rebellions in colonial Vietnam and Lower Burma in 1930 and 1931. Scott notes that the peasant is not troubled so much by economic exploitation so long as there are enough resources to meet subsistence needs. Since reliable subsistence is the "primordial goal of the peasant cultivator," the peasant asks "how much is left before he asks how much is taken" (Scott 1976: 5, 31). Thus, Scott argues that it is not exploitation or deprivation per se that is unsettling to the peasant, but actual or threatened disruptions to the peasants' subsistence routines.

> As peasants experience it, then, the *manner* of exploitation may well make all the difference in the world. Forms of exploitation that tend to offer built-in subsistence security and which, in this sense, adapt themselves to the central dilemma of peasant economies are...far less maligned than claims which are heedless of minimum peasant standards (Scott 1976: 32).

Thus, state taxation and landlord claims to peasant harvests that vary according to the size of the harvest are more palatable to peasants than inflexible, fixed claims and taxes that appropriate the same amount of peasant wealth regardless of harvest size. In Lower Burma, for example, the Saya San rebellion erupted in December 1930 just after an economic crisis hit the region and just before the collection of the capitation tax:

> It was not a question of outright starvation.... Rather it meant a massive and collective decline in a standard of living and an economic security which had for some time been deteriorating. It meant for many a precipitate fall from smallholding or tenancy into the ranks of day labors. It meant for tenants a dramatic worsening of their terms of exchange with landowners as rents held steady against their diminishing income and customary production credit was revoked (Scott 1976: 151).

Based on such observations, Scott concludes that change or exploitation is likely to be particularly volatile when it "threatens existing subsistence arrangements" (1976: 193)—which is to say that collective action, at least in the locates studied, was most likely when, all other things being equal, daily routines were disrupted.

The same dynamic was operative in the food riots and protests of urban and rural poor in early modern Europe (Rudé 1964; Tilly 1975, 1979: Thompson 1971). Writing about the French rural riots of the 18th century, Rudé (1964) notes that they were typically occasioned by food shortages that threatened hunger.

> In fact, whenever harvests were bad, or when the needs of war or a breakdown in communication led to shortage, hoarding, or panic buying, a large part of the rural population, like their fellows in the cities, were threatened with hunger; and on such occasions many would demonstrate in markets or at bakers' shops, or resort to more violent action by stopping food convoys on the roads and rivers, pillaging supplies, or compelling shopkeepers, millers, farmers, and merchants to sell their wares at lower prices, or the authorities to intervene on behalf of the small consumers (1964: 21).

Although Rudé did not explicitly use the language of quotidian disruption, there can be no doubt that is what was at issue. Nothing was more fundamental

to the subsistence of the rural populace of this era than the stable provision of food.

A final illustration of the link between collective action and resource loss is provided by the various farmers' movements that surfaced throughout the south and the midwest in the U.S. in the late 1800s. Although local and regional factors accounted for differences among some of these movements, most were responding in part to broader, national changes that made it increasingly difficult for farmers to pursue their livelihood in a fashion they had grown accustomed to and come to take for granted. As McNall (1988) found in his study of the Farmer's Alliance in Kansas, farmers were confronted with the confluence of forces that altered dramatically the character of their livelihood. The socioeconomic forces included: wealthy railroad companies that charged high rates for transporting farm goods and often monopolized available grain elevators; railroad lines and speculators who controlled so much high quality farm land that farmers often had to buy land from them at inflated prices; and an impersonal market that made the link between hard work and survival even more tenuous than it otherwise would have been. McNall also notes that the situation of farmers was worsened by the demonetization of silver in the mid-1870s which resulted in a six-year depression that lowered the price farmers received for their crops. But McNall makes clear that farmers were responding to more than just a drop in the price of their crops:

> The farmer was reacting to a commodification of land, labor, and money, to the shift from a system in which he produced for local markets to one in which his welfare was dependent on his being a businessman (1988: 45).

In short, what in the past yielded satisfactory subsistence for the midwestern farmer no longer did so. He now had to do things differently in order to survive. The result was the flowering of the Farmer's Alliance movement and support for the burgeoning Populist Party. As in the previous cases, we here see that it is not socioeconomic forces per se that lead to collective action, but primarily dramatic alterations in or loss of the taken-for-granted ways of life.

Together, these illustrations suggest the following proposition about the relationship among resource base, quotidian disruption, and collective action:

> 3. Alteration in taken-for-granted subsistence routines and expectancies due to a declining resource base is likely, all else being equal, to be associated with the emergence of collective action that seeks to restore the previous balance between resource level and subsistence routines.

Claimants Increase But Resources Remain Constant. Collective action may also occur when claimants can no longer pursue their daily routines because their numbers exceed available resources. In other words, because the carrying capacity of the socioeconomic environment has been stretched by an increasing number of claimants, taken-for-granted subsistence routines are disrupted. In many respects, this disjunction between claimants and resources is at the core of Goldstone's (1991) demographic/structural explanation of popular uprisings and state breakdown in Eurasia from 1500 to 1850.

> Put simply, large agrarian states of this period were not equipped to deal with the impact of the steady growth of population that then began throughout northern Eurasia, eventually amounting to population increases in excess of the productivity gains of the land (Goldstone 1991: 24).

This process made it increasingly difficult for large numbers of people to subsist in their accustomed, albeit meager, fashion. As well, certain classes of people could no longer assume their taken-for-granted roles. Employment for the professional classes and state jobs for nobility, for example, became highly uncertain as mounting population pressures taxed state authority. In turn, these disrupted expectancies and routines facilitated the involvement of these classes in revolutionary activity.

This disparity between an increasing number of claimants and their resource base was strikingly evident in our research on homeless social movement activity across American cities in the 1980s and early 1990s. In our fieldwork among fifteen homeless social movement organizations in eight U.S. cities, we found that in ten of the cases initial mobilization was prompted in part or fully by the disruption of either individual or organizational routines.[6]

In the case of the disruption of individual routines, the typical scenario was that one or more homeless individuals found it increasingly difficult to negotiate their daily routines, and that this jolt became a kind of consciousness-raising experience that pushed some in the direction of collective action. Because of increasing numbers of homeless claimants, taken-for-granted routines, such as standing in line at soup kitchens and shelters, no longer guaranteed the expected outcome. One service provider in Philadelphia explained this when discussing a homeless individual who helped begin both the local homeless movement and the National Union of the Homeless:

> To get into the shelter, you had to wait in line, and if they fill up, you're just out of luck. Now these lines were not well supervised, so the bigger guys would fight their way in. Chris is a big guy, and it really ripped him up to have to fight other men so that he could sleep indoors on a floor.

It was in response to this "survival of the fittest" ambience that rendered questionable previously taken-for-granted survival routines that the founder of the Philadelphia movement decided he had enough and began to appeal to other homeless individuals and selected social service providers that the time had come to organize. It was out of this experience that the National Union of the Homeless surfaced in Philadelphia in 1986, and began to reach out to homeless in other cities who were similarly experiencing a disruption of their subsistence routines.

Such cases are particularly interesting because they show that it was not the dire poverty and deprivation of homeless individuals that initially pushed them toward collective action: rather, it was the disruption of habituated survival routines occasioned by the disjunction between resource availability and increasing numbers of claimants. Had some of these individuals been able to continue to subsist in the manner to which they had become accustomed, presumably they would not have become initiators and organizers of collective action.

In the case of the emergence of a number of other homeless SMOs, it was the disruption of extent organizational routines that was pivotal. Street-level social service agencies attending to the subsistence needs of the homeless typically found that they were being overwhelmed by a disjunction between an escalating demand for their services and their ability to meet those demands because of a stagnant or declining resource base. They were experiencing a kind of system overload which made it exceedingly difficult to attend to the needs of their growing client pool and, more generally, to discharge their mission. It was in the face of this organizational disruption that agency leaders in five of the eight cities spearheaded the development of homeless collective action campaigns.

The emergence of the Alliance of the Streets, a homeless SMO in Minneapolis, is a case in point. Minneapolis, like many other cities, witnessed an explosion in its homeless population during the 1980s. While shelter capacity in Minneapolis grew tenfold during the decade, from one hundred beds in 1980 to over one thousand by 1989, the need for shelter space increased steadily each year as well, with most shelters operating at capacity. This was particularly true of "free" shelters, which were not under contract with the county and which were preferred by many homeless because there was less paperwork and they were smaller than the county shelters. As a result, the demand for free shelters often exceeded capacity.

Illustrative of this dilemma was St. Steven's shelter, a free shelter that housed thirty men per night. It first began sheltering homeless people in 1982, and added a meal program two years later, which increased the number of poor and homeless receiving services. But even this expansion was not sufficient, as St. Steven's shelter and food programs became increasingly inundated with poor and homeless people in need of services. Not only was the mission of the church being challenged, but so was the subsistence of its growing constituency. Thus, as the ranks of the homeless increased and the demand for resources exceeded their availability, the need for collective action to help combat the problem became increasingly evident. And it was in this context that Alliance of the Streets was

born in the spring of 1986. Founded with the assistance of St. Steven's and led by homeless residents of the shelter. The SMO immediately began working against the destruction of low-cost housing, for the improvement of police-homeless relations, and for the provision of more resources for facilities such as St. Steven's.

A similar disparity existed in Tueson, where increasing numbers of homeless people during the 1980s overwhelmed the local social service system. The locus of homeless movement activity occurred in the orbit of the local Catholic Worker community known as Casa Maria. As a lay ministry dedicated to living the social gospel, Casa Maria had a history of participation in peace and justice concerns, including the sanctuary movement, the antinuclear movement, and divestment from South Africa. In addition, they operated a soup kitchen and clothing closet for the local poor.

In 1985, three events prompted Casa Maria to redefine the focus of its ministry. First, there was a dramatic increase in the numbers of people eating lunch at the soup kitchen. This coincided with a much publicized United Way report estimating the number of homeless people in Tueson had grown by several thousand. A short time later, another local soup kitchen was closed because of public outcry over "the climate of fear" caused by the increasing numbers of homeless people congregating in the area (Hostetler 1986). This functioned as a significant consciousness-raising event for Casa Maria. As one of its leaders explained: "With the closing of St. Martin's we realized that there was a prevailing hostile attitude toward the homeless and that attitude needed to be fought."

The increasing numbers of homeless people strained the resources of the kitchen, highlighted the dire conditions of Tueson's expanding poor population, and underscored the limitations of service provision for affecting change. These events, coupled with St. Martin's closing, combined to alter business as usual at Casa Maria. The result was a shift in Casa Maria's generalized activism to concentrated concern with the poverty and injustice experienced by the homeless. As another leader put it: "We had been focusing on all these grand global issues like apartheid. But we began to realize that apartheid was happening right here in front of us." Thus, Casa Maria began organizing homeless people in the latter part of 1986. Out of that effort, the Tueson Union of the Homeless was born.

In both Minneapolis and Tueson, as well as in other cities, homeless collective action was spawned by the disruption of organizational routines that resulted from a kind of system overload. These service organizations simply could not accommodate the growing number of homeless given their insufficient resource base.

Thus, in the cases of both homeless individuals and agencies that were initiators of homeless social movement activity, the turning point was those events that disrupted the quotidian. Accordingly, we suggest the following proposition:

> 4. Alteration in taken-for-granted subsistence routines and expectancies due to an increase in claimants (demand) in relation to available resources is likely, all else being equal, to be associated with the emergence of collective action that seeks to redress the imbalance between claimants and resources.

Dramatic Changes in Structures of Social Control

A fourth way in which quotidian disruption may lead to collective action is when everyday routines are shattered by dramatic changes in existing structures of social organization and control. This is especially likely when structures of control are highly regimented, as is typically the case in the context of total institutions, such as asylums and prisons. What makes these contexts vulnerable to changes in the basis of control is that daily routines and rhythms are carefully synchronized with the system of control.

This finely tuned relationship and its vulnerability to disruption by changes in control is evident in research on prison insurrections and riots. Useem and Kimball's (1991) study of U.S. prison riots in the 1970s and 1980s is especially illustrative, as several of the riots studied—Joliet and West Virginia— were clearly triggered by changes in existing structures of control. Inmate life in the Joliet prison in Illinois was controlled informally but fairly tightly by four inmate gungs from late 1969 to December

1974. Prisoners there had more freedoms than in many other prisons, but only insofar as those freedoms were in accord with the interests of the dominant gangs. Moreover, gang members had better lives than non-gang members, who sometimes had to pay protection money, run gang emends, or provide sexual favors to gang members. This system of informal control was rooted in the warden's creation of an inmate council to increase inmate-administration communications. However, the council was dominated by the gangs, and its executive committee members were allowed to move freely throughout the prison. Other gang members were given special privileges such as photo service and soft drinks. Moreover, one gang, the Blackstone Rangers, was able to get itself recognized as a religious organization called Benl-Zaken. Since Joliet allowed inmates unlimited visits with religious leaders, the leader of the Rangers both inside and outside the prison was able to spend eight hours a day, three to four days a week, meeting with non-inmate gang members posing as Beni-Zaken ministers. This allowed the Ranger leader to maintain power in Joliet, as well as in other prisons and on the streets of Chicago. As a result, gang members "openly defied guards…staff was fearful of coming to work" and sometimes, "Joliet officials dismissed disciplinary charges to avoid precipitating a riot" (Useem and Kimball 1991: 62).

A riot occurred in April 1975, however, shortly after a new warden came aboard in December 1974. The new warden immediately began to curtail inmate freedoms and dismantle the structure of informal control by gang members, and soon afterwards prisoners rebelled. As Useem and Kimball note, it was a "reversal of this policy [that] precipitated the rebellion" (1991: 59). Thus, the riot was triggered by changes in the structure of control that altered dramatically the routine grounds of everyday inmate life.

A change in wardens and methods of social control in the West Virginia Penitentiary similarly resulted in the breakdown of everyday routines that culminated in the 1986 inmate takeover of the prison. In 1979 a new warden came aboard after fifteen prisoners had escaped due to extremely lax social control. Although the new warden was very strict, he gained the respect of both inmates and guards because of his scrutiny and enforcement of guard activity. Corrupt guards were fired, abusive treatment of inmates was banned, and inmates were granted more freedom to move about the prison. All of this changed in September 1985, when a stern and uncompromising deputy warden was promoted to warden. Among other things, he instituted a series of changes that included stricter visitation rules, a prohibition on packages from ex-inmates and family members, a new humiliating procedure for inmates in maximum security, and a reduction in the personal property inmates could have in their cells (Useem and Kimball 1991: 176–177). Fearing further changes in their daily prison lives, inmates rebelled and took over the prison on the evening of January 1, 1986.

These two cases clearly demonstrate how the alteration of interconnected systems of formal and informal control and associated daily routines can provide the impetus for collective action. Not only were everyday routines and taken-for-granted privileges disrupted in both prisons, but in one, changes in the structure of social control directly undermined the power of specific gangs and gang members who played a significant role in the eventual riot.

Dramatic changes in the control and policing of noninstitutionalized citizens can also spur mobilization when those changes alter or threaten to alter the routine grounds of everyday life. This was evident in the case of the homeless on a number of occasions in a number of cities. One of the initial mobilizations of homeless people in the Boston area, for example, was sparked by changes in policing practices with respect to the homeless hanging out in the Boston Common. This was explained by a leader of the Homeless Civil Rights Project (HCRP), a social movement organization that originally mobilized over civil liberty violations of the homeless:

> If you were up in the Boston Common and if you were perceived as homeless you were going to get kicked off the benches. You couldn't even sit. You didn't have to be drinking. They kicked you off

the benches because they didn't think it was your park.... The police had a guy who was infamous among homeless circles. He was called Robo Cop. He was a Boston motorcycle cop and his beat was the Common and downtown.... He was convinced that he had the right to kick you out of the park because it was his park and not yours. His other name was Officer Friendly because when he first came on to you, he'd say: "Hi guys, how are your doing today? You know, its a nice day. Listen, I'll be back in 10 minutes and you better be gone, okay?" Very nice, but when he come back 10 minutes later, he'd...manhandle you, arrest ya. And if you said, "Gee, I ain't doing nothing," he'd go into a trash barrel and come out with an empty bottle and say: "public drinking." [...] He absolutely terrorized people.

And in doing so, Robo Cop, along with the transit police who were patrolling the subway stations to keep the homeless out, not only disrupted the routines of the homeless in the Common's area, but made it difficult to establish a new set of routines. It was in response to this escalation of aggressive policing that HCRP was formed, with many of the targeted homeless joining its ranks.

Similarly, when the City Council of Tueson voted in March 1996 to shut down a long-time homeless encampment adjacent to a residential neighborhood, previously apathetic homeless individuals quickly mobilized to protest the decision and salvage their makeshift shantytown: One five-year resident of the camp asked rhetorically:

> What else can we do? If they boot us out, where are we going to go? This is all we have. We can't let the city take it from us without giving us another place to stay!

Taken together, the foregoing observations suggest the following proposition regarding the relationship among changes in structures of social control, quotidian disruption, and collective action:

> 5. Changes in structures of social control that necessitate abandonment or alteration of daily routines, and thereby disrupt the quotidian, are likely, all else being equal, to be associated with the emergence of collective action that seeks to thwart, rescind, or modify the new structure of control

Summary and Conclusions

In the preceding pages we have attempted to reconceptualize the relationship between social breakdown and movement emergence in a fashion that fits better with the realities of the empirical world, which is consistent with strands of cultural theory, phenomenology, and symbolic interactionism, and which resonates with research on the empirical locus of collective action in a diverse array of settings. Specifically, we have argued, first, that the key to understanding the relationship between breakdown and movement emergence resides in the actual or threatened disruption of the "quotidian"—that is, in the taken-for-granted routines of everyday life; and secondly, that four sets of conditions are especially likely to cause quotidian disruption. They include; accidents that throw a community's routines into doubt and/or threaten its existence; the actual or threatened intrusion into and/or violation of citizens sense of privacy, safety, and control; alteration in subsistence routines because of a decrease in the ratio of resources to claimants or demand; and dramatic changes in structures of social control. These events disrupt the quotidian and heighten the prospect of collective action.

Although we have elaborated empirically four sets of conditions that give rise to quotidian disruption and demonstrated their link to collective action, it is reasonable to ask why we should expect quotidian disruption to be an especially potent trigger of collective action, all other things being equal? The answer is provided in part by the conjunction of Tilly's (1978) theorization of the relationship between threat, opportunity, and collective action, and Kahneman and Tversky's prospect theory (1979; Tversky and Kahneman 1981). In exploring the relative contributions of threat and opportunity to collective action, Tilly suggests that the relationship is asymmetrical, with threat likely "to generate more collective action than the 'same' amount of opportunity" (1978: 134–135). From the vantage point of prospect theory, the reason for this is that individuals are especially risk-seeking in contexts of loss because losses are felt much more keenly as disutility than gains are felt as utility (Kahneman and Tversky 1979; Tversky and Kahneman 1981). When

applied to individuals experiencing actual or prospective quotidian disruption—clearly a context of loss—this suggests that they should be powerfully motivated to engage in collective action to reconstitute the quotidian and recoup what they have lost, or preserve the routinized order of things and thus protect what they have.

These observations, in conjunction with our hypotheses regarding quotidian disruption, help us to understand more fully various conditions associated with movement emergence. In particular, they suggest that much of what is theorized and asserted about rationality, political opportunities, framing processes, and collective identity may be subject to modification in the case of collective action that arises out of quotidian disruption and therefore may be overgeneralized.

First, the linkage of prospect theory and our conceptualization of quotidian disruption leads to a more nuanced and contextualized understanding of rationality than has generally been presented in the field. Consistent with Olson's free-rider dilemma (1965), prospect theory suggests that considerable effort is typically necessary to overcome thresholds to most collective action because people are averse to losing what they have in order to risk social movement involvement. Previous research and theory insinuates that situations are framed in a fashion that calls for collective action, collective identities are developed and deployed, and resources are mobilized in order to a overcome the loss aversion that potential participants will presumably experience. When the quotidian is disrupted, however, we suspect the calculus for action is reversed. Instead of movements needing to motivate individuals to overcome the risks often associated with movement participation, quotidian disruption is likely to provide sufficient motivation for participation. As Walder noted in his application of prospect theory to social movements, "those threatened with, or who are experiencing, a loss relative to their accustomed states are more likely than others to feel an acute sense of injustice and moral outrage, and will be more likely to engage in risky contributions to movements of protest" (1994: 9). Thus, prospect theory implies that social movement participants who are motivated by the loss of existing utility will have lower thresholds for collective action than participants in movements which promise the attainment new benefits in the future. At the same time, our hypotheses regarding the link between quotidian disruption and movement emergence refine the hypothesized relationship between prospect theory and collective action by specifying the kinds of contexts or situations in which loss is most likely to be felt.

Turning to the role of political opportunities in movement emergence and participation, our observations suggest that the perception of political opportunities and their objective reality may be quite variable across different categories of social movements. Since most movements that arise for reasons other than quotidian disruption pursue goals which have not yet been realized, individuals and groups are likely to calculate whether to participate by comparing what they stand to lose with what they are likely to gain. Since prospect theory predicts that people will be loss-averse, prospective participants in these movements will, hypothetically, be rather circumspect and conservative in assessing the political opportunities before them. Furthermore, to the extent that cultural work is necessary to alter the tendency to assess political opportunities conservatively and to lower thresholds for participation, movements not based on quotidian disruption should be rich in the cultural work of framing and identity construction. On the other hand, for movements prompted by quotidian disruption, political opportunities may well be exaggerated because of the prospect of loss. This appears to be what Kurzman (1996) found in his study of the Iranian Revolution, in which some participants perceived opportunities that did not objectively exist, end in the process helped to create them. "Liberals." he reports, "were highly sensitive to the structure of opportunities" (1996: 162), modifying their level of protest in tandem with the level of state repression; but the process was often reversed for religious traditionalists, for whom "acts of repression that hit close to home were a major source of revolutionary zeal" and increased militancy (1996: 161). This suggests that the assessment of political opportunities may very

dramatically between those challenging a regime to create a new society and those challenging it to restore a way of life, with the former sensitive to political opportunities due to their aversion to losing what they already have and the latter acting less cautiously towards political opportunities in an effort to restore what they once had.

The foregoing observations also help us to refine and contextunlize our understanding of framing processes in relation to social movements. First, our hypotheses suggest a modification of prospect theory's emphasis on the development of loss frames in relation to the likelihood of collective action (see Berejikian 1992). Inasmuch as individuals are likely to be especially risk-seeking in contexts of loss, we would agree that framing situations in terms of loss may be a necessary precondition for some collective action. However, our hypotheses suggest that such framing activity may be less important in some movement contexts than in others, namely in those situations characterized by quotidian disruption. This is not only because the losses generated by quotidian disruptions are likely to be especially palpable, but also because movements precipitated by quotidian disruption may be able to draw more fully on existing situationally relevant framings since their goals are skewed toward cultural and social restoration rather than broad social change. Because of this latter consideration, the phenomenological constraints or impediments to frame resonance that Snow and Benford (1988) have identified are likely to be less of on issue for movements seeking to defend or reconstitute routines and patterns of everyday life whose cultural validity has already been established. Existing patterns of routines and corresponding natural attitudes are, almost by definition, likely to be empirically credible, experientially commensurate, and consistent with existing cultural narratives.

This is not to suggest, Lawyers, that all framing processes and issues are irrelevant to movements spawned by quotidian disruption. As implied above neither attributional framing, which involves the definition of a condition as problematic and in need of repair, nor motivational framing may be so critical in situations of quotidian disruption. However, prognostic framing, which involves the specification of lines of response and action, probably remains just as problematic in contexts of quotidian disruption as in other situations.

Additionally, the link between quotidian disruption and these core framing tasks may be more pronounced in some situations than others. While quotidian disruption invariably involves a disruption of both routines and the natural attitude, the degree to which each is fractured relative to the other may vary across situations. If the natural attitude is fractured more severely than everyday routines, such that it may not be possible to suspend doubt without first altering previous conditions in novel ways, then diagnostic and prognostic framing may be equally important. The extent to which there may be variability in the degree to which both routines and the natural attitude are fractured is an empirical question. But we suspect that insofar as such variability exists, there will also be differences in the relative importance of the core framing tasks.

Taken together, these observations suggest that processes that are generally assumed to be operative across movements may instead be quite variable in their relative importance. If so, then clearly greater caution should be exercised when specifying or modelling the relationship between movement relevant processes and the emergence and operation of different movements.

In addition to refining our understanding of rationality, political opportunity, and framing processes in relation to social movements, we think that this paper yields a more sophisticated understanding of the relationship between solidarity and breakdown. Rather than conceptualizing the two as a simple dichotomy, our thesis implies that some forms of social breakdown and solidarity are not antithetical, especially as regards mobilization for collective action. As noted at the outset of the paper, our conceptualization of breakdown as quotidian disruption differs from that which Tilly and his associates Jettisoned some twenty years ago (1975). When they spoke critically about "breakdown theory," they were referring to perspectives that argue that social movements are most likely to arise among the disaffiliated and disconnected, those whose social networks and bonds of solidarity have

unraveled and disintegrated. However, when we speak of breakdown or disruption, whether at the organizational or individual level, we do not presume that the actors in question are uprooted, disconnected, or isolated. To the contrary, we assume that they are variously embedded in social networks and bonds of solidarity, or at least situated structurally such that they are available for mobilization, as in the case of the homeless. Thus, what we see as disrupted or broken are patterns of everyday functioning and routinized expectancies associated with those patterns, not associational ties and bonds of solidarity.

However, there are clearly instances of quotidian disruption that so weaken existing social ties and demoralize those effected, as in the case of some forced population transfers and disasters, that collective action of any kind, and particularly sustained movement activity, is unlikely (Erikson 1976, 1994). This suggests that there is a threshold beyond which quotidian disruption and collective action are likely to be negatively related. While the existence of such a threshold remains an empirical question, we have identified four contexts of quotidian disruption that fall beneath that probable threshold and that are clearly associated with collective action.

Finally, our observations address a longstanding and vexing problem with strain theorizing: the failure to specify a determinant relationship between putative strains and social movement activity. By elaborating four sets of conditions as precipitants of quotidian disruption and linking them to a variety of reactive or restorative movements, we have theorized a determinant relationship between concrete, identifiable events, a specific kind of breakdown, and a category of social movements. And in doing so, we have provided a more theoretically refined and empirically grounded understanding of the relationship between a variant of sociocultural strain and social movement emergence, one that indicates that it is not grievances, dissatisfactions, or frustrations per se that are particularly potent for the emergence of collective action, but grievances or frustrations associated with a sense of loss arising from quotidian disruption.

NOTES

This is a revised version of a paper presented at the 67th Meeting of the Pacific Sociological Association, Seattle, Washington, March 21–24, 1996. The research on which the paper is based was supported in part by a grant from the National Science Foundation ISES 90088091. We thank Doug McAdam, Bert Useem, Ed Walsh, and Mayer Zald for their constructive comments on previous drafts of the paper. We are also grateful for helpful suggestions of the anonymous reviewers and the editor.

1. See for example recent edited volumes based on papers presented at social movement conferences (Johnston and Klandermans 1995: Larana, Johnston, and Gusfield 1994: McAdam, McCarthy, and Zald 1996: Morris and Mueller 1992.

2. The concept of "threat" whether actual or perceived, has figured in the work of others. Tilly (1978) regards threat as a trigger for mobilization, defining it in terms of "the extent to which other groups are threatening to make claims which would, if successful, reduce the contender's realization of its interests" (133). The problem, we believe, is that the connection between interests and specific kinds of collective action are left indeterminant. In contrast, we focus on one kind or set of interests—those having to do with everyday routines and their maintenance—and their association with movements thought to be more reactive than proactive.

3. Two considerations guided the literature search: (1) detailed descriptions of collective action and its preceding events; and (2) coverage of a variety of contexts and collective actors, Regarding (2), we were not concerned with exhaustiveness or coverage of the entire corpus of literature associated with a particular context since our interest was in theoretical development and refinement rather than testing. The second data source comes from a national study of homeless protest activity in the U.S. during the 1980s and earlier 1990s. As part of that project, fieldwork was conducted in eight U.S. cities—Boston, Denver, Detroit, Houston, Minneapolis. Oakland, Philadelphia, and Tueston–to understand homeless mobilization. For a detailed discussion of the project, including sampling issues and fieldwork procedures, see Cress and Snow (1996). This field data allowed us to over-come a major shortcoming of most research invoking strain and/or breakdown explanations for emergence; we were able to observe quotidian disruption as they were experienced by homeless individuals and/or organizational representatives. Assessment of classical strain and breakdown work tends to infer the effects of strain on individuals or groups from aggregate indicators. This overlooks the different effects that disruption might have on different segments of a population. If quotidian disruption helps explain at least one variety of movement emergence, then it is imperative to have detailed accounts of the impact of disrupting events on the lives and routines of the individuals and organizations affected. The historical and ethnographic studies on which we draw provide such detailed accounts.

4. For a similar interpretation of Goffman's discussion of the umwelt in relation to humans and human interaction, see Burns (1992). As he writes: "In modern society, the individuals *Umwelt* is often prescribed by the built environment—his room, his house, workplace, office, or some familiar haunt other than these. These are likely to be assumed to be unhazardous and innocent," unless they are invaded, or violated (Burns 1992: 99).

5. Here we focus on the actual fluctuation in resources relative to demand, and not changes in subjective expectations or assessments. The later lead us to consider relative deprivation, which has been found to be tenuously connected to collective action (Finkel and Rile 1986: Gurney and Tierney 1982).

6. Examination of the underlying, precipitating conditions associated with the emergence of each of the fifteen SMOs revealed four sets of such conditions; individual or organizational disruption, diffusion from and sponsorship by another organization, factionalism, and a combination of disruption and one of the other two conditions. The emergence of six of the SMOs was sparked by disruption, three were the direct outgrowth of diffusion and sponsorship, two were factional offsprings, and four emerged as a result of a mixture of disruption and either factionalism or diffusion/sponsorship. Since our focus is on the connection between quotidian disruption and SMO emergence, we elaborate this relationship.

2.
A Demographic/Structural Model of State Breakdown

JACK A. GOLDSTONE

My primary conclusion is quite beautiful in its parsimony. It is that *the periodic state breakdowns in Europe, China, and the Middle East from 1500 to 1850 were the result of a single basic process.* This process unfolded like a fugue, with a major trend giving birth to four related critical trends that combined for a tumultuous conclusion. The main trend was that population growth, in the context of relatively inflexible economic and social structures, led to changes in prices, shifts in resources, and increasing social demands with which agrarian-bureaucratic states could not successfully cope.

The four related critical trends were as follows: (1) Pressures increased on state finances as inflation eroded state income and population growth raised real expenses. States attempted to maintain themselves by raising revenues in a variety of ways, but such attempts alienated elites, peasants, and urban consumers, while failing to prevent increasing debt and eventual bankruptcy. (2) Intra-elite conflicts became more prevalent as larger families and inflation made it more difficult for some families to maintain their status, while expanding population and rising prices lifted other families, creating new aspirants to elite positions. With the state's fiscal weakness limiting its ability to provide for all who sought elite positions, considerable turnover and displacement occurred throughout the elite hierarchy, giving rise to factionalization as different elite groups sought to defend or improve their position. When central authority collapsed, most often as a result of bankruptcy, elite divisions

came to the fore in struggles for power. (3) Popular unrest grew, as competition for land, urban migration, flooded labor markets, declining real wages, and increased youthfulness raised the mass mobilization potential of the populace. Unrest occurred in urban and rural areas and took the various forms of food riots, attacks on landlords and state agents, and land and grain seizures, depending on the autonomy of popular groups and the resources of elites. A heightened mobilization potential made it easy for contending elites to marshal popular action in their conflicts, although in many cases popular actions, having their own motivation and momentum, proved easier to encourage than to control. (4) The ideologies of rectification and transformation became increasingly salient. Spreading poverty and vagrancy, ever more severe and frequent harvest crises and food riots, and state ineffectiveness undermined the credibility of religious leaders associated with states and turned both elites and middling groups to heterodox religious movements in the search for reform, order, and discipline. The conjuncture of these four critical trends—state fiscal distress, intrastate conflicts, heightened mass mobilization potential, and, deriving in part from the other three, increased salience of the folk and elite ideologies of rectification and transformation—combined to undermine stability on *multiple* levels of social organization.

This basic process was triggered all across Eurasia by the periods of sustained population increase that occurred in the sixteenth and early seventeenth centuries and again in the late eighteenth and early nineteenth centuries, thus producing worldwide waves of state breakdown. In contrast, in the late seventeenth and early eighteenth centuries populations did not grow, and the basic process and its four subthemes were absent. Political and social

Goldstone, Jack A. 1991. "A Demographic/Structural Model State Breakdown" pp. 459–475 in *Revolution and Rebellion in the Early Modern World*. Berkeley: University of California Press. Reprinted by permission of the University of California Press.

stability resulted. In the early nineteenth century, one should note, several European states had greatly increased their financial resources; thus, even though population growth initiated a similar pattern, the first critical trend was muted, and the ensuing state crises in 1830 and 1848 were less severe. But their kinship with the earlier wave of state crises, and with contemporary state crises in the Ottoman and Chinese empires, remains clear. After 1850, most western European states had increased the flexibility of their economics through industrialization, and of their administrative and social structures through political revolution or reform; thus, population growth lost its ability to trigger the processes that earlier had led to state breakdown. Russia, China, and the Ottoman empire, however, with their still largely traditional economic, political, and social structures, remained vulnerable to population pressures, which continued through the nineteenth century and led to state breakdowns in the early years of the twentieth.

The power of this argument lies not merely in its ability to explain the timing, and the widespread coincidence, of such crises. It lies especially in displaying the linkages—between population growth and price inflation, and between both these factors and state fiscal crisis, elite mobility and competition, and mass mobilization potential—that shaped the development and key features of these crises. Thus for example, the fact that the English and French revolutions were both preceded by periods of unusual social mobility and triggered by fiscal crises can be understood as similar responses to similar historical situations, rather than as mere coincidence or superficial analogy.

Indeed, it is fascinating to find so many trends that English, or French, or Chinese, or Ottoman specialists have claimed to be the product of unique conditions appearing again and again across time and space. Moreover, this consistency lays to rest many old shibboleths and tortured debates. Thus, we clearly and repeatedly find that revolution and rebellion were *not* due to excessively high taxation by rulers, or to a simple lack of social mobility, or chiefly to class conflict, or to general impoverishment of society as a whole. Instead we find consistently that fiscal crises

were due to *undertaxation* as elites systematically evaded taxes, so that state revenues barely kept pace with inflation, and hence never kept pace with the increasing *real* wealth of their societies. We find everywhere that *high* social mobility—*high* rates of turnover and displacement—preceded crises, while *low* social mobility characterized times of stability. Rapid turnover among high officials, strains on elite education and recruitment, and conflicts over patronage are seen in all states and empires approaching crisis. *Factional conflict within the elites,* over access to office, patronage, and state policy, rather than conflict across classes, led to state paralysis and state breakdown. We also find consistently that elites succeeded in shifting the burden of taxation to the middling classes, and that the conditions of the working classes and peasants declined while elites and commercial classes grew richer. Thus, we consistently see a *polarization* of social wealth in the generations preceding crises. And the combination of declining state effectiveness, heightened conflicts over mobility, and increasing poverty at the bottom of the social scale raised the salience of reformist, disciplined, heterodox moral and philosophical schools, a salience that failed rapidly when these social trends ended. These trends are evident in the sixteenth and early seventeenth centuries, and in the eighteenth and early nineteenth centuries, across Eurasia. Certainly particular conditions in each society shaped the timing and magnitude of these trends. But in light of their near universal character, any claim that such trends were produced *solely* by unique local conditions is thoroughly undermined by the evidence.

Almost two decades ago, Lawrence Stone (1972, 26) wrote that "with both [the English and French] Revolutions, once historians have realized that their Marxist interpretation does not work very much better than the Whig, there has followed a period where there is nothing very secure to put in its place." I hope that the *demographic/structural* model can now take that place, as it explains the key features of both crises in better accord with the known facts than the Marxist or Whig views. It also deals far more effectively with the contemporary crises in China and the Middle East and avoids any of the objectionable teleology characteristic of other analyses.

There is no teleology because, although the basic processes and pressures that led to state breakdown occurred widely, the model allows that the precise responses to these pressures varied with the capacity of states to react, of elites to organize, and of popular groups to mobilize. Moreover, once state breakdown had begun, the struggle for power and the need for state reconstruction gave great scope to distinct ideologies, albeit constrained by existing cultural frameworks, to shape the future course of reaction or revolution. Thus, the same basic causal process gave rise to a range of outcomes, depending on the setting in which that process unfolded.

Historians have long debated whether the main causes of early modern revolutions and rebellions were social, economic, religious, or political cleavages. Such distinctions are illusory. Social and economic conflicts, religious heterodoxy, and political factionalization were not independent factors but related aspects of an underlying causal pattern. For a number of societies, this book demonstrates that the early modern crises were rooted in the simultaneous decline of traditional systems of taxation, elite training and recruitment, and popular living standards; hence, the increased salience and appeal of heterodox ideologies, under the pressure of ecological change.

This model offers several advantages over the Marxist interpretation, its "revisionist" adversaries, and the more recent theories of revolution such as Skocpol's. First, the state appears as an autonomous actor in *three* respects: (1) as an economic actor whose strength is affected by trends in the economy such as inflation and by changing real costs of governance brought by population growth; (2) as a political actor whose strength is affected by the demands of international competition and the demands of domestic elite and popular groups; and (3) as a cultural actor whose strength (and pace of future development) is affected by the tensions—or lack thereof—between state-supported orthodoxy and alternative ideological claims. Marxist interpretation tends to neglect the autonomy of political

actions, the revisionists and Skocpol tend to neglect the impact of key shifts and cycles in economic history, and Skocpol and many Marxists tend to neglect the autonomy of cultural and ideological aspects of social change. The demographic/structural approach to state breakdown—combined with our analysis of the process of revolutionary struggles and their outcome—gives due attention to the economic, political, and cultural aspects of the state's relations with other states, elites, and popular groups.

Second, this analysis of elites identifies a variety of social conflicts, not just those between economically distinct classes. Instead, demographic and economic pressures are seen to create conflicts both *across* classes—between peasants and landlords and between urban artisans and urban oligarchies—and *within* classes—between factions of landed, merchant, professional, and religious groups. Recognition that social mobility can provide absorption or generate displacement and turnover, noting that the latter combination, in particular, generates intra-elite competition and conflict at a *multiplicity* of levels, allows a better understanding of the precise cleavages that broke across the Old Regimes when subjected to demographic pressure: reform versus conservative factions among ministerial, provincial, and town officials; bishops versus curés or preachers; international versus domestic merchants; older versus newer military officers; financiers versus professionals; and orthodox intellectuals versus heterodox reformers.

Understanding how demographic pressure gives rise to heightened elite competition also explains a particular, and heretofore puzzling, phenomenon: the simultaneous "boom" in University enrollments all across Europe and the overburdening of religious schools in the Ottoman Empire and of the imperial examination system in China in the late sixteenth and early seventeenth centuries, followed by the "bust" in those enrollments in Europe and an easing of educational strains in Asia in the late seventeenth and early eighteenth centuries. This sequence was followed by another "boom" in the late eighteenth and early nineteenth centuries. These boom and busts are too extreme to be explained by changes in population size per se. However, we need only recognize that the periods of growing population led to inflation, which created economic opportunities that, in turn, increased the number of people who considered themselves qualified to demand elite positions. At the same time, inflation and sharp resistance to increasing taxation limited each state's ability to increase the supply of elite positions. The result was heightened competition for such positions, which spurred a scramble for credentials. Conversely, periods of stable population give rise to little social mobility, and stable family size allowed much of the demand for elite positions to be satisfied by simple inheritance or family succession. Thus, the demand for formal credentials went "bust." Whether examining education or broad-based elite conflicts, consideration of the *interaction* of demographic, economic, and political relationships is far more fruitful than asserting the centrality of purely class, or purely political, factors.

Third, the demographic/structural approach to popular uprisings allows considerable scope for attention to *regional* differences in conflicts that occur within a crisis. Thus, an awareness of how demographic pressures produce land shortages, rising rents, falling real wages, and a more youthful population helps to explain why banditry, urban riots, and rural rebellions would all become more likely following periods of sustained population increase in agrarian-bureaucratic states. However, the model dictates no particular form of popular unrest. Instead, the precise shape of popular action is determined by the way such pressures impinge on a particular region's distribution of resources and relationships between potential actors. Thus, one would expect different patterns of popular unrest in northern France, southwestern France, and rural England, for in each case the organization of peasants, and the resources of land-lords, differed. Similarly, in China one would expect different patterns of popular unrest in the mountains of the west and in the waterways of the Yangzi delta. Regional differences, as well as international differences, are the logical outcome of a model in which similar *causal* forces, rooted in demographic change, act

on a variety of *social structures* to produce various patterns of conflict.

Fourth, this analysis integrates material and cultural factors in a far richer way than do the Marxist or revisionist analyses, and in a way that rectifies Skocpol's underemphasis on ideologies. I argue that the material causes of state breakdown first give rise to evident decay in state effectiveness and increases in popular and elite discontent. This combination of decay and disaffection raises the salience of ideologies of rectification and transformation which may be longstanding but dormant elements of the political culture. Clear shifts in discourse and the spread of heterodoxy thus precede state breakdown, though these derive primarily from the collision of economic, political, and social structures with demographic change. If state crisis leads to state breakdown, however, the struggle for power polarizes and radicalizes discourse, further shaping and giving vent to ideological conflicts. When a victor emerges and sets a course for state reconstruction, these ideologies have a powerful molding effect on the postrevolutionary state. Moreover, ideologies of state reconstruction reflect not only the struggle for power but also the broader cultural framework of the society at large.

Ideologies reflect the available elements for conceptualizing change. Thus, European societies (as well as non-European societies later affected by European ideas), because of their linear and eschatological notions of time, their stock of apocalyptic imagery, were likely to respond to state breakdown through innovation; whereas Asian societies, with their primarily cyclic notions of time, were likely to respond to state breakdown with conservative state reconstruction. In this argument, both material and ideal factors play a leading role, although they do so in different phases of the process of state breakdown and reconstruction. This model also has the advantage, in regard to the Marxist view of history, of *not* interpreting the relative stagnation of Asia after the seventeenth century as the "absence" of change relative to Europe; instead it is seen as the result of a different *direction* of change, because of its different response to a similar crisis. In this respect, the model suggests parallels between the responses to the seventeenth-century crises in Hapsburg Spain, the Ottoman Empire, and China that merit further study....

Population Growth: A Blessing or a Curse?

There is an old debate in demographic theory about whether there is an "ideal" level of population for a society, and whether increases in population are generally beneficial or detrimental to societal well-being. There have been famous pessimists, from Malthus to Keynes, and famous optimists, most recently Julian Simon and Ester Boserup, who have reiterated Dupréel's argument that "an increase in population is beneficial in itself, because it enhances competition and spurs individual initiative, and is thus a decisive factor in civilization and progress" (cited in Overbeek 1974, 118).

At first glance, the argument in this book appears pessimistic in tone, for population growth in early modern history was strongly associated with mass poverty, elite factionalism, and state crises. But this observation alone would be an excessively simple and misleading characterization of events. The actual matter of interest is not defined by movements of population alone, viewed as a single independent variable, but rather by a set of *balances:* between population and agrarian output, between elite recruitment and eligible aspirants, and between state tax revenues and state expenditures. It was not population growth per se but rather growth beyond the absorptive capacity of early modern economic, social, and political institutions that undid these delicate balances and ruptured the social order. The lesson of early modern history is not that population growth is bad but rather that inflexible social structures are bad, at least in the sense that they become highly unstable in the event of sustained demographic change.

What, then, are the policy implications to be drawn from this book with respect to the pressing issue of population growth in the developing world? Will population growth lead to continued political instability?

The answer is that population increases *probably will* lead to political crises, but they need not. The argument of this book can be neatly divided into two parts. First, there is a theory of the conditions that create a likelihood of state breakdown, drawing on a conjuntural model of crises. This theory asserts that massive state breakdown is likely to occur only when there are *simultaneously* high levels of distress and conflict at *several levels* of society—in the state, among elites, and in the populace. We examined this conjuncture empirically through the *psi* equation, which combined attention to trends in state fiscal distress, elite mobility and competition (including both turnover and displacement), and mass mobilization potential. A sustained rise in all three elements is associated with state breakdown; a rise in two of these elements can produce a state crisis leading to major reforms or modest state breakdown; a rise in any one alone is unlikely to end a regime. This theory can be simply summarized: high *psi* implies a high probability of state crisis. Second, there is a more historically delimited theory that seeks to explain *why psi* rose to high levels in most Eurasian states in the two periods 1550–1660 and 1770–1850, an explanation that rests on the interaction of demography and institutions.

Since the two parts are logically independent, we can approach the problems of contemporary population growth and instability through two questions: Is population growth likely to raise *psi* in today's world? And are there other forces that could raise *psi,* and hence other, more worrisome, sources of state breakdown?

In the early modern world, population growth was a threat to societies that were fundamentally agrarian. As Gellner (1983, 110) has pointed out, "agrarian society...unlike, it would seem, both its predecessor [hunter-gatherer society] and successor [industrial society] is Malthusian." Today, although many developing nations such as India, China, and most nations of Africa and northwest Latin America still have largely agrarian economies, they are no longer purely agrarian *societies.* That is to say, the wealth, political power, and military strength of each depend more on access to capital, technology, information, and often electoral support and foreign assistance than on mere ownership of acreage. Without access to foreign and urban markets, without capital for machinery, fertilizer, fuel, and transportation, large landholdings today are nearly worthless. Without access to national party organizations, large landowners can be, at best, local *caudillos* or bosses; small farmers and tenants can be, at best, restive local forces. Technological improvements that are available in agriculture, production, communication, and transportation dwarf anything that was available in the early modern world. Thus, population growth need not overwhelm modern societies, provided they can harness modern resources to absorb their population increases.

In these circumstances, the question of whether population growth will undo crucial balances that sustain social stability has more to do with government policy, capital availability, and local organization than with the simple arithmetic of bodies and land. Policies of cronyism and corruption that drain or unproductively concentrate capital, and policies of urban investment and price-skewing at the expense of rural infrastructure and economies, are likely to create the same conditions of high mass mobilization potential among impoverished cultivators that simple population growth produced in the seventeenth and nineteenth centuries. Conversely, policies that create a well-capitalized, productive, domestic agriculture, and that can supply employment to the rural sector and food and raw materials to world markets and the urban sector, can cope with quite rapid population growth. Japan under the Meiji oligarchs experienced rapid population increase, but state policies of the latter type served to maintain political stability (Nishikawa 1986, 426; Macpherson 1987).

Development policies often focus on raising GNP per capita. Clearly, this approach need not succeed in reducing *psi,* which is not a simple matter of total social wealth. We have seen that the nations and empires that encountered crisis suffered from *polarization* in their income distribution, from high social mobility that unsettled and divided elites, and from failure of the state to gain resources to cope with rising real expenses. Eighteenth-century France, for example, raised its GNP per capita. But a lagging agricultural sector, and problems in the distribution of income and taxation, still produced a crisis. Thus development policies, if they wish to help counter political instability as well as create growth, need to do more than just raise GNP. Measures such as land reform and support for small farmers, which reduce income polarization and urban migration, and foreign aid aimed at avoiding excessive government debt while providing government resources for housing, education, and other population-linked infrastructural expenses, are more politically stabilizing than investments in concentrated industries. One must also consider the ability of the state, church, business, and social institutions to employ ambitious elites at levels that correspond to their self-perceived qualifications. It is politically risky to create new, professional, educated elites without also creating ample political and economic opportunities for them. It is in these areas that demographic change poses problems to contemporary governments.

In fact, rapid population growth in many Third World countries has had two extremely important political effects: rapid urbanization and the growth of new professional and managerial elites. The extreme urbanization reflects a common economic bias, wherein development policies, pricing policies, and foreign investment increase economic opportunities in cities rather than in the countryside (Bates 1981; Kelley and Williamson 1984; Bradshaw 1985). Unfortunately, such rapid urbanization places enormous strains on the capacity of governments to provide services, political organization and control, and employment for urban residents. Under such conditions, dissident elites may find ready recruits to mobilize in anti-state movements. Tehran and Managua in 1979 thus had the same potential—in terms of mass mobilization in politically crucial sites—as Paris in 1789 or Vienna and Berlin in 1848.

Dissident elites may arise when expanding urban markets offer opportunities to entrepreneurs in manufacturing and services and an expanding educational system produces professional degree holders, while traditional military and landowning elites, or a particular ruler or clique, seeks to monopolize power. Stable balances within a landed oligarchy, or between elite segments under the orchestration of an authoritarian ruler, may be undone by a relatively sudden expansion of urban population and markets.

The demands of traditional elites to preserve their privileged position often clash with the demands of new elites and popular urban and rural groups for broad economic expansion. Development plans must then meet many agendas, from satisfying current and emerging elites to keeping pace with overall population growth. A combination of agrarian reform, guided productive investment, and compensation to traditional elites has sometimes successfully overcome this dilemma, as in Japan during the Meiji era.

However, states with less political clout and fewer resources often seek to defer difficult choices by borrowing. In early modern times, such a course might have led straightforwardly to a state fiscal crisis. But contemporary states have a greater ability to externalize deficits by inviting foreign investment, printing money, and manipulating exchange rates. Thus, in analyzing the "fiscal crisis" component of *psi* for modern states, we may see rising inflation, loss of control of the economy to foreign interests, or wild swings or divergences from parity in the local currency, instead of simple state financial difficulties. Nonetheless, all of these disrupt the flow of resources to states, or to elite and popular groups who look to the state for control of these matters. Thus broadly defined, fiscal or economic crises are a common outcome of states' attempts to utilize borrowing and currency controls to meet foreign competition and the demands of changing elites and growing populations.

Again, we come face to face with the problem of population change and its effects on political and economic *structures*. Early modern states failed to cope with population growth because their economic, fiscal, and social structures—rooted in simple agrarian techniques and in aristocratic status and political systems—lacked sufficient flexibility to deflect or absorb the conflicts produced by that growth. Contemporary states rarely face such simple economic and traditional status institutions, and their attendant constraints. Thus, they often *can* absorb population growth; the question is whether, at a given time, they adopt the policies that will actually allow them to do so (cf. Johnson and Lee 1987).

The tenets that favor stability are simple: do not adopt fiscal policies that rely on debts in excess of what the economy and tax system can reasonably be expected to sustain; do not adopt economic policies that encourage urban growth at a faster rate than housing, services, employment, and civic organization can develop; do not adopt educational policies that produce graduates in excess of the state's and the economy's ability to give them meaningful responsibilities; and do not adopt political policies that exclude from power newly rising groups that are growing in numbers and wealth. States often fail to follow these tenets because it is in the short-term interests of rulers or particular elites to acquire debts, to favor rapid urban expansion, to implement educational expansion, or to seek monopolization of power. The problem is that these short-term, and thus short-sighted, policies undermine political stability in the long run. How a current regime weighs the short-run versus the long-run consequences of its choices is often the key to whether its prospects for stability are brief or extend far into the future.

These tenets are *not* merely matters of economic expansion or development. One can have economically stagnant states that follow these tenets and yet remain politically stable economic backwaters—for example. North Korea. And one can have economically dynamic states that fail to follow these tenets for stability and hence encounter state crisis—for example, Iran.

From 1956 to 1976, the population of Iran increased from just over twenty million inhabitants to nearly thirty-five million, an increase of 75 percent in two decades (B. Clark 1972). During these decades, the Pahlavi regime adopted a rural land reform program that left three-fourths of rural families with inadequate land to support commercial farming, and it adopted pricing and credit policies that starved the rural sector while subsidizing urban populations. The cities were also the focus of development efforts financed by massive borrowing. The state thus drew population to the cities more rapidly than adequate services or regular employment could be supplied, developing a large population of aggrieved urban families who looked to the mosque and bazaar, rather than to the state and modern economic sector, for material benefits, moral authority, and community leadership. The number of university students increased tenfold, many of them educated overseas for lack of domestic facilities (Abrahamian 1980). Witnessing the moral dissolution and poverty in the urban slums, along with the concentration of wealth among the shah's family and associates, many elites and students became dismayed at the moral failures and corruption of the regime.

Counting on future oil wealth, the shah borrowed heavily, and sought to complement his development effort with a military buildup. These expenditures stretched both the state budget and the economy to the limit. The resulting inflation undermined middle- and working-class incomes. Finally, seeking to monopolize power, the shah excluded from politics the professional and managerial groups and civil servants on which his modernization efforts depended, and attacked the bazaar merchants and the traditional religious elite (Keddie 1981; Green 1986).

The result of these policies was mounting state debt, roaring inflation, and political exclusion that made enemies among the salaried middle class and the traditional religious leaders and bazaar merchants. When these elite groups allied and began to mobilize the urban masses against the shah's government, given the questionable ability of the army to act against a broad popular movement (as in France in 1830 and 1848), the breakdown of the shah's regime became imminent (Abrahamian 1980). The shah's fall was thus a product of misguided policies, not an inevitable outcome of rapid development or Islamic fundamentalism. However, once state breakdown had begun, there followed the familiar sequence: an initially moderate, widely supported movement for rectification, then struggles for popular mobilization and power, with victory attained by extremist leaders. These leaders were a formerly marginal elite—the fundamentalist wing of the Shi'ite clergy—who drew on an eschatological ideology. The revolutionary process culminated in an aggressive Iranian nationalism that produced persecution of minorities and other internal "enemies," as well as foreign war.

In sum, population growth does pose problems for modern states. But they are not insoluble problems, as many examples from the newly industrialized countries show. Whether or not population growth will lead to instability depends on the policies adopted by particular regimes. Poor policy choices can create exactly the "high *psi*" conditions—state fiscal crises, elite factionalization and alienation, and rising mass (particularly urban) mobilization potential—that make state crises likely. In contrast, careful policy choices can maintain "low *psi*" conditions, and hence political stability despite rapid economic growth.

Given the explosive population growth that has occurred in the Third World during the twentieth century, often without the benefit of rapid industrialization or flexible political institutions, it is not surprising that this is a "century of revolution" in Third World states. Although a decline in per capita wealth has occasionally been a problem, this has not been the primary factor in modern revolutions. Instead, problems of wealth distribution among the population, weak state finances, and competition among elites, exacerbated by explosive population increases and inappropriate policy responses, have undermined political stability. Wherever rulers or elites have been tempted to put their own short-term interests ahead of long-term political stability for their respective societies, the resulting policy choices have created, over a span of few decades, the ingredients for state crises.

We should thus not be surprised if population growth and state crises, though not inevitably linked, remain companion phenomena in the contemporary Third World.[1]

NOTE

1. For a more detailed consideration of contemporary revolutions, see Goldstone, Gurr, and Moshiri (forthcoming).

3.

Structural Social Change and the Mobilizing Effect of Threat: Explaining Levels of Patriot and Militia Organizing in the United States

NELLA VAN DYKE AND SARAH A. SOULE

Patriot/militia[1] groups came to national attention with the bombing of the Federal Building in Oklahoma City in 1995 and media claims that the chief perpetrator had ties to militia organizations. Throughout the latter half of the 1990s, individuals with connections to militia and/or patriot organizations committed a number of additional acts of violence, many of which also drew national media attention (Berlet and Lyons 2000; Cattarinich 1998; Southern Poverty Law Center 1999). The movement's relatively recent emergence, as well as its potential for violence, makes an exploration of the factors associated with its incidence worthwhile. Both case studies and journalistic accounts of the patriot/militia movement attribute its rise to broad structural changes, including population shifts, economic restructuring, and the increasing political power of previously disenfranchised groups, such as African Americans, women, and Jews (Abanes 1996; Castells 1997; Dyer 1997; Lamy 1996; Snow 1999). Although these explanations are fairly consistent with recent empirical research on social movements, they do not fit neatly into the currently dominant theories of social movement emergence, and thus remain under-theorized.

In this paper, we explore the mobilizing effect of several types of threat produced by structural social change. We consider the possibility that changing economic conditions, demographic shifts, and political competition may all produce threats which inspire *reactive mobilization,* or mobilization in response to the real or perceived loss of power or

Van Dyke, Nella and Sarah A. Soule. 2002. "Structural Social Change and Mobilizing Effect of Threat: Explaining Levels of Patriot and Militia Organizing in the United States." *Social Problems* 49: 497–520, Reprinted by permission of The University of California Press.

resources (Tilly 1978). To evaluate this argument, we conduct a negative binomial regression analysis of state-level counts of patriot/militia organizations and show that economic restructuring, within both the manufacturing and agricultural sectors, explains variation in levels of mobilization of patriot/militia groups in the U.S. in the mid-1990s. We confirm these results with an analysis of 300 U.S. counties. Our findings suggest that scholars of social movements (and especially scholars of reactive social movements) should consider the mobilizing effect of threat alongside other, more commonly theorized, factors that influence the emergence of collective action.

The Mobilizing Effect of Threat and Reactive Social Movements

Scholars of social movements recognize that groups sometimes mobilize in response to threat. Strain theories, which were popular through the 1950s and 1960s, argue that groups mobilize when they face broad-scale social changes, including economic crisis or restructuring, wars, the loss of supporting social institutions, or mass migrations (Bell 1963; Gusfield 1963; Hofstadter 1955; Kornhauser 1959; Lipset 1963). The individual-level component of the theory suggests that socially isolated individuals are more likely to participate in movements, and that participation is a response to psychological distress (Kornhauser 1959; Lang and Lang 1961; Turner and Killian 1987). Although scholars developed the theory based on their studies of the right-wing movements (e.g., Nazism, fascism, McCarthyism) active during the 1940s, 1950s, and early 1960s, they presented it as an explanation of all social movements (Garner 1997).

While strain theory was popular through the mid-1960s, research on the left-oriented movements that emerged in the 1960s generated questions about its utility (Buechler 2000; Garner 1997). Critiques of early individual-level strain theory center on the assertion that social movement participation is irrational and that individuals are more likely to participate in movements when they are socially isolated (Finkel and Rule 1986; Gould 1993; McAdam 1988; McAdam and Paulsen 1993; Tarrow 1996; Taylor 1996). Critiques of the macro-level component of strain theory are based on empirical analyses of left-oriented movements, which consistently demonstrate that groups tend to mobilize when they experience *increased* economic resources, as opposed to *decreased* levels of economic resources (McCarthy and Zald 1977).

While we do not address debates about the utility of the individual-level component of strain theory in this article, we do argue that the macro-level component of the theory is useful in explaining the emergence of reactive forms of mobilization. Resource mobilization and political opportunity theories, the two most dominant theories of movement emergence, do not make predictions about threats produced by macro-level structural change.[2] Classically, resource mobilization theory argues that movements emerge in response to increases in the resources needed to sustain collective action and the availability of organizations to coordinate the effort (for reviews see Jenkins 1983; McAdam 1996; McAdam, McCarthy, and Zald 1988). The political process variant of resource mobilization theory emphasizes the importance of expanding political opportunities as a catalyst to collective action (McAdam 1982 (1999); Tarrow 1989, 1994; Tilly 1978). But, what happens when resources available to those who are generally resource advantaged *decline?* And what happens when political *threats* against those typically in more powerful positions emerge? Groups that have some social power during one period, by virtue of their race or gender or class, may face a loss of power, or at least the perception that they are losing power, during another time period. While we do not advocate a return to the micro-component of strain theory, we suggest here that the threat produced by structural social change may lead to the mobilization of certain social movements, in particular reactive social movements.[3]

Reactive social movements, according to Tilly (1978), involve attempts by a group to reassert claims to political and/or economic resources that they have lost (or that they perceive they have lost, as Beck (2000) suggests). A group may feel threatened when its members perceive that social forces are developing in a way that will prevent them from realizing their interests. As the literature we describe below suggests, groups may mobilize in response to a threatened loss of economic resources and/or political power. The source of the threat may include economic or political developments, or changing majority/minority populations. Political threats may include increased government repression against a group, a loss of rights, or a loss of political power associated with the increased political power by an opposing group (Goldstone and Tilly 2001; Meyer and Staggenborg 1996; Van Dyke forthcoming). Threatening economic developments may include economic restructuring or other economic changes that put at risk a group's ability to economically maintain itself. The same conditions that create favorable conditions for collective action by one movement may present an increased threat for another (McVeigh 1999; Meyer and Staggenborg 1996). Those enjoying the most powerful positions in society may have sufficient economic and organizational resources and political leverage to mobilize, but may only be inspired to do so when faced with a perceived threat to these resources.

The counter-revolutionary mobilization among the Vendée during the French Revolution (Tilly 1964) is a classic example of a reactive social movement. Essentially, the Vendée organized in response to threats produced by the major social changes occurring at the time (including urbanization, industrialization, and demographic changes) that made France ripe for the Revolution. Thus, some segments of the population were affected by social change in a way that inspired them to join the revolution, while others counter-mobilized as they saw the revolution and other social and economic developments threatening their interests. We argue that the patriot/militia movement is a modern day example of a reactive social movement. It is important to note, however, that we do not equate *reactive* social movements with *right-oriented* movements, although there may be considerable overlap between the two. While some recent scholarship suggests that movements on the political right mobilize in response to political or economic threat, other empirical examples provided in the next section demonstrate that *left-oriented* groups may also mobilize in response to threat. Thus, rather than distinguishing between right- and left-leaning movements, we think that a more useful conceptual distinction can be made between reactive and proactive movements.

Structural Social Change and Threat

Recent empirical work shows that reactive mobilization may, at least in part, be a function of threats caused by three types of structural changes: political, economic, and demographic.[4] Tilly (1978) suggests that increased political opportunities or political threats may inspire mobilization. Studies of the American peace movement mobilization in response to the policies of the Reagan administration (Meyer 1990) and the White Separatist movement in the U.S. (Dobratz and Shanks-Meile 1997) support the idea that political threats sometimes inspire mobilization. Similarly, work within the ethnic conflict literature, described below, also suggests that groups mobilize when threatened with a loss of political power.

In addition to political threat, research also demonstrates that changing economic conditions and/or economic restructuring may be perceived to be threatening and thus trigger protest activity. The economic changes of the Nineteenth and Twentieth Centuries triggered mobilization on the part of several different populations. For example, peasants responded to the commercialization of agriculture across Europe with a series of uprisings (Moore 1966; Tarrow 1996), and growing exploitation accompanied by economic insecurity triggered massive peasant unrest in many Asian countries in the same period (Scott 1976). In urban areas, the industrial revolution generated conflict, as workers resisted losing control over production and their increasing dependence on wage labor (Tarrow 1996; Tilly 1993). And, scholars convincingly link economic downturns in the U.S. to the rise of the White Separatist Movement (Dobratz and

Shanks-Meile 1997; Wellman 1993). In all of these cases, factors such as the strength of the state and divisions of power among different groups mediated the success of the insurgency, however, economic restructuring created the underlying social conditions that inspired populations to protest.

Several scholars studying right-wing extremism and racial violence suggest that mobilization is a function of unstable macro-level phenomena such as unemployment and changes in the size of minority populations (Barret 1987; Beck 2000; Koopmans 1996; McVeigh 1999). Research demonstrates that right-wing mobilization in Western Europe is associated with increased minority populations and economic problems (Kitschelt 1995; Koopmans 1996). Indeed, the perception that minority populations are increasing, whether or not the increase is real, may be enough to inspire racist action (Gallagher 1994; Giles 1977; Giles and Evans 1985). Castells (1997) argues that processes of globalization influence the rise of fundamentalist movements, including the patriot/militia movement, in all parts of the world. Increasing globalization and economic restructuring are having a negative economic impact on some segments of society, especially those that do not benefit economically from the changing economy. In locations where minority population levels are increasing, social conflict may ensue.

Finally, work within the ethnic conflict literature also provides strong support for the idea that population changes, when accompanied by scarce economic resources, can lead to mobilization. Political and economic competition theory rests on the idea that competition for scarce economic and/or political resources may trigger ethnic conflict (Blalock 1967; Olzak 1992). Factors that increase contact between ethnic groups (e.g., migration) are likely to trigger conflict, as are factors that decrease the level of available resources (e.g., economic recession). Empirical research provides overwhelming support for arguments from both economic and political competition theories (Beck 2000; Jacobs and Wood 1999; Olzak 1992; Soule 1992; Soule and Van Dyke 1999; Tolnay and Beck 1995).

The empirical evidence from these various traditions supports the idea that structural social changes, including political, economic and demographic shifts, inspire mobilization. Based on these findings, we test hypotheses about how broad structural changes affect levels of organization of a reactive social movement: the patriot/militia movement. Before we turn to a discussion of our cross-sectional analyses, we briefly describe the historical context of the movement and factors that played a role in the emergence of the movement.

The Patriot Movement in the United States

In 1996, there were nearly 800 documented patriot/militia organizations in the U.S. (Southern Poverty Law Center 1996). The number of organizations declined dramatically in subsequent years as these groups and individuals adopted a mode of organization known as "leaderless resistance" whereby they function largely underground in "cells" (Berlet and Lyons 2000; Dobratz and Shanks-Meile 1997; Southern Poverty Law Center 1999, 2002). Nonetheless, in 1996 patriot/militia groups were active all over the country, as shown in Figure 1.

Patriot/militia groups first came to the attention of the U.S. public in 1995, with the bombing of the Oklahoma City Federal Building, however, far right patriot/militia groups were under investigation by the federal government well before this time (Berlet and Lyons 2000; Hamilton 1996). The patriot/militia movement follows a long history of conservative

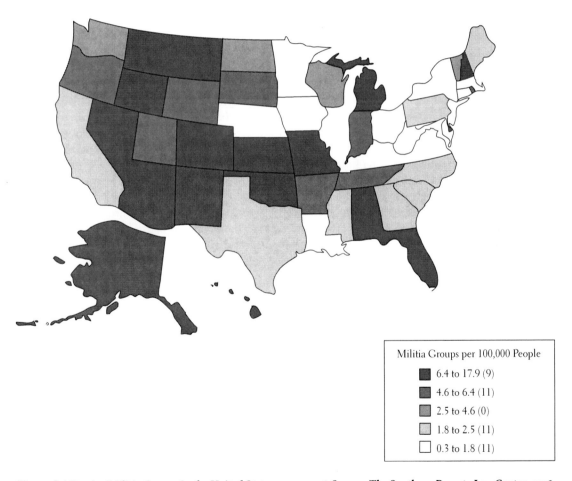

Militia Groups per 100,000 People
- 6.4 to 17.9 (9)
- 4.6 to 6.4 (11)
- 2.5 to 4.6 (0)
- 1.8 to 2.5 (11)
- 0.3 to 1.8 (11)

Figure 3.1 Patriot/Militia Groups in the United States, 1994–1996. Source: The Southern Poverty Law Center, 1996.

political thought and activism in the United States. Its more recent historical antecedents include the Ku Klux Klan, McCarthy-era communist witch-hunts, and the John Birch Society (Berlet and Lyons 2000; Hamilton 1996; Stern 1996). Previous militia initiatives, including that of the Minutemen of the 1960s, the Posse Comitatus, active from the mid-1970s until the mid-1980s, and the Order, active during the early 1980s, also influenced the movement.

Many leaders and members of patriot/militia organizations belonged to other conservative organizations prior to or during their patriot/militia activity (Berlet and Lyons 2000; U.S. Committee on the Judiciary 1997b). Indeed, to separate the patriot/militia movement from other conservative movements is difficult, as members of different right-wing organizations sometimes work together or attend conferences and rallies together (Blee 1996; Neiwert 1999; Stern 1996). On top of this, patriot/militia ideology reflects multiple themes from other conservative organizations and movements (e.g., confrontational anti-abortion, pro-gun, white racist, far right libertarian, and so on) (Berlet and Lyons 2000).

In order to understand the patriot/militia movement, it is important to consider the mobilizing constituency, their identities, and their stated reasons for mobilization. Because the movement is largely underground, it is difficult to obtain representative information regarding the characteristics of patriot/militia members. However extant research suggests that members of the patriot/militia movement are predominantly, though not exclusively, white males (Kimmel and Ferber 2000; Snow 1999; Southern Poverty Law Center 1999). And, other research suggests that patriot/militia groups include individuals who have been hurt by economic restructuring. For example, Abanes (1996) argues that patriot/militia group members are unskilled workers who face increasingly fewer employment opportunities and Snow (1999) adds that, in addition to unemployed working class men, the movement also includes farmers and middle-class individuals who have been hurt by economic restructuring.

At face value, claims about the dismal economic situation faced by members of patriot/militia group seem plausible. While the 1990s were not an especially bad time for the entire U.S. economy, the country experienced profound economic changes in the manufacturing and agricultural sectors. In the U.S. in 1983, 21% of jobs were in manufacturing, but by 1993 that figure had declined to 16% (U.S. Bureau of the Census 1985, 1994). At the same time, the nation experienced what some call the largest farming crisis since the Great Depression (Lobao and Lasley 1995). From 1980 to 1990, between 8 and 12% of farms failed financially, and the farm population fell by 24% (Stam et al. 1991). Individuals with manufacturing and farming skills do not necessarily have the ability to secure positions with comparable pay in the new economy.

One central ideological theme that unifies and galvanizes the movement is the perceived failure of the U.S. government to represent its citizens and uphold the Constitution (Bennet 1995; U.S. Committee of the Judiciary 1997a). Patriot/militia group members believe that the U.S. Government has betrayed the American people by becoming too involved in international politics. In fact, many groups argue that the U.S. is losing sovereignty to a socialist "New World Order," managed by the United Nations and funded primarily by international Jewish financiers (Berlet and Lyons 2000). Many patriot/militia members believe that the "New World Order" is behind a United Nations plan to invade the U.S., overthrow the government, disarm the citizens, and install a dictatorship. As one member of the Militia of Montana states:

> There are individuals in this world, within this country, and in our own government, who would like to rule the world.... These power hungry individuals have corrupted our government and are working on sabotaging our freedom by destroying the Constitution of the United States, in order to establish the "New World Order" (a.k.a. Global Community). (Quoted in Stern 1996:73).

Some patriot/militia members believe that the government actions at Ruby Ridge in 1992 and Waco in 1993 indicate that the U.S. government, in its attempt to disarm people, no longer supports the constitutional rights of its citizens (Berlet and Lyons 2000; Hamilton 1996; Stern 1996). Although we are unable to study the influence of these key events here because of the cross-sectional nature of our data, it seems likely that they played a role in the emergence of the movement, possibly acting as "suddenly-imposed grievances" (Walsh 1981).

According to some patriot/militia groups, part of the government's failure is its apparent secession of power to minority groups and women. Indeed, racism and sexism are two other ideological themes prevalent in the movement. Some movement members are influenced by the Christian Identity religion, which holds that whites are the true chosen people and that Jews are the descendants of the Devil (Hamilton 1996; Neiwert 1999). In a letter to Attorney General Janet Reno, Morris Dees of the Southern Poverty Law Center, states that his organization has "confirmed the active involvement of a number of well-known white supremacists...in the growing militia movement" (U.S. Committee on the Judiciary 1997b:75). This point is echoed in Swomley (1999) as well.

Anti-government rhetoric is often combined with anti-Semitism and racism (Abanes 1996; Dees 1996; Southern Poverty Law Center 1999). One patriot group member. Robert Wangrud, stated:

> There is only one race that founded this country and that is the White Race. The Constitution recognizes this and clearly states that only white people can be citizens of this country. The 14th Amendment changed all that, but we feel it became law illegally and as such is not binding (Quoted in Abanes 1996:33).

Similary, Simpson (1991: 20) argues:

> ...The vast majority of White people have become so befuddled by Jewish propaganda, that they believe this breaking down of barriers can go on without it ending in the destruction of their own race....I am firmly convinced, from a study of history and scripture, that if the White man in America settles down to live side by side with the Black, on any terms, it is only a matter of time— and not a long time—till he will cease to exist as a White man.

Many patriots call for the repeal of the 13th and 14th Amendments and believe that blacks and women should give up the right to vote and own property (Crawford and Burghart 1997; Kimmel

and Ferber 2000; Stern 1996). One book sold by the Militia of Montana argues, "Hillary Clinton and her feminist co-conspirators control the country" (Marrs 1993). Thus, both racism and highly traditional views of gender roles are themes running throughout the movement.

It is important to note, however, that there is some debate in the literature about the extent to which *all* or even *most* patriot/militia members hold racist, anti-Semitic and antifeminist beliefs (Dobratz and Shanks-Meile 1997). The issue is complicated because some groups deliberately seek to distance themselves from overtly racist and anti-Semitic views. As Berlet and Lyons (2000:296) suggest, racist views are clearly "woven into Patriot narrative, but in many cases it is unconscious and unintentional. In other cases far right activists hide their...views to recruit from, or take over, Patriot and militia groups;" These authors also note that the complexity leads some scholars to deem all "...militia members...closet Nazis while others, out of ignorance or expediency, sanitize the movement by trivializing evidence of racism and anti-Semitism" (Berlet and Lyons 2000:296). Thus, while we acknowledge that not all members of these groups hold racist and sexist beliefs, we do not want to ignore the rhetoric espoused by many of these groups.

Research Design, Dependent Variables, and Modeling Technique

In order to explore the factors that influence levels of patriot and militia organizing, we use data on levels of patriot/militia organization, at both the state and county-levels, in the United States. Our data come from the Southern Poverty Law Center's (SPLC) Intelligence Project, a task force that has the goal of identifying all of the patriot/militia groups active in the United States. Since 1994, this organization has been monitoring the activity of all organizations that identify themselves as patriots opposed to a "New World Order" government conspiracy (Southern Poverty Law Center 1996). This includes patriot and armed citizen militia organizations as well as common law courts.[5] The SPLC's Intelligence Project collects data on these groups through several means: field investigations, the study of Internet sites, studies of literature and publications, consultations with law enforcement agencies, and by monitoring news stories. In all, 778 patriot/militia organizations were active between 1994 and 1996, and their distribution across the U.S. can be seen in Figure 1.[6]

While in the state-level analysis we examine all 50 states, we conduct our county-level analysis on three states, California, Georgia, and Michigan. We chose these three states because they are diverse both regionally and in terms of our important independent variables. These states exhibit variation in the extent to which they lost manufacturing jobs, the extent to which they lost farms, and in the composition of their population. For example, Michigan lost approximately 12% of its manufacturing jobs between 1990 and 1993, a level on par with the national average. But, Georgia lost a below average percentage of its manufacturing jobs (5%), while California lost an above average percentage of jobs (24%). The three states exhibit similar variation in the other characteristics especially relevant to this analysis...

In both the state and county-level analyses presented below, our dependent variable is the number (or count) of patriot/militia organizations active in the state or county between 1994 and 1996. While there may be some variation in the *size* of these militia groups, there is evidence that these differences are not substantial. Patriot/militia groups are usually small; it is estimated that even the largest organizations, such as the Militia of Montana, have fewer than 250 members per chapter. Police in Ohio estimate that the state's militia groups have a total membership of approximately 1,000 people, which translates into an average of forty members per group (Winerup 1996). While police estimates of militia group size may be biased, this figure lends support for the argument that patriot/militia organizations tend to be fairly small in size. We argue, then, that the number of organizations is a good indicator of the overall level of mobilization in a state or county.

We also use counts of patriot/militia organizations as our dependent variable for a practical reason; specifically, these are the only data available documenting patriot/militia organization or

activity. We acknowledge that it would be interesting to examine membership numbers in each state, but these data simply are not available. In his testimony before the Senate Subcommittee on Terrorism, Technology, and Government Information in 1995, James L. Brown of the Bureau of Alcohol, Tobacco and Firearms (ATF), notes that *accurate* estimates of membership are not available because the ATF and other federal law enforcement agencies do not collect such data (U.S. Committee of the Judiciary 1997b:51). A similar point was made by Steven Emerson in his testimony before the Senate Subcommittee on Crime in 1996 (U.S. Committee of the Judiciary 1997a:131) wherein he remarked that it is not possible to obtain militia group membership numbers because membership lists are kept secret.

To analyze state and county counts of organizations, we use negative binomial regression, a variant of Poisson regression (Beck and Tolnay 1995), which is the most common method for analyzing event counts (Barron 1992). This form of negative binomial regression corrects for a common problem that occurs when an assumption of the Poisson regression method is violated: overdispersion. A condition of overdispersion exists when the variance of the dependent variable (in this case, the count of patriot/militia organizations) is greater than its mean, and may be caused by unobserved heterogeneity or contagion. Unobserved heterogeneity exists if differences between states on unmeasured variables affect the dependent variable. It is also possible that contagion exists, whereby the occurrence of one event increases the chances of further events. In other words, the existence of one patriot/militia organization in a state or county may inspire the formation of additional militia groups. Because it is possible that both factors are present in our data, we use negative binomial regression, rather than Poisson. The negative binomial method we use effectively takes care of the problem of overdispersion by adding a stochastic component to the model (Beck and Tolnay 1995; Land, McCall, and Nagin 1996). The model calculates coefficient–estimates through maximum likelihood methods, using the following equation:

$$\ln \lambda_i = X_i \beta + \varepsilon, \qquad (1)$$

where In λ_i denotes the natural logarithm of the expected value of the dependent variable, X_i denotes a matrix of covariates, and β represents the regression coefficients for the model. The inclusion of the error term, ε, allows for unexplained randomness in In λ_i.

As noted above, we conduct our analysis at two different levels, the state and county. We do this for two reasons. First, the underground and loose structure of patriot/militia organizations makes them especially difficult to study. Because the groups are somewhat elusive and hard to get a handle on, robustness checks are important. Conducting the analysis at both the state and county-level provides us with confidence that our findings are not an artifact of measurement.

On top of this consideration, certain economic and political processes may operate at the state level, while others may be more local. We think that it is fruitful to pursue research at both levels of analysis because while economic processes do vary within states, they also vary between states. On the one hand, state governments, because of their ability to set economic and political policy, are important (Leicht and Jenkins 1998).[7] On the other hand, aggregate measures of a state's political and economic climate may obscure important differences within states. Within a state, certain local areas may be particularly hard hit by changing economic conditions, but this local variation may wash out when we examine overall state conditions. Similarly, individuals experience changes in the racial composition of the population at the local level (even if their perceptions are affected by higher levels). Thus, although state-level shifts in minority populations may inspire mobilization, these effects may be stronger at the county-level. Because of these reasons, we examine both state-level and county-level variation in levels of patriot/militia organization.

State-Level Hypotheses and Independent Variables

Below, we present four models in order to test whether broad structural changes help explain state-by-state variation in levels of patriot/militia organization.... The first three models include variables to measure three categories of broad social changes that may be perceived of as threatening to patriot/militia members: demographic conditions, political competition, and economic hardship and economic restructuring. The final model includes all significant variables from the previous analysis, along with several controls for the overall political context of the state.[8]

Model 1 includes a measure of demographic change that we expect will affect patriot/militia mobilization based on ethnic competition theory arguments that dominant group members feel threatened if they perceive an increase in the size of minority populations, and based on the racist themes included in patriot/militia group rhetoric. Therefore, the analysis includes a dummy variable coded "1" if there was an above average increase, between 1980 and 1990, in the proportion of the state population that was non-white.[9] Because in this period most states (90%) saw an increase in the proportion of their population that is non-white, we define the dummy based on whether the state saw an increase in its non-white population that was above the mean for all states. We use a dummy variable rather than a continuous variable because we do not expect incremental differences in the non-white population to affect the mobilization of patriot/militia groups. We also use a dummy variable because a continuous measure caused multicollinearity problems in the models. We gathered data on the racial composition of the states from the *Statistical Abstract of the United States* (U.S. Bureau of the Census 1994).[10]

The perception that minorities or women are making political gains may also be threatening to dominant group members, therefore, the second model includes two variables designed to measure political competition. First, we include the percent of the state legislature that was African American in 1993 and second, we include the percent of the state legislature that was female in 1993. Because patriot/militia groups often espouse racist and anti-feminist ideology, we expect to see higher levels of mobilization in those states where political threats are more salient; those which have more African Americans and women in office. It is important to note that, with respect to women in office, we are not arguing that patriot/militia activity is sparked by liberal attitudes of female politicians or that female politicians are inevitably more liberal than their male counterparts. Our argument is about the threat generated by women in non-traditional gender roles holding political power. These data came from the *Statistical Abstract of the United States* (U.S. Bureau of the Census 1994).

Poor economic conditions in a state and economic restructuring may also inspire reactive mobilization, thus, in our third model, we include three variables to measure economic conditions. First, as an overall measure of the economic climate of the state, we include the unemployment rate in 1993. We expect that states with higher levels of unemployment will have higher levels of patriot/militia mobilization, based on prior research suggesting that economic deprivation may inspire reactive mobilization. This measure comes from the *Statistical Abstract of the United States* (U.S. Bureau of the Census 1994).

Second, in order to test the claim that globalization and economic restructuring influence reactive protest activity (Betz 1994; Castells 1997; Lipset 1963), we include a variable in our third model that measures changes in the manufacturing sector. We hypothesize that states that experienced a decline in the number of manufacturing sector jobs between 1990 and 1993 will have higher levels of patriot/militia organizing. Between 1990 and 1993, the number of manufacturing jobs in the U.S. declined by 10% (U.S. Bureau of the Census 1991, 1994). We created a dummy variable coded "1" when the state experienced a decrease in the size of the manufacturing sector, using data from the *Statistical Abstract of the United States* (U.S. Bureau of the Census 1992, 1994). Importantly, we do not expect that the number of manufacturing jobs, *per se,* should affect levels of patriot/militia mobilization, but that a *loss* of these jobs will be indicative of economic restructuring and economic crisis, thus, we employ the dichotomous measure.

In addition to changes in the location of manufacturing jobs, economic restructuring in the U.S. involves a move toward corporate agriculture. The resultant decline in the family farm may influence levels of patriot/militia organization (Abanes

1996; Dyer 1997; Kimmel and Ferber 2000). To tap this, we include a third variable in Model 3 that is coded "1" when a state lost farms between 1990 and 1993. We collected these data from the *Statistical Abstract of the United States* (U.S. Bureau of the Census 1992, 1994). As was the case with manufacturing jobs, we do not expect that the number of farms, *per se,* will affect the number of patriot/militia groups. Rather, we expect that the economic crisis created by a loss of farms will result in higher numbers of militia groups. In this period, 60% of U.S. states lost farms, while 40% either lost no farms or actually gained some. A dummy variable is appropriate due to the bimodal distribution of this measure.

We hypothesize that in addition to demographic, political, and economic threats, levels of militia and patriot organizing respond to the overall political context of the state and the level of preexisting organizational resources. Thus, in our final model, in addition to significant variables from the first three models, we include an additional three variables. First, in Model 4, we include the number of conservative organizations headquartered in each state in 1993 to measure potential organizing bases for the patriot/militia movement. These include white supremacy organizations, anti-taxation groups, historical revisionist groups, and traditionalist conservative organizations. We gathered these data from the *Encyclopedia of Associations* (Burek 1994). We expect to find more patriot/militia organizations in those states with higher levels of indigenous right-wing organization, both because of the overall organizing function these groups may serve, and because of the conservative political climate that they may both reflect and help create within a state.

The second additional variable in the fourth model measures the percent of the state's population that can be considered liberal. Wright and his colleagues (1985) developed this measure, which is a score measuring the percent of individuals in a state who said that they vote liberally. Wright created this measure using the results of 51 opinion polls with over 76,000 respondents. We predict that states with fewer self-proclaimed liberals will have higher levels of patriot/militia organizing.

Our third indicator of the state's political context is a measure of the strength of each state's gun control laws. With data from the Bureau of Alcohol, Tobacco, and Firearms (1989), we create a measure of the number of restrictive gun control laws in each state. Specifically, three laws were considered: whether or not any weapons are banned in the state, whether the state has a waiting period until firearms can be purchased, and whether gun owners must obtain a license before purchasing their guns. Thus, each state could have a value between zero and three for this variable. Political opportunity theory suggests that those states with more restrictive gun control legislation will see lower levels of patriot/militia activity, as stronger gun control laws indicate an institutional political system that is less receptive to claims made by patriot/militia groups. Alternatively, potential militia members may view gun control laws as a threat to their civil liberties, and this may inspire higher levels of organization. We thus include this variable in the analysis but note that there are two different and equally plausible predictions of its effect on patriot/militia organizing.

In all four state-level models presented below, we include two control variables. First, we include a variable representing the overall size of the state's white population, measured in thousands (U.S. Bureau of the Census 1994). Because the membership of patriot/militia organizations is almost exclusively white, we consider the state's white population to be the potential constituency for this movement.[11] We expect that states with larger white populations will have greater levels of patriot/militia organization. Our second control variable measures whether any of the patriot/militia organizations in the state were affiliated with other organizations through a chapter structure (Southern Poverty Law Center 1996). Because this affiliational structure may lead to higher counts of militia groups, we include a dummy variable coded as "1" if there were affiliated organizations in the state. In this way, we are able to ensure that our results are not dependent on assumptions we have made regarding the comparability of affiliated and non-affiliated organizations.

Results of State-Level Analyses

In Model 1, we examine the effect of changing demographic conditions on the number of patriot/militia organizations in a state (see Table 1).

Contrary to our hypothesis based on ethnic competition theory and on the racist rhetoric of some patriot/militia group members, an above average increase in the non-white population is associated with *lower* levels of patriot/militia organizing. However, we note that in the full model (Model 4) the coefficient becomes non-significant. We explore this relationship further in our county-level analysis, as it is possible that demographic changes within smaller geographic areas have more of an impact on levels of patriot/militia organizing.

With respect to the control variables in Table 1, it is not surprising that those states with higher white populations have more patriot/militia organizations. The effect of this measure remains the same across all of the models in Table 1. In Model 1, we do not find a significant relationship between our dummy variable for chapter or affiliated organizational structure, although the coefficient is in the expected positive direction and in subsequent models becomes significant, as we hypothesized.

In Model 2, we find some support for the hypothesis that political threat is associated with higher numbers of patriot/militia organizations. The percent of the state legislature that is female has a positive effect on the number of patriot/militia groups, a finding that is consistent with the argument that women in power pose a threat to patriot/militia group members. In Model 2, each additional percentage of women in the legislature is associated with a 3% higher number of patriot and militia organizations. This effect remains significant in the full model (see Model 4). This finding suggests that the political strength of women may inspire some men to become involved in a movement which calls for more traditional gender roles, as Kimmel and Ferber (2000) propose.

We do not find support, however, for the argument that gains in the political strength of African Americans explain levels of patriot/militia organization, as the coefficient for African American legislators is not significant, although it is in the expected positive direction. This finding, taken alongside the lack of support for our hypothesis regarding an increase in the non-white population (Model 1), indicates that despite the overtly racist rhetoric of many patriot/militia groups, the threat

Table 1. The Effect of Selected Independent Variables on Levels of Patriot Movement Organization in U.S. States. Negative Binomial Regression

	Model 1 Demographic Threat	Model 2 Political Threat	Model 3 Economic Threat	Model 4 Full Model with Controls
Above average increase in non-white population	−0.3736* (0.2136)	—	—	−0.3072 (0.2000)
Percent black legislators	—	0.0106 (0.0222)	—	—
Percent female legislators	—	0.0280* (0.0133)	—	0.0356** (0.0124)
Unemployment rate	—	—	−0.0225 (0.0973)	—
Loss of manufacturing jobs	—	—	0.5364* (0.2595)	0.6667** (0.2387)
Loss of farms	—	—	0.4117* (0.2151)	0.3283* (0.1982)
Number of conservative organizations	—	—	—	0.0170 (0.0423)
Percent liberal voters	—	—	—	−0.0523** (0.0221)
Number of restrictive gun laws	—	—	—	−0.1893* (0.0983)
White population	0.1303*** (0.0278)	0.1100*** (0.0268)	0.0884*** (0.0277)	0.1106*** (0.0306)
Presence of affiliated militia organizations	0.3955 (0.3738)	0.5595* (0.2468)	0.4869* (0.2118)	0.4882** (0.2078)
Intercept	2.0853*** (0.1596)	1.3641*** (0.3401)	1.5024*** (0.5625)	1.7958*** (0.4188)
Dispersion parameter	0.3738 (0.0893)	0.3640 (0.0871)	0.3448 (0.0840)	0.2332 (0.0633)
Chi-square	59.8978	58.0805	59.2893	51.7919
df	46	45	44	40

Note:
* $p < .05$ ** $p < .01$ *** $p < .001$ one-tailed test.
N = 50; standard errors in parentheses.

posed by non-whites (at least at the state level) is not associated with higher levels of organization. Another possibility is that population changes are experienced and, therefore, have an effect at a more local (county) level, as we explore below.

The results presented in Model 3 provide support for the hypothesis that economic restructuring is associated with patriot/militia organizing in the mid-90s. Those states that experienced a loss of jobs in the manufacturing sector saw higher numbers of patriot/militia groups. States where there was a decline in the manufacturing sector had 71% more patriot and militia organizations than those states with a more stable manufacturing economy. Model 3 also shows that those states that lost farms had higher numbers of patriot/militia organizations. A loss of farms is associated with a 51% higher number of patriot/militia organizations. These two findings are consistent with arguments that globalization and the economic dislocations caused by the movement of labor positions overseas and the growth of corporate agribusiness are associated with the rise of the militia/patriot movement (Castells 1997). These results remain significant in the full model.

Contrary to our hypothesis, the coefficient measuring the state's unemployment rate is not significant. When considered alongside the findings for the loss of manufacturing jobs and farms, this finding suggests that the patriot/militia movement is associated with economic crises among certain segments of the population, rather than a general economic downturn. It is also possible that unemployment at the local level affects patriot/militia organizing, but that state-level differences in unemployment do not do so. We explore this possibility in the subsequent county-level analysis.

As noted above, Model 4 includes (in addition to significant variables from prior models) three variables to control for the organizational and political context. The addition of these variables does not significantly change the results for the structural change variables reported above. Both of the two measures designed to capture information about the state's political context are significant in Model 4 in Table 1. The coefficient for the gun control measure is negative and significant, suggesting that more restrictive gun control laws are associated with fewer patriot/militia organizations. The negative coefficient is consistent with political opportunity theory's assertion that movements are less likely to mobilize when they face an unfavorable political climate. In other words, more stringent gun control laws are more likely to exist in more liberal states, and these states are likely to have less favorable political climates for patriot/militia organizations.[12]

The coefficient for the second political context variable, the percentage of the state's population that claims they vote liberally, is also statistically significant and in the expected negative direction. A more liberal populace is associated with fewer patriot/militia organizations. Each additional percentage of the state that is liberal is associated with 5% fewer patriot and militia organizations. This finding resonates with our finding regarding gun control laws; more liberal states are more likely to have stronger gun control laws and fewer patriot/militia organizations.

As we noted earlier, resource mobilization theory predicts that those states with higher levels of indigenous conservative organization should have higher levels of patriot/militia mobilization. We do not find support for this hypothesis, as the coefficient for our measure of preexisting conservative organizations is not statistically significant (however, it is in the expected positive direction). One explanation for the lack of significance of this variable is that we may already be controlling for many of the factors that explain levels of conservative organization. We discuss the implications of our findings after presenting the results of the county-level analysis.

County-Level Hypotheses and Independent Variables

In our county-level analysis, we include independent variables similar to those used in the state-level analysis, although due to a lack of available data, the number of variables is reduced. The first model includes a measure of demographic change consistent with that used in the state-level analysis. We include a dummy variable measuring whether the county saw an increase in its non-white population between 1980 and 1990. On average, counties saw an increase of 1% in the proportion of their population that is non-white (see Appendix, Table A1). The non-white population increased in 67% of counties. This measure comes from the U.S. Census (U.S. Bureau of the Census 1983, 1993).[13]

The second model in the county-level analysis includes variables measuring economic conditions within the county. As was the case in the state-level analysis, the first economic variable measures the county's unemployment rate using data from the *County and City Extra* (1995), a data book that presents data from various government sources. This variable is a continuous measure of the percent of the county population that was unemployed in 1993. We expect to find more patriot/militia organizations in counties with higher unemployment rates.

The second economic variable we include is a dummy variable that indicates whether the size of the manufacturing sector in the county's labor market area saw an above average decline between 1990 and 1993.[14] We use a dummy variable rather than a continuous variable in order to use consistent measures in the two sets of analyses.[15] The manufacturing sector data were also collected from the *County and City Extra* (1992, 1995). Each county in a labor market area has the same value for the change in the size of the manufacturing sector.

We examine the loss of manufacturing jobs within labor market areas rather than counties because research demonstrates that labor markets do not conform to standard geographic units such as SMAs or counties (Tolbert 1989). It is conceptually incorrect to conceive of labor markets as geographic regions such as cities or counties, when they actually consist of relations among buyers and sellers of labor (Tolbert 1989). Therefore, rather than examining changes in the manufacturing sector within a single county, we use labor market areas defined by Tolbert and his colleagues from the Economic Research Service (Tolbert and Sizer 1996). Tolbert and Sizer use census data to define the labor market area relevant to individuals living in different U.S. counties. They define areas based on a hierarchical cluster analysis of county-to-county flows of commuters. Thus, these labor market areas reflect the fact that individuals living in rural areas may commute farther distances to work than individuals

living in more developed areas. For example, research shows that 13% of males who own farms commute more than 100 miles for jobs to supplement their farm income (Deseran 1989).

As was the case in our state-level analysis, we include a measure designed to tap changes in the farming sector between 1987 and 1992.[16] We do not expect an incremental change in the number of farms to explain reactive mobilization, rather, that the economic hardship created by a loss of farms may inspire mobilization. Therefore, this measure is operationalized as a dummy variable coded "1" when a county lost an above average number of farms between the two time periods.[17] These data come from the *County and City Extra* (1994, 1996). We expect the results of the county-level analysis to mirror those of the state-level analysis. We predict that those counties which have suffered as a result of economic restructuring within the manufacturing and agricultural sectors will be the sites of patriot/militia organizations.

The third and final model in the county-level analysis includes a variable measuring the political climate of the county, in addition to the significant variables from the previous models. We include a measure of the percent of voters in the county who voted for a Republican candidate in the 1992 presidential election. These data were collected from *America Votes* (1994).

In all three models, we control for the size of the white population of the county (measured in thousands), using data collected from the U.S. Census (U.S. Bureau of the Census 1993), as we did earlier in the state-level analysis.

Results of County-Level Analyses
Seventy-eight of the 300 counties we examine had a patriot/militia organization within their boundaries. In those 78 counties, the number of patriot/militia groups ranged from 1 to 8. The results of the negative binomial regression analysis provide us with some insight into the question of why some counties have more patriot/militia groups than do others. And, it is important to note that for the most part, our county-level results are consistent with those obtained in our state-level analysis (see Table 1).

In the first county-level model (see Model 1), we find support for the argument that an increasing minority population is associated with a higher number of patriot/militia organizations within a county. Counties whose non-white populations increased have 370% more patriot/militia organizations. This result is consistent with the argument that the patriot/militia movement mobilizes, at least in part, in response to the threat produced by an increase in minority populations. However, as we note above, we do not find this effect in the state-level analysis. One explanation for the discrepancy in findings is that the demographics of their local environment may influence people more so than does the composition of the population at the state level. People experience and interact with people in their local environment more often than they are confronted with the demographics of their state. There can be a great deal of variation between different cities or counties within a state in terms of racial composition, and perhaps state-level data obscure the relationship between the population composition and patriot/militia organization. Given our mixed findings, we are not willing to make a strong argument regarding the relationship between increasing non-white populations and patriot/militia mobilization. Further research is necessary before we will fully understand the relationship.

As was the case in the state-level analysis presented above, counties that experienced a decline in the manufacturing sector and a decline in the number of farms are more likely to have a patriot/militia organization (see Table 2, Model 2). Those counties that experienced an above average decline in the size of the manufacturing sector have 152% more patriot/militia organizations. An above average loss in the number of farms is associated with 107% more patriot/militia organizations. The effects of economic restructuring on levels of patriot/militia mobilization are experienced at both the state and county level.

As in the state-level analysis, the coefficient for the unemployment rate is not significant. As we noted earlier, this finding indicates that a general economic crisis is not associated with increases in patriot/militia mobilization. Rather, patriot/militia mobilization is affected by decreases in the manufacturing and farming sectors, specifically.

The economic and demographic variables in Models 1 and 2 maintain their significance when we add a control for the political climate of the county (see Model 3). Based on political opportunity and resource mobilization theories, we hypothesized that more politically conservative counties, as measured by the percent of the vote going to the Republican presidential candidate, would be more likely to have patriot/militia groups. However, this hypothesis is not supported by the analysis, as the coefficient is not significant, although it is in the expected positive direction. Note, however, that we do find an effect at the state-level; states with more liberal populations had fewer militia group members. One possible explanation for this discrepancy is our use of different measures for the state and county-level analyses. In the state-level analysis, we are able to use a measure of the percent of individuals who said they voted liberally, while in the county-level analysis the only measure available was the percent of people who voted Republican in the prior presidential election. Subsequent research should explore this relationship further.

Conclusion

This paper makes four primary contributions to the literature on social movements and to the study of the patriot/militia movement. First, we emphasize the importance of bringing the notion of threat back into the study of movement emergence. Social movement scholars cast strain theory aside in the 1970s in favor of opportunity and resource-based theories of movement emergence, but they may have thrown the baby out with the bath water. While abandoning strain theory's micro-level focus on irrational individuals may be warranted, scholars were hasty in their rejection of the macro-level component of the theory. We present evidence here supporting strain theory's macro-level argument that structural social changes, including economic and political shifts, influence levels of patriot and militia organization. Our key point then, is that theories of social movement emergence should include structural social change and the threat it engenders

Table 2. The Effect of Selected Independent Variables on the Number of Patriot Movement Organizations in 300 U.S. Counties. Negative Binomial Regression

	Model 1 Demographic Threat	Model 2 Economic Threat	Model 3 Full Model with Controls
Increase in the non-white population	1.5466*** (0.3670)	—	1.3672*** (0.3691)
Unemployment rate	—	0.0203 (0.0463)	—
Above average loss of manufacturing jobs	—	0.9246*** (0.2549)	0.8001*** (0.2533)
Above average loss of farms	—	0.7272** (0.2546)	0.6423** (0.2465)
Percent voting for republican president (1992 election)	—	—	0.0150 (0.0168)
White population	0.0014*** (0.0004)	0.0015*** (0.0005)	0.0011** (0.0004)
Intercept	−2.3136*** (0.3376)	−2.1754*** (0.4319)	−3.6567*** (0.9395)
Dispersion parameter	1.3586 (0.3749)	1.4645 (0.3204)	1.1091 (0.3390)
Chi-square	325.9718	304.7220	298.8925
df	297	295	293

Note:
* $p < .05$ ** $p < .01$ *** $p < .001$ one-tailed test.
N = 300; standard errors in parentheses.

as important mobilizing conditions, particularly for reactive social movements.

While our findings provide empirical support for the argument that reactive movements respond to threat, future research should also consider whether or not structural changes and the threats they create also affect the mobilization of *proactive* and *competitive* movements. If Tilly's (1978) distinction between these three types of movements is to provide us with a useful typology, future research should evaluate whether they emerge in response to different phenomena (Goodwin and Jasper 1999). While research on proactive movements, such as the

civil rights movement, suggests that these respond to an increase in opportunities and resources, it is also possible that some proactive movements respond to both threats and opportunities. In a society as complex as ours, threats and opportunities may come from a variety of social actors within different social arenas. A movement may simultaneously experience opportunities in one arena and threats in another. Thus, future research should explore the emergent conditions associated with each of Tilly's (1978) three movement types.

A second contribution of this paper is our use of empirical analyses at two different levels, states and counties. While we did not obtain consistent results between the two levels of analysis for the effects of non-white population change, we did find similar results for our hypotheses about economic restructuring. The use of analyses at two different levels helps us more fully understand the dynamics of reactive mobilization. While it is not always feasible to study phenomena at two different levels, when data are available, scholars should attempt to do so. This is especially true when studying phenomena as illusive as the patriot/militia movement, where robustness checks are particularly important.

A third contribution of this paper is that we tap the multifaceted nature of threat by including measures of threats spurred by economic restructuring, increases in the political power of formerly less powerful groups, and changing minority group populations. While movement scholars typically focus on threats (such as repression) that are created by actors in the institutional political arena (e.g., Goldstone and Tilly 2001), we show that actors and events outside of the institutional political arena may also create a sense of threat and inspire reactive mobilization. The most robust of these threats for the patriot/militia movement is economic restructuring of the manufacturing and agricultural sectors. Net of an overall economic decline, the loss of manufacturing jobs and farms is associated with higher levels of patriot/militia organizing at both the state and local level. This is an important finding and resonates with the findings from qualitative research and journalistic accounts of the patriot/militia movement, as well as with studies of the white separatist movement (Dobratz and Shanks-Meile 1997). But we also find in our state-level analysis that women's legislative gains are associated with patriot/militia organizing. And, in our county-level analysis, we find that increases in minority group populations are associated with increasing patriot/militia organization. Future research, then, should expand the notion of threat to consider different kinds of threat, including those outside of the institutional political arena.

A final contribution of this paper lies in the implications of our findings regarding the effect of economic restructuring on patriot/militia

organization. Patriot/militia rhetoric is rife with discussions of national sovereignty, the threat of an international conspiracy to take over the U.S., and the failure of the U.S. Government to uphold the Constitution. Why, then, do we find that economic conditions, at the state and local level, have such a powerful impact on patriot/militia organization? Like the working class members studied by Wellman (1993), workers in manufacturing and agricultural sectors may be hit hard by changing economic conditions, and therefore, may find the messages articulated by the patriot/militia movement appealing. Arguments that international interests are gaining power may resonate with those who have experienced a loss of control in their local environment (Castells 1997). Thus, our findings indicate that the rhetoric articulated by the patriot/militia movement is filtered through the personal experiences of individuals. To some, in particular, those hard hit by economic restructuring, the messages will ring true and serve as a call to action.

NOTES

The authors would like to thank Irence R. Beattie, Craig Jenkins, Doug McAdam, and Verta Taylor and anonymous reviewers for their helpful comments on earlier drafts of this article.

1. The *Patriot* movement involves Individuals who Identify themselves as patriots opposed to a "New World Order" government conspiracy. The common theme articulated by the groups we define as belonging to this movement, is the idea that the U.S. government has failed to uphold and protect the Constitution, and that citizen action is necessary for its protection. *Militia* group members are patriots who have formed armed units. We include *both* militia organizations and patriot organizations in our analyses and refer to these as "patriot/militia" organizations in this article. In the section of this article entitled. "The Patriot Movement in the United States." we describe in detail the beliefs that are held, and the ideology articulated, by the movement.

2. They do concede that "suddenly imposed grievances," such as environmental disasters, may trigger mobilization (Walsh 1981). Scholars in this tradition also explore the mobilizing effect of the state's use of repression, which can be considered a type of threat.

3. Tilly (1978:144) classifies collective action based on the forms used and claims articulated by collective actors. In addition to reactive action, he defines competitive and proactive action. Competitive action overlaps with reactive,

and occurs when groups assert the right to resources also claimed by another group. Proactive actions are those that claim resources that have not been previously enjoyed.

4. Environmental crisis is another factor that sometimes inspires reactive mobilization (Walsh 1981), but it is not relevant to our case.

5. The SPLC also includes Identity Churches in their definition, but we exclude these because it is not clear that all patriot/militia organizations are racist and, as we note in the text above, many patriot/militia organizations try to distance themselves from racist organizations.

6. Another potential data source for this project is Wilcox's (1995) *Guide to the American Right*. In order to verify that our findings from the SPLC data are robust, we obtained the 1995 version of this book and ran the same state-level analyses. The results are comparable to those that we present here. We present the results from the SPLC data analysis in this paper because these data are more readily available to the public. (The 1995 edition of the Wilcox book was extremely difficult to obtain, and the 1996 book is no longer available).

7. The economic structure of a state may be unique, for example, if the state offers tax-break incentives to lure corporations within its borders. And, of course, states are also important in setting policy (Earl and Soule 2001; Grattet, Jenness, and Curry 1998; McCammon et al. 2001; Soule and Earl 2001; Soule and Zylan 1997; Zylan and Soule 2000).

8. We include only significant variables in the full model because of our small number of observations and limited degrees of freedom. We performed traditional regression diagnostics, Including variance Inflation factor tests for multi-collinearity. We found no evidence of multicollinearity in the models presented in this article. We also examined whether outliers were driving the results by running the analyses excluding cases with very high numbers of patriot/ militia groups, or with extreme values for important independent variables. Exclusion of outliers did not significantly alter the results.

9. Because patriot/militia members sometimes espouse anti-Semitic rhetoric (Abanes 1996: Berlet and Lyons 2000). we also ran models including three different measures of the Jewish population and organization in each state: the presence or absence of an Anti-Defamation League Office in the state, the number of Jewish Community Centers in the state, and an estimate of the total Jewish population in the state (and the change between 1980 and 1990). None of these

measures was ever significant, and we do not include them in the models we present here because of our small number of observations and limited degrees of freedom.

10. The use of dummy variables in place of continuous variables is appropriate in this case, as in many cases comparing geographic units. The coefficients on continuous measures are calculated at their means, but with this measure (as well as many others used in this paper) the relevant action is not at the variable's mean. Thus, in addition to reducing multicollinearity, using the dummy variable here makes more sense theoretically.

11. We control for the white population rather than the total population of the state for a second, practical reason: we experienced significant multicollinearity problems when controlling for the state's total population.

12. We speculated that gun control laws may be perceived as a threat by patriot/militia members and may therefore inspire their mobilization, however, this does not appear to be the case.

13. Because there is much greater variation in the change in the non-white population at the county-level, this dummy variable is defined differently than at the state-level, where 90% of the cases experienced an increase in their non-white population.

14. Because the vast majority of labor market areas lost manufacturing jobs between 1990 and 1993, we coded this variable "1" when the county's labor market area (LMA) lost an above average percent of jobs, rather than when it lost any manufacturing jobs. In other words, this variable is coded "1" when the county's LMA lost more than the mean value for all states. We should note that we obtain comparable results when we assign the dummy a value of "1" when the county's labor market area lost any manufacturing jobs.

15. We did obtain comparable results when using the continuous measure.

16. We use the change In farms from 1987 to 1992, rather than between 1990 and 1993, as we do in the state-level analysis because farm data were not available for counties for 1990 and 1993.

17. Because a large majority of counties lost farms. we assign this variable a value of "1" when the county lost an above average percentage of its farms. We should note that we obtain comparable results when we assign the dummy a value of "one" when the county lost any farms.

Part 2

Political Opportunities

Writing in 1970, the political scientist Michael Lipsky (1970: 14) urged scholars to be skeptical of:

> system characterizations presumably true for all times and places.... We are accustomed to describing communist systems as "experiencing a thaw" or "going through of process of retrenchment." Should it not be at least an open question as to whether the American political system experiences such stages and fluctuations? Similarly, is it not sensible to assume that the system will be more or less open to specific groups at different times and at different places?

Lipsky believed that the answer to both questions was yes. He assumed that the ebb and flow of protest activity was largely a function of changes that left established authorities newly vulnerable and/or receptive to the demands of particular groups. Three years later, another political scientist, Peter Eisinger (1973: 11), used the phrase *structure of political opportunities* to help account for variation in riot behavior in 43 American cities. Consistent with Lipsky's argument, Eisinger found that "the incidence of protest is...related to the nature of the city's political opportunity structure," which he defined as "the degree to which groups are likely to be able to gain access to power and to manipulate the political system" (Eisinger 1973:5). In 1978, Charles Tilly elaborated on these fragmentary conceptual beginnings by devoting a full chapter of his landmark book, *From Mobilization to Revolution*, to the important facilitative role of "opportunity" in emergent collective action.

Within four years the key premise underlying the work of Lipsky, Eisinger, and Tilly had been incorporated as one of the central tenets into a new *political process* model of social movements (McAdam 1999 [1982]). Proponents of the model saw the timing and ultimate fate of movements as powerfully shaped by the variable opportunities afforded challengers by the shifting institutional structure and ideological disposition of those in power. Though not without its critics (Goodwin and Jasper 1999; Polletta 2004), this central assumption and the related concept of political opportunities has become a staple of social movement research. The emergence and development of movements as diverse as the American women's movement (Costain 1992), liberation theology (Smith 1991), political movements in Central America (Brockett 2005), the nuclear power movement (Meyer 1993), protest waves in El Salvador (Almeida 2003), new social movement activity in Germany (Koopmans 1992), and the variable success of farm worker mobilization in California (Jenkins 1985) have been attributed to changes in the *political opportunity structure*.

The first selection by Craig Jenkins, David Jacobs, and Jon Agnone embodies the oldest tradition in the study of political opportunities and movements. Revisiting the canonical case of African American civil rights (McAdam 1999 [1982]), the authors show that over a 50-year period (1948–1997) the ebb and flow of black protest activity is strongly related to the expansion and contraction in political opportunities. Favorable opportunities in this period include: "divided government, strong northern Democratic Party allies, and, during the 1950s...Cold War foreign policy constraints." The latter factor corroborates narrative treatments of the period by Dudziak (2000;), Layton (2000;), McAdam (1999 [1982]: vii–xlii;), and Skrentny (1998).

In addition to the many studies that have sought to explain the emergence and subsequent development of a single movement on the basis of changes in the vulnerability or receptivity of authorities to movement claims over time, the stress on political opportunities has also spawned a comparative tradition in which researchers have explained the fate of the same movement in a number of countries on the basis of more stable national-level differences in state structure. The aforementioned study by Eisinger exemplifies this tradition. So too does the second piece in this part by Hanspeter Kriesi and colleagues. In this selection, the authors argue that the variable timing, extent, and success of the "new social movements" that arose in most Western European countries in the 1970s and 1980s are largely explained by stable institutional differences that granted movement activists more or less access and influence across these national political systems.

If these two research emphases—changes in political opportunity keying the ebb and flow of movement activity over time and differences in institutional structure shaping cross-national variation in the strength of the same movement— are the oldest in the political opportunity tradition, exciting new lines of theory and research have developed in recent years. Tamara Kay's article

documenting an upsurge in cross-border labor mobilization in the wake of the North American Free Trade Agreement takes up the important issue of how globalization may be reshaping the locus of "political opportunities." Just as the European Union now affords activists any number of new venues in which to press their demands (Marks and McAdam 1996), Kay contends that NAFTA "catalyzed cross-border labor cooperation and collaboration . . . by creating a new opportunity structure at the transnational level."

Finally, in his detailed analysis of protest events in El Salvador between 1962 and 1981, Almeida assesses the simultaneous impact of "opportunity" and "threat" on movement activity. Traditionally, threat and opportunity have been seen as "either or" features of contention, as if movements were catalyzed by one or the other. Although some have speculated that threat and opportunity are not mutually exclusive and, in fact, might interact to shape movement activity (McAdam 1996), virtually no empirical analysis had been adduced to verify or confirm this view. Almeida's work addresses the longstanding neglect of this important issue.

4.
Political Opportunities and African-American Protest, 1948–1997

J. CRAIG JENKINS, DAVID JACOBS, AND JON AGNONE

In response to the general concern that "social movements and the state are seldom treated together as interacting dimensions of the same political process" (Walton 1992, p. 1), a number of scholars have advanced arguments about political opportunities to account for the mobilization, strategies, and outcomes of social movements (Gamson 1990; Piven and Cloward 1977; Jenkins and Perrow 1977; Tilly 1978; Skocpol 1979; McAdam 1996, 1999; Jenkins 1985; Kitschelt 1986; Costain 1992; Kriesi et al. 1995; Koopmans 1995; Della Porta and Diani 1999; McAdam, Tarrow, and Tilly 2001; McAdam and Su 2002). The underlying assumption is that protest is "simply politics by other means" (Gamson 1990, p. 139) and that, for politically excluded groups, new opportunities increase the perceived likelihood of success, thereby encouraging mobilization and collective action.

Political opportunity theory, however, has developed in an ad hoc fashion, in part because of the reliance on historical case studies that lack multivariate tests. This led to debates about the meaning of political opportunities (Gamson and Meyer 1996; McAdam 1996), whether opportunities can be distinguished from other factors that facilitate protest (McAdam 1996; Tarrow 1996), the mechanisms through which opportunities work (Della Porta and Diani 1999, pp. 213–25), and the importance of opportunities versus threats (Goldstone and Tilly 2001; Tarrow 1998, pp. 85–87; Van Dyke and Soule 2002; Van Dyke 2003). Some question whether opportunities (or any other factors) can explain protest across time, arguing that protest can "only be predicted

Jenkins J. Craig, David Jacobs, and Jon Agnoke. 2003 "Political Opportunities and African American Protest, 1948–1997. *American Journal of Sociology* 109: 277–303. Reprinted by permission of The University of Chicago Press. Notes have been renumbered and edited.

from episode to episode" (Turner and Killian 1987, p. 255; Lofland 1993, p. 216). As one might expect from this lack of agreement, research findings sometimes have been contradictory as well.

We focus on how political opportunities affect the frequency of African-American protest between 1948 and 1997. Some contend that elite divisions created by electoral competition and divided government encourage protest (Piven and Cloward 1977; Tilly 1978, pp. 213–14), while others point to the effects of political allies in the form of strong left parties (Rubin, Griffin, and Wallace 1983; Jenkins and Perrow 1977; Jenkins 1985, pp. 225–26; Minkoff 1997) or, alternatively, out-of-power left parties (Kriesi et al. 1995; Della Porta and Diani 1999, pp. 219–22). Other students of social movements and protest argue that political threats are important because, contrary to a simple rational choice calculus, protest is reactive (Goldstone and Tilly 2001).

In this study, we also pursue somewhat neglected topics by assessing the effects of collective grievances and indigenous group organization. While some argue that grievances are "secondary" (McCarthy and Zald 1977, p. 1215) or "relatively constant and pervasive" when protest by politically excluded groups is at issue (Jenkins and Perrow 1977, p. 265), others point to "fraternal" or group-based relative deprivation stemming from racial inequality (Geschwender 1964, 1973; Gurr 1970; Morgan and Clark 1973; Abeles 1976; Smith and Ortiz 2002) and to structural strains stemming from unemployment and the disorganization of everyday life (Piven and Cloward 1977; Useem 1980, 1998; Snow et al. 1998). Indigenous group organization, which provides leadership and organizers, collective solidarity, and social networks for the development and dissemination of injustice frames and tactical innovations (Morris 1984; McAdam 1999, pp. 98–106; McAdam, McCarthy, and Zald 1988), also should contribute to protest frequency. Organized groups are better able to mobilize and act collectively, making protest more likely.

We use time-series analyses of yearly data to examine the frequency of African-American protest from 1948 through 1997. With the exception of Minkoff (1997), past work (McAdam 1983, 1999; Jenkins and Eckert 1986) on African-American protest events has focused on a relatively narrow period by limiting analyses to events between 1955 and 1980. Protest before and after the civil rights era was neglected. By analyzing a longer period, which includes the three decades after the major legal gains of the civil rights movement, we can determine if systematic factors produce these protests or if protest "can only be predicted from episode to episode" (Turner and Killian 1987, p. 255). The multivariate time-series approach we use in this study will furnish independent estimates of the explanatory power of opportunities, threats, collective grievances, and indigenous organization.

Explanations for Protest

We begin with political opportunities, not because we assume that this is the most central factor, but because there has been considerable debate about its definition and its influence on protest. By political opportunities we mean "the probability that social protest actions will lead to success in achieving a desired outcome" (Goldstone and Tilly 2001, p. 182). Opportunity theory assumes rational choice on the part of protesters, who evaluate their political environment and make calculations about the likely impact of their collective action or inaction. Analysts normally distinguish between dynamic and structural opportunities (Gamson and Meyer 1996; Tarrow 1996). In this analysis, we focus on three dynamic processes that varied over a 50-year period: (1) elite divisions; (2) the power of political allies; and (3) political threats. Our research design will not let us explore arguments about regime centralization, bureaucratization, and political institutions because these explanatory factors did not change during the period we study. Such explanations cannot be analyzed with a research design restricted to events in one nation within a 50-year period but instead require a longer time period or

cross-national comparisons (Tilly, Tilly, and Tilly 1975; Kitschelt 1986; Kriesi et al. 1995).

Tilly (1978, pp. 213–14) argues that closely divided, competitive political situations create opportunities for protest. Polity members normally oppose all political challenges by excluded groups, even moderates who are simply pressing for polity membership. For polity members "any change in the makeup of the polity is inherently disruptive of the institutionalized status quo and thus something to be resisted" (McAdam 1999, p. 19). Yet, in a closely divided and competitive situation, polity members may have to tolerate if not actively support political challengers. Several researchers argue that the close and highly competitive presidential elections, coupled with small congressional power margins, in the 1950s and early 1960s led to relaxed repression and civil rights proposals that encouraged African-American protest (Piven and Cloward 1977, pp. 213–21, 231–35; McAdam 1999, pp. 156–60, 169–72; Valelly 1993). Discussing the general protest wave in the 1960s and early 1970s, Jenkins (1985, p. 218) claims, "In the context of a series of closely contested (Presidential) elections, in which the margin of victory was often less than one percent, two swing voting blocs (African-Americans and the new middle class) became increasingly decisive in the electoral calculations of political elites." Costain (1992, pp. 22–24) argues that close presidential elections also created bipartisan tolerance and support for the early women's movement. In a time-series analysis of student protest between 1930 and 1990, Van Dyke (2003) finds that a closely divided federal government leads to greater protest.

HYPOTHESIS 1.—*Electoral competition and resulting elite divisions create opportunities for greater African-American protest.*

A second focus has been political allies. Some contend that strong left parties signal a responsive government that has the power to alter relevant policies, thereby encouraging leftist protest (Piven and Cloward 1977; Jenkins 1985, pp. 217–22). Others argue the opposite view, that out-of-power left parties have a greater stake in supporting protest that promises to strengthen their electoral position whereas strong left parties provide routine political access to challengers, thereby discouraging protest (Katzenstein and Mueller 1987; Kriesi et al. 1995; Della Porta and Diani 1999, pp. 215–22). There is empirical support for both arguments. Studies have found that the congressional strength of the Democratic Party encourages African-American protest (Minkoff 1997) and industrial strikes (Rubin et al. 1983; Isaac and Christiansen 2002). In Japan during the 1960s, the election of environmentalists to the Japanese parliament encouraged the mobilization of local environmental movements (Almeida and Stearns 1998). On the other side, some argue that out-of-power left parties in Western Europe promoted "new social movement" protest in a bid to contest the next election (Koopmans and Rucht 1995, pp. 95–106; Kriesi et al. 1995, chap. 3; Maguire 1995). When researchers studied the U.S. feminist and African-American movements, Minkoff (1997, p. 790) found that Democratic congressional power *reduced* feminist protest but *increased* African-American protest, indicating opposite effects on these two movements. Soule et al. (1999) found that Democratic presidents reduce both feminist protest and conventional political action, while Van Dyke (2003) found that Democratic presidents reduce student protest.

A possible explanation for these inconsistent results concerns the initial political status of the challenging group. African-Americans were politically excluded when they began to protest, so the development of a powerful ally might promise to reduce repression and encourage successful protest. In contrast, the women's movement enjoyed strong political access to Congress and the White House from its early mobilization in the mid- and late 1960s (Freeman 1973; Costain 1992, chap. 2). This may have encouraged the movement to shun protest in favor of institutional methods (Costain 1992) and, when its Democratic Party ally was later out of power, to resort to protest (Soule et al. 1999). The initially excluded status of African-Americans thus leads to

HYPOTHESIS 2.—*Left-party strength creates opportunities for increased African-American protest.*

A related hypothesis focuses on political access. Once a previously excluded group obtains political power, less costly routine political action is favored over more costly protest. Minkoff (1997) found that the growth of African-American congressional representation retarded protest.

HYPOTHESIS 3.—*Increased African-American representation in Congress provides routine political access and thus reduces African-American protest.*

A third political-ally effect may stem from external constraints on elites that lead them to adopt favorable policies. Several scholars argue that Cold War international competition with the Soviet Union for support of newly independent states made Jim Crow racism a major diplomatic liability. This led the Eisenhower administration to promote a civil rights bill in 1956, intervene in the Little Rock, Arkansas, school desegregation conflict in 1957, and promote diplomatic activities abroad that emphasized racial progress (Plummer 1996, pp. 269–73; Skrentny 1998, pp. 272–77). Since political incumbents should have "known" political records that movement supporters can use to gauge their willingness to respond favorably to protest, campaigns by Republican presidential incumbents during this period should signal opportunities. This should have held until 1968, by which time détente, the autonomy of the international nonaligned movement, and the passage of major civil rights laws dismantling Jim Crow eliminated this international diplomatic pressure and Republican presidents shifted to a "Southern strategy" by using symbolic racial appeals to conservative whites to solicit votes (Edsall and Edsall 1991; Skrentny 1998).

HYPOTHESIS 4.—*Campaigns by incumbent Republican presidential candidates between 1947 and 1964 signaled additional opportunities that increased African-American protest.*

Political opportunity theory assumes a rational choice premise that several have criticized for misrepresenting the calculus behind protest. Drawing on prospect theory (Quattrone and Tversky 1988), researchers have argued that negative rewards (or threats) are intrinsically more motivating than their positive counterparts (or opportunities) (Berejikian 1992; Goldstone and Tilly 2001). By threats, we mean "the costs that social groups will incur from protest, or that it expects to suffer if it does not take action" (Goldstone and Tilly 2001, p. 183). Tilly (1978, pp. 134–35) makes the additional point that groups are more responsive to threats because they tend to inflate the value of resources already under control, overestimate the potential negative impact of threats, and can respond more quickly to threats by using existing networks and practices, while, on the other hand, responses to new opportunities demand time-consuming and expensive mobilization.

Several studies document the threat effects of repression and impending negative policies. Francisco (1995) found that state repression in a democratic context stimulates protest rather than reducing it by violating democratic accessibility norms. Rasler (1996) argues that, although repression had short-term negative effects, it also had long-term positive effects on rebellious protest in the autocratic context of the Iranian revolution of 1978–79. "Goading" events (Lofland 1993, p. 220), such as the threat of negative policies or impending governmental changes, may also stimulate protest. In the early 1980s, Reagan administration statements about "limited and survivable nuclear warfare" stimulated nuclear freeze protest, which subsided after Democratic allies adopted a watered-down freeze platform and the Reagan White House tempered its bellicose rhetoric (Meyer 1990, 1993). Van Dyke and Soule (2002) find that the threat of female state legislators mobilized the right-wing patriot/militia movement while Van Dyke (2003) finds that Republican presidents and state governors threatened student protesters, thereby provoking greater protest.

In the African-American case, we can isolate one threat to the movement. Following our earlier reasoning that presidential incumbents should have "known" records that are well understood by movement activists, Republican presidential reelection campaigns beginning in 1968, with the adoption of an anti–civil rights stance, should constitute a threat to the African-American movement.

HYPOTHESIS 5.—*Beginning in 1968, Republican presidential incumbent campaigns constituted a political threat to African-Americans that stimulated additional African-American protests.*

What about collective grievances and group organization? As noted, there has been considerable debate about grievance explanations, with some arguing that grievances are "secondary" (McCarthy and Zald 1977) or that they are too "constant and pervasive" to enhance protest by politically excluded groups (Jenkins and Perrow 1977, p. 265). Earlier research on African-American grievances emphasized "fraternal" or group-based relative deprivation involving negative intergroup comparisons by African-Americans who used whites as a reference group (Pettigrew 1964; Geschwender 1964, 1973; Gurr 1970; Abeles 1976). Although it is impossible to directly tap attitudinal processes in a study based on aggregate data, we can examine objective measures of group inequality that are likely to be interpreted as due to discriminatory treatment. Given the widespread African-American perception that racial discrimination is responsible for differences in the resources of blacks and whites (Jaynes and Williams 1989), racial economic inequality should fuel group relative deprivation and produce an increased willingness to engage in protest. Several studies have found a positive relationship between objective relative deprivation measures and individual protest activity (Geschwender 1964, 1973; Abeles 1976), while studies of the urban riots in the 1960s found a positive relationship between racial inequality and riot severity (Morgan and Clark 1973; Myers 1997, p. 107).

HYPOTHESIS 6.—*Increased economic differences between whites and blacks should produce more substantial African-American grievances and therefore stimulate protests.*

A second source of relative deprivation may be the Vietnam War, which after 1965 was framed by many movement leaders as a racial equity issue. Responding to the Vietnam War buildup in 1965, prominent movement leaders such as Martin Luther King, Jr. (Lewis 1978, pp. 302, 309–12, 359–60), James Farmer and Floyd McKissick of the Congress of Racial Equality (CORE; Meier and Rudwick 1973, pp. 404, 414–15), and Robert Moses, Julian Bond, and Stokely Carmichael of the Student Nonviolent Coordinating Committee (SNCC; Carson 1981, pp. 183–89, 220–21) publicly criticized the war and organized antiwar protests, including draft resistance. Some leaders, such as King, emphasized religious views that justified pacifism and nonviolence. King also stressed the economic costs of the war and its negative effects on the War on Poverty, while others framed their opposition in terms of black nationalism. In 1965, Julian Bond, a SNCC staff member, was barred from assuming his seat in the Georgia state senate because of his antiwar views. These and other events prompted Martin Luther King, Jr., to make public speeches against the war, which gained considerable publicity after he received the Nobel Peace Prize in 1966. In 1967, the heavyweight boxing champion Muhammad Ali was stripped of his title after he refused military induction, claiming that his status as a Nation of Islam minister qualified him for a draft exemption. Vietnam War deaths were the major factor stimulating negative change in public opinion against the war, and African-Americans were significantly more antiwar than whites, with a consistent 10%–20% racial gap in public opinion polls on this issue (Mueller 1973, pp. 142–43). We therefore treat Vietnam War deaths as a source of racial grievances. Because these battle deaths may have varying salience with a greater influence at lower levels and then diminishing returns above a threshold, we test a quadratic function as well as the linear alternative.

HYPOTHESES 7a and 7b.—*The more Vietnam War deaths, the greater African-American grievances and thus protest. This effect may be greater at lower levels but diminish at higher levels.*

There has been a long-standing debate between disorganization theorists, who contend that unemployment creates strains and thereby protests and other civil disorders (Kornhauser 1959; Piven and Cloward 1977; Useem 1980, 1998), and resource mobilization theorists, who contend that unemployment reduces group resources and thus the cohesion required to mobilize protest (Tilly et al. 1975; Snyder and Tilly 1972). The evidence is mixed, with some studies finding no effects of black unemployment on 1960s riots (Spilerman 1976; Myers 1997), others finding positive relationships between (general) unemployment on homeless protests (Cress and Snow 2000) and right-wing patriot/militia mobilization (Van Dyke and Soule 2002), and still others finding negative effects on industrial strikes (Ashenfelter and Johnson 1969; Snyder and Tilly 1972; Hibbs 1976; Franzosi 1995, chaps. 2 and 3).

One possibility is that both theories are valid within specific ranges. Unemployment stimulates protest up to a point, but extremely high joblessness may reduce protest because of its effects on resources in protest prone but relatively poor communities. In addition to a simple hypothesis about linear effects, we also examine the nonlinear hypothesis that, while increased unemployment at low-to-middle levels stimulates protest, at extremely high levels unemployment undermines African-American protest.

HYPOTHESES 8a and 8b.—*African-American unemployment has a linear relationship with African-American protest—that is, African-American unemployment enhances African-American protest—as long as unemployment remains below an inflection point. But unemployment should reduce protest after it goes beyond this point.*

Indigenous African-American organization, ranging from informal networks to community organizations (Tilly 1978, p. 64) and formal social movement organizations (or SMOs), should enhance the incidence of protest by reducing free riding and providing social ties through which mobilizing frames are defined and diffused, leaders and organizers developed, collective incentives enhanced, and collective action coordinated. In general, "the greater the density of social organization, the more likely that social movement activity will develop" (McAdam et al. 1988, p. 793). Historical studies have identified two sources of indigenous organization as critical to African-American protest: (1) the African-American churches, which provided an autonomous institution that "served as the main repository of Black culture... capable of generating, sustaining and culturally energizing large volumes of protest" (Morris 1999, p. 424); and (2) the SMOs created by movement leaders to organize, coordinate, and promote protest. McAdam (1999, pp. 98–100) argues that "the institutional strength embodied in the urban black church... [was critical to] the outbreak of widespread black protest activity in the mid-1950s." Morris (1984) argues that the growth of the African-American church provided the primary networks behind the local movement centers of the protest movement, furnishing leadership, a recruiting ground, and a coordination center for protest. Because the National Association for the Advancement of Colored People (NAACP) was the national SMO most responsible for the long-term development of the African-American movement and because most activists associated with other SMOs were also NAACP members (McAdam 1999, pp. 125–28; Morris 1984), we use this membership.

HYPOTHESIS 9.—*The greater the membership of African-American churches and the NAACP, the greater the level of African-American protest.*

Methods

Research Design and the Dependent Variable

We use time-series estimation to analyze yearly counts of the number of African-American protests from 1948 to 1997. An analysis of a 50-year period provides an opportunity to see if similar factors produced the "rise" and the "decline" of protests. The mean number of protests in the sampled years is 27.66, with a peak of 240 in 1965. Because the log of this series is normally distributed, count estimation using Poisson regression is inappropriate. Such a normal distribution should not be surprising when variable means reach this size (Cameron and Triviedi 1998). It follows that the Jarque-Bera test for a normal distribution does not reject the null hypothesis that the log of this dependent variable is normally distributed, so the factors that produce change in the log transformation of this series are best estimated with least squares. Least squares procedures can be readily corrected for autocorrelation with a generalized least squares (GLS) approach, making this estimator preferable to count alternatives. As we show below, GLS and negative binomial regression (the appropriate count estimator) give similar results.

We have data on the number of African-American protests from 1948 through 1997, so the maximum number of sampled years is 50. Most of our independent variables should have an immediate effect on protest, so, with two exceptions (discussed below), we use unlagged explanatory variables.

Measuring African-American protest.—Figure 1 charts the annual frequency of African-American protests between 1948 and 1997. This series is constructed by combining McAdam's (1983, 1999)

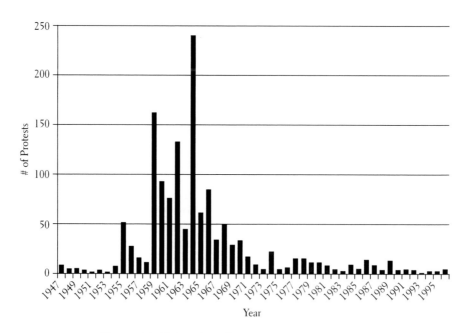

Figure 4.1 African-American protest events, 1947–97.

annual counts for protests for 1955–70 with our own coding of the comparable headings of the news story abstracts provided in the *New York Times Index* for 1948–54 and 1971–97 (*New York Times* 1948–97).[1] To insure coding consistency, we matched our coding for one year on each end of the McAdam portion of the series (1955 and 1970) and, for 1948–54 and 1971–97, used a "double-code" process in which two independent coders coded all events and resolved discrepancies by discussion and the assignment of a consensus code. We use only nonviolent protest by African-Americans, including public demonstrations and marches, sit-ins, rallies, freedom rides, boycotts, and other protest actions. We exclude riots, melees, and racial confrontations that lacked a clear protest quality as well as routine institutional actions (conferences, meetings, press releases, speeches) and *New York Times*–generated events (such as editorials, letters to the editor, news analysis stories). This means our counts differ from the total of "movement-initiated" events that McAdam (1999, pp. 120–25) focused on because he also included conventional political actions such as meetings and press releases. Media coverage is likely more reliable for protests (discussed further below), which favors this measure. We code discrete events, treating multiday protests as a single event unless reported as distinct events with different actors and initiation.

The use of the *New York Times* and news sources in general poses methodological questions. Analyses have shown that newspapers are more likely to cover protests that are large or involve political controversy and violence (McCarthy, McPhail, and Smith 1996; Oliver and Myers 1999; Oliver and Maney 2000). Our aim is to gauge the national trend in the frequency of African-American protest. Several considerations argue for treating this series as the best available method of measuring African-American protest. First, the *New York Times* is the only national newspaper "of record" for our complete period. Introducing multiple news sources for part of our period after 1972 when other national papers become indexed might create inconsistent coverage. Coding a single newspaper increases the likelihood that any selectiveness in reporting is consistent across time. Second, protests

are relatively newsworthy and thus more likely to be reported than conventional actions (Oliver and Myers 1999; Oliver and Maney 2000). Third, least squares is designed to handle random error in the dependent variable while the intercept eliminates the effects of constant errors in the regressand.

Why focus on 1948–97? Although the NAACP was founded in 1909–10 and there were scattered protests associated with Marcus Garvey's Back to Africa movement of the 1920s along with welfare protests in the 1930s (Jaynes and Williams 1989), A. Phillip Randolph's proposed march on Washington in June 1941 was the first planned mass African-American protest. When it became evident that the politically embarrassing march was going to happen, President Roosevelt issued an executive order banning racial discrimination in the defense industries, thus defusing the protest before it could occur (Garfinkel 1969). Our analysis therefore begins with the post–World War II protests, a series of "freedom trains," bus boycotts, and legal actions contesting Jim Crow segregation. The Montgomery bus boycott in 1955–56 demonstrated that thousands of supporters could be mobilized for over a year, and the sit-in campaign in 1959–62 showed that hundreds of committed activists could dismantle Jim Crow laws. Protest peaked in the mid-1960s and then declined, continuing to "percolate" (Lofland 1993) after 1975 at levels roughly double those during the period prior to the 1955 Montgomery bus boycott (3.57 protests per year between 1948 and 1954 compared to an annual mean of 7.05 protests per year for 1976–97). We select 1997 as a cutoff because at the time of the coding it was the last available year of the *New York Times Index*. No years had zero protests. Because this measure is skewed, we use the log transformation in regression. Note as well that problems with simultaneity cannot bias the estimates as long as explanatory variables are lagged and autocorrelation has been removed.

Measuring Explanatory Variables

We assess electoral competition with two measures: (1) the presence of divided government (treated as a dummy variable as discussed below); and (2) the absolute value of the margin of presidential victory (the percentage of the popular vote for the winner minus the percentage of the popular vote for the second major party candidate).[2] Divided government is measured by a dummy variable (0 = no; 1 = yes) representing the presence of divided party control over the Senate, the House of Representatives, and the presidency.

We measure our political ally theses about left-party strength by the sum of northern or nonsouthern Democrats in the Senate and the House (Ornstein, Mann, and Malbin 1982–2002; *Congressional Quarterly* 1947–78) multiplied by a dummy variable (0 = no; 1 = yes) representing the presence of a Democratic president. On questions of race, the Democratic Party has long been regionally divided, with southern Democrats aligning with Republicans on conservative positions. Multiplying the percentage of congressional northern Democrats by the presidential dummy captures the veto power of the president, who can block any effects of northern Democratic strength. This means that all years with a Republican president are scored "0" and the percentage of northern (i.e. non-southern) Democrats in Congress creates positive scores only when the president is a Democrat.

African-American congressional representation is measured by the sum of congressional seats held by African-Americans (Ornstein et al. 1982–2002). This explanatory variable assesses an institutional alternative to protest and therefore should have a negative effect.

During the period in question Republican presidents shifted from being allies of the African-American movement to becoming opponents. In the early part of the Cold War, Republican presidents responded to Cold War international competition by attempting to counter Jim Crow but, beginning in 1968, this became irrelevant as the Southern strategy became paramount. Because incumbents have "known" records, we use an annual dummy coded "1" for those reelection years when Republican presidential incumbents ran for reelection between 1947 and 1964, treating this as an ally effect. Beginning in 1968, this same dummy variable becomes a threat measure. We treat former vice presidents (Nixon in 1960; Bush in 1988) as incumbents, given their strong ties to the previous Republican presidency.

To tap the relative deprivation associated with racial inequality, we use the *ratio of black to white median family income* (USDOC 1948–99).[3] This explanatory variable is reverse coded, so its coefficients should be negative. To capture the racial grievances and movement organizing targeted against the Vietnam War, we use the *number of Vietnam War battle deaths* (USDOC 1948–99, year 1980, p. 365). These deaths are skewed, so they are analyzed in natural log form and, to test the idea that there is a threshold beyond which these deaths have a diminished effect, we test a quadratic function.

To capture the strain and resource effects of unemployment, we use the annual rate of black unemployment in both linear and quadratic form (USDOC 1999). Inasmuch as lower unemployment levels may create grievances and therefore enhance protest, but extremely high levels may reduce resources and protest, we test a quadratic specification.

The organizational base of the African-American movement is measured by the annual membership of the NAACP provided in its *Annual Report* (1947–82) and, after it ceased publication in 1982, the membership reported in the *Encyclopedia of Associations* (Gale Research 1984–98).[4] The NAACP was the main national SMO and most activists from the other SMOs were also NAACP members (McAdam 1999, pp. 125–28; Morris 1984). We use the membership of the National Baptist Convention, which was involved in early African-American protests, including those initiated by the Southern Christian Leadership Conference (Branch 1988, pp. 101–92, 335–39, 500–503). The National Baptist Convention is the most complete denominational series for the African-American churches (Jacquet 1987–98). We use linear interpolation to fill in missing years. Both variables are in two-year moving average form to capture lagged and immediate effects. Appendix table A1 provides the annual values for all these variables in the period we study. To remove the effects of any unmeasured linear effects, we include a linear yearly count measure in all models and, where indicated by the augmented component-plus-residual plots, the square of the yearly count (Mallows 1986).

Results

We begin by controlling for grievances, organization, and political opportunities. Tables 1 and 2 show the results of the regression analysis. We use the Prais Winsten least squares procedure in Stata (ver. 7) to eliminate the effects of autocorrelation because this procedure does not remove the first year.

Model 1 shows that divided government and the two "powerful ally" effects—northern Democratic strength and reelection campaigns by Republican presidential incumbents prior to 1968—increase protests. The results suggest that African-American congressional representation provides political access, thereby reducing protest. As Minkoff (1997) argues, these electoral gains constitute a significant success for the African-American movement and help to channel movement activity into institutionalized political influence methods. In addition to these "expanding opportunity" effects, collective grievances stemming from racial income inequality and Vietnam battle deaths both contribute to protest. We show the quadratic of Vietnam battle deaths, which indicates a positive effect up to a point and then a diminishing effect. In our best-fitting model 5 (below), this threshold is at the eighty-seventh percentile. The simple linear function was also positive and significant, confirming that Vietnam deaths stimulate protest. We find no evidence that the threats associated with reelection bids by incumbent Republican presidents after 1968 had any influence on protests.

Model 2 shows that black church membership does not contribute to protest. Although many of these protests were organized through church networks, the national growth of church membership did not bring about additional protests. Model 3 shows that the absolute value of the presidential vote margin does not matter either. This finding suggests that a divided government, not the margin of party victory in the most recent presidential election, is the key opportunity arising from electoral competition.[5] Model 4 shows that these results hold net of a control for the square of the yearly count, indicated by the augmented component-plus-residual plot.

In model 5 we add black unemployment, but this variable does not account for protests when a linear relationship is tested. Model 6, however, shows that the quadratic is significant. The inflection point is at 12.4%, indicating that unemployment up to that level enhances the likelihood of protest but that after this threshold is reached, the diminished resources emphasized by resource mobilization theorists reduce protest frequencies. The effects we have detected are consistent across a variety of specifications, suggesting that these models are relatively robust.

Robustness tests.—Model 7 shows that a period dummy coded "1" for all years after 1965 is not significant We also tested a similar period dummy for 1971 onward and 1975 onward and both were non-significant. These findings suggest that a structural shift with effects limited to a particular time period is not present. In addition, Ramsey-Reset tests reject the null hypothesis that specification errors are present in the best equations. In the last analysis presented in model 8, we test the explanatory variables in model I using negative binomial count estimator. The results are almost identical to the findings based on least squares, except that reelection campaigns by incumbent Republican presidents have negative effects after 1968 (the reverse of the hypothesized direction) and lagged NAACP membership is just below significance ($P < .053$; $t = 1.62$).

Conclusions

Some students of protest have argued that these events are indeterminate or that they can "only be predicted from episode to episode" (Turner and Killian 1987, p. 255; Lofland 1993, p. 216). While there undoubtedly is a high degree of uncertainty and volatility involved in protest, our findings suggest that a relatively restricted set of hypotheses about political opportunity, collective grievances, and indigenous organization helps account for protest frequencies. We have focused on evaluating the core political process arguments about opportunities and threats, but this analysis also shows that collective grievances and indigenous organization are important. It is not a question of opportunities alone being important, or grievances or organization alone, but of all three contributing to protest.

These results point to the importance of political opportunities that are based on divided government,

Table 1 Annual Determinants of African-American Protest Events, 1948–97

Explanatory Variable	Model 1	Model 2	Model 3	Model 4
Divided government	.8504**	.8186*	.8767**	.9375**
	(.3233)	(.3429)	(.3227)	(.3378)
Northern Democratic Party strength	.0293**	.0289**	.0313***	.0318***
	(.0093)	(.0095)	(.0095)	(.0098)
N blacks in Congress	−.1183***	−.1213***	−.1207***	−.1018***
	(.0204)	(.0230)	(.0204)	(.0272)
1 if Republican incumbent in presidential election:				
1943–64 elections	2.4527***	2.4677***	2.4376***	2.3941***
	(.4241)	(.4304)	(.4227)	(.4297)
1968–97 elections	−.3244	−.3246	−.3383	−.3356
	(.2818)	(.2850)	(.2811)	(.2828)
Black/white median income	−6.3450*	−6.3294*	−6.5275**	−8.5380*
	(2.6944)	(2.7184)	(2.6844)	(3.6104)
ln Vietnam War deaths	.4444***	.4519***	.4828***	.4114***
	(.0933)	(.0974)	(.0990)	(.1003)
ln Vietnam War deaths^2	−.0316**	−.0324**	−.0361**	−.0269*
	(.0107)	(.0111)	(.0114)	(.0119)
ln NAACP members	1.6538**	1.6794**	1.4773*	1.3111*
	(.5990)	(.6103)	(.6168)	(.7076)
ln black church members	...	−.0000	...	...
		(.0000)		
% presidential vote margin (absolute value)	...	...	.0093	
			(.0084)	
Yearly trend variable	.0671***	.0749*	.0708***	.0957**
	(.0167)	(.0311)	(.0170)	(.0354)
Yearly trend variable^2	...	...	...	−.0007
				(.0008)
Intercept	−5.2658	−5.1750	−4.3175	−2.4603
	(3.4224)	(3.4671)	(3.5101)	(4.5999)
R^2 (corrected)	.910***	.908***	.911***	.909***
D-W	2.1556	2.1610	2.1774	2.1703

Note.—$N = 50$ years. NAACP and black church variables are in two-year moving average form. Numbers in parentheses are SEs.

* $P \le .05$, one-tailed tests.

** $P \le .01$.

*** $P \le .001$.

Table 2 Additional Models of Annual Determinants of African–American Protest Events, 1948–97

Explanatory Variable	Model 5	Model 6	Model 7	Model 8
Divided government	.9476**	.8753**	.5916*	.9091*
	(.3394)	(.3013)	(.3430)	(.4988)
Northern Democratic Party strength	.0318***	.0293***	.0191*	.0282*
	(.0098)	(.0087)	(.0098)	(.0142)
N blacks in Congress	−.1000***	−.1024***	−.0562***	−.0926**
	(.0274)	(.0242)	(.0121)	(.0381)
1 if Republican incumbent in presidential election:				
1948–64 elections	2.3073***	2.2881***	2.3510***	1.9592***
	(.4476)	(.4085)	(.4802)	(.3621)
1968–97 elections	−.3258	−.3653	−.4494	−.5344*
	(.2844)	(.2596)	(.3128)	(.3002)
Black/white median income	−9.8472**	−8.1804*	−7.9141*	−7.5716*
	(4.0174)	(3.6255)	(4.0310)	(4.1426)
ln Vietnam War deaths	.3852***	.3436***	.3306***	.3745***
	(.1064)	(.0944)	(.1103)	(.1193)
ln Vietnam War deaths^2	−.0258*	−.0163	−.0129	−.0253*
	(.0120)	(.0111)	(.0136)	(.0138)
ln NAACP members	1.3710*	.9329	1.7466*	1.5111
	(.7146)	(.6559)	(.7336)	(.9347)
% black unemployment	−.0303	.3217**	.4462**	...
	(.0400)	(.1374)	(.1526)	
% black unemployment^2	...	−.0130**	−.0160**	...
		(.0049)	(.0058)	
1 if year = 1965–97	...	...	.3840	...
			(.4345)	
Yearly trend variable	.1173**	.0916*	...	.1015*
	(.0457)	(.0415)		(.0464)
Yearly trend variable^2	−.0011	−.0007	...	−.0011
	(.0009)	(.0008)		(.0010)
Intercept	−1.9919	−2.1081	−6.8753	−3.8759
	(4.6609)	(4.1379)	(4.4493)	(5.6470)
R^2 (corrected or pseudo)	.909***	.932***	.894***	.241***
D-W	2.2336	2.3849	2.0650	...

Note.—N = 50 years, model 8 is estimated with negative binomial count model. NAACP is in two-year moving average form. Numbers in parentheses are SEs.

* $P \leq .05$, one-tailed tests.

** $P \leq .01$.

*** $P \leq .001$.

the political strength of northern Democrats, and Republican presidential incumbents who were pressured by the Cold War to take pro–civil rights stances. These opportunities worked together to expand African-American protest, which grew in response to these forces and contracted when these forces became weaker. At the same time, stronger African-American presence in Congress provided an alternative to protest, discouraging it. Our results also point to the importance of collective grievances and indigenous group organization, by indicating that all three components increase protest. We find that collective grievances stemming from racial income inequality, low-to-high Vietnam War deaths, and low-to-medium unemployment stimulate protest. At the same time, extremely high unemployment attenuates group resources, reducing protest, while greater NAACP membership enhances protest.

Our findings support the classic "expanding opportunity" argument that divided governments and left party strength promote protest. The presence of a divided government creates interparty competition and thus a greater willingness by elites to tolerate or support moderate political challengers who seek political access. Similarly, stronger left party power creates greater opportunities for protest by moderate challengers who seek political access. Yet our results do not support rival hypotheses that out-of-power left parties promote protest or that narrower electoral margins create interparty competition and produce greater support for protest. The first hypothesis may be more relevant in multiparty democracies, where coalition-formation is more complex and out-of-power left parties may have more to gain by playing a "spoiler" role by promoting protest. In a two-party system, however, an out-of-power left party means that excluded groups lack powerful political allies who could reduce repression and create tolerance if not support for protest. In any case, it is important to emphasize that these opportunities are limited to moderate challengers seeking access to a democratic political system. Such processes are unlikely to encourage the mobilization of more radical challengers and counter-cultural or identity movements, whose goals are not primarily political.

How do we reconcile these findings with earlier studies showing that Democratic congressional power reduces feminist protest (Minkoff 1997) and that Democratic presidents reduce both feminist (Soule et al. 1999) and student protest (Van Dyke 2003)? One possible explanation is that our Democratic strength measures differ. Our measure taps the power of northern congressional Democrats combined with Democratic control of the presidency. This measure therefore captures the intense regional divisions among congressional Democrats on racial issues and the importance of the presidential veto. The alternative studies used either the simple percentage of congressional Democrats or the presence of a Democratic president. We also tested these measures, but we find positive if nonsignificant effects.

An alternative possibility is that the "outsider" political status of African-Americans at the initiation of this protest wave created a different left party ally effect. At the start of these protests, African-Americans were politically disadvantaged nationally and, in the South, denied the franchise and basic civil rights. Protest was a critical tool for transforming such exclusions and northern Democratic political power was one of the factors that encouraged this protest. By contrast, at the outset the women's and students' movements enjoyed a degree of political access. Having political access at the start of a movement creates a different calculation about protest. In this circumstance, protest may be seen as challenging one's allies, which would be detrimental, so conventional actions should be less costly and more effective. But a movement that mounts an "outsider" challenge may benefit by having powerful left party allies. Stronger northern congressional Democrats gave African-American protesters a significant ally in their battles against conservative whites. It also meant that protesters were less likely to be repressed and that protest would be tolerated if not supported. This suggests that "outsider" movements respond to favorable opportunities with increased protests, but, for "insider" movements that enjoy political access at the outset, an out-of-power ally may produce more protest. Supporting this contention, as African-American representatives were elected to Congress, protest declined, indicating that the availability of a lower-cost alternative channeled political action into conventional means. This issue deserves further empirical attention using data on diverse movements in different political systems.

The negative relationship between African-American congressional representation and protest raises the complex question of the effects of movement success. While the shift "from protest to politics" means less protest, it also means that African-Americans were more likely to vote (Lawson 1976), to have effective recourse to the courts, to lobby Congress, and to have a greater influence on public policy (Button 1989; Andrews 2001). Congressional representation indicates movement success, but it also reduces the incentives for further protest. Does political success invariably lead to reduced protest? Tarrow (1998, pp. 144–45) argues that minor victories signal greater opportunities, which incite protest (including its diffusion to less organized actors), while major victories that address widespread collective grievances are demobilizing. We have not attempted to deal with the complex question of movement success (see Giugni, Tilly, and McAdam 1999; Andrews 2001; Santoro 2002; McAdam and Su 2002; Jacobs and Helms 2001; and Jenkins and Form, in press), but it is obvious that a full account should examine the accelerating and decelerating effects of different types of movement victories on protest. This would require distinguishing minor from major victories across a wide range of relevant policy arenas, an undertaking for future analysis.

Our analysis also indicates that collective grievances stemming from racial income inequality, Vietnam War deaths, and low-to-moderate black unemployment contribute to African-American protest. These grievances may be "secondary" (McCarthy and Zald 1977) and, at least during the early period of our study, they may have been "relatively constant" (Jenkins and Perrow 1977, p. 265), but they were not constant over the entire period covered by our sample. Summarizing over 350 psychological studies, Smith and Ortiz (2002) found that "fraternal" or group-based relative deprivation has consistently significant effects on individual protest behavior. This influence is strongest in

settings where there is a history of intergroup conflict and discriminatory treatment by the advantaged group that is seen by the disadvantaged as responsible for group subordination. Our findings on the aggregate-level effects of racial income inequality support this explanation. Such results point to a need for further analysis of relative deprivation processes, properly specified in terms of relative group standing and synthesized with political opportunity and resource mobilization arguments (Pettigrew 2002).

We suspect a similar type of group-based relative deprivation may have been at work in the effects of Vietnam War deaths. Mueller (1973, pp. 142–43) shows that African-Americans were consistently more opposed to the Vietnam War than whites and, by the late 1960s, less than a third gave favorable responses toward the war to survey questions. Some saw the mounting casualties and draft call-ups as an "unfair" imposition that was racially discriminatory. African-American leaders also were early critics of the war, some claiming that it contradicted U.S. claims to promote the independence of the newly created "new nations." Others emphasized inconsistencies with their pacifist views and the financial constraints the war in Vietnam imposed on the War on Poverty.

Our findings also support the resource mobilization argument that NAACP organization increased protest. For excluded groups, organization building provides a critical vehicle for mobilization. Protest entails significant risks and leads to problems with free riders and discrepant strategies. Formal organization, especially when it is embedded in a broader set of diffuse informal networks, helps address these problems and thereby contributes to protest.

Our results on black unemployment suggest that the traditional debate between disorganization and resource mobilization is misguided. Instead of viewing this as an "either/or" situation, it may be better to think of it as "both/and." The effects of unemployment depend on its level, with low-to-moderate unemployment creating inducements to protest but high levels of unemployment decreasing resources and thereby reducing protest. Thus, while unemployment is a source of collective grievances, at higher levels it undermines protest. This departure from linearity may account for the conflicting results in prior studies. Some have detected strain effects (Useem 1980, 1998; Cress and Snow 2000; Van Dyke and Soule 2002), while others have found resource effects (Ashenfelter and Johnson 1969; Snyder and Tilly 1972; Hibbs 1976; Franzosi 1995), but these investigators did not test nonlinear relationships.

Our study has significant limits. First, we cannot test arguments about political opportunities linked to the centralization of the state or the capacities of political institutions because such tests would require either a cross-national analysis or a longer time period to capture sufficient variation. Second, we must ignore subnational factors. Because of limitations in the information that is available, we instead treat these outcomes as due to national influences. The data required for a combined analysis of local and national protests would be extremely costly. We nevertheless acknowledge that African-American protest was initially centered in the South, suggesting that local processes are important. The absence of an available control for police violence is another important limitation, despite claims that such acts only encouraged protest in part because they provoked outside sympathizers (Garrow 1978; Barkan 1984). It is possible that the combined effects of national opportunities together with local repression stimulated these protests.

A final question concerns the generalizability of these results. In this study we show that political processes, collective grievances, and formal organization affected the frequency of African-American protest across a 50-year period in the United States. The political opportunities we have examined are most relevant to political challengers seeking moderate political change in a two-party democratic political system. These processes may differ for "insider" movements and in different political systems. Such opportunities are probably of little importance to the mobilization of countercultural and identity movements, whose primary goals are not political, and to movements seeking radical system change (see Kriesi et al. 1995). Political opportunities are expressed differently in nondemocratic regimes, where harsh and arbitrary repression may produce different responses (Rasler 1996; Goodwin 2000). Our findings need to be reinvestigated with additional multivariate studies of protest in other places and times to assess the generality of the patterns we have uncovered. Such a research agenda should produce a more universal theory of political opportunities that better accounts for protest in a variety of conditions.

NOTES

This article has benefited from the advice of Neila van Dyke, Jeff Goodwin, Pam Oliver, Richard Lundman, Bill Form, and the *AJS* reviewers and from the research assistance of Jessica Maguire, Lori King, Linda Powell, and Steve Boutcher.
1. Following McAdam (1999, pp. 235–38), we used the following *New York Times Index* headings: "Negroes, U.S." and "Education, U.S., Racial Issues" for 1946–54; "Blacks, U.S." and "Education and Schools, U.S., Equal Education Opportunities" for 1971–81; and "Blacks, U.S." and "Education and Schools, U.S." for 1982–97 (*New York Times* 1948–97).
2. Because past work (Piven and Cloward 1977, pp. 213–21, 231–35; McAdam 1999, pp. 156–60, 169–72; Valelly 1993; Jenkins 1985, p. 218) has emphasized the presidential vote margin, we focus on this. We also tested the margin of congressional control based on the mean percentage of House and Senate seats held by the congressionally dominant party minus those held by the second party, but this was nonsignificant.
3. The U.S. Census uses inconsistent racial categories across time, comparing "whites" against "nonwhites" from 1948–65 and "whites," "blacks," and "others" for 1966–97. To control for any inconsistency over time associated with the shifting composition of the "black" measure, we estimate the 1948–65 black median family income by multiplying the "nonwhite" score by the 1965 ratio of "black" to other minorities. Inasmuch as the major growth of the nonblack minorities begins after the mid-1960s, this should produce a consistently measured explanatory variable.
4. The NAACP ceased publication of its annual report in 1982 and the national office could not provide annual membership estimates for subsequent years (authors' phone contacts). We therefore used membership estimates for 1983–97 published in the *Encyclopedia of Associations*.
5. As noted in n. 3 above, we also tested a measure of the congressional margin of party control, but it never was significant.

5.
New Social Movements and Political Opportunities in Western Europe

HANSPETER KRIESI, RUUD KOOPMANS, JAN WILLEM DUYVENDAK, AND MARCO G. GIUGNI

Introduction

The crucial contention of the so called "political process" approach to social movements is that social processes impinge indirectly on social protest, via a restructuring of existing power relations (McAdam, 1982). This contention has received considerable support from Skocpol's (1979) analysis of social revolutions. As she has shown, social revolutions are typically triggered by a political crisis that weakens the control on the population exercised by the political system. Similarly, the analysis of a century of collective violence in France, Germany and Italy by Tilly et al. (1975)[1] has indicated that the rhythm of collective violence did not so much depend on structural transformations of society, but was rather directly linked to shifts in the struggle for political power. More recently, the political context has also been shown to be of considerable importance for the mobilization and the impact of different types of new social movement. Thus, in what has probably been the first systematic study of the impact of the political context on the fate of a new social movement, Kitschelt (1986) has shown how the impact of the anti-nuclear movement varied according to specific characteristics of the political context of the countries he studied.

For the systematic analysis of the political context that mediates structural conflicts given as latent political potentials, the notion of *political opportunities structure* (POS) has become fashionable. First introduced by Eisinger (1973), it has been elaborated by Tarrow (1983, 1989). We shall employ a modified version of this concept to show the importance of the

Kriesi Hanspeter, Ruud Koopmans, Jan Willem Duyvendak, and Marco G. Giugni. "New Social Movements and Political Opportunities in Western Europe," *European Journal of Political Research* 22: 219–244.

political context for the mobilization of new social movements (NSMs) to Western Europe. Following the conceptualization of Kriesi (1991), we distinguish three broad sets of properties of a political system: its formal institutional structure, its informal procedures and prevailing strategies with regard to challengers, and the configuration of power relevant for the confrontation with the challengers. The first two sets of properties provide the general setting for the mobilization of collective action; they also constrain the relevant configurations of power. Together with the general setting, the relevant configuration of power specifies the strategies of the "authorities" or the "members of the system" with regard to the mobilization of the "challengers." These strategies, in turn, define (a) the extent to which challenging collective action will be facilitated or repressed by "members of the system," (b) the chances of success such actions may have, and (c) the chances of success if no such actions take place, which may be either positive if the government is reform-oriented, or negative if the government in power is hostile to the movement (Koopmans, 1990a).

In other words, the country-specific mix of facilitation/repression and chances of success and of reform is, in part at least, the result of strategic calculations of the authorities. However, it is not exclusively determined by such strategic calculations, since the general setting also restricts this country-specific mix in a way that is independent of the concrete strategies devised by the authorities. Finally, this country-specific mix determines the set of strategic options available for the mobilization of the "challengers." It provides the crucial link between the POS and the challengers' decision to mobilize or not, their choice of the form of mobilization, the sequence of events to be organized, and the target of their campaign. Figure 1 presents a graphical

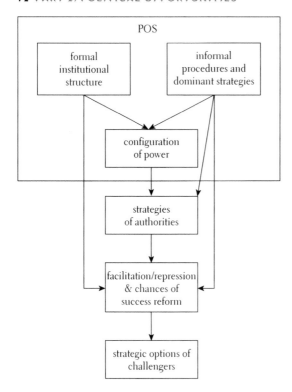

Figure 5.1 Conceptual outline of the general argument.

summary of this argument. As Koopmans (1990a) pointed out, the way the country-specific conditions enter into the challengers' strategic calculations will depend on the type of movement in question.[2]

After a brief discussion of each of these general concepts,[3] we shall test some hypotheses concerning the impact of the various aspects of the POS on the mobilization of NSMs in four Western European countries—France, the Federal Republic of Germany, the Netherlands, and Switzerland. These hypotheses will be tested using data on protest events, collected in a comparative project on the development of NSMs in these four countries in the period from 1975 to 1989. Following the lead of others (Kriesi et al., 1981; McAdam, 1983; Tarrow, 1989a; Tilly et al., 1975), we have collected systematic data on protest events on the basis of a contents analysis of newspapers.[4] In each one of the four countries, we have analyzed the Monday editions of one major newspaper for the period indicated.[5] Protest events

constitute the basic units of an organized, sustained, self-conscious challenge to existing authorities or other political actors. This challenge, in turn, establishes a social movement according to the definition given by Tilly 1978.

We have defined as protest events any kind of public action of a demonstrative, confrontative or violent form which is reported in the newspapers we analyzed. Excluded from this definition are conventional legal actions (such as the filling of a legal suit), conventional political actions (such as participation in a consultation procedure), conventional media-oriented actions (such as press conferences or public resolutions), and strikes. The actions included range from petitions and demonstrations, through boycotts, disturbances and occupations to violent attacks against persons. In the Swiss case, they also include direct-democratic forms of action—initiatives and referenda. In other words, protest events have been defined irrespective of their goal.

For each event, a limited number of characteristics have been coded.[6] On the basis of the goal of the event, we have decided whether it was an event of a given NSM, or of some other movement. Among the NSMs we count the ecology movement (including its anti-nuclear energy branch), the peace movement, the solidarity movement (encompassing various branches mobilizing for humanitarian aid, political refugees, human rights, political regimes in the Third World, and against racism), the autonomous movement (including the squatters movement and the Swiss movement for youth centres), the women's movement, the gay movement, and the citizens' rights movement (mobilizing for democratic participation and against repression).

The General Political Context

For the conceptualization of the overall institutional setting, our approach follows the state-centered theories (Badie & Birnbaum, 1979; Zysman, 1983), which have usefully been applied to the field of new social movements by Kitschelt (1986). In this tradition, a distinction is often made between weak and strong states. Weak states are defined by their openness on the input side and by their lack of a capacity to impose themselves on the output side. Conversely, strong states are defined as closed and having a high capacity to impose themselves. The internal structure of the state institutions—the degree of their internal coherence or fragmentation—is thought to determine the overall strength or weakness of the state. Among our four countries, Switzerland clearly seems to have the weakest state, France the strongest one (see Badie & Birnbaum 1979), with the "semi-sovereign" Federal Republic of Germany (Katzenstein, 1987) coming closer to the Swiss case, and the rather centralized Netherlands more closely resembling the French one (Kriesi, 1990).

The informal procedures and prevailing strategies with respect to challengers are either *exclusive* (repressive, confrontative, polarizing) or *integrative* (facilitative, cooperative, assimilative). It is important to note that such procedures have a long tradition in a given country. According to Scharpf (1984: 260), they develop a powerful logic of their own. Efforts to change them are up against all the "sunk costs" of institutional commitments supporting them. Among our four countries, the French and the German legacy is typically one of exclusion and repression.[7] While the formal institutional structure of the Federal Republic has been completely rebuilt after World War II, the dominant strategy of its ruling elite with regard to challengers from below has continued to be marked by the experience of the

past (Koopmans, 1991). In contrast to France, however, where the exclusive strategy is associated with a strong state, the exclusive strategy in the Federal Republic combines with a relatively weak state, which will result in a different overall setting for social movements in general, and for NSMs in particular. Integrative strategies are typical for the two small, consensual democracies—the Netherlands and Switzerland. Just as in the exclusive case, they are compatible with rather different formal institutional structures. A strong unitary Dutch state, with a system of cabinet government comparable to the "Westminster model," together with a relatively coherent bureaucracy, contrasts with a Swiss state weakened by its federalism, its fragmentation and its direct-democratic institutions.

Combining the distinction between strong and weak states with the distinction between exclusive and integrative dominant strategies, we arrive at four distinct general settings for dealing with challengers. As is indicated in Figure 2, each of these general settings corresponds to one of our four countries. The combination of a strong state with an exclusive dominant strategy we call a situation of *full exclusion*. In such a situation, the challenger can count on neither formal not informal access to the political system. Because of its strength, the state can often choose merely to ignore challenges; if it does react, however, it will most likely confront the challenger

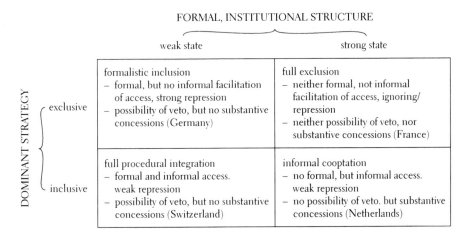

Figure 5.2 The general settings for the approach of members toward challengers.

with repression. Moreover, since the state is a strong one, the challenger is neither likely to have veto power, not is he likely to obtain substantive concessions.[8] This case is represented by France.

In contrast to "full exclusion," we find the case of *full procedural integration,* which is characterized by the combination of a weak state with an inclusive dominant strategy. In such a situation, repression is comparatively weak and the challenger's access to the system is formally as well as informally facilitated. Given the weakness of the system, the challenger cannot count on important substantive concessions, but he may be able to block decisions by exercising a veto. This case is represented by Switzerland. The direct democratic institutions as well as the federalist structure of Switzerland provide for a large number of formal access points for challengers. The traditionally integrative strategy enhances the general effect of the formal structure.

Germany represents one of the two intermediate cases, that of *formalistic inclusion.* In this situation, the challenger can count on formal, but not on informal, facilitation of access. Moreover, he tends to be met with strong repression. There is a possibility of veto, but no concessions can be expected. The federal structure of the German Republic allows for a multiplication of points of access. Moreover, the strong position of the German judiciary provides the challengers with another set of independent access points. Compared to Switzerland, the number of formal regional and local access points is, however, more limited, because—apart from some exceptions[9]—the Federal Republic does not have direct democratic institutions. Moreover, the repressive legacy of the system implies that those who articulate themselves outside of the formally available channels will be confronted with strong repression.

The second intermediary case, of *informal cooptation,* is represented by the Netherlands. In such a general setting, challengers do not have a lot of formal access, but they can count on informal facilitation. Such informal measures may not go as far as the overt facilitation of action campaigns of social movements, but they may imply the facilitation of their organizational infrastructure. This includes public recognition, consultation, and even subsidization of SMOs. Since the Dutch state is also quite

strong, it is able to make considerable substantive concessions, and it can prevent challengers from exerting a veto. Concessions have actually been forthcoming in the Dutch case, because of the prevailing inclusive strategies, which serve to preempt challengers.

These general settings can be expected to have a country-specific impact on all challenging mobilizations, not only on those of the NSMs, with respect to the general level of mobilization, the general form and strategy of the challenging mobilizations, and the system level at which mobilizations are typically oriented.

It is difficult to make predictions about *the general level of mobilization.* On the one hand, as we have just argued, inclusive strategies have a tendency to preempt protest. However, it also seems plausible to argue that inclusive strategies imply elaborate decision-making processes which increase the chances for challengers to intervene and to exercise a veto. A most telling example is provided by a series of non-decisions by the Dutch government with regard to the stationing of the cruise missiles in the early 1980s, which has given the Dutch peace movement ample opportunities to continue its anti-missiles campaign. On the other hand, one may argue that repressive strategies generally raise the costs of collective action, and thereby serve to limit its scope in a general way.

However, strong repression may also stimulate collective action. As is pointed out by Koopmans (1990a), there are at least three ways in which this may happen. First, repression reinforces the identity of countercultural movements, which may stimulate offensive reactions of a rather radical type on the part of these movements. Second, repression may itself become a crucial issue for the challengers. Finally and related to this second point, repression may focus media attention on the challengers, which may result in the support of third parties that would otherwise not have supported the movement. Such supportive mobilization, in turn, may be expected to be of a rather moderate type.

Although it is thus very hard to say anything about the amount of unconventional mobilization, we can be more specific about two types of more conventional mass mobilization, that require relatively little effort from the participants: petitions and direct-democratic actions. The latter, like petitions, amount to the collection and presentation of signatures, but they are different from petitions in that they formally compel the authorities to take a position and to submit the proposition to a vote by all the citizens. The possibility for this type of action is, as we have seen, restricted to the Swiss case, and offers an extra channel of mobilization to the citizens of that country. We may, therefore, expect that the existence of this possibility in Switzerland leads to a higher overall participation in protest events. Petitions, although of course equally possible in all countries, are not likely to be equally important in all of them. A petition is a very moderate form of action which entails only a small amount of direct pressure on the authorities. It is, therefore, a more likely form of mobilization in those countries where authorities can be expected to react favorably even to such a friendly show of public discontent. This means that petitions are expected to be most frequent in the two countries with inclusive informal strategies: Switzerland and the Netherlands.

To arrive at a comparable indicator of the general level of mobilization in each country, we have calculated the total number of persons mobilized in the events represented in our newspaper file per million inhabitants; that is, we have taken the sum of all participants[10] in the events we have recorded over the 15 years period, multiplied this by one million and divided by the total population of the country in question. For the events where we did not have any information about the number of participants, we calculated estimates on the basis of the median of the number of participants in comparable events in the same country.[11] In Table 1 the

value of this rough indicator of the general level of mobilization is given for three types of mobilization: unconventional events mobilizing people in the streets (ranging from demonstrations to violent events), petitions, and direct-democratic events.

If we look at the first column, we notice that the general level of unconventional mobilization is of the same order of magnitude in each of the four countries. This result reflects the difficulties we had in formulating hypotheses concerning this aspect of mobilization. We find the result quite puzzling. It suggests that there might be something like a "natural" level of unconventional mobilization which is attained—in different ways of course—in each country, irrespective of the POS or the level of structural problems. Of course, we have no way of knowing whether this finding is only accidental. It seems clear, however, that such a "natural level" can at the most extend to comparable, democratic countries. Dictatorial regimes, at least in the short and medium run, often succeed in limiting protest to a very low level.

However, turning to the more moderate forms of mass mobilization, significant differences emerge even between the countries under study. The more moderate forms are clearly more popular in the two inclusive, consensual democracies. Due to its additional direct-democratic possibilities, Switzerland now emerges with the highest level of overall mass mobilization. Strikingly, even outside of direct-democratic channels, quite a lot of petitioning is going on in this country, although the Netherlands rank even higher on this. In the two countries with exclusive dominant strategies, Germany and France, petitions are much less popular, especially in the fully exclusive French case, where people

Table 1 General Level of Mobilization (Participants/Millions)

Country	Unconventional Mobilisation	Petitions	Direct Democracy
The Netherlands	216,000	304,000	—
Germany	232,000	140,000	—
France	237,000	24,000	—
Switzerland	234,000	207,000	198,000

apparently do not have much faith in the effectiveness of such a moderate form of protest.

In line with the above considerations, we hypothesize that, with regard to *the general forms and strategies of action* typically used by challengers in the different countries, the French context of "full exclusion" invites disruptive strategies on the part of the challengers. As Wilson (1987: 283) observed, the strength of the French state gives rise to its greatest weakness; unable to allow challengers to articulate their concerns through formal or informal channels of access, it is periodically confronted by large scale explosions of discontent. By contrast, the highly accessible Swiss system is expected to invite moderate, conventional strategies on the part of the challengers. Such a system functions much like a sponge; it absorbs all kinds of protest without granting much in the way of concessions to meet the demands of the challengers. In spite of a conspicuous lack of concessions, challengers may continue to mobilize in moderate ways, because procedural success is to some extent a functional equivalent of substantive success (Epple, 1988), and because occasionally the challenges may still exert a veto power. We may expect, however, that there will be considerable variation of this general theme within Switzerland, given that the informal procedures to deal with challengers vary quite substantially from one region to the other.

In the general setting of informal cooptation in the Netherlands, we may also expect collective action to be moderate. The Dutch tradition of pillarization will especially stimulate the growth of social movement organizations, working through conventional channels, that will be treated in much the same way as are the religious minorities for which the system was set up. This implies large scale subsidization, integration into advisory bodies, and even some relatively autonomous role in the implementation of government policies. On the other hand, the possibilities to influence policies will not be as large as in Switzerland, most importantly because of the lack of possibilities for direct-democratic intervention and because of the relative strength of the Dutch state. Therefore, the Dutch action repertoire may be expected to include a considerable amount of more radical, confrontative forms of action as well. The low level of repression

enables social movements to use such forms but at the same time will ensure that the actions involved remain mainly of a non-violent nature.

Finally, in the case of Germany we may expect the relatively large number of formal access channels, and the possibility of blocking political decisions through such channels, to invite moderate mobilization. On the other hand, the level of state facilitation of social movements will be quite low, due to the repressive legacy of the German state. While this legacy may also be expected to push the bulk of the activists to more moderate, less risky forms of action, it will at the same time probably lead to the radicalization of another, smaller group that will turn to more radical, violent forms of action.

In our newspaper analysis, we have distinguished five broad forms of protest events of increasing radicalness: direct democratic events, demonstrative events (such as petitions and demonstrations), confrontative events (such as blockades and occupations), events of light violence (such as violent demonstrations and limited damage to objects) and of heavy violence (bombings, arson and violence against persons). For each of the four countries, Table 2 presents the distribution of events over these five forms of action. The distributions are given separately for NSMs and for other movements.

As the table indicates, collective protest in France is, indeed, more disruptive than elsewhere. Heavy violence clearly plays a larger role among French NSMs than among those in other countries. Such violence is not as prominent among the NSMs in France, however, (17.8% of their events belong to this category) as it is among the other French movements, for which it constitutes almost a third (31.4%) of the events. The other movements mainly associated with these violent actions are the French regional movements, especially those in Corsica and the Basque country.

Mobilization in Switzerland, on the other hand, is most moderate—given the possibility of mobilization in direct democratic channels. The direct-democratic possibilities turn out to be less frequently used by NSMs (4.8% of events) than by others (13.3%). In spite of the generally moderate character of the Swiss action repertoire, we also find a considerable amount of light violence (10.6%

Table 2 Form of Protest Events (in Percentages)

Level	Netherlands	Germany	France	Switzerland
New Social Movements				
I. Direct Democracy	–	–	–	4.8
2. Demonstrative	57.4	66.7	58.8	68.I
3. Confrontative	30.5	19.3	18.7	12.7
4. Light Violence	6.5	7.I	4.8	10.6
5. Heavy Violence	5.6	6.7	17.8	3.8
Total	100.0	100.0	100.0	100.0
n	(881)	(1795)	(811)	(811)
Other Movements				
I. Direct Democracy	–	–	–	13.3
2. Demonstrative	48.2	62.3	34.6	63.0
3. Confrontative	42.9	18.3	27.5	14.5
4. Light Violence	2.2	3.1	6.5	3.1
5. Heavy Violence	6.7	16.3	31.4	6.1
Total	100.0	100.0	100.0	100.0
n	(450)	(541)	(1430)	(511)

of events) among Swiss NSMs, and some heavy violence (6.1%) among the events produced by other movements. These violent events are largely caused by the urban autonomous movement of Zurich and by the regional movement of the Jura, and are thus explained by regionally specific factors.

In the case of the Netherlands, confrontative mobilization plays, indeed, the important role that we expected. A total of 30.5% of the events of NSMs and fully 42.9% of the events of other movements can be classified in this category. The Dutch action repertoire is thus clearly more radical than the Swiss, but it is still a moderate kind of radicalism that prevails.

In the German case, the overall repertoire of protest is quite moderate, and comparable to the Swiss. However, heavy violence plays a considerable role among the other movements (16.3% of the

events). In fact, the same is true for the NSMs as well. Although the 6.7% of heavy violence is not that much higher than in the Netherlands (5.6%) and in Switzerland (3.8%), it includes very heavy acts of violence (among others committed by the Rote Armee Fraktion), in which several dozens of persons have been killed. The existence of such a violent minority in a generally moderate social movement sector is in line with our above expectations regarding the effect of repression; moderating most and radicalizing a minority of protestors.

Highly conventional forms of action, such as lobbying and judicial action are not included in the above figures because such forms only rarely reach the newspaper columns. For the NSMs we have, however, an additional indicator that laps the extent to which such actions are undertaken. This is strength of formal, professionalized movement

Table 3 Membership of New Social Movement Organisations (per Million Inhabitants)

Level	Netherlands	Germany	France	Switzerland
Ecological Movement	85,000	34,000	17,000	78,000
Solidarity Movement	18,000	2,000	2,000	18,000
Peace Movement	3,000	1,000	1,000	3,000
Total	106,000	37,000	19,000	100,000

organizations (SMOs). In Table 3, the total SMO membership per million inhabitants is presented for the three most important NSMs.[12]

The international differences here are quite remarkable and fully in line with what we expected. In the two consensual democracies with integrative strategies, SMOs of NSMs turn out to be much larger than in the two exclusive countries. In both the Netherlands and Switzerland, SMOs receive considerable state subsidies and have a whole range of channels of access available to them. By contrast, in Germany and even more so in France, SMOs have only limited access to the decision-making process, which makes them less attractive for possible members. Moreover, facilitation by the state is much less important in those countries. The differences among the four countries can also be seen when we consider the national branches of international SMOs only. Thus, for instance, the national chapters of Amnesty International and the World Wildlife Fund have, even in absolute terms, a larger membership in the Netherlands and in Switzerland than in Germany and France, although the number of inhabitants of the latter two countries is much higher. Equally remarkable are the differences between the three movements. The same pattern emerges in all four countries, with the ecology movement having by far the strongest organizational infrastructure, the solidarity movement being already a lot less organized and, finally, the peace movement being quite weak as far as its formalized organizations are concerned.

With regard to the system level at which mobilization is typically oriented, our hypothesis is simple. We maintain that mobilization is predominantly oriented at the national level in centralized states, while being above all oriented at the regional or local level in decentralized states. Table 4 largely confirms this hypothesis.

In the two federalist countries—Germany and Switzerland—mobilization is much more decentralized than in the two centralized ones—the Netherlands and France. The Swiss NSMs in particular are by far the most locally-oriented ones—43.5% of their events are locally oriented—whereas the German NSMs are about as locally oriented (25.3% of their events) as they are oriented toward the regional level (22.1%). The very limited regional orientation of the Swiss NSMs (3.8% of their events) is striking compared to the remarkably strong regional focus of the other Swiss movements (33.7%). Given the great weight of the regional, (cantonal) level in Swiss politics, the absence of a regional orientation of the Swiss NSMs is all the more astonishing. The concentration of the events of the French NSMs, as well as of the other French movements, on the national level corresponds to the far-reaching centralization of the French state. What also distinguishes the French movements from those in the other three countries is their lack of international orientation.

Summarizing, we conclude that the French pattern of mobilization is the most centralized, the least formally organized—and the most radical. As a result of their overall radicalism and lack of formal organization, the French movements also mobilize a comparatively small number of people in moderate forms. Thus, the French pattern of social movement mobilization mirrors the situation of "full exclusion" movements have to face in the same country. The Swiss pattern, by contrast, is the most decentralized and the most moderate one, mobilizing the

Table 4 System Level Towards Which Protest Events are Oriented (in Percentages)

Level	Netherlands	Germany	France	Switzerland
New Social Movements				
1. International	25.9	12.8	8.7	22.8
2. National	51.7	38.8	66.6	29.8
3. Regional	3.7	22.1	17.6	3.8
4. Local	18.7	25.3	7.2	43.5
Total	100.0	100.0	100.0	100.0
n	(870)	(1789)	(809)	(811)
Other Movements				
1. International	16.4	16.5	4.1	19.4
2. National	56.0	40.2	74.7	15.1
3. Regional	5.5	11.8	10.1	33.7
4. Local	21.9	31.4	11.1	31.8
Total	100.0	100.0	100.0	100.0
n	(439)	(532)	(1422)	(510)

comparatively largest number of people. Moreover, formalized SMOs operating through conventional channels are very strong in Switzerland, reflecting the characteristics of "full procedural integration" prevailing in this case. The Dutch and German patterns, finally, correspond to the contradictory situations the social movements are confronted with in these countries. Integrative strategies coupled with a strong state result in a centralized, but otherwise hybrid mobilization pattern in the Dutch case. This pattern combines strong formalized, fully integrated SMOs mobilizing comparatively large numbers of people in rather conventional forms with a moderate, non-violent radicalism of those protesting in the streets. "Formalistic inclusion" in the German case, finally, results in an equally hybrid, but nevertheless distinct pattern that combines a largely decentralized mobilization of the majority of protesters by relatively moderate, but little formally organized means with a far-reaching radicalization of a small violent minority.

The Configuration of Power in the Party System

We shall now turn to the third broad set of properties of the POS: the configuration of power. We shall here focus on the configuration of power in the party system. A more complete treatment should also take into account the corresponding configuration in the system of interest-intermediation, especially that in the union system. Moreover, the opportunities for a specific movement or set of movements (like the NSMs) will also depend on the composition of the social movement sector (SMS) at large. Compared to the configuration of power in the party system, these factors are in our opinion, however, of only secondary importance for the mobilization of NSMs, which is the main reason why we do not treat them systematically here.

The configuration of power in the party system refers to the distribution of power among the various parties as well as to the relations which exist between these parties. As is indicated in Figure 1, the configuration of power in a given political system can be thought of as an element of the POS that intervenes between the formal institutional structure and the system's general strategic legacy on one hand, and the country-specific mix of strategies applied to challengers on the other. Itself constrained by the general systemic context (such as the electoral system), the configuration of power in turn sets more specific limits to the strategies available to the authorities with regard to given challengers.[13] It modifies the openness of access channels and the system's capacity to act, and it modulates the general strategic legacy.

Not all the established parties have been of equal significance for the mobilization of NSMs in Western Europe. The supporters of NSMs typically belong to the electoral potential of the left (see Müller-Rommel, 1985, 1989; Kriesi & van Praag Jr., 1987). Therefore, we have to pay particular attention to the *configuration of power on the left*. As has been indicated in more detail elsewhere (Kriesi, 1991), two aspects of this configuration are of particular importance in the present context: whether or not the left is divided between a major Communist current and a Social Democratic/Socialist one, and whether or not the left participates in government.

Following Brand (1985: 322), we propose that under conditions of a *split left,* there will be relatively little action space for the NSMs in general, and that support for their mobilization by the Social Democrats will be strongly conditioned by their struggle for the hegemony on the left. By contrast, in a setting where the left has *not been divided* and where the class conflict has been pacified by the time of the emergence of the NSMs, there will be more action space for the NSMs and the Social Democrats can be expected to be much more likely to support the mobilization of these new challengers. To what extent they will be prepared to do so depends, however, on a second set of factors.[14]

With regard to this second set, we expect the Social Democrats to profit, if they are *in the opposition,* from the challenges that NSMs direct at the government. These challenges weaken their major opponents in the next elections. Moreover, since the supporters of NSMs also form part of the electoral potential of the left, the Social Democrats

will appeal to them in the frame-work of a general strategy designed to build as broad an electoral coalition as possible. Being in the opposition, they will therefore tend to facilitate the mobilization of NSMs. On the other hand, being in the opposition, they have of course no possibility to make any material concessions to the NSMs. If *in government,* the Social Democrats will be much less amenable to the mobilization of NSMs, even if they may be willing to make limited concessions to some of them. The details of the strategy chosen by a Social Democratic governing party depend on its position in the government. If the Social Democrats govern alone, then they will be more able to make concessions than if they depend on a coalition partner. If they are only a minority partner in coalition governments, then they may not be able to make any concessions at all.

These considerations imply decisive changes in the POS of NSMs, when the left becomes part of the government, and when it resigns from government. If the left takes power, the necessity for mobilization decreases for NSMs, because of anticipated chances of reform in their favor. At the same time, their mobilization is no longer facilitated by their most powerful ally. The net result predicted is a clear cut decrease in the mobilization of NSMs, but not necessarily for other movements that are not dependent on the support of the left. Conversely, if the left resigns from government, the necessity for mobilization increases for NSMs, because the chances of reform in their favor become much more limited. Moreover, their mobilization is now facilitated by their most powerful ally. The net result to be expected in this case is a clear-cut increase in the mobilization of NSMs, but not necessarily of other movements that are not dependent on the support of the left.[15] The impact of these changes in the POS of NSMs may not exactly coincide with the change in government. We have to allow for some measure of anticipation or delay. For example, the deterioration of a government coalition where the left participates may already improve the POS of NSMs before the effective collapse of the coalition. Similarly, prolonged coalition formation and unstable prospects of a newly-formed center-right coalition may delay the mobilization of the left against the new government.

The general outline of the configuration of power on the left is given by the two crucial dimensions discussed so far—split/unified left, left in/out of government. It is also, finally, modified by the extent to which *new forces on the left* (the New Left, and Green parties in particular) have constituted themselves as new actors within the party system, and by the extent to which the traditional major parties on the left—Communists and Social Democrats—have been open with regard to these new forces.

We should briefly like to discuss the strategies chosen by the Social Democrats with regard to NSMs in the four selected countries in the light of these general theoretical expectations. Figure 3 indicates the situation of the Social Democrats in the four countries in the course of the last twenty years.

Let us first take a look at the French Social Democrats. Among the four countries selected, these are the only ones who have been faced by a major Communist party. In the early 1970s, the Communists were definitively the dominant force on the left. It was at that time that President Pompidou predicted that, as a result of the bipolar dynamics of the presidential system, only two political forces would survive in French politics—the Gaullists and the Communists. He has, of course, been wrong. By the early 1980s, the Socialist Party (PS) has become the dominant force on the left.[16] To gain predominance on the left, the PS has opened itself to various leftist militants since the early 1970s. It has attracted important groups of militants from the CFDT, the PSU, left wing Catholics, and also from the NSMs. At that time, the PS appeared to be

the best of all possible choices for NSM-supporters and activists (Ladrech, 1989). But, for the PS, the integration of the concerns of the NSMs remained superficial. It constituted a tactical choice rather than a fundamental reorientation.

As the renewed party rapidly gained success, it became increasingly less accessible to outside forces such as the NSMs (Lewis & Sferza, 1987). In the course of the late 1970s, the party's strategy has become less facilitative, although it has remained generally favorable to the NSMs. Not soon after the PS came to power in 1981, its strategy has changed again, in line with what we would have expected. The party abandoned the concerns of NSMs which would have imperiled its short-term management of the economy. Thus, it completely gave up its—admittedly always quite limited—anti-nuclear position (von Oppeln, 1989). Depending on the issues raised by NSMs, the PS in power has, at worst, followed a fully exclusive strategy, at best one of cooptation by material concessions and procedural integration. The only exception from this general pattern is the anti-racist movement, which received strong support from the socialists, even when they were in government.

The German Social Democratic party (SPD) has traversed a trajectory exactly opposite to that of the French PS. All through the 1970s and up to 1982, the SPD was the dominant partner in a coalition with the FDP. During this period, it followed a strategy which comes close to full exclusion—close to the one of the French socialists in power. To understand why, we should, first, note that the SPD had to govern in coalition with the FDP, which imposed

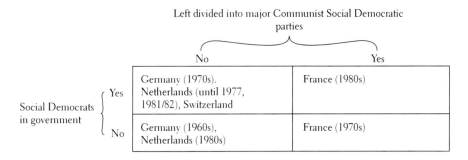

Figure 5.3 Situation of the Social Democratic parties in the countries under study.

a constraint on the amount of concessions they could have made to the NSMs. Second, the generally repressive legacy prevented the governing SPD from taking a more integrative stance toward the NSMs. Third, the terrorist attacks during the 1970s, while being themselves in part a result of the generally repressive mood, reinforced the tendency of the governing SPD to resort to repression once again. Finally, although there was no Communist competition in Germany, the SPD nevertheless was under pressure from the strong union movement to stick to the traditional goals of the labor movement. However, contrary to the PS, the leadership of the SPD was not able to centralize debate on the new issues, or to keep internal discussions under control. This greater openness of the SPD can be attributed to a number of factors (von Oppeln, 1989): the federal structure of the German political system; the relatively strong position of the party's youth organization (Juso's); the challenge by a vigorous Green party since 1979; and the programmatic disorientation of the SPD in the final stages of the left-liberal coalition. When the coalition finally broke down in 1982 and the SPD had to join the ranks of the opposition, these factors resulted in a much more facilitative strategy with regard to the new challengers.

In line with the integrative strategy of the Dutch political system, the Dutch Social Democrats (PvdA) have been open to NSMs since the early 1970s. Under the impact of the depillarization of the Dutch political system and significant competition from New Left parties in the late 1960s and early 1970s, the PvdA had radicalized and attracted many New Left militants, who eventually gained control over the party (Kriesi, 1989b). Being the dominant government party from 1973 to 1977 tempered its support for NSM mobilization provisionally. But after its change into the opposition in 1977, the PvdA came even closer to the NSMs than it had already been. It joined the antinuclear power camp in 1979—after the Haltrisburg accident (Cramer, 1989: 66)—and, most importantly, it embraced the goals of the peace movement (Kriesi, 1989b). Except for its brief spell in government in 1981–82, one may describe the strategy of the PvdA with respect to NSMs during the first half of the 1980s as one of strong facilitation. This situation changed radically,

however, after 1985. In this year, the PvdA's liaison with the peace movement finally proved to be a failure, when the government decided to deploy cruise missiles after all. When this decision did not lead to the hoped for electoral gains for the PvdA in the 1986 elections, the Social Democrats' close link to the NSMs was almost completely severed. This was the result of a new party strategy (finally successful in 1989) designed to make the PvdA acceptable to the Christian Democrats as a government partner once more. This example shows that there may be conditions under which even a Social Democratic party in opposition may refrain from supporting the NSMs.

The Swiss Social Democrats (SP/PS), finally, have had an ambiguous position with regard to NSMs. Having been part of the grand-coalition that has governed Switzerland since 1959, they shared the formal responsibility for the government's policies against which the NSMs mobilize. Having always been in a clear minority position within the governing coalition, they have at the same time been opposed to the government on specific issues, including several issues of concern to NSMs. The ambiguity of the party's position is reflected by its internal division into a party left and a party right. As a result of the most fragmented character of the Swiss party system, the specific configuration of power within the party has varied from one canton to the other.

Given the situations described, we first maintain that the NSMs have generally played a less important role in France than in the other three countries. The split in the left in France, as well as the absence of a pacification of class and other traditional conflicts,[17] are expected to have limited the action space of NSMs to a greater extent than elsewhere. The results presented in Table 5 confirm this hypothesis.

The percentage of protest events caused by NSMs is considerably lower in France (36.1%) than elsewhere. Measured by the share of protest events, the preponderance of NSMs turns out to be particularly impressive in Germany (76.9%), but they dominate also in the two smaller countries where they cause around two-thirds of the events. Except for Switzerland, we get largely similar results if we

Table 5 The Relative Level Mobilisation of NSMs and Other Movements in the Four Countries

Country	Percentage of Events Caused by NSMs	Percentage of Participants Mobilised by NSMs
The Netherlands	66.1 (n = 1331)	72.9
Germany	76.9 (n = 2336)	81.4
France	36.1 (n = 2241)	81.4
Switzerland		
(without direct dem.)	63.7 (n = 1215)	47.7

measure the relative importance of the NSMs by the share of participants they have mobilized in each country. In the case of Switzerland, the share of participants (47.7%), turns out to be considerably smaller than the share of the number of events (63.7%). This means that, on the average, the events caused by Swiss NSMs are clearly less massive than those caused by other Swiss movements and that, in relative terms, they are also less massive than those generated by the NSMs in the other countries. Among the other Swiss movements, the regional movement of the Jura, in particular, has been able to mobilize large numbers of people over an extended period of time—much larger numbers than any of the NSMs of the country. Moreover, the fact that events associated with Swiss NSMs turn out to be less massive than those of other countries is clearly linked to their predominantly local orientation. Local events are typically smaller than events targeted at higher system levels in all the countries.

Second, following the above considerations about the effect of the Social Democrats' acceding to or resigning from government, we expect a clear decline in France in the level of mobilization of NSMs since 1981, the moment the left came to power. The mobilization of the labor movement is also likely to have declined, but not the mobilization of the other movements. Conversely, for Germany we expect an increase in the level of mobilization of NSMs, starting in the early 1980s. The left had lost power in 1982, but the coalition had already started to get into difficulties before that date, and competition from the Greens had set in since 1979. No corresponding increase is expected for the other movements—with the possible exception of the labor movement. In the Netherlands, the mobilization of NSMs, but not necessarily that of other movements, should have started to increase in 1978. For Switzerland, predictions are more difficult, since there has never been an explicit change in government as in the other countries. Alternatively, one might argue that the takeover of the Social Democratic party organization by its left wing in some cantons during the late 1970s may have had a clear mobilization effect on the NSMs in the regions concerned.

Figure 4 allows for a test of these expectations. It contains four diagrams, one for each country. In each diagram, the evolution of the number of events caused by NSMs and the one caused by all the other movements are shown.[18] Let us first look at the two large countries. The contrasting evolution of the number of NSM events in the two countries starting in the early 1980s is striking: whereas Germany experiences a surge of NSM activity after 1980, there is a decline of their mobilization in France. This contrast corresponds to our hypothesis about the impact of the loss of power of the left in Germany, and of its access to power in France. The level of mobilization of the other movements has hardly at all been affected by this change in the configuration of power, which also corresponds to our expectations. Here however, the aggregation of all other movements obscures important differences. Whereas left-wing mobilization follows the same declining pattern as the NSMs, mobilization from the right increases after the coming to power of the socialists.

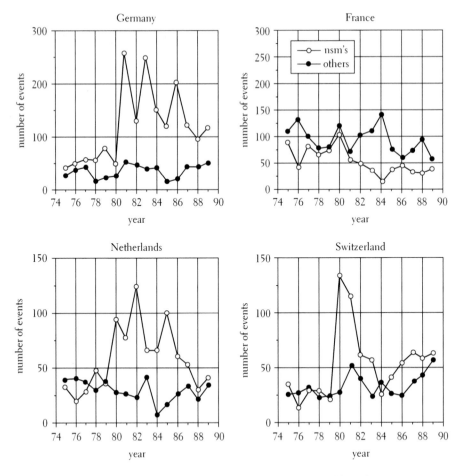

Figure 5.4 Evolution of the number of events caused by NSMs and by other movements in the four countries between 1975 and 1989.

Turning to the two smaller countries, the case of the Netherlands confirms the general hypothesis once again. After the Social Democrats lost power, the level of mobilization of NSMs started to increase and reached impressive peaks in the early 1980s. The reaction to the change in power has not been as rapid as in France or Germany, but the general pattern conforms to what we have expected. Also as predicted, after 1985 the Dutch NSMs experience a relatively strong decline that coincides with the changes in the strategy of the Social Democrats. As in France and Germany, the other movements have once more not been affected by such changes in the configuration of power. In the Swiss case, we also

find a substantial increase in the mobilization of NSMs at the beginning of the 1980s. This increase has, however, been almost exclusively a result of the mobilization of the urban autonomous movement at Zurich. This lends some support to our hypothesis that the change in power within the regional and local Social Democratic party may have been conducive to the enormous increase in the overall level of mobilization. Concerning the other Swiss movements, they have again hardly been affected by such changes in the configuration of power on the local level.

To conclude this section, we should draw the reader's attention to the fact that we have not offered any hypotheses about the course of the events once the mobilization of NSMs has reacted to a change in the configuration of power. The basic idea is that the initial change in the level of mobilization caused by a basic change in the configuration of power will establish a specific interaction context which will follow its own auto-dynamic course. Karstedt-Henke (1980), Tarrow (1989a, 1989b) and Koopmans (1990b) have presented some theoretical arguments about how such interaction contexts may develop. Finally, the argument presented has not taken into account differences between various NSMs with regard to their dependence on POS either. More detailed analyses show that not all NSMs react to the same extent to a change in the configuration of power (Duyvendak, 1990b; Giugni & Kriesi, 1990).

Conclusion

In this paper we have tried to elaborate the notion that "politics matter," even in the field of new social movements. In stressing the importance of conventional politics for movement politics, we have implicitly taken issue with the mainstream of NSM analyses in Western Europe, for which aspects of social and cultural change are central to the understanding of the evolution of NSM mobilization. In our view, social and cultural change only become relevant for the mobilization of social movements to the extent that they are mediated by politics. In focusing on politics we do not deny the relevance of other factors for the explanation of the origins and the development of social movements in general, and of NSMs in particular. However, we maintain that the overt collective action that constitutes the organized, sustained, self-conscious challenge to existing authorities is best understood if it is related to political institutions, and to what happens in arenas of conventional party and interest group politics. We interpret the general thrust of our results as a confirmation of this basic point.

The invisible side of social movements, the activity which does not become public and is not reported in the newspapers, is probably less related to the factors of POS. To stress the overt challenge of social movements is not to deny that movements have a less visible side as well. Since it does not treat

the latent side of social movements at all, the theory presented here obviously is only a partial one. However, in our view, the crucial element of a social movement is its overt challenge to authorities—it is the series of action campaigns, constituted in interaction with the authorities, that defines a social movement in Tilly's (1978) terms.

As indicated, the argument presented in this paper presumes that the most relevant level of the POS is the national one. The other levels have entered into our argument only in a subsidiary way. This raises, finally, the question as to whether the theoretical argument is not only partial, but also one that is no longer pertinent for the explanation of the evolution of contemporary movements mobilizing in a world that increasingly becomes determined by international politics. The international POS certainly is becoming more relevant for movement politics as well. Today, changes in the international POS may have a structural impact on the level of the national POS. Thus, the breakdown of the formerly communist states in Eastern Europe and the end of the divide between East and West introduce fundamental changes in the POS of NSMs in the countries with a traditionally divided left. The end of the divide between East and West implies, in the not too long run, the end of the divided left in these countries. In this case, it is still the national POS which ultimately determines the mobilization of NSMs, although a national POS of an entirely different make-up. The relevance of the national POS may, however, decline in an even more fundamental way, if the nation-state loses its prominence in conventional politics in a unified and/or regionalized Europe. There certainly are strong tendencies towards the decline of the nation-state, but we believe that they should not be exaggerated at this point. They do not yet challenge the crucial importance of the national-level POS for the mobilization of NSMs.

NOTES

1. We adopt here the simple distinction between "members" and "challengers" as it has been made by Tilly (1978). While it is not always possible to separate members from challengers neatly, we stick to this distinction to simplify the exposition. We shall frequently refer to the "members" in terms of "authorities," that is, the two terms are used interchangeably.

2. We are aware of the fact that both types of strategy—those of the authorities and those of the challengers—are to some extent mutually independent. This interdependence does, however, not enter into the present discussion because the focus is on those aspects of the political context that have to be taken as given by the challenging actors. The mutually interdependent aspects of the political context belong to what we propose to call the "interaction context" of a specific challenge. The interaction context follows its own logic which will not be treated here.

3. For a more detailed account of these concepts and their implications, see Kriesi (1991).

4. For more details about this methodology and the problems it involves we refer the reader to the presentation of Tarrow (1989: 27–31, 349–66) and to the summary discussion of Olzak (1989a).

5. We used *Le Monde* for France, *Frankfurter Rundschau* for Germany, *NRC* for the Netherlands, and the *NZZ* for Switzerland. To limit the amount of work, we restricted ourselves to one issue per week. We chose the Monday edition, because a large number of protest events take place over the weekends, which means that we get at a larger number of events than if we had picked a day at random.

6. These characteristics include the location of the event in time and space, its form and thematic focus, the number of participants (if possible as reported by the organizers of the event), the organizations participating, the reactions of the authorities and the possible location of the event within larger action campaigns of the movements concerned.

7. As other Southern European countries, France has a long legacy of repression of the labor movement (Golden, 1986; Gallie, 1983).

8. We did not enter here into the discussion of the different forms of success. For a more detailed discussion of this point, see Gamson (1975: 28ff.), Kitschelt (1986: 66f.) and Kriesi (1991).

9. There are direct-democratic procedures *(Volksbegehren)* in one member state of the Federal Republic—Bavaria—and on the community level in Baden-Württemberg.

10. In case the newspaper reports contained more than one estimate of the number of participants, we have chosen the highest figure reported, which is of course usually the version of the organizers.

11. The number of events with missing data about participants were not evenly distributed among our four countries: the percentage of missing data range from 4% for Germany, though 16% for the Netherlands and 20% for France to 28% for Switzerland. A comparable event was defined as an event of the same form (e.g., demonstration) in the same country (e.g., a demonstration in France).

12. The figures have been computed by adding the 1989 (or the year for which figures were available closest to that year) membership figures of all large formalized organizations for each movement, as reported by the organizations themselves. The figures have been rounded to whole thousands.

13. The configuration of power is, of course, also a function of the cleavage structure of a given society (see Lipset & Rokkan, 1967). We acknowledge this determinant factor, but we want to restrict our attention here to the interrelationships among the elements of the political system.

14. The structure of the union system also plays a role in this context. Thus, a strong union system may exert pressure on the Social Democrats to give priority to the traditional labor concerns, even if they do not face a serious trade-off in electoral terms.

15. The labor movement may be an exception, because it may also have a greater incentive to mobilize under these circumstances.

16. On the right, the Gaullists soon had to contend with a second major conservative force (UDF), not to talk about the rise of the Front National.

17. Apart from class conflict, other "traditional" conflicts still play an important role in French politics. In the whole period under study, regional conflicts played an important role in the social movement sector (responsible for 17.9% of all unconventional events), and in the 1980s conflicts around the position of religious education mobilized hundreds of thousands (responsible for 9.3% of all events and 17.5% of all participants).

18. Among the other movements, the labor movement is included. Since we have not taken strikes into account in our analysis, the number of events caused by the labor movement is relatively small in all the countries—it varies between 3.6% for Switzerland and 9.8% for France. In order to keep the presentation in Figure 5 as simple as possible, we have not shown the evolution of the labor movements separately.

6.

Labor Transnationalism and Global Governance: The Impact of NAFTA on Transnational Labor Relationships in North America

TAMARA KAY

Introduction

The 1993 passage of the North American Free Trade Agreement (NAFTA) institutionalized processes of globalization that had been occurring since the 19th century into North American policy, better enabling transnational companies to traverse the planet in search of new markets, untapped natural resources, and cheap labor.[1] NAFTA embodied an emergent "multilateral regime,"[2] that is, a particular kind of global governance institution that many predicted would intensify animosity among North American unions by forcing them to compete for a diminishing number of manufacturing jobs.[3] An examination of the aftermath of the struggle against free trade in North America, however, reveals that far from polarizing workers, NAFTA had the unanticipated consequence of stimulating labor cooperation and collaboration among many North American unions.

In this article, I will examine the emergence of labor transnationalism (i.e., ongoing cooperation and collaboration across national borders on substantive issues) in North America and its relationship to a new global governance institution, NAFTA.[4] To measure labor transnationalism, I employ as my unit of analysis the emergence of transnational *relationships* among unions,[5] and focus on one trinational relationship that developed in the 1990s among the United Electrical,

Radio and Machine Workers of America (UE), the Authentic Labor Front (Frente Auténtico del Trabajo, or FAT), and the Canadian Steelworkers of America (CUSWA).[6] These were not the only unions to engage in transnationalism as a result of NAFTA; however, I focus on this triad because the relationship was the earliest to emerge and is the most developed.[7] I argue that NAFTA and its labor side agreement, the North American Agreement on Labor Cooperation (NAALC), stimulated the relationship among these unions by constituting a new transnational political opportunity structure through which labor activists could engage each other.[8] Using this case, I will reveal the process by which NAFTA created a new political opportunity structure at the transnational level that facilitated the creation of a nascent transnational political action field.[9]

While North American unions had contact with each other for years prior to NAFTA through various institutions and organizations (e.g., the World Federation of Trade Unions, the International Confederation of Free Trade Unions, and international trade secretariats, among others), these interactions did not rise to the level of transnational relationships according to my definition because in general they were not equitable, were not based on efforts to create and nurture long-term programs based on mutual interests, and usually only involved union leaders and elites.[10] Moreover the anticommunist activities (particularly in Latin America) of the American Federation of Labor and Congress of Industrial Organization (AFL-CIO), and the tendency of the U.S. labor movement to employ racist rhetoric and policies to scapegoat foreign workers and immigrants for job losses in the United States, tainted relations among

Kay, Tamara. 2005. "Labor Transnationalism and Global Governance: The impact of NAFTA on Transnational Labor Relation ships in North America." *American Journal of Sociology* 111: 715–756. Reprinted by permission of The University of Chicago Press. Notes have been renumbered and edited.

North American unions.[11] When asked about the AFL-CIO's involvement in transnationalism prior to NAFTA, a leader in the federation's international department explained: "Basically there was nothing, or very little before NAFTA. The AFL was involved with the CTM and worked mostly through the International Labor Organization on issues not related to the U.S. or Mexico, but on other Latin American countries, problems.... The transnational activities that existed prior to 1990 were not really linked to national unions, but rather were carried out by progressive locals, or dissident northern movements, and did not involve long-term relationships usually."[12] The relationships among unions and federations that emerged in NAFTA's wake were new and unique in North America.[13] This presents a compelling puzzle: How did NAFTA, the concrete manifestation of globalization processes in North America, help deepen labor solidarity on the continent?

I argue that NAFTA catalyzed labor transnationalism in two ways. First, it stimulated political mobilization. Labor unions in Canada, the United States, and Mexico, which for years had been isolated and estranged from each other, came together to try to kill the free trade agreement and what they deemed a weak and ineffectual labor side agreement. They created and nurtured new ties of cooperation and networks of protest during the NAFTA negotiations.

Second, NAFTA created nascent institutions through which labor activists could build transnational relationships. The NAALC established new rules, procedures, and venues to adjudicate complaints of labor rights violations in North America. It established National Administrative Offices (NAOs) in each of the three NAFTA countries to handle complaints of labor rights violations (called public submissions or communications). The NAALC stipulates that complaints may be filed against the government of any NAFTA country through an NAO in a country other than the one in which the alleged labor violation occurred. Because it requires submitters to file complaints outside their home countries, the NAALC forces labor unions to search for allies in other NAFTA

countries with whom to collaborate on submissions. By facilitating cooperation and collaboration through its procedural rules, the NAALC catalyzed transnational relationships that had not previously existed.

An examination of NAFTA not only offers empirical insights into the nature of global governance institutions and labor transnationalism, but also provides rich theoretical contributions to the social movements literature. Substantively, this analysis illuminates the process by which global governance institutions constitute transnational political opportunity structures. It shows that changes in transnational rather than national political systems and institutions stimulated the alliance among the UE, FAT, and CUSWA. This is not to suggest that nation-states become irrelevant as a transnational political action field emerges. To the contrary, national labor movements continue to be oriented to and gain leverage through nation-states while simultaneously exploring the strategic possibilities of the transnational arena. To the extent that transnational relationships emerged in North America, however, they did so in response to a nascent transnational political opportunity structure, which is the focus of this article.[14]

An analysis of NAFTA also enables us to expand our theoretical understanding of national political opportunity structures to the transnational arena in order to explain how power is constituted at the transnational level. Moreover it contributes to our theoretical understanding of transnational social movement emergence.[15] That is, it demonstrates how global governance institutions stimulate the emergence of transnational social movements by creating new political opportunity structures, which together with the social actors that engage them, constitute an emergent political action field. If, as Tilly (1984) argues, the development of national social movements can only take place in the context of the nation-state, the case of NAFTA implies that statelike entities in the international arena can play a pivotal role in the development of transnational social movements.[16] Thus, the creation of new global governance institutions like the

NAALC should help stimulate the growth of transnational social movements.

National and Transnational Political Opportunity Structures

The nature and salience of the political process theory of social movements has been widely debated during the last decade (see Tilly 1995; Tarrow 1994; McAdam, McCarthy, and Zald 1996; Gamson and Meyer 1996; Goodwin and Jasper 1999, and responses in *Sociological Forum* 1999; Jenkins, Jacobs, and Agnone 2003). The intellectual debate centers on how well the key concepts of political opportunity and political opportunity structure explain the emergence, strategic repertoires and trajectories, and success of social movements.[17] But despite the intellectual skirmishes, political process theory remains part of the holy trinity of social movement theory (along with resource mobilization and framing), and has given birth to numerous analyses of national social movements.

Political process theory, however, developed almost exclusively in relationship to national social movements and nation-states. While scholars have dissected the nuances of national power structures, international or transnational power structures and their relationship to political opportunities have not been examined in the same depth. Thus with the rapid progression of globalization processes, a new debate surfaces about how well political process theory explains the emergence and strategic nuances of transnational social movements (see Keck and Sikkink 1998; Tarrow 2005, 1998b, chap. 11; Khagram, Riker, and Sikkink 2002). In particular, can theories of national political opportunity structures simply be applied whole cloth to regional, transnational, or international political opportunity structures, or do those theories need refinement to account for the particularities of transnational social movements and their unique relationship to nation-states and global governance institutions?

Khagram et al. point out that some social movement theorists acknowledge the existence of "multilayered" opportunity structures and "multi-level polities" (2002, p. 18). But, they suggest that scholars tend to dismiss the idea of transnational political opportunity structures because social movement actors target institutionalized power (as embodied by and leveraged through nation-states), which is rare in transnational contexts (2002, p. 18). While other scholars articulate the importance of transnational political opportunity structures (Stillerman 2003), few studies examine and theorize the nature of transnational political opportunity structures.

Keck and Sikkink (1998) provide the primary exception in their nuanced analysis of the relationship between global governance institutions, nation-states, and transnational social movements (other work includes Ayres 1998, Dreiling 2001, and Khagram 2004). They describe how globalization processes create political openings that enable social activists to leverage states and provoke changes in state policies and practices. While Keck and Sikkink's work is an important contribution to our understanding of the relationship between social movements and global governance institutions, they do not articulate a theory of the *emergence* of transnational labor movements in relationship to global governance institutions. And because they do not analyze networks of labor activists, they cannot illuminate the processes by which transnational labor movements develop in response to globalization processes and how and why they coalesce transnationally.[18]

Here I argue that global governance institutions constitute transnational power structures that provide new political opportunity structures for emergent transnational social movements. Although there are some similarities between national and transnational political opportunity structures, I argue that there are critical differences in the way power is constituted at the transnational and national levels. Thus the model of national political opportunity structures cannot simply be mapped onto a transnational political action field.

Synthesizing key scholars' conceptualization of the term, McAdam (1996, p. 27) highlights four primary dimensions of political opportunity at the national level: (1) the relative openness or closure of the institutionalized political system, (2) the stability or instability of elite political alignments,

(3) the presence or absence of elite allies, and (4) the state's capacity and propensity for repression. While these variables allow for a rich analysis of national social movements, they lack explanatory power when applied to the transnational arena. Unlike nation-states, global governance institutions have neither democratic electoral accountability nor repressive capacity. A polity's relative accessibility is therefore largely irrelevant at the transnational level. Electoral politics, which Tilly (1984) cites as the primary engine behind national social movements' engagement with the nation-state, also lacks relevance in the transnational arena. Transnational elites are not elected, nor do they belong to transnational parties subject to voter sanction. At this stage of labor transnationalism in North America, the effects of transnational elites are therefore minimal.[19]

And finally, while power at the national level can be constituted through repression, global governance institutions lack repressive powers. NAFTA and the NAALC, for example, have no military power and little ability to impose severe sanctions. Moreover all four dimensions of political opportunity structure at the national level presume the existence of one nation-state. But what if the political opportunity structure involves three nation-states (in North America) and one nascent global governance institution (e.g., NAFTA)?

Here I offer three primary dimensions of political opportunity structure at the transnational level that explain how power is established at the transnational level: (1) the constitution of transnational actors and interests, (2) the definition and recognition of transnational rights, and (3) adjudication of rights at the transnational level. The first dimension of transnational political opportunity structures highlights the importance of constituting regional or North American actors with North American interests (as opposed to national actors with national interests).[20] Actors in the transnational arena often have opposed interests that stem from varied geographical, cultural, economic, and political experiences and positionings. Some scholars suggest that these differences are particularly difficult for labor movements to overcome because the interests of labor unions in developed and developing

countries are antagonistic (Bhagwati 2000). That is, the global economy forces workers in different countries to compete for jobs.

In this article I show how global governance institutions facilitate a process that constitutes transnational actors and interests. NAFTA forced labor unions in all three countries to recognize the common threat to North American workers if the free trade agreement stimulated a reduction in jobs and wages and in health, safety, and environmental standards. Although it is commonly thought that NAFTA only created a common market, my data suggest that it also created a transnational political opportunity structure through which national unions in North America could identify their common interests as *North American unions* and advocate for them by developing a transnational political action field.

The second dimension of transnational political opportunity structures expands upon the first by emphasizing the importance of defining and recognizing transnational actors' and social movements' rights in the transnational arena. This dimension is similar to Tilly's (1984) assertion that national social movements target nation-states because they have the power to grant or deny legitimacy. In the transnational arena, global governance institutions have the same power. That is, they make and enforce rules that, however weak, establish transnational rights, standards, and norms. By laying out 11 North American labor principles and recognizing transnational social movements' right of standing through the NAO submission process, the NAALC creates a set of *North American labor rights* that must be protected in all three countries. Moreover their violation allows for redress by any North American "citizen."[21] Thus the NAALC grants a legitimacy to North American labor unions and their grievances that did not exist before NAFTA's passage.

The third dimension of transnational political opportunity structures emphasizes the importance of adjudicating grievances at the transnational level. The NAALC, for example, not only defines and recognizes transnational rights, but also adjudicates complaints of labor rights violations at the transnational level. And its procedural rules facilitate cooperation among North American labor unions in that adjudicative process. While national political opportunity structures have both electoral and adjudicative dimensions, transnational political opportunity structures lack the former. At the transnational level, political opportunity structures are embedded in rules and bureaucratic processes rather than electoral processes. This is another reason for the minimal role of the polity and elite alignments at the transnational level.

Figure 1 presents my schematic model of the ways in which NAFTA helped catalyze labor transnationalism by forging a new transnational political opportunity structure. As figure 1 shows, NAFTA catalyzed labor transnationalism in two ways. First, between 1989 and 1993, it stimulated unions to mobilize politically in order to prevent its passage. In so doing, it constituted North American unions as transnational actors with common interests (the first dimension of transnational political opportunity structures). I call this NAFTA's *political mobilization effect*. Second, between 1994 and 2001, NAFTA had an institutional effect because it created new institutions through which labor activists could nurture transnational relationships. These new institutions define and recognize transnational rights, and adjudicate violations of these rights at the transnational level (the second and third dimensions of transnational political opportunity structures). It is important to empha-size that both effects serve a constitutive function; during the political mobilization period, because new interests are created, and during the period of institutionalization, because actors are legitimized. Thus power is constituted at the transnational level during both periods, but in different ways.[22]

By examining NAFTA as a case of a global governance institution that spurred three unions to collaborate across North American borders, we can develop a more rigorous model of the relationship between global governance institutions, the emergence of labor transnationalism, and the development and idiosyncrasies of a transnational political opportunity structure.

Research Design

Using the transnational relationship as my unit of analysis enables me to illuminate labor transnationalism not only as an outcome, but also as a process of relationship and institution building. That is, it is a process of creating a transnational union culture based on cooperative complementary identities, defined as a shared recognition of mutual interest coupled with a commitment to joint action. I identify five stages in this process: (1) contact, (2) interaction and the coalescing of interests, (3) growth of confidence and trust, (4) action (e.g., joint activities and actions to address mutual needs and interests), and (5) identification (e.g., recognizing mutual interests).

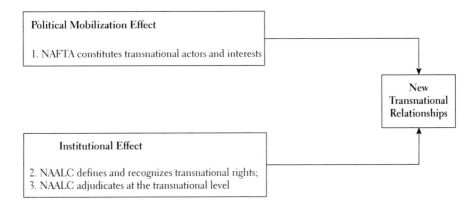

Figure 6.1 NAFTA's effects on labor transnationalism

My analysis centers on one set of North American unions that developed a relationship after 1989 in response to NAFTA—the United Electrical, Radio and Machine Workers of America (UE), the Authentic Labor Front (Frente Auténtico del Trabajo, or FAT), and the Canadian Steelworkers of America (CUSWA). This case emerged out of a larger sample of unions that developed transnational relationships in the post-NAFTA (1989–2001) period.[23] I focus on this case because it has achieved all five stages in the process and is therefore the most robust.

The FAT was formed in 1960 as an independent federation of Mexican labor unions, worker-owned cooperatives, farm workers, and community organizations. It is a progressive organization, promulgating gender equity and democratic values in each of its affiliates. The UE was born in 1936 and was the first union chartered by the CIO. In 1949 it broke with the CIO to protest red baiting and has maintained its focus on democratic unionism ever since. The CUSWA formed in 1942. Though part of the United Steelworkers of America (USWA), it remains extremely independent and autonomous. In 2000, the CUSWA had 190,000 members. That year the UE had 35,000 members, and the FAT claimed approximately 30,000 members.

In order to determine the catalyst of the relationship among these three unions and to evaluate the relationship's nature and quality, I employed a qualitative approach that included in-depth interviews, ethnographic fieldwork, and the analysis of a variety of secondary sources and archival materials. I interviewed key informants at each of the unions, including the UE's director of organization, political action director, and director of international labor affairs; a founding director and executive director of the CUSWA Humanity Fund; and four (current and former) national coordinators of the FAT. In addition, I interviewed one former and two current attorneys for the FAT, and two FAT organizers. Interviews lasted between one and four hours.

I conducted interviews with UE and CUSWA officials between May 2000 and March 2001 in Washington, D.C., Pittsburgh, Toronto, and Ottawa. I completed interviews with FAT officials in Mexico City between June 1999 and August 2000. All FAT interviews were conducted in Spanish. In addition to interviews, I conducted ethnographic fieldwork in the FAT offices in Mexico City between February and July 2000. While working as a volunteer with the FAT.[24] I observed various meetings, conferences, protests, strategy sessions, and rank-and-file union exchanges (including one held jointly with the UE). I was also given access to FAT archives.

In addition to conducting in-depth interviews and fieldwork, I examined the union newspapers/magazines of the FAT, UE, and CUSWA. I examined all available issues of the *UE News* published between 1987 and 1999, *Steelabour* (Canadian version) published between 1986 and 1999, and the FAT's *Resistencia Obrera*, published between 1978 and 2000. I also examined archived documents from each union, including press releases, internal memoranda, educational materials, newsletters, position papers, policy statements, and correspondence. And finally, I reviewed the 23 NAO public submissions filed between 1994 and May 2001 and legal documents associated with them.

Findings
Constituting Transnational Actors and Interests
Despite all they had in common, the FAT, UE, and CUSWA did not have a relationship before 1991. Bertha Luján, formerly a FAT national co-ordinator, explained that before NAFTA, the FAT did not have transnational relationships with other North American unions:[25] "I think there was little interest on the part of American unions and also on our part to establish relations...the United States was not a priority, it was not in our strategy, nor on the part of American unions was there interest in Mexico" (Bertha Luján: FAT, 8/29/00). During this period few unions had transnational contacts, and those that existed were transient and inequitable (as between the AFL-CIO and official Mexican unions). There were no ongoing programs of action, nor coordinated efforts of solidarity. Permanent transnational relationships based on mutual support through actions and assistance did not exist before NAFTA.

But the trade agreement presented a "shock" to the landscape of international union relations that forced unions to reevaluate their previous strategies. Suddenly, with NAFTA's introduction, the priorities of North American unions shifted. Institutional scholars have long recognized that severe shocks to stable organizational fields in the form of legal or policy shifts can force organizations to change their own policies and strategies (see Fligstein 1985, 1991). Labor scholars have recently examined how shocks impact organizational transformations within labor unions (Voss and Sherman 2000).

Social movement scholars also recognize that social movements often emerge in response to threats (Berejikian 1992; Goldstone and Tilly 2001; Jenkins et al. 2003).[26] Here I will argue that NAFTA presented a shock or a threat that helped constitute a transnational political opportunity structure by mobilizing labor unions in two ways. First, it constituted transnational actors and interests by making economic globalization processes tangible, and forcing labor activists to recognize their common plight in the face of regional economic integration. While processes of regional economic integration had been occurring for over a decade, NAFTA embodied them in a way that was concrete and transparent. UE members, for example, knew that a significant amount of their work had been transferred to Mexico in the 1980s. Mexican labor activists realized the plethora of well-paid jobs promised by freer trade and border factories (called maquiladoras) had not materialized. And Canadian activists witnessed free-trade inspired downward harmonization that they had predicted and fought against during negotiations over the Canada-U.S. Free Trade Agreement in the mid-1980s.

According to Luján, NAFTA had profound effects on Mexican unionists. She explained that the trade agreement helped to change the consciousness of Mexican activists; that is, it altered the way they viewed their northern neighbors and the process of economic integration: "NAFTA permitted us to understand that we were all a part of the same strategy and process of economic integration. It helped us to see that we have the same problems. Globalization has provoked the fall of labor standards and salaries in the three countries. The consequences have been for us to realize that the same labor and economic policies apply in the three countries, and that we're facing the same enemies" (Bertha Luján: FAT, 8/3/99).

Second, NAFTA brought labor activists into contact with each other and helped coalesce their interests as North American unions. Labor leaders realized that it would be difficult to combat the forces of global capital as individual and isolated labor unions. The struggle against NAFTA would have to be a collaborative one, a uniquely North American one. Before NAFTA, North American unions saw their struggles as isolated and particular to their own nations. But NAFTA's negotiation and subsequent passage created a transnational political opportunity structure that helped them constitute a transnational political action field in North America. In this field, labor unions struggled to defeat the free trade agreement and came to see their interests and futures as inextricably linked. The surfeit of joint meetings, conferences, and strategy sessions during the NAFTA battle reflects NAFTA's ability to constitute North American actors and interests.[27]

The first contact between the UE and FAT occurred in 1991. Canadian organizations (which organized their own struggle in the mid-1980s against the Canada-U.S. Free Trade Agreement)[28] approached U.S. and Mexican organizations to join their efforts against NAFTA (Arroyo and Monroy 1996). In October 1991, the trade ministers of the three North American countries met in Zacatecas, Mexico, to negotiate the free trade agreement. A trinational group opposed to free trade convened a forum in the same city; they dubbed their meeting "Public Opinion and the NAFTA Negotiations: Citizen Alternatives." It was through participation in this forum that FAT and UE representatives first met. Thus NAFTA provided the political impetus for labor activists to begin to mobilize transnationally. According to Luján, "In reality the majority of relationships with unions in the United States began with NAFTA, and our activities against NAFTA" (Bertha Luján: FAT, 8/29/00). NAFTA therefore provided the three unions an opportunity to solidify their positions and push common agendas. Gerry Barr, formerly of the CUSWA explained, "because of the context created by NAFTA there were lots of opportunities for relevant discussions and sort of common policy discussions and so on. I mean someone once said about NAFTA that one of its best byproducts was the sort of solidarity platform it created for social movement actors and trade unionists and I think there is some truth in that. And one of the important pieces of that theory is that the FAT is a great believer in it, they themselves think that" (Gerry Barr: CUSWA, 3/1/01).

The UE viewed the Zacatecas forum as an opportunity to create more solidary relationships with Mexican unions. Bob Kingsley, the UE's director of organization, explained that in the months leading up to the forum UE leaders worried that a free trade agreement would intensify the flight of UE jobs to Mexico. In order to deal with the loss of UE jobs, which had been decreasing since the 1980s, the UE hoped to begin a dialogue with the FAT.

> I had come down after discussions with the leadership of our union to try to figure out what else we could do to try to make a link to the FAT that would be more than just the cordial distant relationship that existed at that time. We knew of them, we had perhaps corresponded with them but we hadn't done much with them. So during the course of it I was able to get together with Bertha Luján and a couple of other leaders of the FAT.... To sit down and talk about what is possible in terms of a relationship between the UE and FAT that takes our unions forward, that takes international solidarity work forward. (Bob Kingsley: UE, 1/23/01)

One of FAT's three national coordinators confirmed this account of how the FAT-UE relationship began: "Before NAFTA certain unions in the United States suggested we start to work together in the face of the negotiations that were going on over NAFTA. The UE was one of them. So we started to create alliances and solidary mechanisms with the idea of creating them by sector. So through events in both countries, support for our organizations, we have developed relationships that are more tight and solid, beginning with our compañeros from the UE" (Alfredo Dominguez: FAT, 4/3/00). Another FAT leader explained that the UE distinguished itself from other North American unions during the NAFTA struggle by not promulgating a nationalistic, protectionist rhetoric: "Originally, during the initial fight over NAFTA negotiations, the attitude of American and Canadian unions was protectionistic. They wanted to prevent American companies from leaving the U.S. After NAFTA

there was a difference. We wanted to create real collaboration and solidarity and the great majority of U.S. unions were very protectionistic. The UE was an exception" (Alfredo Dominguez: FAT, 4/3/00).

The UE's stance on NAFTA, then, facilitated its relationship with the FAT. Its view that NAFTA was a threat to North American unions, not simply to U.S. unions, helped build a common agenda and trust with the FAT. The two unions embarked on a historic relationship. They created a Strategic Organizing Alliance that survived despite NAFTA's ultimate passage. As the UE proclaims on its Web site, "UE works to give new meaning to *international solidarity* through its 'Strategic Organizing Alliance' with Mexico's independent Authentic Labor Front (FAT). The first-of-its-kind cross-border approach to organizing developed out of the two organizations' opposition to the North American Free Trade Agreement (NAFTA)."[29]

The first project the two unions undertook through their alliance was to attempt to organize a General Electric (GE) plant in Juárez, Mexico. They chose GE because the company had relocated plants with UE membership to Mexico. But the goal of the campaign was not to keep jobs in the United States; rather, it was to maintain decent labor rights and standards in North America. The UE's Bob Kingsley explained: "The idea that we could form an organizing alliance with the idea that rather than just publicly condemn what was going on, we would try to fight it by identifying locations where our jobs had moved and targeting them for organization. And undertaking actual campaigns to improve wages and conditions in those locations, knowing that the result would not be that the work would return to the United States but trying to take the edge of exploitation out of what's going on here by raising wages and conditions for workers in the Mexican facilities" (Bob Kingsley: UE, 1/23/01).

Although the GE organizing campaign was not successful (due to the strength of employer and Mexican government opposition), it was instrumental in strengthening the bonds between the FAT and the UE. The failure provided activists from both unions an opportunity to reevaluate the project together and ultimately to change the project's strategy. As the director of international affairs for the UE explained, the UE and FAT realized that their failure stemmed, in part, from a lack of worker education and knowledge in northern Mexico. To remedy this problem, they opened a workers' center, the Education Center and Labor Workshop (CETLAC by its Spanish acronym) in Ciudad Juárez in 1996. Robin Alexander, the UE's director of international labor affairs explained: "The response to that [failure] was that we needed to take a few steps back and do some of the basic education in a way that would begin to educate workers and prepare them for a different kind of struggle where they weren't just seeking some quick bucks and moving on, but really seeking to gain some control within a plant" (Robin Alexander: UE, 12/21/00).

Since 1992, the FAT and UE's joint actions have included organizing multiple worker and organizer exchanges, opening additional worker education centers, implementing an adopt-an-organizer program, and completing mural projects in both countries. In addition, some UE locals support FAT through a voluntary supplementary dues checkoff and monthly contributions. The UE and FAT also collaborate on an online bimonthly periodical titled "Mexican Labor News and Analysis," created on January 1, 1996. The FAT and UE are in weekly, and often daily, contact.

Activists have definitely achieved the fifth and final stage in the process of labor transnationalism, identification. They see themselves as connected and have a strong sense of mutual interest. Arturo Alcalde, one of the FAT's lawyers, was forceful in his defense of labor transnationalism based on mutual interest and concrete action, "After this process of identification, which brings information and confidence, trust, it is very important to work on common agendas" (Arturo Alcalde: FAT, 3/29/00). A former FAT national coordinator explained that while differences persist between the unions, the two organizations focus on building upon common problems and concerns: "So I think there are differences and areas of convergence. And it is those areas of convergence which are common interests, there is where we must find and construct things in common" (Bertha Luján: FAT, 8/3/99).

This commitment is made manifest in the symmetry of the relationships. That is, they are not one-sided (with northern unions simply offering money and "expert" advice to Mexican unions), as many contacts between U.S., Canadian, and Mexican unions have historically been. FAT's Alcalde explained:

> And international solidarity isn't just about the United States and Canada helping us, the poorer less developed country, because the United States is not a haven of labor freedom. There are many obstacles there. And here is the double sidedness of international solidarity, the old international solidarity which people criticized as being protectionist. We can't judge Americans in general, we committed many errors in the past because we lacked information. The Americans also committed an error because they assumed all Mexican unions were corrupt. They lacked information. So information is a central point in creating specific common programs and collaborating, the exchanging of realities in a more simple manner is a good path to follow. (Arturo Alcalde: FAT, 3/29/00)

In 1994, the two unions' theoretical commitment to mutualism was put into practice when the UE requested assistance from FAT to organize Latino workers as part of its organizing drive in a Wisconsin plant. The UE's political action director, Chris Townsend, explained the reasons for the UE's decision to request a FAT organizer: "But it is an interesting tactic. To me, it was a little bit of turnabout. I was talking earlier about U.S. labor people running all over the planet giving out free advice and this was an example of where we had some turnabout and invite somebody to come here. But it came out of a practical necessity" (Chris Townsend: UE, 12/18/00).

With FAT's assistance, the UE won the election by 12 votes. Townsend suggested that the collaborative strategy was more important than the victory itself because it reflected an historic shift in the direction of aid across the continent. A FAT national coordinator agreed that the strategy was significant because it marked a change in attitude and method for North American unions:

> We need to create organizations that look beyond their borders and have respect for the idiosyncrasies of each country. I can't tell labor leaders in the U.S. what they need and they can't come here and

teach me what I need. Labor leaders used to come here and try to tell us what we needed. We need to give each other support. We sent some organizers from here to go and help organize a plant in [Wisconsin] because they needed help organizing Latino workers, some were undocumented. This organizer went and they won the election. We need to say where do you need our help and what kind of help do you need. (Benedicto Martínez: FAT, 7/27/99)

The alliance between the UE and FAT is strengthened by regular exchanges among their members. The UE's Robin Alexander explained the importance of the exchanges for institutionalizing labor transnationalism within her union:

I think the time and effort that we put into the worker-to-worker exchanges are really important, too. Part of the thinking behind them was we need to understand each other and each other's realities and it's not just a question of doing support for organizing work, but there has to be a deeper understanding within our organizations of what's going on and what the realities are. Because otherwise we're not really able to talk to each other.... But it's a wonderful thing to watch because you really visibly see people's mindsets shift within a 10-day period, and it's pretty extraordinary. And it happens on both sides of the border. (Robin Alexander: UE, 12/21/00)

When asked the most significant lessons workers on both sides of the border learn from the exchanges, Alexander replied:

I think people on both sides are just astounded by the similarities, that they expect things to be very different and yet they find that the details may be different, but in the broad strokes it's sort of the same. It's that organizing is hard in both places. I think people here tend to kind of assume that folks in Mexico probably don't really know what they're doing...and they get down there and it's like, ah, these people are really good, they work really hard, they're very dedicated...and they run into problems that are not all that dissimilar to what we confront, that workers are afraid to organize because they're afraid they're going to lose their jobs. That bosses are nasty. It's very familiar stuff. (Robin Alexander: UE, 12/21/00)

Alexander's description suggests that the UE and FAT's joint participation in a transnational political action field solidified the process of constituting regional actors and interests, and helped undermine racial stereotypes and assumptions.[30]

Although the CUSWA developed a relationship with the FAT after NAFTA's passage, the union's decision to seek out a Mexican partner was a direct result of the free trade agreement. The Canadian Steelworkers' Humanity Fund, created to assist with the African food crisis in the mid-1980s, began to devote attention to labor solidarity work in the early 1990s. One of its founders described how regional economic integration made relationships with Mexican unions more relevant and how the fund's directors identified the FAT as a partner in this new context:

A number of the people who were working in the Humanity Fund had long histories in solidarity work, and it was because of that that we were aware of the FAT...and as we thought our way through the question of involvement in Mexico, and Mexico was increasingly relevant particularly with the arrival of NAFTA, it seemed to us that—I mean you talk about tricky labor terrains in which to work Mexico was a classic example of that—and we needed I think a kind of relatively secure sort of anteroom to the world of labor and labor politics in Mexico, we needed a sort of safe place from which to...a relatively safe place in developmental terms I mean in terms of integrity in programming.... And the FAT was an obvious candidate for that, they were solid, they had survived, they were thoughtful, they had careful analysis, they believed a lot in solidarity so it was just sort of a no-brainer for us. (Gerry Barr: CUSWA, 3/1/01)

Like the UE, the CUSWA strengthened their relationship with the FAT in the wake of NAFTA. The CUSWA and FAT regularly hold joint meetings and exchanges. The two unions have also devoted significant resources to collaborations on health and safety issues. In 1994, the unions embarked on an innovative project to build a strike fund for the FAT, which previously had no access to emergency funds. David Mackenzie, who administered the

Humanity Fund, explained the project, known by its Spanish acronym, FOSAM:

> What's unique about our relationship with the FAT, the Canadian Steelworkers, is that we have built through the Humanity Fund a specific mutual support fund with them which they can access as a kind of emergency strike fund or emergency organizing relief fund in situations that are, well emergency situations basically or extremely stressful ones. They needed long term support mechanisms to support people at strikes like the Morelos print shop that's been going on for four years. So that's been a concrete way we can help them and we've been working with them to build this assistance fund. And we've funded it up front, and we're funding it for a five year period, it will end in a couple of years. And the FAT meanwhile have assigned people ... to work full time getting the FAT locals and co-ops and other organizing members paying into the Fund at their end so that after a while when we stop paying into it will be self sustaining, it will feel like part of joining the FAT is joining this mutual support fund. (David Mackenzie: CUSWA, 2/16/01)

In addition to the FOSAM project, the CUSWA also began to fund a project to support FAT's expansion and consolidation efforts. As the Steelworkers Humanity Fund Programme describes, "This is a two-year project meant to increase membership in iron, steel, metal-mechanic and textile sectors in the Valle de Mexico. It is carrying out organising campaigns and offering educational, legal and technical support for groups of workers in non-union workplaces or workplaces with 'official,' government-linked unions" ("Steelworkers Humanity Fund's Programme," n.d., p. 8).

Like the UE, the CUSWA also institutionalized its ties to FAT by educating members about the value of labor transnationalism. CUSWA's Mackenzie described the development of the union's "Thinking North-South" project:

> Over time, as people got increasingly proud of [the Humanity Fund], it compelled us to do a couple of things. One of the things was to ramp up our ... international solidarity program education internally. We basically created a new one. We

used to have a kind of half-assed course that we borrowed bits and pieces from other people, but we starting using our Humanity Fund assisting our Education Department developing a program we called "Thinking North-South," a week long program that was very popular. And we find that it's very useful to have local union people in that who then go back to their locals all charged up who want to bargain the Fund and get involved. So we've created a network through the Fund and through the Education Department, a network of international solidarity activists right in our local unions who are on top of these issues and extremely knowledgeable and constantly pressuring the union to do things. Like all unions have networks of health and safety activists, and we've got this really good group of international solidarity activists. (David Mackenzie: CUSWA, 2/16/01)

CUSWA's Barr explained that the relationship between his union and the FAT, and the UE and the FAT, ultimately led to interactions between CUSWA and the UE. He described how, through their engagement in a North American political action field on labor rights, the three unions' relationship began to coalesce trinationally:

> So the FAT was keenly interested in and valued the international tie and as a result of that interest as well, I mean I think that moved us forward to a much more mature kind of level of participation with each other's work. And then of course there were—simultaneously and preceding our sort of formal connection with the FAT—there had been other ties of course that the FAT had created with unions in the United States and elsewhere but certainly in the United States. And one of the most obvious points of connection is their relationship with the small but very valiant United Electrical Workers. And so they had created a very high quality point of contact and very thoughtful, very careful, very long-term. And naturally we became involved in three-way discussions between sort of Canada—the Steelworkers in Canada—the UE and the FAT. (Gerry Barr: CUSWA, 3/1/01)

As will be discussed below, the relationship among the three unions became trinational through their joint participation in a significant NAO submission. But the construction of a nascent transnational political action field enabled these unions to build trust, collaborate, and lay the groundwork for a robust transnational relationship.

The data clearly demonstrate that NAFTA provided a new transnational political opportunity structure for FAT, UE, and CUSWA. The free trade agreement had a significant political mobilization effect—it made manifest processes of regional economic integration and brought the unions into contact for the first time. It also allowed them to interact and exchange information as they came together to fight NAFTA. The plethora of joint meetings, conferences, and strategy sessions during the NAFTA battle attests to the substantive nature of their interaction. NAFTA, then, catalyzed a new kind of North American labor struggle by constituting transnational actors whose complementary interests transcended physical and cultural borders. A FAT official explained: "I would say that one of the great benefits of NAFTA is that it obligates us-unions and organizations—to seek out relations and strengthen them, and to create alliances. Now relations do not result from mere circumstance, but from a recognition of mutual interests. I think that before NAFTA there was not an understanding of the reality and the phenomenon of globalization" (Benedicto Martínez: FAT, 7/27/99). After they failed to prevent the ratification of NAFTA, the three unions did not abandon their relationships; rather they continued to nurture and develop them.

Defining, Recognizing, and Adjudicating Transnational Rights

While the fight over NAFTA constituted transnational actors and interests and provided a foundation for transnational relationships between the FAT and its U.S. and Canadian counterparts, the NAALC created a new institutional context for transnational collaboration and cooperation. The NAALC laid out 11 labor principles that defined and recognized the key labor rights of North American "citizens." It also established new adjudicatory venues and procedures for filing complaints of labor violations in each of the three signatory countries, based on the 11 labor principles. The NAO process therefore enables us to gauge the effects of a nascent global governance institution on the development of a transnational political opportunity structure.

I argue that the NAO process allowed activists to deepen their relationships and increase their activities in two ways. First, it legitimized labor activists and their grievances through the joint filing of NAO submissions. And second, the NAO process allowed them to collaborate in concrete and meaningful ways. The FAT's attorney explained that being able to engage an international venue was particularly important for independent Mexican unions such as FAT.[31]

> Now when we have a submission someone in the Mexican government will call and want to know why this, why that. They don't ignore it anymore, and this didn't exist before. We spoke but they didn't listen, we existed but they didn't see us. I think now that they listen, and they listen because what we do hurts them. And what we do is within the law. So there's a balance, in general terms things have been very positive, educational. And I am confident that the government will have to change its labor policies. Not of their own volition, but because of the pressure we've been putting on them. Because more and more the governments of the U.S. and Canada question the labor policies of the Mexican government. (Benedicto Martínez: FAT, 7/27/99)

A former UE attorney who worked on numerous NAO submissions concurred that the NAO process legitimized and strengthened the hand of independent Mexican unionists: "And in Mexico I think it went a long way to overcome the isolation of the independent union forces, I mean they became real players because they had this. They were able to invoke this international mechanism. In the last year of the PRI government Bertha Luján was a regular visitor at the secretary of labor's office, he would consult her because she was now a player" (Lance Compa, 12/19/00).

In describing her participation in one of the first NAO cases, the UE's director of international labor affairs explained how an international platform to address labor rights violations was important for U.S. and Mexican activists: "But at the point where we first filed the NAO cases, there was no official platform that independent lawyers or trade unionists could use to talk about what was going on" (Robin Alexander: UE, 12/21/00).

In addition to legitimizing labor activists and their grievances, the NAO process also provided them with a new institutional arena in which the rules of regional economic integration and by extension, those of the global economy, could be contested. The NAALC provides a tangible institution to engage. Labor activists and lawyers told consistent and compelling stories about how the NAALC's procedural rules facilitate labor transnationalism. These procedural rules make it extremely difficult for a union to file a submission with a "foreign" NAO without the assistance of "foreign" unions/organizations. The NAALC stipulates submissions may be filed against the government (not individual employers or corporations) of any NAFTA country through an NAO established in each country. Public submissions may be filed with an NAO other than the one in which the alleged labor violation occurred. The FAT's lawyer explained how this procedural rule generates labor transnationalism: "I think the side agreement facilitates relations among unions, there is an intimate relation between these submissions and international relations. In our experience one of the most important sources of relations has precisely been this type of submission because above all else you must present them in another country. If you don't have contacts you can't submit complaints" (Arturo Alcalde: FAT, 3/29/00).

Steve Herzenberg, assistant to the U.S. chief negotiator of the NAALC, concurred that the NAO process resulted in increased labor transnationalism: "The side agreement contributed to that increase because it created new venues through which you could act in solidarity and support one another" (Steve Herzenberg: U.S. Department of Labor, fall 2000). FAT's Luján argued that the NAO process also stimulated labor transnationalism by forcing unions to recognize the problems workers face in other countries: "Does the NAO process stimulate transnational labor solidarity? Yes, obviously yes. The submission process has increased the solidarity between unions because it obliges unions to recognize the violations that occur in the other countries and obliges them to mobilize themselves. This is a form of solidarity and support that is very concrete between unions. It's a concrete way of establishing a relationship. It's not theory, it's something very concrete" (Bertha Luján: FAT, 8/3/99).

Luján suggested that labor activists could no longer dismiss or claim to be ignorant about the problems of their NAFTA counterparts. The NAO process forced interaction and the dissemination of information about conditions in other countries. Luján made this claim more specific by arguing that the NAO process helped unions make achieving labor freedom a "unifying goal" in North America:

> In general our participation in submissions has been very interesting. It's allowed us to construct stronger relationships with unions in the U.S. and Canada. It means that to file submissions, U.S. and Canadian unions must learn more about the situation in Mexico, and we must learn more about what is going on in those countries, for example the forms of labor repression and discrimination that exist in those countries. It's allowed us to construct an agenda in common. Through the submissions, for example, labor freedom has become a unifying goal among unions in the three countries. We realize that the only way to rectify violations of union liberty which occur in the three countries is through unity. The side agreements have helped us strengthen our efforts toward this goal. (Bertha Luján: FAT, 8/3/99)

Labor Lawyer Lance Compa suggested that the process by which the NAO grants legitimacy and generates concrete collaboration is inextricably linked:

> And what the NAALC has created is this kind of framework for a lot of rich interaction between union activists in the countries...like when the flight attendants came up from Taesa [a Mexican airline] to testify at the public hearing in Washington, D.C., they were just—ecstatic might be overstating it—but they thought it was great because until this forum was available, this would have been just some...a silent suffering in Mexico, and nobody would have ever heard of it. Even in Mexico it would be, kind of a few people on the left would know about it, but it would be totally ignored otherwise. And here they've got high level officials from the U.S. government sitting in a public hearing listening to them tell the story of what

happened to them, and what Taesa did to them and what the government did to them. And they said, this is great...it's just great that somebody will take us seriously and hear our story. And for the two unions—the flight attendants in the United States, and ASSA, the union in Mexico—the people from those unions also told me, this is great, it's given us a chance to really work together and get to know each other better. What they did before was send each other resolutions of support, or telegrams of support, and that was it. And now they've got something very concrete to work on. And in the long run that's going to pay off, even if it doesn't pay off in some magical judgment under the NAALC to rehire the workers that got fired. (Lance Compa, 12/19/00).

For the UE, FAT, and CUSWA, the NAO process not only gave them legitimacy, it also catalyzed their relationship into a trinational one. In 1997, a group of six U.S. and Canadian unions (including the UE and CUSWA), and FAT, formed the Echlin Workers Alliance. These unions had previously worked together in various coalitions to defeat NAFTA. The alliance was created to support workers employed by the Echlin Corporation (which later became Dana), a U.S.-based transnational auto parts manufacturer. Member unions represent workers in Echlin/Dana plants in all three NAFTA countries.

One of the primary objectives of the Echlin alliance was to support Mexican workers in their struggle to improve the working conditions in Echlin plants. A statement adopted at its founding meeting read, "We will make a special effort to support Echlin workers in Mexico who suffer the lowest wages and worst conditions and who face the worst repression when they stand up for their rights" (Hathaway 2000, p. 191). The Echlin alliance, then, was created because the unions viewed protecting workers' rights in plants in all three NAFTA countries as their common interest and goal. Soon after the alliance's founding, STIMAHCS, a FAT-affiliated independent metal workers union, requested assistance for an organizing drive at a Dana-owned plant called ITAPSA in Mexico City. The alliance pledged its mutual support for STIMAHCS's organizing campaign at ITAPSA. Bob Kingsley of the UE described how unions from the three NAFTA

countries came together to support the ITAPSA struggle:

> Before very long even though the initial organizational vision was sort of a broader one about how we were going to go out and cooperatively by comparing notes and joining forces—Canada, Mexico, and the United States—attempt organization throughout this chain, the thing became focused on ITAPSA because the Mexicans were first out of the gate. They went to the factory, they tried to organize it, [and] you know they faced horrible repression, of course this new organization then closed ranks behind the workers involved in that struggle and made that the prime piece of our work. And that work took a number of forms, from activities we tried to organize in the various organized shops to protest the company's actions, our first instinct being to involve the rank-and-file Echlin workers to take on this company. And we were able to undertake activities in Canada, in the United States, in support of what was going on at ITAPSA in Mexico. (Bob Kingsley: UE, 1/23/01)

Echlin did not relent and in December, 1997, the Echlin Workers Alliance filed a public submission with the U.S. NAO office that accused the corporation of labor rights violations in Mexico and demanded that the Mexican government remedy the situation. Over 50 organizations from all three NAFTA countries, including seven unions that represent Echlin workers in the United States and Canada, signed the submission. The UE, FAT, and CUSWA were among the submitters. The submission was reinforced by concrete actions, including demonstrations in front of the company's headquarters and actions at their shareholders meeting. At the shareholder's meeting, the alliance demanded that the company sign a code of conduct which would apply in Echlin's plants in Mexico, the United States, and Canada. The UE's director of organization described the action at the shareholder's meeting this way:

> And it was just right. It was the scene that ought to be. Here's their corporate headquarters, this palatial setup overlooking this beautiful lake, comfortable location used by these overpaid executives that run this outfit. And here we are, a nasty bunch of skunks attending their garden party and bust up this meeting by raising the Echlin issue and

demanding that they respond to us on this topic, that they contemplate adopting a corporate code of conduct, that justice be done for these people who've been done wrong. And it was a good day for us, was a good day for us when we were able to do that. (Bob Kingsley: UE, 1/23/01)

Despite the alliance's efforts, the U.S. NAO submission and joint actions failed to remedy the problem at ITAPSA. Thus, a year later the CUSWA spearheaded another NAO submission against Echlin and submitted it to the Canadian NAO in April 1998. Gerry Barr, formerly of the CUSWA, explained that although Canadian unions were hesitant to use the NAO submission process, his union decided to participate in the case in order to support the FAT:

> In Canada this turned out to be the first time that a union aimed at using the side agreement. The view with respect to the NAFTA side agreement had been very very harshly negative and we thought and to some extent still think that this is a procedure designed to not work and designed to be inaccessible and designed for inefficacy not efficacy and to some extent we still think that. But it does remain true that it was a venue, right? It was a place to engage and so because the FAT was interested in that we became interested in it. And because they valued it we suspended some of the critique with respect to the nonutility of the platform and were prepared to accompany them, their interest and to sort of give some weight to their interest in having it aired in Canada and we became the lead agency as it were. (Gerry Barr: CUSWA, 3/1/01)

Barr's comments reflect how his union came to see its interests as linked to those of the FAT. The CUSWA therefore supported (and helped fund) the NAO complaint even though the case did not involve Canadian workers.

It was through this process, with the FAT as an intermediary, that the CUWSA developed a relationship with the UE. When asked to describe the benefits of the NAO case, the UE's Robin Alexander responded, "I think that one benefit for us is we really did get to know the Canadian Steelworkers much better as a result of all of this" (Robin Alexander: UE, 12/21/00). Alexander described how the relationship with the CUSWA developed through participation in the case:

> There had been no NAO cases filed in Canada. And so the [Canadian] Steelworkers agreed to really be the point people on that case, because of their relationship with the FAT, and the FAT had through the Echlin Workers Alliance asked for assistance, and so a decision was made to file cases both here and in Canada and so the Canadian Steelworkers agreed to really coordinate that work…I wound up working very very closely with people in their Humanity Fund and with their lawyers and got to know them. (Robin Alexander: UE, 12/21/00)

The Echlin NAO case demonstrates that through the NAO submission process, the NAALC provided a concrete mechanism to stimulate new relationships and direct and galvanize established relationships in the wake of NAFTA's passage. It also shows how the NAALC helped constitute transnational actors with uniquely North American interests. The unions that formed the Echlin alliance were those that had worked together to defeat NAFTA, and through this process they came to see their fates as intertwined. The UE-FAT-CUSWA relationship served as a model and signaled a significant shift in the way many unions deal with shocks such as free trade. Instead of relying on protectionistic and nationalistic strategies to deal with the crisis, these three unions decided to fight against the threat together by creating a relationship that was beneficial to all participants. One FAT leader explained that although the relationship requires constant negotiation to ensure that the needs of all are being met, it is a step in the right direction:

> This is not a relation of agreements and declarations, of good intentions. This is a relation based on action and from here we have to work very hard. But for good reason because these are new experiences, and each side has distinct needs. Therefore the process goes slowly. But we are on this path. And we need to do the same thing with unions in Europe. And it takes a lot of work due to differences in culture, standards of living, etc. But we have confidence in this path and that like capital, we will create global unionism. That we will not have to be an individual union confronting capital where it appears in our country. (Benedicto Martínez: FAT, 7/27/99)

NAFTA's effects transcend the specific case of the FAT, UE, and CUSWA. An analysis of the NAO submissions filed during the period under (1994–2001) study reveals a general trend toward increased joint participation on submission cases. While only the one or two submitting unions participated in joint actions to support the first few NAO cases, over 50 unions and NGOs participated in the NAO Echlin/ITAPSA submission. Many of these unions had no previous contact.[32]

Conclusion

An examination of NAFTA and the emergence of labor transnationalism suggests that the dimensions of political opportunity structure articulated by social movement theorists cannot adequately explain how political opportunity structures operate at the transnational level. Because political process theory developed almost exclusively in relationship to nation-states and national political processes and institutions, the processes by which power is constituted at the transnational level have not been fully theorized. I show that just as the nation-state constitutes a national power structure that provides political opportunities for national social movements, transnational global governance institutions (such as NAFTA and the NAALC) constitute transnational power structures that provide new political opportunities for emergent transnational social movements. I therefore identify a relationship between the development of a transnational power structure and the *emergence* of transnational social movements.

But an analysis of NAFTA as a *case* of a new global governance institution enables us to do more than simply illuminate the link between it and the emergence of labor transnationalism; it also allows us to unearth the process by which this reaction occurred. Here I illuminate the *process* by which global governance institutions create new transnational political opportunity structures for transnational social movements. I offer three dimensions of transnational political opportunity structures that global governance institutions affect in order to constitute power transnationally.

First, global governance institutions constitute transnational actors and interests in the transnational arena. NAFTA forced labor unions in North America to see the common threat NAFTA posed to the continent's living and working conditions. Through their common struggle to define and defeat the threat of regional economic integration, national unions in North America came to identify and organize around their collective interests as *North American unions*. Second, in the transnational arena global governance institutions have the power to define and recognize transnational rights and grant legitimacy to transnational actors and their claims. While nation-states have the power to define and grant the rights of national "citizens," global governance institutions define and recognize the rights of transnational or regional social actors and their organizations. That is, global governance institutions constitute them as "citizens of standing" in transnational adjudicative arenas. They do so by making and enforcing rules that establish transnational rights, standards, and norms. The NAALC, for example, codifies North American labor principles.

And finally, global governance institutions provide a formal political-institutional structure that makes rules and provides mechanisms for expressing and adjudicating grievances when rules are violated at the transnational level. Although the NAALC's enforcement mechanisms are weak, the creation of transnational standards and norms is useful to labor activists whose grievances are legitimized at the transnational level. Moreover by engaging the NAO process and collaborating on submissions, North American labor unions solidify their common interests. NAFTA's stimulation of transnational labor relationships demonstrates that global governance institutions catalyze labor transnationalism by both galvanizing resistance to and providing venues for contesting the rules governing the global economy.

These findings have several implications for the study of transnational social movement emergence. First, they suggest that the literature on social movements and state building needs to be refined and extended to the transnational level. At the center of this analysis should be global governance institutions that create shifts in national and transnational political opportunity structures.

As the FAT-UE-CUSWA case demonstrates, it was not changes in national political systems and institutions that stimulated this trinational alliance, but rather, changes in the transnational arena. Moreover, it was not a change in an existing *national* political institution that created a shift in the North American political opportunity structure, but rather the introduction of new global governance institutions—NAFTA, the NAALC, the NAOs—that opened new political possibilities in the transnational sphere.[33]

Second, this analysis demonstrates that processes of globalization need not undermine labor movements.[34] While leaders of the FAT, UE, and CUWSA unanimously criticize the NAALC for failing to provide sufficient remedies for labor rights violations in North America, they agree that by providing a new transnational political arena, the NAALC is quite valuable. That is, although they do not see the NAALC as an effective mechanism to eliminate labor abuses, they do see it as useful insofar as it gives them standing and legitimacy in a transnational arena and facilitates their continued cooperation. Thus, it is possible that as the transnational political opportunity structure develops, labor activists can build their capacity to take advantage of it, to amend their strategic repertoires, and to begin to shape how the rules governing the regional economy are made. This possibility may not have existed were it not for the initial contacts and relationships stimulated by NAFTA.

Finally, a case analysis of NAFTA and its transnational progeny offers much needed insight into the obstacles to labor transnationalism. A dearth of global governance institutions that have meaningful participatory mechanisms could explain a corresponding lack of transnational social movements, while the existence of the NAALC, a statelike global governance regime, explains transnational emergence. Excavating the mechanisms by which NAFTA and the NAALC stimulated labor transnationalism suggests that global governance institutions that grant legitimacy and provide mechanisms for expressing and redressing grievances when rules are violated, are critical to the development of transnational social movements. NAFTA serves these functions in North America, thus it

galvanizes resistance to globalization processes in different ways than global governance institutions that lack these functions, such as the World Trade Organization (WTO) and World Bank (WB). For example, popular resistance to WTO and WB policies is usually manifested in large transnational demonstrations precisely because these institutions have no public adjudicative processes that activists can engage. Activists cannot file complaints of labor rights violations with the WTO or WB; there is no transnational legal rights mechanism to engage. Indeed, activists' primary criticism of these institutions is their lack of transparency and democratic participatory processes.

This study indicates that future research that pursues negative and positive cases of labor transnationalism would be invaluable to our understanding of transnational social movement emergence. In addition, it would be useful to compare the effects of global governance institutions of long standing (such as the International Labour Organization, or ILO), with emergent transnational institutions (such as the NAALC) on transnational social movement development. The dimensions of transnational political opportunity structures and global governance institutions I identify as being the most salient to labor transnationalism provide a useful yardstick by which to measure other global governance institutions and their potential to serve as catalysts for various types of transnational social movements. It is probable that the role of transnational social movements poised to contest inequalities wrought by processes of globalization will only become more important as these processes proceed.

NOTES

1. I thank Avri Beard, Joshua Bloom, Jennifer Chun, Michael Dreiling, Rhonda Evans, Peter Evans, Neil Fligstein, Leslie Gates, Sanjeev Khagram, Isaac Martin, Simone Pulver, Robyn Rodriguez, Akos Rona-Tas, Harley Shaiken, Sidney Tarrow, Harold Toro Tulla, Kim Voss, Chris Woodruff, and the *AJS* reviewers for their insightful and helpful comments. An earlier version of this article was presented at the University of California, San Diego, the University of California, Berkeley, the University of Oregon, Rutgers University, Cornell University, and Harvard University. Many thanks to all of those who, at each of these institutions, offered invaluable suggestions and ideas. NAFTA was passed

by the U.S. Congress in September 1993; it entered into force on January 1, 1994.

2. For a discussion of multilateral regimes see Krasner (1983) and Ruggie (1993).

3. NAFTA is more accurately a regional governance institution, but for simplicity and consistency with the term used in the literature, I will refer to it as a global governance institution.

4. The practices of labor tansnationalism can include grassroots and labor organizing, political lobbying and mobilization, strategic planning, campaign organizing, invoking legal bodies, creating new institutions, etc.

5. Scholars distinguish among several types of transnational contention or political activity, including cross-border diffusion and political exchange, transnational social movements, and transnational advocacy networks (see Keck and Sikkink 1998; Tarrow 2005, 1998b, chap. 11). Here I add the term "transnational relationship," defined as ongoing interactions based on equality, long-term goals, and mutual interest, with rank-and-file involvement.

6. The Canadian steelworkers are known by USWA, but to distinguish them from their U.S. counterpart, I use CUSWA in this discussion.

7. Other relationships include the largest unions in the telecommunications industries in each country: the Communication Workers of America (CWA, U.S.), the Communications, Energy, and Paperworkers Union (CEP, Canada), and the Mexican Telephone Workers' Union (STRM); and among North American labor federations the AFL-CIO, the Canadian Labour Congress (CLC), and independent Mexican union federations (those not controlled by the ruling party), including the FAT and National Union of Workers (UNT). For a discussion see Boswell and Stevis (1997), Cohen and Early (1998), Kay (2004b).

8. Here I utilize political opportunity structure as a set of independent variables that facilitates the *emergence* of labor transnationalism, not its success and failure (see Gamson and Meyer 1996). I adopt Tarrow's definition of political opportunity structure as "consistent—but not necessarily formal, permanent, or national—signals to social or political actors which either encourage or discourage them to use their internal resources to form social movements" (Tarrow 1996, p. 54). I use the term political opportunities to identify those opportunities that emanate from a political opportunity structure. Thus, in the transnational arena, a transnational political opportunity structure would emerge first, allowing for the creation of a transnational political action field.

9. Fligstein defines fields as "local social orders" in which "actors gather and frame their actions vis-à-vis one another" (Fligstein 1998, pp. 2, 6). See also DiMaggio (1986), Scott (1995), DiMaggio and Powell (1991), and Fligstein (2001). For a discussion of political action fields, see Evans (2002).

For a discussion of the related concept "transnational social fields," see Khagram (2004), and Levitt and Schiller (2003). Here I define a transnational political action field as an arena that crosses national boundaries in which social actors and their organizations frame issues, mobilize, and contest or advocate particular policies or practices.

10. For a discussion of the history and limitations of international labor organizations, see Stevis (1998) and Boswell and Stevis (1997). I characterize union relations in the pre-NAFTA era as similar to what Tarrow (1998a) terms "contingent political alliances," which are based on ephemeral transnational "relays" or exchanges between social activists.

11. For more on the anticommunist activities of U.S. labor, see Cantor and Schor (1987), Spalding (1992), Morris (1967), and Herod (1997). U.S. labor's xenophobic tendencies are discussed by Bustamante (1972) and Frank (1999). I have examined how NAFTA helped facilitate the process of rupturing racist rhetoric and policies among North American labor unions (Kay 2003b, 2004a, 2004b).

12. The Confederation of Mexican Workers (CTM) is the major Mexican union federation with historic ties to the ruling party (the Institutional Revolutionary Party, or PRI). The quote comes from a personal interview with an AFL-CIO representative, February 29, 2000, in Washington, D.C.

13. For discussions of changes in the landscape of union relations in response to NAFTA, see Kay (2000), Stillerman (2003), Robinson (2002), Kidder (2002), and Hinojosa-Ojeda (2002).

14. The relevance of the nation-state to labor movements is unique among social movements because their tactical options are constrained by labor laws that force them to engage the nation-state and employers through institutionalized processes (see Kay 2003a; Stillerman 2003). Unlike other social movements that can focus primarily or solely on disruptive politics (such as the antiglobalization movement), the labor movement must invoke legal mechanisms as part of its tactical repertoire, or risk legal sanction. Of course, the labor movement also benefits from institutional access to power, and guarantees of particular kinds of state protection. It is therefore highly unlikely that, in an international system composed of nation-states, labor movement activists would embrace transnational strategies to the full exclusion of national or local strategies. Elsewhere, I discuss how national labor movements' continued orientation toward their nation-states presents significant obstacles to labor transnationalism (Kay 2004b).

15. Here I examine one transnational relationship that emerged among many in the struggle against NAFTA that together constituted a transnational social movement; elsewhere I provide a more detailed discussion (Kay 2004b).

16. My argument is not that North American labor activists should applaud the passage of NAFTA and the NAALC. The free trade agreement undermined labor's bargaining power

and stimulated capital flight in North America (see Scott et al. 2001; Bronfenbrenner 1997). The argument I make here is that despite the negative effects of free trade, NAFTA provided new political openings that, if exploited, could be used strategically to improve workers' lives and working conditions in North America.

17. In this article I am concerned with how political opportunity structures explain the emergence, not the success or failure, of social movements.

18. The burgeoning literature on labor transnationalism tends to focus on the history of labor transnationalism (Sikkink and Smith 2002; Herod 1997; Stevis 1998; Howard 1995), and the causes of success and failure of particular transnational campaigns (see Armbruster 1995, 1998a, 1998b; Cohen and Early 1998; Jessup and Gordon 2002; Kidder 2002; Zinn 2002; Anner 2002; Wilson 2002). See Evans (2000, 2005), Tarrow (2005), Waterman (1991; 1998) for theoretical analyses of labor transnationalism. Some scholars have suggested that NAFTA's labor side agreement facilitates labor transnationalism (Alexander 1999; Bouzas 1999; Carr 1999; Damgaard 1999a, 1999b; de Buen 1999; Compa 1999; Cook 1997; Kay 2000; Kidder 2002; Luján 1999; Stillerman 2003; Thorup 1993). Here I extend these analyses by introducing new empirical data and providing a theoretical analysis of the process by which NAFTA and the NAALC constituted regional actors, interests, and rights.

19. National elites were critical to the passage and structure of NAFTA and the NAALC (see Evans 2002).

20. I do not mean to imply that social movement actors no longer retain national identities and interests, but that these exist simultaneously and are compatible with their nascent transnational identities and interests.

21. The NAALC actually allows any party, regardless of national origin, to file public submissions. As of this printing, no party outside North America has filed a public submission.

22. The period when NAFTA was introduced and was being negotiated was critical to unions because the trade and labor side agreement architectures would be crucial components of the transnational power structure. That unions and other civil society organizations (e.g., environmental, fair trade, farmers, indigenous rights groups, etc.) contested them so vehemently at local, national, and transnational levels shows how much they believed was at stake with the passage of these multilateral accords (see Evans 2002). Thus, power was constituted during this period despite the lack of institutional mechanisms, as unions participated across borders in the process of determining the nature of the transnational mechanisms and institutions that would emerge. And they

did so because they began to see themselves as transnational actors with regional interests. Unions' collective demand that the trade agreement include labor protections helped ensure that a labor side agreement was passed, although North American unions had little influence on the structure of the NAALC and the level of labor protections it would provide (Evans 2002). Theoretically, this case suggests that transnational political mobilization can precede transnational institutionalization and can occur without institutionalization. Indeed, many unions began to organize transnationally during this mobilization period (see Evans 2002; Carr 1999; Compa 1999; Cook 1997; Kidder 2002). But, the two institutional effects help reinforce the political mobilization effect by underlining the constituted interests and offering a remedy based on those interests.

23. Although NAFTA was formally passed in 1994, I consider the period during which it was debated and negotiated part of the post-NAFTA period because NAFTA had an effect on union mobilization during this prepassage period.

24. As a volunteer, I assisted with translations and helped organize FAT archives.

25. With the exception of the Quebec-based National Union Confederation (CSN) that, like the FAT, was affiliated with the World Federation of Labor and had links to the Catholic Church.

26. Although their origins vary, threats and political opportunities often generate similar responses. Both can force social movement actors to decide what is worth fighting for and to mobilize.

27. For a discussion of these early collaborations see Evans (2002).

28. See Ayres (1998) for an excellent discussion of Canadian social movements' struggles against free trade.

29. http://www.ranknfile-ue.org/uewho4.html.

30. In other work, I give a detailed discussion of how NAFTA helped undermine racial stereotypes (Kay 2004a, 2004b, 2003b).

31. Independent Mexican unions are those not officially linked to the government or ruling party. Historically, the organizing efforts of independent Mexican unions such as the FAT have been thwarted by government authorities.

32. I discuss this in detail elsewhere (Kay 2004b).

33. It is plausible that labor transnationalism could also emerge as a result of significant changes in existing global governance institutions (such as the International Labour Organization) that encourage transnational collaboration and cooperation.

34. For discussions of counterhegemonic globalization, see Carr (1999) and Evans (2000, 2005).

7.

Opportunity Organizations and Threat-Induced Contention: Protest Waves in Authoritarian Settings

PAUL D. ALMEIDA

Introduction

The political process model has reached near canonical stature in the study of social movements. The theoretical framework focuses on the specific political opportunities in a movement's environment that facilitate collective action by providing incentives such as institutional access, electoral realignments, elite conflict, external allies, and relaxation in state repression (Tarrow 1994; McAdam 1996). Yet, even with the recent gains in explaining social movement emergence and outcomes, we still know relatively little about these same processes in authoritarian states, which tend to be much less homogeneous than core democracies (McAdam, McCarthy, and Zald 1996; Tarrow 1999; Meyer 2002; Wickham 2002; McAdam 2003).

Scholars taking up the challenge to apply the political process model in nondemocratic contexts find support for the framework with core political opportunities associated with changes in protest levels and outcomes (Cook 1996; Hipsher 1998; Bunce 1999). These important studies often emphasize authoritarian situations in which a polity experiences a period of liberalization and/or democratization (Osa 2001). Selecting cases that allow for variation in the nondemocratic context may yield different sources and patterns of contention. For example, what conditions are linked to the outbreak of protest waves in extremely repressive authoritarian settings where political opportunities are scarce?

The present article addresses such questions and contributes to social movement theory by analyzing

Almeida, Paul D. 2003. "Opportunity Organizations and Threat-Induced Contention: Protest waves in Authoritarian Settings." *American Journal of Sociology* 109: 345–400. Reprinted by permission of The University of Chicago Press. Notes have been renumbered and edited.

the temporal sequencing of political opportunity, organizational infrastructure, and threat in shaping the *level* and *form* of collective action in a changing authoritarian context. Specifically, I analyze the onset of two protest waves in El Salvador between 1960 and 1981 (see figs. 1 and 2).[1] The study begins with the conceptual distinction between political opportunity and threat and is followed by a sequential theoretical model that outlines the shift from an opportunity environment to a threatening political environment.

Distinguishing Threat from Political Opportunity

Tilly's (1978, pp. 133–38) and Goldstone and Tilly's (2001) mobilization models maintain that *two* general paths drive expanded collective action: (1) *political opportunity* and (2) *threat*. In recent years political opportunity variables have received much more attention than threat variables in the social movement literature (see McAdam [1982] 1999, pp. x–xi; Tarrow 2001, p. 12; McAdam, Tarrow, and Tilly 2001, pp. 42–43). In addition, in standard political process models threat (e.g., state repression) is often incorporated *within* the concept of political opportunity as the negative side of opportunity associated with declining protest (Goldstone and Tilly 2001). However, with the move to extend political process theory to authoritarian contexts, we find that protest is not driven solely by responsive political institutions and relatively facilitative governments.

In order to analyze the roles of political opportunity and threat dimensions in contributing to increased contention we need to conceptually separate them and develop indicators of threat as political process scholars have previously done for political opportunity. Tilly (1978) defines *opportunity*

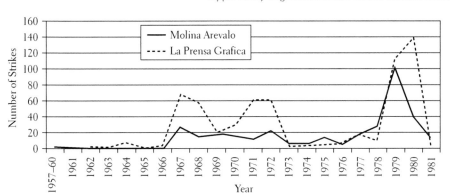

Figure 7.1 Reported strikes in El Salvador, 1957–81. (Sources: *La Prensa Gráfica* **1962–81; Molina Arévalo 1988.)**

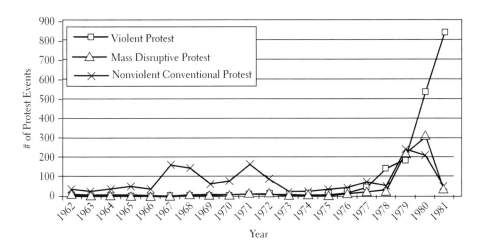

Figure 7.2 Forms of protest in El Salvador, 1962–81. Nonviolent conventional protests were defined as street marches, strikes, public gatherings, demonstrations, petitions, spray-painting political graffiti, handing out political literature, hunger strikes, and public statements. Mass disruptive protests were coded as occupations of buildings and land, constructing barricades, cutting off power, sit-ins, and disseminating political propaganda via homemade explosives (*las bombas de propaganda*). Violent protests include armed attacks, bombings, kidnappings, arson, sabotage, armed occupations of radio stations and towns, and robberies by political groups. (Source: *La Prensa Gráfica* **1962–81)**

as the likelihood that challengers will enhance their interests or extend existing benefits if they act collectively. In contrast, *threat* denotes the probability that existing benefits will be taken away or new harms inflicted if challenging groups fail to act collectively (Tilly 1978; Koopmans 1995; Jasper 1997; Goldstone and Tilly 2001; Van Dyke and Soule 2002). Viewing opportunity and threat as ideal types, groups may either be driven by positive environmental cues and institutional incentives to push forward new demands and extend benefits (i.e., political opportunity) or be pressed into action in fear of losing current goods, rights, and safety (i.e., threat). In the following sections, a sequential theoretical framework is provided that conceptually links political opportunity and threat to the outbreak of protest waves in authoritarian settings.[2]

The Political Opportunity Environment in Authoritarian Settings

The political opportunity model is largely a theory of protest driven by a relatively more responsive institutional setting and political context. That is, the political environment opens in a manner conducive to the pressing of demands by multiple groups (Tarrow 1989; Koopmans 1993; Mueller 1999; Beissinger 2001). In Tilly's (1978) initial conceptualization of opportunity, groups have a greater probability of realizing their interests or gaining new advantages if they decide to act collectively. The state and state managers are probably the most important actors in organizing this changing political environment (Jenkins 1995; Goodwin 1997).

While political opportunities increase the likelihood for movement emergence in democratic settings, in nondemocratic contexts they *first* encourage the formation of challenger organizations. To realize an escalation in protest requires a certain level of such organizational resources (McCarthy and Zald 1977) and cognitive attributions that assess and interpret the political environment (Snow et al. 1986; McAdam 1999). Without organizational structures collective action will likely be short-lived (Oberschall 1973). Organizational resources include sympathetic institutions, associational networks, and civic organizations (McCarthy 1996). These informal and formal organizational elements constitute an *organizational infrastructure* for multiple groups to link previously unconnected collectivities, exchange resources and information, and launch protest campaigns resulting in a protest wave or cycle (Walton and Seddon 1994; Gould 1995; Minkoff 1997; McAdam 1999).

Although various challenger organizations and their building blocks of associational networks

and sympathetic institutions serve as important covariates in explaining protest dynamics in democratic settings, their mere existence must be accounted for in authoritarian contexts where basic civil liberties and rights of free association have been historically restricted (Wickham 2002). Two political opportunity dimensions salient in overcoming these restrictions and encouraging challenger organizational formation include (1) *institutional access* and (2) *competitive elections* (Tarrow 1989, 1994; Jenkins 1995; Markoff 1996; Linz and Stepan 1996). Below, these two political opportunity dimensions are analyzed in relation to the emergence of an organizational infrastructure in authoritarian settings.

Institutional Access

New laws, state agencies, resource commitments, and symbolic gestures emitted by liberalizing states to civil society act as positive forces for disempowered groups (Almeida and Stearns 1998; Amenta and Young 1999). When new laws are passed and written down, they provide an increasingly stable, predictable, and consistent system of political incentives for challengers to form organizations (Stinchcombe 1965; Weber 1968; McCarthy 1996; Wiktorowicz 2001). Also, officially registering and legalizing nongovernmental entities (e.g., political parties, labor unions, professional and civic associations, rural cooperatives) in authoritarian contexts provide a state-sanctioned and legitimated organizational form (DiMaggio and Powell 1983) in which to support collective claim making. A more competitive electoral system ensures the reliability of this widening institutional access for organization building.

Competitive Elections

One of the most important ways in which authoritarian states vary resides in the relative openness of the electoral process (Cook 1996; Markoff 1996; Linz and Stepan 1996). Democratization efforts allowing increasingly *competitive elections* in authoritarian regimes supply previously excluded groups with an arena in which to begin organizing drives. These nationally generalized conditions of permitting relatively open elections contribute to the formation of organizations and associations by protecting multiple challengers (Tilly 1978).

By convoking multiparty elections, the ruling political party's legitimacy becomes linked to the election process and outcome. As a result, severe repression of emerging civic organizations can place state legitimacy and future electoral competitiveness in question. The state's new incentive to restrain from repressive acts gives challengers the opportunity to access organizational resources and sympathetic institutions to found and maintain new organizations around specific issues affecting their constituencies. Excluded groups calculate that they have a greater chance of successfully organizing and exerting political pressure without being physically threatened or extinguished.

Once opposition parties secure some representation in a democratizing polity, they have an interest in forming alliances with challenging groups and organizations outside to increase their own electoral power (Przeworski 1991; Markoff 1996). Electoral opposition parties may encourage and view emerging challenger organizations as a vital component of their own constituency. With allies in the polity, challengers increase the likelihood that their investments in organizing result in new advantages and organizational survival. Boosting challenger organizing efforts include such opposition party actions as supporting and financing civic organizations, and securing a hearing/parliamentary debate for demands and more neutral state arbitration for conflicts with the private sector. Challenger organizations under these conditions want to reform the state, get new policies, expand existing benefits, or change public attitudes (Tilly 1978; Jenkins and Klandermans 1995; Goldstone 1998). In accord with this liberalizing trend in state practices and the larger political environment, more nonviolent and civil forms of protest are predicted since institutional channels of conflict resolution are more available and legitimated (Goodwin 1997; Goldstone 1998; McAdam, Tarrow, and Tilly 2001).

Organizational Infrastructure as Political Opportunity "Holdovers"

A period of expanded political opportunity in authoritarian contexts also permits the survival of an organizational infrastructure after the political opportunities responsible for its emergence diminish. In other words, political opportunity periods deposit lasting organizational remnants or "holdovers" that persist in the political environment (Taylor 1989; Meyer and Whittier 1994; Minkoff 1997). Indeed, the maintenance and survival of challenger organizations may be the most important outcome of a political opportunity–generated protest wave in authoritarian contexts. Such enduring organizations provide a fungible resource infrastructure from which protest waves may emerge in much different political environments. One such political context is that of threat, whereby a set of *negative* environmental conditions pushes groups into collective claim making.

Environmental Transition from Opportunity to Threat

A political environment that transitions from political opportunity to threat will likely initially throw the entire social movement sector off guard. After years of investing time and resources in organizational founding, membership recruitment, and strategies consonant with a liberalizing authoritarian state, challengers facing a transition to a threatening environment find that the old ways of organizing and seeking political influence are inadequate. These challenger sunk costs will likely cause organizational inertia and a lag effect in responding and adapting to a more repressive political environment (Stinchcombe 1965; Hannan and Freeman 1989).

However, if the political environment continues to transition in a consistent direction over time (i.e., a more threatening trajectory), challengers are once again signaled by the state to change their organizing structures and strategies. For example, petitioning a national parliament that assumed power via electoral fraud or engaging in orderly street marches while security forces repeatedly disperse them with live ammunition motivates well-organized and resourceful challengers to radicalize their organizational structures and strategies. Having access to a preexisting organizational infrastructure allows challengers to adopt new organizational forms and practices (i.e., growth in radical organizations and disruptive protest) *over time* in response to a threatening environment.

With an organizational infrastructure already in place, challengers more easily employ bloc recruitment, while "the presence of numerous organizations ensures a pre-established communications network, resources already partially mobilized, the presence of individuals with leadership skills, and a tradition of participation among members of the collectivity" (Oberschall 1973, p. 125). Without the previous buildup of an organizational infrastructure or political opportunity "holdovers," threat-induced collective action will likely be weak to nonexistent.

The Threatening Political Environment

We can partition threat into more precise dimensions. Three principal threats that apply to authoritarian states in the global periphery include (1) *state-attributed economic problems,* (2) *erosion of rights,* and (3) *state repression* (Tilly 1978; Walton and Seddon 1994; Goldstone and Tilly 2001; Goodwin 2001; Almeida 2002). These forms of threat in most times and places increase the costs of collective action and deter protest (Tilly 1978; Jasper 1997). However, if the recipients of these threats are well-organized, resourceful groups with an elaborate organizational infrastructure, greater levels of collective action and resistance are expected (Jenkins 1983; Gould 1991; Walton and Seddon 1994; McAdam 2003). Challenger organizations boost confidence, exchange information and resources, link disconnected groups, and provide a collective vehicle to resist unwanted changes via popular contention. Thus, organizational infrastructures surviving past a period of political opportunity in which they were founded perform a key task in determining if threats will deter or escalate collective dissent.

State-Attributed Economic Problems

As the resource mobilization perspective suggests, economic grievances alone are usually not sufficient to explain escalating levels of contention since they are ubiquitous while protest is not (McCarthy and Zald 1977; Jenkins 1983). Nonetheless, when *organized* groups convincingly attribute to specific agents

the responsibility for a decline in their economic conditions they may initiate campaigns to resist unwanted changes (e.g., middle-class organizations in Argentina—*los ahorristas*—protesting throughout 2002 against the loss of their savings accounts because of state-initiated bank freezes and currency devaluations). The administrative expansion of the nation-state as regulator of economic life and vital resources makes it a common target for redress of economic problems (Tilly 1984; Walton and Seddon 1994; Goodwin 1997). Two specific state-attributed economic problems in the global periphery include land access (Wickham-Crowley 1992) and basic price increases (Goldstone 1986 and 2001).

When state-sponsored agro-export policies expel peasants from subsistence plots and fail to institute highly publicized agrarian reform or when basic prices rise abruptly, incentives increase for networked and resourceful groups to resist. For example, state-initiated structural adjustment programs and price increases are likely to trigger severe protests in developing countries with dense urban populations and high rates of labor unionization (Walton and Ragin 1990; Walton and Shefner 1994; Auyero 2002). In sum, state-attributed economic problems experienced directly in the immediate lives of resourceful groups may be a threat incentive to join in resistant collective action.[3] Even though state-attributed economic problems increase the probability of heightened protest among organized groups, the form of protest will likely only become more radicalized and violent when combined with an erosion of rights and escalating state repression.

Erosion of Rights

After a period of extending civil rights, taking away voting and a sense of citizenship blocks the conventional means to individual political participation (Useem 1985; Olzak, Beasley, and Olivier 2003). Alternative, nonconventional political strategies and organizations appear much more attractive under these circumstances (Amenta and Young 1999). In particular, when competitive national elections are nullified, canceled, and/or perceived as fraudulent and meaningless, the state announces the closure of the polity on a national scale and calls into question its legitimacy. This sends a strong message to challenger organizations that the state as an audience and arbiter to reform-type demands is greatly restricted (if not outright hostile). Over time, challengers will likely use their in-place organizational infrastructure to form extraparliamentary and revolutionary organizations and attempt more disruptive and violent strategies to exercise political influence. Unresponsive state managers that are perceived to be no longer publicly accountable drive this radicalization in the form of protest, when petitioning authorities through routine conflict resolution channels appears futile (White 1989; Goodwin 1997; Jenkins and Bond 2001).

State Repression

State repression may also be a critical component in igniting further protest. A number of empirical studies outside of advanced industrialized democracies have shown positive effects of state repression on aggregate and group-specific protest activities (Olivier 1991; Khawaja 1993; Francisco 1995; Rasler 1996; Loveman 1998; Schock 1999; Moore 2000; Beissinger 2001). State repression may generate moral shocks and suddenly imposed grievances for both the general public and activist groups (White 1989; Loveman 1998; McAdam, Tarrow, and Tilly 2001; Wood 2003). Coercive state behavior breaks publicly held norms of expected state–civil society relations—especially when the repressive acts are way out of proportion to the type of demands and claims protesters pursue (Goldstone 1998).

Activists can use state repressive acts as empirical verifications of the unworthiness of state managers to rule as well as for motivational appeals within organizations and interorganizational units to participate in future protest actions. These organizational settings provide solidary incentives, normative pressures, and shared activist identities to engage in high-risk protest (Loveman 1998; Snow and McAdam 2000; Petersen 2001).[4] In addition, repressive acts grant occasions for emotionally charged focal events, such as funeral processions and homage ceremonies for fallen victims of state violence, to rally challengers.[5] State repression, as erosion of rights, also pushes well-networked challengers into more radical forms of organization and dissent as repeated outrageous acts of state violence convince challengers that a fundamental reorganization of the state and society is a desirable goal (Brockett 1993; Goodwin 1997; Goldstone 1998).

Theoretical Summary: Two Paths to Protest Waves

Figure 3 summarizes the temporal relationships conditioning alternate pathways to protest waves in authoritarian contexts. The schematic model should be viewed as a probabilistic causal chain (Ganz 2000; Tilly 2002) that sequentially links political

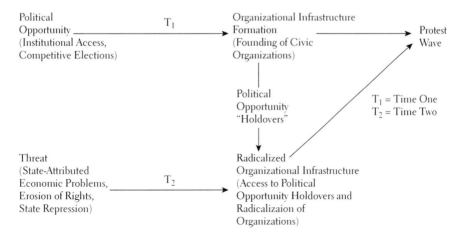

Figure 7.3 Pathways to protest wave outbreaks in authoritarian settings

opportunity, organizational infrastructure, and threats to the outbreak of protest waves. An authoritarian regime that liberalizes with institutional access and competitive elections (i.e., time 1) brings about the development of an organizational infrastructure (i.e., formation and legalization of civic organizations, cooperatives, and unions). As challengers interpret the relatively positive cues emitted from the opening political environment, they use their newly formed organizational infrastructure and launch protest campaigns leading to the outbreak of a protest wave. Under these conditions, multiple groups press the state for new advantages and benefits, using more orderly and non-violent tactics.

When political opportunities contract and the protest wave descends, an organizational infrastructure is left in place (i.e., opportunity "hold-overs"). If, following the political opportunity–induced protest episode, challengers receive consistent environmental feedback indicating that the political climate has shifted to one potentially more injurious if they fail to mobilize (i.e., loss of goods, rights, and safety in time 2), they are motivated to adapt their organizational infrastructure to the threatening environment over time and create more radical organizations. Once the organizational infrastructure is radicalized, another protest wave is triggered by repeated threat incentives. Radical challenger organizations employ more disruptive and violent forms of protest as institutional channels to defend rights erode and state repression decreases the national government's credibility.

Data and Methods

This study employs a dynamic political process method that tracks changes over time (Gamson and Meyer 1996) in El Salvador's political environment to explain variations in the *level* and *form* of protest activity. The analysis centers on the sequential relationship between political opportunity, organizational infrastructure, and threat in generating the outbreak of protest waves. The case draws on protest events collected and coded from the daily El Salvadoran newspaper *La Prensa Gráfica* between 1962 and 1981.[6] The number of protest events identified and coded over the 20-year period (January 1, 1962–December 31, 1981) totaled 4,151. Protest events

were defined as collective challenges of three or more people making claims on political or economic elites (Rucht and Ohlemacher 1992; McAdam, Tarrow, and Tilly 1996). Protests were coded into 25 different forms, ranging from petitions and street marches to factory occupations and armed attacks. Other properties of the protest events were also coded, including use of conventional nonviolence, disruption and violence by protesters, and presence and type of challenger organization(s) in protest events.

Two Protest Waves Compared
El Salvador, 1932 to Mid-1960s

Between 1932 and the mid-1960s El Salvador's political system was restricted to conservative military governance (Guidos Véjar 1980; Baloyra 1982; Wood 2000; Mahoney 2001). The military regime originated in 1932 in the context of a peasant uprising in the western coffee-growing departments. The security forces swiftly suppressed the revolt and carried out in retribution a massacre of a reported 8,000–30,000 peasants in a three-week period (Anderson 1970; Zamosc 1989; Pérez Brignoli 1995; Paige 1997). Following the massacre, from the 1930s to the mid-1960s, there were only sporadic outbreaks of urban unrest. Though at times large enough to bring down the existing government and usher in a new military regime (e.g., 1944 and 1960; Turcios 1993), popular contention never lasted for more than a few months. Restrictions on union organization, noncompetitive elections, general fear in the countryside, and a series of quasimartial laws and state repressive actions (e.g., 1944–48, 1952–56, 1960, and 1961) prevented the formation of durable civic organizations (Larín 1972). For example, the urban labor movement failed on several occasions to form an enduring labor federation after the 1932 crackdown (Larín 1972).[7] The political climate, though, changed in the mid-1960s, becoming favorable to the emergence of an organizational infrastructure capable of sustaining multiple social movements.

Political Opportunities in El Salvador, 1960–72

Institutional access.—The Salvadoran military regime that emerged in the early 1960s was under enormous international and domestic pressure to implement moderately reformist measures. Its liberalizing efforts could most clearly be observed in the institutional access it provided to three key sectors of civil society: (1) the labor sector, (2) the educational sector, and (3) the church sector. The national government promoted a number of unprecedented initiatives in the sphere of state-labor relations. The state provided greater autonomy and investment in the educational sector by expanding the public education system and legalizing school teachers' associations. In the church sector, the state actively supported the formation of cooperative associations allowing entry to the Catholic Church in the countryside. This increasing institutional access (along with multiparty elections) encouraged a dramatic upsurge in the formation of civic organizations in all three social sectors.

Labor sector access.—To better regulate the industrialization process, the Salvadoran state revised and instituted a number of labor laws in the early 1960s that acted as a catalyst for the mobilization of urban labor organizations. In 1962 the liberalizing Rivera military regime allowed governmental and semi-governmental employees the right to form associations with state recognition (Molina Arévalo 1988; Arriola Palomares and Candray Alvarado 1994). In 1963, Rivera enacted a labor code. Unprecedented for modern El Salvador, a set of legalized labor standards was put into place in which worker grievances could be settled (Arriola Palomares and Candray Alvarado 1994). The labor code recognized the right to form labor federations and confederations as well as a jurisdictional body (ministry of labor and labor courts) in which to place claims for adjudication. These opening gestures in the sphere of state-labor relations reactivated a number of clandestine and semilegal union confederations (CGTS, CGS) and were responsible for the foundation of several new labor federations and unions organizations (e.g., FUSS, STISSS, STUS, SETA, FESTIAVTCES, UNOC, FESINCONTRANS). Table 1 summarizes the principal legislative actions in the early 1960s opening the way for urban labor organization.

The Law of Collective Labor Conflicts, passed in 1961, created the potential that the state would become a more neutral arbiter in disputes with private employers. The right of public employees to unionize also mobilized thousands of teachers, social security institute workers, state-industry and administration workers, and university workers to form union organizations and associations in the mid to late 1960s. Legislation authorizing the right of urban workers to strike was ratified in the 1962 constitution as well as in the labor code of 1963. This legally sanctioned an important pressure tactic for urban workers. With these state actions, the size of the union sector grew considerably in the 1960s. In 1960 there were 64 unions with 21,000 affiliates and by 1971 there were 127 unions with 64,186 members (Menívar 1982; Molina Arévalo 1988).

Educational sector access.—A major institution in Salvadoran society historically supporting oppositional activity is the National University of El Salvador (UES) (Parkman 1988; Grenier 1999). In 1950 the national government implemented a university autonomy law that was not activated until the elections of the 1960s (Webre 1979; security forces invaded and occupied the university in 1952 and 1960). In the 1960s, the central government permitted self-management of the university with little interference (Grenier 1999). As part of the state's liberalization drive in the 1960s, it greatly increased funding for postsecondary education. In 1960, the national government budget for higher education was $800,000 and it grew to over $6.5 million by 1970 (U.S. AID 1973). The proportion of the total education budget allocated to universities also grew significantly in these same years, from 7% to 22% (U.S. AID 1973).

In the context of these new state resource commitments to higher education, university student enrollment expanded markedly. Between 1955 and 1968, the university student population more than quadrupled, from 1,393 to 6,500 students (Wickham Crowley 1989; Valle 1993). The UES also relocated its academic schools previously dispersed throughout the capital to a centralized location in a northern San Salvador suburb (Ciudad Universitaria). The physical size of the new main campus tripled between 1963 and 1968 (Valle 1993).

In addition, new UES campuses opened in Santa Ana in 1965 and San Miguel in 1969—the second and third largest cities in the nation. In 1965 the Jesuit-run Catholic university (Universidad Centroamericana José Simeón Cañas) was founded in the capital as a public corporation and reached an enrollment of more than 1,300 students by 1970 (Beirne 1996). Instead of counting the number of potentially mobilizable university students in the hundreds on a small, single decentralized campus, as in the pre-1960s, students now numbered in the thousands in four centralized universities in the three largest cities. This development created favorable ecological conditions for the building of university-based organizations (Zhao 1998).

The government also nearly tripled its investment in primary and secondary public education between 1960 and 1970, from a budget of $9.14 million to a budget of $26.58 million (U.S. AID 1973). In this same period, the number of enrolled junior high and high school students more than doubled (U.S. AID 1973). During this rapid educational expansion, the state tolerated the formation of public sector teachers' associations, whose leadership had in part been exiled after a 1961 military coup.

Church sector access.—Beyond the new urban labor laws and educational expansion, institutional access spread to the countryside via the Catholic Church. In the 1960s, the central government started to encourage the formation of rural cooperative associations, giving increased jurisdiction and resources for this purpose to the Ministry of Agriculture and the Regional Colonization Institute (Guerra Calderon 1976). At the same time, the state permitted the Catholic Church to initiate cooperatives in rural zones with small landholders and poor peasants. The government granted legal recognition to the Catholic Church Cooperative program in 1967 (FUNPROCOOP) and formed its own cooperative institute in 1969 (INSAFOCOOP; Guerra Calderon 1976). Though modest in intentions, the cooperative programs, according to one participant observer, "broke the ice of fear, distrust, and passivity" that had existed between the peasantry and the state since the 1932 massacre (Guerra Calderon 1976, p. 231).

In 1961, the church formed the Inter-Diocesan Social Secretariat (ISS), which was funded by the central government from 1962 to 1967 (Vega 1994). The ISS sponsored rural cooperatives for small landowning and landless peasants under the FUNPROCOOP program (Guerra Calderon 1976). Church-sponsored cooperatives spread rapidly, starting in 1963 with 98 members in 2 cooperatives and reaching 37 cooperatives in 1969 with 10,500 members; by 1971 there were 54 cooperatives (Guerra Calderon 1976). In these cooperatives, peasants learned valuable farming and leadership skills, while at the same time they received training in community organizing and civil rights (Vega 1994). The church also used the legal protection of the cooperative program as a springboard to organize peasant leagues, Christian base communities, and peasant training centers. The opening electoral system added another layer of pressure on the state to sustain institutional access in the labor, educational, and church sectors.

Competitive elections.—In 1963, following 32 years of one-party military rule, the Salvadoran

Table 1 National Labor Legislation Promoting Institutional Access

Law or Legal Action	Year of Enactment
Labor Tribunal Law	1960
Law of Collective Labor Conflicts	1961
Revision of Retirement and Pensions Law	1961
Legalization of Public Employees to Form Unions/Associations	1962
Right of Urban Workers to Strike	1962, 1963
Right of Unions to Form Federations and Confederations	1963

Source.—Molina Arévalo (1988).

government changed the electoral system to proportional representation—partly as a result of Colonel Rivera's embarrassment at running unopposed in the 1962 presidential elections as well as pressure brought to bear by the newly formed Partido Demócrata Cristiana (Christian Democratic Party, or PDC, founded in 1960). The new proportional system allotted a fixed number of national deputies (the equivalent of U.S. House and Senate seats) in El Salvador's unicameral legislative assembly to each of the 14 departments (the equivalent of U.S. states) based on its population size. This dramatically transformed the system of political competition for nearly a decade.

The 1964 parliamentary elections staged the first test for the new system of proportional representation. The oppositional PDC performed strongly, winning 14 seats in the unicameral legislature and taking the mayorship in the nation's capital, San Salvador. Table 2 illustrates the increasing electoral strength of opposition parties (especially the Christian Democrats) in the parliamentary elections between 1950 and 1970. At the local level the opposition parties made inroads as well. In 1968, the Christian Democrats won the mayoral races in the three largest cities. The opening of the electoral system was a trend that continued until the presidential and legislative assembly elections in the first quarter of 1972 (Gordon 1989). It marked a sharp break from the personalist military rule of General Martínez (1931–44) and the one-party rule of the PRUD and PCN military governments up to 1964—a period Rubén Zamora (1998, p. 26) calls *monopartidismo* ("one partyism").

Under the new context of competitive elections, opposition parties encouraged the formation of challenger organizations as supportive constituencies outside the polity. The opposition parties such as the PDC, PAR, and MNR often used their new power in the parliament to call hearings and investigations supporting challenger organization demands (e.g., labor codes, promotional systems, university budgets, retirement packages, rural unionization, and land reform) and they served as advocates for worker and teacher organizations during these groups' strike campaigns. In September 1964, newly elected oppositional politicians began

to lobby for a national teachers' pension plan as part of a larger debate on a retirement system for government employees (Ruiz Abarca 1967). This action assisted in the foundation of the public school teachers' union (ANDES-21 de Junio) by unifying teachers around the content of the retirement plan.

During the mid-1960s, the Christian Democratic Party played a leading role with the church in founding or greatly expanding Catholic-based organizations such as the Catholic university (Whitfield 1994), a labor union (UNOC), a peasant federation (FECCAS), youth organizations in the city and countryside (JEC, JOC, and JAC), neighborhood action associations, and university student organizations (ACUS and FRUSC). Emerging challenger organizations also benefited from the relative respite in state repression, owing to the necessity for the official government party to remain competitive in elections and protect its public image.

In sum, the liberalization of the military regime ushered in two key political opportunities in the form of *institutional access* and *competitive elections*, which provided incentives and a protective cover allowing the labor, educational, and church sectors to establish civic organizations. In the late 1960s, excluded social sectors that had suffered from ongoing repressive state actions over the previous 30 years found that they could sustain themselves via the legalization of their organizations and support from newly elected oppositional political parties.

Birth of an Organizational Infrastructure

By the end of the 1960s, regime liberalization motivated political activists to form a wide variety of civic organizations in workplaces, schools, and churches to press for political and economic reform. These nascent challenger organizations learned to develop long-term and reciprocal network relationships with one another (Powell 1990). The increase in organizational foundation and interorganizational relationships constituted an organizational infrastructure in the labor, educational, and church sectors.

Labor sector organizations.—Both the progovernment labor confederation (CGS) and the smaller communist-influenced labor confederation (CGTS)

Table 2 Political Party Representation in Salvadoran National Assembly, 1950–70 (by Absolute Number of Deputies)

	Year										
Deputy's Party	1950	1952	1954	1956	1958	1960	1961	1964	1966	1968	1970
PRUD/PCN*	54	54	54	54	54	54	54	32	31	27	34
PDC†								14	15	19	16
PAR								6	4		
PPS									1	4	1
PREN									1		
MNR										2	
UDN											1
Total	54	54	54	54	54	54	54	52	52	52	52

Sources.—McDonald (1969) and Webre (1979).

* The military party.

† Christian Democrats.

were formed in the late 1950s and secured legal recognition by the mid-1960s. In 1965, the fledgling CGTS merged with seven independent unions to form the Federación Unitaria Sindical de El Salvador (FUSS). The CGTS was a semiclandestine labor organization since its emergence in 1957 and frequently persecuted by security forces. In the fall of 1965, in an unprecedented move, the liberalizing military government gave legal recognition to the FUSS, which led or was involved in most of the major urban strikes between 1967 and 1972. In 1965 FUSS had only 14 affiliated unions, but by 1971 it had 24 with more than 9,500 members (Menjívar 1982; Carpio 1982). The FUSS leadership sensed that the opening electoral process offered a favorable occasion to test how far it could push demands for its affiliates in the urban working class. Indeed, within FUSS a subunit was organized called Comité Obrero de Acción Política (COAP). The purpose of COAP was to infiltrate proregime unions, direct protest activities, and campaign for opposition candidates in the 1966, 1967, and 1968 parliamentary and presidential elections (Menjívar 1982).

In 1968 FUSS also encouraged the development of a second militant trade union organization: the Federation of Workers in Food, Clothing, Textile, and Related Industries (FESTIAVTCES). By 1971, FUSS and FESTIAVTCES together controlled 41 unions. In the early 1970s, they mobilized rural workers in favor of unionization and founded a peasant organization (ATACES). Using stipulations in the 1963 labor code, other public sector employees in this period established unions such as the national university workers (STUS) in 1966 (Valle 1993) and, in 1968, the Water and Aqueduct Service Employees (SETA), Municipal Employees (AGEPYM), Social Security Workers (STISSS), and Electrical Workers (STIES), and in 1972 the Hydroelectric Commission Workers (STECEL) (Richter 1980; Bollinger 1987). The legal recognition alone of these newly created unions by the state was a major victory. Ten years prior, left-of-center unions had had virtually no legal standing while many labor leaders were in exile (Webre 1979).

Educational sector organizations.—In the university sector, the main student organization, the Asociación General de Estudiantes Universitarios Salvadoreños (AGEUS), increased its ranks with the government's university expansion program. Groups within AGEUS showed signs of political differentiation with the formation of such organizations as the communist-influenced Frente Estudiantiles Universitarios Revolucionarios (FEUR), Catholic students in the Federación Revolucionaria de Universitarios Social Cristianos (FRUSC) and Acción Católica Universitaria Salvadoreña (ACUS), and the social democratic Frente Socialista Demócrata (FSD). These organizations established subunits in each of the seven academic colleges of the national university (Valle 1993). By the end of the 1960s even high school students formed organizations such as El Consejo General de Bienestar Estudiantil (CGBE) and La Asociación de los Estudiantes de Secundaria (AES).

One of the most important challenger organizations to form in the 1960s was the public school teachers' union, La Asociación National de Educadores Salvadoreños (ANDES–21 de Junio). ANDES began internally organizing in 1964 and made a public presence in 1965, when an estimated 11,000 teachers marched (dressed in their finest attire) through San Salvador to the presidential palace demanding their own teacher-specific retirement system and exclusion from the government's general program for state employees. Symbolically planned, the mass street march occurred a day before the traditional teacher's day, June 22, and hence, the teachers named their new organization ANDES–21 de Junio. Two years later (in June 1967), ANDES–21 received legal recognition from the national government. The formation and self-entitlement of ANDES–21 signified a move toward greater autonomy for public education workers.

The new teachers' organization had the support of more than 80% of the 10,000–14,000 teachers working in El Salvador at the time. ANDES–21 organized nationally, with regional organizations in each of El Salvador's 14 departments. The association evidenced a strong break with the past; previous military governments had carried on a paternalistic relationship with public educators, busing them en masse into the capital for progovernment parades and election rallies (Anaya Montes 1972; Bevan 1981). ANDES-21 also organized the first national high school student organizations between 1968 and 1971 (CGBE and AES).

Church sector organizations.—The Catholic Church was motivated to form organizations via the government's rural cooperative program and its close relations with the newly elected Christian Democratic Party (PDC) in parliament and city governments. In 1964 the Catholic Church and the PDC reactivated the Catholic UNOC and founded a federation of peasant leagues (FECCAS) that would become a focal organization for widespread rural protest in the 1970s. FECCAS held a series of annual peasant conferences beginning in 1965. During these gatherings, FECCAS publicly pressured the state for land reform and the right to form rural unions (Guerra Calderon 1976). FECCAS grew to about a thousand members by 1970.

The Archdiocese of San Salvador in collaboration with the Christian Democratic Party created the organization Centro de Estudios Sociales y Promoción Popular (CESPROP; 1967–72), which trained youth groups to work in urban shantytowns and in the countryside (with FECCAS). CESPROP also published a number of reports supporting social reforms such as land redistribution and peasant unionization. Using the new access points in the countryside, priests and pastoral teams arrived in rural communities where they organized peasants in Las Comunidades Cristianas de Base (CCBs). The CCBs performed traditional religious practices (e.g., singing, praying, and reading scripture) with *active* peasant participation. In these small and intimate organizational settings (of 10 to 30 people) new interpretations of biblical passages emerged that provided the moral and spiritual bases to seek greater social and economic parity in the everyday lives of El Salvador's urban and rural poor (Wood 2003). In 1970 the Archdiocese of San Salvador sponsored the Semana Pastoral (Pastoral Week) where it committed itself to forming Christian base communities nationally, meeting periodically to coordinate these efforts, and to publishing newsletters sharing CCB experiences around the country.

A related organizational product of the new commitment of the Catholic Church to the rural poor was the formation between 1968 and 1972 of seven major peasant-training centers (Vega 1994). An estimated 15,000 peasants received technical and religious training (theology of the new social doctrine) in the centers (Montgomery 1982). By the late 1960s and early to mid 1970s, as an outgrowth of the church cooperatives, peasant leagues, CCBs, and rural training centers, peasants were beginning to organize around land and unionization issues.

Political Opportunity Deposits Enduring Organizational Infrastructure

By the late 1960s, under the encouragement of widening institutional access and protection of the liberalizing electoral system, challengers used sympathetic institutions and organizations in the labor, educational, and church sectors to create an unprecedented network of civic organizations and associations. This organizational infrastructure was accessible to groups (especially unionized workers, teachers, students, and a growing number of church-organized peasants) to draw upon and initiate social movement protest campaigns. The newly established organizational infrastructure permitted by expanded political opportunity culminated in the outbreak of a protest wave between 1967 and 1972—the longest period of sustained contention since the late 1920s and early 1930s.

Political Opportunity–Driven Protest Wave, 1967–72

Between 1967 and 1972 popular contention increased, as witnessed by the total number of strikes and protest events, which eventuated in a full-blown protest wave (see figs. 1 and 2). The most important outcome of this protest wave was that multiple challenger organizations and groups learned how to maintain the organizational infrastructure permitted by expanding political opportunity. Another feature of the 1967–72 protest wave was its orderly and nonviolent character (see fig. 2). Popular contention focused on pushing the state to pass new reforms or alter existing policies. Between 1965 and 1971 nearly one out of every five protest events targeted the legislative assembly, which challenger organizations viewed as legitimate and autonomous enough to receive movement demands and at times pass favorable legislation.

The 1967–72 protest wave began with a series of bus drivers' strikes and teacher mobilizing efforts from 1965 to 1967 (organized by FUSS and

ANDES-21). A string of urban labor strikes in the first third of 1967 shook San Salvador, Santa Ana, and Zacatecoluca, terminating with a progressive general strike in April involving 35,000 workers (Carpio 1980). The general labor strike enlisted the public support of student and peasant organizations. In late 1967 and early 1968, ANDES-21 unleashed a major public school teachers' strike targeting the Ministry of Education and Legislative Assembly to consider a teacher-proposed retirement program. The 58-day teachers' strike included several mass marches of over 20,000 protesters (some reaching over 80,000); a month-long occupation of the patio in front of the National Library, where the Ministry of Education offices were housed; and several solidarity strikes by FUSS-affiliated unions. This particular campaign was reportedly the largest protest mobilization to date in modern El Salvador (Monteforte Toledo 1972).

There was a lull in contentious activity during the second half of 1969, which was linked to hostilities between El Salvador and Honduras. Major challenger organizations such as FUSS and AGEUS temporarily placed their resources into supporting the government's war mobilization efforts. Labor activities and gains occurred in 1969, nevertheless, as Richter (1980, p. 123) reports from research using FUSS primary documents: "During the first eight months of 1969 there were thirteen major strikes in El Salvador and several related job actions, of which eight were won outright by the workers—a fact that indicates a continued escalation of the level of trade-union struggle and organization."

During the summer of 1971, ANDES-21 initiated another major two-month-long teachers' strike, demanding a modernized salary scale corresponding to rank and seniority—which again included numerous mass marches and the pacific occupation of the Palacio National during parliamentary debate on the salary legislation. The 1971 teachers' strike tapped into the organizational infrastructure support of Catholic labor unions, public sector unions, high school and university student associations, oppositional political parties, and even the incipient peasant movement (Anaya Montes 1972). The university community raised $5,200 for the teachers and donated their printing services to publish

ANDES-21 pamphlets and newspapers (Anaya Montes 1972), while thousands of church-organized peasants in Suchitoto protested and secured the release of arrested teachers held in the local jail (Pearce 1986).

In the late 1960s and early 1970s, in addition to protests by urban workers and teachers, student organizations began to sustain protest (as opposed to intermittent outbursts) as part of a larger protest wave. First, university student organizations supported the major strikes of ANDES-21 in the form of solidarity strikes, marches, and fundraising drives. Anaya Montes (1972) reports that up to 80% of UES students were actively supporting the ANDES-21 strike in the summer of 1971. UES student organizations launched their own strikes and building occupations between 1970 and 1972, in protest over how general education requirements (*areas comunes*) were implemented. Even the traditional student *bufo* marches (costume parades lampooning government officials; Dunkerly 1982) were now taking place on the streets outside of the newly created UES campuses in the cities of Santa Ana and San Miguel, providing stinging political satire well beyond the capital.

The long dormant peasantry benefited from widening political opportunity created by attempts of the church, labor unions, and opposition political parties to press the liberalizing state to extend the right to unionize to rural workers (Larín 1972). Most importantly, peasants profited from the Catholic Church's rural cooperative program and from the foundation of the Christian Federation of Peasants (FECCAS) in 1964. In turn, FECCAS-affiliated peasants publicly supported the 1967 general labor strike and the ANDES-21 teachers' strikes (Guerra Calderon 1976; Cardenal 1987).

The protest wave rapidly descended in 1972 after mass protests against the electoral fraud of presidential and parliamentary elections. The failure of these mass-based nonviolent protests to prevent electoral fraud threw the entire organizational infrastructure off balance in terms of developing a viable strategy to exercise political influence in a transitioning political environment. As political opportunities contracted with electoral obstruction and narrowing institutional access in the early to mid 1970s, there were markedly fewer inducements to initiate social movement activity. However, the organizational infrastructure founded in the labor, educational, and church-based sectors persisted, creating the potential for subsequent rounds of mobilization if pushed by new incentives from the state.

Environmental Transition from Opportunity to Threat

The period from mid-1972 to 1981 was one in which the threats of state-attributed economic problems, erosion of rights, and state repression increasingly characterized El Salvador's political environment. Beginning in 1972, the key political opportunities driving the 1960s' wave of protest, institutional access and the practice of competitive elections, narrowed. This contraction in political opportunity effectively ended the 1967–72 wave of protest and dampened the level of contentious activity between mid-1972 and 1976 (see figs. 1 and 2). In place of political opportunity, rising threats began to push challengers to radicalize their organizational infrastructure. By 1977, the combination of mounting threats with the dominance of revolutionary organizations in the social movement sector contributed to a much more disruptive and violent cycle of protest.

Declining Political Opportunities, 1972–81

Institutional access.—Between 1972 and 1977 the Salvadoran regime narrowed the institutional access that it opened to challenger organizations in the labor, education, and church sectors in the 1960s. By the mid-1970s, only labor, peasant, and civic organizations closely aligned with the ruling military party (PCN) enjoyed institutional access or received support from state agencies. State controlled peasant groups and construction unions held the largest demonstrations and strikes in the period between 1973 and 1976 (Lungo 1987). The ruling military party tried to form a corporatist base while excluding organizations that had participated in the 1967–72 protest wave, such as the independent students' and teachers' associations and the center-left unions. By 1977, with the state's inability to implement a moderate land reform proposal and the ascendancy of General Humberto Romero (formerly the minister of defense and public security) to the presidency, the attempt at narrow corporatism had failed and the official military party focused much more on state repression than on co-optation or restricted institutional access (Guidos Véjar 1979; Stanley 1996). Institutional access also became more meaningless with the closing of multiparty elections.

Competitive elections.—In late 1971, the three left-of-center opposition parties (UDN, MNR, and PDC) united forces in an electoral coalition (Unión National Opositora, or UNO) for the upcoming presidential elections in February 1972. The 1972 elections were of colossal political importance because it was a scheduled year in which presidential, legislative, and local elections all took place within three weeks of each other. Preoccupied with a potential UNO electoral victory, the ruling military party returned to using the Comisión Central de las Elecciones (CCE)—in which it had appointed all three directors—the national police, and the National Guard to obstruct electoral participation, imitating the military regimes before the mid-1960s. In February 1972 the opposition coalition reportedly won the presidential elections, but, according to a detailed study by the newly created Catholic University, the ruling military party (PCN) committed electoral obstruction and refused to investigate the opposition's allegations of fraud (Hernandez Pico et al. 1973).[8]

On March 12, 1972, during parliamentary elections, 74,000 voters defaced their ballots in San Salvador in protest of the CCE decision to disqualify UNO candidates running for the legislature in the departments of San Salvador, Sonsonate, San Miguel, San Vicente, and La Unión (Hernandez Pico et al. 1973; *El Diario de Hoy*, March 15, 1972, pp. 2, 55). The opposition used a technical loophole in the electoral code that stated if a majority of null ballots were cast, the election would be voided. However, the CCE refused to decertify the parliamentary elections and the PCN gained a large parliamentary majority through electoral obstruction. In a three-week period (February 20–March 12, 1972) the Salvadoran state effectively erased more than eight years of unprecedented political

liberalization via competitive elections. By implementing a number of electoral manipulations, the state initiated the gradual closure of the political system at the national level by impeding both the presidential and parliamentary elections.

After the fraudulent 1972 presidential and assembly elections, UNO remained in the parliament as a marginalized legal opposition. UNO had 8 deputies between 1972 and 1974. In the 1974 parliamentary elections UNO gained 15 assembly seats, though the official results were never publicly released (Webre 1979) and widespread fraud was reported during balloting (Dunkerly 1982). UNO boycotted the 1976 elections after the CCE once again attempted to block the registration of its candidates in the largest cities. Between 1972 and 1978 the official military party employed a variety of tactics to prevent opposition parties from either gaining a parliamentary majority or winning the executive. These tactics included using the electoral commission to change vote totals and decertify opposition party candidates, ballot stuffing at the local level, and extralegal intimidation of opposition members. The reduction in electoral competitiveness was also closely associated with an erosion of rights and increasing levels of state repression during this period. The orderly forms of protest, such as strikes, marches, and massive public rallies, that characterized the 1967–72 protest wave proved ineffective in confronting the regime as it deliberalized. This changed the dynamic of popular movement–state interaction for the remainder of the decade, as the political environment shifted from opportunity to threat.

Political Opportunity Organizations in a Transitioning Environment

Despite the contraction in political opportunities that attended the narrowing of institutional access and fraudulent elections, the organizational infrastructure established in the late 1960s endured in the shifting political environment of the early to mid-1970s. The key social sectors benefiting from political opportunity in labor, education, and church-sponsored circles were largely able to keep their organizations and ongoing relationships intact regardless of fewer incentives to engage in orderly protest for new benefits and advantages. These political opportunity holdovers provided the building blocks for the more radical and revolutionary organizational infrastructure emerging in the mid to late 1970s. Observing the evolution of each of the three key social sectors from the early to mid 1970s demonstrates their organizational persistence.

Labor sector organizations.—By the mid-1970s, the traditional progovernment trade union federation (CGS) lost support as multiple unions broke off, forming federations and confederations with a more radical leadership such as FENASTRAS and CUTS (Arriola Palomares and Candray Alvarado 1994). By 1976 the CGS accounted for only 19% of unionized workers, down from 42% in 1971 (Dunkerley 1982). El Salvadoran Ministry of Labor data demonstrate that by the mid-1970s the majority of union membership was affiliated with autonomous, left-of-center unions (Anner 1996). Many of the unions that joined in radical political contention in the late 1970s were first legalized in the 1960s and came from strategic economic and governmental sectors that benefited from their power to disrupt public services and economic activity such as the nation's ports, electricity, water, transportation, judicial, and educational systems (Montgomery 1982). Beginning in 1976, the three largest revolutionary organizations created clandestine labor-organizing committees within the existing union infrastructure to coordinate disruptive labor actions (which often included wildcat strikes and factory occupations) across different work sites (Molina Arévalo 1988; Guidos Véjar 1990).

Educational sector organizations.—As political opportunities contracted, public school teachers' associations and high school– and university-based organizations endured. ANDES-21 officially counted a national dues-paying membership of 4,000 in 1974 and 5,500 in 1975 (ANDES-21 1974; Makofsky 1978). By the late 1970s, ANDES-21 had the organizational capacity to mobilize 15,000–18,000 teachers nationally for work stoppages and strikes. Growth in university enrollment continued through the 1970s. Indeed, El Salvador university enrollment rates were the second highest in Latin America between 1965 and 1975 (Wickham-Crowley 1989). By 1979, the university student population soared to 26,000 (where as recently as 1960 only 2,200 university students were enrolled) (Ministerio de Economia 1981). However, the government violated the autonomy it had allowed in the 1960s by occupying the university on three separate occasions (1972, 1976, and 1980) and imposing its own governance structure in 1973 (CAPUES). Nonetheless, Salvadoran universities persisted as a central source of challenger organizational recruitment throughout the 1970s, with all five competing mass revolutionary organizations counting at least one university (and high school) student protest organization in its ranks.

Church sector organizations.—The Catholic Church had created a successful template for organizing the rural sector in the late 1960s and early 1970s under the protection of the state-sanctioned peasant cooperative program and support from the Christian Democratic Party. Peasant training centers, cooperatives, retreat bases, workshops, and monthly news-letters all demonstrated the ongoing commitment of the Catholic Church to the rural poor.

Already, in the late 1960s and early 1970s in regions around Suchitoto, Aguilares, Ilopango, Ciudad Arce, Quezaltepeque, San Salvador, San Antonio Abad; Ayutuxtepeque, Mejicanos, Zacamil, Guazapa, Cojutepeque, Los Ranchos, La Palma, Chalatenango, Tecoluca, and Gotera, religious experiments were under way in the form of the CCBs (Rivera Damas 1977). This work was carried out in rural parishes (and in some urban shantytowns), beginning during the period of expanded political opportunity. It built on the church's pre-existing cooperative program (FUNPROCOOP), which grew to 15,000 members in 1976 (*Justicia y Paz,* October 1976). It was further promoted by the 1970 Semana Pastoral, whereby the church encouraged the formation of CCBs to promote the principles stipulated in Vatican II (1962–65) and the 1968 Medellín bishops' conference—the Latin American church's official call to actively "accompany" the region's poor in their pursuit of social and economic justice (Cáceres Prendes 1989; Smith 1991).

Vega (1994) reports an estimated 50,000–60,000 Salvadorans participating in hundreds of CCBs by the mid-1970s, and the monthly newsletter for rural

CCBs, *Justicia y Paz,* circulating between 6,000 and 8,000 copies of each issue in the period from 1972 to 1979. The monthly newsletter highlighted the state's responsibility regarding inflation, land access, and political persecution in a format in which semiliterate peasants could easily identify (e.g., use of the peasant vernacular, peasant narration, discussion questions, and humor with cartoon caricatures; see app. B for an example of a 1974 issue of *Justicia y Paz* attributing responsibility for carrying out land reform and maintaining viable prices to the state). The seven church-based peasant training centers founded around the country between 1968 and 1972 also continued teaching organizational and leadership skills until they were shut down by state repression in 1980 (Peterson 1997).

Many of El Salvador's top peasant organization leaders and recruiters in the 1970s, such as Apolinario Serrano of the Christian Federation of Salvadoran Peasants (FECCAS) and Justo Mejía of the Union of Rural Workers (UTC), began their political careers as Christian base community and cooperative leaders in the late 1960s (Rivera Damas 1977; Alvarado López and Cruz Olmedo 1978; Cabarrús 1983; Pearce 1986; Cardenal 1987). In short, the early organizational work of the Catholic Church (and the Christian Democratic Party) in promoting rural cooperatives, peasant organizations, Christian base communities, youth groups, peasant training centers, and community organizing in the late 1960s and early 1970s endured into a vast recruitment pool for more radical and revolutionary organizations in the late 1970s (though this was certainly not the intention of the original founders).

The organizational infrastructure was thus firmly established even after political opportunities had faded. This increased the probability of subsequent rounds of mobilization motivated by new environmental stimuli such as state-attributed threats. These kinds of negative environmental incentives occurred with greater frequency by the mid-1970s. Threat-induced mobilization, though, was a time-dependent process as challengers reinterpreted their environment and radicalized preexisting organizational structures and strategies.

Threats, 1972–81

The mid-1970s witnessed the return of higher levels of threat in the Salvadoran political environment. By 1974, the world economic slowdown and rising international petroleum prices initiated high rates of consumer inflation, exacerbating land access tensions in the countryside. The closing of competitive elections improved the likelihood that the Salvadoran state would return to an institutional legacy of denying basic civil rights and applying repression to real and suspected opponents of its authoritarian rule. At first, the entire organizational infrastructure was knocked off balance in trying to respond to a changing and contradictory political environment (e.g., elections with fraud). Over time, though, as the state moved onto a consistent trajectory of increasing threats, challengers radicalized their leftover organizational infrastructure.

Already, in 1976, one could observe in speeches, street demonstrations, and written propaganda by oppositional organizations the litany of references to skyrocketing inflation, the electoral frauds of 1972 and 1974, and rural state massacres in Chinamequita (April–May 1974), La Cayetana (November 1974), Tres Calles (June 1975), Hacienda Santa Barbara (October 1975), and the killing of university students in the capital (July 1975). Thus, increasing threats were not just objective changes in the political environment but were also actively interpreted and attributed to the state by regime challengers (McAdam, Tarrow, and Tilly 2001).

A political pamphlet distributed in January 1976 from one of the largest mass-based extraparliamentary organizations (FAPU) synthesizes the perception of mounting threats:

> The Unified Popular Action Front (F.A.P.U.), since its formation in June 1974, has been proposing to the Salvadoran people the necessity to sustain an energetic and combative struggle against the high cost of living in the economic sphere and against the Molina military dictatorship's fascist escalation in the political sphere; these are the tasks of the moment, the immediate struggles.... We are all witnesses to the relentless increase in the cost of basic necessities (food, clothing, shoes, medicine, etc.) as we are witnesses to the increasing shameless repression that the government unleashes against

the population; it's enough to remember the peasant massacres in Chinamequita, La Cayetana, Tres Calles, etc; the savage slaughter of students on July 30, 1975; the assassination and capture of many union leaders that in one form or another contribute to the Salvadoran working-class struggle. These two social processes (the economic crisis and the increase in antipopular repression) are marked within a process of fascist escalation that since 1972 has been developing in the womb of our society. (FAPU 1976, p. 1; author's translation)

The above litany of economic and repressive threats attributed to the state, as acting against the labor, educational, and church-organized peasant sectors, slowly radicalized the challenger organizational infrastructure created in the 1960s as such processes intensified and repeated themselves on an expanding scale. By 1977, challengers radicalized the leftover organizational infrastructure to the point that the increasingly threatening environment fueled more disruptive and violent forms of contention. Underlying this new round of mobilization stood the specific threat incentives of state-attributed economic problems, the erosion of rights, and state repression.

State-attributed economic problems.—By 1974, the global economic recession plagued El Salvador with high imported fuel prices and inflationary pressures. Table 3 shows the consumer price index for the years between 1958 and 1979. Real wages also declined for manufacturing workers in the 1970s as unemployment increased, intensifying the effects of consumer inflation (Dunkerley 1982; Argueta Antillón 1983; Booth 1991; Kirby 1992; Smith 1996). In contrast, during the 1960s, El Salvador had experienced the lowest consumer inflation rates in Latin America (Sheahan 1990). Already, by 1974, pressuring the government to implement price controls on basic consumer goods was a major demand of regime challengers (Cabarrús 1983). In 1975, the leading Catholic figure in the country, Archbishop Monsignor Luis Chávez y González, released his Fiftieth Pastoral Letter ("La Inflación en El Salvador ante la Conciencia Cristiana"), urging the

Table 3 Consumer Price Index in El Salvador, 1958–79

Year	General Index	Food	Housing	Clothing	Other Consumer Goods
1958...	107.7	108.7	119.1	83.9	112.3
1962...	104.1	105.3	98.9	88.7	117.9
1966...	106.8	107.6	102.6	91.7	120.5
1972...	116.3	124	107.8	85.4	125
1973...	123.7	133.3	115.9	87.9	129.7
1974...	144.6	156.4	137.7	95.9	153
1975...	172.2	188.5	163.5	123.7	167.5
1976...	184.4	201.6	177.8	138.1	172.2
1977...	206.1	219.1	205	150.5	210.5
1978...	233.5	242.5	251.8	163.8	240.9
1979...	280	287.3	294.9	229.9	285.8

Source.—López (1983, p. 165).
Note. —Based on June 1954 standard of living for urban workers (1954 = 100).

government to take measures to reduce inflation on basic consumer items and land rents (Alas 1982; Vega 1997).

Besides price increases, land access was another state-attributed economic problem becoming more acute with over 40% of rural families classified as landless in 1975 and up to 65% in 1980 (Kirby 1992; Williams 1986)—up from 12% in 1962 (Cabarrús 1983) and less than 8.6% in 1950 (Castellanos 2001). The land situation was compounded in the early 1970s by the forced repatriation of 130,000 Salvadoran peasants from Honduras as a result of the Soccer War (Durham 1979).[9] Nearly 60% of the population lived in rural areas at the time. Land access increasingly became a state-attributed problem for peasants in the 1970s because of failed government attempts to implement an agrarian reform on two separate and highly publicized occasions in January of 1970 and the summer of 1976 (Vega 1994). Ethnographic fieldwork in church-organized rural zones in the 1970s (e.g., northern San Salvador, Cuscatián, San Vicente, and Chalatenango) consistently reports land access and inflation as central peasant grievances (Rodríguez 1976; Durham 1979; Samaniego 1980; Cabarrús 1983; Pearce 1986; Cardenal 1987; Paige 1996; Hammond 1998). In brief, consumer price increases and land access acted as major state-attributed economic problems pushing well-networked urban and rural groups into sustained collective action by the mid-1970s. Often, land access issues were the source of rural unrest that led to the first government massacres in the mid-1970s, such as in the community of La Cayetana, San Vicente Department.

Erosion of rights.—Citizenship rights eroded throughout the 1970s. Table 4 illustrates the eroding electoral process between 1972 and 1978. In contrast to the late 1960s and early 1970s, challenger organizations had little protection from inside the polity to defend their interests. In addition, the state intermittently implemented a series of quasi-martial laws throughout the 1970s (e.g., spring 1972, part of 1977, all of 1978, early 1979, and the second half of 1980). These declarations of special states of emergency denied a number of constitutional rights

Table 4 Erosion of National Elections, 1972–78

Election	Outcome
1972 presidential elections	Government fraud. Military party (PCN) remains in power.
1972 parliamentary elections	Electoral Commission refuses to certify opposition candidates in San Salvador, San Miguel, Sonsonate, and Usulután. Opposition parties in San Salvador have supporters deface ballots, resulting in a majority of null votes. Electoral Commission refuses to acknowledge a majority of null votes and hold new elections as called for in its own electoral code. Government allows UNO 8 seats in 52-member parliament.
1974 parliamentary elections	Reported government fraud. No official/public release of vote count. Government allows 15 opposition seats in parliament.
1976 parliamentary elections	Opposition parties boycott elections after Electoral Commission impedes the registration of two-thirds of their candidates. For the first time since 1964, the parliament returns to one-party rule, with all 52 seats taken by the official military party.
1977 presidential elections	Reported government fraud. Legal opposition sent into exile after elections, government massacre of opposition supporters in San Salvador.
1978 parliamentary elections	Opposition boycotts elections. Official military party retains all 52 parliamentary seats.

such as public assembly, the right to associate, right to habeas corpus, and public dissent. In effect, the state outlawed many of the orderly forms of protest used in the 1967–72 protest wave, providing a disincentive for their continued use.

Between mid-1972 and 1981 there was an erosion in the state's commitment to binding consultation with civil society. By mid-1976 Salvadoran citizens no longer elected their own representatives in the legislative and executive branches. This shift in state practices encouraged previously organized challengers to radicalize their organizational forms as institutionalized channels to press demands closed. Indeed, many of El Salvador's senior revolutionary leaders in the 1970s and 1980s date their incorporation into more radical organizations to the 1972 fraudulent elections (see McClintock 1998 for multiple cases). In turn, the national government now demonstrated much less restraint in implementing repression against its opponents.

Stale repression.—By the mid-1970s a shift took place in state–civil society relations. The government became more repressive, harassing, exiling, and even killing leaders of the electoral opposition and firing live ammunition at demonstrators during relatively peaceful urban and rural protests.[10] The rising number of massacres in the mid-1970s clearly indicated a greater willingness by military state managers in the employment of repression against organized challengers.

UNO opposition deputies attempted to initiate parliamentary investigations of both the La Cayetana peasant massacre in 1974 and a university student massacre in 1975. The military party–controlled legislative assembly rebuffed their efforts on two separate occasions. State repression continued to escalate in the late 1970s. A pattern of "disappearing" (forced abduction in which the subsequent whereabouts of the victims are unknown to relatives) suspected political activists emerged after 1975. By 1979 Salvadoran security forces and associated paramilitary groups were responsible for dozens of political deaths per month. During 1980 and 1981, when state repression peaked, security forces and paramilitaries reportedly killed an average of nearly 1,000 civilians per month. Human rights data available on arrests, torture, and other forms of state-sponsored abuse also show a marked annual increase between 1973 and 1981 (see fig. 4).

There was a gradual ratcheting up of state repression throughout the 1970s. Reformist political parties and challenger organizations were the first targets of repression, and the state intermittently exiled, killed, or "disappeared" some of their members. By the late 1970s, repression was becoming much more intensive and continuous. Across segments of the labor, educational, and church-organized sectors, activists (suspected and real) were increasingly detained, tortured, killed, and/or disappeared (Stanley 1996). Human rights abuse

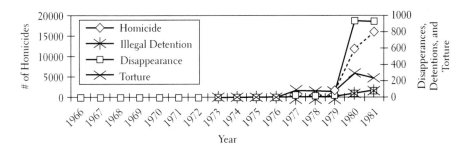

Figure 7.4 Reported number of political disappearances and homicides by government and paramilitary groups 1966–81, and reported illegal detentions and tortures, 1973–81. (Data are drawn from Socorro Jurídico Cristiano 1981, 1984; Morales Velado et al. 1988; *La Prensa Gráfica*; IDHUCA 1997; Ball 2000; Latin American Bureau 1977; Anaya Montes 1972.)

records indicate that it was precisely these three organized sectors (i.e., unionized workers; students and ANDES-affiliated teachers; and church-organized peasants and religious workers) that bore the brunt of state repression in terms of their over-representation among the occupational statuses of the victims listed (Socorro Jurídico Cristiano 1981; Delgado Tobar and Peña Rosales 1989). Since the state opted for a gradual escalation of repression approach over the decade, it failed to dismantle the organizational infrastructure founded in the liberalizing 1960s and rapidly radicalizing in the 1970s.

From Opportunity Organizations to a Radicalized Organizational Infrastructure

The key supporting institutions and challenger organizations in the labor, educational, and church sectors that cohered into an organizational infrastructure in the liberalizing 1960s persisted in the transitioning political environment in the mid-1970s. While the government sporadically attempted to disband- or impede the continuance of challenger organizations (by such threatening actions as occupying the national university and intimidating urban unions and church-organized peasant communities), the process of widening political opportunity in the 1960s made it difficult to control the rich array of organizations now available to challenging groups. Indeed, efforts by the state to dismantle the organizational infrastructure led more often to radicalizing it. The radicalization of organizations was a time-dependent process as the state responded to orderly protest against various threats by ignoring challengers or repressing them. In turn, the labor movement, educational sector, and church-based groups used their organizations and established relationships to sustain the radicalizing organizational infrastructure. Hence, the revolutionary organizations emerging in the mid-1970s were clearly stamped by the political opportunity organizations created in the late 1960s (see table 5).

Table 5 lists the largest and most important extraparliamentary and revolutionary organizations to emerge in El Salvador in the mid-1970s. The table demonstrates a clear dynamic in which organizations, leaders and participants from the 1967–72

protest wave founded more radical and revolutionary organizations in the 1970s. Once established, the new radical organizations secured continued support from the preexisting organizational infrastructure (i.e., political opportunity organizations) in terms of resources, bloc and individual recruitment, and protection. The labor, educational, and church-based sectors each contributed organizational resources and/or cadre to the radicalizing organizational infrastructure of the mid to late 1970s.

Three of the most prominent and high-ranking FUSS labor leaders who directed the 1967 progressive general strike founded the radical revolutionary organization Popular Liberation Forces (FPL) in the early 1970s. Arguably, the most important revolutionary leader in the 1970s and trade union leader in the 1960s, Salvador Cayetano Carpio, describes labor activists abandoning the FUSS leadership in the early 1970s in order to construct the FPL:

> The most clear-sighted people, who at that moment understood the needs of the revolutionary struggle in our country, had to withdraw from the organizations to which they had virtually devoted their lives, with a great deal of pain but with great realism in taking the step....To do so it was necessary to leave posts of great responsibility and honor in those other organizations. Several of our members who later joined the Farabundo Martí People's Liberation Forces as founding members were esteemed leaders of the workers' movement. For instance, José Dimas Alas was the secretary general of the Labor Unity Federation [FUSS] and one of its founders; Comrade Ernesto Morales was the youth secretary of the same Federation: and there were others who were also labor leaders who had to leave the traditional organizations to be able to develop in the new revolutionary school. (Tricontinental Society 1980, p. 25)

The revolutionary leaders sustained their new radical organizations by recruiting from the national university, teachers' union, and church-organized student and peasant sectors (Harnecker 1993). The public school teachers' association (ANDES-21) united other social sectors, including peasants, shantytown dwellers, and students, into common radical organizations such as the Popular

Table 5 Political Opportunity Organizations and Their Radicalization into El Salvador's Revolutionary Organizational Infrastructure, 1972–81

Radical Organization and Year Formed	1967–72 POLITICAL OPPORTUNITY ORGANIZATIONS			
	Labor-Sector Opportunity Organizations	Educational-Sector Opportunity Organizations	Church-Sector Opportunity Organizations	
Popular Forces of Liberation (FPL) (1970–72)	Formed by leaders of FUSS (which launched strike wave of 1967)	Some ANDES-21 leaders align with the FPL in mid-1970s; University students from the UES form initial cells of FPL	Early members also come out of high school and university Catholic organizations (JEC and FRUSC)	
People's Revolutionary Army (ERP) (1972)		UES students form initial cells	Some early members also participated in high school and university Catholic organizations (JEC and FRUSC) and Christian Democratic youth movement	
Unified Popular Action Front (FAPU) (1974)	FUSS and FESTIAVTCES participate in the founding of FAPU, later strengthened by alliance with FENASTRAS (a large break-off labor federation from Catholic UNOC and progovernment CGS)	ANDES-21, Catholic University students and UES students participate in the founding of FAPU	Initially founded by Christian base communities in Suchitoto and by FECCAS	
Union of Rural Workers (UTC) (1974)			Early members come from Cathotic Cooperative Movement	
National Resistance (RN) (1975)		Break-off of ERP-UES students	Some members of Catholic Youth Organizations (JEC)	

(Continued)

Table 5 (*Continued*)

	1967–72 POLITICAL OPPORTUNITY ORGANIZATIONS		
Radical Organization and Year Formed	Labor-Sector Opportunity Organizations	Educational-Sector Opportunity Organizations	Church-Sector Opportunity Organizations
Popular Revolutionary Bloc (BPR) (1975)		Founded by ANDES-21, Catholic University students, UES students, high school students	Members of FECCAS, Christian base community priests, and church/Christian Democrat-organized slum dwellers participate in founding
Revolutionary Party of Central American Workers (PRTC) (1976)		UES students (leaders in 1970 *areas comunes* student strike, ANDES-21 leaders)	Some early leaders work in Christian Democratic community action program
Popular Leagues "28th of February" (LP-28) (1977)		Formed largely by UES students	Some participation of Christian base communities connected to peasant training center in eastern El Salvador.
Popular Liberation Movement (MLP) (1979)		Formed by 1960s leaders of teachers' union ANDES-21 and former rector of National University in the 1960s	

Sources.—Alas (1982); Henriquez (1988); Cienfuegos (1993); Harnecker (1993); Ueltzen (1994); McClintock (1998); Binford (1999).

Revolutionary Bloc (BPR). ANDES-21 leaders from the 1960s also played a major role in the formation of the mass revolutionary organization MLP (Alas 1982). University of El Salvador student leaders from the 1970 Areas Comunes strike committee were central actors in founding the revolutionary organizations ERP, RN, and PRTC (McClintock 1998).

From the church-organized sector, Christian base community members and priests initiated the formation of the mass-based extraparliamentary organization the Unified Popular Action Front (FAPU) in 1974 and participated in the forming of the Popular Revolutionary Bloc in 1975. Both of these mass radical organizations were officially inaugurated in churches (Montgomery 1982; Pearce 1986). The Catholic-based student organizations (JEC, FRUSC, and PDC youth) that formed in the 1960s also contributed to the ERP, RN, and FPL some of their early and/or founding revolutionaries (Henriquez 1988; Harnecker 1993). The church's organizing efforts were so successful that the secular Marxist-Leninist revolutionary organization, the (FPL), bent ideological protocol and distributed a special pamphlet in 1974 inviting the Christian community to join the revolutionary struggle. Without this modification, revolutionary leaders confessed it would have been "impossible" to align with parts of the church-organized peasant sector (Harnecker 1993, p. 128).[11]

One movement leader, active in both the BPR and the UTC, illustrates through his personal account the role of the 1960s organizational infrastructure in subsequent radical organizational participation in the mid-1970s. He first describes the sequence of opportunity organizations that he and fellow peasants passed through in the Chalatenango region before they joined the revolutionary movement in the 1970s:

> I arrived to the [revolutionary] movement through two paths...one path, because I was an activist in the Christian Democratic Party since I was very young, and, later, by the cooperative movement sponsored by the Church in which I also participated. Through this route I began to link myself with peasant organizations. This was also the history for the majority of us. Many of us came from the ranks of the Christian Democratic Party, we

> were people that had lost all hope in finding an alternative solution through this political party; we were people that had developed our human and social consciousness through the Christian movement. (Harnecker 1993, pp. 153–54; see also McClintock 1998, p. 258)

This same activist then discusses why preorganized groups left over from the 1967–72 organizational infrastructure were targeted for partial appropriation by more radical organizations in the mid-1970s:

> We had the ability to sense that we should not try and work with whatever social sector, but only the most receptive ones. We did not search out or collaborate with workers in general, nor with peasants in general, but we had already begun working openly with ANDES, the teachers' organization, that was the most combative organization in the early 1970s. Their experience demonstrated to us that we could expand the movement and that is what happened. ANDES played, in fact, an extremely important role in the organization of peasants and high school students, the students were another very receptive sector....The same thing occurred in the countryside. The situation was explosive because of the crisis it was experiencing in terms of the scarcity of land in which to work, credit and material for production, commercialization of production, and low salary levels during the harvesting season. In the countryside there were a lot of expressions of spontaneous mass rebellion. We were convinced that the peasantry was another sector ripe for organization, for mobilization. The university sector was another receptive group....In reference to the work with the peasantry, our [revolutionary] organization began to influence the Christian Federation of Salvadoran Peasants (FECCAS) directed in this period by the Christian Democrats and the Catholic Church. (Harnecker 1993, pp. 125–26; see also Grenier 1999, pp. 45, 137, and 178 n. 28)

The early revolutionaries realized the stakes of operating in a high-risk/threat environment and substantially cut their organizing costs by searching out the specific social sectors *already* organized (i.e., the most "receptive" or "ripe" sectors) from the 1967–72 protest wave, as opposed to trying to collaborate with "whatever social sector" or with workers and peasants "in general." The ability of revolutionary challengers to partially appropriate the leftover organizational infrastructure is due to the fact that they came out of it themselves and continued ongoing interorganizational relationships (Grenier 1999). Indeed, by the mid-1970s, many leaders and organizers maintained multiple overlapping memberships in trade union, student, or peasant organizations while simultaneously participating in more clandestine revolutionary organizations (see Harnecker 1993 for multiple accounts).

Threats penetrated the labor, educational, and church-based sectors to such a degree by the mid-1970s that key radical organizations formed and/or named themselves in direct response to specific threatening events. Four out of the nine principal radical/revolutionary organizations listed in table 5 mark their origins to specific threats. The first mass-based radical organization, FAPU, was formed in June 1974 to struggle against the threats of price increases, state repression, and fraudulent elections (Alas 1982; Montgomery 1982; Cardenal 1987).[12] FAPU was a coalition of labor, education, and church-based organizations founded during the institutional opening in the 1960s; it included the teachers' union ANDES-21, the labor federations FUSS and FESTIAVTCES, Christian base communities (CCBs) from Suchitoto, the church- and PDC-organized peasant league FECCAS, along with young clerics and university students. A similar coalition of opportunity holdover organizations formed the largest extraparliamentary organization in August 1975—the Popular Revolutionary Bloc (BPR)—in response to a government massacre of university students on July 30, 1975. By the late 1970s, FAPU and BPR served as focal organizational units in which thousands of workers, students, teachers, and church-organized peasants could unite by linking their respective subunit challenger organizations under a single organizational umbrella.

At the end of 1974, a major radical peasant organization was formed out of the church-based cooperative movement in San Vicente and Chalatenango within weeks of the La Cayetana massacre—the Union of Rural Workers (UTC) (Pearce 1986; Berryman 1987). Another radical organization, the Popular Leagues "28th of February" (LP-28), named

itself in homage to the victims of a state massacre of a massive nonviolent demonstration in downtown San Salvador protesting government fraud on February 28, following the 1977 presidential elections (between 50 and 100 people were killed). LP-28 and BPR also titled many of their affiliated subunit organizations after the exact dates of repressive events (e.g., military occupation of the university and 1975 student massacre) or after the names of fellow members killed by the security forces; these served as rallying cries for future mobilization and organizational recruitment.

In contrast to the reformist late 1960s, challenger interpretations of the political environment that emerged by the mid-1970s were much more antisystemic. The Salvadoran state was no longer viewed as a *relatively* legitimate jurisdictional body in which to present claims for new advantages and benefits. Rather, the state was now viewed by opponents as economically harmful, exclusive, and repressive. Military state managers were seen as unworthy of ruling and serving only the narrow interests of the agro-export elite, as evidenced by their inability to implement land reform (Stanley 1996; Griffith and González 2002), reduce inflation, convoke competitive elections, or tolerate public dissent.[13] These emerging perceptions generated much more radical organizing strategies whereby coercive actions and tactics (e.g., building, factory, and land occupations and barricade construction) were encouraged to seek political influence in the increasingly threatening political environment.

By 1977, the challenger organizational infrastructure had been radicalized, as measured by the higher ratio of revolutionary organizations to reformist organizations present in protest events (see fig. 5). The dominance of revolutionary organizations in the social movement sector provided a "tipping point" (Petersen 2001) where increasing threats triggered a much more disruptive and violent protest wave between 1977 and 1981.

Threat-Induced Protest Wave, 1977–81

Regime challengers modified their organizational infrastructure in this period by changing their strategy from reformist organizations to radical and revolutionary organizations as the political

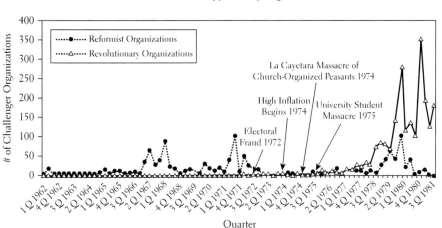

Figure 7.5 Quarterly presence of reformist and revolutionary challenger organizations in protest events, 1962–81. Reformist organizations were coded as those organizations that had reformist goals (i.e., group-specific policy changes) and did not make claims for the overthrow of the state. Revolutionary organizations were coded as all organizations that were explicitly revolutionary and/or extraparliamentary with the replacement of the government as a central goal (i.e., the revolutionary organizations listed in table 5, their affiliates, and guerrilla organizations). (Source: *La Prensa Gráfica* 1962–81)

system slowly shut down following the fraudulent 1972 presidential and parliamentary elections (see fig. 5). Several indicators of contentious activity, including total protests and strikes, show a marked decline between 1973 and 1976 (see figs. 1 and 2) as challengers reinterpreted the changing political environment and radicalized their organizational infrastructure. In 1977 a second protest wave ascended, reaching more than 1,000 protest events a year by 1980. This second protest cycle exhibited much more disruptive and violent properties, nearly overthrowing the regime between 1980 and 1981.

By 1977, revolutionary-based organizations acquired the capacity to mobilize frequent protest events in response to escalating threats. The most publicized and notorious acts of human rights violations and state repression—such as the July 30, 1975, student massacre, the February 28, 1977, massacre of UNO supporters protesting electoral fraud, and the assassination of Father Rutilio Grande in March 1977 (a popularly supported Jesuit organizing CCBs)—were each immediately followed by large demonstrations in repudiation and then

commemorated annually with massive homage ceremonies. Other rights-violating and repressive acts, such as arrests of organizational leaders or the violent dispersion of street demonstrations, led to more coercive tactics that included building occupations (especially churches, embassies, and government offices) to demand the release of political prisoners and the whereabouts of the "disappeared." Revolutionary organizations also increasingly launched armed attacks on the state security forces.

Figure 2 demonstrates the widespread employment of mass disruptive protest and violence during the second wave (1977–81) of political contention. Between 1979 and 1980 there were 161 reported farm invasions by organized land-poor peasants. In 1979, nearly half (43%) of the 114 reported labor strikes (see fig. 1) also included factory occupations. At the peak of the strike wave in 1980, 50% of worker actions demanded higher wages to match exorbitant inflation rates while another 25% of labor strikes centered on issues of state repression (Delgado Tobar and Peña Rosales 1989). In contrast to the nonviolent and orderly 1967–72 protest wave, over 60% of reported protest events were violent between 1977 and 1981 (see fig. 2). Mass nonviolent and disruptive protests peaked in the first half of 1980. State repression reached such alarming levels in 1980 that the presence of reformist organizations and mass protest declined rapidly by the end of the year, while armed attacks by revolutionary organizations remained high throughout the early 1980s as the country spiraled into civil war.

Summary

El Salvador's authoritarian political environment varied considerably in the mid to late 20th century. The protracted political opening in the 1960s characterized by institutional access and competitive elections benefited organizational entrepreneurs in the labor, educational, and church sectors. During the liberalization period the state and oppositional political parties actively encouraged the formation of a wide variety of civic organizations and associations. The result was an organizational infrastructure in which multiple challenger organizations loosely coalesced, developed ongoing relations, and pressed the state for new advantages and benefits. This process culminated in an orderly and nonviolent protest wave where challengers viewed the liberalizing state as a *relatively* legitimate jurisdictional body to which claims could be presented. The wave of demonstrations and strikes that rocked El Salvador between 1967 and 1972 was the longest sustained period of popular contention since the 1932 peasant uprising and state massacre.

The reform-oriented protest wave came to an end when the state held successive fraudulent presidential and parliamentary elections in 1972. Even with this closing in opportunities, the organizational infrastructure founded in the late 1960s endured in both the countryside and cities through the 1970s. Few of the key organizations or associations created in the 1960s were effectively dismantled by the state (i.e., teachers' union, labor federations, universities, student groups, and Catholic Church organizational initiatives) until the height of state repression in 1980 and 1981. In brief, a sustained period of political opportunity deposited an organizational infrastructure that persisted after opportunities diminished.

From 1972 to 1981 the Salvadoran state gradually became more exclusive and repressive, which combined with state-attributed economic problems (price increases and land shortage) to create an increasingly threatening political environment. Responding to these increasing threats, challenger organizations left over from regime liberalization radicalized. The decision of military state managers to close down institutionalized channels of dissent, convoke repeated electoral frauds, and commit outrageous acts of state repression motivated regime challengers to adopt more coercive protest strategies. By 1977 revolutionary organizations had launched a much wider, disruptive, and violent protest wave eventuating in El Salvador's civil war in the 1980s.

Discussion

The case of El Salvador offers insight into a central theoretical puzzle in current research on protest waves and revolutions in authoritarian contexts that employ political process/opportunity models: How is large-scale rebellion possible in repressive regimes when the most often cited conditions in the political environment are the exact reverse of those associated with mass protest in democratic states? For instance, Goodwin (2001, p. 177) states, "Far from being a response to political openings, the revolutionary mobilization that occurred in Central America during the 1970s and 1980s was generally a response to political exclusion and violent repression—the *contraction* of political opportunities and the *closing down* of 'political space'" (emphasis in the original).

This investigation suggests that the explanation resides in a sequential model of political opportunity and threat. Such a framework highlights periods of political liberalization/political opportunity and organization building before a regime becomes exclusive and repressive. With the exception of an infusion of resources from elite allies, transnational networks, or foreign states, it would otherwise be extraordinarily difficult for regime challengers to establish organizational infrastructures capable of sustained resistance to authoritarian rule. Political opportunity periods not only encourage an escalation in orderly forms of protest activities in authoritarian settings, as shown in previous research, but also stimulate the formation of enduring civic organizations. These organizational infrastructures persevere in the political environment long after the political reforms responsible for their establishment fade away.

Originally founded to act as collective vehicles to pursue group interests in a liberalizing authoritarian regime, these units and their memberships are likely to radically change goals, strategies, and alliances when the political environment no longer matches their organizational structures and endangers their survival. Increasing threats are one set of environmental incentives in which this organizational transformation/radicalization occurs. As a corollary, resistance to mounting threats is unlikely without the previous buildup and appropriation of an organizational infrastructure by regime challengers.

The present study maintains more precisely that the political opportunity features of regime liberalization periods (state-initiated practices of institutional access and competitive elections) selectively encourage the formation of civic organizations in particular social sectors. Future research may want to investigate additionally the role of persisting ideational elements created by prolonged periods of liberalization, such as notions of entitlements and emergent norms of state–civil society relations. These nonorganizational forces may also contribute to increased popular dissent when the state de-democratizes.

A related strategy in this line of study would be to recognize the leading social sectors participating in mass rebellion against a repressive regime. Once identified, the organizational genealogy should be traced for these sectors to determine the political context in which they first originated. For example, Chile's urban shantytown dwellers were a key sector demonstrating against the Pinochet military dictatorship in the mid-1980s, but their organizational founding dates back to the predictatorship period (1960–73), when there was support from the state and competing electoral political parties (Schneider 1995). The Front Islamic du Salut (FIS), which dominated extreme Algerian contention in the 1990s, evolved from a mass-based electoral

party that was denied victory by the state in early 1992 (Martinez 2000). In other words, preceding liberalization periods appear to generate organizational building blocks for radical challenger groups operating in more authoritarian contests. The case of El Salvador offers one striking example that revolutionary movements in repressive settings are organizationally constructed from earlier political opportunity periods.

Finally, this article proposes that social movement theories should give more attention to negative environmental incentives and threats—the underdeveloped side of political process models—as inducements to increase contentious activity (Goldstone and Tilly 2001; Van Dyke and Soule 2002) and/or radicalize organizations. However, caution is in order. First, this study suggests that when threats occur without a preexisting organizational infrastructure, they will likely deter challengers from sustained contention (as in El Salvador between 1932 and the mid-1960s). Second, not all threats are equivalent. State-attributed economic problems may lead to increased contention for well-networked groups but probably will not create radical forms of conflict unless combined with an erosion of rights and/or state repression. These latter two threats are more often found in authoritarian states than in democratic ones, making the emergence of mass-based revolutionary movements much more likely in non-democratic settings (Goodwin 2001). Nonetheless, much more work needs to be done (in democratic and authoritarian contexts) on the role of political environments characterized by varying combinations of political opportunity and threat and how the nature and sequencing of those combinations produce particular forms of organization and contention.

NOTES

A previous version of this article was presented at the American Sociological Association annual meetings in Anaheim, August 2001. The author acknowledges Edna Bonacich, Eduardo Bonilla-Silva, Linda Brewster Stearns, Steve Brint, Sam Cohn, Ed Collom, Christian Davenport, Bob Hanneman, Mark Lichbach, Harland Prechel, Jose Rutilio Quezada, and the *AJS* reviewers for helpful comments on earlier drafts of this article. The project benefited from grants awarded by the Graduate Division and the Ernesto

Galarza Research Center at the University of California, Riverside.

1. I use the term "protest wave" interchangeably with "protest cycle" in this work. Protest waves or cycles are defined as periods of widespread protest activity across multiple social groups and often encompass much of the national territory (Tarrow 1989, pp. 48–49).

2. In the present article political opportunity and threat are treated as distinct (but sequentially related) political contexts in authoritarian settings. For an excellent theoretical discussion and formal model of a "mixed" political environment where various levels of political opportunity and threat occur simultaneously, see Goldstone and Tilly (2001).

3. Tilly (1978) originally gives the examples of rural resistance to tax collection and land dispossession as episodes of threat-induced collective action (i.e., state-attributed economic problems). In more recent works, analysts have focused more on the threat of state repression (Goldstone and Tilly 2001).

4. The sense of harm, though, has upper boundaries on escalating protest. At some point protest will likely appear too dangerous as the state's repressive actions turn outrage into fear (Brockett 1993). Much of the large-sample, cross-national literature on state repression and political violence finds evidence for a curvilinear relationship with semirepressive regimes generating the highest levels of political discontent (Muller 1985; Muller and Seligson 1987; Boswell and Dixon 1990; Muller and Weede 1994).

5. The three largest protest campaigns in Argentina in 2002 took place in Buenos Aires on June 27, July 3, and December 20 to publicly denounce the police killings on June 26 of two unemployed protesters (*los piqueteros*) (Fernández Moores 2002) and commemorate the one-year anniversary of the 28 antiausterity protesters killed in late December 2001.

6. When *La Prensa Gráfica* was unavailable or additional information was needed about a particular event, a Salvadoran newspaper—*Diario Latino, El Diario de Hoy, El Mundo,* or *El Tiempo*—was used.

7. The Salvadoran labor and legal historian Augusto Larin (1972, p. 18) states that between 1932 and 1944 (during the General Martínez dictatorship) even mentioning the words "labor union" could be considered a public offense.

8. At least three massive public demonstrations and a general strike attempt were held in late February 1972 to protest the electoral fraud. These would be the largest acts of civil disobedience until the late 1970s.

9. The Soccer War was a five-day military conflict between El Salvador and Honduras in July 1969 that resulted in 3,000–4,000 deaths; the hostilities were in part related to Salvadoran immigration to Honduras and inequities within the Central American Common Market.

10. In 1972 martial law was declared from March 25 until April 10 and then extended until June 2, in response to a failed coup attempt. During the first three weeks of the martial law period, at least 22 civilians were killed (most of whom were associated in some way to the electoral opposition) by agents linked to the state (Morales Velado et al. 1988). On July 19, 1972, the military occupied the national university (UES) on all three campuses, which resulted in 800 student and faculty arrests and the banishment of the administration (including the rector) into exile in Nicaragua. The UES was shut down for over an entire year until September 1973 (after which the government installed intimidating security agents inside; the students called them "verdes" for their olive militarylike uniforms). In September 1972, the government sent 21 union and opposition party members into exile (Morales Velado et al. 1988). Then again, in January 1973, 18 more dissidents were exiled. Increasingly, by the middle of the 1970s state repression was targeted not only against UNO supporters, unions, the UES, and other urban sectors but also against the Catholic Church and the church-organized peasantry. On April 30, 1974, the security forces killed at least four people protesting electoral fraud in the rural town of Chimanequita, La Paz. On November 29, 1974, six peasants were massacred in La Cayetana, San Vicente, by the National Guard. During the operation an additional 25 peasants were arrested, out of which 13 "disappeared." On June 2, 1975, 40 soldiers and members of the paramilitary patrol ORDEN reportedly killed four peasants in Tres Calles, Usulután. On July 30, 1975, the National Guard killed as many as 37 UES students during a peaceful march in San Salvador. On September 26, 1975, a UDN member of parliament (and FUSS labor leader) was murdered by a death squad. In October 1975, the National Guard fired on striking farmworkers on Santa Barbara Estate in Chalatenango, killing at least two peasants, disappearing four, and injuring many others (Latin American Bureau 1977; Socorro Jurídico Cristiano 1981).

11. Henriquez (1988) further suggests that radical organizations such as the BPR would not likely have been able to penetrate urban shantytown communities (*los tugurios*) in the mid-1970s without the preestablished organizational work of the Catholic Church and Christian Democratic Party in these same areas in the late 1960s and early 1970s.

12. One of FAPU's first campaigns was to press the state to develop an anti-inflationary policy (Cabarrús 1983). Consumer goods prices rose rapidly between 1974 and 1977 for such basic items as cooking oil, rice, red beans, cheese, and bus fares (Ministerio de Economia 1978).

13. After 1976, the credibility of the regime had fallen to such a low level that virtually no protests targeted the legislative branch of government, as opposed to about 20% of protests during the 1967–72 protest wave. In a public opinion survey of 335 Salvadoran citizens in the mid-1980s, only 8% of respondents believed that General Romero came to power in 1977 through free elections (Morales Velado et al. 1988).

PART 3

Resources and Organization

In Part 2 we focused on the ways in which systems of institutionalized politics shape the emergence, development, and ultimate fate of social movements. These systems—in both their stable features and variable aspects—condition collective action by posing new threats to, or opportunities for, the advancement of group interests. But threats and opportunities alone do not make a movement. Even the most favorable political environment only creates a certain structural potential for successful collective action. Among the most important factors determining whether this potential will be realized is the organizational capacity of any group that would challenge the system. In the absence of sufficient organization and resources, a challenger is unlikely to act no matter the intensity of the grievance or the actual or perceived availability of opportunity to do so.

This fundamental insight is at the heart of the resource mobilization perspective on social movements. As first articulated by John McCarthy and Mayer Zald (1973, 1977), resource mobilization theory accented the role of resource acquisition and deployment. It is the mobilization of new resources, they contended, that keys the emergence and development of social movements. In particular, they stressed the importance of formal social movement organizations (SMOs) and external resources in affording traditionally powerless groups the capacity to sustain movement activity.

Initially some critics charged that the emphases on formal organization and external resources obscured the critical role played by informal grassroots groups and the human resources of indigenous communities in the creation of insurgency (McAdam 1999 [1982]; Morris 1984; Piven and Cloward 1979). In time, however, the distinction between these two emphases has evolved into a more general stress on the importance of organization and resources, with greater appreciation and empirical attention paid to variation in the nature and source of organization and resources. Part 4 includes selections that focus more on the ways in which the informal networks and ecological/spatial structure of aggrieved communities facilitate movement emergence. In Part 3, however, we focus more on work in the resource mobilization tradition—work that underscores the importance of formal organization and external resources in the generation and sustenance of movement activity.

In an article out of their groundbreaking comparative study of homeless mobilization in eight U.S. cities, Dan Cress and David Snow document the critically important role of external "benefactors" in accounting for variation in the viability of homeless SMOs. Of the 15 SMOs they studied, the authors deemed seven "viable" and eight "nonviable." Five of the seven viable organizations managed to attract the support of external sponsors or "benefactors." None of the eight nonviables were able to do so. The article also differentiates between types of resources and analyzes the combinations that appear to be most important in helping to sustain viable SMOs.

The second selection, by Elizabeth Armstrong, documents and provides a compelling account of the "the crystallization of a field of lesbian/gay organizations in San Francisco, 1969–1973." Drawing on both institutional theory and social movement scholarship, Armstrong argues that the simultaneous temporal embedding of the embryonic gay liberation movement in both the late New Left and increasingly conservative political establishment powerfully shaped the initial emergence and subsequent "settlement" of the movement in San Francisco. Emerging near the peak of the late New

Left in 1969, the gay liberation movement initially reflected both the radical rhetoric and multiple, conflicted, possibilities inherent in those turbulent times. But as the political establishment lurched to the right in the wake of Richard Nixon's ascension to the White House in 1968, a new generation of movement leaders—attuned to the more limited possibilities—fashioned a more moderate organizational vision for the movement. The result was the rapid expansion of the field of isomorphic gay and lesbian organizations documented by Armstrong in her article.

Consistent with one of the major emphases in this volume, the final selection in Part 3 sheds light on another of the ways in which globalization is altering the structure and dynamics of social movements. In that selection, Jackie Smith documents the rapid expansion in transnational social movement organizations (TSMOs) in several issue areas (e.g., human rights, environment, women's rights) between 1973 and 2000.

8.

Mobilization at the Margins: Resources, Benefactors, and the Viability of Homeless Social Movement Organizations

DANIEL M. CRESS AND DAVID A. SNOW

Nearly two decades after the flowering of the resource mobilization perspective on social movements, many of the perspective's assumptions have been "assimilated as the routine and unstated grounds of much contemporary work" (Zald 1992:327). One such taken-for-granted assumption is that resources are a sine qua non determinant of the course and character of social movement organizations (SMOs) and their activities. Indeed, no other assumption is so fundamental to the resource mobilization perspective and a plethora of derivative work. Yet there is little definitive understanding of several resource-related issues relevant to the dynamics of SMOs. One such issue concerns the conceptualization and identification of resources; a second issue addresses whether some types of resources are more important than others for mobilization and collective action; the third issue concerns resource derivation, particularly the relative importance of externally derived versus internally derived resources; and the fourth issue concerns the implications of external support for SMO viability and tactical actions. We address these four issues with data on 15 homeless SMOs in eight U.S. cities, and we explore the implications of our findings for a more nuanced understanding of social movements of the poor.

Unresolved Issues in the Study of Resource Mobilization

Resource mobilization theory generally has been regarded as the dominant perspective on social movements since the mid-1970s. Its central premise is that the principal antecedent task to collective action is

Cress, Daniel M, and David A. Snow. 1996. "Resources, Benefactors, and the Viability of Homeless SMOs." *American Sociological Review* 61: 1089–1109. Reprinted by permission of American Sociological Association.

resource aggregation and that fluctuation in the level of discretionary resources accounts, in large part, for variation in the activity levels of social movements (Jenkins and Perrow 1977; McCarthy and Zald 1973, 1977; Oberschall 1973). Despite all the research generated under the rubric of resource mobilization,[1] our understanding of the presumed relationship between resources and social movement activity is surprisingly limited. This is due largely to three oversights: (1) the failure to clarify and empirically ground the resource concept, (2) the failure to examine the link between types of resources and various mobilization processes or outcomes, and (3) the failure to clarify empirically competing claims about the sources of resources, in particular whether sources are external or internal. These three oversights give rise to the four issues we seek to explore.

Conceptualizing Resources

The resource concept is surprisingly slippery and vague given its ubiquity in the social movement literature. This ambiguity has been a source of concern among students of social movements for several years (Freeman 1979; Jenkins 1983a; Marx and Wood 1975; Morris and Herring 1988; Piven and Cloward 1977; Zurcher and Snow 1981), but little headway has been made in anchoring resources conceptually or empirically. Conceptually, the tendency has been to include as resources anything that SMOs need to mobilize and deploy in pursuit of their goals (McAdam, McCarthy, and Zald 1988; McCarthy and Zald 1977; Oberschall 1973; Tilly 1978). Attempts have been made to add greater specificity to the concept by considering how resources are used (Gamson, Fireman, and Rytina 1982; Jenkins 1983b; Rogers 1974), but this overlooks the plasticity of many resources (Jenkins 1983a). Thus, most researchers merely list the resources used by the SMOs they study. The problem with this strategy is that it seldom goes beyond identifying the general categories of money, legitimacy, people, and occasionally expertise (Freeman 1979; Gamson et al. 1982; Lofland 1993; McCarthy and Zald 1977; Oliver and Marwell 1992; Tilly 1978). As a consequence, it is usually unclear whether the listed resources include all resources mobilized or only those deemed critical by the researcher. Thus, the resource concept remains nearly as ambiguous as it did when it was introduced more than 20 years ago. We empirically identify all resources mobilized by the 15 homeless SMOs we study and assess their relevance for the viability of the SMOs.

Resources and Mobilization Outcomes

Given the assumption that resources are a necessary condition for successful mobilization, a detailed understanding of the link between specific types and combinations of resources and mobilization outcomes should be a matter of course. This, however, is not the case. Instead, understanding of the relationship between resources and mobilization remains mired at a very general level. For example, McCarthy and Zald (1973, 1977) argue that general levels of movement activity are related to overall levels of discretionary resources in a society. Likewise, Jenkins and Perrow (1977) contend that changes in the external sponsorship of the farm workers' movement account for the successful mobilization campaign of the late 1960s in contrast to the unsuccessful efforts to organize farm workers in the late 1940s.

More recently, Oliver and Marwell (1992) examined the consequences of mobilizing one type of resource rather than another (labor versus money), arguing that the resources pursued constrain tactical action. Their research takes a step in the right direction because attention is focused on the consequences of mobilizing particular types of resources. We extend this line of inquiry by examining the significance of a variety of resources and resource combinations for SMO viability.

Resource Derivation

A third issue concerns the source of resources. One argument sees resources as emanating primarily from external sources, namely "conscience constituents" (those who support movement activity without benefiting directly from attainment of its objectives) and extramovement organizations (McCarthy and Zald 1973, 1977). A second argument focuses on the indigenous character of resources, arguing that they are provided mainly by an SMO's constituency (McAdam 1982; Morris 1981).[2] We explore two questions: Are the resources mobilized by homeless SMO's derived externally or internally? And does their source affect SMO viability?

External Support and Control

The fourth issue we examine flows from the resource derivation debate: Does external support or patronage lead to co-optation or control? There are two overlapping hypotheses: The social control hypothesis argues that external sponsorship moderates SMO goals and tactics, thus dampening the prospect of militant collective action (Haines 1984; McAdam 1982; Piven and Cloward 1977). A second hypothesis contends that external patronage does not necessarily mute radical dissent, but channels it into more professional and publicly palatable forms (Jenkins and Eckert 1986). Although these two hypotheses provide a useful point of departure concerning the effects of external support on SMO activities, they focus exclusively on support from elite external organizations. Thus, the effects of sponsorship by nonelite organizations remains an empirical question.

Context, Data, and Procedures

We examine the foregoing issues with data derived from fieldwork conducted between 1989 and 1992 on 15 homeless SMOs and their organizational supporters and antagonists in eight U.S. cities. Homeless activists and their SMOs are particularly well-suited for addressing the issues we have identified. Given their overwhelming poverty, homeless individuals are able to provide little more than their voices and physical presence to SMOs. Consequently, differences in the durability and accomplishments of homeless SMOs across the country must be partly the result of differential success in mobilizing resources, presumably from external organizations. Thus, a comparative study of homeless SMOs provides a unique opportunity to assess the importance of specified resources in relation to mobilization outcomes.

The 15 SMOs were local variants of a larger social movement that emerged in the 1980s with the proliferation of homelessness throughout the United States, and this issue generated a voluminous research literature and a great deal of public interest during the decade (Burt 1992; Rosenthal 1994; Rossi 1989; Snow and Anderson 1993; Wagner 1993; Wright 1989). Relatively little was done, however, on the state or federal level to remedy the problem. In part because of this apparent indifference and because policy initiatives did little more than expand the nation's network of shelters, the homeless began to mobilize in one city after another in the 1980s. Although it is difficult to pinpoint the emergence of this movement, it first gained national visibility in 1983 with Mitch Snyder's 60-day fast and the Community for Creative Non-Violence's embrace of homelessness as its focal concern. The pinnacle of the movement's mobilization occurred in October 1989 when an estimated 250,000 homeless individuals and their supporters assembled at the foot of the nation's capitol under the banner of "Housing Now!" Although these two events gained national visibility for the homeless movement, most collective actions by homeless people, such as protest rallies, marches, housing takeovers, and encampments on government property, were local. These local activities, however, were widespread, as collective actions occurred in over 50 cities in the 1980s.[3] Although attempts were made to coordinate some of these local mobilizations by the National Union of the Homeless, which surfaced in 1986 in Philadelphia, and although approximately 15 local SMOs affiliated with the National Union, the movement was primarily a city-level phenomenon.

Because of the local character of the movement, we focused our research on homeless SMOs in eight cities: Boston, Denver, Detroit, Houston, Minneapolis, Oakland, Philadelphia, and Tucson. Two factors influenced our selection of these eight cities. First, given our interest in the relationship between resource aggregation and mobilization outcomes, the cities needed to vary in level of mobilization. We determined this by a content analysis of newspaper accounts of homeless collective actions in 18 U.S. cities that had a daily newspaper indexed throughout the 1980s.[4] Thus, the eight cities had to be selected from these 18 cities. We were also constrained by time and access. Because of funding requirements, the fieldwork had to be conducted during a three-year period. To avoid having to gain access anew in each city—a time-consuming process—we selected cities in which we already had contacts with leaders of the local homeless SMOs. These contacts were made during a year of pilot fieldwork in Minneapolis, Philadelphia, and Tucson.

The eight sampled cities and the 15 SMOs analyzed are shown in Table 1. The cities sampled are among the 50 largest cities in the United States, and the sample appears to be representative of these cities in size, region, and homeless rate. Our primary concern, however, is not with generalizing to the universe of homeless SMOs, but with using our case findings to address the unresolved theoretical issues we identified earlier.[5]

The principal objectives of our fieldwork were to map the organizational field in which the SMOs were embedded in each city and to discern patterns of interaction, such as resource flows, within these fields.[6] We employed an "onion-snowball" strategy that began with an SMO and moved outward in a layered fashion contingent on the information and referrals received. Thus, in each city we began with a homeless SMO with which we had already established contact. We interviewed its leaders and cadre, attended meetings, and participated in collective actions when they occurred. Based on these contacts, we then moved to the facilitative organizations—service providers, churches, and activist organizations—that provided information regarding their ties to the homeless SMO and their resource contributions. Next, we gathered information on the targets of the SMOs, such as mayors' offices, city councils, police departments, and the Department of Housing and Urban Development (HUD). In addition to allowing us to map the relevant organizational field, this onion-snowball strategy provided us with several validity checks on our various sources of information.

Table I Cities and Homeless SMOs Used in the Analysis

City	Population Rank Among 50 Largest Cities, 1988	Region of Country	Homeless Rate per 10,000 in 1989[a]	Homeless SMOs
Boston	19	Northeast	46.7	Boston Union of the Homeless Homefront Homeless Civil Rights Project
Denver	25	West	29.7	Denver Union of the Homeless Homeless People United
Detroit	7	Midwest	12.2	Detroit Union of the Homeless
Houston	4	South	8.7	Heads Up! Houston Union of the Homeless
Minneapolis	46	Midwest	32.8	Alliance of the Streets Minneapolis Union of the Homeless People United for Economic Justice
Oakland	44	West	11.7	Oakland Union of the Homeless Membership Caucus
Philadelphia	5	Northeast	32.3	Philadelphia Union of the Homeless
Tucson	35	Southwest	27.2	Tucson Union of the Homeless

[a] Derived from Burt (1992, app. A)

Note: Other cities that comprised the initial sampling frame include: Atlanta, Chicago, Cleveland, District of Columbia, Honolulu, Los Angeles, New Orleans, New York, SL Louis, and San Francisco.

We also used this onion-snowball strategy to gather information on homeless SMOs no longer in existence. In each case, former members and affiliates of other relevant organizations were tracked down and interviewed. Ultimately, data were gathered on 15 homeless SMOs that were active between 1984 and the end of 1992 in the eight cities. Nine of the SMOs were still active during the course of our fieldwork from 1989 through 1991.[7] The 15 homeless SMOs varied in size, ranging from organizations with a half-dozen active homeless members to those with 30 or more active members. All claimed broad support among their local homeless constituents but differed in their abilities to mobilize homeless people for collective actions: Some SMOs drew upward of 500 homeless people to their rallies and protests, while others managed to attract only a handful. Such differences were partly due to their differential success in mobilizing other resources we identify shortly.

Table 2 provides a composite typology of the organizational field in which the SMOs were embedded and in which homeless mobilizations occurred. The typology classifies organizations that constitute the field in terms of their general responses to homelessness and their specific operating perspectives, which reflect what they actually do rather than their official objectives or proclamations. Theoretically, any of these organizations could be and indeed were targets of homeless collective

Table 2 Composite Organizational Field of Homeless SMOs

Orientation	Operating Perspective	Examples
Caretaker	Accommodative	Shelters, soup kitchens, clothes closets
	Restorative: Medical Salvationist Service provision	 Detoxification, mental health, and health care facilities Skid row missions, 12-step substance abuse programs Transitional housing programs, job training and referral programs
Market	Exploitative	Plasma centers, day labor operations, liquor stores, single-room occupancy
Activist	Advocacy	Service provider coalitions (e.g., Community for Creative Nonviolence; National Coalition for the Homeless)
	Empowerment: Humanist Social gospelite	 Jobs with Peace, Welfare Rights, Urban League Catholic Workers, American Friends Service Committee
Social control	Expulsionist Containment	Merchants, universities, residential neighborhoods Police departments
Apathy/indifference	Lip service and foot-dragging	Housing and Urban Development, Department of Labor, Veterans Administration

actions, with the exception of activists. In contrast to the targets of SMO attacks, the facilitative organizations were associated solely with an activist or caretaker orientation.

Our fieldwork roles resembled those assumed by Snow and Anderson (1993) in their research on the homeless in Austin, Texas: a buddy-researcher role when dealing with the homeless and their SMOs, and the role of credentialed expert when dealing with other organizations.[8] In addition to the data gathered via these fieldwork roles, we examined documents from the homeless SMOs, facilitative organizations, and target organizations, as well as newspaper accounts of the SMOs and their collective actions in each city. These additional data sources provided greater understanding of the SMOs and allowed us to cross-check informants' claims and to compare documents against one another.

Our observations and interviews yielded over 1,500 pages of field notes. The data were coded into master empirical and conceptual categories that dovetailed with issues in the study of social movements. For example, one category included all information pertaining to the goals of the homeless SMOs; another category included all data relevant to relationships with facilitative organizations. The materials in the master categories were then coded to highlight the variation within each category. This process helped to organize and make sense of the data and clarified the organizational dynamics and resource relationships in each city.

Findings

A Taxonomy of Resources

Previous discussions of resources tend to overlook their fungibility and emphasize the generic categories of money, people, and legitimacy. We attempted to avoid these problems by identifying the range of resources mobilized by the 15 SMOs and then noting their specific uses or functions—drawing on the resource-type and resource-use strategies while avoiding their shortcomings. We grouped the resources we identified into four categories: moral, material, informational, and human. These categories are exhaustive in that they contain the range of specific resources that the homeless SMOs mobilized; they are also mutually exclusive inasmuch as the specific resources fit logically into only one category. Table 3 describes the resource categories and the specific resources included within each.

The resource categories build on prior conceptualizations. For example, the *moral resources category* dovetails with the concept of legitimacy used by others in that external legitimation may be a consequence of sympathetic or solidaristic support. But our conceptualization also emphasizes the internal validation and support that external endorsements

provide for the homeless SMO. The sense that other organizations shared their concerns and supported their actions was an important morale boost for many of the homeless SMOs. Likewise, the *material resources category* includes mundane items that are typically overlooked or subsumed under the category of money. Although money is a frequently noted resource in the social movement literature (Jenkins and Eckert 1986; Lofland 1993; McCarthy and Zald 1977; Oliver and Marwell 1992), we were more concerned with the specific resources that money was used to acquire. Moreover, the homeless SMOs seldom received funds directly, and when they did, the funds were used to acquire the resources listed in this category.

Our *informational resources category* builds on other conceptualizations of "know-how" (Gamson

Table 3 Types of Resources Mobilized by Homeless SMOs

Type of Resource	Description
MORAL	Endorsements by external organization of the aims and actions of homeless SMOs.
(A) Sympathetic support	Statements by external organization that are supportive of the aims and actions of homeless SMOs.
(B) Solidaristic support	Participation by an external organization in the collective actions of the SMO.
MATERIAL	Tangible goods and services mobilized by homeless SMOs.
(C) Supplies	Basic goods that help maintain the SMO (e.g., paper, posterboard, telephones).
(D) Meeting space	Area controlled by external organization used by homeless SMOs.
(E) Office space	Areas controlled by homeless SMOs to conduct business.
(F) Transportation	Use of cars and buses to take the homeless to meetings and collective actions.
(G) Employment	Provision of jobs for members of SMOs.
(H) Money	Cash received by SMOs.
INFORMATIONAL	Knowledge capital pertinent to the organization's maintenance and mobilization.
(I) Strategic support	Knowledge that facilitates goal-attainment collective actions, like sit-ins and housing takeovers.
(J) Technical support	Knowledge that facilitates organizational development and maintenance (e.g., how to run a meeting and delegate tasks).
(K) Referrals	Provision of connections to potential external organization for resources.
HUMAN	People who donate resources, time, and energy to the SMO.
(L) Captive audiences	Constituency and bystander populations assembled for recruitment and resource appeals.
(M) Leaders	Individuals who provide relatively stable organizational guidance and who function as spokespersons.
(N) Cadre	Individuals who function as lieutenants on a relatively permanent basis.

et al. 1982; Oliver and Mar-well 1992) by including knowledge relevant to conducting collective actions. But we also include knowledge about building and maintaining the organization and knowledge about potential supporters in the homeless organizational field.[9] Finally, our *human resources category* elaborates on general references to people power or labor by noting three types of human resources: captive audiences, leaders, and cadre.[10] Thus, the resource categories presented in Table 3 are empirically grounded in the homeless SMOs we studied, but are linked to and extend previous conceptualizations of resources.

Resources and Viability

We begin our examination of the relationship between the resources mobilized and SMO viability by first conceptualizing viability. The baseline barometer for viability is *survival,* which is consistent with the emphasis in the organizational literature on survival as the primary goal of organizations (DiMaggio and Powell 1983; Hannan and Freeman 1989; Pfeffer and Salancik 1978; Stinchcomb 1965). We operationalize survival by whether an SMO existed for one year or more. The one-year criteria is used because it elicited the most reliable responses from our informants when assessing the longevity of SMOs that were not in existence while we were in the field.

Because organizations may persist without engaging in much activity, we also measured viability by considering the core *activities* of the SMOs: meetings and collective actions. We looked at how frequently an SMO met and categorized SMOs by whether they met at least twice a month. We also examined whether SMOs planned and conducted protest campaigns. Protest campaigns refer to packages of collective actions organized around particular issues. All homeless SMOs protested, but much protest was reactive and short-lived. Protest campaigns represent a higher order of viability in that they are proactive and more complex to execute because they involve a series of interrelated events. Thus, we conceptualize SMO viability in terms of temporal survival, meeting frequency, and the capacity to conduct collective action campaigns.

Social movement organizations that meet all three criteria are categorized as viable.

How did the homeless SMOs do in terms of resource acquisition and viability? Table 4 identifies the array of resources mobilized by the 15 SMOs and indicates whether they were viable. A homeless SMO was credited with a particular resource if it reported ongoing access to that resource.[11]

Table 4 indicates that the SMOs demonstrate a wide range of success in securing different resources. One-third of the SMOs received 5 or fewer resource types, one-third secured 8 to 12 resource types, and one-third acquired 13 or more of the resources. Table 4 also suggests that those SMOs with more resources were more likely to be viable. But we are also interested in whether some resources were more important than others to the viability of an SMO. What resources and resource combinations were necessary and sufficient for SMO viability?

To address this question, we employ qualitative comparative analysis (Ragin 1987). This analytic framework, which is based on the logic and techniques of Boolean algebra, identifies the multiple and conjunctural causes of an event when comparing a relatively small number of cases. More specifically, it identifies the necessary and sufficient conditions for an event to occur, and is especially suited to situations with complex patterns of interactions among the specified conditions. In addition, the product of Boolean equations represents the conjunction or interaction of present and absent conditions. Thus, qualitative comparative analysis allows us to identify the simplest combinations of resources that lead to viability from among the many possible resource combinations.[12]

What resources were most important for SMO viability? Using Boolean reduction, we can simplify Table 4 for viable organizations with the following equation:

$$V = (ABCDEUKM) (fghln + FGHin + FHLN).$$

where V is viability, and the remaining letters correspond to the specific resources listed in Table 3. In Boolean equations, capital letters indicate the presence of a condition, while lowercase letters

Table 4 Resources Received by SMOs and SMO Viability

SMO	Moral			Material					Information			Human			Viability[a]
	A	B	C	D	E	F	G	H	I	J	K	L	M	N	
Alliance of the Streets	1	1	1	1	1	1	1	1	1	1	1	1	1	1	1
Oakland Union of the Homeless	1	1	1	1	1	1	1	1	1	1	1	1	1	1	1
Philadelphia Union of the Homeless	1	1	1	1	1	1	1	1	1	1	1	1	1	1	1
Detroit Union of the Homeless	1	1	1	1	1	1	1	1	1	1	1	1	1	1	1
Tucson Union of the Homeless	1	1	1	1	1	1	0	1	1	1	1	1	1	1	1
Homeless Civil Rights Project	1	1	1	1	1	1	1	1	1	1	1	0	1	0	1
People United for Economic Justice	1	1	1	1	1	0	0	1	1	1	1	1	1	0	1
Boston Union of the Homeless	1	1	1	1	0	0	0	0	1	1	1	1	0	0	0
Homeless People United	1	1	1	1	1	0	0	0	1	1	1	0	0	1	0
Denver Union of the Homeless	1	1	1	1	0	0	0	0	1	1	1	1	0	0	0
Homefront	1	1	0	0	0	0	0	1	1	0	0	0	0	0	0
Heads Up!	1	1	1	1	0	0	0	0	0	0	0	0	1	0	0
Houston Union of the Homeless	1	1	0	1	0	0	0	0	0	0	0	1	0	0	0
Minneapolis Union of the Homeless	0	0	1	1	1	0	0	0	0	0	0	1	0	0	0
Membership Caucus	1	0	1	1	0	0	0	0	1	0	0	0	0	0	0

[a] An SMO is viable if it survives at least one year, holds meetings at least twice a month, and sponsors collective action campaigns.

Note: In this table, 1 indicates that an SMO received the resource/was viable; 0 indicates that it did not receive the resource/was not viable.

indicate the absence of a condition. Letters not present in an equation indicate that a condition is irrelevant.[13] Indicators of multiplication are read as "and," while indicators of addition are read as "or." Thus, the nine resources in the first term after the equal sign (ABCDEIJKM) are necessary for viability as all viable SMOs received these resources; and these resources are sufficient in conjunction with one of the three resource combinations that follow. Table 5 lists the three possible pathways to viability and the SMOs associated with each. We illustrate each of these pathways and discuss how the resources contributed to the viability of the respective SMOs.

A combination of nine resources was necessary for each viable SMO. Each of the viable SMOs mobilized the moral backing of other organizations, receiving both statements of support (resource A) and active participation in their collective actions (resource B). The leader of the Oakland Union of the Homeless provides an example of this support when discussing a Christmas Day protest:

> We had a bunch of ministers from all over the Bay Area come and their basic statement was, "I'm not here to say that our church can solve homelessness; I'm here to say our church can stand in solidarity with the homeless." And so they all stood there and pledged that night that even though their churches needed them on Christmas, they would commit civil disobedience with us.

Moral support facilitated viability in two ways. First, the backing of organizations like churches and labor unions provided legitimacy for the homeless SMOs among other entities in the organizational field. Second, moral support gave the SMO a sense that others were behind them, an important morale booster for a population that typically endures a pariah-like status.

The viable SMOs also mobilized three of the six material resources: supplies (C), meeting space (D), and office space (E). A regular place to meet and adequate supplies are requisites for doing regular organizational business. A supporter of the Detroit Union of the Homeless discussed the importance of these resources:

> Well, I think that giving people space makes life possible. You know, I mean what's the difference between a person who is homeless and a person who isn't homeless? The person who isn't homeless has a home. Well the Homeless Union when it was homeless had a different character than when it had some place to be. There is a kind of franticness when you don't really have a place where you can invite anybody into. But when you do, people can find you. Strategies can be developed. You can get a sense of your own identity.

There are three reasons for the salience of these material resources in relation to SMO viability. First, having a reliable place to meet centralizes an SMO's day-to-day operations and lessens the prospect that the SMO may be harassed for conducting its business in public spaces intended for other activities. Second, a regular meeting space is important symbolically in that it signifies the acquisition and control of a rare commodity for the homeless: physically bounded, private space. Third,

Table 5 Resource Paths to Viability for Homeless SMOs

Path	Necessary Resources	Additional Resources	Homeless SMOs
I	(ABCDEIJKM)	(fghin)	People United for Economic Justice
2	(ABCDEIJKM)	(FGHin)	Homeless Civil Rights Project
3	(ABCDEIJKM)	(FHLN)	Alliance of the Streets, Detroit Union of the Homeless, Oakland Union of the Homeless. Philadelphia Union of the Homeless, and Tucson Union of the Homeless

the provision of office space by a facilitative organization strengthens its commitment to the SMO and helps legitimate the SMO.

All three informational resources—strategic support (I), technical support (J), and referrals (K)—were also necessary for viability. The importance of these resources to SMO viability is not difficult to understand given the general resource deprivation among the homeless. Most homeless people come from backgrounds of extreme poverty (Burt 1992; Rossi 1989; Shinn and Gillespie 1994), they typically have lower educational levels than the general population (Rossi 1989; Snow and Anderson 1993), and their employment experience and skills are usually associated with jobs at the bottom of the occupational structure (Rossi 1989; Snow and Anderson 1993). Additionally, the growing professionalization of the social movement arena (Jenkins and Eckert 1986; McCarthy and Zald 1973, 1977) has placed greater emphasis on managerial skills and organizational abilities—talents that are in short supply among homeless people.

Because of these deficits, the survival of homeless SMOs is partly contingent on their abilities to mobilize the requisite informational resources. Thus, the Detroit Union of the Homeless established an advisory board of sympathetic organizations that could be called upon to provide informational assistance. The director of the United Housing Coalition, a member of the advisory board, explained how it worked:

> If the president of the Detroit Union calls and needs something, we try to assist him. For example, right now they are working with HUD to obtain some houses. They wanted to put together the application form. The president called us last week to meet with the new head of the Union Business School that's going to provide all the labor. So, you know, we help provide what is needed on an on-call basis.

Similarly, the director of the Women's Economic Agenda Project in Oakland explained how her organization assists poor people's movements, like the Oakland Union of the Homeless:

> Well, we try to assist (them) from the stand-point of helping them with technical assistance....It

can be anything from sitting down with people and showing them how to make an agenda, to helping them with an outline for a speech for someone who knows how to raise hell but, you know, never intended to be involved politically, but needs that confidence there. We also try helping them to do research, putting their issues into a broader topic.

And a lawyer for a Philadelphia law firm that specializes in civil rights and property law and does pro bono work for the Philadelphia Union of the Homeless described the strategic assistance he provided:

> My role is to assist them in how to use the law affirmatively, like in terms of lawsuits; how to force the city to comply with certain terms and agreements they've made. I also work on defense cases for their civil disobedience trials.

These comments from personnel in facilitative organizations in three cities illustrate informational assistance and underscore its importance for the viability of resource-impoverished SMOs.

Finally, all viable organizations had relatively strong leaders (M), one of the three human resources. Leaders contributed to the viability of homeless SMOs in several ways. Often they were the primary source for the critical informational resources mobilized by the organization. As an organizer with a local community center in Denver noted when discussing how the lack of leadership contributed to the demise of the failed Homeless People United:

> I'm convinced that had there been somebody who could have worked with that group full time, some things could have happened differently. I was doing it as a part-time kind of thing, doing other stuff as well, and it was real clear to me that doesn't work. We had a core group of people who politically, at least, and ideologically, had a sense of things that needed to be done. But I think they had to have more support there. I think they needed somebody who understood organizing well, who could spend the time working with them to do that....They needed someone who had more time than an hour per day. [and then] Homeless People United could have developed.

In addition, leaders provided continuity for the organization and helped counter the persistent problem of turnover among the ranks. Although all movements confront this problem, it is particularly pressing for homeless SMOs, whose adherents are often tenuously committed because of the uncertainty of meeting their basic survival needs and/or the necessity of looking for opportunities to get off the streets.

These nine resources represent the minimum resources necessary for viability, as six of the seven viable organizations needed to mobilize additional resources. The exception to this tendency was People United for Economic Justice in Minneapolis, an example of the first pathway listed in Table 5. This organization was somewhat distinctive in two ways. First, as a splinter SMO from another viable Minneapolis SMO (the Alliance of the Streets), People United for Economic Justice operated in a context of ongoing homeless activism. Second, and perhaps most important, it benefited from an experienced and tenacious leadership. Its president had been active in the Alliance of the Streets, and he was sufficiently skilled and aggressive that he affected a coup that elevated him to the chairmanship of the local coalition of social service providers to the homeless. Once this happened, the resource situation of the SMO improved. But before that, because of their prior experience in homeless activism and their leadership skills, he and a few associates were able to steer the SMO through an eight-month period without any external support—a period that included meeting in parks and libraries. Knowing some of the inherent difficulties in organizing the homeless enabled them to foresee and weather resource deficits that discouraged and sometimes doomed novice activists.

The other two pathways to viability required the mobilization of additional resources. One path is illustrated by the Homeless Civil Rights Project in Boston, which acquired the additional material resources of transportation (F), employment (G), and money (H) from a facilitative organization that was attempting to organize the homeless in Boston. A leader of a local activist group that helped form the Homeless Civil Rights Project explained their involvement with mobilizing the homeless:

We thought that the best way we could organize the homeless was to essentially come up with the funding to back a homeless-run organization and, you know, allow for homeless people to build their own organization from the ground up, and that is what we wound up doing.

The activist organization provided transportation for SMO members to organizational meetings and collective actions, which contributed to viability by increasing participation. In addition, the provision of transportation enabled the SMO to demonstrate in different locations across the Boston metropolitan area and the New England region, which increased their visibility and stature in the eyes of the local homeless.

Perhaps even more important was the facilitative organization's hiring of a homeless activist—the job enabled him to devote his full attention to the SMO. The leader of the activist organization elaborated:

With Jack, we had the foundation for recruiting homeless people into the Homeless Civil Rights Project. He was able to do the outreach and be there to do the work to draw people into the organization. So after a couple of weeks, I hired him. And that was how Civil Rights Project started.[14]

Providing a job for the homeless leader facilitated organizational viability by maintaining the involvement of a skilled homeless activist who might otherwise have been sidetracked by subsistence activities. It also provided leadership stability and continuity—a necessary resource for viability. Thus, for the Homeless Civil Rights Project, the additional material resources of transportation, employment, and money (used primarily for supplies) in combination with the necessary resources was sufficient for viability.

The third pathway to viability also involved securing the additional material resources of transportation (F) and money (H). But pathway 3 is distinguished from pathway 2 by the need for the two additional human resources—captive audiences (L) and an activist cadre (N)—and the irrelevance of employment if both of these were secured. This was the most common pathway—five of the viable SMOs followed this track. Since we have illustrated how money and transportation influenced SMO viability, we focus on the contribution of human resources to viability, as exemplified by the Tucson Union of the Homeless.

The Tucson Union of the Homeless (TUH) was led by an activist from a local Catholic Worker community. Although there was high turnover among the homeless rank and file, there was typically a cadre of a half-dozen homeless people who were the core active members in the organization. This cadre exercised strong influence on the issues that the Union pursued, and they carried out the day-to-day work of the organization. They played key roles in executing collective actions—developing and distributing fliers, mobilizing other homeless people, preparing food for demonstrations, speaking, and getting arrested. Thus, the cadre contributed to the viability of the Union by providing membership continuity as well as providing the muscle behind the work of the organization.

In addition to a cadre of homeless activists, the TUH had access to a captive audience of homeless who ate the only noonday meal served in Tucson at a soup kitchen run by the Catholic Workers. This resource facilitated viability by supplying the SMO with a pool of homeless to offer feedback on their concerns and grievances and the issues they wanted the Union to pursue. It also provided a relatively large and concentrated group of homeless who could be targeted for mobilization.

Having identified the three resource pathways of the viable homeless SMOs, and suggested how the resources contributed to their respective viability, the question arises as to the causal order of the resource-viability relationship: Is viability a function of the mobilization of a pool of salient resources? Or do viable SMOs attract salient resources? We suspect both processes occur, but we are certain about the first—that the acquisition of salient resources is a necessary condition for SMO viability. We say this not only because of the impoverished condition of the SMOs' homeless constituents, but also because we consistently observed that SMOs with fewer resources held fewer meetings and engaged less frequently in protest actions. Meetings and protest actions were essential to maintaining connections

and a semblance of solidarity among the homeless, whose street relationships and agency ties tend to be highly tenuous and transient (Snow and Anderson 1993). Particular resources, such as meeting space, transportation, and strategic and technical support, clearly increased the probability that regular meetings and collective actions would take place. In turn, SMOs that conducted these activities were more likely to survive. The case of the Denver Union of the Homeless is illustrative. In the early days, it was barely able to survive because it had no regular place to meet. As its president explained:

> We were meeting in the shelter still, and we'd get other people to come in. We'd go and talk to them, like on the street, and tell them we're meeting at this place at a certain time, you know, and then we'd try to meet outside a few times. And a lot of things didn't work out. We'd try different things and they didn't work out. It was exhausting sometimes, and sometimes we couldn't get anybody to meet.

But its fate changed when a sympathetic supporter provided a house to be used as its organizational base. This enabled the SMO to enjoy a relatively stable period in which it engaged in a number of collective actions, the last being a highly publicized housing takeover. Because of the attention this takeover attracted, however, the supporter evicted the SMO and closed the house. Lacking a regular meeting place, the SMO soon dissolved.

In this case, the failure to secure essential resources signaled the demise of the SMO. Thus, for the homeless SMOs we observed, organizational viability was contingent on the acquisition of the resource combinations identified. Viability was initially a function of successful resource mobilization, but once visibility was achieved, it facilitated the acquisition of subsequent support.

Resource Derivation, Organizational Benefactors, and Viability

There are two lines of argument regarding the sources of acquired resources: One focuses on external sources such as conscience constituents (McCarthy and Zald 1973, 1977); the other stresses the role of indigenous constituencies (McAdam 1982; Morris 1981). Are the resources mobilized by homeless SMOs externally or internally derived? Do SMOs' external relationships affect their viability?

Table 6 indicates whether the resources mobilized by the 15 SMOs were externally or internally derived. Resources coming primarily from external sources are indicated with an E; those derived internally from the SMO constituency are signified by an I. Dashes indicate that the resource was not mobilized by the SMO.

Although the homeless SMOs secured resources from both external and internal sources, 75 percent (104 of 139) of the resource types were derived from external sources. In addition, all but one of the viable SMOs mobilized the majority of their resource types from external supporters, thus highlighting the importance of facilitative organizational support for homeless SMOs. The only exception to this pattern was again the People United for Economic Justice (PUEJ), which relied heavily on the meager resources of its members to remain viable. However, this was not by choice, as PUEJ competed with two other homeless SMOs, the Alliance of the Streets and the Minneapolis Union of the Homeless, for external support. PUEJ had a difficult time distinguishing itself from the better-known Alliance of the Streets when it sought resource support in the community and often had to explain why it was not affiliated with the Alliance. Thus, the lack of external support was more a result of competition with other SMOs in the organizational field than a lack of PUEJ effort or need.[15]

Our findings underscore the importance of external support for homeless activism. Almost all SMOs studied, whether viable or not, mobilized most of their support from external sources. What distinguishes viable from nonviable SMOs is the range of resource types provided by external supporters: Viable SMOs mobilized an average of 9.7 external resources, while nonviable SMOs mobilized an average of only 4.5 external resources (p = .08, using Levene's test for equality of variances).

Given this dependence on external resources, what accounts for variation in the levels of external support? One factor that stands out from our field observations is the type of relationship established with facilitative organizations: Five of the seven viable SMOs were involved in relationships with a single facilitative organization that supplied at least 50 percent of the resource types mobilized by the SMO, whereas none of the nonviable organizations had such a relationship. We refer to this type of relationship, summarized in Table 7, as a "benefactor relationship."

Although the relationship between organizational patronage and (social movements has received considerable attention (Gamson [1975] 1990; Jenkins forthcoming; Jenkins and Eckert 1986), such patronage typically refers to any type of external support or sponsorship. Our conceptualization for "benefactor" is more specific.

Benefactors facilitated SMO viability not only by providing resources but by providing those resources necessary for viability. This finding was underscored by the leader of the Boston Homeless Civil Rights Project:

> We've been trying to create a homeless empowerment organization but it's tough to figure out; it's a really tough thing to do. So we looked at the successful models, and we found certain things that were in common. And what they were was that you had leadership development, ownership of the project by homeless people, and you had a sponsoring organization that was able to provide the sort of resources and financial backup that made the thing go. All the successful organizations had sort-of-like parent organizations that provided the resources.

A benefactor produces stable resource flows that facilitate viability by allowing the SMO to devote more time to collective actions. SMOs depended on sustained protests to maintain mobilization among the local homeless population. Because of the tenuous ties in this constituency, periods of inactivity usually resulted in membership attrition. SMOs that were less preoccupied with resource concerns could concentrate on organizing collective actions that in turn enhanced the prospect of viability. Thus, having a benefactor within its organizational field greatly increased the chances of an SMO's survival.[16]

The two viable SMOs that lacked a benefactor relationship were the People United for Economic

Table 6 Source of Resources and Presence of Benefactor for Homeless SMOs

					Resource											
	Moral		Material						Informational			Human			Benefactor[a]	Viable
SMO	A	B	C	D	E	F	G	H	I	J	K	L	M	N		
Alliance of the Streets	E	E	E	E	E	E	E	I	E	E	E	E	E	I	1	1
Oakland Union of the Homeless	E	E	E	E	E	E	E	E	E	E	E	E	E	I	1	1
Philadelphia Union of the Homeless	E	E	E	E	E	I	E	E	I	I	E	I	I	I	0	1
Detroit Union of the Homeless	E	E	E	E	E	E	E	I	I	I	I	I	I	I	1	1
Tucson Union of the Homeless	E	E	E	E	E	E	–	E	E	E	E	E	I	I	1	1
Homeless Civil Rights Project	E	E	E	E	E	E	E	E	E	E	E	–	I	–	1	1
People United for Economic Justice	E	E	I	I	E	–	–	–	I	I	I	–	I	–	0	1
Boston Union of the Homeless	E	E	E	E	E	–	–	I	I	I	I	E	I	–	0	1
Homeless People United	E	E	E	E	E	–	–	–	E	E	E	–	–	I	0	0
Denver Union of the Homeless	E	E	E	E	–	–	–	–	I	I	I	–	I	–	0	0
Homefront	E	E	–	E	–	–	–	E	I	I	–	–	–	–	0	0
Heads Up!	E	E	E	E	–	–	–	–	–	–	–	–	I	–	0	0
Houston Union of the Homeless	E	E	–	E	–	–	–	–	–	–	–	–	I	–	0	0
Minneapolis Union of the Homeless	–	–	E	E	E	–	–	–	–	–	–	–	I	–	0	0
Membership Caucus	E	–	E	–	–	–	–	–	E	E	–	–	–	–	0	0

[a] A supporting organization that supplies at least one-half of the resource types used by an HMO.

Note: E = resource externally derived; I = resource indigenous or internally derived; l = situation present; 0 = situation absent.

Table 7 Viability by Benefactor Relationship for Homeless SMOs

Presence of Benefactor	Viable SMO	Nonviable SMO	Total
Yes	5	0	5
No	2	8	10
Totals	7	8	15

$\chi^2 = 8.57$, d.f. $= 1$, $p < .05$

Justice and the Philadelphia Union of the Homeless. The Philadelphia Union of the Homeless was also an anomaly. Shortly after its formation by two homeless men, the SMO applied for and received a $21,000 grant from the city to open its own shelter—the first in the nation to be operated solely by the homeless—and to purchase necessary supplies. However, we did not classify the Philadelphia Union of the Homeless as being involved in a benefactor relationship for several reasons. First, it did not meet our benefactor criterion: The external provider did not supply at least one-half of the resource types. Additionally, having its own base of operations early in its career, it was less dependent on subsequent organizational support than other homeless SMOs. Furthermore, the SMO's collective actions often targeted the city, so it is equally plausible to interpret the city's "support" as a collective action outcome. In each of these ways, the Philadelphia Union of the Homeless did not have the type of interactive relationship with the city that the other SMOs had with their benefactors.

Benefactors were not scattered at random throughout each SMO's respective organizational field, but were concentrated among the activist empowerment-oriented organizations. Two types of empowerment organizations worked closely with the homeless. One type was characterized by a general "humanist" objective of securing dignity and equality for all people. Because of the breadth of this mandate, local examples of such organizations—such as the Urban League, Jobs with Peace, and Welfare Rights—were committed to a range of issues in addition to empowering the homeless. The second type of empowerment organization working among the homeless we termed "social gospelites"

because of their commitment to the Christian ethic to "stand with the poor." This ethic typically manifests itself through what the leader of the Catholic Worker house in Tucson called "acts of mercy" and "acts of justice." "Acts of mercy" refer to charitable work conducted for the poor; "acts of justice" refer to empowerment efforts. Acts of justice distinguish the social gospelites from other religiously oriented caretaker agencies that service the homeless, such as the Salvation Army and the spate of missions and soup kitchens.

Of the two types of empowerment organizations, the social gospelites were clearly more prominent, as they accounted for four of the five benefactor relationships. The social gospelites established benefactor relationships with homeless SMOs because their calling to stand with the poor placed them in greater association with the homeless and their SMOs than was the case for the humanist organizations. Furthermore, commitment to this "calling" provided the social gospelites with greater staying power, because assisting the homeless and other impoverished groups was seen as an end in itself. In contrast, most humanist organizations, with their broader mandate, tend to work on behalf of a greater variety of causes and SMOs, and thus tend to be more diffuse in their focus and action.

Patronage and SMO Control

The literature suggests that external support comes with a cost: generally a loss of SMO autonomy; more particularly, a moderating influence with respect to SMO objectives and strategic actions (Jenkins and Eckert 1986; McAdam 1982; Piven and Cloward 1977). If the general thrust of the literature is correct, these tempering influences should be even

Table 8 Militancy Among Homeless SMOs by Benefactor Relationship

Presence of Benefactor	Use of Militant Tactics	Use of Nonmilitant Tactics	Total
Yes	3	2	5
No	5	5	10
Totals	8	7	15

$\chi^2 = .135$ (not significant)

more pronounced among those SMOs with greater resource dependency. Thus, we should expect to find less stridency or militancy among homeless SMOs involved in benefactor relationships.

Table 8 assesses the relationship between the presence of a benefactor relationship and the use of militant tactics. We define militant tactics as those that intentionally break laws and involve the risk of arrest for participants—blockades, sit-ins, housing takeovers, and unauthorized encampments. In contrast, non-militant tactical actions include petitions, rallies, and demonstrations that typically have been/negotiated and sanctioned in advance.[17] Dividing the range of tactical actions engaged in by the 15 SMOs into these two categories, we discern no significant relationship between the establishment of a benefactor relationship and a propensity of SMOs to engage in militant action: 3 of the 5 SMOs with a benefactor engaged in militant action, as did 5 of the 10 SMOs without a benefactor. Thus, a benefactor relationship appears to enhance the viability of SMOs representing homeless constituents, but does not necessarily moderate tactical actions.

Discussion and Implications

Current understanding of the resource mobilization process in social movements has been plagued by a lack of specification of the resources that SMOs commonly mobilize, by the absence of an empirically based understanding of the relationship between different types and combinations of resources and mobilization outcomes, by empirical and conceptual ambiguity regarding the relative importance of externally derived versus internally derived resources, and by the dearth of research on the consequences of different relationships with

facilitative organizations for SMO viability and tactical actions. We have attempted to shed empirical and conceptual light on these ambiguities using data drawn from our research on 15 homeless SMOs in eight U.S. cities.

We summarize our findings below in the course of discussing their implications for understanding four broader issues in the study of social movements: the role resources play more generally in the careers of SMOs; the importance of externally derived versus internally derived resources; the role of benefactors; and the relevance of resources and organization to movements of the poor.

Resources

Two general implications regarding the relationship between resources and social movements can be drawn from our findings. First, some SMOs clearly require a broader array of resources then do others. Most of the literature has focused on money, labor, and legitimacy, and even some dimensions of these resources typically have been glossed over. The underspecified conceptualization of resources is largely the result of schemes that are too narrow or too general. We proceeded inductively to identify the range of resources accumulated by the 15 homeless SMOs and then categorize them around common functional dimensions. Although the resultant categories—moral, material, human, and informational—and their variants pertain directly to the homeless SMOs we studied, they build on and extend prior conceptualizations. Thus, we believe our elaborated typology is sufficiently general to be applicable to other movements and contexts. As well, our expanded taxonomy of resources underscores the utility of conducting more refined empirically grounded analyses of the resources SMOs need and secure than has been customary in the research literature.

Second, our findings affirm the cornerstone assumption of the resource mobilization perspective: The mobilization of resources profoundly affects the course and character of SMOs. Although this seems self-evident, this has been a link based more on theoretic assertion than on empirical demonstration. We extend this cornerstone assumption in several ways. Concerning the relationship between the number of resources mobilized and SMO viability, we found that nine of the resources, when joined with other resource combinations, yielded three pathways to viability. Thus, it may not be the absolute number of resources that determines the viability of an SMO but the type of resources and the way they combine and interact.

Regarding the relative importance of some kinds of resources vis-à-vis others, we found that informational resources, leadership, and having a place to meet were the most important in relation to viability. However, the salience of any particular resource or set of resources probably varies by type of SMO, the class or socioeconomic status of its constituents, and desired outcomes. Again, these issues beg for further empirical examination. It is clear, however, given our findings, that analyses that focus solely on the link between the availability of broad categories of resources and mobilization miss an important part of the resource mobilization dynamic.

Resource Derivation

Our findings are also relevant to the debate between the variant of resource mobilization theory that accents the externally derived character of resources (McCarthy and Zald 1973, 1977) and the political process model, which emphasizes the indigenous or constituency-based character of resources (McAdam 1982; Morris 1981; Tilly 1978). Our findings indicate that the debate may be overstated as the homeless SMOs secured both external and indigenous support. However, the bulk of resources acquired by 14 of the 15 SMOs came from nonconstituent facilitative organizations, indicating the greater salience of external support for homeless SMOs.

This finding hardly seems surprising. Not only do the homeless suffer extreme resource impoverishment, but it would seem that the greater the resource deprivation, the greater the dependence on external sources for resource mobilization. Yet those who have argued for the importance of internally derived resources have typically focused on movements of the poor to make their case (McAdam 1982; Morris 1981; Piven and Cloward 1977). What distinguishes their arguments from our findings is that they assumed the presence of resources (i.e., indigenous organization and leadership) that are in short supply among the homeless as well as necessary for organizational viability. Thus, the relative importance of external or internal support may vary considerably across movements within a particular category of movements, such as poor people's movements.

Patronage, Benefactor Relationships, and Control

Documentation of external organizational support, and particularly the existence of benefactor relationships, raises the question of co-optation or control: Does resource dependency transform SMO goals and tactics? Or, more colloquially, does the piper call the tune? One argument noted earlier is that resource dependence alters an SMO's original goals and tactical proclivities (Haines 1984; McAdam 1982; Piven and Cloward 1977). An alternative argument is the "channeling" thesis: External support or elite patronage may modify the appearance of an SMO, dressing it up a bit and professionalizing it, but not necessarily changing its objectives (Jenkins and Eckert 1986); the means change, but not so much the ends.

Neither scenario fits our findings neatly: Militant and nonmilitant actions were pursued regardless of a benefactor relationship. This is not to say that the benefactor did not affect the SMO. To the contrary, we observed that both the SMO and the organizational benefactor often marched to the same tune, but in some cases it was moderate and in other cases it was more radical and militant. Such findings fit the resource dependency perspective in the broader organizational literature, which argues that the goals and actions of resource-dependent organizations are likely to resemble those of the organizations on which they depend (Pfeffer and Salancik 1978). Thus, the acquisition of resources from facilitative organizations does not automatically alter an SMO's objectives or course of action. Rather, it depends in large part on how radical the resource provider is. This suggests a "correspondence thesis:" one which posits that the character of tactical action is a function of the perspective of the facilitative organization rather than of resource dependency per se. Hence, radical SMOs tend to be associated with radical supporters.

This finding suggests that the traditional conceptualization of patronage is too narrow. Patronage typically has been associated with "elite" support and has been viewed, in part, as a mechanism of control. But benefactors of homeless SMOs, typically social gospelite organizations located within the homeless organizational field, were not elite organizations. This suggests that patrons may be motivated by interests other than control or co-optation. It calls for more careful research on different levels or types of patronage and corresponding differences in effects. We know a good deal about the influence of elite sponsorship on SMO tactics from research on the support of national foundations, but relatively little about the character and consequences of local activist patronage of the kind we have examined. For example, one important distinction between elite patronage and benefactor patronage concerns the timing of support. Jenkins and his colleagues (Jenkins forthcoming; Jenkins and Eckert 1986) have shown that patronage by national foundations typically follows heightened periods of protest. This is contrary to McCarthy and Zald's (1977) assertion that resources precede protest, and it directs attention to the social control motives associated with the support. In contrast, the benefactor organizations in our study actively supported homeless SMOs prior to enhanced protest activity, suggesting that there may be important distinctions in intent and outcome between local and national patronage as well as between different types of patronage organizations.

Organization, Resources, and Movements of the Poor

Finally, our findings shed light on movements of the poor, particularly with respect to the role of organization. Much has been made of Piven and Cloward's (1977) thesis that building mass organizations is antithetical to the interests of movements among the poor (Cloward and Piven 1984; Gamson and Schmeidler 1984; Hobsbawm 1984; Piven and Cloward 1992; Zald 1992). Their argument has often been interpreted as suggesting that the poor should not organize (Gamson and Schmeidler 1984; Hobsbawm 1984). But Piven and Cloward's concern is not so much with organization per se as with the consequences of alternative forms of organizing. They are pessimistic about building mass organizations because they are skeptical about the effectiveness of what they see as interest-group approaches to improving the conditions of the poor (Cloward and Piven 1984; Piven and Cloward 1977). They argue that the political power of the poor resides in their ability to disrupt the routine functioning of political and economic institutions, and that the most effective organization for doing so is centralized but loosely structured "cadre organizations." These organizations are coalitions of leaders that activate people in existing networks and institutions. Thus, the issue is "not about organization versus no organization; it is about the political effectiveness of different kinds of organizations" (Cloward and Piven 1984: 588).

Our findings complement and challenge some implications of Piven and Cloward's work. The homeless in our study typically were not in the types of preexisting networks and institutions that are assumed by Piven and Cloward. Thus, organization-building was a necessary substitute for the absence of everyday connections in order for the mobilization of disruption to occur. Furthermore, rather than organization following and dampening disruption as Piven and Cloward suggest, homeless organization typically preceded protest because of the resource poverty of the homeless. Yet Piven and Cloward (1992) downplay the role of resources in protest activity. Citing Oberschall (1973), they contend that the necessary resources for protest consist simply of shared grievances and a common target. Although few resources may be required for episodic outbursts of protest, like rioting, to sustain mobilization over time as a social movement, like the SMOs we studied, requires a significant number of different types of resources.

Given the relatively nonproblematic role of resources in Piven and Cloward's approach to insurgency among the poor and their corresponding skepticism about external sponsorship, they must assume that the requisite resources exist within indigenous communities. Our findings clearly challenge both assumptions. Not only did the homeless SMOs depend on external support to organize protest, but those that established relationships with benefactors were much more likely to remain viable and be involved in sustained protest because it allowed them to focus on protest activity rather than on resource mobilization.

In sum, sustained, effective protest for the poor requires strong organizations predicated on the mobilization of essential resources. For impoverished constituencies, this typically requires support from nonconstituency-based facilitative organizations. While we do not discount the potential moderating influence of conscience-constituent support, we argue that moderation is far from inevitable. Thus, regarding movements of the poor, the real issue is not whether the poor should organize, but in what ways and with whom?

NOTES

The research was supported in part by a grant from the National Science Foundation (SES 9008809, David A. Snow, principal investigator). We thank Theron Quist and Kelly Smith for their assistance on the project, and Peter Adler, Andrew Jones, Doug McAdam, Fred Pampel, and Yvonne Zylan for their constructive comments on an earlier draft, as well as the other members of the informal Social Movement Seminars at the University of Arizona and the University of Colorado at Boulder. We are also grateful for the constructive comments of the three anonymous *ASR* reviewers, the Editor, and Deputy Editor Charles Tilly.

1. For a summary of this literature, see Buechler (1993), Jenkins (1983a), and Pichardo (1988).

2. For further discussion of these contrasting positions, see Pichardo (1988).

3. This figure is based on our inspection of newspaper reports assembled through the 1980s by the NewsBank Newspaper Index, which collects selected articles from over 400 newspapers in the United States. Little research has been published on these protest events or on the homeless movement in general (but see Rosenthal 1994; Wagner 1993; and Wright 1995).

4. We had hoped to take a random sample of the 50 largest U.S. cities, and use the New York Times Index and Newsbank Index to determine the incidence and intensity of homeless

collective actions across the cities sampled. However, fieldwork in Minneapolis, Philadelphia, and Tucson, including a summer spent working with the National Union of the Homeless in Philadelphia, indicated that accounts of homeless mobilization were underrepresented in these two indexes. Thus, we turned to local dailies for information on homeless mobilization and collective action across U.S. cities. Our content analysis of the 18 dailies found over 500 homeless protest events during the 1980s across the 18 cities, ranging from a low of 5 to a high of 74, with a mean of 32.

5. The use of case studies to extend and refine existing theoretical positions is consistent with a growing literature exploring the rationale and uses of case studies (see Burawoy 1991; Feagin, Orum, and Sjoberg 1991; Glaser and Strauss 1967; and Ragin 1987).

6. By organizational field we mean a set of organizations that share overlapping constituencies and/or interests and that recognize one another's activities as relevant to those concerns. This conceptualization encompasses all facilitative and antagonistic organizations with which links might be established. It is consistent with the institutional perspective on organizations (DiMaggio and Powell 1983) and with work on multiorganizational fields in the study of social movements (Klandermans 1992).

7. Since it is reasonable to wonder if the founding and careers of each of the 15 SMOs were affected by different period effects, it is important to note that all 15 were founded between 1984 and 1989. This was a period in which homelessness escalated and became increasingly visible in the United States (Burt 1992; Jencks 1994; Rossi 1989), and in which public interest in the problem intensified, judging from media coverage of the problem (Bunis, Yancik, and Snow 1996). It has been speculated that homelessness has declined since the end of the 1980s (Jencks 1994) and that public interest in the problem has dwindled owing to a combination of compassion fatigue and issue competition (Bunis et al. 1996). However accurate these hypothesized changes, they would not appear to account for variation in the careers of the SMOs in our sample as they were all founded during the same time period before 1990.

8. Whereas the buddy-researcher assumes a sympathetic but curious stance, the credentialed expert assumes a nonpartisan stance in which his or her professional identity legitimates the research inquiry (Snow, Benford, and Anderson 1986).

9. Oliver and Marwell (1992) identify mobilization technologies as intraorganizational know-how, but this is limited to knowledge about resource acquisition.

10. We did not include turnout at collective actions as a labor resource in part because we conceptualized it as an outcome of SMO mobilization activity. Most SMOs could not predict how many people an action might draw, so it was an unstable resource at best. We felt that leadership and cadre best captured the labor resources of the SMO.

11. We were unable to distinguish SMOs by amount of each resource mobilized. This was unavoidable because the SMOs did not have systematic accounting procedures. Also, because different resources have different utilities, comparisons of resource amounts among particular types of resources (e.g., material versus informational) are inappropriate (Freeman 1979).

12. Research employing qualitative comparative analysis has typically used fewer independent conditions than we use (Amenta and Poulsen 1994; Ragin 1987). The greater the number of independent conditions, the greater the likelihood that the number of possible combinations will increase, thus making it more difficult to discern patterns among the cases. This would be problematic for our analysis if each SMO had a unique resource combination. However, our SMOs cluster into relatively few resource combinations.

13. Equations that are identical in all but one aspect can be reduced by that aspect. For example, if two viable SMOs have the same pattern of resource acquisition except that one provides employment and the other does not (e.g., FGHLN and FgHLN), employment can be dropped as a necessary causal condition. Stated another way, in the presence of the other resources mobilized, it does not matter if employment is present or not. This is indicated by the absence of the appropriate symbol in the equation (e.g., FHLN). This is similar to experimental controls in which only one aspect is allowed to vary while others are held constant.

14. This is a striking example of employment serving as a selective incentive for participation, but it was not common across the 15 SMOs we studied. Moreover, it was a necessary condition only for the Homeless Civil Rights Project.

15. This finding, coupled with the fact that all but 3 of the 15 SMOs were situated in cities with 2 or more homeless SMOs, raises two confounding propositions. First, the presence of 2 or more homeless SMOs in a city may overtax the carrying capacity for such movements and increase the competition for limited resources. We cannot assess this proposition directly, but our data do not appear to support it, as viable SMOs are found in cities with 1 SMO (Detroit, Philadelphia, and Tucson), 2 SMOs (Oakland), and 3 SMOs (Boston and Minneapolis). A second proposition raises the possibility of a "radical flank effect," which suggests that the presence of more radical or extremist SMOs in a movement industry encourages support for the more moderate SMOs (Haines 1984). We find little support for this proposition, as the more radical SMOs in cities with multiple SMOs were often the more viable ones (e.g., the Oakland Union of the Homeless and the Homeless Civil Rights Project in Boston).

16. The high level of resource support that characterized the benefactor relationship raises the issue of organizational boundaries. Are the homeless SMOs in these relationships merely "front organizations" for their organizational benefactors? We believe that the SMOs involved in these relationships were essentially autonomous organizations operating on their own initiatives. Even in the cases of Alliance of the Streets and the Homeless Civil Rights Project, in which benefactors created the SMOs, there were deliberate attempts to keep separate the SMO and the benefactor. Also, SMOs formed by benefactors did not differ in viability from those that were not.

17. Although there is no single, accepted scheme for distinguishing radical/militant tactics from negotiated or less institutionally threatening forms of protest, our distinctions are consistent with other treatments of this issue (Lofland 1985:260–69; Piven and Cloward 1992; Sharp 1973; Tarrow 1994:100–17).

9.

From Struggle to Settlement: The Crystallization of a Field of Lesbian/Gay Organizations in San Francisco, 1969–1973

ELIZABETH A. ARMSTRONG

In 1969 gay liberation was new and exciting. The collision between existing homosexual organizing and the New Left had transformed activists' understandings of what could and should be accomplished by organizing on behalf of homosexuals. In this moment of intense energy the ideologies of the movement were contradictory. Gay liberationists wanted both to solidify gay identity and to demolish sexual identity categories altogether. They wanted both revolution and civil rights. By 1972 the revolutionary and anti-identity currents of the movement were on the wane. Many scholars have remarked upon the transformation of gay liberation from a radical movement into one focused on identity building and gay rights (Altman 1982; Bernstein 1997; Epstein 1987; Escoffier 1985; Gamson 1998; Seidman 1993; Vaid 1995). Affirming gay identity and celebrating diversity replaced societal transformation as goals. This turn toward identity building was accompanied by rapid political consolidation and the explosive growth of a commercial subculture oriented around sex. For the first time, gay organizations agreed upon a national gay rights agenda and moved aggressively to pursue common goals in the political arena.

This sudden transformation of the movement is puzzling. How did the movement come to settle in this way at this moment? How, in general, does settlement occur? This question, in both its general and specific forms, can best be addressed by drawing on both social movement and organizational theory, as "weaknesses in one field…might be redressed

Armstrong, E.A. 2005. "From Struggle to Settlement: The Crystallization of a Field of Lesbian/Gay Organizations in San Francisco, 1969–1973." Pp. 161–187 in *Social Movements and Organization Theory*, edited by Gerald Davis, Doug McAdam, W. Richard Scott, and Mayer Zald, New York: Cambridge University Press. Reprinted by permission.

by insights from the other" (McAdam and Scott 2005. Institutionalists have studied institutional reproduction, social movement scholars have studied challenges, but few have examined the role of conflict in producing new orders.[1] Scholars of revolutions and social movements have focused on the sources of revolutions and social movements, while treating the return of order after a cycle of social protest as a natural consequence of the decline of factors facilitating movements.[2] Along with other scholars, many of whom are represented in this volume, I attempt to integrate organizational and social movement scholarship in order to advance our understanding of institutional change.

McAdam and Scott, and Campbell, argue in this volume that integrating organizational and social movement theory is eased by overlap and commonality between the fields. Campbell 2005: 42 points out that organizational and social movement literatures theorize the "mechanisms by which organizations and social movements develop and change" in similar terms. Thus, both literatures would expect political opportunities, framing, and strategic leadership to be factors in field crystallization 2005. And they are, as I will show. However, both social movement and organizational sociologists often implicitly assume a stable political opportunity structure. I argue that framing and strategic leadership operate differently in unstable institutional environments, and that understanding how they do so is central to understanding processes of field crystallization. Stable political environments encourage, discourage, and channel action more predictably than unstable environments. Framing is a more difficult task when it is unclear with what actors should resonate. Unstable situations often bring multiple cultural strands into contact and generate feelings of possibility that allow for more creative cultural recombination, or bricolage. And, as Fligstein argues, strategic leadership is both more important and more difficult under conditions of uncertainty (Fligstein 1997a, 1997b, 2001b; Swidler 1986, 2001).

In addition, neither social movement nor organizational sociology pays sufficient attention to temporal processes. While Campbell 2005 does not claim that the mechanisms he discusses are exhaustive, his neglect of temporality might lead others to neglect it as well. The unfolding of process over time plays an important role in both of the cases that McAdam and Scott (2005) discuss, but the theoretical importance of time is not highlighted in their analyses. Elsewhere McAdam reveals that he is highly cognizant of the importance of temporality in social movement processes. In a coauthored piece, McAdam and Sewell argue that "the precise sequencing of actions over the course of a few hours or days and the particular contingencies faced by actors at particular times may have structuring effects over a very long run" (2001: 102). Historians and historical institutionalists have also emphasized the importance of temporality (Buthe 2002; Pierson 2000a; Sewell 1996; Thelen 2000). Events unfold and occur in time, in particular sequences and over long or short durations.

In the pages that follow I demonstrate the power of environmental, framing, strategic leadership and temporal mechanisms by employing them to explain how and why the field of lesbian/gay organizations crystallized as an identity and rights movement instead of a revolutionary one.

Explaining Field Settlement

Studying institutional crisis is central to the study of social change. Durable social arrangements often consolidate as periods of upheaval come to a close. In 1991 Walter W. Powell hypothesized that, "when change does occur…it is likely to be episodic, highlighted by a brief period of crisis or critical intervention, and followed by longer periods of stability or path-dependent development" (1991: 197; Stinchcombe 1965). Similarly, William H. Sewell, Jr. (1996) has observed that major changes tend to occur around dramatic crises and monumental historical events. This section discusses existing theories of field crystallization, contrasting structural

approaches with more process-oriented approaches. Before describing these competing theories of field crystallization, I first discuss the concept of the "field" and the identification of stable and unstable fields.

Identifying Crisis and Stability

Stable fields are "organized around local rules of action and conceptions of membership" (Fligstein and McAdam 1995: 2–3).[3] These local rules are institutionalized; they are "stable and self-reproducing," and provide shared understandings about the goals of an enterprise, who can participate in it, and how the enterprise is to be pursued (Jepperson 1991: 145; Swidler 2001: 202). Actors' identities and interests are produced by and stabilized by fields. These "rules of the game" benefit some actors more than others, providing some with more resources and power than others. Differences in power are created by and depend upon fields. Fligstein argues that "preexisting rules of interaction and resource distributions operate as sources of power" (2001b: 5).

A field is in crisis, is "unsettled" (Swidler 1986, 2001), or experiencing a "structural dislocation," "rupture," (Sewell 1996: 845) or "critical juncture" (Campbell, 2005) if "major groups are having difficulty reproducing their privilege, as the rules that have governed interaction are no longer working" (Fligstein 2001b: 26). Sewell sees such moments as characterized by uncertainty about how to proceed, because "no one [can] be entirely sure what actions [are] safe or dangerous, moral or wicked, advantageous or foolish, rational or irrational" (1996: 848). Actors often experience these crises as emotionally unsettling (Sewell 1996: 865).

The process of moving an arena from a state of disorganization to a state of organization has been referred to variously as field structuration, consolidation, institutionalization, or crystallization (DiMaggio and Powell 1983). Zysman (1994) refers to the process of arriving at new institutional settlements. Campbell (2005) refers to "lock in." Unsettled moments are usually, but not always, brief and quickly resolved. Established rules enable actors to pursue orderly lines of action with a reasonable degree of certainty about the consequences of action (Swidler 1986, 2001).

Because fields do not exist independently of actors' collective conceptions of them, the stability of a field is always at risk. Small ruptures are usually "repressed, pointedly ignored, or explained away" (Sewell 1996: 843), but there always exists the possibility that ruptures might escalate and become threatening. DiMaggio explains that "large-scale cultural changes may be caused by large-scale, more-or-less simultaneous frame switches by many interdependent actors" (1997: 15). The wholesale abandonment of the rules of the game is relatively rare because those who benefit usually continue to engage "in actions that have always worked to their advantage" until (and often beyond) the point when it is clear that their old strategies no longer work (Fligstein 2001b: 37). This devotion to the rules of the game sometimes operates as a self-fulfilling prophecy. By acting as if the rules of the game still apply, dominant actors are sometimes able to restabilize the field.

"The distinction between continuity and change [in fields] is one of degree, not of kind" (McAdam and Sewell 2001:121), which makes the task of distinguishing between stable and unstable fields difficult. Fields also evolve through "the accumulation of small revisions" in the course of institutional reproduction (Sewell 1996: 843; see also Clemens and Cook 1999). Stable fields are dynamic; they must be able to "neutralize" and "reabsorb" challenges presented by changing environments (Sewell 1996: 843).

Processes Producing Field Settlement
Most research on how political opportunities, framing, and strategic leadership shape movements and organizations assumes relatively stable arenas. However, understanding field crystallization requires theorizing action under conditions of uncertainty. How does order reemerge when it is no longer possible for actors to determine what the consequences of action are likely to be? This section discusses how framing and strategic leadership operate differently in unstable institutional environments, and how both are dependent upon temporal processes.

Arguments about political opportunity structures' effects on organizations and movements rest on the premise that environmental rigidities enable some possibilities and block others. While the influence of political opportunity structures on action is viewed as indirect (as actors must first define opportunities in order to act), scholars generally assume that the strategy and structure of movements will reflect environmental constraints and opportunities.

Political process models are intended to analyze how actors respond to political environments in flux. Authors such as Doug McAdam (1982) have demonstrated that it is often when environments shift, opening up new opportunities, that movements emerge. But even models attentive to the dynamism of political opportunities often assume that the evolving environment continues to be predictable and transparent. In short, political opportunity structure models assume institutionalized environments.

Existing explanations of field crystallization tend to refer to a background institutionalized order to account for the shape of the new field (Brint and Karabel 1991: 346; Carruthers and Babb 1996: 1578–9; Rao 1998: 918; Starr 1982; 8). As Rao explains, "when multiple frames and forms vie with each other, why one form is chosen and why other roads are not pursued hinge on larger constellations of power and social structure" (1998; 912). Brint and Karabel found that the field of American community colleges developed in relationship to four-year colleges and business organizations (1991).

But in times of severe upheaval it is often not clear what is possible and what it is not. These are situations in which the rules of the game are called into question. The more thoroughly the rules have broken down, the more challenging it is for actors to reach agreement, because the more uncertainty there is about how to disagree, and the less binding the results of contestation (Morrill 1991; Stinchcombe 1999).

Just as actors organize their action in response to environmental rigidity, they also respond to environmental uncertainty. Action is less predictable when it is not clear which strategies are likely to be effective and which are not. Actors tend to experience these moments of environmental uncertainty as "crisis." Crises tend to generate extreme emotion, both positive and negative (Sewell 1996). Sometimes cognitive restraints on imagining alternative ways of doing things lift, opening up a moment of collective creativity (Armstrong 2002a; Sewell 1996). The high emotion and collective creativity of the moment can generate action that appears irrational once order is reestablished. These moments are sometimes characterized by the intersection of cultural currents usually kept distinct (Armstrong 2002a). The combination of a sense of possibility and the presence of multiple cultural options generates particularly creative forms of bricolage. Bricolage refers to the "innovative recombination of elements that constitute a new way of configuring organizations, movements, institutions, and other forms of social activity" (Campbell 2005; see also Clemens and Cook 1999). However, the lack of clear environmental signals about the consequences of action may generate conflict about how to proceed. Thus, crisis may be highly creative but also paralyzing. In general, the desire for action to have predictable results leads most actors to have an investment in the reestablishment of order.

Research on framing typically has assumed the existence of stable cultural repertoires which strategic actors attempt to resonate with in order to accomplish their goals (Benford and Snow 2000; Snow and Benford 1988, 1992; Snow et al. 1986). Framing is based on the notion that "activists must frame issues in ways that resonate with...supporters....Frames mediate between opportunity structures and action because they provide the means with which people can interpret the political opportunities before them and, thus, decide how best to pursue their objectives" (Campbell 2005: 48–49). This suggests that a stable political opportunity structure exists to be interpreted. Framing is more difficult when the environment is uncertain. Actors may find it useful to build a variety of ambiguous frames, investing little in any of them, in situations where it is not yet clear which coalition or set of rules will organize the arena. In these circumstances, successful framing activity may not be so much about resonating with a stable aspect of culture, but about being able to "realign" and shift allegiances rapidly. The activity of framing under conditions of uncertainty may involve guesswork, intuition, and rapid adjustment.

Consequently, strategic leadership is more difficult under conditions of uncertainly (Fligstein 1997a, 1997b, 2001b; Swidler 1986, 2001). Social skill is "the ability to induce cooperation among others. Skilled social actors empathetically relate to the situations of other people and in doing so, are able to provide

those people with reasons to cooperate" (Fligstein 2001b: 112). "Some social actors are more capable at inducing cooperation than others" (Fligstein 2001b: 112). Fligstein points out that "in fields where there is little internal turbulence or external threat, it is possible that social skill matters less for the reproduction of groups" (2001b: 117). When fields are in crisis, actors struggle to clarify differences, forge agreements, and mobilize consensus. They circulate a variety of different possible solutions. Coalitions try to convince others to get behind the frame they have proposed. The ability of new groups to consolidate fields depends "on their being able to convince a large number of actors that changing the rules is in their interest" (Fligstein 1997b: 403).

Temporality matters by shaping the ways in which actors and frames intersect with shifting political opportunities. Whether or not a field "locks in" may depend on whether actors and frames manage to come together before a particular window of opportunity closes. If actors with the right cultural tools happen to be in place when an opportunity emerges, a field may form. Political opportunities are not static but active, flowing, changing processes. Opportunities have to be grabbed when and where they present themselves. Thus, it matters precisely where and when opportunities occur in time and space. They are moments of possibility that may or may not present themselves to actors again in precisely the same form.

Sewell's work on revolutionary France vividly demonstrates how temporality matters. He found that without a unique confluence of circumstances, the taking of the Bastille would not have been a "world-shaping" event. This outcome depended on what Sewell refers to as "conditions peculiar to the circumstance." Sewell builds his understanding of the importance of particular conditions on the work of Marshall Sahlins, who used "the term 'structure of the conjuncture' to refer to the particular meanings, accidents, and causal forces that shape events—the small but locally determining conditions whose interaction in a particular place and time may seal the fates of whole societies" (Sewell 1996: 862; see also Sahlins 1981 and Jacobs 1996). While Sewell does not refer to "fields" or "field settlement" in his work, his theory can be seen as illustrating the role of contingent sequences of historical events in field crystallization.

The Study

One question motivating the collection of the data analyzed here was why lesbian/gay organizations in San Francisco seemed to be diversifying over time instead of homogenizing, as predicted by DiMaggio and Powell (1983). I created a database of all lesbian/gay organizations existing in San Francisco from the years 1950 to 1994 by coding listings of organizations in periodicals, resource guides, and directories.[4] This data set provided an exhaustive record of the forms of organization extant at each point in time.

After constructing the data set, I attempted to measure the diversification of the field. It gradually became clear that the organizations were not similar enough to each other even to identify dimensions along which it was meaningful to measure diversity and homogeneity. Comparing homosexual organizations founded in the 1960s with those founded in the 1970s was like comparing apples and oranges. However, if I looked only at organizations formed after 1972 it was possible to measure their homogenization and diversification. This indicated a relatively sudden increase in the coherence of this collective project in the early 1970s.

Once I realized this, I turned to describing and explaining the crystallization of this field. Stinchcombe noted in 1965 that "organizational types generally originate rapidly in a relatively short historical period, to grow and change slowly after that period" (1965: 168). The forging of new fields tends to be associated with the development of new organizational forms and the rapid proliferation of these organizations. The sudden proliferation of organizations in this case provided a vivid picture of field founding: the emergence of guides to lesbian/gay nonprofit organizations provided another indicator of field crystallization.[5]

To those familiar with the history of the lesbian/gay movement in the United States, the notion that there was a rupture in the late 1960s and early 1970s is hardly surprising. All accounts of the development of the gay movement confirm the existence and importance of this rupture. I analyzed both archival and secondary sources to provide a detailed description of the shift. Once I described the crystallization of the field, I turned to primary and secondary sources to analyze why it crystallized when and how it did.

Successful institutionalization tends to produce the view that the resulting settlement was natural or inevitable—that the outcome could not have been otherwise (Clemens 1997). Sometimes the fact that a particular arena was ever organized differently is forgotten. I attempt to dislodge the assumption of inevitability in this case by developing counterfactuals—by pointing out the various paths the gay movement might have taken if events had unfolded differently. To reconstruct the feel of open-endedness that characterizes social life on the ground and in the moment—when actors do not know how things are going to turn out, and when, in fact, outcomes are not yet determined—it is important to rely on evidentiary materials created in the heat of the moment, and to be skeptical of accounts constructed after the fact.

The Crystallization of the Lesbian/Gay Movement

Homophile organizations that were formed in the 1950s mark the beginning of a continuous thread of organizing on behalf of homosexuals in the United States (D'Emilio 1983; Licata 1981; Marotta 1981; Martin and Lyon 1991).[6] They hoped to improve life for homosexuals by educating the mainstream public (Bernstein 1997, 2002; D'Emilio 1983; Epstein 1999). After brief experimentation with secretive structures borrowed from Communist Party organizations, homophile organizations modeled themselves on public nonprofit organizations (D'Emilio 1983). They adopted names that conveyed little explicit information about sexual identity, such as the Society for Individual Rights, the Daughters of Bilitis, and the Mattachine Society. By adopting conventional organizational forms, particularly winning legal incorporation, they endeavored to enhance the legitimacy of their cause (D'Emilio 1983). Homophile activist Marvin Cutler boasted in 1956 that Mattachine was "incorporated under the strict requirements of California law, to insure impeccable propriety and civic nonpartisanship at all times" (1956: 10).

Although usually dated from the Stonewall riots that took place in New York in late June 1969, the gay liberation movement had been under way in San Francisco since at least April of that year (Armstrong 2002b; Murray 1996; Stryker and Van Buskirk 1996). Often treated as merely another outgrowth of the

New Left, gay liberation was deeply influenced by and embattled with the preexisting homophile movement (D'Emilio 1983; Duberman 1993; Marotta 1981; Stein 2000). Contemporary accounts focus on gay liberation as the source of a politics of gay pride centered on "coming out," but at the peak of the movement gay liberation also saw itself as part of a broader New Left coalition bringing about a revolutionary transformation of society (D'Emilio 1983; Jay and Young 1992 [1972]; Kissack 1995).

At its peak, gay liberation was composed of three analytically distinct currents.[7] Gay power sought the overthrow of capitalism and the creation of a liberated society in which sexual identity categories would no longer be necessary. Gay power activists, who saw themselves as gay revolutionaries, fought for sexual liberation for all, not just for rights for gay-identified people. This strain of gay liberation, organized around a redistributive political logic, was deeply indebted to the socialist ideas of the New Left. Gay power activists saw themselves as a vanguard, as part of a movement that would improve society for everyone, not just for a particular group. While gay power activists endorsed coming out, they did not see the affirmation of gay identity as the end goal of sexual politics. They saw the creation of gay identity as merely a step toward the goal of getting rid of sexual identity categories altogether (Altman 1993: 239). Gay power activists believed that "everyone is gay, everyone is straight," and that gay liberation should lead to "a far greater acceptance of human sexuality and with that...a decrease in the stigma attached to unorthodox sex and a corresponding increase in overt bisexuality" (Altman 1993: 246). Consequently, in their view, "Gay, in its most far-reaching sense, means not homosexual, but sexually free" (Young 1992 [1972]: 28).

In contrast, a second strain of gay liberation, which I refer to as gay pride, saw the solidification of gay identity as the primary goal of gay politics. Gay pride endeavored to build gay culture and community through forming support groups and other kinds of gay organizations. Dennis Altman (1993: 242) described the difference between gay pride and gay power as follows: "The liberal sees homosexuals as a minority to be assisted into a full place in society. The radical sees homosexuality as a component of all people including her- or himself." Gay power

activists thought all revolutionaries should come out as gay, thus contributing to the blurring of sexual identity categories. Gay pride activists felt that only those individuals sincerely interested in same-gender sexual relations should come out.

The third current, inherited from the homophile movement, believed that the situation of gays could be improved through single-issue interest group politics seeking rights. Gay rights activists identified themselves primarily as gay and worked to improve life for gay people. Gay rights activists were never convinced that revolution was the answer. Indeed, they were often skeptical about how homosexuals would fare under socialism.[8] They believed in the reform of the current system, and advocated working within mainstream institutions. Gay rights activists criticized gay power's attention to issues other than those of concern for homosexuals. They questioned whether other radicals would reciprocate and take up homosexual issues. Gay rights activists rejected violent means in favor of working within the political system and engaging in clever cultural "zaps." Gay rights activists tended to see the building of identity as a necessary precursor to institutional politics, while gay pride activists saw engaging in gay rights politics as a way to build gay identity.

Radical gay liberation fell into disarray in 1970 (D'Emilio 1992a; Humphreys 1972). As it disintegrated, a more moderate gay movement crystallized. In the early 1970s, observers noted that it seemed like something new was forming. Sociologist Laud Humphreys noted that in 1970, "the old-line, civil-libertarian thesis and the gay liberationist antithesis began to produce a synthesis" (Humphreys 1972: 123). *The Advocate,* a prominent Los Angeles gay newspaper, proclaimed in September 1971 that

Between the hard conservatives and the intolerant radicals, young Gays are finding the middle ground productive. From coast to coast, they are building new organizations modeled after New York's highly successful and active Gay Activists Alliance. The formula; just enough structure and planning to have a sound foundation but not so much that action is impossible. Also, most new groups are limiting their activity to gay-oriented issues, rather than tackling all the world's ills at once. It seems to be a formula that can win the widespread support that the GLF's (Gay Liberation Front) were never able to get.

This new coherence in the gay political project manifested itself in a variety of ways. It sparked the rapid proliferation of a diversity of new gay organizations. These new organizations had more specialized names reflecting a continuously unfolding variety of new identities and subidentities, such as Affirmation Gay/Lesbian Mormons, Gay Asian Pacific Alliance, Straights for Gay Rights, Gay American Indians, Digital Queers, and the Bay Area Bisexual Network (1995). Organization names included elaborate identity information and represented specialized subidentities. These organizations included gay religious organizations (e.g., the Metropolitan Community Church, founded 1970), gay self-help organizations (e.g., Gay Alcoholics Anonymous, founded 1971), gay hobby organizations (e.g., San Francisco Front Runners, founded 1974), and gay parenting groups (e.g., Lesbian Mothers' Union, founded in 1971). The use of bold sexual identity terminology in organizations'

names illustrated their new devotion to pride and identity building. The sudden explosion of support groups, which were unheard of before 1970, created contexts in which individuals could discover and express themselves.

The changing density of various kinds of homosexual organizations provided another confirmation of the timing of the consolidation of the gay identity movement. Figure 1 shows the decline of both homophile and gay liberation organizations and the proliferation of gay rights and gay pride organizations. The existence of multiple kinds of organizations in the years from 1969 to 1972 indicates the unsettled nature of the field, which coalesced in the early 1970s.

The creation of resource guides in the early seventies also indicated field crystallization. While the community published bar guides throughout the 1960s, the first guides to list both nonprofit and commercial organizations were published, in

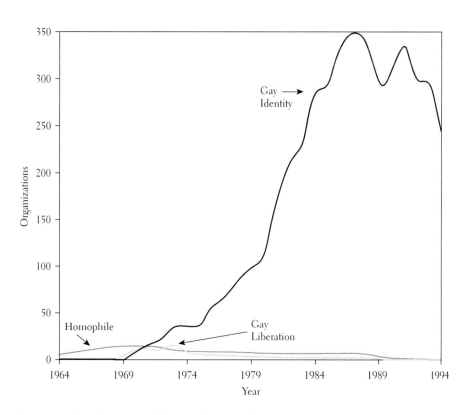

Figure 9.1 Total Number of Homophile, Gay Liberation, and Gay Identity Organizations in San Francisco, 1964–1994

1972. *Gayellow Pages,* the first national guide to both nonprofit and commercial organizations to be published annually, was first published in 1973. These guides listed bars and bathhouses as well as political and cultural organizations, revealing that gay activists saw their project in terms of the expansion of all kinds of gay social space.

Today, lesbian/gay freedom day parades occur in all major U.S. cities and some small towns each June. The intent of the founders of the parades was to commemorate the June 1969 Stonewall uprisings in New York. Organizers of the first parade in New York in 1970 defined the event as an opportunity for the gay community to show its pride, its unity, and its diversity. San Francisco organized its first freedom day parade in 1972, and has had a parade every year since. Each year the original language of "pride," "celebration," "unity," and "diversity" appears in parade themes and mission statements.

The year 1972 also marked the first time, after years of effort, that a national conference of homosexual organizations reached a consensus on a political platform (Humphreys 1972: 165). In February 1972, at a National Coalition of Gay Organizations, jointly sponsored by New York's Gay Activists Alliance and Chicago's Gay Alliance, eighty-five organizations from eighteen states agreed on a Gay Rights Platform in preparation for the 1972 elections (Humphreys 1972: 162). Never before had a national conference of gay organizations been able to agree on a gay stance. Throughout the late 1960s multiple attempts had failed to produce such a consensus (Humphreys 1972: 165). Together, these indicators provide strong evidence of field consolidation in the early 1970s. The next section explains how this outcome came to pass.

Explaining Field Crystallization

The movement that developed in the 1970s and 1980s was not the only kind of movement that could have been organized on behalf of homosexuals. Even in 1969, when much of the groundwork for the contemporary lesbian/gay movement was in place, the shape (and even the existence) of the future movement was not fully determined. Activists might have endorsed a more revolutionary option, as did some aspects of the New Left. Or the movement could have split off into different wings, as

did the women's movement. It is also possible to imagine internal conflict destroying the movement altogether. The crystallization of a field of lesbian/gay organizations was not inevitable, but a result of political decisions made within a historically specific context. Below I demonstrate that framing and strategic leadership were much more difficult at the peak of the New Left. Thus, the decline of the New Left, which made the political environment more transparent, rapidly changed the environment in which activists struggled to arrive at the best way to proceed. The timing of the intersection of homosexual organizing with the New Left, and of the decline of the New Left, played a crucial role in determining what actors, political approaches, and possibilities intersected. Even slight differences in the way events unfolded might have led to different convergences among actors, political models, and political possibilities that could have channeled the movement in a different direction.

How Possibility Paralyzes

Few would dispute that the 1960s was a time of great cultural and political upheaval in the United States. The generalized nature of the cultural crisis called into question the rules of multiple arenas. Debra Minkoff described "an open environment for social action that was (and is) unmatched in U.S. history" (1999: 1669). Todd Gitlin, who was deeply involved in the New Left, described "the hallucinatory giddiness of the late Sixties...whose sheer wildness, even now, seems the stuff of another century...people were living with a supercharged density: lives were bound up with one another, making claims on one another, drawing one another into the common project." The expansive feeling of possibility expanded the boundaries of the thinkable, producing "unraveling, rethinking, refusing to take for granted, thinking without limits..." (Gitlin 1987: 7). Wini Breines, also an activist, echoed Gitlin's description of the moment: "We believed that we were going to make a revolution. We were convinced that we could transform America through our political activity and insights....A deep enthusiasm characterized our faith in our own political and social power....The new left opened everything to scrutiny" (1989: xxi-xxii).

The relaxation of beliefs about the impossibility of major structural change in the United States, combined with the intense interaction characteristic of crisis and the intersection of distinct cultural traditions, created an unusual context of collective creativity (Armstrong 2002a). The encounter with the New Left introduced homosexual activists to new ways of thinking about organizing around sexuality. Introduction to an identity logic generated new strategies such as coming out, pride parades, rap groups, and cultural zaps. Coming out, the practice of revealing one's sexual identity for psychological, cultural, and political gain, seems obvious now. However, until homosexual activists were able to conceive of the public revelation of sexuality as politically productive, the practice did not and would not have developed. These new strategies developed through bricolage, in this case the combining of elements of the New Left with homosexual movement approaches.

The encounter between the New Left and the homophile movement was historically contingent. Had homophile politics not collided with the New Left, say, because of an earlier decline of the New Left, it is not certain that strategies such as coming out would have been created. Cornerstone assumptions of contemporary gay politics owe much to the fact that an existing homosexual movement collided with the New Left early enough in the New Left's lifespan for the gay movement to experience the full creative benefit of involvement with this encounter. The cultural tools needed to forge the lesbian/gay movement field were created in the encounter between existing homophile organizations and the New Left.

However, this moment of creativity also generated political conflict. The intersection of the New Left and a preexisting homophile movement generated the view that gay liberation could not be achieved without simultaneously addressing class, race, and gender inequality. In 1969, it was very difficult for activists to assess what was politically possible. The fate of the New Left was not yet clear. Some still felt that revolutionary change was possible, while others had lost faith, and still others had never been convinced. Activists fought about what was politically possible as well as about what

was politically desirable. It was difficult to ascertain whether it made more sense to support the gay power frame which aligned the gay movement with the New Left and its revolutionary project, or to support gay rights and gay pride frames which resonated more readily with fundamental features of the American political environment. In 1969, though, in the midst of the excitement of the moment, the limits of the politically possible were opaque.

Throughout the fall of 1969 and the spring of 1970, conflict between the various strands of gay liberation escalated. In November 1969, a faction of New York's Gay Liberation Front (GLF) split off to found the Gay Activists Alliance (Dong 1995; Marotta 1981: 142). The issue which brought the crisis to a head was whether the Gay Liberation Front should support the Black Panthers (Dong 1995; Marotta 1981: 135, 142; Teal 1995: 78). Gay liberation activists on the West Coast also faced the Black Panther issue. According to Rt. Rev. Michael Irkin, the November 15, 1969, March for Peace revealed

> a clear division in the ranks of the Homosexual Liberation Movement as represented by the Committee for Homosexual Freedom, the Gay Liberation Theatre, the Gay Liberation Front, and some other groups. [This] became clear to all during the rally at the Polo Grounds when, during the speech of David Hilliard of the Black Panther Party, dissension broke out when some of our members, among them the author of this article and some others under our banner, joined with other pacifists in shouting down David Hilliard's speech with cries of "Peace, Now!" while others showed their support of his statements with clenched-fist salutes and cries of enthusiasm (Irkin 1969: 8).

Irkin was critical of the Black Panther Party, while the gay power activists were enthusiastic supporters. Irkin felt that "under the pretense of speaking for peace, [Hilliard had] called for violence.... We cannot see that violence, in any man's hand, is any less violence" (Irkin 1969:9). In response, Irkin clarified the ideological differences internal to gay liberation: "[The Committee for Homosexual Freedom] at present has among its members many who have not come to any particular socio-economic or political philosophy. While the majority of our members...call themselves socialists, I know personally of at least a few members who believe that capitalism should continue in some modified form" (Irkin 1969: 8). Similar conflicts about related issues occurred in late 1969 and 1970.

Thus, the encounter between the New Left and the homophile movement created potentially paralyzing internal conflict. The intensity of the conflict could have become debilitating, as it did for other parts of the New Left. By introducing new cultural possibilities and making the context difficult to read, this unsettled moment escalated the social skill required to arrive at a stable way of organizing around sexuality. This provides an example of how unstable political environments influence action differently than stable environments. In stable environments actors may be able to assess opportunities and constraints with reasonable accuracy. In unstable environments this is less possible. Uncertainty may generate intense conflict about how to proceed, as it did among gay activists in 1969. However, this particular case does not allow us the opportunity to see if and how activists are able to stabilize political projects in uncertain environments, as the environment grew more predictable with the rapid demise of the New Left in 1970 and 1971.

The Timing and Rapidity of the Decline of the New Left

In the 1960s many movement activists believed the United States was on the verge of radical social change (Gitlin 1987). This optimism faded quickly as the sixties came to a close. Scholars point to the election of Richard Nixon as a political turning point: "The 1968 election of Richard Nixon signaled a turn away from the supportive political agendas associated with the Kennedy-Johnson decades, and as antiwar and student movements escalated, a period of intensive political retrenchment began" (Minkoff 1995: 65). By the early seventies, it was clear that revolutionary change was not likely.

Students for a Democratic Society (SDS) "burned up and out in a spectacular fashion" in 1969 and 1970 (Echols 1992: 22; Polletta 2002). Echols noted that "the conventional sixties' story line," developed by white male leaders who have written on the New Left, tends to equate the disintegration of the SDS with the end of "radicalism," finalized by

the "February 1970 Greenwich Village townhouse explosion" (1992: 23). Humphreys and Echols also pointed to the Kent State killings later that year as a common marker for the end of radicalism (Echols 1992: 23; Gitlin 1987; Humphreys 1972).

Feminists Wini Breines and Alice Echols de-emphasized SDS in their accounts of the radicalism of the times and claimed that male leaders exaggerated "the significance of the collapse of SDS at the end of the decade" (Breines 1989: xv; Echols 1992).

> What is overlooked in accounts that focus on the fate of SDS as an organization is the mass movement after 1968, regional and local activity not dependent upon a national organization, students organizing and grass-roots activists (including women and people of color), the counterculture, and the significance of the birth of other movements such as the women's liberation and gay movements. (Breines 1989: xv)

Alice Echols argued, "if one's narrative is conceptualized around the idea that radicalism was simply played out by the decade's end, then there really is only token narrative space available for women's liberation (or for the Chicano, Native American, or gay and lesbian movements)" (1992: 13). Breines and Echols have a point. Radicalism did survive beyond 1970, but the demise of the SDS in 1970 marked a fundamental shift in the nature of activism and the optimism associated with it. Activism shifted away from an effort to bring about a socialist transformation of society, and away from Marxist-influenced, class-oriented, redistributive politics.

While opportunities for some forms of political action contracted in the late sixties and early seventies, other opportunities began to expand. Debra Minkoff has shown in her work on women's and racial-ethnic organizations that while it became more difficult to form and maintain protest organizations, the environment improved for more moderate service and policy advocacy organizations. She argues that: "The increasing efforts at law and order during the Nixon administration and into the 1980s did not so much repress collective action as channel it into more institutionally acceptable organizational activity" (Minkoff 1995: 74).[9] Minkoff, drawing on the work of Jenkins and Walker, pointed to the improved "funding opportunities" for "interest groups and a broader range of policy advocacy organizations" in the seventies (1995: 55).[10] Foundations increased their level of support for nonprofit organizing. "Congressional reforms that began in the early 1960s gradually decentralized authority, creating broader opportunities for non-profit advocacy" (Jenkins 1987:301). In 1969 and 1976 the tax deductibility of contributions to nonprofit organizations involved in political advocacy were liberalized (Jenkins 1987: 301). McCarthy, Britt, and Wolfson (1991) describe the emergence of a "tangle of incentives" pushing movements toward nonprofit organizational forms.

While more radical socialist ideologies lost their luster, the pursuit of ethnic group equality and civil rights remained viable. Together, the Civil Rights Act of 1964, the Voting Rights Act of 1965, and the Equal Employment Opportunity Act of 1972 enhanced the political utility of an ethnic self-characterization. An ethnic framing of gay identity and an orientation toward gay civil rights fit nicely with the structure of American politics (D'Emilio 1992 [1972]: xxvii; Epstein 1987: 2; Gamson 1998: 20). Epstein noted that "This 'ethnic' self-characterization by gays and lesbians has a clear political utility, for it has permitted a form of group organizing that is particularly suited to the American experience, with its history of civil-rights struggles and ethnic-based, interest-group competition" (1987: 2).

In addition, the cultural permissiveness introduced by the 1960s survived well into the 1970s. A revolution in the sexual mores of heterosexual Americans, particularly the young, was ongoing. The broader cultural focus on authenticity, therapy, self-actualization, and "doing your own thing" supported an acceptance of gay identity and lifestyle as one possible result of a search for a "true self."

How the Rapid Decline of the New Left Mattered

The most commonsensical story about how the decline of the New Left mattered for the gay movement is that it simply accommodated to a political environment growing more conservative. In an essay drafted in 1991, historian John D'Emilio argued that

> one reason [for the demise of gay power] is that the soil that fertilized GLF, the radicalism of the 1960s,

was drying up rapidly. The belief that a revolution was imminent and that gays and lesbians should get on board was fast losing whatever momentary plausibility it had. By the early 1970s, the nation was entering a long period of political conservatism and economic retrenchment. With every new proclamation of revolutionary intentions, radicals compromised their credibility. (D'Emilio 1992b: 245)

The plausibility of this account is difficult to dispute. And, indeed, it is part of the story. The decline of the New Left revealed a political environment more transparent and more conservative than what had gone before. In this new context, gay activists found gay power's revolutionary vision less plausible than gay rights or gay pride approaches.

However, simply pointing to the implausibility of revolutionary change is an incomplete explanation. Not all parts of the New Left responded to the change in the political environment by modulating their notions of what was possible and desirable. Some parts of the New Left remained committed to revolutionary visions. Some even turned to violence. Why gay activists found it relatively easy, compared to other New Left activists, to turn away from a multi-issue social justice vision still must be explained. The answer lies partially with the timing and rapidity of the decline of the New Left. Gay activism intersected with the New Left long enough to benefit from the tremendous creativity of the moment but not so long as to enable many gay activists to become deeply invested in the more radical political project.

As mentioned above, the encounter between the homophile movement and the New Left provided the crucible in which the gay pride model, emphasizing coming out and identity expression, was forged. The existence of this model provided an alternative to the radical gay power approach—an alternative that became increasingly appealing as its mobilizing power started to become obvious. In New York, the Gay Activists Alliance (GAA) staged highly successful cultural zaps. The GAA, tailored to the "'hip' homosexual mainstream" was "activist but nonviolent, imaginative, cool, and very successful" (Humphreys 1972: 160; Marotta 1981: 146). In San Francisco, the Society for Individual Rights (SIR) was aware of the successes of the GAA in New

York. In June 1971, the SIR's publication, *Vector,* expressed admiration for New York's GAA, while criticizing New York's GLF. The *Vector* editor indicated that the SIR needed to adapt to stay vital: "Gay liberation is on the move and if SIR does not stay aboard it will go the way of the Mattachine Society" (*Vector* 1971: 4). SIR organizers situated themselves in a parallel position to New York's GAA. Activists observed what seemed to work and imitated it.

The SIR experienced immediate success with the gay pride formulation. In June 1971 the SIR organized a "work-in" at the. San Francisco Federal Building. This ingenious demonstration involved homosexuals (with signs on their lapels identifying themselves as such) volunteering their services to the government "until they were 'fired' by the Security Guards. For a time, Uncle Sam had homosexuals working for free in the IRS, Federal Employment Information Center, the US Printing Office Book Store, and homosexuals working as Indian Guides, and elevator operators. The Federals went into a 'panic' when a homosexual tried to be a janitor, by pushing a broom across the lobby" (Broshears 1971: 1). This demonstration was organized to protest "what SIR's president, Bill Plath, called 'an unjust government policy in refusing to employ homosexuals'" (Broshears 1971: 1).

Thus, part of the reason that gay activists turned away from gay power was that an exciting alternative existed. That this alternative existed, and was beginning to reveal its potential, is a consequence of the timing of the intersection between homophile and New Left movements. People are less likely to abandon a line of action, even one that is doomed, if they do not have an alternative available. However, people do not always support even the most exciting alternatives if they are already deeply committed to another approach (Wilde 2004). And, here, timing played a role in gay activists' relative lack of commitment to radical politics.

The intersection between homosexual organizing and the New Left was brief, limiting homosexual commitment to a revolutionary agenda. By the time gay liberation emerged in 1969, signs of the decline of the New Left were evident. Gay activists witnessed the pitfalls of revolutionary politics without experiencing the series of events that led other

movements down that path. Some gay leaders, such as New York's Jim Owles, were self-conscious in their efforts to try to prevent the gay movement from repeating what they saw as the mistakes of other branches of the New Left. In a 1971 statement, Owles made the case that trying to create an ideologically homogenous movement would be a mistake. He asserted that "few of us are anxious to see a uniform and monolithic movement develop out of the foundations we have laid. We have seen other mass movements develop in this direction in the past, only to be torn apart by internal struggles over ideology and leadership, eventually to fail in achieving their goals" (Humphreys 1972: 126–7). Owles saw efforts to develop ideological consensus to be dangerous, potentially leading to movement fictionalization. Thus, the relatively late emergence of gay liberation in the cycle of protest, combined with the very rapid decline of the New Left, helped protect the gay movement from the fate of kindred movements.

The enthusiasm of gay activists for the gay power perspective also was reduced by the reaction of other movements to this attempted alliance. Gay activists reported painful experiences of homophobia within the New Left. Jim Owles, one of the founders of New York's GAA, experienced the New Left as "viciously antihomosexual":

> When [gay liberationists] did go out to other actions—let's say a support rally for the Panthers or the Young Lords or the more radical groups – ... they were still getting spit at. The word faggot was still being used at them. They were relegated to 'back' roles, and were told, 'Don't come out in front! We don't want our groups to become known as homosexual things.' That happened in other groups; in women's lib the lesbians are told, 'Get in the back, We don't want women's lib to be identified as a lesbian movement.' It was just one put-down, spit-in-the-face thing all the way. And I just couldn't do that.... (Teal 1995: 297–8)

Owles was explicit that this treatment contributed to his desire to work in a single-issue organization because in this brief moment of experimentation activists learned that linking homosexual interests with those of other minorities could lead to rejection. The New Left never fully incorporated gay liberation because of the challenge it posed to its gender and sexual politics.

Even with the mixed reception gay liberation received from the women's movement, women's liberation was, of all the various strands of the New Left, most akin to gay liberation. Women's liberationists were already discussing the need to break away from a male-dominated New Left movement by the time gay liberation emerged (Echols 1989: chap. 3). The separation of women's liberation from the New Left decreased the likelihood that gay activists would make a deep commitment to revolutionary politics. If the New Left would not take women's issues seriously, what hope could gay activists have that homosexuality would be taken seriously? In addition, by splitting off from the New Left, the women's movement modeled a possible path for the gay movement and shaped the relationship between women's and gay movements. Just as the women's movement separated from the Left, lesbians turned away from participation in gay politics toward a separatist lesbian feminism (Martin 1970). The departure of women from the gay movement increased the likelihood that the gay movement would turn to a single-issue rights politics. Lesbian involvement in gay liberation militated toward a multi-issue politics because women were more likely to argue that issues of gender and sexuality both needed to be addressed.

Thus, the abandonment of the gay power agenda by gay activists was partly a pragmatic response to a changing environment. Activists wanted the gay movement to survive this tumultuous moment. In this moment when multi-issue movements were floundering, gay activists saw the turn away from multi-issue politics as key to survival. However, pragmatism cannot fully explain the abandonment of gay power. A lack of commitment to radical politics, partially a result of the timing of the decline of the New Left, also played a role. The late development of gay liberation in the cycle of protest meant that the intersection between the homophile movement and the New Left was brief. This, in turn, meant that the vision of gay interest as inextricably connected to the interests of those oppressed in terms of gender, race, and class was tentative. This vision did not stand much of a chance as

gay activists witnessed the failures of more radical approaches, and the successes of the gay pride and gay rights approaches. All of these features of the situation guided activists away from gay power approaches. The lack of appeal of gay power was not inevitable, but a result of the specific historical circumstances.

The fact that white middle-class men created and experimented with gay power politics suggests that a different formulation of gay interest was possible. Interests are constructed and reconstructed, and do not emerge directly from identity, which is itself an historical and political accomplishment. Some gay men were, and still are, advocates of a multiracial, multi-issue social justice politics. A view that assumes that the way actors interpret their interests can be derived from an objective analysis of social structure cannot explain the existence of the many middle-class white men who were and are devoted political radicals.

The abandonment of gay power by many (although not all) gay activists had both immediate and long-term consequences for the movement. In the short run, it reduced conflict internal to the gay movement, and thus, the social skill needed to forge agreements. Given the intensity of the conflict internal to gay liberation in 1969 and 1970, the continuation of those conflicts could have destroyed the movement. Attempting to reach agreement on goals and strategy in an uncertain political context might have led to a slow, contentious movement death. The timing and rapidity of the decline of the New Left meant that activists encountered this new (albeit more conservative) environment in a highly mobilized state. For most, turning to the more moderate gay pride and gay rights approaches did not feel like "selling out," but felt ripe with fresh possibilities. Thus, the rapid decline of the New Left in the early 1970s meant that the political environment became more transparent before activists were worn down by years of disagreement. Thus, the sharp decline of the New Left and the associated rejection of gay power played a pivotal role in the dramatic crystallization of a gay rights/pride agenda and the explosive growth of the gay movement in the 1970s.

Because of the sharpness of the rejection of the gay power agenda, the gay movement became more aggressively single issue than it might otherwise have become. This has had long-term consequences for the inclusivity of the movement. The turn away from gay power meant the abandonment of a politics that saw race, class, and gender politics as inextricably linked with sexual liberation. The race, class, and gender implications of this turn were not lost on activists at the time. The split of the GLF in New York occurred around the issue of the Black Panthers, giving the conflict between gay pride and gay power a distinctively racial cast. When interviewed in the 1990s for the documentary *Out Rage '69,* African American activist Bob Kohler talked about his feelings about the founding of the GAA as if the events had happened yesterday. He explained that, in his view:

> [The Gay Activists Alliance] was formed as a class thing. It was formed because of class and because of race.... The dirty little secret of the gay movement is how and why the GAA was formed.... They wanted white power. And so they let the freaks, the artists, the poets, the drag queens, the street people, the street queens, the blacks, and the colored people keep the GLF. We're going to go form this thing that is going to change laws. That is a good idea. Change laws. But it was mainly reformist. The vision was broken. The vision went. (Dong 1995)

Kohler's palpable sense of loss was fueled by the knowledge that for a brief moment the possibility of a fundamentally different kind of gay identity and movement existed. Middle-class white men experimented with a way of thinking about sexual identity and interest that would have aligned their interests with those disadvantaged in terms of gender, race, and class. But this experimentation had little time to develop. The decline of the New Left shut this conversation down by resolidifying earlier formulations of class, race, and gender interest and identity.

The rapid response of gay activists to the restabilizing of the political environment suggests how much easier it is for people to act collectively (or to agree that it is too dangerous to act collectively) when they receive clear signals from stable environments about the likely consequences of action. Framing and strategic leadership are difficult in unstable environments. This case also provides

an example of the role of temporality in field settlement. While the gay movement abandoned gay power partially because of the pragmatic assessment of political possibility, activists also were guided away from gay power because of *the particular timing and sequence of events.* Had the decline of the New Left unfolded in a different way, activists might have built a more radical (and unsuccessful) movement, or perhaps no movement at all. What we take for granted as the obvious and inevitable way of organizing around sexuality is only one possible outcome.

Discussion and Conclusion

A historically specific sequence of events enabled the crystallization of the lesbian/gay field in San Francisco in the early 1970s. A rapidly changing political environment in the late 1960s engendered a sense of nearly infinite possibility, which, in turn, generated both creative bricolage and internal conflict within the gay movement. Many ways of framing the movement seemed possible and it was difficult to assess which would resonate with surrounding movements and the larger political environment. Thus, strategic leadership at this moment was extremely difficult.

This moment of possibility ended abruptly, when actors suddenly found themselves in a much more predictable environment in the very early 1970s. The task of framing then became easier as it was more obvious which frames were likely to resonate with the larger political environment. While the stabilization of the environment curtailed creativity, the earlier period had generated many creative ideas about how to organize around sexuality. Strategic leadership in this case involved accurately reading the environment and acting to streamline the movement to take advantage of political possibility. Thus, the highly uncertain environment generated creative ideas but also conflict and paralysis, while the more transparent environment curtailed creative activity, but encouraged strategic thinking by allowing activists to select which frames would resonate in the new context. The rapid change in the political environment meant that possibilities that existed in one moment did not in the next. In order to take advantage of these fleeting possibilities it was necessary for actors to be there with cultural tools ready. Actors and frames intersect in contexts created by the unfolding of events over time.

The use of social movement and institutional theory in the explanation of field crystallization has implications for future theoretical development and empirical scholarship. Theoretically, the analysis here suggests that common mechanisms identified by organizational and social movement scholars are a powerful starting point in the analysis of organizational and social movement development and change. However, the analysis here also suggests that both intellectual arenas are much better at understanding social action under conditions of social order than in conditions of serious social upheaval. Both social movement and organizational scholars should attend more closely to the problem of action in conditions of uncertainty, and to sources of innovation and creativity. The analysis also suggests the importance of temporality to processes of field transformation. A variety of social movement theorists currently are focusing on such issues as the roles of place, identity, and emotion in movements (Goodwin, Jasper, and Polletta 2001; Polletta and Jasper 2001; Sewell 2001). It would be a mistake if the intersection between social movement and organizational theory neglected the insights of these scholars and developed an approach based on the shared resource/rationalist basis of much social movement and organizational theory. The third party to this new intersection between social movement and organizational sociology is culture. Attending to culture means attending not only to framing processes, but also to the sources of cultural repertoires, and the ways in which culture is constitutive of structures, institutions, identities, interests, grievances, goals, and strategies.

A focus on processes also has methodological implications. New settlements form through contentious social and political processes. The more that established arrangements are disrupted, the more contentious the process is likely to be. This approach suggests the examination of questions such as: what the rules of the game were before the field was thrown into crisis, how the field became unsettled, who the various actors with stakes in new framings of the field were, how the interests and identities of these actors were reconstructed through the political process, how actors constructed events to be consequential, what the alternatives were that actors were promoting, how one solution or another succeeded at organizing the field, and how the processes unfolded through time.

Studying field transformation and using theory from both institutional and social movements is consistent with the suggestion that social movement scholarship move away from narrow studies of the internal processes of movements (McAdam, Tarrow, and Tilly 2001). Social movement and institutional processes and theories are inextricably connected: we need to understand change to understand social order, and vice versa. Drawing simultaneously on the theories developed in both of these sociological traditions provides a powerful set of analytical tools. These approaches enable the explanation of field transformation in a variety of arenas in society, including economic, political, cultural, medical, educational, and sexual arenas.

NOTES

Thanks to Doug McAdam, Mayer Zald, Huggy Rao, Ann Mische, and Melissa Wilde for comments on earlier versions of this paper.

1. Institutionalists have noted the weakness of their theories in accounting for change. See Brint and Karabel (1991), DiMaggio (1988, 1991), Fligstein (1997a: 29), McAdam and Scott (2005), and Powell (1991: 197). In recent years, scholars have begun explaining institutional change. For examples, see Clemens (1999), Clemens and Cook 1999, Fligstein (1990, 2001a), and Rao (1998).

2. Stinchcombe (1999) criticizes this tendency in research on revolutions.

3. For definitions and discussions of fields see Bourdieu (1977), DiMaggio (1983), DiMaggio and Powell (1983), Fligstein (1990, 1996, 2001b), Fligstein and McAdam (1995), McAdam and Scott (2005), Meyer and Rowan (1977), Mohr (1992), and Scott (1994, 1995).

4. See Armstrong (1998, 2002b) for more details on the construction of the data set.

5. Organizational researchers see resource guides as an indicator of the existence of a field (DiMaggio and Powell 1991; Mohr 1992: 42). Guides provide evidence that participants are aware of being involved in a common enterprise, and evidence of the ways that participants conceive of their enterprise. Guides to nonprofit lesbian/gay organizations did not exist before the early 1970s.

6. Homosexual organizations formed in the 1950s were not the very first such organizations in the United States. Adam

discusses a homosexual rights organization which existed briefly in the 1920s (1987: 42). See also FitzGerald (1986 [1981]), Blasius and Phelan (1997), and Stein (2000).

7. Marotta (1981) developed a more complex categorization of the strains of gay liberation ideology. I borrow the distinction between gay power and gay pride from Teal (1995: 68).

8. This concern manifested itself in a debate within gay liberation about the quality of gay life in Cuba. See Jay and Young (1992 [1972], section 6) and Teal (1995: 77).

9. Minkoff (1995) cites Haines (1984), Jenkins and Ekert (1986), and McAdam (1982). See also McCarthy, Britt, and Wolfson (1991) and Meyer and Imig (1993).

10. See Jenkins (1985a, 1987) and Walker (1983).

10.
Globalization and Transnational Social Movement Organizations

JACKIE SMITH

The transnational integration of markets and political institutions, especially prevalent in recent decades, presents new challenges for organizations of activists seeking to protect their existing rights or entitlements or to advance new claims against power holders. As national markets dissolve into a growing global marketplace, national governments have turned increasingly to international organizations to negotiate new rules about the boundaries of state authority. These interdependent and parallel processes of "globalization" (global market integration) and "internationalization" (the increasing importance of relations between nations)[1] substantially transform the character of the organizational fields in which social movements seek to pursue their interests. This chapter draws from the insights of social movement and organizational scholarship to analyze the changes in the global political economy that are most relevant for social movement actors. It explores whether and how these changes have influenced the character of the population of transnational social movement organizations.

The expansion of the global economy reduces the capacities of states (some more than others) to

Smith Jackie, 2005. "Globalization and Transnational Social Movement Organizations," Pp. 226–248 in *Social Movements and Organizational Theory,* edited, by Gerad Daus, Doug McAdam, W. Richard Scott, and Mayer Zald. New york: Cambridge University Press. Reprinted by permission.

define and enact their own internal economic policies. It thereby prevents the state from carrying out its traditional functions of regulating the national economy and ensuring the welfare of its citizens. Moreover, the global legal and political environments increasingly constrain the range of policy choices available to national decision makers. As the effective sources of authority in the global polity shift from the national level, groups seeking to challenge existing policies and distributions of power must adapt their strategies and structures to this transformed organizational field.

Globalization forces states to reduce their role in economic planning and decision making in favor of global "free market" forces as reflected in international trade agreements such as the General Agreement on Tariffs and Trade (GATT) and now the World Trade Organization (WTO). This is especially true for the poor states of the global South. By reducing the state's role in the economy, globalization undermines national democratic decision making, because it removes important decisions about things such as labor or environmental standards and even government purchasing choices from local political control (for review, see Wallach and Sforza 1999).

Internationalization also shifts policy decisions from local and national to transnational settings by producing agreements among national governments to address shared problems such as environmental degradation, crime, weapons trading, and disease.

As states enter such agreements, they effectively shift some of their authority to supranational institutions. An important difference between the global political institutions and those defining the global economic order, however, is that the WTO and international financial institutions such as the International Monetary Fund (IMF) and the World Bank have far greater enforcement capacities than do institutions such as the United Nations and the treaty bodies under it.[2] Also, the latter two organizations are governed by a system of voting that is weighted by a country's financial stake. Thus, the richer countries have an obvious advantage here and have sought to move key policy decisions into those bodies.

This increasing formalization of transnational economic and political relations through the expansion of global treaties and international organizations has occurred during a time of rapid growth in the organization of all sorts of social relations both within and across national boundaries (see, e.g., Boli and Thomas 1999; McCarthy and Zald 1977; 2001; Minkoff 1995; Walker 1991). Thus, as governments have developed new ways to coordinate their policies and address transnational problems, private sector and civil society groups have evolved in similar ways to maximize their goals and to respond to their changing social environments (cf. Powell and DiMaggio 1991).

The following section examines the ways that expanding political institutions affect the organizational field and therefore the strategic options available to social movement actors and how they alter the organizational demands of political challengers. Next, I describe the population of transnationally organized social movement organizations, or TSMOs, to establish whether we do indeed see adaptations to this changing environment. Finally, using survey data from selected subsets of TSMOs, I explore some of the key organizing challenges for transnational organizations face as they attempt to mobilize across national boundaries and affect change in the global polity.

Organizational Imperatives of Globalization

As governments turn increasingly to global institutions such as the World Trade Organization and the United Nations to resolve shared problems, social movement actors seeking to change local and national practices find that they must look beyond their national boundaries to do so. The global political context both expands and complicates the strategic choices available to those hoping to promote political and social change. In the terms of organizational theorists, we should expect that the nesting of states within a broader and increasingly influential interstate system—which itself introduces new institutional actors and governance structures— would change the broader *institutional logic* that governs the organizational field in which social movements operate (see, e.g., chapter by McAdam and Scott, 2005). This means that we also should see changes in the ways social movement actors carry out their struggles.

In particular, we can expect that social movement organizations—viewed by many as key building blocks of social movements—will become increasingly transnational in structure. This process parallels the transformation of contentious politics during the rise of national states (cf. McAdam, Tarrow, and Tilly 2001; Tilly 1984). For instance, within a global institutional setting, efforts to shape the practices of a particular government require international legal or scientific expertise, understandings of the rivalries and practices of interstate political bargaining, and capacities for mobilizing protests and otherwise bringing simultaneous pressure against multiple national governments.[3] Interstate politics, in other words, has a dynamic and logic of its own, and social movement scholars need to refocus their analytical lens to account for an organizational field that transcends national boundaries.

The logic that drives interstate politics requires that activists develop organizations that can facilitate broad, cross-cultural communication while managing diversity and coordinating joint action around a shared agenda. These demands differ sharply from those required of most national-level movement organizations. We should not be surprised, therefore, to find that social movement organizations devoted especially to transnational-level organizing and political action play key roles in global-level contentious politics. A growing body of empirical evidence on transnational protests allows us to evaluate this assumption. For instance, a growing number of case studies point to the presence of transnationally organized groups or at least transnational coalitions of associations in major global change campaigns (see, e.g., Fox and Brown 1998; Keck and Sikkink 1998; Khagram, Riker, and Sikkink 2002). To explore in detail the relations between transnational and national SMOs, we must examine key "episodes" in transnational or global contentious politics and analyze relationships among the key organizations. Table 1 does this by summarizing some of the central organizational actors and their various roles in the 1999 "Battle of Seattle" against the expansion of the WTO. This event has come to represent the first major—though by no means the first—confrontational protest at a global political site.

I have categorized each organization according to the extensiveness of its transnational ties. If there are any transnational ties, are they informal and sporadic or are they somehow formalized and routinized within the organization? Are these transnational ties peripheral or central to the day-to-day operations of the organization? Thus, we can distinguish among the organizational participants in the Seattle mobilization in terms of how exposed they were to regular and direct transnational exchanges. The next question then is whether or not the extensiveness of transnational ties was associated with different forms of participation in this particular episode of collective action. Do transnational organizations perform different tasks than do more locally organized SMOs?

The general pattern that emerges from this table is that groups with less routinized and formalized transnational ties were indeed more involved in mobilizing local participation in the Seattle protest event. The educational activities in which they engaged drew largely from the strategic framing and information dissemination done by groups with more extensive transnational ties. In contrast, more of the work of groups with routine transnational ties or with transnational organizational structures was devoted to facilitating such mobilizing work by other groups. Groups with transnational ties enabled transnational exchange of

various kinds by producing newsletters and Web sites that provided information about the work of activists in various countries, as well as by bringing activists from different countries for speaking tours and other forms of direct transnational contacts. In the Battle of Seattle, for instance, People's Global Action organized a "People's Caravan" that traveled across the United States in the weeks before Seattle to participate in local teach-ins on the WTO and its effects on various peoples around the world. The People's Caravan relied upon and complemented local organizations, which provided the meeting venues, audiences, and resting places along their route. Groups such as the Women's Environment and Development Organization (WEDO) provided funds, training, and otherwise enabled activists from poor countries to attend global meetings and to speak at public rallies and to participate in organizing workshops such as those held during the 1999 WTO meeting.

Broad changes in the organization of the state and society are seen as having substantial impacts on the ways that people might wage political struggles, and they have contributed to the professionalization of social movement organizations and to the now widespread formation of social movement organizations to advance these struggles (see McCarthy and Zald 1977; Tilly 1984).[4] Alongside globalization processes, we find an expansion in the numbers of SMOs (and other types of organizations) that incorporate members from different countries (Boli and Thomas 1997; Smith 1997). SMOs and their transnational counterparts (TSMOs)[5] are carriers of movement ideas, cultures, and skills. They are not the only actors in social movements; they are joined during times of movement expansion by church and school groups, unions, and other social groups (see McCarthy 1996). But by understanding their structures and discourses we can gain insights into broader social movement dynamics and capabilities. The consistent rise in the numbers of TSMOs during the latter half of the twentieth century suggests that political challengers see sufficient benefits in developing and formalizing transnational ties to justify the relatively higher costs of long-distance organizing. As was seen with the rise of national SMOs in the eighteenth century, we

Table 1 Mobilizing Structures and Divisions of Labor in the "Battle of Seattle"

Type of Transnational Tie	Movement Mobilizing Structures*	Major Roles
No formal transnational ties	Local Chapters of National SMOs (e.g., NOW)	Public education
		Mobilizing participation in protest
	Neighborhood Committees United for a Fair Economy	Localizing global frames
Diffuse transnational ties	Direct Action Network	Public education
	Reclaim the Streets	Mobilizing participation in protest
	Ruckus Society	Localizing global frames
	Coalition for Campus Organizing	Tactical innovations and diffusion
Routine transnational ties	Public Citizen	Public education
	Global Exchange	Facilitating local mobilization by others
	Rainforest Action Network	
	United Students Against Sweatshops	Tactical innovations and diffusion
		Articulating and disseminating global strategic frames
	Council of Canadians	
	Sierra Club	Research/publication of organizing materials
		Facilitating transnational exchanges
		Monitoring international institutions
Formal transnational organization	Greenpeace	Public education
	Friends of the Earth International Forum on Globalization	Facilitating local mobilization by others
		Articulating and disseminating global strategic frames
	Third World Network	
	Peoples Global Action	Research/publication of organizing materials
	50 Years is Enough Network	
	Women's Environment and Development Organization	Facilitating transnational exchanges
		Monitoring of international institutions
		Coordinating transnational cooperation
		Cultivating and maintaining global constituency
		Global symbolic actions

Note: This list is illustrative, not comprehensive.

* Organizations vary a great deal in their levels of formalization and hierarchy. For instance, Friends of the Earth and Greenpeace have well-defined organizational structures and institutional presences while groups such as Peoples Global Action resist forming an organizational headquarters, and Reclaim the Streets seeks to sustain a loose, network-like structure relying heavily on electronic communications.

Source: Adapted from Smith (2002b).

would expect that these transnational organizations and their interactions with other global actors will have important influences on the ways that people engage in politics in the global political arena (cf. McAdam, Tarrow, and Tilly 2001).

The Changing Population of Transnational SMOs, 1970s–2000

The argument outlined above would lead us to expect that the quickening pace of global integration and the related changes to the relevant organizational field will generate more extensive efforts by social movement actors to develop formal transnational organizations to defend against unwanted forms of global integration and to shape global processes in ways that complement their goals. Below we examine changes in the population of TSMOs in order to assess the extent to which this expectation is borne out. Table 2 presents the counts of TSMOs identified in various editions of the *Yearbook of International Associations* (Union of International Associations), the most comprehensive census of all international organizations, including governmental, business, and civil society groups.[6]

The population of TSMOs has expanded dramatically, especially in the past three decades.[7] While fewer than 200 TSMOs existed in the 1970s, there were nearly one thousand such organizations by 2000. However, the data for 2000 suggests that the very rapid growth of TMSOs in the population that was seen during the 1970s and 1980s has slowed. We examine some reasons for this below, but first we should consider the issues around which these TSMOs organize. Human rights TSMOs constitute the largest segment of the TSMO population, and they consistently remain around 25 percent of all TSMOs during the four periods examined here. In contrast, we found fairly rapid growth in the environmental and economic justice movement "industries," particularly in the most recent decades. The most dramatic change, however, is in the number of TSMOs that adopted "multi-issue" goals such as "environment and development" or "human rights to development" rather than the more traditional, single-issue focus. The number of multi-issue groups doubled during the 1990s (growing at twice the rate of the overall TSMO population), and in percentage terms, they rose from less than

Table 2 Growth and Issue Focus of Transnational Social Movement Organizations

	1973 N = 183		1983 N = 348		1993 N = 711		2000 N = 959	
	No.	%	No.	%	No.	%	No.	%
Human rights	41	22	89	26	200	28	247	26
Environment	17	9	43	12	126	18	167	17
Peace	21	12	37	11	82	11	98	10
Women's rights	16	9	25	7	64	9	94	9
Development/Empowerment	8	4	15	4	52	7	95	10
Global justice/Environment	7	4	13	4	30	4	109	11
Multi-issue organizations*	18	7	43	12	82	12	161	17
% change from prior decade	30		90		104		42 (est. to 2003)	

* This categorization overlaps some of the categories above—especially the global justice category.
Source: Yearbook of International Associations.

10 percent of all groups in the 1970s to 17 percent in 2000.

I want to explore some of the reasons why we are seeing these two broad shifts in the TSMO population, namely, a declining rate of growth and a shift from single-issue to multi-issue organizing frames. When considering why the population's growth rate has slowed, we must account for the important development at the 1992 United Nations Conference on Environment and Development that produced a change in the *environmental mechanisms* relevant to social movement actors. This institutional change allowed more direct access by national and subnational groups to United Nations forums. Before that time, only international organizations could obtain "consultative status" with the UN, which allowed them access to international meetings as well as to important documents on international negotiations and UN practices (see Willetts 1999). This effectively reduced the benefits of transnational association for some groups, which may have found it easier to make direct appeals to international organizations rather than to submerge their own organizational interests within a broader transnational framework. Moreover, once the UN began to credential national and subnational groups, this paved the way for their greater access to other international organizations.

The shift to multi-issue organizing frames is another interesting development, and one that might be explained by changes in the *relational mechanisms* that are at work in this organizational field. Specifically, over time we see a growing number of organizations representing a growing number of individual activists engaging in more international meetings and other exchanges, often with the self-conscious aim of generating networks of ties to other activists and organizations. These networks and the exchanges they produce have contributed to a growing awareness of global interdependencies (see, e.g., Young 1991) or a transformed understanding of movement issues that arises from the experience of activism itself. We might categorize this changed awareness as a *cognitive mechanism* that contributes to the changes in the broader environment.

Such cognitive processes have been documented in other, national, movements as well. For instance, Marullo and his colleagues (1996) found that peace movement organizations in the United States tended to adopt more complex, multi-issue frames over time. They interpreted these frame shifts as attempts by SMOs to maintain the interest of activists who had confronted the limitations of previous organizing frames (in this case, the nuclear freeze) and whose activism had led to a greater appreciation for the complex relationships between U.S. military spending and its interventionist foreign policy. Multi-issue organizations may also be a response to attempts to build transnational ties that can include activists with quite different political and cultural backgrounds. As groups form and extend inter-group and inter-personal ties across national boundaries, they find that they must re-frame their ideas about the causes of and solutions to the problems they hope to address. In many cases, we see processes of *diffusion, translation, and bricolage* at work (see, e.g., Bandy and Smith 2005). These processes are also well documented in Rothman and Oliver's (2002) analysis of transnational environmental and indigenous rights coalitions in Brazil, in the work of Alison Brysk (1996, 2000), and in Rupp's (1997) analysis of the international women's movement.

Another factor in the slowing TSMO growth may be the organizational structures adopted by TSMOs. Transnational organizing requires substantially greater resources than does more locally oriented action. Not only is this due to larger communication and transportation costs, but it also results from the need to bridge linguistic and cultural distances within the organization. We can expect to find organizational structures aimed at limiting these transaction costs. The *Yearbook* data allows us to determine the ways that TSMOs structure their relationships with members. Table 3 displays the changes in these organizational structures. The more centralized, "federated" structure involves the division of the organization into national sections that are certified by the international secretariat. Typically national sections have a national monopoly on the organization's name (e.g., Amnesty International-USA), contribute

Table 3 Organizational Structures of TSMOs

	1973%	1983%	1993%	2000%
Federation structure	50	38	28	18
Coalition structure	25	31	43	60

Source: Yearbook of International Associations.

a predetermined share of their resources to the international secretariat, send national delegates to international meetings, and agree to follow a set of international guidelines regarding political claims, governance, and activities. In contrast, what I refer to here as the "coalition" form reflects a more *decentralized* and informal structure. There are fewer requirements for conformity with a broad set of organizational rules, goals, and procedures as defined in the organization's secretariat or international office. While coalitions vary tremendously in the extensiveness of their shared commitments and in the ties between organizational affiliates and the international headquarters, the main feature of this form is that affiliates are asked to adopt a relatively limited shared ideological framework, and they maintain fairly wide autonomy within the coalition framework.

The most dramatic change in the TSMO population over the past three decades is that these groups are adopting the more decentralized and informal coalition form. It is probably no coincidence that this same phenomenon is happening in the corporate sector, as firms seek to maximize the ability of their diverse regional and national operations to adapt quickly to changing market forces (see, e.g., Sklair 2001). The coalition form accelerates decision making and therefore adaptability of groups by decentralizing authority within the organization. In a rapidly changing and uncertain political context, such flexibility is essential.

How can these changes in the organizational structure of TSMOs help explain the patterns of growth we found in Table 2? First, the more common, decentralized coalition structure would allow more national groups to participate in transnational associations without major changes in their preexisting routines and agendas. Joining transnational coalitions brings rather minimal financial costs,

and for many groups the commitments of time and other organizational resources can be determined by the affiliate organization itself. The returns on coalition membership include access to strategic information and frames, access to policymakers, and the enhanced solidarity that comes from being part of a transnational collectivity of diverse local struggles (see, e.g., Cullen 2003). For some groups, there may be even greater benefits such as assistance with global-level mobilization and attendance at international conferences, financial and strategic resources for global work, greater local and international legitimacy, and enhanced opportunities to participate in transnational meetings. In sum, given the logics governing the global organizational field, the coalition form can reduce the start-up costs to groups seeking to extend their work into the global arena. With an almost unlimited capacity for expansion, coalitions can absorb new participants more readily than can the more rigid and centralized federation structure (see, e.g., Murphy 2002).[8]

Coalition structures also encourage the framing of goals and issues in ways that extend their possibilities for attracting the broadest possible base of affiliates. Thus, the shift to multi-issue frames may reflect this need to organize from a constituency of activists that crosses major geographic, political, cultural, and ideological divides. By limiting the degree of ideological conformity among affiliates to a limited consensus around a specific set of aims, coalitions create spaces where a more diverse range of organizations can join transnational collective efforts without abandoning their own organizational constituencies and missions. Thus, with fewer organizations, coalitions can accommodate a broader and more diverse constituency.[9]

Another dimension of TSMO organizational structure is the extent to which they are organized on a global versus a regional level.[10] Boli and Thomas's analysis of the more general category of international nongovernmental organizations (INGOs) showed a growing tendency for these groups to organize along regional lines. They argued that regional organizing enjoyed the "practical advantages of shared language, culture, and history as tools for mobilization with respect to the larger world." In their view, the broader world culture and its institutional artifacts define an overarching framework within which "world culture authorizes and compels organization at diverse levels" (1999: 31–2). The question remains, however, as to whether this pattern is reproduced among that segment of the INGO population that is devoted to social change goals. To evaluate this, I examined TSMO memberships in terms of their locations within the global North, the global South, or in both Northern and Southern regions. While various regional categorizations are possible, this North-South division distinguishes between the "core" of the global economic and political order (the North) and the "periphery" states that have more recently been incorporated into this world order. It assumes, generally, that the central interests and histories of each region differ in ways that are likely to affect the shape of political mobilization. Table 4 presents the distribution of TSMOs according to their regional scope.

We see in this table that most TSMOs are organized interregionally, that is they incorporate members from both the global North and the South. However, the growth rates among *intra*-regional organizations exceed those of the interregional groups. While nearly one half of North-only TSMOs and more than one third of South-only TSMOs were formed during the 1990s, only one fifth of all interregional TSMOs began their work in the 1990s. This pattern could reflect a growing *polarization* among transnational social movement organizations along the major structural divide in the world system, meaning that social movement actors have been unable to mitigate or overcome the major lines of inequality in the global system.

On the other hand, this pattern could also reflect a change in the relevant relational mechanisms, as we may find that more regional organizations play a *bridging* role for transnational organizations. This would be consistent with the expectations of Boli and Thomas and other world culture theorists. Regional structures facilitate the aggregation of diverse interests of local actors in order to more effectively integrate local and regional interests into global-level negotiations. They make it easier, in particular, for groups whose language or historical experiences differ most dramatically from the dominant Western influences on world culture to define their interests within the world cultural framework and to devise strategies for fostering their regional interests. Indeed, intergovernmental conferences may encourage region-specific organizing by the fact that they hold regionally based preparatory meetings before major global conferences and by their emphasis on regional representation in their formal structures and negotiation processes. Further research is needed to assess the underlying dynamics behind this organizing pattern, but certainly this regionalization of TSMO structures will impact the nature of transnational mobilizations yet to come.[11]

Table 4 Subregional Versus Transregional Organizations

	North Only	South Only	Both North and South
Number of organizations	211	87	531
% of all organizations (N = 829)	25	10	64
Age (mean years)	18.6	17.5	32.6
(median)	12	13	22
% formed during 1990s	45	36	20

Source: Yearbook of International Associations, 2000.

Organizational Integration and Its Challenges

The net effect of the changes in the global organizational field and the changing mechanisms at work here is that a much larger societal infrastructure exists for the transnational dissemination of information and exchanges between people from different national backgrounds.[12] If we can view each organizational unit as an indicator of a variety of social interactions across national borders, then these figures reveal substantially more frequent transnational communication and dialogue in the 1990s than in earlier decades. Such transnational dialogue is essential to cultivating ideologies and identities that will appeal to an international movement constituency.

But how *global* are these associations? Do they serve to reinforce the "opportunity hoarding" (Tilly 1998) found across many societies, where already privileged groups reinforce their influence and advantages, while weaker groups see minimal gains as they fall farther behind? Western Europeans and North Americans are clearly overrepresented in TSMOs, and most organizational headquarters are based in those regions (principally in Western Europe). However, there is some evidence of a gradual shift towards greater representation of Southern citizens in TSMOs (Sikkink and Smith 2002; Jackie Smith 1997). Case studies also suggest that, within TSMOs and other transnational coalitions, the influence of Southern activists has been increasing (Fox 2002; Gray 1998; Wirth 1998).

Regardless of their geographic scope, the extent to which TSMOs can produce transnational relationships that are meaningful for political contention depends upon the types of activities taking place within them. Does the transnational character of these associations trickle down to affiliates in different countries? International organizations in particular must over-come distinct challenges to cultivating a unified organizational purpose that can motivate collective action. Organizational *integration,* in other words, cannot be assumed by the mere presence of a transnational organizational structure, but rather varies in the degrees to which an organization produces the cognitive shifts necessary to overcome diversity, distance, economic barriers, and political fragmentation (Young 1991). Young argues that both technological advances and changes in perceptions of global interdependence will make the internal cohesion of transnational associations less problematic.

To assess the internal dynamics of transnational SMOs, this study draws from two different mailed surveys of TSMO leaders and their local and national affiliate organizations.[13] One survey addressed leaders of transnational human rights SMOs and the other focused on the organizational affiliates of EarthAction, a TSMO working on global environment, development, and human rights issues. The human rights survey, conducted during 1996, examines the transnational headquarters of all human rights TSMOs, providing evidence about their human rights frames, contacts with interstate institutions, resources, and geographic makeup. The survey response rate was just over 50 percent (144 responses), and there was no systematic difference in the response rates of groups based in the global South as compared with Northern-based groups (see Smith, Pagnucco, and Lopez 1998). However, most human rights TSMOs were based in the North (103 versus 41 Southern TSMO respondents).

EarthAction's principal focus is on supporting multilateral solutions for global environmental and economic justice problems. It distributes "action kits" to its affiliate or "Partner Organizations," providing them with background information and action suggestions. EarthAction actively solicits input from affiliates as it plans its campaigns, which include global negotiations such as those on climate change and local struggles such as the Ogoni people's resistance to the Nigerian government and multinational oil companies. The survey was conducted during 1998, and achieved a response rate of 52 percent (209 responses). Comparisons of the pool of respondents with nonrespondents found no systematic differences in organizational location, size, structure, or duration of ties with EarthAction. However, as one might expect, respondents tended to be somewhat more active partners than were nonrespondents.[14]

Internal Communications

Transnational SMOs vary tremendously in the intensity of interactions they represent. Some TSMOs may have only quadrennial meetings of national representatives of their members, while others may have bi-weekly conference calls among leaders and/ or frequent electronic communications with local individual or organizational members. Some may have the resources to conduct extensive electronic and mailed communications, while others may have more uneven electronic contacts and infrequent postal exchanges. For instance, the frequency of EarthAction contacts depends to a large extent upon its success at fundraising for its various campaigns. So what can we say generally about the significance of the transnational linkages represented by this collection of groups? Table 5 displays the responses of human rights TSMOs to questions about the frequency of contacts with organizational affiliates.

This table shows that most groups maintain fairly frequent contact with their affiliates at the local and national levels. Ninety percent of all transnational human rights organizations responding indicated that they have at least quarterly contacts with members through background papers, action alerts, or other contacts. Seventy-nine percent indicated contact with members beyond quarterly communications. In addition, most TSMOs are actively engaging in contacts with other organizations in their environment. The human rights survey showed that more than half of all groups engage in at least monthly contact with other nongovernmental organizations. Such contacts indicate relationships that link actors and identities to global human rights frames and arenas.

Certainly the rise of electronic communications over recent years has facilitated transnational organizing. Indeed, Warkentin (2001) argued that progressive groups advancing global agendas helped pioneer the application of these technologies in the service of a global civil society. Nevertheless, given the wide disparities in access to Internet communications even within the highly industrialized countries, we should expect great inequity in the use of electronic communications by Northern and Southern TSMOs and their affiliates. The data we have in these surveys supports this contention, although the gaps may not be as wide as some might anticipate. Among the human rights TSMOs surveyed in 1996, just 44 percent reported use of electronic communications (e-mail and/or Internet). Comparing geographic differences, we see that 30 percent of Southern-based groups and 49 percent of Northern-based groups reported access to electronic communications.[15] A somewhat higher percentage of EarthAction affiliates reported access to electronic communications.[16] Overall, 59 percent of respondents reported that they used e-mail, and 50 percent reported use of the Internet. Here again, geographic differences were not as great as one might expect. While 80 percent of Northern groups used e-mail, about half (51 percent) of Southern affiliates reported doing so. Disparities on Internet usage were greater: 77 percent of Northern groups, compared with 39 percent of Southern ones, reported using the Internet. Eighty-two percent of European and 79 percent of North American partners reported that they used e-mail; African partners reported the least access to e-mail, 35 percent. Asian groups were next at 41 percent. Nearly three-quarters of Latin American

Table 5 Frequency of Transnational Communications

Activity	Number of Times Group Engaged in Activity During 1995*	
	Quarterly or Less (%)	Monthly or More (%)
Issue background papers or action alerts to members	40	23
Contact organizational sections or members	28	40
Contact other nongovernmental organizations	20	54

* No statistically significant differences were found between groups based in the global North and those in the global South.
Source: Human Rights TSMO survey (N = 144).

Partners and 62 percent of partners in the Pacific have e-mail.[17]

One thing that is clear is that the "digital divide" between Northern-based and Southern-based TSMOs is far smaller than that for the general society. The 1999 UN *Human Development Report* showed that more than 26 percent of the U.S. population and around 7 percent of the populations of other industrialized Northern countries were Internet users, compared to less than 1 percent of the populations of countries in the South (UNDP 1999: 63). But without further knowledge of the class backgrounds of groups with access to communications technologies, we cannot say whether or not the comparatively small technology gap between Northern and Southern TSMOs is simply a result of their location within an educated cosmopolitan middle class (see, e.g., Tarrow 2001b).

It is also worth emphasizing that new communications technology alone cannot produce the kinds of commitment and understanding that are essential for sustained collective action. "The revolution will not be e-mailed," according to People's Global Action (2000). Jocelyn Dow, founder of a women's organization in Guyana and a board member of the international Women's Environment and Development Organization, argued that "if we are not careful, we lose the texture of information. One of the most important things for women is to continue to meet globally, because there is nothing that better challenges any misguided notion you might have than to meet a person in her actual skin. We have to live each other's reality. [Global] conferences have a capacity for energizing what I call the agenda of defiance" (quoted in Thom 2000: 32).

My own contacts with affiliates of transnational organizations corroborate this widespread desire for human connections and its importance to solidarity building. EarthAction affiliates, for instance, quite frequently ask the organization to organize conferences for their partners to meet each other. Directories of affiliates have been very popular within the organization as a means of promoting more direct exchange.[18] Despite the vase distances between activists, the need for personal contact remains important for motivating and sustaining

collective action. Transnational organizations facilitate this contact.

In sum, despite the higher costs of transnational activity, this evidence suggests at least a capacity for fairly routine transnational communications between the headquarters and the local or national affiliates of TSMOs. Without more qualitative data we cannot say much about the content of these communications, but at the very least they suggest that TSMOs actively incorporate routine information exchanges that are necessary for effective transnational cooperation to develop.

Perceived Obstacles to International Cooperation

The following two tables explore some of the obstacles that participants in transnational organizations perceive in their efforts to build transnational cooperation around social and political change goals. Table 6 lists items from the survey of transnational headquarters of human rights groups regarding perceptions of financial, linguistic, and cultural obstacles. Responses to similar questions by EarthAction affiliates appear in Table 7.

These responses indicate that financial limitations are perceived as a relatively small obstacle to transnational work by human rights groups. In contrast, the EarthAction affiliates were more likely to report strong financial constraints on their abilities to participate in transnational campaigns. The contrast between the two surveys is probably explained by the fact that the human rights groups are transnational associations whose principal purpose is to promote global organizing around human rights goals. Therefore, their organizational budgets are likely to account for the expenses involved in maintaining regular contact with widely dispersed affiliates. In contrast, many affiliates of EarthAction are small, local groups attempting to address the global dimensions of their local concerns or trying to connect their local efforts with those of other activists. Few have very large budgets, and much of the efforts taken on behalf of global campaigns must come out of regular organizational budgets that leave little room for new outreach or campaign efforts.

Not surprisingly, Southern affiliates were considerably more likely to report having financial limitations on their activities than were Northern groups. This is atleast partially related to the fact that Southern groups were more likely than Northern ones to be local or national in orientation and that the more locally oriented groups also tended to report greater financial limitations on their transnational participation.[19] Organizations oriented towards local and national activities can be expected to face difficulties in shifting scarce organizational resources to global campaign efforts.

Linguistic differences were reported to be a much smaller problem for all groups involved. This may be because EarthAction produces materials in three languages, and many human rights organizations reported the use of multiple working languages. One additional reason may be that the infrequent and written communications representing many of the interactions taking place within most TSMOs do not require the same facility with language that direct interactions or verbal exchanges do. It might also reflect a rather limited engagement of affiliates or members in decision making or complex negotiations about organization strategy and activities.[20] Further research is needed to assess the relevance of language differences as a barrier to organizational integration.

A greater difficulty for transnational affiliates was in relating their local concerns to global campaigns. Southern affiliates and local groups especially reported much more frequent difficulties in this area. Certainly this disparity hinders equitable North-South integration into transnational organizations. It suggests a need for greater efforts

Table 6 Organizational Integration Survey Items: Human Rights TSMOs

	% "Often or Always True"
Our organization has difficulty maintaining contact with some members because of the costs of transportation and communication	20
It is difficult to involve many of our members in decision making because of language differences	10
Cultural differences among our members make it difficult to agree on joint statements or actions	6

Source: Human Rights TSMO Survey (N = 144).

Table 7 Organizational Integration Survey Items: TSMO Affiliates

	% "Often or Always True"			
	North N = 56	South N = 156	Reg./Global N = 79	Local/Nat'l N = 130
Financial limitations prevent us from taking action on EarthAction campaigns	51	64	44	62
Language differences make it difficult for us to use EarthAction materials	14	14	12	15
We have difficulties relating global issues to people's everyday concerns	26	42	27	45

Source: EarthAction Survey (N = 209).

to articulate and develop strategic connections between local interests and relevant global political processes. In other words, if they are to better integrate groups that are most dependent upon their transnational organizing work—local and Southern affiliates—TSMOs such as EarthAction must make efforts to enhance strategic frames so that they better demonstrate local-global connections and suggest feasible local actions. Comparing responses to this question by groups that were less active in EarthAction campaigns with those that were more engaged revealed that groups engaging more frequently in global campaigns found fewer difficulties making global-local connections. Thus, efforts to assist groups to make such connections may encourage them to take more concerted action on EarthAction's transnational campaigns.[21]

Conclusion

This study set out to explore the ways that a changing global environment affects the dynamics of social movement organization. The processes of global political and economic integration alter the organizational field in which social movements operate, and even locally oriented social movements require some level of awareness about, if not involvement in, global-level political institutions. This is especially true for activists in the global South, at the periphery of the global economy, where the policy autonomy of national governments is increasingly limited (see, e.g., Robinson 1996; Walton and Seddon 1994). Thus, we expected that transnationally organized SMOs would fill a particular niche in the social movement sector[22] by providing specialized information and articulating global strategic frames.

The expansion of global institutions has encouraged the rapid growth of transnationally organized social movement organizations. These TSMOs reflect the key conflicts at work in the global political economy, as most groups focus on issues of human rights, environmental preservation, and economic empowerment/justice. Over the past several decades, the form of transnational SMOs has become more decentralized and adaptive, indicating that these organizations are responding to a changing and uncertain global environment.

Within transnational SMOs, we find that language and cultural differences constitute a relatively minor obstacle for organizers, suggesting that these groups have internalized effective cognitive mechanisms to bridge their internal differences. But while cognitive matters were less problematic, financial limitations were of greatest significance to the affiliates of TSMOs rather than to the transnational organizations themselves. Moreover, affiliates in the global South and locally organized affiliates–those on the periphery of this organizational field–had the most difficulty relating to global organizational initiatives.

We might ask, in closing this chapter, about the extent to which the population of TSMOs can be expected to grow or shrink in relation to major galvanizing events (such as the September 11, 2001, attacks, the anti-WTO protests in Seattle, or the outbreak of a major war). Do old groups respond to new issues and conditions that emerge, or must new groups be formed to accommodate new surges of interest in an issue? Analysts of organizations and of world culture (see the contributions in Boli and Thomas 1999) have argued that global institutions themselves motivate new transnational organizing efforts by restructuring institutional logics and by staging international conferences and other fora where governments reflect on major global problems and their possible solutions. Indeed, we see surges of new organizational formations in the years immediately preceding and following these kinds of events. My focus on more recent years prevents a systematic analysis of this question, but it supports the world cultural theorists' expectations that organizational growth will follow changes in the broad institutional and cultural framework of the world polity. In this sense, organizational growth likely will be more tied to institutional events or transformations than to more contingent events such as the September 11 attacks. Of course, to the extent that the September 11 tragedy has generated collective responses within international organizations, it too could have consequences for the population of transnational organizations advocating for social and political change.

In short, the global political context has important consequences for social movement challengers, not the least of which is the problem of devising organizations that are effective at mobilizing a broad and diverse global constituency and providing them with significant avenues for participation in global political debates and decision making. The protests against the global trade regime in Seattle showed the extent of popular interest in expanding democratic input into policy that is increasingly made in international organizations. But we lack the infrastructure for formal democratic participation in global-level policy debates. TSMOs have attempted to fill this institutional vacuum by providing some of the few opportunities for popular scrutiny of and participation in decisions that increasingly affect our day-to-day lives.

Understanding these organizations and their operations will help uncover the likely dynamics of global change and of the routes to greater democratization of global institutions, perhaps along lines similar to those seen with the rise of the modern democratic states of the West. However, as social movement actors strive to promote greater "internationalization," or the strengthening of democratic institutional structures that make interstate policies more transparent and accountable to popular constituencies, they must face the competing process of "globalization." The concentration of resources in the hands of a few multinational corporations and the class of elites that controls them alters the nature of the struggle between the holders of capital and those demanding greater popular input into the actions of states. The work reflected in this volume, and in the broader literatures in organizational studies and social movements, has provided some useful tools for helping discover the dynamics that drive change in this global polity and for providing us with some insights into the types of organizational structures and strategies that are likely to be most effective in this political arena.

NOTES

Support for this research was provided by the American Sociological Association-National Science Foundation Funds for Advancing the Discipline Program, the World Society Foundation, the Joyce Mertz-Gilmore Foundation (human rights organization survey), and by the Aspen Institute Non-profit Sector Research Fund (survey of transnational affiliates).

1. This distinction between internationalization and globalization is drawn from Daly (2002).

2. The WTO and NAFTA, have built-in dispute settlement mechanisms that allow for the automatic enforcement—through economic sanctions and/or fines—of decisions put forth by their panels of judges. In contrast, the United Nations requires proactive responses by member governments to take action to enforce international law.

3. For more on the political dynamics of social movements within nested national and interstate politics see Rothman and Oliver (2002), Smith, Chatfield, and Pagnucco (1997), and Tarrow (2001a).

4. In practice, social movement organizations vary tremendously in the extent to which they adopt formal bureaucratic structures and hierarchical leadership. My use of the term "organization" includes both highly bureaucratic groups such as Amnesty International and self-consciously decentralized and nonformalized groups such as People Global Action.

5. TSMOs are at least minimally formalized organizations that involve participants from more than one country whose purpose is to "change some elements of the social structure or reward distribution, or both, of a society" (McCarthy and Zald 1977: 1218). Prominent examples of TSMOs are Greenpeace and Amnesty International.

6. For more details on this source and its relevance to these claims, see Boli and Thomas (1999) and Smith (1997).

7. This pattern parallels the growth of other international nongovernmental organizations (INGOs). It also likely is influenced by the expansion of national-level social movement sectors. Although we lack systematic data with which to compare growth in national and transnational SMO populations, existing theories and research (see, e.g., Fisher 1993; Minkoff 1995) support the claim the past three decades have seen an expansion in the numbers of both national and transnational organizations. Moreover, research on transnational organizing suggests that this is dependent upon strong national-level movements (e.g., Lewis 2002; Sikkink 1993).

8. Interestingly, an unsystematic survey of the foundings of transnational groups suggests that quite a few of them were formed by activists who began their careers in major transnational federations such as Amnesty International or the International Confederation of the Red Cross, but left these groups because of their rigid and hierarchical structures. The former helped spawn many groups, including Equality Now and Peace Brigades International, and the latter inspired Medécins Sans Frontierès (see, e.g., Smith, Pagnucco, and Romeril 1994).

9. Whether or not this enhances political effectiveness is a separate question. Looking at national groups, for instance, Gamson (1990) found that more formalized and centralized organizations (i.e., federations in this study) were more successful at achieving their goals.

10. This section is based upon a similar discussion in Smith 2004.

11. A slightly higher percentage of intraregional groups were organized in the area of human rights, and this is an issue along which Northern and Southern activists tend to be divided between an emphasis on civil and political rights versus economic and social rights. More North-only groups were organized around environmental issues, whereas South-only groups were more likely to focus on development and economic justice issues. This may signal that highly contentious issues create the strongest incentives for actors to organize within similar cultural, ideological, or geographic groupings.

12. This section draws from analyses reported in Smith (2002b).

13. Further details on these surveys and additional findings from them are available in Smith (2002b).

14. The measure used here was a dummy variable indicating whether or not the group had made any contact with EarthAction (e.g., by sending newsletters or news clippings about their campaigns or returning postcards indicating that they took action on an EarthAction campaign) or responded to earlier attempts by EarthAction to contact them prior to the survey. Thirty-five percent of respondents and 22 percent of nonrespondents had made prior contact with EarthAction international offices, a significant difference.

15. Differences were statistically significant at the .05 level ($t = 2.13$).

16. Some of this difference might be due to expanding access to electronic communications as the 1990s progressed. The different sampling frames of these two studies also may account for some differences. The transnational organizations may be more heavily reliant upon electronic communications than some of the many more locally organized groups in the EarthAction survey. Indeed, a comparison of EarthAction affiliates that transcend national boundaries shows that a significantly higher percentage of transnational affiliates than local and national affiliates used email (72 percent vs. 52 percent) and the Internet (69 percent vs. 41 percent). (Mean differences are significant at .01 level for both comparisons.)

17. Use of the Internet was again less common: only one-quarter of African and Asian partners reported use of the Internet, while around three-quarters of European, Latin American, and North American partners were Internet users.

18. Brown and Fox (1998: 455–6) reported similar conclusions from their study of transnational coalitions working to oppose World Bank projects and policies.

19. Seventy-two percent of the survey sample of Southern affiliates, compared with 38 percent of Northern affiliates, were organized at the local or national levels.

20. The finding could also be a result of the fact that response to the surveys was more likely from groups with leaders who speak or read English, French, or Spanish.

21. Comparisons of mean responses by groups taking part in at least half of the campaigns listed in the survey with those taking up fewer than half suggest, not surprisingly, that more active groups found greater benefits from EarthAction resources and campaigns. Differences between the more and less active affiliates reached or approached significance on the following claims: that "EarthAction helps us link local issues to global negotiations," ($p < 10$); that their work relating to the UN has increased since joining EarthAction ($p < .05$); and that EarthAction materials aided their work with other NGOs and the media ($p < .10$).

22. I use the term "social movement sector," following McCarthy and Zald (1977), to refer to the aggregate of all organizational and individual actors that are advocates for *any* social movement industry.

Part 4

Facilitative Spaces and Contexts

In addition to unsettling disruptions or threats, some degree of political opportunity, and the accumulation of some variety of resources, the prospect and character of movement emergence and mobilization is often affected by various ecological factors and the existence of "free spaces." The concept of *ecological factors* directs attention to the spatial arrangement of aggrieved populations and physical places that may facilitate or impede the development and character of movement challenges to authority. The importance of ecological factors in relation to student movements worldwide has long been noted in research on student movements. Two campus ecological factors are especially prominent worldwide: the spatial or territorial segregation of youth creating what has been called "youth ghettos" (Lofland 1968) and spatial arrangements that channel the daily comings and goings of students and often aggregate them in particular places at particular times, such as student unions or centers, campus quads that students crisscross between classes, and the administratively designated and ecologically marked "free speech" areas that were created on university campuses in the United States in the 1970s and 1980s to centralize and control student rallies and protest. But ecological factors are relevant to protest and movements beyond the college and university campus. Illustrative is a study of the distribution of peasant radicalism in Chile in the 1960s that found that spatial proximity to highly organized and politically radical mining municipalities located in the countryside was the main determinant of variation in the degree of peasant radicalism (Petras and Zeitlin 1967). In other words, those peasants most ecologically proximate to the mining municipalities became the most radical because of increased exposure to the miners' leadership and ideology.

The first reading in this section, by Dingxin Zhao, provides further elaboration and illustration of the significance of ecological factors to movement mobilization in an in-depth analysis of the spring 1989 Beijing student movement that flourished for nearly two months prior to the Tiananmen Square massacre. According to Zhao's analysis of the movement, the unique ecology of Beijing's universities, concentrating as it did large numbers of students in a very small and insulated area, greatly facilitated mobilization and "the formation of many ecology-dependent" tactics among the students (see also Zhao 2001).

Free spaces are a specific ecological factor that has been linked to movement emergence by numerous analysts. Free spaces are small-scale community or social settings beyond the surveillance and control of institutionalized authorities in which dissidents and system complainants can fashion the kinds of adversarial narratives and frames that precede or accompany mobilization (see Evans and Boyte 1986; Polletta 1999; and Scott 1990, who uses the parallel term "hidden arbors"). Examples of free spaces include quasi-public places like coffee houses, neighborhood bars, student lounges, class rooms, religious institutions such as churches and mosques, and more private places like one's home, apartment, dormitory room, and office or place of work. Two factors make spaces relatively free in the sense of being safe or protected: they are typically beyond the direct gaze and earshot of authorities, and they are controlled by movement sponsors or friends or appropriated and colonized by the dissidents themselves.

The importance of free spaces to the development and nurturing of adversarial sentiments and mobilization is clearly illustrated by the other selections in this section. In his analysis of the black student sit-in movement that spread across 69 cities in February and March of 1960, mostly in the South, Aldon Morris chronicles the role of black churches and colleges in facilitating the emergence and diffusion of the movement. How so? By providing the organizational infrastructure, associational connections, and free spaces in which to organize, strategize, and mobilize.

In the final selection, Robert Futrell and Pete Simi examine how free spaces contribute to the persistence of the U.S. White Power Movement (WPM). Drawing on observational and interview data gathered on WPM activities between 1996 and 2003, the authors explore how different types of free spaces enable and inhibit different social ties and practices and how they enhance movement persistence. They find that the persistence of the WPM is based in large part on an infrastructure of free spaces that maintain activist networks and movement identity, albeit precariously, within a generally hostile environment.

II.
Ecologies of Social Movements: Student Mobilization During the 1989 Prodemocracy Movement in Beijing

DINGXIN ZHAO

After the late 1960s, social movement studies gradually moved away from traditional breakdown theories to resource mobilization approaches that emphasized the role of organizations and interpersonal networks in movement participation. The transition started with Pinard (1971) and von Eschen, Kirk, and Pinard (1971) who criticized Kornhauser's (1959) mass society theory and argued that organizational membership does not always draw people into routine politics while discouraging people's participation in social movements. Then, Oberschall (1973) proposed a model that argues that both communal and associational ties facilitate movement mobilization. In turn, Tilly's (1978) mobilization model emphasized organizations, and McAdam's (1982) political process model noted the importance of black churches and black college groups during the Civil Rights movement in America. Since then, this perspective—variously named resource mobilization model I (Jenkins 1987; Perrow 1979), political process model (McAdam 1982), or solidarity model (Useem 1980)—has prevailed in social movement studies.[1]

When it came to the 1980s, studies of movement mobilization began to focus on microlevel issues and network-based mobilization. Most studies in this tradition suggest that people are recruited into social movements through social movement organizations or activist and friendship networks and that the number of ties with movement activists are correlated with movement participation (Klandermans and Oegema 1987; Marwell, Oliver, and Prahl 1988; McAdam 1986; McAdam and

Zhao, Dingxin. 1989. "Ecologies of Social Movements: Student Mobilization During the 1989 Pro-Democracy Movement in Beijing, *Americal Journal of Sociology* 103: 1493–1529. Reprinted by permission of The University of Chicago Press. Notes have been renumbered and edited.

Paulsen 1993; McCarthy 1987; Opp and Gern 1993; Snow, Zurcher, and Ekland-Olson 1980; Walsh and Warland 1983). Recent studies by Gould (1991, 1993, 1995) used not only network ideas but also more advanced network techniques to reveal things that would remain uncovered with the conventional "counting the number of ties" type of studies.

The publications above, and most other works that were not discussed here, did not have the same agendas, and indeed there were many debates among them. Yet, because of this collective effort, one idea gradually formed and has now become conventional wisdom. That is, organizations and preexisting networks are the basis of movement mobilization.[2] As a child of this tradition, I never intended to deviate from it. Especially, by 1992 and 1993, the time when this research was conducted, scholars had tried to explain the uprising in China and the East European revolutions in terms of the rise of civil society in totalitarian states.[3] Although most of these analyses are very thin, they resonate with the resource mobilization paradigm. Thus, in interviews, I designed several questions to probe in that direction. As expected, I found many signs of network-based communication and mobilization. Yet, many of these instances could not be understood without taking campus ecology into account. Moreover, the campus ecology had facilitated student mobilization beyond movement organizations and student networks.[4] Let me provide an example.

Almost all campuses in Beijing are separated from the outside by brick walls with only a few entrances guarded by the university's own security forces. During the 1989 Beijing student movement (BSM), no police or soldiers had ever gone inside campuses to repress students. After talking to students, I found that the existence of campus walls was important for the development of the movement. Because of the walls, roads on campus are no longer part of the public road system, and police cannot get inside a campus without clear consent from school authorities. Here, even if some school authorities in Beijing were unsympathetic to the movement, they might not be interested in calling police to handle students. If they did so, they would alienate the students and would have more troubles in dealing with students after the police left. Therefore, the simple existence of walls has created a low-risk environment and facilitated student mobilization.

Discrepancies between the theories that guided my data collection and empirical results pushed me to look more seriously at the role of campus ecology in student mobilization. I found that the campus ecology affected student mobilization during the 1989 BSM in the following ways. (1) It facilitated the spread of dissident ideas before the movement and the transmission of news about a particular event during the movement. (2) It nurtured many dormitory-based student networks. These networks were the basis of mutual influence, even coercion, among students and, therefore, sustained a high rate of student participation. (3) It shaped students' spatial activities on the campus, creating a few places that most students had to pass or stay daily. These places became centers of student mobilization. (4) The concentration of many universities in one district encouraged mutual imitation and interuniversity competition for activism among students from different universities. (5) The ecology also facilitated the formation of many ecology-dependent strategies of collective action. Those actions patterned the dynamics of the movement.[5] The above findings and their theoretical implications will be the focus of this article.

Scattered mentions of the impact of campus environment on movement mobilization have appeared in social movement literature. It was noticed that the campus environment had facilitated student movements in the United States during the 1960s (e.g., Berk 1974; Heirich 1971; Lofland 1970) and student movements in Russia (Kassow 1989) and China (Chow 1967; Wasserstrom 1991). For example, Heirich (1971, pp. 59–65) describes how changes in campus layout at Berkeley since the 1950s made Berkeley students more available for political recruitment during the 1960s. Kassow (1989) reports that the dining halls built by Nicholas II for students in Moscow to get cheap meals became meeting places where students could trade news, make new contacts, and hold assemblies. Chow (1967) and Wasserstrom (1991) note that the congested living condition on Chinese campuses facilitated student activism in early modern China. There are other nonstudent movement examples as well. In the 19th century in Western Europe, a nascent civil society coexisted with traditional communities, and most social movements ocurring in that period, such as Chartism in England and the Paris Commune in Paris, were organized by formal organizations that relied heavily on the infrastructure of traditional community (with ecology implied) to extend their mobilizing potential (Gould 1995; Mann 1993, chap. 15). Additionally, community movements in the contemporary West (e.g., Delgado 1986; Perry, Gillespie, and Parker 1976) or the black riots in America also tended to have an ecology-dependent process of mobilization. As Feagin and Hahn (1973) and Fogelson (1971) mention, the sudden and massive black riots in some American cities were made possible partly because of the densely populated black ghettos and the fact that residents in those areas tended to spend a great deal of their leisure time on the street. However, these and other writers treated the ecological impact on movement mobilization in passing without much elaboration. Even Lofland's article, which may be considered an exception, only deals with the issue of homogeneity in an abstract way.

Nevertheless, ecological perspectives are not new in sociology.[6] The approach adopted here resonates with human ecology, a paradigmatic perspective of early American sociologists. However, human ecologists have been interested in the forces behind the spatial order of urban communities, such as land values and the logistics requirements of an economy (Burgess 1925; McKenzie 1924; Park 1915, 1936; Warner 1963) or the conflict between peoples with different cultural, ethnic, and class backgrounds (Lofland 1973; Suttles 1968, 1972). In short, in these perspectives spatial relations have been treated as expressions of social relations.[7] In contrast, the starting point of this article is a given spatial relation. I insist that while a spatial form of a community is socially constructed and reflects socioeconomic relations, once it is formed, it can act functionally as a social structure and its impact on social actions cannot always be reduced to social and/or class relations.

Here, my line of thinking is close to one of Simmel's ideas. In his discussion of mobile/immobile artifacts, Simmel concluded that when an artifact is immobile, certain social relationships must be ordered around it, and therefore, the artifact becomes a socially important pivot of human interaction (Spykman 1964, chap. 4). This Simmelian idea is the basis for research scattered on urban studies (Beckham 1973; Duncan and Duncan 1955; Fischer 1977; Krupat 1985), human geography (Garling and Evans 1991; Gold 1980; Gollege and Timmermans 1988; Werlen 1993), small group ecology (Baldassare 1975, 1977; Case 1981; Sommer 1967, 1969), and environmental psychology (Barker 1968; Loo 1972; Osmond 1957; Saegert and Winkel 1990; Schoggen 1989). It has been shown that design factors of houses and their overall spatial arrangements can encourage as well as discourage people's mutual interaction and communication. In general, other factors being equal, the closer a number of people live together (in both physical and functional terms), the greater the chance of unintentional contacts and active group making (e.g., Case 1981; Festinger, Schachter, and Back 1950; Michelson 1976; Whyte 1956), especially when there is a homogeneous population (e.g., Gans 1967; Michelson 1976; Newcomb 1961).[8] However, high-density housing, especially high-rise housing, tends to discourage neighborly interactions (McCarthy and Saegert 1978; Mitchell 1971). The design factors and spatial distribution of houses also shape the opportunity structure of social action. Therefore, the crime rate of an area is strongly related to the spatial characteristics of physical settings (Newman 1973; Taylor 1987).

However, previous studies on relationships between physical environment and social action have been on elementary network relations or psychological mechanisms. This article demonstrates that ecological conditions can be important to a political process as complex as a large-scale social movement and that its impact extends beyond networks and solidarities.

Before moving on, I would like to make clear that this article only intends to explain student mobilization (especially during the early stage of the 1989 BSM), not the later mass mobilization centered on Tiananmen Square. This is, in part, because early mobilization faced stronger repression and involved more uncertainties, so the campus ecology was then crucial to sustain it. After students successfully challenged the regime, the perceived risk to join a movement greatly declined. In fact, it was so diminished that, after mid-May, going to Tiananmen Square became a common pastime and a fun activity.

The 1989 BSM

In the late 1980s, China's economic reform was in a deep crisis. Many Chinese, especially intellectuals and university students, were demoralized by emerging social problems such as high inflation, rampant official corruption, the decreasing economic status of intellectuals and students, and the slow process of political reform. In 1988 alone, over 200 demonstrations and other protest activities occurred at Beijing university campuses (Ren 1990). These early actions were contained by the government, yet social problems deepened into 1989.

On April 15, 1989, Beijing students seized the opportunity of Hu Yaobang's sudden death and started protest activities.[9] The government's initial reaction to the movement was restrained. However, as the scale of the movement expanded, the government toughened its attitude by publishing a *People's Daily* editorial on April 26, which labeled the movement as an antirevolutionary turmoil agitated by a small number of people behind the scenes. Heretofore, people were discouraged by similar messages, which indicated an impending government repression. Yet to most people's surprise, instead of backing off, Beijing students defied the editorial with a large-scale demonstration on April 27. The success of the demonstration caused the government to adopt a soft strategy, which initially worked well. With a limited compromise from the government, the movement quickly declined during early May.

The effectiveness of this soft government strategy, however, caused a small group of students to adopt more radical tactics. On May 13, around 300 students, mostly from Beijing University, staged a hunger strike in Tiananmen Square. Throughout the movement, the government's knowledge about the movement was superficial. Without knowing exactly what was going on, the government started to negotiate with a group of student activists who could neither agree with each other nor represent the hunger strikers. The fruitless negotiation went on for two days while the scale of the Tiananmen Square occupation quickly expanded. By May 15, when Mikhail Gorbachev, then leader of the Soviet Union, arrived at Beijing, students still occupied the square. Since many activities of the state visit had been originally arranged inside or around Tiananmen Square, the hunger strike interrupted the Sino-Soviet summit and insulted the government. During this period, the top state leaders in China became increasingly split. Since a limited soft-liner approach did not work, most of them wanted to return to a hard-liner strategy, whereas Zhao Ziyang, the general secretary of the Communist Party, insisted on a more substantial compromise. Eventually the hard-liners won and Zhao Ziyang lost his power. Martial law began on May 20.

In the meantime, the hunger strikers' health conditions were deteriorating. After May 15, more and more hunger strikers fainted, and the sirens could be heard almost everywhere in downtown Beijing. Most people in Beijing, including lesser government leaders, were concerned about the students' health and greatly annoyed by a silent central government. They were also greatly moved by the heroism that the hunger strikers had expressed. Since May 16, from factories up to the State Council, almost all the government, public, and private institutions in Beijing had semiofficially organized demonstrations to support the students and to urge the central government to negotiate with them.[10] The number of demonstrators rocketed to well above a million on both May 17 and 18. Students ended the hunger strike in the night of May 19, after they heard the news of the martial law, yet, the Tiananmen Square occupation continued.

During the night of May 19, even before the martial law was formally announced, about seven or eight divisions of troops (10,000–15,000 each) advanced on Beijing from all directions. The government might have expected that the sheer size of the army itself would be enough to deter any attempt at resistance. On the contrary, under a popular belief that the soldiers were going to hurt the students in the square, people went out in the hundreds of thousands and successfully stopped the army.[11] The troops had to withdraw after two days of stalemate; the Tiananmen Square occupation was preserved. The army invaded Beijing once again in the night of June 3. They met a violent resistance, yet with a resolute order from the government, the troops pushed their way to the square, leaving behind several hundred dead and thousands more wounded. Students managed to leave the square peacefully after more and more soldiers arrived. The movement was suppressed.

Methodology

The data used in this article were obtained from original interviews conducted between late 1992 and early 1993. Informants were recruited through a snowball method: after each interview, an informant was asked to suggest friends who might be willing to participate. The 1989 BSM has been a politically sensitive topic to most Chinese. A snowball method was thus appropriate because Chinese tend to put a lot of trust in friends. To ensure the representativeness of informants and to maintain efficiency in data collection, I made some decisions as to whether or not a suggested candidate should be interviewed. For example, I tried not to recruit two informants who were classmates (especially roommates) at the time of the BSM to minimize redundant information. Prior to the interview, I was also aware that undergraduates, students in key universities, and students of the social sciences and humanities were more active in the movement. I decided that my informants should reflect this fact.

Seventy people were interviewed in my study, 40 in Beijing and 30 in Montreal. Of the 70 informants, social science and humanities majors made up 44% ($n = 31$), compared to an 18.5% national average. At the time of 1989, 37 informants were undergraduate students, 11 were graduate students, 16 were political control cadres or teachers, and six worked in various cultural and academic institutions. In terms of the level of movement participation, six informants were student leaders, 21 had actively participated in the whole process of the movement (six of them were also hunger strikers), 17 were actively involved in the movement for a significant period of time, 20 participated in some movement activities, and six were nonparticipant adherents of the movement. The informants were from 18 universities and four cultural and academic institutions. Most of them were from Beijing University ($n = 12$), People's University ($n = 12$), Qinghua University ($n = 10$), Beijing Normal University ($n = 8$), the University of Political Sciences and Law ($n = 4$), and Beijing Chemical University ($n = 4$). Except for Beijing Chemical, the rest were also the most active universities during the 1989 BSM.

A set of questions was prepared before the interview. These questions served as a guideline for further probing. In the interview, informants were asked slightly different questions and probed differently. Therefore, the sample size for statistics extracted from the interview is usually smaller than the number of informants interviewed. Before each interview, I explained the purposes of the study and the anonymity of their information. I also told them that they could refuse to answer a question if it made them uncomfortable for whatever reasons. In fact, very few informants refused to answer any questions, and the Beijing informants showed no more restraint than the Montreal informants.

The interviews were conducted between late 1992 and early 1993, while the movement occurred in 1989. So there is the possibility of forgetting and distorting as the result of their current state of mind. These problems cannot be totally eliminated, but I have tried to minimize their impact by avoiding questions that probe into personal views, impressions, or experiences of a short-term nature. After the interview, I cross-checked the precision of an informant's narrative by the other informants' descriptions of the same event. Sometimes, when an informant's description was part of a major event, the published accounts were also used to

check reliability. Possibly because the period before and during the 1989 BSM was so dramatic in most informants' lives, the narratives of my informants showed a strong consistency.

The interviews were carried out in Chinese. All the quotes in this article are my translations. Each quote was labeled by a number to mark the source of information while maintaining anonymity.

Universities and Student Life in Beijing
The Haidian University District
In Beijing, most universities are located in and around the Haidian District. As a legacy of state planning, the giant university compound acquired its current shape in two separate efforts during the 1950s. The first step was to restructure the existing universities and to establish People's University, while the second effort was to build a large number of Soviet-style polytechnic institutions (Du 1992). By 1956 Beijing had 31 universities with an enrollment of 76,700, compared with 13 universities and a total enrollment of 17,442 in 1949 (Zhang and Zhou 1989). This tendency continued. By 1989, Beijing had 67 institutions of higher learning with 162,576 boarding students at undergraduate and graduate levels (*Educational Statistics Yearbook of China* 1989; *Zhongguo gaodeng jiaoyu daquan* 1989).

Campuses in Beijing
University campuses in China are structurally similar. Since Beijing University is the center of student activism in Beijing as well as in China as a whole, this section uses Beijing University to illustrate the campus in Beijing.

As shown on the map of Beijing University (fig. 1), most universities in China are separated from the outside by a brick wall. Within a university, there are restaurants, student dining rooms, a cinema, a hospital, a post office, barber's shops, grocery stores, sports facilities, recreational areas, and so forth. It is so self-contained that hard-working students can live on campus for a whole semester without going outside once.

Most university students in China board and live in campus dormitories. Classmates are usually assigned to several connected rooms in a dormitory. In Beijing University, student dormitories occupy

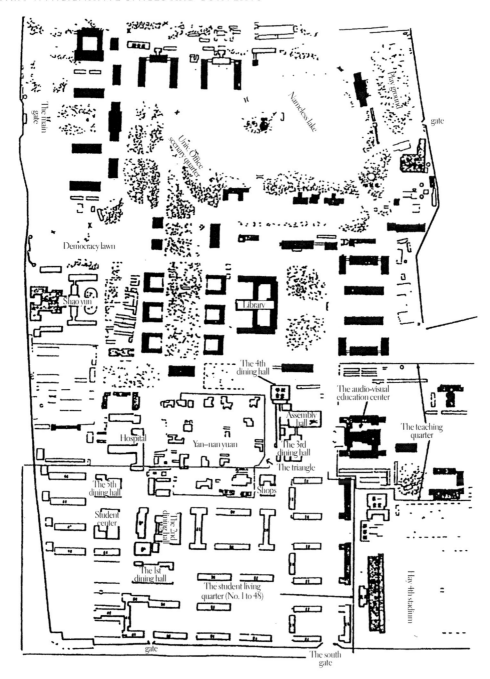

Figure 11.1 The map of Beijing University, showing the ecological concentration of students on campus.

49 buildings. They are located at the lower right side of figure 1. Buildings 28–43 are for undergraduate students. With six to eight students living in each dormitory room, these dormitories held a total of 9,271 students in 1988. Buildings 45–47 are for master's students, whereas doctoral students live in dormitories 25 and 26. With four master's students or two doctoral students living in each dormitory room, 2,893 students lived in these five buildings in 1988. Finally, buildings 16–24 are dormitories for young unmarried teachers. The remaining dormitories housed foreign and special students in short-term training programs.

Student Life on Campus

According to my informants, in the late 1980s, many students in Beijing University (and in other universities as well) did not study hard. The first class in Beijing University started at 8:00 A.M., but some students got up as late as 10:00. Some students would stay in the dormitory until lunch at about noon. A nap was common after lunch. The diligent students got up at 2:00 P.M., but others might get up at 3:00 or even 4:00. Dinner started at 5:00 P.M. Activities after dinner varied. Some went to the library or to conferences. Others went to dances, movies, or out with their boyfriends or girlfriends. Still others remained in the dormitory rooms chatting, playing poker, or mah-jongg. Most students returned to dormitories around 10:00. Curfew was at 11:00. Chatting after curfew was a common pastime; students called this *wotanhui,* which means meeting while laying on bed. This *wotanhui* could go on as late as 2:00 in the morning.

Campus Ecology and Patterns of Mobilization

In the interviews, I found that the campus ecology in Beijing had facilitated the transmission of dissident ideas and information about movement activities. It squeezed students into many small dormitory-based student networks, which sustained a high level of student participation, encouraged interuniversity competition for activism, and upheld many ecology-dependent strategies of collective action. I will discuss them in turn in this section. In the next section, I will present a case study of the April 27

student demonstration to show how ecology-based mobilization mechanisms manifested themselves in one of the most important events of the 1989 BSM. I will take the impact of homogeneity as an established fact and focus only on how design factors of Beijing universities shaped the density, distribution, and spatial movement of Beijing students in a way that facilitated student mobilization.

Dissident Ideas and Movement Information Transmission

Most students live in campus dormitories. Six to eight students live in each dormitory room, a few dozen classmates of the same sex live in several closely located dormitory rooms, and several hundred students stay in each building. A dormitory area of a university in Beijing can accommodate up to 10,000 students. Without the knowledge of student dormitories, the patterns of communication and mobilization on campuses during the BSM cannot really be understood.

Many informants reported that they usually chatted in the dormitory room for one to several hours each day. Although politics and political grievances were not always the topic, they did constitute a major theme when the socioeconomic situation in China worsened. Dormitory rooms were the primary location where nonconforming ideologies spread and achieved dominance. Frequent chatting among students of the same or nearby dormitory rooms narrowed students' attention. Dormitories also nurtured the friendship networks necessary for student mobilization.

During the 1980s, enthusiasm for newly introduced or reintroduced Western philosophies and political thought occurred repeatedly on campus, thereby forming numerous "fevers" such as Freud fever, Nietzsche fever, Sartre fever, cultural fever, and political reform fever. Almost every fever involved a large number of students in its heyday. Some fevers, such as the Nietzsche fever, even attracted the majority of students in some major universities. Yet, in a study of 2,005 students in eight universities, Li (1988) reported that only about one-third of the students tried to read original books by Nietzsche during the Nietzsche fever. Most students got to know Nietzsche and his ideas when students in the same or nearby dormitory room who were reading Nietzsche shared their reading in dormitory conversations. During the 1980s, many students got new ideas also from various conferences held on campus.[12] Students in the same or nearby dormitory rooms frequently informed one another and went to conferences together.

During this period, nonconforming intellectuals in China spread their ideas by publishing student-oriented books and holding conferences in universities. Those students who were sensitized by them then spread the ideas through dormitory rooms. When a student got interested in politically related matters, his/her reading would probably be a recurring topic of discussion in his/her dormitory room. As one student (no. 54) reported: "The major topic in our dormitory room was reform,...mainly market economy and privatization. One student in our dormitory room strongly supported the market economy. He read the *World Economic Herald* a lot.[13] He also read many books by Fang Lizhi and Li Yining. When he read those books, he passed these messages to us [in the dormitory room]. We then debated [these ideas]." Here, dormitory rooms have a convergence function but not in the sense that students would eventually agree with each other. The same informant continued: "During the debate, I and another student were strongly against his idea, while one student supported him. The rest were in the middle." Students seldom simply agreed with each other. However, continuing discussions of similar issues, which were often social problems that had no easy solutions, made students more sensitive to these issues, and gradually they came to some consensus on a few basic points as the social problems were prolonged or even worsened. Therefore, during the late 1980s, more and more students believed that democracy and capitalism were better solutions for China and had lost hope for the reform (Liu 1990).

Communication of dissident ideas was also facilitated by the ecology of the Haidian District. The distance between most universities in Beijing is less than half an hour by bicycle. Such short distances made interuniversity communication extremely easy. Before the 1989 BSM, famous dissidents and liberal intellectuals were often invited to give talks in various universities. If a talk was held by someone famous, students from the other universities would go there by bicycle. As soon as the movement was started, the very first action of many activists was to go to other universities (especially the major ones) to see what was happening. They went there to read big character posters, listen to speeches, and establish connections. Thus, campus ecology made a largely spontaneous movement look like a coordinated action from the very beginning.

Sanction to Free Riders

In his study of the 1989 BSM, Calhoun (1994, p. 170) noticed that students often marched together during a demonstration by school, class, and often major. According to Calhoun, this manifested Chinese culture, which encourages solidarity, loyalty, and friendship. Calhoun's observation and explanation are not without any foundation. However, explaining a sign of group solidarity in terms of a group culture is tautological. More important, this line of reasoning neglects the structural basis of the solidarity and runs the danger of assuming that all the students participated in the movement for the same reason. In my study, I found that students not only often marched together by school, class, and major but also by dormitory room. However, they did this not just out of a sense of group solidarity but because the campus ecology and dormitory-based student networks were the basis of mutual influence, persuasion, and even coercion among students.

The key here is the dense living environment on campus, especially dormitory rooms. With six to eight students living in the same dormitory room for a period of four years, it is as if every student was forced to play an Axelrodian game in which cooperation is the only optimum long-term solution.[14] Therefore, once movement participation was regarded by most students as a moral action, avoiding participation became very difficult for those who actually did not intend to do so in the beginning. Among 56 student informants, 14 reported open attacks of active participants on less active ones in dormitories. Students in the same or nearby dormitory rooms often checked each other's behavior. As one student commented: "All students joined the movement after several demonstrations. Students who did not go would feel isolated and hated. For example, when the government asked us to resume class, only one student went to class. As a result, that student was accused of being a renegade" (no. 4).

Another student described what happened in his dormitory room on the evening of April 26, which made him eventually join the April 27 student demonstration:

> [When the April 26 *People's Daily* editorial was published,] students in our dormitory room were very angry. Many of them decided to go to demonstrate. They asked me. I said I did not want to go....They were mad at me....They quarreled with me angrily. I found this unbearable and thought that we were fellow students, why should you talk to me like this?...There was a party member in our dormitory room who did not want to go either....He told us that they just had a meeting. It was explained in the meeting that there would be a lot of policemen on the way the next day. He asked the other students not to go....Then people poured their anger toward him. (no. 42)

Because of high student density in a dormitory building, coercion among students could sometimes go beyond a dormitory room. One student (no. 62) had given a vivid account of this:

> During the whole process of the movement, one event left me with a very deep impression. In the law department, there were quite a few graduate students of the 1989 class who did not care about the movement at all and played mah-jongg in their dormitory rooms everyday. I knew this from a notice board in no. 46 building. It read: "Since the hunger strike, several scoundrels on the fifth floor have not cared about the movement at all and have lost all their consciousness. They have been locking themselves in their dorms and playing mah-jongg everyday. We belittle them very very much...." I also remembered a line in a big character post. It said: "Those red noses and black hearts are playing mah-jongg even when the other students are on a hunger strike. Beware of your dog noses!"

However, most pressure was more subtle. When a follow-up question was asked ("What did you think of those students who did not participate in

the movement at all?"), the following was a rather typical response: "We did not care about those students. Because these people did not interact with classmates even at regular times, no one paid much attention to them" (no. 37).

These students were labeled as deviants by their classmates. Obviously, such mutual checking and comparing for activism could effectively sustain movement participation largely because of the particular living condition.

Interuniversity Competition for Activism

Most of the 67 universities in Beijing are located close to one another. The close distance between universities facilitated mutual imitation and interuniversity competition for activism, which also sustained student participation.[15] In the interviews, I found that some students from People's University were proud of being the leading troop in the April 27 demonstration, which was considered a highly risky action. Students from Fada [University of Political Science and Law] were proud of their numerous firsts earned during the movement, despite being a small university: "Later, we calculated that Fada owned 13 firsts. We were the first university that went to demonstrate on the street and went on a class strike. The first chairman of the Autonomous Student Union was our student. The headquarters of the dialogue delegation was located in our university, and many others.... We were very proud of that The fame of Fada has grown thereafter" (no. 59).

Finally, when students from Beijing University talked about their activities during the 1989 BSM, they talked as if they were the unquestionable leaders of the movement. Their most elegant slogan was "The whole nation does not fall asleep as long as Beijing University is still awake" (no. 51). One student leader in Fada commented on Beijing University in a Fada-centric way: "When Fada demonstrated on the street on April 17, Beijing University rushed to Tiananmen the same evening.... Students in Beijing University always feel they are different from other universities. Therefore, when they felt they might lose the leadership [as in early May] they came out with the radical tactic, that was the hunger strike" (no. 60).

Comments as such may not be taken too literally. However, it does reveal an intensive interuniversity competition during the 1989 BSM. It was the ecology of the Haidian District—the concentration of so many universities in such a small area—that made such competition detailed, instantaneous, and interactive.

The Development of Ecology-Dependent Strategies of Mobilization

So far, I have shown how the campus ecology facilitated student mobilization and why patterns of student mobilization during the 1989 BSM cannot be properly understood without the knowledge of campus ecology. At this level, my analysis still points to student solidarities and, therefore, supports resource mobilization theories and especially Gould's analysis on mobilization during the Paris Commune. In the following, however, I will present another set of findings that is equally important to the student mobilization but is, nevertheless, not clearly related to student networks.

Most universities in Beijing have a similar spatial layout The design factors regulate the daily life and spatial movement of students on a campus, which in turn facilitated the formation of many ecology-dependent strategies of student mobilization. For example, in each university, big character posters and announcements were concentrated and mobilization was initiated only in specific places. These places emerged because they were central to students' daily life. The famous Triangle in Beijing University, the third student dining hall in People's University, and the tenth dining hall in Qinghua University are such places. For example, the Triangle is located between student dormitories, the library, classrooms, and several dining halls (fig. 1). The post office, bookstore, and several other shops are also in the vicinity. Whenever students go to the classroom, library, dining hall, post office, or back to dormitories, they have to pass the Triangle.

This kind of spatial layout makes mobilization extremely simple. In Beijing University, for example, when student activists wanted to organize a demonstration, all they needed to do was just "put several posters at the Triangle, write down the time, location of gathering, and purposes of the demonstration and slogans to be used, and then waited in the place and brought students out on that day" (no. 69). In case not enough students showed up, the activists usually brought those who had come to march inside the campus on the avenues between dormitory buildings. In my study, I found that marching through avenues between dormitories before demonstrating on the street was a standard way that Beijing students used to achieve a high level of mobilization, and this is another example of the ecology-dependent strategy of mobilization. For instance, in the evening of April 17, 1989, around 200 students of Beijing University initiated a demonstration at the Triangle. They marched inside the dormitory area first. As they were chanting and making noises, more and more students were attracted and came out. The size of the formation swelled from a few hundred to between 5,000 and 6,000, and eventually the students marched out of the campus. This was the first large-scale student demonstration by the students of Beijing University.

Now, to what extent can this type of mobilization process be understood in terms of networks and solidarities? The closest network explanation of this event is that Beijing University had two types of networks during the 1989 BSM; an activist-based movement network and many structurally equivalent dormitory-based friend networks. Strong ties existed in each type of network. Within each dormitory-based network, some students were exposed to dissident ideas earlier and were sympathetic to the movement. Thus, when they saw the demonstration outside, they persuaded and even coerced their fellow roommates to join in. Here, campus ecology was important only to the extent that it simultaneously bridged a social movement network with all the dormitory-based networks. If one is preoccupied with modeling movement mobilization as a networking process, one may consider the ecological linkage as "structure holes" (Burt 1992) or weak ties (Granovetter 1973).

The network explanation is not totally unreasonable. Even with the size of Beijing University, it could still be argued that all students might be in the same network through either chains of friends or a certain structural equivalency. However, this explanation has two problems. First, it is very difficult to conceive chanting and making noise in a place as a network mode of communication to those who can hear it. Social networks are commonly defined as a finite set of nodes (actors) linked by lines (social relations) (Laumann and Pappi 1976; Wasserman and Faust 1997). To make network analysis a meaningful tool in sociology, those lines are usually confined to social relations that are relatively stable and can be specified prior to a study. They are also restricted to privileged and specific information and resources exchanges or boundary overlapping among actors (Laumann and Pappi 1976; Laumann and Knoke 1987, pp. 12–13). For example, if there is a loud clap of thunder in the middle of the night that wakes up many people, it cannot be said that these people acquire information of the storm through social networks. However, if someone is not wakened by the thunder and does not know about the storm until informed by a friend, it can comfortably be said that the latter acquires this piece of information through a network relation.[16] Obviously, in that evening those students who chanted outside targeted everyone who lived in the dormitories rather than a specific group of people. In other words, information about the demonstration was not passed through prior existing ties but through a near simultaneous direct contact with all who lived on campus. The mode of information transmission was thus diffused and nonprivileged. Network analysis loses its analytical power if information transmission of this kind is interpreted as networks.

Second, the role of networks in movement mobilization is not just communication but solidarity. In other words, if it is argued that students were mobilized that evening through networks, then the students who came out of their dormitories should be roughly of two categories: most came out of a sense of solidarity and some came out because they were persuaded or coerced by their roommates. However, this was not the case that evening. This was still April 17, two days after Hu Yaobang's sudden death. At this stage, most students in Beijing had not been mobilized politically. Therefore, in that evening while some joined the march out of various grievances or a sense of solidarity, most followed the

march without a political reason.[17] In fact, according to one of my informants (no. 63), more than half of the students came out of dormitories and followed the march wearing slippers and gradually left the march before it arrived at Tiananmen Square, and many of his friends including himself followed the demonstration simply because they wanted to *kanrenao* (literally, watch the fun).[18] In short, there was no clear evidence of persuasion and coercion among students that evening. No common grievances, identity, or network-based mobilization could be constructed.

What about the intensive persuasion and coercion inside the dormitory, which I discussed earlier? There was a threshold: the majority of students only acted as sympathetic audiences most of the time during the movement, and they did not care about their fellow roommates' decisions about movement participation. However, on some occasions the state's reaction to the movement was deemed unreasonable by most students. At that point, students started to share their anger in dormitories, and more committed students also started to persuade and even coerce the less active ones to join protest activities.[19] Students' reaction to the April 26 *People's Daily* editorial is one such occasion.

The April 27 Demonstration

I chose the April 27 student demonstration as a case study to illustrate the importance of campus ecology in the process of mobilization. The demonstration was one of the most important events of the 1989 BSM. It marked the first large-scale open defiance of Chinese to the state since the Communists took power. The success of the demonstration in many ways shaped the subsequent dynamics of the movement, which finally led to the crackdown. Equally important, the demonstration was perceived by many students as extremely risky, perhaps even more so than the protest activities on the night of June 3. Some students even wrote wills before joining the demonstration. Though the demonstration was not suppressed, the state did set up many police lines to try to stop the students from entering Tiananmen Square. The existence of state force and the perceived danger pushed students to utilize any possible resources, including ecological conditions, to make the demonstration successful.

Background

Since the movement started as mourning for Hu Yaobang's death, the government was unable to take any major action before Hu Yaobang's state funeral on April 22. On April 24, a politburo meeting was held to deal with the movement. The result of that meeting was the April 26 *People's Daily* editorial, which labeled the movement as a turmoil instigated by a small number of antirevolutionaries. Major excerpts of the editorial were broadcast on the April 25 evening news. Students in Beijing were deeply alienated by the outdated language that the editorial used. The Autonomous Student Union decided to defy the editorial by a demonstration on April 27.

The government tried to prevent the coming demonstration. It demanded that university authorities, including student control organizations, prevent students from going to the street. Their efforts failed to stop students. The government also mobilized all the police forces in Beijing, including some troops, and set many police lines on the street to try to stop the demonstrators from entering Tiananmen Square. The major police lines are marked on figure 2.

The Demonstration

After hearing the editorial and the news of the proposed demonstration, students as well as activists gathered in dormitory rooms to express their anger and to discuss what would happen if they went out. Most expected a harsh crackdown, but many still decided to participate. The feeling of injustice was too strong for students to succumb to threats.

However, most students were also extremely worried. Here, except for the coercion that I discussed earlier, more determined roommates also acted as counselors to the less committed ones. As one student (no. 59) recalled:

> Several of my roommates were extremely worried about possible consequences of the next day's demonstration. I had to comfort them. They said that I was very persuasive and should share my ideas with other students in the university. They suggested

that I use the intercom in the porter's room. The intercom was installed for the porter to get a particular student when there was a phone call for her or him....We turned on all the switches so that people in every dormitory room could hear but no one outside would know.

Meanwhile, the Autonomous Student Union broadcast stations in many universities repeatedly aired speeches from student activists, young teachers, and famous dissidents to denounce the editorial and the government, and to boost the morale of students. Places like the Triangle in Beijing University were crowded with people for the whole day of April 26. They made speeches, chanted slogans, and sang songs. Activists' emotions were kept high.

The demonstration took three routes to Tiananmen Square. Beijing University, People's University, Qinghua University, Northern Communication University, and Beijing Agriculture University took the west route. The Fada University, Beijing Normal University, and eight big institutions of higher learning took the middle route. Finally, a few other universities took the east route (Wu 1990). Figure 2 illustrates the paths of the demonstration of the west and middle route.

However, students did not march to Tiananmen Square directly. They zigzagged. In what follows, by centering on People's University and Fada's path of demonstration, I will explain how and why students marched this way, as well as other ecology-related issues.

In the morning of April 27, some students appeared at People's University. Yet, under enormous pressure, no one dared to march out of the campus as planned. One informant (no. 39) even saw a student leader with a red microphone announcing that the demonstration was canceled, but many students remained. After quite some time, one student came out and suggested marching inside the university. Many followed. However, after marching and chanting for five or six rounds in the university, more and more people were attracted and joined in. Students also became increasingly excited. Eventually they rushed out of the gate. However, when they were out, they did not march directly to Tiananmen Square. A police line was at the Friendship Hotel intersection, which was not

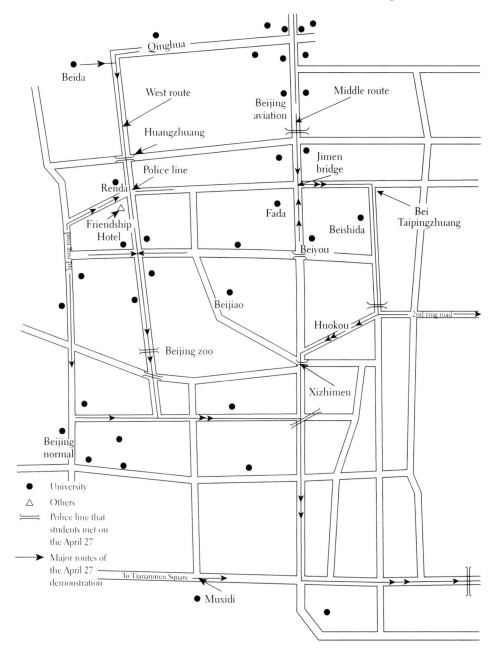

Figure 11.2 The west and middle route of student protest and police lines during the April 27 demonstration.

far away from People's University. Students were too afraid to encounter the police, so they marched in the opposite direction to try to meet the students from Beijing University and Qinghua University.

Here, many liaison men played an important role. Most liaison men were not assigned to do the job by movement organizers. These were students (almost all of them were male) who wanted to see more of the demonstration. When they saw that students of People's University had come out, the liaison men rushed to Beijing University on bicycles and chanted in front of the gate of Beijing University: "People's University has come out What are you waiting for?" Students in Beijing University then came out.

There was a police line at the Huangzhuang intersection. However, with students from Beijing University, Qinghua University, and People's University on two sides of it, the police line collapsed. The students joined and marched back to the Friendship Hotel intersection. This time, the Northern Communication students and students from some other universities also arrived at the southern side of the intersection but dared not push away the police line. With students from Beijing University and Qinghua University at the back and students from many other universities at the other side of the police line, the students led by People's University students easily pushed away the police line at the Friendship Hotel intersection.

This was a historical push for students of the west route as well as the middle route. Many students who had stayed outside the formation joined in.[20] Liaison men spread in different directions to inform the students of their own universities. The size of the formation expanded enormously. An informant (no. 70) vividly described what was happening at the Friendship Hotel intersection:

> When students of People's University met the police lines, they dared not march forward and asked students from Beijing University to go first. But students of Beijing University did not want to go either.... At the moment, quite a few self-appointed organizers from the outside stepped in and commanded demonstrators to line up well, to keep a good order, and so on. As the intersection became more and more crowded, people from the outside

repeatedly chanted: Go...go...Let's go together! Finally students of People's University started to move forward. When they confronted the police lines, students talked to policemen about constitutional rights. The policemen had no reaction. Then students started to push. The police lines collapsed soon after. On seeing this, organizers and students from different universities rushed back to get their own students. I heard a student from Beijing Industrial University say, "We lost face today," and rushed back quickly.[21] Students from those universities then waited at different intersections. The scale of the demonstration expanded enormously.

During that morning, many liaison men rode their own bicycles from one university to another. On their way, they passed the news of what was happening elsewhere. By doing this, they had consciously or unconsciously coordinated the movement. One of my informants (no. 57) was one of them on that day:

> When I got up in the morning, I saw students in Beijing Teacher's were already marching at the campus stadium. I wanted to know what was happening in People's University. I went there by bicycle. At the time that I arrived, students of People's University had gone north to meet students from Beijing University. I then followed. By the time that I met with students of People's University they had already joined with students from Beijing University and moved back again. I then rode back to the Friendship Hotel intersection and watched. There were police lines there and students from Northern Communication were stopped by them on the south side. When the big troops [of students] arrived, with the efforts from both sides, the police line soon collapsed....As soon as students pushed policemen aside, I rode back to Beijing Teacher's to see what they were doing. I saw that students were sitting on the sidewalk outside their university. I passed the message: go quickly in Chegongzhuang direction, students from other universities are coming.

Fada University took the middle route in the April 27 demonstration. Initially, students in Fada were not able to get out. The president and a few other university authorities were standing in front of the gate. They claimed that it was too dangerous to go outside. They requested that the students confine their activities on the campus for their own safety. The president even begged the students. However, a few students had already gone to other universities to see what was happening there. When the news came back that Beijing Aviation had broken one police line and were marching in their direction, students in Fada rushed out and moved south in the direction of Tiananmen Square. Meanwhile, picket lines were formed outside the demonstrators. Only about 200 students were inside the picket lines. Including followers, the formation was no greater than 600 or 700 people.

When they marched to Mingguanchun, a police line stopped them. Fada students dared not march further. They withdrew and moved north to the University of Posts and Telecommunication. As one student (no. 60) recalled: "When we arrived at the University of Posts and Telecommunication, we chanted loudly outside their campus. I saw a lot of students who were stopped inside their gate by some teachers. Many students were waving at us over the window of their dormitory rooms. We shouted: Come down! Come down! Then more and more students jumped over the campus wall. Eventually students inside the University of Posts and Telecommunication pushed their way out of the gate."

Meanwhile, many Fada students came over from the campus and more and more students outside the picket lines joined in. Students within the picket lines increased to some 700 or 800. Some other universities from the south such as the Central Finance University also joined. They then continued to march north. At Jimen bridge they met with students from Beijing Aviation University, Beijing Medical University, and many other universities. The above quoted informant (no. 60) recalled that he was already unable to see the two ends of the student formation after the merging. Together they moved east to Taipingzhuang then south to meet with students of Beijing Normal University.

During this entire time, liaison men continuously passed news on what had happened in the west route, a route taken by several of the most prestigious universities. As they arrived at Beijing Normal University, news came from the west that students of Beijing University and People's University had broken the Friendship Hotel police line. Students in the middle route cheered. They decided to join the west route. So they marched southwest, pushed away a police line at Huokou, and eventually met the west route after Xizhimen.

Several witnesses recalled the moment as unforgettable. By the time the two groups met, all the intersections were filled with students and civilians. People who stood on the Xizhimen overpass could not see where the crowds ended in all the directions. A renowned student leader (no. 69) told me with emotion that he had never seen such a magnificent scene in his life. At this point, most students were no longer worried about their safety. But it was not until they broke the last police line at Liubukou and entered Tiananmen Square that they realized that the government was totally defeated. Their joy was fully expressed on their way back to their universities as they cried, chanted, and sang songs. Many students walked back. By the time they got back it was already midnight. They had walked for nearly 20 hours.

What had made the April 27 demonstration so successful? Higher levels of grievances and government restraint did play a role here. However, the dormitory factors, the campus environment, and, most important, students' successful use of ecology-dependent strategies were also crucial. Often, students did not march directly out of the campus. If they did so, not many students would follow. The crowd size was still not large enough, people were not yet excited, students were too afraid. Instead, they marched inside the campus first. By marching and shouting, not only did they attract more and more students but they also created an atmosphere of excitement and heightened the pitch of their anger. Finally, they built up enough courage to march out.

Although full of anger, students felt deadly afraid once on the street They avoided confronting the police when they did not feel strong enough. Therefore, they tried to bypass the police line and get more students from other universities. With so many universities around, they were always able to do so. When they had to confront the policemen, the police lines were already overwhelmed by the masses of students coming from all over.

Finally, the instantaneous interactions among universities were also very important. Students in many universities would never demonstrate outside the campus if liaison men had not passed the news that other universities were already on the street. On the other hand, students who were already outside of their campuses might not go very far if students from other universities did not join in. These ecology-dependent strategies were highly effective exactly because of the physical environment of the campuses and the whole university district.

Discussion

Is my emphasis on the importance of the physical environment in movement mobilization a new insight? If this article is summarized into the following two propositions suggested by a reviewer— (a) when organizations of a similar type (e.g., schools or factories) are clustered geographically, collective protest among the groups in them will be more common; and (b) when communities are tightly knit and physically isolated, they have a higher capacity to protest—then the arguments may not seem to be really new. These are the founding insights of the resource mobilization perspective developed by Charles Tilly. Even Marx (1985a, pp. 227–28) has argued in the *Communist Manifesto* that the concentration of workers into a small number of factories will enhance the political capacity of the proletariat. However, the ecological model presented here differs from these two propositions.

First, this article is not so much about density and homogeneity as it is about the spatial distribution and patterned spatial movement of a population caused by design factors—which have been neglected by resource mobilization theorists. Moreover, one should not misconstrue resource mobilization theory and Marx. The key insight of resource mobilization theory (and Marx) is that the density and homogeneity of a population matters to movement mobilization *only* to the extent that they facilitate group solidarity. Therefore, when Tilly (1978, p. 62) discussed "netness," he referred to group solidarity created by "a specific kind of interpersonal bond." When he put "catness" and "netness" together, he equated them to organization. Finally, when Tilly and his associates measured the

level of mobilization, what was actually measured was the level of organization (Tilly 1978, pp. 69–84). This is understandable because what is implied in the resource mobilization theory is that high density and homogeneity actually lead to a low mobilization potential if a population is assembled simply as "a sack of potatoes" as Marx (1985b, p. 317) commented about the 19th-century French peasants.

This article is by no means trying to undermine the importance of organizations and networks in the mobilization process. However, it does show that the design factors of Beijing universities, the accompanying density and distribution of a population, and its patterned spatial movement had great importance to the formation of student networks on campus. This importance cannot be properly understood without the knowledge of campus ecology.[22] Therefore, the analysis at this level bears similarities to Festinger et al.'s (1950) classic study, a perspective that has not been adopted by many resource mobilization scholars.

Moreover, my study suggests that some ecology-dependent process of mobilization cannot be reduced to networks and organizations. The zigzag route of demonstration, the specific places where students put their big character posters and made speeches, the march inside the dormitory areas, and so forth had much more to do with the spatial layout of the campus and university district than the organizations and networks of the movement. Trying to explain these kinds of mobilizing strategies in terms of networks and solidarities will not only blur our sensitivity toward variations behind the seemingly similar process of movement mobilization, but also stretch the common definition of social networks to an extent that every kind of social relation becomes a network relation and every kind of knowledge transmission is network-based communication.

The importance of ecology to movement mobilization lies in the fact that, other factors being equal, the mobilizing potential of a population will be different if the same population is spatially arranged in even a slightly different way. During the 1980s, student movements in Beijing had two rather consistent patterns: Students who came to the universities from places outside Beijing had a higher participation rate than students from Beijing, and graduate students had a lower participation rate than undergraduates.[23] The patterns can be interpreted in a few ways, yet both can be simply explained in terms of the spatial positions that different categories of students were in: Beijing students were able to go home after the April 22 class strike so they were not exposed as much to movement activities as were students who remained in the dormitories. On the other hand, each graduate student dormitory room housed only two to four students. As some were married and lived off campus, the real occupancy was often lower than the capacity. Therefore, it was more difficult, if not impossible, to form any kind of majority in a room.

I also found that when a university had two campuses with one inside and another outside the Haidian District, the one outside the district had a much lower rate of movement participation. For example, Beijing Normal University had two campuses, and the one outside had a much lower rate of participation than the one located inside the university district. The following narrative from a student of that university explains why: "My first year university life was spent on the campus near Beihai. We did not join in the class boycott. We also participated in very few demonstrations. We did not go to the main campus very often. We knew little about what was going on over there" (no. 33).

In other words, to participate in the movement, one had to be at least exposed to the environment. This is a very good controlled case. Since the differentiated participation occurred at the same university, it is very difficult to imagine that factors other than the spatial location of campuses contributed to the level of student participation.

It is possible to see affinities between my work and Gould's work on mobilization during the June uprising in 1848 in Paris and the Paris Commune in 1871. Gould essentially argues that, because of the Haussmann projects, the new Paris residential areas were no longer class based. Consequently, the mobilizing base of the Paris Commune was no longer working-class consciousness, as was the case of the June uprising in 1848, but neighborhood solidarity.[24] To the extent that both Gould and I intend to show how the spatial arrangement

of people contributed to movement mobilization, our works share similarities. However, while Gould focuses on the impact of the macrodesign factors of the Haussmann project on movement mobilization, this article studies the ecological impact not only at the level of the university district, but also at the level of individual campuses and even dormitories. These microlevel ecological dimensions determined the mobilizing potential as well as the strategies of the movement. Moreover, Gould intends to let networks speak for an ecologically embedded social structure. His idea is, thus, tied to the conventional—group solidarity—wisdom. My strategy, on the other hand, is to let the ecology speak for the mobilization, and I have shown that the mobilization during the 1989 BSM was assisted not only by ecology-based student networks but also directly by the campus ecology itself.

Recently, resource mobilization theories started to move away from a narrow perspective that emphasizes only the role of formal organizations and social movement networks in movement mobilization to a more flexible concept called "mobilizing structures" (McCarthy 1996; Tarrow 1994, chap. 8). At this stage, the concept of mobilizing structures is still confined to organic social relations, namely, the formal and informal ties between people that "can serve as solidarity and communication facilitating structure" (McCarthy 1996, p. 143). This article may be viewed as a further development along this direction. I have shown that the spatial layout of a physical environment has a significant impact on the mobilizing potential of the population that lives in it, yet such an impact cannot always be reduced to interpersonal ties and solidarities.

Now, as a mobilizing structure, how important is ecological mobilization to a social movement in general (obviously, a perspective with little generalizability is not desirable)? Here, I argue that the importance of ecology to social movement mobilization depends on the nature of the movement as well as types of regime.[25] Some social movement mobilization is done primarily through formal organizations. This happens, for example, in mainstream society of the contemporary West where associational life is highly developed and politically sensitive individuals are situated under what scholars call "multiorganizational fields" (Curtis and Zurcher 1973; Fernandez and McAdam 1989; McAdam and Paulsen 1993; Rosenthal et al. 1985). Since most organizations of this kind are not territory based and have more effective infrastructures to reach their members, ecological conditions are less likely to be heavily used in movement mobilization. Some social movements in the contemporary West, especially some of the new social movements, have a mobilization process approximate to this ideal type.

Most mobilizing processes, however, involve a mixture of formal organizations, interpersonal networks centered around people's immediate living and working environment, and direct ecological exposures. No systematic research has been conducted. However, as mentioned in the beginning of this article, studies on student movements, social movements in 19th-century Europe, community movements, and black riots in America do point to the importance of ecological conditions to movement mobilization.

Finally, mobilizing processes of some social movements seem mainly ecologically based. It typically occurs in places where intermediate associations are underdeveloped and associations beyond state control are illegal. In such cases, the ecology and ecology-based networks and communications become the only means that a movement mobilization can count on. Many social movements in strong authoritarian regimes have a mobilizing process close to this extreme because those states suppress volunteer associations. In a sense, the 1989 BSM is an ideal case to study the impact of ecology on movement mobilization. As a student movement and, more important, as a movement occurring in an authoritarian regime where associational life was sanctioned, ecology became critical. By studying a movement of this kind, the extent to which a physical environment can influence movement mobilization can be explored.

A final issue that I would like to bring out is that an environment that allows easy communication and mobilization may also facilitate state control. Therefore, I must also explain why the same university environment that contributed to the repeated rise of student movements in the 1980s,

did not lead to any sizable student uprising during Mao's era.[26]

The answer lies in the weakening of the student control system in universities. Different from the control system in most East European countries, political control in Chinese universities depended mainly on the cooperation of students with nonprofessional political workers, which is also known as "internal control" (Schurmann 1968). As I have argued elsewhere (Zhao 1997), this control method is particularly sensitive to the ideological legitimation of the state and the economic and political reward patterns in the larger society. In the 1950s and 1960s, many students who more or less believed in communism felt it was moral to turn in students who expressed independent thinking. Moreover, during that time every university student was assigned jobs upon graduation by the state. Students who were politically more active (including checking upon other students' political conduct) usually got better positions. Therefore, during Mao's era, the high student density and other spatial characteristics of the campus had actually extended the effectiveness of student control. After the economic reform, however, the ideological legitimation of the Communist state greatly declined while other avenues of status attainment outside the realm of state control opened up.[27] Participating actively in mutual supervision became neither a moral nor necessarily a profitable activity. Therefore, the campus environment, which once facilitated political control over students, became conducive to student mobilization.

Conclusion

To date, scholars who are interested in the impact of the physical environment on social action have focused on elementary social relations or psychological mechanisms, and scholars of social movements have tended to believe that formal movement organizations and interpersonal networks are the primary base for movement mobilization. They both have neglected the fact that ecological conditions—in the sense of the spatial characteristics of a physical environment and the accompanying density, distribution, composition, place-based relations, and routine spatial activities of a given population—could function as a "social structure" and achieve predominance in the mobilization.

This article argues that ecology is relevant to movement mobilization because it determines the structure and strength of social networks as well as the spatial position and routine activities of people in a community. It shows that, as a result of state planning of higher education, most universities in Beijing are located in one area and have a similar structure, and most students live in dormitories located at one corner of the campus and have similar rhythmic spatial movement. During the 1989 BSM, this campus ecology greatly assisted the information transmission and mobilization of Beijing students at the dormitory, university, and the Haidian District levels. As illustrated by the April 27 student demonstration, students also actively made use of the campus ecology, so that it encouraged movement participation and invalidated the normal state control measures. They had also created a rather stable set of ecology-dependent strategies of collective action which gave many unique characteristics to and, to some extent, patterned the dynamics of the 1989 BSM.

In the past, scholars generally thought that communist regimes were highly stable because their repression was assisted by modern infrastructural and military technologies. This totalitarian myth was broken after revolutions swept across Eastern Europe in the late 1980s. Thereafter the question, "How can autocratic regimes that appear to have such awesome power over their citizens collapse so quickly?" (Olson 1990, p. 16), became a puzzle. Restricted by conventional wisdom, most scholars have tried to address the question by emphasizing the role of civil society during East European revolutions. In the light of this article, these studies are possibly limited. Judging by the nature of the former East European regimes, it is conceivable that even in Hungary, Czechoslovakia, and Poland, where civil society was more developed, their initial movement mobilization might depend more on ecology and ecology-dependent strategies than on formal organizations or political networks.

For instance, similarities can be seen between the mobilizing strategies of the Beijing students and the Polish workers during the Gdansk and Gdynia strike in 1970 as described Laba's (1991) book on the root of the Solidarity movement. At the initial stage of the strike, a few activists chanted from one workplace to another to attract followers; they also pushed a sound car to different shipyards to draw more people (Laba 1991, chap. 2). The existing organizations such as the Workers' Defense Committee (KOR) or the Catholic Church had nothing to do with the strike at this stage. The importance of shipyard ecology is clearly revealed even though Laba does not mainly focus on the issue of movement mobilization.

An authoritarian regime may crush intermediate associations, but it is not able to destroy ecology-centered human interactions. In fact, as it is revealed in this article, the process of centralization under an authoritarian regime often strengthens ecology-based human interactions. The huge capacity of ecology-centered mobilization at the time of political crisis explains, in part, why the seemingly mighty Communist regime is actually fragile.

NOTES

The author would like to thank Maurice Pinard, Steven Rytina, Donald von Eschen, Suzanne Staggenborg, Robert Sampson, William Parish, John McCarthy, Craig Jenkins, Qin Chen, and the *AJS* reviewers for their insightful comments on the early versions of this article.

1. The phrase *resource mobilization I theory* was coined to distinguish it from McCarthy and Zald's (1973, 1977) version of resource mobilization theory, which attributed the rise of social movements in the 1960s to the increased supply of resources (particularly discretionary time and money).

2. In this article, I define *organization* as a social group that is constructed to seek specific goals through coordinated effort. It usually has a nonrandom division of labor, power, and communication responsibilities (Etzioni 1964). Churches, unions, neighborhood associations, student and professional associations, and social movement organizations are some examples. I will discuss the concept of social networks later in this article.

3. For the Chinese case, see Huan (1989), Strand (1993), and Sullivan (1990), and for East European cases, see Di Palma (1991), Ost (1990), Poznanski (1992), and Tismaneanu (1990).

4. By *ecology,* I mean the impact of the campus physical environment on students and the reaction of students toward the environment. By *physical environment,* I refer to design factors of the architecture in each university and the layout of the entire university district in Beijing. The physical environment determines the spatial distribution and daily

spatial activities of students, which shape student interactions through passive encounters and active networking.

5. *Ecology-dependent strategies* are a relatively stable set of mobilizing strategies. Their effectiveness and their likelihood to be adopted by movement activists are based largely on particular ecological conditions.

6. Beyond the ones that I discuss below, ecological perspectives have been adopted in the study of populations of organizations (Hannan and Freeman 1989). Also, in *Union Democracy,* Lipset, Trow, and Coleman (1956) have analyzed how the ecology of work, such as the substitute worker system, the activity pattern of workers on the night shift, and the structure of larger printing plants, facilitated the formation of social networks and print workers' participation in union activities.

7. Similarly, Marxists also assume that human spatial relations reflect the reality of class domination (Castells 1978; Harvey 1985; Molotch 1979).

8. Festinger et al.'s (1950) work is particularly interesting. They found that people tend to make friends with immediate neighbors. Moreover, the design factor of a housing project such as the location of mailboxes and stairways, the position of an apartment in a courtyard or a building, and the door that an apartment faces would determine people's daily spatial movement, ability to make friends, and group formation in a community. Blau (1977) has also formalized similar ecology-centered propositions into theorems.

9. Hu Yaobang was the general secretary of the Chinese Communist Party between 1981 and 1987. Forced to resign his position because of his soft attitude toward the student unrest in 1986, Hu became a widely respected figure among students and intellectuals.

10. Most demonstrations during the hunger strike were semiofficial in the sense that the organizers could freely use public resources, the participants were given paid leave, and the whole action was either tacitly approved or directly led by the authorities of work units.

11. At this stage, most troops were unarmed. After being stopped, soldiers usually did not push their way through.

12. In 1988 and early 1989, major Chinese universities were the sites of numerous antiestablishment conferences held by dissidents or liberal intellectuals. My informants referred to this as "conference fever."

13. *World Economic Herald* was an outspoken newspaper published in Shanghai during the 1980s. It has stopped publishing since 1989.

14. In game theory language, this is a prisoner's dilemma game involving a small number of people and with a large number of iterations. As Axelrod (1984) has nicely demonstrated, repeated encounters between two players in this game make cooperation the only robust and optimum long-term solution. In other words, it is actually unnecessary to introduce Chinese culture at this point because a sense of

group solidarity or friendship will at most only function as an initial condition of the Axelrodian game to speed up the rise and dominance of conformist behavior.

15. The interuniversity competition was induced also because, when the ideological legitimacy of the state greatly declined, some students took activism as a point of honor and equated the level of activism with the prestige of their university.

16. In reality, the distinction is not always that clear. A general rule is that the more the linkages among the nodes are privileged and specific, the more such linkages are subject to meaningful sociological analysis.

17. The demonstration was spontaneously initiated when someone came back from downtown and announced at the Triangle that Fada students had demonstrated at Tiananmen Square in the afternoon. The activists who gathered at the Triangle did not plan this demonstration beforehand, nor did they have a clear purpose. Several hours after the march (they almost arrived at Tiananmen Square), student leader Zhang Boli was still asking Wang Dan about the purpose of the demonstration, and Wang Dan replied: "I do not know. It is you guys who started this" (Zhang and Bai 1993, pp. 49–51).

18. When they arrived at Tiananmen Square, the size of the demonstration was only around 2,000, which also included many students that they picked up from other universities along the way.

19. The distinction made here bears similarities with Tilly's (1978, p. 73) defensive and offensive style of mobilization.

20. The student demonstration was separated from urban residents by picket lines on each side. In the past, the government often charged that student demonstrations created riots and looting in Beijing. Therefore, students developed this strategy to make sure the demonstrators were bona fide students.

21. Here, the student said his university lost face because students in his university did not participate in the Friendship Hotel incident for it was perceived as too dangerous. See the section on interuniversity competition for activism for more discussion on this issue.

22. For example, as I have discussed earlier, without a clear awareness of the campus ecology in Beijing, Calhoun was led to explain the phenomenon he found in terms of students' sense of solidarity rooted in Chinese culture (Calhoun 1991, 1994).

23. A study conducted in Beijing University also indicated that the participation rate of an earlier student movement in 1986 was 49.6% for city students, 58.9% for rural students, and 68.2% for small-town students (Liu and Huang 1989). The same article also reported that graduate students participated considerably less than undergraduates.

24. For example, Gould (1991, 1995) shows that the recruitment system of the National Guard during the Paris Commune was residentially based, and thus, guardsmen in two districts shared a certain level of neighborhood ties. He

is able to find that when the resistance at one district was strong and a large number of guardsmen in that district was recruited from another district (implying more ties with the people in another district), then the resistance of the other district would also tend to be strong, even if these two districts were spatially remote.

25. Scholars generally agree that the mobilizing structures of a social movement are primarily shaped by the nature of a state and state-society relations (Kriesi 1996; Rucht 1996; Tarrow 1994).

26. I exclude the Red Guard movement during the 1960s because it was mainly a state-sponsored mobilization.

27. For example, during the 1980s many students preferred to go abroad, to work in better paid foreign and joint venture companies, than to work in the state-controlled public sector.

12.
Black Southern Student Sit-in Movement: An Analysis of Internal Organization

ALDON MORRIS

Scholars of the Civil Rights movement (Zinn, 1964; Oppenheimer, 1964; Matthews and Prothro, 1966; Meier and Rudwick, 1973; Oberschall, 1973; McAdam, 1979) and Civil Rights activists agree that the black Southern student sit-in movement of 1960 was a crucial development. The sit-ins pumped new life into the Civil Rights movement and enabled it to win unprecedented victories. Moreover, the sit-ins exercised a profound tactical and strategic influence over the entire course of social and political upheavals of the 1960s.

Apart from having a jarring impact on race relations, the sit-ins signaled the possibility of militant action at both Northern and Southern white campuses (Haber, 1966; Obear, 1970; Sale, 1973). A critical mass of the early leaders of the white student movement acquired much of their training, organizing skills, and tactics from the black activists of the student sit-in movement (Sale, 1973; Westby, 1976). Thus, the beginning of the white student movement as well as the quickened pace of Civil Rights activity can be traced to the black student sit-in movement.

Morris, Aldon D. 1981. "Black Southern Sit-in Movement: An Analysis of Internal Organization." *American Sociological Review* 46: 744–767. Reprinted by permission of American Sociological Association.

The sit-ins were important because their rapid spread across the South crystalized the conflict of the period and pulled many people directly into the movement. How is such a "burst" of collective action to be explained? A standard account of the sit-ins has emerged which maintains that the sit-ins were the product of an independent black student movement which represented a radical break from previous civil rights activities, organizations, and leadership of the Black community (e.g. Lomax, 1962; Zinn, 1964; Oppenheimer, 1964; Matthews and Prothro, 1966; Meier and Rudwick, 1973; Oberschall, 1973; Piven and Cloward, 1977).

In the standard account, various factors are argued to be the driving force behind the sit-ins, including impatience of the young, mass media coverage, outside resources made available by the liberal white community of the North, and support from the Federal Government. Although these writers differ over the proximate causes of the sit-ins, they nevertheless concur that the sit-ins broke from the organizational and institutional framework of the emerging Civil Rights movement. The data for the present study do not fit this standard account and suggest that a different account and interpretation of the sit-ins is warranted. The purpose of this paper is to present new data on the Southern student sit-in movement of 1960, and to provide a framework that will theoretically order the empirical findings.

Theoretical Context and Propositions

Classical collective behavior theory and the recently formulated resource mobilization theory are the major sociological frameworks that attempt to provide explanations of the origins, development, and outcomes of social movements. Classical collective behavior theory (e.g. Blumer, 1946; Turner and Killian, 1957; Lang and Lang, 1961; and Smesler, 1963) maintains that social movements differ substantially from institutionalized behavior. Social movements are theorized to be relatively spontaneous and unstructured. Movement participants are often portrayed as nonrational actors functioning outside of normative constraints and propelled by high levels of strain.

Classical collective behavior theorists do not deny that organizations and institutional processes play a role in collective behavior. Rather, organizations and institutional processes emerge in the course of movements and become important in their later stages. The standard account of the sit-ins fits the collective behavior imagery. Indeed, it can be argued that the diverse proponents of the "standard account" have been unduly influenced by classical collective behavior theory; their account largely ignores the organizational and institutional framework out of which the sit-ins emerged and spread.

The resource mobilization explanation (e.g. Oberschall, 1973; Gamson, 1975; Tilly, 1978; McCarthy and Zald, 1973) of social movements differs markedly from classical collective behavior theory. In this view, social movements have no distinct inner logic and are not fundamentally different from institutionalized behavior. Organizations, institutions, pre-existing communication networks, and rational actors are all seen as important resources playing crucial roles in the emergence and outcome of collective action. In contrast to classical collective behavior theory, organizational and institutional structures are argued to be central throughout the entire process of collective action.

In its present formulation, resource mobilization theory is unclear about the type of organization and resources that are crucial for the initiation and spread of collective action. Some theorists (Oberschall, 1973; McCarthy and Zald, 1973; Jenkins and Perrow, 1977) argue that resources and organizations outside the protest group are crucial in determining the scope and outcomes of collective action. External groups and resources are argued to be especially critical for movements of the poor. In other formulations of this approach (e.g. Gamson, 1975; Tilly, 1978), emphasis is placed on the important role that internal organization plays in collective action. However, internal organization is but one of several variables (e.g. repression, bureaucracy, opportunity) that are investigated. In my view such an approach fails to capture the degree to which collective action is dependent on internal organization.

This paper focuses on the central function that internal organization played in the emergence and development of the sit-in movement. My analysis suggests that one-sided emphases on spontaneous processes or outside resources can lead to unwarranted neglect of internal structure. A case will be made that the diffusion of the 1960 sit-ins cannot be understood without treating internal organization as a central variable. The analysis will be guided by three propositions.

Proposition 1. Pre-existing social structures provide the resources and organizations that are crucial to the initiation and spread of collective action. Following Tilly (1978), collective action is defined here as joint action by protest groups in pursuit of common ends. This proposition maintains that collective action is rooted in organizational structure and carried out by rational actors attempting to realize their ends. This proposition is central to resource-mobilization theory and has received considerable support from a number of empirical studies (Oberschall, 1973; Gamson, 1975; Tilly, 1975).

Proposition 2. The extent and distribution of internal social organization will determine the extent to which innovations in collective strategy and tactics are adopted, spread, and sustained. This proposition directs attention to a protest group's internal organization—its "local movement centers." A local movement center is that component of social structure within a local community that organizes and coordinates collective action. A local movement center has two major properties. First, it includes all protest organizations and leaders of a specific community that are actively engaged in organizing and producing collective action. During the sit-ins, the Southern Christian Leadership Conference (SCLC), Youth Councils of the National Association for the Advancement of Colored People (NAACP), Congress of Racial Equality (CORE), and "direct action" churches existed in numerous Southern black communities. A local center within the Civil Rights movement included all these organizations and leaders. Second, a local movement center contains a unit that coordinates protest activities within the local movement and between the local center and other institutions of the larger community. During the Civil Rights movement, a particular church usually served as the local coordinating unit. Through this unit the protest activities of the church community, college community, activist organizations, and their leaders were mobilized and coordinated. Thus, movement centers provide the organization and coordination capable of sustaining and spreading collective action.

Proposition 3. There is an interaction between the type of pre-existing internal organization and the type of innovations in strategy and tactics that can be rapidly adopted and spread by a protest group. This proposition addresses the issue of why a protest group adopts a particular tactical innovation rather than another.[1] Whereas Proposition II maintains that diffusion of an innovation in strategy is a function of the development and spread of internal social organization, Proposition III specifies that certain types of organization are more conducive than others to the diffusion and adoption of certain types of tactical innovation.

In short, the framework for the analysis of the 1960 sit-ins consists of three interrelated propositions. One, collective action is initiated through pre-existing structures. Two, tactical innovation within a movement is a function of well-developed and widespread internal organization. Three, the type of innovation in strategy and tactics which can be rapidly disseminated and sustained is largely determined by the characteristic internal organization of a protest group.

Data

This study of the sit-ins is part of a larger study on the origins of the Civil Rights movement (Morris,

forthcoming). A substantial part of the data were collected from primary sources—archives and interviews with Civil Rights participants. The archival research was conducted at various sites between May and September of 1978.[2] Thousands of original documents (i.e. memoranda, letters, field reports, organizational histories and directives, interorganizational correspondences, etc.) generated by movement participants were examined. These data contained a wealth of information pertaining to key variables—organization, mobilization, finance, rationality, spontaneity—relevant to the study of movements.

Interviews with participants of the movement constituted the second source of data. Detailed interviews with over 50 Civil Rights leaders were conducted. Interviews made it possible to follow-up on many issues raised by the archival data; and, since these interviews were semi-open-ended, they revealed unexpected insights into the movement. Whenever statements were heard that seemed novel or promising, interviewees were given freedom to speak their piece.

Methods

The strategy for the archival research was straightforward. The researcher examined every document possible within the time allocated for a particular site.[3] The main objective was to examine the roles played in the sit-ins by variables associated with Weberian theory and theories of collective behavior and resource mobilization. Following collective behavior theory, I was concerned with the extent to which the sit-ins were spontaneous and discontinuous with established social structure. From Weberian theory I was interested in whether a charismatic attraction between a leader and followers was sufficient to produce the heavy volume of collective action in the 1960 sit-ins. Finally, several issues addressed by resource mobilization theory were of interest. I examined archival sources to ascertain the role of social organization and resources in the sit-ins. Also, I was concerned with whether the leadership, money, and skills behind the sit-ins were supplied by outsiders or by the indigenous Southern black community.

Three strategies were employed in the interview process. First, the researcher attempted to learn as much as possible about the movement from extensive library and archival sources before conducting interviews. This prior knowledge enabled the interviewer to ask specific questions and to assist interviewees in rooting their memories in the social, temporal, and geographical context of their actions twenty years earlier. Prior knowledge enabled the interviewer to gain the respect of interviewees and increased the likelihood that they would approach the interview in a serious manner.

Second, the interviews were semistructured, usually lasting two or three hours. An extended list of questions structured around the variables used in the archival research were formulated beforehand. The interviewees were instructed to feel free to deviate from the questions and to discuss what they thought to be important. Their "diversions" produced new information.

Third, the interview sample was assembled in two ways. While examining the archival material, the names of leaders associated with various activities turned up constantly. These were the initial individuals contacted for interviews. Once the interview process was underway, interviewees would invariably remark, often in response to queries, "you know, you really should speak to [so-and-so] regarding that matter." Subsequent interviews were arranged with many of these individuals. Thus, the snowball effect was central to the sampling process. Although the activists interviewed came from numerous organizations and represented different, if not conflicting, viewpoints, to our surprise they agreed on many basic issues.

Given that the sit-in movement occurred twenty years ago, it is reasonable to wonder whether interview accounts are reliable and valid. Moreover, there is the suspicion that participants might have vested interests in presenting the "facts" in such a way as to enhance their own status. Such problems of recall and vested interest have been minimized in this research because the analysis is not based on any one source. Rather, it is built on an array of published material, archival sources, and accounts of individuals who participated in and were eyewitnesses to the same events. Furthermore, cross references were made throughout the data collection process. Follow-up phone calls were made to clarify ambiguity and to obtain a comprehensive view of the sit-in movement. It appears that neither of these potential trouble spots produced fundamental defects in the data.

Early Sit-ins: Forerunners

The first myth regarding the sit-in movement is that it started in Greensboro, North Carolina, on February 1, 1960. This research documents that Civil Rights activists conducted sit-ins between 1957 and 1960 in at least fifteen cities: St. Louis, Missouri; Wichita and Kansas City, Kansas; Oklahoma City, Enid, Tulsa, and Stillwater, Oklahoma; Lexington and Louisville, Kentucky; Miami, Florida; Charleston, West Virginia; Sumter, South Carolina; East St. Louis, Illinois; Nashville, Tennessee; and Durham, North Carolina.[4] The Greensboro sit-ins are important because they represent a unique link in a long chain of sit-ins. Although this paper concentrates on the uniqueness of the Greensboro link, there were important similarities in the entire chain. While other studies (Southern Regional Council, 1960; Oppenheimer, 1964; Matthews and Prothro, 1966; Meier and Rudwick, 1973) have not totally overlooked these earlier sit-ins, they fail to reveal their scope, connections, and extensive organizational base.

The early sit-ins were initiated by direct-action organizations. From interviews with participants in the early sit-ins (Moore, 1978; McCain, 1978; Lawson, 1978; Smith, 1978; McKissick, 1978, 1979; Luper, 1981; Randolph, 1981; Lewis, 1981) and published works (Southern Regional Council, 1960; Meier and Rudwick, 1973), I found that Civil Rights organizations initiated sit-ins in fourteen of the fifteen cities I have identified. The NAACP, primarily its Youth Councils, either initiated or co-initiated sit-ins in nine of the fifteen cities. CORE, usually working with the NAACP, played an important initiating role in seven of the fifteen cities. The SCLC initiated one case and was involved in another. Finally, the Durham Committee on Negro Affairs, working with the NAACP, initiated sit-ins in that city. From this data, we can conclude that these early sit-ins were a result of a multi-faceted organizational effort.

These sit-ins received substantial backing from their respective communities. The black church served as the major institutional force behind the sit-ins. Over two decades ago, E. Franklin Frazier argued that "for the Negro masses, in their social and moral isolation in American society, the Negro church community has been a nation within a nation" (Frazier, 1963:49). He argued that the church functioned as the central political arena in black society. Nearly all of the direct-action organizations that initiated these early sit-ins were closely associated with the church. The church supplied these organizations not only with an established communication network, but also leaders and organized masses, finances, and a safe environment in which to hold political meetings. Direct-action organizations clung to the church because their survival depended on it.

Not all black churches supported the sit-ins. The many that did often supported sit-ins in a critical but "invisible" manner. Thus, Mrs. Clara Luper, the organizer of the 1958 Oklahoma City sit-ins, wrote that the black church did not want to get involved, but church leaders told organizers, "we could meet in their churches. They would take up a collection for us and make announcements concerning our worthwhile activities" (Luper, 1979:3). This "covert" role was central. Interviewed activists revealed that clusters of churches were usually directly involved with the sit-ins. In addition to community support generated through the churches, these activists also received support from parents whose children were participating in demonstrations.

These sit-ins were organized by established leaders of the black community. The leaders did not spontaneously emerge in response to a crisis, but were organizational actors in the full sense of the word. Some sit-in leaders were also church leaders, taught school, and headed up the local direct-action organization; their extensive organizational linkages provided blocks of individuals to serve as demonstrators. Clara Luper wrote, "The fact that I was teaching American History at Dungee High School in Spencer, Oklahoma and was a member of the First Street Baptist Church furnished me with an ample number of young people who would become the nucleus of the Youth Council" (Luper,

1979:1). Mrs. Luper's case is not isolated; leaders of the early sit-ins were enmeshed in organizational networks and were integral members of the black community.

Rational planning was evident in this early wave of sit-ins. During the late fifties, the Revs. James Lawson and Kelly Miller Smith, both leaders of a direct-action organization—Nashville Christian Leadership Council—formed what they called a "nonviolent workshop." In these workshops, Lawson meticulously taught local college students the philosophy and tactics of nonviolent protest (D. Bevel, 1978; Lewis, 1978).[5] In 1959, these students held "test" sit-ins in two department stores. Earlier, in 1957, members of the Oklahoma City NAACP Youth Council created what they called their "project," whose aim was to eliminate segregation in public accommodations (Luper, 1979:3). The project consisted of various committees and groups who planned sit-in strategies. After a year of planning, this group walked into the local Katz Drug Store and initiated their sit-in. In St. Louis in 1955, William Clay organized an NAACP Youth Council. Through careful planning and twelve months of demonstrations, members of this organization were able to desegregate dining facilities at department stores (Meier and Rudwick, 1973:93). In Durham, North Carolina in 1958, black activists of the Durham Committee on Negro Affairs conducted a survey of 5-and-10-cent stores in Durham (Southern Regional Council, 1960). The survey revealed that these stores were heavily dependent on black trade. Clearly, the sit-ins initiated by this group were based on rational planning. A similar picture emerges in Sumter, South Carolina and for all the early sit-ins.

Finally, these early sit-ins were sponsored by indigenous resources of the black community; the leadership was black, the bulk of the demonstrators were black, the strategies and tactics were formulated by blacks, and the finances came out of the pockets of blacks, while their serene spirituals echoed through the churches.[6]

Most of the organizers of the early sit-ins knew each other and were well aware of each other's strategies of confrontation. Many of these activists were part of the militant wing of the NAACP. Following the Montgomery bus boycott, this group began to reorganize NAACP Youth Councils with the explicit purpose of initiating direct-action projects. This group of activists (e.g., Floyd McKissick, Daisy Bates, Ronald Walters, Hosea Williams, Barbara Posey, Clara Luper, etc.) viewed themselves as a distinct group, because the national NAACP usually did not approve of their direct-action approach or took a very ambivalent stance.

These militants of the NAACP built networks that detoured the conservative channels and organizational positions of their superiors. At NAACP meetings and conferences, they selected situations where they could present freely their plans and desires to engage in confrontational politics. At these gatherings, information regarding strategies was exchanged. Once acquainted, the activists remained in touch by phone and mail.

Thus, it is no accident that the early sit-ins occurred between 1957 and 1960. Other instances of 'direct action' also occurred during this period. For example, Mrs. Daisy Bates led black students affiliated with her NAACP Youth Council into the all-white Little Rock Central High School and forced President Eisenhower to send in National Guards. CORE, beginning to gain a foothold in the South, had the explicit goal of initiating direct-action projects. We have already noted that CORE activists were in close contact with other activists of the period. Though these early sit-ins and related activities were not part of a grandiose scheme, their joint occurrences, timing, and approaches were connected via organizational and personal networks.

Sit-in Cluster

Organizational and personal networks produced the first cluster of sit-ins in Oklahoma in 1958. By tracing these networks, we can arrive at a basic understanding of this cluster and a clue to understanding the entire sit-in movement.

In August of 1958, the NAACP Youth Council of Wichita, Kansas, headed by Ronald Walters, initiated sit-ins at the lunch counters of a local drug store (Lewis, 1981). At the same time, Clara Luper and the young people in her NAACP Youth Council were training to conduct sit-ins in Oklahoma City. The adult leaders of these two groups knew each other: in addition to working for the same organization, several members of the two groups were personal friends. Following the initial sit-ins in Wichita, members of the two groups made numerous phone calls, exchanged information, and discussed mutual support. This direct contact was important because the local press refused to cover the sit-ins. In less than a week, Clara Luper's group in Oklahoma City initiated their planned sit-ins.

Shortly thereafter, sit-ins were conducted in Tulsa, Enid, and Stillwater, Oklahoma. Working through CORE and the local NAACP Youth Council, Clara Luper's personal friend, Mrs. Shirley Scaggins, organized the sit-ins in Tulsa (Luper, 1981). Mrs. Scaggins had recently lived in Oklahoma City and knew the details of Mrs. Luper's sit-in project. The two leaders worked in concert. At the same time, the NAACP Youth Council in Enid began to conduct sit-ins. A Mr. Mitchell who led that group (Luper, 1981) knew Mrs. Luper well. He had visited the Oklahoma Youth Council at the outset of their sit-in and discussed with them sit-in tactics and mutual support. The Stillwater sit-ins appear to have been conducted independently by black college students.

A process similar to that in Oklahoma occurred in East St. Louis, Illinois. Homer Randolph, who in late 1958 organized the East St. Louis sit-ins, had previously lived in Oklahoma City, knew Mrs. Luper well, and had young relatives who participated in the Oklahoma City sit-ins.

In short, the first sit-in cluster occurred in Oklahoma in 1958 and spread to cities within a hundred-mile radius via established organizational and personal networks. The majority of these early sit-ins were (1) connected rather than isolated, (2) initiated through organizations and personal ties, (3) rationally planned and led by established leaders, and (4) supported by indigenous resources. Thus, the Greensboro sit-ins did not mark the movement's beginning, but were links in the chain. But the Greensboro sit-ins were a unique link which triggered sit-ins across the South at an incredible pace. What happened in the black community between the late 1950s and early 1960s to produce such a movement?

Emergence of Internal Organization

During the mid-fifties the extensive internal organization of the Civil Rights movement began to crystalize in communities across the South. During this period "direct action" organizations were being built by local activists. Community institutions—especially the black church—were becoming political. The "mass meeting" with political oratory and protest music became institutionalized. During the same period, CORE entered the South with intentions of initiating protest, and NAACP Youth Councils were reorganized by young militant adults who desired to engage in confrontational politics.

However, neither CORE nor the NAACP Youth Councils were capable of mobilizing wide-scale protest such as the sit-ins of 1960, because neither had a mass base in the black community. CORE was small, Northern-based, and white-led, largely unknown to Southern blacks. Historically, the NAACP had been unable to persuade more than 2% of the black population to become members. Furthermore, the national NAACP was oriented to legal strategies, not sit-ins. Following the 1954 school desegregation decision, the NAACP was further weakened by a severe attack by local white power structures. Members of the Southern white power structures attempted to drive local branches of NAACP out of existence by labeling them subversive and demanding they make their membership public. NAACP officials usually refused to comply with this demand because their members might suffer physical and economic reprisals if identified. NAACP's opponents argued in the local courts that this noncompliance confirmed their suspicion that NAACP was subversive, and the courts responded by issuing injunctions which prevented NAACP from operating in a number of Southern states. For example the NAACP was outlawed in the state of Alabama from 1956 to 1965 (Morris, 1980). This repression forced the NAACP to become defensively-oriented and to commit its resources to court battles designed to save itself. Thus, neither CORE nor NAACP Youth Councils were able to provide the political base required to launch the massive sit-ins of 1960.

Nevertheless, between 1955 and 1960 new organizational and protest efforts were stirring in Southern black communities. The efforts attracted CORE southward and inspired the direct-action groups in the NAACP to reorganize its Youth Councils. The Montgomery bus boycott was the watershed. The importance of that boycott was that it revealed to the black community that mass protests could be successfully organized and initiated through indigenous resources and institutions.

The Montgomery bus boycott gave rise to both the Montgomery Improvement Association (MIA) and the Southern Christian Leadership Conference (SCLC). The MIA was organized in December 1955 to coordinate the activities of the mass bus boycott against segregated buses and to serve as the boycott's official decision-making body. The MIA was a local church-based Southern organization. Its leadership was dominated by local ministers of Montgomery, with the Rev. Martin Luther King serving as its first president. The dramatic Montgomery boycott triggered similar boycotts in a number of Southern cities. As in Montgomery, these boycotts were organized through the churches, with a local minister typically becoming the official leader. SCLC was organized in 1957 by activist clergymen from across the South to coordinate and consolidate the various local movements. SCLC's leadership was dominated by black ministers with King elected as its first president, and the major organizational posts were filled by ministers who led local movements. Thus, SCLC was organized to accomplish across the South what the MIA had in Montgomery. The emergence of MIA and SCLC reflected the dominant role that churches began to play in confrontational politics by the late 1950s.

The Montgomery bus boycott demonstrated the political potential of the black church and church-related direct-action organizations. By 1955 the massive migration of blacks from rural to urban areas was well underway, and many Southern cities had substantial black populations. The black urban churches that emerged in these cities were quite different from their rural counterparts. The urban churches were larger, more numerous, and better financed, and were presided over by ministers who were better educated and whose sole occupation was the ministry (Mays and Nicholson, 1933; McAdam, 1979; Morris, 1980). Moreover, urban churches were owned, operated, and controlled by the black community.

These churches functioned as the institutional base of the Montgomery bus boycott. They supplied the movement with money, organized masses, leaders, highly developed communications, and relatively safe environments where mass meetings could be held to plan confrontations. This institutional base was in place prior to the boycott. Movement leaders transformed the churches into political resources and committed them to the ends of the movement. The new duty of the church finance committee was to collect money for the movement. The minister's new role was to use the pulpit to articulate the political responsibilities of the church community. The new role of the choir was to weave political messages into the serene spirituals. Regular church meetings were transformed into the "mass meeting" where blacks joined committees to guide protests, offered up collections to the movement, and acquired reliable information of the movement, which local radio and television stations refused to broadcast. The resources necessary to initiate a black movement were present in Montgomery and other communities. They were transformed into political resources and used to launch the first highly visible mass protest of the modern Civil Rights movement.

The important role of the MIA in the emergence of the modern Civil Rights movement is seldom grasped. As a non-bureaucratic, church-based organization, MIA's organizational affairs were conducted like church services rather than by rigid bureaucratic rules, as in the case of the NAACP. Ministers presided over the MIA the way they presided over their congregations. Ultimate authority inhered in the president, Dr. King. Decisions pertaining to local matters could be reached immediately. Diverse organizational tasks were delegated to the rank-and-file on the spot. Rules and procedures emerged by trial and error and could be altered when they inhibited direct action. Oratory, music, and charismatic personalities energized MIA's organizational affairs. The structure of the organization was designed to allow masses to participate directly in protest activities. The MIA proved to be appropriate for confrontational politics because it was mass-based, nonbureaucratic, Southern-led, and able to transform pre-existing church resources into political power.

Southern blacks took notice of the Montgomery movement. Activists from across the South visited Montgomery to observe the political roles of the church and the MIA. For example, when Hosea Williams (at the time, an activist associated with the NAACP in Savannah, Georgia) visited the Montgomery movement, he marvelled at its dynamics:

> You had had NAACP lawsuits, you'd had NAACP chapters, who had much less than 5% participation anyplace. But here's a place [Montgomery] where they got masses of blacks—they couldn't get a church big enough where they could hold mass rallies. And then, none of them [masses] were riding the buses. I was interested in these strategies and their implementation and in learning how to mobilize the masses to move in concert. [Williams, 1978]

Williams, like countless others, did more than marvel. In his words, "I went back to Savannah and organized the Youth Council and nonviolent movement." Thus, another direct-action organization emerged.

Black ministers were in the best position to organize church-related direct-action organizations in the South. Even while the Montgomery movement was in progress, ministers in other cities (e.g., Steele in Tallahassee, Shuttlesworth in Birmingham, and Davis in New Orleans) began to build mass-based movements patterned after the Montgomery movement: These ministers were not only in a position to organize and commit church resources to protest efforts, they were also linked to each other and the larger community via ministerial alliances. In short, between 1955 and 1960 a profound change in Southern black communities had begun. Confrontational politics were thrust to the foreground through new direct-action organizations closely allied with the church.

SCLC and Movement Centers

The creation of the Southern Christian Leadership Conference (SCLC) in 1957 marked a critical organizational shift for the Civil Rights movement. The ministers who organized SCLC clearly understood the historic and central institutional importance of the church in black society. They knew that the church nurtured and produced most of the indigenous leaders, raised finances, and organized masses, as well as being a major force in other aspects of black culture. By 1957 these ministers, many of whom were leading movements in their local communities, consciously and explicitly concluded that the church was capable of functioning as the institutional vanguard of a mass-based black movement. Hence, they organized SCLC to be a Southern-wide, church-based protest organization.

Prior to SCLC, the major black protest organization—NAACP—had been closely linked with the church. Yet, before SCLC was created, the NAACP, and not the church, functioned as the organization through which protest was initiated. With the emergence of SCLC, the critical shift occurred whereby the church itself, rather than groups closely linked to it, began to function as the institutional center of protest.

In 1957 the organizers of SCLC sent out a call to fellow clergymen of the South to organize their congregations and communities for collective protest. The remarks of Rev. Smith of Nashville typified the action of protest-oriented ministers:

> After the meeting [SCLC organizing meeting] and after the discussion that we had and all that, it became clear to me that we needed something in addition to NAACP. So I came back and I called some people together and formed what we named the Nashville Christian Leadership Council in order to address the same kind of issues that SCLC would be addressing. [Smith. 1978]

Hundreds of ministers across the South took similar action.

From this collective effort resulted what can best be conceptualized as local movement centers of the Civil Rights movement, which usually had the following seven characteristics:

1. A cadre of social-change-oriented ministers and their congregations. Often one minister would become the local leader of a given center and his church would serve as the coordinating unit.

2. Direct action organizations of varied complexity. In many cities local churches served as quasi-direct-action organizations, while in others ministers built complex, church-related organizations (e.g., United Defense League of Baton Rouge, Montgomery Improvement Association, Alabama Christian Movement for Human Rights of Birmingham, Petersburg Improvement Association). NAACP Youth Councils and CORE affiliates also were components of the local centers.

3. Indigenous financing coordinated through the church.

4. Weekly mass meetings, which served as forums and where local residents were informed of relevant information and strategies regarding the movement. These meetings also built solidarity among the participants.

5. Dissemination of nonviolent tactics and strategies. The leaders articulated to the black community the message that social change would occur only through non-violent direct action carried out by masses.

6. Adaptation of a rich church culture to political purposes. The black spirituals, sermons, and prayers were used to deepen the participants commitment to the struggle.

7. A mass-based oñentation, rooted in the black community, through the church.

See Figure 1 for a schematic diagram of a typical local movement center.

Most scholars of the movement are silent about the period between the Montgomery bus boycott and the 1960 sit-ins. My analysis emphasizes that the organizational foundation of the Civil Rights movement was built during this period and active local movement centers were created in numerous Southern black communities. For instance, between 1957 and 1960 many local centers emerged in Virginia. Ministers such as Reverends Milton Reid, L. C. Johnson, Virgil Wood, Curtis Harris, and Wyatt Walker operated out of centers in Hopewell, Lynchburg, Portsmouth, and Petersburg. The direct action organizations of these cities were named Improvement Associations and were

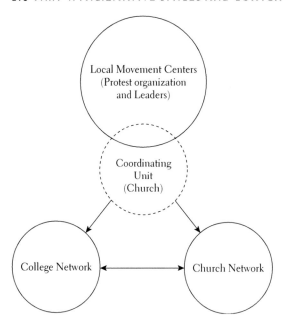

Figure 12.1 Structure of a Typical Local Movement Center

patterned after the original MIA. South Carolina also had its movement centers. For example, in 1955–1956, after whites began exerting economic pressure against blacks desiring school integration, the black community of Orangeburg initiated an economic boycott against twenty-three local firms. This extended boycott resulted in a vibrant movement center led by the Reverends Matthew McCollom, William Sample, and Alfred Issac and their congregations. Movement centers emerged in other South Carolina cities, such as Sumter, Columbia, and Florence, organized by James McCain of CORE and activist clergymen.

In Durham, North Carolina, churches that made up the movement center were Union Baptist, pastored by Rev. Grady Davis; Ashbury Temple, pastored by Rev. Douglas Moore; Mount Zion, pastored by Rev. Fuller; St. Marks, pastored by Rev. Speaks; and St. Josephs, pastored by Rev. Swann. Movement centers were also to be found in cities of the deep South such as Montgomery and Birmingham, Alabama; Baton Rouge, Louisiana; and Tallahassee, Florida.

So prevalent were these centers throughout the South that when Gordon Carey, a CORE field investigator, surveyed the situation in 1959, he reported:

> In some Southern cities such as Montgomery, Orangeburg, Tallahassee, and Birmingham nonviolent movements have been and are being carried on. But most of the South, with its near total segregation, has not been touched. Many places have *felt* the *spirit* of Martin Luther King, Jr. but too often this spirit has not been turned into positive action. [Carey, 1959, emphasis added]

The "spirit" to which Carey referred was in fact the church-based movement centers he found throughout the South, most of which were affiliated with or patterned after SCLC.

Elsewhere (Morris, 1980), I have analyzed how, in the late 1950s, these centers were perfecting confrontation strategies, building organizations, leading marches, organizing voter drives, and radicalizing members of the community. Scholars (e.g., Oberschall, 1973:223) persistently dismiss these centers as weak, limited, and unwilling to confront the white power structure. Yet the evidence suggests a different interpretation. For example, Rev. Fred Shuttlesworth and his mass-based movement center continually confronted Bull Connor and the white power structure of Birmingham throughout the late fifties. As a consequence, Shuttlesworth's home and church were repeatedly bombed.

In short, between 1955 and 1960 many local movement centers were formed and hardened. These centers, which included NAACP Youth Councils and CORE chapters, constituted the new political reality of Southern black communities on the eve of the 1960 sit-ins. It was these structures that were able to generate and sustain a heavy volume of collective action.

The Greensboro Connection

On February 1, 1960 Ezell Blair Jr., Franklin McCain, Joe McNeil, and David Richmond, all students at North Carolina Agricultural and Technical College, sat-in at the Woolworth's lunch counter in Greensboro, North Carolina. Though most commentators mark this as the first sit-in, the four protesters knew that they were not the first to sit-in in the state of North Carolina. Sit-in activity in the state had begun in the late fifties, when a young black attorney, Floyd McKissick, and a young Board member of SCLC, Rev. Douglas Moore, and a small group of other young people (including a few whites from Duke University) began conducting sit-ins in Durham.

These early Durham sit-ins were part of the network of sit-ins which occured between 1957 and 1960. The activists involved in the early sit-ins belonged to the NAACP Youth Division, which McKissick headed, and their own direct-action organization called the Durham Committee on Negro Affairs. During the late fifties, McKissick and Moore's group conducted sit-ins at local bus stations, waiting rooms, parks, hotels, and other places (McKissick, 1978). In 1957, Rev. Moore and others were arrested for sitting-in at a local ice-cream parlor. The subsequent legal case became known as the "Royal Ice Cream Case." McKissick, who also headed the local Boy Scout organization, periodically would take the young "all-American" scouts into segregated restaurants and order food. In short, this Durham group persistently confronted the white power structure in the late fifties.

The four students who sat-in at Greensboro and sparked the widespread sit-in movement had been members of the NAACP Youth Council, headed by McKissick. According to McKissick, he knew them all well and they knew all about the Durham activities. Martin Oppenheimer (1964:398), an early historian of the sit-ins, confirms this: "All of the boys were, or at some time had been members of an NAACP Youth Council." Indeed, the four students had participated in numerous meetings in social-action oriented churches in Durham. Involvement with the NAACP Youth Council meant that they were not only informed about the Durham sit-ins, but also knew about many of the sit-ins conducted prior to 1960. Thus, the myth that four college students got up one day and sat-in at Woolworth's—and sparked the movement—dries up like a "raisin in the sun" when confronted with the evidence.

The National office of the NAACP and many conservative ministers refused to back the Greensboro sit-ins. The NAACP's renowned team of lawyers did not defend the "Greensboro Four." Nevertheless, on the same day they sat-in, the students contacted a lawyer whom they considered to be their friend, and Floyd McKissick became the lawyer for the "Greensboro Four." The network of college students and adult activists had begun to operate in earnest.

Well-forged networks existed between and among black churches and colleges in North Carolina, facilitated by the large number of colleges concentrated in the state. Indeed, ten black colleges existed within a ten-mile radius of Greensboro (Wolff, 1970:590). Interactions between colleges and churches were both frequent and intense; many colleges were originally founded by the churches. A number of North Carolina churches were referred to as "college churches" because they had large student memberships. These two sets of social organizations were also linked through college seminaries where black ministers received their theological training.

These church-student networks enabled activist-oriented students to become familiar with the emerging Civil Rights movement via local movement centers and made it possible for adult activists to tap the organizational resources of the colleges. Leaders of student governments and other campus groups facilitated student mobilization because they, like the ministers, had organizing skills and access to blocs of people. Moreover, the concentration of colleges in the state provided an extensive network of contacts. Fraternity and sorority chapters linked students within and between campuses, as did dating patterns and joint cultural and athletic events. Finally, intercollegiate kinship and friendship networks were widespread, and student leaders were squarely tied to these networks. Similarly, black communities across North Carolina could be rapidly mobilized through the churches, since churches were linked through ministerial alliances and other networks. By 1960 these diverse and interlocking networks were capable of being politicized and coordinated through existing movement centers, making North Carolina an ideal state for the rapid diffusion of collective action.

Within a week of the Greensboro protest, sit-ins rapidly spread across the South. In an extensive study, the Southern Regional Council (1960) reported that between February 1 and March 31

Table 1 Number of Cities with Sit-ins and Related Protest Activities, February-March 1960, by State

State	Number
North Carolina	18
Florida	11
Virginia	9
South Carolina	7
Texas	5
Tennessee	4
Alabama	4
Georgia	2
West Virginia	2
Louisiana	2
Arkansas	2
Maryland	1
Ohio	1
Kentucky	1
Total	69

Compiled from: Southern Regional Council. "The student protest movement, winter 1960." SRC-13, April 1 1960 (revised)

of 1960, major sit-in demonstrations and related activity had been conducted in at least sixty-nine Southern cities (see Table 1).[7]

Beyond Greensboro

As soon as the sit-ins started in Greensboro, the network of movement centers was activated. In the first week of February, 1960, students continued to sit-in daily at the local Woolworth's, and the protest population began to grow. The original four protesters were joined by hundreds of students from A & T College and several other local black colleges. Black high-school students and a few white college students also joined the protest. Influential local whites decided to close the Woolworth's in Greensboro, hoping to take the steam out of the developing mass-movement. It was too late.

Floyd McKissick, Rev. Douglas Moore, and others who had conducted previous sit-ins formulated plans to spread the movement across the state. They were joined by CORE's white field secretary, Gordon Carey, whose services had been requested by the local NAACP president. Carey arrived in Durham from New York on February the 7th and went directly to McKissick's home, where the sit-ins were being planned. Carey was a good choice because he had knowledge of nonviolent resistance and because of his earlier contact with movement centers in Southern black communities.

On February 8th—exactly one week after the Greensboro sit-ins—the demonstrations spread to nearby Durham and Winston-Salem. McKissick, Moore, Carey, and others helped organize these sit-ins, bringing students from the local colleges to churches where they were trained to conduct sit-ins. For example, the Durham students were trained at the same churches through which McKissick and Moore had planned direct action in the late 1950s. Following training and strategy sessions, the students went to the local lunch counters and sat-in.

The organizing effort was not limited to these two nearby cities. Within the first week of the Greensboro sit-in, McKissick, Carey, and Rev. Moore made contact with activists in movement centers throughout North Carolina, South Carolina, and Virginia, urging them to train students for sit-ins. They not only phoned these activists, but traveled to various cities to provide assistance. Upon arrival they often found sit-in planning sessions already underway. According to Carey (1978), "when we reached these cities we went directly to the movement oriented churches." When asked why, Carey replied, "Well, that's where the protest activities were being planned and organized." Thus, these sit-ins were largely organized at the movement churches rather than on the campuses. To understand the sit-in movement, one must abandon the assumption that it was a collegiate phenomenon. For different reasons, Rev. Moore attempted to convey this same idea in the early days of the sit-ins: "If Woolworth and other stores think this is just another panty raid, they haven't had their sociologists in the field recently" (Moore, 1960). The sit-ins grew out of a context of organized movement centers.

As anticipated above, the Southern Christian Leadership Conference was central to the rise of the 1960 sit-in movement. It is critical to remember that when Rev. Moore and other organizers visited churches in North and South Carolina and Virginia, they discovered that church leaders were already training students for sit-ins. Speaking of the ministers who headed these movement churches, Carey (1978) reported, "All of these ministers were active in the Southern Christian Leadership Conference. At least 75% were getting inspiration from King." Additionally, these ministers had contacts with and often were leaders of both CORE and the activist wing of the NAACP.

Since the movement centers were already in place, they served as both receiving and transmitting "antennas" for the sit-ins. As receivers they gathered information of the sit-ins, and as transmitters they rebroadcast information throughout the networks. Because this internal network already existed, information was rapidly channeled to groups prepared to engage in nonviolent collective action.

During the second week of February 1960, plans were formulated to conduct sit-ins in a number of Southern cities. Communication and coordination between the cities was intensified. For example, early in the second week of February, the Rev. B. Elton Cox of High Point, North Carolina, and Rev. C. A. Ivory of Rock Hill, South Carolina, phoned McKissick and other leaders, informing them that their groups were "ready to go" (McKissick, 1978). Cox's group sat-in on February 11th and Ivory's on February 12th. Rev. Ivory organized and directed the Rock Hill sit-ins from his wheelchair. Within the week, sit-ins were being conducted in several cities in Virginia, most of them organized through the dense network of SCLC movement centers in that state (Southern Regional Council, 1960; Walker, 1978).

The movement hot lines reached far beyond the border states of North Carolina, South Carolina, and Virginia. Rev. Fred Shuttlesworth, an active leader of the Birmingham, Alabama, movement center, happened to be in North Carolina when the first wave of sit-ins occurred, fulfilling a speaking engagement for the leader of the High Point sit-ins—Rev. Cox. According to Shuttlesworth, "He [Rev. Cox] carried me by where these people were going to sit-in...I called back to Atlanta, and told Ella [Baker] what was going on. I said, 'this is the thing. You must tell Martin [King] that we must get with this, and really this can shake up the world'" (Shuttlesworth, 1978). Baker, the Executive Director of SCLC, immediately began calling her contacts at various colleges, asking them, "What are you all going to do? It is time to move" (Baker, 1978).

Carey and Rev. Moore phoned the movement center in Nashville, Tennessee, and asked Rev. Lawson if they were ready to move. The student and church communities coordinated by the Nashville Christian Leadership Conference answered in the affirmative. According to Lawson,

> Of course there was organizing because after the sit-in, the first one in February, people like Doug Moore, Ella Baker, myself, did call around to places that we knew, said, 'Can you start? Are you ready? Can you go? And how can we help you? So there was some of that too that went on. Even there the sit-in movement did not just spread spontaneously. I mean there was a readiness. And then there were, there were phone calls that went out to various communities where we knew people and where we knew student groups and where we knew minister groups, and said, you know, 'this is it, let's go.' [Lawson, 1978]

When asked, "Why did the student sit-in movement occur?" Lawson replied,

> Because King and the Montgomery boycott and the whole development of that leadership that clustered around King had emerged and was ready and was preaching and teaching direct action, nonviolent action, and was clearly ready to act, ready to seed any movement that needed sustenance and growth. So there was...in other words, the soil had been prepared. [Lawson, 1978]

These data provide insight into how a political movement can rapidly spread between geographically distant communities. The sit-ins spread across the South in a short period of time because activists, working through local movement centers, planned, coordinated, and sustained them. They spread despite the swinging billy clubs of policemen, despite Ku Klux Klansmen, white mobs, murderers, tear gas, and economic reprisals (Southern Regional Council, 1960; Matthews and Prothro, 1966; Oberschall, 1973). The pre-existing movement centers provided the resources and organization required to sustain the sit-ins in the face of opposition.

Sit-in Clusters of 1960
The organizational and personal networks that produced the first cluster of sit-ins in Oklahoma in 1958 have already been described. The cluster concept can be applied to the entire set of sit-ins of February and March 1960. Many of the cities where sit-ins occurred can be grouped by geographic and temporal proximity. A cluster is defined as two or more cities within 75 miles of each other where sit-in activity took place within a span of 14 days. In Table 2, forty-one of the sixty-nine cities having sit-ins during this two-month period have been grouped because they meet these criteria. Within this period 59% of the cities that had sit-ins and related activity were part of clusters. The percentage of these cities forming sit-in clusters is even more striking in the first month: during February, 76% of cities having sit-ins were part of clusters, while during March the percentage dropped to 44%.

The clustering differentials between the two months can be explained by taking region into account as shown in Table 3. In the first month (February) 85% of the cities having sit-ins were located in Southeastern and border states. This pattern had been established earlier, when most of the pre-1960 sit-ins occurred in border states. Most of the February sit-ins took place in cities of border states because repression against blacks was not as severe there as in the deep South. This made it possible for activists in border states to build dense networks of movement centers. We have already seen that North Carolina, South Carolina, and Virginia had numerous social-action churches and direct-action organizations. By the time the sit-ins occurred in Virginia, SCLC had affiliates throughout the state, and Rev. Wyatt

Walker, who was the leader of Virginia's movement centers, was also the state Director of CORE and President of the local NAACP. Similar patterns existed in the other border states. Small wonder that in the month of February, 73% of cities having sit-ins were located in Virginia, North Carolina, and South Carolina. Similarly, these cities produced 88% of the February clusters. This clustering reflected both the great density of movement centers and a system of domination less stringent than that of the deep South.

Table 3 reveals that in March a major change took place: the majority of the sit-ins occurred in cities of the deep South. With a few exceptions, the sit-ins in the deep South did not occur in clusters. They occurred almost exclusively in Southern cities where movement centers were already established: Montgomery and Birmingham, Alabama; Baton Rouge and New Orleans, Louisiana; Tallahassee, Florida; Nashville and Memphis, Tennessee; and Atlanta and Savannah, Georgia. Repression would have been too great on student protesters operating outside of the protection of such centers in the deep South. Thus, the decrease in clustering in the deep South reflected both the high level of repression and the absence of dense networks of movement centers. Focusing on the internal movement centers enables us to explain both the clustering phenomenon and its absence.

Given the large proportion of sit-ins occurring in clusters, we can say that they did not spread randomly. The clusters represented the social and temporal space in which sit-ins were organized, coordinated, spread, and financed by the black community.[8] Within these clusters, cars filled with organizers from SCLC, NAACP, and CORE raced between sit-in points relaying valuable information. Telephone lines and the community "grapevine" sent forth protest instructions and plans. These clusters were the sites of numerous midday and late night meetings where the black community assembled in the churches, filled the collection plates, and vowed to mortgage their homes to raise the necessary bail-bond money in case the protesting students were jailed. Black lawyers pledged their legal services to the movement and black physicians made their services available to injured

Table 2 Clusters of Cities with Sit-ins and Related Activities, February–March 1960

Cluster	Number of days between first sit-ins within cluster	Maximum number of miles between farthest two cities within cluster
Fayetteville, Raleigh, N.C. (2/9/60–2/10/60)	1	50
Tampa, St. Petersburg, Sarasota, Fla. (2/29/60–3/2/60)	2	50
Montgomery, Tuskegee, Ala. (2/25/60–2/27/60)	2	25
Columbia, Florence, Sumter, S.C. (3/2/60–3/4/60)	2	70
Austin, San Antonio, Tx. (3/11/60–3/13/60)	2	75
Salisbury, Shelby, N.C. (2/16/60–2/18/60)	2	60
Wilmington, New Bern, N.C. (3/17/60–3/19/60)	2	75
Charlotte, N.C., Concord, Rock Hill, S.C. (2/9/60–2/12/60)	3	50
Durham, Winston-Salem, High Point, N.C. (2/8/60–2/11/60)	3	75
Chapel Hill, Henderson, N.C. (2/25/60–2/28/60)	3	50
Jacksonville, St. Augustine, Fla. (3/12/60–3/15/60)	3	40
Charleston, Orangeburg, Denmark, S.C. (2/25/60–2/29/60)	4	70
Daytona Beach, Sanford, Orlando, Fla. (3/2/60–3/7/60)	5	54
Houston, Galveston, Tx. (3/5/60–3/11/60)	6	65
Richmond, Petersburg, Va. (2/20/60–2/27/60)	7	30
Hampton, Norfolk, Portsmouth, Suffolk, Newport News (2/11/60–2/22/60)	11	35

Compiled from: Southern Regional Council. "The student protest movement, winter 1960." SRC-13, April 1 1960

demonstrators. Amidst these exciting scenes, black spirituals that had grown out of slavery calmed and deepened the participants' commitment. A detailed view of the Nashville sit-ins provides an example of these dynamics, because the Nashville movement epitomized the sit-ins whether they occurred singularly or in clusters.

The Nashville Sit-in Movement

A well-developed, church-based movement center headed by Rev. Kelly Miller Smith was organized in Nashville during the late 1950s. The center, an affiliate of SCLC, was called the Nashville Christian

Leadership Council (NCLC). Rev. James Lawson, an expert tactician of nonviolent protest, was in charge of NCLC's directaction committee. Lawson received a call from Rev. Douglas Moore about two days after the Greensboro sit-ins began. The Nashville group was ready to act because a cadre of students had already received training in nonviolent direct action. They had conducted "test sit-ins" in two large department stores in downtown Nashville prior to the 1959 Christmas holidays. Moreover, the group had already made plans in late 1959 to begin continuous sit-ins in 1960 with the explicit intention of desegregating Nashville (Smith,

Table 3 Cities with Sit-ins and Related Activities. February–March 1960, by Geographic Region

	Deep South	Southeastern and Border States	Non-South	All States
February–March 1960				
Number of cities with sit-ins, 2-month total	26	42	1	69
Region's % of 2-month total	38	61	1	100
February 1960				
Number of cities with sit-ins	5	28	0	33
Region's % of Feb. total	15	85	0	100
% of 2-month total occurring in Feb.	19	67	0	48
March 1960				
Number of cities with sit-ins	21	14	1	36
Region's % of March total	58	39	3	100
% of 2-month total occurring in March	81	33	100	52

Compiled from: Southern Regional Council. "The student protest movement, winter 1960." SRC-13, April 1 1960
Note: Deep South states are Alabama, Florida, Georgia, Texas, Arkansas, and Louisiana. Southeastern and Border states are South Carolina, North Carolina, Virginia, Tennessee, Maryland, Kentucky, and West Virginia. The non-South state is Ohio.

1978; D. Bevel, 1978). Thus, Greensboro provided the impetus for the Nashville group to carry out its pre-existing strategy.

Rev. Smith's First Baptist Church became the coordinating unit of the Nashville sit-in movement. A decision to sit-in at local lunch counters on Saturday, February 13 1960, was arrived at after much debate. The adults (mostly ministers) of the NCLC met with the students at movement headquarters and tried to convince them to postpone the demonstrations for a couple of days until money could be raised. According to Rev. Smith (1978), "NCLC had $87.50 in the treasury. We had no lawyers, and we felt kind of a parental responsibility for those college kids. And we knew they were gonna be put in jail, and we didn't know what else would happen. And so some of us said, 'we need to wait until we get a lawyer, until we raise some funds.'"

NCLC leaders told the students that they could collect the money through the churches within a week. Then, according to Rev. Smith:

James Bevel, then a student at American Baptist Theological Seminary, said that, 'I'm sick and tired of waiting,' which was a strange thing to come from a kid who was only about nineteen years old. You see, the rest of us were older... [Bevel said] 'If you asked us to wait until next week, then next week something would come up and you'd say wait until the next week and maybe we never will get our freedom.' He said this, 'I believe that something will happen in the situation that will make for the solution to some of these problems we're talking about.' So we decided to go on. [Smith, 1978]

The proximity of four black colleges in Nashville—Fisk University, Tennessee State College, American Baptist Theological Seminary, and Meharry Medical School—facilitated the mobilization of large numbers of students. In its extensive ties between students and churches, Nashville resembled the state of North Carolina. Indeed, John Lewis, James Bevel, and Bernard Lafayette, who became major sit-in leaders, were students at the American Baptist Theological Seminary and were taught there by Rev. Smith. Furthermore, they were student leaders:

> John Lewis, Bernard and myself were the major participants in the seminary. All of us were like the top student leaders in our schools. I think John at the time was the president of the Student Council. I was a member of the Student Council. I was one of the editors of the yearbook. Bernard was an editor of the yearbook. So all of us were like the top leaders in our school. [J. Bevel, 1978]

Thus the student leaders could rapidly mobilize other students because they already had access to organized groups. Other writers (Von Eschen et al., 1971; McAdam, 1979) have pointed out that these college networks played a key role in sit-in mobilization. However, the sit-in movement cannot be explained without also noting the crucial interaction between black college students and local movement centers. Speaking of Rev. Smith and his church, Bevel recalled, "the First Baptist basically had the Baptist people who went to Fisk and Meharry and Tennessee State, and the Seminary were basically members of his church" (J. Bevel, 1978). These students had been introduced to the Civil Rights movement while they attended church.

On the first day of the sit-ins in Nashville, students gathered in front of their respective campuses. NCLC sent cars to each college to transport the students to Rev. Smith's church. Again, the major organizational tasks were performed in the church which served as the coordinating unit of the local movement center, rather than on the campuses. Coordination of sit-in activity between the college community and the churches was made less difficult because many of the students (especially student leaders) were immersed in the local movement centers prior to the sit-ins. The pattern of close connection between student demonstrators and adult leaders had already existed in places

such as Greensboro and even Oklahoma City in 1958; indeed, this pattern undergirded the entire movement. Rev. Jemison's (1978) remark that the Baton Rouge sit-in demonstrators "were schooled right over there at our church; they were sent out from here to go to the lunch counters" typifies the relationship between the students and the local movement centers.[9] Jemison continued, "The student leaders attended church here. We had close ties because they were worshipping with us while we were working together."

Once the Nashville students arrived at movement headquarters, they participated in workshops where they learned the strategies of nonviolent confrontation from experts like Rev. Lawson, Rev. Metz Rollins, Rev. C. T. Vivian, and the core group of students that Lawson had already trained. This pool of trained leaders was a pre-existing resource housed by NCLC. After the workshops, the students were organized into groups with specific protest responsibilities, each having a spokesperson who had been trained by Lawson during the late 1950s. They then marched off to confront Nashville's segregated lunch counters and agents of social control.

The adult black community immediately mobilized to support the students. Shortly after the demonstrations began, large numbers of students were arrested. According to Rev. Smith,

> We just launched out on something that looked perfectly crazy and scores of people were being arrested, and paddy wagons were full and the people out in downtown couldn't understand what was going on, people just welcoming being arrested, that ran against everything they had ever seen.... I've forgotten how much we needed that day, and we got everything we needed. [That particular day?] Yes, sir. About $40,000. We needed something like $40,000 in fives. And we had all the money. Not in fives, but in bail. Every bit of it came up. You know—property and this kind of thing...and there were fourteen black lawyers in this town. Every black lawyer made himself available to us. [Smith, 1978]

Thus, basic, pre-existing resources in the dominated community were used to accomplish political goals. It was suggested to Rev. Smith that a massive movement such as that in Nashville would need outside resources. He replied,

> Now let me quickly say to you that in early 1960, when we were really out there on the line, the community stood up. We stood together. This community had proven that this stereotyped notion of black folk can't work together is just false. We worked together a lot better than the white organizations. So those people fell in line. [Smith, 1978]

Rev. Smith's comments are applicable beyond Nashville. For example, in Orangeburg, after hundreds of students were arrested and brutalized, the adult black community came solidly to their aid. Bond was set at $200 per student, and 388 students were arrested. Over $75,000 was needed, and adults came forth to put up their homes and property in order to get students out of jail. Rev. McCollom, the leader of the Orangeburg movement center, remarked that, "there was no schism between the student community and the adult community in Orangeburg" (McCollom, 1978). Jim McCain (1978) of CORE, who played a central role in organizing sit-ins across South Carolina and in Florida, reported that community support was widespread. According to Julian Bond (1980), a student leader of Atlanta's sit-ins, "black property owners put up bond which probably amounted to $100,000" to get sit-in demonstrators released from jail.

These patterns were repeated across the South. This community support should not be surprising, considering the number of ministers and congregations involved before and during the movement. Yet, Zinn, an eyewitness to many of these events, wrote, "Spontaneity and self-sufficiency were the hallmarks of the sitins; without adult advice or consent, the students planned and carried them through" (1964:29). This myopia illustrates the inadequacies of analyses that neglect or ignore the internal structure of oppressed communities and protest movements.

The continuing development of the Nashville sit-ins sheds further light on the interdependence of the movement and the black community. A formal structure called the Nashville Nonviolent Movement was developed to direct sit-in activities. Its two substructures, the Student Central Committee and the Nashville Christian Leadership Council, worked closely together and had overlapping membership (Reverends Lawson and Vivian were members of both groups). The Central Committee usually consisted of 25 to 30 students drawn from all the local colleges. NCLC represented adult ministers and the black community. The two groups established committees to accomplish specific tasks, including a finance committee, a telephone, publicity, and news committee, and a work committee. The work committee had subgroups responsible for painting protest signs and providing food and transportation. The city's black lawyers became the movement's defense team, students from Meharry Medical School were the medical team.

This intricate structure propelled and guided the sit-in movement of Nashville. A clear-cut division of labor developed between the Central Committee and the NCLC. The Central Committee's major responsibilities were to train, organize, and coordinate the demonstration. The NCLC developed the movement's financial structure and coordinated relations between the community and the student movement. Diane Nash Bevel, a major student leader of the Nashville sit-ins, was asked why the students did not take care of their own finances and build their own relationships with the larger community. She replied,

> We didn't want to be bothered keeping track of money that was collected at the rallies and stuff. We were just pleased that NCLC would do that, and would handle the book-keeping and all that trouble that went along with having money.... Besides, we were much too busy sitting-in and going to jail and that kind of thing. There wasn't really the stability of a bookkeeper, for instance. We didn't want to be bothered with developing that kind of stability.... We were very pleased to form this alliance with NCLC who would sponsor the rallies and coordinate the community support among the adults and keep track of the money, while we sat-in and...well, it took all our time, and we were really totally immersed in it. My day would sometimes start...well we'd have meetings in the morning at six o'clock, before classes, and work steady to extremely late at night, organizing the sit-ins, getting publicity out to the students that we were having a sit-in, and where and what time we would meet. Convincing people, and talking to people, calming people's fears, going to class, at the same time. It was a really busy, busy time for all of the

people on the Central Committee. We were try-ing to teach nonviolence, maintain order among a large, large number of people. That was about all we could handle. [D. Bevel, 1978]

Students are ideal participants in protest activi-ties. Usually they do not have families to support, employer's rules and dictates to follow, and crystal-lized ideas as to what is "impossible" and "unrealis-tic." Students have free time and boundless energy to pursue causes they consider worthwhile and imperative (Lipset and Wolin, 1965:3; McCarthy and Zald, 1973:10). McPhail's (1971:1069) finding that young, single, unemployed males were ideal partic-ipants in civil disorders and McPhail and Millers (1973:726) discussion of availability for participa-tion in the assembly process parallels this notion that students are ideal participants in protest activ-ities. Nevertheless, although black students were able to engage in protest activities continuously because of their student status, a one-sided focus on them diverts attention from the larger community, which had undergone considerable radicalization. Speaking of the adults, James Bevel (1978), a student organizer of the Nashville sit-ins, remarked, "But when you talk to each individual, they talked just like we talked-the students. They had jobs and they were adults. But basically, their position would be just like ours. They played different roles because they were in different—they had to relate based on where they were in the community" (J. Bevel, 1978).

The adults of the NCLC organized the black community to support the militant student sit-in movement. Once the movement began, NCLC insti-tuted weekly and sometimes daily mass meetings in the churches. Rev. Smith (1978) recalled,

Sometimes we had them more than once a week if we needed to. When things were really hot we called a meeting at eight o'clock in the morning. We'd call one for twelve that day, twelve noon, and the place would be full. We had what we called our wire service. People got on telephones, that was our wire service, and they would fill that building. They'd fill that building in just a matter of rela-tively short time."

At these mass meetings, ministers from across the city turned over the money that their respective churches had donated to the movement. Thousands of dollars were collected at the mass meetings while black adults, ministers, and students sang such lyr-ics as "Before I'd be a slave, I'd rather be buried in my grave." Then too, bundles of leaflets were given to adults at mass meetings who then distributed them throughout the black community. This shows how the movement built communication channels through which vital information, strategies, and plans were disseminated.

During the Nashville sit-ins, word went out to the black community not to shop downtown.

We didn't organize the boycott. We did not orga-nize the boycott. The boycott came about. We don't know how it happened. I tell you there are a lot of little mystical elements in there, little spots that defy rational explanation.…Now, we promoted it. We adopted it. But we did not sit down one day and organize a boycott…ninety-nine percent of the black people in this community stayed away from downtown during the boycott. It was a fantastic thing—successful. It was fantastically successful. [Smith, 1978]

Yet the boycott was largely organized by NCLC. According to Bevel, Dr. Vivian Henderson, who was head of Fisk University's economic department and a member of NCLC, played a key role in the boycott, because

Vivian Henderson was basically responsible for calling the boycott. He got up at a mass meeting and said, 'at least what we could do to support students, if we've got any decency, we can just stop paying bills and just don't shop until this thing is resolved.' A very indignant type of speech he made. It just caught on. All the bourgeois women would come to the meeting, and they just got on the phone and called up everybody, all the doctors' wives and things. They just got on the phone and called 300 or 400 people and told them don't shop downtown. Finally there was just a total boycott downtown. There would be no black people downtown at all. [J. Bevel, 1978]

Activists were stationed downtown to insure that blacks knew not to shop. According to Rev. Smith, shortly after the boycott was initiated, merchants began coming to his home wanting to talk. Diane Nash Bevel attributed the boycott's effectiveness to reduced profits during the Easter shopping season. It also changed the merchant's attitude toward the sit-ins.

> It was interesting the difference that [the boycott] made in terms of how the managers were willing to talk with us, because see we had talked with the managers of the stores. We had a meeting at the very beginning and they had kind of listened to us politely, and said, 'well, we just can't do it. We can't desegregate the counters because we will lose money and that's the end of it.' So, after the economic withdrawal, they were eager to talk with us, and try to work up some solution. [D. Bevel, 1978]

In early 1960 the white power structure of Nashville was forced to desegregate a number of private establishments and public transportation facilities. SNCC's *Student Voice* reported that in Nashville, "A long series of negotiations followed the demonstrations, and on May 10, 6 downtown stores integrated their lunch counters. Since this time others have followed suit, and some stores have hired Negroes in positions other than those of menial workers for the first time" (*Student Voice,* August, 1960). Daily demonstrations by hundred of students refusing to accept bond so that they could be released from jail, coupled with the boycott, gave blacks the upper hand in the conflict situation. Careful organization and planning was the hallmark of the Nashville sit-in movement.

Discussion and Conclusions

Consistent with Proposition 1, I have presented evidence that pre-existing social strctures played a central role in the 1960 sit-in movement. Pre-existing activist groups, formal movement organizations, colleges, and overlapping personal networks provided the framework through which the sit-ins emerged and spread. Previous writings on the sit-ins (e.g., Lomax, 1962; Zinn, 1964; Matthews and Prothro, 1966; Killian, 1968; Meier and Rudwick, 1973; Piven and Cloward, 1977) have persistently portrayed pre-existing organization as an after-the-fact accretion on student spontaneity. The dominant view is that SCLC, CORE, NAACP, and community leaders rushed into a dynamic campus movement after it was well underway, while my data provide evidence that those organizational and community forces were at the core of the sit-in movement from its beginning. Thus, preexisting organizations provided the sit-ins with the resources and communication networks needed for their emergence and development.

Prior to 1960 the sit-in was far from being the dominant tactic of the Civil Rights movement, yet in early 1960, sit-in demonstrations swept through thirteen states and hundreds of communities within two months. Almost instantly sit-ins became the major tactic and focus of the movement. A tactical innovation had occurred.

Consistent with Proposition 2, the data strongly suggest that the 1960 Greensboro sit-in occurred at the time when the necessary and sufficient condition for the rapid diffusion of sit-ins was present. That condition was the existence of well-developed and widespread internal organization. Because this internal organization was already firmly in place prior to 1960, activist groups across the South were in a position to quickly initiate sit-ins. The rapidity with which sit-ins were organized gave the appearance that they were spontaneous. This appearance was accentuated because most demonstrators were students rather than veteran Civil Rights activists.

Yet the data show that the student organizers of the sit-ins were closely tied to the internal organization of the emerging Civil Rights movement. Prior student/activist ties had been formed through church affiliations and youth wings of Civil Rights organizations. In short, students and seasoned activists were able to rapidly coordinate the sit-ins because both were anchored to the same organization.

Innovations in political movements arise in the context of an active opposition. The organization of the Civil Rights movement provided the resources that sustained diffusion of the sit-ins in the face of attack. This vast internal organization consisted of local movement centers, experienced activists who had amassed organizing skills, direct-action organizations, communication systems between centers, pre-existing strategies for dealing with the opposition, workshops and training procedures, fund-raising techniques, and community mobilization techniques.

The pre-existing internal organization enabled organizers to quickly disseminate the "sit-in" idea to groups already favorably disposed toward direct action. In the innovation/diffusion literature (e.g., Coleman et al., 1957; Lionberger, 1960; Rogers, 1962) a positive decision by numerous actors to adopt a new item is treated as a central problem. In the case of the sit-ins, the adoption problem was largely solved by the pre-existing organization. Since that organization housed groups that had already identified with "confrontational politics," little time was lost on debates as to whether sit-ins should be adopted. Thus, the diffusion process did not become bogged down at the adoption stage.

Repression might have prevented the diffusion process. The authorities and white extremist groups attempted to prevent the spread of the sit-ins by immediately arresting the demonstrators, employing brutal force, and refusing to report the sit-ins in the local press. The organizational efficiency of the movement centers prevailed against the opposition. Existing recruiting and training procedures made it possible for jailed demonstrators to be instantly replaced. When heavy fines were leveled against the movement, activists were able generally to raise large sums of money through their pre-existing community contacts. The pre-existing communication networks easily overcame the problems imposed by news blackouts. Moreover, skilled activists were able to weaken the stance of the opposition by rapidly organizing economic boycotts. Because the internal organization was widespread, these effective counter measures were employed in Black communities across the South. Thus, it was well-developed and wide-spread internal organization that enabled the 1960 sit-ins to rapidly diffuse into a major tactical innovation of the Civil Rights movement.

Propositon 3 maintains that pre-existing internal organization establishes the types of innovations that can occur within movements. The internal organization that gave rise to the sit-ins specialized in what was called nonviolent direct action. This approach consisted of a battery of tactics that were disruptive but peaceful. The nonviolent approach readily fitted into the ideological and organizational framework of the black church, and provided ministers, students, and ordinary working people with a method for entering directly into the political process.

The movement centers that emerged following the Montgomery bus boycott were developed around nonviolent approaches to social change. Indeed, the primary goal of these centers was to build nonviolent movements. Yet, nonviolent confrontations as a disciplined form of collective action was relatively new to the black masses of the South. The activists within the movement centers systematically introduced blacks to the non-violent approach. They organized non-violent workshops and conducted them on a routine basis in the churches and protest organizations. Literature from organizations (e.g., Fellowship of Reconciliation and CORE) that specialized in the non-violent approach was made available through the centers. Skilled nonviolent strategists (e.g., Bayard Rustin, James Lawson, and Glenn Smiley) travelled between centers training leaders how to conduct nonviolent campaigns. The varied tactics—mass marches, negotiations, boycotts, sit-ins—associated with direct action became common knowledge to activists in the centers. Moreover, in the late fifties activists began experimenting with these tactics and urging the community to become involved with nonviolent confrontations. Meier and Rudwick (1976) have shown that sit-ins at segregated facilities were conducted by black activists in the nineteen forties and late fifties. But this tactic remained relatively isolated and sporadic and did not diffuse throughout the larger community. Meier and Rudwick (1976:384) conclude that diffusion did not occur before 1960 because the white mass-media failed to cover sit-ins. My analysis suggests another explanation: sit-ins prior to 1960 did not spread because the internal organization required for such a spread did not exist. In short, without viable internal social organization, innovations will remain sporadic and isolated. With organization, innovations can spread and be sustained. By 1960 the internal organization of the Civil Rights movement had amassed resources and organization specifically designed to execute nonviolent confrontations.

The sit-in tactic was well suited to the existing internal organization of the Civil Rights movement. It did not conflict with the procedures, ideology, or resources of the movement centers. Indeed, because the sit-in method was a legitimate tactic of the direct-action approach, it was quickly embraced by activists situated in the movement centers. Because these activists were already attempting to build nonviolent movements, they instantly realized that massive sit-ins could have a wide impact. Furthermore, they were well aware that they were in command of precisely the kinds of resources through which the sit-ins could be rapidly diffused. This is why they phoned activist groups and said, "This is it, let's go!" That is, the sit-ins became a tactical innovation within the movement because they fit into the framework of the existing internal organization.

In conclusion, this paper has attempted to demonstrate the important role that internal organization played in the sit-in movement. It is becoming commonplace for writers (e.g., Hubbard, 1968; Lipsky, 1968; Marx and Useem, 1971; McCarthy and Zald, 1973; Oberschall, 1973) to assert that the Civil Rights movement was dependent on outside resources: elites, courts, Northern white liberals, mass media, and the Federal Government. The present analysis suggests that this assertion may be premature, especially when the role of internal organization is ignored. Future research on collective action that treats internal organization as a topic in its own right will further increase our knowledge of the dynamics of social movements.

NOTES

I would like to thank Kim Myles, Walter Allen, Michael Schwartz, Charles Perrow, Lewis Coser, Doug McAdam, Mayer Zald, William Gamson, and Charles Tilly for their helpful comments on this paper. The debt that I owe movement participants who consented to be interviewed will be obvious. A special thanks to Sheila Wilder and Debbie Snovak who labored through several drafts of this paper. Finally I thank two anonymous ASR Reviewers for extremely valuable comments. This research was partially supported by the ASA Minority Fellowship Program and a grant from the National Science Foundation SOC 76-20171.

1 Why, for example, did the "teach-ins" spread rapidly between college campuses during the mid-sixties? This proposition suggests that the teach-in tactic was especially suited to the university-based internal organization of the white student movement. In its essentials the teach-in innovation was academically oriented and could be implemented by academic types who were entrenched in the "movement centers" of the various universities involved in the movement. Lecture halls, libraries, film clips, study groups, seminar notes, etc. were the pre-existing indigenous resources used by agents of the movement via the teach-ins.

2 King papers at Boston University; SCLC papers at the Southern Christian Leadership Conference headquartered in Atlanta: Rev. Kelly Miller Smith's papers housed at First Baptist Church of Nashville.

3 All of the King papers at Boston University and all of SCLC's files in Atlanta were examined, as well as the portion of Rev. Smith's papers dealing with the sit-ins.

4 I suspect that further research will reveal that sit-ins occurred in more than these fifteen cities between 1957 and 1960.

5 Actual names of movement participants are used in this study rather than pseudonyms. I decided to use actual names because my study focuses on real places, movements, and activists. This approach will assist other researchers in evaluating the interview data, since they will know who said what and can conduct further interviews if the need arises. In addition, the respondents had a story to convey and expressed no desires to remain anonymous.

6 It could legitimately be argued that outside resources were central to these early sit-ins, given that in some cases CORE was involved. However, it seems that the emerging black; direct-action organizations of the late 1950s and the church served as a resource base for CORE. Thus, CORE, which was very small at the time, "piggybacked" on indigenous resources of the black community. Elsewhere (1980) I have presented supporting data for this argument. Meier and Rudwick's account of early CORE suggests a similar conclusion.

7 To appreciate the volume of protest activity engendered by the sit-ins, it is necessary to note that the total number of cities (69) is not a count of actual day-to-day demonstrations, which during these first two months ran into the hundreds if not thousands.

8 Cities identified as part of a particular cluster may actually be part of another cluster(s). I assume that the probability of shared organization and coordination of sit-ins is high if two or more cities within a 75-mile radius had sit-ins within a two-week period. My data and analysis generally confirm this assumption.

9 For further evidence of the centrality of student-church ties in other cities that had sit-ins see Morris, forthcoming.

13.
Free Spaces, Collective Identity, and the Persistence of U.S. White Power Activism

ROBERT FUTRELL AND PETE SIMI

Culturalist approaches to social movements emphasize the social construction of collective identity as an essential part of activism (Polletta and Jasper 2001). Collective identity refers to the actors' shared sense of "we"; it is around these perceptions of commonality and solidarity that actors mobilize (Calhoun 1993; Cohen 1985; Friedman and McAdam 1992; Hunt, Benford, and Snow 1994; Klandermans 1997, 1994; Larana, Johnston, and Gusfield 1994; Melucci 1989, 1996; Mueller 1994; Pizzorno 1978; Snow 2001; Snow and McAdam 2000; Taylor and Whittier 1992; Touraine 1981). One area of considerable interest is the physical and social contexts within which members forge and sustain their sense of collective identity (Buechler 1990; Evans and Boyte 1992; Fantasia 1988; Hirsch 1990; Johnston and Snow 1998; Polletta 1999; Rupp and Taylor 1987; Taylor 1989; Taylor and Raeburn 1995). As Francesca Polletta (1997, 1999) observes, "free spaces" (Couto 1993; Evans and Boyte 1992), along with "abeyance structures" (Taylor 1989), "protected spaces" (Tetreault 1993), "safe spaces" (Gamson 1996), "sequestered social sites" (Scott 1990), "submerged networks" and "cultural laboratories" (Melucci 1989, 1996; Mueller 1994), "havens" (Hirsch 1990), and "spatial preserves" (Fantasia and Hirsch 1995), all describe small-scale settings that provide activists autonomy from dominant groups where they can nurture oppositional movement identities.

While the free space concept is useful for highlighting the contexts where members develop movement identities, it remains unclear exactly *how* free spaces facilitate identity work (Polletta

Futrell, Robert and Pete Simi. 2004. "Free Spaces, Collective Identity, and the Persistence of U.S. White Power Activism." *Social Problems* 51: 16–42. Reprinted by permission of The University of California Press.

1999). Some scholars suggest that it is mainly the structural isolation from control by the powerful that explains the role of free spaces in generating collective identities (Evans and Boyte 1992; Fantasia and Hirsch 1995; Hirsch 1990; Morris 1984). But, this "simply posits a 'space' wherein [identity work] occur[s], without specifying how, why, and when certain patterns of relations [and cultural practices] produce" (Polletta 1999:8) or sustain oppositional cultures in free spaces. Polletta (1999) proposes that we recognize that different *types* of free spaces play different *roles* in mobilization. To concretize this idea, she surveys prior scholarship on free spaces and identifies three general types—indigenous, transmovement, and prefigurative—which, she argues, are effective in different ways for mobilization.

Although useful, this schema is limited in two ways. First, prefigurative politics—i.e., practices and relationships that model the society a movement seeks to build—is not necessarily a quality constituting an autonomous free space type, but can be understood as a continuous quality of both indigenous and transmovement spaces and critical to sustaining collective identity in those spaces. Second, as she herself admits, the schema is limited because it is informed exclusively by research on left-wing, progressive movements (Pichardo 1997; Polletta 1999). In contrast, the role(s) of free spaces in "regressive," revolutionary right-wing movements remains largely ignored.

This article extends Polletta's formulation by examining free spaces in the U.S. white power movement (WPM) and seeks to understand their specific roles in enabling members to materialize, communicate, and sustain collective identity. Drawing primarily upon observational and interview field data gathered on WPM activities between 1996 and 2003, we contrast the different social ties and cultural practices that various types of free spaces both enable and inhibit. We also describe how these spaces contribute together to enhance movement persistence. Specifically, we observe two types of prefigurative cultural spaces that draw upon indigenous and transmovement networks. "Indigenous-prefigurative" spaces are small, locally-bound, interpersonal networks where members engage in political socialization, boundary marking, and other cultural practices which create prefigurative Aryan relationships. Many of these practices are relatively hidden as otherwise unexceptional, mundane activities performed in private settings such as families and homes, Bible study groups, and crash-pads. Local in reach and scope, indigenous-prefigurative spaces cannot alone provide the network connections activists require to maintain their culture beyond the bounds of small local networks. In contrast, the "transmovement-prefigurative space" draws these otherwise unconnected local networks into broader webs of white power culture and identity. Intentional Aryan communities, music festivals, and cyberspace link local activist networks and extra-local movement networks through both physical and virtual spaces, and provide participants with prefigurative experiences. By participating in these spaces, local activists feel they are not alone but rather part of a larger, ongoing movement culture, which helps reinforce their solidarity, faith, and commitment to the cause. These free spaces create a bi-leveled *infrastructure of spaces* that contribute to the persistence of white power activism by encouraging distinct network ties and activities through which members sustain collective identity. Maintaining this infrastructure of free spaces is critical to WPM persistence, for without the contributions of both free space types the networks that sustain activism would atrophy significantly—a point that has implications for social control efforts to dismantle white power networks.

The U.S. White Power Movement

The white power movement in the United States is generally portrayed as a "fragmented, decentralized, and often sectarian network" (Burris, Smith, and Strahm 2000:218) of overlapping groups such as the Ku Klux Klan (KKK). Christian Identity sects, neo-Nazis, and white power skinheads (Dobratz and Shanks-Meile 1997). The Klan is the oldest and, historically, the most influential organization in the WPM, with roots dating to late-nineteenth century Reconstruction. In the 1920s, Klan membership expanded to a high of between 1.5 and 5 million followers of the group's anti-immigrant, anti-Catholic, social purity ideals (MacLean 1994; Moore 1991). The civil rights movement of the 1960s sparked another wave of KKK activism and violence (Chalmers 1987; Dobratz and Shanks-Meile 1997; Wade 1987), which gave way to (mostly failed) attempts at creating a more polished, legitimate, politically viable Klan in the 1970s and 1980s (e.g., Klan leader David Duke's entry into electoral politics. Also, see Berbrier 1998 on WPM efforts at rhetorical legitimation). The roots of Christian Identity groups can be traced back to nineteenth century British Israelism, which claimed that the "true" Israelites were Anglo-Saxons and that Anglo Christians are God's chosen race (Barkun 1994). The U.S. neo-Nazi branch of the WPM is rooted in the American Nazi Party, which organized around Adolf Hitler's racial purity ideals. Umbrella groups such as the Aryan Nations (AN) have led Klan members, skinheads, and others increasingly to embrace Nazi symbols and ideology, along with Christian Identity theology, as compatible with their white power sensibilities (Burris et al. 2000:218). White power skinheads constitute the fourth, and newest, major wing of the WPM. The members are linked together by such cultural symbols and practices as shaven heads, white power music, racist politics, and a propensity for racial violence (Hamm 1993; Moore 1993).[1]

Although differences exist between these various wings of the WPM, they all agree on fundamental doctrines (Burris et al. 2000). Abby Ferber (1998) explains, they "...share common ideologies and goals and an overriding commitment to maintaining white supremacy. There are ongoing debates among the groups, but also sustained efforts to forge shared objectives..." (p. 49). Foremost is the commitment to white power and defending the "white race" from "genocide." The future world they envision is racially exclusive, one in which "non-whites" are vanquished, segregated, or at least subordinated to Aryan authority. This is the world imagined, for example, in the "14 Words" statement ("We must secure the existence of our people and a future for white children") which has become a "master frame" (Snow and Benford 1992) for the movement (Dobratz 2001). More specifically, many WPM members are strongly anti-Semitic and support Aryan militarist nationalism which seeks to create and defend a white homeland. Members concretize this aim by wearing movement uniforms and symbols (Nazi military dress. KKK robes, national socialist symbols, etc.) which many envision to be parts of the standard dress in the future Aryan state. Members abhor inter-racial sex, marriage, and procreation, and idealize conservative traditional patriarchal family forms and community relations dominated by Aryan kinship. Women are celebrated for domesticity, particularly for rearing committed white power children who will become the early risers of the racial revolution and prominent members of the future Aryan nation. Although the everyday practices and rituals differ across the movement wings (e.g., young skinheads versus veteran Aryan Nations or National Alliance activists) it is this general "…agreement on basic ideas [which] is the glue that holds the movement together…" (Ezekiel 1995: xxix). WPM members develop these particular social relationships, rituals, discourse, and other practices that we discuss below, as prefigurative experiences of an anticipated Aryan dominated future. By concretizing this vision through everyday activities in the movement's free spaces, members create a powerful social context where they nourish their solidarity and commitment to white power ideals. To be clear, we are not implying that the WPM is without cleavages. As we explain below, members of different wings of the movement construct space in accordance with their specific ideological needs.

A rich WPM culture endures despite the fact that overt white power activism is on the margins of contemporary politics and society.[2] Since the late 1950s, integrationist policies and multi-cultural ethics isolated the WPM by increasing the public stigma attached to racist ideologies and those who espouse them (Barkun 1994; Bennett 1995; Blee 2002; Diamond 1995; Dobratz and Shanks-Meile

1997; Kaplan 1995; Wellman 1993). Although racist tendencies certainly persist in many forms and among many people (Feagin and Vera 1995), there are now "strong codes against the direct expression of racist views" (Billig 2001:270; Van Dijk 1992). Media accounts and some scholarly work intensifies the symbolic trivialization of WPM activists (Roberts and Kloss, 1979 [1974]) by frequently dismissing them as "buffoons," "wackos on the fringe," and "pathologically evil" (for similar arguments, see Aho 1990; Blee 2002; and Kaplan 1995). Simultaneously, state repression is strong. Infiltration by government agents has been a major concern of activists since the 1960s, when the FBI began the "White Hate Group Program" which included both overt (e.g., search and seizures) and covert (e.g., agent provocateurs, wire taps) strategies to subvert the groups (O'Reilly 1989). Non-governmental organizations (e.g., Southern Poverty Law Center, Simon Wiesenthal Center, Anti-Defamation League) also act as social control agents through infiltration operations and lawsuits, which have resulted in the bankruptcy of influential white power organizations such as the United Klans of America, White Aryan Resistance, and Aryan Nations (Southern Poverty Law Center 2000). Counter-movement demonstrations at white power rallies, marches, and other public events represent some of the most visible expressions of hostility and repression toward white power activism. Anti-racist groups typically mobilize much larger numbers for such events than white power factions (Blee 2002; Dobratz and Shanks-Meile 1997; Kaplan 1995), and public opinion data indicates low approval ratings among Americans for the most overt racist activities of WPM members (Lewis and Serbu 1999).[3]

Because they are marginalized, WPM members face difficult choices about their willingness to communicate their beliefs publically and engage in activism. Many believe that expressing their ideas publically is risky as it might disrupt their personal relationships with non-WPM members (e.g., neighbors picketing activist residences once beliefs are revealed) and result in job loss (Bjorgo 1998; Blee 2002, 1996; Kaplan 1995; Southern Poverty Law Center 2001a). More than half the participants we interviewed attribute their loss of a job to an employer's opposition to their white power beliefs. While we cannot verify those claims, it is clear that the activists *perceive* themselves to be severely repressed and almost all our informants acknowledged they were worried about losing their jobs, being shunned, or even put under surveillance and arrested, if their activism became known (for similar findings, see Blee 2002; Dobratz and Shanks-Meile 1997:23). As Blee (2002) notes, many activists now see "those who use overtly racist symbols in public or who adopt an exaggerated racist style as movement novices…" (p. 167). Yet white power activism persists. Some studies even suggest a gradual growth in the total number of WPM organizations over the past decade, and rising membership in groups such as the National Alliance, World Church of the Creator, and Hammerskin Nation (Anti-Defamation League 1998; Dobratz and Shanks-Meile 1997:25; Southern Poverty Law Center 1999, 2002). The recent growth of white power music during the late 1990s (Center for New Community n.d.; Southern Poverty Law Center 2001c) also suggests an enduring white power movement culture. Our own data also confirm the persistence of WPM networks and a rich, albeit hidden, activist subculture. At first glance, such persistence seems to contradict expectations. Repression, stigma, and fear ought to raise the costs of movement participation and diminish people's disposition to participate in it, especially when that repression is considered legitimate and warranted by most (Della Porta and Diani 1999:211). The crucial question then is precisely *how* white power activism persists.

Free Spaces, Collective Identity, and WPM Persistence

One useful strategy to explain the persistence of white power activism is to focus on the settings where members forge and sustain their movement identities. Lying at least partially outside the direct control of dominant groups, free spaces are environments where participants nurture oppositional identities that challenge prevailing social arrangements and cultural codes. Free spaces are critical for cultivating the social networks that anchor oppositional subcultures, as participants feel safer to openly express and enact their beliefs than in other settings (Larana,

Johnston, and Gusfield 1994; Polletta 1999). The WPM persists largely because of the intense commitment, rich and variegated culture, and strong activist networks that members cultivate in the movement's free spaces. But to claim that free spaces are important for developing and sustaining collective identities in the WPM, or any other movement, does not explain much beyond the opportunities they provide for identity construction (Polletta 1999). As Polletta (1999:8) points out, furthering our understanding of free spaces requires a better sense of their various *subtypes*, their specific cultural and structural arrangements, and, we argue, their respective contributions to movement *persistence*.

Polletta (1999) provides a starting point for addressing these issues. Drawing widely from prior scholarship on free spaces, she distinguishes between three types of free spaces—indigenous, transmovement, and prefigurative—which differ by the type of associational ties that characterize them, and by the practices they support. First, indigenous spaces are comprised of dense ties among small, locally-based cadres of activists. Highly-integrated interpersonal networks provide strong solidary incentives and facilitate recruitment based on pre-existing ties (Polletta 1999:11). At the same time, however, the local reach of these spaces limits their effectiveness in fostering connections that tie local activists to wider movement networks. For example, Polletta (1999) notes that while the Southern black churches in the U.S. civil rights movement provided early leaders, strong solidary incentives, and mobilizing frames that anchored local movement identities, alternate structures were required to draw locals into a broader coalition that could coordinate actions beyond individual locales (see also McAdam 1986; Morris 1984). Second, transmovement spaces draw together activists from across existing local movement networks, thereby facilitating contacts between them and providing newer activists exposure to movement veterans and other historical links to the movement (Polletta 1999:9). These are spaces where activists regularly congregate for training in organizing and protest strategies and solidarity-building events (e.g., Highlander Folk School in the civil rights movement or Belmont House in the feminist movement). The extensive network contacts members cultivate in transmovement spaces are important for linking isolated actors and local cadres into broader activist networks. Third, prefigurative spaces are settings where actors attempt to "prefigure the society that the movement is seeking to build by modeling relationships that differ from those characterizing mainstream society" (Polletta 1999:11). Prefigurative action is critical for transformative social movements as it anticipates the ways and means of the new society they seek and incorporates those practices into movement spaces as, for example, did the egalitarian democratic relationships that prevailed in the New Left (Breines 1989). Other examples range from the women's only spaces of 1970's radical feminism to a broad array of social experiments including organic farms and alternative service organizations such as food coops, community credit unions, health clinics, and schools which have become some of the most enduring movement institutions from the 1960s and 1970s protest cycle (Polletta 1999:11–12).

Polletta's three-part schema is an important step toward distinguishing differences among free space types, as it gives significantly more analytic hold on understanding the distinct roles and effects of free spaces on mobilization. Yet, some issues are undertheorized. For instance, her rigid distinctions among free space types obscure the issues we highlight below—specifically, the ways that prefigurative practices may be tightly-coupled with indigenous and transmovement spaces, and what this means for movement persistence. By relegating prefigurative politics to a wholly separate *type* of free space. Polletta neglects the ways that prefiguration can play a critical role in cultural practices that occur in indigenous and transmovement spaces. This distinction reflects a longstanding tendency in social movement scholarship to separate cultural (or expressive) dimensions from structural dimensions of movements. As Steven Buechler (2000:209) points out, this separation often obscures more than it reveals about movement dynamics (see also Breines 1989). Instead, we should be exploring both the range of cultural expressions in movements and the interplay between their cultural and structural dimensions (McAdam 1994). If, as Wini Breines (1989:6) explains, prefigurative practices "create

and sustain within the live practice of the movement relationships and political forms that prefigure and embody the desired society," then these practices should be analyzed as part and parcel of the activist networks and activities in indigenous and transmovement spaces, rather than existing apart from them. Prefigurative politics recursively builds movement goals into the members' daily activities and movement networks in ways that symbolize who they are and what they want not just as an end, but as a daily guide to movement practice (Buechler 2000:207). It is important, then, to explain how members' prefigurative practices nurture, reflect, and sustain collective identity within both the dense, isolated activist networks of a movement's indigenous spaces, and in the transmovement spaces that draw members from across movement networks.

We focus on WPM free spaces to evaluate how the cultural practices that support them help *sustain* activist communities anchored in white power political identity and ideals. We find that prefigurative practices in the WPM cut across indigenous and transmovement spaces in ways not captured by the mutually exclusive categories that Polletta provides. While the degree of prefiguration varies across the spaces we observe, it is always present. WPM prefigurative practices include the communication of revolutionary racist discourse; the promotion of traditional patriarchal gender relations; participation in solidarity rituals such as cross-lightings and commitment ceremonies; and the wearing of racist regalia. WPM members envision each of these actions as facets of the future white power society they imagine—i.e., a racially-exclusive, male-dominated society centered around white militarist nationalism and celebrated in ceremonies and rituals. Thus, instead of the three discrete free space types described by Polletta, we see prefigurative practices collapsed in the WPM's indigenous and transmovement spaces (see Table 1). Whether such free space formations are exclusive to the WPM or other highly-marginalized reactionary movements, or are an over-looked dimension of many social movement spaces, is an issue we take up in the conclusion. For now, the crucial point is that the spaces we identify contribute to movement persistence by

Table 1 Free Spaces in the U.S. White Power Movement (adapted from Polletta 1999)

	Character of Ties and Practices	Role in Movement Persistence	Examples
Indigenous-prefigurative	Dense ties, insular networks. Private, local narratives and practices that prefigure the specific white power visions/ relationships active in the local network.	Reinforces collective identity through strong interpersonal ties. Opportunities to recruit through local networks. Sustains movement in varied locales.	Intergenerational family socialization, homeschooling, informal gatherings/ritual parties, Bible study groups, skinhead crashpads.
Transmovement-prefigurative	Extensive ties, sporadically organized. Practices prefigure general WPM goals.	Network intersections that link otherwise isolated activist networks through physical and virtual spaces. Demonstrate WPM continuity to members.	Intentional Aryan communities, music shows, cyberspace.

creating a bi-leveled infrastructure of free spaces in which prefigurative practices are woven into a variety of indigenous and transmovement spaces.

Method and Data

Our analysis is grounded primarily in the ethnographic data we collected on a variety of white power activists and groups between 1996 and 2003. We used a multi-method approach (Snow and Anderson 1993) which included participant observation in a variety of settings and one to three hour in-depth face-to-face and telephone interviews with 56 WPM activists.[4] Of those, 14 were movement leaders and 42 were rank-and-file activists. We conducted 39 follow-up interviews with the primary movement contacts, for a total of 95 interviews. We also performed a content analysis of WPM texts such as newsletters, websites, Internet discussion groups, and radio broadcasts. In addition, we collected information about the WPM from public authorities such as law enforcement sources, research groups (e.g. Anti-Defamation League, Southern Poverty Law Center), and both print and broadcast media (newspaper articles and television segments).[5]

We conducted participant observation with Christian Identity activists in the Southwest. Aryan Nations activists in Idaho, and a variety of WPM participants in Southern California, including major leaders such as Tom Metzger (originator of the White Aryan Resistance), and several white power music promoters and band members. The range of events we observed with the skinheads in Utah and Arizona included 23 house visits lasting from one to three days, social gatherings (e.g., parties), other leisure activities (e.g., hiking), and various other forms of interaction and participation (e.g., court hearings). Additionally, we visited the Aryan Nations former headquarters on four different occasions for three to five days in length, which provided us with the opportunities to observe three Aryan Nations World Congresses, cross lightings and other Aryan rituals, a wedding, numerous prayer services, speeches, press conferences, marches, and rallies. Our contacts with Southern California WPM groups included two live website/ radio broadcast productions, additional social gatherings, white power music concerts, and 21 home visits with activists ranging from one to four days.

We selected interview subjects through snowball and purposive sampling strategies which enabled us to access a wide range of activists, networks, and groups within the WPM. The sample included members of networks active in 18 states.[6] Specific organizations represented include White Aryan Resistance, Aryan Nations and local branches of Aryan Nations (AN), Hammerskins,

National Alliance, Ku Klux Klan, Southwest Aryan Separatists (SWAS), and various smaller skinhead groups (e.g., Aryan Front, Bayside Skins, Independent Skins, L.A. County Skins, and Orange County Skins).[7] Our interviews focused on the types of activism individuals had engaged in, the movement strategies advocated within and across the groups, and the meanings activists attached to various types of movement participation. Participant observation and interviewing allowed for the close examination of a wide-range of political activism which is not available through sole reliance on secondary sources and movement propaganda (Blee 1996). We also analyzed secondary sources for evidence that would either corroborate or contradict the insights about the movement we gleaned through primary interview and observational data. Our multi-method approach allowed for triangulation across an array of data (Denzin 1978).

While our data is rich, it is not perfect. We encountered methodological difficulties which we mainly attribute to WPM members' preference for secrecy and, at times, for illegal activity. We relied on non-probability sampling due to the hidden character of the population (see Heckathorn 1997, 2002, for an alternate respondent-driven sampling approach for hidden populations). Entry into the movement's groups is difficult and we obtained many of our interviewees through introduction by our initial movement contacts. In addition, as the white power movement appears to be diversely structured with multiple centers and levels of activism, our generalizations about the movement will remain modest and tentative. At the same time, we accept Val Burris, Emory Smith, and Ann Strahm's (2000) remark that there do not appear to be sharp doctrinal cleavages across different factions of the movement and that there is a significant degree of ideological continuity among its various wings. Accordingly, we find that there are affinities across white power groups that allow us strong analytic hold on the nature and role of free spaces in the WPM.

Sustaining WPM Identity in Indigenous-Prefigurative Spaces

Indigenous-prefigurative spaces in the WPM are characterized by dense, interpersonal ties and insular, hidden networks where members reinforce their collective identity by participating in various prefigurative symbolic practices. We include here families and a range of small informal domestic gatherings, such as study groups, ritual parties, and skinhead crash-pads, as the main settings where members reaffirm and transmit commitment to the movement's goals and discourage sympathy toward mainstream cultural codes. These settings share similar structural characteristics: they are small in size, exclusive, intimate, and rooted in enduring relationships—all qualities that encourage members to safely and openly express their radical racist ideologies. More concretely, many members see the family as one of the earliest means of racial socialization and thereby assign it a critical role in ensuring the persistence of white power identity across generations. Family and home constitute a space where parents unequivocally trace in-group-out-group boundaries and transmit white power sentiments across generations. Other types of informal gatherings provide a space where members enact prefigurative relationships that reinforce commitment and boundaries between WPM activists and nonmovement "others," and also recruit new members.

Family and Intergenerational Movement Socialization

That family plays a central role in political socialization in the WPM should not be surprising, as primary ties are generally fundamental to socialization. As Hank Johnston (1991, 1994) has shown, the intergenerational transmission of collective identity is essential for movement endurance in repressive contexts, and the control and anonymity available in the home ensures that identity work can proceed relatively unchallenged. Likewise, Richard Couto (1993:61) notes that when the chance of repression is high for overt resistance, identity work occurs "in carefully guarded free spaces, such as the family." The importance of the family as a free space vital to movement persistence is also clear to WPM activists.

> [The role of the family] is central, no doubt about it. You can't get anywhere without a solid foundation.

The movement has to have stronger families to survive. If we can raise our children to be racially conscious and white families pull together, then maybe there's hope. It's really the only hope we have. (AN activist, 5/23/97a)

Naming children, and even pets, with symbols of Aryan ideology is one of the earliest means of instilling parents' vision of "racial politics" to their progeny. For instance, a skin-head parent we interviewed named his first-born son Hunter after a fictional character in William Pierce's white power fantasy novel of the same name. Hunter is a sniper who murders interracial couples and Jews to "cleanse" America and save the future of white civilization (McDonald [Pierce] 1989). In this case, parents have assigned Hunter a symbolic anchor in order to establish links between his individual sense of self and the collective WPM identity. Similarly, names associated with Nordic mythology are also common among our respondents. Examples include Valkyries (winged warriors of Nordic mythology), Thor (mythological Nordic warrior), Valhalla (Nordic heaven in Odinist mythology), and other names rooted in the "Aryan" word (e.g., Ariana). As a veteran white power activist explained:

> It's not gonna start a revolution or anything, but names are like a lot of other things, it's what they symbolize that's important. They tell you something about what's in a person's heart and they help remind us what's in our own hearts and what the future holds. It's kind of like the 14 Words, they may just be words but they're also a lot more than that. (Orange County skinhead, 8/20/02)

Embracing a collective identity requires merging the self with a wider set of shared attitudes and commitments (Friedman and McAdam 1992). Names that signify movement ideals not yet attained and prescriptions for future action can be exceedingly powerful when assigned to children who may carry out future actions in support of the heritage to which they are so overtly linked. Naming family pets with symbols of Aryan resistance further extends these symbolic connections. A SWAS activist boasted, "We [have] a full-blood German Shepherd. We named him Deutschland Glory, call him Dutch for

short" (Interview, 1/17/99a). Like Hunter, the meaning of Dutch is not obvious to the uninitiated, but can be invoked as a symbolic referent of the WPM among family and in other situations where those meanings are openly supported.

Activists also establish family rituals which promote racial politics in their private family space. Before-meal prayers in Christian Identity families typically celebrate patriarchal family ideals, promote racial separation and the white homeland, and reveal expectations of an impending race war. Members also use birthday celebrations and other rites of passage such as graduations, hunting trips, and commitment ceremonies to initiate children into adult white power groups and further link individual and collective Aryan identity. Birthdays are particularly infused with Aryan symbolism; cakes are decorated with swastikas, KKK images, and the phrases "14 Words." or "white power." Members also frame birthday gifts within an Aryan ideology when, for instance, they refer to toys such as G.I. Joe as "G.I. Nazis who will help save the white race" (SWAS activist, 3/6/98), or when they explain that gifts such as guns and camouflage are survivalist equipment essential for the race war. Relatedly, hunting trips are particularly significant rituals fathers use to educate their sons about an idealized Aryan vision of naturalism and about the need for survivalist skills in racial conflict.

Movement memorabilia around the home, such as pictures, posters, cards, newsletters, racist comic and coloring books, and movement uniforms (e.g., adult and children's Klan robes, T-shirts, fatigues), also reinforce political identity in unambiguous ways. Family members wear T-shirts emblazoned with Hitler, Nazi soldiers, hooded Klansmen, and insignia of white power music bands to signify their affiliation with the WPM. Also, photos or paintings of Adolf Hitler often hang on living room walls, and pictures of children wearing Aryan garb or photo collages of children surrounded by WPM insignia are also common. For instance, in a SWAS member's living room, a display of a newsletter showed his daughter's picture on the front page. He explained,

> This . . . is our collectors item. It has a picture of my daughter, we tell her she's a poster girl for the movement (next to the baby picture of his daughter on

the front page, the headline read "Life—The White Choice"). (SWAS activist, 6/27/97b)

Like naming, children's pictures constitute frames of reference which parents use to reinforce their identification with the movement and, hence, to guide future political sensibilities. Similarly, at another house several Ku Klux Klan holiday cards were displayed, one of which read:

"Have a White Christmas and a Jew-free New Year"
   "Wishing you all the blessings of this beautiful holiday season." (SWAS activist, 6/28/97c)

Articulating a racial discourse, such messages are a form of bricolage whereby members tinker with dominant objects, practices, and ideas in order to subvert their traditional meanings and impose the central WPM ideological beliefs on them (Hebdige 1979). Like naming, these symbols are used by members to establish a radically racist, Aryan dominant setting to aid intergenerational socialization of WPM children.

The most systematic approach to political socialization engineered in WPM families is homeschooling, which allows WPM families both direct control over the dissemination of white power ideology and practices and the suppression and/or delegitimation of alternative worldviews. Women are typically responsible for the duties of homeschooling as part of their idealized domestic role. All those we spoke to enthusiastically saw the rearing of ideologically aligned children as their essential contribution to sustaining the movement. Discussion on the Stormfront listserv is indicative of the general sentiment toward homeschool:

Education is a key component to our survival, however, the conventional ideas of education, i.e.: one provided by an institution such as college or university is not sufficient, because of the liberal, Jewish bias that is imposed on most learning materials, as well as assignments, with questionable content. (Stormfront.org. listserv. 1/7/01)

According to this view, "proper education" requires free spaces where adults can teach children WPM ideals and negate multicultural ones.

For our children to be properly educated we must have places to teach them the accomplishments of white Europeans, and the greatness of their cultures, survival skills, morality, and the importance of staying true to one's race, because almost all of these will be ignored or discouraged in (secular) schools. If we don't take the time to show them the way, they will be brainwashed by ignorant liberal teachers…that encourage race-mixing and degeneracy. (Stormfront.org, 1/3/02)

WPM members argue that homeschooling is intended to protect their children from mainstream schools which they perceive as brainwashing institutions that perpetuate myths about the "wonders of race-mixing" and force a "Jewish-liberal ideology" upon children. Parents consistently expressed to us their worries about school officials victimizing ideologically aligned Aryan children because of their racist views, and about non-whites bullying their children because of their "whiteness." In fact, many adult activists described to us their own school experiences as those of "racial dispossession" which ignited their interest in white power politics and homeschooling for their children (also see Blee 2002, 1996). Homeschooling provides adults and children the opportunity to "re-center" European-American racial consciousness, while simultaneously subverting multicultural values, thus prefiguring core white power ideals, practices, and relationships within the privacy of their homes.

Homeschool is the best. You provide the information, they live it. I'm not about to put my child in public school. Homeschool allows me to know that my children will get the truth and not all this liberal propaganda. (SWAS activist, 1/19/99d)

While many WPM families live in urban and suburban settings, others make concerted attempts to withdraw from "the system"—to escape both physically and psychologically from the mainstream. Accordingly, geographic isolation is another strategy activists use to carve private family spaces where they can more easily submerge themselves in the white power worldview and practices that prefigure that world. Many activists explain their withdrawal as motivated precisely by the sort of freedom that most analysts argue free spaces provide.

[The biggest joy out here in rural Utah is] living free, the freedom. I just wanna live off the land, live by the scripture, raise my family, raise my crops, just live…I'm doing what it takes to get out of the system, it takes a lot more than saying forget the system or the system sucks, you know everyone knows that, but unless you got a plan B then you're gonna go with the system. (SWAS activist, 8/13/97e)

Like homeschooling, members opt for geographic isolation in order to insulate the family, resist incursion by mainstream authorities and anti-Aryan perspectives, and nurture the survivalist sensibilities required for the expected race war.

White power families are, then, ideological shelters where minorities are excluded, patriarchal gender relations are maintained, ideals and practices of militant Aryan nationalism are promoted, and, ideally, a supply of young adherents to the WPM is created. Naming, rituals, and other movement symbolism, homeschool, and physical isolation help to prefigure a world in which radical racist meanings are normalized and become a basis for understanding fundamental relations between oneself and others—i.e., between self, movement members, and the movement's many designated "others." According to James Aho (1999), this racial socialization reifies racial hierarchy and "embed[s]…race consciousness in the minds of new generations" (p. 67). One of the most remarkable and potentially powerful features of these practices, and those we discuss below, is the degree to which they are interwoven with the mundane items and routines of daily life. This interweaving reduces the psychological distance between everyday life and virulent racist activism. Thus, it is not merely the practices, but what they intend to symbolize, that is critical for sustaining collective identity. For instance, while there are many recreational hunters, few hunt explicitly to practice survivalist training for an expected race war. Likewise, homeschooling is a rapidly growing alternative to established educational settings, but few homeschool with the explicit purpose of instilling and preserving Aryan nationalist identity among young WPM members.

There is some debate among scholars on the role of the family as free space. On one hand, some argue that the small size and intimacy of family increases safety and the possibility of free expression

(Scott 1990). Especially among the most marginalized groups, "narratives are preserved in the most private of free spaces, the family…" (Couto 1993:77). However, Polletta (1999:6) observes that intimacy offers no guarantees that families will be free spaces where activism is encouraged. Indeed, family pressures are likely to restrict radical political action among members, especially activism that may bring repression of the activist or their kin (Polletta 1999:35). Our findings support the former view. As an indigenous-prefigurative space, WPM families clearly preserve narratives, symbols, and experiences of white power resistance in ways that are hoped will further the movement by nurturing new cadres of white power activists. Moreover, WPM families knowingly encourage the type of virulent racist identity and practices that may well bring reprisals from authorities and others opposing Aryan activism.

Identity Work in Informal Gatherings: Boundary Marking and Commitment

Informal symbolic gatherings represent a second type of indigenous-prefigurative space in the WPM. Members purposefully design these gatherings as interaction sites where they can nurture white power identity. These gatherings provide opportunities to meet with other local movement members and to participate in "cultural havens" (Hirsch 1990) where prefigurative relations abound and where activists reinforce the boundaries between themselves and the mainstream. While deeply imbued with white power ideology and ritual performances, these encounters are most often organized under the auspices of, or combined with, mundane social functions such as parties and Bible study groups. The casual and private nature of these spaces reduces the possibility of external social control, thereby increasing members' sense of safety and, thus, participation.

Many white power activists depend upon small independent churches and Bible study meetings in activists' homes for gatherings where participants can practice what they believe is the "true" Biblical insight inspired by Aryan ideals, and undiluted by the watered-down *"Jew*deo-Christian" rhetoric found in other religious settings. In these contexts, members experience a great deal of autonomy to elaborate and refine white power ideologies and enjoy the affective support of like-minded activists under the guise of ordinary theological study. Members often pledge their allegiance to the movement in elaborate rituals that bestow a sacred quality to their racist practices. While some Bible studies are organized in formal church settings and draw up to 50 members, smaller gatherings that join between 5 to 20 members are conducted in members' homes or combined with outings to places identified as spiritually and racially pure.

> We have Bible study classes once a week or whenever I can get people together. You know we meet at someone's house or go to Zion [National Park] and study the scripture. (SWAS activist, 1/21/97d)

Zion National Park is especially charged with ideological meaning for Southwest Aryan groups because of highly racialized religious meanings they invest in the area, as well as the freedom, anonymity, and purity this space provides for their activities. When asked about the importance of Zion, a SWAS member explained,

> It's when you come here and stop and look around, that's when you realize your racial destiny and heritage. This is what we struggle for. For the right to maintain this kind of purity. You know, the way things are going, thanks to the multi-cultural third world invasion, if it continues there won't be places like this for much longer. That's why I'd sacrifice my life to keep that from happening. (SWAS activist, 3/13/99b)

Similarly, Aryan Nations activists invest areas of northern Idaho with racialized and religious meanings, and describe them as free spaces which are both physically and ideologically isolated from the "polluted" mainstream.

> This part of the country is still white and we're trying to keep it this way. We appreciate the tranquility. These are God-fearing people who don't live like the rest of the country, like a sewer. You come up here and you thank God there are still a few places like this.... (AN activist, 7/9/97b)

Members construe excursions into these areas as bonding and commitment rituals that enable them to transcend what they perceive to be an overly constraining, "impure," multiethnic society.

> We consider the hikes and campouts like a kind of racial and religious retreat. We look at them as much more than just having fun on the side of a mountain. These are our opportunities to come together. It's a time for us to be together, understand ourselves, and each of these trips helps our commitment grow more and more. (SWAS activist, 1/21/97f)

Although the particularities of place wherein identity work occurs is significant for many white power activists, this aspect of collective identity is not yet well understood in the literature (Polletta and Jasper 2001). Our observations suggest that these places are important to members both on strategic and symbolic grounds. Strategically, because they allow members to discuss white power themes and openly bond with other racists away from the public eye. Symbolically, because of the particular meanings members invest in them, especially regarding the "purity" of racial separation that members reportedly experience.

Parties, from backyard patio get-togethers to bonfire gatherings, are also spaces where activists explore, experiment with, and enact various dimensions of white power ideology. These informal gatherings typically draw between 15 to 50 WPM sympathizers, with most typically averaging 20–25 members. As we describe below, members attend them to establish and nurture common ideological ground with fellow activists through talk that dramatizes their plight and ritual performances intended to model the type of racially-exclusive relationships they seek. In short, these parties ensure a space where members can freely discuss Aryan ideas and enact prefigurative Aryan relationships.

> When you live in a world like we do, you have to find places where you don't have to hold back on being racist; where other people feel and act the same way you do. The parties are definitely part of it. The parties, the dinners. You get a chance to come together in a small setting where it's easier to know people and build friendships. (SoCal skinhead 9/7/02)

To have people over, get the bonfire going, the more people come around the more they want to be here. We're building the community we desire. (SWAS activist. 6/13/98)

Freeing up discussion around movement themes is a primary part of the oppositional cultures that free spaces encourage (Polletta 1999:6). Talk is integral to identity work in WPM parties. Movement "fortifying myths" (Voss 1996:252), which celebrate the efficacy and persistence of the WPM, are customary, as are stories of racial dispossession and the emergence of racial consciousness. The excerpt of conversation below between a long-time white power skinhead and two initiates is a typical and concise example. The experienced activist explains,

> We are the warriors…that's our God-given racially determined destiny. We have to remain strong. We have to keep healthy. That's why I love hanging out with my brothers because that's what this docs, it keeps me proud, it keeps me strong. (Hammerskin, 7/19/01c)

Aspects of fortifying myths like this offer strong beliefs about the movement's efficacy through ideas about inevitable destiny, righteousness, and preparation to struggle for Aryan dominance. These sentiments are often validated and reciprocated by others. A young activist confirmed the message and offered examples of racial dispossession that fueled her Aryan activism.

> It was in school…it was always these poor blacks, these poor so and so. I got so sick of hearing all this shit and then when I started seeing these signs on the side of the freeway that show how we have to watch out for the illegals running across the roads, oh my God, what the fuck! And now they're dropping these food and first aid kits in the desert so if they get stranded. (Women's Aryan Unity activist. 7/19/Ole)

And a third member contributed his own stories of perceived injustice regarding space for cultural expression to illustrate his experience of Aryan racial dispossession.

> Yeah and everyone else is able to play a show [music concert], the blacks, the Asians, the Mexicans, but when we try and create our music and try and find a place where we can get together, drink a few beers and actually listen to the music, we're committing a federal offense, the media gets involved, the police are all over the place, and of course the JDL (Jewish Defense League) and those fucks start screaming racism…Hell, these rappers can go around talking about killing cops and that's o.k. We just want the simple rights that everyone else is able to exercise. (Aryan Front skinhead, 7/19/old)

The multigenerational character of many informal gatherings allows younger activists to interact with more seasoned members who act as role models as they share stories of their white power activities and visions. Like family gatherings, these spaces also function as sites for intergenerational movement socialization.

Identity talk also defines racial boundaries and the parameters of white power lifestyles. Many members find these parties to be safe places where they can not only express white power ideals, but also explore, question, and clarify specific features of white power identity. For instance, in a discussion over the proper racial boundaries for intermarriage, an Aryan activist claimed that he "might be willing to marry an Indian or Mexican, but not a Black that's just wrong" (SWAS activist, 8/7/98). Others immediately countered that the practice would be "disgusting" and proceeded through extensive discussion and negotiation to clarify the boundaries of exogamy along strict Anglo lines. Through such vigorous identity work members not only clarify group norms and bring the offending member back into the fold, but also prefigure the group's vision on marriage to all those involved.

Ritualistic performances, elaborate morality tales, and jokes are also prominent aspects of the identity work members perform in these informal gatherings. At some parties, time is allocated to WPM commitment pledges, group "Sieg Heil" salutes, and dramatic performances such as hanging Blacks, Hispanics, or Jews in effigy, or hooded executioners symbolically beheading WPM "actors" who have painted their faces black. The morality tales typically revolve around non-whites' culpability for societal problems and small victories for Aryanism, and often have a ritualistic character. Prominent activists are the center of attention as they recount events that idealize commitment to the white power vision. The story-telling cues others to offer similar tales as mutual reinforcement of white power norms and group solidarity. These stories also instruct listeners about unobtrusive tactics of recruitment and resistance, which others can adapt in their repertoire of white power activism. The racist jokes that permeate conversations also provide a language for activists' understandings of racist politics. As Michael Billig (2001) notes, such jokes intentionally dehumanize the subjects and often compel tellers and listeners to imagine extreme racist violence against them, the type of which is seen as both precursor to and normative activity in an Aryan-dominated world that activists foresee. Jokes also communicate ideological themes to less experienced activists in more accessible and less demanding formats than formal speeches. In this sense, humor expresses the same political sentiments as more serious forms of rhetoric, while sparing members the usual gloom and doom tone.

Some informal gatherings occur in more public settings, and have a more tentative, emergent quality than the private gatherings described above. Particular bars and restaurants that are accommodating to white-power activists, although not always explicitly aligned with the WPM, have become "safe spaces" (Gamson 1996) for activists. Some of these settings have overt symbolic importance. For instance, "Deutschland Restaurant" (pseudonym) in Southern California offers neo-Nazi activists a symbolic connection to a cultural heritage they identify with white power ideals; some have designated it as a *de facto* gathering place for the faithful. Although this restaurant neither openly publicizes nor advocates the patronage of this clientele, some Southern California activists understand that there is a good chance of finding like-minded people under its roof. A young skinhead recalled an evening at the restaurant where interaction between two groups slowly progressed from modest introduction and conversation, to rounds of animated storytelling, and culminated in open expressions of white power rituals.

We were at Deutschland's once and there was a table of old WWII vets from Germany. We bought a

few rounds of beer and later they also told us about their time in the German army. By the end of the night they were giving us sieg heils. (SoCal skinhead, 8/7/01f)

Taverns in other communities sometimes also function as *de facto* public gathering places for WPM sympathizers. While in the field, one author observed the emergent nature of racialized interactions in a Utah tavern. While standing at the bar with two activists, an unidentified man approached and asked one of the activists for a white power newsletter. The activist left and then returned shortly thereafter with several documents which he sold for five dollars. After thanking this man for his purchase, the activist then proceeded to engage him in a lengthy discussion about the Ruby Ridge saga. After the man left, the activist commented, "see we're a household name around this town. They know where to find us" (SWAS activist, 1/16/97a).

Skinheads typically converge on core members' homes, or "crash pads." Like family and parties, these "pads" are spaces where members develop, enact, and sustain an elaborate and expressive white power culture through talk, rituals, and symbolic displays (see also Hamm 2002). Typically, 4 to 12 skinheads will converge at any one time on members' homes to commiserate and live there for a few days, sometimes a week or two, and occasionally longer. Crashpads are usually decorated with Nazi banners and movement slogans such as 14 Words, 88 (i.e., "h" is the eighth letter in the alphabet, 88 is code for "Heil Hitler"), and SWP (Supreme White Power). Racist media (literature, music) is available for reading, listening, and distributing, and racialized talk is pervasive.

While an Aryan lifestyle is promoted at all times in the free space of crashpads, one of the most prominent ritual occasions is tattooing. Being tattooed with white power insignia is one of the most important means of initiation and commitment to both the group and the larger movement. A swastika on the temple or forehead, a German iron cross, a Confederate flag, Hitler, German soldiers, crossed hammers, a clenched fist with slogans such as, "White Power," "White Pride," "SKIN," "14 Words," and "Proud To Be White" underneath are all common. Like many exclusive groups that dominate members' identities and roles, commitment is anchored symbolically through visual symbols (Coser 1974). Strikingly similar to the college sorority members who take on totems of their group as a symbol of their rebirth as members of the organization (Arthur 1997), white power tattoos demonstrate skinhead initiates' commitment, consciousness, and degree of self-completion as Aryan skinheads.

> Why do skinheads want tats? We want to tell a story, to establish who we are, and what we've done or will do. We want people to know we're down for our race and down for the cause. (Hammerskin 8/17/02)

Tattooing is neither a one-time ritual nor for initiates only. Long-time members are often tattooed on repeat occasions in crashpads as a bonding experience with the group and the wider movement; every successive tattoo is a physical symbol of their intensifying identification with the movement, and their increasing separation from the mainstream.

> Well, they're (tattoos) about displaying your racial pride, making sure there's no doubt. As you get more and more, it's a way of reinforcing who you are and drawing that line a little harder each time. (SoCal Skin 11/17/02)
>
> This was my first tattoo (German Iron Cross). I have seven since that one and with each one you feel a little more committed. You know you're never going back, that you're never going to lose your racialist feelings. (SWAS activist 6/23/99)

Fellow WPM members typically etch these tattoos in crashpads, and some white power tattoo artists consider Aryan tattooing as their most important contribution to the movement.

> I'm most proud about the work I do on other skins. I get to see young ones who are getting their first one and will always remember that one, but I also get to give my brothers who've been out here for years their fifteenth or whatever tattoo. Either way, I'm doing my little bit to help the movement where I can. In the world we live in we have to use symbols. We use this art to fuel our love for our race. (L.A. County skinhead 8/19/02)

The free space of crashpads is critical for the ritualistic aspects that are not allowed in most licensed tattoo businesses. For instance, white power tattoos are often completed in the company of other skinheads who, as a form of hazing, will slap the tattooed area to cause pain and, combined with chants and songs, help to reinforce ideals of rugged masculinity and brotherly solidarity with other skins. Finally, while many Aryan skinheads hide tattoos with their clothes in settings where the symbols might evoke unwanted attention, in the free space of the crashpads, they openly model them for others and converse about the meaning and the commitments the symbols represent.

All the gatherings identified here enable individuals to enact and participate in white power culture largely through otherwise innocuous everyday practices within submerged networks (Melucci 1989, 1996). WPM free spaces cannot be separated into indigenous and prefigurative spaces. Instead, activists blend prefigurative practices in their indigenous "networks of recognition" (Emirbayer 1997; Pizzorno 1986) to intensify members' commitments and forge a shared racist agenda. Aryan narratives provide members historical precedents of individual and collective resistance, explanations of the group's conditions, and an exposition of group virtues to legitimate their efforts. Rituals and excursions enhance solidarity by nurturing exclusively Aryan relationships that predict the future they envision. Yet, these indigenous-prefigurative spaces cannot sustain an activist culture beyond their local boundaries. The WPM's transmovement-prefigurative spaces fill this void as members tie local networks to broader ones and create opportunities to participate in prefigurative relationships with a wider range of members. As we discuss below, intentional Aryan communities, music festivals, and cyberspace represent the other layer of the bi-level infrastructure of free spaces that sustains the WPM.

Transmovement-Prefigurative Spaces in the WPM

Transmovement-prefigurative spaces play a critical role in sustaining the WPM because they gather adherents from across the movement's fragmented networks and branches together in both physical and virtual spaces; here, members engage in prefigurative practices and develop broad-based "cultures of solidarity" (Fantasia 1988). In these spaces, adherents whose activism is otherwise limited to the private orbits of home and immediate networks of friends find opportunities to participate in wider movement networks. These networks typically increase members' perceptions of an ongoing, vibrant movement "out there" that they can access and support. Members learn the full extent to which their claims and ideals are shared by others with whom they are not in direct contact (Scott 1990). Intentional Aryan communities and white power music events are concrete settings where extended networks of activists congregate and elaborate prefigurative relationships and rituals. Cyberspace provides myriad virtual networking sites which are unconstrained by the space and time limits (Gamson 1996) of indigenous and other transmovement spaces. Both forms establish the type of network intersections which are crucial for sustaining broad-based movement identities.

Solidarity Networks in Intentional Aryan Communities and Music Shows

A small number of intentional Aryan communities organized over the last few decades serve as transmovement-prefigurative spaces. These settlements contain as few as a dozen members to around 100 activists, and are located in various spots across the country including the 20 acre Aryan Nations compound in Hayden Lake, Idaho, the 346 acre National Alliance grounds near Hillsboro, West Virginia, and in Elohim City, a 1,000 acre white separatist community in eastern Oklahoma. The prefigurative dimensions of most communities are unambiguous, as they are organized as model Aryan societies. Devoutly racist, they typically exclude non-whites, provide Aryan worship centers, archives of white power literature, music and movement paraphernalia, and paramilitary training. They are also hubs for white power networking. Activists outside the communities often pilgrimage to them to attend large gatherings held at some of the sites or simply to visit and experience an active Aryan settlement. Many are also way stations for traveling WPM activists or those eluding authorities (Hamm 2002). The communities differ in their insularity, economic autonomy, and the degree to which members express their racism to outsiders. For instance, Elohim City maintains an extremely low public profile and, according to Somer Shook, Wesley Delano, and Robert W. Balch (1999) "is close to being institutionally complete," with a sawmill, trucking company, school, church, community medical service, calendar, armed patrol unit, and construction firm supporting the 85-person community (see also Southern Poverty Law Center 1997). Elohim City community members do not proselytize and instead prefer to shield their racialism from outsiders (Shook et al. 1999). By contrast, the Aryan Nations settlement draws much more notoriety, especially during the annual Aryan World Congresses which at their peak in the mid-1990s drew up to 300 WPM leaders and activists and widespread media attention. Between congresses, the Aryan Nations settlement housed a very small number of permanent community members (6–15 during our research) but provided a haven for WPM activists to retreat, worship, and invigorate their racist commitments. On the whole, WPM members create thorough prefigurative experiences by establishing intentional communities where white dominance is paramount. As one activist explains,

> Living here (Aryan Nations) is the best thing we can do. It's so peaceful and white. We're able to teach our daughter the way we see fit, and we live next to the Pastor (Richard Butler) and get to be around him which is a real gift. Pretty soon we'll start building another home here. (Aryan Nations community member, 4/22/97)

The Aryan Nations (AN) settlement, once known throughout the WPM as the "international headquarters of the white race," is the community where we collected most of our observational data. Between the early 1980s through 2000, World Aryan Congresses brought WPM activists from a wide range of domestic and international groups together at the AN property. Our data indicate that WPM members attending the AN compound originated from various National Socialist organizations (e.g., National Socialist Vanguard, National Socialist Workers), Aryan Nations, National Alliance, KKK and skinhead groups from more than 18 states and several European countries. Regarding international connections, Jeffery Kaplan and Leonard Weinberg (1998) explain:

> [Aryan Nations and their annual congresses] provide a relatively stable communal experiment.... Pastor [Richard] Butler established important connections with European movement activists, especially in Germany, that will continue to flourish long after the Hayden Lake compound is but a memory. (P. 150)

Accordingly, the congresses were one of the few places where movement activists could experience a large, extended community of white power adherents who exemplified the qualities of the "racially-cleansed" society they imagined. Speeches by WPM leaders would stress the "normality" of racism, which attendees could immediately experience in the free space of the compound. Seminars offered lessons in movement ideology, recruitment strategies, and for a time even guerilla warfare. In short, the AN congresses joined together WPM activists from many wings of the movement and encouraged the concrete articulation of the white power vision in the company of supportive peers (Blee 2002:196; Kaplan and Weinberg 1998).

The rituals performed in these settings intensify activists' prefigurative experience by providing opportunities to practice the virulent racist relationships and routines that are to be normative in the future Aryan nation. Singing racialized hymns, wearing regalia symbolizing the respective white power beliefs present at the congress, playing Aryan national anthems, and engaging in sacred cross lightings, commitment ceremonies, and crude military exercises are all parts of the congress' internal spectacle. This spectacle is aimed at strengthening activists' commitment by producing excitement, reaffirmations of collective grievances, and the type of solidarity "high" which Doug McAdam (1988) describes as an integral part of sustaining activism in the face of high risks (for a similar description of Aryan National Congress rituals, see also Aho 1999, 1993).[8]

> These (congresses) are a good time for us to come together in one place where we can feel some comfort being around proud white people. These few

days make it possible to get through the rest of the year. With good speakers and all the literature, I feel real fortunate to make these. (AN activist, 7/22/98c)

> Right now we're here together as a people and, you know, that's what's going to allow us to defeat the Zionist occupational government. These [congresses] help us build our solidarity and bring people together. It gives us time away from everything else. (AN activist 7/2/99d)

According to Aryan Nations leader, Richard Butler, the gatherings are one of the few places where WPM members openly enact and experience what they perceive as their essential whiteness.

> [The Congresses] allow us to be *true* white men. We can say nigger and not have to worry about losing a job and having someone scream racist. It used to be this way in all of America not just places like here. (AN leader Richard Butler, speech at Aryan Nations Congress, 7/8/97)

As the congresses gained notoriety during the 1990s, surveillance and repression increased, making it increasingly difficult for the AN compound to insulate attendees from external social controls. As William Gamson (1996) points out, "one of the most effective means of social control is the prevention of autonomous space" (p. 27). Legal actions against Aryan Nations by local civil rights activists and the Southern Poverty Law Center stripped the group of its compound in 2000, forcing a hiatus on the annual events. But in late June 2003, approximately 75 activists from Aryan Nations, KKK, National Socialist Movement, and White Revolution reorganized the World Congress in a state park near the former Aryan Nations compound (Huus 2003).

White power music festivals are now a leading form of large white power activist gatherings. Although initiated in the late 1980s, the festivals did not become a consistent part of the WPM until the late 1990s. Since 1998, they have increased in both frequency and size. The two most prominent festivals are *Hammerfest*, which is sponsored by the skinhead group Hammerskin Nation, and *Nordic Fest*, which is organized by Imperial Klans of America. Both occur annually and reportedly draw between 300 and 600 activists from both the U.S. and Europe (Anti-Defamation League 2002).

The 2002 *Rocky Mountain Heritage Festival* featured bands and activists from various skinhead groups, the National Alliance, and KKK affiliates based in 12 states, Great Britain, Germany, Poland, and the Netherlands (field notes, 7/15/02). The festivals explicitly cater to several generations of white power activists, from teens and young adults to much older veterans, thereby creating a powerful context for the transmission of movement identity and practices, as well as for the recruitment and retention of nascent members (for similar findings, see Hamm 2002:85–93). These gatherings typically feature up to a dozen bands, speeches from WPM leaders, white power merchandise vendors, and ritual swastika and cross lightings.

Organizers attempt to limit attendance to WPM sympathizers. Skinhead groups, such as the Hammerskins, who organize many of these festivals, welcome all Aryan activists regardless of affiliation, but especially those who might be wary of attending a predominately skinhead event. As one organizer explained:

> Everyone seems to understand how important it is for us to be able to leave behind any confrontational mindset to come together with our people and celebrate the growth of the white racialist movement. (SoCal skinhead, 8/13/00)

Like the Aryan congresses, these events are opportunities for fellowshipping with a wide range of activist peers in a free space devoted solely to white power ideals. The festivals are often organized on remote, private lands, the exact location of which is announced via movement websites only days before the event to help ensure privacy from authorities and counterprotesters. For instance, tickets and information about *Hammerfest 2000* were available to activists only through a password-protected website. Tickets were required for entry and all patrons were thoroughly observed at the gates to insure the festival was a safe haven. As a California skinhead explains, these gatherings offer an intensity of experience in a vibrant white power culture that might otherwise be unavailable to recruits.

> Going to *Hammerfest* was the best thing I could have ever done. Before that, I really didn't know anyone [outside my small group]. I knew what I

wanted to be doing, but I wasn't part of anything big. When I went there, I met a bunch of bros. After that my life really started changing. (SoCal skinhead, 1/25/02)

Another remarked,

> Before '93 I didn't really hang out with others [in the WPM] much. I pretty much did my own thing and hung out with [white power] people around the neighborhood and in college. But then I went [to a festival] and that's when it started to change. That show helped build so much unity. We really came together after that. There were people from all over. California, Arizona, Nevada, from all over, even from other countries. It was all 'cause of this show. (L.A. County skinhead, 3/28/02)

More frequent, albeit smaller, than festivals are bar concerts, which usually draw between 50 and 200 people. Most events are organized as private parties where attendees' names are checked by bar and WPM security personnel against a list compiled by the show's organizers. Typically, the concerts include 4 to 7 bands playing a set each, with brief speeches from WPM activists between sets. Most of the audience is composed of young male and female adults (under 30), although some veteran activists also attend. At the concerts we observed, attendees were members of diverse movement networks such as the Hammerskins, KKK, National Alliance, Women for Aryan Unity, Aryan Front, Orange County Skins, World Church of the Creator, Blood and Honour, and Aryan Nations. White Aryan Resistance, Panzerfaust Records, Vinland, and National Alliance provide attendees with direct access to movement materials by stocking the bar with literature, white power CDs and cassettes, and other paraphernalia. While organizers attempt as much as possible to keep the concerts secret, they still sometimes draw protesters and media attention. At the concerts we attended, media and hostile outsiders were never knowingly allowed into the shows in order to maintain ideological continuity and safety within the space.

Intentional Aryan communities, congresses, festivals, and bar concerts provide a level of organization, camaraderie, and extensive networking that smaller informal gatherings and the family simply cannot. The events bring a much wider range of people together in settings that create a sense of movement strength and endurance. WPM members preserve ideals such as racial exclusivity and the open expression of racism by recursively building these utopian goals into the relationships they routinely advocate and practice in these spaces. Music events are especially important as one of the few settings where WPM activists participate in collective prefigurative relationships anchored in Ayran ideals which help reaffirm their ties to the wider movement.

> When you're at a show you get to do things you normally can't do and it just feels great to let go and be what you are [audience members are simultaneously sieg heiling during the performance]. You know, be a racist with everyone else who's here. We're all here because we're white and we want to be somewhere where that's not a crime and you don't have to be ashamed of it and that's hard to find today. It's hard to find places where you can do that. (Aryan musician/activist, 7/15/02)

Virtual Networks in Cyberspace

The transmovement-prefigurative space which has shown the most significant growth over the last decade is cyberspace (Southern Poverty Law Center 2001b). Cyberspace enables a wide range of white power groups and activists to create dense interorganizational channels through which information about the movement travels quickly and unimpeded (Burris et al. 2000). Links are especially common between Klan and neo-Nazi skinhead websites, and between Christian and non-Christian websites, both nationally and internationally (Burris et al. 2000). Aryan websites provide information about the movement, white power music, literature, and other movement symbols. Importantly, many of these websites are not just information clearinghouses, but provide space for real-time communication through list-serves, chat rooms, and bulletin boards where virtual members create and sustain virtual white power communities. Some sites intersect very closely with the home to enhance the racial socialization that occurs there. For instance, sites offer opportunities for white singles networking,

homeschooling newsletters and discussion groups, and a "Mothers of the Movement" website provides parenting advice and a space for parents to discuss strategies for indoctrinating their children into the movement. Other virtual spaces are designed explicitly for children and provide racist crossword puzzles, coloring pages, children's white power literature, and acidly racist interactive video games (e.g.. Shoot the Blacks, SA-Mann). The latter have become particularly popular, attracting both young and old Aryan members to interactive role playing in an explicitly violent, racist virtual environment where whites rule. Set against medieval or contemporary urban backdrops, the games focus on themes of racial holy war, genocide, and attaining a white homeland. Participating in these games alone or with others helps activists sustain their commitment to the movement and offers a strategy to draw in potential recruits.

> [Virtual games] are a great idea for the movement. We need more of it too. It's planting a seed. It's like pollination. When we make these games we're like bees. [The games] may not cause every person who plays to get active, but a certain percentage will realize that it's not just a game this is the real shit, that we already live in cities with black savages raping white women and children, it happens everyday, and that the race war is coming, no doubt about it.... [We] need these games, it helps keep us going.... there's just something about the video games that's awesome... the visual part and being able to really get into it...." (Southeastern Aryan Activist, 6/28/03)

Many WPM members see cyberspace as the most critical free space for overcoming obstacles that prevent greater communication among Aryan activists.

> The technological restrictions that have kept us from communicating with other Whites is rapidly coming to an end.... Broadcasting stations own or at least control the transmission of media between sender and receiver, but Internet radio uses the common infrastructure of the Internet for transmission which is not controlled by anyone.... Radio broadcasting is usually restricted to a certain geographic area, the Internet is a global network, making Internet radio stations available to every [white

power activist] in the world who has access to the Internet.... (Stormfront.com, 3/13/03)

We need access to our own people through any medium available, music, the Internet, television, literature, personal outreach...We think a lot about how to reach a wider audience with the [mainstream] media pushing all this anti-white propaganda. We can't let that media define us. We've got to find ways to get the message out and with the Internet we've had some success. [Aryan websites] are forums that help connect people to something larger that's out there. Some will be happy sitting home in comfort and surfing the web, but for others [Internet participation] will serve as a springboard. (Southeastern Aryan activist 12/15/02)

In addition to advocating Aryan values and linking indigenous movement networks, several sites also provide space for logistical planning of movement events, such as festivals, concerts, and congresses. According to the Anti-Defamation League's (2002) review of sites selected for the planning of music event *Nordic Fest 2000*, the messages "evinced a spirit of cooperation among extremists, and it seems that those who posted [them] would not have connected with each other had they not gone online." More generally, the Anti-Defamation League argues that the Internet presents opportunities for networking that simply did not exist before by offering a private form of communication and "bring[ing] distant isolated groups and individuals together. [It] has the potential to reach an audience far beyond any they could reach with their traditional propaganda" (Hoffman 1996:72). WPM activists express similar ideas:

Since we've been able to access the Internet and email Hammers in other countries it's changed everything. We really see ourselves as part of an international movement. We communicate with each other on a regular basis, we coordinate events, we share our views on issues and what we're doing to fight for the cause. The Internet has helped us in the direction of seeing other skinheads as international brothers fighting for the same cause. I've been around a long time and it is really a lot different than before we had the Internet. We knew about [skinheads in other parts of the world], but it was more word of mouth and now we're actually working together. (Northern Hammerskin, 7/13/02)

Streaming Internet radio stations, such as Radiowhite.com and Resistance.com, broadcast white power music and interviews with movement leaders to a wide range of WPM networks.

You can really do a lot with the Internet. With our website we're trying to combine different aspects so that we don't just appeal to younger or older racists. We want it to be both educational and entertaining and that's why we have the music but also do interviews with people who are respected role models for our movement. I love doing our show live online and talking with all these people about white power music about the movement. We get instant messages from all over the world, we're always getting free CDs and interviewing [movement leaders] like Metzger and Butler. We just sit back; let them talk, and take it all in. (SoCal Skinhead and Radiowhite DJ, 8/17/02)

The growing range of white power websites from "soft-core" to "hard-core" enables potential recruits to find their way into the movement through the group whose ideology they feel most affinity with (Burris et al. 2000:231). Kaplan and Weinberg (1998:159) describe the importance of the Internet for building movement networks.

The popularity of [cyberspace] as a medium of communication has, by the mid-1990s, brought the transnational movement online and into constant communication.... The availability of a mode of communication that connects the continents instantaneously opens a number of fascinating possibilities undreamed of...but a scant few years ago.... No longer do even the most isolated individuals...need to feel alone [as] they may become an interactive part of a seemingly vast community of adherents.

Yet observers are divided on the effectiveness of the Internet for the purposes of recruitment and identity reinforcement. For instance, Devon Burghart (1996) argues that cyberspace cannot effectively substitute for face-to-face interaction and doubts that it adds much to building WPM ties. More generally, Gamson (1996) also suggests that cyberspace is "not a particularly useful kind of space when it comes to building commitment, solidarity, and a strong sense of collective identity" (p. 35) because it lacks direct physical contact and concrete action settings that he feels are crucial. But the WPM creates other indigenous and transmovement spaces that do provide for precisely the type of face-to-face encounters that cyberspace lacks. Thus, we agree with David Hoffman (1996), and Burris, Smith, and Strahm (2000), who argue that cyberspace is a qualitatively new and effective channel for reaching existing members and potential recruits. WPM websites tie members into broader movement networks which, *in conjunction with other free space forms,* create a submerged infrastructure of movement spaces where white power identity persists.

What cyberspace offers, then, is opportunities to participate in white power activism relatively free from the risks posed by publicly identifying with the WPM. Internet forums are not time-bound (Gamson 1996) and they allow for discussion and dissemination of information with a high degree of discretion and anonymity. This drastically "reduce[s] the perceived risk of contacting these groups. If you have to go to a [white power] rally or actually write to [white power groups] to get involved in hate, that's a big barrier to overcome" (Todd Schroer, qtd. in Southern Poverty Law Center 2001b). As a result, virtual transmovement spaces may play a crucial role in attracting new activists, pulling peripheral members closer to the movement, and maintaining the commitment of already active participants. It seems certain, however, that if "virtual activism" (Back, Keith, and Solomos 1998) became the primary form of movement participation, we could well see a dissolution of face-to-face movement networks resulting in a withering of the movement (Kaplan and Weinberg 1998). Presently, indigenous and other transmovement-prefigurative spaces provide the contexts for face-to-face interaction which is lacking in cyberspace.

Together, WPM's physical and virtual transmovement-prefigurative spaces establish the network connections required to sustain activist culture beyond the bounds of indigenous networks. Indeed, these spaces draw otherwise unconnected local networks into much broader webs of white power culture and identity and importantly, convey to members a sense of participating in a much larger movement culture, which helps reinforce solidarity and commitment to the cause. They also offer

members some of the very few prefigurative Aryan relationships and experiences available to them. Combined with the WPM's indigenous-prefigurative spaces, these transmovement-prefigurative spaces create a bi-leveled *infrastructure of spaces* supporting distinct kinds of network ties and activities that enable activists to sustain collective white power identity.

Conclusion

Throughout this article, we have discussed the issue of precisely *how* free spaces contribute to the persistence of the U.S. White Power Movement. Our study shows that the WPM relies upon an infrastructure of free spaces to maintain activist networks and movement identity within a generally hostile context. The idea of an infrastructure of free spaces is important for highlighting the undertheorized issue of how different types of free spaces contribute to movements in different ways. In the WPM, indigenous-prefigurative spaces allow for the kind of network connections that help nurture strong interpersonal solidarity among small, local cadres of activists, thereby increasing participation in white power culture. Prefigurative practices in these spaces establish intergenerational movement ties and build commitments among adherents through symbolic rituals that mark boundaries between activists and their opponents. Embedding these practices in otherwise innocuous activities (e.g., homeschooling, study groups, hikes, parties) reduces the distance between daily life and white power activism which, in turn, helps "normalize" these practices and the beliefs they articulate. However, the insular character of these spaces reduces their effectiveness in maintaining an activist culture beyond the bounds of the local network. Transmovement-prefigurative spaces create network connections that link otherwise disconnected local networks into broader webs of white power culture. Participation in these spaces links activists to a more widespread, vibrant, and enduring movement culture in ways that indigenous spaces cannot do alone. Maintaining the indigenous pockets of collective identity and linking them through transmovement spaces is critical to the WPM's ability to sustain a rich variegated movement culture.

In other words, for the WPM, these free spaces *are* the movement.

Our observations also suggest that rather than understanding prefigurative politics as characteristic of a wholly separate *type* of free space, prefigurative cultural practices may instead permeate activities in indigenous and transmovement free spaces. In the WPM, prefigurative practices are built upon, reflect, and sustain collective identity and member commitments within activist networks participating in indigenous and transmovement spaces. Social relationships predicated on ideals of racial exclusivity, anti-Semitism, patriarchy, and Aryan nationalism, and articulated in talk, symbolism, and movement rituals, exemplify to members the types of people, ideas, and experiences they should seek in their desired social world. These ideals are materialized in the WPM's free spaces recurrently, if only briefly, not just as ends, but as guides to daily practice. It is likely that this intertwining of prefiguration with indigenous and transmovement spaces is also a characteristic of many other movements. There is some evidence that indigenous and transmovement spaces in the women's movement (Buechler 2000:205; Ferree and Hess 2000), the U.S. Civil Rights Movement (e.g., activist homes, churches, freedom schools) (McAdam 1988; Morris 1984), and the New Left (Breines 1989) always included strong expressions of prefigurative politics. Advancing our understanding of free spaces requires more research on the linkages between the cultural and structural dimensions of free spaces in movements on both the right and left. Likewise, we should develop more precise distinctions between the various intensities of these linkages and their various effects on movement mobilization and persistence.

While the WPM presently persists within its indigenous and transmovement-prefigurative spaces, long-term endurance is precarious. Betty Dobratz (2001) predicts that ideological schisms internal to the movement may be the most difficult obstacle members will have to overcome if they are to sustain the movement over the long-term. While we do not disagree that these internal conflicts are important, we also wish to point out that the movement's infrastructure of free spaces may help

to mitigate this destabilizing trend. The wide range of physical and virtual spaces in the movement appear to provide ample room for variation on specific beliefs and practices, while still promoting the basic doctrines that anchor white power identities across the movement's wings. Our analysis leads us to suggest that long-term movement persistence may be just as threatened by limitations of the types of free spaces that members are able to create. Indigenous and transmovement-prefigurative spaces create strong contexts for identity work and provide network intersections that join together otherwise fragmented activists. The WPM's marginality works strongly against activists' ability to establish the type of autonomous prefigurative spaces that Polletta (1999) notes are critical for sustaining movements over the long-term.

Not surprisingly, agents of social control and countermovement groups aim at eliminating the WPM's transmovement spaces. The successful efforts by federal authorities and the Southern Poverty Law Center to strip Aryan Nations of their compound and halt the Aryan World Congresses will undoubtedly lead to more concerted efforts to eradicate other transmovement spaces. Whether such efforts are justified is a political question outside the scope of this article. But it appears that, if successful, these efforts may eliminate an element of the movement critical to its persistence. Without the robust network intersections (Polletta 1999:2) created by transmovement structures, the activist base nurtured in the WPM's indigenous spaces would further fragment and deplete much of the movement's remaining vitality. On the other hand, if this infrastructure of free spaces can be sustained, WPM mobilization could increase in a less hostile climate (Taylor 1989).

While the persistence of the WPM is precarious, it seems unadvisable to discount the enduring viability of the movement—a tendency suggested by most social movement scholarship, which pays little attention to contemporary radical right-wing movements (Esseveld and Eyerman 1992), especially regarding the dimensions of free spaces (Polletta 1999) and collective identity (Pichardo 1997). Movements such as the WPM that have been "more successful at [cultivating free spaces and] structuring their own activities along [ideological-ly-appropriate] lines than at restructuring the larger society along such lines" (Buechler 2000:208) are too often dismissed by social movement scholars as not worthy of serious attention (see also Taylor and Whittier 1992:105). But an important variable in assessing movement viability is the capacity to establish free spaces where members communicate, reinforce, materialize, and celebrate their ideology and collective identity. As Buechler (2000) observes, the free space concept precisely emphasizes that "the sheer maintenance of a cultural community of activists who [sustain radical discourse and practices is an inherently political act and sometimes] the outer limit of what is possible under some...circumstances" (p. 208; see also Johnston 1994; Taylor 1989). In our view, social movement scholars will advance the field by paying more attention to right-wing movements generally, especially the most radical ones, and particularly to the various contexts in which members cultivate their commitment and develop networks which sustain a broad movement culture.

NOTES

Equal authors. The authors wish to thank Simon Gottschalk, the Huntridge Writers Group. *Social Problems* reviewers, and Editor Holstein for their insightful suggestions on improving the article. Research support for this project was provided by the National Science Foundation (SES-0202129) and the UNLV Graduate College.

1. Not all skinheads hold white power beliefs. We refer only to those involved in white power activities.

2. The WPM was popular in earlier periods, especially the Ku Klux Klan during the 1920s. For more on early white power activism, see Chalmers 1987; Moore 1991: and MacLean 1994.

3. Ferber (1998) argues that mainstream racial thinking shares some important assumptions with white supremacist ideology. We agree, but there are some important distinctions to be made. As Blee (2002) explains, "the difference between everyday racism and extraordinary racism is the difference between being prejudiced against Jews and believing that there is a Jewish conspiracy that determines the fate of individual Aryans, or between thinking that African Americans

are inferior to whites and seeing African Americans as an imminent threat to the white race" (p. 76). Moreover, notions of an impending "race war," a "Zionist Occupational Government," and the current "genocide of the white race" are core beliefs that are widely shared by WPM adherents, but have little salience with the general public (Blee 2002; Kaplan 1995). Indeed, as one white power activist explains, part of the WPM goals is, "to wake people up. We're trying to make people realize who they are and the place that they need to take in their society" (qtd. in Blee 2002:67). Perhaps the most telling indication of the WPM's marginalization from the mainstream is the tendency among "everyday" racists to disavow and disassociate themselves from the Klan, skinheads, neo-Nazis, and other openly racist groups (Blee 2002; Feagin and Vera 1995). "The paradoxical phenomenon of whites who claim not to be racist perpetrating racially harmful acts can be explained in part by the fact that 'racism' has come to be held in such opprobrium that few whites are willing to accept 'racist' as a personal trait" (Feagin and Vera 1995:13).

4. Of the 56 interviewees, 40 were with male activists, 16 with female activists. The activists' ages ranged from 15–25 years (n = 7), 26–35 years (n = 26), 36–45 years (n = 8), 46–55 years (n = 9), and 55 and over (n = 6).

5. Newspaper articles on the WPM were drawn primarily from the *Los Angeles Times, The Salt Lake Tribune, The Spectrum* (St. George, Utah), and the *Las Vegas Review Journal*. Articles were selected through a structured, exhaustive search of the Lexus-Nexus database and microfilm indexes of the *Los Angeles Times* and *Las Vegas Review Journal* to 1985 using search terms such as skinhead, neo-Nazi, white supremacy, white power, and hate (including hate-crime, hate group, etc.). Other articles are drawn from data provided by watchdog groups (e.g., Southern Poverty Law Center, Political Research Associates). We also examined 48 white power movement websites.

6. The states are: Alabama, Arizona, California, Georgia, Idaho, Illinois, Kansas, Maine, Michigan, Montana, New Jersey, New York, Ohio, Oregon, Pennsylvania, Texas, and Washington.

7. In the case of widely known white power groups, the names of the organizations and their representatives are left unchanged. In other cases, pseudonyms are used.

8. For instance, although we did not observe this, Aho (1999) describes another prefigurative practice, "Nigger Shooting" contests, during which Aryan World conferees shot at, "among other targets, crude facsimiles of running black men and enlarged photos of despised Jewish faces" (p. 68).

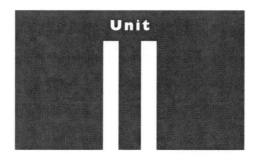

Unit

Processes of
Micromobilization

Part 5

Social Networks

Prior to the mid-1970s, explanations of differential recruitment and participation tended to cluster under the canopy of a "dispositional" perspective. Emphasis was placed on the ways in which "psychological traits or states render individuals more or less susceptible to participation in crowds and social movement activities. The underlying assumption (was) that certain personality characteristics and/or cognitive and emotional states are likely to make the appeal of some movements especially attractive, thus predisposing some individuals to participation" (Rohlinger and Snow 2003: 505).

Included among the various psychological traits or states posited as key correlates or causes of participation were heightened frustration (Dollard et al. 1939), authoritarian personalities (Adorno et al. 1950), and unresolved emotional conflicts with parents (Feuer 1969). Today such dispositional hypotheses have little traction among students of recruitment and participation for two reasons: first, research examining the relationship between dispositional factors and movement participation has provided little empirical support for the connection; and second, there was a paradigmatic shift, between the mid-1970s and -1980s, that emphasized the rationality of social movement actors and the socially embedded and structured character of recruitment and participation. It is this recognition that differential recruitment and participation is partly socially structured that is the focus of this section.

This shift was prompted in large part by the observation that movement recruitment is generally unlikely to occur in the absence of prior connections to one or more recruitment agents. As Snow, Zurcher, and Ekland-Olson (1980) framed the issue in their initial call for a microstructural approach to differential recruitment:

(E)ven if one accepts the…contention that some individuals are predisposed social-psychologically to movement participation, the following question still remains: What determines which potential participants are most likely to come into contact with and be recruited into one movement rather than another, if any movement at all? (1980: 789)

Their answer, based on analysis of data on the recruitment paths of participants in two religious movements and of University of Texas students in various forms of activism, was straightforward. In their words, "the probability of being recruited into a particular movement is largely a function of two conditions: (1) links to one or more movement members through a preexisting or emergent interpersonal tie; and (2) the absence of countervailing ties" (1980: 798).

This and much subsequent research on social networks—the operative term for links, ties, and connections between two or more units of analysis—focuses on interpersonal networks as a key variable accounting for differential recruitment. But it is important to understand that such network ties are usually embedded in community and organizational contexts, and that some such contexts may be more facilitative of recruitment and participation than others. Thus, in the first selection, Marc Dixon and Vincent Roscigno's study of striking workers at Ohio State University in 2000 shows that those workers who were embedded in a striking unit were more likely to participate in the strike than other workers because those "workplace networks" functioned as critical conduits for "grievance sharing and identity formation prior to the strike" and influenced "individual decision making and calculations at a pivotal point" in the process.

In the second selection, Doug McAdam and Ronnelle Paulsen focus not only on organizational affiliation or embeddedness, but also on the intersection of network associations with other factors that can affect participation. They do so by comparing those who took part in the 1964 Mississippi Freedom Summer Project with those who applied and were accepted by project organizers, but did not participate. Using original project applications and follow-up surveys, they highlight a particular confluence of factors that greatly increased the likelihood of involvement in the summer project. More specifically, they show that those applicants who were overwhelmingly likely to make it to Mississippi were those who framed project participation in terms of a salient prior identity (e.g., "Christian," "teacher," etc.), who were members of organizations supportive of this link between identity and action, and who encountered little opposition from parents or other significant others.

The selections by Dixon and Roscigno and McAdam and Paulsen not only provide further confirmation of the importance of network embeddedness for recruitment and participation, but they also hint at why social ties matter with their parallel findings regarding the participatory efficacy of networks that develop or sustain individual and group identities. In the final reading in this section, David Smilde pursues more directly this important issue of why and how networks matter through his study of conversion to Pentecostalism among a sample of Venezuelan men. He finds, among other things, that while network links are strong determinants of who converts, other factors also matter, such as an individual's experience with life problems.

Together, the three readings in this section clearly demonstrate the salience of social networks in relation to differential recruitment and participation. They also suggest why and in what ways networks matter. As well, they reflect how this line of research has become increasingly more sophisticated and nuanced both theoretically and methodologically (See Diani 2004, and Diani and McAdam 2003, for overviews and further work).

Do these observations add up to the conclusion that psychological factors are irrelevant to the study of differential recruitment and participation? Certainly not! In our view, various cognitive, motivational, and emotional factors figure prominently in the determination of initial and sustained participation, but the nature of the relations is more complex than theorized in earlier work. The importance of cognitive and motivational factors to participation and the complexity of the relationship will be taken up in the next two parts of this section.

14.

Status, Networks, and Social Movement Participation: The Case of Striking Workers

MARC DIXON AND VINCENT J. ROSCIGNO

Individual participation and its determinants are at the core of social movement analyses. While movement formation and persistence are certainly shaped by more aggregate processes, such as historical junctures of subordinate group opportunity (Jenkins 1983; Tilly 1978) and tactical innovations of insurgent groups and elites (McAdam 1983), mobilization itself is ultimately dependent on individual participation and related status, cultural, and microstructural dynamics (Fantasia 1988; Klandermans 1984; Snow, Zurcher, and Eckland-Olson 1980; Taylor and Whittier 1992).

In recent years, a growing body of work has applied insights from social movement theory to the American labor movement (e.g., Ganz 2000; Isaac and Christiansen 2002; Johnston 1994, 2001; Voss and Sherman 2000). Yet little of this work has addressed individual participation in industrial actions, strike activity in particular. This is unfortunate. Successful union organizing drives in the United States involve nearly 250,000 workers annually, and more than 200,000 workers take part in strike events each year (Bureau of Labor Statistics 2002; Clawson and Clawson 1999). But what influences who participates in work-based collective action? Is involvement shaped by rational decision making by actors, each of whom weighs the costs of participation relative to their own status position? Might social networks—a key focus in social movement theory—also persuade or dissuade worker involvement in strikes?

Building on rational choice conceptions of social action and movement participation (e.g.,

Dixon, Marc and Vincent J. Roscigno. 2003. "Status, Networks, and Social Movement Participation: The Case of Striking Workers." *American Journal of Sociology* 108: 1292–1327. Reprinted by permission of the University of Chicago Press. Notes have been renumbered and edited.

Huber 1997; Marini 1992; Oberschall 1980, 1994) and research on potentially influential status distinctions between workers (e.g., Cornfield and Kim 1994; Form 1985; Wright 1985), this article extends the literature on social movement participation and strike activity.[1] We also consider more aggregate network processes that may condition the costs and benefits of participating in the first place. Indeed, rather than existing in a social or cultural vacuum, individual decision making is ultimately bounded and conditioned by social attachments and associations (Blau 1964; Oberschall 1994). Our data and analyses, which focus on an actual strike in 2000 by the Communications Workers of America (CWA), are appropriate for addressing these questions. They are also unique relative to much prior work in that they include participants and nonparticipants and allow for the inclusion of both individual status distinctions and potentially influential network dynamics. We conclude by discussing our findings relative to existing research on worker insurgency and more general perspectives pertaining to social movement participation and formation.

Status, Social Movement Participation, and Labor Insurgency

The importance of individual status to social movement participation has been at the center of historical arguments and analyses pertaining to the civil rights, women's rights, and antiwar movements. Grounded in assumptions regarding rational decision making, this literature holds, most generally, that individuals of markedly low status or those with greater autonomy from institutional or political constraint will be more likely to participate, since the costs of involvement (be they social, political, or economic) will be lower and the rewards arguably higher. Such a premise, usually implicit, is not too far removed from the relatively straightforward costs-benefits analyses put forth by classical rational choice and exchange theorists (e.g., Homans 1961).

Notably, however, a tension exists regarding individual status, costs/benefits, and the choice to participate—a tension that becomes apparent upon closer inspection of the social movement literature. On the one hand, some analyses suggest that aggrieved groups and subordinated individuals will be more likely to participate in a mobilization campaign given that it is in their rational interest to do so. Classic social movement literature, such as Piven and Cloward's *Poor People's Movements* (1977), as well as some resource mobilization accounts (e.g., Klandermans 1984; McCarthy and Zald 1977) certainly rest on this assumption. Yet, we also find examples of advantaged individuals taking part, leading, or even becoming a protest core in movements given greater autonomy from structural constraint and, arguably, the lower political and social costs that participation might entail. McAdam's (1988) Freedom Summer activists, more highly educated, middle-class whites involved in women's movements (Higginbotham 1992; Mathews 1982), and the high-status participants in environmental and peace movements (Oliver 1984; Oskamp, Bordin, and Edwards 1992; Walsh and Warland 1983) serve as cases in point.

Participant status differences across movements certainly exist and may be a function of historical era (see Melucci 1985). In this regard, some have highlighted the tendency of "old" social movements to recruit on the basis of, and appeal to, material grievances. Lower-status groups are thus more likely to participate. "New" social movements, in contrast, are more likely to organize and mobilize on the basis of identity (Taylor and Whittier 1992). This strategy generates a following among those for whom the identity is salient, including especially those of advantaged status positions. Despite such historical tendencies *across* movements, it is equally important to recognize that status divides exist *within* both historical and contemporary movements, with serious implications for movement cohesion and success.

The question of status and status divides likewise exists, both theoretically and empirically, in

research dealing specifically with the labor movement. Research on historical labor mobilizations, and that pertaining to union membership more generally, has highlighted the tendency of not just workers but especially poor, low-status, and racial and ethnic minority workers to be the most fervent in terms of class-conscious attitudes, activism in organizing campaigns, and the unfolding of actual strike events (e.g., Letwin 1998; Roscigno and Kimble 1995; Zingraff and Schulman 1984). Status divisions among workers (be they race, gender, skill, occupation, etc.) and their relation to labor organization, development, and cohesion are, nevertheless, complex and often historically contingent (Baron 1991; Cornfield 1989; Goldfield 1997; Gordon, Edwards and Reich 1982). Indeed, any resulting labor organization and mobilization can vary considerably in type and character depending on the degree of elite cohesion, specific workplace grievances, and strategies formulated at the point of production (Brown and Boswell 1995; Kimeldorf 1999; Kimeldorf and Stepan-Norris 1992).

In contrast to work highlighting the central role of low-status workers, other labor research denotes significant participation in, and initiation of, collective action by more advantaged, skilled workers. Rather than being driven strictly by material grievances, skilled workers' participation is related to a historically forged class identity, solidarity-generating labor processes, and greater workplace power and autonomy (Form 1985; Lichtenstein 1980; Zetka 1992, 1995). Just who becomes the protest core may thus reflect a divide between worker mobilizations based on heightened material grievances and those tied to an advantaged labor market position (Cornfield 1985; Fantasia 1988). The contemporary labor movement and related recruitment strategies arguably embody both tendencies. This is evidenced by the recent upsurge in organizing activity among predominantly low-paid immigrant and racial and ethnic minority service workers, as well as in that of somewhat more privileged professionals (Milkman 2000; Waldinger et al. 1998; Cornfield and Fletcher 2001).

Individual status is undoubtedly influential for movement participation, via rational calculation processes, and this association continues to be important for labor organization and strike activity. The possibility of somewhat contradictory status pulls and tensions, however, remains. Those of the lowest status probably have the least to lose in absolute terms and, therefore, should be more likely to collectively mobilize. In contrast, higher-status individuals may exhibit greater participation since they will hold some power and autonomy relative to existing power structures and oftentimes hold an already established, historically driven, class-based identity. In our view, both scenarios are plausible— that is, there may exist a bipolar effect of status on involvement. Such a possibility has been difficult to address because of a lack of data on status attributes and *variations between social movement participants and nonparticipants.*

McAdam and Paulsen's (1993) analysis of Freedom Summer begins to get at the question by analyzing activists' relatively advantaged status, although the comparison group is not young adults or even college students generally, but rather those who applied to the Freedom Summer project (i.e., those who wanted to participate). Hodson, Ziegler, and Bump (1987) similarly analyze worker status effects relative to a particular strike campaign, yet the workers they examine are quite homogeneous in terms of status attributes. As a consequence of these data limitations, social movement and labor analyses have tended to focus on participants and processes pertaining to mobilization, rather than comparing participants and nonparticipants on various status dimensions.

Networks, Social Movement Culture, and Participation

Along with being patterned by individual status attributes, social movement participation is also a function of the networks one is embedded in and of related normative, cultural, and cognitive processes that translate movement issues into the day-to-day experiences of individuals. Indeed, networks are necessary for the recruitment and coordination of individual participants (Kim and Bearman 1997; Klandermans 1984; Myers 2000; Oberschall 1994; Oliver 1984; Opp 1988; Zhao 1998), and they serve as the conduit for identity building, framing, and dissemination of social movement culture (Fantasia

1988; Gamson 1995; Melucci 1985; Snow et al. 1986; Taylor and Whittier 1992). Networks and what they disseminate may, in fact, alter calculations and either facilitate or hinder individual involvement.

Network accounts can inform the question of why individuals participate and are intuitively linked to discussions of social movement culture, identity, and framing. Oppositional cultural formation and identity, in fact, are salient only to the extent that they are somehow transmitted to group members and potential participants. Conversely, networks will be influential to the extent that they are disseminating something of consequence (Roscigno and Danaher 2001) or are altering actors' calculations at some temporally proximate moment (Maxwell and Oliver 1993; Oberschall 1980). Network accounts thus tend to focus on the conduit itself and the resulting spread of social movements across time, place, and population, while research on framing, social movement culture, and identity delineate what precisely is being transmitted. Both aspects, certainly interdependent, are important for mobilizing individuals (Strang and Soule 1998).

Although little labor research has dealt specifically with network effects and potentially related social movement cultural and identity processes, there is good reason to suspect that these foci are important. Fantasia's (1988) analyses of contemporary strike campaigns, for instance, suggests that transportation and communication networks provide a necessary conduit for strikers and that "cultures of solidarity" emerge and are disseminated with clear implications for individual involvement and commitment (see also Letwin 1998). In a more recent analysis of textile worker mobilization in the U.S. South during the 1920s and 1930s, Roscigno and Danaher (2001) explicate the role of radio networks in the activism that occurred, along with the cultural content that was transmitted and that arguably fostered necessary dimensions of identity, interpretation, and collective political efficacy. Certain key questions nevertheless remain. To what degree might network processes pattern worker identity and action, regardless of individual status attributes? And, what forms of network processes might occur, particularly at the point of economic production, with implications for worker resistance?

In the next section, we address these questions within the context of contemporary workplace divisions and structures. For many workers, we suggest, status position and related calculations may be directly influential, although they are also often tied to, if not embedded within, relevant network processes.

The Case of Striking Workers

Understanding worker mobilization requires attention to influential status distinctions, potentially relevant network processes, and their respective associations. The most obvious starting point in these regards is literature pertaining to class status in the United States—a literature that highlights the complexities of the working class and their implications for collective and political efficacy (Grusky and Sorensen 1998; Rubin 1986). Such foci are central to Wright's (1978, 1985) work on contradictory class locations, whereby individuals are conceived of as holding power in occupational hierarchies without necessarily owning or controlling assets within the structure of production. Although this is especially pertinent to the case of the contemporary middle class, Form (1985, 1995) has delineated increasing segmentation among the working class as well, resulting in cleavages most notably between skilled and nonskilled workers. Such divides, he suggests, have implications for, and if anything undermine, class mobilization and political efficacy.

While occupational and skill divisions contribute to the complex and possibly fragmented nature of the working class, status divisions of race/ethnicity and gender may also be important for understanding worker mobilization and strike campaigns. Race and gender represent meaningful background statuses in and of themselves, patterned within and outside the economic arena, with implications for mobilization generally and class-based action (Cornfield and Kim 1994; Zingraff and Schulman 1984). These status attributes and associated inequalities may be commensurate with worker grievances and, thus, can enhance the capacity to organize on a class basis. At the same time, however, and as made clear in historical and social movement literatures, such divisions may also undermine cohesion and the ability

to organize working class individuals and groups. This is particularly true when the specific grievances of subordinate group participants within a movement are overlooked or neglected (Gabin 1990; Gilroy 1991; Geschwender 1971; Roscigno and Anderson 1995). Cornfield and Kim's (1994) analysis of union support provides some conceptual clarity on these issues, denoting how worker status should be conceptualized of as multifaceted and measured both at the workplace level (i.e., occupation, skill, income, etc.) and in terms of more ascriptive background attributes (i.e., race/ethnicity, gender, etc.). But how and why might particular statuses prove to be influential in the case of labor organization? And, might not status variations undermine efforts toward collective action?

In relation to the first question, one might expect workers with high occupational status to have greater allegiance to, and identify more with, their employer than the union (Cornfield and Kim 1994). This tendency will be driven by prestige associated with skill level, possibly greater seniority, and higher relative wages. Such a straightforward prediction, however, lacks clear delineation of historical context and the complexities of class. Skilled workers should indeed exhibit greater commitment to employers and a diminished likelihood of striking, given their relatively high pay and prestige. At the same time, however, these very same workers have a historical legacy of successfully organizing and striking (Form 1985). Such *intrastatus* tension, between higher rewards on the one hand and a historical union legacy on the other, leads to the expectation that wages and job status may have countervailing effects, particularly for skilled workers.

In contrast to highly skilled workers, who may experience contradictory pulls in the process of labor organizing and mobilization, those of low workplace and subordinate race/ethnic and gender statuses may have an overall greater propensity to participate (see Cornfield and Kim 1994). We see this as partially driven by lower relative status inside and outside the economic arena and, consequently, heightened material grievances. It is also likely that historical exclusion, persistent segregation, and a legacy of action through collective, informal political channels, especially for African-Americans and Hispanics in the United States, will play a role in fostering participation among what Oberschall (1993) calls "negatively privileged groups" (see also Tilly 1975; Zingraff and Schulman 1984). It is for these reasons that unions, at least in the contemporary era, have been more inclined to recruit and mobilize based on background statuses.

Rational calculations pertaining to movement involvement or, in our case, strike action are thus structurally patterned by status distinctions. Equally important is the recognition that potential actors and their decision making are fundamentally bounded by, and linked to, social attachments and network processes. Making explicit the social milieu within which decision making unfolds or is even constrained is not only useful but necessary (Blau 1964; Huber 1997; Oberschall 1994). It is usually the case, for instance, that movements themselves introduce grievance frames, collective identity processes, and even repertoires in a manner that alters potential participants' calculations and that can bridge status divides (Fink 1985; Letwin 1998; Snow et al. 1986). Actors' embeddedness within social networks may or may not be, strictly speaking, related to a movement or mobilization campaign. Such networks nevertheless may condition the terms, rewards, and/or costs of individual involvement (Calhoun 1982).

Network and cultural processes are issues not entirely distinct from the topic of individual statuses, rational calculations, or identities. The structuralist perspective in social movements (e.g., Gould 1995; Wellman and Berkowitz 1988), in fact, typically assumes an isomorphism between individual processes and structural location. Constructionists, in contrast, suggest there is "considerable indeterminancy between identities and their roots in either personality or social structure" (Snow and McAdam 2000, p. 46). Rather than adopting either extreme, Snow and McAdam (2000) suggest that the task is to identify situations in which identity convergence—a situation wherein individual identities and calculations correspond to the goals and framing of a movement—occurs. This process, they continue, unfolds in part through solidarity networks or through networks of individuals "who are

not only linked together structurally in some fashion or another but also share common social relations, a common lifestyle, and a common fate and who therefore are likely to share a common identity" (p. 48). To successfully recruit, a movement must tap into such networks and make effective use of grievance frames—grievance frames that are relatively consistent with already established identities and that bridge potential status divides (e.g., see Fink 1985; McAdam 1982; Morris 1984). If successful on these counts, rapid mobilization is more likely since "bloc recruitment" (as opposed to individual recruitment) will be possible (Oberschall 1973; Snow and McAdam 2000).

Although little research directly addresses the relevance of networks and their interplay with calculations among workers, there are several pieces of work from which we can draw. Notable in this regard is the early work by Kerr and Siegel (1954) on interindustry strike propensity, wherein the authors suggest that preexisting social relations among workers are crucial. Especially important, they continue, are situations in which members of an aggrieved group are linked to one another by conditions and concentration in their lives and at work. Lincoln (1978, p. 217) similarly suggests that employment concentration increases strike activity because it "defines the actual organizational boundaries in which interaction networks among workers are formed" (see also Shorter and Tilly 1974).

It is conceivable that there exists considerable capacity for the formation of influential networks at the workplace itself, as opposed to those occurring across broader communities or through autonomous institutions or organizations highlighted elsewhere in the social movement literature (Minkoff 1993; Morris 1984; Taylor 1989). Prior research on worker grievances, communication, and insurgency suggest that the workplace itself is the arena within which individuals formulate impressions about their jobs, the adequacy of rewards, and their capacity to demand change (Burawoy 1979; Hodson 1996, 2001; Vallas 1987). What this suggests to us is that networks occurring naturally at the point of production, while certainly not the only network a worker may be embedded in, may be most influential for shaping individual involvement in strike action. Indeed, sociohistorical accounts of union involvement and striking suggest that rather than being shaped by the goals, strategies, or networks of a larger union or broader-based class mobilization, worker grievances and insurgency are often formulated and fostered more proximately to the point of production (e.g., Fantasia 1988; Kimeldorf 1999).

But how might networks be forged at work, and why might they be influential in shaping mobilization and individual strike support specifically? Workers tend to be segregated by skill level and by race and sex (Kilbourne, England, and Beron 1994; Okamoto and England 1999; Tomaskovic-Devey 1993), and concentration of workers of similar statuses may have implications for identity and consciousness. Such segregation in large organizations typically occurs across the lines of work unit, with certain units being comprised of lower-skilled or race- or gender-specific employees. And, it is within such units and via job segregation that several processes with implications for insurgency may unfold.

First, if concentration within a workplace, or within units of a given workplace, is particularly intense, those of similar statuses (advantaged or disadvantaged) will be working alongside one another, communicating, and possibly sharing grievances (see Oberschall 1973). Here, the work unit becomes the natural network conduit, and within such a unit lies the potential that consciousness, working class identity, and grievances will homogenize among unit members despite possible status variations that exist. If greater union or class loyalty manifests within a unit, for instance, this may encourage individual support of a union or actual strike participation above and beyond the impact of one's own pay, seniority, or feelings toward unions or strikes. If racial segregation within work units is evident, one might expect racial identity to become salient. This may help or hinder the unfolding of class action depending on whether the movement can successfully frame and negotiate identity differences across work units. That is, grievance framing within a movement, if effective, will bridge potential status divides among workers of various structural locations.

A second possibility is that networks may be influential not simply because of potential information, identity, or oppositional culture that is shared but, rather, through their effects on rational calculation at a given, arguably pivotal, point in time (Marwell and Oliver 1993; Oberschall 1980). Such might be the case during a walkout, when an individual must choose to stay behind on her job or walk out with fellow workers. While such on-the-spot decision making will undoubtedly be patterned by an individual's particular statuses, it will also be weighted by the immediate and/or future costs associated with not walking out with one's coworkers. Although actors may garner such information informally through their networks days or even weeks prior to the mobilization, there is often on-the-spot "milling" that occurs, where actors assess the immediate likelihood that others will participate (Brown 1965; Oberschall 1993). What this means is not only that rational calculation will make its way into individual status effects, but that such calculation also typically occurs within a context of network position and group affiliation. In either scenario—the first, where identity building and grievance sharing occur informally and prior to a mobilization campaign, or the second, where momentary calculations are made—one's workplace networks will be crucial. The analyses that follow attempt to delineate which, if either, is occurring, although we do not view the two possibilities outlined as mutually exclusive but perhaps instead reinforcing.

The data, the case, and measurement
Our analyses draw from data on a strike by the Communications Workers of America (CWA) that occurred in the spring of 2000 at Ohio State University. This data, which includes a variety of relevant indicators pertaining to the background and workplace status of the 1,681 full-time dues-paying university workers covered by the CWA collective bargaining agreement, was provided to us by CWA Local 4501 immediately following the strike.[2] Also included are work unit identifiers and university time records for each employee over the three-week strike period. These allow for the computation of several aggregated network measures and an indicator of individual strike participation. We supplement this quantitative data with ethnographic

material, including our own interviews with strikers and union officials, observational notes of protest events and pickets, and archived media accounts.[3]

The significance of this particular strike and the more general usefulness of case analyses are worth highlighting. Although detailed, historical analyses of unique cases may undermine efforts toward generalizable conclusions, cases that lend themselves to assessment of theoretically meaningful questions have been essential to the development and understanding of common social processes (Ragin 1991; Ragin and Becker 1992). Indeed, rigorous sociological analyses of a single case provide the benefits of both theoretical generality and "situational groundedness" (Harper 1992, p. 139; see also Kimeldorf 1985). We thus bring to this analysis general theoretical questions pertaining to mobilization, in-depth knowledge of the specific context within which the strike at Ohio State University (OSU) unfolded, and the explicit goal of informing theoretical understanding of mobilization outside the context of this one case.[4]

The strike by CWA workers at OSU was the first walkout in 33 years, and it marked a breaking point from generally conciliatory labor relations with the university. In the context of the city of Columbus, where the labor movement has been historically inactive and poorly integrated relative to other industrial strongholds in the region (Form 1995; Hirsch and Macpherson 2000), the three-week strike at one of the largest and most well-known employers in the area was indeed a significant action. Despite voting to strike at the expiration of numerous contracts over the past 25 years, all previous efforts to strike were eventually averted, with the union consistently conceding on wages, health care, and the contracting out of jobs to nonunion employees (Devault 1975; Doulin 1990; Flood 1994; Helsel 1988). In the case of the 2000 strike, however, workers did not concede.

The service, skilled trades, and maintenance workers at OSU made clear to a reluctant union leadership and a disbelieving administration that they were fed up, underpaid, and ready to walk out. As a veteran female custodian put it: "This has been 30 years in the coming. Let 30 years of frustration build up and when they walk, they're not going to

come back until they get what they want" (Marx and Thomas 2000, p. 1).

Under the banner of "2 for 2000" (or the demand for an immediate two dollar raise across the board in the year 2000), nearly 80% of all CWA members walked out and stayed out for the duration of the three-week strike. What resulted was a general upheaval at the relatively quiet Mid-western campus, known more for its football than for its activism. Picket stations and noisemakers dotted the campus, workers and students staged nearly a monthlong sit-in of the administrative offices, and many faculty and graduate instructors orchestrated teach-ins and held classes outside as a showing of solidarity. The administration responded by cancelling strikers' health insurance that was already paid for, taking away employee building keys before the strike even unfolded, bringing in temporary workers (often students), and threatening wayward instructors through mass e-mails and a full-page ad in the student newspaper (Marx and Thomas 2000; Thomas 2000).

Rallies and meetings, complete with chants and slogans highlighting wage grievances and economic inequalities, kept workers tied to one another, garnered sympathizers, and also rekindled excitement every few days. According to one striker,

> The last rally we had was a shot in the arm for all of us. After talking to everyone, and listening to everyone who we don't see but are our friends, there's a lot of students, and there were faculty, which really surprised me too. They put their necks on the line, and hopefully there won't be any repercussions after this is all settled on them...for speaking their minds....Everybody walked away from it feeling like we can get back out there, and we can keep the fight going, so that was really positive.

The introduction of new tactics generated excitement and greater public awareness as well. In one of the most visible of protest events, strikers (with student support) shut down the $187 million dollar construction project at the university football stadium, thus highlighting their material grievances in the midst of seemingly abundant wealth. In the process, national attention was focused on the OSU case (Meatto 2000). The Teamsters responded by offering support and by helping to shut down campus mail services, vending machines, and deliveries. The Construction and Building Trades Union followed suit by refusing to cross picket lines, and poet Maya Angelou and NAACP President Kwiesi Mfume canceled previously scheduled appearances on the campus. Local, regional, and national visibility escalated as strike events were reported daily by the student newspaper and the Columbus city papers. The strike action would eventually receive coverage in the *New York Times* and *Washington Post* and would be counted in *Mother Jones* magazine as one of the top 10 campus protests of 2000.

The strike by CWA workers at OSU was particularly impressive given the diversity across race and ethnicity, as well as across status distinctions of skill, occupation, and rewards. In the previous section we noted the theoretical implications of such segmentation for worker mobilization. We suggested that the impact of status distinctions, and potential divides across them, may vary depending on network dynamics and the ability of the movement to frame issues broadly. In terms of the latter, the dominant frame was clearly a material one. The 2 for 2000 slogan, which became ubiquitous across campus, demanded an immediate and universal rectification of years of inadequate wage practices. This struck a chord for workers across the board, high and low status, black and white, male and female. As an African-American custodial worker noted,

> We need the money. Wages plus cost of living, everything is going up. They don't want to give us that, the two dollars, they don't want to give us that. They want to give us lower wages, and people ain't gonna' go for that, man. We want more, this is a new millennium. Year 2000 now, things are changing now, that's why we are out here. To make them understand that we ain't gonna' go for that no more. No more low wages and stuff, that's pennies, nickels, and dimes, man.

The issue of wages resonated with skilled workers as well, as suggested to us by a white male electrician, employed by OSU for nearly 24 years:

> The university keeps taking more and more away from us, as a whole, and it's got to a point where they have got our backs against the wall. Uh, first they took away longevity, which they used to have step raises and longevity, they took away the step raises, and they took away the longevity, so now the only raises I would get would be, uh, the annual raises.

There was certainly some potential for racial division and the emergence of an overriding racial injustice frame, given the disparate concentration of African-Americans in the least skilled and lowest paying jobs on campus (discussed momentarily). Such framing might have alienated the disproportionately white, skilled workers on the campus. Although periodic slogans and chants emphasized racism by the university, this never became the overriding theme during the strike or for workers themselves. Instead, the focus on low wages, the use of the 2 for 2000 slogan, the tactical and verbal emphasis on university multimillion dollar spending on a football stadium, and the contrast between OSU's wages and those of other public sector employees off campus, all of which were played out in the local media and during rallies, kept levels of solidarity high.

With high levels of participation throughout the three-week period and strong student and community support, workers at OSU made some meaningful financial gains (averaging raises of more than 18%), although the final contract included contentious pay differentials between north campus and medical center employees.[5] Equally important to financial gain was the statement workers made to the administration by walking out for the first time in three decades. As one union official described, "People who had been ignored for a long time got heard" (Marx 2000, p. 11E).

In the context of this strike, framed largely in material terms, the following analyses attempt to disentangle and more fully understand the impact of pertinent status distinctions among workers and their structural location in the workplace hierarchy. We also examine more aggregate processes occurring in worker networks and their impact on individual strike involvement. Our analyses and the data from which they draw are quite unique relative to prior studies, which have been limited to a single occupation or a relatively homogeneous population. Furthermore, and unlike many social movement analyses, these data include not only participants in the mobilization *but also nonparticipants.* Ideally, such data would be longitudinal and allow for measurement of predictors at an earlier time point relative to the outcome of interest. Although the analyses that follow are cross-sectional,[6] confidence in causal ordering is bolstered to some degree by firsthand accounts by strikers and by the media and archival sources from which we draw.

Strike Participation

Our indicator of strike participation measures in dichotomous fashion whether an individual took part in striking over the entire three-week period. Approximately 80% of the 1,681 workers did so, while the remainder continued to work during this period. Of the nonstrikers, about half crossed the picket line at some point during the strike (most at the conclusion of the first week), while the other half worked the entire period. Rather then treating nonstrikers as a homogeneous category, we ran models of strike participation using a continuous measure of total hours worked during the strike. We also analyzed strikers, strikebreakers, and nonstrikers in multinomial logistic regression. The patterns, however, were consistent with findings derived from the dichotomous indicator reported in the forthcoming tables, suggesting that nonstrikers and strikebreakers are more similar than distinct, relative to those striking over the three-week period. Table 1 presents descriptions, means, and standard deviations for our dichotomous indicator of strike participation, along with key individual and network explanatory variables.

Background and Workplace Status

Consistent with Cornfield and Kim (1994), we include measures of an individual's background and workplace statuses. Among background status indicators are age of the employee, measured in years, and sex (1 = male). Race is coded as African-American and other, with white as the referent.

The data provide relatively specific measures of workplace status, the most important of these being occupation. Occupational categories include custodial worker, hospital service worker, maintenance/manual worker, and skilled worker, with service

worker as the referent in the analyses. Note the substantial occupational heterogeneity within the sample, with custodial workers making up the largest portion of workers, followed by the service workers (the referent and 28% of the sample), skilled workers, maintenance/manual workers, and hospital service workers, respectively.[7]

While background and workplace status may have direct effects on participation, it is also likely that they may be influential through associated reward structures and/or individual class identity. For these reasons, we include measures of income (hourly wage), seniority, and card-carrying union member status. Rational choice perspectives would suggest a depressant effect of income on participation, while the impact of seniority is less clear-cut. On the one hand, seniority may reflect an organizational commitment to the employer. At the same time, seniority may be related to higher commitment to the work group itself and, thus, may facilitate action (Burawoy 1979; Hodson et al. 1987).

Card-carrying status, an indicator of individual, class-based identity, should have a positive impact on individual strike involvement. Upon hire, workers have the option to become a card-carrying union member or a "fair-share" member, the latter meaning that they pay dues but do not identify with the union. Although perhaps a symbolic gesture upon being hired, the decision to be card-carrying likely reflects commitment to the union, class-based attitudes, and an overall greater propensity to act during a strike. Our quantitative findings along with qualitative insights, discussed momentarily, support these possibilities.

Networks

To gauge network and associated collective identity processes, we use aggregate workplace unit data. The work unit sets the organizational boundaries in which workers interact on the job and thus can be a conduit for information flow and communication. The union's shop steward system is also built around work unit organization. Shop stewards are, among other things, responsible for disseminating information between union leadership and rank-and-file members for each work unit. Importantly

Table 1 Variable Names, Variable Descriptions, and Means and Standard Deviations

Variable	Description	Mean	SD
Dependent variable:			
Strike participation	Dichotomous measure of whether an individual worker took part in the strike (0 = no; 1 = yes)	.80	.29
Background status:			
Age	Age in years	43.25	11.24
Race/ethnicity	Reference = white		
African-American	1 = African-American; 0 = other	.57	.50
Other	1 = Asian, Hispanic, and Native American; 0 = other	.10	.30
Sex	1 = male; 0 = female	.66	.47
Workplace status:			
Occupation	Reference = service worker		
Custodial	1 = custodian	.38	.48
Hospital service	1 = hospital service workers	.07	.26
Maintenance/manual	1 = maintenance/manual workers	.10	.29
Skilled	1 = skilled workers	.17	.38
Income	Hourly wage in dollars	10.48	2.64
Seniority	Seniority in years	9.63	9.37
Card-carrying	Individual, class-based identity as denoted by the worker's union card-carrying status (1 = yes; 0 = no)	.65	.48
Network measures:			
% card-carrying in unit	% employee's work unit that is card-carrying, not including specific employee	65.43	16.41
% African-American in unit	% employee's work unit that is African-American, not including specific employee	56.63	21.92
% striking in unit	% employee's work unit that went on strike, not including specific employee	80.13	17.12

for prestrike mobilization, shop stewards were responsible for bringing to workers the pragmatic details of a potential strike (information on legal rights, potential picket locations, how strike pay works, etc.) as well as reports from prestrike informational meetings, which grew considerably in attendance and contentiousness toward the end of the negotiations period.[8] The 1,681 employees in the data are spread out across 82 workplace units on the campus, ranging in size from 1 to 368. More than three-quarters of these individuals are concentrated in 13 units of 30 or more people.[9]

Earlier we suggested that the concentration of individuals of a similar status may have implications

for identity, consciousness, and strike action. Moreover, networks at the point of production may be influential through their effects on decision making at a temporal point in time. To address the first of these possibilities, we use the percentage of an individual's work unit that is card-carrying and the percentage of the individual's work unit that is African-American as indicators of aggregate class- and race-based identity within the work unit. The percentage of a workplace unit that went on strike is used as a proxy for social pressure to strike within the network and offers insight into the temporal component. Figure 1 reports the distribution of work activism across work units in our study.

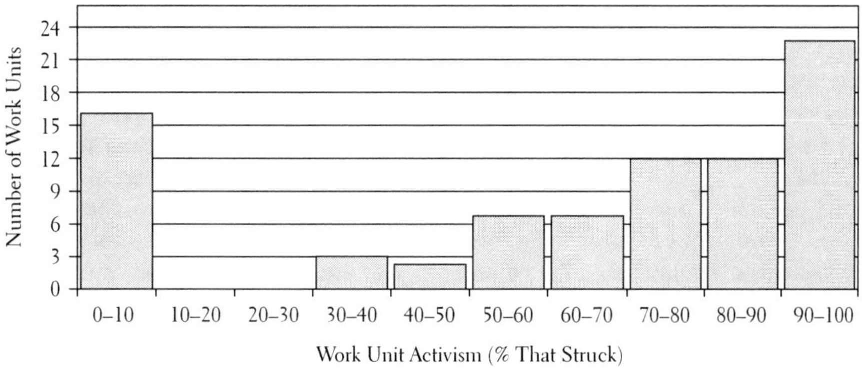

Figure 14.1 Distribution of work unit activism across work units (*N* = 82)

Given the possibility of nonlinear pressure associated with workers in one's unit walking off the job, we use the natural log function of this indicator—something we discuss in our analytic strategy section and graphically display in our results.[10] The variable itself, as the reader will note in figure 1, is negatively skewed to begin with: a fact that is not remedied by the log transformation being used. This should not raise concern, however, given that logistic regression makes no assumption and has no restrictions pertaining to the distribution of independent variables (von Hippel 2003). We nevertheless undertook several steps to bolster confidence that the negative skew was not altering the patterns or associations we report.[11] Potentially influential outliers were eliminated, as were small and low activism units, resulting in a more normal distribution. Results pertaining to the impact of work unit activism and its slope, however, did not change.

Importantly, the actual individual under examination was excluded from the three network computations pertaining to his unit. This was done to insure that findings are not influenced by collinearity artificially created during aggregation. Workers in one-person units (*N* = 11), by virtue of our measurement strategy, automatically receive a score of 0 for network activism (given that they do not have any immediate union coworkers). To insure that this coding scheme and especially its application to very small work units were not altering our

findings, we controlled for individuals in units of 1–3 people; introduced a dummy control for units of fewer than 10 workers, and also excluded small units from the analyses altogether. None of these procedures altered the results, thus bolstering confidence in our measures and findings.[12]

Analytic Strategy and Results

The analyses proceed in two steps. We first illustrate linkages between background and workplace statuses and their respective associations with individual strike participation. This provides insight into the relations and varying effects of status described by Cornfield and Kim (1994), although it is an extension in two regards. First, by delineating associations between background and workplace statuses, we acknowledge that such statuses are often interdependent and consequential for understanding race/sex disparities in pay and occupational segregation—something clearly noted in recent stratification research (e.g., Tomaskovic-Devey 1993). Second, we extend the analytic focus not to union support, which is typically done, but rather to mobilization in the form of strike participation. For strike participation models, we introduce background status, workplace status, and then individual income, seniority, and card-carrying status. Declines in coefficient magnitudes and significance across equations highlight the degree to which background status matters through occupational disparities and whether occupational rewards (i.e., income), class-based identities (i.e., card-carrying), or seniority mediate some of the status effects we find. Quantitative findings are supplemented throughout with qualitative, open-ended interview material, gathered by the authors during the strike.

The second portion of our analyses highlights the importance of network processes for individual strike involvement. We introduce the percentage of card-carrying members in the employee's work unit, the percentage of African-Americans in the work unit, and the percentage in the work unit that struck. These are examined in separate equations and then simultaneously, while controlling for status, income, identity, and seniority measures specified earlier. Declines in significance for the percentage of card-carrying members and the percentage of African-Americans in the final equation, when network strike participation is included, is suggestive of a network identity process, played out through action (i.e., strike participation in the network).

Persistent and nonlinear effects of work unit strike support on individual strike participation may be driven by prestrike network identity processes or by more temporally proximate calculations of individuals based on whether those in their work unit walked out when the strike unfolded. Indeed, decision making with regard to collective action does not occur in a vacuum but rather is interdependent with the attitudes and actions of those in close proximity (Granovetter 1978; Klandermans 1984; Oberschall 1980). Especially important may be the existence and impact of an initial, critical mass of strike supporters within the network (see Marwell and Oliver 1993).[13] It is for this reason that we utilize a nonlinear function of work unit activism in our modeling and plot the relationship in figure 2 (displayed later on) for the distinct subgroups highlighted in our initial findings.

Admittedly, most employees fall in work units with high levels of activism, providing less than ideal variation at the lower end of the work unit activism continuum. Dropping low activism units from the analyses, however, does not alter our results. Moreover, while confidence intervals around the average effect (also illustrated below in fig. 2) are understandably wider for low activism units, given their limited representation in the data, the general pattern and interpretation do not differ significantly. Such data limitations notwithstanding, our finding of a nonlinear effect of work unit activism, its actual graphical pattern, and our own interviews with strikers and union leaders suggest that on-the-spot calculations were made by many workers.

Individual Status, Income, and Identity

Table 2 reports associations between workplace occupational status, the background statuses of race and sex, and income, seniority, and union support measured by card-carrying status. Consistent with much research on work organization and stratification, the workforce at OSU is relatively segregated across occupational lines. Minority groups tend to be concentrated in lower-status service and custodial jobs. White males, in contrast, are concentrated in the skilled trades and in maintenance and manual work. This pattern of segregation is most pronounced among skilled workers, nearly three-quarters of whom are white and virtually all male. As denoted in the table, it is within these higher-skilled and maintenance jobs that wages are higher, as is the general level of union support. These workers, as we suggested earlier, may consequently experience intrastatus contradictory pulls when it comes to strike action.

Disparate occupational concentration may also hold consequences for reward structures across race and gender lines. The resulting wage gaps between minority and white workers and between male and female workers, reported in table 3, are both considerable and statistically significant. On average, whites receive over two dollars more in hourly wages than blacks and others, and men receive about a dollar and a half more an hour than women in the sample. Arguably, this deficit in wages should increase minority and female involvement in protest action since the absolute wage costs of participation will be lower and material grievances probably more pronounced.[14]

Table 4 reports the consequences of background status, workplace status, income, seniority, and

Table 2 Worker Attributes by Occupation

Occupation (N)	% Minority	% Female	% Card-Carrying	Average Hourly Wage	Average Seniority
Custodial (646)	84.20	40.10	65.00	8.95	7.17
Hospital service (126)	80.90	65.10	57.00	10.34	9.52
Maintenance/manual (161)	38.60	1.90	71.00	11.89	10.93
Skilled (296)	25.10	1.40	70.00	13.71	13.60
Service (452)	73.60	49.20	64.00	10.10	10.18

Table 3 Average Hourly Wage by Race and Sex

Category	Hourly Wage
Race:	
Black	9.84
White	12.01
Other	8.83
Sex:	
Male	11.02
Female	9.42

card-carrying status for strike participation among 1,681 workers over the three-week strike period. Consistently, African-Americans and other racial/ethnic minorities are significantly more likely to strike relative to whites. For African-Americans specifically, the likelihood is nearly double that of white workers ($P < .001$). Although there is no apparent gender influence, workplace status clearly matters. Occupational differences in the likelihood of striking are reported in equation (2) of table 4. Custodians, skilled workers, and maintenance and manual workers are all more likely to strike than service workers generally, as well as hospital service workers.

Equation (3) of table 4 introduces potential mediators—individual income, seniority, and card-carrying status. Income, in the form of hourly wage, has an expected, negative effect on striking. For each dollar per hour in wages, the average likelihood of an individual's striking declines by approximately 25% ($P < .001$).

In contrast to income, seniority and union identity (measured by card-carrying status) positively shape the likelihood of striking. A card-carrying union member is about four times more likely to strike than a counterpart without similar union identification ($P < .001$). We proposed initially that card-carrying status implied a more general commitment to the union and that this might foster strike participation. Although many striking workers noted that their reasons for striking were strictly economic, several high-skilled workers with considerable seniority highlighted their commitment to the union. Such was the case with the following white male technician, with 23 years of service to the university: "I support the union as a union card-carrying member. They all voted to strike. I have to follow suit with their decisions....When you're a card-carrying union member you got to honor what they decide and it was a 98% strike vote."

Intrastatus contradictory tensions are apparent, however, with the addition of wages, seniority, and card-carrying status in equation (3) and in conjunction with the descriptive associations reported earlier. Skilled and maintenance/manual workers experience the highest wages and strongest union identity, yet wages and union identity have countervailing effects. The depressant effects of wages on striking explains why occupational status effects among skilled and maintenance workers actually increase in equation (3). These occupational groups are likely to support collective action because of individual union identity and probably recognition of broader union and strike history and

Table 4 Logistic Regression Estimates of Strike Participation on Individual Background and Workplace Status Measures

	Equation		
Variable	(1)	(2)	(3)
Background status:			
Age	−.003 (.006)	−.006 (.006)	−.014 (.007)*
Race/ethnicity:			
African-American	.675 (.137)***	.718 (.151)***	.527 (.161)**
Other	.482 (.228)*	.473 (.238)*	.450 (.254)
Sex	.071 (.139)	−.184 (.152)	−.057 (.159)
Workplace status:			
Custodial		.820 (.163)***	.572 (.176)**
Hospital service		−.475 (.223)*	−.324 (.236)
Maintenance/manual		.761 (.245)**	1.108 (.274)***
Skilled		.655 (.200)**	1.454 (.265)***
Income			−.299 (.058)***
Seniority			.031(.013)*
Card-carrying			1.448 (.153)***
Constant	1.095	.924	3.237

Note.—N = 1,681; nos. in parentheses are SEs. Two-tailed tests of significance.
* P <.05.
** P <.01.
*** P <.001.

potential—something captured by the persistent, strong, and significant effects of these occupational designations. Yet, their higher incomes mitigate, to some degree, their likelihood of actual participation. This important finding highlights some level of discontinuity between subjective and objective criteria informing individual decisions pertaining to work-based actions.[15]

Custodial workers, whose ranks tend to be disproportionately African-American, display persistent and positive strike support. The coefficient decline suggests that this is partially a function of lower pay and, in all likelihood, clearer-cut wage grievances. When asked why he was participating, a custodial worker with eight years experience suggested that it was

for better wages. Because like right now, just paying off my insurance and all that, and child support, I bring home $230 every two weeks. And that's

nothing. You see, so I'm struggling, and I like to spend a lot of time with my children. If I have to go out and get another job, then we won't have time at all. You see, and I need this raise, bad.

Notable as well in table 4 is the persistent effect of being African-American even with workplace status and other potential mediators included. As suggested earlier, this lingering effect may be tied to the history of collective action in the African-American community and its viability, even in the contemporary era, for addressing workplace grievances. This is consistent with the reflections of a black male worker, given while out on the picket line: "Well, I'm kind of like a '60s child, kind of, I was back in the '60s where you protested for what you wanted. A lot of that's there. A lot of it is actually, uh, feeling for other people."

Findings presented thus far denote a strong effect of both background and workplace status attributes on individual strike participation. For background status, race is clearly the most meaningful. While part of its impact is tied to occupational concentration, the impact of African-American status remains strong and stands alone. Among workplace status attributes, occupational designations clearly make a difference. Although some of the impact is tied to differences in income and union identity, these effects remain. Simply, occupational designations and identities are meaningful for workers and for their strike involvement (see also Klandermans and de Weerd 2000). Although skilled workers may have a stronger union identification and, consequently, a relatively high propensity for involvement, their higher incomes appear to seriously mitigate this potential. Nevertheless, results suggest that along with lower-status African-American custodial workers, high-skilled, mostly white, workers remain more likely on average to mobilize. The implication is that there is a heightened capacity for action, even within a single labor campaign, among low- and high-status mobilizers.

The Impact of Networks

The preceding analyses illustrated the impact of background and workplace status on strike participation and the partial mediation of these effects through income, seniority, and individual union identity. In table 5, we analyze the impact of workplace network dynamics, with controls for the status, income, and individual union identity indicators specified earlier. We also account for unit size throughout.

Equation (1) suggests important effects of work unit class identity on individual strike participation. Recall that the computation of this work unit network measure does not include the individual under consideration. The influence of individual card-carrying status, reported in the lower portion of the table, remains significant and virtually unchanged relative to the earlier, individual model. This suggests to us an identity dynamic occurring in the network, not reducible to individual preferences or individual union affinity.

Work unit racial composition exhibits no apparent influence on the likelihood of individual striking (eq. [2]). The effect of having strikers in one's work unit, however, is quite sizable and

significant ($P < .001$). Social movement scholars have debated for some time over the issue of potential protestors' calculations within the context of social connections and network embeddedness, suggesting possible exponential costs of not participating when others do or an initial and strong pull to participate once a core takes action (Marwell and Oliver 1993). Our use and finding of a nonlinear effect lends some weight to these claims. Figure 2 displays the pattern graphically for the two high-activism groups of workers, highlighted in the first portion of our analyses, relative to all other employees. The figure reports the predicted probabilities of striking derived from equation (3) of table 5.[16] In the lower right corner, the reader will note the average impact of work unit activism on striking, with confidence intervals surrounding the mean effect.

What we find in figure 2 is an initial and quite strong slope for all three groups of workers. The impact of unit activism on the probability of individual strike participation continues to increase at higher percentages but at a decelerating rate. Notably, and consistent with our expectations and findings reported earlier in table 4, both low- and high-status mobilizers start out with a greater likelihood of striking relative to other employees. It is interesting to note, however, variations in the slopes for the three groups and, specifically, a steeper initial slope especially for African-American custodial workers—a pattern that seems to suggest that these workers may be more amenable to activism when there is already support in the network. The same seems to be the case for high-status white workers, although their higher incomes have a mitigating effect (see also tables 2 and 4).

The finding of a stronger initial slope is most consistent with an "initial activist core" interpretation, while the persistent but decreasing coefficient at higher levels of network strike support seems congruous with the "decelerating production function" argument posed by Marwell and Oliver (1993; see also Oliver, Marwell, and Teixeira 1985). These two possibilities may exist simultaneously. An initial core of workers who walk off the job reduces for others *the potential costs of striking*. The fact that the positive influence does not completely tail off or reverse implies that there are also *costs associated*

Table 5 Logistic Regression Estimates of Strike Participation on Work Unit
Attributes, with Individual Controls

	Equation			
Variable	(1)	(2)	(3)	(4)
% Card-carrying in unit	.009			.003
	(.004)*			(.004)
% African-American in unit		.005		−.001
		(.004)		(.004)
(ln) % striking in unit			.682	.663
			(.124)***	(.131)***
Background status:				
Age	−.014	−.014	−.015	−.015
	(.007)*	(.007)*	(.007)*	(.007)*
Race/ethnicity:				
African-American	.562	.524	.505	.514
	(.162)**	(.162)**	(.165)**	(.166)**
Other	.476	.436	.408	.416
	(.254)	(.255)	(.258)	(.259)
Sex	−.074	−.052	−.007	−.012
	(.160)	(.161)	(.163)	(.164)
Workplace status:				
Custodial	.629	.646	.498	.495
	(.180)**	(.180)**	(.184)**	(.184)**
Hospital service	−.426	−.520	−.365	−.346
	(.249)	(.250)*	(.259)	(.263)
Maintenance/manual	1.217	1.306	1.115	1.101
	(.285)***	(.285)***	(.291)***	(.294)***
Skilled	1.461	1.653	1.293	1.262
	(.270)***	(.284)***	(.275)***	(.297)***
Income	−.314	−.314	−.305	−.304
	(.059)***	(.059)***	(.060)***	(.060)***
Seniority	.029	.032	.033	.032
	(.014)*	(.014)*	(.014)*	(.014)*
Card-carrying	1.460	1.489	1.461	1.453
	(.155)***	(.155)***	(.157)***	(.158)***
Control for work unit size	−.001	−.001	−.001	−.001
	(.0005)*	(.0005)*	(.0005)*	(.0005)*
Constant	3.016	3.209	.687	.630

Note.—$N = 1,681$; nos. in parentheses are SEs. Two-tailed tests of significance.
* $P < .05$.
** $P < .01$.
*** $P < .001$.

with not striking when those in one's work unit are doing so at high percentages. These conclusions are nevertheless tempered by our recognition of data limitations, especially the fact that most workers in our case fall into units with high activism. That the mean effect and the confidence intervals surrounding it remain largely consistent do, however, offer some empirical leverage relative to our interpretation (see fig. 2, lower right-hand corner).

Our conclusions regarding on-the-spot calculations relative to one's network associations are also tentative given that the data represents a cross-section of workers who either walked off the job or did not (as opposed to a longitudinal account of workers striking and their coworkers following

afterward). Our discussions with participants and union officials nevertheless do substantiate our interpretations and the possibility of an immediate effect. As late as the evening before the strike, for instance, union officials were only sure that about half the workers who actually walked out would in fact go. The decision whether or not to strike was especially instantaneous for many third-shift workers. Having already reported to work the evening prior to the strike, these employees were faced with the immediate decision of whether or not to walk out at midnight. Many, it turned out, actually *ran* out at midnight despite the negotiations being extended until 2:00 A.M. the morning of the strike (McKinney 2000).[17]

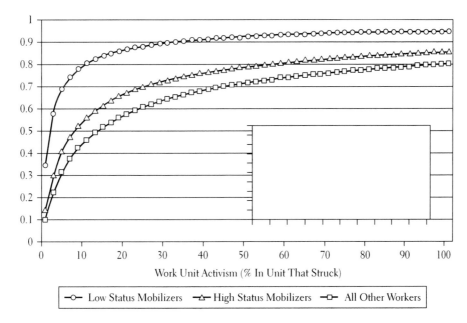

Figure 14.2 Predicted probabilities of individual strike participation by work unit activism for low-status mobilizers, high-status mobilizers, and all other workers (lower right corner, average impact of unit activism and 95% confidence intervals). Groups of workers are defined as follows: (1) low-status mobilizers are African-American, custodial, card-carrying workers with the average custodial hourly wage ($8.95); (2) high-status mobilizers are the white, skilled workers who are card-carrying union members with the average wage for skilled workers ($13.71); (3) the last group (all other workers) represents the average values for all workers not included in the first two occupational categories.

One rank-and-file activist summed up these possibilities by suggesting that while workers were signing up for picket duty in the week leading up to the strike, and certainly talking to one another and "sizing each other up," many made up their minds at the last possible moment. Most workers signed up for picket duty in locations proximate to their actual work sites. This produced a situation across campus on the first strike day whereby employees coming to work saw their very own coworkers picketing: a scene that generated tremendous social pressure. More pointedly, as this employee recalled, workers were all of a sudden struck with the reality that "oh shit, everybody else in my department walked out." Both of the possibilities we have described—grievance sharing prior to the strike and temporally proximate decision making—were forged by worker networks and were important in this particular mobilization.

The final equation of table 5 introduces the three network indicators simultaneously. The impact of percentage card-carrying declines to the point of nonsignificance once work unit strike action is included. Since card-carrying status was determined well before the strike, we interpret this decline to be reflective of the importance of class identity in the work unit, but only through strike action. This is not to suggest, however, that strike action in the unit is purely a function of identity dynamics. The persistent and strong effect of strike action in the unit, in conjunction with the actual pattern displayed in figure 2 and our ethnographic material, suggest to us that much of the impact was more temporally immediate.

Conclusion

This article extends the understanding of social movement participation, and strike action specifically. Building on prior social movement and labor analyses, we suggested that participation in collective action will be patterned by both calculations associated with status position and the embeddedness of actors in networks—networks that may condition decision-making processes through information, grievance sharing, and identity building or that may more directly pressure individuals to act. The case of a labor strike on a large university campus provided the opportunity to address these questions with appropriate and unique data. These data include straightforward measures of participation, demographics on participants and nonparticipants alike, and network indicators that are meaningful given our population of interest and the actual form of mobilization examined.

Findings revealed the importance of background and workplace status, and their associations, for individual strike involvement. African-American and other racial and ethnic minority employees displayed higher levels of strike participation relative to whites. This is partially attributable to their disparate concentration in lower-paying custodial work. Here, the absolute income costs of participation are lower and wage grievances arguably more pronounced—something quite evident in our qualitative observations of protest events and pickets. Maintenance and especially skilled workers, in contrast, experienced a contradictory intrastatus tension between rewards on the one hand (which decrease strike support) and union loyalty and history (which increase strike support) on the other. Indeed, once we accounted for the depressant effect of their higher incomes, these workers were the most likely to strike. Importantly, as noted in our background discussion, this particular mobilization framed issues broadly and mostly in material terms. This served to bridge potential interstatus divides between black and white workers and between low- and high-skilled workers.

Such findings inform labor and social movement research given the explicit focus on the complexities of class and other background statuses in relation to action. Labor research, because of data limitations, has been somewhat limited in this regard to examinations of single occupations or relatively homogeneous workforces. Thus, variation in status impact and mobilization potential among advantaged and disadvantaged groups is often overlooked. This is unfortunate, as the status divisions and pulls specified here are relevant not just to labor mobilization but to social movement participation and persistence generally. Most movements, in fact, attempt to appeal to distinct social groups. In order to persist, they must also successfully negotiate internal status divisions.

Equally, if not more important, is our finding that strike participation is shaped by more than individual status, income, and identity. Networks, too, are influential. Results indicated that, above and beyond individual causes, class identity within networks and especially strike action among those in one's unit have implications for individual involvement. Both quantitative results and supplemental ethnographic material suggest that workplace networks are crucial through grievance sharing and identity formation prior to the strike, as well as through individual decision making and calculations at a pivotal point. Here, an initial core of strikers in the unit appeared to be influential for engaging others in strike mobilization. The results also suggested, through a declining but persistent positive effect of network strike support, a possibility that there are lingering costs associated with not striking when others in one's unit do.

The impact of networks on involvement has been noted by social movement researchers for some time. Networks, this literature suggests, are essential to both the diffusion of insurgency across geographic space and in the recruiting and mobilizing of individual participants. Consistent with our focus, recent theorizing attempts to explicitly bridge discussions of individual status and decision making with those pertaining to network processes and impact (Snow and McAdam 2000). Our analyses build upon and apply these insights and recent developments in the social movement literature to labor mobilization specifically. Workers, we have argued, are typically embedded in networks at the point of production. The status composition of such networks, the potential information and identity shared among members, and the degree of protest involvement within, as findings revealed, may all have consequences for individual calculations and strike propensity beyond the impact of individual attributes.

Our conclusions are nevertheless tempered by recognition of data limitations. These include the inability to measure network dynamics outside the work environment, as well as limited detail pertaining to coworker interactional processes and potential friendship networks within the workplace. Consequently, the effects of networks on strike action presented here may be somewhat understated. Equally important, the generalizability of findings from our particular case must be considered, relative to other labor actions and social movements. Here, it is important to be explicit that our theoretical discussion and predictions are conditioned by the historically variable relevance of particular statuses, discussed previously, as well as by the university, public sector, and institutional context within which the mobilization we have described unfolded.

The employment setting on a large university campus likely entails more diversity than most workplaces and social movements.[18] This particular university setting also represents public sector employment, where elite countermobilization may be somewhat constrained and where employers, historically speaking, have been more receptive to labor representation. Finally, the fact that the strike examined occurred within one institution also makes it somewhat unique relative to many social movements or industrywide strikes, which must recruit and forge networks in a broader geographic sense. One consequence is spatial and structural proximity of potential participants: something that lends itself to significant bloc recruitment (Zhao 1998). This may contribute to the high level of participation, relative to that of other social movements. Although variations in levels of activism were less than ideal, our data and analyses nevertheless reflect an important extension in a literature that typically examines *only* participants.

Despite these qualifications, most movements and workplaces have some internal status variations that may, to a greater or lesser degree, impact the capacity to mobilize. Furthermore, most social movements and labor mobilizations, be they intra- or interinstitutional, or public or private sector, typically rely on preexistent networks to recruit, share information and social movement culture, and alter potential participants' decision making. In the case of the analysis presented in this article, we combined analytical rigor with in-depth detail and background to address general theoretical questions pertaining to status distinctions among workers, their social networks, and their implications for individual participation. We thus have confidence in our findings and conclusions, and their utility for understanding more general strike and movement processes, and we see them as unique contributions to, and extensions of, prior work. The labor movement's multidimensional character as both a social movement and labor market institution, in fact, provides an ideal setting for studying the processes outlined and represents a rich, yet relatively untapped arena for social movement scholars.

NOTES

We are grateful to Randy Hodson, Craig Jenkins, Verta Taylor, and the anonymous *AJS* reviewers for their comments on earlier versions of this article, and to William Form, James Moody, Pamela Paxton, Zhenchao Qian, and Paul von Hippel for their helpful advice. We also thank the members of the Communication Workers of America Local 4501, whose cooperation made this research possible.

1. Rather than the typical formulation of utility maximization employed in economics, we adopt a less restrictive model of purposive and conscious choice that may include utility maximization in the economic sense, but that also recognizes the role that values, beliefs, trust, friendship, and group and network affiliations may play in goal-directed decision making (see also Blau 1964). This is made more explicit in our theoretical development section, where we discuss historically forged status identities as well as the ways in which network and group affiliations may impact individuals' choices, calculations, and actions.

2. The bargaining unit covers all skilled trades, service, and maintenance workers on the main campus in Columbus. Skilled trades include electricians, carpenters, plumbers, pipe fitters, etc.

3. All quotations are from interviews the authors conducted during and after the strike unless otherwise noted.

4. We nevertheless recognize that, in the face of attempting to draw generalizable conclusions, it is important to define or even constrain the theoretical scope of the questions and the theoretical generalities we can make given the specifics of the case we analyze. For this reason, we have made explicit in our literature review and theoretical development section that the impact of various status attributes, such as race, tensions between status groups (i.e., skilled vs. unskilled workers), and union recruitment strategies will vary by historical era and that our case is reflective of labor and recruitment in the modern day. We return to issues of generalizability in our concluding discussion.

5. While many regarded the new contract as the best in recent years, the union conceded on a 10 pay differential separating north campus and medical center workers.

6. To model the processes described longitudinally would require detailed, daily, individual records of worker action starting on the first day of the strike, which we do not have.

7. Hospital service workers, while not at the top of the wage scale, faced a number of normative challenges to striking. This included emphasis by the university on "patient care and well-being."

8. According to union officials and rank-and-file activists, the informational meetings held during the negotiations period drew unanticipatedly high attendance (200–300 in attendance vs. the 20–50 at typical union meetings). While attendance at meetings typically increases during contract talks, this was substantially more than in recent years and thus meant that, in addition to the shop stewards, there were more rank-and-file members bringing back information to their work units. In fact, it was during these meetings that rank-and-file members demanded that union leadership ask for more at the bargaining table and coined the 2 for 2000 slogan that was used throughout the mobilization. It was also during this period that some rank-and-file activists (given a degree of autonomy on their jobs that allowed them to move across campus) began to spread information on negotiations, grievances, strike possibilities, and the like across work units on the campus.

9. One of our initial concerns was whether work unit size itself was conditioning the individual likelihood of striking. For this reasons, we include work unit size in our analyses of network effects. The influence appears to be mild and slightly negative. We also introduced dummy indicators for small, medium, and large work unit size, which confirmed the general, linear relationship reported in our findings section.

10. We use the natural log of this indicator given the theoretically derived expectation not only that the effect may be nonlinear but that its initial impact may be significantly more pronounced, followed by a tailing off.

11. There are 16 work units between 0% and 10% when it comes to work unit activism. Predictably, these units are small, ranging from one employee to 12. Combined, these work units have 36 workers.

12. We recognize that our work unit network measures may not capture potentially influential network processes manifested outside the workplace. Little work, however, has incorporated network and identity dynamics into strike analyses to begin with. Thus, despite the limitations of these measures, they are the best proxy for network processes occurring at the point of production.

13. This implies a nonlinear effect, or what Marwell and Oliver (1993) refer to as a "decelerating production function," where returns decrease at increasing levels of X_i.

14. Although this is not reported in the table, African-Americans are somewhat more likely than whites to be card-carrying union members. This difference is statistically significant below the .05 level. Other racial/ethnic minorities did not differ significantly from whites, and men and women displayed no apparent difference on this indicator.

15. More broadly, this finding reflects a division between conceptions of worker resistance focused on heightened subjective grievances (or consciousness-based approaches) versus accounts more informed by resource mobilization theory, which tend to highlight the structural capacity of workers in more advantaged labor market positions and their ability to withdraw labor without fear of replacement.

16. Figure 2 is generated from eq. (3) of table 5, using the coefficient for work unit activism and discrete attributes of groups of workers informed by the patterns suggested in our analyses of individual attributes (table 4). High-status mobilizers are white skilled workers who are card-carrying union members, and who earn one standard deviation above the mean in hourly wages. Low-status mobilizers are African-American custodial workers who are card-carrying union members, and who earn a standard deviation below the mean in hourly wages. All other workers are represented who do not hold these attributes. Although bivariate associations suggest that levels of participation

may be somewhat higher in larger work units, this association becomes weak and slightly negative once controls for individual status attributes and network identity and strike support measures are included. Consequently, the actual slope effects and our interpretations did not vary when we ran separate models for small, medium, and large work units.

17. The vast majority of CWA members work on the first shift. The third shift workers, however, who reported to work on the evening before the strike faced an immediate on-the-spot decision of whether or not to walk out. According to one of our informants, many came with picket signs and noisemakers at hand and actually ran out of the facilities in a jubilant display at midnight.

18. This arguably makes such a setting ideal for case analyses of mobilization. The significant variation in statuses denoted throughout, on the other hand, may make our case more complicated than some mobilization campaigns that organize around a unique identity or a singular status.

15.
Specifying the Relationship Between Social Ties and Activism

DOUG MCADAM AND RONNELLE PAULSEN

In recent years much attention in the social-movements literature has been focused on the role of social or organizational ties in movement recruitment. The result has been a growing body of studies that appear to attest to the causal importance of organizational ties (Barnes and Kaase 1979; Curtis and Zurcher 1973; Fernandez and McAdam 1988; Gould 1991; McAdam 1986; Rosenthal et al. 1985; Orum 1972; Walsh and Warland 1983) or prior contact with a movement participant (Bolton 1972; Briët, Klandermans, and Kroon 1987; Gerlach and Hine 1970; McAdam 1986; Snow, Zurcher, and Ekland-Olson 1980; Zurcher and Kirkpatrick 1976) as strong predictors of individual activism. But while they remain important, these studies are

McAdam, Doug and Ronnelle Paulsen. 1993. "Specifying the relationship Between Social Ties and Activism." *American Journal of Sociology* 99: 640–667. Reprinted by permission of The University of Chicago Press. Notes have been renumbered and edited.

nonetheless plagued by a troubling theoretical and empirical imprecision that raises important questions about their ultimate utility. This imprecision stems from three sources.

First these studies are generally silent on the basic sociological dynamics that account for the reported findings. That is, in most cases, no theory is offered to explain the observed effects of social ties on activism (for exceptions, see Opp 1989; Fernandez and McAdam 1988; and Gould 1993, 1991). So there remains a fundamental question about what the findings mean.

A second source of imprecision stems from the failure of movement scholars to specify and test the precise dimensions of social ties that seem to account for their role as facilitators of activism. As Marwell, Oliver, and Prahl (1988, p. 502) note, "it is widely agreed that participants in social movement organizations are usually recruited through preexisting social ties.... But exactly how and why social ties are important is less well established."[1]

This second problem is very much related to the first. Having failed to advance a theory that specifies the precise link between social ties and activism, empirical researchers have been content to assess the basic strength of the relationship instead of testing the causal power of the various dimensions of social ties. Accordingly, we do not really know whether it is the presence of a tie, the number of ties, or the salience, centrality, or strength of a tie that determines its effectiveness as a recruitment agent.

Finally, and perhaps most important, the existing studies fail to acknowledge conceptually or treat empirically the fact that individuals are invariably embedded in many organizational or associational networks or individual relationships that may expose the individual to conflicting behavioral pressures. This weakness is due to all the well-known dangers of sampling on the dependent variable. Almost invariably, the studies of movement recruitment start by surveying activists after their entrance into the movement. But showing that these activists were linked to the movement by some preexisting network tie does not *prove* the causal potency of that tie. No doubt there are many others who also had ties to the movement but did not participate in its activities. We suspect one of the principal reasons for the failure of the tie to impel participation in these cases is the existence of other, perhaps more salient, ties that are constraining involvement. But, to date, our lack of conceptual models of the recruitment process and the tendency to study activists after the fact of their participation has left the effects of these "multiple embeddings" unexamined.

In this article we hope to address these shortcomings in the network literature on recruitment. We will begin by briefly reviewing the existing literature on recruitment to activism and placing the recent emphasis on structural or network factors in the context of a broader discussion of other possible causal influences. We will then sketch a very rudimentary model of recruitment as mediated by social ties. In doing so we will take conceptual account of the multiple embeddings typical of social life. We will then use this model as a basis for examining the role of social ties in mediating individual recruitment

to the 1964 Mississippi Freedom Summer Project. Specifically, we will seek to determine (a) which dimensions of social ties (e.g., salience, strong vs. weak, etc.) have the most causal potency and (b) how competing ties affect the decision of whether or not to participate in the project.

Review of the Literature
Among the topics that have most concerned researchers in the field of social movements is that of "differential recruitment" (Jenkins 1983, p. 528; Zurcher and Snow 1981, p. 449). What accounts for individual variation in movement participation? Why does one individual get involved while another remains inactive? Until recently, researchers have sought to answer these questions on the basis of individual characteristics of movement activists.

Psychological or Attitudinal Accounts of Activism
The basic assumption underlying such accounts is that it is some psychological or attitudinal "fit" with the movement that either compels participation or, at the very least, renders the individual susceptible to recruiting appeals.

For all their apparent theoretical sophistication, empirical support for all of these individually based psychological or attitudinal accounts of participation has proved elusive. Summarizing his exhaustive survey of the literature on the relationship between activism and various psychological factors, Mueller (1980, p. 69) concludes that "psychological attributes of individuals, such as frustration and alienation, have minimal direct impact for explaining the occurrence of rebellion and revolution per se." Much the same conclusion has been reached as regards the link between attitudes and activism. On the basis of his analysis of 215 studies of the relationship between individual attitudes and riot participation, McPhail (1971) concludes that "individual predispositions are, at best, insufficient to account" for participation in collective action.[2]

Does this mean that psychological characteristics or attitudes are irrelevant to the study of individual activism? Certainly not. In our view, both remain important insofar as they demarcate a "latitude of rejection" (Petty and Cacioppo 1981) within which individuals are highly unlikely to get involved in a given movement. However, in the case of most movements the size of the pool of recruits—the "latitude of acceptance"—is still many times larger than the actual number of persons who take part in any given instance of activism. Klandermans and Oegema (1987) provide an interesting illustration of the size of these respective groups in their study of recruitment to a major peace demonstration in the Netherlands. On the basis of before-and-after interviews with a sample of 114 persons, the authors conclude that 26% of those interviewed were unavailable for recruitment because of their basic disagreement with the goals of the demonstration. That left nearly three-quarters of the sample as potentially available for recruitment. Yet only 4% actually attended the rally. It is precisely this disparity between attitudinal affinity and actual participation that, of course, requires explanation. One thing seems clear, however; given the size of this disparity, the role of individual attitudes (or the psychological factors from which they derive) in shaping activism must be regarded as fairly limited. If 96% of all those who are attitudinally or psychologically disposed to activism choose, as they did in this case, not to participate, then clearly some other factor or set of factors is mediating the recruitment process.

Microstructural Accounts of Activism

Since psychological and attitudinal explanations of individual participation have been weak, there has been increased usage of alternative microstructural explanations. The microstructural account posits that it is relatively unimportant if a person is ideologically or psychologically predisposed to participation when they lack the structural location that facilitates participation. Without structural factors that expose the individual to participation opportunities or pull them into activity, the individual will remain inactive. A number of recent studies appear to demonstrate the strength of structural or network factors in accounting for activism (Fernandez and McAdam 1989; Gould 1990, 1991; Marwell et al. 1988; McAdam 1986; McCarthy 1987; Orum 1972; Paulsen 1990; Rosenthal et al. 1985; Snow et al. 1980). These studies tend to focus on two sources

of the link between the potential recruit and social movement activity: interpersonal ties and membership in organizations.

Interpersonal ties—Knowing someone who is already involved in social movement activity is one of the strongest predictors of recruitment into the membership (Briët et al. 1987; Gerlach and Hine 1970; Heirich 1977; McAdam 1986; Orum 1972; Snow 1976; Snow et al. 1980; Von Eschen, Kirk, and Pinard 1971; Zurcher and Kirkpatrick 1976; Bolton 1972). Strong or dense interpersonal networks encourage the extension of an invitation to participate and they ease the uncertainty of mobilization. Oliver (1984), for example, finds that one of the best predictors of participation in neighborhood organizations is residence in the same area as one's closest friends or relatives. Oliver also states that "social ties may be thought of as indicators of subjective interest in the neighborhood, as factors influencing the availability of solidarity incentives for participation in collective action or as factors reducing the cost of action by making communication easier" (1984, p. 604). These notions elaborate on why social ties are an important measure in the prediction of participation.

Membership in organizations—Organizational membership is another microstructural factor that has been linked to individual activism. There are two possible explanations for the relationship, the first of which has already been mentioned. Membership in organizations is an extension of the interpersonal social tie. Acquaintances made in the formal setting of the organization form elaborate structures of interpersonal ties. In other words, belonging to an organization is a good way to meet people and the likelihood of being pulled into social-movement activity increases through this contact with others. Movement organizers have long appreciated how difficult it is to recruit single isolated individuals and therefore expend most of their energies on mobilizing support within existing organizations.

The alternative explanation draws on the relationship between organizational membership and feelings of personal efficacy. It appears that individuals who hold membership in several organizations have a stronger sense of efficacy than those who have few or no memberships (Finkel 1985; Neal and Seeman 1964; Sayre 1980). A strong sense of efficacy is also a good predictor of participation in collective action (Craig 1979; Paulsen 1990, 1991; Sutherland 1981; Travers 1982).

Whether the positive relationship between membership in organizations and activism is explained using networks of interpersonal ties or the development of a sense of efficacy, its existence is well established. Empirical evidence supporting the relationship is clear in a wide variety of social-movement contexts including the civil rights movement (McAdam 1986), student sit-ins (Orum 1972), and the antinuclear movement (Walsh and Warland 1983).

Toward an Elaborated Microstructural Model of Recruitment

In our view, the recent emphasis on structural or network factors in movement recruitment represents a welcome corrective to the earlier individualistic accounts of activism. And certainly the empirical evidence linking individual or organizational ties to movement participation appears to be stronger than the simple association between either psychological attributes or attitudes and individual activism.

Not discounting this progress, serious conceptual and methodological lacunae continue to plague the structural network approaches to the study of movement recruitment. Three such problems were noted above. First, we still lack a general sociological explanation of the empirical effects reported in these studies. In short, we have demonstrated a strong association between social ties and activism, but have largely failed to account for the relationship theoretically. Second, perhaps owing to the absence of any real social structural theory of recruitment, with a few notable exceptions (Fernandez and McAdam 1988; Gould 1991, 1993; Marwell et al. 1988) researchers have failed to distinguish empirically between various dimensions of social ties. So it remains unclear which aspect(s) of a social tie (e.g., strength, salience, centrality) accounts for its effectiveness as a recruitment agent. Finally, as both Roger Gould (1991, 1993) and Andrew Marchant-Shapiro (1990) have perceptively noted, our efforts

to assess the link between social ties and activism have thus far been seriously hampered by a highly truncated view of this relationship. As Gould (1990, p. 14) notes, these studies rest on "the presupposition that existing social relations exert an unconditionally positive influence on a group's capacity to mobilize for collective action." In point of fact, social ties may constrain as well as encourage activism. Our failure to acknowledge the variable impact of social ties is due, in turn, to our failure to take account of the "multiple embeddings" that characterize people's lives. The effect of these two limiting presumptions has been to structure empirical analysis in ways that virtually assure positive effects. First, we have tended only to study activists, thereby inflating the positive influence of existing social ties. And second, instead of examining a range of social ties, we have restricted our attention to a single class of ties: those linking the subject to others in the movement. This leaves unexamined (*a*) all those nonactivists who also had ties to the movement and (*b*) the effect of other social ties—parents, peers, and so forth—on the recruitment process. To truly test the utility of a structural/network account of activism we must take account of both phenomena. To do so, however, first requires a fuller conceptualization of the role of social ties in the recruitment process. In sketching such a conceptualization, we will begin by stressing the importance of two concepts: *multiple ties* and Sheldon Stryker's notion of *identity salience* (1968).

All of us, except perhaps for the occasional hermit, are embedded in many relationships. Some of these are mediated by formal organizational processes; the rest by informal interpersonal dynamics involving one or more persons. The presence of these multiple ties points up the fundamental flaw in most existing studies of movement recruitment, which focus solely on the presence or absence of a prior tie between the subject and someone in the movement. The question is, Why should this tie be granted causal primacy? Why should it be examined in the absence of all others? The fact that we are embedded in many relationships means that any major decision we are contemplating will likely be mediated by a significant subset of those relationships. This, of course, would apply to participation in any significant forms of activism, especially those of the "high-risk" variety (McAdam 1986; Wiltfang and McAdam 1991). The fact that the recruitment decision is likely to be influenced by a number of people, in turn, raises the critical question of how the individual goes about aggregating the advice she or he receives. It is unlikely that all the advice will be consistent. It is more likely that the contemplated action will invite a range of responses from those party to the decision-making process. We thus need a model of how these responses are aggregated to yield a final decision.

Here is where Stryker's (1968) notion of *identity salience* may prove useful.[3] For Stryker (1981, pp. 23–24), "identities are conceptualized as being organized into a hierarchy of salience defined by the probability of the various identities being invoked in a given situation or over many situations." In turn, the salience of any particular identity is a function of the individual's "commitment" to it, defined "as the degree to which the individual's relationships to specified sets of other persons depends on his or her being a particular kind of person" (1981, p. 24). So, for Stryker, it is the centrality and importance of our relationships with others that serve to establish and sustain the salience of various identities.

When applied to the recruitment process, the perspective above suggests that the decision to join or not join a movement will be mediated by the salience of the identity invoked by the movement and by the support or lack thereof that the prospective recruit receives from those persons who normally serve to sustain or reinforce the identity in question. This suggests a three-step recruitment process by which a prospective recruit brings the intended behavior—in this case, movement participation—into alignment with their existing hierarchy of identities. First, the individual must be the object of a recruiting appeal (whether direct or, in the case of the media, indirect) that succeeds in creating a positive association between the movement and a highly salient identity. This linkage creates the initial disposition to participate in the movement. Second, the recruit discusses this disposition with those persons who normally sustain the identity in question. In effect, the recruit is seeking to confirm the linkage between movement and

identity and thus the ultimate "correctness" of the intention to participate. Should the recruit receive this confirmation, she or he would still need to reconcile the intended action with the demands of any countervailing identities that may be even more salient. This would again open the individual up to influence attempts by those persons on whose support these more salient identities rest. The ultimate decision to participate, then, would depend on the confluence of four limiting conditions: (1) the occurrence of a specific recruiting attempt, (2) the conceptualization of a tentative linkage between movement participation and identity, (3) support for that linkage from persons who normally serve to sustain the identity in question, and (4) the absence of strong opposition from others on whom other salient identities depend. The prohibitive nature of these conditions may help explain why so few of those whose attitudes place them in the "latitude of acceptance" (Petty and Cacioppo 1981) actually engage in activism.

This perspective would also help to account for the oft-noted role of established organizations (Curtis and Zurcher 1973; McAdam 1982; Morris 1984; Oberschall 1973; Rosenthal et al. 1985) in the recruitment process. Provided that the identity invoked by the organization (e.g., "Christian," "feminist," etc.) is highly salient to its members, it would be hard to imagine a more efficient way to recruit movement adherents.[4] In effect, when organizations serve as recruiting agents, the three-step process outlined above is reduced to a two-step process. The initial recruiting appeal is immediately merged with efforts to confirm the "correctness" of the link between member status and movement participation. Moreover, the organization may well retain a virtual monopoly on those significant others who have long sustained the identity in question. To the extent that these referent others have affiliated with the movement, it will be difficult for the individual in question not to do so as well.

But the ultimate utility of this perspective will not derive from the plausible interpretation it affords past findings, but rather from how well it accords with data designed to test its merits. This is what we hope to do in the remainder of the article.

The Study

In seeking to assess the role of social ties in movement recruitment, we will focus on a single instance of high-risk activism: participation in the 1964 Mississippi Freedom Summer Project. That campaign brought hundreds of primarily white, northern college students to Mississippi for all, or part of, the summer of 1964 to help staff "Freedom Schools," register black voters, and dramatize the continued denial of civil rights throughout the South. As instances of activism go, the summer project was time-consuming, physically demanding, and highly newsworthy.

The project itself began in early June with the first contingent of volunteers arriving in Mississippi fresh from a week of training at Oxford, Ohio. Within ten days, three project members, Mickey Schwerner, James Chaney, and Andrew Goodman, had been kidnapped and killed by a group of segregationists led by Mississippi law-enforcement officers. That event set the tone for the summer as the remaining volunteers endured beatings, bombings, and arrests. Moreover, most did so while sharing the grinding poverty and unrelieved tension that was the daily lot of the black families that housed them.

Preliminary to their participation in the campaign, all prospective volunteers filled out detailed applications providing information on, among other topics, their organizational affiliations, previous civil rights activities, and reasons for volunteering. On the basis of these applications (and, on occasion, subsequent interviews), the prospective volunteer was either accepted or rejected. Acceptance did not necessarily mean participation in the campaign, however. In advance of the summer, many of the accepted applicants informed campaign staffers that they would not be taking part in the summer effort after all. Completed applications for all three groups—rejects, participants, and "no-shows"—were copied from the originals which are now housed in the archives of the Martin Luther King, Jr., Center for the Study of Non-violence in Atlanta, and the New Mississippi Foundation in Jackson, Mississippi.[5] A total of 1,068 applications were coded in connection with this study. The breakdown of these applications by group is as

follows: 720 participants, 239 no-shows, 55 rejections, and 54 whose status as regards the summer project is unclear.

Besides the five pages of information included on these forms, the applications also served as the methodological starting point for a follow-up survey of those who applied to the project. Specifically, several items of information from the original applications—alma mater, parents' address, major in school—functioned as crucial leads in efforts to obtain current addresses for as many of the applicants as possible.

The result of these efforts were verified current addresses for 556 of the 959 participants and withdrawals for whom there were applications. Of these, 382 (of a total of 720) had been participants in the project, while another 174 (of 239) had withdrawn in advance of the summer. Separate questionnaires were then prepared and sent to the participants and to the no-shows. Participants were questioned about the influences that led them to apply, their activities immediately preceding the summer, as well as their personal and political experiences during and since the project. The questionnaire sent to the no-shows dealt with these topics as well as the reasons why they withdrew from the project. In all, 212 (or 56%) of the participants and 118 (or 68%) of the no-shows returned completed questionnaires. In addition, in-depth interviews were conducted with 40 volunteers and another 40 no-shows to flesh out the information gleaned from the questionnaires. Together, the applications, questionnaires, and interviews provide a rich source of data for an analysis of the ways in which social ties mediated the decision of whether or not to take part in the project.

Results

In seeking to learn more about the relationship between social ties and movement recruitment, we will address two principal topics. First, we will take up the issue of multiple ties by examining for each applicant the breadth of support they received for participation across five categories of possible ties (parents, friends, civil rights organizations, other volunteers, and religious groups or figures). Second, we will seek to determine which dimensions of social ties appear to account for their important role in recruitment. Specifically, we will look at three such dimensions: (1) the strength of the tie (weak vs. strong), (2) the locus of the tie (face-to-face or geographically removed), and (3) the salience of the tie.

Multiple Ties

As Gould (1991) and Marchant-Shapiro (1990) have argued, prior network studies of recruitment have failed to take account of the multiple ties that comprise a person's social world. Instead, researchers have focused on the presence or absence of a particular type of tie—prior contact between the recruit and another activist—as the crucial relationship mediating entrance into the movement.[6] An earlier analysis of recruitment to the Freedom Summer project shares this deficiency (see McAdam 1986). To illustrate the point as well as to provide a statistical baseline for what is to follow, we have rerun, using updated data, the final logit regression from the earlier paper.[7] Table 1 reports the results of this analysis.

The dependent variable in the analysis is participation/nonparticipation in the summer project. The independent variables include a variety of measures, among which are the applicant's gender, race, age, college major, highest grade completed, and home and college regions. But the single best predictor of participation is the existence of a prior strong tie linking the applicant to another volunteer. However, this is the lone network or social-tie item included in the analysis. No effort has been made to assess the impact of other kinds of ties on the recruitment process. The result is precisely the kind of truncated analysis of the relationship between social ties and activism about which critics such as Gould and Marchant-Shapiro have rightly complained.

To remedy this deficiency we have sought in the present analysis to assess the effect of various types of ties on the decision to take part in the Freedom Summer project. Specifically, we have differentiated the applicants on the basis of whether or not they report having received support for participation from each of five categories of others: parents, friends, religious groups or figures, civil rights organizations, or another volunteer. The data on the first three support categories were taken from

a single item on the follow-up survey distributed to the applicants. The item asked respondents to rank order, from a fixed list, all those groups or individuals who "*positively* influenced your decision to apply to the Freedom Summer Project." The first three support categories listed above were included in the responses provided to subjects.[8] The subject's responses to these three support categories were coded separately to yield three dichotomous variables. For example, subject's responses to the category "parents" were coded "0" and "1" to create the variable "parental support." Listing parents as a positive influence resulted in a code of "1"; failure to list was coded as "0." The same coding procedures were used in regard to the other two categories of ties as well.

The fourth support category, civil rights organizations, was generated using the list of organizational affiliations provided on the original applications. Those subjects reporting membership in a civil rights organizations were coded as "1" on this variable; those lacking such an affiliation were coded as "0." The final support category, "other volunteers," makes use of the variable, "strong tie to another volunteer," included in the earlier logit regression (see table 1). This variable was created using information provided on the original project applications. One item on the application asked the subjects to list at least 10 persons whom they wished to be kept informed of their summer activities. The most common categories of names supplied by the applicants were those of parents, parents' friends, professors, ministers, and any other noteworthy or influential adults they had contact with. Quite often, however, applicants would list another applicant. This enabled us to construct a measure of the interpersonal ties connecting the applicant to (*a*) other Freedom Summer volunteers and (*b*) no-shows. In doing so, we were careful to distinguish between "strong" and "weak" ties (Granovetter 1973). Persons listed directly on the subject's application were designated as strong ties. Weak ties were defined as persons who, although not listed on the subject's application, were nonetheless linked to them by way of an intervening strong tie.

The applicant's responses to this application then were coded to produce a fifth dichotomous variable,

Table 1 Logit Regression Predicting Freedom Summer Participation by Various Independent Variables

Independent Variables	Dependent Variable (b)	Summer Status SE(b)[a]
Level of prior activism	.020	.039
N of organizational affiliations	.118*	.059
Strong tie to a volunteer	.491**	.191
Weak tie to a volunteer	.141	.098
Strong tie to a no-show	−.169	.325
Major:		
Social science	.167	.324
Other	−.137	.182
Home region:		
West north central	−.204	.324
New England	−.372	.387
Mid-Atlantic	.294	.583
East north central	−.517	.486
West	.694	.468
South	−.411	.484
College region:		
West north central	−.144	.297
New England	−.447	.327
Mid-Atlantic	−.251	.555
East north central	.439	.486
West	−.444	.358
South	.748*	.333
Race = white	−.135	.218
Gender = female	−.446**	.178
Age	.022+	.013
Highest grade completed	−.014	.022
Distance from home to Mississippi	−.0003	.0002
Constant	1.039	.636

Note.—N = 766.

[a] No-shows = 0; volunteers = 1.

+ P < .10.

* P < .05.

** P < .01.

termed "volunteer support." Only those applicants who reported a strong tie to a volunteer were coded as "1" on this variable. All other responses, including weak ties, were coded as "0."

Table 2 reports the percentage of volunteers and no-shows who received support from each of these five support categories. The percentage difference between volunteers and no-shows was significant in regard to the following forms of support: that from parents, civil rights organizations, and other volunteers. Moreover the differences are in the expected direction. The differences are especially great in regard to the first and last of these categories. The percentage of volunteers reporting support from parents was nearly double the figure for the no-shows. And the proportion of volunteers reporting support—in the form of strong ties—from other volunteers was 75% greater than the comparable figure for no-shows. But these simple bivariate comparisons tell us little about the impact of these various forms of support, either in relation to each other or to the other significant variables shown in table 1. For that we turn to table 3, which reports the results of a second logit regression predicting participation.

Included in the analysis shown in table 3 is a pared-down version of the model reported in table 1 (including all the significant relationships from the earlier analysis), plus the five support variables. The results generally mirror the findings reported for table 1, while simultaneously confirming the suggestion contained in table 2.[9] That is, in the aggregate, those who made it to Mississippi *did* have the benefit of greater support from parents and project peers. Or, if one prefers the negative interpretation, the no-shows were handicapped by relatively low levels of support from these two important groups. Whichever interpretation one prefers—and both are probably operative—the results support a complex, differentiated view of the role of social ties in movement recruitment. Ties to persons not in the movement—in this case, to parents—may also influence recruitment decisions. And, those ties may, as in the case of the no-shows and their parents, constrain as well as encourage participation.

Table 2 Percentage of Volunteers and No-Shows Reporting Support from Various Sources

	Volunteers		No-Shows	
	%	N	%	N
Parents	26**	55	14	17
Friends	46	98	52	61
Religious groups or figures	14	30	19	22
Civil rights groups	43+	313	37	89
Other volunteers	41**	210	24	36

+ $P < .10$.
* $P < .05$.
** $P < .01$.

Prior Contact with Another Volunteer: Interpreting the Relationship

While our efforts to broaden the study of the relationship between social ties and activism have produced results suggesting the importance of various types of ties (e.g., to parents), they have done nothing to undermine the special significance previously ascribed to contact with another activist, in this case, another Freedom Summer volunteer. On the contrary, regardless of what other ties or additional variables are introduced into the analysis, a strong tie to another volunteer remains, to this point, the best predictor of participation in the summer project. The robustness of this finding suggests a conclusion that is both interesting and perhaps broadly relevant in seeking to make a behavioral decision in the face of conflicting advice from multiple others: *behavioral,* as opposed to rhetorical or attitudinal, support is likely to prove decisive. That is, in supporting with their own actions the applicant's original behavioral intention, other volunteers provided a more dramatic and, perhaps, more meaningful form of support than the other ties whose influence we have sought to measure.

But apart from this generalization, we do not really know what it is about these ties to other volunteers that accounts for their predictive significance. What dimensions of these ties are especially facilitative of activism? In the remainder of

Table 3 Logit Regression Predicting Freedom Summer Participation by Various Independent Variables, Including Tie Categories

Independent Variables	Dependent Variable (b)	Summer Status SE(b)[a]
Level of prior activism	.085*	.041
N of organizational affiliations	.217+	.129
Weak tie to a volunteer	−.524	.403
Strong tie to a no-show	−.504	.546
Race = white	−.026	.522
Gender = female	−.555+	.338
Age	.192*	.069
Highest grade completed	.016	.056
Distance from home to Mississippi	.0004	.0003
Support categories:		
Parent	1.223*	.497
Friends	−.491	.368
Religious groups	−.548	.526
Civil rights groups	.149	.433
Other volunteers	1.360**	.455
Constant	−4.810**	1.850

Note.—$N = 206$.
[a] No-shows = 0; volunteers = 1.
+ $P < .10$.
* $P < .05$.
** $P < .01$.

this article, we will explore this question in some detail. Specifically, we will take up two dimensions of these ties: "strength" and salience.

1. *Strength of ties.*—Much has been made in the movement literature of the "strength of weak ties" (Granovetter 1973) as a force for the diffusion of collective action. Numerous studies have shown that movements often spread by means of diffuse networks of weak bridging ties (Freeman 1973; McAdam 1982; Oppenheimer 1989) or die for lack of such ties (Jackson et al. 1960). These findings suggest that, at the meso level, the critical function performed by social ties for a movement is one of communication. However, the findings reported

earlier in tables 1 and 3 suggest a very different role for social ties at the individual level. The significant positive relationship between strong ties and participation and the absence of any relationship between weak ties and involvement suggests that, at the microlevel, ties are less important as conduits of information than as sources of social influence. And the stronger the tie, the stronger the influence exerted on the potential recruit. This implies that the ultimate network structure for a movement would be one in which dense networks of weak bridging ties linked numerous local groups bound together by means of strong interpersonal bonds. But for our purposes, the mesolevel structure of a movement is irrelevant. Our concern is solely with the microlevel function of social ties. And in this regard, our results support a strong conclusion: as dimensions go, the strength of a social tie appears to account for much of its power as a predictor of activism. But before we pronounce certainty on this issue, let us turn our attention to one other dimension of social ties.

2. *Salience of ties.*—Given the theoretical importance ascribed to the salience of a tie at the outset of the paper, it is especially important that we try to assess the significance of this dimension in shaping the applicant's decision regarding the summer project. To do so we will make use of several items from the original project applications. The principal item is an open-ended question asking the individual to explain why they "would like to work in Mississippi this summer." These answers were content-coded along a number of dimensions. But the important dimension for our purposes concerns the extent to which, in their statements, the applicants explicitly aligned themselves with a specific community or reference group. Some examples of these types of "aligning" statements follow:[10]

> If I'm to continue *calling myself a Christian,* I must act NOW to put my abstract conception of brotherhood into practice.
> *All of us in the movement* must join forces if the Summer Project is to succeed.
> *In my group of future teachers* I make it a point to ask each of them, "Why do you want to go into education?"

When combined with the organizational affiliations listed on the application, these statements allowed us to create the variable, "recruitment context," to capture the principal communities/identities that served to draw people into the project. Five such communities emerged from our reading of the open-ended question. These were teachers, religious community, socialists/leftists, liberal Democrats, and the civil rights movement. Along with the category, "no discernible group," these five communities or reference groups comprised the coding scheme for the variable, "recruitment context." But to be coded as belonging to any of these communities, it was not enough that the applicants express

identification with the group in their statements. They also had to include among the organizational affiliations listed on their applications at least one organization tied to the community in question. So, for example, to be coded as belonging to the "liberal Democratic community," the applicants would have had to assert this identity in their statements *and* report membership in either their campus chapter of Young Democrats or in a similar group. The variable, then, has both a subjective identification and objective organizational dimension.

The significant, but hardly surprising, finding from our perspective concerns the much higher rates of participation among those embedded in all five of the aforementioned recruitment contexts. Table 4 reports the percentages of no-shows and volunteers in each of the five contexts with the comparable figures for those not identified with any discernible context.

Only 65% of those lacking an identifiable recruitment "community" made it to Mississippi, as compared to from 83% to 87% of those so embedded.[11] The apparent causal influence of these recruitment contexts would appear to be due to two factors. First, the subject's expressed identification with these communities suggests a high degree of salience for the identities embodied in each. And second, their membership in organizations associated with these communities no doubt afforded these subjects strong support for their expressed identity as well as for the link between that identity and participation in the Freedom Summer project. This is exactly the combination of a highly salient identity and strong social support for activism based on that identity that we stressed at the outset as crucial to the process of movement recruitment. But one might complain that organizational membership alone could well predict activism and that combining it with subjective identification makes it impossible to tease out the effects of each. We will turn to this issue in our final analysis.

Assessing the combined effects of these dimensions.—So far we have sought to assess the independent effects of various factors or dimensions on the relationship between social ties and activism. But what of the combined effects? When taken together, which of these factors or dimensions

Table 4 Recruitment Context by Status on the Summer Project*

		Recruitment Contexts												
	Church/Religious		Civil Rights		Liberal Democrats		Socialist/Leftist		Teachers		No Context		Total	
	%	N	%	N	%	N	%	N	%	N	%	N	%	N
Volunteers	83	94	87	82	85	51	83	93	87	87	65	320	75	727
No-shows	17	19	13	12	15	9	17	19	13	13	35	169	25	241
Total	100	113	100	94	100	60	100	112	100	100	100	489	100	968

* Only two applicants were coded as affiliated with more than one recruitment context. Rather than lose data by excluding these subjects, we coded them as being affiliated with whatever context they first aligned themselves in their response to the open-ended item.

appear to account for the role of social ties in constraining or facilitating activism? To answer this question, we report the results of four logistic models incorporating all but one of the significant variables touched on previously.[12]

The results reported in table 5 serve to underscore the importance of the combination of a highly salient identity and structural support for same in encouraging activism. Three specific results from the table bear comment. First, membership in any of the five recruitment contexts is shown in the full model (model 4) to bear a strong, positive relationship to participation in Freedom Summer.[13] Second, none of the simple organizational variables—including number of organizational affiliations, as well as the specific categories of organizational membership—are predictive of participation when included in the same model as the recruitment contexts. Finally, even the heretofore significant effect of a strong tie to another volunteer washes out in the face of the predictive power of the context variables.

The conclusion is unmistakable: neither organizational embeddedness nor strong ties to another volunteer are themselves predictive of high-risk activism. Instead it is a strong subjective identification with a particular identity, *reinforced by organizational or individual ties*, that is especially likely to encourage participation. Does this mean that organizational or individual ties are irrelevant to the recruitment process? Hardly; it does, however, suggest that if the identity sustained by the tie is neither linked to participation nor particularly salient to the person in question, it is not likely to encourage activism. What about the opposite question? Is strong identification with a particular identity enough to promote involvement in the absence of structural support for same? It is significant that we cannot directly answer this question with our data. None of our subjects expressed strong identification with any of these five identities without also being structurally embedded in the relevant organizational community supportive of that identity. That is, identity salience would itself seem to be a social product.

We are left, then, with the kind of necessary but not sufficient relationship sociologists are so fond

of. Prior ties—either through organizations or particular others—would seem to be necessary, but not sufficient, for recruitment to high-risk activism. In the absence of (*a*) a strong identification with the identity sustained by the tie and (*b*) a link between that identity and the movement in question, prior ties are no more productive of participation than the absence of ties. Such prior ties provide the crucial social context in which identities *may* achieve salience and the linkage between identity and activism *can* be forged, but the existence of such ties does not ensure that these crucial processes will, in fact, take place.

Before concluding with a discussion of the significance of these findings, a few words are in order regarding the strength of the relationship linking integration into the "teaching context" with participation. Of the five contexts it would appear to be the one with the least relevance for an explicitly political project such as Freedom Summer. In point of fact, however, the relationship is entirely consistent with the contemporary "framing" (Snow and Benford 1988) of the project and, as such, represents a nice nonintuitive example of the broader social psychological dynamic sketched earlier.

As noted earlier, one of the two principal components of the project was the campaign to establish a network of "freedom schools" throughout the state. These schools were to expose students to a broader range of subjects and more information on African-American history than they typically got in the historically impoverished "separate but equal" institutions they normally attended. The prominence accorded the freedom school effort in planning for the summer (see Holt 1965; McAdam 1988), made the recruitment of qualified teachers a major goal of project organizers. Toward this end they sought and received official endorsement for the project from the major national teacher's associations, including the American Federation of Teachers and the National Educational Association.

These endorsements, coupled with the specific steps taken by organizers to recruit upper-division education majors on campus, represent exactly the kinds of efforts to link a particular identity with participation that we expect to be especially effective in encouraging participation. Though historically

Table 5 The Effects of Various Independent Variables on Participation in Freedom Summer Project

Independent Variables	Model 1 (b)	SE(b)	Model 2 (b)	SE(b)	Model 3 (b)	SE(b)	Model 4 (b)	SE(b)
Level of prior activism	.037*	.015	.024	.171	.030+	.018	.001	.020
Race = white	-.144	.189	-.097	.192	-.051	.196	-.006	.200
Gender = female	-.291+	.157	-.311*	.158	-.338*	.161	-.311+	.165
Age	.064**	.016	.066**	.017	.061**	.017	.048**	.018
Highest grade completed	-.042*	.019	-.036+	.019	-.037+	.019	-.032+	.019
Distance from home to Mississippi	.00008	.0001	.00009	.0001	.0001	.0001	.00009	.0001
N of organizational affiliations	.110*	.051	.102*	.052	.089	.056	.050	.057
Weak tie to volunteer	.504**	.190	.119	.261	.145	.264	.090	.269
Strong tie to a no-show	-.260	.340	-.290	.353	-.239	.353	-.352	.361
Support categories:								
Civil rights group			-.277	.189				
Other volunteers			.570+	.336	.561+	.339	.524	.349
Proximity of tie:								
Proximal			-.013	.176	-.028	.177	-.017	.181
Distal			.238	.189	.237	.190	.241	.194

Membership:								
Religious organization					−.429+	.242	−.271	.296
Civil rights organization					−.241	.197	−.354+	.202
Democratic Party organization					.198	.253	.362	.282
Socialist or New Left organization					.074	.228	.143	.277
Teachers organization					−.434	.372	−.270	.431
Recruitment context:								
Religious							.723*	.341
Civil rights							1.057**	.390
Liberal Democrat							1.210**	.414
New left							.798*	.344
Teaching							.867*	.382
Constant	−.177	.481	.104	.603	1.258	1.129	.426	1.000

Note.—N = 766.
+ P < .10.
* P < .05.
** P < .01.

not as disposed to political action as those integrated into the other four recruitment contexts, prospective teachers were, in this case, the object of specific recruiting appeals that sought to link their future occupational identity to involvement in the Freedom Summer project.

Discussion and Conclusion

All of this calls to mind the model of movement recruitment outlined at the outset of this article. We suggested that the ultimate decision to participate in a movement would depend on four *limiting conditions:* (1) the occurrence of a specific recruiting attempt, (2) the successful linkage of movement and identity, (3) support for that linkage from persons who normally serve to sustain the identity in question, and (4) the absence of strong opposition from others on whom other salient identities depend.

The results reported in table 5 can certainly be interpreted as consistent with the above account of recruitment. All of our subjects—no-shows and volunteers alike—shared the first two limiting conditions noted above. Clearly they were aware of the project (condition 1) and, given their willingness to apply, appear to have viewed the project as consistent with some salient identity (condition 2). In our view, what differentiates the volunteers from the no-shows is the extent of support they received for this linkage (condition 3) and the relative absence of opposition from salient others (condition 4). Not only were the volunteers embedded in more organizations, but also in ones—civil rights organizations, teacher associations, and so forth—ideally suited to reinforcing the linkage between identity and action. Moreover, as the greater support from parents suggests, the volunteers also appear to have received less opposition (or more support) from other salient relationships in which they were involved.

All of this may help to explain the surprising lack of statistical significance of the relationship linking a strong tie to another volunteer with participation. While this relationship had been significant in all previous analyses, it appears that it was merely a proxy for the recruitment contexts included in table 5. That is, the volunteers' ties to other volunteers were themselves a function of the participants'

greater integration into specific recruitment contexts that served as the microstructural basis for their decisions to take part in the project.

If this is the case, then, the analyses presented here do more than simply support the general model of recruitment outlined earlier. Our findings also argue for a much stronger effect of organizational (or otherwise collective) as opposed to individual ties in mediating entrance into collective action. Clearly much work remains to confirm this conclusion, but it is an intriguing one and one that accords with "bloc recruitment" accounts of the emergence and rapid spread of collective action (Ober-schall 1973). Ties to individuals may well mediate the recruitment process, but they appear to do so with special force and significance when the tie is embedded in a broader organizational or collective context linking both parties to the movement in question.

We would be remiss, however, if we closed the article on the structural note above. Clearly, the most important implication of this research is as much sociopsychological as structural. Network analysts of movement recruitment have been overly concerned with assessing the structure of the subject's relationship to the movement without paying sufficient attention to the social psychological processes that mediate the link between network structure and activism. As Gould has recently argued, "It is risky to make generalizations about the impact of network structure in the absence of detailed information about collective action settings" and the "influence process" by which people come to participate in a social movement (1993, p. 195).

More specifically, prior ties would appear to encourage activism only when they (*a*) reinforce the potential recruit's identification with a particular identity and (*b*) help to establish a strong linkage between that identity and the movement in question. When these processes of identity amplification and identity/movement linkage take place, activism is likely to follow. In the absence of these processes, prior ties do not appear to be predictive of participation. Movement analysts, then, need to be as attuned to the *content* of network processes as to the *structures* themselves.

NOTES

This article was completed while the first author was a fellow at the Center for Advanced Study in the Behavioral Sciences. Partial support for the year at the center was provided by National Science Foundation grant BNS-8700864. The research on which this article is based has been supported by several awards given to the first author. These include a Guggenheim Fellowship, National Science Foundation grant SES-8309988, and various forms of support from the Social and Behavioral Sciences Research Institute at the University of Arizona. In addition, we would like to thank Carol Diem and Phil Wiseley for their research assistance on the paper, and Bert Klandermans and Karl-Dieter Opp for their helpful comments on an earlier draft of the article.

1. The paper by Marwell et al. (1988) is perhaps the only empirical work to date that takes seriously the need to distinguish and test the causal significance of various dimensions of social ties.

2. In general, the discrepancy between attitudes and behavior has been borne out by countless studies conducted over the years. In summarizing the results of these studies, Wicker (1969) offered what remains the definitive word on the subject. Said Wicker, there exists, "little evidence to support the postulated existence of stable, underlying attitudes within the individual which influence both his verbal expressions and his actions" (p. 75).

3. Stryker is hardly alone in stressing the idea that the self is made up of a hierarchy of identities. McCall and Simmons's (1978) notion of "role salience" and Rosenberg's (1979) concept of "psychological centrality" also rest on this fundamental premise.

4. For a slightly different but highly compatible argument, see Taylor and Whittier (1992).

5. Our deep appreciation goes to Louise Cook, the former head librarian and archivist at the King Center, and to Jan Hillegas—herself a Freedom Summer volunteer—of the New Mississippi Foundation, for all their help in locating and copying the application materials used in this project.

6. The work of David Snow and several of his colleagues provide an important exception to this general assessment. In their pioneering theoretical work on the role of social ties and social networks in recruitment, Snow et al. (1980) acknowledge the importance of "multiple embeddings" in structuring a person's "differential availability" for movement participation. Later, Snow and Rochford (1983), in their study of recruitment into the Hare Krishna movement, sought to analyze the effect of various social ties on the recruit. They conclude that "a substantial majority of…recruits had few countervailing ties which might have served to constrain their participation in the movement." In his later book on the movement, Rochford (1985) provided additional data consistent with this conclusion.

7. Since the publication of this analysis in 1986, the first author has acquired additional data that has allowed for a recoding of the network items (strong tie to a volunteer, weak tie to a volunteer, and strong tie to a no-show). Table 1 is included, then, not only to provide a baseline model for the results to follow in this paper but to update the key analysis from the earlier paper.

8. The other responses included in the list given respondents were "spokespersons for movement groups," "movement literature," and "other."

9. The reader should note that the N for the analysis reported in table 3 is only 206, as compared to 630 for table 1. The reason for the reduced N has to do with a shift in the sources of data used in computing tables 1 and 3. All the variables in table 1 were generated using data taken from the original project applications. Excluding those whose applications were rejected and those whose project status could not be determined, the number of such applications was 959. However, the data from which the support variables shown in table 3 were constructed were taken from the 330 follow-up surveys returned by project applicants. In order to test to see what effect, if any, reducing the N would have on the magnitude of all variables other than the support categories, a separate logit regression was run. It is reassuring to note that a comparison of these two logits (the original with an N of 206 and the one described above with an N of 630) revealed no significant differences in the direction or magnitude of the other coefficients.

10. These quotes were taken from the summer project applications. In each case the emphasis is my addition.

11. When we use an overall chi-square test, these differences are significant at the .01 level.

12. The one exception is the measure of parental support used in table 3. Given that the measure was based on information taken from the follow-up survey, including it here would have reduced the overall N for the analysis from some 600 to 200.

13. "Recruitment context" is a single categorical variable in the logit regression. The coefficient for each context reflects the effect that is in addition to the base category, "no discernible group."

16.

A Qualitative Comparative Analysis of Conversion to Venezuelan Evangelicalism: How Networks Matter

DAVID SMILDE

Why do people join new religious movements? Are they pushed by their problems or pulled by their social contacts? While conventional wisdom usually speaks in terms of the former, sociologists of religion have decisively opted for the latter. Indeed, recruitment through network ties is one of the most established findings in the sociology of religion (Lofland and Stark 1965; Stark and Bainbridge 1980; Stark 1996; Stark and Iannaccone 1997; Snow, Zurcher, and Ekland-Olson 1980; Snow and Phillips 1980; Sherkat and Wilson 1995; Hoge, Johnson, and Luidens 1995; Mears and Ellison 2000; Nepstad and Smith 2001; Becker and Dhingra 2001). But what do networks do? The theory generally used by sociologists of religion is that of social psychological conformity (Marsden and Friedkin 1994; Festinger 1962). In this view, all humans have a fundamental need for social relationships, and they cultivate and conserve those relationships. Thus individuals adopt new cultural meanings and practices, such as those provided by new religious movements, not because of any inherent characteristics of the latter, but rather to the degree that they reduce dissonance in important relationships. "Conversion is not about seeking or embracing an ideology; it is about bringing one's religious behavior into alignment with that of one's friends and family members" (Stark 1996, pp. 16–17). Networks, then, are the real causes of conversion, and any "deprivations" addressed by the new religious beliefs and practices are better seen as emergent, ex post rationalizations, or, at best, general limiting conditions not very useful in causal explanation (see Stark and Finke 2000).

Religious conversion is a subset of recruitment to social movements, and similar formulations have been influential in studies of how persons join movements. Rather than looking at social psychological dispositions or individual motivations, scholars look at ties to movement members that mean an individual is more likely to be contacted and recruited (see Snow et al. [1980] for the seminal statement). But social movement scholars have increasingly taken issue with existing network approaches and are pushing toward reformulation. Critics have argued that it is unclear how or even why networks function. The late Roger Gould wrote that unless we have information to the contrary there is no reason to think a network tie between a social movement participator and a nonparticipator would lead to participation by the latter rather than nonparticipation by the former. "Unless they are strongly asymmetric, friendships, like marriages, are bilateral monopolies" such that any threat to the relationship would be felt equally by ego and alter and therefore be neutral in effect. Gould argued that we need to know more before attributing any causal significance to a network tie (Gould 2003, p. 244). Second, critics accuse network analysts of repeating errors past in portraying an "oversocialized" human being. Empirically driven, network research typically rests on a default conceptualization of human beings acted upon by networks rather than acting on them and through them. "Network analysis all too often denies in practice the crucial notion that social structure, culture, and human agency presuppose one another; it either neglects or inadequately conceptualizes the crucial dimension of subjective meaning and motivation—including the normative commitments of actors—and thereby fails to show exactly how it is that intentional, creative human action serves in part to constitute those

Smilde, David. 2005, "A Qualitative Comparative Analysis of Conversion to Venezuelan Evangelicalism: How Networks Matter." *American Journal of Sociology* 111: 757–796. Reprinted by permission of The University of Chicago Press. Notes have been renumbered and edited.

very social networks that so powerfully constrain actors in turn" (Emirbayer and Goodwin 1994, p. 1413; see also McAdam 2003; Gould 2003; McAdam and Paulsen 1993; Cook and Whitmeyer 1992).

Much of this criticism suggests that different research methods might advance our conceptual understanding. First, samples need to actually vary on the independent and dependent variables. Typically recruits are studied, they are seen to have networks, and these networks are accorded causal status. The possibility that there are others with the same network ties that did not participate or that the existence of conflicting ties could work against mobilization is not generally considered. "No doubt there are also many non-activists with ties to someone in the movement who did not participate, perhaps because salient others outside the movement put pressure on them to remain uninvolved" (McAdam 2003, p. 286). To actually establish the causal importance of network effects, participators and nonparticipators, as well as the existence of multiple networks need to be taken into account. Second, qualitative studies are needed to examine how network ties actually work. We know *that* networks matter, now it is time to understand *how* they matter (Diani 2003, pp. 2–3; see also Diani 2002; Mische 2003; McAdam 2003; Emirbayer and Goodwin 1994; Wellman 1988).

This article addresses these issues through a study of evangelical conversion in Venezuela. Using a sample of converts and nonconverts and a diversity-oriented methodology that combines the thick description of qualitative methods with the data reduction of quantitative methods, I find the social conformity theorization most often used in network analysis to be important but incomplete. Network ties frequently influence despite little or no direct contact between ego and alter and little or no motivation to conform. Similarly, "structural availability" works not only by freeing an actor from conformity-inducing constraints. It also indicates a relative absence of social and cultural support, which motivates individuals for religious innovation. Finally, while network location strongly determines who converts, the individual experience of life problems remains a causal factor, and, in a small but irreducible number of cases,

actors clearly exercise agency over their network locations.

Evangelicalism in Latin America

Evangelical Protestantism is the fastest growing religion in Latin America and arguably its most dynamic form of civil society.[1] Approximately 10% of the region's 400 million people are now evangelical Protestants (Freston 2001). Given the large role attributed to Protestantism in the historical rise of capitalism and democracy in the West (Weber 1958; Halévy 1924; Eisenstadt 1968) this growth has attracted considerable attention from social scientists (Martin 1990; Bastian 1994; Freston 2001). Venezuela was long an exception to this growth. But this has changed in the past 15 years with the dramatic decline of its petroleum-fed economy and state institutions as well as the diversification of its civil society (Smilde 2004). Approximately 5% of Venezuela's population is evangelical. However, this small percentage surprises many Venezuelans, as their social presence, in the form of street preaching and door-to-door evangelization, is much greater than their actual numbers would suggest.

The empirical material in this article comes from three years of participant observation with two evangelical churches whose membership draws primarily from the poor barrios that surround the Venezuelan capital of Caracas. Evangelicalism has developed in Venezuela primarily since World War II through a process of indigenization whereby members of churches founded by Baptist, Methodist, and Presbyterian missionaries branched off to create churches tending more toward Pentecostal theology and forms of worship (see Steigenga 2001; and Smith 1998). Evangelical churches generally have some sort of service every day of the week, and membership is considered an all-encompassing identity that should sharply distinguish the adherent from "the world." The defining characteristics of evangelical theology are beliefs in spirit possession and divine healing. However, these are not necessarily the most important characteristics of every church. Indeed in the churches I studied, more attention is paid to "perfectionism": the ability of believers to fulfill God's dictates and live a life of sainthood.

In the evangelical meaning system, one is either "in the way of the Lord" (*en el camino del Señor*) or "in the world" (*en el mundo*). Being "in the world" one lives "in the flesh," freely engaging in sin, and preoccupies oneself with "worldly concerns"; that is, material and status interests, rather than spiritual concerns, resulting in alienation from God. Being "in the world" results in a spiritual void where God should be that is promptly filled by Satan. "The Enemy" takes control of the unbeliever's life and uses that person to do evil; this Satan-driven existence leads to conflict, suffering, and pain for others and the sinner. In addition, those outside God's path may be directly harmed by Satan or subjected to God's wrath if He decides to "claim His proper place." Being "in the way of the Lord," on the other hand, the believer lives "in the spirit," avoiding "sins" such as marital infidelity, smoking, gambling, conflict, cheating, and, most important, alcohol. The believer must congregate with other Christians to praise the Lord and read the Bible, bring the word to those who "don't know the Lord," and engage in activities that continually renew and maintain the connection to God, such as prayer, vigil, and fasting. When the Christian engages in these practices, God protects him or her from the devil, controls his or her life (either directly or by communicating his will to the individual), and blesses him or her, resulting in well-being, peace, and happiness (Smilde 1998).

As a sociological phenomena, the growth of Latin American evangelicalism is ripe for network analysis since existing explanations generally use "deprivation-congruence" explanations in which individuals convert because they seek to overcome problems. Conversion is seen as a "cultural strategy" with which poor Latin Americans address the "pathogens of poverty" (Mariz 1994; Chestnut 1997; Burdick 1993; Martin 1990). Nevertheless, the problems that Latin American evangelicalism purportedly addresses—addictive behavior, violence, gender conflict, and unemployment—are much more widespread among Latin America's poor than among its evangelical membership, and as causal variables do not, therefore, successfully distinguish between those who convert and those who do not (see Stark and Bainbridge 1980).

Life History Interviews

I began my research by interviewing 55 men from the two churches I studied.[2] My interviews aimed to understand the conditions that precipitated conversion in each individual case.[3] The central methodological challenge in working with life histories, of course, is to find a way to get at "the facts" in order to construct a causal account. Life history is not only a data collection method for social scientists, it is a medium through which social actors construct the self, and their narratives are necessarily partial and embellished. This leads many researchers to argue that you simply cannot use life histories to obtain objective facts, and can only treat them as cultural objects (see, e.g., Irvine 1999; Blee 2002). And the problem can only be worse in the case of religious conversion, since this experience often accentuates narrative reconstruction of biographies (Csordas 1994; Smilde 2003). In the case of Pentecostalism, for example, the "once was lost, but now am found" narrative structure could well lead to an exaggeration or even fabrication of problems in the respondent's past, leading to an overestimation of their causal importance.

Nevertheless, while they are reinterpreted, reconstructed, and overlaid with meaning, biographical facts such as addiction, divorce, and household composition do exist, and causal accounts can be constructed if they are painstakingly uncovered. Furthermore, in most field settings, there are cultural tendencies that, if comprehended, can facilitate the sociologists' task. Among the respondents studied here, there were two such characteristics. First, while these evangelicals indeed exert much energy reconstructing and reconfiguring their past, they also place a high premium on honesty in the sense that an exposed, outright lie would result in a tremendous loss of esteem. Distortions of the past, therefore, are usually produced through abstract scripted narratives that selectively omit specific facts, or strategically obfuscate sequences of events. My interview strategy focused on making this difficult by getting as concrete as possible. I did not ask them what caused them to convert, to tell me their life history, or what their life was like before their conversion. Rather, I guided respondents through the time period under study using a month-by-month event-history calendar to track 21 variables from three years before their conversion (or seven years before our interview in the case of nonconverts): religious participation, residence, education, employment, wife's employment, nonreligious participatory organization, relationship, personal health, family health, death of friends or family, family evangelical contact, nonfamily evangelical contact, victim of crime, alcohol abuse, drug abuse, gambling, problems with police/law, betrayal by or loss of friends, financial problems, fear for safety, family problems (Freedman et al. 1988). We would start with those aspects of life, such as residence and conjugal relationships, about which memory was most likely to be accurate. Where memory faltered, I used temporal landmarks common to all, such as the riots in February 1989, the two coup attempts in 1992, the World Cup soccer tournaments of 1990 and 1994, or life events such as the birth of a child. The clearing up of temporal ambiguity was the source of many modifications of personal history.[4]

There was a second characteristic of cultural context that facilitated my task. I found that the "once was lost" narrative had a competitor. In what I call the "chosen by God" narrative, a respondent cultivates an image of having converted beyond any self-interest or intention when he was abruptly chosen by God. This is a source of spiritual legitimacy just as powerful as the "once was lost" narrative. As a result, I found no systematic bias. It was just as common for me to find, by getting concrete, that a respondent had failed to mention an important life problem preceding conversion as it was to find that a respondent had exaggerated the role of a life problem.

After collecting the evangelical life histories, I collected a control sample with 29 nonevangelical men from similar socioeconomic circumstances.

Qualitative Comparative Analysis

To analyze this data I used "qualitative comparative analysis" (QCA) as developed by Charles Ragin (1987, 2000). QCA uses Boolean algebra to penetrate bodies of data that are not large enough for multivariate statistical analyses, yet are too large for simple eyeballing. Yet it also facilitates the dialogue between ideas and evidence that is the strength of qualitative data analysis. It works by presenting every possible combination of dichotomous independent variables in a truth table to see how these combinations line up with the dependent variable. Independent variables are tried and discarded, defined and redefined to increase fit. Focusing on contradictory cases, QCA amounts to a multi-iterated process of inference and updating. Its sensitivity to multiple causality well suits it to the task of this article. Rather than trying to find which variable wins the battle of main effects, QCA can portray multiple causal combinations including minority effects.

Not surprisingly, looking at the evangelical life histories in isolation seems to corroborate views of their conversions as caused by the experience of life problems.[5] Fully 85% of the conversions to evangelicalism among my respondents were preceded by addictive behavior, involvement in violence, relationship problems, or problems of personal adjustment. These life problems and how they are addressed by evangelical practice and belief are briefly summarized in table 1.[6] But the fact that these respondents appear to convert in order to address life problems does not mean these problems *explain* conversion. Other men with similar problems may address them in different ways or not address them at all. To figure out what factors can provide a causal account we need to include the sample of nonconverts.

To work with this life-history data in QCA, I segmented it into "spells" as used in event-history analysis (Allison 1984). A spell is a time segment whose duration is determined by unique combinations of the independent variables under review. In other words when any one of the independent variables changes, the old spell ends and the new spell begins. Of course, the duration of spells varies—in this study anywhere from one month to several years—and the total number of spells depends on which and how many independent variables you work with.

As QCA is a multi-iterated process of causal discovery that I can only partially present in an article of this length, I will briefly narrate the first several stages of this analysis and then pick it up in full.[7] Since problem-solving behavior is the most

Table 1 Problems Addressed by Evangelical Practice and Belief

Problem	Description
Addictive behavior	Approximately 40% of evangelical respondents reported experiencing serious difficulties with addictive behavior—either alcohol, drugs, or gambling—when they became evangelical. Problems with addiction are resolved in a very direct way since drinking, taking drugs, and gambling are explicitly anathema to the evangelical lifestyle. Abstinence from them is seen as both a cause and an effect of being evangelical and tantamount to maintaining communion with God. And when one is in communion with God, evangelicals believe, God "takes control" of the person and keeps dangerous influences at bay. Beyond ideas, the substance abuser or gambler participates in a social group in which many people have had similar problems, in which there is a discourse of caring, and in which the meaning system is continually reaffirmed through discourse and ritual.
Violence	Approximately one-third of the evangelical respondents reported having experienced serious problems with violence, either as victim or victimizer, Immediately before their conversion. Evangelicalism provides a socially recognized means of stepping out of the logic of violent conflict, a sense of protection to those who daily have to navigate violence-ridden contexts, as well as a vocabulary through which to implicitly or explicitly engage potential aggressors.
Social problems	A significant number of evangelical respondents had experienced important problems of a social nature immediately before their conversion, either in terms of male-female relationships, family relationships, or peer social life. Evangelicalism provides a vocabulary and discourse that can help resolve interpersonal problems related to questions of authority and trust. It can provide victims of the highly aggressive interpersonal atmosphere of Caracas's popular sectors with an atmosphere of acceptance and support. And for individuals involved in problematic relationships, it can provide them with a vocabulary and sense of legitimacy in their interactions with their partners or family, regardless of whether these latter are themselves evangelical.
Personal development	A significant number of evangelical respondents had experienced economic difficulties, frustrated desires for personal growth, or recurring emotional difficulties immediately before their conversions. People in these situations find in evangelical discourse and the alternative social network it provides, a means to facilitate the personal change and development they seek.

commonly used explanation of conversion to evangelicalism in Latin America, I began by looking into cases in which conversion took place in the absence of problems. In all of these cases the person lived with another evangelical. I then combined these two explanatory variables and followed up the contradictions among those cases in which the respondent was experiencing a problem but did not live with an evangelical. Looking at a number of different variables, I found here that whether or not the person was living with family of origin at the time was the one condition that distinguished, at a statistically significant level, between those who committed and those who

did not. It is with this three-variable model that I will pick up the analysis for more detailed presentation.

Table 2 is a truth table of every combination of the three independent variables, the total number of cases in each combination, the number of conversions among these, the proportion this represents, and a judgment on the output value. Comparing the proportion of conversions that occur in each causal combination to the overall proportion of .431, we get clear, statistically significant tendencies in all but one combination: ~PFE (men who are not experiencing life problems, live with their family of origin, live with an evangelical).

Table 2 Truth Table of Combinations of Life Problems, Living with Family of Origin, and Living with an Evangelical

P	F	E	Total	~C	C	Proportion of C	Output
~P	~F	~E	10	10	0	.000**	~C
~P	~F	E	7	1	6	.857*	C
~P	F	~E	30	30	0	.000**	~C
~P	F	E	6	3	3	.500	?
P	~F	~E	40	10	30	.750**	C
P	~F	E	10	1	9	.900**	C
P	F	~E	30	25	5	.167**	~C
P	F	E	11	2	9	.818**	C
			144	82	62	.431	

Note.—P = life problems; F = living with at least one member of family of origin; E = spatially present evangelical; C = conversion.
* Binomial probability < .05.
** Binomial probability < .01.

If, for the time being, we disregard the ambiguous row (Ragin 1987, pp. 116–17) and reduce the truth table asking which combinations constitute *clear* causes of conversion, we get three causal combinations that can be used to guide qualitative analysis:

> *Combination* 1: ~P~FE and P~FE can be reduced to ~FE.
> *Combination* 2: P~F~E and P~FE can be reduced to P~F.
> *Combination* 3: P~FE and PFE can be reduced to PE.
>
> C = ~FE + P ~ F + PE.

Put substantively, conversion (C) results from spells in which men (1) do not live with family of origin and live with an evangelical (~FE) or (2) are experiencing life problems and do not live with family of origin (P~F) or (3) are experiencing life problems and live with an evangelical (PE). Preliminary analysis, then, shows that the experience of life problems is part of the story, but is neither sufficient nor necessary for conversion. Rather, two variables fill out the picture by pointing toward a respondent's network position.

In what follows, I will first look at the two network variables to try to gain a glimpse of how they function. Then I will return to the issues surrounding the impact of life problems. The goal is not to figure out which variable individually explains the most, but rather to see how they work together.

The Mechanics of Influence

Explanations resting on network influence are generally treated as *alternatives* to cultural explanations that focus on individual-level motivations. In their study of conversion to Mormonism, for example, Stark and Bainbridge (1980, p. 1378) use their network results to show that "rather than being drawn to the group because of the appeal of its ideology, people were drawn to the ideology because of their ties to the group." Emirbayer and Goodwin argue that such views transform "the important theoretical distinction between a structure of social relations, on the one hand, and cultural formations, on the other, into an ontological dualism" (Emirbayer and Goodwin 1994, p. 1427). Here I will offer an interpretation in which networks as social structures and evangelical meanings and practices as cultural structures are analytically distinct yet frequently interrelated.

Conformity Effects

As mentioned above, the simple conformity model of network influence has been increasingly criticized. Clearly network influence happens. But we need more information to establish why it works in one direction rather than another (Gould 2003). We can begin by refraining from viewing network ties as direct transmitters of influence but rather as culturally constituted, frequently contested, sites of interaction (McAdam 2003, p. 290; Mische 2003; see also Sherkat and Wilson 1995). Within these sites of interaction, we will see situations in which network influence leads in the direction of evangelical participation because there is a clear asymmetry of power or number, or because aspects of the evangelical meaning system interact with features of the interactions that take place.

In a number of cases of conversion, network influence clearly occurred in an asymmetric social context. Teodoro returned to his family in the interior from military service to find that the majority of them had converted to evangelicalism and attended the evangelical church across the road from their home. They no longer would go to parties and social occasions with him. So when they invited him to attend a young adults' program at their church, he gladly went and ended up converting as well. When Pedro split up with his wife, the two members of his family that still lived in Caracas and on whom he had to rely were evangelical—having converted some time before. First he lived with his sister, then with his brother. In the latter setting, Pedro suffered a bout of depression that eventually led to his own conversion. He said this depression was caused in large part because of the fact that his brother would no longer drink and wrestle with him—a form of male bonding not uncommon in Venezuela. When he converted, his relationship with his sister and brother improved. When Gregorio moved to Caracas after losing his job in the interior, he moved in with four evangelicals he had previously met. They brought him

to church with them, and his conversion process began. Finally, four of the conversions under network influence happened while the respondent was in jail. Venezuela's prisons are internationally infamous for violence, and these respondents quickly converted when they were assigned to a cell block that was predominantly evangelical. Jose Gregorio went through three cycles of converting and then discontinuing his practice as he was transferred between evangelical and nonevangelical cell blocks.[8] While specific aspects of evangelical meanings or practices may have been important in any of these cases, the asymmetric social context was probably more important. In most of these cases one could imagine almost any subcultural meaning system functioning in a largely similar way.

A number of cases of network influence, however, present precisely the situation of bilateral monopoly that Gould problematizes. In five cases a respondent converted through spatial ties to a romantic interest. Juan Miguel came to Caracas after his life had fallen apart in his hometown in the interior. He soon met an evangelical woman whom he married. "I was unconverted when I married her and the Lord, through her, ministered to me. He 'tamed the lamb' as they say." Henry converted the very same day that he began to live with the woman he would eventually marry. They had developed a friendship at the lunch counter where she worked. When she invited him to rent a room from her in her house—a common practice given the lack of affordable housing in Caracas—he immediately took her up on it. That same afternoon she invited him to a plaza service. "And that same Saturday there was a revival in the metro [subway station plaza] and she invited me 'come on, let's go so that you can see how nice it is.' So I went and that's where—She also invited me...to go up [to the altar call] she said 'let's go up front so that you can see how beautiful it is, let's go see!' She was the one who invited me to go up when they made the altar call." Here we can ask Gould's question: Why did the network tie lead the man to convert instead of the woman to discontinue her participation? Gould argues that, frequently, social movement participation in itself can provide additional value to the relationship, thereby outweighing the alternative of nonparticipation. In each of these five cases either the relationship was new or the couple was experiencing relationship problems. Given evangelicalism's strong association with family and conjugal relationships among adherents (Brusco 1995; Smilde 1997), participation likely added value to these new or troubled ties.

There is another possibility for understanding how network influence occurs in cases of bilateral monopoly. Events and contingencies can revalue existing discourses and determine the direction they take and the symbolic elements that dominate (Ellingson 1995; Sahlins 1985). When an evangelical and a nonevangelical share living space, there is a continual potential for "interanimation": the forced recognition of alternative, competing discourses (Mische and White 1998; Bahktin 1981).[9] In my field-work, evangelicals who lived with nonevangelicals tend to engage the latter in a low-intensity but persistent way by continually providing evangelical conceptualizations of the situations and dilemmas the nonevangelical confronts. This requires response from the nonevangelical, who develops a repertoire of ways to deflect the confrontation. The equilibrium is often broken when a moment of sickness, mishap, or misfortune arises that tips the interpretive balance of power toward the evangelizer, who inevitably provides an evangelical analysis of the nonevangelical's misfortune. The meaning system gains life for the evangelized, and he assents to adopting that system (Brusco 1995).

Seven years after Juan Santiago and his wife married, they began attending together one of the churches I studied. But while his wife went through indoctrination classes and baptism, his interest flagged. "She would say to me 'C'mon let's take this more seriously!' You can't take God lightly," Juan recounted. When, in the span of one month, he twice spent a couple of nights in jail for disputes with neighbors, he made a deal with God and became a participating member. "God calls us with love. But when we don't pay attention, he calls us in other ways. What happened was that I was implicated in a robbery and went to jail. After three days I spoke to the Lord and said 'If you get me out of here, it will be different.' That's what it took for me to actually accept Christ. He let me out under oath."

In this case Juan's going to jail broke the standoff with his wife, and he indeed decided to "take God seriously."

The case of Darton and his wife's conversion while living with the latter's evangelical mother provides an even more striking example. Darton's mother-in-law continually tried to get them to convert to evangelicalism, and they would occasionally go to church with her. However, they never attended regularly until their child almost died from a respiratory problem. When he was revived after he stopped breathing, they viewed it as a miracle. And Darton's mother-in-law did not miss the opportunity to interpret the occurrence as a message from God.

Q: So after that happened, what did your mother-in-law say about it?
A: She wasn't surprised because she knows that God truly is a God of miracles. But she deplored us. [She said] it had happened to us because we were disobedient before God.... Because we knew,... We would always go and ask for prayers when she was pregnant [but] we didn't serve him. So she said that God did that so that we would understand that he really is a living God and that we weren't serving him...that perhaps he was calling us through our child since we weren't going [to church] on our own accord. He started calling us through our child.

The case of Eric is ostensibly similar, but differs in a way that will lead us into the next section. In it we will see direct interaction that only indirectly leads to conversion. Eric's years of conflict with his female partner peaked when her pregnancy ended in a stillbirth. This produced a tremendous amount of resentment toward Eric on her part, and guilt in Eric since, while she was pregnant, his wife had wanted to see a shamanistic healer to protect the child, and Eric had balked at the hefty fee. They both became evangelical shortly afterward and "learned" that he was not guilty of any misdeed since the healer represented a "false" religion. However, in the following we can see how this interpretation had already been transmitted to him from his Adventist sister.

Q: In the years from 1989 [beginning point for the life history], did you have contact with any family member who was evangelical, someone who would talk to you about the Gospel?

A: Yes, my sister.

Q: Did she live in the same house as you?

A: She still lives in the same house as me!

Q: Has she been evangelical for a long time?

A: Oh yeah, since 1985 or so.

Q: And what types of things did she say to you. What types of things would you [two] talk about?

A: Well she would give me magazines, because she was [Seventh Day] Adventist. Magazines about tobacco addiction, alcoholism, sexual diseases, she would give me magazines and would always invite me to her church. I went with her once on a Saturday when they have their day of rest. I went with her.

Q: And when your child died, did she talk to you about that?

A: My sister? She wouldn't say anything because it had happened and that was that. It died because the Lord... We would always talk and we believed that if God had permitted it, it was because it [the baby] wasn't meant to be born.

Eric's sister clearly had an important role in his conversion. Nevertheless, it would be a stretch to represent this as Eric's attempt to achieve conformity with her. Eric had lived with his sister for years before he became evangelical. His parents were not evangelical; nor was his female partner. Furthermore, he converts not to Adventism with his sister, but to Pentecostalism with a friend. It seems clear that he was under no social pressure to convert in order to be on the same wavelength as a family member. Eric's sister had transmitted religious meanings to him—including a reinterpretation of his child's death—that at a key crisis moment in his life brought him to think of religious innovation as a possible solution.

Theoretically such contingencies can work with any cultural practice or discourse; however, Venezuelan evangelicalism seems especially adept at building on them. Evangelicalism specializes in predicating precisely the types of misfortune lower-class Venezuelans are most likely to experience, and this fact, combined with the relative inattention by the mass media and popular culture, means that when such a misfortune occurs, it constitutes prima facie evidence for the validity of evangelical discourse. Furthermore, while we know that actors frequently use highly general and ambiguous meanings to avoid an interanimation of competing or contradictory discourses that might undermine their network (Mische 2003; Ansell 1997; Padgett and Ansell 1993; McLean 1998), here we see the opposite. In the cases of Juan Santiago, Darton, and Eric, the clear and unambiguous meanings of Venezuelan evangelicalism turn misfortune into an interanimation of conversion and foot-dragging discourses. This interanimation effectively highlights the opposition between spiritual choices to a degree that a decision becomes necessary.

Vector Effects

Portraying network explanations as alternatives to cultural explanations leads to an overemphasis on conformity effects. In many of my cases, network influence either worked through direct interaction in which conformity was irrelevant, or it came through unilateral observation in which conformity was not at issue. Kenneth Burke (1989) wrote that the primary attribute of symbols is precisely that they provided an intersubjective vehicle in which sentiments, ideas, and discoveries could find a life beyond the experience or intentions of a single "genius." A spatially copresent evangelical provides a living bearer of meanings and practices that can be observed, considered, and tried on by a nonevangelical, regardless of whether there is direct interaction between ego and alter. In my data, such indirect effects fit into two general categories: modeling and ecological influence.

Modeling.—In a number of cases the respondent became evangelical not through any apparent attempt to achieve network harmony, but through intimate spatial exposure to meanings and practices that came to make sense for his or her life at a critical juncture. This is frequently referred to as "behavioral contagion" (Marsden and Friedkin

1994). I refer to it as "modeling" because the idea of providing a good "witness" is an explicit part of evangelical thought. Evangelicals are enjoined to evangelize not only through direct interaction, but by behaving in exemplary ways and overtly "wearing their faith on their sleeve."

Bartolo, who converted in the midst of a crisis deriving from his life of violence and drugs, had one evangelical brother. When I asked him whether his brother had talked to him about evangelicalism before his conversion, he said he gave him Bible tracts once in a while but not much else. When I asked him why not, he said that not everybody was close with everybody else in his large family. He could count on this evangelical brother in times of necessity. "But in sharing and confiding with each other we weren't close. I was close with one brother, and he was with another. But we weren't close with each other like 'hey, try this.' No, that was rare. Lack of communication, I guess that's why." Nevertheless, when Bartolo reached a crisis point in his life, he had a rudimentary knowledge of evangelicalism that made it a possible solution.

An even more striking case is that of Ugeth. He converted as a result of a crack addiction that was undermining his relationship with his wife and children. During his problem period he lived in the same house with two brothers who had already converted a couple of years before because of a similar drug problem. However, so problematic was his sibling relationship with them that he said they never once tried to evangelize him.

> No, they didn't talk to me [about the Gospel]. One time I remember, I was consuming [drugs] in my room alone, they came in and instead of talking to me [about the Gospel] they started mocking me, throwing barbs at me. They would say "Are you going to keep on [consuming drugs]?" They didn't say "Christ loves you" or preach to me. They never called out to me.

Nevertheless, when he actually did convert, his brothers' example was important for him.

> The Lord had manifested himself in them and pulled them out of where they were. Because they were terrible. One would rob in the street. The other would steal at home. But the Lord, I mean,

Glory to God; I'll give their testimony. I involve them here in this interview because they were an inspiration for me, seeing how the Lord had rescued them from the things they would do...and inspired, seeing everything that the Gospel was doing in the lives of those who were close to me, I realized that it was something supernatural, that it wasn't normal. And I said "Hey, I have to try this."

I noted with interest that while his conversion did get Ugeth over his crack addiction, it seemed to have little effect on his distant relationship with his brothers. While I knew the three of them, his brothers came to church and even sat together with their respective families in the pews. Ugeth had an entirely different circle of friends and sat elsewhere in the church. Ugeth clearly did not convert in order to conserve a relationship. Rather, his brothers' spatially present religious practice presented him with the chance to consider closely its appropriateness for his life.

Ecological effects.—There are other mechanisms through which network influence can occur beyond social conformity. Alter's practice may change the conditions to which ego responds (Marsden and Friedkin 1994). Winklenman converted at age 18. Being a quiet, intellectual boy in one of the toughest, most violent neighborhoods in Caracas, he suffered severe problems of personal and social adjustment. As a boy, his mother separated from his father and began a new family. Because of acute conflict between his mother and stepfather, Winklenman frequently moved between his "more-or-less" evangelical mother's house and his evangelical grandmother's house. In his description his mother was engrossed in her new family and small children and paid little attention to him. Winklenman had no friends and would spend hours drawing or watching action movies on television. However his mother and grandmother would both put Christian radio on at home. Once he started to listen, Winklenman was hooked. He would spend hours listening and even calling in to radio talk programs until he finally decided that becoming evangelical would solve his problems. He went to church with his grandmother a few times and then started to go to evangelical concerts and events that were advertised on the radio programs he listened to. In this case, Winklenman reports no attempts at evangelization by his mother or grandmother— indeed he eventually joined not his grandmother's church but the one he found with the most active youth program. Rather he worked through the possibility of religious innovation in engagement with his radio. "It's the Holy Spirit that ministers to you through the radio. So I would listen to the church programs that were on at 9 p.m. and that talked about Venezuela's problems, people's problems, and Christ's solutions, how glorious the Lord is, this and that about the Lord. With the testimonies I heard, I found that Christ was the solution."

Roberto Alfonzo lives in his own house built as an addition to his mother's house—a common arrangement in Venezuela's densely populated barrios. His brother and sister-in-law, who lived with Roberto Alfonzo's mother, converted to evangelicalism before he did. When I asked Roberto Alfonzo if his brother talked to him about the Gospel he said "Yeah, he talked to me about the Gospel. But not much. We come from a family where we respect each other a lot. When he'd go too far I'd say—in 'worldly' terms—'get lost' and he would stop immediately because there was personal respect in our family." Nevertheless, his brother and sister-in-law would have services in their home, and Roberto Alfonzo would listen. "They would have services in my Mother's house and my house is below hers. So when they had their services, I would listen. They would have the [sound] equipment turned on and you could hear it since there is just one wall that separates us."[10] These services piqued his interest and led him to buy a Bible to study. He "surrendered" in a plaza service that he visited by himself one day on his way home from work.

The point of the cases of Bartolo, Ugeth, Winklenman, and Roberto Alfonzo is not that spatially present evangelical family members were irrelevant, but rather *how* they were relevant. In these cases, as well as others, describing the mechanism as social conformity seems false to the phenomena. In none of these cases did the person appear preoccupied by coming into line with the beliefs of their spatially present evangelicals. Rather, either through modeling or by changing ecological conditions, spatially present evangelicals exposed these respondents to evangelical meanings and practices that came to make sense to them in their lives. In these data, such cases of indirect influence constitute a substantial minority of 11 of the 27 (40.7%) of cases of network influence.

Countervailing Networks and Structural Availability

It is not entirely accurate to indict sociologists with ignoring countervailing networks (Diani 2002; McAdam 2003; McAdam and Paulsen 1993), as their *absence* has received significant attention virtually since the discipline's classic statements. Hobbes's (1962) "masterless men," Machiavelli's (1950) "adventurer-prince," Simmel's (1971) "stranger," and Durkheim's (1951) state of anomie all underlined the sociological importance of *freedom from* some or all network ties. Current social movements research addresses the absence of countervailing networks through the concept of "structural availability." In their seminal study Snow et al. (1980, p. 794) argued that individuals who are structurally available "can follow their interests and/or engage in exploratory behavior to a greater extent than individuals who are bound to existing lines of action" by their network obligations. Rodney Stark (1996) says that recruitment to a new religious movement occurs when the potential recruit has more significant ties to members of the movement than to nonmembers. This is a variant of the "control theory" of deviant behavior, which says that people generally do not deviate because they have "stakes in conformity." "Most of us conform in order to retain the good opinion of our friends and family. But some people lack such attachments. Their rates of deviance are much higher than are those of people with an abundance of attachments" (Stark and Finke 2000, pp. 117–18). In essence, the existing concept of structural availability amounts to a logical transposition of the conformity model of network influence. However, here as well, we will find important substantive aspects of structural availability that move us beyond the conformity model. In the first section of what follows I will use negative examples—cases in which network influence did not work as it normally does—to infer how spatially present family of origin enforces conformity and thereby prevents religious innovation. In the second section I will look at more substantive functions of networks by comparing the experience of men who confront life problems without spatially present family of origin, to men who confront problems with them.

Conformity

According to McAdam and Paulsen (1993), the most relevant network ties in studying social movement recruitment are those that an individual uses to sustain his or her identity. In Venezuela, these ties are most often family ties. While the Venezuelan family nucleus is often fatherless, people communicate, associate, collaborate, and simply spend time with members of their family of origin to a degree that citizens of the industrialized West would find difficult to imagine. Children usually live with their parents until they form their own family or need to move for reasons of work or study. If none of these occur, it is common for individuals to live with their parents well into their thirties or forties. Furthermore, housing costs lead many to stay at home well after their first union is formed. A parent's home is often considered the main inheritance for offspring, and it is common, after parents have died, for several brothers and sisters to live together in the home with their own families. In Venezuelan society there is a moral expectation that individuals will support and defend their family of origin above and beyond any other social group or ideology. In sum, family ties in Venezuela provide identity, belonging, and a web of social support.

Venezuelans of the popular classes rarely object to evangelicalism as a threat to their Catholicism. Rather, they object to the way evangelical practice breaks with the pragmatic, flexible, context-dependent, and personalistic morality characteristic of Venezuelan culture. Fervent religious beliefs and rigorous adherence to ethical standards are occasionally admired as manifestations of a principled character. But more commonly they are distrusted, viewed as antisocial, or seen as a signs of personal maladjustment. A family member's becoming evangelical may be considered an embarrassment, a rebuke, or simply a loss. For example, when Juan Betancourt returned to his hometown after converting in Caracas, his father broke down and cried

because Juan would no longer drink with him. Above we saw that one cause of the depression that preceded Pablo's conversion was the fact that his newly evangelical brother would no longer drink and wrestle with him.

Such distancing is a powerful reason not to convert if there is valued and frequent rapport with nonevangelical family members. Nevertheless, such processes are not easily uncovered. In my life histories, converts rarely discussed the absence of pressures to conform during their conversion, and nonconverts rarely discussed pressure to conform as a reason not to convert. Where these quiet and subtle effects are most visible is in the anomalous cases in which they did not work in their usual way and therefore broke to the surface of conscious interaction.

Of the 60 cases in which young men lived with their nonevangelical families (rows PF~E and ~PF~E combined), there were only five conversions. In four of them the respondent reported considerable conflict created by converting in such a context. I had the following exchange with Henry.

> Q: Since you became evangelical, has your relationship with your family changed?
> A: Yeah it's changed, but for the worse. I mean there are more differences now because there is conflict because they want to separate me from my ideals.
> Q: For example, what do they do?
> A: Yeah they always talk to me and say that the Gospel is for people with problems, who are crazy or whatever, that feel unsatisfied with themselves.

Ernesto converted after his mother and father both died, leaving him to enter adulthood while living with his older brothers and sisters. When he converted they tried to prohibit him from participating. "[They would tell me] that I was going to go crazy, that they were going to call the police and have them put me in the military. They would pressure me a lot to stop [participating]. One time they burned my Bible."

In these cases, instead of staying in the background, conformity-inducing pressures were exposed because conversion happened. But why did these pressures not prevent it in the first place? Upon examination, in four of the five cases, either one of the respondent's major problems was *with* family authority figures or the respondent was in some sense alienated from his family. Henry, for example, lived with his family and became evangelical after the rock-and-roll band he led and had heavily invested in broke up, and after he met an evangelical woman whom he found attractive. The context of all these issues was long-term family problems.

> Q: And how was your relationship with your family from the time you finished high school [the starting point for our interview]. I mean did you get along well with them? Did you have conflicts with them?
> A: Yeah, the same conflicts continued.
> Q: Yeah? Why? I mean, what were the "same conflicts"?
> A: I mean it was a sort of—I was sealed off in everything. I stayed in my shell and didn't give my family any space to enter. What I would do outside of the house my family knew nothing about. I was completely closed off.
> Q: Was that when you were in high school?
> A: Yes, I mean it was always that way.

The conflict with Henry's family stemmed not only from his late-night activity in rock-and-roll dubs, but also, as he put it, from his mother's continual "enmity" toward any girlfriend he might have. He described his usual reaction to his mother's rejection as greater attraction to the girl in question. We can assume then, that Henry's coexistence with his family was not an impediment to becoming evangelical when his new romantic relationship presented the opportunity.

Juan Zerpa's life began to fall apart when he quit his good job as a waiter in hopes of using his severance pay to go into business for himself. He never got around to launching his new endeavor, and before he knew it he was broke and unable to secure another good job. These economic problems undermined his identity as an efficacious male upon which his relationship with his girlfriend seemed to have been based, as well as his economic contribution to his impoverished family. When I followed up on his mention of conflict with his family, I was struck by the lack of rapport he felt.

> Q: So did you already have family problems before you surrendered to the Gospel?
> A: I did, but they didn't really come out since I would close myself off. They hadn't come out since I would come go to my room and shut the door, leave, come back and do the same. I don't have my own room, I share it with my brothers. But they didn't spend much time there. So I would come home and shut myself in my room. At that time I wasn't a Christian. I was unemployed but I had the Bible that the Lord had given me and from the beginning when all this began, from the beginning of my being unemployed, I began to read it.

What is clear in the cases of both Henry and Juan is that they did not have the type of rapport with their families that could have prevented their conversions.

Such a lack of rapport works the same way in evangelical households. The ambiguous row we previously set aside, ~PFE, appears to contradict what we would expect from everything that has been said so far regarding networks. If living with an evangelical (E), and living with family of origin (F), each constitute causally important sources of conformity, one would think that living with an evangelical family of origin would be doubly effective. Indeed in the three cases of conversion, the respondent converted shortly after family members converted. What happened in the other three cases? Venezuela is no different than the rest of the world insofar as young people frequently are at odds with their family or for some reason feel the need to individuate away from its influence. Two cases of nonconversion, Manuel and Pablo, demonstrate precisely this. Each of them grew up in evangelical homes and stopped participating in church in their teens. Each expressed that they had rebelled against something that had been forced upon them. Pablo, for example, grew up in an evangelical household and was forced to attend church with his mother. "It got to the point that I couldn't stand church anymore and the small part that I did like about it—the prayers—started to disgust me. So when I started high school it was like a liberation. The girls would say things like 'that's nerdy,' 'that's for adults, for old people,' 'that's boring.' So they put those ideas in my head when I was already disliking it because of my mom's pressure. So I decided not to go anymore. I disobeyed my mother's orders and I stopped going."

It is extremely common for children in evangelical families to stop participating as young adults as a form of rebellion against their parents. Besides the cases of Manuel and Pablo, three more of the evangelical respondents in the sample were socialized in evangelical families, rejected it during adolescence or young adulthood, and then came back to it when confronted by serious life problems.[11] Certainly many such individuals never return to evangelical practice. Others do, especially when they confront life problems and recall meanings imparted to them in their religious socialization.

In sum, a spatially present family of origin exercises a strong conservative impact that works against cultural innovation. Men who live with nonevangelical families rarely convert even when they experience life problems, unless those problems are with the family or they lack rapport with family members. Similarly, men who live with evangelical families strongly tend toward conversion unless they have a lack of rapport with family members, most commonly their parents. This supports the view that men who did not live with their nonevangelical family members were left open to explore religious options.

Social and Cultural Support

Existing conceptualizations of structural availability rarely move beyond logical transposition of the conformity view of network influence. In this section I will show that spatially present families of origin not only enforce conformity, they provide important social and cultural support to their members that can help them navigate the problem situations they encounter. Conversely, those men who face problem situations without spatially present family of origin do not receive this support and are more likely to seek religious innovation. First I will relate some stories of the way young men not living with their families of origin experienced

the problems that preceded their conversion. Then I will look at some young men who experienced problems while living with their family of origin. Both through absence and presence, we will see that family of origin helps young men confront problem situations by providing social support as well as helping them make meaning regarding these situations.

Whether a young man separates from his family of origin out of desire or necessity, being autonomous and self-sufficient can be an important aspect of self-esteem. After Henrique finished his military service he did not return to the family home in the interior but stayed in Caracas working and living on his own. After tiring of his job because of low salary and demanding working conditions, he quit before finding another. He subsequently spent a year unemployed and ended up selling many of his possessions to get by. He converted to evangelicalism at the tail end of his economic crisis as he went through a training program for a job at a bank. I asked him if any friends or family would lend him money, and his answer demonstrated how he experienced financial independence. "Well, family, I had one uncle here but I never went to him and told him about the situation because he lives in a place here in Caracas that is hard to get to. I didn't go frequently. But sometimes I did go to, say, spend a weekend. But I didn't tell him about the problem openly. I would just sort of swallow it and try to solve my problem some other way so that they wouldn't see that I was in such a critical situation." What is interesting about Henrique's case is not only that he suffers problems of subsistence, but that he does not feel it appropriate to ask extended family for help, and does not even mention the possibility of asking friends or his spatially distant family of origin.

Willian is an example of one of those who lives apart from his family of origin for economic necessity. He lucidly describes the impact of this isolation in terms surely experienced by others. He had explained to me that when he converted, he was "loaded with problems," and I asked him what type. He responded as follows:

I had personal afflictions, moments of loneliness. Those were tough times. Being here [in Caracas] without your family is tough. You tend to have economic problems. I also had problems with sickness, moments of loneliness. And sometimes you feel that there isn't anyone who can talk to you to raise your spirits. Because when you look at them [people you don't know very well], they have more problems than you do. So I couldn't trust them, their advice. I was always taught that my family was God, that my family would solve my problems. And I got close to some people where I would have lunch. I would eat lunch at an evangelical kiosk and was able to place my trust in them.

Of course, it's unlikely that Willian thought his "family was God" before he converted. This is clearly an evangelical reconceptualization of what he did think before he converted: that his family was his main resource for solving his problems. What is interesting in Willian's case is not just that he experienced the normal problems of a young man living on his own for the first time, but the emphasis he puts on not having anyone to talk to. In effect, Willian did not have trusted interlocutors who could, through dialogue, help him make meaning of the situations he was going through. When he came across such a satisfying interactive space in the form of an evangelical kiosk where he would eat lunch, he cultivated this network.

We can further circumscribe the phenomenon by looking at the support family provides to an individual facing life problems. These examples will be taken from cases in which a respondent experienced life problems, but was living with family of origin (PF~E). Two years prior to our interview, some neighborhood thugs shot Jose Luis. He was taking a spin on a friend's new motorcycle and rode past a group of guys gathered by the side of the road. One, whom he had met before, called him over. He stopped but, perceiving that their intentions were not good, took off again on the motorcycle. The one who called out to him pulled out a gun and opened fire. One bullet entered his thigh, another his buttock. However, he managed to stay on the motorcycle and get back home and then to a hospital. Recovering from his wounds, he was not out of danger. For in the institutional vacuum of Caracas's lower-class barrios, justice functions

through the logic of vendetta. Having been shot by someone meant that others, including the victimizer, expected Jose Luis to seek revenge. And this in turn meant that Jose Luis was a prime target for a preemptive strike (Hardin 1995; Nisbett and Cohen 1996). This was the exact situation in which several of my evangelical respondents had converted. For example, an evangelical respondent named Ramiro was involved in a months' long vendetta chain in the same neighborhood which left seven people dead and several others in jail. "The situation got so bad that I converted to the Gospel" he told me. Jose Luis, however, was able to resist involvement in vendetta. In the following exchange, we can get a sense of the role played by his strong family life.

> After I was shot, I was afraid that he [his assailant] would—I thought he was going to think that I was going to do something bad to him, I mean seek revenge. And I never at any time thought about revenge because I'm not part of that malicious environment.
>
> Q: So you thought that he thought that?
> A: Yeah, I mean the day after I was shot, I was sitting in the door [of my house] and he walked by and had his gun on him.
> Q: How did you know he had his gun on him?
> A: Because he had it hanging out of his back pocket and he stared at me. My Dad was there next to me.
> Q: And you were in your house?
> A: Yeah, I was right in the door. We had the door open.
> Q: Oh, okay, and nobody said to you that you had to fix things, that you had to seek revenge or anything like that?
> A: Well my brother thought about doing something to the guy. The [brother] who is away.
> Q: The one who is Mormon now?
> A: Yeah, exactly. With Frank, you know Frank [a neighbor also interviewed for this study]. They thought about doing something and I said no, to leave it at that, that people would think it was me since the only one who had problems with him in that sector was me.
> Q: And what about people in the barrio. Didn't they laugh at you. I mean saying that you didn't make him pay?

A: Yeah, a lot of people said, "Man, you're a loser. You should have done something to him. You should have done something." But I thought no, that that would just put more wood on the fire.

Q: And what did your family say?

A: No, my Moth…what they did was advise me to leave it at that, let it die out.

In the case of Jose Luis, the avenues open to him were (1) seek revenge at risk of continuing the vendetta, (2) opt out of the logic by becoming evangelical as Ramiro did, or (3) let it peter out at the risk of falling to a preemptive strike and with the assurance of a loss of esteem among others in the barrio. As Jose Luis tells the story, he took the last option. If this is true, it is clear that the influence of his family encouraged this solution. But it is interesting that he mentions that his brother wanted to seek revenge. Previously in the interview he mentioned both that his victimizer was no longer around and that his brother had become Mormon and moved to Utah. It could well be that his brother sought revenge and then converted to Mormonism in the aftermath of guilt and fear. But in either case, Jose Luis's story provides a nice example of how the material and cultural support of a spatially present family of origin helps individuals navigate problem situations and how that support precludes the need for network innovation. Had Jose Luis lived without his family of origin, he most likely would have taken a more open role in the vendetta or become evangelical.

Aurelio is a 40-year-old man living in his parents' house. Two years before our interview, he began to organize residents to close off their sector of the barrio with locked gates to which only the residents would have keys. This is one of a number of ways that residents of Venezuela's barrios have found to reduce crime and violence. However, the prospect of gates often causes conflict with those who—usually involved in the drug economy—benefit from disorganization. And neighborhood organizers are frequently the targets of violence. Indeed in Aurelio's barrio just three years earlier, a neighborhood activist had been brutally murdered in the middle of the night by hooded gunmen. With this in mind, Aurelio was reluctant about the

leadership role he had taken in this tense process. He expressed resentment at his neighbors for what happened when some of his opponents tried to intimidate him through violence. The story reveals the strength of familial versus extrafamilial ties: "Because it's happened to me! I put the gates up and I had a problem with one of the families. So they brought a *malandro* [gangbanger] to fuck me up and I ended up letting *him* have it because I have a lot of family too! Who defended me? My family. What everyone else did was wash their hands [of the problem]. Everyone ran into their houses to hide and watch the fight."

In the data presented here, "stakes in conformity" work against religious innovation not only because of the desire to correspond with significant others and maintain their good opinion. These significant others also provide important social support as well as help in making meaning regarding a problem situation. Those young men who do not live with their family of origin not only have more freedom to innovate; they are more likely to have more motivation to innovate, since they are left to their own devices when confronting a problem situation. None of this should surprise, as a large part of the literature on the positive effects of religious practice on psychological and physical health focuses on social support networks (Fraser 2002; Foley, McCarthy, and Chaves 2001; Ebaugh and Pipes 2001; Ellison 1997; Bankston and Zhou 1996; Haines, Hurlbert, and Beggs 1996), as does an important tradition in community studies (Walker, Wasserman, and Wellman 1994; Wellman 1982; Silveira and Allebeck 2001; Warren, Thompson, and Saegert 2001). However, this support function rarely figures in studies of conversion because of a lack of sustained attention to countervailing networks.

Problems, Agency, and Purposes

The strong program in network analysis seeks to explain sociological phenomena by focusing on patterns of social relations—that is, social structure—and regards attributes of individuals such as their problems, agency, and purposes as spuriously significant (see Emirbayer and Goodwin [1994] for a review of this position). Nevertheless, as argued in the introduction, scholars have persuasively argued that this tendency reifies the structure—agency dyad, ignoring more dynamic conceptualizations of social structure by Giddens (1979), Bourdieu (1977), and others (e.g., Sewell 1992; Emirbayer and Mische 1998). There are a couple of overlapping but distinct issues involved in the desire to bring actors back into network explanations. In this section I will look at the roles of problems, agency, and purposes.

Problems.—In the data analyzed here, the significance of the two network variables just reviewed provides strong support for structural approaches. Nevertheless, the individual experience of life problems (P) stubbornly stays in the equation (see table 2). Even if we were to code the output of ambiguous combination ~PFE as conversion, the causal significance of life problems would remain. While "living with an evangelical" (E) would become a sufficient condition, "not living with family of origin" (~F) would still need to combine with P to cause conversion.

But it is still possible to question the causal importance of problems. QCA is oriented toward diversity and counts all causal relationships with the same output as equal no matter their numeric frequency. Thus the reason P does not drop out of the equation describing conversion is the very clear, but not terribly common, tendency for combination ~P~F~E not to lead to conversion; ~P~F~E describes only 10 cases. Of the 50 total cases in which a man does not live with family of origin and does not live with an evangelical (~F~E), 40 experience problems. Indeed combination P~F~E accounts for close to half of the conversions in the entire sample. We could hypothesize that while ~F is neither a necessary nor sufficient cause of P, there could well be a *strong tendency* for ~F to cause P. If this were the case, problems would still not be spurious, for without them ~F does not lead to conversion. But P would look more like a mediating variable. From this perspective, problems could be seen as a function of structural availability and therefore not as causally important as we previously thought. A simple cross-tabulation of all cases according to whether they were living with family of origin

and whether they experienced life problems indeed shows a statistically significant relationship (see table 3).

But, of course, correlation does not establish direction of causation, and there is another possibility. It is normally assumed that structural availability is the product of happenstance or at least issues irrelevant to the outcome of interest. So, for example, Snow et al. (1980) use the example of a 25-year-old male whose luggage was lost on his flight to Los Angeles and who wound up living on the streets. This contingent misfortune left him open and receptive to recruitment to a religious movement. In most of my cases, structural availability was indeed caused by life course characteristics or contingencies. However, it should come as no surprise that, frequently, structural availability was *itself* caused by a problem involved in the conversion project. Below we will see how Lenin moved away from his family of origin because of inconformity and conflict. Alberto, Jhonny, and Melvin all lived on the street as a result of their involvement in drugs and crime. In other cases, the respondent had been thrown out of the family home. Martin's mother forced him and his wife to leave because of their incessant, frequently violent fighting. Ernesto's mother threw him out of the house when she believed neighbors who implicated him in a murder, rather than his proclamations of innocence. Jose Gregorio became structurally available when going to jail meant he was forced to be away from his mother's home. In 15 of the 50 cases of P~F, it was the problem that would eventually lead to conversion that itself caused structural availability.

Table 3 Cross-Tabulation of the Experience of Life Problems While Not Living with Family of Origin

	F	~F	Total
P	41	50	91
~P	36	17	53
Total	77	67	144

Note.—$\chi^2 = 7.04$ ($P \leq .01$.); P = experience of life problems; F = living with family of origin.

If I exclude these cases from the sample in order to simply compare cases in which life problems clearly arise and are experienced while living *with* family of origin with cases in which life problems clearly arise and are experienced while living *apart from* family of origin.[12] I can demonstrate that the connection does not meet generally accepted standards of significance for a sample of this size (see table 4). This finding leads to the conclusion that ~F is causally important not because it causes P but because of what happens when P occurs. It also provides some sociological content to the common belief that an individual must "hit bottom" before getting serious about overcoming an addiction or other problem of the self (Irvine 1999, pp. 56–57). In these data "hitting bottom" often amounted to an individual losing his or her most valued social relationships, which in turn simultaneously left them to their own problem-solving devices and freed them up for innovation.

Agency and purposes.—The most fundamental difference between structural and voluntaristic approaches to social action is precisely that the former takes into account the unacknowledged conditions and unintended consequences of action (Giddens 1979, p. 59). Structural explanations focus on the notion that actors do not usually know why they do what they do and do not fully understand the consequences their action will produce. So trying to demonstrate agency by focusing on Willian's case (he found some evangelicals to talk to at a lunch kiosk and cultivated the network) or the case of Juan Zerpa (he was too broke to take the bus, so he walked miles from his home to a plaza where he knew evangelicals were preaching), would miss the mark. Structural approaches do not deny that actors experience agency in what they do, nor that they can provide agentive stories about what agents have done. Rather these approaches argue that these "vocabularies of motive" are spurious because the real causes work behind actors' backs (Emirbayer and Goodwin 1994; Burt 1986). It is understandable from this perspective, then, that the desire to bring agency into network explanations looks like wanting to have your cake and eat it too.

However, there are two possible responses to this view. First, in contemporary theorizations, agency does not imply an integral relationship between intentions and consequences. Anthony Giddens defines agency as "the stream of actual or contemplated causal interventions of corporeal beings in the ongoing process of events-in-the-world," which is not confined to the intended consequences of an actor's action (Giddens 1976, p. 77; see also Sewell 1992; Emirbayer and Mische 1998). Defined in these terms, the data show that in 61% of cases of conversion in which either E or ~F was causally effective, we can see respondents' agency in the construction of their network location (see table 5). In the great majority of the cases of ~F, the respondent had intentionally moved away from his family due to life course considerations: either he had gotten married and was able to move out, or he had moved from the

Table 4 Cross-Tabulation of the Experience of Life Problems While Not Living with Family of Origin, Excluding Cases in which P Caused ~F

	F	~F	Total
P	41	35	76
~P	36	17	52
Total	77	52	129

Note.— $\chi^2 = 2.54$; P = experience of life problems; F = living with family of origin. For all coefficients, $P \leq .20$.

Table 5 Agency in Construction of Network Locations

	Intentional	Not Intentional	Total
Not living with family of origin (~F)	34	11	45
Living with an evangelical (E)	10	17	27
Total	44	28	72

interior for employment reasons. In contrast, most cases of E were not intentionally brought about—the respondent lived with a spatially copresent evangelical not by choice but because that was his family of origin or because the evangelical in question converted after the respondent had joined the household. However, there were 10 cases in which the person intentionally moved into a household with an evangelical resident. Agency, thus defined, is quite compatible with the traditional network program. For networks to be key causal characteristics of social phenomena, it is not necessary that they be uncaused, or even that they be uncaused by the actors that eventually are constrained by them. Rather, the core claim is that they have important effects that function beyond (even contrary to) the conscious interests and intentions of actors. In effect, an actor switches on the light to illuminate the room and unintentionally alerts the prowler (Giddens 1976, p. 77).

A second, more direct challenge to the exclusion of agency in network explanations would be a purposive account in which there *is* an integral relationship between intentions and consequences—the actor switches on the light to illuminate the room *in order to* alert the prowler. In other words, a more direct challenge would be an empirical demonstration of action in which agents not only intentionally create network locations, they do so because they perceive potential network effects. To inquire into this possibility, I looked at the 44 cases in which the respondent intentionally created the network location to see if this agency was an integral part of the same project of change that resulted in conversion. In seven cases I found evidence of such a process (see table 6).

Gregorio converted while living away from family of origin and with a group of evangelical men (~FE). However, he actively sought these conditions as part of a project of change. Two problems were affecting his life before his conversion. First he had long suffered bouts of depression, and second he had just lost his job. While living at home with his family he became familiar with evangelicalism through a revival and even had a religious experience. Nevertheless, while he was interested, he did not participate in a church. He did meet a number of evangelicals from Caracas, and they invited him to stay with them if he ever came their way. Indeed he was already considering moving to the capital to launch a music career. When he did, he looked up his evangelical friends, and they found him a place to stay with several other evangelicals. He immediately began to attend church with them. When his music career sputtered, he put all of his energies into this evangelical church. In this case, moving away from family of origin to Caracas to live with some evangelicals and pursue a music career were all part of a project of change, a new start that eventually led to religious conversion.

When Jose Gregorio went to prison for a cocaine binge that involved a car theft and a shoot-out with police, he was assigned, beyond any intention of his own, to an evangelical-controlled cell block. There he converted within several weeks of arriving. However, some months later he developed an attraction to a woman who frequently visited another inmate on weekends. When that inmate changed to a nonevangelical cell block, Jose Gregorio changed along with him and promptly discontinued his religious practice. However, when the relationship with the woman did not lead anywhere, he intentionally

Table 6 Purposive Action in Construction of Network Locations

	Intentional		
	Not Integral	Integral	Total
Not living with family of origin (~F)	31	3	34
Living with an evangelical (E)	6	4	10
Total	37	7	44

moved back to the evangelical cell block in order to recover his evangelical participation. "The Devil tricked me and that girl got me to leave. She trapped me—I mean she captured me and I decided to change cellblocks, in order to maintain contact with her. And when I changed cellblocks and left the Gospel, she didn't visit the jail anymore. So she was an instrument intended to derail me. But I understood, and I went back."

Lenin speaks, dresses, and carries himself with moderation and care. His manner and appearance belie his humble origins and tough upbringing. While he has always been close to his mother, he has experienced serious problems with his two younger brothers. When Lenin and I discussed the nature of this conflict, he emphasized that, like his father, his brothers would drink at home, did not respect him or his mother, and behaved violently. He finally moved out in August 1995 because of his frustration at not being able to deal with them effectively. "The situation got so bad that I decided to just leave and not have to see it. My anger would consume me." During the three months he was away from his mother's house he lived in three different locations. At the end of the first month, Lenin "surrendered" to the Lord and began indoctrination classes in one of the churches I participated in. As he studied the Bible he focused on verses that said he should not harbor anger toward others. This led him to visit home in September and converse with his brothers to resolve his issues with them. In October he returned to his mother's house as an evangelical, continuing his participation until he was baptized in December. In Lenin's case, acute family conflict and the ire it produced in him led him to leave home. Being away from home gave Lenin the opportunity to reflect and to address this issue, among others. By the time he returned home he had been able to gain a familiarity with and confidence in the new meaning system and use it to confront his problem.

These are cases in which network location ends up looking like a mediating variable between individual motivations and conversion. It clearly has a causal impact, but the respondents themselves created that impact as part of a conscious project of change. The respondents did not necessarily see that a change in network location would lead to conversion in particular. But they did correctly perceive that, in more general terms, it would facilitate a project of change. While this is a clear challenge to structural approaches that oppose the network project to voluntaristic explanations, it should be underlined that this happened in less than 10% of conversions (7 of 72) related to networks. In more than 90% of cases there was no integral relationship between actors' intentions and network effects.

Conclusion

As this article uses a diversity-oriented methodology designed to probe beyond main effects, the findings have been multiple. Therefore they merit brief recapitulation.

Problems.—In contrast to dominant portrayals of conversion to evangelicalism in Latin America, and consistent with contemporary sociological explanations of conversion, the life problems experienced by respondents were neither necessary nor sufficient causes of religious conversion.

Network influence.—(a) Direct effects functioning through social conformity are central in this data analysis. In most cases, such conformity works because of an asymmetric relational context. In other cases it appears to work because it adds value to new or troubled romantic relationships, or because a contingent misfortune tips the interpretive equilibrium between ego and alter. (b) However, there is a significant minority of cases of network influence that did not fit this portrayal. These indirect effects worked through modeling or ecological influences, which in turn underline the autonomy and mobility of meaning and practices.

Structural availability.—(a) The data reveal that young men who live with their family of origin face significant conflict when they convert. Such countervailing networks, then, likely play an important conformity-inducing role. (b) However, there are important substantive aspects of structural availability that move us beyond the conformity model. Comparing the experience of men who confront life problems without spatially present families of origin to men who confront problems with them, we saw the important social and cultural support that likely reduces motivation for religious innovation.

Problems, agency, and purposes.—(*a*) While problems are neither necessary nor sufficient causes of conversion, their causal role does not disappear. They are not a simple function of structural availability. Indeed they are highly correlated with structural availability precisely because they often *result in* structural availability when addiction, violence, or inconformity creates conflict in the home. (*b*) Agency in the broadest sense is evident in the majority of cases of conversion in which network locations were in play. In most cases, actors had a hand in creating the network locations that then constrained their action. (*c*) Agency in the more narrow sense of purposive action integrally related to the eventual effect of the network location was also evident in a small minority of cases.

This analysis, of course, is confined to understanding conversion to Pentecostalism among Venezuelan men, as the substantive dynamics I describe will likely vary according to social, cultural, gender, or religious contexts. However, the theoretical and methodological directions taken can provide orientation for future study. Existing biases in network explanations are not without foundation. In most cases, social conformity is indeed the mechanism that underlies network influence as well as structural availability, and in general, structural determination trumps actors' purposive behavior. Nevertheless, moving beyond main effects to a focus on causal diversity demonstrates irreducible divergences from these emphases. Networks work not only through conformity; they work through the transportability of meaning. Lack of networks not only creates freedom, it creates needs that make religious innovation more appealing. Finally, while in most cases networks constrain actors, actors actively create network positions and, in a small number of cases, clearly perceive the same consequences sociologists do. This portrait does not muddy the waters of the network project; it puts it on footing more consistent with contemporary theorizations of social structure. These grant structure causal primacy but simply see it as the crystallization of human actions which, at any subsequent moment, can constrain or be affected by further human action (Bourdieu 1977; Giddens 1979; Sewell 1992; Emirbayer and Mische 1998).

NOTES

Versions of this paper were presented at the 2001 and 2002 annual meetings of the American Sociological Association, the 2002 meetings of the Eastern Sociological Association, the 2004 Latin American Studies Association Congress, the Helen Kellogg Institute for International Studies at the University of Notre Dame, the sociology departments at Duke University, the University of Pennsylvania, and the University of Georgia, the Georgia Workshop on Culture and Institutions, and the Department of Religion at the University of Florida. It was also improved by the individual comments of David Gibson, Julian Go, Wendy Griswold, Daniel Levine, Scott Mainwaring, Paul McLean, Ann Mische, William Parish, Linda Renzulli, Barry Schwartz, Martin Riesebrodt, Timothy Steigenga, Richard Wood, David Yamane, and the *AJS* reviewers. The fieldwork this article is based on was supported by a U.S. Department of Education Fulbright-Hays dissertation fellowship.

1. There is no easy solution to the terminological difficulties of studying non–Catholic Christianity in Latin America. At least two-thirds of Protestantism in Latin America is what in North America would be called Pentecostal. Latin American Pentecostals themselves do not dislike the term Pentecostal but generally refer to themselves as *Evangélicos,* to denote their professed prioritization of the Gospels, i.e., the first four books of the New Testament telling the story of Jesus, or *Cristianos* to denote their christocentrism and to imply that Catholics are not true Christians. Baptists and other historic Protestant denominations usually refer to themselves as evangelical as well. To complicate matters further, Catholic Latin Americans generally refer to all new religious movements as "evangelicals," while Mormons, Jehovah's Witnesses, and Seventh Day Adventists do not use the term to refer to themselves. Here I will favor their self-definition.

2. These interviews frequently led to discussion of intimate subjects. Among these people in this context, this intimacy made my carrying them out with women a practical impossibility. I therefore restricted my sample to men. Only further study would reveal whether the dynamics revealed here function in the same way with women.

3. I agree with criticisms of the term "conversion" that say it generates expectations of a rapid and radical transformation that is rarely the case in individual religious change (Stark and Bainbridge 1987; Comaroff and Comaroff 1991). However, alternatives also stack the conceptual deck. "Affiliation" directs our attention away from belief and personal experience and toward organizational membership. "Recruitment" places agency with the organization or movement rather than the person who joins. The term "commitment" directs our attention to personal assent to the meaning system. Here I will simply use the term "conversion" and rely on my substantive descriptions to make clear that radical change is not necessarily involved.

4. This methodological strategy closely resembles "objective hermeneutics" (Reichertz 2002). I disagree with Denzin's (1989) view that such an approach necessarily conflates data, sociological texts, and subjects' lives. Misplaced concreteness is not the weakness of any one methodological approach, but a general pitfall that all sociological thinking needs to avoid. I also disagree that it implies a linear view of biography. As I will show in this article, it is precisely biographical facts that often help us demonstrate contingency despite respondents' efforts to construct linear narratives.

5. I use "problems" instead of alternative terms often used in studies of conversion or social movement mobilization. "Deprivations" only makes sense from a structural functional perspective in which one can make sense of a baseline equilibrium of need fulfillment. This is rarely feasible and even less so in a cross-cultural study. Instead I view problems as a persisting sense of "dis-ease" in an individual's experience (Chesnut 1997; see appendix for coding rules). "Complaints" makes most sense when there is an adversary that has authority over or responsibility for the problem in question. That is rarely the case with the problems described here.

6. For reasons of space, I cannot elaborate the pragmatist view of culture as a "strategy for dealing with situations," that I use in this article (see Smilde 2003, in press.)

7. I give a fuller quantitative account of these stages elsewhere (Smilde, in press, app. C).

8. While this makes it tempting to conclude that Jose Gregorio's conversions were expedient and therefore superficial, he continued with his evangelical participation after being released from jail, married an evangelical woman, and, several years later, became the youth pastor of one of the churches in which I conducted fieldwork.

9. This is essentially the same process as "frame alignment" as developed by Snow and others (see, e.g., Snow, Rochford, Worden, and Benford 1986). Here I use the more general and flexible term "interanimation" as it seems more appropriate to this type of everyday interaction.

10. It is customary for Venezuelan evangelicals to use sound amplification even when doing a service with only a handful of people in a small space precisely to get their message to others who might be interested but not attending the service.

11. Each of these respondents had already moved away from home and so converted from combination P~F~E.

12. An alternative strategy would be to recode these cases as living with family of origin which would reduce the significance even further. However this would become substantively unintelligible in cases like that of Jose Angel, who was in jail.

Part 6

Interpretive Factors: Framing Processes

In the introduction to Part 1, we noted that people rarely respond to disrupting and threatening trends and events in an automatic or stimulus/response fashion because trends, events, and situations are subject to differential interpretation. The same situation or event may be defined or perceived differently depending on the meanings attached to it, which, in turn, often depends on how it is framed. Framing, within the context of social movements, refers to the signifying work or meaning construction engaged in by movement adherents (e.g., leaders, activists, and rank-and-file participants) and other actors (e.g., adversaries, institutional elites, media, countermovements) relevant to the interests of movements and the challenges they mount in pursuit of those interests. The concept of framing is borrowed from Erving Goffman's *Frame Analysis* (1974) and is rooted in the symbolic interactionist and constructionist principle that meanings do not naturally or automatically attach themselves to the objects, events, or experiences we encounter, but arise, instead, through interpretive processes mediated by culture. Applied to social movements, the concept of framing problematizes the meanings associated with relevant events, activities, places, and actors, suggesting that those meanings are typically contestable and negotiable and thus open to debate and differential interpretation. From this vantage point, mobilizing grievances are seen neither as naturally occurring sentiments nor as arising automatically from specifiable material conditions, but as the result of interactively based interpretation or signifying work. The verb framing conceptualizes this signifying work, which is one of the activities that social movement leaders and participants, as well as their adversaries, do on a regular basis.

The link between framing and social movements was first noted in an experimental study of the conditions under which authority is defined as unjust and challenged (Gamson, Fireman, and Rytina, 1982) and than developed more fully in a 1986 article that offered a more systematic conceptualization and elaboration of "frame alignment processes" (Snow, Rochford, Worden, and Benford, 1986). Since then there has been a rapid proliferation of research on framing and social movements, with much of the work congealing into what is now called the framing perspective on social movements (Benford and Snow 2000; Snow 2004). The analytic appeal and utility of this perspective is based largely on the conjunction of three factors. The first is the relative neglect of the relationship between meaning and mobilization, and the role of interpretative processes in mediating that relationship, by the dominant perspectives on social movements that emerged in the 1970s; the second is the rediscovery of culture and the so-called discursive turn in the social sciences that occurred during the 1980s; and the third is the development of a conceptual architecture or scaffolding which has facilitated more systematic theorization and empirical assessment of framing processes and effects. The four selections in this part elaborate several key aspects of this conceptual architecture and illustrate the analytic relevance of framing in understanding social movement activity in a number of different contexts.

In the first selection, David Snow and Scott Bryd explore the relationship between ideology and framing processes in relation to Islamic terrorist movements. They argue that the monolithic use and application of the concept of ideology to Islamic terrorist movements, as many national leaders have done, is of questionable analytic utility because it not only ignores ideological variation and flexibility among these movements, but also glosses over the ways in which ideas, beliefs, and values – the stuff of ideology – and various on-the-ground social events are strategically linked together via the discursive mechanisms of frame articulation and elaboration and the core framing tasks of diagnostic, prognostic, and motivational framing. It is through these processes that elements of Islamic ideology and events are linked together in ways that have helped to justify and inspire Islamic terrorist movements and their activities.

In the second selection in this section, Mario Diani draws on and links the concepts of master frames and political opportunity structures in his assessment of the electoral success of the Northern League in Italy in comparison to a number of competing groups in the same region in the early 1990s. He finds that different master frames – which are collective action frames that come to function like master algorithms in the sense that they color and constrain the orientations and activities of other movements within particular periods – helped to account for the electoral success, but not independent of the political context and particularly the political opportunity structure. However, his findings go beyond suggesting that political context can constrain framing to arguing that different configurations of political opportunity favor some master frames over others and that this synchronization may affect various aspects of the operation of social movements, such as the use and effectiveness of organizational resources.

The third selection, by Myra Marx Ferree, extends analysis of framing processes by showing how feminist framing in the abortion debates, from 1970–1994, in the U.S. and Germany varies in terms of whether it is culturally or institutionally resonant or radical, and how such differences are affected by different "discursive opportunity structures" in the two countries (see also, Ferree et al. 2002). Aside from informing understanding of cross-national and historical differences in the framing of abortion, this selection makes two

important contributions: it provides a corrective to the presumption that framing activity is generally geared towards cultural resonance, and it suggests that framing processes are likely to be embedded in and thus constrained by discursive opportunity structures.

Merging insights from theorizing and research on framing in the study of social movements and from the sociology of law, the final selection, by Nicholas Pedriana, argues that law is a highly resonant master frame that affected how the women's movement was framed in the 1960s. Specifically, he contends that transformations in the women's movement and women's employment practices were largely attributable to a framing contest involving three frame alignment processes – amplification, extension, and transformation – between competing cultural constructions of gender ("protective" vs. "equal treatment") in the workplace and in society at large. The analysis not only illustrates the concept of legal framing, but suggests that the symbols and categories of law may often function more generally to affect how movements frame their grievances, identities, and objectives.

Together, the four selections invoke and illustrate the analytic utility of a number of key framing concepts – master frames, resonance, and frame alignment processes—as well as the core framing tasks of diagnostic, prognostic, and motivational framing. The readings also show how framing processes and the resultant collective action or master frames are connected to other key concepts or processes – ideology, political opportunity structures, discursive opportunity structures, and law – in ways that both constrain and facilitate framing processes. In doing so, these selections not only highlight the importance of framing process to movement mobilization, but also indicate that a more thoroughgoing and nuanced understanding of movement mobilization nay best be achieved though theoretically integrative analyses.

17.
Ideology, Framing Processes, and Islamic Terrorist Movements

DAVID A. SNOW AND SCOTT C. BYRD

Leaders of Western democracies have tended to homogenize their descriptions of terrorist movements around the world and the motivations of their adherents. British Prime Minister Tony Blair has described the struggle against global terror as a confrontation with "an evil ideology" (BBC 2005). And U.S. President George Bush has declared repeatedly that global terrorism is fueled by a "totalitarian ideology that hates freedom" (CNN 2006a). Furthermore, these monochromatic descriptions have permeated our media reports and have been extended to other conflicts. For example, CNN correspondent John Roberts said, referring to the Israeli-Hezbollah conflict in the summer of 2006, "this is a conflict that breaks with the traditional mold of Middle East wars—not about territory, but ideology." An Israeli Defense Force spokesman, Doron Spielman, stated similarly that "this is part of the same conflict of the U.S. against bin Laden—this is the same war we are up against today. This is the global war on terror." (CNN 2006b).

This homogenizing tendency is not peculiar to the combatants in the current "war on terror," but is commonplace when two or more parties, whatever their form, are embroiled in intense conflict. Not only are one's antagonists or combatants likely to be seen as "perfidious, insolent, sordid, cruel, degenerate, and lacking in compassion" (Shibutani 1973: 226), but differences among them are overlooked as they tend be seen in terms of a common collective identity (Hunt, Benford, and Snow 1994). While this homogenizing tendency may facilitate in-group mobilization, it is simultaneously

counterproductive because it glosses over diversity among one's adversaries, thereby limiting understanding of them and indirectly affecting one's strategies for effectively combating and coping with the threats they pose.

In this article, we focus on one dimension of this homogenizing impulse in relation to the current wave[1] of Islamic terrorist movements: the tendency to view them as being ideologically equivalent and coherent. We proceed by first problematizing descriptively and analytically the ideology(ies) associated with contemporary Islamic terrorist movements, and then seeking to inform understanding of that relationship by drawing on the framing perspective in the study of social movements. The argument we present contains two core threads. The first is that the concept of ideology, as often used and applied in monolithic terms with respect to terrorist movements in particular and social movements more generally, is of questionable analytic utility because its treatment tends not only to ignore ideological variation, but also glosses over the kind of discursive work required to articulate and elaborate the array of possible links between ideas, events, and action. And, as a consequence, an alternative conceptual scheme is required that focuses attention on this discursive work, which, as we will argue, is what the framing perspective provides.

Undergirding this inquiry are two orienting assumptions: the first is that there is no single, generic Islamic terrorist movement but instead a variety of such movements that, taxonomically considered, are similar in some respects and yet different in others; and second, that the corpus of theorizing and research associated with the substantive study of social movements can facilitate analytically our understanding of the character and course of terrorist movements. We mention

Snow, David, A. and Scott C. Byrd. 2007. "Ideology, Framing Processes, and Islamic Terrorist Movements." *Mobilization: An International Journal* 12: 119–136. Reprinted by permission.

these assumptions at the outset because they are not necessarily obvious in light of the occasional reference to the "Islamic movement,"[2] as if it were a unified and coherent enterprise, and to Islam's incomparable, incommensurable character as a religion,[3] which, if it were so, would make it impervious to analysis via extant theoretical perspectives grounded in research on other religions and movements. An additional caveat should be mentioned as well: we make no claim of expertise about any particular Islamic terrorist movement.[4] At the same time, we do claim a general understanding of Islamic movements and terrorist organizations based on examination of a variety of secondary sources (e.g., Jansen 1979; Reich 1990; Juergensmeyer 2000; Kepel 2002; Lewis 2002; Pape 2005; Rashid 2000, 2002; Sterns 2003; Nasr 2006), as well as a measure of theoretical and empirical expertise about the study of social movements in general, and particularly about religious movements and the framing perspective. We draw on this knowledge in exploring the connection among ideology, framing processes, and contemporary Islamic terrorist movements.

This article is organized into four parts. First, we review and problematize the concept of ideology and its application to the study of Islamic terrorist movements. Then, in the next two sections, we explore the framing perspective, as applied to issues of mobilization and collective action frames. Finally, we summarize the arguments, emphasizing their conceptual and theoretical yield. To illustrate particular points, we draw mainly on the work of others on the Iranian revolution of the late 1970s, on the more recent militant Islamic movements and terrorist activity originating within the Middle East and Central Asia, on the post-9/11 Islamic terrorist activities and groups, and on relations among these movements and episodes.

Deconstructing Ideology

One of the themes that surfaces in the literature on social movements and Islamic terrorist movements is the importance of ideology in relation to movement emergence and dynamics. In the study of social movements, ideology is generally invoked as a cover term for the values, beliefs, and goals associated with a movement or a broader, encompassing social entity, and is assumed to provide the rationale for individual and collective action (Garner 1996; Oliver and Johnston 2000; Turner and Killian 1987; Wilson 1973). Thus, scholars suggest that social movements be conceptualized as "ideologically structured action" (Zald 2000). Although a case can be made that there is an ideological dimension to much social movement activity, there are other dimensions that are equally, if not more, important in determining the course and character of social movements. As well, it can be argued, according to some conceptualizations of ideology (e.g., Geertz 1973), that most social action is structured in some way by ideology. If so, then there is little analytic purchase in claiming that social movements can be best understood as ideologically structured action in contrast to social action outside of the context of the social movement arena. An equally serious issue in the social movement literature has been the tendency to treat ideology descriptively rather than analytically, and statically rather than dynamically. Among the various criticisms that can be leveled at this treatment of ideology, two are relevant here: (1) the ideas and bundles of meaning that are supposedly constitutive of ideology are treated as given, as if they are derived automatically from some sacred text, cultural narrative, or traumatic experience; and (2) the use and application of ideology is viewed in an almost mechanistic fashion rather than as a social production that evolves during the course of interactive or dialogic processes among activists, targets, and events in the world.[5]

Not coincidentally, these same questionable tendencies regarding the use and application of ideology are evident in much of the literature on Islamic terrorist movements. Consider the following sampling of commentary from scholars of Islamic movements. In his essay on "the emergence of Islamic political ideologies," Arjomand concludes that "the distinctiveness of the contemporary movements in Islamic history is due to the centrality of *ideology* and to their preoccupation with the Islamic state...." (1989: 122). Although not stated quite as definitively, Salehi, in his essay on radical Islamic insurgency in the Iranian revolution, accents the importance of ideological factors by contending that the development of a strategy that facilitated the 1978–79 national uprising "relied heavily on religious and symbolic means" (1996: 48–49). In Bill's (1984) overview of factors under-girding "resurgent Islam in the Persian Gulf," ideology is acknowledged as being of considerable importance, and especially the ideology of Shi'ism. And in Moaddel's analysis of the Iranian revolution, he contends not only that ideology was the ingredient "required to transform Iran's economic and political problems into a revolutionary crisis," but also that ideology "distinguishes revolution from routine contention for power" (1992). Pretty powerful stuff this ideology!

Turning to the most recent surge in Islamic terrorism, there has been a tendency for researchers similarly to treat it as of one cloth ideologically. For example, Rapoport (1990: 109) traces the emergence of contemporary "Islamic sacred terror" as a means to create a world governed by Sharia or Islamic law. He explores the evolution of *jihad* from a traditional interpretation of "spiritual struggle against one's own evil nature" towards a more fundamentalist struggle designed to defend Islam from outside assaults. But as we will see, not all Islamic movements are driven towards the establishment of a Sharia-governed world. Nor is it reasonable to assume that all adherents of any particular Islamic movement necessarily subscribe to identical ideas and appeals, in spite of occasional scholarly claims to the contrary, as is evident in Hellmich's contention regarding al-Qaeda:

> Bin Laden's rhetoric, with its appeal to powerful imagery embedded in the collective consciousness of the Muslim community, and its juxtaposition of political goals with the teachings of the Quran, inspires followers to commit terrible acts of destruction while being fully convinced that they are fulfilling the ordained will of Allah. (2005:53)

We have no problem with the contention that the values, beliefs, and ideas that are said to be constitutive of ideology figure prominently not just in al-Qaeda but in all Islamic terrorist movements, just as in all social movements. However, we do have a number of questions about the way in which ideology is used that raise doubts about its explanatory utility in accounting for the emergence and operation of religious militants.

First, ideology is either invoked without offering a working conceptualization or, if one is provided, the rationale for its use over alternative conceptualizations is typically glossed over. In either case, it is unclear which of the views on ideology prevail. Is it the more general and neutral conception (Geertz 1973: Seliger 1976; Gouldner 1976)? Or, is it the more critical conception wherein ideology is an instrument of social control, functioning to sustain class structures and relations of domination and in which distortion, mystification, false consciousness, and hegemony flourish (Gramsci 1971; Marx and Engels 1989: Thompson 1984)? Or, is it the view of ideology as an agent of social change (Garner 1996; Mannheim 1985; Zald 2000)? Noting these different conceptualizations is not inconsequential inasmuch as they provide reason to question the analytic utility of a concept that has been viewed historically in such strikingly different ways.

Second, whichever of these general, orienting conceptualizations is used, there is still the problem of reconciling the common view that ideology is a fairly coherent and integrated set of values and beliefs that affects one's orientation not only to politics but to everyday life more generally, which is a feature of all three conceptualizations, with various contradictory strands of research. For example, research shows that in the United States not only do individuals acknowledge a range of values and beliefs that often are contradictory or in conflict, but that these rarely cohere in an integrated manner (Converse 1964; Rokeach 1973; Williams 1970). This point is made quite clearly by research on the "cultural wars" thesis in the U.S., which shows that American political opinions, attitudes, and values do not cluster neatly or tightly together at any one ideological pole (DiMaggio, Evans, and Bryson 1996; Davis and Robinson 1996; Fiorina, Abrams and Pope 2005).

Insofar as values and beliefs constitute salient components of ideology, then such observations suggest that perhaps their presumed integration with respect to any particular ideology should be problematized and thus explored empirically rather than assumed. This tack is also consistent with the frequent observation that movements on different sides of the political spectrum can find sustenance in the same broader cultural ideology, as amply illustrated by movements on "the right" and "the left" in the United States.

Although the above observations come from the U.S, they do raise an important question: Should we expect ideology to function differently—that is, in a more integrative and coherent fashion—in and across Islamic societies? Assuming agreement can be reached as to the key constituent elements of Islamic ideology, should we presume that it is necessarily or inherently more coherent and integrated than other major religious and political ideologies? To say that "advocates of Islamic ideology understand it to be a conception of Islam as a total unified sociopolitical system and a total way of life based on the full unity of doctrine and practice" (Arjomand 1989: 109) is to assert an ideological understanding. But such an assertion does not demonstrate the impact and influence of the ideology. While all Muslim believers may assert that there is only one God and only one Islam, there are different combinations and permutations of how this actually works itself out politically in terms of everyday life both within and across Islamic societies. This ideological variance is due not only to the existence of different Islamic traditions (e.g., Sunni, Shi'a, and Sufi) and different strands or sects within those traditions (e.g., Deobandism, Jadidism, Salafism, and Wahhabism), but also to differences in both the history and current state of the economies, polities, and cultures of the different Islamic countries.[6] Because of these factors and the different ways in which they interact in different countries, it is reasonable, historically and sociologically, to presume that the character and course of Islamic terrorist movements in one part of the world, say in Central Asia, are likely to be different in important ways from Islamic movements in other parts of the world, such as in the Middle East or in Indonesia. And if so, then it follows that the Islamic ideological undercurrent of these movements is sufficiently pliable and elastic as to be amenable to adaptation to differences in sociocultural and political-economic contexts. Thus, as Ahmed Rashid (2002: 121–22) writes in his analysis of militant Islam in Central Asia:

Whereas the Ikhwan-based movements (anchored in the Muslim Brotherhood that surfaced in the 1930s in Egypt) seek to seize state power and then transform each country into an Islamic state, movements such as the Taliban, HT (Hizb ut-Tahrir), and even the IMU (Islamic Movement of Usbekistan) come from the new Deobandi-Wahhabi tradition, which sees the seizure of power only as a way to impose sharia (Islamic legal system and code derived from the Koran and the hadith [sayings] of the Prophet Muhammad) and transform social behavior. Once that is done, they believe, an Islamic state will evolve by itself.

Even among the movements rooted in a blend of the Deobandi and Wahhabi traditions, there can be striking differences, with the IMU described as more violent and inclined to resort to guerrilla and terrorist tactics than Hizb ut-Tahrir, which reportedly "envisages a moment when millions of its supporters will simply rise up and topple the Central Asia governments...by sheer force of numbers" (Rashid 2002: 124).

The point, then, is that even among movements that share a common ideological base, it is difficult to foretell their course and character across time. A further example is provided by recent currents of unrest and change in Iran today.

These days, it is not uncommon to hear Iranians whisper the shah's name with shades of nostalgia, even reverence, "God bless the shah," they will tell a foreigner, glancing about nervously as they tour the preserved magnificence inside Neyavaran Palace in Teheran.... This is not to say that Iranians have forgotten...the brutality of the shah's secret police, his modernizer's insensitivity to Iran's 1,350-year embrace of Islam or the corruption he tolerated.

Rather, it is a measure of how anguished Iranians have become after nearly a generation under "the government of God" and of their desperate yearning for change (Bums 2000: Sec. 4, 1).

According to this observer, the grafting of "the political ideals of democratic liberalism onto the ancient beliefs of Islam" is likely. This will require, of course, a reframing "within Islam of the relationship between state and religion" (Burns 2000: Sec. 4, 1 & 4).[7]

These observations suggest that how we conceptualize ideology might be softened to allow for variance in the scope of its application, in how tightly coupled its constituent beliefs and values are, and in the extent to which it facilitates or constrains challenge. Rather than conceptualize ideology as a fairly pervasive and coherent set of beliefs and values that functions in a programmatic and doctrinaire fashion, we are closer to the mark when we view ideology as a variable phenomenon that ranges on a continuum from a tightly and rigidly connected set of values and beliefs at one end to a loosely coupled set of values and beliefs at the other end, and that functions, in either case, as both a constraint on and a resource for constructing and making sense of the so-called "imaginary." Conceptualizing ideology in this more flexible, elastic, and less programmatic way makes it a more agentic-friendly concept in several ways. First, it provides an empirically and theoretically based counterpoint to approaches that portray individuals as passive, mimetic recipients. Second, it allows, more readily, for the development of emergent sets of ideas and values that function either as innovative amplifications and extensions of existing ideologies or as antidotes to them. And, third, in turn, it calls for an alternative conceptualization and understanding of the process through which these innovative amplifications and extensions, or antidotes, arise.

The framing perspective in the study of social movements, which has evolved in recognition of the importance of these issues, focuses attention on the process of framing in relation to the development of innovative amplifications and extensions of, or antidotes to, existing ideologies or discourses, which, in turn, are conceptualized as collective action frames.[8] We turn now to a brief discussion of these concepts and the enveloping framing perspective, and then elaborate aspects of the perspective that provide, we believe, analytic leverage for securing a better understanding of the ideological dimension of Islamic terrorist movements.

Collective Action Frames and Core Framing Tasks

The framing perspective on collective action and social movements views movements not merely as carriers of existing ideas and meanings, but as signifying agents actively engaged in producing and maintaining meaning for constituents, antagonists, and bystanders (Benford and Snow 2000; Gamson 1992; Johnston and Noakes 2005; Polletta and Ho 2006; Snow and Benford 1988, 1992; Snow, Rochford, Worden, and Benford 1986; Snow 2004, Tarrow 1998). The verb *framing* is used to conceptualize this signifying work, which is one of the activities that social movement leaders and their adherents do on a regular basis. In elaborating the relevance of framing processes to movement participant mobilization, Snow and Benford (1988: 199) argue that variations in success, both within and across movements, depend in part on the degree to which movements attend to problems of consensus and action mobilization through the core framing tasks of diagnostic, prognostic, and motivational framing.[9] The problem of consensus mobilization concerns the generation of ideational and attitudinal support among prospective adherents; the problem of action mobilization concerns the activation of adherents for engagement in the cause (Klandermans 1984). Furthermore, collective action frames may serve an interpretive function by focusing, articulating, and exening meanings to activate adherents, transform bystanders into supporters, exact concessions from targets, and demobilize antagonists (Snow 2004), and the extent to which collective action frames are used in these ways suggest that they have a "strategic imperative" (Westby 2004: 287).

Diagnostic Framing

Diagnostic framing addresses the problem of consensus mobilization by diagnosing some event or aspect of social life or system of government as problematic and in need of repair or change, and attributes blame or responsibility. In the context of social movements, diagnostic frames provide answers to the questions of "What is or went wrong?" and "Who or what is to blame?" in a fashion not dissimilar from Bernard Lewis's book-length essay (2002) on the eclipse of the Islamic Middle East over the last three centuries. In general, the answers to such questions recast features of political or social life that were previously seen as misfortunes or unpleasant but tolerable facts of life as intolerable injustices or abominations that demand transformation. The commentary of Islamic movement leaders and pamphleteers are filled with such diagnostic rhetoric. In one work on Islamic militancy in the modern world, for example, its eternal enemy is said to be "the cosmopolitan free-thinking Westernized liberals, who are heavily represented in the ruling elites" (Jansen 1979: 46). As to what it is about these Westernized elites that makes them reprehensible and the target of hostility, a former minister of education in Pakistan and vice-chancellor of Karachi University claimed that:

> [They] impose systems of education, economy, social institutions and mores to perpetuate the stranglehold that they have established over the entire area of national life. All of this is done in the name of progress, which is identified with Westernization. The Muslim peoples cannot come into their own until they dethrone these elite groups which are the creators of all the misery and have led their nations into a deep psychosis of an inferiority complex that paralyzes their thought and action alike (Qureshi 1978:243–244).

The only hope for those under this stranglehold, he concluded, was "to revive the sense of national identity and uniqueness of Islam."

Such remarks suggest that the ruling class in some Islamic societies is held in disdain not solely or merely because of their superior economic position, but because of what they symbolize—Westernization and its consumerism and moral laxity. That this seemed to be the case in Iran was reflected repeatedly in the rhetoric of not only the Ayatollah Khomeini, whose scathing denunciations of Western culture were widely publicized (see Xaviere 1980, and Nasir 2006), but also in the remarks of others involved in varying degrees in the Iranian revolution. As a post-revolutionary official complained about the Shah's policies:

> [They] made a little shah out of every Iranian. Look at Iran today. The major concern of every Iranian is the pursuit of materialism. Those who do not have a car or a house think of nothing else but cars and houses. Those who have them want bigger cars and houses. Iranian Muslims have forgotten the values of their religion. Modesty, contentment, integrity, kindness, and fairness to others have been replaced by greed. We have to change all of this. This revolution has just begun (Ibrahim 1979: 78).

In light of Osama bin Laden's February 1998 announcement of the creation of a transnational movement called the International Front for Jihad Against Jews and Crusaders, the transnational spread of his al Qaeda movement, and the events of September 11, the contention that the Iranian revolution was the beginning rather than the end of Islamic revolt now appears to be a prophetic statement. As bin Laden declared in his 1998 edict:

> For over seven years the United States has been occupying the lands of Islam in the holiest of places, the Arabian Peninsula, plundering its riches, dictating to its rulers, humiliating its people, terrorizing its neighbors, and turning its bases in the Peninsula into a spearhead through which to fight the neighboring Muslim peoples....Despite the great devastation inflicted on the Iraqi people by the crusader-Zionist alliance, and despite the huge number of people killed, which has exceeded 1 million...despite also of this, the Americans are once again trying to repeat the horrific massacres. (Osama bin Laden 2002; 1998: 1)

Such bellicose diagnostic framings notwithstanding, there is now emerging an alternative, internal, diagnostic framing of the problems confronting the Islamic world. Referring to the attribution component of diagnostic framing as "the blame game," Lewis (2002: 159) observes that while it "continues, and shows little sign of abating...for growing numbers of Middle Easterners it is giving way to a more self-critical approach." This self-critical, inward-looking approach has not displaced the virulent, anti-Western diagnostic framing promulgated by some militant Islamic movement leaders, such as the late Ayatollah Khomeini and Osama bin Laden, and parroted in the remarks of some rank-and-file Middle Eastern Muslims, such as those of a 45-year-old Palestinian drywall installer issued on September 11, 2002: "What happened to America was righteous repayment for America's arrogance in the world. How could I feel badly? Inasmuch as Osama bin Laden did what he did to fight American injustice, then he is a hero" (Nickerson 2002: 5). Yet, the diagnostic frames of all contemporary Islamic terrorist movements are not focused on the U.S.

or the West as the primary source of their grievances. Instead, a number of them are nationalistically focused, as has been the case with the major Palestinian movements and the Islamic Movement of Uzbekistan. As one of the founders and leaders of the IMU explained:

> The goals of IMU activities are firstly fighting against oppression within our country, against bribery, against the inequities and also the freeing of our Muslim brothers from prison.... Who will avenge those Muslims who have died in the prisons of the regime? Of course we will. We consider it our obligation to avenge them.... We do not repent our declaration of jihad against the Uzbek government. (quoted in Rashid 2002:148)

This nationalist thrust is also evident in the case of Hezbollah, although it is often glossed over by adversaries who tend to see it in the same light as al Qaeda, as evidenced by the assertion of an IDF spokesman that the 33-day conflict between Israeli and Hezbollah in 2006 is the same as the U.S. struggle against al Qaeda. Such a reading of Hezbollah is perhaps understandable in light of its origins in the mid-1980s as a Shi'a resistance movement supported by Syria and Iran and rooted ideologically in the preaching of the late Ayatollah Khomeini (Nasir 2006).[10] Indeed, Hezbollah's objectives seem to be derived from the ideological rhetoric associated with the Iranian Revolution:

> We are an *umma* linked to the Muslims of the whole world by the solid doctrinal and religious connection of Islam, whose message God wanted to be fulfilled by the Seal of the Prophets, i.e., Muhammad. This is why whatever touches or strikes the Muslims in Afghanistan, Iraq, the Philippines and elsewhere reverberates throughout the whole Muslim *umma* of which we are an integral part.... We see in Israel the vanguard of the United States in our Islamic world. It is the hated enemy that must be fought until the hated ones get what they deserve. (Hezbollah Program 1985: 1)

Yet, Hezbollah has become more nationalist in orientation over the last decade by seeking a more prominent role in Lebanon's government, and therefore conventional politics; something which al Qaeda's leadership has no aspirations to emulate.

Hezbollah also has been "cultivating good relations with Palestinian resistance groups, including Hamas" (Wright 2006: 57; Nasir 2006) to enhance the prospect of liberating itself from the claimed regional injustices perpetuated by Israel with the support of the U.S. (Hezbollah Program 1985). Interestingly, this alliance is of concern not only for Israel and the U.S., but also for the Sunni aligned al Qaeda, whose diagnostic appeals seek to bring Palestinian struggles under the umbrella of their global network. This can be seen in the diagnostic video statement by Ayman al-Zawahiri [al Qaeda's second in command] in the summer of 2006 addressing the Hezbollah-Israeli conflict and the Gaza strip:

> The whole world is an open field for us. As they attack us everywhere, we will attack them everywhere. As their armies got together to wage war on us, our nation will get together to fight them.... The shells and missiles that tear apart the bodies of Muslims in Gaza and Lebanon are not purely Israeli. Rather, they come from and are financed by all countries of the Crusader alliance. Thus, all those who took part in the crime should pay the price. We cannot just stand idly by in humiliation while we see all these shells fall on our brothers in Gaza and Lebanon (BBC 2006: 1).

Here we see that al-Zawahiri is not only trying to win the hearts and minds of Palestinian organizations and militants, but is also taking up common cause with Hezbollah, though he casts a much wider net by blaming the "crusader alliance."

While there is certainly overlap between the ideological framings of al Qaeda and Hezbollah, akin to the overlapping circles of a Venn diagram, they are not identical or isomorphic ideologically. As well, caution needs to be exercised so as not to presume there is ideological coherence within these various movements if not between them. Considering al Qaeda, a counterterrorism strategist at the U.S. State Department has noted that while al Qaeda's leadership may paint its media edicts with wide strokes in terms of who is to blame, "It's important to realize that there are numerous competing points of view within the movement [al Qaeda]" (Wright 2006: 53). This strategist explains that although "Al Qaeda propagates a 'single narrative' aimed at influencing the West…each faction within the jihadi movement has its own version of this narrative, often sharply different from the message put forward by bin Laden or al-Zawahiri" (2006: 59). Such tensions, or frames disputes (Benford 1993), have been especially apparent in Iraq, for example between Shi'a and Sunni groups and between al-Zarqawi, al Queda's now-deceased Iraqi leader, and its leadership elsewhere. But the foregoing suffices to illustrate varying degrees of ideological heterogeneity between and within Islamic militant and terrorist movements, and thus suggests that ideology is much more pliable and elastic than often presumed. Ideological tensions and framing disputes notwithstanding, clarification of the character of some problem or issue and who or what is culpable is a necessary condition for targeted collective action. But diagnostic framing alone does not automatically translate into a solution or plan of attack; also important is prognostic framing, the second core framing task.

Prognostic Framing

Prognostic framing primarily addresses the previously mentioned problem of action mobilization by stipulating specific remedies or solutions and the general means or tactics for achieving these objectives. In essence, prognostic framing address the Leninesque question of "What is to be done?" The answer for bin Laden and presumably his al Qaeda followers is unequivocal and now well known:

> We—with God's help—call on every Muslim…to kill the Americans and plunder their money wherever and whenever they find it. We also call on Muslim *ulema,* leaders, youths, and soldiers to launch the raid on Satan's U.S. troops and the devil's supporters allying with them, and to displace those who are behind them so that they may learn a lesson (Osama bin Laden 2002).

Although bin Laden's prognostic framing appears to flow almost seamlessly from his mentioned diagnostic framing of the problems confronting Muslim peoples, the answer to Lenin's question probably rarely flows whole-cloth in a clear and incontestable manner from some extant ideology or diagnostic framing. Certainly the history of the fractious and rancorous debates associated with Lenin's question suggests that prognostic frames do not necessarily spring naturally or clearly from preceding diagnostics framings. Several analyses of the Iranian revolution suggest that the issue of prognostic framing was a contestable and contentious one in this case as well. Noting, whether rightly or wrongly, that the Iranian masses "were already quite prepared for an uprising," Salehi insinuates that the problem of prognostic framing was a serious one.

> The question one would hear in private circles was *how* was it to happen. Political groups were also deeply concerned with the question of strategy. Their underground documents reflect how much they were involved in discussing this issue. No one expected a simple answer. They had learned by experience that the system was quite alert and was well prepared to crush any opposition movement (1996:49, emphasis in original).

The problem of strategy or "what to do" continued to loom, even after the shah's regime was overthrown. Now, however, the problem was not with overthrowing the regime but with consolidating control and moving forward to establish a viable post-revolutionary order. As Moaddel has observed, "when concrete plans emerged for building the post-revolutionary 'Islamic' order," disputes arose among three rival groups: "liberal Muslims, headed by Mehdi Bazargan," who called for "a form of parliamentary democracy within the existing capitalist relationship guided by the moral values of Islam"; "the ulama followers of Ayatollah Khomeini," who championed "the governance of Islamic jurisprudence (*velayat-i faqih*)"; and "the Mojahedin, radical Islamic political organization" that "advanced a sort of Islamic socialism" (Moaddel 1992:368).

Similarly, the invasion of Iraq posed a prognostic dilemma for al Qaeda, as the population of Iraq is majority Shi'a which the Sunni considers heretics (Wright 2006). In Iraq Sunni and Shi'a militants have fought not only to expel the coalition troops but also each other; a reality that cannot be separated from larger ideological rifts existing between the two sects as they have vied for control of the country's government and future. In his final video recorded statement to his followers, Mosaab al-Zarqawi, the Jordanian-born self-ascribed leader of al Qaeda in Iraq, declares that "the Muslims will have no victory or superiority over the aggressive infidels such as the Jews and the Christians until there is a total annihilation of those under them such as the apostate agents headed by the *rafidhah*" (derogatory term meaning Twelfth Imamist Shi'a who follow the Ja'fari creed) (Quoted in Kazimi 2006: 1). Nibras Kazimi writing on the anti-Shi'a brand of Sunni terrorism promoted by Masub al-Zarqawi in Iraq asserts that:

> Zarqawi is mapping out the next phase of *jihad* as he sees it: in order to strike at Islam's perceived enemies such as the United States of America, Europe and Israel, the jihadists must also do battle with the Shi'a who are serving as agents of the forces that are hostile to the faith. In a doctrinal sense, Zarqawi asserts early on that "the *rawafidh* is a religion wholly different from the Islam…and that [*rawafidh*] has no other purpose than to destroy Islam." According to Zarqawi, the Shi'a perpetrate this perceived conspiracy by casting doubts upon the tenets of Islam, and through sowing sedition against Muslim rulers (Kazami 2006: 2).

There is no doubt that the anti-Shi'a rhetoric and extreme tactics of al-Zarqawi posed difficulties for the al Qaeda leadership that sought to unite the Muslim world against Western influence and exploitation. Hoping to steer al Zarqawi closer to al Qaeda's long-term religious and political objectives, al-Zawahiri sent him a letter in the summer of 2005 containing a prognostic laundry list for Iraq:

> The first stage: Expel the Americans from Iraq. The second stage: Establish an Islamic authority or emirate, then develop it and support it until it achieves the level of caliphate. The third stage: Extend the jihad wave to the secular countries neighboring Iraq. The fourth stage: It may coincide with what came before—the clash with Israel, because Israel was established only to challenge any new Islamic entity (quoted in Wright 2006).

Ultimately, al-Zarqawi did not heed the advice given by al Qaeda's ideological leader to moderate his tactics, and partly as a consequence Iraq descended into sectarian barbarism. Partly because of this, the movement's leaders and strategists began paying closer attention to the way its message

was communicated to the Islamic world, especially through the media, as they believed the "barbaric" and sensational attacks in Iraq were undermining al Qaeda's ability to promulgate a rational plan for justifiable action.

What such observations underscore is that reference to or use of "Islamic ideology" as a critical variable in an explanatory account of the Iranian revolution, Palestinian-Israeli conflict, and recent terrorist activity in Iraq and elsewhere may well gloss over more than it illuminates. Even if the generation of a coherent and compelling diagnosis is achieved in a relatively consensual manner—which does not appear to have been the case in the preceding examples—there is no guarantee that the business of prognostic framing will occur in a harmonious or noncontentious fashion. More likely, there will be competing arguments as to what should be done and how, which is reflected in recent debates not only about the meaning of "jihad," but about its appropriate targets as well.

Motivational Framing

However the diagnostic and prognostic framing tasks are attended to for any particular movement, the problem of action mobilization is not completely solved, as the activation or mobilization of ideological adherents—that is, those who subscribe to the diagnostic and prognostic framings—remains. Metaphorically, constituents have to be moved from the balcony to the barricades. This takes us to what has been conceptualized as motivational framing, which involves "the elaboration of a call to arms or rationale for action that goes beyond the diagnosis and prognosis" (Snow and Benford 1988: 202). More concretely, motivational framing entails the construction of "vocabularies of motive" (Mills 1940) that provide prods to action by, among other things, overcoming both the fear of risks often associated with collective action and Olson's (1965) vaunted "free-rider" problem (e.g., why work for a goal that is a "public good" in the sense of being an indivisible and nonexcludable benefit?).

Salehi's analysis of the Iranian revolution shows the importance of motivational framing. He contends that "mere dissatisfaction with the regime was not sufficient to inspire people to want to risk their lives. A strong commitment was essential to downplay any attachment to fear that had ordinarily prevented people from joining the movement" (1996: 50). How was this fear neutralized such that "an army of well-disciplined protesters came into existence"? According to Salehi, among others, the answer resided in large part in the motivational framing by clerical leaders. As he notes, they "made the protest a religious obligation by subjecting the political situation to religious definitions and interpretations" such that the struggle was portrayed as "the equivalent of a holy war" and death as constitutive of "martyrdom" (Salehi 1996: 51).

In a similar vein, bin Laden appealed to religious duty and obligation in his 1998 fatwa, declaring that the "the ruling to kill Americans and their allies . . . is an *individual duty for every Muslim* who can do it in any country in which it is possible to do it." (Osama bin Laden 1998, emphasis added). Although such a calling is likely to seem especially sinister or evil to the putative targets, appeals to religious or moral duty as the basis for perpetrating violence is fairly commonplace across movements anchored in different religions.[11]

But appeals to religious or moral duty are not always sufficient to impel adherents to engage in violence for the sake of the cause. The case of Palestinian suicide bombers is instructive. Although reference is made to moral obligation, greater weight appears to be placed on the special rewards and status enhancement that awaits the suicide bomber or "martyr," as he or she is called in the Islamic world, because suicide is generally understood as being contrary to the teachings of Muhammad. Among the special rewards awaiting the martyr, much is made of the "72 black-eyed virgins." But "more basic," according to one investigative report on suicide bombers, "is the omnibus promise of divine favor rewarding them for righteous deeds" (Lelyveld 2001: 54). As noted by a member of Hamas[12] involved in the recruitment and training of martyrs:

> We focus attention on paradise, on being in the presence of Allah, on meeting the Prophet Muhammad, on interceding for his loved ones so that they, too, can be saved from the agonies of hell, on the houris, and on fighting the Israeli

occupation and removing it from the Islamic trust that is Palestine (Hassan 2001: 40).

In addition to the promise of divine rewards that accompany ascent to paradise, there are various earthly enticements, such as the enhancement, indeed elevated reconstitution, of the martyr's former identity: their pictures are plastered on public walls, their deaths announced in the press and media as weddings rather than as obituaries; their families have received visits from political officials and sometimes even given money, and they have been praised in mosques and at rallies (Lelyveld 2001; Wilkinson 2002). Thus, not only are the incentives for martyrdom multifaceted, but they are not merely theologically or ideologically based.

In suggesting and illustrating the relevance of the three core framing tasks of diagnostic, prognostic, and motivational framing to understanding Islamic terrorist movements, primarily in the Middle East and Central Asia, we argue that reference to a general conceptualization of ideology glosses over these core framing functions, thereby making the problems of consensus and action mobilization appear less complicated than is often, and probably typically, the case. As well, whether one uses the language of movement ideology or collective action frames, we suggest that these three core framing tasks provide an analytic handle for comparing and contrasting movements in terms of ideational factors and meaning—constructionist processes relevant to their life histories.

Now let us be more concrete about this contention. Although the foregoing discussion presents a rather static conception of the three components of a collective action frame, they can be quite variable and dynamic. Specifically, they can vary in at least four ways. First, the relevance and salience of each component may vary by the type of movement or the conditions underlying the movement, such that diagnostic framing may not be as important for movements rooted in "moral shocks" (Jasper 1997) or "quotidian disruptions" (Snow et al 1998), but that prognostic framing may still be quite important. Second, their relevance or salience may vary at different critical junctures in a movement's career, depending on the specific tasks at hand, such as mobilizing participants for engagement in high-risk activity, or on the kinds of opposition encountered or support secured. Third, there may be variance in terms of the substantive development of each component, such that some diagnostic and prognostic frames are more focused and coherent, and thus articulate, than others. And finally, each of these components may vary in their resonance with or relevance to their intended targets or audience.[13]

Thus, we might expect to find that differences in the spread and mobilization efficacy of a number of movements within the same category, such as Islamic movements, may be due in part to variation in one or more of the above possibilities. To date, such fine-tuned comparative analysis of the ideological realm across movements has rarely been conducted. As a consequence, we are left with highly descriptive accounts of movement ideologies and questionable claims about their relative influence vis-à-vis other explanatory schemes, such as resource mobilization and political opportunity. Our argument is that the analysis of mobilizing ideas and meanings in terms of the core framing tasks elaborated above and the ways in which they can vary should provide increased analytic purchase with respect to our understanding of the role ideational factors and meanings play in relation to the course and character of both specific genres of movements and of movements in general.

Frame Articulation and Elaboration

In elaborating and illustrating the core framing tasks and suggesting their analytic utility, we have said nothing about their derivation and their relation to the broader cultural ideologies to which they are connected in varying degrees. The question is thus: From whence or where do collective action frames come?

The traditional answer is that they are given by or pulled whole cloth from a broader cultural ideology, much as if a piece of clothing is plucked from the closet depending on the weather forecast. Such is not the case, however, as there is mounting evidence that collective action frames (or movement-specific ideologies) are not identical to, or isomorphic with, existing ideologies, but are novel blends of the old and the new, the past and the present. As Tarrow observes:

The lessons of the civil rights movement is that the symbols of revolt are not drawn like musty costumes from a cultural closet and arrayed before the public. Nor are new meanings unrolled out of whole cloth. The costumes of revolt are woven from a blend of inherited and invented fibers into collective action frames in confrontation with opponents and elites (1998: 118).

The implication here is that extant ideologies constitute cultural resources from which collective frames are partly derived, but not in a determinative fashion. Rather, cultural or religious ideologies function much like established vineyards from which different varietals can be innovatively grafted together to generate a new yield. To understand how this metaphorical blending, weaving, and grafting process works with respect to the generation of collective action frames, we turn to a consideration of two highly agentic, interactive, discursive processes: frame articulation and elaboration. *Frame articulation* involves the connection and alignment of events, experience, and strands of moral codes so that they hang together in a relatively unified and compelling way. Slices of observed and experienced "reality" and moral directives or callings are assembled, collated and packaged. What gives the resultant collective action frame or one of its components their novelty is not so much the originality or newness of its ideational elements, but the manner in which they are spliced together and articulated, such that a new angle of vision, interpretation, or understanding is provided. *Frame elaboration,* on the other hand, involves accenting and highlighting some events, issues, or beliefs as being more important than others. These punctuated or accented elements may function in the service of the articulation process by providing a conceptual handle or peg for linking together various events and issues. In turn, these elaborated elements may function much like synecdoches, bringing into sharp relief and symbolizing the larger frame or movement of which it is a part, as was arguably the case with such movement slogans as "Liberté, Fraternité, and Egalité" in the case of the French Revolution, "Power to the People" in the case of the student, antiwar movement of the 1960s and 1970s, "We Shall Overcome" in the case of the civil rights movement, and "Death to the Shah" in the Iranian revolution.

The Iranian revolution and the role played by the Ayatollah Khomeini, his clerical followers, and the structure of their organizational base not only illuminate the above processes and questions, but also that these processes and questions can help to gain analytic leverage in thinking about differences in Islamic movements, both within and across different countries. Consider, for example, the relationship between so-called Islamic ideology and the Iranian revolution. Although some assessments of that association foster the impression that the ideological basis for the Islamic revolution issued full-cloth from Shi'ite ideology, there also are those who have argued that Khomeini's framings did not flow directly from Shi'ite ideology but were the result of his and his core followers' innovative constructions. For instance, Rose (1983) and Moaddel (1992: 366) argue, pointing to disagreement among numerous grand ayatollahs, that "there was no ideological precedent to justify ulama direct rule in society." And, as a consequence, Moaddel contends that the ideology associated with the Iranian revolution "was not simply a preexisting ideology resting on Shi'ite political theory or ulama institutional development, ready to be used by discontented groups and classes against the Shah" (1992: 375). This suggests the importance of frame articulation and elaboration processes.

Both processes are also relevant to understanding suicide bombings in Palestine, Iraq and presumably elsewhere. Although the knee-jerk reaction in some circles is to view such acts as rooted in a kind of madness based on a blend of deep frustration and ideological single-mindedness, there is little evidence that suicide bombers are deranged or psychologically damaged individuals who readily assume the identity of a suicide bomber once a certain threshold of personal and ideological rage is reached. Instead, available accounts and analyses of suicide bombing, especially in Palestine, indicate that neither psychological nor ideological explanations are very useful in understanding these bombings (Pape 2005). This is because, as one Middle Eastern academic observer emphasized, "it is not a phenomenon of individual psychology [but] an organizational phenomenon" (quoted in Lelyveld 2001: 52). Unpacked, this suggests that what we need to know, among other things, is not so much the psychology of why bombers do it but how they are recruited and trained. To be sure, "the bombers themselves (are) weapons." However, "they were [and are] available to skillful and compelling recruiters who...knew [and still know] how to weave interpretations of history, religion and present injustice, personal or national, into a tactical imperative" (Lelyveld 2001: 52). It is this weaving, this blending, this knitting or stitching together of strands of history, religious beliefs or ideology, conceptions of injustice, and selected events by movement and other sponsoring organizations that is the essence of the processes of frame articulation and elaboration.

A concrete example of these interpretative processes at work is found in the transformation of suicide bombing into an act of martyrdom. As noted earlier, suicide is generally understood as being contrary to the teachings of Muhammad, and thus antithetical to the tenets of Islam, unless conducted under special circumstances, which themselves are open to interpretative debate. Thus, in order to avoid the negative implications and questions associated with suicide, suicide bombers are referred to as *shaheed,* or martyrs, and their deaths may be celebrated as weddings rather than as funerals, as in the announcement in the Palestinian press of "The Wedding of Martyr Ali Khadr Al-Yassini to Black-Eyed in Eternal Paradise" (Lelyveld, 2001: 51). But the interpretative work does not stop here. Some observers suggest that a cult of martyrdom has evolved that has, as its focus, the glorification of the martyr (Wilkinson 2002: All), as illustrated by the distribution of "copies of the martyr's audiocassette or video to the media and to local organizations as a record of their success and encouragement to other young men" and by naming children "for *shaheed batal*—martyr heros" (Hassan 2001: 441, 36). Considered together these various observations suggest that suicide bombers are developed and nurtured through the interaction of various social processes, including frame articulation and elaboration.

Orchestrating the recruitment and development of suicide bombers, including much of the interpretive work, are the efforts of various local social movement organizations, such as Hamas and Islamic Jihad in Palestine. Although prospective martyrs are generally volunteers, there is no guarantee that all volunteers will end up as martyrs. This is because their reasons or motives have to be "acceptable to Allah" and the volunteers have to undergo training or preparation for the special moment. According to a planner-trainer for the Islamic Jihad, the motives of a potential martyr are examined closely:

> We ask this young man, and we ask ourselves, why he wishes so badly to become a human bomb. What are his real motives? *Our questions are aimed at clarifying* first and foremost for the boy himself *his real reasons and the strength of his commitment.* Even if he is a long-term member of our group and has always wanted to become a martyr, he needs to be very clear that in such an operation there is no drawing back. Preparation bolsters his conviction, which supports his certitude. It removes fear (Quoted in Hassan 2001: 40, emphasis added).

Even here, in the initial meeting, frame articulation and elaboration are at work. And once the individual is accepted, this interpretive, shaping, preparatory work is continued in the context of a martyrdom cell, which tends to be "tightly compartmentalized and secret" and generally "consists of a leader and two or three young men" (Hassan 2001: 41). Herein the prospective martyr assumes the identity of *al shaheed al hayy,* "the living martyr" or "he who is waiting for martyrdom" (Hasan 2001: 41).

Taken together, the foregoing observations indicate that becoming a suicide bomber, at least in Palestine, is largely the result of an organizationally embedded process in which the articulation and elaboration of strips of history, biographical experience, selected segments of the Koran, group-specific beliefs, and various contemporary events are woven together in a fashion that ultimately provides a compelling rationale for martyrdom. A case can be made that both religious and movement-specific ideology come into play, but not in a determinative or mechanistic way. Instead, broader Islamic beliefs and more group-specific ones are drawn on and blended with other relevant factors. Thus, to understand suicide bombing, as well as other aspects of the course and character of Islamic terrorist movements, one has to investigate, among other things, the processes of frame articulation and elaboration as organizationally embedded activities.

Conclusion

In this article we attempt to inform understanding of contemporary Islamic terrorist movements by drawing on work on ideology and framing processes within the context of social movements. We examine the ideological dimension of selected terrorist movements in the Middle East and Central Asia by focusing on framing processes as the key discursive mechanism through which ideas, beliefs, and values—the stuff of ideology—and various social events are strategically linked together in a fashion that facilitates the mobilization or support of targeted constituents and even bystanders. This strategic framing provides the ideational basis for not only becoming a jihadi militant, but also provides the motivation to commit sensational acts of violence, such as suicide bombings, and to be a vehicle for carrying and delivering the message to others. In this sense, al Qaeda "inspired" events such as the London train bombings and Madrid train attacks provide interesting cases for further exploration and application of this process. Perhaps the success of al Qaeda on the global scale may be partly attributable to the ability of its leaders to adapt the diagnostic and prognostic components of its master frame to local contexts.

We argue that the use of the concept of ideology is often encumbered by two misguided tendencies: the first is to view ideology in a homogenized, monochromatic manner; the second is to conceptualize it as a tightly coupled, inelastic set of values, beliefs, and ideas. Both of these tendencies cloud our understanding of social movements in general and terrorist movements in particular. This is not because ideology is irrelevant, but because it is seldom automatically clear which aspects or strands of an ideology best apply to and inform the flow of events and various categories of actors or political geographies that might be relevant to any particular movement in a manner that attends to the problems of mobilization or, more concretely, the challenges of diagnostic, prognostic, and motivational framing. If the link between the tenets of any particular ideology and events in the world were as direct and self-evident as often assumed, then there would be less diversity among Islamic terrorist movements, fewer internal debates among movement participants, and more congruency among national organizations such as Hamas and Hezbollah compared with global organizations like al Qaeda, which also is not immune from internal framing disputes.

In sum, the basic problem with the conventional use of ideology as a kind of explanatory variable is that it tends to be reified and treated as a given rather than as a topic for analysis, and thus glosses over the discursive ideological work required to articulate and elaborate the array of possible links between ideas, events, and action. In this article, we problematize ideology accordingly, treating it and its link to events and actions associated with Islamic terrorist movements, as topics for analysis, and show the utility of the framing perspective in unpacking and illuminating these links by focusing on various core framing tasks and the processes of frame articulation and elaboration. It is through these processes that ideas, beliefs, and events are connected in ways that has helped to justify and inspire terrorist movements and their activities.

NOTES

This is an extensively updated and revised version of a paper initially presented at a New York University conference on Islam and Social Movements in 2000. We would like to thank Mayer Zald and Al Bergesen for their helpful comments.

1. For a discussion of the historical waves of terrorism see Bergesen and Lizardo (2004).

2. See, for example, a three-part series titled "The Spread of the Islamic Movement" in the *Austin American-Statesman* (March 1, 8, and 15, 1987).

3. See, for example, the statement of the leader of the Iraqi Muslim Brothers, as quoted in Arjomand (1989: 111).

4. Although the senior author has coauthored a published paper on "cultural imperialism, social movements, and the Islamic revival" (Snow and Marshall 1984), we would not use this publication as the basis for claiming expertise on Islamic movements.

5. There are a few exceptions to this mechanistic view. See, for example, Fine and Sandstrom (1993), who take an interactionist approach, and Steinberg (1993, 1994), who approaches ideology from a dialogic perspective.

6. For a rich and detailed account of ideological variation in the Islamic world, see Moaddel's (2005) sociological and historical analysis of Islamic modernism, nationalism, and fundamentalism.

7. For further illustration of not only the yearning for change in Iran but actual currents of change, see Murphy's account of how "disaffected young Iranians are reshaping the country with a force as irresistible as their parent's revolution" (2002: 42).

8. Collective action frames refer to action-oriented sets of beliefs and meanings that call forth and legitimate social movement activities and campaigns. This conceptualization derives from the work of Gamson (1992), Snow and Benford (1988, 1992) and Tarrow (1998).

9. These three framing tasks are derived from Wilson's (1973) decomposition of ideology into three parallel functions: diagnosis, prognosis, and motivation. The value-added contribution of considering these functions from a framing perspective is that it focuses attention on how their ongoing construction and elaboration, and on how the diagnostic, prognostic, and motivational components of frames can very significantly both within and across movements.

10. There is much consternation throughout the global community as to whether or not Hezbollah should be considered a terrorist organization. It is regarded as a resistance movement throughout the Arab world. The United States, Israel, Netherlands, Australia, U.K., and Canada consider Hezbollah wholly or partly a terrorist organization. The United Nations Security Council resolutions call for armed militia groups like Hezbollah to disarm. The EU has yet to classify them as a terrorist group.

11. A recent example in the U.S. are the shootings and bombings associated with the militant wing of the antiabortion movement. For a discussion of the global rise of religious violence, see Juergensmeyer (2000).

12. Hamas is a militant Palestinian movement born in the late 1980s during the first intifada. It seeks to displace Israel from the land it regards as Palestine's, and it is a major sponsor of suicide bombing, routinely claiming responsibility for a significant number of such bombings.

13. For a discussion of the factors hypothesized to account for variation in the resonance of proffered framings, see Benford and Snow (2000) and Snow and Benford (1988: 207–11).

18.

Linking Mobilization Frames and Political Opportunities: Insights from Regional Populism in Italy

MARIO DIANI

The regionalist parties that form the Northern League[1] have played a major role in recent Italian politics. Their impressive electoral growth between 1990 and 1993 has undermined support for traditional parties, including oppositional parties, and has paved the way for the advent of Mr. Berlusconi's party, Forza Italia. In this paper I do not discuss the events that have followed the general election of March 1994. In particular, I ignore both the League's troubled relationship with Forza Italia and Alleanza Nazionale-MSI, which resulted in the collapse of the right-wing government led by Mr. Berlusconi in December 1994, and its recent shift toward explicit secessionist goals, which led to the proclamation of an "Independence Declaration" in September 1995. Instead I focus on the process that in the early 1990s led to the success of a new political organization and placed a whole polity in jeopardy despite powerful opposition from established political actors.

Italian leagues present an interesting case study for students of collective action for several reasons. First, their growth has not been an isolated event. Rather, they have been one of the most successful examples of a broader trend toward the promarket and antipolitical orientations that have challenged social-democratic arrangements in western political systems since the late 1970s. Moreover, although it is debatable whether the leagues should be regarded as right-wing phenomena (Betz 1993; Corbetta 1993; Mannheimer and Sani 1994; Poche 1994), they are certainly distant from the "new

Diani, Mario. 1996. "Linking Mobilization Frames and Political Opportunities: Insights from Regional Populism in Italy." *American Sociological Review* 61: 1053–1069. Reprinted by permission of American Sociological Association.

social movements" that have inspired most recent theorizing in the field (Dalton and Kuechler 1990; Morris and Mueller 1992). A proper understanding of the leagues requires (and at the same time stimulates) a finer tuning of interpretations and concepts that have been elaborated largely by reference to other empirical objects.[2]

The success of the leagues challenges current theoretical approaches to collective action. The leagues could not rely on large organizational resources, especially in comparison with established political parties. Similarly, most of their activists had no significant political experience. Also, although opinion-makers have often attributed the success of the leagues to their leaders' communication skills, those leaders had no direct control of mass media and hardly any familiarity with advertising technologies. Finally, success came in spite of a political context that, according to current paradigms, could not be viewed as particularly favorable. These inconsistencies prompt analysts to reconsider the relationship between organizational resources, symbolic production, and political opportunities in collective action theory. I integrate these different layers of analysis by addressing the following question: Under which structural (particularly, political) conditions will some mobilizing messages by "challengers" (Tilly 1978) be more effective than others?[3]

First, I propose a typology of opportunity structures based on a reformulation of Sidney Tarrow's (1994) definition. I relate each type to a specific dominant representation of the political environment, which, following Snow and Benford (1988), I call the "master frame." I argue that one can expect mobilization messages to be more or less successful in different political settings, depending on their congruence with the master frames dominant in a given political phase. As an example, I illustrate how the leagues' "regional populism" has managed to represent within a single frame certain processes and social changes that in principle also could have been represented in other, sometimes very different, ways. Why regional populism has succeeded where other competing frames have failed is explained by the congruence between the leagues' message and the master frame that characterized the political opportunity structure of the early 1990s in Italy. Next, I show how different degrees of consistency between the opportunity structure and actors' frames can render organizational resources more or less valuable and effective, and how in particular this situation created greater opportunities for the leagues than for their competitors. Finally, I provide some examples showing how this framework contributes to the comparison of mobilization dynamics across time.

Throughout this paper I draw on the substantial secondary evidence that has been gathered to date about the Northern League. This includes survey data about voters (Mannheimer et al. 1991; Corbetta 1993; Cartocci 1994; Mannheimer and Sani 1994), activists (Segatti 1992), or both (Diamanti 1992, 1993); content analyses of political documents (Allievi 1992); electoral posters (Todesco 1992); excerpts from journalistic surveys (Pajetta 1994); and accounts by leaders (Bossi and Vimercati 1992).

Accounting for Challengers' Successes: Relating Frames to Political Opportunities

To date, the determinants of successful collective action have followed two major lines of investigation. One has highlighted, albeit in different ways, the role of challengers in converting grievances and issues into actual mobilization. Resource mobilization theorists (Zald and McCarthy 1987; Gamson 1990) have treated the success of social movement organizations mainly as the product of skillful political entrepreneurs acting on the basis of a rationality paradigm. From the second perspective, advocates of constructionist approaches to collective action have identified the sources of successful mobilization in the actors' capacities to mount "symbolic challenges" to dominant definitions of reality by reshaping available symbols and

creating new systems of meaning (Melucci 1989; Eyerman and Jamison 1991; Johnston 1991; Benford and Hunt 1992). In particular, Snow and associates have pointed out that mobilization attempts are successful if leaders manage to carry on "frame alignment" processes: "…the linkage of individual and SMO interpretive orientations, such that some set of individual interests, values, and beliefs and SMO activities, goals, and ideology are congruent and complementary" (Snow et al. 1986: 464).

Although several theoretical disagreements separate resource mobilization from constructionist approaches, these approaches share a critique of structural determinism and an emphasis on the challengers' creative role.[4] In contrast, recent structural approaches have explained successful mobilization in the light of processes that are largely beyond actors' direct control. Some observers have pointed out how mobilization is affected by variables such as differential access to status and power, structural changes in the labor force, and urban renewal (Feagin and Capek 1991; Piven and Cloward 1992). Others have related the spread of collective action and protest to the possibilities created by the political system. In this connection, the notion of "political opportunity structure" has gained increasing popularity (Eisinger 1973; Tilly 1978). This notion has been defined in terms of those "dimensions of the political environment that provide incentives for people to undertake collective action by affecting their expectations for success or failure" (Tarrow 1994:85). According to Tarrow, these dimensions are the stability of political alignments, the formal channels of access to the political system, the availability of allies within the polity, and intra-elite conflict.

Recently, many scholars have related symbolic production to political conditions more explicitly. Snow and Benford (1992) have focused on the link between framing activity and protest cycles, arguing that success will be easier for those movements whose frames are most consistent with the "master frame" that shapes the whole protest cycle. Gamson and Meyer (1996) have shown that the political opportunity structure itself is the outcome of negotiations about meaning between different actors, often within the same movement or even the same movement organization. Taking a different point of departure, Tarrow (1994) explicitly has incorporated the role of symbolic production into his theory of the political opportunity structure. Although the latter, in the last analysis, remains the key explanatory variable in his model, challengers, by careful use of rhetorical devices, may take advantage of changes in the political context to increase their opportunities to act.[5]

These contributions have substantially improved our understanding of mobilization dynamics, but they also have left some questions unresolved. Resource mobilization approaches have been criticized for failing to identify the structural inequalities underlying differential access to mobilization resources (Piven and Cloward 1992); cultural approaches have been faulted for failing to connect systematically symbolic production with political and economic structures (Bartholomew and Mayer 1992). Most important, from my point of view, critics have emphasized the risks of indeterminacy (and, I would add, ad hoc explanations) inherent in these perspectives. Given the multiplicity of mobilization resources and cultural symbols that characterize societies at any one time, it would not be difficult for any successful challenger to identify the specific "discourse" with which its frame is aligned or the specific resource that its leaders have managed to mobilize.

Similar remarks apply to analysts of political opportunities. Generally these analysts produce lists of political variables that might be expected to affect protesters' behaviors and chances of success. Then they explain specific episodes of mobilization by selecting from that list those dimensions that best fit the case under investigation. They account for challengers' successes by pointing out one or more facilitating conditions; they account for their failures by stressing the absence of opportunities. Usually, however, they omit a systematic analysis of those situations in which some opportunities are clearly available while others are clearly not. This situation is problematic inasmuch as the absence of some opportunities could compensate for the presence of others and could decrease people's "expectation for success" (see, for example, Tarrow 1994:18, 84, 163, 183–84).[6]

The question, then, is how to account systematically for the several potential configurations of the opportunity structure while expanding on current attempts to integrate different theoretical perspectives. I start with a reformulation of the concept of political opportunity structure that draws on two distinct dimensions. One dimension corresponds to Tarrow's "stability of political alignments" and measures the *opportunities created by the crisis of dominant cleavages.* The other dimension is defined as *opportunities for autonomous action within the polity.* By the latter term I mean the political conditions that foster among challengers the perception that they may engage in independent action within the political system. Opportunities will be greater in this respect, the more conspicuous the presence of one or more of the other dimensions identified by Tarrow (1994:85–9): increasing access, influential allies, divided elites. The combination of these two variables defines four different configurations of opportunity structures (see Figure 1). Each reflects

Opportunities for Autonomous
Action within the Polity

		HIGH	LOW
Opportunities Created by the Crisis of Dominant Cleavages	HIGH	Realignment Frames	Antisystem Frames
	LOW	Inclusion Frames	Revitalization Frames

Figure 18.1 Most Successful Framing Strategies, According to Different Configurations of the Political Opportunity Structure

a different perception of the political environment and can be expected to be most conducive to a particular type of framing strategy.

A favorable context for challengers is provided, in principle, by an opportunity structure that combines the perception of ample opportunities for independent action with the decreasing capacity of traditional alignments to support collective identities and to structure political action. Here in particular we find the best conditions for the success of what I would call *realignment frames*. Such conditions emphasize the need to restructure political systems on the basis of new collective identities without a global delegitimation of the established members and procedures of the polity. This environment probably has been the most favorable for the success of the new social movements, at least those (the large majority, I suggest) which have adopted a "democratic populist" perspective (Kitschelt 1993).

In another configuration of the opportunity structure, high opportunities for autonomous action combine with low opportunities created by the stability of political cleavages. In this case we shall expect *inclusion frames* to be those whose mobilization efforts are most likely to succeed. By this expression I mean rhetorical devices emphasizing new political actors' aspirations to be recognized as legitimate members of a polity, in which definitions of the major actors are not altered. Political innovation following the inclusion of new actors thus affects the composition of the political system rather than its symbolic structure. One should expect greater chances to be offered to challengers who emphasize their continuity with established political actors as much as the differences, rather than to challengers who are willing to introduce new, different cleavages in the polity.

In the most difficult situation for the emergence of new political actors, the capacity of traditional alignments to structure political conflicts is not contested and few chances are available for newcomers to play an autonomous political role. In such a context, *revitalization frames* are likely to be the most successful—or the least unsuccessful. This expression reflects the fact that the most reasonable option open to challengers is that of entering established political organizations in order to

redirect their goals and revitalize their structures from within.

Yet, another configuration best fits the Italian politics of the 1990s and the emergence of the League. It is characterized both by global crises of traditional alignments and by poor opportunities for autonomous action by challengers. This configuration can be regarded as particularly favorable for what I call *antisystem frames*. The mobilizing messages that fall under this heading challenge both fundamental traits of a political system: its dominant cleavages and identities, and its capacity to accommodate heterogeneous and often conflicting interests and orientations within the political process. Antisystem frames therefore advocate a radical transformation of the polity. One should not associate their dominance with the greatest likelihood of confrontational events, political violence, or even revolutionary outcomes. Whether or not representations emphasizing the need for radical change ultimately result in disruption, revolution, or reform (however deep) depends largely on intervening variables, particularly, the mediating role of political elites (Tarrow 1989a, 1994; Tilly 1993). By antisystem frame I simply mean here any representation of political reality that defines political actors along lines other than established cleavages and denies legitimacy to the routinized functioning of the political process.[7]

The case of the Northern League provides an empirical illustration of this argument. Before we look at this example in greater detail, however, some qualifications are necessary.

First, the political opportunity structure here depends less on objective facts than on actors' perceptions that chances for successful action are opening up (Gamson and Meyer 1996). Admittedly, the properties of specific events may be expected to affect actors' interpretations of the available opportunities (McAdam 1994). Nevertheless, the easier it is to associate specific events with broader cultural frames, the greater will be the impact of those events.

Second, elites' policy responsiveness is excluded from the determination of the opportunity structure. Potential members of protest groups are always largely unhappy with the performance of political elites. Ultimately, agency always presupposes feelings of injustice (Gamson 1992). Also, full policy responsiveness may be as conducive to demobilization as is fierce repression (Tilly 1978; Rüdig 1990). What matters is whether the behavior of elites creates chances to develop effective collective action, not whether those elites are effective problem solvers.

Third, I posit the existence of a dominant perception of the political context (i.e., a "master frame"), for each political phase. This is not a return to the untenable assumption that each country shares a single political culture. Nor should one forget that controversies about interpretations of the political context arise regularly even among and within movement organizations (Gamson and Meyer 1996). I borrow Snow and Benford's (1992) idea of the "master frame" to stress the importance of representations of reality, which in a given phase are perceived as more compelling and "realistic" than other, competing representations. Although specific master frames may not be strong enough to attract people socialized in an alternative political tradition, they may weaken those individuals' beliefs, thus reducing their likelihood of mounting effective counter-frames.[8]

Fourth, I view frames here as abstract forms of political rhetoric rather than as belief systems anchored to specific contents. For example, the success of the League's populism is related to its consistency with a broader, strongly critical perception of the political opportunity structure rather than to the peculiar themes and symbols of populism as such.[9]

Fifth, and most important, the notion of frame alignment is redefined here. Usually this notion refers to the connection between movement entrepreneurs' values and goals, on one hand, and their potential constituents' culture, on the other, where culture is understood in the broad sense of the term (Snow et al. 1986; Tarrow 1994:123). Here I interpret frame alignment in a more limited sense—as the integration of mobilizing messages with dominant representations of the political environment.

Grievances and Frames
The Structural Roots of the Leagues
The new regional leagues were established in Italy in the 1970s and early 1980s. At first their electoral strength was negligible. The strongest of these parties, the Lombard League, and its counterparts in other northern regions, including Piedmont and Veneto, made their first significant appearance in the national political arena only in 1987. For the Lombard League, this was the first participation in any national election. On that occasion the various leagues ran independently for parliamentary seats and polled overall about 1.5 percent of the national vote. In 1990 the regional parties formed the Northern League under the leadership of the Lombard League.[10] Two years later their support in the new general elections rose to 8.6 percent, an outstanding result if one considers that their constituencies are restricted to the northern areas of the country. The two MPs (members of Parliament) who had been elected in 1987 were joined by 78 new MPs. In the national elections of March 1994 the League registered for the first time a slight reduction in its electoral support, polling 8.4 percent on the national level. However, as a result of the new majoritarian electoral system and their alliance with Forza Italia, the number of its MPs increased to more than 150.[11]

The League's strongholds in northern Italy display a peculiar socioeconomic profile. Regardless of the individual voters' class and status (Mannheimer et al. 1991), the League developed in social milieus with a strong small-industry, petite bourgeoisie profile (Diamanti 1993:35–40). After growing at extraordinary rates throughout most of the 1980s, these sectors faced the recession of the late 1980s and early 1990s. Fears about the economy were paralleled by the growth of other typical sources of middle-class resentment: public corruption, Third-World immigration, the growth of criminal activities, particularly in southern Italy, and spreading fears such as those related to drug addiction or AIDS.[12] Widespread anger over the misfunctioning and corruption of the state fuelled traditional hostility between northern and southern Italians.[13] The striking differences in economic and institutional performance between northern and southern Italy (Putnam 1993) also played a role.

The Northern League's Populism
Major sources of grievance in the Italian society of the late 1980s, however, hardly explain why the

regionalist leaders managed to mobilize such massive support. Indeed, social problems have long been recognized as the outcome of social construction processes and struggles over meaning (Hilgartner and Bosk 1988; Best 1989). Therefore, far from "creating" the Northern League, changes in Italian society provided new opportunities for political groups willing to assert themselves as "problem owners" (Gusfield 1963) through their peculiar definitions of the issues at stake.

In this conflict over meaning, the League developed its own approach. To link references to as many sources of grievance as possible within a coherent interpretative frame without losing its distinctness from established political actors, the Northern League increasingly adopted what most observers regard as a (regional) populist frame (Biorcio 1991, 1992; Betz 1993; Leonardi and Kowacs 1993; but see Segatti 1992). Providing a precise definition of populism is not simple: Populism is not a coherent and systematic ideology and it can take several forms (Wiles 1969). Still, we can associate it broadly with "those political beliefs that draw their major inspiration and legitimacy from 'the people.' People are seen as an homogeneous social aggregate as well as the only depository of peculiar, positive, and everlasting values" (Incisa 1983:859). Careful analysis of the electoral communications of the Lombard League and later of the Northern League (Todesco 1992) shows that these parties actually adopted most of the 24 distinctive traits of populist discourse identified by Wiles (1969) in his seminal contribution. For simplicity, however, these traits can be grouped under three broad themes.

The first theme focused[14] on the definition of the actor. Northern Italians did not differ from other people on strong cultural or ethnic grounds: The northern Italian identity had no clear, positive defining quality except for the *voglia di lavorare* (commitment to work), which cut across all layers of local society (Confalonieri 1990). Consistently, no class divisions were recognized in northern Italy. Class struggle was rejected in favor of cooperative attitudes between employers and employees, inasmuch as

> ...all social classes in Lombardy share a quest for freedom, and all wish to liberate themselves from

their subordinate position, according to which they are exploited as animals, and treated like a Roman colony. (From *Lombardia Autonomista*, November 1985, as quoted in Allievi 1992:18)

Rather, identity was defined mostly by opposition to those groups and actors who did not belong to the people—that is, whose behavior ran counter to the ordinary person's values and aspirations. This theme was articulated in both an upward and a downward direction. Considerable hostility was expressed toward the political and economic elites. Although in broad terms the League's approach was quite distant from the anticapitalist positions of traditional agrarian populism (Poggio 1994), hostility toward the economic elites often surfaced.

> I live nearby a FIAT car dealer.... When I pass by I always think the same thing: "You may be big and powerful, but even a little man can sometimes put empires into jeopardy if he is backed by the people."...No, life will not be easy for FIAT when the League is in power. (Umberto Bossi, as quoted in Bossi and Vimercati 1992:295; also see Pajetta 1994:59)

The harshest polemics, however, were directed against politicians. They were singled out because of their pervasive control over Italian society, their involvement in corruption, and their waste of the resources originating from people's work. Traditional political elites were described as having lost all touch with ordinary people and were contrasted with the League's leaders, who had proved capable of perceiving and giving voice to their people's beliefs and aspirations (see, for example, Gianfranco Miglio's foreword to Bossi and Vimercati 1992).

Rather than taking an autonomous form, antisouthern sentiments were framed largely within the antipolitician perspective:[15]

> We aim at the transformation of the current, centralized state, that is in the hands of the Southern ethnic majority, whose dominant position is enforced by "Roman" parties. (*Lombardia Autonomista*, January 1986, as quoted in Allievi 1992:38; see also Leonardi and Kowacs 1993)

Anti-elite sentiments also resulted in the strongest disregard for intellectuals and journalists, usually described as the servants of rulers. Sometimes these sentiments even took the form of overt hostility toward the Catholic hierarchy (Pajetta 1994).

The second basic theme of regional populism consisted of suspicion and hostility toward marginal social groups. One major polemical target was the ethnic underclass from Third-World countries. To be fair, the leagues never adopted a strictly racist approach, nor did their electoral success increase overt acts of intolerance. In a few cases, such as in Varese, some positive steps even were taken to facilitate the integration of non-White immigrants (Pajetta 1994, chap. 3). As a rule, however, the leagues were extremely critical of current immigration policies, which they judged to be too "loose." They viewed immigrants as a problem rather than as an opportunity (in both cultural and economic terms) for Italian society.[16] Hostility toward immigrants was often paralleled by similar attitudes toward individuals with unconventional lifestyles. This was not restricted to drug addicts or other marginal groups, but also applied to people who violated conventional social norms regarding sexual behavior, "regular" work, or "normal" family life; for example, a member of a local branch of the Northern League in the Northeast was expelled from the party because of his homosexuality.

The third major theme in the League's populism was a generally suspicious attitude toward political activity. It went well beyond the stigmatization of specific politicians' illegal behaviors. Rather, it entailed a wholesale rejection of the mediating role of political parties:

> The League's roots are in the local communities, and in their strong quests for autonomy…the League is the most straightforward expression of those claims, and rejects the intermediating role of traditional parties. (*Consulta Cattolica-Lega Nord,* as quoted in Poggio 1994:151)

In contrast to democratic populism as it was embodied in many contemporary movements (Boyte 1980; Kitschelt 1993), in the League little emphasis was placed on participatory democracy.[17] The function of democracy was reduced largely to the selection, by electoral means, of a new political elite. Being the true expression of the northern people, the "powerful League" would have automatically found

the best way to promote northern Italy's interests (Biorcio 1991; Todesco 1992).

The leagues also showed themselves frequently to be indifferent toward or even intolerant of democratic procedures and the formal requirements of government. Calls for greater respect for procedural rules coming from the center and left-wing opposition in those local councils where the Northern League was now in control usually were dismissed as mere efforts to slow down the "revolutionary" action of the new administrators. Democracy often was viewed as an obstacle to the achievement of practical results, rather than as a set of practices deserving respect as such. According to the League's former ideologue, Gianfranco Miglio,

> [E]ven when they belong to the upper-middle classes, [the supporters of the League] usually do not waste time with doubts, discussions, and sophisticated analyses; they much prefer simple diagnoses and basic values. (Bossi and Vimercati 1992:3)

Each of these aspects of the League's populism was reflected clearly in its political communication, as demonstrated by a content analysis of 43 electoral posters between 1987 and 1992 (Todesco 1992). In four-fifths of these posters, emphasis was placed exclusively on external enemies rather than on positive goals or proactive policies. The most frequently cited targets of hostility were "political parties" (mentioned in 16 posters), the "mafia" (15), and "thieves and corrupted people" (i.e., politicians and civil servants) (12). "Rome" (taken as the symbol of centralized, inefficient power), "the state," and "southern Italy" also were mentioned with some frequency (9, 9, and 6 times respectively). In agreement with other findings about the League's monthly magazine, southern Italy was not treated as an adversarial target in itself, but as part of a broader message (Segatti 1992). In the League's electoral posters, the Mafia and the south occurred together only twice, while the mafia was associated with politicians, the state, and political parties 14 times (Todesco 1992:284–90).

The Political Opportunities of Regional Populism

One might suggest that the League's populism is a reasonable explanation of its success. After all, it allowed it to incorporate into a single discourse a hatred of political parties and state bureaucracies, suspicion of deviants and Third-World immigrants, and resentment of privileges granted to economic elites. Therefore it could be regarded as an example of successful "frame alignment." This conclusion, however, would prevent us from understanding why the League's mobilizing messages succeeded where competing frames failed. For this purpose we need a more systematic treatment of the connection between the League's frame and the political opportunity structure.

How well do the various dimensions of the political opportunity structure fit the case of the Northern League? Traditional alignments certainly were crumbling in Italy in the early 1990s. According to Eurobarometer surveys, the proportion of those refusing any (even weak) identification with the left-right cleavage had risen from 12 percent in 1977 to 27 percent in 1992 (Martinotti and Stefanizzi 1994). This situation facilitated the spread of alternative points of view, which stressed the emergence of a new cleavage based on territorial differences within the country. It also created opportunities for groups supporting promarket and antiwelfare views.

In this respect, one should note the peculiarities of the Italian left-right cleavage as it emerged after World War II. In contrast to other Western countries, the major rightwing political party in Italy was not a committed advocate of free-market and deregulation policies. Both the left and the Christian Democrats recognized the importance of welfare policies to counterbalance the social costs of market competition. At least in the political rhetoric, emphasis was placed on collective rather than individual responsibility. The ideological differences lay in the definition of the criteria by which citizenship rights should be allocated or in the role assigned to traditional institutions (such as the family or the Catholic Church) in addition to state welfare agencies in the provision of welfare benefits (Ascoli 1985; Zincone 1992).

In such a context, a greater stability in traditional political identities would have drastically reduced the potential appeal of the League's message. For example, a persisting shared emphasis on social solidarity and co-operation might have discouraged at least some of those who sympathized with goals of decentralization and federalism from supporting the League. These persons were perceived (and stigmatized by opponents) as concerned only with selfish individual achievement and as largely hostile to welfare policies and disadvantaged social groups such as Third-World immigrants. Stronger moral objections would have been voiced against some of the key ideas of the populist frame, and those receiving the message would have perceived more of the internal inconsistencies.[18] Indeed, the only northern Italian areas where the League largely failed to break through were the "red regions" of Emilia-Romagna and Tuscany (Diamanti 1993:35–40); traditional cleavages there have maintained some vitality, even after the dissolution of the old Communist Party (Baccetti and Caciagli 1992).[19]

The relationship between the crisis of dominant alignments and the spread of populism is consistent with the broader arguments that associate the former with the success of challengers of any kind. In other aspects of the political opportunity structure, however, this connection is hardly present. To begin with, the regional leagues could not rely on support from, or alliances with, any established member of the polity; they faced fierce opposition from all traditional political actors across the left-right spectrum. Moreover, the regional leagues developed in a context where patterned inter- and intra-elite conflicts were hard to detect and understand in political terms. Although a number of conflicts shook Italian elites during the 1980s, their implications were not easily grasped by ordinary people. Therefore, their impact on citizens' broad perceptions of the political context was quite small, and they did not create new opportunities for challengers attempting to gain political recognition.[20] In addition, the regional leagues achieved an impressive degree of success in a political system where institutional channels granted little access to the polity to nonrepresented or poorly represented interests. On the one hand, there were—and still are—few opportunities for interest groups in terms of access to litigation procedures or involvement in consultation forums, hearings, and the like (Diani

1995, chap. 2). On the other hand, until 1993 it was quite easy for challengers to obtain parliamentary or local council seats, thanks to the proportional electoral system.[21] Even so, the general hostility of the established parties toward the Northern League denied the League any capacity for coalition (Sartori 1976). Its chances for autonomous action within the polity were therefore reduced, even from the viewpoint of electoral participation.

Finally, available options for representing interests also depended largely on the new challengers' connections within the system, and on their leaders' political skills. The lack of significant political experience among many League activists and sympathizers, which emerges from preliminary accounts (Diamanti 1992: Segatti 1992), may have largely prevented them from exploiting even those limited options.

Citizens' opinions reflected growing perceptions of a generally hostile political environment. According to surveys conducted in 1985 and 1992, the proportion who felt that "all parties are the same" increased from 25 percent to 50 percent, while the proportion who felt that political parties were essential for democracy declined from 74 percent to 42 percent (Mannheimer and Sani 1994:8–9). Admittedly, massive mistrust of political elites has been a constant trait of Italian society (Cartocci 1994). Yet the reduction in the early 1990s in the proportion who expressed loyalty to at least one party demonstrates the increasing deficit in representation. No political actor was thought any longer to be reliable, even as a patron of private interests. Moreover, those who rejected left-right differences were also the most strongly disillusioned with political actors in general (Martinotti and Stefanizzi 1994). Most significantly, a strong correlation has been found between electoral support for the League, mistrust of traditional politicians, and refusal to identify with the left-right scheme (Mannheimer and Sani 1994, chap. 4).

If we had treated these dimensions as individual predictors of successful action, our interpretation of the League's success would have been rather weak. The League's expansion should have been prevented, not supported, by the lack of potential reliable allies within the polity, by the absence of

patterned conflicts between elites and by the limited number of institutional opportunities for interest representation offered by the polity. We can explain why this was not the case only if we accept that different types of opportunity structures exist, and that the League's populism was aligned with the general perception of politics dominant among significant sectors of Italian public opinion in that period. The League's emphasis on regional differences was wholly consistent with the decreasing salience of traditional political identities, which presupposed in contrast the existence of class or religious cleavages within the Italian population. Similarly, the League's disregard for political elites and institutions matched citizens' perceptions of the political system as a generally closed and hostile milieu, which offered no opportunities for action from within. The League's mobilization message, in other words, was consistent with a widespread antisystem master frame.

Competition Between Challengers: Organizational Resources and Narrative Fidelity

Regional populists, however, were not the only challengers to emerge in that context. Between 1990 and 1993, strong criticism of the old system was also expressed by small parties such as the Greens (who ran in national elections for the first time in 1987) or La Rete (who first ran in 1990). These organizations also were involved in broader coalitions of old and new parties, movement organizations, and public interest groups, which in the 1993 local elections ran under the slogan "reforming politics."

Both the Greens and La Rete shared with the League a peripheral position in the parliamentary arena. Like the League, they had been very active in fighting public corruption and promoting mobilizations against the spread of criminal groups across the country. In principle they were credible alternatives to the League. In many respects their messages also were rather similar: They, too, advocated the replacement of the old political class with new representatives, and believed in overcoming the traditional barriers between left and right. Ultimately, however, they profited far less than the League from the crisis of traditional parties. In the crucial 1992 national elections, La Rete polled 1.9 percent and the Greens polled 2.8 percent, both well below the 8.6 percent polled by the League even though they were not restricted like the League to the northern regions (Istat 1993a).

One of the causes of their failure was the lack of consistency between their messages and antisystem frames. First of all, although the goals and frames of both the Greens and La Rete were difficult to place on a traditional left-right continuum, the majority of their most prominent figures had a background of militancy in left-wing parties or movements. As a result, these leaders were not perceived as reliable sources, or "validators" (Oberschall 1993), of messages advocating the overcoming of the left-right cleavage. This situation was not helped by their frequent association, in local elections and other political events, with traditional left-wing parties such as the PDS (Biorcio 1994). Moreover, regardless of their specific alliances, neither the Greens nor La Rete were prepared to take stances as fully anti-political as those of the League. Although they were strongly critical of the old parties, their leaders continued to emphasize the specificity of political activity and to accord it a degree of dignity. They also tended to differentiate between the responsibilities of ruling parties (especially the Christian Democrats and Socialists) and oppositional parties (especially the former Communists).

In contrast, as we have seen, the League attacked the political system as a whole. It also strongly criticized notions of political activity as patient mediation between diverging interests, and was scarcely interested in developing internal democratic procedures. Coupled with its activists' lack of involvement in the traditional political class (Diamanti 1992), these attitudes gave its frames stronger "narrative fidelity" (Snow and Benford 1988) than its competitors' in the eyes of prospective constituents with explicit antipolitical sentiments.[22]

In contrast, it is doubtful whether organizational resources mattered in this respect. Admittedly we lack conclusive evidence about the League's real strength. In November 1991, for example, Mr. Bossi claimed about 135,000 members and 300 local branches; in the following May, however, the party's newsletter, mailed to all members, reported only 50,000 copies and 132 branches (Todesco 1992:158–62). Even if the higher figure were the correct one—which I doubt—it would not suggest an organizational structure that was overwhelmingly stronger than that of the League's competitors, especially in light of the small mobilizing capacity demonstrated by most local chapters (Todesco 1992). For example, when the Federation of the Green Lists was established in 1987, it had 125 local branches, not much different from the League (Farro 1991:181).[23]

In any case, the fact that the League became the major "carrier" (Hilgartner and Bosk 1988) of antisystem sentiments cannot be causally related to the existence of a powerful organization. Even the League's use of media and its communication skills were rather poor in technical terms (Todesco 1992). The spread of its messages was not due to an efficient staff or a generous budget, but rather to "free media exposure" (Hilgartner and Bosk 1988:60). As a radically novel phenomenon, the League received increasing media attention, especially TV coverage.[24] This treatment often reflected negative evaluations of the new party. Especially in the case of public TV, however, the sources of those judgments were either full-time politicians or media professionals usually perceived as close to traditional parties. Rather than undermining public perception of the League as a credible challenger, this negative coverage reinforced it. Moreover, media of all political perspectives gave increasing attention to the very issues on which the League was focusing, thus, once again, facilitating consistency between their priorities and the overall public agenda.[25]

Resources mattered, however, in the 1994 elections, when the League faced electoral competition from the newly created party, Forza Italia.[26] In contrast to the leaders of La Rete or the Greens, Mr. Berlusconi was one of Italy's best known entrepreneurs and the chairman of a world-class soccer club; this fact made his claims to be a radical alternative to the *"partitocrazia"* ("partitocracy") highly plausible. Also, Berlusconi's emphasis on individual achievement and the virtues of entrepreneurship separated his party from both sides of the old left-right cleavage.[27] These traits made Forza Italia as credible as the League with respect to the production of antisystem frames, and a much stronger actor in organizational terms. In this case, differences in resources were a decisive factor. Although in 1994 the League obtained roughly the same share of votes as they had polled two years earlier, it lost virtually all the new votes it had gained between the national elections of 1992 and the local elections of 1993. In 1993 it reached, or exceeded, 40 percent of valid votes virtually everywhere in northern Italy (Istat 1993b; Biorcio 1994).

Thus, although resources are important for mobilizing consensus, they do not guarantee success (Tarrow 1994:150). Their ultimate effect varies according to the congruence between the challengers' specific frames and the opportunity structure. This congruence converts potential assets into effective assets (Moaddel 1992). Specifically, the effectiveness of organizational resources is increased substantially if the actors' strategies are framed so as to be consistent with the master frames, and if they characterize the opportunity structure at a given time.

Conclusions

I have focused on mobilization attempts conducted in a single period. The framework presented here may help to clarify why, in a given political period, some frames are less effective than others, although they appear just as plausible at first glance. At the same time, it enables us to capture the differences between opportunity structures at different points in time, and their effects on the likelihood of different mobilizing messages. In conclusion I provide a brief, preliminary illustration of this argument, showing how opportunities for challengers have changed in Italian politics in recent decades.

The 1980s, especially the first half of the decade, were particularly conducive to mobilization attempts framed in terms of political realignment. For example, although the Italian environmental movement failed to displace fully the left-right "materialist" cleavage, its strength was clearly greater in that period, when traditional identities had started to crumble, than in the late 1960s and early 1970s, when industrial conflict played a greater role in the new wave of social struggles. Also, the environmental groups could rely on a

number of opportunities for alliances with established members of the polity. The environmentalists' overall political influence consistently increased when the political ecology organizations abandoned their antisystem orientation in the early 1980s and emphasized in their ideological statements the need to interact with political elites and to take institutional constraints into account (Diani 1995). Both changes were consistent with broader transformations of environmental collective action at the European level (Rüdig 1990; Dalton 1994). Most important, both reflected a tendency to frame political reality in a way consistent with "realignment" master frames: a crisis of traditional alignments along with perceptions of opportunities for autonomous action within the polity.

In contrast, the 1965 to 1973 cycle of protest in Italy (see Tarrow 1989a; Ginsborg 1990; and Lumley 1990 for accurate reconstructions of those years of contention) provides a good example of the dominance of inclusion frames (also emphasizing opportunities for autonomous action, but in the context of stable political identities). On a superficial level, these years might well be regarded as the most favorable period for the prevalence of antisystem orientations. This idea would be consistent with the observation that the social movements of the time often supported very radical views. Both students' movements and new, radical workers' organizations openly criticized established political actors. They also aimed at the revolutionary overthrowing of the "bourgeois state" (Lumley 1990).

This was not the reaction, however, to a generally closed altitude of the political establishment toward new demands. Careful analysis of the protest wave has shown that the rise of autonomous mobilizations was encouraged by changes and innovations among traditional political actors (Tarrow 1989a). Significant sectors of the elite were willing to engage in dialogues with challenging groups; they also mobilized against attempts to increase the costs of participation by means of police repression, as became clear in the aftermath of the 1969 bombings in Milan.

Moreover, despite efforts to drastically reframe the traditional left-right opposition, and to place a new emphasis on the leading role of the working class and on social actors' autonomy in relation to old left organizations (Tarrow 1989b), the centrality of the left-right cleavage was never questioned. In that period the issue was the rule of the Christian Democrats and their allies rather than the cleavage as such. Indeed, as the cycle progressed, reform-oriented policies began to be implemented. Traditional left-wing parties and unions strengthened their links with the oppositional movements and ultimately regained their leadership over these movements (Tarrow 1989a).

This approach explains why the bearers of anti-system frames—namely the most radical new left parties and movement organizations—largely failed to establish themselves as powerful political actors in the mid-1970s, despite the favorable electoral system and the impressive amount of unconventional protest activities occurring at that time. Most of their potential constituents continued to identify with traditional alignments; they still believed that traditional left-wing organizations had a positive role in the representation process. The new left leaders often adopted frames that portrayed the old left organizations as betrayers of the working class and advocated their replacement by the new left groups (Bobbio 1990). This may have provided their core activists with strong symbolic incentives, but it ran counter to the dominant views among their prospective supporters and thus rendered frame alignment more problematic.

The years preceding 1968 were different again, in that the political system was shaped by Communist-Socialist and Catholic identities and was reluctant to offer challengers opportunities for autonomous action. In such a context, "revitalization" frames proved the most appropriate option. For example, new ideas started to spread within the Catholic Church well before the 1968 protest cycle began (Tarrow 1989a). However, obstacles to explicit contestation of the Church hierarchies encouraged concealment of attempts to innovate. At first, support for new ideas was not expressed in openly critical terms; support took the form of arguments that suggested new and different interpretations of doctrinal principles while it formally reconfirmed loyalty to these principles. Opportunities for independent, explicit action were perceived by

those favoring a more socially concerned Church only later, when ideas originating from the Second Vatican Ecumenical Council became more diffuse and a fragmentation of the hierarchy began. At that point the number of independent religious communities increased, and even explicitly left-wing Catholic political organizations such as *Cristiani per il Socialismo* (Christians for Socialism) were created (Cuminetti 1983). Revitalization frames remind us that collective action often originates within institutions rather than outside and against them (Tarrow 1994).

One additional advantage of this framework, therefore, is its capacity to identify the differences between political phases, particularly those phases which were characterized by similar attitudes toward politics and the political class. As these examples suggest, harsh criticism of the establishment and of government policies was found in Italy both in the period 1968 to 1973 and in the early 1990s, but the two periods differed both in the opportunities perceived by challengers and in the impact of different mobilizing frames. Similarly, both the early 1960s and the 1980s were characterized in broad terms by a decrease of interest in politics and a greater political consensus. Once again, however, differences in the salience of traditional identities and perceptions of opportunities for autonomous action created chances for somewhat different types of frames.

Swidler (1986) has remarked that "...in unsettled cultural periods, explicit ideologies directly govern action, but structural opportunities for action determine which among competing ideologies survive in the long run" (p. 273). The framework described here offers us a clearer way of specifying those opportunities. It also reminds us, however, that challengers' mobilizing messages may be effective in any political structure, albeit in different guises, and that their impact need not be restricted to the effervescent, unsettled periods on which most analysts of collective action usually focus.

NOTES

Preliminary versions of this paper were presented to seminars at the Universities of Lund, California–San Diego, Padua, and Milan. I acknowledge criticism and help from participants in those seminars, and from Francesco Battegazzorre,

Ian Carter, Paolo Donati, Alberto Melucci, Sandro Segre, Judith Stepan-Norris, and Mario Stoppino. I am also most grateful to the *ASR* Editor, Deputy Editor Charles Tilly, and reviewers.

1. The Northern League includes regionalist parties originally formed as independent organizations from Veneto (Liga Veneta), Lombardy (Lega Lombarda), and Piedmont (Piemont Autonomista), plus three newly constituted leagues in Liguria, Emilia-Romagna, and Tuscany. In this paper I occasionally use expressions such as "the League" as synonymous with the "Northern League."

2. This is true in spite of the recent rise of interest in conservative and right-wing politics among students of collective action (Oliver and Furman 1989; Lo 1990; Oberschall 1993, chap. 13).

3. I refer to challengers, rather than to movements, to emphasize that social movements should not be equated with organizations (Tilly 1978; Diani 1992). In practice, however, most of the theoretical contributions I discuss here have taken social movements, and particularly organizations acting within those movements, as their empirical object.

4. Substantial divergences especially occur between those who view symbols mainly as a "tool" for political action (McCarthy 1987) and those who see struggles over symbolic production as the major conflictual issue in postindustrial society (Melucci 1989; Benford and Hunt 1992). Differences between the two fields are not always so sharp, however. Even leading proponents of the frame approach to collective action tend in their research to conceive of frames largely as symbolic resources to be used along with more material resources as a means of increasing challengers' mobilization capacities (Snow et al. 1986; Gamson 1990, 1992).

5. Other recent contributions in the same direction include Zuo and Benford (1994) and Koopmans and Duyvendak (1995).

6. At the same time, however, scholars who take this line are well aware of the problem. Tarrow observes that the dimensions of the opportunity structure "are arrayed differentially in various systems and change over time, often independently of one another, but sometimes in close connection" (1994:89).

7. Here I come close to Sartori's (1976:132–33, 1982:299–303) definition of antisystem parties as political actors challenging the legitimacy of a given political regime without necessarily aiming at revolutionary outcomes or acting violently.

8. For example, the emphasis on social welfare shared by major political actors in Italy in the 1970s made it very difficult to disseminate frames emphasizing the need to keep public expenditure under control; such frames immediately would have been labelled "antisolidaristic." In contrast, widespread distrust of public agencies in the early 1990s has rendered it virtually impossible to oppose the privatization of public services without being stigmatized as supporting "inefficient and corrupted bureaucracies."

9. The distinction between these two notions of "frames" is discussed by Donati (1992). Most analysts of collective action, however, refer to frames in either sense (Snow et al. 1986).

10. See Diamanti (1993) for a documented reconstruction of the early phases of the leagues, as well as for an introduction to the persistent differences between these parties.

11. In the new electoral system, three-quarters of the parliamentary seats are assigned on a first-past-the-post basis; the remaining seats are assigned on a proportional basis.

12. A broad picture of recent changes and problems in Italian society and politics may be found in Ginsborg (1994).

13. As a result of clientelistic public employment policies, southern Italians are overrepresented in the rank-and-file positions of the public administration (Woods 1991; Leonardi and Kowacs 1993).

14. Use of the past tense throughout this section does not imply that this picture of the League's discourse is totally, or even partially, outdated. Rather, I wish to stress that I focus on the period that preceded the League's access to—and later, withdrawal from—government.

15. This, however, should not lead one to overlook the role of antisouthern attitudes among the League's supporters. For example, according to a survey conducted in late 1992 and early 1993 among 590 residents in Lombardy and Veneto, one in two Northern League supporters stood for limiting in some way the presence of people of southern origin in their regions, versus 26 percent of the total respondents; hostility toward southerners actually was identified as the most influential variable explaining individual support for the Northern League (Diamanti 1993:105; also see Mannheimer and Sani 1994, chap. 4).

16. One telling example comes from a meeting held in Milan in September 1994, which was called to launch a campaign for stricter immigration policies. It was advertised by posters carrying the headline "Public Order-Third World Immigrants," thus implying a strong connection between the two. Opinion polls confirm the special appeal of the League for those sectors of the northern Italian population which are most sensitive to these issues. Almost three-quarters of League supporters (72 percent) regard Third-World immigrants as causes of social and cultural conflicts, versus 58 percent of the general public (Diamanti 1993:105).

17. The only exception was during a phase of the Berlusconi government, when Mr. Bossi appointed himself as protector of democracy, presumably as a means of differentiating the leagues from their coalition partners, and later as a way of providing their electors with a rationale for the breakdown of the coalition.

18. For a broader, theoretical argument along related lines, see Friedman and McAdam 1992.

19. Diamanti (1993) shows in particular that 70 percent of the variance in support for the League at a provincial level may be explained by the strength of the Communist Party (later, PDS) in those provinces. The persistence of the Communist identity in those regions may have been facilitated by the opposition between local left-wing councils and the central Christian-Democratic government. As a result, it may have been easier for the Communist Party to frame the center-periphery conflict (particularly, the northern "periphery" versus Rome) in keeping with a left-right perspective.

20. This point applies, for instance, to the struggles in the late 1980s, in which Silvio Berlusconi's and Carlo De Benedetti's groups fought for control of Mondadori, the most important publisher in the country. Although these struggles had important political implications, the general public could hardly grasp their political relevance (Giglioli and Mazzoleni 1992).

21. The new majoritarian electoral system was not put into effect until summer 1993.

22. For discussions of recent developments in Italian politics see Diamanti and Mannheimer (1994), Ginsborg (1994), and Mannheimer and Sani (1994).

23. Also, according to surveys conducted in 1992 in Lombardy, overall membership in political parties in the region exceeded 500,000, while environmental organizations had 150,000 members (Biorcio and Diani 1993).

24. The same did not happen to the Greens or La Rete, possibly because they were closer to traditional political styles in spite of the new issues they raised.

25. Analysis of the most influential "centre-left" daily paper in the country, *la Repubblica,* has shown for instance that editorials addressing issues of political corruption, inefficiencies in the public administration and the political system, the waste of public resources, large regional differences, and immigration-related problems increased from 22 in 1980 to 105 in 1990 (Ruzza and Schmidtke 1993).

26. I do not consider the new role of the post-fascist Alleanza Nazionale-MSI except to point out that they were also able to put forward credible antisystem frames, having been in the opposition and, at least for the past 30 years, having had no involvement with consociational agreements, as had been the case with the Communist Party (Ignazi 1994).

27. Even later, when Berlusconi's largely rightwing views surfaced, the revitalization of the left-right conflict that he fuelled—already in late 1994—nonetheless differed radically from the previous version of the same cleavage. Above all, he introduced a far more secularized notion of the political right than that which the Christian Democrats had embodied (Ginsborg 1994:667–70).

19.

Resonance and Radicalism: Feminist Framing in the Abortion Debates of the United States and Germany

MYRA MARX FERREE

Where once American social movement theories could be criticized for a narrow view of rationality that assumed that strategic choice was simply a matter of objective opportunities and organizational efficiency, it is now largely acknowledged that a movement's objectives, opportunities, and choices are socially constructed and culturally variable. This "cultural turn" in social movement theory

Ferree, Myra Marx. 2003. "Resonance and Radicalism: Feminist Framing in the Abortion Debates of the United States and Germany." *American Journal of Sociology* 109: 304–344. Reprinted by permission of The University of Chicago Press. Notes have been renumbered and edited.

emphasizes the role of discourse. In particular, the focus has shifted to how issues are framed discursively, and the cultural resonance of such framing strategies is often seen as a sine qua non of movement success (Benford 1997; Benford and Snow 2000).

Yet the concept of cultural resonance is still problematic. First, it has not been operationally defined independently of the outcomes it is claimed to produce. Most studies approach cultural resonance by describing the framing of a single movement and arguing that the resonance of this framing contributed to its success (e.g., Čapek 1993; Diani 1996) or that its failures can be explained by the shortcomings of the frame or framing work of the organization (e.g., Babb 1996). Because cultural resonance and movement success are both seen as outcomes, it is easy to lose sight of the distinction between them; any idea that gains ground becomes defined as having been culturally resonant.

Second, framing language can obscure how power relations shape the dominant discourses and through them affect movement speech, channeling what challengers will attempt to say and how they say it, as well as affecting how they are heard (Steinberg 1999; Ellingson 1995). Certain ideas are likely to be structurally disadvantaged by the terms of the dominant discourse. When cultural resonance is interpreted as success in conforming to these more advantaged frames, the "best" movement speech will appear to be that which is most co-opted into this discourse. Analyzing the framing process as if it were merely the search for cultural resonance reduces it to a marketing process rather than one in which principles and ideological considerations play a significant role (Oliver and Johnston 2000).

Third, speakers within the same movement have reasons for framing issues differently. Short-term strategic effectiveness is not the only goal of movement speech, but it is a more important goal for some speakers than for others. Speakers who persist in raising nonresonant issues may be ineffective in the short-term and even dangerous to the movement, but, even so, not all speakers seek resonance. Looking at which speakers are discursively marginalized and the strategic risks they represent to the movement provides important clues to the power relations institutionalized in the hegemonic framing of issues. The use of nonresonant frames is by definition radical.

The main argument of this article is that institutionalized forms of discourse offer opportunities to speakers but do not force the choice of the most resonant framing; the gradient of opportunity still allows actors to opt for radicalism rather than resonance. Although resonant ideas appear mainstream and offer conventional forms of success, such as winning popular support and elite allies, radical ideas are attractive to movement actors who

seek a restructuring of hegemonic ideas and the interests they express and support. Just which ideas and interests are radical and which are resonant will depend on the local structuring of discourses. This is illustrated in comparing the feminist arguments for abortion rights in the United States and in Germany. Although both privacy and protection are part of the feminist repertoire of discourse available to speakers in both countries, they are selectively advantaged differently in each country. In the United States the discursive opportunity structure privileges individual privacy, and in Germany state protection is institutionally anchored in the discourse.

But such resonance is only half the story. All discursive opportunity structures are inherently selective, such that openings for ideas taking certain directions also are obstacles to other ways of thinking about a problem. When movements seek the advantages resonance offers they also accept political costs, particularly in marginalizing alternative frames, the speakers who offer them, and the constituencies whose concerns they express. Narrowing public framing of feminist claims to those that are most *resonant* is expedient for the purposes of influencing policy, gaining public support, and forestalling countermovement attacks; however, such strategic framing also excludes interests and needs that—while no less feminist in principle—are *radical,* that is, less defensible in that discursive context, but whose success implies more fundamental change. Because the discursive opportunity structure of each country is different, these strategic inclusions and exclusions follow different lines. What is mainstream feminism in one country is marginalized in the other, and vice versa.

After clarifying the concepts of frames, ideologies, and discursive opportunity structures, the article shows how constitutional court decisions in both countries in the 1970s institutionally anchored discourse about abortion in two different ways of understanding women's needs. In Germany, the court affirmed a fetus's right to life but also the social needs of women and the moral obligations of the welfare state; in the United States, the court affirmed a right to privacy for all abstract individuals, including pregnant women in the category of persons who could exercise free moral choice within that zone of privacy and excluding state consideration of women's social circumstances. The article empirically demonstrates the effect of these differences in discursive opportunity on men and women abortion-rights speakers in both countries, showing how those who enter each media mainstream, including those representing feminist organizations, highlight the ideas that resonate with those that are institutionally anchored in their particular setting. The second half of the article explores the exclusions that result from the search for resonance by comparing mainstream ideas with those marginalized by the movements in each country. Seeking resonance is in both cases a costly choice, sacrificing portions of the feminist repertoire of ideas as well as failing to represent the interests of some potential constituencies.

Movement Discourses and Their Contexts

There is little disagreement today that social movements' objectives, opportunities, and organizational choices are socially constructed and culturally variable (McAdam, McCarthy and Zald 1996; Della Porta and Diani 1999). Rather than merely conducting strategic arguments about the most effective ways to achieve specific goals (the rational actor model), movements struggle to define the meaning of specific policies and practices (Gamson 1992; Melucci 1995; Della Porta and Diani 1999). Recognizing such cultural work as important, increasing attention is paid to the role of discourse in how actors perceive political opportunities, construct collective identities, and define their available choices (Johnston and Klandermans 1995; Gamson and Meyer 1996). This literature offers insights into both movement discourses and the political fields in which they operate.

Frames and Discourses

Snow and his colleagues (Snow et al. 1986; Snow and Benford 1988) offered the most generally influential approach to studying social movement discourses by reviving and applying the Goffmanian concept of "framing" to the cultural work movements do. Their central concept is "cultural resonance," by which they mean an objective congruence with society's values and principles, understood as reflecting properties of the frame itself (its narrative fidelity, experiential commensurability, and empirical credibility; Snow and Benford 1988, p. 208). Because this view of framing removes it from an analysis of power relations, discourse does not appear to express or institutionalize inequalities (Gamson 1992; Steinberg 1999). It also casts a movement, perceived as singular and unitary, as always trying to achieve resonance, and it presents frames as a stock of resources for the movement to deploy.

Critics of this approach have stressed instead the dialogic nature of the interaction between authorities and challengers (Gamson and Meyer 1996), and define "the production of meaning as essentially contested collective action" (Steinberg 1999, p. 737), which includes both themes and counterthemes (Gamson and Modigliani 1989). Despite the opportunity to read new meanings into dominant discourses such indeterminacy presents, challengers are "always partly captive" to meanings already present and thus cannot "simply readily and instrumentally manipulate" them as cynical means to be effective within the status quo (Steinberg 1999, p. 753).

Advocates of more attention to the relation of power to framing argue that when frames are cut loose from the relations to other actors and ideas that specify their wider social meaning, the concept of "frame" becomes problematic. Oliver and Johnston (2000) contrast *frames,* which they see as discrete packages of meaning that can be "marketed" by movement actors, and *ideologies,* defined as socially imbedded and complex systems of values, norms and beliefs, usually with historical roots in ongoing power struggles. Thinking about frames as resources, they suggest, leads to seeing movements as merely seeking appealing "sound bites," a valid but distinctively modern concern. Steinberg (1999, pp. 746–47) stresses that the *discursive hegemony* power holders exercise by virtue of their institutional control can at least partially limit what discourses are perceived to be empirically effective and experientially valid and thus shape the practical repertoire of ideas available. He argues that the concept of a *repertoire* should substitute for that of a frame, to emphasize how discourses are "relational products of contention between challengers and powerholders, which limits both the strategic choice of performances as well as the conceptual mapping of possibilities for action" (Steinberg 1999, p. 750). However, this move loses the useful sense of frames as the narrower "interpretive schemata" or "packages" that are part of a larger interpretive repertoire or stock of contested codes and meanings (Gamson and Modigliani 1989).

The concept of a frame as an "interpretive package" with an internal structure organized around a central idea (Gamson and Modigliani 1989, pp. 2–3) provides a unit of analysis to track over time and in specific contests over meaning. Situating the concept of frame as an interpretive package in a dynamic model of interaction between challengers and power holders links frames to hegemonic ideas (discursive opportunity structures), to the historical contention of groups over codes (repertoires), and to the core values, identities, and interpretation of material interests of social groups (ideologies) that guide their use. A feminist repertoire, for example, includes all the frames grounded in the core principle of women's self-determination that are used within a particular historical struggle. But as this paper will show, not all frames in the repertoire will be similarly advantaged by a particular discursive opportunity structure.

Discursive Opportunities

Ideologies, repertoires, and frames do not exist in a vacuum. Discursive opportunities are structured, both in the sense of having pattern and form and in the sense of being anchored in key political institutions (Sewell 1992).[1] While the concept of political opportunity structures is popular in current social movement scholarship, the idea of discursive opportunity structure advanced here is not just an extension of this global and sometimes seemingly all-encompassing concept still further, but an attempt to more clearly specify the structured and institutionalized nature of what Steinberg calls discursive hegemony.[2] Discursive opportunity structures are *institutionally anchored ways of thinking that provide a gradient of relative political*

acceptability to specific packages of ideas (Ferree et al. 2002; cf. Koopmans and Olzack 2002). As institutionally anchored patterns of interpretation, discursive opportunity structures in modern democracies can be found in major court decisions, as well as in the prior constitutional principles they invoke and in subsequent legislation written to be consistent with these principles. These texts provide concrete ways of understanding what an issue means politically in that particular place and time.

Comparisons of similar frames in different contexts help to separate the role of such structured discourses (the gradient of opportunity) from agency (the strategic choices made among available frames). Although institutionalized interpretations provide greater openings in some directions than in others, at the extremes making some ideas "unthinkable" and others "common sense," not all movement speakers always respond opportunistically to hegemonic discourses. When challengers battle on this common terrain by looking for "gaps, contradictions and silences" and by seeking to "appropriate pieces to inflect…with their own subversive meanings" (Steinberg 1999, p. 751), not all of them will seek success in the terms that the dominant discourse defines. Their claims are never fully freely chosen, but also not institutionally dictated. Some movement speakers attempt to redefine the meaning of words, revalue their connotations and create new ways of perceiving the world (Staggenborg 1995).

Cultural resonance is thus not simply a property of the frames themselves, a tool movements can adopt for success, a resource waiting to be discovered, or the outcome all speakers are seeking, but an interaction of a certain package of ideas with the variable structure of an institutionally anchored discourse. In this article, *resonance* is defined as the *mutually affirming interaction of a frame with a discursive opportunity structure supportive of the terms of its argument,* while *radicalism* is similarly defined as a *mutually contradictory relationship between this structure and a frame.*[3] Institutional anchoring is the concrete manifestation of the symbolic power that makes certain ideas hegemonic and others not. Just what ideas are hegemonic will differ both across cultures and over time.

Radical Identities and Discourses

Although some would argue that ideas that are not resonant will necessarily be changed (Ellingson 1995, p. 109), it would seem foolish to suggest that there are no persistently radical streams of thought in social movements nor speakers who deliberately choose radicalism over accepting the terms of a dominant discourse. Indeed, Ryan's (1992) study of feminist ideology in National Organization for Women (NOW) groups in the 1970s and Katzenstein's (1998) study of feminist mobilization within the Catholic Church and military establishment indicate that identity as a "radical" and struggling against the terms of the hegemonic discourse are closely related choices, selectively embraced by some collective actors. The choice to use resonance with the dominant discourse strategically can offer certain kinds of success to certain speakers, but the choice to persist in making radical claims can also be justified, particularly by the hope for a longer-term success in changing the terms of the discourse (Staggenborg 1995; Katzenstein 1998).

Ultimately, the strategic choice to seek resonance is stripped of effective agency if it is defined as the inevitable direction that all framing efforts will take. The strategic implications of framing decisions are constructed from the interaction between frames and structures of discursive opportunity, but movement speakers make different trade-offs between their effectiveness in influencing policy makers and in articulating needs and interests marginalized by the status quo. Casting movement arguments in the terms of the dominant discourse creates both winners and losers, because a resonant version of the issues will echo at least some of the exclusions assumed by the terms of this discourse. Who wins and who loses, however, depends on the specifics of each case.

Media and Movement Discourses

Discourses also do not speak themselves; however reified they may appear in the form of texts, they are authored from a specific standpoint in social structure that is more than merely discursive (Smith 1999). Public discourse in contemporary societies is largely—though not exclusively—mediated through the institutions collectively known as "mass media" that also contribute their own interests and standpoints in selecting and diffusing what becomes the "mainstream" of ideas and claims (Ferree et al. 2002). Achieving representation in the media is a prerequisite to reaching a popular constituency with a movement message and thus is an important form of success for particular speakers.

But journalists also select speakers whom they view as responsible and important. The construction of the media mainstream is influenced by—though not directly determined by, nor defined as—the discursive opportunity structure laid down in law, court decisions, or other institutionally anchored interpretative action. The relative representation of certain sorts of speakers (and the views they express) and a movement's success or failure in entering this media mainstream of discourse must be separated analytically from the extent of congruence between an institutionally anchored discourse and specific frames in a movement's repertoire.[4] By definition, "mainstream" speakers in a movement are those who have achieved media visibility. Marginalized speakers have not; they are the "losers" in the struggle for cultural influence in and through the mass media. As we will see, some feminist speakers make it into the mainstream and others do not, but what they have to say differs dramatically by national context.

Constitutional Interpretation of Abortion in Germany and the United States

Germany and the United States offer two very different discursive opportunity structures for dealing with women's autonomy in making abortion decisions. Both countries' constitutional courts made key decisions about abortion in the mid-1970s, but the two decisions could not have been framed more differently.

In the United States, the Supreme Court in *Roe v. Wade* in 1973 drew upon ideas about individualism and privacy to conclude that the state had no right to intervene in the first trimester (and a limited right to do so in later stages) in women's abortion decisions. This individualist understanding of rights was codified in further decisions. As Justice Powell, writing for the Supreme Court majority in *Maher v. Roe* in 1977, averred: "We are not unsympathetic to the plight of an indigent woman who desires an abortion, but the Constitution does not provide judicial remedies for every social and economic ill" (432 U.S. 464). Social and economic problems that do not arise directly from state action are seen as outside the purview of the rights secured by *Roe v. Wade,* just as the Court had historically viewed the inequalities of bargaining position between employers and employees as merely private. When the Supreme Court revisited *Roe* in the *Webster* (1989) and *Casey* (1992) decisions, it allowed the state more latitude in intervening to protect the fetus but continued to define women's right as that of making an individual choice.

In West Germany, the 1974 effort by the legislature to legalize abortion in the first trimester was overthrown by the West German constitutional court in 1975 by finding there was "a consensus" that the fetus was a human life that the state had an obligation to protect. At the same time, the court acknowledged that there might be conditions in which it went beyond the bounds of decency to require a woman to carry the fetus to term. In the law that went into effect in 1976, the "indications" that would make the state's insistence on her continuing the pregnancy intolerable (*unzumutbar*) included threats to her own life or health, rape, fetal deformity, and an unspecified condition of "social need" (*soziale Not*) determined by a doctor.[5]

Although by 1977 the issue was seen as settled, two matters returned abortion to the parliamentary agenda. First, the 1988 widely publicized trial of a doctor in Memmingen (in the southern, conservative Catholic state of Bavaria) for performing abortions without adequate "indications" put judges in the position of second-guessing his decisions. Second, the fall of the Berlin Wall in 1989 and subsequent unification of West and East Germany raised the issue of reconciling two different abortion laws, since East German law had allowed legal abortion in the first trimester since 1972. East German protests kept the 1990 unification treaty from simply extending the West's abortion law. In writing the new law in the now unified parliament, West German women legislators played a leading role, crafting the cross-party coalition effort (the so-called *Gruppenantrag,* or group bill) that passed (Young 1999). This 1992 law was again overturned

by the constitutional court, which sent it back to be refashioned in a more "pro-life" direction. The text of the final 1994 law requires state-licensed counseling to be "pro-life-oriented but outcome-open"; it defines abortion as a crime and forbids health insurers to pay for it for that reason. In the law, the state defines its responsibility as being to "help not punish" the pregnant woman. While defining all abortions as criminal, it gives a woman the right to make a nonprosecutable decision in the first trimester without disclosing her reasons to her counselor, offers state funding for abortions for women on welfare, and promises increases in state support for kindergartens and other aid to child rearers.

Thus, in the late 1980s and early 1990s, both countries' courts revisited the abortion issue and modified but did not reject the distinctive principles of their original decisions. Although the court decisions provide the institutional anchors for identifying the different discursive opportunities facing feminists, the rationales each court used also drew upon longer-standing political traditions of liberal individualism and social protection that distinguish each country.

O'Connor, Orloff, and Shaver (1999) point out that the liberal individualism that makes the United States so noteworthy for its miserliness in social welfare policy also puts it in the fore in respecting women's autonomy in making abortion decisions. In contrast, German law, like European abortion laws more generally, emphasizes public health or humanitarian justifications (Githens and Stetson 1996; Lovenduski and Outshoorn 1986). Protecting women from the psychic and social burdens an unwanted pregnancy imposes, particularly on the poor, as well as from the health risks that illegal abortion might carry, offers a framework in these countries for offering conditional access to legal abortion that is institutionally anchored in their self-definition as welfare states.

Liberal individualism as a principle of social policy in the United States emphasizes "negative liberty," shielding individuals and markets from interference by the state. As applied to abortion by the Supreme Court, U.S. social policy places particular emphasis on the freedom of the individual woman to decide for herself whether abortion is appropriate, but it also specifically exempts the state from any obligation to pay for abortions except in exceptional circumstances (when the life of the mother is at risk or in a situation of rape or incest) and, in recent welfare reform legislation, also releases the state from the obligation to support poor mothers' child rearing (Colker 1992; O'Connor et al. 1999). Liberal individualism positions women as citizens who, like men, are in control of their own persons and assumes that women should have the opportunity to make their own way in the labor market, without any special regard for the children for whom they are likely to be responsible.

Germany is a sharply contrasting case, being a strongly protectionist policy regime. Classical liberalism was never a strong political force, and the main axis of political debate in West Germany since World War II lies between social democrats and Christian conservatives, both of whom agree that protecting women as wives and mothers is an obligation of the state (Moeller 1993). The German welfare state offers a variety of economic supports for male breadwinners and for single mothers and their children, and the German constitutional court has held that the state has a positive obligation to support families (Ostner 2002). Applied to the abortion question, the protectionist policy approach emphasizes the positive moral obligation of the state, simultaneously affirming the fetus as a human life deserving state protection and acknowledging the state's responsibility to offer the "practical social and economic support" women need to be able to bear and rear children (Berghahn 1995).

In sum, the discursive opportunities institutionally anchored in these contrasting court decisions reflect long-standing legal principles of liberal individualism in the United States and social protection in Germany. Despite differences in the chances for success given by these differing opportunity structures, when feminists in both countries mobilized to claim reproductive rights, the repertoire of frames available to them included both individualist and protectionist framing of women's autonomy.

Individualist and Protectionist Frames in the Feminist Repertoire

Autonomy is a core value for feminists. Feminist thinking about how to use abortion rights to achieve greater autonomy for women (what Gordon [1990] calls actual birth control) in both the United States and Germany offers two types of ideologically justified claims related to feminist arguments in other situations. The first framing situates abortion as a matter of choice, which women, like men, should be able to exercise freely as rights-bearing citizens, and is squarely situated in the mainstream of liberal political theory (Bordo 1993; O'Connor et al. 1999). By acknowledging women's moral competence to make abortion decisions, a state not only withdraws its coercive power from a significant arena of women's life but also symbolically recognizes women's full personhood. While this is more than a merely negative liberty, it falls short of providing a means to realize rights to exercise choice in practice through positive state intervention (Roberts 1997). Within this framing, women's similarity to men is stressed, not their specific social position as women or their particular race and class.

The second framing of autonomy assumes the need for women to be protected from social coercion to be free. Insofar as abortion is understood not merely as a consumer choice but as an aspect of control over the conditions in which women's life chances are structured—birth control, in Gordon's terms—then male dominance and the risk of exploitation must be considered. Rosalind Petchesky offers a telling analysis of the politics of "taking risks," arguing that the "need to balance the dangers of individualism (exposure to exploitation or unfair risk) against the dangers of protection (invasion of privacy, paternalism, exclusion)...lives and breathes" in the history of feminism. She notes that

> it has re-surfaced from time to time around issues relating to sexuality—prostitution, rape, pornography—where one group of feminists fought to expose and regulate the dangers to women in the trafficking and exploitation of their bodies...while others foresaw the dangers of protection, its tendency to be used as a pretext for denying women their capacity to be sexual, to work, or even to walk on the street. And, of course, both groups have been right...neither individualism—formulated as the 'right to privacy' in liberal constitutional tradition—nor paternalism has ever provided

adequate solutions to women's collective oppression. (Petchesky 1984, pp. 190–91)

Petchesky raises the question of when and how state protection might contribute positively to women's self-determination.

Thus, both individualism and protectionism are ways of thinking about women's self-determination that are fully consistent with a feminist emphasis on women's autonomy as a core ideological value. Whether rights or risks are emphasized in any particular case is part of a complex ideological elaboration of feminist principles. As Oliver and Johnston (2000) argue, such ideological work is very different from framing in the strategic sense of offering arguments aimed to influence policy makers, sway bystanders, or motivate adherents to action. The specific elaborations of feminist principles are often grouped in categories such as radical, liberal, or socialist "feminisms" or defined as core debates within feminism, such as those between equality and difference (Tong 1989; Lorber 2001).

Similarities and Differences in Feminist Repertoires

These different ideological orientations provide a broad repertoire for feminist thinking about a variety of issues, and both are available to frame abortion rights. Studies done in both Germany and the United States point to complexity in the frames used within each country. Central to the American abortion debate, according to studies of activists on both sides, are contrasting notions of gender relations that focus on reconciling work and motherhood in women's lives (Luker 1984; Ginsberg 1990; Staggenborg 1991). Condit (1990) shows how the American print media from 1960 to 1985 created support for legal abortion through strategic appeals to choice and individual freedom, connecting abortion to women's ability to be good mothers who would limit their families in order to invest more care in fewer children. The gender relations that feature most centrally are liberal individualist ideas of opportunity and the freedom to enter into labor markets, and these are the "needs" that legal abortion apparently addresses.

However, attitudes about sexuality also play a significant role in public support for women's abortion rights in the United States (Granberg 1982, 1991). In matters of sexuality other than abortion, issues of (sexual) risks rather than (economic) opportunity have generated significant protectionist discourses among critics of pornography and prostitution (Barry 1979; Dworkin 1989; MacKinnon and Dworkin 1997). Press and Cole (1999) find American women's responses to media presentations of abortion reflect attitudes toward sexual pleasure and danger in women's lives. Women who take risks by pursuing sexual pleasure as men have done are seen as being "punished" by pregnancy for their "carelessness." Protective attitudes toward sexual risk vie with individualist beliefs about family and work to shape how American abortion discourses invoke gender relations.

In some regards like radical feminists in the United States, many German feminists stress the risks and dangers to women in the domain of sexuality, ranging from pornography to the international traffic in women's bodies (Ullrich 1998).[6] Yet, in the late 1960s and early 1970s, feminist groups in Germany typically protested the criminalization of all abortions (via sec. 218 of the criminal code) with assertions that "my belly belongs to me," arguing that there was no legitimate basis for the state to regulate abortion. The demand for the complete and unconditional abolition of section 218 was the touchstone of feminist politics at that time (Schenk 1980, Ferree 1987). As feminists became ambivalent about reproductive interventions and pessimistic about being able to challenge the constitutional principle of fetal protection established in 1975, grassroots groups in West Germany had difficulty in mobilizing against section 218 (Wuerth 1999; Young 1999). Yet it is clear that both individualist and protectionist ways of thinking about what women need to be self-determining are part of the repertoire of West German feminist thought.

In practice, most German abortion-rights mobilization in the early 1990s came either from the former East Germany or from feminists in conventional party politics. After 1989, East German framing of abortion rights emphasized how they were a protective accomplishment of the former socialist state that should not be discarded (by those sympathetic to the former Communist Party) or that they were a marker of individual freedom of conscience in the newly democratic state (by those sympathetic to the former opposition) (Maleck-Lewy and Ferree 2000). In the West, women in all political parties were vocal about the need for abortion reform after the Memmingen trial in 1988. Feminists in parliament saw the unification process as a chance to make legislative gains for women and grassroots feminists in the West deferred to them to make that case (Sauer 1995; Mushaben, Lennox, and Giles 1997).

In the following analysis, I argue that strategically chosen American and German feminist discourses have successfully entered the mainstream of media discourse in each country. But by tailoring their demands to be resonant within the discursive opportunity structure, mainstream feminist speakers also limited their conceptualization of autonomy to a more onesided claim than the overall repertoire of feminist beliefs defines as what women need. When demanding individual liberty or protection from exploitation, mainstream feminism (the type best represented in the mass media) in each country selectively offers frames that resonate with their own national discursive opportunity structure.

But in highlighting the strategic choices of the mainstream, it is a mistake to disregard the feminists in each country who take other positions. Such radical speakers are unlikely to win short-term policy gains and may even open the movement to strategic attack from its opponents. In the second part of the analysis, I contrast the mainstream to the concerns that are strategically marginalized (both by the media and by the movement's own preferred speakers) in each country. In constructing the discursive boundaries that exclude certain frames from the mainstream, the interactive process between audiences and speakers defines radicalism along lines that are reverse images of resonance. The frames that are excluded, even attacked, differ such that what is radical in one country is mainstream in the other and vice versa.

The analysis that follows (1) identifies the interactions between national discursive opportunities and the strategic choices of frames by men and women who support women's autonomy to show how individualism and protectionism characterize

the media mainstream in each country; (2) compares how feminist speakers in each country define abortion, showing how they, too, incorporate hegemonic ideas about individualism and protection in their framing; and (3) examines the discourse of feminist speakers that does not appear in the media and is rejected by the mainstream advocates to see how counterhegemonic concerns are marginalized.

Data and Measures

Analysis of who and what is represented in the media discourses of both countries is based on newspaper data collected by a project comparing German and American abortion discourse from 1970 to 1994 (Ferree et al. 2002). The newspaper data encompass 2,618 articles on the subject of abortion, including news reports, commentary, and features but excluding letters to the editor and book and movie reviews, published in the *New York Times,* the *Los Angeles Times,* the *Süddeutsche Zeitung,* and the *Frankfurter Allgemeine Zeitung.* Within these coded articles, each speaker (an individual or organization quoted or paraphrased in a single article) was also coded as to gender, party, organizational affiliation, stance on abortion restrictions, and on the details of ideas she or he expressed about abortion (if any). Media selection of such speakers defines them as having achieved some degree of *mainstream* status, and their work with the media also indicates that effectiveness in shaping public perception or influencing policy makers is likely to be their goal.

In the qualitative analysis of mainstream and marginalized feminist frames, I draw on interviews conducted with spokespersons for 14 U.S. and 11 German organizations engaged on the abortion-rights side of the debate, feminist arguments offered in texts and documents about abortion provided by these organizations, and feminist writings in U.S. and German publications. The interviews were done with a purposive sample of groups that offered distinctive arguments or media strategies; their spokespeople were treated as informants about strategic choice.

The qualitative analysis focuses on two types of "excluded arguments": the mainstream German feminist one (which is missing from the American mainstream) and the "radical" arguments in each country that its mainstream speakers reject.[7] The stenographic transcripts of the German legislative debates in 1992 (Bundestag, Ninety-ninth Session) are analyzed to see how the connection between protection for women and women's self-determination is made in Germany. These transcripts capture mainstream German feminist arguments, since the grassroots feminist organizations in the West explicitly deferred to the leadership of women in parliament in the late 1980s and early 1990s (Young 1999; Mushaben et al. 1997). The interviews and documents in both countries as well as the German legislative transcripts were also analyzed for evidence of framing that is rejected by feminists, to see what points of view are marginalized by those looking to be strategically effective.

Quantitative Coding

In the newspaper database, all ideas were coded in terms of a three-digit code that grouped arguments hierarchically in terms of core concerns (frames), policy directions (supporting greater restrictions on abortion [anti], fewer restrictions [pro], or neutral), and detailed specific claims. Thus, for example, the frame of "fetal life" included arguments in pro, neutral, and anti directions that revolved around whether the fetus was to be defined as a human life or not and that could take a variety of specific forms (science says it is a human life, it is a human life at some stage but not before, abortion is murder, etc.) reliably distinguishable by the coders.[8] First-digit frames were also divided into distinctive clusters at the third-digit level. The individual and state frame, for example, included clusters of ideas about religious freedom, individual privacy, states' rights, and the moral role of the state (for examples of these frames and clusters, see Ferree et al. 2002).

Each argument offered in a single utterance (paragraph or uninterrupted quote) by a speaker was coded separately, so that individual utterances could contain multiple ideas. Speakers were classified as pro, neutral, or anti based on the directional balance of their frames in each article. Overall, there were 4,762 U.S. speakers and 3,737 German speakers, of whom 3,593 in the United States and 2,267 in Germany offered codable ideas about abortion.[9] In this article, speakers who do not offer any framing ideas or who oppose abortion rights are excluded from the analysis, since the focus is on differences between feminist and nonfeminist frames for abortion rights. This analysis examines 469 neutral and 1,791 pro-abortion-rights speakers in the United States and 293 neutral and 836 pro speakers in Germany.[10]

The full three-digit codes are used to identify four types of arguments in favor of abortion rights: (1) an argument for individual rights (against state intervention) not explicitly about gender; (2) an argument for women's specific self-determination as women; (3) an argument for protection of the needy, the exploited, and those at risk without specific mention of gender; (4) an argument for specific protection for women in the risks and problems they face as women. There is thus a liberal individualist argument (1) and a gendered self-determination argument (2) that frame the core feminist value of autonomy in significantly different ways. There is also an ungendered and gendered form of a protectionist argument (3 and 4). The ungendered version of protectionism for example, argues that the poor are the ones victimized by making abortion illegal, that counseling is necessary to get informed consent, or that health care for teens is undermined by parental consent rules, while the gendered version of protection explicitly names women as the ones in need—women's victimization as women through rape, women's needs as mothers to care for the children they have, women's need for counseling to know their options, or good health care for women as specifically demanding access to abortion.

Measures.—Two measures of framing use are constructed, each of which is independent of the presence or absence of other ideas in the argument and both of which rely on aggregation to the speaker level (within an individual article). First, the rate per utterance measure counts the frequency of use of any one of these types of arguments, regardless of the number of other idea types also included in the speakers' utterances. The second measure counts the proportion of speakers of a given type who include any argument in this category, regardless of what other arguments they may also use. The degree to which the four types of claims are empirically distinct or related is thus an analytic question, not an artifact of a coding procedure.

Speakers for abortion rights are divided into four basic types: (1) those who represent a feminist organization or grassroots group, (2) those who speak for other pro-abortion-rights organizations, (3) those who represent pro-abortion-rights political parties, and (4) all other pro and neutral speakers. Speakers are also identified as women or men, with non-gender-identified speakers (such as non-bylined journalists and collective actors with no named spokesperson) as the omitted group. Finally, change over time in framing is not conceptualized as a year-by-year linear trend but as a broad shift between periods. The three periods used for this analysis are the years before 1977 (when the first wave of constitutional interpretation and legislation was being done in both countries),[11] the 1977–88 phase of response to this reform, and the 1989–94 period when the law was revisited and revised by the courts in both countries.

Media Analysis

Analysis of the newspaper data focuses on how the interaction between discursive opportunity and speakers' efforts to achieve resonance with it leads to distinctively different patterns in the mainstream of discourse among abortion-rights advocates. This leads first to examining individualism, protectionism, and the interaction between them in each country's mainstream media discourse. The second part of the analysis indicates how the speakers who are organizationally defined as "feminists" conform to and differ from this overall mainstream.

Autonomy as Individualism or Women's Right

Looking first at how autonomy is framed, we see a sharp difference between the two countries. German abortion-rights speakers, especially women, make claims for self-determination that are specifically gendered as women's right, and U.S. speakers, both men and women, advocate abortion rights in non-gendered language that refers to the rights of the "individual" (and her doctor, and her family) to be free from state interference. As figure 1 indicates, German women speakers include a gendered argument for women's self-determination more than

three times as often as they make abstract claims for individual rights (51% vs. 16%), while U.S. women speakers are more likely to prefer abstract individualism to gendered arguments, though not by nearly as wide a margin (41% vs. 35%). American men speakers show a dramatic preference for the individualist argument over the gendered one (45% vs. 21%), while German men tend to share the German women speakers' preference for including an argument about women's rights as women, though not as strongly preferring it (28% vs. 19%). There is thus a dominant form of discourse in both countries for making claims about self-determination. The mainstream German version is explicitly gendered and the American version is not, yet in both countries women speakers show more preference than men do for making the argument in gendered terms.[12] The abstract individualism of American liberal discourse seems to frame the debate in terms men prefer.

Protection frames.—Framed in liberal individualist terms, American rhetoric downplays arguments about the need for the state to protect women, and German rhetoric overall is more likely to draw upon protectionist claims, as would be expected. Yet differences in use of protectionist framing are also active responses to changes in the discursive opportunity structures that abortion-rights advocates confronted in each country. Figure 2 shows the effects of divergent court interpretations on speakers in both countries in the changes by period that it reveals. The shift in discursive opportunity produced by controversial court decisions in the 1970s leads mainstream speakers in both countries to become more distinctive in their framing, each in the direction that seeking resonance would lead one to expect.

In the early period of the debate, both German men and American women tend to include an argument about the need for social protection somewhat more often (about 50% do) than either American men or German women (about 40%). Initially, in fact, German women are a little less likely to make protectionist arguments than comparable Americans are. This is the period in which they were claiming "my belly belongs to me," a phase that speakers on all sides now agree is over, while American speakers

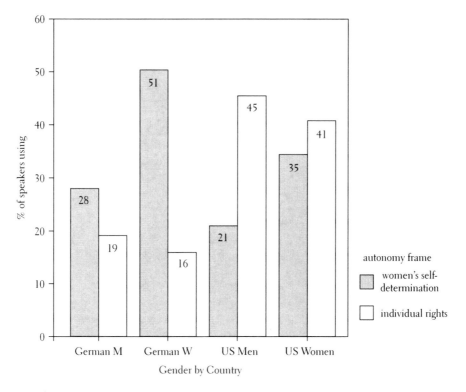

Figure 19.1 Percentage of speakers who include any pro-abortion-rights claim in the women's self-determination and individualism frames by country and gender. Note: The weighted *N* of cases is 368 for German men, 403 for German women, 964 for U.S. men, and 731 for U.S. women, with 160 cases where no gender is given excluded along with all speakers who are either antiabortion overall in their framing in an article or neutral but speaking for an antiabortion party or organization.

in the pre-*Roe* period included many claims about the risks and dangers of illegal abortion from which legalization would protect women. However, by 1977, the German constitutional court had affirmed paying attention to special circumstances ("indications" justifying abortion are required and social necessity, financial or otherwise, is a legal indication) and the U.S. court had rejected the idea that the "private social and economic ills" of pregnant women justify state funding for abortion. Once these contrasting rationales are anchored in jurisprudence, the inclusion of protectionist arguments goes up markedly among German women and down among both men and women abortion-rights speakers in the United States, as figure 2 shows. In

the third time period, the period of reconsideration (prompted by the *Webster* decision in the United States and by unification in Germany) that begins in 1989, American abortion-rights discourse in these newspapers remains unlikely to address the need for social protection.

Overall, in both countries, men speakers consistently differ from women speakers but in opposite, proresonance directions. Compared to women, men who support abortion rights are more likely to be protectionist in Germany and less likely in the United States, just as we earlier saw U.S. men as framing abortion more as a matter of liberal self-determination than as women's rights. However, the marked interactive effect on protectionist discourse

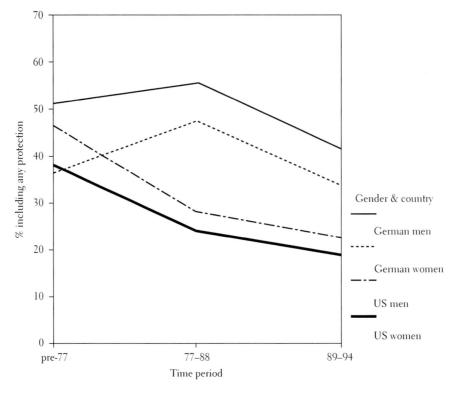

Figure 19.2 Inclusion of protection frames among pro and neutral men and women speakers by country and time period. Note: Weighted *N* of cases by period for each group: German men, 147, 52, 170; German women, 63, 74, 266; U.S. men, 194, 354, 416; U.S. women, 85, 257, 389. In all periods speakers who are on balance antiabortion in an article or neutral and representing an antiabortion party or organization are omitted.

in reaction to the court's framing of abortion was not found when liberal individualism was similarly examined over time. Although individualist frames increase slightly for American men and drop some among German men over time, the primary differences in the use of this frame (rather than a more gendered framing of autonomy) are those between countries and genders depicted in figure 1.

Combining autonomy frames with protection.— Although liberal individualism and women's rights frames the argument for autonomy differently, this does not mean that the claim for self-determination is necessarily any stronger or more prevalent in either country. In fact, the overall degree of emphasis on the issue of autonomy is similar for women advocates in both countries, as figure 1 also shows,

although German men lag behind American men in their support. Nonetheless, the use of these two different languages of justification matters for reasons beyond liberalism's relatively greater resonance for men.

Since active protection by the state is inherently at odds with self-determination when it is understood as the right of an individual to be let alone by the state, one would expect liberal individualist framing to be less consistent with advocating women's need for state protection than a women's rights framing of autonomy would be. Indeed, the choice of rhetoric for claims for autonomy goes along with a strong difference in the extent to which abortion-rights discourse accommodates claims for protection. Figure 3 shows the rate of use per utterance of

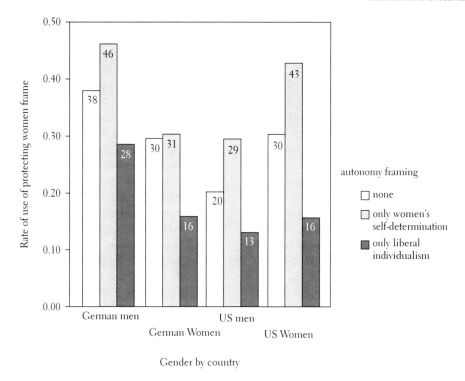

Figure 19.3 Rate of use of protecting women frame by framing as individual or women's rights by gender and country. Note: Cases here are utterances rather than speakers, with speakers averaging more than one utterance per article. Weighted *N* of cases for German men of each type, 224, 73, 40; for German women, 163, 176, 36; for U.S. men, 417, 109, 344; and for U.S. women, 281, 153, 197. Excluded speakers are those with no gender given (922 utterances) and those using both liberal individual and women's rights frames (346 utterances), as well as all antiabortion speakers as previously defined.

the argument that women need protection by three groups of speakers—those who frame autonomy as women's rights, or as liberal individualism, or who include neither form of autonomy frame.

As figure 3 shows, compared to those speakers who do not frame abortion as being a matter of autonomy at all, women's rights framers more often include claims about women's needing protection. For example, German men who use the women's rights frame include an average of .46 frames about protecting women compared to an average of .38 for German men who include no claim about autonomy in their speech. However, the effect of framing abortion rights as a matter of individual freedom from

state interference is precisely the opposite, reducing the average frequency with which speakers claim women need protection. Thus, German men who use a liberal individualist argument include an average of only .29 protectionist frames. This same relationship holds for all four groups of speakers, indicating that how self-determination is framed, the more stable feature of the discourse, encourages or discourages speakers from also drawing on feminist rhetoric about women's needing protection from exploitation.[13] The women's rights frame, which we saw was much more common both in Germany and among women, supports the inclusion of ideas about protecting women. The liberal individualism frame tends instead to reduce the likelihood that women will be framed as needing protection.

Overall, we find (1) both country and gender affect the choice of the liberal individual or women's rights frame for autonomy; (2) including protection frames interacts over time with the discursive opportunity structure offered by the court; and (3) the specific framing for autonomy affects speakers' use of protection arguments. These results indicate that framing is both responsive to discursive opportunities and strategically consequential. Both stable and changing aspects of discursive opportunity affect framing, while, strategically, all speakers who choose liberal individualist frames, as a desire for resonance in the U.S. context would encourage them to do, say less about protecting women.

Specifically Feminist Frames

The extent of differences among speakers based on their organizational affiliations also varies between countries, confirming that speakers identified as feminist are affected by these differences in discursive opportunities. In table 1 speakers affiliated with a specifically feminist organization (e.g., NOW, local groups, feminist coalitions) are distinguished from those with pro-choice social movement affiliation that is not explicitly feminist (in Germany, the Green Party and ProFamilia account for most of these speakers; in the United States these speakers represent groups such as NARAL [formerly the National Abortion Rights Action League], Planned Parenthood, and the American Civil Liberties Union [ACLU]) and from speakers with a mainstream pro-choice party identification (in Germany, the Social Democrats [SPD] and Liberals [FDP], and in the United States, the Democratic Party). These three types of organizational representatives are compared to the baseline of other speakers. These other abortion-rights speakers largely represent medical, religious, and legal groups; journalists; experts; and

Table 1 Framing Strategies by Organizational Type and Country for Pro and Neutral Speakers

	TYPE OF ORGANIZATION							
	Feminist Group or Network		Abortion Rights Advocacy and Counseling		Pro-Abortion-Rights Political Party		Other Pro and Neutral Speakers	
Speakers and Utterances	U.S.	Germany	U.S.	Germany	U.S.	Germany	U.S.	Germany
Proportion of speakers who include any gender-specific self-determination (%)	37	81	22	56	17	37	20	28
Proportion of speakers, including any nongendered individualism (%)	51	11	41	18	49	15	44	16
Rate of use:								
Autonomy ideas per utterance	.77	.71	.75	.81	.60	.52	.68	.55
Protection ideas per utterance	.28	.62	.31	.38	.23	.43	.51	.90
Protecting women per utterance	.17	.29	.23	.23	.17	.25	.29	.56
N of speakers	80	17	344	80	164	401	1,619	524

Note.—Only speakers who are on balance pro or neutral in an article and who do not represent antiabortion parties (Republicans, Christian Democrats) or antiabortion movements are included.

non-party-affiliated government speakers such as judges.

In Germany, speakers for autonomous feminist groups characteristically argue for women's self-determination as women (81% of these 17 speakers include this argument). The pro-choice organizations are in turn more likely to use gendered language than those in the pro-choice parties, and the latter are in turn more likely to do so than the other speakers. Thus organizational representatives in Germany line up so that those representing types of groups that more consistently support abortion rights include proportionately more gendered self-determination arguments. In contrast, the inclusion of individualist framing is always relatively low and is especially so among the small number of feminists who appear in the media. What distinguishes those who more strongly advocate abortion rights from others in Germany is the degree to which they include arguments that specifically raise women's self-determination as a gendered right, not their use of liberal individualist arguments, and in this feminists lead the way. They can be said to have succeeded in making a core feminist frame mainstream.

By contrast, all groups in the United States, including feminist spokespeople, make their arguments in the media predominantly using non-gender-specific individual rights ideas. Speakers representing feminist organizations are at least equally likely to use the liberal individualism frame as other American groups are, though they are more likely to include one or more women's rights ideas, too. Nonetheless, their use of ungendered framing still outweighs their use of language referring specifically to women's rights. In fact, compared to the huge differences among groups in Germany, there is but a small tendency for American feminists to include women's self-determination more than other groups do among their ideas (37% of feminists do, compared to a range of 17%–22% among other abortion-rights speakers). In both countries it is clear that women's self-determination can be characterized as a specifically feminist argument, although even feminist speakers in the United States do not emphasize it as much as they do abstract individualism (37% vs. 51%).

In terms of overall support for autonomy, which combines both liberal individualism and women's rights frames, feminist speakers in both Germany and the United States are quite similar to each other (.77 and .71 autonomy claims per utterance respectively). They are also similar to other pro-choice movement organizations (with mean rates of use of .81 and .75), but more likely than the pro-choice parties and the "other" pro and neutral speakers to make autonomy their concern. It would therefore not be accurate to see either German or U.S. feminists as being more concerned about women's autonomy than speakers in the other country; instead, they express these concerns in different languages of justification, women's self-determination in Germany and abstract individualism in the United States.

It is not surprising also to see in table 1 that protection arguments are far more common among all four types of German organizational representatives, even feminists, than among spokespeople for comparable U.S. organizations. Comparing just the "other" speakers (who are the majority of abortion-rights speakers), autonomy is more frequently used than protection in the U.S. discourse (.68 to .51) while the reverse is true in Germany (.55 for autonomy vs. .90 for protection). But it is the relative significance of protectionist language in specifically feminist discourse in Germany that is most striking. Autonomy and protection both figure strongly in how German feminist speakers speak about abortion (.71 and .62 respectively), while American feminists emphasize autonomy without also making protection-based claims (.77 vs. .28). Thus feminist arguments in the United States do not merely take on a discursive cloak of nongendered individualist rhetoric. As the suppressor effect of individualist frames for autonomy on the inclusion of protection that was found in the overall discourse makes unsurprising, American feminists who have voice in the mass media frame women's autonomy in a way that only rarely involves considering women as needing state help and protection.

This comparison establishes that a sharp difference in framing between Germany and the United States has emerged in relation to their differences in discursive opportunity, while there are also differences between feminists and other framers. U.S. feminist groups who enter mass media discourse argue in the nationally dominant and institutionally anchored language of abstract individualism that the Supreme Court affirmed. German feminists make a case for gendered rights for women as women in matters of reproduction, yet also talk about protecting women. One can therefore speak of a mainstream feminist position that is distinctive to each country. As we will see below, each mainstream framing is not merely a view selected by the media for presentation to the public, but also is part of how feminist organizations and representatives present themselves.

Mainstream Feminist Discourses

Interviews with activists in feminist and pro-choice organizations in the United States and examination of legislative discourse in Germany illuminate just how feminists have adapted to the discursive constraints they faced, and what this also implies about the rhetorical exclusions they adopted.

The U.S. Feminist Mainstream

U.S. feminist organizations criticize the overall "pro-choice" media strategy of stressing abstract "choice" and view the choice approach as leaving out certain groups of women. They nonetheless say they have to adopt such rhetoric in order to be "effective" in defending abortion rights. When they criticize "choice" rhetoric, they particularly focus on the stigma associated with the choice of abortion and the obstacles to access to abortion, not on the social coercions, such as poverty, that can push women to have abortions they do not really want. From this perspective, the issue is a society that is insufficiently supportive of women having abortions, not one that is insufficiently supportive of women having children.

Feminist groups express concern about the negativity toward both actual women and their abortions in the media's "pro-choice" rhetoric. The spokeswoman for NOW, for example, acknowledges pressure to conform to the usual way of talking about abortion rights:

> We don't say pro-choice. We don't use that term . . . we say supporter of abortion rights. Because

I think you have to claim the word. . . . If you can't bring yourself to say it you must believe in your heart of hearts that it's a really horrible thing. It's a really sad situation so you have to call it something else. You have to think of a euphemism, because it's so. . . . And, for a while, we did do that. I mean, we started to do that. (Interview, July 1997)

Within the general abortion-rights movement in the United States, feminist organizations specifically emphasized that their difference from other groups lay in viewing abortion itself in less morally negative terms, as something that was not necessarily traumatic in women's lives. As the spokeswoman for the Feminist Majority put it,

> We were very concerned about how even abortion-rights groups themselves were playing the abortion issue. We were very much against the sort of characterization of abortion as like this really horrible thing that women, after they scrutinized having to do this horrible thing, should have the right to do this horrible thing. And that's still framing it as a horrible thing. And I think it just undermines your cause dramatically. (Interview, September 1997)

Overall, the feminist critique is that abortion is not "this horrible thing" and women should not feel any need for an "apology" for having had an abortion. In their view, "pro-choice" rhetoric already concedes too much ground by suggesting that abortion is something that can be morally disapproved while still permitted legally as a "private" decision.

But they also admit that being effective implies this rhetorical separation. A spokesperson for the Communications Consortium, a consulting group that worked with the "Core Group" of feminist and abortion-rights organizations, affirmed that separating the abstract choice from the content of what was chosen was the movement strategy throughout the 1980s and 1990s:

> That's why, after all these years, and all the millions and millions of dollars of research, NARAL still sticks to messages about choice. People say, "Oh, you need some new messages." But the thing is, that's the one that works. That's the one where people say, "Well, I wouldn't do this, BUT that's not my business, you know. And I don't think people should interfere." That's why it doesn't change. (Interview, March 1998)

She conceded that privacy language was problematic because "vulnerable women" were left out of the debate. She detailed efforts to address women of color and specifically acknowledged that "the things that the groups decide not to go after are those things that affect poor women, a disproportionate number of whom are women of color." She particularly singled out funding for abortion as something these groups no longer pursued. She viewed this as something "they [pro-abortion-rights groups] couldn't win" and hence "politically I won't say it's the wrong decision" but also saw it as a reason that "they lost the moral high ground" (interview, March 1998).

The Feminist Majority spokeswoman said that her organization's emphasis on social protection for women could be found in the feminist defense of clinics from anti-abortion violence, stressing that it was poor women and women of color who disproportionately relied on them, She noted that "most of the clinics, especially the ones most under siege are ones that service especially young poor and women of color populations.... I think higher income, more white populations tend not to go to clinics, they tend to go to private physicians" (interview, September 1997). In this way, by continuing to battle for greater abortion access, even if no longer for funding, feminists defended the practical right to secure an abortion.

But this right of access is a very narrow conception of what protection the state might offer to women in need. Within the movement, in writings directed to scholars and activists, feminists are critical of the state's strongly limited role in financing abortion and child rearing in the United States (Roth 2000; McDonagh 1996; Petchesky 1984). Even when it is acknowledged that practical political alternatives for challenging the limits of liberal individualism are lacking (Fried 1990; Solinger 1998), the "moral high ground" of advocating funding abortions for the poor and also supporting a definition of reproductive rights that includes government support for helping poor women have children, not only abortions, is widely present in academic feminist discourse in the United States (Copelon 1990). But as William Saletan (1998) argues, this narrowly strategic framing is a defensive move in a climate that is seen as putting the formal legal right at risk, and it sacrifices the needs of more socially vulnerable groups for wider state protection of the right to have children as well as abortions. As these organizational spokespeople admit, expanding the concept of reproductive rights is not today what the mainstream movement is seeking to achieve.

The U.S. feminist emphases on destigmatizing abortion and resisting limits on access are very different from mainstream German feminist discourse, which places women's self-determination in a context in which the choice of abortion is portrayed as morally troubling and often less than fully autonomous, but still speaks of self-determination as women's right. This discourse is so rare in the U.S. context that it may be difficult for Americans to recognize it as feminist at all.

German Mainstream Feminist Discourse

There are three basic arguments offered by the women legislators who represented the public face of feminism in the German 1990s abortion debate, and to whom (most) grassroots feminists deferred in the hope of being influential. All these mainstream arguments are shaped by the constitutional court's finding that the fetus is a life to protect and also by feminists' desire to be effective in shaping the 1992 legislation, recognizing that a compromise bill was the best they could win, though not what they considered an ideal solution.

First, there is the claim that women will have (illegal) abortions in any case, so that it is only possible "to protect the fetus with the woman and not against her." Thus, any government action to protect the fetus (the appropriateness of which is not challenged) can only do so by helping women to want to have children and to be able to welcome a particular pregnancy ("to say yes to the child"). In this argument, women choose, but if a social context is "child-friendly" and supportive of women's personal aspirations, women will choose to have children rather than not. As Inge Wettig-Danielmeier, one of the SPD leaders in formulating the coalition bill, argued, "We don't undervalue developing life because we put changes in this society in absolute first place among protective measures, for only when women are finally equal, finally have the same rights and duties, finally know that their lives do not stand every day at the disposition of their partners and children, will they be able to decide to have children with pure joy and full inner conviction" (8225A).[14] Rather than the stick of criminal law, the carrot of equality for women, including benefits for child rearing, will be the only really effective form of government intervention, and "a politics that is against women, to whom developing life is entrusted in the first place, is at the same time a politics against developing life" (Edith Niehuis, SPD, 8269A).[15]

Given this premise, help and protection for women are a means to the end of protecting the fetus, since a child-friendly society is one in which women have the means to "combine work and family." Antidiscrimination provisions and better wages for women workers are encouragements for women to see having a child as something they can literally afford to do; expanded state provision of kindergartens and full-day schools will help eliminate the conflict in women's lives that gives rise to "conflict pregnancies" in which abortion is even considered.

Second, there is the claim that pregnant women are essentially mothers and so are inseparably joined to the fetus emotionally. Not only do women really want to be mothers if they can be, so that any decision to terminate a pregnancy is difficult and a "conflict" for the woman, but abortion is a fundamental assault on the woman herself, by her own hand, even a form of "suicide." Dorle Marx (SPD), first pointing out that she herself was pregnant, made this analogy explicit, saying, "I assert that every termination of pregnancy is a kind of partial suicide for the mother, a destruction of a piece of her own self and is also perceived to be exactly this by the pregnant woman" (8257D), a statement that was interrupted by applause from the SPD and FDP representatives. The fetus is not just a "developing child" but the pregnant woman is portrayed as a "developing mother" (*werdende Mutter*). This argument stresses the continuity between the fetus as part of the woman's body and the woman herself, not presenting the fetus as "tissue" or as the property of the woman, but as a part of her "self." Because of the continuity between fetus and self, a decision to end a pregnancy is portrayed difficult, traumatic, and only undertaken when the woman can see no other way out of a situation.

While affirming thereby that women only choose abortions for serious reasons, not as easily or lightheartedly as abortion opponents might suggest, this line of argument also readily accepts the idea that women need psychological counseling and help to see their alternatives. Feminist speakers in the legislature largely framed even mandatory counseling as fundamentally helpful to women. But giving women the final say over abortion is, in this argument, giving the choice to the person who is most sympathetically identified with the interests of the fetus. Should she decide that a continuation of the pregnancy is not desirable, it must really be inadvisable, since she literally loves the baby "as herself."

The third strategy is to argue that "only the woman can know" the actual circumstances in which her motherhood would occur. Playing particularly upon the fear that women's decisions could be second-guessed by a court and found to be insufficient, as they were in the Memmingen trial, this argument is that courts, judges, and even doctors are privy only to a limited view of the circumstances in which women find themselves. They must rely on what women are willing to disclose to them about the details of their life situation, and so third parties are by definition less, rather than more, capable of assessing the situation. As Uta Würfel, the FDP leader of the coalition effort, put this argument, "This situation of need, this situation of conflict is something she alone can grasp and is not something a third party can evaluate on her behalf" (8230D).

Unlike the typical U.S. "choice" argument for noninterference in a woman's own decision making, this argument does not frame the decision as inherently individual or private but rather as social and complex. The involvement of others in her life is critical, but something that only she has sufficient knowledge to evaluate. Since she will (the argument presumes) be the one who will be responsible for actually caring for the child over the long haul, she is the one best able to evaluate what resources she has and needs to carry out that task. Rita Süssmuth, a self-described feminist and leader of the faction of the Christian Democratic Union (CDU) that split from the rest of the party to support the coalition bill, explicitly accepted the right-to-life position that "there is no self-determination as a right over another human life" but then qualified it: "A termination of pregnancy can only be considered in a situation of need and conflict in which there is no way out. I wonder why a doctor, or a judge or prosecutor second-guessing him, would be granted more competence or responsibility to make this decision than the woman, who not only now, but lifelong, takes on the responsibility for the child, the children. Let us finally stop thinking of women as incapable of decision, incapable of responsibility" (8291B). This argument was greeted by applause coming from all the parties.

Overall, these three strategies combine to both assert a position of women as socially vulnerable and victimized but also as self-determining in practice and by right. Abortion is in no way destigmatized, but alternatives to abortion are offered to rather than forced upon women. The emphasis is on a society that would support childbirth, even for unmarried and poor women.

There is a sharp contrast between the two discourses sketched out here. The dominant American one emphasizes an abstract choice, and it is further pushed by feminist organizations not to see abortion as "a horrible thing" when women choose it. Destigmatizing abortion and focusing on abortion access rather than supports for motherhood are strategic feminist responses to the opportunity structure of American liberal individualism. German feminist discourse in the legislature instead strategically casts abortion as deeply undesired, especially by women, who are nonetheless entitled to make this decision by being the "ones most deeply affected."[16]

Both strategic ways of framing the abortion issue marginalize alternative points of view that are part of the more complex feminist ideological repertoire. The logical consequence of the contrasting discursive opportunity structures of these two countries is that the frames that are marginalized among self-described feminists in one country most resemble the feminist perspective typical of the other.

Marginalized Feminist Discourses

In the United States, one part of this excluded discourse is a "feminist pro-life" position. Serrin Foster, of Feminists for Life, would be quite mainstream in the German context but is attacked by both sides in the American debate when she makes claims for helping women avoid abortion that are based on women's oppression. Like many of the German women legislators, she says that "we believe that no woman chooses abortion freely...that it is a last resort, that it's a reflection that there is a problem in society." She explains that many of her pro-life allies reject her perspective:

> They hate the word feminism. [They say that] women were having abortions because they wanted to be free, you know, that it was the changing dynamics of the family structure that caused women to have abortions, and [we] were saying "No, women were not having abortions because they want to be in control of their own lives and whatever.... They were having abortions because women were abandoned by men and, in some cases, threatened and coerced by men into having abortions." (Interview, July 1997)

At the same time, she is unconvinced that pro-choice feminists are really supportive of the choice to have a child, pointing out that on college campuses "if there's such a free choice, then where's the housing, where's the day care, where's the maternity coverage for women [students]?...If everybody has such a free choice, why would they only choose abortion?" (interview, July 1997).

American pro-choice speakers are reluctant to acknowledge the social coercion that may coexist with formal legal freedoms and to admit that the "free choice" may not be experienced as a choice at all. In doing so, American abortion-rights discourse marginalizes those women who are in reality victims, and who have been "left alone" by the state to deal with the economic, personal, and social crisis they are experiencing with their pregnancy. Poor women and women of color are disproportionately among the women who do not feel that they have a choice to bear a child and who may feel instead compelled and coerced into sterilization, adoption, or abortion (Solinger 2001; Roberts 1997). The Black Women's Health Network and other women of color groups try to speak for these women but virtually never have voice in the media and are (with regret) abandoned on their "moral high ground" by mainstream women's groups. Their radical positions do not make it into the mainstream of media representation.

The virtual absence of a protectionist discourse within the American abortion-rights movement does not eliminate the actual experience of women who would indeed choose to have a child if there were "such a free choice." It does leave these more economically vulnerable and socially abused women open to a gendered antiabortion mobilization that takes up themes of women's exploitation and victimization and uses them, paradoxically enough, against feminism. Women's groups in the pro-life movement, such as American Victims of Abortion, Birthright, and Project Rachel as well as Feminists for Life, strategically seek to take advantage of this discursive exclusion. They appeal to this constituency by positing a "postabortion syndrome" of guilt and remorse, which can make sense of some women's regrets over a decision that they felt was not a real choice in practice.

In unified Germany, the radical discourse that is marginalized and rejected by mainstream feminists primarily comes from women who were raised in East Germany and so experienced abortion rights in a "child friendly" society. The East German state after 1972 did not have recourse to mandatory pro-life counseling, stigmatizing indications, or punitive criminalization to deter women from abortion, but actually relied on the "carrots" that West German reformers said they wanted.[17] Women from the (former) East and the small number of West German grassroots feminists who took to the streets to demand self-determination—whose voices virtually never appeared in the West German newspaper sample—did not speak of the absence of discrimination against women or benefits for child rearing as protections that would allow women the freedom to be self-determining, but assumed that women were already free and independent actors. Their rhetoric distinguished itself from that of mainstream German feminists by insisting that women could not only choose motherhood but also nonmotherhood without guilt or apology. Their desire

to destigmatize abortion resembles the mainstream American feminist discourse, even though it is renounced and ridiculed in Germany.

These feminist speakers and their allies among Bündnis 90/Green and PDS legislators made claims to self-determination that resembled the scope of what the *Roe* decision guaranteed for American women.[18] For example, the National Coalition against Section 218, the umbrella organization coordinating grassroots feminist protest, in 1990–91 featured a sign demanding "Abolish Section 218" on the cover of its political pamphlet *Women Demand Self-Determination*. Waltraud Schoppe, identified with feminist causes and one of the first women's affairs ministers in West Germany, argued against mandatory counseling that "apparently no other country sees women in pregnancy conflicts as morally and ethically collapsed persons like this...fixing women in a victim role, [counseling is] a conservative political idea that refuses to admit that women have decisiveness and determination" (8265C). She drew neither applause from the representatives nor coverage from the press.

The PDS, the successor party to the Communist Party in the East and a strong advocate of the view that abortion rights were one of the accomplishments of that regime, offered a bill that simply stated "a woman and the fruit of her womb are one physical and social unit. Every woman has the right to decide for herself if she will bear a pregnancy to term or not." PDS speakers such as Petra Bläss praised the social supports for children and mothers that the German Democratic Republic (GDR) had offered, sometimes facing catcalls from other representatives that "then you must want to go back there" (8236B). PDS remarks were not applauded by legislators in other parties, reflecting the overall disapproval in which they were (and are) held.

The Bündnis 90/Green legislators, all also from East Germany, also argued against stigmatizing abortion. Christina Schenk put the argument starkly:

> Only when the freedom [of women's decision] is guaranteed and when the one decision is as socially accepted as the other can you say that women's dignity is truly recognized...it is absurd to think that pregnancy termination is fundamentally

wrong and must be treated with disapproval by the state.... This law criminalizes East German women...and by saying that through counseling women will be put in the position to make a responsible self-determined decision it tells them...that because there was no mandatory counseling rule, women in the GDR did not act responsibly. (8234B)

She and other East German speakers emphasized the insult that mandatory counseling regulation conveyed to them and defended the importance of asserting the principle of state noninterference, but also acknowledged that their parliamentary position was not going to be effective.

Neither the PDS nor the Bündis 90/Green bills garnered the least support in the legislature, nor were significant numbers of feminists in West Germany willing to take to the street on their behalf. Unlike Americans who advocate simply leaving women alone to make a free decision, these East German feminists were occasionally ridiculed, more often simply ignored.

Conclusions

As this comparative-historical analysis has shown, some movement speakers do seek resonance within a specific discursive opportunity structure and frame their arguments in ways that respond strategically to the chance to be effective in influencing popular and elite discourses. Both American and German feminists in the mainstream media present arguments for abortion rights that express the dominant framing of the issue as privacy in the United States and protection in Germany. But other feminist speakers still frame the issue in ways at odds with the hegemonic discourse of their particular place and time. While these radical speakers are discursively marginalized in their home country, their frames are quite mainstream in a different context. The destigmatizing claims that are most ridiculed and excluded in German feminism are among the most acceptable in the United States, and the unattainable "moral high ground" of state support for reproductive rights in the United States is part of the protectionist mainstream in Germany.

To make sense of this finding, analysis of framing in general and of resonance in particular needs

to be more explicitly connected with the analysis of power relations. The concept of discursive opportunity structure as an institutionally anchored gradient of opportunity provides this missing link between discourse and power, and it also clarifies the difference between discursive context and strategic choice. When movement speakers seek to be effective within the bounds set by the hegemonic discourse, they will strategically choose to make claims in terms that are resonant with it. Because discursive opportunity structures are part of the arrangements of power and status in society, it is socially disadvantaged groups that have the most interest in the frames marginalized by hegemonic discourse. Excluding ideas has consequences for group inclusion, just as excluding groups limits the range of ideas that are expressed. This analysis explains, then, why social movement groups that seek resonance will tend to downplay the needs of their more disadvantaged constituents and representatives of these groups will tend to advance arguments that are more radical than resonant.

We should thus never expect all movement speakers to seek resonance; some speakers will persist in offering arguments that are radical, contradicting rather than affirming the premises of the discursive opportunity structure. Their radicalism lies in the challenge they pose to the institutionalized ways of thinking about an issue and the power relations embedded in these symbolic conventions. Analytically, therefore, radicalism is something different from either violent and confrontational behaviors or some theoretically defined set of "fundamental" social demands that are constant across context. Like resonance, radicalism is an *interaction* between discursive opportunity and the frames that are chosen, but it is oppositional rather than supportive in nature. Just who is a radical depends on the discursive context in which they speak. This context differs by time and place, which explains the apparent paradox that some radical ideas of the past now seem commonplace (and vice versa).

Feminist experience with individualist and protectionist discourses in Germany and the United States also shows that frames are not simply inert resources used to construct winning strategies by and for a particular movement. Framing is an interactive process that is inherently about inclusion and exclusion of ideas, so the choice of what ideas "the" movement endorses sets boundaries on its collective identity and on the definition of what losses would count as a movement failure. Choosing language that conforms to hegemonic discourse, feminists who want to be "effective" limit the range of claims that they consider "feminist" as well as drop certain goals as simply "unrealistic," rather than admitting they have lost this fight. Thus mainstream feminists in Germany accept a definition of victory as women's limited right to self-determination in the face of a variety of state protections such as mandatory counseling, and mainstream feminists in the United States define winning as defending a formal legal right to abortion without any state funding for either abortion or childbirth. As political radicals in every social movement have always recognized, choosing resonance implies sacrificing ideals for which the movement has stood, limiting the demands that the movement places on authorities, and potentially excluding significant constituent groups and their needs from movement representation. In fact, using "effectiveness" as a criterion for deciding on what frame to use may be the critical underlying mechanism that produces what movements call "co-optation." Seeking longer-term change in hegemonic ideas is radical, and while it may decrease effectiveness in the short term or in relation to the formal political institutions of the state, it may be the only route to cultural transformations that delegitimate existing power relations.

In addition to such general conclusions about social movement rhetoric and strategies, this comparative-historical analysis also offers insights into the gender order and the gaps in feminist abortion frames in each of these specific national contexts. The definitions of what kinds of needs enter the public arena are different in Europe and the United States, and these discursive contours of the political field are themselves part of how the institutional gender order is differentially structured in each. Where the American political organization of gender maintains gender inequalities more by "privatizing" them, the German tradition more often institutionalizes gender inequality in the way it paternalistically brings in the state. Thus, the

exclusions seen in regard to abortion discourse are likely to be found on a range of issues.

Unlike German discourse, American abortion-rights rhetoric does not particularly stress women as embodied (or connected to the fetus with any distinctive psychological identification), socially located in a distinctive context that can be supportive or oppressive to her as a woman (through violent or unsupportive partners, for example), or facing discriminations in her job, education, or personal life should she become a mother. It therefore has little connection to the protectionist "radical feminist" discourse that is often found, in the United States on other issues of sexuality such as rape, pornography, and prostitution. The women who are, and feel themselves to be, victimized by oppressive social conditions—including not only poverty and racism but also parents, husbands, or boyfriends who pressure them into abortions they personally do not want—thus form a constituency that is not being addressed by feminists. Their regrets and sense of victimization present a strategic opportunity that women's groups in the antiabortion movement have taken up. These strategically produced exclusions may relate to the race and social class differences in pro- and anti-abortion-rights mobilization observed by Luker (1984) and others.

But German discourse, while collectively affirming a variety of supportive policies that allow women "to say yes to the child" in ways that American social policy does not, equally narrowly draws boundaries around acceptable "needs" that women have. The personal desire to say no to becoming a mother remains discrediting and unnatural in the frame of reference for West German speakers. Abortion in this view has to be understood to be a "horrible thing" if women are not to be seen as horrible people. Women's "choice" to reject motherhood is not admitted within the boundaries of what women authentically might choose for themselves. Like pornography and prostitution, abortion is seen as always forced upon women who should not be further punished for the necessity that a hostile society lays upon them; "help, don't punish" defines the range of options for responding to women who can be thought of only as victims. Women in former East Germany are insulted to find their experiences with legal abortion being framed as victimization rather than their autonomous decision making, and many American women would feel equally affronted if *Roe* were replaced by a protectionist policy like Germany's.

If legal abortion is, as Gordon argues, only a means to the end of authentic birth control, fostering the conditions under which women can choose either a yes *or* a no autonomously would also include acknowledging a wider range of experiences in women's lives, including those discursively marginalized in each country. But the power relations structuring discursive opportunity in the United States and in Germany make such a widening of feminist frames highly unlikely. Incorporating structurally marginalized perspectives would mean advancing arguments that are not merely less likely to have a policy impact but are actively dangerous politically to the movement. By being at cross-purposes with the way feminists have adapted their arguments to the prevailing structure of discursive opportunity, they offer inviting targets for the opposition to attack.

In the end, for all social movements, discursive opportunity structures will create both losers and winners. Seeking to be successful in terms used by institutional power holders will always carry costs in marginalizing certain frames and the real needs they express. This may explain why some movement groups, including some feminist framers, still prefer to be radical.

NOTES

This article is based on work supported by the National Science Foundation (grant no. SBR9301617). Thanks are extended for the many useful comments and suggestions provided by Ann Taylor Allen, Christine Bose, Lisa D. Brush, Jane Collins, Shelley Correll, Linda Gordon, Richard Hiskes, Joya Misra, Victoria Mayer, Silke Roth, Elizabeth Rudd, Leila Rupp, Kristen Springer, and Joan Twiggs on an earlier and much less focused draft of this article, as well as to the *AJS* reviewers for their constructive theoretical contributions.

1. The concept of *discursive opportunity structure* acknowledges that limits and opportunities to which movements are strategically responding include both stable and variable elements, as well as features that may be specific to a particular issue or more widely available across issue domains (Gamson and Meyer 1996; Ferree et al. 2002). While the *production* of a discursive opportunity structure and its change over time surely requires examination of the effects of both movements and countermovements on it, this article focuses on the *effects* it has on one movement, feminism.

2. Discursive opportunity structures are certainly political but are not usefully conceptualized as merely a subtype of state-centered political opportunity structure. By advantaging certain ways of speaking that are at least potentially open to anyone, discursive opportunity structures deploy power to shape ideas directly (and group access indirectly) while other forms of political opportunity structure shape group access directly (and the expression of ideas indirectly). In the sense of seeing the symbolic as itself a domain of power, the term "hegemonic discourse" comes closer to what the term covers but does not emphasize the structural and institutional character it has. Although anchored in institutionalized texts, the effects of privileging a certain way of framing are expressed in a "capillary" way in expert discourses, media presentations, and popular culture, not only in what is recognized as formal politics.

3. National and local contexts vary, and long-term transformations of material interests and ideologies, as Babb (1996) shows, can undercut the appeal of once popular frames. Events may also create new opportunities for formerly radical ideas (Ellingson 1995; Gamson and Modigliani 1989).

4. Yet it should not be surprising to find that ideas that conflict with institutionally dominant frames might enter the media's representation of a movement, especially when a movement is being presented as a danger or threat to society (see Davenport and Eads 2001). It might be hypothesized that the more radical a movement is perceived to be by the public is a direct function of such representations, but testing this hypothesis is beyond the scope of this article.

5. Approximately 90% of all abortions in Germany are estimated to have been performed under the "social need" indication.

6. Ullrich (1998) also shows that German feminist discourse in women's studies publications from 1985 to 1992 has become more protectionist, portraying women who "appeared to choose" new reproductive technologies as victims or dupes. Self-determination appears as a dangerous "spirit that we summoned" for the 1970s abortion debate that is "coming back to haunt" 1990s feminist politics (pp. 191–98).

7. The American mainstream is least emphasized here because it is by far the most familiar argument; indeed, it is difficult even to discuss the debate in English without resorting to the language of "pro-choice" institutionalized in the United States. But because the terminology of "choice" is the result of a specific discursive strategy, as I later discuss, I have tried to avoid the term "pro-choice" as much as is possible and thus not to assimilate other frames to this mainstream U.S. definition of the issue. Although for brevity I have sometimes substituted the term "pro-choice" for the more accurate term "pro-abortion rights" to describe the political position (although not the frame), these are not

wholly synonymous concepts and "pro-choice" is potentially misleading as a label if taken too literally.

8. Ideas coded as neutral in policy direction included some that would lead in different directions in each country (e.g., asserting that the fetus is a life at a particular stage and not before would imply lesser regulation in Germany but not in the United States) as well as ideas with no directional implication (e.g., "I wonder whether this is a human life").

9. These numbers reflect weighted figures corrected for differences in sampling fractions by newspaper, year, and country. For details of the weighting procedure see Ferree et al. (2002).

10. Neutral as well as pro-abortion-rights speakers are included since speakers coded as neutral include those whose organizational position clearly locates them on one side or the other but whose utterance taken at face value in the article did not. For example, the rhetorical question "Is this a human life?" means something different, even if it is the only statement offered in an article, depending on whether it is uttered by the director of the National Right to Life Committee or the director of the National Abortion Federation, but both were coded as neutral. In addition, arguments that were contextually different (mandatory counseling for teens only was restrictive in the United States but more liberal in Germany) were also coded as neutral. Many feminist speakers in both countries were coded as neutral, making it more valid to include than to exclude them from this analysis. However, any speakers who were discursively neutral in the article but represented antiabortion parties or antiabortion social movement organizations were excluded from the analysis in this article.

11. In the United States the constitutional interpretation in *Roe* triggered a wave of state legislation and constitutional argument, while in Germany the order was reversed, with federal legislation in 1974 being referred to the constitutional court and then modified when the court rejected the initial legalization. But by 1977 in both countries the nature of the court's institutional framing was established.

12. The effect of gender on the speaker's inclusion of a women's self-determination frame outweighs that of country (βs

are .17 and −.07 respectively; the difference is significant [P <.05]), but the effect of country outweighs that of gender for the inclusion of an abstract individualism argument (βs are .20 and −.03 respectively [P <.05]).

13. Speakers who include both types of autonomy frames look more like women's rights framers than like liberal individualists, suggesting that it is the *exclusive* reliance on the ungendered frame that makes the use of protection frames less likely.

14. This and all quotations from the German are my own translations. The citation is to the location within the stenographic transcript of the Bundestag debates.

15. A subsidiary argument to this central theme is the claim that women have and always will have the option to have an illegal abortion, and so criminalization is powerless to really prevent abortion. This presents the state as weak and women as strong and self-determining as a matter of historical fact (e.g., Christina Lucyga, SPD 8345B; Ingrid Matthäus-Maier, SPD 8356D).

16. *Betroffenheit,* the German term for being the ones who are affected, was a central claim raised by radical feminists for voice in decisions of all kinds.

17. This does not mean that abortion was actually destigmatized or discussed freely. See Maleck-Lewy and Ferree (2000) for a discussion of the East German experience.

18. The PDS is the Party of Democratic Socialism, or reformed Communist Party, of East Germany. The Bündnis 90/Green legislative coalition was assembled from among the many dissident groups active in the East directly before the fall of the wall. Although the Green Party in general represents "new social movement" constituencies in West Germany, in this immediate postunification election it failed to win sufficient votes in the West to get seats (there is a 5% minimum hurdle) and was represented only by East German dissidents allied with it. Note, too, that because, especially in the East in this period, the Green Party represented social movements rather than an institutionalized party, it is grouped in the quantitative analysis as a "pro-choice organization or movement" rather than as a political party.

20.
From Protective to Equal Treatment: Legal Framing Processes and Transformation of the Women's Movement in the 1960s

NICHOLAS PEDRIANA

Introduction

In the mid-1960s, the women's movement found itself at an organizational and ideological crossroads. When Title VII of the 1964 Civil Rights Act suddenly and unexpectedly prohibited employment discrimination on the basis of sex, women's groups responded with ambivalence. On the one hand, women's advocates were generally pleased with the new law; just a year earlier, the President's Commission on the Status of Women (PCSW)—created in 1961 to offer policy advice on women's issues—promoted an end to most gender-specific employment classifications. On the other hand, protective labor laws exclusively for women had historically been a legislative cornerstone of the women's movement. From the early 1900s into the 1960s, activists fought to enact and consolidate policies that shielded women from dangerous and unfair working conditions.[1] Title VII thus set into motion a political and cultural debate, both inside and outside the women's movement, about traditional gender stereotypes, women's employment rights, and the meaning of equal opportunity for women in American society more generally. When the dust settled a few years later, the women's movement had been organizationally and philosophically transformed. From a loose collection of leaders organized primarily within government-sponsored "status-of-women" committees emerged an independent and far more politically aggressive social movement organization—the National Organization for Women (NOW). Unlike its predecessors, NOW rejected *all* sex-specific employment classifications and was ideologically committed to a full-blown equal treatment standard for women in the workplace. NOW's immediate political identity centered on the destruction of gender-specific legal categories, including those that for decades had required and legitimated protective labor policies exclusively for women. And just a few years later, protective laws for women were legally invalidated, never to return. Thus the title of this article simultaneously describes fundamental changes in sex discrimination policy and a transformation in the identity and objectives of the women's movement itself.

This article takes off from a central premise: transformations in the women's movement and women's employment policies were largely attributable to a framing contest between competing cultural constructions of gender in the workplace and in society more generally. Moreover, this framing contest—what I call "protective" versus "equal" treatment—was waged in explicitly legal terms. Analyzing legal framing of the women's movement in the 1960s presents an opportunity to further develop theoretical knowledge on the cultural and symbolic processes that enable, constrain, and transform social movements. I begin by revisiting the idea of cultural framing, a conceptual staple of social movement theory and research (see, e.g., Benford and Snow 2000; McAdam, McCarthy, and Zald 1996; Snow et al. 1986). I suggest that the general absence of law from framing research (and from social movement theory more broadly) limits conceptual and theoretical understanding on how—and with what consequences—challenger groups socially construct their grievances, identities, and objectives. To address this theoretical shortcoming,

Pedriana, Nicholas. 2006. "From Protective to Equal Treatment: Legal Framing Processes and Transformation of the Women's Movement in the 1960s." *American Journal of Sociology* 111: 1718–1761. Reprinted by permission of the University of Chicago Press. Notes have been renumbered and edited.

I integrate a key strand of law and society scholarship that focuses on how law's deeply embedded "constitutive" symbols and categories influence cultural framing processes. I make no claim that cultural framing of social movements should be understood in exclusively legal terms. However, development of a legal framing perspective offers a theoretically novel framework for analyzing the repertoires of meaning that movement actors construct and mobilize in their quest for social and political change.

I develop my theoretical arguments about legal framing through a historical-narrative analysis of the women's movement and the debate over protective labor policies in the 1960s. I focus on a series of key events and sequences, each of which corresponded to specific legal changes in equal employment policy for women. My analysis illustrates several distinct "frame alignment" processes— amplification, extension, and transformation— originally identified by Snow et al. (1986; see also Benford and Snow 2000). I conclude with a summary of my historical findings and discuss more general implications of a legal framing perspective for theory and research on cultural framing processes and social movements.

Social Movements, Cultural Framing, and Law

Up to the late 1980s, the lion's share of social movement scholarship concentrated on the organizational resources or political-institutional constellations that enabled and constrained collective actors. Thus "resource mobilization" theory (Jenkins 1983; McCarthy and Zald 1977) explored how a movement's fortunes were tied to organizational command of instrumental resources, including money, personnel, expertise, third-party support, access to mass media, and so on. Meanwhile, political process models (McAdam 1982; Tarrow 1994; Tilly 1978) focused analytic attention on "political opportunity structures"—broader institutional features of states, parties, and interest representation systems—that conditioned social movement emergence, development, and outcomes (see Kitschelt 1986; Kriesi 2004; McAdam et al. 1996; McAdam, Tarrow, and Tilly 2001). Thus, the bulk of social movement theory and research was concerned with the *structural* conditions and resources that encouraged or inhibited challenger groups.

Yet like the broader "cultural turn" (Steinmetz 1999; Williams 2004) in the social sciences more generally, social movement scholars became increasingly aware of the symbolic and social-constructionist dimensions of collective action. Social mobilization requires in part that actors perceive a common identity and sense of shared grievances. Researchers thus developed the concept of "collective action frames," "action-oriented sets of beliefs and meanings that inspire and legitimate the activities and campaigns of a social movement organization" (Benford and Snow 2000, p. 614). Accordingly, the process through which movements mobilize "symbols, claims, and even identities in the pursuit of activism" is generally known as *framing* (Williams 2004, p. 93; see also, e.g., Benford 1993; Benford and Snow 2000; Gamson and Meyer 1996; McAdam et al. 1996; Polletta 1999; Snow 2004; Snow and McAdam 2000; Snow et al. 1986; Zald 1996). Building on Erving Goffman's (1974, pp. 464–66) concept of frame as "schemata of interpretation," the seminal work of David Snow et al. (1986, pp. 464, 466) summarized the importance of framing for the study of social movements: "By rendering events or occurrences meaningful, frames function to organize experience and guide action, whether individual or collective....What is at issue is not merely the presence or absence of grievances, but the manner in which grievances are interpreted and the generation and diffusion of those interpretations."

Frame analysis has established a solid empirical base "with respect to a broad range of movements in a variety of contexts and countries" (Snow 2004, p. 387, and summary table, pp. 388–89), and has generally been used to complement, not supplant, "structural" approaches to social movements (see, e.g., Benford and Snow 2000; Cornfield and Fletcher 1998; Ferree et al. 2002; Gamson and Meyer 1996; Polletta 1999; Snow et al. 1986; but see Goodwin and Jasper 1999, 2004).[2] For both reasons, cultural framing has earned its rightful place as a central theoretical perspective in social movement theory and research.

Even so, I argue that the literature as a whole has been weakened by an important omission: law and legal institutions have not been central components of social movement theory generally, nor of cultural framing scholarship specifically.[3] This is somewhat peculiar. Legal institutions, including administrative agencies and courts, are important sites of political conflict among challengers, dominant social groups, and the state (Bernstein 2001; Handler 1978; Pedriana 2004; Pedriana and Stryker 2004). Both sociologists of law and law and society scholars have long argued that legal rules and norms, statutory texts, administrative regulations and guidelines, and judicial rulings are key resources for social action (see, e.g., Bernstein 2001; Burstein 1991; Edelman 1992; McCann 1994; McIntyre 1994; Stryker 1994). Moreover, nearly all social movement objectives are at least in part *legal* objectives. Whether challengers demand recognition of previously denied rights (e.g., right to same-sex marriage), expansion of existing rights or benefits (e.g., affirmative action as opposed to passive nondiscrimination), or government regulation of social and economic behavior (e.g., legal limits on industrial pollution), social movements routinely draw upon law and seek legal change.

To be sure, some studies of social movements and collective behavior have made reference to law. Olzak and Shanahan (2003), for example, examined the enabling impact of court rulings upholding the legitimacy of racial segregation on heightened collective violence against racial minorities in the post–Civil War United States. Oliver and Maney (2000) found that protest about legal/legislative issues receives more media coverage than other types of protest issues. In her analysis of public discourse over same-sex marriage in Hawaii, Hull (1997) found that elite actors were more likely than nonelite actors to frame the issue in terms of legal rights. Woliver (1998) traced the effects of Supreme Court abortion rulings on the framing strategies of both the pro-choice and pro-life movements. And numerous studies of the Civil Rights Movement have considered how court rulings both enabled and constrained subsequent mobilization, including the creation of new symbolic frames (see, e.g., McAdam 1982; Pedriana and Stryker 1997).

Thus, I am *not* arguing that law and legal issues have been altogether missing from the social movement literature. Rather, my basic claim is that law has not as yet been systematically incorporated—as a fundamental concept and theoretical mechanism—into social movement theory generally, and into the cultural framing perspective specifically (for initial attempts to do so, see Marshall [2003] and Pedriana [2004]). I maintain also that this has limited knowledge of cultural framing processes because law is a central *meaning-making* institution within which challengers do "interpretive work" (Snow 2004, p. 380) and socially construct their grievances, identity, and objectives. I therefore attempt to integrate the cultural framing literature with key insights from law and society scholarship. Specifically, "constitutive" approaches to law offer a powerful theoretical vehicle for understanding how legally embedded symbols and categories shape social actors' interpretive capacities in ways that enable and constrain movements in their competition with dominant groups and the state.

Law's Constitutive Effects and Cultural Framing

Constitutive perspectives are unified by the organizing principle that "law provides social actors with a powerful set of interpretive tools" (Marshall 2003, p. 661) that influence patterns of social conflict and action (see, e.g., Bernstein 2001; Calavita 2001; Ewick and Silbey 1998; Marshall 2003; Nielsen 2000; Sarat and Kearns 1993; Yngvesson 1988). Legal symbols and categories act as cognitive lenses through which individuals and groups construct the relationships, practices, and knowledge that make up, or "constitute" social life. Rather than viewing law solely as a tool or instrument of social control, constitutivists explore how law affects society from the "inside out, by providing the principal categories that make social life seem natural, normal, cohesive, and coherent" (Sarat and Kearns 1993, p. 22). People often construct and understand social relationships—even those relationships that are not explicitly legal—through conceptual prisms of property, contract, rights, obligations, due process, and so on. Each of these ideas is rooted in a symbolic framework organized around *legal* concepts and categories.

A great deal of constitutive scholarship looks broadly at people's use of law to frame "everyday" perceptions, actions, and experiences (see, e.g., Ewick and Silbey 1998; Marshall 2003; Merry 1990; Nielsen 2000; Sarat and Kearns 1993). Other work explores law's constitutive influence more specifically on social movements and patterns of collective action (e.g., Lazarus-Black and Hirsch 1994; McCann 1994). As John Brigham (1988) noted, "[Law] infuse[s] and inform[s] [social] movements themselves by becoming an essential part of their thought, their identity, and their social boundaries" (p. 304). Indeed, since law provides social actors with key interpretive resources, constructing and mobilizing legally embedded cultural symbols is one central theoretical mechanism through which challengers frame their grievances, identity, and objectives. For example, the principle of color-blind equal treatment under law embedded in the Fourteenth Amendment's equal protection clause was one dominant legal frame of the 1960s Civil Rights Movement. It was a successful frame in part because it drew upon widely shared—and legally codified—cultural principles about equal opportunity in American society.

Moreover, because "law may be the source of new expectations for existing relations" (McIntyre 1994, p. 113), aggrieved groups can also sustain successful challenges by *reframing* a movement's grievances and objectives around new or alternative legal symbols. As Bryant Garth and Austin Sarat (1998) wrote, "Progressive struggle for social change...comes in part through resistance and transformation of seemingly taken-for-granted [legal] categories and terms" (p. 8). To continue with the civil rights example, the movement was—with some success— later able to push for affirmative action policies in part by culturally redefining the *legal* meaning of equal opportunity to include race-conscious remedies for historical discrimination against minority groups (see Graham 1990; Pedriana and Stryker 1997, 2004; Skrentny 1996).[4]

In short, law's constitutive symbols and categories are central elements of a social movement's interpretive repertoire. Exploring how challengers frame social movements in legal terms may expand general theoretical knowledge on the cultural framing processes that enable, constrain, and (sometimes) transform social movements. My legal framing approach builds on a small body of empirical work that has begun to merge constitutive legal scholarship with research on social movements and cultural framing. For example, Anna-Maria Marshall (2003) showed how women create and mobilize legal frames to make sense of their perceptions and experiences of sexual harassment in the workplace. Michael McCann's (1994) seminal work explored law's symbolic impact on development of the women's pay-equity movement in the 1980s. McCann analyzed in part "the constitutive role of legal rights both as a strategic resource and as a constraint for collective efforts to transform or 'reconstitute' relationships among social groups" (McCann 1994, p. 7).

The Theoretical Novelty of Legal Framing

Given the now-voluminous scholarship on cultural framing and the ever-growing taxonomy of frames identified in particular case studies, one might be reasonably skeptical about the conceptual novelty of legal frames and a constitutive approach to framing processes. In his "insider's critique" of the framing literature, Robert Benford (1997) pointed to a "descriptive bias" in which "a major thrust of the research agenda has been to identify the universe of specific frames... [resulting] in a rather long laundry list of types of frames" (p. 414). Viewed from this standpoint, legal frames may indeed appear to be little more than the proverbial kitchen sink, throwing yet another frame type onto the pile. I argue, however, that legal frames are not on equal footing with other types of frames. Instead, law and legal symbols are "master frames" with a theoretical power and importance that goes well beyond the case-specific frames unique to a given social movement.

Law as a Master Frame

Master frames serve as dominant "algorithms" (Benford and Snow 2000, p. 618) that resonate deeply across social movements and protest cycles. As Benford (1997) wrote, "[Master frames] serve the field well because they are clearly applicable across a variety of movements and cultural contexts"

(p. 414). Hull (1997) added "the scope and duration of whole cycles of social movement activity may in part depend on the potency of their underlying master frames" (p. 209). Conceiving of law as a master frame finds theoretical justification in the social movement literature specifically, and in the sociology of law more generally.

Although the current list of identified master frames is small, the legal "rights" frame is invariably among them (see e.g., Benford 1997; Hull 1997; Valocchi 1996). Hull provides a summary statement:

> Because its emphasis on equal rights and opportunities resonates with core American values, the civil rights master frame has inspired the specific collective action-frames of a diverse array of recent social movements in the United States, including the women's movement, the disability movement, the animal rights movement and the gay rights movement....The civil rights master frame arguably has been the single most dominant master frame in U.S. movements over the last three to four decades. (Hull 1997, p. 209)

But if the master status of the rights frame has been duly acknowledged, framing scholars have not systematically attempted to explain, conceptually and theoretically, *why* the rights frame resonates so strongly among collective actors, especially in the United States.[5] The reason, I argue, is that rights are fundamental *legal* symbols with a powerful impact on how grievances and objectives are conceived, legitimized, and acted upon in the American political system. Both classical and more recent law and society scholarship strongly support this claim.

Tracing the development and centrality of legal-rational authority in Western society was of course one of Weber's crowning intellectual achievements. Codified legal rules and individual rights, consistently applied and enforced by technically skilled officials working within well-defined bureaucratic hierarchies is the foundation of state legitimacy in modern complex societies. Yet Weber himself did not conceive of law solely as a collection of formal/instrumental rules, rights, incentives, and penalties; the idea of "legality" also functioned as a dominant belief system in which social actors constructed and legitimated social relationships increasingly in terms of formally articulated rights and obligations

enforceable through the state's coercive apparatus (Weber 1978; see also Marshall 2003; McIntyre 1994; Stryker 1994). Legality has also almost fully permeated social expectations and behavior in extralegal organizational settings, including the workplace, schools, hospitals, universities, and so on (Edelman and Suchman 1997; Stryker 2003).

The legalization of society—in both formal-structural and cultural terms—has arguably found one of its purest expressions in the U.S. constitutional system. As early as the mid-1800s, Toqueville (2000) observed the remarkable extent to which social and political conflicts in the United States eventually became judicially resolved legal questions. More recently, Stuart Scheingold's (1974) seminal book *The Politics of Rights* forcefully argued that law in the United States cannot be properly understood as a formal, neutral system under which all individuals are abstractly equal and legal reasoning is disinterestedly applied case by case. Instead, the "legal paradigm" of officially enforceable rules, rights, and obligations is itself a political ideology; it provides a template, or blueprint of belief and action that directly influences the forms of political conflict available to collective actors, and "furnishes American politics with its most visible symbols of legitimacy" (Scheingold 1974, p. 13).

Legitimacy conferred through law on social and political behavior has been a central point of emphasis among sociologists of law (e.g., Dobbin and Sutton 1998; Edelman 1992; Stryker 1994, 2003; Suchman 1995). Law and organizations scholars, for example, have built a comprehensive research agenda focused in part on how employers legitimate their own organizational practices through symbolic compliance with legal commands regulating the employment relationship (Dobbin and Sutton 1998; Edelman 1992). Likewise, Stryker (2003) promoted a rule-resource institutional framework for analyzing law's mutually reinforcing relationship with economy and society. Such a perspective emphasizes law's dual resource value as instrumental incentives and penalties, on the one hand, and socially constructed legitimating scripts and schemas, on the other.

Conceiving of law as both enabling resource and constitutive symbolic package partly addresses a common critique that the framing literature betrays an inherently instrumental bias; that is, framing scholars have a tendency to treat culture as simply one of many tools (money, organization, elite support, etc.) at a movement's disposal (see, e.g., Goodwin and Jasper 1999; Steinberg 1995, 2002; Naples 1997, 2002). But as some critics have argued, the very raw materials of cultural frames—language, rhetoric, narratives, and meanings—structure and constrain activists' capacity to construct and mobilize frames for instrumental purposes. Some have thus promoted a more discourse-centered or "dialogic" approach (Steinberg 2002; see also Naples 1997; Ferree et al. 2002): "Cultures constructed through contention are only partly the product of calculated action. Discourse…is partly bounded by the cultural practices available for them to make meaning.…This means focusing on the discourse through which people make claims, articulate senses of justice, and express their identities" (Steinberg 2002, p. 208).

Constitutive legal frames conceptually and theoretically appreciate the importance of discourse. Indeed, law is itself a language system. The vernacular staples of law—rights, duties, privileges, prohibitions, remedies, and so on—construct and express ideas of social conflict and their resolution. And for exactly this reason, master legal frames can set rigid and enduring boundaries on the very words and discourses available to challengers in their attempt to produce and mobilize resonant cultural frames toward instrumental ends.

In short, because social movements draw on deeply resonant cultural symbols to define and legitimate their grievances and goals, and because law provides one of the deepest reservoirs of symbolic resources, discourses, and institutionalized scripts available to collective actors of all sorts, social movements—especially in highly legalized societies such as the United States—typically (though not exclusively) frame their cause in explicitly legal terms.

Law, Legal Frames, and Framing Processes

The novelty of legal framing also stems from its potential to further develop theoretical understanding of the *processes* through which social movement frames are constructed and mobilized. Yet while there is a clear scholarly consensus acknowledging the inherently dynamic nature of cultural framing, some have lamented the literature's "static tendencies," focusing on "frames as 'things' rather than on the dynamic processes associated with their social construction, negotiation, contestation, and transformation" (Benford 1997, p. 415).

A legal framing perspective offers an ideal theoretical mechanism to explore systematically these interactive and emergent processes *because* of law's status as a master frame. Law, by its very nature, is contested terrain. Yet because law's dominant symbolic framework of rules, rights, and obligations sets boundaries on how collective actors conceive of their grievances and goals, ongoing *disputes* over the proper construction of legal symbols is likely to take place both within a given movement itself and between the movement and its external environment. Disputes over the meaning or existence of *rights* provide perhaps the best illustration of such contested processes.

The interactive, dynamic nature of legal framing can also be seen in how it answers the call by some framing scholars for greater analytic attention to the "multiorganizational" fields within which framing processes and contests occur (Benford 1997; Benford and Snow 2000; Evans 1997). Like all collective action frames, legal frames engage counter-movement organizations, bystanders, mass media, and political, economic, and cultural elites. However, *legal institutions*—including courts and administrative agencies—are typically left off such lists and are generally undertheorized in analyses of multiorganizational fields. But, just as legal frames have greater influence than particular, case-specific frames, legal institutions have a capacity to further illuminate and expand the impact of collective action frames in ways that other components of the multi-organizational field cannot. Put simply, courts and enforcement agencies are unique in that they are the only institutional/organizational sites within which legal frames can be directly translated into rights claims *authoritatively recognized, codified, and enforced by the state.*

Indeed, this leads to a final way in which a legal framing perspective can make novel theoretical contributions to an already rich and comprehensive literature: it can shed substantial theoretical light on the potentially transformative impact of social movements—through their framing strategies—on social and political relationships in ways that significantly increase the opportunities and life chances of challengers and the often disadvantaged groups they represent. This directly addresses Benford and Snow's (2000) concern that "there have been few systematic studies of the actual contribution of framing processes,... [which] calls for further investigation of the relationship between framing processes and the goal attainment efforts of different varieties of movements" (p. 632).

As I have argued throughout this section, law is a unique type of symbolic resource; it is not only a *means* by which a movement can, by appealing to deeply resonant legal symbols, garner legitimacy and support for the movement. Law in part also represents the *ends* of that process. In other words, translating a cultural frame into an officially recognized legal *right* is itself one of the central objectives of social movements. Typically (but not exclusively), this happens through litigation. Access to courts allows aggrieved groups to turn a symbolic frame into a legal claim. And courts have the power to codify—or refuse to codify—those claims. If successful, such legal changes not only further enhance a movement's symbolic framing efforts; legal change also transforms social and political relationships, and thus has the capacity to exert power and influence beyond the movement itself. Thus, while law is central to a movement's framing strategies, it is also an endpoint in a political contest that uses frames in ways that can foster progressive social change more generally.

In sum, a legal framing perspective has the capacity to produce more systematic theoretical knowledge on the cultural and symbolic processes through which—and with what consequences— social movements frame their grievances, identities, and objectives. Analyzing battles within the women's movement over protective labor laws in the mid-to-late 1960s is an ideal case to explore, illustrate, and further develop such a perspective. As discussed above, a growing tension between the protective and equal treatment visions of women's

employment opportunities was one of the defining events leading to transformations in the both the movement and the law. And to be sure, there were several interrelated yet distinct frames available to women's advocates including (but not limited to) women as workers versus women as mothers and homemakers, gender identity versus individual identity, women as different versus women as the same, and women as individuals with expectations of privacy in personal decisions involving work and family life. Each of these would be a reasonable representation of the debate over the general direction of the women's movement, and the debate over protective labor policies, specifically. Yet as my legal framing perspective suggests, each of these frames can be subsumed under the broader category of a legal/rights frame. For the women's movement was not simply trying to further engage cultural debate over women's proper roles at work, in the family, and in society more broadly; it was also attempting to enshrine those competing cultural constructions of gender into *law* officially recognized and enforced by the state's judicial and administrative apparatus.

A Caveat

Although this study focuses on legal framing processes in the women's movement in the 1960s, I neither claim nor attempt to produce a "total explanation" (see Kiser 1996) of the movement. Clearly the women's movement was wide reaching, and certainly not all of its activities were discussed or framed in explicitly legal terms. Thus, it is *not* my intention in the analysis that follows to somehow isolate legal frames as the single, central variable that explains all of the debates, conflicts, and processes driving the women's movement during this period. Nor do I juxtapose legal frames against other potentially relevant ("nonlegal") frames that one could possibly identify for this case, and then attempt to determine which among them was the "winner" (i.e., legal frames vs. nonlegal frames) in transforming the movement. Instead, my central objective is to analyze a crucial sequence of events in the mid-to-late 1960s as a way of both illustrating *and* further developing the central concepts and theoretical mechanisms of an explicitly legal framing perspective on social movements. And, law's status as a master frame notwithstanding, the law/legal rights frame cannot be expected to become everything for our, knowledge of cultural framing processes, but it can significantly expand our general understanding of those processes, especially in highly legalized societies.

All that said, both the primary historical record and secondary analyses *do* strongly justify my empirical emphasis on law and legal frames for exploring transformations in the women's movement in the 1960s. Movement scholars in the social sciences, history, and law almost unanimously concur that, whatever else was going on, the enactment of Title VII—and the interpretations, debates, and conflicts over that law that ensued—were among *the* defining events that accelerated basic rethinking of women's roles in the workforce and in society and thus greatly influenced future directions in the movement (see, e.g., Eastwood and Murray 1965; Freeman 1975; Graham 1990; Harrison 1988; Pedriana 2004). The central actors themselves, both at the time and in subsequent in-depth interviews, concur with this basic contention (see generally Florer 1973).

Methods and Data

I develop a legal framing perspective through historical-narrative analysis of the women's movement in the 1960s.[6] I focus on several major legal/policy "events" surrounding Title VII generally, and the debate over protective labor classifications in particular. Analysis of each event corresponds to three "frame alignment" processes originally outlined by Snow et al. (1986). Specifically, I analyze a sequence of framing strategies within the women's movement that began with frame "amplification," moved on to frame "extension" (see also Cornfield and Fletcher 1998), and culminated with frame "transformation."

My methodological strategy is "analytic" narrative (see, e.g., Abbott 1992; Bates et al. 1998; Goldstone 1998; Pedriana 2005; Sewell 1996; Stryker 1996). Analytic narratives are theoretically informed "stories" that focus on social actors, the alternatives for action they construct, the actions they take, and the consequences of those decisions. In addition, chronology and sequence are central methodological tools. Narratives "present and analyze

historical data as temporally linked sequences of action [organized] into a meaningful analytic whole" (Pedriana 2005, p. 351; see also Griffin 1992; Stryker 1996). Analytic narrative is an appropriate strategy for this study because legal framing of the women's movement was a temporally unfolding *process;* women's efforts proceeded through a series of key frame alignment "stages," each influenced by, and building upon, those that preceded them.

Narratives rely to a great extent on primary, historical sources.[7] Archival data allows the researcher to place social actors and groups at the center of the analysis by revealing information about their perception of situations and events, negotiation of choices and alternatives, and why certain actions are taken rather than others. My analysis thus mines heavily archival documents from the women's movement in the 1960s. Sources include the papers of the major women's organizations at the time, including the PCSW, the Interdepartmental Commission on the Status of Women (ICSW), the Citizens Advisory Council on the Status of Women (CACSW), and NOW. Since Title VII of the 1964 Civil Rights Act was the central law/policy at issue, I also draw frequently on the public and private documents of the Equal Employment Opportunity Commission (EEOC), the agency created to enforce Title VII. Sources include press releases, transcripts of internal EEOC commissioners' meetings, legal documents, annual reports, transcripts of conferences and hearings, and internal administrative histories. Journalistic accounts from major national newspapers, especially the *New York Times* and the *Wall Street Journal* were also key primary data sources. And finally, a number of secondary works, including—but not limited to—Brauer (1983), Florer (1973), Freeman (1975), Graham (1990), and Harrison (1988) were key sources of historical information. Secondary sources also helped identify additional primary documents and served as a "check" on my own interpretations and conclusions about the historical record.

Frame Amplification: Enactment of Title VII and the Women's Movement

"Amplification" is one major frame alignment process, defined by Snow et al. (1986) as "clarification and invigoration of an interpretive frame that bears on a particular issue, problem, or set of events" (p. 469). The first part of my historical-narrative analysis explores how enactment of Title VII of the 1964 Civil Rights Act gave women's leaders an opportunity to illuminate or "amplify" the political debate and cultural symbols surrounding women's employment rights. Women's advocates used explicitly legal symbols and categories embedded in Title VII to frame that renewed debate.

Equal employment historians generally concur that. Title VII's sex provision was something of a historical accident (see, e.g., Brauer 1983; Graham 1990; Harrison 1988; but see Freeman [1991] for an alternative interpretation). There was little debate in Congress over equal employment opportunity for women; *racial* discrimination was the primary focus of the civil rights bill. Nor did the established women's organizations seriously lobby to include women under Title VII's protection (but see discussions in Brauer [1983] and Freeman [1991]). Nonetheless, Representative Howard Smith (D-Va.)—a Southern opponent of civil rights—devised a ruse to erode support for the entire legislative package. On the House floor, Smith offered an amendment barring employment discrimination against "the women" (U.S. Congress 1964, p. 2577). Aware that "women's rights were generally not taken seriously then" (Brauer 1983, p. 38), Smith hoped that including sex in Title VII would sink the bill (see Graham 1990; Harrison 1988; Miller 1967). But while Smith's male colleagues (of both parties) met his proposal with laughter, jokes, and facetious debate, several women members rose up in support of the sex amendment (U.S. Congress 1964, pp. 2577–84). Unexpectedly, the amendment was passed, later cleared the Senate with little discussion, and was signed into law.

Response of "Status-of-Women" Groups

At the time of Title VII's enactment, progressive women's advocates were organized primarily within "status-of-women" commissions. In 1961, President Kennedy formed the PCSW. The PCSW was created in part to offset demands for an equal rights amendment by a small but vocal group of feminists in the National Women's Party (or NWP;

Brauer 1983; Harrison 1980, 1988). The commission's major task was to "develop recommendations for overcoming discriminations [*sic*] in government and private employment on the basis of sex and for developing recommendations for services which will enable women to continue their role as wives and mothers while making a maximum contribution to the world around them" (PCSW 1961). PCSW members came from women's civic organizations, labor unions, educational institutions, and other government agencies associated with the Women's Bureau located in the U.S. Department of Labor (see e.g., Duerst-Lahti 1989; Graham 1990). Committed to class justice for women—as opposed to formal equal rights—this coalition's political identity and legislative objectives historically centered on protective labor policies to shield women from long hours and dangerous working conditions (see Costain 1992; Freeman 1975; Harrison 1988; Skocpol 1992). By 1965, most states had enacted protective laws for women. Whether they involved maximum hours, weight-lifting restrictions, limits on night work, "special" facilities for women, or some other gender-specific rule, such laws were expressly designed to provide "protection from hazards to health and safety" and to "enable women more adequately to fulfill their roles as both workers and homemakers" (PCSW 1963*b*, p. 22).

The PCSW published its findings and recommendations in its 1963 report to the president titled *American Women* (PCSW 1963*a*). On the one hand, the report promoted equal treatment for women workers. It called for equal opportunity in public and private employment, gender-neutral minimum wage laws, equal pay for equal work policies, and equal access to unions and collective bargaining (PCSW 1963*a*, pp. 27–39). On the other hand, the PCSW remained staunchly committed to protective legislation. Rejecting claims that protective laws restricted women's opportunities, the PCSW's Committee on Protective Labor Legislation wrote, "differences between men and women and the dual role of women as mothers and homemakers, and of workers, are realities that distinguish their needs from the needs of men" (PCSW 1962, p. 3).

Upon publication of *American Women*, President Kennedy immediately created two new commissions to carry on the work of the PCSW: the ICSW and the CACSW.[8] Since the ICSW and CACSW were "continuations of the president's commission not only in spirit, but also in personnel," there was "no sharp departure...from the agenda described by the commission report [*American Women*]" (Harrison 1988, p. 174).

So when Congress unexpectedly added sex to Title VII, the status-of-women groups still officially embraced some sex classifications under law that allowed protective policies exclusively for women. As summarized by Esther Peterson, assistant secretary of labor and former head of the Women's Bureau, "discriminations [*sic*] based on sex involve problems sufficiently different from those based on other factors to make separate treatment preferable" (quoted in Smith 1964, p. B4). Yet equal treatment language was embedded in Title VII, making it illegal to "segregate, classify, or otherwise discriminate" on the basis of sex.[9] Nowhere did the new law exempt protective labor policies, which by definition required sex-specific classifications.

The status-of-women commissions immediately questioned the legal consequences of Title VII for protective laws. "Many states have laws...which set...standards for female workers which do not apply to male workers," some women's advocates wondered, "How will challenges be met that allege State [protective] laws discriminate on the basis of sex? Will they be invalidated?" (Women's Bureau 1964, p. 4). At a February 1965 meeting, the ICSW echoed these concerns, asking, "Is any labor law which requires a difference in treatment of the sexes discriminatory in and of itself?...Does the [protective] law discriminate against men in denying them the same...protection it grants women?" (CACSW, n.d., p. 6).

In short, Title VII's ban on sex discrimination amplified an uneasy frame alignment between competing cultural symbols of gender, both of which were constructed largely around constitutive legal categories. One frame—"equal treatment"—favored the end of unnecessary and draconian sex classifications under law that restricted women's employment opportunities. The other legal frame—"protective treatment"—simultaneously wished to retain sex classifications that offered genuine protections exclusively for women. Either way, Title VII's explicit legal language seemed to require equal treatment of women and suggested that both frames could not peacefully coexist for long. This became increasingly apparent as the women's movement steadily "extended" the equal treatment frame to other widely accepted—and gender-specific—employment practices quickly coming under Title VII's purview.

Frame Extension: Bona Fide Occupational Qualifications, Help-Wanted Ads, and the EEOC

While amplification can illuminate a particular interpretive frame, it may not be sufficient to draw in other potential allies. A central activity of social movements is to expand their influence by broadening the movement's scope and organization. One way this is accomplished is through frame "extension," defined as the process through which a movement "extend[s] the boundaries of its primary framework...to enlarge its adherent pool by portraying its objectives or activities as...being congruent with the values or interests of potential adherents" (Snow et al. 1986, p. 472; see also Cornfield and Fletcher 1998). My narrative continues by analyzing how the EEOC's contradictory legal rulings on Title VII's sex provision provided an opening to extend the equal treatment frame to other advocates—advocates who were still committed to protective treatment of women.

The Bona Fide Occupational Qualification and Protective Legislation

Given the peculiar origins of Title VII's sex provision, neither the EEOC nor women's groups were sure how to deal with sex discrimination. The *New York Times* reported "the word 'sex'...is expected to create some problems for the agency [EEOC]" (*New York Times* 1965a, p. A32). When asked about the sex provision, EEOC chairman Franklin Delano Roosevelt, Jr., responded, "We can't foretell what problems there will be in this area. We will have to learn as we go along" (*New York Times* 1965a, p. A32). Mixed messages from women's advocates contributed to general ambivalence over sex discrimination. In August 1965, the White House held a two-day conference on equal employment opportunity. An entire panel was dedicated to "discrimination because of sex," and included representatives from government, women's groups, industry, and organized labor. The first major issue involved "sex as a bona fide occupational qualification" (EEOC 1965b, p. 12). Section 703(e) of Title VII permitted sex discrimination if "sex...is a *bona fide occupational qualification* (BFOQ) reasonably necessary to normal operation of that particular business or enterprise."[10]

Just several days before the conference, secretary of labor—and chairman of the ICSW—Willard Wirtz wrote EEOC chairman Roosevelt that the BFOQ "should be narrowly construed" (Wirtz 1965a, p. 2). Accordingly, ICSW member Evelyn Harrison told conferees that the BFOQ exception should be applied only in "those certain instances where it is reasonably necessary to the normal operation of that particular business" (EEOC 1965b, p. 6). Examples included a bikini model, a women's bathroom attendant, a wet nurse, and other jobs that, by their very nature, required a sex classification. Harrison was adamant, however, that the BFOQ not be allowed on the basis of traditional gender stereotypes: "The application of a loose definition [of the BFOQ] could result in categorizing jobs...as 'his' or 'hers' contrary to the specific intent of the law" (EEOC 1965a, p. 6). Women's Bureau director Mary Keyserling concurred that the BFOQ "be limited to...where sex is a natural correlative to the natural performance of the job" (EEOC 1965b, p. 18). Citing a recent U.S. Civil Service Commission finding that in just 40 of 35,000 federal job listings "was sex held to be truly relevant to the job" (EEOC 1965b, p. 182), Keyserling concluded "the categories that could be established where sex is a [BFOQ] would be exceedingly narrow" (EEOC 1965a, p. 183).

When it came to protective laws, however, the status-of-women groups switched gears. ICSW chairman Wirtz wrote that the relationship between Title VII and state protective laws "was not clearly spelled out by Congress," and therefore it was the ICSW's opinion that "nothing in the provisions of...Title VII...has the effect of a general invalidation of these laws" (Wirtz 1965a, p. 3). At the White House conference, Keyserling restated the

ICSW's (and CACSW's) position. A stalwart of the Women's Bureau alliance committed to class justice for women, Keyserling strongly defended protective policies. Reminding conference participants that "these laws were put on the books by women's organizations in the interest of women...[and] sought to eliminate the real abuses which prevailed widely in industry" (EEOC 1965b, p. 22), she argued "the freeing of women from employment discrimination does not demand that they all have identical treatment" (EEOC 1965b, p. 26). Speaking for the Department of Labor and the Women's Bureau, Keyserling suggested that the EEOC "should follow a general policy of preserving these laws wherever possible" (EEOC 1965b, p. 27). Major women's organizations, including the YWCA, the American Association of University Women, the national councils of Jewish, Catholic, and Negro women, and the National Consumers League, all concurred (EEOC 1965b, p. 28).

Even so, the debate over protective polices was itself in transition. Status-of-women representatives acknowledged that many "protective" laws were pretexts for discrimination. Maximum hours and weight-lifting limits, for example, restricted women's advancement opportunities. Caroline Davis of the AFL-CIO Women's Department testified at the White House conference that "we have had many...cases where women are not allowed to move up on to better paying jobs because there is a law which says she cannot work overtime occasionally, or she cannot lift beyond [certain amounts]....These state laws have proved discriminatory in many instances" (EEOC 1965b, pp. 31–32). Keyserling agreed "many of these laws are exceedingly out-dated and are in need of rigorous change" (EEOC 1965b, p. 33). ICSW chairman Wirtz informed the EEOC: "Commissions on the Status of Women are now in the process of re-examining these laws in the light of current developments. Many legislatures have already amended them to apply, where feasible and appropriate, to *men as well as women*" (Wirtz 1965a, p. 3; emphasis added).

Thus, initial debates over Title VII's sex provision saw the status-of-women committees steadily extending the equal treatment frame. Title VII's equal treatment language gave women's advocates an opportunity to rethink their historical identity constructed largely around protective legal classifications. Women's leaders unanimously favored a very narrow interpretation of the BFOQ exception so that employers could not use traditional gender stereotypes to restrict women's employment opportunities. Equal treatment—in all but the most narrow of circumstances—should be the general rule. Even protective policies themselves had come under greater scrutiny. The status-of-women groups began to argue for retention of laws that offered protections to *all* workers, while those used for discriminatory purposes should be eliminated.

Nonetheless, constitutive legal categories also constrained the effort to extend the equal treatment frame. The political and cultural identity of the women's movement had for so long been symbolized by protective policies for women that advocates were not yet prepared to abandon them flatly. And even though the status-of-women groups had begun to reexamine many sex-specific protective laws, the protective treatment frame hung on, roughed up, but still intact. As the next section explains, the tension between the equal and protective treatment frames was then exacerbated by the EEOC's inconsistent legal guidelines on Title VII's sex provision. The result was further extension of the equal treatment frame.

EEOC Guidelines on Sex Discrimination

The EEOC's early administrative guidelines on sex discrimination imported nearly wholesale the contradictions between the equal and protective treatment frames. Consistent with the ICSW's recommendation that the BFOQ be narrowly interpreted, the EEOC ruled "the bona fide occupational qualification will not be allowed on the bases of assumptions or employment characteristics in general or stereotyped images of the sexes" (EEOC 1968*b*, p. 239; see also *Wall Street Journal* 1965). The commission listed a number of unlawful discriminatory practices, including refusal to hire women for jobs requiring interstate travel, clerical positions open to females only, separate seniority lines, classifying jobs as "light" or "heavy," refusal to hire women in departments staffed mostly by males, longer break periods for women than men, offering supervisory training

to men but not women, policies restricting employment of married women but not married men, and refusal to hire women with children younger than six years old (EEOC 1966*c*, pp. 15–20).

But if the EEOC followed the consensus of status-of-women groups on the BFOQ, the ambivalence surrounding protective policies was also apparent. The agency seemed truly baffled about the relationship between Title VII and state protective legislation. One EEOC commissioner, citing the EEOC's position that "it is the opinion of the Commission that Congress did not intend to disturb state laws," stated "I have no deep feeling one way or the other" (EEOC 1966*b*, p. 7). In its first compilation of legal interpretations, the EEOC's general counsel concluded that it would not violate Title VII if "refusal to hire women for certain work is based on a state law which precludes the employment of women for such work, provided that the employer is acting in good faith and that the law in question is reasonably adapted to protect women rather than to subject them to discrimination" (EEOC 1966*c*, p. 23; see also 1968*b*, pp. 243–44; 1966*e*, p. 2). The commission did call for states to "rescind outdated state protective legislation" (EEOC 1968*b*, p. 244) and warned that "if the state law...is not to protect women but to subject them to discrimination, it won't be considered valid" [*Wall Street Journal* 1965, p. 3). But the EEOC did not elaborate on how the agency would determine—procedurally or substantively—whether a challenged law was discriminatory or truly protective. Less than a year later, the commission tried to distance itself altogether from the issue. The agency's revised policy in August 1966 stated that the "EEOC will not make determinations on the merits in cases which present a conflict between Title VII and state protective legislation" (EEOC 1966*c*, p. 23). Instead, the commission decided to let the federal courts deal with it. The EEOC would simply advise the complainant of her right to sue "to secure a judicial determination as to the validity of the state law" (EEOC 1966*c*, p. 23).

Thus, like the framing contest between equal and protective treatment itself, the EEOC's early guidelines betrayed a legal double standard that prohibited sex classifications in most instances, while allowing them in others. By this time, the equal treatment frame had extended to a growing number of women's advocates who had become disillusioned with these lingering legal inconsistencies. Ongoing debate over protective legislation revealed a widening fissure among status-of-women members. Mary Eastwood, a Justice Department official who had worked closely with status-of-women commissions, "had become convinced that protective labor laws hampered women's opportunities" and recommended that "in a case of conflict between state laws and Title VII, the state laws should be ruled inoperative" (Harrison 1988, p. 187). In 1965, Eastwood and Pauli Murray of Yale University published a seminal paper in the *George Washington Law Review* entitled "Jane Crow and the Law: Sex Discrimination and Title VII" (Eastwood and Murray 1965). Their paper called for a broad equal treatment interpretation of Title VII's sex provision, and recommended abolition of sex-specific protective policies. "In view of the waning utility of these state protective laws that make compliance with Title VII difficult, relatively little harm would result if employers were relieved of complying with the state laws" (Eastwood and Murray 1965, p. 253).

Yet those calling for a full-blown equal treatment standard were still a minority in the status-of-women alliance officially connected to the Johnson Administration and the Department of Labor. While the committees puzzled earnestly over Title VII's relationship to state protective laws, there was as yet no official push to abolish *all* sex-specific legal classifications. Nonetheless, the EEOC's subsequent rulings on sex-segregated help-wanted ads extended the equal treatment frame further still and pushed its framing contest with protective treatment to the breaking point.

The Conflict over Help-Wanted Ads

Section 704(b) of Title VII prohibited, absent a BFOQ, job advertisements stating a gender preference.[11] The traditional and widespread practice of placing job ads under separate "male" and "female" columns clearly appeared to violate the letter and spirit of the law. The EEOC's own ruling that conventional gender norms and stereotypes did not qualify as a BFOQ seemed consistent with this interpretation. If employers could no longer classify

jobs—except in narrow instances—by sex, then they certainly could not advertise for "men's" jobs and "women's" jobs. The EEOC, however, said that they could. In its first guidelines on sex discrimination— the same guidelines that outlined the commission's BFOQ interpretation—the agency ruled that employers could continue to place ads in sex-specific columns entitled "jobs of interest—male" and "jobs of interest—female...for the convenience of readers." The only caveat was a required disclaimer stating that ads "specifically state that the job is open to males and females" and "are not intended to exclude or discourage applications for persons of the other sex" (EEOC 1965a; see also *New York Times* 1965b, p. 4; Pedriana 2004; Zelman 1980, pp. 98–99).

The EEOC's ruling on help-wanted ads stunned status-of-women groups and helped further extend the equal treatment frame to the normally politically cautious ICSW and CACSW. In October 1965, the CACSW released a memorandum titled "Equal Employment Opportunities for Women under Title VII of the 1964 Civil Rights Act." Noting "the Council considers Title VII a Congressional mandate for full economic opportunity for women," it was essential that Title VII "be vigorously administered and enforced" (Wirtz 1965b, p. 1). On the EEOC's help-wanted guidelines, the CACSW lamented: "The council is alarmed at the lack of compliance with this provision....Separate...columns in newspapers serve only to advise prospective job applicants not to apply where they are not wanted....The council urges that the EEOC make clear to employers that the law prohibits placing an employment advertisement in a newspaper column that indicates a sex preference" (Wirtz 1965b, p. 8).

Despite criticism from status-of-women groups, the commission took its original ruling on help-wanted ads a step further. Some commissioners suggested "that we remove this [disclaimer] obligation of the newspaper and make it entirely the responsibility of the advertiser to indicate that he is not making an unlawful expression of preference based on sex" (EEOC 1966a, p. 2). Less than a month later, the EEOC officially lifted the disclaimer requirement for ads listed in male or female columns. "Advertisers covered by [Title VII] may place advertisements for jobs open to both sexes in columns classified by publishers under 'Male' or 'Female' headings to indicate that some occupations are considered more attractive to persons of one sex than the other" (EEOC 1966d). Nor, ruled the agency, would employers be required "to state specifically that both sexes may apply" (*Wall Street Journal* 1966, p. 5).

Some women's leaders quickly mobilized against the EEOC's new guidelines. The status-of women committees stepped up their complaints against the agency and demanded that the EEOC rescind its discriminatory ruling on help-wanted ads (Harrison 1988; Pedriana 2004). Congresswoman Martha Griffiths (D-Mich.) spoke for most women's advocates when she took to the House floor and lashed out at the Commission: "The Commission...reached the peak of contempt for women's rights when it issued its 'guideline' of April 22, 1966, interpreting the advertising provision of the law....Permitting job advertising in separate columns for men and women encourages violation of the law which the EEOC was set up to enforce" (U.S. Congress 1966, pp. 13689–92).

In short, the EEOC's help-wanted guidelines extended the equal treatment frame even further. Permitting sex-segregated job advertisements contradicted the agency's own ruling—fully endorsed by the status-of-women groups—that traditional gender stereotypes could not legally justify unequal treatment of women. This in part convinced many women's advocates that the legal double standards that continued to govern sex discrimination policy were untenable, and thus the equal and protective treatment frames could no longer coexist. Protective classifications—despite the historical benefits they offered women workers—would probably have to go. As the final section of my narrative explains, these developments contributed greatly to a new, independent, and far more aggressive social movement organization—one whose political and cultural identity was legally framed exclusively and unequivocally around equal treatment.

Frame Transformation: Formation of NOW and the Legal Assault on Protective Policies

When a cultural frame fails to resonate adequately with collective actors, "new values may have to

be...nurtured, old meanings...jettisoned, and erroneous beliefs...reframed" in a process referred to as frame "transformation" (Snow et al. 1986, p. 473). As discussed above, the EEOC's guidelines on sex-segregated job advertisements earned the disdain of women's advocates—even those who were still genuinely pondering the wisdom of protective classifications. The help-wanted controversy convinced a growing number of status-of-women members that the current legal framework permitting some sex-specific classifications perpetuated traditional gender stereotypes that continued to justify discriminatory treatment of women. What was needed, in short, was a frame transformation: destruction of the protective treatment frame altogether in favor of a global, across-the-board equal treatment frame.

When the ICSW and CACSW met for the annual status-of-women conference in June 1966, "practically all of the delegates came with the feeling that [Title VII's] sex provision was not being taken seriously" (statement of Assistant Secretary of Labor Esther Peterson, quoted in Florer 1973, p. 41). Still, status-of-women officials—mindful of their official obligations to the Department of Labor—rejected some members' call for a resolution demanding aggressive enforcement of Title VII's sex provision (NOW, n.d., p. 1; Florer 1973, p. 51). When it became clear that no official action would be taken, several women's leaders concluded that the time had finally come to break away from the government-embedded status-of-women organizations. Sitting among conference delegates, this small group created NOW (see Friedan 1991, p. 104; Harrison 1988, pp. 194–95; Florer 1973, pp. 39–59).[12]

That NOW was created at the June 1966 status-of-women conference is well documented by primary and secondary evidence (see, e.g., NOW, n.d.; Freeman 1975; Friedan 1991; Harrison 1988; Pedriana 2004). Women's movement historians—and the participants themselves—further concur that anger over EEOC enforcement of the sex provision generally, and the agency's ruling on help-wanted ads specifically, was a driving force behind NOW's formation (see Florer 1973). From a legal framing perspective, the emergence of NOW is theoretically meaningful not only because it was a major organizational change in the women's movement; NOW also *reframed* the women's movement from one that clung to some sex-specific legal classifications to one that rejected *all* such classifications. As I explain below, NOW's immediate assault on protective policies helped complete this frame transformation process.

NOW's Legal Attack on Protective Policies

NOW's own internal documents strongly suggest that the new organization's central identity was constructed around a universal equal treatment frame. NOW's immediate political objectives focused on women's *legal* status under Title VII. At its first organizing conference in October 1966, NOW created a "Task Force on Equal Opportunity in Employment," and demanded "rigorous enforcement of Title VII" (NOW papers, n.d., p. 1). NOW further called for "replacement of the EEOC guidelines on employment advertising which affirmatively permits discrimination based on sex with a guideline prohibiting such discriminatory advertising" (NOW papers, n.d., p. 2). Two months later NOW prepared a lengthy legal petition demanding the EEOC rescind its help-wanted guidelines (NOW 1966).

On the one hand, NOW's attacks on the EEOC were simply a continuation of what most status-of-women members had already begun the preceding year. On the other hand—unlike the official status-of-women position—NOW was dedicated to a universal equal treatment standard under law that included elimination of protective polices. Absent were the traditional arguments on the benefits of protecting women or technical-legal distinctions between discrimination and genuine protection. For NOW, sex-specific protective classifications were inherently discriminatory and thus unlawful. Moreover, because NOW was not beholden to any government agency or commission, its political and legal agenda was not hampered by the same institutional constraints faced by status-of-women groups. Officially tied to the Department of Labor, combined with a historical commitment to protective policies, the ICSW and CACSW stopped short of a political agenda framed exclusively around equal treatment. But NOW confronted no such

obstacles. In its initial mission statement, press releases, correspondences, and memorandums, NOW aggressively promoted equal treatment for all employment practices, including protective laws. In a letter circulated to President Johnson and secretary of labor and ICSW chairman Willard Wirtz, NOW cited a current case involving California's eight-hour maximum work law. "This case involves the conflict between Title VII...which prohibits discrimination on the basis of sex, and a state law which discriminates on the basis of sex. The State [law]...which prohibits women (but does not prohibit men) from working more than eight hours a day...is clearly in violation of the...Title VII provisions against sex discrimination" (Wirtz 1966a, p. 3).

NOW also demanded that the EEOC follow its own tepid guidelines on Title VII/state law conflicts. Just several months earlier, the commission announced that it would let the federal courts deal with the issue. In a November letter to the EEOC, NOW urged "that the Commission take a more active position in...cases involving conflict between Title VII and state laws [by] appearing as amicus curiae in future judicial proceedings" (Wirtz 1966b, p. 4). By mid-1967, several major lawsuits involving state protective laws were pending in federal court. But the EEOC had still not made its position clear and had produced no overall strategy. In April, the agency published in the *Federal Register* only "proposed interpretive rules," stating, "The Commission is presently considering whether to indicate by rule or decision the extent, if any, to which State protective legislation is affected by Title VII" (*Federal Register* 1967, p. 5999). The EEOC then announced public hearings on sex discrimination, including state protective legislation, scheduled for early May (*Federal Register* 1967, p. 5999; see also EEOC 1967a, 1967b). At the hearings, NOW boldly stated its position:

N.O.W. strongly supports modern labor standards legislation which protects ALL WORKERS, men as well as women....On the other hand, NOW strongly opposes and considers outmoded and unnecessary, 3 types of state laws, deceivingly described as "protective" laws which conflict with the guarantee against sex discrimination under

[Title VII], namely: laws imposing arbitrary hours restrictions, laws restricting night work and weight lifting limits, imposed only upon women workers. Such laws prevent women from being hired, promoted, transferred, and recalled to work after layoff. (NOW 1967)

NOW attacked protective laws in the courts and in the streets. Seeking "a public redefinition of discrimination based on sex through support or initiation of legal cases," NOW represented plaintiffs and filed amicus briefs in cases challenging hours laws and weight-lifting restrictions (NOW, n.d., p. 16). NOW also organized demonstrations protesting sex discrimination. In 1968, the New York chapter organized a nationwide boycott of Colgate-Palmolive "to protest the company's long-standing job discrimination against female employees" including its policy excluding women from lifting over 35 pounds—"i.e., the weight of a small child" (NOW 1968). Several months later, NOW won a major legal victory in a case challenging Georgia's 30-pound weight-lifting limit for women. The district court had ruled that the Georgia law was "reasonable and makes sex a bona fide occupational qualification for the job at issue in this case" (*Weeks v. Southern Bell* 277 F. Supp. 117 [1967], p. 119). The Fifth Circuit reversed, using strong equal treatment language:

> Southern Bell…would have us "assume" on the basis of a "stereotyped" characterization, that few or no women can safely lift 30 pounds, while all men are treated as if they can.…What does seem clear is that using these class stereotypes denies desirable positions to a great many women perfectly capable of performing the duties involved.…Title VII…rejects this type of romantic paternalism as unduly Victorian and instead vests individual women with the power to decide whether or not to take on unromantic tasks. (Quoted in NOW 1969, p. 23)

NOW celebrated the decision, writing "After two years of courtroom battling, street demonstrations, and strongly worded correspondence," women now had the right to "bid for so-called 'men's' jobs which had been denied them under the guise of protecting them from strenuous (and higher paid) work" (NOW, n.d., p. 15).

As more cases challenging protective policies reached the federal courts, the EEOC began to play a more active role in resolving the Title VII/state law conflict. In 1967, several district courts relied on the EEOC's opinion that Congress did not intend to overturn state laws designed to protect women, and thus that "the Commission will consider…such state laws…to be bona fide occupational qualifications…not in conflict with Title VII" (EEOC 1966c). In two key cases, courts cited this language to uphold weight-lifting limits for women.[13]

But by this time the EEOC, influenced in part by the May hearings on sex discrimination, was rethinking its guidelines on protective legislation. Rescinding its 1966 decision not to rule on cases involving Title VII/state law conflicts, the agency in early 1968 announced that in cases "where the effect of state protective legislation appears to be discriminatory rather than protective [the Commission] will decide whether that state legislation is superceded by [Title VII]" (EEOC 1969, p. 15; 1968c). Thus, NOW's protests notwithstanding, protective policies were still permissible, so long as their intent was not to discriminate. The EEOC would now make that determination on a case-by-case basis (NOW 1968a).

Later that year, the commission submitted an amicus brief in a case challenging the California labor code's 25-pound lifting limit for women.[14] The EEOC argued that the 25-pound limit was unnecessarily low and therefore—according to commission guidelines—discriminated unlawfully on the basis of sex. The district court agreed "the effect of the California…legislation is to subject women to discrimination and…establishes standards which are 'unreasonably low.'"[15] But the court then went on to make a broader legal point: "The California…legislation violates the provisions of the Civil Rights Act of 1964. Accordingly, such legislation is contrary to the Supremacy Clause of the United States Constitution and, therefore, is void and of no force and effect.…To the extent…the EEOC 'Guidelines on Discrimination Because of Sex'…is contrary to, or inconsistent with [these] conclusions…[the guidelines are] void and of no force and effect."[16] In other words, it did not matter whether or not the state law fell within EEOC guidelines: sex-specific protective classifications were by their very nature discriminatory and illegal under Title VII. As summarized by an appeals court citing the case a few months later, "*even if* 25 pounds did not constitute an unreasonably low level within the meaning of those guidelines, such restrictions are *still* contrary to Title VII...and must yield."[17] The ruling was upheld by the ninth circuit;[18] it and was not appealed to the Supreme Court.

The federal courts thus resolved ongoing debate over the legality of state protective legislation. Title VII's prohibition of sex discrimination superseded *all* state laws that required sex classifications. The EEOC referred to the *Rosenfeld* decision as an "important legal advance....[The] California hours and weights legislation was [ruled] contrary to [Title VII's] provisions in that it discriminated against women" (EEOC 1970, p. 15). So important, in fact, that the commission quickly revised its guidelines on state protective legislation *again*.[19] This time, however, there was no ambiguous language, no disclaimers or caveats, no promises of case-by-case investigations. Instead, "the Commission has found that such laws and regulations do not take into account the capacities, preferences, and abilities of individual females and therefore discriminate on the basis of sex...such laws and regulations conflict with are superseded by Title VII of the 1964 Civil Rights Act....Accordingly, such laws will not be considered...a basis for the application of the bona fide occupational qualification exception" (*Federal Register* 1969, p. 13367).

In short, equal treatment emerged both as the dominant legal rule governing sex discrimination under Title VII *and* as the dominant symbolic frame that defined NOW and the women's movement. Key administrative and judicial decisions on state protective policies converged with—and were greatly influenced by—NOW's political and cultural identity organized predominantly around an equal treatment frame. NOW mobilized on a platform of equal treatment and the abolition of traditional sex stereotypes embedded in gender-specific employment practices and legal classifications. Using both institutionalized and disruptive tactics, NOW pressured the EEOC and the federal courts to strike down discriminatory state protective laws. When both then announced that such laws were illegal under Title VII, the frame

transformation from protective to equal treatment was largely complete.[20]

Summary and Discussion

This article's central objective is to expand theoretical knowledge on the cultural and symbolic processes that enable, constrain, and transform social movements. Historical analysis of the framing contest between protective and equal treatment contributed to this goal by illustrating and further developing the concept of *legal* framing. Building on both classical and more recent law and society scholarship, I argued that law should properly be thought of as a highly resonant master frame. Then, tying together insights from social movement theory and the "constitutive" perspective on law, I proposed that law's deeply embedded symbols and categories have a major—sometimes dominant—impact on how challengers construct and mobilize their grievances, identities, and objectives. Exploring three distinct frame alignment processes—amplification, extension, and transformation—my analysis showed that the framing contest between protective and equal treatment was waged in explicitly legal terms (see table 1).

Legal Framing of the Women's Movement: Amplification, Extension, and Transformation

An emerging framing contest within the women's movement was already evident in the early 1960s, *before* enactment of Title VII. As written in the PCSW's comprehensive 1963 report *American Women,* status-of-women groups simultaneously promoted protective *and* equal treatment of women workers. Both frames were constructed—to a large extent—around constitutive legal symbols and categories. Protective treatment was informed by sex-specific legal classifications that understood women primarily as mothers and homemakers less able than men to defend themselves from the dangers and difficulties of the workplace. Equal treatment was in many ways the opposite: women were individuals with diverse preferences, abilities, and aspirations. Gender-based employment categories were thus unnecessary, discriminatory, and *illegal.*

Title VII's unexpected prohibition of sex discrimination immediately amplified and accelerated the tension between the protective and equal

Table 1 Summary of Legal Frame Alignment Processes

Alignment Process	Major Events	Central Legal Issues	Key Institutional and Organizational Actors	Outcomes
Amplification	Enactment of Title VII	Does Title VII require equal treatment of women in all circumstances?	U.S. Congress, status-of-women groups, the media, EEOC	Enhanced debate about equal vs. protective treatment and equal employment opportunity for women
Extension	Early interpretations of the BFOQ and the prohibition of sex-segregated help-wanted ads	Do sex stereotypes legally qualify as a BFOQ? Are sex-specific job ads illegal under Title VII? If so, what are the implications for protective labor classifications?	Status-of-women groups, EEOC	Legal double standard leads to anger and resentment among women's advocates; women's groups extend the equal treatment frame to address protective classifications; organizational transformation in the women's movement: formation of NOW
Transformation	NOW takes aggressive equal treatment position; protective laws challenged administratively and judicially	Are state protective laws superceded by Title VII's ban on sex discrimination?	NOW, EEOC, individual, states, federal courts, employers	All protective classifications ruled illegal under Title VII; equal treatment frame triumphs over protective treatment frame

treatment frames. Because Title VII's plain language seemed to require equal treatment of men and women, it gave some women's advocates an opportunity to further illuminate the equal treatment frame. At the same time, other women's leaders feared that Title VII's equal treatment language might immediately undo the movement's decades' long effort to enact and consolidate protective legal classifications exclusively for women.

Either way, Title VII offered new symbolic resources to *extend* the equal treatment frame. For example, women's groups generally favored, and the EEOC endorsed, a very narrow interpretation

of the BFOQ defense. Employers would not be allowed to use traditional sex stereotypes as a legal justification for gender-specific job classifications. This extended the equal treatment frame by legally invalidating outdated and draconian employment practices that overtly discriminated against women. Moreover, equal treatment's growing momentum—both within the women's movement and from a legal standpoint—gave women's advocates additional interpretive/symbolic tools to combat the EEOC's partial rollback of equal treatment by upholding the legality of sex-segregated job advertisements. The fight over help-wanted ads further emboldened the women's movement *because* of the emerging symbolic power of the equal treatment frame codified in Title VII generally, and in the narrow BFOQ interpretation specifically. The result was yet further extension of the equal treatment frame. So much so, in fact, that it led directly to an organizational transformation within the women's movement committed exclusively and unequivocally to an equal treatment frame.

The historical record confirms that resentment among women's advocates—including those who had traditionally defended sex-specific legal classifications—over the EEOC's anti–equal treatment ruling on help-wanted ads was a direct contributor to NOW's formation in 1966. And since NOW's central identity was constructed around a full-blown equal treatment frame, it immediately mobilized that identity to attack *all* sex-specific legal classifications. Despite women's advocates' long-standing efforts to shield women from the dangers of the workplace, the movement's now exclusive commitment to equal treatment could no longer accommodate protective labor policies and could no longer coexist with the protective treatment frame. By the early 1970s, equal treatment emerged as the hands-down winner in the legal framing contest between protective and equal treatment.

Legal Framing and Social Movements: Some Further Theoretical Implications

Extracting more general theoretical knowledge from case studies always requires caution and humility. Indeed, this article did not attempt to offer a "total explanation" of the women's movement in the 1960s, nor was it designed to produce a universal perspective on all cultural framing processes. Yet the central framing contest between protective and equal treatment *was* largely a battle over legal symbols and categories. And although it was not my objective to systematically analyze *every* frame that may have partially represented the movement, this does not mean that other frames were nonexistent or unimportant. Indeed, women's issues during this period were also framed in terms of marital relationships, income security, education, childcare, political citizenship, and women's health (PCSW 1963*b;* NOW, n.d.). Even so, there were empirical

justifications for placing law and legal framing processes front and center in this case. Historically, the transformations outlined in my analysis—including the formation of NOW and the subsequent prohibition of protective classifications—were driven above all else by the enactment of Title VII and the legal conflicts that emerged over the proper interpretation of that law regarding women's employment opportunities. In this way, women's advocates were increasingly encouraged to frame the movement around legal rights—equal versus protective treatment—each of which incorporated competing cultural constructions of women's roles at work and in society more generally.

All that said, this article's central arguments and findings do suggest some broader theoretical implications for social movement theory and research. I consider several specific, and interrelated, issues central to framing scholars' recent calls and attempts to further develop theoretical knowledge on cultural framing processes: the *diffusion* of master frames, frame *transformation,* and the relationship between cultural frames and *social change.*

Diffusion of the Legal Rights Frame

As this article has consistently argued, legal frames are not simply another bundle of symbolic resources in a social movement's cultural tool kit. Legal concepts and categories are often so central to how challengers understand and construct social relationships that law and law's constitutive symbols are a type of master frame with a potentially dominant influence on a movement's framing efforts. This ties into a growing body of work on "diffusion" processes across social movements and protest cycles (see, e.g., Benford and Snow 2000; McAdam 1995; Soule 2004). Diffusion refers generally to the contagion effects of earlier social movements on other movements, or on subsequent cycles of protest within the same movement. When a movement employs a set of mobilization strategies or protest tactics proven, or perceived to be, successful, other movements are likely to imitate them (Soule 2004).

The impact of master legal frames—especially those centered on legal rights—is a primary example of such diffusion processes. Tarrow (1994), for example, argued that the Civil Rights Movement initiated a master frame focused on "rights" that quickly spread to a wide range of movements throughout the 1960s and 1970s. John Skrentny's (2002) recent book *The Minority Rights Revolution* further supports this diffusion argument. Skrentny persuasively demonstrates how, once the Civil Rights Movement won legal recognition of its rights claims, the rights model created an immediate bandwagon effect and encouraged other ascriptive groups—including women, Hispanics, Asians, Native Americans, and even white ethnics—to make new demands and claims on the state. And while neither Tarrow nor Skrentny explicitly discussed the concept of legal frames, rights by their nature constitute a *legal* relationship between individuals, groups, and the state. Once a movement's interests and identities become widely understood as legal rights, they significantly expand the cultural and symbolic resources available to challenger groups by further legitimating their grievances and objectives. It is thus not surprising that subsequent movements—including the women's movement—actively constructed cultural frames focused on legal rights successfully employed by prior movements.

Indeed, the ascendance of the rights frame greatly contributed to the framing contest within the women's movement outlined in this article. Where women's advocates in the early 1960s were slowly initiating a renewed national debate about women's roles in modern American society, by the end of the decade that debate had become an aggressive appeal to the state to authoritatively recognize and enforce women's claims for legal rights in the workplace and elsewhere.

On the other hand, the ascendance of the equal treatment legal frame itself had important diffusion effects for subsequent developments in the women's movement.

By the early 1970s, the women's movement steadily expanded its focus from equal treatment in the workplace to questions of personal autonomy and reproductive rights. The equal treatment frame was consistent with these central concerns because it represented women as individuals entitled to make personal choices about work, family, and the general direction of their lives. Even so, reproductive health, contraception, and abortion decisions tended to be exclusively women's issues. The equal treatment frame may thus not have been sufficient because questions of reproductive rights were generally inapplicable to men in the first place. Instead, the women's movement built on its successful rights-centered strategy over protective polices by framing the debate over reproductive rights around the individual right to privacy—another broad *legal* right steadily expanded by the federal courts throughout the 1960s.[21] The right to privacy thus emerged as an additional legal frame more strategically equipped to symbolically represent the burgeoning national debate over abortion, and the women's movement's interest in expanding reproductive rights. Yet the right to privacy frame did not *replace* the equal treatment frame altogether; it built upon and complemented equal treatment in ways that further expanded the movement's cultural and symbolic resources as it confronted new issues and articulated new objectives. Just as the concrete debate over protective policies was framed around broader legal symbols and categories (equal treatment), the struggle over reproductive rights and abortion was also constructed around more abstract legal principles (individual right to privacy).

Frame Transformation and Social Change

This study also makes further theoretical and empirical contributions to the somewhat skimpy research on frame transformation processes and the consequences of those transformations for broader patters of social change. As Snow (2004) pointed out, although frame transformation is the most "dramatic and systematic form of frame alignment, [it] has received less explicit attention than other strategic alignment processes.... This is somewhat puzzling in light of ... the fact that social movements are in the business of affecting change" (Snow 2004, p. 393).

My analysis demonstrated two interrelated frame transformation processes identified in the literature: agent driven and event driven (see Snow 2004). I showed in part that emergence of the equal treatment frame resulted from dynamic interaction between the women's movement and its changing political and legal environment. The transformation from protective to equal treatment would not have been possible without the active interpretive work and framing efforts of women's advocates. At the same time, enactment of Title VII—and the EEOC's legal interpretations of Title VII—were central events that at once enabled and constrained the movement's steady push to further mobilize and legitimate the equal treatment frame. This back and forth between the movement and its political/legal environment drove the process forward until courts and administrators were forced to settle the debate one way or another. Nonetheless, *had* the equal treatment frame not won official endorsement from the federal courts—and eventually the EEOC—the capacities and consequences of the movement's legal framing efforts would likely have been far more limited.

Consider, for example, what might have happened if NOW had been unsuccessful in legally invalidating protective labor policies. Had the federal courts interpreted Title VII's prohibition of sex discrimination to *not* require elimination of sex-specific employment classifications that were considered "protective," the resource value of law for both the movement and for broader social change would have been reduced significantly. It would have partly undermined the movement's aggressive attempt to erode long-standing cultural stereotypes about women's abilities and roles in society. If so, the movement may have had to rethink how to strategically frame their grievances and goals in ways more resonant with the idea that women were fundamentally different than men, and thus that unequal treatment was warranted in certain key areas of social life. As it was, official endorsement of the equal treatment frame further emboldened the movement and allowed it to forge ahead with a set of legal resources—both symbolic and substantive—that could be successfully mobilized to other major issues, including the right to reproductive freedom. Thus legal change had direct implications for the internal symbolic resources available to the women's movement for future struggle. At the same time, this case further demonstrates that law is a unique type of cultural resource because it has the potential to enshrine symbolic visions of a movement's grievances and identities into officially recognized legal rights enforceable through the state's coercive apparatus.

This then leads to perhaps the most important theoretical implication of a legal framing perspective: it contributes to our growing but still insufficient understanding of a movement's ability to produce social change. Notwithstanding the ever-expanding breadth and volume of the social movement literature, the fundamental goal of this entire scholarly enterprise is, and has always been, to produce general knowledge on how, in what forms, and under what conditions social movements become a force for social and political change. Legal frames and legal framing processes offer a unique analytic framework for exploring the link between social movements and social change because *law is simultaneously a collective action frame and a collective action goal.* This suggests a jointly constructed, mutually reinforcing connection between challengers and the state, a conclusion fully consistent with the literature's repeated acknowledgement that the relationship between social movements and social change is not linear, but interactive.

When a movement successfully translates a master legal frame into an officially recognized legal right, it can lead to broader social change in two key interrelated ways. First, it transforms—through substantive legal change—the formal-structural relationships between challengers and dominant groups. For example, the legally codified frame transformation outlined in this article had real consequences for women's opportunities and life chances beyond the women's movement itself. A tremendous number of jobs and occupations previously off-limits to women were now legally required to be opened; hours limitations could no longer systematically hinder women's desire and ability to seek promotions; restrictions on night work or overnight travel that once cemented images of women as the weaker, more virtuous sex were increasingly eroded. And notwithstanding ongoing scholarly debate over precisely *how much* equality women have achieved in the workplace since these legal changes took effect, the legal shift from protective to equal treatment was undoubtedly a crucial step forward.

Second, when a legal frame becomes a legal right, it also transforms the *political environment* within which future struggles among movements, countermovements, and the state must take place. Because of the cultural and symbolic resonance of law, official recognition of legal rights expands the legitimacy of the movement's grievances and goals. This makes it more difficult (but of course not impossible) for a movement's opponents to successfully roll back achieved gains. Thus for example, when the pro-life movement mobilizes against abortion, it is taking head-on a judicially recognized constitutional right that a majority of citizens (albeit a slim one) views as legitimate. This places opponents at a political disadvantage *because* it places them at a legal disadvantage. It is thus perhaps not surprising that, despite decades of backlash against abortion rights, and the steady emergence of a solid conservative majority, antiabortion forces—at least to this point—have been unable to achieve their fundamental objective of retracting a woman's legal right to terminate a pregnancy. Moreover, judicial endorsement of legal rights *requires* that opponents and countermovements—at least in part—appeal for change to those same legal institutions that recognize and enforce the very rights that are being protested. In such situations, opponents cannot rely solely on the democratic process or calls to broader moral principles; they also typically have to go to court.[22]

In sum, because law is a master frame, and because a social movement's goals nearly always invoke law in some way, strategic framing of law's constitutive symbols offers a powerful conceptual and theoretical framework for exploring the processes though which, and with what consequences, social movements culturally frame their grievances, identity, and goals. Social movement scholars generally, and frame researchers specifically, should thus pay close attention to the culturally embedded legal meanings and categories that enable, constrain, and sometimes transform social movements in their broader struggle for social and political change.

NOTES

This research was supported in part by a research grant from the John F. Kennedy Library, Boston. An earlier version of this article was presented at the annual meeting of the American Sociological Association, August 2004, in San Francisco, California. I would like to thank Michael McCann, Sarah Soule, Doug McAdam, Robin Stryker, Stacia Haynie, Anna-Maria Marshall, Mary Bernstein, Teri Fritsma, and the *AJS* reviewers for their valuable criticisms and suggestions.

1. Although the number and type of protective labor laws varied state by state, common examples included—but were not limited to—maximum hours and prohibition of overtime, weight-lifting restrictions, limits on night work, no overnight travel, separate facilities for female employees, and outright exclusion from some dangerous jobs.

2. Frame analysis is not the only way in which culture has been incorporated into social movement theory and research. Scholars have focused on other cultural dimensions, including—but not limited to—semiotics, emotions, narratives and storytelling, ideologies, and discursive structures or "fields." And while there is a great deal of conceptual overlap among these different cultural dimensions, framing has arguably emerged as the central cultural perspective on social movements. Moreover, although this article is theoretically focused on cultural framing processes, it is *not* intended to be a "cultural" vs. "structural" analysis. Nor does it attempt to provide a total explanation (i.e., a fully integrated cultural *and* structural analysis) of social movements generally, or of the women's movement specifically. While fully appreciating the importance of structural forces in shaping social movements—and wholly acknowledging the vast literature upon which structural explanations are based—my theoretical objectives are more modest: to refine and further develop frame theory in social movement research.

3. By "social movement theory," I am referring to a specific body of literature in sociology (and sometimes political science) that has focused, either separately or together, on the resources, opportunity structures, and cultural processes that influence social movement emergence and development (for recent overviews, see McAdam et al. 1996; McAdam et al. 2001; Meyer 1999; Snow, Soule, and Kriesi 2004). This should be distinguished from an important literature in law and society scholarship that *does* explore the relationship between law and social movements (see, e.g., Bernstein 2001; Bumiller 1988; Burstein 1991; Burstein and Monaghan 1986; Handler 1978; McCann 1994). This body of work generally focuses on legal mobilization, including, but not limited to, litigation as a social movement tactic to achieve tangible economic and social benefits for challengers or other traditionally disadvantaged groups. This latter work—some conceptual overlap notwithstanding—is not normally associated with social movement theory as I refer to it here.

4. This is not to say that legal framing is always a successful social movement strategy. Some law and society scholars are more pessimistic about a movement's reliance on legal frames. They argue that law's constitutive symbols and categories

often pigeonhole a movement's transformative possibilities into abstract, narrowly defined legal concepts and frameworks (see, e.g., Bernstein 2001; Calavita 2001; Hunt 1990; Lazarus-Black and Hirsch 1994; Merry 1990). Dominant legal ideas—e.g., equal treatment, due process, and individual rights—can thus have a "conservatizing effect on social movements" (Bernstein 2001, p. 421) by restricting the range of political and social visions available to challenger groups. Thus for example, while some constitutivists view the Civil Rights Movement's successful color-blind frame as contributing to progressive change, others would argue the opposite: that framing race relations largely in terms of abstract legal principles, in which all individuals were hypothetically equal, obscured—and thus failed to remedy—the systemic, institutionalized nature of racial disadvantage in American society.

5. Exceptions include McCann (1994) and, among sociologists, Hull (1997). But while Hull does focus on framing conflicts between the civil rights frame and alternative frames that eschewed rights, developing a broader theory on legal frames or legal framing processes is not her author's central objective.

6. My analysis is limited to key changes that took place within the women's movement within a relatively brief time period between the mid-1960s and early 1970s. I make no attempt to explain or chronicle emergence and development of the entire "women's movement," going back to its origins in the 1920s (or perhaps earlier). Nor do I deal with major subsequent changes in the movement that took place in the 1970s—especially over the abortion issue—and beyond.

7. Unfortunately, there is no formal decision rule for choosing which historical documents to examine and which to ignore. In making those decisions, I relied on the totality of my knowledge of this entire historical sequence. This included identifying all of the major actors and organizations who played an important role in the event's unfolding, and, whenever possible, locating their own internal papers and documents. Also, while I did look at journalistic accounts from several of the nation's most influential newspapers, I did not systematically analyze all potential journalistic sources. The emerging national story over the women's movement and Title VII was, however, consistently and comprehensively covered by key outlets such as the *New York Times* and *Wall Street Journal,* and thus they were a crucial, though not exclusive, source of primary journalistic data. Comprehensive secondary accounts also led me to the most relevant and important sources of historical documents on which others have systematically relied in their own analyses of these events. Finally, by clearly acknowledging up front which sources were used, why, and where they are located, other researchers can check the "reliability" of my chosen sources and my interpretation of them.

8. A number of individual states also created their own status-of-women groups around this time.

9. More precisely, section 703(a) of Title VII states: "It shall be an unlawful employment practice for an employer—(1) to fail or refuse to hire or to discharge any individual, or otherwise to discriminate against any individual with respect to his compensation, terms, conditions, or privileges of employment, because of such individual's race, color, religion, sex, or national origin; or (2) to limit, segregate, or classify his employees in any way which would deprive or tend to deprive any individual of employment opportunities or otherwise adversely affect his status as an employee, because of such individual's race, color, religion, sex, or national origin" (U.S. Const. 42, 2000e-2[a]).

10. U.S. Const. 42, 2000e-2[e]; emphasis added. The BFOQ exemption also applied to discrimination on the basis of religion or national origin, but *not* to race.

11. Section 704(b) of Title VII stated: "[It] shall be an unlawful employment practice of an employer, labor organization of employment agency to print or publish...any notice or advertisement relating to employment...indicating any preference, limitation, specification, or discrimination, based on race, color, religion, sex, or national origin, except that such a notice or advertisement may indicate a preference, limitation, specification, or discrimination based on religion, sex, or national origin when religion, sex, or national origin is a bona fide occupational qualification" (U.S. Const. 42, 2000e-3[b]).

12. NOW's own internal documents, in-depth interviews with NOW's original members, and secondary accounts all concur that NOW was officially created at the June 1966 status-of-women conference, and that anger toward the EEOC was the immediate cause. As NOW cofounder Mary Eastwood recalled, "the issue of sex-segregated job advertisements was one of the major reasons NOW was established" (quoted in Florer 1973, p. 72). However, NOW's formation was not completely spontaneous. Betty Friedan and several other delegates had been quietly meeting behind the scenes during the conference, pondering the possibility of a new organization (see NOW, n.d., p. 1; Friedan 1991; Florer 1973; Freeman 1975; Harrison 1988).

13. *Weeks v. Southern Bell* 277 F. Supp. 117 [1967]; *Bowe v. Colgate-Palmolive* 272 F. Supp. 332 [1967]).

14. *Rosenfeld v. Southern Pacific Company* 293 F. Supp. 1219 [1968].

15. Ibid., p. 1224

16. Ibid.

17. *Weeks v. Southern Bell* 408 F.2d 228 [1969], p. 233; emphasis added.

18. 444 F.2d 1219 [1971]

19. Women's movement scholar Jo Freeman confirms that "the EEOC was forced to change its interpretations to keep them in accord with judicial rulings on Title VII" (Freeman 1975, p. 187; see also Davidson, Ginsburg, and Kay 1974). Freeman also quotes EEOC commissioner Elizabeth

Kuck: "This Guideline revision followed the reasoning of the case of *Rosenfeld v. Southern Pacific Company*" (speech by Kuck, November 1969; quoted in Freeman 1975, p. 187).

20. For example, in 1969, 46 states had laws restricting women's hours of work. By 1973, just six states had not revised or repealed their hours-of-work laws, and by 1975, Nevada was the sole holdout (Davidson et al. 1974, pp. 650–51; Freeman 1975, p. 187). As Freeman (1975) concluded, EEOC and court interpretation of the Title VII/state law relationship "has had a devastating effect on state protective legislation" (p. 187).

21. In *Griswold v. Connecticut* the U.S Supreme Court ruled that the Bill of Rights and the due process clause of the Fourteenth Amendment included a substantive right to privacy. Although Griswold dealt specifically with the right of married couples to use contraception, the right to privacy became the doctrinal foundation of *Roe v. Wade's* central holding that women had a constitutional right to terminate a pregnancy.

22. This brief example of the pro-life movement brings up a final important point on this study's implications for future research on cultural framing processes. Given this article's overall focus on gender inequalities and the legal/rights frame, one might conclude that perhaps my framework's applicability is restricted to social movements from below that represent traditionally disadvantaged groups (racial minorities, women, the disabled, homosexuals, etc.). Yet a legal framing perspective need not be limited to challenges over resource distributions (legal or otherwise) between haves and have-nots. For example, the environmental movement has been increasingly framed around citizens' right to "environmental justice" and has routinely used litigation to promote those rights (Marshall 2003). Movements organized around issues of morality, privacy, and/or religious faith can also be analyzed from a legal framing perspective. Thus the pro-life, pro-choice, right to die, Christian conservative, and other such movements have also frequently found themselves framing their grievances and goals in terms of legal and constitutional rights, and have consistently turned to state and federal courts to promote their symbolic and legal visions of deeply held moral principles. Key examples include, but are not limited to, rights of the fetus vs. rights of personal autonomy, right to die vs. right to physician-assisted suicide, and right to free exercise of religion in public institutions vs. right against governmental establishment of religion.

Part 7

The Social Psychology of Participation: Grievance, Identity, and Emotion

We saw in Part 5 how social networks, whether interpersonal or organizationally based, constitute a key factor in accounting for differential recruitment and participation. Yet, it is important to bear in mind that while participation usually is unlikely to occur in the absence of a network tie to a movement member or organization, not all individuals who receive invitations from acquaintances, friends, or family will participate. This is because networks facilitate rather than determine recruitment and participation. Equally important is whether individuals sympathize or identify with the causes that movements champion. Recall from Part 5 that several of the selections accented the importance of the intersection of networks and identity. Also, we learned in Part 6 that framing may function to amplify and align this connection and/ or generate sympathy for a movement's cause. But even sympathy coupled with an invitation to participate in a movement does not guarantee participation. This is because there are at least two kinds of individual-level mobilization: consensus mobilization and action mobilization (see Klandermans 1984). The former indicates shared grievances or sympathies; the latter indicates willingness to act on those shared sentiments. That consensus mobilization does not necessarily lead to action mobilization was clearly illustrated in a study by Bert Klandermans and Dirk Oegema (1987) of the efforts of the Dutch peace movement to mobilize citizens against the deployment of the cruise missile in the mid-1980s. They found that while three-quarters of a random sample of community residents were sympathetic to the movement's goals, not many of them (only 1 out of 20) ended up participating

in a protest event for the cause. This high rate of nonparticipation was due to three factors: first, not all of the sympathizers were targeted or recruited (60 percent); second, only one-sixth (10 percent) of those targeted expressed sufficient motivation to participate; and third, only one-third of those who intended to participate actually ended up doing so, largely because of different obstacles that popped up, such as having to work or attend to a sick family member.

Such findings not only underscore the importance of looking beyond network ties and shared grievances to understand the determinants of movement participation, they also focus attention on the variable of individual motivation. What social psychological factors generate the motivation sufficient to devote some portion of time and energy to movement activities? What, in other words, contributes to action mobilization? And what factors contribute to sustained participation? Of course, the character of participation varies across social movements, with some movements demanding relatively little time, energy, and personal resources, while others are comparatively greedy, demanding a great deal from their members (Coser 1967; Turner and Killian 1987; Wiltfang and McAdam 1991). Wherever a movement falls on this continuum of participation demands, however, its relative success in securing and retaining adherents depends in part on the adherent's motivation. The four readings in this section address this issue.

In the first selection, Bert Klandermans, Marlene Roefs, and Johan Olivier explore the sources of mobilizing grievances in South Africa between 1994 and 1998. The apartheid policies of the pre-1994 government yielded a deeply segregated and divided society, but social movement protest among black South Africans was not as widespread or persistent as one might expect given the depths of race-based inequalities. Clearly this was not due to the absence of grievances among black South Africans. The highly repressive measures of the South African government no doubt functioned to suppress the mobilizing potential of those grievances, as political opportunity theorists would argue. However, Klandermans and his colleagues found—based on interviews with a large sample of South Africans over a five-year period—that the effects of objective, material disparities were modified by subjective assessments, such as comparative evaluation of one's situation with others and the level of trust in the government. In other words, the character and depth of grievance among South Africans was not an automatic artifact of their racial category or socioeconomic situation, but was influenced by various social psychological factors that, in turn, affected the prospect of action mobilization.

In the second selection, Francesca Polletta examines students' narrative accounts of the 1960 sit-in movement that occurred predominantly in the South. Polletta's article highlights the role of narrative as a key mechanism in motivating action, especially through helping to generate a shared, collective identity and sense of passion among sit-in participants. One of the features of Polletta's analysis that we find particularly noteworthy is that it shows how, in some instances of movement activity, the motivation for passionate engagement does not precede the action but is generated during the course of the action itself.

Collective identity and emotion also figure prominently in the third reading in this section, by Rachel Einwohner. However, in contrast to most research, which is conducted in settings wherein activists have considerable elbow room to pursue various identity strategies, Einwohner uses the case of the Warsaw Ghetto uprising of 1943 to explore activists' identity work in a highly repressive context. She finds that a "strong sense of collective identity, coupled with emotional responses to Nazi persecution of European Jews, helped motivate the Ghetto fighters to take action," but they had to take care to hide or suppress their identity and emotion at certain times because of the dangerous, repressive conditions in which they operated. As a result, the resistance fighters identity work was "characterized by the simultaneous amplification and suppression of identity work and emotion," thus reminding us how movement-related social psychological processes may operate somewhat differently in different contexts.

In this section's final article, Sharon Erickson Nepstad shifts attention from recruitment and action mobilization to membership persistence or retention over time. Using the case of the Catholic Left Plowshares peace movement, she identifies various community-based rituals and practices that, on the one hand, reinforce activists' identities and strengthen various types of commitment while, on the other hand, strategically neutralizing tendencies that can lead to disaffection. Here we see that organizationally embedded social psychological processes are as important to understanding membership retention as they are in accounting for differential recruitment and participation.

21.
Grievance Formation in a Country in Transition: South Africa, 1994–1998

BERT KLANDERMANS, MARLENE ROEFS, AND JOHAN OLIVIER

The apartheid policies of the pre-1994 South African government resulted in a deeply divided society (Sisk 1995). Racial cleavages ran through every sector of society: South Africans were classified as either black, colored, Indian, or white. This classification in turn determined one's life chances: where one was allowed to live, with whom one was allowed to associate, where one was allowed to go to school, the kind of work one could get, the church to which one belonged. Apartheid politics had imposed race upon the South Africans as the overpowering identity (Marx 1998). Africans (blacks) occupied the lowest status of all four categories; the coloreds were next lowest, the Indians were next highest. The whites reserved the highest status in South African society for themselves.

Obviously, many years must pass before the racial cleavage loses its significance. Differential treatment of citizens will continue to be based on racial categorization for a long time, not only as a legacy from the past, but also because of the affirmative action programs that have been implemented to correct past injustices (South Africa Survey 1996/1997). Will the enduring existence of the racial cleavage continue to generate grievances? This question is vitally important for the country.

It is a well-documented social phenomenon that differential treatment is not necessarily converted into grievances. In the past, the racial cleavage obviously did generate grievances, as witnessed by the long-lasting struggle against apartheid. Will it continue to do so, now that the political landscape has been altered so dramatically? Or will cleavages

other than the racial divide come to determine grievances in South African society?

These questions about the formation of grievances are not trivial. They possess not only tremendous political importance, but also great theoretical significance. As for the political importance, in a country that is socioculturally as heterogeneous as South Africa, any grievance defined along sociocultural lines poses a potential political threat. As long as grievances are distributed randomly in a society, they are politically neutral. If members of a group feel that their *group* is treated unjustly, however, group-based grievances will develop. Such grievances become politically relevant because aggrieved groups may—and often do—mobilize and demand change.

Grievance theory has little to say about such mobilization processes. Relative deprivation and social justice theories—two well-known families of grievance theories in social psychology—give little attention to mobilization, even though protest is mentioned as a behavioral consequence of relative deprivation and feelings of injustice (Hegtvedt and Markovsky 1995; Tyler et al. 1997). Traditionally, the mobilization of aggrieved people has been the subject of social movement research. Today's "ruling" paradigms—resource mobilization and political process theory—have always concentrated on why and how aggrieved people mobilize (for an overview, see Tarrow 1998). The question of why and how people become aggrieved has received much less attention. This is not to say that students of social movements regard grievances as irrelevant; rather, as protagonists of resource mobilization and political process theory argue, grievances are so ubiquitous in a society that their mere presence is not sufficient to explain the emergence of social movements.

Because of this lack of interest in the formation of grievances, relative deprivation theory, a grievance

Klandermans, Bert, Marlene Roefs, and Johan Olivier. 2001. "Grievance Formation in a Country in Transition: South Africa, 1994–1998." *Social Psychology Quarterly* 64: 41–54. Reprinted by permission of American Sociological Association.

theory that formerly was important in the social movement domain, has lost its relevance for students of social movements. In general, very little systematic theorizing has been undertaken on the formation of grievances in the social movement literature. To be sure, the concept of a *collective action frame,* especially its component injustice frame, resulted in a renewed focus on grievances (for a synthetic treatment, see Klandermans 1997). Even so, very little has been said to date about the formation of such frames. Grievance theory in the social movement domain became enmeshed in ever more highly elaborated taxonomies of grievances, but how such grievances are formed remained largely unspecified.

As for the theoretical significance, the case of South Africa is interesting precisely because it is the situation in which we may expect that the racial divide will continue to exist, but in a political context that has changed dramatically. The South Africa case provides a unique opportunity to investigate questions about the formation of grievances that cannot be studied in relatively stable societies. On the one hand, in a society in transition, changes in the sociopolitical context may trigger the formation of new grievances. On the other, old grievances may disappear because people may feel that their situation is improving or because they are optimistic about the future.

In this paper we define grievances as feelings of dissatisfaction with important aspects of life such as housing, living standard, income, employment, health care, human rights, safety, and education. We will show that such feelings of dissatisfaction are not linked to objective outcomes in a simple way. Two literatures are proposed to clarify the reason: relative deprivation and social justice. The reasoning we develop here is applied to a description and an understanding of the changing patterns of grievances in South Africa. We hope we can demonstrate that sophisticated grievance theory—specifically, relative deprivation and social justice theory—remains relevant for the study of social movements.

The Formation of Grievances

Differential treatment of citizens does not necessarily generate grievances. Obviously, grievances are the result of some kind of evaluation. Relative

deprivation theory emphasizes the importance of comparisons in determining outcome evaluations (for overviews, see Hegtvedt and Markovsky 1995; Tyler et al. 1997; Tyler and Smith 1998). Stouffer et al. (1949) were the first to point out that people compare their rewards with those of others in a comparison group and that the outcome of this comparison determines their evaluation.

Other classic varieties of relative deprivation theory were proposed by Davies (1962) and Gurr (1970), who have concentrated on people's comparisons with themselves at different points in time. People compare their current situation with either their past experiences or their future expectations. Objectively a group may be in a disadvantaged situation, but its members may feel that the situation has improved in comparison with the past. As a consequence, they may be satisfied. They will be more satisfied if they expect that the situation will continue to improve in the future. Indeed, both Davies and Gurr explain contention by citing people's growing concern that the experienced improvements will *not* continue. Davies' famous J-curve hypothesis and the various types of relative deprivation distinguished by Gurr are all about the concern that future outcomes will no longer meet expectations for the future.

An important conceptual distinction, that between individual and group relative deprivation, was introduced by Runciman (1966)—egoistic and fraternalistic deprivation, in Runciman's terminology. People (1) may feel personally deprived or (2) may feel that the group to which they belong is deprived. Research suggests that feelings of group relative deprivation increase the likelihood of collective behavior, whereas feelings of individual relative deprivation increase the likelihood of individual-level behavior (Martin 1986).

Later versions of relative deprivation theory (Crosby 1982; Muller 1980) introduced the concepts of deserved and entitled outcomes. The most recent versions (Atkinson 1986; Folger 1987; Masters and Smith 1987) attempt to build conceptual bridges to other social psychological approaches such as social comparison and social cognition. These versions try to resolve the ambiguities surrounding the choice of different bases of comparison.

In their review, Tyler and Smith (1998) suggest that sociological versions of relative deprivation theory have placed more emphasis on *intrapersonal* comparisons with the past or the future, whereas social psychological theories of relative deprivation emphasize *interpersonal* comparisons with other people or groups. Research suggests that people often prefer to make downward comparisons with people who are worse off in order to enhance or protect their own feelings of self-worth, rather than making upward comparisons with people who are better off, which can lead to feelings of relative deprivation (Tyler and Smith 1998). Therefore inequality often fails to generate grievances simply because people are not making the "right" comparisons (Major 1994).

Contrary to what Tyler and Smith suggest, time also plays a role in social psychological relative deprivation theories. These theories emphasize the significance of optimism: that is, grievances are reduced by the expectation that the situation will improve in the future. Results from laboratory studies provide evidence supporting this assumption (Folger 1987).

Hegtvedt and Markovsky (1995) point out that relative deprivation theory concentrates on a comparison of output without taking differences in input into account. Equity theory, however, proposes that outcomes are evaluated in terms of the associated input: people who have invested more should receive more. In fact, most people in Western societies believe that economic inequality is justified because they believe they live in a just world, where people deserve what they get and get what they deserve (Lerner 1980). Yet according to Hegtvedt and Markovsky (1995), the evaluator's position in society tempers the perceived fairness of equality. Individuals occupying lower positions in the stratification system seem less likely to judge inequality as fair; instead they favor a more equal distribution. Indeed, individuals in lower positions seem to prefer equality to equity, whereas individuals in higher positions seem to prefer equity to equality.

Procedural Justice

Perceived fairness of procedures is a core variable in theories of social justice (Tyler and Smith 1998; Tyler

et al. 1997; for an application in the South African context, see Roefs, Klandermans, and Olivier 1998). These theories distinguish distributive justice from procedural justice. Distributive justice concerns the distribution of outcomes, whereas procedural justice concerns the procedure used for distributing outcomes. Obviously, relative deprivation theory is about outcome distributions that are deemed unjust.

According to social justice theory, an important reason for considering outcome distributions unjust is that people doubt the fairness of the procedures employed to arrive at that distribution. People are more satisfied with a specific distribution of public goods if they regard the distribution procedures as fair. Thibaut and Walker (1975) argue that the key procedural characteristic shaping people's views about the fairness of procedures is the distribution of control between the parties. If people actually have been involved in the decision-making process, procedures are more likely to be deemed fair (Tyler and Lind 1992). Thus, for the South African case, we hypothesize that grievances are more likely to develop if people feel that they have no influence on the new authorities in South Africa.

Tyler and his colleagues (Tyler and Lind 1992; Tyler and Smith 1998), in their evaluation of the fairness of procedures, argue that people are not driven only by *instrumental* motives—that is, by the extent to which they have been able to influence the outcomes—but also by *relational* issues. Such issues include people's evaluation of the decision-making process as unbiased and honest, the trustworthiness of others in the relationship (in particular, authorities), and the degree to which people feel that they are respected. Evidence suggests that trustworthiness is typically the most important factor shaping evaluations of authorities (Tyler and Smith 1998): people seem to place great weight on their inferences about the motives and intentions of the authorities with whom they deal.

In the South African situation, this point leads us to hypothesize that grievance formation depends on the trustworthiness of the new authorities in the eyes of the people. Thus grievances will be more likely to develop in South Africa if people feel that the unequal distribution of outcomes between social groups results from procedures that they deem unfair. People's view of the fairness of procedures is affected by the extent to which they feel that they have been able to influence the new authorities, and by the degree to which they feel that the new authorities can be trusted.

Summary

Our brief tour of relative deprivation and social justice theory results in a few hypotheses about grievance formation. First, we assume that people will be aggrieved if they occupy a low position in society (Hyp. 1). Basically, this hypothesis proposes that objective conditions affect grievance formation.

Our second hypothesis capitalizes on the effect of comparison. We hypothesized that, *net of the impact of objective conditions, comparison adds to the process of grievance formation*: regardless of their objective situation, people will be aggrieved if (a) they feel that their situation is worse than that of others and/or (b) worse now than in the past, and/or (c) if they expect that it will not improve in the future (Hyp. 2a, 2b, 2c).

Our third hypothesis concerns the combined effect of objective conditions and comparisons. We hypothesize that the grievances generated by poor objective conditions will intensify if people feel (a) that they are worse off than others, *or* (b) that their situation has declined over the past few years, *or* (c) that their situation will not improve in the future (Hyp. 3a, 3b, 3c).

Our fourth hypothesis concerns the moderating effect of the evaluation of the government as the authority in control of distributing wealth in a society. We hypothesize that the grievances generated by poor objective conditions will intensify if people (a) don't trust government and/or (b) don't feel that they have an influence on government (Hyp. 4a, 4b).

In the remainder of this paper we test these hypotheses with data collected in South Africa between 1994 and 1998.

Methods
Design

Annual surveys in random samples of the South African population have been conducted since 1994. Face-to-face interviews were conducted in people's homes by trained interviewers of the interviewees' ethnic background, who spoke their language. The interviews were based on structured questionnaires. The first interviews took place in February 1994, the period just before South Africa's first democratic elections. The subsequent waves of data were collected in March 1995, 1996, 1997, and 1998. The five waves are based on separate samples of 2,286, 2,226, 2,228, 2,220 and 2,227 respondents respectively.

Respondents

The respondents were drawn by means of a multiple-stage cluster probability sample design. The population the sample was drawn from were all South African residents age 18 and older. We stratified the sample according to provinces[1] and by a classification of socioeconomic regions: tribal, traditional rural areas in former homelands; squatter areas; hostels, hotels, and boarding schools in urban areas both metropolitan and non-metropolitan;[2] townships for coloreds, Indians, and Africans, metropolitan and non-metropolitan; town and cities, metropolitan and nonmetropolitan; and rural areas excluding former homelands. The sampling allocation to these strata was made proportionally to the 1991 population figures, with a few exceptions: provinces were given a minimum of 120 respondents; the minimum number of Indians was fixed at 120; and we introduced an additional sub-sample for live-in domestic workers.[3]

As a consequence of the sampling procedures, unweighted results are not representative of the South African population. For our purposes, however, it is more important that the samples are drawn according to the same principles and thus are comparable. For that matter, the sampling design guarantees that the regional breakdowns of the samples are almost identical. The differences between the sampling design of the first survey and the latter four surveys, however, result in different proportions of Africans, coloreds, Indians, and whites in the first survey than in the latter four. Over-time comparisons of the samples' four racial groups on age, gender, and education reveal that these groups are similar as to gender, but slightly different in age and level of education. Yet MANOVAs with the key variables of our study as dependent variables (measures b, c, d, and e; see below) and with age, education, and time as factors reveal no significant interactions. Hence there is no indication that the observed age and educational differences between our samples explain the variation over time in these key variables.

Measures

a. *Demographics*. These measures are population group (African, colored, Indian, white), age, gender, education, income, employment status, occupation, language, and religion.

b. *Outcome distribution*. We developed a living standard measure based on the availability, in the household, of a variety of items ranging from electricity and running water to a microwave oven.

c. *Grievances*. We assessed grievances by asking our respondents how satisfied they were with their general personal situation, the neighborhood they live in, the job they have or their chances to get a job, the educational opportunities in their communities, their standard of living, the health care available, the recognition of their human rights, and the safety in the area where they live (answered on a seven-point scale ranging from "extremely dissatisfied" to "extremely satisfied"). We combined the eight questions into a scale of distributive grievances ranging from 1 ("not at all aggrieved") to 7 ("very much aggrieved") (Cronbach's alpha = .84).

d. *Relative deprivation and future expectations*. We asked our respondents (1) whether their general personal situation is better or worse than that of other people in South Africa; (2) whether their general personal situation is better or worse than it was about five years ago; and (3) what they think their general personal situation will be five years from now. The questions were answered on a seven-point scale from 1 ("very much better") to 7 ("very much worse").

e. *Influence on and trust in authorities*. We assessed this variable with two questions. The first question tapped perceived influence on government: "Do you agree or disagree with the statement 'people like you can have an influence on governmental decisions'?" (on a seven-point scale

ranging from "disagree very strongly" to "agree very strongly"). The second tapped trust in government: "How often do you trust the government to do what is right for people like you?" (never, seldom, sometimes, mostly, always). The two questions are correlated at $r = .36$.

Results

Our first hypothesis states that people occupying a low position in society will be aggrieved. We have tested this hypothesis for race and class, the two main stratification criteria in South Africa.

Figure 1 maps the mean scores of the four racial categories on our grievance scale. In 1994 the four groups' relative positions were what one would expect: the Africans were the most aggrieved and the whites the least; the coloreds and the Indians occupied an intermediate position. After 1994, however, race became less important in explaining grievances: Africans became less aggrieved and whites became more aggrieved, while the relative position of the coloreds and Indians remained more or less stable. By 1998 the grievance levels of Africans, coloreds, and Indians were identical. Although whites were more aggrieved than in the past, they were still less aggrieved than any other group.[4]

Our findings for class are what one would expect and seem to be more stable. As our indicator of class, we used outcome distributions as indicated by income and living standard. The zero-order correlation between grievances (on the one hand) and income and living standard (on the other) remained fairly stable through the years and hovered around −.30. That is, the lower people's income and living standard, the more aggrieved they are. Not surprisingly, income and living standard are highly correlated: the correlations throughout the five years under study vary between .60 and .70. Because the results for income and for living standard are essentially the same, we restrict ourselves in the remaining analyses to living standard as our indicator of outcome distribution.

Even today, race and class are social categories that overlap strongly in South Africa. Our data also reveal this point unequivocally. In 1998, 42 percent of the variance in income and living standard was still explained by race; hence, we had to disentangle

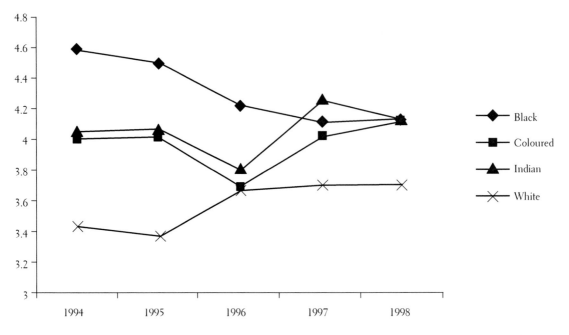

Figure 21.1 Dissatisfaction. *Note.* **Dissatisfaction scores are based on a scale comprising levels of dissatisfaction with the neighborhood, employment, education, living standard, health care, human rights, and safety. A score of I means "very much satisfied"; a score of 7 means "very much dissatisfied."**

the effects of the two. To do so, we conducted regression analyses with race and class as the independent variables and grievances as the dependent variable.

Table 1 presents the results of these regression analyses. Blacks, coloreds, and Indians are contrasted with white South Africans, and we employed living standard as our indicator for class. The pattern that emerges is extremely interesting. Over the five years under study, race became almost irrelevant, whereas living standard gained in significance. In 1994, race explained 23 percent of the variance in grievances while living standard explained nil, but these percentages were 3 percent and 6 percent respectively in 1998.[5]

Thus, net of race, living standard became *more* important over the years as a predictor of grievances. This is illustrated in Table 2, where the living standard measure is broken down into three levels: low, medium, and high.[6] The means are provided for distributive grievances for the racial categories at these three levels for the first and the last year.

In 1994, grievance levels were determined by racial categories, whereas living standard was less relevant. By 1998, it was the other way around: racial categories were less relevant and living standard made the difference.

Thus, after 1994, the *direct* effect of race on people's sense of grievances decreased; the *indirect* effect via living standard became more significant. In other words, race seems to be replaced by class. To be sure, class is linked closely to race, but class seems to have become more important than racial categorization in regard to satisfaction or dissatisfaction with outcome distributions. Grievances are now determined by "what people have" and no longer by "who they are."

In summary, the results confirm our first hypothesis. People who occupy lower positions in the South African society are more aggrieved than those in higher positions, although the impact of objective conditions on grievance formation has declined over the years. Our most important

Table 1 Grievances Regressed on Race and Living Standard: Unstandardized Coefficients

	1994		1995		1996		1997		1998	
	Model 1	Model 2	Model 1	Model 2	Model 1	Model 2	Model 1	Model 2	Model 1	Model 2
African	1.31	1.31	1.12	.96	.58	.31	.36	.07	.45	.00
	(.06)	(.07)	(.06)	(.08)	(.06)	(.07)	(.05)	(.06)	(.06)	(.08)
Colored	.68	.71	.62	.61	.26	.01	.40	.20	.36	.19
	(.08)	(.08)	(.10)	(.09)	(.09)	(.09)	(.09)	(.07)	(.11)	(.06)
Indian	.71	.68	.68	.58	−.04	.28	.29	.33	.43	.27
	(.08)	(.08)	(.09)	(.10)	(.09)	(.09)	(.07)	(.09)	(.09)	(.11)
Living Standard		−.02		−.05		−.08		−.09		−.14
		(.02)		(.02)		(.01)		(.01)		(.01)
R^2	.23	.23	.18	.19	.07	.09	.02	.05	.03	.09

Note: Standard errors in parentheses.

Table 2 Grievances: Race and Living Standard

	1994 Living Standard			1998 Living Standard		
	Low	Medium	High	Low	Medium	High
African	4.70	4.68	4.58	4.27	3.88	3.76
Colored	3.84	4.10	4.23	4.18	4.10	3.97
Indian	—	4.07	3.98	—	4.32	3.85
White	—	3.45	3.26	—	4.03	3.63

Note: Only very few Indians and whites report a low living standard.

finding, however, concerns the changes in the relative significance of race and class. The objective conditions of living standard (class) have come to matter more than the objective conditions of political rights (race) in explaining a person's sense of grievance.

Intra-Versus Interpersonal Comparisons

Our second hypothesis links grievance formation to choice of comparison. We made a distinction between interpersonal comparison (comparison with others) and intrapersonal comparison

(comparison over time). We assumed that net of the impact of objective conditions, people will be aggrieved if (a) they feel that their situation is worse than that of others and/or (b) worse now than in the past, and/or (c) if they fear that it will decline in the future. Each of these hypothesized effects was observed, as revealed by the regression analyses in Table 3.

In this table the three types of comparisons are entered in the equation in a second step after the effects of race and living standard have been determined. They add considerably to the variance

Table 3. Grievances Regressed on Race, Living Standard, and Inter-and Intrapersonal Comparisons: Unstandardized Coefficients

	1994		1995		1996		1997		1998	
	Model 1	Model 2	Model 1	Model 2	Model 1	Model 2	Model 1	Model 2	Model 1	Model 2
African	1.29	.85	.97	.91	.32	.46	.08	.22	.02	.19
	(.07)	(.06)	(.08)	(.06)	(.07)	(.07)	(.07)	(.06)	(.07)	(.06)
Colored	.71	.38	.63	.51	.02	.06	.13	.11	.19	.23
	(.08)	(.06)	(.09)	(.07)	(.09)	(.08)	(.07)	(.06)	(.09)	(.05)
Indian	.69	.48	.60	.50	.31	.32	.32	.25	.28	.26
	(.09)	(.07)	(.10)	(.08)	(.09)	(.08)	(.09)	(.08)	(.11)	(.05)
Living Standard	.01	.01	-.04	.00	-.07	-.02	-.08	-.03	-.14	-.07
	(.02)	(.01)	(.01)	(.01)	(.01)	(.01)	(.01)	(.01)	(.01)	(.01)
Comparisons with Others		.43		.36		.31		.29		.27
		(.02)		(.02)		(.02)		(.02)		(.02)
Comparisons with the Past		.18		.15		.10		.08		.15
		(.02)		(.02)		(.02)		(.02)		(.02)
Expectations for the Future		-.00		.09		.07		.09		.13
		(.02)		(.02)		(.02)		(.02)		(.02)
R^2	.23	.56	.19	.50	.09	.34	.05	.34	.09	.39

Note: Standard errors in parentheses.

in grievances explained, as the figures indicate. Obviously people feel aggrieved because they regard their situation as worse than that of others and/or worse than their own situation in the past, and/or because they expect that it will decline. Each of these comparisons contributes independently of the other comparisons to people's sense of grievance. All three effects are fairly stable. Together the three comparisons add some 30 percent to the variance in dissatisfaction explained by race and class in each equation.

Interpersonal comparisons, however, are far more important than intrapersonal comparisons. Apparently a sense of grievance about the distribution of outcomes is determined especially by the assessment that one's situation is worse than that of others and, to a lesser extent, by the assessment that the situation is worse now than five years ago or will decline in the next five years. This finding makes sense: grievance, as we assessed it, pertains to the *distribution* of outcomes in a society, and interpersonal comparisons obviously are more informative about that distribution than intrapersonal comparisons. Yet intrapersonal comparisons add explanatory power. Regardless of how their outcomes relate to those of others, people feel aggrieved if their position has declined in relation to the past or if they fear that it will decline in the future. On the other hand, people also feel more satisfied if their position has improved or if they expect it to improve, even if it is currently worse than that of comparison others.

Moderating Grievance Formation

The moderating effect of comparisons. Our third hypothesis concerns the moderating effects of inter- and intrapersonal comparison on grievance formation. We hypothesized that the outcomes of such comparisons may sharpen or soften someone's sense of grievance. That is, disappointing outcomes become even more disappointing if people believe that others are better off, or that current outcomes have declined, or that future outcomes will not improve.

To test these assumptions, we broke down the total sample on the basis of the scores for the three types of comparisons in groups of approximately the same size: (1) a group of people who feel that their situation is better than that of others, a group of people who feel that their situation is more or less the same as that of others, and a group of people who feel that their situation is worse than that of others; (2) a group of people who feel that their situation has improved from the past, a group who feel that their situation has remained more or less the same, and a group of people who feel that their situation has declined; and (3) a group of people who expect their situation to improve in the future, a group who expect that their situation will remain more or less the same, and a group who expect their situation to decline. We then conducted regression analyses for each group in each of the five years, with race and living standard as independent variables and grievances as dependent variable (Table 4). In this way we could assess whether the effect of objective conditions on grievance formation was moderated by the outcomes of comparisons.

Table 4 gives the R^2 values for race and for race and living standard. The relative size of these values for the three groups is important for our discussion, both within a given year and as they develop over time. Expectations for the future especially moderate the link between objective conditions and grievances: objective conditions continue to exert a considerable effect on grievances only for people who fear that their situation will decline. In fact, in 1998 the impact of race and class on grievances is higher than for the previous years. At the same time, objective conditions lose their influence on grievance formation among those who expect that their situation will improve. People who believe that their situation will remain the same occupy an intermediate position.

Comparisons with the past exert a similar but less dramatic effect, while interpersonal comparisons do not seem to matter. This suggests that a low position in society especially affects grievance formation among people who fear that their situation will not improve, and/or who find that it has not improved thus far. For all groups, the impact of living standard increases in relation to that of race. Apparently our earlier finding that class became more important than race holds in combination with the various outcomes of these comparisons.

Intrapersonal comparison (comparison of time) seems to moderate the formation of grievances, and to do so much more strongly than interpersonal comparison. Apparently quite a few South Africans feel that they are part of an ongoing process of change which has brought improvements in the past and is expected to continue doing so. The reverse is also true, of course: those who feel that they are in a

Table 4. Race, Living Standard, and Grievances Moderated by Comparions with Others and Comparison with the Past, and by Expectations for the Future: R^2 Values

	1994	1995	1996	1997	1998
Comparison with Others					
Better:					
Race	.15	.14	.04	.01	.02
Race + liv.std.	.16	.14	.04	.01	.04
Same:					
Race	.22	.20	.09	.06	.01
Race + liv.std.	.22	.20	.09	.08	.05
Worse:					
Race	.05	.05	.03	.00	.01
Race + liv.std.	.05	.05	.03	.03	.05
Comparison with the Past					
Better:					
Race	.17	.12	.06	.03	.01
Race + liv.std.	.19	.12	.06	.03	.05
Same:					
Race	.33	.31	.13	.12	.07
Race + liv.std.	.34	.32	.13	.17	.11
Worse:					
Race:	.21	.31	.13	.04	.09
Race + liv.std.	.22	.31	.13	.06	.15
Expectations for the Future					
Better:					
Race	.27	.12	.05	.02	.01
Race + liv.std.	.27	.12	.06	.02	.04
Same:					
Race:	.38	.34	.19	.16	.06
Race + liv.std.	.38	.35	.19	.21	.10
Worse:					
Race	.20	.48	.19	.14	.25
Race + liv.std.	.20	.49	.20	.17	.30

climate of decline–seem to translate their objective conditions more rapidly into grievances.

The moderating effect of beliefs about government. As we mentioned in our theoretical introduction, grievances may sharpen or soften for yet another reason. Procedures that have led to the existing distribution of outcomes may be considered fair or unfair; depending on such evaluations, distributive justice may be evaluated more or less favorably. We assumed that people's evaluation of authorities influences their assessment of their situation. Perceived influence on authorities and trustworthiness are two important aspects of such an evaluation: Authorities who are perceived to be open to influence attempts and to be trustworthy supposedly make people more optimistic about the future (Tyler and Lind 1992).

We begin our discussion of the results with the latter assumption. Indeed, trust in government and perceived influence over government are related to future expectations (Table 5).

The more positively people evaluate the South African government, the more optimistic they are about the future. The correlations for expectations about the future are considerably higher than those for relative deprivation, based on comparisons with others. They are also higher than those for relative deprivation, based on comparisons with the past, but here the differences are smaller. Comparisons of trust and influence reveal that trust has the stronger relationship to expectations for the future.

This confirms Tyler and Lind's (1992) observation that trustworthiness is the most important factor shaping evaluations of authorities.

Apparently, trust in and influence over government are more relevant for comparisons over time than for comparisons with others; of the two comparisons over time (comparisons with the past and expectations for the future), future expectations are influenced more strongly. Trust in authorities is like a blank check, as Barnes and Kaase (1979) remarked. It is the feeling that one's interests receive attention even if the authorities are subject to little supervision or scrutiny. Such trustworthiness makes people optimistic about the future, and such optimism, as we noted in our previous section, softens current distributive grievances.

Do trust and influence also moderate the relationship between living standard and distributive grievances, as our fourth hypothesis suggests? Table 6 reports results from analyses that address this question. For these analyses we executed a median split to create two groups that were high and low on both trust and influence. For these groups, again, we conducted regression analyses with race and living standard as independent variables and grievances as the dependent variable.

The R^2 values largely confirm our expectations: correlations are higher if trust and influence are low than if trust and influence are high. The first year is the exception: in 1994 we found the reverse pattern. That was a volatile year, however. Our interviews

Table 5. Comparison with Others and with the Past, and Expectations for the Future, with Trust in Government and Influence on Government Pearson's *r*s

	1994	1995	1996	1997	1998
Trust in Government					
Others	−.20	−.11	−.16	−.09	−.11
Past	−.16	−.19	−.30	−.22	−.22
Future	−.09	−.35	−.39	−.34	−.39
Influence on Government					
Others	−.03	−.06	−.14	−.11	−.05
Past	−.07	−.15	−.19	−.17	−.15
Future	−.13	−.25	−.29	−.29	−.17

Table 6. Race, Living Standard, and Grievances Moderated by Trust in Government and Influence on Government: R^2 Values

	1994	1995	1996	1997	1998
Trust in Government					
Low					
Race	.17	.29	.09	.09	.08
Race + liv.std.	.17	.29	.11	.13	.14
High					
Race	.27	.17	.09	.02	.03
Race + liv.std.	.28	.17	.10	.04	.07
Influence on Government					
Low					
Race	.17	.24	.10	.07	.06
Race + liv.std.	.17	.26	.11	.11	.15
High					
Race	.27	.15	.06	.02	.02
Race + liv.std.	.27	.15	.08	.02	.04

were conducted in the months before the elections, the old government was still in place, and nobody knew what the elections would bring.

In those days of uncertainty, half of our respondents feared that their situation would decline, whereas the other half was divided approximately equally between people who expected everything to stay the same and people who expected their situation to improve. Under these circumstances, expectations about the future acquired a different meaning, related much more closely to the country's political future and much less closely to individual outcomes.

For the remaining four years, R^2 values for those who trust government or feel that they can influence government are considerably lower than for those who do not trust government and who do not feel able to influence government. In other words, objective conditions are more likely to lead to grievances if people do not trust government or feel that they have no influence on government. Also in these analyses, the effect of living standard gradually replaces that of race.

Conclusions

Our study has produced interesting results. First, we found that racial categorization has lost its

relevance for the formation of grievances, despite its unabated significance for differences in living standards. In 1998, 42 percent of the variance in living standard still could be explained by racial categories. In the explanation of a sense of grievance, however, race was replaced by class as indicated by income and living standard. The direct effect of race disappeared and was replaced by an indirect effect via class.

Second, net of objective conditions interpersonal and intrapersonal comparisons were shown to be important for the formation of grievances, explaining 30 percent of the variance in grievances. Of the two types, interpersonal comparison appeared to be by far the more important. In regard to moderating effects, however, intrapersonal comparisons (especially expectations for the future) were more important. Being worse off than a comparison other generates a strong sense of grievance, but occupying a low position also generates a sense of grievance, especially if such a position is due to a decline from past circumstances and/or is unlikely to improve in the near future.

Third, trust in government and perceived influence on government affect comparisons over time (intrapersonal comparison), but not comparisons with others (interpersonal comparison). The more people trust government, and the more they feel able to influence government, the more they feel that they have improved their situation over the past five years and the greater their optimism about the future.

Fourth, trust in government and perceived influence on government moderate the translation of low outcomes into grievances. Among people who do not trust government or who feel unable to influence the government, chances are high that low outcomes will generate a sense of grievance. On the other hand, among those who are high in trust and perceived influence, low outcomes are less likely to result in grievances.

Obviously the racial cleavage did not disappear in South Africa; nobody would have expected it to do so in only a few years (Marais 1998). Our findings, however, suggest that the racial cleavage no longer defines people's sense of grievance. Grievances now are related more closely to actual income and living standard—in other words, to social class. Of course, class coincides with race, but over the years class also has become more important as a distinction within race. This distinction has gained significance for the explanation of grievances.

The transition from race to class as a determinant of distributive grievances is an intriguing phenomenon. Indeed, one could argue that the South African society has begun to normalize. A sense of grievance about the distribution of wealth in society is now determined less by apartheid's racial categorization and more by the actual distribution of wealth in the country. The importance of objective conditions for grievance formation declined over the years, however. Certainly, class has become more important, but not important enough to compensate for the declining impact of race.

Grievances not only are formed by objective conditions such as race or class, but also depend on the comparisons made in assessing the objective situation. In fact, the effect of comparisons by far outweighs the effect of objective conditions. The subjective component of grievance formation, as determined by comparison, played an important role in the formation of grievances throughout the whole period. Regardless of the objective conditions, comparisons suggesting that one is worse off than others or worse off than in the past, or the expectation that one's situation will be worse in the future, are powerful generators of grievances. The outcomes of such comparisons explain a considerable proportion of the variance in grievances; in addition, comparisons (especially comparisons over time) moderate the translation of objective conditions (whether caused by race or by class) into grievances.

The choice of basis for comparison makes a difference. Comparison with others (interpersonal comparison) has a strong direct impact on people's sense of grievance, much stronger than comparison over time (intrapersonal comparison with past or future). Comparisons over time, however, are much stronger moderators than comparison with others. Apparently it is easier to cope with a low position that results from an improvement over the past than with a low position that has stayed the same or even is worse than in the past. Similarly, a low position that is expected to improve is easier to cope with than a low position that is expected to stay the same or even to decline further. Thus, depending on the choice of basis for comparison, it is not only the evaluation of the situation that varies; the dynamics of grievance formation vary as well.

With inequalities of the size that one finds in South Africa, comparisons can easily generate high levels of relative deprivation either directly or indirectly. Depending on the kind of comparisons made, this reaction can be politically dangerous if people feel that the group they identify with is disadvantaged. On the other hand, large proportions of the population—especially the African population—are optimistic about the future, trust their government, and believe they can influence its decisions. That attitude makes it easier to cope with low outcomes. If people feel that the authorities have their hearts in the right place, they are not only more prepared to accept the existing situation but also inclined to believe that it will improve. After all, they believe, government is doing its utmost to change the situation. That belief, in its turn, makes it easier to live with the current situation. For that matter, it is helpful that the Africans—who objectively are the most deprived—are the most optimistic and the most positive about the government.

Findings like these raise a question: how long will the disadvantaged maintain their trust in government and their optimism? That depends on the extent to which the government actually can improve their situation. Our findings suggest two possible scenarios.

In the first, the government works to reduce inequality. In doing so, it not only reduces dissatisfaction—because fewer people feel deprived—but also makes itself more trustworthy and creates more optimism about the future. These feelings in turn make more bearable the inequality that continues to exist.

In the second scenario, the government fails to reduce inequality, forfeits trust, and makes people pessimistic about the future. This combination of inequality, lack of trust, and pessimism intensifies dissatisfaction. Let us recall the classic scenario that Davies projected with his J-curve of the improvements which make people expect that their situation will continue to improve. This scenario may materialize if the government fails to deliver what it promised.

These findings suggest the continued relevance of relative deprivation theory and social justice theory—or, more generally, grievance theory—for the social movement domain. Provided that more sophisticated conceptualizations, measurements, and analyses are employed, relative deprivation still is relevant for understanding political protest. To be sure, grievances are not sufficient conditions for the occurrence of protest. On the other hand, people who are protesting *are* aggrieved. Understanding how such grievances are formed remains a constructive endeavor.

NOTES

The authors want to thank the reviewers of this journal for their comments. This research was supported by the Human Science Research Council, Pretoria, and by the South Africa-Netherlands Programme on Alternatives in Development(SAN-PAD).
1. The stratification for the African population was conducted differently for the first survey because at that time South Africa was still divided into former homelands and the rest of the country. In the first survey, we stratified the African sample into these areas and into metropolitan and nonmetropolitan areas. The regional distribution of the 1994 sample is very similar to those of the later samples, however.
2. Metropolitan areas are those around cities such as Johannesburg, Cape Town, Durban, and Pretoria. Nonmetropolitan areas surround the smaller cities.
3. In the 1994 sample design, we stated no fixed minimum per region. Numbers were fixed, however, for the population groups: 1,252 Africans, 600 whites, 300 coloreds, and 200 Asians.
4. Indeed, regression analyses revealed that the variance in grievances explained by race declined from 23 percent in 1994 to 3 percent in 1998. A two-way analysis of variance with time and race as factors revealed no main effect of time, a main effect of race ($F = 13.56$, df = 3, $p < .001$), and a significant interaction of race with time ($F = 23.91$, df = 12, $p < .001$).
5. We checked these and all other regression analyses for normality, homoscedasticity, and excessively influential data points, applying SPSS residual statistics and plots. We found no problems in that regard.
6. We broke down the total sample into three groups of approximately the same size.

22.
"It Was Like A Fever..." Narrative and Identity in Social Protest

FRANCESCA POLLETTA

On February 1 1960, four Black students sat-in at a segregated lunch counter in Greensboro, North Carolina and touched off a wave of similar demonstrations around the South. Two months later, Harvard graduate student Michael Walzer returned from a tour of Southern colleges to report that "every student" he met had given the same account of the first day of protest on his or her campus. "'It was like a fever. Everyone wanted to go'" (Walzer 1960a:111).

Metaphors of wildfire, fever, and contagion were common in early accounts of the sit-ins. The *New Republic* reported in April 1960: "No outside organization masterminded the recent uprisings.…In almost every instance, they were planned and carried out by students, without outside advice or even contact between schools except by way of press and radio news" (Fuller 1960:13). The *Nation* in May: "Up to this point, the student demonstrations have been spontaneous." *Harper's* (Wakefield 1960:404) in June quoted an NAACP branch president: "How can I correlate anything when I don't know where and when it's going to happen" (Lomax 1960:47). Paul Wehr (1960), one of the first academic observers of the sit-ins, was surprised by the "absence of any effective liaison" among sit-in groups on eight campuses (quoted in Oberschall 1989:35). Martin Oppenheimer, in another early study, dismissed prior organizational links as explanation for the spread of the sit-ins, arguing that "the sit-ins caught on in the manner of a grass fire, moving from the center outward" (1989:40; see also Carson 1981; Matthews and Prothro 1966; Piven and Cloward 1977; Zinn 1964).

Polletta, Francesca. 1998. "'It was Like a Fever…' Narrative and Identity in Social Protest." *Social Problems* 45: 137–159. Reprinted by permission of the University of California Press.

A grass fire indeed: by the end of February, demonstrations had spread to thirty cities in seven states; by the end of March to fifty-four cities in nine states. By mid-April, fifty thousand people had taken part in the sit-ins (Carson 1981; Chafe 1980).

Twenty years later Aldon Morris persuasively challenged the alleged spontaneity of the student sit-ins. As part of a broader assault on sociologists' neglect of the activist traditions and networks that precede social protest, Morris revealed that the Greensboro sit-inners were members of an NAACP Youth Council and had close ties with people who had conducted sit-ins in Durham in the late 1950s. Their discussions of nonviolence and direct action were pursued in an organizational context of skilled strategists. After the sit-in began, a network of ministers, NAACP officials, and other activists swung into action, contacting colleagues to spread the news, training students in sit-in techniques, and persuading adults to support the protests. The church was the linchpin of student activism, Morris argued, supplying leaders and guidance, training and inspiration. "To understand the sit-in movement, one must abandon the assumption that it was a college phenomenon.… The sit-ins spread across the South in a short period because [adult] activists, working through local movement centers, planned, coordinated, and sustained them," he concluded (1984:200, 202).

Subsequent chroniclers have taken Morris's lead in detailing the extensive adult networks that preceded the sit-ins (Blumberg 1984; Chafe 1980; Powledge 1991). Why then did Walzer's interviewees say they had been "like a fever"? Why, in interviews with reporters, statements to Congress, letters to friends, articles and editorials in campus newspapers and in the *Student Voice*—organ of the brand new Student Nonviolent Coordinating Committee—did sit-inners describe the protests as sudden, impulsive, and unplanned? Certainly, there were good strategic reasons for conveying that image to the American public. Spontaneity deflected charges of communist influence, and were likelier to garner public support for a "home-grown" protest. But students also referred to the spontaneity of the sit-ins in less public statements, in articles and letters in campus newspapers, and in communications with each other. One would imagine that the chief aim in these communications would be to make sense of unfolding events and to inspire and mobilize fellow students. Why then emphasize the *absence* of planning, represent the sit-ins as driven not by concerted student action, but by a zeitgeist over which students had no control? Would not the latter undermine the sense of collective efficacy essential to successful mobilization (Benford 1993a; Gamson 1992, 1995; Klandermans 1988, 1997; McAdam 1982; Piven and Cloward 1979)?

My examination of students' descriptions of the sit-ins as they were occurring suggests that "spontaneous" did not mean "unplanned." In the stories that students told and retold about the sit-ins, spontaneity denoted independence from adult leadership, urgency, local initiative, and action by moral imperative rather than bureaucratic planning. Narratives of the sit-ins, told by many tellers, in more and less public settings, and in which spontaneity was a central theme, described student activists and potential activists to themselves and, in the process, helped to create the collective identity on behalf of which students took high-risk action. Sit-in stories—and their narrative form was crucial—also motivated action by their *failure* to specify the mechanics of mobilization. Their *ambiguity* about agents and agency, not their clarity, successfully engaged listeners.

The analysis that I present here draws on cognitive psychology and literary theory as well as the sociology of social movements to respond more broadly, to two lacunae in theories of collective action "framing." Framing has been defined as how "social movement organizations and their agents...assign meaning to and interpret relevant events and conditions in ways that are intended to mobilize potential adherents and constituents, to garner bystander support, and to demobilize antagonists" (Snow and Benford 1988:198; see also Benford 1993a, b; Gamson 1988; McAdam, McCarthy and Zald 1996; Tarrow 1994). As such, it has been limited to the persuasive efforts of already established movement organizations. This neglects the discursive processes that precede the formation of movement organizations or that take place outside their auspices. We still know little about how the interpretive processes occurring in oppositional subcultures and indigenous institutions, and occurring *during* Initial episodes of collective action (strikes, marches, occupations, etc.) yield movement identities on behalf of which people are willing to sacrifice their personal welfare (Klandermans 1988, 1992; Oberschall 1989; but see Hirsch 1990; Steinberg 1996; Taylor and Whittier 1992).

I argue that narrative is prominent in such interpretive processes because its temporally configurative capacity equips it to integrate past, present, and future events and to align individual and collective identities during periods of change. Narrative's reliance on emplotment rather than explanation further engages potential activists precisely by its *ambiguity* about the causes of collective action. These features distinguish narratives from frames, which are said to contribute to identity-formation through taxonomic atemporal and discursive processes of analogy and difference. Frames' mobilizing capacity, moreover, is allegedly dependent on clear, not ambiguous, specification of the agents, intentions, and efficacy of protest. My purpose in this article is thus to show how narrative identification supplies powerful incentives to participate.

To make my case, I draw on accounts of the sit-ins that appeared in: articles, editorials, and letters to the editor culled from eight campus newspapers;[1] articles, letters, and personal narratives published in the *Student Voice*, a monthly that began publication in May 1960, and newsletters, speeches, personal correspondence, and memos circulated among sit-in leaders and participants beginning in February 1960 that were deposited in SNCC's extensive files (which contain more than 93,000 pages of documents). Materials included communications to small audiences as well as large ones, to friends and family as well as strangers, and to fellow activists as well as funders, the media, and government. Together, these data help to counter the instrumentalist and organizational biases of recent social movement theorizing by elucidating the social-psychological and discursive processes involved in recruitment that takes place outside of formal organizations.

In the rest of the paper, I will more fully distinguish the concept of "narrative" from that of "frame," make several propositions about the mobilizing role of narratives in conditions of "loose structure" (Oberschall 1989), and then turn to an analysis of students' accounts of the sit-ins.

Frames, Plots, and Protest

Mancur Olson's (1965) identification of the "free rider" problem set the challenge for sociologists of collective action. Under what circumstances will people overcome their rational reluctance to participate? When and why do their cost-benefit calculations tip in favor of participation in spite of the fact that they will lose little from non-participation?

Concepts of "frames" and "framing" have proved useful in answering these questions. Frames are "interpretive schemata that enable individuals to locate, perceive, identify, and label occurrences within their life space and the world at large" (Snow and Benford 1992:137; Snow et al. 1986:464; see also Tarrow 1994; Zald 1996). Frames combine a *diagnosis* of the social condition in need of remedy, a *prognosis* for how to do that, and a *rationale* for action (Benford and Hunt 1992; Snow and Benford 1988). Gamson (1992, 1995) identifies injustice, identity, and agency components of frames. The Injustice component refers to the cognition that a situation is wrong and that it is political rather than merely personal, or "situational" rather than "individual" (Klandermans 1988:179). The agency component denotes a sense of collective efficacy, a belief that the situation is not immutable and that "we" can change it. The identity component refers to this "we," and to the "they"—human antagonists rather than impersonal forces like hunger or poverty—against which collective action must be mobilized.[2] Other

theorists emphasize discursive processes of "association and disassociation" (Hunt and Benford 1994), "typification" (Benford and Hunt 1992), "comparison" (Klandermans 1988, 1997:18), and "categorizing and labeling" (Klandermans 1992:83) in developing the collective identities on behalf of which people participate.

What makes for successful frames? At a minimum, say McAdam, McCarthy and Zald, "people need to feel both aggrieved about some aspect of their lives and optimistic that, acting collectively, they can redress the problem" (1996:5). Snow and Benford argue that the diagnosis, prognosis, and rationale for action provided by frames must be "richly developed and interconnected" (1988:199), empirically credible, and congruent with potential adherents" beliefs and broad cultural understandings (see also Gamson 1988). Successful frames connect information and experiences in new ways, or in ways never before "clearly articulated" (Snow and Benford 1992:138). They foster "a sense of severity, urgency, efficacy and propriety" (Benford 1993a:209), supply a "clearly interpretable" rationale for participation, and discourage "fatalism" (Snow and Benford 1988:203). They convince people "that they have the power to change their condition. Such a conviction presupposes the presence of agents that impress people as politically efficacious, by virtue of either their success in the past or their potential efficacy" (Klandermans 1997:18). In each of these accounts, then, frames motivate participation by persuasively distinguishing insurgents ("us") from antagonists and irrelevant others ("them"), and by clearly representing the possibility, necessity, and efficacy of collective action by deliberate actors.

Recently, framing theorists have included narratives—stories, tales, anecdotes, allegories—in their discussions of framing (Benford 1993a; Fine 1995; Hunt and Benford 1994).[3] Narrative is treated as a discursive form through which frames are "expressed and made concrete" (Fine 1995:134), and "exemplified" (Benford 1993a:196). However, subsuming "narrative," under the broader category of "frame" obscures distinctive features of narrative. Indeed, an analysis of movement narratives, understood as chronicles invested with moral meaning through emplotment (White 1980), can fill some significant gaps in recent framing analyses.

First, narratives' configuration of events over time makes them important to the construction and maintenance of individual and collective identities. This temporal dimension of identity has been underemphasized by theories of framing which, again, represent identities as developed through discursive processes of analogy and difference.[4] Narrative understandings of identity, by contrast, emphasize the structuring of events into evolving wholes. Life events are "rendered intelligible" say Gergen and Gergen, "by locating them in a sequence or 'unfolding process'" (1997:162; see also Ricoeur 1984). Narratives not only make sense of the past and present but, since the story's chronological end is also its end in the sense of moral, purpose or telos, they project a future. This is the basis for self-identity and action. We act not after the kind of categorization that frames imply (in Polkinghorne's (1988] example, "I am 40 years old; I should buy life insurance"), but by locating events within an unfolding life-story ("I felt out of breath last week, I really should start thinking about life insurance").

These features point to narratives' role in the development of collective as well as individual identities. In telling the story of our becoming—as an individual, a nation, a people—we establish who we are. Narratives may be employed strategically to strengthen a collective identity but they also may precede and make possible the development of a coherent community, or nation, or collective actor (Carr 1997; Ginsburg 1989; Hart 1992; Sewell 1992; Somers 1992, 1994). They may be especially important during periods of ongoing or potential social transformation. Narratives retain continuity in change, preserve the self or collectivity through change (as in cases of serious illness [Williams 1997], recovery [Denzin 1987], and politicization [Ginsburg 1989]). They connect through narrative reversal the group under conditions of oppression and the group under conditions of liberation. Stories thus explain what is going on in a way that makes an evolving identity part of the explanation.

A second difference between narratives and frames centers more specifically on how events are linked to outcomes in each one. What makes a frame successful, say Gamson (1988, 1992), Snow and Benford (1988, 1992), and Klandermans (1997), is clear specification not only of the injustice against which protest must be mounted but the agents and likely efficacy of that protest. People must be shown that deliberate action will have its intended effect. But individual intention is just one among the principles that may link events in a story. The question in a story is often just what the linkage is: are things happening because of chance or divine intervention, conscious intention or subliminal drive? This is what grips us, what keeps us listening or reading. A story whose end was immediately apparent would be no story at all—would be the moral without the story. Narratives which "underspecify" (Leitch 1986) risk unintelligibility; those which overspecify risk the loss of narrativity, of readers' or hearers' engagement with the text. Wolfgang Iser writes that, "It is only through inevitable omissions that a story will gain its dynamism" (1972:285; see also Bruner 1986). Narrative necessitates our interpretive participation, requires that we struggle to fill the gaps and resolve the ambiguities. We struggle because the story's end is consequential—not only as the outcome but as the moral of the events which precede it.

Literary critic J. Hillis Miller argues that even the story's conclusion may not resolve the ambiguity—another reason for narrative's hold. Along with plot and personification, all narratives are characterized by repetition of a "complex word," Miller argues, a word with multiple, indeed incongruous, meanings, as "right" may mean to have the right, to be right, or to be straight (as in "right angle"). Each of those meanings may or may not be simultaneously operative in the same story; this indeterminacy is both what compels our attention and calls for more stories. "[W]e always need more stories because in some way they do not satisfy," Miller suggests (1990:72). I will expand on the argument later. For now, my point is that the difficulty of logically explaining some events (because they are unfamiliar or defy conventional rationales for action)[5] may compel a narrative explanation, which in turn preserves the ambiguity that calls for more stories.

To illustrate, let me turn to the "Hundredth Monkey Story" which, according to Benford (1993a), demonstrates the importance of severity, urgency, propriety, and efficacy components of frames. The book, which became a powerfully persuasive tool for the American antinuclear movement, opens with an allegory:

> The Japanese monkey. Macaca fuscata, has been observed in the wild for a period of over 30 years. In 1952, on the island of Koshima, scientists were providing monkeys with sweet potatoes, but they found the dirt unpleasant. An 18-month-old female named Imo found she could solve the problem by washing the potatoes in a nearby stream. She taught this trick to her mother. Her playmates also learned this new way and they taught their mothers too.
>
> This cultural innovation was gradually picked up by various monkeys before the eyes of the scientists. Between 1952 and 1958, all the young monkeys learned to wash the sandy sweet potatoes to make them more palatable.... [sic]
>
> Then something startling took place. In the autumn of 1958, a certain number of Koshima monkeys were washing sweet potatoes—the exact number is not known. Let us suppose that when the sun rose one morning there were 99 monkeys on Koshima Island who had learned to wash their sweet potatoes. Let's further suppose that later that morning, the hundredth monkey learned to wash potatoes. THEN IT HAPPENED!
>
> By that evening almost everyone in the tribe was washing sweet potatoes before eating them. The added energy of this hundredth monkey somehow created an ideological breakthrough!
>
> But notice. The most surprising thing observed by the scientists was that the habit of washing sweet potatoes then spontaneously jumped over the sea—Colonies of monkeys on other islands and the mainland troop of monkeys at Takasakiyama began washing their sweet potatoes!
>
> Thus, when a certain critical number achieves an awareness, this new awareness may be communicated from mind to mind.... You may furnish the added consciousness energy [sic] to create the shared awareness of the urgent necessity to rapidly achieve a nuclear free world. (quoted in Benford 1993a:196)

Benford argues that the story promotes efficacy by demonstrating "the power of the new awareness and your role in the unfolding drama" (196). Yet the story's demonstration of the power of conscious individual action is not at all clear. "THEN IT HAPPENED," the story goes, but it is not clear just *what* happened, nor why all the Koshima monkeys and monkeys in distant tribes suddenly, "spontaneously," began washing potatoes. How did monkeys that were not in contact with the original tribe learn the practice? The story raises more questions than it answers, indeed, seems to attribute the spread of the practice to some force beyond rational control. Contrary, then, to Benford's contention that a successful frame specifies agents and agency, it seems that this story was successful precisely by its failure to supply a logical explanation for action. It promises to explain the link between action and outcome but then simply places us, the reader/listener, at the victorious end. Penetrating the mystery of collective action requires more stories, and indeed, requires not only stories, but that we ourselves act.

Of course, self- and collective narratives are *social* narratives, created not solipsistically but from the wider narratives at hand (Somers (1994) similarly distinguishes between "ontological" and "public" narratives). We can as little imagine a nineteenth century thief narrating his life in terms of a lack of self-esteem as we can imagine him lodging that defense in a court of law. This points to a third critical difference between narratives and frames. To be effective, say framing theorists, frames must resonate with extant "ideology, values, belief systems" (Gamson 1988:220). But since "every coin has two sides; every argument has its opposite arguments" (Klandermans 1992:84), there is still plenty of room for ideological maneuver. Framing theorists thus emphasize the multiplicity of coexisting, often contradictory value positions that can be mobilized by activists. By contrast, narrative's dependence on a limited stock of culturally resonant plots—on a canon—emphasizes the *constraints* levied by dominant cultural understandings. Narrative theorists differ on just how many plots there are, and just how universal they are. But there is agreement that stories not conforming to a cultural stock of plots typically are either not stories or are unintelligible. Activists' very understandings of "strategy," "interest," "identity," and "politics" may be structured by the oppositions and hierarchies that come from familiar stories. Thus, if part of the power of mobilizing narratives lies in their polyvalence of meaning, oppositional meanings must always contend with more conventional ones. In the case of the student sit-in narrative. I will show how the anchoring theme of "spontaneity" both galvanized action and weighted subsequent strategic options unequally. Spontaneous protest—sitting-in—was represented as moral, urgent, and radical (contrary to the amoral, gradualist, and moderate protest of adult activists). But it was also characterized, by implication, as *non*-political and *non*-strategic.

Mobilizing Identities in Fledgling Movements

Narratives' capacity to make sense of unfamiliar events, to engage as they explain, and to sustain identity during periods of rapid change suggests that they would be especially prominent in movement discourse that develops before movement organizations have been consolidated or that occurs outside their auspices. This phase of protest remains generally understudied. Indeed, says Oberschall, analysts have tended to project the aims of the formally organized phase of the movement backward to explain its beginnings. So, for example, "they write about a civil rights movement when there was yet only sporadic and disjointed challenge to segregation.... Black leaders and participants in the 1960 sit-ins were not yet conscious of forming a civil rights movement nor creating one according to some well thought-out master plan" (1989:46).

Oberschall's "diffusion model" responds to this bias by describing mechanisms of recruitment in "loose structures," collectivities where there is no prior overarching organization, ideology, or dependable flow of resources. In these circumstances, actors tend to overestimate the likelihood of repression and underestimate the possibility for success. But "[s]uppose that in a similar social milieu protest is initiated by people much like oneself, with whom one shares a common identity, and that the outcome and conflict circumstances become widely known" (41). When widely diffused, for example via media coverage, such perceptions cause people to

revise their calculations of success and to participate. Applied to the sit-in movement, this scenario has students learning about the Greensboro protest through friendship networks, basketball leagues, and media coverage, then planning their own campus meetings, and rallying their fellow students to demonstrate. Against political process analyses, Oberschall argues that church networks and movement organizations such as the NAACP, SCLC, and CORE responded to the sit-ins and helped to sustain them, but did not initiate them.

Oberschall's model is persuasive but it leaves underspecified several key mechanisms. How is it that protesters elsewhere come to be seen as "much like oneself," and worthy in their efforts? How does a common identity come to be shared and to compel participation? Are perceptions that retaliation and repression are less severe than originally thought enough to explain activism that is still physically demanding and dangerous? Friedman and McAdam (1992) provide answers to these questions by emphasizing the normative dimension of participation. Highly regarded roles within communities may come to be linked with activism in a way that makes participation a requirement of the role. In the early part of the civil rights movement, activism was linked with—normatively required of—churchgoers; in 1960, *student* became linked to activist, became a "prized social identity" that supplied the selective incentives to participation.

Contemporaneous and retrospective accounts suggest that in 1960 activism did become normative for Black college students. As Tallahassee sit-in leader Charles Smith put it: "a spirit of competition has found its way into the civil rights arena, and no college or university wants to be left behind or be found wanting in this kind of courage or conviction" (Killian 1984:781). In his survey of sit-inners on eight college campuses shortly after the wave of sit-ins began, Wehr (1960) found that "one common response to the question 'Why did the movement start at your school?' was 'we wanted to jump into the movement before [another school]" (quoted in Oberschall 1989:35). Laue noted similarly that:

[T]he response of Negro students to Greensboro was almost always phrased in terms of "keeping up" with the other students. "When students came to me to talk about their protest plans," recalls Tuskegee Dean Charles Gomillion. "I asked them, 'Where are you going to sit-in here?' [in predominantly rural Macon County, Alabama.] 'We *have* to go,' they said. 'What will other colleges think of us if we don't?'" (1989:82)

Friedman and McAdam's claim that student and activist identities had become normatively fused is persuasive but their explanation for it is unclear. "In the first stage, the emerging movement grows out of but remains dependent upon preexisting institutions and organizations...*established groups* redefine group membership to include commitment to the movement as one of its obligations" (1992:162–163, emphasis mine). If they mean that Southern college officials deliberately promoted an activist identity, such an assertion is belied by the evidence.[6] According to Orbell (1972), most student sit-inners experienced their college administrations and faculties as unsupportive of the sit-ins (46% of sit-inners enrolled at private colleges reported support from both administration and faculty; 50% of state college demonstrators reported that faculty was supportive of their efforts, but only 15% reported that administrations were). By the end of the 1960 spring term, over a hundred students had been expelled from Black colleges for their participation (Laue 1989:77).[7] My own examination of campus newspapers showed that many made no mention of sit-ins in which their own students were participating; archivists attributed this lacuna to the conservatism of campus administrations.

If Friedman and McAdam mean instead that the equation of student and activist was effected by students themselves through informal framing processes that were as much about making sense of current developments and trends as they were about persuading people to mobilize, then we need a better understanding of those processes. To account for the emergence of a mobilizing identity on Black college campuses, and the development of such identities more broadly, we need to examine not only the instrumental framing efforts of indigenous and formal movement organizations but also: (a) the larger social and cultural context in which an idiom of student activism made sense

(cf. Emirbayer and Goodwin 1994); and, (b) the diffuse, noninstitutionalized discursive processes by which people's efforts to make sense of initial protests turned into a rationale for participation.

With respect to the first, Black college students in 1960 could not but be affected by the association of student and activist that was occurring on a world historical stage. "There was a feeling that it was the 'dawn of a new era,'" SNCC founder and advisor Ella Baker recalled, "that something new and great was happening and that only [students] could chart the course of history" (see also Flacks 1971).[8] The sit-ins came at a time when students were playing visible and dramatic roles in regime changes around the world: they had toppled military regimes in Turkey and South Korea, and had blocked President Eisenhower's visit to Japan (participants at the 1960 National Student Association conference heard from student movement representatives from all three countries).[9] It was not only students, but *Black* students who were the change makers. "Sure we identified with the Blacks in Africa," Nashville sit-in leader John Lewis said later, "and we were thrilled by what was going on. Here were Black people, talking of freedom and liberation and independence, thousands of miles away. We could hardly miss the lesson for ourselves" (quoted in Viorst 1979:116). African students studying at Black colleges participated in the Nashville sit-ins, Lewis recalls. Representatives of the Republic of Cameroon, Kenya, Nigeria, and other nations visited Black college campuses in 1959 and 1960, and Black campus newspapers devoted considerable coverage to events in Africa during this period. "Today, the dark people on the other side of the earth are protesting and dying for their freedom," a Howard University student noted in calling for student activism in early 1960. "All over the world a new generation of leadership is emerging." wrote a Fisk student. And another, "We realize that students can play an important role in the development and redevelopment of society."[10]

Students at Black colleges were thus exposed to students as change-makers through their direct contacts with international student activists, through national media accounts, and through their own campus press. At the same time, campus newspapers in 1959 and early 1960 referred frequently to the problems of student "apathy," and editorials chastised students for their lack of political and intellectual engagement: "The majority of our students are now apathetic toward student government;" "General student apathy towards affairs pertaining to them—political, social or otherwise—is a 'campus disease' badly in need of therapy;" "Throughout American education there is a growing concern for what has been labeled by some 'student apathy.'" The "beatniks" were discussed critically in several editorials, and their repudiation of middle-class conventionality was attributed to a pervasive normlessness. The cultural media to which students were most directly exposed thus offered and evaluated two modes of being a student, with the revolutionary aspirations of the international students lauded and the deviance of the beats condemned.[11]

The dynamic involved in the "fusion of prized role and activism" that Friedman and McAdam (1992) describe seems to have been less an established organization pitching a role than students perceiving it on a world historical stage. But how did a collective identity of student activist come to be associated with a particular set of expected *behaviors*? Even after news spread of the Greensboro protest, one can imagine "student activism" meaning rallying financial and moral support for the sit-inners, or organizing campus discussions about race relations or about the upcoming Presidential election. How and why did "student activist" come to mean "putting one's body on the line," participating directly in nonviolent desegregation efforts?

The equation of student and sit-inner on a wide scale was in part the result of strategic framing efforts by representatives of the Student Nonviolent Coordinating Committee (SNCC), the campus coordinating group formed when SCLC activist Ella Baker convened 200 sit-in leaders to discuss strategy in April 1960. In the following, I describe SNCC representatives' efforts to legitimate and promote participation. But SNCC was given only a modest role by campus groups who were insistent on maintaining autonomy. And characteristic of a loose structure, SNCC's voice was only one of many. In the weeks and months after the Greensboro sit-ins, spokespeople for the fledgling movement were

legion: sit-in leaders and rank and file, participants and supporters, Northerners and Southerners told stories of the sit-ins in letters to the editor of the *Student Voice* and to SNCC, letters to the editors of Black campus newspapers and letters among members of student groups such as the National Student Association, the YMCA, and YWCA. These stories, along with movement organizations' strategic framing efforts and a consciousness of students' international political role, contributed to the development of mobilizing identities.

Stories Versus Frames

Story-tellers had diverse aims: garnering adult support; urging federal intervention; commenting on the larger significance and likely course of the movement; and mobilizing participants. Did they, as framing theorists would suggest, emphasize the injustice of their situation, cast their identity in terms of their differences from clearly specified antagonists, and assert their own capacity to bring about the changes they sought? My examination of students' discussions suggests not. The injustices they described were often vague: denial of "the humane aspects of the American dream;" of "equality and dignity;" "dignity;" the injustice of "a passively immoral society;" not only "the existing conditions, but...the snail-like pace at which they are being ameliorated;" and the "accumulated indignities suffered by Negro Americans since Reconstruction days." Sit-inners pitted themselves against "apathy"—a condition that seems more unfortunate than unjust.[12]

Contrary to framing theorists' contention that successful frames make protest's agents and agency clear, in these accounts, students' control over their own actions was ambiguous. The students acted, powerfully, transgressively, with immediate, real consequence. And yet they were simply the carriers of a force beyond them. The sit-ins came from nowhere—"boom"—and were the culmination of "centuries of accumulated anger." Narrators were as likely to deny conscious intent as to assert it (when one group of students launched a demonstration, "[t]his was a surprise (and shock) not only to the whole town but to themselves as well"), to declare themselves followers rather than leaders ("Some great leaders are present today," a student wrote in the Morris Brown College *Wolverine.* "Let us follow them wherever they go"), to predict rather than claim their own activism ("As soon as the movement broke. I knew I would get into it"). "No one started it..." a sit-inner insisted—his claim denying collective identity altogether.[13] Students attributed the sit-ins not to conscious, collective intent, but to forces over which they had no control. Rather than planning, they emphasized spontaneity.

Sit-In Narratives

The narrative form of students' representations of the sit-ins is striking. They told stories, and similar stories, over and over again. A piece published in the Shaw College campus newspaper in May 1960 opened:

> It was night time Tuesday, Feb. 9. Radio and television commentators had announced that 'it' was not expected to happen in Raleigh. Wednesday morning. Feb. 10. 10:30—BOOMI—'it' hit with an unawareness that rocked the capital city from its usual sedateness to a state of glaring frenzy.[14]

The same month, from a letter sent by the just-formed Student Nonviolent Coordinating Committee to Congressmen:

> The sit-ins began February 1st in Greensboro N.C. when four freshmen at Negro North Carolina A and T sat down at a variety store lunch counter after purchasing several items in other departments of the store. They were refused service. Their action was a spontaneous rebellion against the accumulated indignities suffered by Negro Americans since Reconstruction days. "Why must we be continually under tension and indignity when we want to eat, or find a lodging place, or use a rest room?" they asked. Their action has led others to ask the same question—and to do something about it. Since February, the sit-Ins have spread to almost 100 cities in every southern state.[15]

One can imagine other ways of representing the sit-ins. Writers or speakers might have first described the current state and scale of the sit-ins in snapshot rather than chronological form (for example, "there are students currently sitting-in in fifty cities"). They might have begun by questioning or

advocating the future course of the demonstrations ("we must build on the sit-in movement to fight for more radical changes," "after the sit-ins, what next?"), or by appealing directly to fellow students' commitment ("your fellow students are putting their lives on the line. Where are you?"). Instead, they recounted events in chronological order from "the beginning," with the moral of the story conveyed by the events themselves. Newspaper accounts are more likely to recount events in narrative form than are speeches or personal letters, and I cite more of the former than the latter. But newspaper stories typically do not display the degree of suspense, moral as well as temporal directionality, and ambiguity around causality that the sit-in narratives did. Interestingly, the very first campus newspaper accounts of the Greensboro sit-in, which appeared in the Agricultural and Technical College *Register,* used much more conventionally journalistic and editorial formats. The difference between these and subsequent accounts suggest that the narrative representation of the sit-ins took some time to develop.[16]

Students' narratives of the sit-ins exhibited each of the elements that Miller (1990) sees as characteristic of the form: plot ("an initial situation, a sequence leading to a change or reversal of that situation, and a revelation made possible by the reversal of the situation" [75]); personification ("a protagonist, an antagonist, and a witness who learns" [75]); and repetition of a complex word. With respect to plot, the sit-ins reversed a situation of student apathy and a movement dominated by adult gradualism; they created a new, student-led, action-oriented movement. The revelations generated by the reversal were multiple. To the country, they showed the level of Black discontent, to mainstream civil rights organizations, they showed the inadequacy of a moderate agenda, to students themselves, they showed the potency of students' collective agency. "Saint Paul College students have been jokingly awakened to the fact that we must do our part as thinking Negro Americans, and take a definite stand in the fight for equal rights," a student writer ended his account. "Because of [the sit-ins] Baltimore will never be the same," another concluded. "When, in the future we look back on the 60's may it be remembered as the years in which the American Youth forced the nation to dedicate itself to turning the American Dream into a Reality."[17]

The successful plot makes the familiar unfamiliar or, as Roman Jakobson puts it, "the ordinary strange" (quoted in Bruner 1991:13). We read because we sense that the story we know will transpire differently on this occasion. The sit-in narrative made the quotidian act of sitting down at a lunch counter and ordering a cup of coffee—what should have been a non-political act—a dangerous and unpredictable epic. In conversations with North Carolinian students, Michael Walzer observed that they "told one story after another about…minor but to them terribly important incidents in the buses, in stores, on the job. The stories usually ended with some version of 'I ran out of that store. I almost cried…'" (Walzer 1960a). The sit-in narrative thus transformed a too-common story of humiliation into one of triumph. In several accounts, the adventure was funny as well as exciting. Editors of a college newspaper wrote, "Here were two harmless young people sauntering through a store…stalking them in true dragnetness were no less than half a dozen police officers, while customers and managers hovered in corners as if the invasion from Mars had come!" A Knoxville College writer composed an "Ode To A Lunch Counter:" "Little lunch counter with your many stools/And your nervous pacing manager fools/How do you feel amid this confusion and strife?/Do you object to a change inevitable in life?"[18]

Students who did not participate in the demonstrations constructed narratives in which the sit-ins were a subplot of their own larger story. For example, a White high-school student wrote to sit-inners of his experience in a race relations-themed summer camp:

> And now it is September. For many of us we will return to homes and schools which will irritate us even more after knowing and living what we have learned and what we have lived. But we do seem to agree that we cannot behave quite the way we did before we came to this camp. We have talked so much about what the sit-in movement means to us. It would be almost impossible to know how much it means to you. To us it is an affirmation

of so many things. Of the courage of our young people. Of the miracle of spontaneity. Of the faith in people who will do something about what they believe.[19]

Conversations about the sit-ins, about "the miracle of spontaneity" were thus integrated into campers' own story of enlightenment. Swarthmore College editors wrote in the same vein, "Because our minds are knit into a web, the agitation of a few will tremble in all dimensions. Students cannot control, they can only communicate, in a Tokyo snake dance demonstration, a Nashville sit-in, or a chorus behind their printed word."[20]

Personification was a second key feature of the sit-in narrative. The witness role that Miller (1990) refers to was fulfilled by at least four players: the sit-inners themselves who realized their own capacity for transformative action; adult movement leaders; the national public; and potential student activists who would recognize their potential selves in the sit-in story. Dramatis personae expressed a set of appropriate emotions. Sit-inners were "weary" of oppression and the slow pace of change, "tired" of waiting for the "American dream to materialize." They were "apprehensive" about the repercussions of their actions, plagued by "butterflies." Yet, they were "all so very happy that we were (and are) able to do this to help our city, state and nation." and "maintain[ed] high enthusiasm." None of the stories represented the sit-inners as angry, cynical, or calculating. SNCC's Jane Stembridge wrote to a sit-inner that she had "read and re-read" his story "with the deepest pain, joy, laughter, and chills.…You have written a story of Life." she observed. "We can write fact after fact about the movement, and never touch the real element."[21] Narrative made "real" the movement in a way that non-narrative "facts" could not.

Miller's (1990) third narrative feature, repetition of a complex word, occurs in the repeated reference to the spontaneity of the sit-ins. Again, in these communications aimed at mobilizing fellow students as well as understanding what had happened, why would students draw attention to—indeed, celebrate—the unplanned character of the protest? There were good strategic reasons for representing the sit-ins that way. Spontaneity offered some defense against charges that the demonstrations were led by "outside agitators"—read communists. The students' image as eager, impatient, and fearless also may have allayed potential financial supporters' fears of communist inspiration, and gave older leaders a valuable bargaining chip in their threat of disruption.[22] But an exclusively instrumental account is belied by the fact that students represented the sit-ins as spontaneous in communications with each other as well as in more public settings.

It is unlikely that if asked, they would have denied the involvement of specific adults and organizations in helping to plan the sit-ins. Referring to the spontaneity of campus mobilization was not at odds with the existence of planning networks. For example, one group of sit-inners described their action as "the result of spontaneous combustion," then went on to chronicle the planning that had preceded it. They emphasized, however—and this seems to be the point of using the term "spontaneous combustion"—that "there was no organizational tie-in of any kind, either local or national." But they also acknowledged "in order to make the story complete" that members of the sit-organizing group had previously received a "Letter to Christian Students" from the National Student Christian Federation urging them to seek ways to participate.[23] This insistence on spontaneity in spite of evidence and acknowledgment of planning suggests that the term meant something other than that the sit-ins were unplanned. Closer examination of student sit-in narratives suggests three meanings.

First, the sit-ins' spontaneity signaled a decisive break, both with students' prior apathy, and with adults' moderation. Howard University's newspaper. *The Hilltop* ran a story titled "Students Picket in Spontaneous Move" which opened: "A group of 130 Howard students did much recently to destroy the myth of student 'apathy.'" Editors of a new campus journal wrote: "No longer may students be called the 'Silent Generation.' Dissatisfied with a passively immoral society, they are increasingly involved in the world they want to change." "Our impatience with the token efforts of responsible adult leaders, was manifest in the spontaneous protest demonstrations which, after February

1, spread rapidly across the entire South," SNCC's chair Marion Barry told Platform committees at the Democratic and Republican national conventions.[24] The sit-ins were thus represented as signaling the death of an old movement and the birth of a new. Commending the formation of a new Black periodical, SNCC wrote to its editors, "There is no longer a way to rationalize gradualism. It did die on February 1, 1960, in Woolworth's of Greensboro. It will die again and again when every individual rises to his responsibility....We hope for [the continuation of the *Atlanta Inquirer*] and its effectiveness as a death blow to apathy, fear, and gradualism." A piece published in the *Student Voice* referred to the student sit-ins as giving "birth" to a "freedom child." "The Baltimore Sitdowner," read a flyer for that city's movement, "was born on a bitter, cold night in March."[25]

A second prominent theme in the sit-in narrative, one again evoked by the term spontaneity, represented the demonstrations as motivated by a moral imperative rather than a strategic plan, a directive to lay one's body on the line that did not admit of negotiation. "Despite fears, the sit-ins will continue for a long time," one story concluded. "Many more tears will be shed, and perhaps many of my friends will be hurt. They feel that they must go on." A piece in the *Student Voice* opened. "It is really strange—to do things alone. Sometimes we have no alternative," then described student Henry Thomas's frustrated efforts to mobilize students in St. Augustine, Florida. "'I decided to make another try at it,' Thomas was quoted. "Still thinking of the opposition I would have, I decided to carry out my plans regardless if there was no one but me—I did it alone.'" "Hank Thomas road a train South"—now the editor's voice. "He had to do this thing now. People on the train talked, said go slow, said don't try too hard, said no to Henry...but the train did not stop till it got home and Hank was on it." The story combined agency and zeitgeist: Hank acted on his own and yet was just a passenger on a freedom train.[26] Seven of the thirteen students interviewed by sociologist James Laue in 1962 attributed the start and spread of the sit-ins to the "tenor of the times," or called them "inevitable." "Your relationship with the movement is just like a love affair," said one. "You can't explain it. All you know is it's something you have to do" (quoted in Laue 1989:62, 78).

Howard University's Lawrence Henry related the story of that campus's sit-ins: "Who started it? No one started it. What united us was the American principle of freedom and equality and the fact that we want to be free." Jane Stembridge told members of the National Student Association, "The fact that the protest broke out overnight and spread with fantastic speed said simply this: the Negro, despite the thoughts of too many Whites, is NOT content.... And *nobody* could escape this." For students at Penn State, the sit-ins were "symbolic of a new era in race relations and of a new Negro—one who is unwilling to wait until the sweet by-and-by." "We had been ready to do something like this for a long time;" "We have been planning it all our lives;" "We're living in a jet age and we're tired of moving at an ox-cart pace;" "Sure we've been influenced by outsiders, outsiders like Thoreau and Gandhi. But our biggest influence has been inside—all those years of second-class citizenship;" "We have 'taken it' since the day we were born;" "After 95 years of discussions, delays, postponements, procrastination, denials, and second-class citizenship, the Negro of today wants his full citizenship in his day"—formulations like these peppered the sit-in narratives. Editors of Shaw University's newspaper wrote, "[T]he students say—and it is reasonable to believe them—that they are tired of waiting for the humane aspects of the American dream to materialize."[27]

Students of Philander Smith College in Little Rock, Arkansas wrote, "The spirit reached the boiling point at 11:00 a.m., March 10, 1960. It was on this day that the students of Philander Smith College cast their lots into the New Student Movement." On this rendering, protest was an expression of centuries of frustration. SNCC's letter to Congressmen said of the sit-inners: "Their action was a spontaneous rebellion against the accumulated indignities suffered by Negro Americans since Reconstruction days." Third, then, the sit-ins were represented as driven by an imperative over which individuals had no control, as expression of a world historical force. "This situation was inevitable," a speaker told

Howard University students. "Negroes are in the process of discovering a new self-image; and they are no longer willing to accept the injustices done to them." The "current wave of demonstrations is the spontaneous ground swell of the profound determination of young Negroes to be first-class citizens" wrote students at Vanderbilt University. From SNCC: "We know now that we must inexorably win the battle against injustice."[28]

Descriptions of the student protest "burst[ing]," "breaking," "exploding," "sweeping," "surging," "unleashed," "rip[ping] through the city like an epidemic," of students "fired" by the "spark of the sit-ins," of "released waves of damned-up energy," of a "chain reaction" were common and suggested again an unstoppable moral impetus. Attacks on desegregated accommodations were just one manifestation of a protest that could expand in myriad ways. "It was not the coffee that caused an unbelievable wave of demonstrations to arise spontaneously and, within weeks, to cover the entire South. It was, as the Atlanta students wrote, 'an Appeal for Human rights.' " [29]

If the twentieth century American "standard story" is one in which significant actions occur as consequences of the deliberations and impulses of independent, conscious, and self-motivated actors (Tilly 1998), then students' representations of the sit-ins as spontaneous challenged that rationale for action, along with its connotations of adult gradualism and amoral instrumentalism. Students narratively constructed what was happening in order to make sense of it, but also to signal its significance. In the process, they created a new collective identity of student activist. "The sit-ins," SNCC Chair Charles McDew said in October 1960, "have inspired us to build a new image of ourselves in our own minds" (McDew 1967). That identity supplied the selective incentives that made "high risk activism" (McAdam 1986) attractive.

Narratives of the sit-ins also motivated by their very failure to convey a single meaning. References to the sit-ins' spontaneity simultaneously explained and failed to explain the sit-ins in a way that called for the story's retelling—and reenactment. To clarify, I return to the third feature of Miller's (1990) characterization of narrative. Again, the complex word at the heart of all narratives is not only poly-valent but finally indeterminate, Miller argues; its core meaning is unfixable. The impossibility of a conclusive meaning calls for more stories that reca-pitulate the dilemma, but differently. All stories both explain and fail to explain, Miller goes on, but the dynamic is clearest in stories of human-kind's origins. The point at which man separates himself from beasts is unknowable, since "what-ever is chosen as the moment of origination always presupposes some earlier moment when man first appeared" (72). The question cannot be answered logically, and the alternative is a mythical narrative whose illogical premises will nevertheless require that it be retold. Thus Sophocles' *Oedipus the King* depicts a man who both has and has not broken the incest taboo—that which separates humans from all other species—and is punished (punishes him-self) for that which he did not know. The enigma is revealed but unresolved; hence the need for more stories—for Shakespeare's *Hamlet,* for Faulkner's *Absalom, Absalom.* "What cannot be expressed logically, one is tempted to say, we then tell stories about," Miller concludes (74).

The question of origins is just as unanswer-able in the case of social movements. When does protest begin? In this case, did it begin when the first students were arrested? Did it begin with the Montgomery bus boycott? With *Brown v. Board?* Did it begin with the first slave rebellion? With the first song sung, or African tradition preserved, or Christian ritual reinterpreted in what James Scott (1990) calls an "infrapolitics of dissent" stretching back to Africans' enslavement in this country? The question of origins is historical but also personal. When does collective action begin? When can I call myself an activist? The sit-in narrative posed those questions and resolved them in a way that called for their re-asking. The students acted, and yet it was a force that made students act, an impetus that acted through the students.

The word "spontaneity" means both volun-tary and instinctual (involuntary)—contradictory meanings contained in the same (complex) word. In the sit-in narratives, spontaneity functioned as a kind of narrative ellipsis in which the movement's "beginning" occurred; "IT HAPPENED," and the

non-narratable shift from observer to participant took place. This ellipsis or ambiguity strengthened the engagement of the listener/hearer in one of two ways. Either, following Iser (1972) and Leitch (1986), its underspecification of the mechanisms of partici-pation forced listeners/hearers to fill in the missing links, to become co-authors of the story. Or, fol-lowing Miller (1990), the story could not establish, could not fix the motivation for participation and so required its retelling. And since the story was a true one, retelling required reenactment of the events already described. Either way, ambiguity was crucial to narrativity, to readers' engagement and identification with the story.

A concept of narrative thus captures the action-compelling character of the discourse around the sit-ins better than does the concept of frames by virtue of narrative's combination of familiarity and undecidability, convention and novelty, and truth (representing reality) and fiction (constituting real-ity). It was not the sit-in narratives' clarity about the antagonists, protagonists, stakes, and mechanics of struggle that made them so compelling but rather their containment of ambiguity, risk, and mystery within a familiar discursive form.

Institutionalizing Spontaneity

How compelling were the sit-in narratives? In addi-tion to the number of students who joined the sit-ins (70,000 by September 1961 [Oberschall 1989]), the challenges created for SNCC as a fledgling organi-zation by the sit-in narratives suggests their potency. Spontaneity, emblematic of students' indepen-dence and their unique contribution to the move-ment, became organizational commitments which both animated and constrained strategic action. Students called for coordination but were resistant to direction, wanted the movement to speak to the nation but were wary of leaders, wanted to expand the scope of protest but distrusted adult advice. Southern Regional Council official Margaret Long advised SNCC workers on their fundraising activi-ties: "I wonder if it is really true, as this brochure says, that you 'seek to be a coordinating agency.' I see a great deal of uprising and brave and impec-cable and successful marches on the Bastille, but I don't see any coordinated movement by you or anybody else. And I don't know that there should be."[30] SNCC leaders apparently took Long's advice, for in funding appeals, newsletters, and speeches, they represented the group as extension of the spontaneity of the sit-ins, and of the values of moral imperative, local autonomy, and radicalism that spontaneity connoted. A narrative of the sit-ins warranted SNCC as a kind of "anti-organization," as observers would later call it, an organization that sought not so much to guide the struggle as to go where people were "moving;" that was less interested in executing a well-planned agenda than in enacting in its own operation the society it envisaged, and that privileged direct and moral action over political maneuvering.[31]

The strength of the sit-in narrative, and its equation of student protest with moral—as opposed to political—action, is also suggested by the Internal conflict SNCC faced the following year in moving from direct action (sit-ins and freedom rides) to voter registration. Proponents of voter registration within SNCC were careful to emphasize that "the only group that could do a complete voter registration program southwide was a student group,"[32] thus asserting SNCC's distinctive identity as a *student* organization. But they still met with fierce resistance (Carson 1981; Zinn 1964). Detractors were wary of the federal administration's support for a voter registration campaign and worried about cooptation. They also saw electoral politics as "immoral," and as antithetical to the moral protest that had animated SNCC's activism thus far (Stoper 1989).

An organizational split was averted only through the intervention of advisor Ella Baker, who persuaded the group to form direct action and voter registration wings, an arrangement abandoned as some direct action proponents left the organization and others shifted to voter registration. SNCC workers were also discovering, as one put it later, that "voter registration *was* direct action" (Charles Jones quoted in Stoper 1989:197). Accompanying Black people to southern courthouses to register provoked the same violence and disruption as had the sit-ins and served equally well to dramatize to the nation the denial of African-Americans' constitutional rights. Marches and demonstrations to protest the harassment of civil rights workers drew

new members to local movement organizations; "Freedom Days" where people went to the courthouse en masse built solidarity; and public facilities-testing through direct action did both (Carson 1981; Payne 1995).

Yet SNCC workers never fully integrated direct action with political organizing, a failure evident in field reports that allude to conflicts between residents' desires to test public accommodations and SNCC directives to focus on electoral mobilization.[33] Organizers' commitment to "letting the people decide" the direction and methods of struggle sat uncomfortably with their persistent suspicion of direct action as not properly *political*. In 1963, for example, SNCC workers framed the choice between voter registration and direct action as whether "the emphasis should be political or religious, spontaneous or rigidly political."[34] The formulation is revealing. "Spontaneous" had come to refer to action not oriented to electoral politics, action motivated by religious commitment rather than strategic calculation, and action orchestrated by local groups rather than national committee. Its meaning went far beyond an absence of planning, but remained locked within a set of dualities: spontaneous versus political; political versus moral; moral versus instrumental. Since even proponents of direct action accepted these dualities, they were ill-equipped to challenge direct action's relegation to the sphere of the personally satisfying but politically ineffectual. The problem thus lay in the power of the canonical narrative to shape strategic options. In this movement, like in others, the conventional storyline that has people acting out their moral commitments in emotional and impulsive protest overwhelmed one in which people acted emotionally, morally, *and* in politically instrumental ways.[35]

Conclusion

I have argued that although the sit-ins and the groups they galvanized were not without prior organizational affiliation, their narrative construction as spontaneous was central to an emerging collective identity. The Black students who launched the sit-ins, then kneel-ins, wade-ins, and pray-ins, and who founded SNCC, departed from the existing civil rights organizations not so much in long-term goals (integration), nor even in strategy (nonviolent resistance) as in militancy and organizational form. The sit-ins were represented as a break with the gradualism of prior Black protest forms (spontaneity denoted urgency), a break with the incomplete engagement of adult leaders (spontaneity denoted a moral imperative to act) and a break with the hierarchy and bureaucracy of existing organizations (spontaneity denoted local initiative). Narratives of the sit-ins helped make normative a physically demanding and dangerous form of activism.

To be sure, representing the surge of student protest as spontaneous defused charges of outside planning by left-wing groups. And tying SNCC to the sit-ins legitimated it as organizational expression of the sit-ins. However, my account suggests that this kind of instrumentalist view is limited. Representations of the sit-ins as spontaneous coincided with rather than followed the establishment of a student protest organization. My account thus builds on Oberschall's (1989) theory of the diffusion of protest by showing how high rates of participation can occur by means other than the formal recruitment strategies of already established movement organizations. But contrary to Oberschall's argument that it is simply information about the reduced costs of participation that leads people to join fledgling movements, I have argued that narratives of the sit-ins, told in formal and informal settings, made participation normative. Rather than simply persuasive devices deployed by strategic collective actors, narratives help to *constitute* new strategic actors. After a formal movement organization was consolidated, the sit-in narratives shaped contests over legitimate strategies within it.

Further examination of the role of narrative in mobilization promises several analytical pay-offs. First, it will help us to better understand the dynamics of mobilization before the consolidation of a formally organized movement. As Klandermans (1988, 1992) observes, we still know little about how collective identities emerge from "subcultural networks and indigenous structures" and emerge during episodes of collective action. Further investigation of the discursive processes that unfold in such settings should detail the causal schemes that underpin popular vocabularies of motive. Is the dominant logic one of individual intention and collective efficacy, as framing theorists maintain? Or are events

represented as unfolding by narrative necessity, as I have suggested? Is a critical discursive ellipsis, a point in the story where the non-narratable movement beginning takes place, a characteristic feature of movement-founding stories?

Activists do more than tell stories, of course. They storm barricades, negotiate with authorities, evaluate past tactics, march. They use referential, persuasive, and expressive modes of discourse as well as narrative ones (Polkinghorne 1988). Under what other circumstances, then, are they likely to turn to narrative? This is a second important line of research. After formal organizations have been established, activists probably continue to tell stories in order to sustain and strengthen members" commitment since, as Stephen Cornell puts it, in telling stories, "we not only make sense of ourselves; through stories we create ourselves: we become subjects" (1996:3). Movements in which the goal is self-transformation as much as political reform may see personal story-telling *as* activism. Narratives undoubtedly figure more in movement decision making than classical rational models would have us believe (March and Olson 1976; Meyer and Rowan 1977). Activists may legitimate and evaluate drastic transformations in agenda or strategy by telling stories that configure past decisions in a broader narrative of enlightenment. Veteran activists may stake their authority on a superior knowledge of the movement's history. However, stories are not only legitimating but evaluative, they are lenses through which opportunities and obstacles, costs and benefits, and success and failure are assessed (King 1986). Jo Freeman argues that "past experiences" constrain the resources available to movement groups for action (1979:177). But experience is filtered through discursive frames, among them stories. This suggests more attention to the role of narrative in movement decision making.

Narratives' dependence on a stock of plots, on a canon, suggests a point of conceptual entry into the relationship between the hegemonic and subversive features of (movement) culture. Rather than counterpoising oppositional stories to hegemonic ones, we should ask whether there are features of narrative—not shared by other discursive forms—that make it prone to reproducing hegemonic understandings even when used by oppositional movements.

Drawing on Ewick and Silbey's (1995) study of legal narratives, we can identify several such features. Since narratives rely for their intelligibility on their conformity to familiar plots, modern Western movement stories may tend to attribute insurgency to individual, independent actors rather than to the relationships that social movement scholars know are so important in generating and sustaining participation. It may be easier to tell a story of short-term triumph than one of long-term endurance.[36] Since narratives do not lay out the grounds for their credibility, relying on emotional identification and familiar plots rather than on testing or adjudication of truth claims, they are better able than other discursive forms to rule out challenge. This may be a good way to stifle internal dissent, but if leaders seek to prefigure a fully democratic society within the movement itself, then this feature of narrative surely proves a hindrance. Finally, narratives often work by "effac[ing] the connections between the particular and the general" (Ewick and Silbey 1995:218). A compelling story seems to speak to a shared experience but without demonstrating its representativeness. The danger for movements is that my particular story is too easily seen as that of "women" or "gays," in a way that erases difference within the group.

Stories, like other cultural forms, both reproduce the existing and provide tools for changing it. The key, of course, is to understand how and when they do each. And that requires grasping not only the formal features of narrative that distinguish it from other discursive forms, but the social conditions in which stories are more and less familiar, easily communicated, and authoritative.

NOTES

Research was supported by a grant from the Columbia University Humanities and Social Sciences Council. Thanks to Marc Steinberg, Gregory Polletta, two anonymous reviewers, the editorial staff of *Social Problems,* members of the City University of New York Graduate Center Sociology Colloquium, and of the Great Barrington Theory Group for their comments on previous drafts. Thanks also to Linda Catalano and Joyce Robbins for research assistance, and to the many archivists who helped to locate and search campus newspapers, especially Ms. Kafhy Jenkins of Howard University's Moorland-Splngam Research Center, Ms. Tanya Moye of Atlanta University's Robert W. Woodruff Library, and Ms. Ledell B. Smith of Southern University.

1. In twelve other campus periodicals examined by me or by college archivists, there was no mention of the student demonstrations in 1960 or 1961, this despite the fact that students from those institutions had been Involved In sit-ins. One former student at Lincoln University remembers the administration prohibiting coverage of the sit-ins in the campus newspaper (Interview with Elizabeth Wilson by Linda Catalano, September 29, 1997).

2. Gamson suggests that although the identity of the "they" in an adversarial ("us and they") frame may be elusive ("In the pursuit of cultural change, the target is often diffused throughout the whole civil society and the they being pursued is structurally elusive" [1992:85]), the "we" must be dearly specified ("In sum, frames with a dear we and an elusive they are quite capable of being fully collective and adversarial" [85]).

3. Interest In narrative in sociology, anthropology, political science, history, psychology, and law is burgeoning. For an extensive bibliography of work on narrative in the social sciences see Hinchman and Hinchman (1997). For sophisticated treatments in sociology see the essays collected in a special issue of Social Science History, Vol. 16, no. 3 (1992), as well as Somers (1994); and Polkinghorne (1988). There is also renewed interest in narrative as a mode of presentation as well as object of investigation. See the Hinchman and Hinchman (1997) bibliography, Polkinghorne (1988). and for an interesting critique, Tilly (1998).

4. Drawing on Goffman's (1959) dramaturgical perspective. Hunt and Benford (1994: see also Benford and Hunt 1992) argue that frames configure Identities in dramatic form. Listeners/readers are encouraged to see themselves in the role of hero, to see movement antagonists as villains. This would seem to suggest the narrative configuration that I'm describing. However, as Polkinghome points out. "To play a social role is not the same as configuring one's life into a plot that is one's personal identity." Distinguishing a narrative perspective from a Goffmanian dramaturgical one, Polkinghorne argues that roles rather "take on meaning from the perspective of the single adventure that is one person, as defined by the life plot" (1988:153).

5. Psychologist A. E. Michone (1963) found that when presented with small colored rectangles moving on a screen, viewers constructed elaborate narrative plots: "It is as if A's approach frightened B and B ran away."It is as if A, in touching B induced an electric current which set B going.'" 'The arrival of A by the side of B acts as a sort of signal to B....' 'It is as if A touched off a mechanism inside B and thus set it going'" (quoted In Sarbln 1986:13). Observers often laughed at the rectangles' movements. The experiment suggests our proclivity to turn to narrative to make phenomena intelligible.

6. Johnston, Larana and Gusfield (1994) thus paraphrase and criticize Friedman and McAdam: "there are leaders, committees, or cabals that plot the best collective identity for a movement, much like marketing executives strategize the

best way to present a product. It is a "top down" approach to collective identity that seems to be more useful...when SMOs are established and likely to be thinking in these strategic terms. At earlier stages, however...it makes sense that a more "bottom up" approach is, if not the entire answer, then at least deserving of a place in the theoretical equation" (1994:18).

7. SNCC reported that near 200 students had been expelled during that period ("from you know who..." NA. ND [July 1960], SNCC microfilm reel 1 #291). Michael Walzer (1960b) wrote that the sit-ins had galvanized a surge of church-based adult movement organizations. But "the students, for the most part, do not attend the weekly meetings in the churches. Embarrassing moments often follow suggestions that students present rise and be applauded. They turn out to have stayed on campus for a meeting of their own."

8. Ella Baker Interview in Stoper 1989.

9. "Theopolis Fair, John Baker, Jerry Byrd. Henrietta Eppse Represent Fisk." *Fisk Forum*. September 30, 1960.

10. Joan Bun to the editor; *Hilltop*. May 31, 1960: *Fisk Forum*. October 28, 1960: "Retreat Best In History of School, Declares Dean Green." *Fisk Forum*, September 30, 1960. On African students and representatives at Southern colleges, see transcript of John Lewis interview, Moorland-Spingam Research Center; "Cameroun's (sic) Foreign Minister Visits Xavier U. Campus," *Xavier Herald* October 1960. SNCC invited the brother of Tom Mboya to be keynote speaker at its first conference, addressing the "relationship of the African freedom movement to our own fight" (Marion S. Barry, Chairman, to Dear Friend. October 10, 1960. SNCC microfilm reel 4 #920).

11. "Campus Politics." *Xavier Herald*, January 1960; "Student Sloth," *Xavier Herald*, October 1960: *Fisk Forum*. September 30, 1960: "Like—Being Way Out," *Aurora* (Knoxville College). March 1960. The fact that some of these characterizations appeared when the sit-ins were well under way, and at the same time as some were referring to 1960 as "the year of the student" [*Fisk Forum*, September 30. 1960] suggests that accusations of student apathy continued a powerful challenge.

12. "Sitdown Protest in Pictorial Retrospect," *Shaw Journal*, May 1960; "Justifiable Recalcitrance," *Shaw Journal*, March-April 1960; "The New Freedom." SNCC microfilm reel 4 #108; "An Appeal for Dignity." *Student Voice*. November 1960, reprinted in Carson. 1990: 23; "Call for Unity in Struggle for Freedom." *Hilltop*, March 7, 1960.

13. "A Report on the Student Direst Action Movement at Penn State as of March 31, 1960," SNCC microfilm reel 44 #22; "The price for Freedom." *Wolverine Observer*. October-November 1960; Jane to Dave. August 14, 1960, SNCC microfilm reel 4 #810; "Call for Unity in Struggle for Freedom," *Hilltop*, March 7, 1960.

14. "Drama of the Sitdown." *Shaw Journal*, March-April 1960.

15. "Newsletter to Congressmen." August 1960, SNCC microfilm reel 1 #291-2.

16. The latter used an explicitly persuasive mode—"you as students can believe me when I tell you this will benefit every one of us who sit at the Woolworth counter"—and emphasized nor transformation but continuity: "The waitress ignored us and kept serving the White customers. However, this is no great surprise to me because I have been exposed to segregation at lunch counters for 15 years and the situation is predominately unchanged" (*Register* February 5, 1960).

17. Saint Paul's college (Virginia) *Student Journal*, May 1960; "The Sitdowns came in 1960, But They Remain for 1961" by George Collins, SNCC microfilm reel 44 #98; Joan Burt to Dear Editor, *Hilltop*, May 31, 1960.

18. "Column from Cambridge Correspondent." SNCC microfilm reel 62 #130 (ellipses in original); "Ode to Lunch Counter" by Robert Booker. *Aurara*. June 1960.

19. Sidney Simon to Dear Friend. September 8, 1960. SNCC microfilm reel 4 #1230.

20. *Albatross* (Swarthmore College).

21. Marion S. Barry to Congressman Byron L. Johnson, August 22, 1960. SNCC microfilm reel 1 #285: "Sitdown Protest in Pictorial Retrospect." *Shaw Journal*, May 1960: Edward King to Dear Friend. September 12. 1960. SNCC microfilm reel 4 #920. NT, Henry Thomas report. ND (July 1960). SNCC micorfilm reel 5 #170: Fuller, 1960:16: "Civic Interest Group Progress Report." October 13, 1960, SNCC microfilm reel 4 #1279; Jane Stembridge to Henry James Thomas, July 20, 1960, SNCC microfilm reel 5 #174.

22. NAACP head Roy Wilkins announced a nationwide economic boycott as the sit-ins spread, explaining. "We have always used persuasion through various means of political and economic pressure, but now we're going to use It much more intensively than in the past because the membership has become restless over the slow pace of the civil rights proceedings" (Bennett 1960). Lewis Killian argues that the need to deflect red-baiting charges led the organizations assisting the sit-inners in Tallahassee. Florida to deny their own involvement (1984:782).

23. "A Report on the Student Direct Action Movement at Penn State as of March 31, 1960." SNCC microfilm reel 44 # 22.

24. *Hilltop*, March 7, 1960; "The New Freedom." SNCC microfilm reel 4 #108; "Statement submitted by SNCC to the Platform Committee of the National Democratic Convention." July 7, 1960, SNCC microfilm reel 1 #243–248.

25. The Student Nonviolent Coordinating Committee to Mr. Bill Strong. July 31, 1960. SNCC microfilm reel 1 #207; Bob Moses. "A Freedom Child," ND (July 1960), SNCC microfilm reel 4 #939; "Inside the Sitdowner," ND, SNCC microfilm reel 44 #100.

26. Stephen Henderson "A White Student Sits-in." *Social Progress*. February 1961; Jane Stembridge to Henry Thomas, July 20, 1960. SNCC microfilm reel 5 #174; SNCC newsletter entry, 1960. SNCC microfilm reel 5 #190.

27. "Call for Unity in Struggle for Freedom." *Hilltop*, March 7, 1960; Speech to NSA by Jane Stembridge, SNCC microfilm

reel 44 #1280–1283; "A Report on the Student Direct Action Movement at Penn State as of March 31, 1960," SNCC microfilm reel 44 #22; Fuller 1960:13; Walzer 1960a; Dykeman and Stokely 1960:10. "Justifiable Recalcitrance," *Shaw Journal,* March-April 1960; Letter to the editor, *Aurora,* April 1960; "Sitdown Protest in Pictorial Retrospect." *Shaw Journal.* May 1960.

28. "Up Against the Obstacles." NA. ND, SNCC microfilm reel 4 #980; "Newsletter to Congressmen." August 1960, SNCC microfilm reel 1 #291–2; "Author Says Sit-Ins Were Inevitable," *Hilltop,* April 29, 1960; "This is important," ND, SNCC microfilm reel 44 #113; Edward B. King to Dear Friend, September 20, 1960, SNCC microfilm reel 4 #920.

29. Jane Stembridge to Lillian Lipsen, August 18, 1960. SNCC microfilm reel 4 #207; Sample Fund-Raising Letter for Student Nonviolent Coordinating Committee, SNCC microfilm reel 3 #785; Bennett 1960:35; "An Appeal for Dignity." *Student Voice.* November 1960, reprinted in Carson 1990:23: "Across the Editor's Desk," *Student Voice.* November 1960, reprinted in Carson 1990:22; *Student Voice.* special supplementary Issue, November 1960, reprinted in Carson 1990:20; "Drama of the Sitdown," *Shaw Journal,* March-April 1960; "Students Continue Woolworth Picket." *Hilltop;* April 8, 1960; "Dear Congressmen, from the Student Nonviolent Coordinating Committee." August 12, 1960. SNCC microfilm reel 12.

30. Letter to Julian Bond from Margaret Long; Heirich to Jane Stembridge, SNCC microfilm reel 4 #122.

31. *Student Voice.* April and May 1961, reprinted in Carson 1990:2.

32. SNCC Minutes. July 14–16 1961, SNCC microfilm reel 3 #792–5.

33. See, for example, Meridian Report, November 23, 1964, SNCC microfilm reel 66 #1259–1230; Field Report: Perry County, Alabama, Jan. 16–25, 1965, SNCC microfilm reel 37. #123; Overall Report, Southwest Georgia, February 1965, SNCC microfilm reel 37 #839b-843.

34. Summary of Selma Workshop, December 13–16, 1963, SNCC microfilm reel 9 #382–389. Among White new leftists, the skepticism was even greater. In 1961, Tom Hayden of Students for a Democratic Society praised SNCC's "new emphasis on the vote" as "signal[ing] the decline of the short-sighted view that 'discrimination' can be isolated from related social problems." "The moral darity of the movement has not always been accompanied by precise political vision," he went on, "and sometimes not even by a real political consciousness." Another SDS leader concluded in 1962 that, "The focus of action on Negro campuses in the non-violent protest movement has been largely 'non-political.'" (To SDS, From Hayden Re: Race and Politics Conference, ND [1961], SNCC microfilm reel 9 #1142; "For Dixie with Love and Squalor," by Robb Burlage, ND [1962], SNCC microfilm reel 9.)

35. Rosenthal and Schwartz (1989) note that a tendency to associate spontaneity with expressive, even irrational action is common in sociological accounts of collective action.

36. Kim Voss argues that Poland's Solidarity movement was sustained in periods of defeat by activists' invocation of the "Catholic belief in the successive stations of the 'via dolorosa' to explain failures, the implication being that while early uprisings resulted in Crucifixion, eventually insurgency would bring Resurrection and Life" (1996:8). Derrick Bell (1992) has described similarly sustaining narratives among African Americans.

23.

Identity Work and Collective Action in a Repressive Context: Jewish Resistance on the "Aryan Side" of the Warsaw Ghetto

RACHEL L. EINWOHNER

Debates about the meaning and utility of the term "identity politics" notwithstanding, scholars have recognized that identity is central to social move-

Einwohner, Rachel L. 2006. "Identity Work and Collective Action in a Repressive Context: Jewish Resistance on the 'Aryan Side' of the Warsaw Ghetto." *Social Problems* 53: 38–56. Reprinted by permission of The University of California Press.

ments and political action of all kinds (Bernstein 2005). The well-established research literature on identity and social movements demonstrates that identity processes shape all aspects of the protest experience, from movement emergence to outcomes (for reviews, see Polletta and Jasper 2001; Snow 2001; Stryker, Owens, and White 2000). One line of Inquiry within that broad literature focuses on the strategic use of identity. As scholars have shown, protesters often make strategic decisions about how to present themselves to best advantage in the political arena in order to achieve their goals. Indeed, various strategies of "identity deployment" (Bernstein 1997) have been shown to be useful in a number of movement settings, including the gay and lesbian movement (Bernstein 1997; Dugan 2003), the animal rights movement (Einwohner 1999; Groves 1997), and the breast cancer movement (Montini 1996), among others.

This paper addresses the strategic role of identity in social movements with an examination of the collective Jewish resistance in Nazi-occupied Warsaw that culminated in the Warsaw Ghetto Uprising of 1943.[1] While this case might not be what usually comes to mind when one thinks of "identity politics," there is no question that issues of identity were central to Warsaw Jews' struggle. Like other Jews throughout Nazi-occupied Europe, Warsaw Jews were persecuted because of their Jewish identity. However, the extreme costs associated with the display of Jewish identity in this setting set this case apart from other studies of activists' identity strategies. Under the Nazi regime, all individuals who were identified as Jewish were at risk for great personal harm, whether they were activists or not. Furthermore, Jewishness was a highly visible identity, marked by a number of physical and behavioral traits. The following analysis therefore asks: Given the fact that their activism took place in a setting in which Jewish identity was both visible and costly, to what extent could Jewish resistance fighters in Warsaw use that identity strategically? Did their "identity work" (Snow and Anderson 1987; Snow and McAdam 2000) differ from that of activists working in other contexts? If so, what can this case teach us about the role of identity in social movements more generally?

Some readers might be surprised or even offended by my use of a case of Jewish resistance during the Holocaust to further scholarly understanding of social movements and collective action. The Holocaust was an episode of such unimaginable horror and suffering that some consider it unique and, therefore, incomparable; indeed, some scholars suggest that comparing the Holocaust

to other cases of genocide robs it of its meaning and lends credence to those who deny that the Holocaust happened at all (for more on the debate about the uniqueness of the Holocaust, see Bauer 2001; Gerson 2001; Melson 1992; Rosenbaum 2001). Although my analysis does not explicitly compare the Warsaw Ghetto Uprising with other cases of collective action, I do use it to draw implications for social movement research. Therefore, I also implicitly argue that collective resistance during the Holocaust may be meaningfully compared to collective resistance in other contexts. However, in doing so, I do not intend to diminish in any way the terrible tragedy of the Holocaust or the immense suffering of its victims. By presenting a sociological account of the Holocaust, I follow the lead of other scholars who have performed similar analyses using other research literatures (e.g., Berger 1995, 2002; Berger, Green, and Kreiser 1998; Gallant and Cross 1992; Gross 1994; for more on sociological approaches to the Holocaust, see also Gerson and Wolf, forthcoming).

On the other hand, some readers may accept the notion of social scientific work on the Holocaust in general but might not see the Warsaw Ghetto Uprising as a social movement and, therefore, may take exception to my application of social movement theory and research to this case. I justify my use of this case as a social movement or, more broadly, as a case of "contentious politics" (McAdam, Tarrow, and Tilly 2001) for several reasons. Although there is no single definition of a social movement, most scholars agree that movements are organized, sustained, collective attempts to further the goals of some group, typically in opposition to some government or authoritative structure (Tarrow 1994; see also Jasper 1997; McAdam 1982). Collective resistance in the Warsaw Ghetto was planned and organized, with clear leadership and an organizational structure (Gutman 1994; Kurzman 1993; Zuckerman 1993). Jewish resistance in the Warsaw Ghetto was socially and politically motivated as well; the organizers of the Warsaw Ghetto Uprising staged collective resistance not to escape from the confines of the Ghetto, but to preserve the honor of the Jewish people as a whole (Gutman 1982, 1994). Moreover, this case shares many of the attributes of other, recognized, social movements. For instance, like many other cases that have been the subject of social movement research, participants in the resistance movement in the Warsaw Ghetto were active in other political organizations and movements prior to their involvement in the resistance and were recruited through these pre-existing activist networks (Cochavi 1995; Zuckerman 1993). Although these activists did not use tactics traditionally associated with contemporary protest in the West, such as marches and demonstrations, one must remember that the setting in which they worked rendered such tactics useless. Since Jews living under the Nazi regime lacked both citizenship rights and public support, mass marches and similar actions would not have been effective and, indeed, probably would have led to increased repression. The tactics these activists chose (i.e., armed resistance) made sense, given their situation. Moreover, such tactics have been featured in other cases of collective action that have been studied by movement scholars, including Jeff Goodwin's (1997) analysis of the Huk rebellion and Robert White and Michael Fraser's (2000) study of the Irish Republican movement. For these reasons, the Warsaw Ghetto Uprising can be appropriately defined as a social movement and may, therefore, be used to make a scholarly contribution to the field. (For other applications of social movement theory to this case, see also Einwohner 2003.)

My inquiry focuses on the experiences of those Jewish activists in Warsaw whose physical features and language skills allowed them to "pass" as non-Jews. Such individuals were able to move in and out of the walled ghetto in which all Warsaw Jews were interned. They participated in collective resistance efforts by smuggling weapons and other resources into the Ghetto and making contact with members of the Polish underground. These activists shared a strong Jewish identity, yet for obvious reasons, they had to mask that identity in order to carry out their work outside the Ghetto, on the so-called "Aryan side." Not only did circumstances force these individuals into identity displays that they otherwise might not have chosen, but their identity work featured a dissonant set of identities, Jewish and Gentile, both of which were enacted during collective action. Their strategies therefore featured, and

were shaped by, identity in ways that were distinct from the other identity-based strategies identified by social movement research. Furthermore, I suggest that such forced, dissonant identity work is particularly likely to be featured in protest in extremely repressive contexts.

Certainly, "passing" on the Aryan side was not an identity strategy used solely by members of the resistance movement; other, non-activist Jews who fled the Ghetto for the relative safety of the Aryan side had to hide their identity as well (Engelking 2001). Thus, while passing may be seen as an act of resistance in general, in the sense that it helped save Jewish lives and therefore worked against the Nazis' genocidal agenda (see Shneldman 2002), the use of this identity strategy did not distinguish participants from non-participants in the resistance movement. Nonetheless, because activists could not carry out their tasks on the Aryan side without also passing as non-Jews, I argue that this identity work was a crucial component of their collective activist experience and is, therefore, worthy of inquiry, in light of theory and of research on identity and social movements.

The goal, therefore, is not to use social movement theory to explain why Jews "chose" to hide their identity on the Aryan side. Instead, examining the experience of Jewish resistance work on the Aryan side illustrates a type of activist identity work that is qualitatively different from what has been previously identified and may be used to draw some broader implications for the study of social movements. More generally, by bringing the case of Jewish resistance fighters in the Warsaw Ghetto to the attention of social movement scholars, I hope to broaden the range of cases and movement settings beyond those typically explored by social movement research.

I begin with a discussion of strategic identity work in social movements. I then draw on both primary and secondary historical sources to examine the identity strategies used by Jewish activists on the Aryan side of the Warsaw Ghetto walls. I conclude by drawing some implications for future research.

Identity and Strategy in Social Movements
Social movement scholars generally agree that protest is undertaken for the purpose of achieving

some goal (Burstein, Einwohner, and Hollander 1995). Activists, therefore, face any number of strategic choices in the pursuit of their objectives (Jasper 2004). Strategic action in social movements includes various tactical choices, such as the use of either violence or non-violence (Gamson 1990) or tactical innovations in response to the actions of targets (Barkan 1984; McAdam 1983; Morris 1993). Activists may also recruit strategically, that is, by attempting to attract high-status participants (McAdam 1988) and may choose either to mobilize or to "lay low," depending on the the broader sociopolitical environment and public receptivity to their cause (Meyer 2004; Taylor 1989). In addition, virtually all movement communications, including messages geared toward the general public and internal communiqués, are carefully and strategically composed. For instance, activists use a variety of framing techniques to garner public support (Snow et al. 1986) and to keep members mobilized despite apparent failures (Einwohner 2002; Voss 1998; see Jasper 2004 for more on strategic choices in social movements).

In many situations, protesters also incorporate aspects of their identity into their strategy. Protesters choosing nonviolence, for instance, not only perform nonviolent acts but in so doing, effectively state to onlookers: "We are non-violent people" (Polletta and Jasper 2001). Identity can also be an explicit feature of social movement strategy, as Mary Bernstein (1997) demonstrates. Her study of "identity deployment" in the gay and lesbian movement shows how activists in a number of states used different strategies of self-portrayal in pursuit of their policy goals, either by stressing their similarities to or differences from the heterosexual mainstream. Kimberly B. Dugan's (2003) discussion of activity surrounding an anti-gay ballot initiative in Cincinnati also illustrates activists' strategic use of identity. As she shows, both the gay and lesbian activists who opposed the initiative, and the members of the Christian right who supported it, sought to portray themselves in certain ways in order to persuade the voting public. These studies emphasize the strategic portrayal of identity through the news media and policy statements. Other work shows how activists use additional means and media to

present a particular image of themselves to others, including self-framings posted on the Internet (Schroer 2003) and the careful management of emotion in formal settings such as courtrooms and public hearings (Einwohner 1999; Montini 1996; Whittler 2001).

While the works cited above do not adopt an interactionist perspective per se, identity deployment may be thought of as a form of "impression management," Erving Goffman's (1959) term for the performative strategies used by social actors to foster certain images of themselves in the eyes of others. Goffman's influence is seen more explicitly in the work of other movement scholars who have theorized about the role of identity in social movements. Chief among these is David Snow, who, in work with Leon Anderson and with Doug McAdam (Snow and Anderson 1987; Snow and McAdam 2000), outlines the concept of "identity work." This term illustrates the range of activities in which movement actors engage to construct, promote, and maintain their identities, both as individuals and as members of a collective. "Identity work" is, therefore, a broader category than "identity deployment." The former refers to strategic identity displays intended for external audiences and to a variety of other identity oriented tasks, including intragroup discussions about "who we are," which result in the construction of collective identity within a movement (Gamson 1996; Hunt and Benford 1994; Hunt et al. 1994; Lichterman 1999; Reger 2002; Taylor and Wittier 1992; Wittier 1995). The term also includes the work done by individuals to align the personal sense of self with the collective (Snow and McAdam 2000). Finally, "identity work" also refers to the work required to make sense of each person's multiple identities and group memberships (Brekhus 2003; King 2004; for more on identity work in social movements, see also Einwohner, Reger, and Myers unpublished).

Although extant theory and research have uncovered many examples of identity work in social movements, I suggest that this research suffers from two biases. First, studies of the type of identity work described as "identity deployment" or "impression management" assume that activists have the freedom to choose which aspect of self they want to promote. Having such freedom implies, in turn, that protest occurs in the context of relatively safety. In such a situation, it is not terribly costly to reveal (or to hide) one identity or another (for an exception see Taylor and Raeburn 1995, who note explicitly that revealing one's identity as a gay or lesbian activist can be quite costly). However, such assumptions about identity might not hold for protests in extremely hostile or repressive situations, where the costs associated with identity displays can limit activists' choices about how they want to appear to others. While all protest activity carries with it some cost (McAdam 1986), activists who are members of stigmatized or oppressed groups cannot always afford the costs that may accrue when group membership is revealed or portrayed in a particular light. For instance, mothers and grandmothers protesting the disappearances of their loved ones during the "Dirty War" in Argentina emphasized their maternal identity, which, as a highly valued status in Latin America, afforded them a certain amount of protection from the military regime. However, those activists who were also members of minority religions or who identified as leftist or Communist were much more hesitant to deploy those identities, for fear of reprisal (Arditti 1999; Fisher 1989).

A second bias of current work is that it focuses mostly on what can be called "harmonic" identity work. That is, many types of identity work are described as tasks that are performed in order to organize or align diverse identities into a coherent unit of some kind. The harmonic nature of identity work is most clearly visible in the examples provided by Snow and colleagues (Snow and Anderson 1987; Snow and McAdam 2000), who outline the work involved in the "convergence" between an activist's individual identity and the collective identity of the protest group or the movement as a whole. Other research has approached identity work as something intended to achieve identity "harmony." Many studies of the construction of collective identity in social movements emphasize how activists arrive at a shared definition of "we-ness" (Gamson 1992; Taylor and Whittier 1992). Although multiple collective identities may exist within a single movement (Reger 2002; Whittier 1995), the work involved in identity construction is still seen as something

that is done to draw together diverse individuals into a coherent collective. This process also takes place at the individual level. For instance, Debra King (2004) describes the processes by which long-time activists manage their identities as activists and their nonmovement identities (e.g., those based on work or family) in order to sustain their activism over time.

Wayne H. Brekhus's (2003) analysis of identity construction and performance among suburban gay men provides another example. He shows how individuals use different "identity grammars"—which refer to seeing gayness as a verb, noun, or adjective—in order to manage their identities and, thereby, to reconcile two statuses (being gay, and living in the suburbs) not generally perceived as compatible by outsiders. Although his is not a social movement analysis per se, it is intended as an overall theory of identity and can therefore apply to identity in social movements as well (2003:7). According to the foregoing research, then, the activist's task in performing identity work is to align different aspects of her identity or to join others in constructing a coherent collective identity that incorporates diverse constituencies.

Yet, this portrayal may only be accurate in certain settings. In other words, I argue that identity work in social movements is not always, or not solely, harmonic. Specifically, I suggest that protest in extremely repressive contexts can feature other, different kinds of identity work. I base this hypothesis on other research on "high-risk" activism, which shows that activism that carries with it great dangers can operate in different ways than "safer," less risky acts (Loveman 1998; McAdam 1986; Wiltfang and McAdam 1991). It is not unreasonable to expect, therefore, that the demands of high-risk settings might force activists into different types of identity work than those that have been described by current research.

Nazi-occupied Warsaw provides such a setting. In what follows, I examine the identity work performed by Jewish resistance fighters operating on the "Aryan side" of the walls of the Warsaw Ghetto. Despite the highly visible and "marked" nature of Jewish identity in Nazi-occupied Europe, these activists were able to use identity strategically in pursuit of their goals. However, instead of freely choosing some aspect of self to deploy strategically, Jewish resistance fighters were forced by circumstance into passing as Gentiles, thereby hiding, rather than displaying, their identity. Moreover, since their activism heightened their Jewish identity at the same time, their identity work was characterized by dissonance rather than harmony, due to the simultaneous enactment of situationally-contradictory identities.

In addition, my account of these activists' identity strategies highlights the ways in which emotion can be used to display identity strategically. As I explain, in the context of Nazi-occupied Warsaw certain emotions (notably, fear and sadness) were situationally specific indicators of Jewishness and therefore required careful management. This discussion of emotion and identity work borrows heavily from Arlie Hochschild's (1979, 1983) concept of "emotion work." Following Hochschild, I conceptualize emotion not as an automatic, largely passive reaction to an external stimulus but as an active process of recognizing one's reaction to some stimulus, labeling that reaction in terms of emotion, and actively displaying the appropriate response. Therefore, my analysis also shows how emotional management can be used to perform activists' identity work in repressive settings.

Case Selection and Data

Although I focus on Jewish resistance activities in Warsaw, it is important to note that Jewish resistance was not limited to that city; indeed, resistance took place in ghettos, camps, and forests throughout Nazi-occupied Europe (Bauer 1989; Grubsztein 1971; Marrus 1989; Tec 1993). However, I choose the case of the Warsaw Ghetto Uprising because it is the best known and best documented instance of collective Jewish resistance during World War II. Thanks to the meticulous record-keeping efforts of Jews interned in the Ghetto and of the Germans who persecuted them, an impressive array of data exist that describe both the Ghetto and the uprising that took place there. This analysis uses both primary and secondary historical sources. The former include twenty published diaries and memoirs written by Ghetto residents, some who survived the

Ghetto and others who perished, yet were still able to preserve their diaries, either by hiding them or by entrusting them to those who did survive (see Corni 2002 on the advantages of such data for describing ghetto life). In addition, I draw on two published collections of documents such as letters, diaries, and reports retrieved after the Ghetto's destruction (Grynberg 2002; Kermish 1986). While most of these sources have been edited and translated, I treat them as primary data and use them to examine activist experiences on the Aryan side of the Ghetto walls. Using these sources affords the opportunity to describe the ways in which these activists used their Jewish identity strategically, in the course of their activist work. When analyzing the data I used the concept of identity work as a guide, reading the materials repeatedly and paying particular attention to quotes and other data that made reference to the activists' Jewish identity and to the ways in which that identity was featured in their resistance activities. I also cite a number of secondary sources, primarily to describe relevant events from the Ghetto's establishment in 1940 until its destruction in May 1943.

The Warsaw Ghetto, 1940–1943

Thirteen months after Germany's invasion of Poland in September 1939, Nazi officials decreed the establishment of a Jewish Ghetto in Warsaw (Gutman 1982, 1994). Located in the city's traditional Jewish Quarter, the Ghetto encompassed a little over one square mile and was completely enclosed by a ten foot high wall, topped with, in various places, barbed wired and/or broken glass. The Ghetto was to become home not only to Warsaw's Jewish population, which consisted of some 360,000 in August 1939, but also to Jews who were relocated from smaller towns and villages in the region around Warsaw, after Nazi edicts forced them from their homes (Ainsztein 1979; Gutman 1982). The Nazis publicly claimed that the Warsaw Ghetto was established in order to protect Jews from anti-Semitic Poles. However, in claims to the Polish population, the stated reason was to isolate the Jewish community in order to prevent outbreaks of typhus among the rest of the city's inhabitants. In practice, the creation of the Ghetto was an efficient means of concentrating the Jewish population in preparation for subjecting them to forced labor, confiscation of property, and eventual deportation to the death camps (Gutman 1982; Hilberg 1979). This process of ghettoization took place throughout Nazi-occupied Poland, with major ghettos constructed in fifty-three cities (Gutman 1994:51).

Conditions in the Warsaw Ghetto were difficult from its inception and grew more dire with time. Extreme crowding coupled with a lack of sufficient food and water caused widespread hunger, disease, and death.[2] For example, there were 898 deaths in the Ghetto in January 1941 but 5,560 in August 1941; overall, ten percent of the Ghetto population died during that year (Gutman 1982:64). Despite these grievances, resistance did not emerge at first. While the topic of resistance was debated at a number of community meetings, many segments of the Ghetto population believed that attempts at resistance would only increase the harsh treatment that residents received at the hands of German soldiers. Already, the soldiers beset Ghetto residents with beatings, forced labor, and a variety of humiliations such as being forced to strip in public and engage in sex acts (Ainsztein 1979; Gutman 1982). Perhaps more importantly, the idea of resistance was not widely embraced because many Warsaw Jews maintained the hope that Germany would lose the war (Gutman 1994). In other words, as long as there was some hope that Warsaw Jews would survive the war, collective resistance was seen as unnecessarily risky. Such perceptions changed greatly in the summer of 1942, however, when German soldiers began daily deportations of Jews from the Warsaw Ghetto to the death camp Treblinka. By the end of September, roughly seventy-five percent of the Ghetto population had either been deported or murdered in the streets (Gutman 1982:213). This unmistakable evidence of the Nazis' genocidal plans ushered in a new mood among Jews in the Ghetto: If everyone was bound to die anyway, it was more honorable to die while fighting than to allow the Nazis to murder Jews unopposed (Gutman 1994). Furthermore, armed resistance against the Nazis would affirm not only the dignity of the Ghetto fighters themselves, but of the Jewish people as a whole (Ainsztein 1979; Cochavi 1995; Gutman 1982, 1994; Kurzman

1993; Lubetkin 1981). The diary of Hirsch Berlinski (quoted in Ainsztein 1979), who became one of the Ghetto fighters, described these views:

> In one way or another, deportation means annihilation. It is therefore better to die with dignity and not like hunted animals. There is no other way out, all that remains to us is to fight...By acting in this manner we shall show the world that we stood up to the enemy, that we did not go passively to our slaughter. Let our desperate act be a protest flung into the face of the world, which has reacted so feebly against the crimes committed by the Nazis against hundreds of thousands of Polish Jews. (Pp. 36–37)

While the majority of Ghetto residents who remained after the deportations in the summer of 1942 eventually came to support the idea of resistance, calls for resistance were strongest among a certain segment of the population: young activists from a number of political organizations and youth movements that pre-dated the war (Cochavi 1995; Gutman 1982, 1994). Pre-existing networks among these activists led to the establishment of two organizations dedicated to armed resistance in the Warsaw Ghetto: the Jewish Fighting Organization (*Żydowska Organizacja Bojowa*, or ŻOB) and the Jewish Military Union (*Żydowski Związek Wojskowy*, or ŻZW). My analysis focuses on the experiences of ŻOB activists, since a lack of archival records on the ŻZW has limited scholarly knowledge about that organization (Gutman 1982:293). In particular, I examine one distinct group of ŻOB activists: those whose work took them beyond the confines of the Ghetto, to the "Aryan side." The tasks of these organizers and couriers included making contact with the Polish underground and other resistance groups outside the Ghetto in order to obtain weapons, supplies, and documents and deliver those goods safely to the Ghetto. Not surprisingly, such work was extremely dangerous: Not only did these individuals put themselves at risk by transporting contraband material, they risked their lives simply by venturing beyond the Ghetto walls—an act that, by Nazi edict, was punishable by death (Engelking 2001; Gutman 1982). Their activist task—which were crucial to the resistance movement as a whole—could not be carried out unless these individuals hid their Jewish identity by passing as non-Jewish Poles. This identity work was, therefore, a strategic means to an end, and an important component of these individuals' activism. In fact, as I demonstrate below, these activists did not want to pass as non-Jews and would have preferred to remain in the Ghetto; the primary goal of their identity work was not personal survival but collective resistance. In what follows, I use the experiences of these individuals to examine activist identity work in the context of extreme repression.

Forced Identity Work: Passing on the Aryan Side

The ŻOB's plans for resistance required a distinct division of labor among activists. Within the Ghetto, small fighting cells were organized, each comprised of activists belonging to a particular youth movement or political organization (Ainsztein 1979; Gutman 1982; Kurzman 1993). Some activists also assumed specific roles; for example, Michal Kiepfisz became an explosives expert responsible for constructing homemade bombs (Gutman 1982; Meed 1979). Another crucial task involved generating the funds needed to pay for weapons and supplies. Despite several years of hardship in the Ghetto, some of those who remained after the deportations had managed either to hold on to some valuables or to amass them (e.g., through selling smuggled goods). Some ŻOB activists engaged in aggressive fundraising efforts—in many cases, exacting funds through coercive taxes and "expropriations" from smugglers and others who had profited from the war—in order to purchase guns (Gutman 1982; Meed 1979; Rotem 1994; Zuckerman 1993). Although they were somewhat successful in these efforts, the high cost and low availability of weapons—all of which had to be purchased outside of the Ghetto and smuggled in—meant that the ŻOB was able to obtain relatively few arms (Gutman 1982; Kurzman 1993).

The purchase and transport of weapons was the responsibility of another distinct group of ŻOB activists, individuals who had to be able to sneak out of the Ghetto and move freely on the Aryan side in order to carry out their tasks. In the context of Nazi-occupied Warsaw, however, Jewishness was a highly visible identity. For instance, all Jews over

the age of ten were forced to wear white arm bands with a blue Star of David, clearly illustrating their identity (Engelking 2001; Gutman 1982). Jewish men's bodies were also marked by their circumcisions (a practice not shared by most other religious and ethnic groups in Europe at that time), and certain facial features and styles of dress were also stereotypically associated with Jewishness. Finally, because Yiddish was the first language of most Jews in Poland, having poor Polish language skills and/or speaking Polish with a Yiddish accent were clear markers of Jewish identity as well (Engelking 2001; Gutman 1982; Rotem 1994). Activists working on the Aryan side therefore had to have "good looks"—i.e., non-Semitic features—and the ability to speak perfect, unaccented Polish in order to pass successfully as non-Jewish Poles. Indeed, such traits determined which individuals went to the Aryan side. For example, activist Vladka Meed wrote (1979) that she was hand-picked for courier work because a ŻOB leader told her that she "looked like a Gentile" (p. 73). ŻOB courier Adina Szwajger possessed similar characteristics, as noted in her memoirs (1990):

> I didn't want to go, because I wanted to stay with everyone else. [But] Marek [Edelman, a ŻOB leader] explained that I had "good" looks—I had blonde hair and blue eyes—that I had no accent when I spoke Polish, which meant that I could walk around town freely, and that I would be of more use to them there than here. (P. 74)

While having "good" features protected these activists somewhat while on the Aryan side, the risk of being discovered was exacerbated by the presence of blackmailers (also referred to, in various sources, as *shmaltsovniks, szmalcovny* or *szmalcownicy*) among the Polish population. These individuals' familiarity with Polish Jews allowed them to detect traces of accents and other subtle features that could go unnoticed by German soldiers; armed with this information, they harassed and extorted fees from their victims in exchange for not turning them in to the Gestapo (Engelking 2001; Rotem 1994; Zuckerman 1993). The memoirs of Simha ("Kazik") Rotem (1994), a ŻOB activist who worked on both sides of the wall, describe several encounters with blackmailers. On one occasion, he and other activists were caught leaving the Ghetto, an act that revealed their Jewish identity:

> We hadn't gone far when we were joined by a group of blackmailers who had immediately recognized that we were Jews and who tried to extort whatever we had. We didn't have anything valuable and I realized that unless we got rid of them, they would turn us over to the Germans. I glanced around and thought quickly. As I looked, a truck passing by in the street came into my field of vision. At once we ran and climbed on from behind. By the time the blackmailers understood what was going on, we were far away, (P. 45)

Working in a setting in which revealing their identity as Jews meant both betraying their fellow activists and being put to death themselves, ŻOB couriers and organizers working outside of the Ghetto, therefore, had to hide their identity at all costs. They did so by strategically deploying an assumed identity: that of a non-Jewish Pole. As noted above, certain physical characteristics and language skills were put to use during these strategic identity displays. Passing as non-Jewish Poles also required church attendance and/or the demonstration of knowledge of Roman Catholic religious rites and practices (Engelking 2001). Additional strategies for masking Jewish identity included obtaining forged identification papers and assuming Polish, non-Jewish names and nicknames. For instance, Vladka Meed's real name was Feigel Peltel; "Vladka" was a nickname for her assumed name of Wladyslawa Kowalska, Similarly, ŻOB activists Simha Rotem, Arieh Wilner, Yitzhak Zuckerman, and Tovye Shaingut went by Polish nicknames "Kazik," "Jurek," "Antek," and "Tadek," respectively (Meed 1979; Rotem 1994; Zuckerman 1993).

Another performative strategy used by ŻOB activists on the Aryan side illustrated the connection between identity and emotion for Jews in Nazi-occupied Warsaw. Given the constant dangers that they faced, many activists on the Aryan side experienced a great deal of fear. For example, describing her daily work as a courier, Szwajger (1990) wrote,

> From the moment that I hid the scraps of paper in my handbag or tucked them into my clothes the shivering began—a sort of fear or anxiety. It was a cold feeling beneath the skin—an awareness that from that moment on every accidental search in the street might be the end. And the day was just beginning. (P. 81)

In the context in which these activists worked, then, public displays of fear—especially during everyday activities such as walking down the street, which no non-Jewish, "regular" Pole should have feared—also stood in as highly visible indicators of one's Jewishness. As Meed (1979) explained.

> "Your eyes give you away," our Gentile friends would tell us. "Make them look livelier, merrier. You won't attract so much attention then." But our eyes kept constantly watching, searching the shadows ahead, glancing quickly behind, seeing our own misfortune and foreseeing even worse to come. Haunted by fear of betrayal, our eyes betrayed us and this knowledge only increased our fear. (P. 194)

These activists' identity work therefore required explicit emotional management to control the emotions that could reveal their Jewish identity (Hochschild 1983; see also Goodwin and Pfaff 2001). One common strategy for hiding fear (and, therefore, for strategically displaying non-Jewishness) was to act confidently, even brashly (Engelking 2001). This strategy is illustrated in a passage from Rotem's memoirs (1994) that describes an exchange between him and his landlady on the Aryan side:

> One evening as I returned home, the landlady asked me, "Are you really a Pole? I think you're also a Jew." She looked at me obliquely. I burst out laughing and replied on the spot. "I'm willing to prove it to you, madam." She said, "Please, sir, prove it!" I unbuckled my belt, unbuttoned my fly, and pulled down my pants: when I was down to my underwear, she turned around and walked out. This was the kind of "existential problem" you came across on a normal day; it was not unique at all. (P. 85)

Given the marked nature of Jewish men's bodies, had the landlady gone through with calling Rotem's bluff his true identity as a Jew would have been clear; apparently, his confidence (as evidenced by the burst of laughter, the lack of hesitation, and his willingness to expose his body) was sufficient to establish his identity as a Pole in her eyes. On the other hand, a display of fear—with or without the removal of his clothes—would have enhanced her suspicions of his Jewishness. Thus identity work performed by ŻOB activists on the Aryan side also required that the activists pay attention to what Hochschild (1979, 1983) calls "feeling rules," or rules that "govern how people try or try not to feel in ways 'appropriate to the situation'" (1979:552). Because these rules differed for Jews and Gentiles, following them correctly could help one "perform" as a member of one group or the other.

Like fear, sadness was an emotion that could reveal Jewishness and, therefore, had to be managed carefully during interactions with others. Many accounts note instances in which an activist experienced grief and sadness—typically, when witnessing harm to another Jew—yet could not display that emotion. For example, the diary entry of ŻOB activist Tuvia Borzykowski (1976), who survived both the January and April Uprisings, read on May 17, 1943:

> We came close to the ghetto wall, a long high wall topped with broken glass...I could see behind the wall naked chimneys which remained standing after the houses were burned. Thick smoke was still rising in the distance. I felt an overwhelming need to make some kind of gesture which would signify that I was passing a sacred site. However, I could not allow myself such a luxury...I had to look like the majority of passersby who were either oblivious to the sight, or wore an expression of malicious satisfaction. (P. 116)

Another activist quoted in Engelking (2001) made a similar remark about her experiences on the Aryan side during the April Uprising:

> It was for me the most painful experience on "the Aryan side." It was quite simply a cataclysm. It was the time of the Easter holiday. There were crowds in the streets going on foot to pay visits to their family or friends...I heard passers-by say, "The Yids are frying, they're spoiling our holiday, it's because of them that we have to walk"...I walked and wept. I suddenly realized that I might give myself away. I got a grip on myself. (P. 55)

Other diaries and memoirs describe additional strategies for managing fear and sadness as a means of masking Jewish identity. Working in pairs was one such strategy; for example, Szwajger (1990) notes that it was important for her to be with another young woman at all times when in public, for "if one of us went out alone, she might forget herself, and have 'sad eyes,' eyes that betrayed the pain within" (p. 83). Telling jokes in order to force laughter during times of emotional stress was another strategy illustrated in Szwajger's account. Also a witness to the April Uprising from the Aryan side, she wrote,

> We stood in Krasinski square and told each other jokes to make ourselves laugh...We stood holding our flowers listening to the explosions, while Swietojerska street burnt and we stood laughing. I saw my own house burning. And I kept laughing. (P. 89)

Hochschild's theory of emotion (1983) suggests that all emotions are managed to some extent. According to her, emotion is first experienced as a "signal" that tells us how we feel about a situation and cues an appropriate course of action to manage and display that feeling; as she writes, "Feeling is something we *do* by attending to inner sensation in a given way, by defining situations in a given way, by managing in given ways...The very act of managing emotion can be seen as part of what the emotion becomes" (p. 27; emphasis in original). As the above quotes suggest, the experiences of ŻOB activists on the Aryan side illustrate a particularly stark example of emotional management, through which activists suppressed their true emotions and forced themselves to publicly display the opposite of what they actually felt. While this suppression of emotion certainly took a lot of work, it is not what Hochschild (1979:560) calls "emotion work," or individuals' efforts to *change* their emotions. Activists on the Aryan side carefully managed their emotional displays in order to maintain their appearance as non-Jews; they did not attempt to change their true feelings. Their work with their own emotions is therefore closer to what Hochschild terms "surface acting," or impression management, than "deep acting," or true emotion work.

Many accounts also refer to explicit ŻOB instructions that activists on the other side of the wall were simply forbidden to cry in public. Privately, however, Jews could unleash their anguish. The memoirs of ŻOB leader Yitzhak Zuckerman (1993), whose Aryan features made him well suited to work outside the Ghetto, describe how a vulnerable moment shared with his Armenian landlady helped each identify the other as "safe":

> One night, I woke up with a hand stroking me. It turns out I had been crying, talking and shouting in Yiddish in my sleep. And here was that "Armenian" woman sitting next to me and weeping…I asked myself if the "Armenian" woman really was Armenian, since she cried like a *Yidishe mama* [Jewish mother]. I didn't ask because there was no need to ask. (P. 380; emphasis in original)

"Passing" as non-Jews was therefore a form of strategic identity work; Jewish activists staged "performances" (Goffman 1959) by strategically deploying what was actually a false identity in order to be able to move freely on the Aryan side long enough to carry out the rest of their activist tasks. They did so by following a number of culturally and situationally relevant codes that indicated Jewishness and non-Jewishness. The choice of which identity to deploy (and, consequently, which one to suppress) was not made freely, however. On the contrary, Jewish activists on the Aryan side *had* to present themselves as non-Jews, given the demands of a highly repressive context that made any display of Jewishness too costly.

Dissonant Identity Work: The Simultaneous Amplification and Suppression of Identity

While the situational demands of the Aryan side required that Jewish activists suppress their true identity, the activist experience actually heightened that identity at the same time. Because of the simultaneous amplification and suppression of identity, these activists' identity work may be described as dissonant as well as forced.

Jewish identity was heightened for the activists on the Aryan side in a number of ways. First, all members of the ŻOB consciously drew on themes of honor and identity when framing their resistance. For instance, during the April Uprising they posted flyers throughout the Ghetto saying. "To fight, to

die, for the honor of our people!" (Kurzman 1993). The memoirs of ŻOB activist Zivia Lubetkin (1981) corroborate these themes:

> We said to ourselves: "We must see the truth for what it is. The Germans want to annihilate us. It is our duty to organize ourselves for defense, and struggle for our honor and the honor of the Jewish people"…We would not go helplessly off to the slaughter. We would no longer die without a struggle. We would wage a battle for ourselves, for the Jews in the Homeland, for the Jews in the Diaspora. (P. 91)

Hence, participation in the resistance can be understood as an expression of collective identity. By resisting, these activists were able to express their membership in a collective that they defined as a strong, proud, and honorable people. In this respect, their resistance was similar to many other instances of collective action which have also been understood as expressions of identity. For example, see Craig Calhoun (1994) on the democracy movement in Tiananmen Square, Rick Fantasia (1988) on the U.S. labor movement, and Kevin Neuhouser (1998) on women's activism in Brazil. Thus, even though activists on the Aryan side could not openly display their Jewish identity, their resistance activity expressed that identity nonetheless.

Because the ŻOB activists understood their resistance as a fight to preserve the honor of the Jewish people, their strong identification with and commitment to the Jewish community is clear. For those activists on the Aryan side, their separation from the rest of the community may have heightened this sense of collective identity even further. Another piece of evidence suggesting that the activist experience intensified their sense of identity as Jews was these activists' oft-expressed desire to be back in the Ghetto. That is, although the individuals working on the Aryan side understood the importance of their work and performed their tasks willingly, many longed to be in the back in the Ghetto with their comrades, "where they belonged." Furthermore, they only intended to stay on the Aryan side long enough to complete their tasks, after which they expected to return to the Ghetto to participate in battle. For instance, Michal Grynberg's (2002) description of Gustawa Wilner's writings about her brother Arieh, a ŻOB activist who worked on the Aryan side, noted that "His sister recalled a conversation after the war with his close friend and comrade-in-arms Maria Jiruska. When Jiruska tried to convince him not to go back to the ghetto, since that would mean certain death, Wilner replied, 'That's where my place is, rather you should wish me an honorable death'" (p. 473). Similarly, Szwajger (1990) wrote:

> All of our feelings were concentrated on what was happening within the ghetto walls. I often went up to the walls with "deliveries"—we would throw things across, or receive things from the other side—and I remember how I dreamt at times that they might let me go back there. (Pp. 84–85)

Activist work on the Aryan side was characterized by simultaneous, yet opposing, identity effects: activists experienced a heightened sense of identity as Jews at the same time that they had to do everything they could to keep that identity hidden.

Not surprisingly, a number of emotions accompanied these activists' strong identification with other Jews. For instance, emotions such as rage and a desire for revenge were prevalent among the activists. These emotions are evident in the following passage from Meed's (1979) memoirs, which describe her reactions to hearing ŻOB leader Abrasha Blum explain the organization's plans for resistance:

> His address was like a wave that both uplifted and engulfed me...I listened breathlessly as he spoke. More than once, since the deportation of my mother, my brother and sister, I had had to suppress the impulse to strike out at the Germans; a passion for revenge raged within me. Now, preparations for direct action were underway. That ungratified desire for revenge which each of us harbored was now to be given outlet. The idea of death had become integrated into our outlook; we knew that all the roads led toward it. Our faces now bore expressions of grim determination. (Pp. 72–73)

Here again, these activists' experiences are similar to those of activists working in other settings, as the growing literature on emotions and social movements has demonstrated (see Goodwin et al. 2001; Jasper 1998; Taylor 2000). What is different about this case is the dissonant nature of the resistance fighters' identity work, which was characterized

by the simultaneous amplification and suppression of both identity and emotion. In the course of their activism, these individuals felt certain emotions (sadness, fear, anger, rage) that compelled their activism. However, as discussed previously, in order to maintain the identity displays on which their activism depended, they had to display other emotions (e.g., happiness) that were quite the opposite of what they actually felt.

Further examination into the role of emotion in the activist experience on the Aryan side shows that nor only was the activists, identity work dissonant, but it appears to have been painful as well. As she quotes in the preceding section suggest, hiding one's identity—and especially in a sociopolitical context that heightened the salience of that identity—was emotionally difficult, leading to feelings of guilt and sadness. Another example from Meed's (1979) memoirs illustrates the emotional costs of hiding her identity from a fellow Jew:

> I looked as his bowed figure, his tattered clothes, his grimy, scratched hands, and the beggar's sack dangling over his shoulders. I yearned to reveal to this sorrowing fellow Jew how deeply I fell with him, but I had to maintain a detached air, without showing the least sign of kinship, posing as a total stranger, lest suspicion be aroused and all of us endangered. (P. 173)

Similarly, Rotem's (1994) memoirs note:

> To pretend all the time, not to identify yourself to anyone—that's not easy to live with. I was often gripped by a strong desire to confess. In general it isn't easy to step into someone's shoes, to project a borrowed image, the image of a Pole. (P. 62)

ŻOB activists on the Aryan side therefore faced a difficult task: They had to publicly downplay and even deny an identity that was strongly felt. Instead of bringing different aspects of self into some coherent whole or achieving some other kind of identity "harmony," their identity work was characterized by dissonance and discomfort.

Discussion: Identity Work, Repression, and the Costs and Risks of Activism

As described in activists' memoirs and other materials, the identity work performed by members of the ŻOB working on the Aryan side of the Warsaw Ghetto was both forced and dissonant. I have argued that their identity work took this form because of the demands of the highly repressive context in which they were working, one that simultaneously increased the salience of their Jewish identity and forced them to hide it.

Admittedly, this analysis is based on an extreme case, one characterized by very high levels of repression. This case was chosen for exactly that reason. As I argued in the beginning of this paper, little is known about identity work in highly repressive contexts. In addition, other specific features of the Warsaw Ghetto make this case especially useful for an analysis of activists' identity work. For instance, the clear demarcation between the Ghetto and the Aryan side provided obvious staging areas for the activists' identity displays (as Jews within the Ghetto, and as non-Jews on the Aryan side). The rules for identity work were also quite clear in that setting; to pass as non-Jews, activists' performances had to feature the proper combination of physical traits and social behaviors (in addition to other displays, such as removing and hiding their identifying armbands). Finally, the genocidal practices of the Nazi regime made the costs for unsuccessful identity performances painfully dear.

Because the extreme costs and risks associated wish Jewish resistance on the Aryan side (and especially with activists' identity work) are such an important aspect of this case, they deserve more discussion here. According to Doug McAdam (1986; Wiltfang and McAdam 1991) and Sharon Erickson Nepstad and Christian Smith (1999), activist work on the Aryan side can be considered both "high-risk" and "high-cost." The costs of activism are the sacrifices a person makes, in order to carry out the action in question; these include "the expenditures of time, money, and energy that are required of a person engaged in any particular form of activism" (McAdam 1986:67). Risks, in contrast, are the costs that *might* result from activism, or "the anticipated dangers—whether legal, social, physical, financial, and so forth—of engaging in a particular type of activity" (McAdam 1986:67; see also Shriver 2000). Gregory Wiltfang and Doug McAdam (1991) also argue that while an activist may have a certain

expectation of risks, she may be unaware of (or even in denial about) all the risks that may actually stem from her activities. They therefore differentiate further between the subjective and objective risks of activism, and suggest that long-term participation in high-risk movements may "toughen" activists or otherwise help to reduce the perceptions about the risks involved in their activities (see also Hollander 1997, 2001 and Linneman 2003 for more on perceptions of risk).

As this analysis has demonstrated, the costs of activism on the Aryan side were quite high. Resistance work in that setting required a great deal of time and energy, not simply to obtain and transport weapons and other necessary items but also to perform the careful, and painful, identity work needed in order to be able to move freely around the city. These findings, therefore, show that the costs of activism can be emotional and identity-based as well as physical and material. Further, by calling attention to these costs, this analysis also suggests that the term "high-cost" can apply to a broader range of acts than previously thought. Thus, activism that takes little time or money an still be "high-cost" if it requires high expenditures of emotion such as sadness or identity work that involves pain and dissonance. Examples of such acts in less repressive contexts than I have discussed here might include having to boycott one's family business or destroying a beloved antique or family heirloom (e.g., a fur coat) in the course of one's activism.

Clearly, the risks of activism on the Aryan side were high as well, since ŻOB members, risked death by leaving the Ghetto. However, these findings also illustrate an aspect of risk that has been inadequately explored by previous work. Although Wiltfang and McAdam (1991) emphasize the potential discrepancies between perceived risks and actual risks, in the case of the Warsaw Ghetto Uprising, ŻOB activists appear to have had a fairly accurate sense of what they risked with their activities. More importantly, these individuals were quite certain that those risks would eventually be realized. Indeed, as noted above, expectations of death were a large part of what motivated resistance in the first place. The strong likelihood—both actual and perceived—of being killed if identified a Jewish meant that activists on the Aryan side had to use multiple strategies of identity management (based on language and appearance as well as emotion) in order to survive long enough to carry our their activist tasks.[3] This case therefore suggests that the probability associated with risk is also important to the dynamic of collective action and deserves mote scholarly attention.

Summary and Conclusions

This paper has used the case of the Warsaw Ghetto Uprising of 1943 to explore activists' strategic identity work in a highly repressive setting. However, the ŻOB activists working as couriers and organizers on the "Aryan side" of the Ghetto walls also had to suppress that identity and emotion in order to survive the dangerous conditions long enough to do their work. Their identity work was therefore characterized by the simultaneous amplification and suppression of identity and emotion, the combination of which increased the costs of activism, beyond the time and energy needed for these individuals to carry out their tasks. Importantly, this identity work differed from the identity strategies identified by current research. For Jews living in Nazi-occupied Warsaw, the choice of which aspect of self to deploy was taken away; instead of being freely chosen, their identity work was forced. Furthermore, in order to stage collective action, activists had to downplay their true identity during their activist work. The nature of that work, and the context in which they were working, highlighted that identity at the same time. In addition to their identity work being forced, therefore, their work was also dissonant. Activists had to simultaneously "be and not be" themselves in order to carry out their resistance activities. For them, identity work was not intended to align one's self-concept with a collective identity or to manage diversity in movements, but to maintain dissonant identities.[4]

What, then, can an examination of this extreme case teach us about identity and social movements more generally? First, despite the highly visible nature of Jewish identity in Nazi-occupied Poland and the costs associated with being Jewish, it is notable that members of the ŻOB whose work took them to the Aryan side of the Warsaw Ghetto were

able to use their identity strategically in the course of their activism. By illustrating the strategic use of identity in a setting that would seem to preclude it, this analysis demonstrates the robustness of identity work in social movements. At the same time, however, these activists' identity work was quite different than the "free" and "harmonic" work described by current research, differences that can be attributed to the highly repressive setting in which these activists worked. This study also illustrates another important, if basic, point: Identity work reflects and is shaped by the context in which it is performed. Additional examples of forced and dissonant identity work used to facilitate collective resistance in other repressive settings might include light-skinned African American slaves passing as white in order to mobilize resources for slave rebellions or to help ferry others along the Underground Railroad, or women crossdressing as men in order to participate in battle to further some broader political cause (regarding the latter, see Young 1996).

As previously noted, this analysis also has implications for the costs and risks of activism. I suggest that the multiple strategies of identity management used by ŻOB activists on the Aryan side of the walls of the Warsaw Ghetto were not only the result of what these activists risked—specifically, death—but were also a response to the absolute certainty that they would be put to death if identified as Jewish. Because of that certainty, identity management was a necessity. In contrast, if there had been less danger—that is, if there were some way for Jews to live freely as Jews on the Aryan side—identity management might have been something that activists could choose for reasons other than survival (e.g., to gain Polish support for the resistance), which would be closer to the "free" identity work characteristic of most social movement research.

Finally, although I have argued that forced and dissonant identity work is characteristic of activism in highly repressive settings, it is important to remember that activists face repression in a wide variety of contexts. While it is unlikely that these findings would be replicated in a study of activism in a setting with little or no repression, they nonetheless point to the existence of a wider range of types of identity work than has been discussed by research to date. It is therefore worth exploring identity work in less repressive settings to see if any features of the external environment make that work "forced" or "dissonant" to any extent at all. Additional studies of activism in both high-risk and low-risk settings will help document and explain the strategic use of identity in social movements more fully.

NOTES

An earlier version of this paper was presented at the annual meetings of the Midwest Sociological Society, Chicago, IL., April 2003. The author wishes to thank the audience at that session, along with Jim Holstein, Dan Myers, Jocelyn Hollander, Viktor Gecas, Diane Wolf, and several anonymous reviewers, for their comments on previous drafts. This research was supported by a PRF Summer Faculty Grant, a College of Liberal Arts Dean's Incentive Grant, and a Library Scholar's Grant, all from Purdue University.

1. There were actually two armed uprisings in the Warsaw Ghetto: the first was a four-day battle between Jews and Nazis in January 1943, and the second began on April 19, 1943 and lasted until mid-May, at which point the Ghetto was razed (Gutman 1994; Kurzman 1993). Together, these episodes are referred to as the Warsaw Ghetto Uprising. These events are distinct from the Warsaw Uprising of 1944, a city-wide uprising against Nazi occupying forces.

2. While historians agree that the Ghetto was crowded, they disagree on the exact size of the population. For instance, Kurzman (1993) writes that the population peaked at 500,000 in the summer of 1941, while Gutman (1982) estimates that the Ghetto reached its maximum size in March 1941 with a population of 445,000.

3. The probability of death was, of course, high for all Jews in Warsaw (as well as throughout Nazi-occupied Poland), whether or not they participated in collective resistance. However, my goal in calling attention to the strong likelihood of being killed is not to explain why some people resisted and others did not. Instead, it is to describe the experiences of the activists themselves.

4. Though not a social movements analysis, Gallant and Cross (1992) provide another example of identity work performed by Jews during the Holocaust. Focusing on Jews in concentration camps, they use the concept of "challenged identity" to refer to the transformative process through which individuals who had been dehumanized by the disruption and horror of camp life managed to recapture their sense of self and, by forging connections with others, instill in themselves a will to survive, However, because the construction of a "challenged identity" builds on the individual's core, true self, it is distinct from the identity work I have described here and is in fact closer to the "harmonic" identity work characteristic of previous research.

24.
Persistent Resistance: Commitment and Community in the Plowshares Movement

SHARON ERICKSON NEPSTAD

A considerable amount of research has focused on how individuals become involved in social movements. Few studies, however, examine how people maintain an activist commitment once they have been successfully recruited. This gap in the literature is surprising, given that a movement's vitality

Nepstad, Sharon Erickson. 2004. "Persistent Resistance: Commitment and Community in the Plowshares Movement." *Social Problems* 51: 43–60. Reprinted by Permission of The University of California Press.

and longevity are dependent on its ability to attract *and* retain members. The lack of research on activist retention may be due to the assumption that once enlisted, individuals remain engaged until the movement's demise. Yet studies have documented that some activists leave a movement before protest subsides. (Klandermans 1997), while others are able to sustain their resistance even after movement organizations cease to operate (Taylor 1989). There is a need for more systematic attention to the question of how movement commitment endures

over time, fostering persistence among some protestors.

In this article, I examine long-term activist
commitment in the Plowshares movement. This is
a pacifist movement instigated by members of the
Catholic Left who gained notoriety for draft board
raids during the Vietnam War. As the war ended,
they used similar controversial tactics to resist the
expanding nuclear arms race. Their first action
occurred in 1980, when eight people entered a
General Electric (GE) plant outside of Philadelphia,
armed with household hammers and bottles of
their own blood. Upon locating GE's Mark 12A
nuclear missiles, they enacted the vision of the
prophet Isaiah, who spoke of a day when "nations
shall beat their swords into plowshares and their
spears into pruning hooks; one nation shall not
raise the sword against another, nor shall they train
for war again" (Isaiah 4:2). The group hammered
on the missiles, poured blood on security documents, and shredded blueprints. Afterwards, they
prayed for peace until they were arrested, charged,
and taken to jail. They were eventually convicted
of burglary, conspiracy, and criminal mischief and
given sentences that ranged from five to ten years
(Laffin and Montgomery 1987).

The Plowshares movement is a useful case for
exploring persistent activist commitment for several reasons. First, the movement has demonstrated
endurance while many other peace groups have disbanded. Roughly a quarter-century after the first
action at General Electric, Plowshares campaigns
continue and have expanded internationally. To
date, close to 200 people from nine different countries have engaged in approximately 70 Plowshares
actions. This is remarkable considering the broader
movement against nuclear weapons subsided in
the early 1990s as the Berlin Wall fell, the Soviet
Union collapsed, and the Cold War ended. In fact,
35 percent of all peace organizations had ceased
operations by 1992 (Edwards and Marullo 1995) due
to dissipating public concern about nuclear arms.
Second, this is an appropriate case because many
Plowshares participants demonstrate a high degree
of commitment. Survey responses indicate that 100
percent are still involved in anti-war activism today.
Naturally, there is likely a self-selection bias in the

sample that makes this percentage unusually high;
the respondents may well reflect the most committed Plowshares activists. However, since I am
focusing on the mechanisms that enable people to
persistently resist over time, these are the precise
individuals who can shed light on the topic, as most
respondents have been involved in the movement
for ten or more years. Finally, their ongoing commitment is even more noteworthy in light of the
costs associated with their unique tactics of resistance. Although the average time served for these
acts of symbolic disarmament is 1.5 years, some
have received sentences as high as 18 years. Despite
the risks and consequences, many remain active in
the movement.

Movement Recruitment, Exiting, and Persistence

Theories of activist persistence ought to be connected to the broader dynamics of recruitment,
exiting, or retention. Of these three processes, we
know the most about differential recruitment—
that is, the factors that distinguish activists from
the rest of the population. Many recruitment studies substantiate the ideas of the micromobilization
model developed by David Snow, Louis Zurcher,
and Sheldon Ekland-Olson (1980). This model
posits that recruitment is primarily determined
by structural availability rather than psychological disposition. In other words, whether one participates in collective action is mainly a reflection of
organizational ties to the movement, relational ties
to other activists, and the absence of countervailing
pressures.

In a study of high-risk activism in the Mississippi
Freedom Summer campaign, Doug McAdam (1986)
expands upon this micromobilization model. As
portrayed in Figure 1, he argues that receptive attitudes predispose some individuals toward a movement. While such receptivity is necessary, it does
not sufficiently account for recruitment. Openness
translates into participation when sympathizers are
pulled into the movement by social ties to activists.
New recruits subsequently begin playing the activist role by engaging in low-risk forms of protest.
Those who are "biographically available"—that
is, relatively free from life responsibilities such as

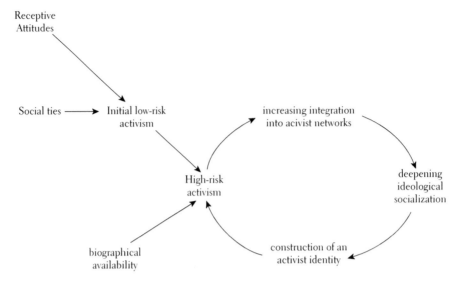

Figure 24.1 McAdam's (1986) Model of High-Risk Activism

full-time employment and family obligations—may be willing to increase their level of involvement by engaging in high-risk actions. This in turn leads to greater integration into activist networks, deepening ideological socialization, and the construction of an activist identity.

The micromobilization model provides insight into the recruitment process, but does not give much attention to the factors that contribute to activist disengagement. Since Freedom Summer was a short-term, one shot campaign, the issue of retention over time is irrelevant. Yet many movements endure for years, entail multiple campaigns, and have no clear end point. Under these circumstances, some participants inevitably become less committed or drop out completely. This is likely to happen when members' convictions weaken and their relational and organizational ties to the movement wane. These trends are often related. As beliefs abate, activists may withdraw from movement networks; similarly, if members are not strongly integrated into activist groups, the intensity of their convictions may dissipate. Social ties to movement outsiders can also facilitate disengagement, especially if these relationships are with significant others who oppose this type of activism

(Aho 1994). Other studies document that activist termination may be attributed to increase in life responsibilities (Downton and Wehr 1997), competition from other voluntary associations (Cress. McPherson, and Rotolo 1997), or burnout, which Bert Klandermans (1997) describes as high levels of psychological tension combined with strong commitment and the incursion of significant costs. Thus, looking at activist commitment over time, we must amend McAdam's model to include the parallel influences that can derail participation, as conveyed in Figure 2.

While all these factors can undermine long-term activism, not everyone who is exposed to such countervailing forces quits protesting. So what distinguishes those who leave a movement from those who remain engaged? In a comparative study of "persisters," "terminators," and "shifters" in the Dutch peace movement, Klandermans (1997) found that persistent activists possessed higher levels of commitment than those who dropped out. Steven Barkan, Steven Cohn, and William Whitaker (1993, 1995) elaborate on the factors that foster an enduring movement commitment. They posit that activists are more likely to exhibit firm allegiance when their overarching beliefs and values are compatible

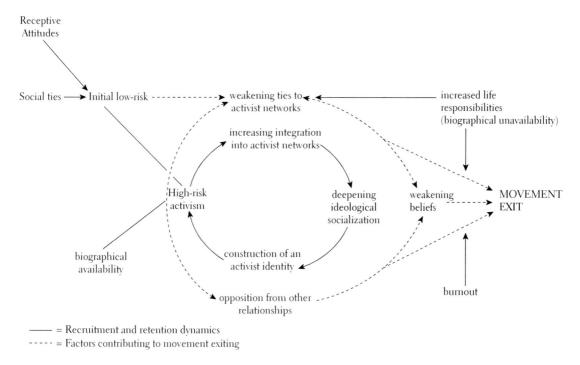

Receptive
Attitudes

Social ties ⟶ Initial low-risk ---------→ weakening ties to ◄———— increased life
activist networks responsibilities
(biographical unavailability)

increasing integration
into activist networks

High-risk
activism

deepening
ideological
socialization

weakening
beliefs

MOVEMENT
EXIT

biographical
availability

construction of an
activist identity

opposition from other
relationships

burnout

———— = Recruitment and retention dynamics
- - - - = Factors contributing to movement exiting

Figure 24.2 Model of Movement Recruitment and Exiting

with a social movement organization (SMO). They note that while "interest in achieving SMO goals and agreement with SMO ideologies often go hand in hand, that is not always the case. For example, although many feminists might agree with the goal of an anti-pornography SMO led by religious fundamentalists, the two groups would disagree on their reasons for opposing pornography and many other points" (p. 364). Feminist members of this organization, therefore, are likely to be less dedicated than their fundamentalist counterparts. Barkan and associates also argue that those who have close friendships with other activists and with leaders are more devoted to a movement. Finally, they maintain that social-psychological perceptions partly condition members' level of involvement. Those who trust movement leaders and feel that the movement is effective demonstrate higher degrees of commitment.

While Barkan, Cohn, and Whitaker delineate the elements that promote an enduring activist

commitment, Klandermans draws our attention to the fact that commitment is a multifaceted phenomenon. He notes that it is comprised of an *affective* component, reflecting the degree of emotional attachment to a movement, a *continuance* component—referring to the costs associated with leaving a movement that consequently encourage ongoing involvement—and a *normative* component, indicating the moral obligation individuals feel to continue working for movement goals (Allen and Meyer 1990; Meyer and Allen 1991; Meyer, Allen, and Gellatly 1993).

These three forms of commitment emerge from independent sources. Affective commitment develops through pleasurable interactions with fellow activists and through material or cultural rewards gained from movement participation. Hence people are more likely to be loyal to a union, for instance, when they enjoy working with other members and the union wins concessions from employers. Verta Taylor (1989) also found that the commitment of a small cadre of feminists remained strong from 1945–1960, despite the decline of the broader women's movement and the inhospitable conditions of that era. She argues that this was partly due to the close friendships and the rich cultural life that developed at the National Women's Party (NWP) headquarters in Washington, DC. Through NWP events and celebrations, a strong affective commitment was forged that sustained the women's movement in this abeyance phase.

Normative commitment emerges from long-term socialization processes that instill beliefs that are consistent with the movement, as well as the moral imperative to fight injustices. Klandermans believes there is little that movement leaders can do to affect this type of commitment, since people either have a preexisting affinity to a movement or not, but he does state that organizers can engage in "framing" (Snow et al. 1986) to increase the degree of congruence between individual values and movement goals. Yet he portrays beliefs, values, and moral obligations as static and fixed. I suggest that normative commitment can fluctuate, since convictions, particularly militant ones, may diminish with time if they are not continually reinforced. Therefore, leaders may need to develop strategies and practices that rejuvenate moral beliefs in order to keep normative commitment strong.

Continuance commitment is formed when activists make extraordinary sacrifices for a movement, such as risking their own safety or forfeiting careers and relationships for a cause. According to Klandermans, this makes members more invested in the movement since a movement's failure would render these sacrifices worthless. Donatella della Porta (1992) concurs. In a study of Italian and German underground groups, she argues that "the militants' very high initial investment reduced the likelihood that they would leave their organization… They persisted in their involvement because surrendering implied 'losing' everything they had already paid as the costs for entering the underground" (p. 284). This finding is further supported by Rosabeth Moss Kanter's (1968) comparison of successful and failed utopian communities. She found that those communes that survived required some degree of sacrifice and personal investment from their members, giving them a greater stake in the fate of the group. Although this helps us understand *why* activists may persist in their resistance, most studies of high-risk activism do not sufficiently explain *how* movements help people make the sacrifices that create continuance commitment.

These three forms of commitment are positively associated with persistent activism, yet the factors that undermine support must also be addressed. James Downton and Paul Wehr (1991, 1997) examine the obstacles to long-term engagement in a comparative study of activists in the U.S. peace movement. They found that a key characteristic distinguishing persisters from terminators is the capacity to manage issues that disrupt movement participation. Persisters were able to minimize the effects of opposition to their political work through a variety of coping mechanisms, such as humor and meditation. They also countered the impact of cross-pressures—negative reactions and criticism from significant others—by finding alternative sources of support. They implemented strategies to avoid burnout, such as regularly scheduled time for recreation. Moreover, they arranged their lives to accommodate their activism, often pursuing careers in social change organizations or only accepting employment that offered a flexible schedule. Those who successfully managed these threats to commitment were more likely to remain involved in peace activism over time.

These studies advance our knowledge of long-term movement commitment. However, these researchers do not adequately address a number of issues. First, since their emphasis is on delineating the differences between movement persisters and dropouts, they give less attention to the specific mechanisms employed to sustain commitment over time. That is, their theories explain *why* persisters are able to remain active but do not convey as much information about *how* movements cultivate long-term engagement. Precisely how do radical groups reinforce members' militant beliefs when widespread protest has ceased? How do they keep emotional bonds strong decade after decade? What cultural practices do they implement to rejuvenate moral convictions and the willingness to act on them, regardless of the cost? Second, the issue of obstacle management is only addressed at the individual level. Downton and Wehr imply that the ability to minimize the factors that contribute to commitment erosion—namely burnout, opposition, and life responsibilities—is primarily a reflection of personal skills. They do not explore how movement organizations and leaders may institutionalize strategies for reinforcing commitment and overcoming barriers to long-term activism. Finally, none of these studies address the unique challenges involved in ongoing participation in high-risk campaigns. Barkan, Cohn, and Whitaker (1993) acknowledge this limitation, stating that "the sources of commitment in...decidedly low-risk activism may be different from those in SMOs advocating more risky forms of political action" (p. 372). McAdam's study of the short-term, high-risk Freedom Summer campaign only examines the recruitment process; consequently, we have no knowledge of the factors that sustain high-risk activism over the long run.

To address these issues, I focus on persisters in the Plowshares movement with the aim of explaining how their normative, affective, and continuance commitment is maintained over the long run. I examine the practices developed by movement leaders to sustain radical beliefs and revitalize affective ties that, without maintenance, can easily atrophy with time. I also explore how Plowshares organizers have formed structures of support that help persisters overcome obstacles to long-term, high-risk activism, enabling them to make significant sacrifices for the movement.

Methodology

To explore persistent resistance in the Plowshares movement, I draw upon data collected using a triangulated methodology that incorporates a variety of research methods and data sources (Denzin 1978). I began by engaging in participant observation at Jonah House, an intentional community formed by leaders of the Catholic Left and the center of many Plowshares actions. I also attended the gatherings of the Atlantic Life Community, a network of Catholic Left anti-war activists (including many Plowshares participants) who meet for weekend retreats several times a year. Before participating, I spoke with movement leaders about my research interests and made no attempt to conceal my academic role. During this time, I took extensive field notes on community practices and informal conversations I had with Plowshares activists.

Based on this qualitative data, I designed a mail survey that addressed basic demographic information, religious beliefs and practices, prior history of activism, participation in community, and so forth. To locate activists, I used movement documents to compile a list of individuals who participated in Plowshares actions between September 1980 and June 2001. Since the movement has no formal organization or membership, I contacted the editors of *The Nuclear Resister,* a newsletter that provides information on prisoners of conscience. They gave me addresses for many Plowshares activists. When I reached these individuals, I asked them to assist me in contacting others. Out of 161 living activists, I was able to locate 112 people. I sent the surveys, along with follow-up reminders two months later. This resulted in 54 individuals participating in the project, reflecting a 48 percent response rate and roughly one-third of the entire movement. Although this rate is not strong, the unique circumstances of the project must be taken into consideration. A number of activists were serving sentences at the time. Prison authorities examine incoming and outgoing mail and some facilities prohibit the sending of self-addressed, stamped envelopes to inmates. This may have decreased the response rate. Additionally, the Plowshares movement has at times experienced severe repression and government infiltration (Polner and O'Grady 1997). This might justifiably make activists reluctant to share their experiences with an unknown researcher. Lower response rates are not unusual in studies of deviant groups.

To clarify the survey responses, I conducted follow-up interviews with approximately 40 activists. These individuals were selected from the sample based on their availability and legal status. Those who were incarcerated or facing impending criminal charges were not interviewed. The interviews lasted between one and three hours, and were tape recorded and transcribed. Finally, I also draw upon archival documents that include court transcripts, public statements, prison journals, and letters of Plowshares activists as well as newspaper articles, letters, and books.

Background

To understand the practices of the Plowshares movement requires some background information. The movement is heavily shaped by the Catholic Worker tradition started by Dorothy Day in the 1930s. Working as a reporter for a socialist newspaper, Day covered issues of poverty, labor, and immigration. Although she fought for women's suffrage, Day was influenced by anarchism and she felt voting had little value since the country needed a comprehensive social revolution. Eventually, she converted to Catholicism and combined her political commitments with her religious beliefs. Together with Peter Maurin, she began publishing a newspaper called *The Catholic Worker* (mimicking the communist *Daily Worker*) that integrated labor issues with Catholic teachings. They also established "houses of hospitality" that provide food and shelter to the destitute and homeless (Klejment 1996; McNeal 1992).

The Catholic Worker movement advocates more than works of mercy, however. It offers a radical interpretation of the gospel that includes a commitment to pacifism, voluntary poverty, communal living, and reconstruction of the social order. It aims to create a more just society by withdrawing from the capitalist system as much as possible, by dialoguing on a variety of issues—from labor practices to militarism—and by confronting those who perpetuate exploitative practices. It holds that it is not enough to feed the poor and shelter the homeless; the cause of these social ills must also be addressed (Chatfield 1996). One of Day's renowned acts of resistance occurred in 1955 when New York held mandatory defense drills in preparation for a nuclear attack. Anyone who did not participate risked a one-year prison sentence. Yet when the drills began—with sirens signaling people to go to their designated fall-out shelter—Day and several Catholic Workers refused to cooperate, gathering in City Hall Park in protest. They were arrested but the scene was re-enacted the following year, and again in 1957. Each passing year, public sympathy for

the protest expanded so that by 1961, nearly 2,000 people of various affiliations joined the Catholic Worker crowd in the park. New York papers proclaimed the civil defense drills an exercise in futility and city officials eventually ended the practice (Forest 1997).

Day provided a model of commitment that combines spirituality, works of mercy, activism, and communal living. She also legitimized civil disobedience as an appropriate Catholic response to unjust laws. Her influence on a younger generation of radical Catholics was evident during the Vietnam War when Catholic Workers participated in rallies and sit-ins. Yet despite expanding opposition, the White House did not change its foreign policy. Out of this context, two priests—Phil Berrigan and his brother, Daniel—emerged as passionate and eloquent critics of the Vietnam War. They argued that protest was not stopping the war and more effective means of nonviolent resistance were needed. They instigated a shift from protest to revolt in October 1967, when Phil Berrigan and three others raided a Selective Service office in Baltimore and poured blood over draft files. Several months later, Dan Berrigan joined his brother and seven others in a second action. They broke into another Maryland draft board office and removed hundreds of conscription files, burning them with napalm made from instructions found in a Special Forces handbook. These actions propelled the Berrigans into positions of leadership, establishing them as the architects of a new type of Catholic resistance (Klejment and Roberts 1996; McNeal 1992).

These brother priests spent several years in federal penitentiaries for the draft board raids. In prison, they formed communities with other anti-war activists. They met regularly for Bible study, prayer, political discussion and action, including fasting and refusing to work in war-related prison industries. They came to appreciate the value of community, acknowledging it as a key factor that sustained their resistance during incarceration. Phil Berrigan (1996) wrote:

> During my years behind bars, I had seen young men succumb to despair. Arriving with high ideals, they broke under the strain of prison life...Others withdrew into sullen shells, devoured

by anger and loneliness. They had taken a principled stand, but without the support of a loving community they couldn't withstand the brutality of prison. . . . *Resisters cannot persist and survive without community.* Sooner or later, they will be frustrated and crushed. That is why we invested so much time, effort, and money into starting Jonah House. We wanted a place where people could share meals and ideas, study scripture together, and support one another through the long haul. (Pp. 166–7, my emphasis)

Upon his release from prison in 1973, Phil Berrigan returned to Baltimore where he announced that he had married another Catholic Left activist, Elizabeth McAlister. They were promptly excommunicated from the church since both were members of religious orders at the time and had not been released from their vows. They rented a house with several others, forming a community known as Jonah House. Following the Catholic Worker tradition, the community places a strong emphasis on voluntary poverty, recognizing that it is the U.S. population's obsession with possessions and property that has led to the stockpiling of weapons to protect them. Members hold all resources in common, working as independent painting contractors when necessary to earn funds for basic living expenses. Yet Jonah House differs from the Catholic Worker tradition in that its primary emphasis is on resistance to war and militarism rather than serving the poor. So as the Vietnam War ended, members of Jonah House planned acts of revolt against the nuclear arms race. Those plans culminated in 1980 when the Berrigans and six others entered the General Electric plant in Pennsylvania to "beat swords into plowshares" and

to challenge GE's motto. "We bring good things to life."

The General Electric action inspired others and soon Catholic Left activists around the country were engaged in symbolic disarmament at military facilities and weapons production sites. Many visited or lived at Jonah House in preparation for their action. Although McAlister and Berrigan welcomed people to stay at Jonah House, they quickly realized that the broader network of Catholic Left activists would need to meet regularly to sustain anti-war resistance and to assist each other with the logistics and consequences of these high-risk campaigns. Thus, they organized regularly scheduled retreats, drawing people throughout the Northeast and mid-Atlantic region. Consequently, they named this activist network the Atlantic Life Community.

Commitment and Community in the Plowshares Movement

According to long-term Plowshares activists, the Atlantic Life Community and Jonah House serve a central role in sustaining movement engagement. Survey responses indicate that most persisters are linked to these Catholic Left communities. Table 1 reveals that 97 percent of respondents have visited Jonah House, almost 94 percent of respondents have attended an Atlantic Life Community retreat, and over 80 percent have volunteered at a Catholic Worker House. Table 2 indicates that Plowshares activists feel these ties are essential to the longevity of their commitment to war resistance. Nearly 91 percent stated that Jonah House is extremely or very important in sustaining their faith and activism, and almost 90 percent shared the same sentiments

Table 1 Plowshares Activists' Participation in Catholic Left Communities (percentages)

	Yes	No	Total
Volunteered at Catholic Worker	81.3	18.7	100
Attended Atlantic Life Community gatherings	93.8	6.2	100
Visited Jonah House	96.9	3.1	100

N = 54.

Table 2. Importance of Catholic Left Communities in Sustaining Plowshares Activism (percentages)

	Extremely Important	Very Important	Somewhat Important	Not Very Important	Not At All Important	Total
Jonah House	68.8	21.9	9.3	0	0	100
Catholic Worker	55.2	34.5	6.9	3.4	0	100
Atlantic Life Community	43.4	20.0	23.3	3.3	10	100

N = 54.

about Catholic Worker communities. Close to two-thirds believe that the Atlantic Life Community is extremely or very important in maintaining their resistance to militarism. But why? What occurs in these communities that sustains commitment and counters the tendency toward exiting?

Community as a Plausibility Structure that Reinforces Beliefs

Catholic Left communities strengthen normative commitment to the movement by functioning as "plausibility structures." This term was developed by Peter Berger, who argued that beliefs about the supernatural, as well as other views at odds with mainstream society, would weaken under social pressures that deem such perspectives untenable. To maintain faith, people must form groups where they "huddle together with like-minded fellow deviants—and huddle very closely indeed. Only in a counter-community of considerable strength does cognitive deviance have a chance to maintain itself" (Berger 1969:19). Berger's claim is supported by studies of doomsday groups such as *When Prophecy Fails* (Festinger, Riecken, and Schachter 1956). This work chronicles the events surrounding a woman who claimed to be receiving messages from outer space about an impending flood. On the predicted day of disaster, her prophecy failed to materialize. As a result, some of her followers lost faith, but others did not. The factor distinguishing the ongoing believers from the former believers was social support. One group had awaited the flood together; when the disaster did not transpire, the leader reportedly received another extraterrestrial message stating that the city was saved because of their

faithfulness. These participants not only accepted the explanation, they also became active proselytizers. Those who were isolated from the group, however, relinquished their faith in the prophetess.

Community, therefore, can sustain even highly improbable beliefs. It does so by providing interaction with "confirming others" and by offering explanations that legitimate beliefs and assuage doubts. Plausibility structures often use rituals as well, such as prayer and group singing, to regularly reinforce alternative values and views (Billings 1990). Berger (1969) maintains that "it is only as the individual remains within this structure that the conception of the world in question will remain plausible to him" (p. 40). Plowshares activists agree. One stated:

> My family doesn't support me at all. I've also gone through hard times with church leaders [because of my Plowshares actions]. But I have a community that says, "You're not crazy. What you're doing is right." I have friends who are behind me 100 percent...You have to meet with like-minded activists. All of the long-haul activists have learned that. It simply isn't possible to continue working for peace without community.

As plausibility structures, Catholic Left communities have succeeded in keeping robust many activists' commitment to Plowshares goals and values. This is evident in the responses to a survey question that asked respondents to rank the importance of various activities from war resistance and fighting injustice to prayer, charitable giving, and voting. The results are summarized in Table 3. Not surprisingly, "resisting war," "resisting injustice," and "fighting for the poor and oppressed" were ranked

Table 3. Beliefs and Values of Plowshares Activists (percentages)

	Extremely Important	Very Important	Moderately Important	Somewhat Important	Not Important At All	Total
Resist war	87.1	9.7	3.2	0	0	100
Resist injustice	87.1	9.7	0	0	3.2	100
Fight for poor & oppressed	87.1	9.7	3.2	0	0	100
Follow one's conscience	86.7	10	0	3.3	0	100
Environmental protection	74.2	22.6	0	0	3.2	100
Prayer	74.2	19.4	3.2	3.2	0	100
Works of mercy	67.7	29.0	3.3	0	0	100
Support fair labor practices	62.1	31.0	6.9	0	0	100
Change the social order	61.5	15.4	19.2	3.9	0	100
Bible study	60.0	23.3	10	6.7	0	100
Simple lifestyle	58.1	29.0	9.7	0	3.2	100
Withdraw from capitalism	51.7	13.8	13.8	13.8	6.9	100
Proselytizing	15.4	0	3.9	19.2	61.5	100
Giving to charity	10.7	14.3	21.4	21.4	32.2	100
Sexual purity	8	8	36	12	36	100
Attend church regularly	0	3.8	23.1	23.1	50	100
Theological orthodoxy	0	3.6	7.1	14.3	75	100
Voting	0	0	13.8	17.2	69	100

the highest, with 96.8 percent indicating that it is extremely or very important. Nearly the same number (96.7 percent) share this sentiment about "following one's conscience, even when it means going against the church." Although respondents gave high marks to the defining traits of the Catholic Worker movement—i.e., works of mercy, supporting fair labor practices, and changing the social order—they are clearly secondary. This finding reflects continuity with the values of the Catholic Worker movement, but also a stronger connection to Jonah House and the Plowshares movement's emphasis on resistance. Voting was ranked the least important, which also reflects Catholic Left beliefs.

Recall that Dorothy Day placed little value on voting, instead calling for a social revolution. Phil Berrigan also argued that "voting only encourages [politicians]. Vote with your actions." This view is still prevalent, as nearly 70 percent of respondents indicated that voting is not important at all. Thus, persistent activists retain a strong normative commitment, even decades after the movement began.

Yet what type of cultural practices do Catholic Left communities employ to reinforce these beliefs over time? To address this question, I draw upon my participant, observation research at the 2002 Feast of Innocents retreat of the Atlantic Life Community. This retreat occurs several days after Christmas, on the liturgical commemoration of events described in the gospel of Matthew. The scripture recounts the story of Jesus' birth and the Magi's search for the Christ child. Herod, the regional ruler, hears reports of a newborn king, a messiah, and fears that the child poses a threat to his rule, so he orders the slaying of all male children under two years of age. Retreat organizers built off this biblical story. Throughout the weekend, contemporary leaders were compared to Herod and the slaughter of children in the Middle East was linked to the massacre of innocents at the time of Christ's birth. U.S. actions toward Iraq were portrayed as a reflection of gospel themes, reinforcing the moral obligation to resist.

The Atlantic Life Community also uses rituals to underscore movement beliefs and goals. Each morning and evening, participants gather for singing, prayer, and biblical reflection. At the start of the retreat, a nun shared her thoughts on the scriptural account of the slaughter of the innocents. She discussed biblical commentaries that describe Herod as a manipulative, ambitious leader who was willing to crush any challenges to his authority. She spoke of the parallels between the behavior of current world leaders and Herod, stating that violence and oppression arise from the lust for power. She concluded by calling all to look at the Herod within themselves and their society, and asking each person to make a commitment to eradicate these violent impulses. After the meditation, the group sang. Given the proximity to Christmas, many of the songs were holiday carols that had been changed to reflect the retreat theme and movement goals. For instance, we sang "The Twelve Days of Christmas" using the following alternative lyrics:

On the first day of invasion my leader said
to me,
    "They're the most dangerous nation in
    the world."
On the second day's invasion my leader said
to me,
    "They have weapons of mass destruction;
    They're the most dangerous nation in the
    world."
On the third day's invasion my leader said
to me,
    "They won't allow inspections;

They have weapons of mass destruction;
    They're the most dangerous nation in the
    world."
On the fourth day of invasion my leader said
to me,
    "They didn't sign the biological weapons
    treaty;
    won't allow inspections; weapons of mass
    destruction;
    They're the most dangerous nation in the
    world."
On the fifth day's invasion my leader said
to me,
    "DEMAND REGIME CHANGE NOW!
    Didn't sign the biological weapons treaty;
    won't allow inspections;
    Weapons of mass destruction; they're the
    most dangerous nation in the world."
On the sixth day (etc.)....

Similarly, we sang "Silent Night, Holy Night" with the following words:

> Silent night, holy night
> All is not calm
> All is not right
> Millions die from war and poverty
> Children living in misery
> Stop the violence, choose life
> Stop the violence, choose life.

The evening closed with a prayer written by three nuns imprisoned for a Plowshares action. Like the biblical meditation, the prayer reflects the retreat's theme of crying out against the state's (Herod's) slaughter of the innocents. The following excerpt illustrates how this ritual reinforces Catholic Left beliefs in fighting for justice and resisting militarism, thereby strengthening normative commitment.

All: Oh God, hear the voice of your servant.
    Hear the cry of your people.
Leader: Philip Berrigan has been present in the
    wilderness of these Washington. DC sites for
    decades. Listen to his voice crying. "Disarm!
    Disarm!"
All: We join our voices to his, to Dorothy
    Day, Catholic Workers, and Jonah House.

Disarm! Disarm! Oh God, hear the voice of
your servant. Hear the cry of your people.

Leader: Kathy Kelly has been present in
Iraq many times since 1990. Listen to her
voice crying. "Stop the sanctions! Stop the
bombing!"

All: We join our voices to hers and to Voices in
the Wilderness. Stop the sanctions! Stop the
bombing!...

Leader: Bruce Gagnon has begun the
international movement to keep outer space
as the sacred heavens. Listen to his voice
crying: "No wars into space! No wars from
space! No wars through space!"

All: We join our voices to his and to the Global
Network against the Nuclearization and
Militarization of Space. No wars into space!
No wars from space! No wars through
space!...

Leader: Cry out prophets of our times. Cry out
at the top of your voice, herald the good
news. Fear not to cry out and say to the cities
of the world. "Here is your God in the midst
of your struggle for justice, for peace."

All: Amen. So be it.

Such ritualistic reinforcement is particularly crucial since Plowshares activists often see no measurable results from their efforts. After decades
of resistance, war has not been eradicated and
nations have not dismantled their weapons of mass
destruction. And, it is unlikely that these goals will
be accomplished in the near future. Under these
circumstances, it might be easy to lose faith in the
movement's goals and the necessity of action. As
a plausibility structure, Catholic Left communities must therefore provide an alternative explanation that underscores the importance of resistance
regardless of the outcome. This type of legitimation
was evident during one retreat when an activist
named John (pseudonym) reflected on a biblical
passage in which Ezekiel had a vision of God giving
him a scroll and commanding him to eat it. God
said to him, "Go now and speak my words to the
people...But they will not listen to you because
they are not willing to listen to me, for they are
hardened and obstinate" (Ezekiel 3: 4, 7). John commented that Phil Berrigan, who had recently died,

was similar to Ezekiel. He prophesied even though
the world did not listen and he called each person
to be a prophet, claiming that every Christian has a
duty to denounce war.

The belief that they are part of a prophetic tradition helps Plowshares activists overcome doubts
about the importance of their sacrifices and the need
for ongoing resistance. It also demonstrates that
perceived effectiveness is not necessarily essential
for maintaining a strong movement commitment,
contrary to the research findings of Barkan, Cohn,
and Whitaker (1993, 1995). As one man stated: "Our
goal, our purpose, our approach is not primarily to
have an effect. It is first of all to be faithful. When
you follow the gospel, it's not in order to be a success. It's an attempt to be faithful to God, to God's
will for today, to be the voice of conscience."

Community as a Mechanism for Strengthening Relationships

Community practices also sustain activism by reinforcing the affective component of commitment. By
regularly sponsoring retreats, Plowshares leaders
keep activist networks and relational ties strong. One
activist, for instance, stated that the Atlantic Life
Community gatherings are like a family reunion. In
fact, he said he felt more at home at these retreats
than he did during a recent family reunion where a
cousin thanked him, saying that as a multiple felon
and a married (former) priest, he made everyone else
in the family look comparatively good. As this statement reveals, the sacrifices that Plowshares activists
make for the movement often give them a sense of
distinction from the rest of the population. Catholic
Left communities provide activists a place where
like-minded individuals surround them and they
have a sense of belonging. When people develop an
awareness of the beliefs, values, and life-styles they
share with others, bonds of solidarity are forged
(Jasper 1998). Moreover, affective commitment is
strengthened through the pleasurable interactions
that occur during these retreats. One activist stated.
'I've experienced an enormous amount of fun and
warmth and friendship. These gatherings, the people, have helped me and...never fail to inspire me.
It's like getting my batteries recharged."

Emotional ties to movement leaders are also
important, as previous research indicates that

rank-and-file activists who closely interact with leaders have higher levels of commitment (Barkan et al. 1993). In the Plowshares movement, such interaction occurs during retreats but also through visits to Jonah House. As stated earlier, 97 percent of Plowshares activists have spent time at Jonah House (see Table 1) and many claim that this experience instilled deep respect for the leaders' tenacious life of resistance. This affection can be heard in one man's comments:

> Philip Berrigan, Liz McAlister, Carl Kabat—their lives, actions, friendships, commitment to peace, and their sacrifices have deeply influenced my faith and activism. They have the ability to bring joy, hope, and love in this dying world. It is comforting to know that they aren't going to run away from the responsibilities of being human, of being Christians, and living up to the command to love. I wouldn't trade our time together for all the money the Pentagon protects.

As activists become acquainted with leaders, many are inspired to emulate their example. Rank-and-file participants also feel greater pressure to remain involved in resistance; not only is there direct accountability to live out one's convictions, but failure to do so might cause disappointment among the leaders they so admire.

Although these relationships may initially form in community, ongoing contact is necessary to sustain these bonds over time. Lack of communication, distance, and infrequent interaction can undermine friendships and deplete affective commitment. If the exiting literature is correct that weakened ties to movement networks foster termination, then we would expect persisters to regularly spend time at Catholic Left communities so that emotional ties can be rejuvenated. As conveyed in Table 4, survey respondents do demonstrate a strong degree of involvement in these communities. Nearly 60 percent have lived at a Catholic Worker house for more than a year and roughly 30 percent have lived at Jonah House for one or more years. The extent of continued contact can be roughly gauged by the number of Atlantic Life Community retreats that persisters have attended. According to the survey, almost three-quarters have participated in four or more Atlantic Life Community retreats; about one-third have been to 15 or more. Although comparative

Table 4 Extent of Plowshares Activists' Involvement in Catholic Left Communities (percentages)

Catholic Worker	
Involved in a Catholic Worker House for:	
One month or less	18.2
2–6 months	9.1
6–12 months	13.6
1–5 years	13.6
5–10 years	13.6
10+ years	32.0
Total	100.1
Jonah House	
Visited 1–4 times (but did not reside there)	24.1
Visited 5–10 times (but did not reside there)	20.7
Resided for 1–5 months	10.3
Resided for 6–12 months	13.8
Resided for 1–2 years	3.5
Resided for 3 or more years	27.6
Total	100.0
Atlantic Life Community	
Attended 1–3 gatherings	26.7
Attended 4–7 gatherings	23.3
Attended 8–14 gatherings	20.0
Attended 15 or more	30.0
Total	100.0

N = 54.

data with movement dropouts is needed to substantiate the importance of regular community contact in sustaining affective commitment, these numbers at least indicate that persisters spend a fair amount of time with other Catholic Left activists.

Community Deepens Activist Identity

In addition to strengthening normative and affective commitment, community practices also intensity activist identity, which is derived from action, not simply identification with an ideological position or a political group. Jonah House and Catholic Worker houses routinely organize protest events and protests are a ritualized part of the Atlantic Life Community retreats. At each gathering, "witness actions" are conducted at the White House and the Pentagon. Every retreat participant is involved in the planning process and given a specific task, from leafleting to being the designated spokesperson.

During one retreat I attended, the group staged a silent vigil and a die-in in front of the White House. Some members committed civil disobedience, "dying" in the restricted area and pouring blood. Later, the group reconvened to evaluate the action. The conversation centered on differential treatment by the police. Specifically, several people poured blood but only one was charged with the more serious felony of defacing government property. One of the blood throwers commented that, "I felt like Peter denying Christ because I didn't come forward to say that I had done it, too." He struggled between not wanting to give information to the police but not wanting to abandon the individual who was singled out. A Plowshares leader responded that it is typical police practice to try to divide the group. She then led community members in a brainstorming session on different methods of handling this situation. This discussion reflected movement socialization, learning the appropriate rules and protocol of protest. The planning, implementation, and evaluation of the White House witness not only taught people how to be activists, it gave them a chance to engage this role, thus deepening their activist identity.

Communal Support for Overcoming the Barriers to Long-Term Activism

To foster activist persistence, movements must deal with both sides of the retention equation—that is, they must reinforce commitment *and* address the barriers to long-term movement participation. One common obstacle is life responsibilities that render people biographically unavailable. Several studies, however, indicate that while full-time employment and family obligations can be a barrier, those who have a strong activist identity and are deeply motivated may structure their lives to accommodate movement engagement (Downton and Wehr 1997; Lichterman 1996). Yet this need not only be a personal, individual-level effort; movement communities can help activists with these responsibilities.

In the Plowshares movement, Catholic Left communities provide material assistance and family support so protesters are free to go to

prison if necessary. This is important because unlike McAdam's Freedom Summer volunteers, Plowshares activists are not, for the most part, young students who are biographically available. The average age of U.S. Plowshares activists at the time of their first action is 42 years old, and many have adult obligations. However, like the persisters in Downton and Wehr's study, most have placed such a high priority on resistance that they have organized their lives to accommodate activism. Although 44 percent have graduate degrees, many have given up professional careers in order to devote more time to the movement. Survey results show that only 29 percent have full-time jobs, while over 58 percent are full-time volunteer activists. Roughly 13 percent work part-time; most are self-employed or contract workers in manual labor or social service fields. This provides for basic living expenses while offering flexibility for protest activities. As a result, 90 percent of Plowshares activists responded that they did not lose their job due to their acts of resistance.

Although the potential loss of employment is not a serious barrier to activism for most in the Plowshares movement, family responsibilities can be. Approximately 45 percent of Plowshares activists had children at the time of their arrest. Consequently, concern about their family's well-being has led many to rely on community support while they are incarcerated. Members of Jonah House jointly raise their children so parents can go to prison knowing that their sons and daughters are well cared for. Berrigan and McAlister (1989) described how this aspect of communal life freed them to make sacrifices for the movement but also provided a motivation.

> [Our children] were born in a community committed to nonviolent resistance. They have been surrounded by people who love them, people who are...committed, self-sacrificing, deeply spiritual women and men. Each of the adults has developed a unique relationship with the children, has shared in their upbringing, has become co-responsible for them....So many experiences have taught us that children need to see commitment lived out by those who love them. We recall the terrible dislocation and alienation of German youth after World War II as they realized that their parents were silent in face

of Hitler's crimes in order to "protect" them...Our resistance is perhaps our only armor against the hard "why" they will ask. (Pp. 34–5)

In addition to childcare, Catholic Left communities assist with other logistic such as housing for activists during trials and after incarceration. For instance, one woman was granted an early prison release on the grounds that she not return to Jonah House since the court felt that the community would encourage her to violate the law again. Since her husband and child resided there, the family needed to find a new place to live for the duration of her probation term. They were immediately taken in by a Catholic Worker house in Minnesota. Thus, community can foster continuance commitment by assuring that the material needs of protesters, including food and shelter, will be readily available to those who make sacrifices for the movement's cause.

The type of high-risk activism that characterizes the Plowshares movement also requires emotional support. Those planning to participate in a campaign of symbolic disarmament know that they may receive a long prison sentence and could be injured or killed by security forces. Thus, they have to deal with emotions, such as fear, which can paralyze people from acting on their convictions and pose a serious barrier to participation (Goodwin, Jasper, and Polletta 2000, 2001). Community support is one of the primary means of managing fear. Pre-action preparations include prayer, strategizing, and role-playing, but also time to openly discuss emotions. One activist describes how these meetings helped him cope with his fears:

> I found our meetings very helpful for preparing and talking about our fears. One of the sessions was on preparing for death. We could be killed while doing these actions because the security is there and they would be justified, probably honored and rewarded, if they shot someone. So we try to prepare for that.... And, of course, we face the question: are you ready for 20 years in jail? Dan [Berrigan] says that our lives, inside and outside prison, are in some ways very similar. We study nonviolence, we pray, we try to build community. So I accepted that if I got 20 years, okay, I would trust God and believe God would be working through us and it

would be a benefit to society. So it involved preparing concretely for those possibilities.

Catholic Left communities also practically prepare Plowshares activists for prison by establishing a lifestyle of austerity and sacrifice. Those who live in Catholic Worker houses or Jonah House relinquish their property, resources, and nuclear family living arrangements in favor of a life of voluntary poverty and community. These norms reflect, to some degree, the tradition of religious orders. This is not surprising since many Catholic Left communities were established by priests and nuns and the survey data indicate that approximately one-third of Plowshares activists in the United States are, or previously were, members of religious orders. Many claim that their experience in religious life has helped them face the challenges of prison. Father Carl Kabat, an Oblate priest, described how he handled an 18-year prison sentence. He said, "For me it wasn't so hard. I was trained in the old church, back before Vatican II. The major seminary helped prepare me because in many ways, it's like prison. When I was in seminary, you didn't leave the grounds for five or six years." Phil Berrigan and Elizabeth McAlister (1989) also stated:

> In so many ways, religious life prepared us well for prison. Indeed, in many ways, prison life seemed easier than the religious formation we recall. The parallels deserve some mention: There is in both a radical displacement from home and loved ones and periodic, formalized visiting time with them. There is in both the enclosure, the cell, and authorization to move about. One's possessions are as limited and circumscribed in prison as they are in religious life. We were prepared for the enforced celibacy of prison life and had learned better ways to live with that special kind of pain. One obeys in prison or meets heavy consequences of lock-down and privation. There are sanctions in religious life, too, for disobedience.... One prays in prison and in religious life or rapidly meets a death of spirit. And there are few diversions with which to excuse the failure to pray. (Pp. 192–3)

Experience in religious orders enhanced the ability of Plowshares leaders to endure lengthy prison sentences. This, in turn, sets an example to which others aspire. As one lay activist stated, "Those who were in religious orders are accustomed to lives of austerity, community and sacrifice. The rest of us have to adjust." However, once they do make a sacrifice, they develop continuance commitment. After giving up their possessions and enduring prison sentences, they—like Kanter's utopian community members or the underground militants described by della Porta—are reluctant to abandon the movement since they have invested so much. They will be more devoted to its survival since it would be difficult to accept that the sacrifice of one's career, the absence from family, and the years in prison served no purpose. Yet it is important to recognize that the material, emotional, and logistical assistance of Catholic Left communities enabled these individuals to engage in high-risk activism in the first place, leading to the initial formation of continuance commitment.

Conclusion

Plowshares participants' ability to mount action after action, returning to prison repeatedly, is proof that they have found effective methods for maintaining commitment to high-risk activism. Although limited generalizations can be drawn from a single case and comparative research with movement dropouts is needed to confirm my findings, this study suggests that activist retention is not only a reflection of individual tenacity. Rather, the Plowshares movement has managed to sustain itself, even as the broader peace movement subsided, because leaders have intentionally implemented practices to reinforce commitment. By forming Catholic Left communities, they created plausibility structures where normative commitment is strengthened through rituals such as biblical meditations, prayer, and singing. These communities also offer answers when doubts arise regarding the efficacy of protest, and they function as a site for ongoing political socialization that deepens activist identities. Moreover, they bring like-minded individuals together on a regular basis, rejuvenating the emotional bonds and relational ties that strengthen affective commitment and keep people integrated into activist networks. Finally, Catholic

Left communities assist with life responsibilities so activists can engage in high-risk campaigns. Once they make a sacrifice for the movement, continuance commitment forms.

In addition to strengthening these three types of commitment. Catholic Left communities offer various forms of support that neutralize exiting influences and help individuals overcome barriers to long-term participation. First, they offer social support that counteracts the effects of cross-pressures. This is essential because Plowshares activists often face significant opposition from loved ones. For example, one woman stated, "My husband thought I had been mesmerized by this group of people who were controlling my mind. He was really determined to stop me. My friends and my brothers and sisters thought I'd gone cuckoo." However, the affirmation and moral reassurance she received from other Catholic Left activists was sufficient to sustain her commitment despite her family's disapproval. Second, these communities provide emotional support that minimizes the psychological tension that accompanies high-risk activism and contributes to burnout. One activist priest noted. "We've seen thousands of people walk away from the broader peace movement because they burned out. They were on their own and when they got distressed or despairing, they didn't have people to help them." Finally, Jonah House and Catholic Worker communities further diminish psychological stress by offering material and practical support to Plowshares activists, alleviating concerns about shelter, family obligations, and other responsibilities.

Activist retention, therefore, reflects two processes—regularly reinforcing commitment and addressing the issues that foster exiting. While previous studies document that some individuals manage this on their own (Downton and Wehr 1997; Lichterman 1996), movements can enhance activist persistence by building structures of support and establishing cultural practices that help maintain participation over time. This type of communal support is probably more important in high-risk campaigns where the consequences are serious, family opposition is likely, the potential for burnout is high, and doubts about efficacy may arise.

NOTE

Completion of this article was made possible through grants from the Philip H. and Betty L. Wimmer Family Foundation at Duquesne University and the National Endowment for the Humanities. The views expressed here are solely the author's and do not necessarily reflect those of the granting agencies. The author wishes to thank Bert Klandermans, Robert Wuthnow, Paul Lichterman, John Markoff, Neil Smelser, Diedre Crumbley, James Holstein, members of the Religion and Culture Workshop at Princeton's Center for the Study of Religion and the Pittsburgh Social Movements Forum, and several anonymous reviewers for comments on earlier versions of this article.

Unit

Movement Dynamics

Strategies and Tactics

In Part 8 we examine one of the most interesting and dynamic aspects of social movements: the use of various tactics and strategies to advance movement aims. Besides its intrinsic scholarly appeal, the topic is critically important to movements and those who would seek to direct them. Consider the stark challenge that confronts most movements. They arise to challenge established authority in a given institutional realm—religious, educational, economic, political, etc. Moreover, in challenging these authorities, movements typically eschew the "proper [decision-making] channels" of the institution in question. They typically do this for two reasons. First, as suggested above, movement groups often do not have access to these "proper channels" or experience with the forms of action (e.g., lobbying, electoral politics) associated with them. Second, as relatively powerless groups, they may fear that their aims will be compromised by pursuing them through the arenas or settings that ordinarily are controlled or dominated by established institutional elites.

This rejection of conventional institutional or political means may make sense for movement groups, but it nonetheless poses a dilemma. By opting for politics "by other means," movement groups must answer a difficult question: What should these "other means" be? How can movements hope to overcome their relative powerlessness and press effectively for the realization of their goals?

What do we know about this crucial topic? Perhaps not as much as we know about the dynamics of movement emergence or differential recruitment, but as the selections in Part 8 show, there is now a rich and growing body of work on the broad topic of movement tactics and strategies. Work in this area has focused on a range of specific issues including how tactics are chosen, how interaction with authorities shapes their actual use, and the

relative effectiveness of different strategies in achieving movement goals. We illustrate all three of these emphases in this section. We begin with the determinants that shape the choice of tactics and strategies deployed by movement groups.

How do activists select from among all possible tactics theoretically available to them? No doubt a number of factors influence the selection process, but among the most important is cultural knowledge of any given tactic. The fact is, for all the seeming spontaneity and unpredictability of emergent political contention, the selection of tactics by challenging groups is culturally constrained and, thus, fairly predictable. At any given historical moment, activists—especially those sharing a general ideological orientation—have available to them only that fairly narrow "tool kit" of action forms with which they are already familiar. The late Charles Tilly coined the term *repertoires of contention* to refer to those established means of popular protest that are culturally known and regarded as legitimate within a given social milieu. The initial selection in Part 8 reproduces the 1977 *Theory and Society* article in which Tilly first introduced the concept of repertoires and theorized their importance in shaping the dynamics of contention.

But surely movements are not entirely bound by the conventional forms of protest characteristic of the historical period in which they develop. If movements were truly restricted in their selection of action forms, we would never be able to account for change in these repertoires of contention. And change does, indeed, occur. Movements are themselves sources of innovation in protest forms, expanding, through their actions, the forms of contention that will be available to succeeding generations of activists.

How does this innovation occur? What are the dynamics that give rise to new protest tactics? In the second selection, McAdam takes up this important question. Part of the answer to the question, he contends, lies in the ongoing tactical interaction between movement groups and their opponents, both within and outside of the state. The portrait that emerges from McAdam's study of the civil rights movement is that of an elaborate tactical chess match that, by fits and starts, gradually expands the available repertoires of contention. But what is the dynamic that drives the creation of new tactical forms? According to the author, it is the movement's ongoing efforts to offset the enormous disparity in coercive power that characterizes its relationship with its opponents. To do this it must keep its foes off guard by finding new ways to disrupt "business as usual" and temporarily neutralize the superior repressive capacity of authorities.

In the case of the civil rights movement, McAdam shows that the ebb and flow of protest activity and major movement victories was closely related to the introduction of a series of significant *tactical innovations* that temporarily afforded the movement the leverage needed to wrest concessions from the federal government. But each innovation eventually produced a *tactical adaptation* by southern segregationists that effectively countered the original innovation and sent movement activists back to the drawing board. According to McAdam, this iterative tactical "dance" powerfully shapes not only the creation of new tactics, but the overall trajectory and fate of the movement.

Mary Bernstein's landmark 1997 article on "the strategic uses of identity by the lesbian and gay movement" betrays much the same interest in movement/environment interaction as the previous selection. Comparing a half dozen or so city- or state-level campaigns for gay and lesbian rights ordinances in the 1970s and 1980s, Bernstein convincingly accounts for the varying identity strategies employed in each case on the basis of differences in the political environments in which they were operating. For the author variation in "political access [and] movement interactions with opposing movements and the state" powerfully shaped the strategic choices made by movement groups. But besides its rich analysis of movement/environment interaction, the article is important for the valuable corrective it offers to the tendency of scholars to simplistically differentiate between "expressive" and "instrumental" movements. As Bernstein shows, gay and lesbian identities were manifest in varying degrees in these campaigns as both expressive ends and instrumental means, making the aforementioned distinction hard to apply in practice.

Finally, there is the all-important question of effectiveness. What do we know about the impact of various tactics? McAdam's selection contains the provocative and perhaps counterintuitive suggestion that movement success depends, at least in part, on the innovative and temporarily disruptive force of movement tactics. In a political system that has long stressed playing by the rules, what are we to make of this suggestion? The classic article by William Gamson, which brings the section to a close, systematically addresses this question.

In his comparative study of 53 "challenging groups," Gamson sought to relate various dimensions of these groups to their success in gaining "new advantages" and "acceptance" by political elites. Among the dimensions he studied were the tactics employed by these groups. The results may surprise you. On average, those groups who used "disruptive" forms of protest were more successful in gaining new advantages and acceptance than those who eschewed such tactics. On the issue of violence, Gamson is more equivocal. While groups who used violence had slightly higher rates of success than those who did not, Gamson is cautious in interpreting the finding. It may be that only those groups that are strong enough on other dimensions use violence in the first place, thus making it hard to know whether it is their general strength or their use of violence that accounts for their higher success rates. However you interpret this latter finding, the overall thrust of Gamson's results is clear: like it or not, a degree of disruption may be functional for movement success. In the arena of social movements, as in other aspects of life, the squeaky wheel may, indeed, get the grease.

25.
Getting It Together in Burgundy, 1675–1975

CHARLES TILLY

What the Archives Say

The municipal archives of Dijon occupy several cluttered rooms in the grand old palace of the Dukes of Burgundy. The archives' main door looks out onto the elegant semicircle of the Place de la Libération, built in the late seventeenth century as the Place Royale. Readers in the high-ceilinged *salle de travail* have no trouble tallying arrivals and departures. A strident bell sounds in the room so long as the outside door is open. The interruption usually lasts five to ten seconds, as the newcomer closes the street door, crosses the anteroom, fumbles with the inner door, and enters. In bad weather arrivals are more disruptive; after the long bell stops sounding, visitors stomp their feet unseen, remove their boots and hang up their raincoats before presenting themselves for inspection. Exists are equally distracting, for they mirror the entries precisely: thud, shuffle, stomp, ring.

Distractions, however, are few. Not many people come to the archives: a few city employees, an antiquarian or two, an occasional student from the university, now and then an itinerant historian. Those few have riches before them. They have the surviving papers of the capital of Burgundy, both as an independent power and as a major French province. The archives are especially full up to the point at which the centralization of the Revolution shifted the balance of power, and paperwork, toward the state's own bureaucracy.

Among the thousands of bundles in the pre-revolutionary collection, 167 fall into series I. Series I includes Police, in the broad old-regime meaning of defense against all manner of public ills. Its topics are sanitation, public health, fire protection, asylums, pursuit of beggars, vagrants and criminals, control of games, gatherings and public ceremonies. Nineteenth-century archivists sorted the papers by subject matter, by rough time period and then usually by affair, event, session, or whatever other subdivision the organization producing the records had used in its own work.

The series contains reports of the activities of the *chassecoquins,* the seventeenth-century officials assigned, literally, to chase *coquins* (scalawags and ne'r-do-wells) from the city. It includes more details than most of us would care to read concerning the official surveillance of the wine-harvest, in that great wine region, from 1290 onward. It has a great mass of reports—and, especially, of invoices—from four centuries of publicly-sponsored celebrations. We see the elaborate preparations for the annual fireworks of St. John the Baptist Day, including a note from 1642 on the "Malefactors who set off the fireworks when the mayor was going to light them himself as usual…" (A. M. [Archives Municipales] Dijon I 43). We watch the great funeral processions, including the sixty musicians who played and sang the funeral mass composed for the Dauphin in 1711 (A. M. Dijon 148). We witness incessant pompous entries into the city of dukes, duchesses, queens, kings, princes and ambassadors: King Charles VI in 1387, Duke Charles the Bold in 1470, King Henry IV in 1595, Louis XIV and the Queen in 1674, and dozens of others (A. M. Dijon 15–36). In short, the very tapestry of Dijon's public life.

Those concerned less with kings and more with the participation of ordinary people in the city's public life also find much to think about in series I. The fifty-four affairs in bundle I 119, for example, deal with "seditions" and other serious offenses against public order between 1639 and 1775. In the

Tilly, Charles. 1977. "Getting It Together in Burgundy, 1675–1975. *Theory and Society* 4: 479–504.

century before the Revolution, "sedition," "emotion," and "mutiny" were common terms for events which later observers would probably have called "riots" or "disturbances." Unsympathetic observers, that is. "Sedition," "emotion," "mutiny," "riot" and "disturbance" are terms of disapproval, power-holders' words. The documents of Bundle I 119 breathe life into the shapeless words. In 1668, for example, they show the municipality issuing a warning against unnamed people who had spread the rumor that the major tax, the *taille*, was to be increased, and forbidding the populace "to assemble or form a crowd day or night on any pretext, or to incite the people to sedition, on pain of death…" The anonymous enemies of the people had allegedly said "they needed a Lanturelu."

Lanturelu was a popular song of the 1620s which gave its name to a popular rebellion of the 1630s. Back then, Richelieu and Louis XIII had announced the elimination of Burgundy's privileged tax status. On the 27th and 28th of February 1630, a hundred-odd armed men led by winegrower Anatoire Changenet, plus a crowd of unarmed women, men and children, gathered in the streets of Dijon. (*Gens de bas étage*—lowly folk—city officials called them later. Anatoire Changenet himself had just served as King of Fools in the city's Mardi Gras festivities.) Among other things, the crowd sounded the tocsin, sacked the houses of royal officials, and burned a portrait of Louis XIII. They are supposed to have shouted "Long live the Emperor"—the Habsburg descendant of Burgundian Charles the Bold, and mortal rival of the French king. Dijon's mayor hesitated a day before calling out the militia, which killed ten or twelve of the rebels in the process of dispersing the crowd. The King retaliated by imposing a state of siege, ordering the winegrowers to move outside the city walls, requiring a large payment to the victims of property damage, further abridging the city's privileges, and staging, in April 1630, a humiliating confrontation with local dignitaries. The Parlement of Burgundy, doing its part, condemned two leaders of the rebellion to hang. That was a Lanturelu.

No Lanturelu occurred in 1668, yet seventeenth-century Dijon had its share of seditions, emotions

and mutinies. In February 1684 the winegrowers again took their turn. The public prosecutor described the event as "…a popular sedition that three or four hundred winegrowers wanted to start in the city by their enterprise of gathering together, marching through the city with beating drum and unfurled banner without any authorization to do so…" Later details in the prosecutor's own account set the number of marchers at something over a hundred. (The exaggeration at the start of the account may well reflect the fact that in an encounter between city officials and the winegrowers at the Guillaume Gate, as the prosecutor tells the story, "it was only by some sort of miracle that none of them was assaulted, notably the aforesaid public prosecutor by one of the seditioners, who was at the head of the crowd and got ready to strike him with his pruning-knife.") The wine-growers assembled to the drumroll, as people often assembled for special occasions in those days. Among the leaders, as in 1630, was a winegrower named Changenet–this one the Jean Changenet who later described himself as "winegrower in Dijon, rue Chanoine, twenty-nine years old, professing the Apostolic Roman Catholic religion."

The winegrowers went *en masse* to Champmoron wood, which belonged to the nearby Carthusian monastery. There they gathered firewood, then returned to the city. They were on their way back through the gate when they met the small band of officials who had come to stop them. Hilaire Edouard Demouchy (*conseiller du roi, trésorier de France* and, most important, leaseholder of Champmoron wood) filed a formal complaint asking for redress, prosecution and official rejection of the winegrowers' claim to the firewood. The authorities clapped a dozen leaders of the march, including Jean Changenet, in jail. A few days later the mayor and council received a petition reading:

> You are asked by some of the poor winegrowers and some of your most faithful servants among the poor people of this city to have pity and compassion for the poor wretches who are in jail here for having assembled at the sound of the drum to go to the woods, which was done without any thought of offending you but only to give the group strength

against those who wanted to stop it from cutting wood…

In their own petition, the twelve imprisoned winegrowers said they had been arrested "…while returning from Champmoron wood where they had gone to cut firewood, along with many other winegrowers from the city who claimed they had the right to do so as a result of concessions granted to the winegrowers by the Duke of Burgundy, as has often been practiced in the past when required by bad weather and hard winter, as in the present year where the need is great." Part of the transcript from the interrogation of forty-year-old Pierre Reignaut runs as follows:

> Asked why they banded together thus to go to the wood if they already had the right to cut there.
>
> Replies that the reason they went to the aforesaid wood in large numbers was that the first persons to go had been chased out by the valets of the Carthusian fathers and in the fear that the same thing would happen again the greater part of the winegrowers had assembled in order to maintain their right to cut in the aforesaid wood.

After some weeks in jail, the twelve prisoners went free on their promise of good behavior. Their action apparently stirred the municipality: the following year the city sued the Carthusians for enforcement of the winegrowers' right to gather wood.

The traces of many other events appear in that rich bundle of seditions: another confrontation over firewood in 1696 (but this one over the royal toll on wood entering the city); threatening, demanding gatherings of women during the great hungers of 1693 and 1709; seizure of grain wagons by a crowd of "more than a thousand" in 1770; still others earlier and later. The events portray a Dijon in which some issue brought crowds to the street and into confrontation with the authorities every three or four years.

The Seventeenth Century Confronts the Twentieth

As I pored over the papers of Bundle I 119 one day in the spring of 1975, Monsieur Savouret, Madame Jacquette and Monsieur Benoist, the staff of the Dijon archives, were busy about their work in the reading room. Gradually a muffled sound outside resolved itself into chanting, *crescendo*. "What is it?" I stupidly asked my companions. We went to the windows, which gave us a view into the Place de la Libération through the great barred gate of the palace. People were marching outside.

I rushed to the exit. The indefatigable bell signaled my translation from the seventeenth century to the twentieth. Up the street came several hundred young men and women, in uneven ranks. Some carried an effigy of a man, others hoisted signs and banners. They continued to chant loudly. A marcher thrust a handbill at me. The issue, it turned out, was the future of students preparing to teach sports and physical education. The dummy appeared to represent M. Mazeaud, the Secretary of Youth, Sports and Leisure, who was proposing a tiny budget for physical education as well as the removal of compulsory sports from public schools. That would seriously curtail these students' job prospects. The demonstrators were on their way to the Place de la République for a rally, as students in other French cities were likewise on the way to their Place de la République for rallies. An hour or so later, they passed the archives again, on the way back to the university area. The undisciplined ranks and disciplined chants had dissolved, but the demonstrators still shouted and cheered. Gradually their voices gave way to the ordinary noises of the street. My thoughts turned back three centuries to 1675.

Are the turbulent events of 1675 and 1975 knots on the same long thread? The event in the archives and the event on the street both consist of people banding together to act on their shared grievances, hopes and interests. That banding together—let us call it collective action for short—has its own history. As people's grievances, hopes and interests change, and as their opportunities for acting on them change, obviously their ways of acting collectively change as well. In between interest and opportunity, and less obviously, comes a third factor: organization. Whether we are watching seventeenth-century winegrowers or twentieth-century students, we notice that they do not seize every opportunity to act on their interests, and do not react to every opportunity in the same way. How they are tied to each other, what ways of acting together are already familiar to them, and which sorts of news they have alerted themselves to, affect how much they act, in what manner, and how effectively.

The Dijon winegrowers had a pressing need for firewood that cold winter. Indeed, wood shortage was becoming a critical problem in all Burgundy as forests passed into private hands and small wood-burning forges multiplied. The winegrowers had the slim opportunity offered by their claim to a privilege granted by the Dukes of Burgundy; that opportunity was disappearing as the rise of bourgeois property squeezed out the old shared rights to glean, pasture, forage or fish on local territory. Compared with other groups of poor people in Dijon, winegrowers had the advantages of coherent organization: extensive ties sustained by daily contact, relatively effective leadership, previous experience in acting together. The history of collective action clearly has four components: interest, opportunity, organization and action itself. All four vary from group to group, place to place, time to time, problem to problem.

Interest, opportunity, organization and action: a large, rich historical agenda. The turbulent events whose traces have survived in seventeenth-century police archives are obviously a peculiar sample of all the century's collective action, and therefore of the interests, opportunities and organization at work. Nevertheless those events immediately identify lineaments of seventeenth-century French collective action, and its context, which differ significantly from those of the twentieth century.

Collective Action in Seventeenth-Century Burgundy

Dijon and Burgundy had come to the French crown with Louis XI's defeat of Charles the Bold, Duke of Burgundy, at the end of the fifteenth century. Charles' successors, the Habsburg emperors, continued to press their claims by word and sword. Adjacent to the Habsburg lands of Franche-Comté, Burgundy was a military frontier and a favorite sixteenth-century battleground. After the decline of the direct military threat from outside

came a division from within; Burgundy ran red with the blood of sixteenth-century wars between Protestants and Catholics. The wars of the League, the dynastic struggles for control of the duchy which blended into the Thirty Years War, popular insurrections continued through the tumultuous time of Lanturelu to the mid-seventeenth-century rebellion of the Fronde. During the early years of the Fronde, many Burgundian notables sympathized, and even conspired, with the insurgent governor of Burgundy, the Prince of Condé. From 1651 to 1653 the supporters of Condé raised an armed rebellion which only ended with the royal siege of Dijon and the conquest of the fort of Bellegarde, at Seurre. With the victory of Louis XIV and Mazarin over the *Frondeurs* came the end of Burgundy's age of war and large-scale rebellion.

Thus the middle of the seventeenth century marks an important transition. The transition shaped the development of popular collective action in Burgundy as well as the province's general political history. Before, every popular movement provided an opportunity for some fragment of the ruling classes to press its advantage against the Crown. The clientele of one great noble or another were frequently the basic units among the warriors or rebels. Crowds which moved against royal exactions, such as the crowd led by Anatoire Changenet in 1630, found sympathy or even support among the local authorities. With the decisive subordination of local officials to royal power in the later seventeenth century the chances for implicit or explicit alliance between officials and plebeian rebels greatly diminished. Ordinary people continued to act. But the shift of the process of extension of royal power from a stage of great uncertainty and cross-class alliances to a stage of crunching but inexorable growth left ordinary people to act alone in the name of their particular rights and privileges. The authorities, quelled or coopted, increasingly treated popular gatherings as dangerous sources of "sedition."

During that seventeenth century, then, the interests, opportunities, organization and collective action of Burgundy's ordinary people were changing. Their interests shifted as a warmaking monarchy pressed them increasingly for taxes to support its growing armies, and as the bourgeois of Dijon increased their domination of the region's land and economic activity. Their opportunities to act on those 'interests altered, mostly for the worse, as the importance of patronage and the possibility of alliance with regional power-holders declined. Their organization changed with the increasing proportion of landless workers and the stratification of rural communities. As a result, the collective action of ordinary people changed as well.

In the years after the winegrowers' invasion of Champmoron wood, a number of the incidents which left their remains in Dossier I 199 and adjacent archives involved popular resistance to demands of the state. In 1691, a royal edict prescribed yet another creation and sale of offices for the profit of the Crown. This time there were two offices of *jurés crieurs des obsèques et enterrements:* public registrars of funerals and burials. They sold for 6,000 livres. Word spread that the funeral fees of the poor would therefore rise prohibitively. Menacing crowds formed outside the home of the purchasers of the offices, insulted them, and called again for a Lanturelu (A. M. Dijon B 329). In 1696, firewood was again the issue, and the Porte Guillaume again the site of the crucial confrontation. This time countrymen delivering wood to the city pried open the gate with pokers and crowbars, in order to avoid paying the new tax of eight sous per bundle (A. M. Dijon I 199). During the last years of the century, as Louis XIV pursued his wars against Spain, we see rising complaints and resistance against conscription, impressment, billeting and military foraging among the reports of *Te Deums* for royal victories.

During those same years the food riot elbowed its way to the leading position among the more turbulent forms of popular collective action. From the 1690s to the 1840s, some form of the food riot was no doubt the most common setting for violent conflict above the scale of the barroom brawl in Burgundy, as in the rest of France. 1693 and 1694 brought Burgundy innumerable instances of the food riot in all three of its major forms: the popular inventory and seizure of grain held in storage by dealers and private parties; the forced sale of grain or bread at a price below the current market; the blockage of grain shipments destined to leave or pass through

on their way to other markets. In 1693, the combination of an inferior harvest and the pressure to supply the French armies at war in Germany emptied the Burgundian markets, drove prices up and squeezed the poor. When they could, the authorities of Dijon and other cities responded to the rioters in kind: they inventoried and commandeered the grain on hand, blocked shipments, and arranged the public sale of food below the market price.

For the most part, the so-called rioters were either substituting themselves for the authorities or forcing them to do their duty. Sometimes, however, the crowd wreaked or threatened vengeance. A declaration of the Parlement posted on the 20th of August 1693 stated that "…yesterday from 8 to 10 P.M. many wives of winegrowers and laborers gathered together and threatened to kill and to set fire to houses because there is only a small amount of grain in aforesaid city, and it cannot be enough to feed all the residents…" As usual, the poster went on to forbid "…all inhabitants of Dijon, of whatever sex or age, to gather in the streets or any place else by day or night, or to use threats, violence or inflammatory language, on pain of death…" (A. M. Dijon I 119).

Food riots flourished in the next century. One of the greatest struggles over subsistences in French history occurred in 1709. Again the coincidence of a bad harvest and extraordinary demand from armies abroad put acute pressure on local supplies. Again the crisis gave merchants and local officials a hard choice: give priority to the local poor by commandeering the local stocks and selling them at controlled and subsidized prices, or accede to the higher-priced, and officially-backed, demand from outside. As the eighteenth century moved on, royal policy favored the armies and the national market with increasing zeal and effectiveness; the desire of merchants and officials to favor the locals wilted obligingly. Since the landless poor were actually increasing as a proportion of the general population, the pressure on local communities increased despite a slow rise in agricultural productivity. The widespread food riots of the eighteenth century replied to that pressure.

The structure of the classic food riot–commandeering, blocking and/or selling below market–makes it clear that it was a means of forcing the merchants and officials to favor the locality over the armies and the national market. The procedure often worked. The structure of the individual event does not make it quite so clear that it was a tool to block the advance of mercantile capitalism. In that regard, it was at best a monkey wrench in the machinery: stopping the gears now and then, knocking out a few teeth, but also encouraging the development of tougher machines and protective screens.

The form of food riot that grew up in the late seventeenth century nicely illustrates the place of changing interests, opportunities and organization in changes of collective action. The interest of the local poor (and, to some extent, their patrons) in local priority over the food supply was growing as the interest of the Crown and larger merchants in freeing it from the local grasp increased. The opportunities of the poor were mainly negative, since they consisted of official failures to intervene in the local market as local authorities were supposed to. The change in organization in this case is relatively unimportant although there are some signs that groups such as Dijon's winegrowers were becoming more clearly aware of their distinctive and threatened class position. What is important is the *persistence* of local organization on the basis of which poor people pressed their claims to the food supply. This changing combination of interests, opportunities and organization produced the food riot as naturally as other combinations produced the tax rebellion, concerted resistance to conscription and attacks on enclosing landlords.

To the Revolution

If we were to inch forward through the eighteenth century, further changes in the surface of popular collective action would give us more indications of shifts in interest, opportunity and organization. To get a stronger sense of the changes still in store, however, let us leap a century from the 1690s to the Dijon of the early Revolution. A National Guard report informs us:

> Today 23 August 1790, on the complaints brought by a number of citizens to the commander of the Volunteers' post at the Logis du Roy around 11 P.M. that someone (to the great scandal of right-thinking

folk) had just sung, to the accompaniment of several instruments, a Romance or Complaint containing a funeral ode to the Marquis de Favras, outside the home of M. Frantin, a city official. We, Jean-Baptiste Roy, captain of Volunteers commanding the aforesaid post at the Logis du Roy, thought proper to form immediately a patrol to follow the group of musicians who we had been informed were heading toward the rue du Gouvernement and therefore led the aforesaid patrol to that street where we did in fact find the aforesaid group of musicians at the hour of midnight, stopped before the door of M. Chartraire, mayor of this city. Among them we recognized, and heard, M. Roche, a lawyer, singing to the accompaniment of a guitar and of several violins in the hands of MM. Propiac, Pasquirer and a number of others unknown to us, the Complaint of the aforesaid Favras, in which we noticed the language of the enemies of the Revolution, in that the author of the Complaint in his delirium dares to accuse the Parisian people of madness, and taking a prophetic tone announces that the people will get rid of the new system. Considering that a text of that type in which one is not ashamed to favor a traitor to the people such as the King's friend, sung at improper times in the most frequented neighborhoods of the city could only have for its object to incite the people to insurrection, and considering that it is urgent to prevent that mishap, we thought it was our duty to report the event to the general staff...(A. D. [Archives Départementales] Côte d'Or L 386).

The comrade-in-arms of our commander at the City Hall post informs us that:

> ...a number of citizens of the city of Dijon, following a musical ensemble, passed before the City Hall; eight of the riflemen of the post of the aforesaid City Hall, drawn by the melody, followed the line of march, which ended in front of the home of the Mayor; there the musicians, seating themselves, sang a Complaint or Romance which seemed quite improper to the riflemen, in that they heard some words which could overturn public order...
> (A. D. Côte d'Or L 386).

And as "seditious song" itself? The surviving text includes this verse:

> Since you must have a victim
> Blind and cruel people,

Strike, I forgive your crime,
But fear eternal remorse;
You will recover from madness;
And tired of a new system
You will see my innocence
You will cry on my tomb.

Now, the Marquis of Favras was part of a plot to seize the King and spirit him away from the grasp of the Revolution. Betrayed by his fellow conspirators, Favras was hanged in the Place de Grève, in Paris, on 18 February 1790. One could hardly have a more counter-revolutionary hero. Confronted with such evidence of subversive activity, the National Guard's general staff leapfrogged the city council to make its report on the incident directly to the Department's administration; it appears that among the serenaders were some members of the city council itself.

The counter-revolutionary musicale connected with a whole series of demonstrations of opposition to the leaders and the symbols of the revolutionary movement in Dijon. There is, for example, that group of forty-odd citizens who "struck down the national cockade" in November, and who "provoked all the citizens" at the cafe Richard (A. D. Côte d'Or L 386). There is the group of customers at the Old Monastery cabaret who, two days later, insisted that three young men take off their national cockades (that is, their red, white and blue ribbons) before being served (A. D. Côte d'Or L 386). At that time the National Guard, municipal guardian not only of public safety but also of revolutionary sentiment, was campaigning for the obligatory wearing of the cockade. (The city council, at its meeting of 8 November 1790, declared the request that its members wear the cockade on their chests "illegal and harassing": A. M. Dijon 1 D).

We should not conclude from these little run-ins, however, that Dijon was simply a counter-revolutionary haven. The capital of Burgundy had undergone a local revolution thirteen months before the mayor's serenade: an impeccably bourgeois revolutionary committee seized power from a council which was strongly attached to the Parlement, and therefore to old-regime institutions. A more conservative municipality came to office in the elections

of January 1790. It faced an active patriotic Club speaking for the National Guard's leaders and the revolutionary committee of 1789.[1] Other events displayed the revolutionary spirit in Dijon: the popular demonstrations of December 1790 against the so-called Fifth Section of the Amis de la Constitution, a reactionary club; the workers' gatherings around the municipal offices at the opening of the relief-work program in March 1791; the crowds of April 1791 which "formed in front of the churches of La Madeleine and La Visitation and went through the city to tear down coats of arms, pillars and ornaments attached to private houses and public buildings…" (A. M. Dijon I D; A. D. Côte d'Or L444). Dijon was a divided city, like many other French cities of its time.

The conflicts which divided Dijon reappeared throughout France. Rather than flowing from a unanimous desire of the French people, the Revolution we know emerged from ferocious struggles in place after place. Their form, their combatants and their results varied with local social structure. The Revolution which occurred in Paris during July 1789 started a vast effort to centralize political power, opened up great opportunities for the organized segments of the bourgeoisie, stirred an unprecedented popular mobilization, encouraged a politicization of all sorts of conflicts. But the ramifications of the Revolution outside Paris posed particular problems in each locality, depending on the existing interests and organization. In the Loire, for example, the fundamental cleavage which led to the department's participation in the anti-Jacobin Federalist revolt separated two well-defined groups: the Montagnards, composed largely of workers and a bourgeois fragment, and a moderate majority coalition led mainly by the region's landholders.[2] In the Vendée, a compact nucleus of merchants and manufacturers faced a formidable coalition of nobles, priests, peasants and rural workers.[3] In Burgundy, the bourgeois fought against the resistance of the Parlement's adherents and the relatively radical demands of winegrowers.

Despite the diversity of these alignments, from them developed certain deep, common consequences: intense political participation on the part of the general population; a decline in the influence (and especially the official position) of priests and nobles; a rise in the political significance of the regional bourgeoisie; a promotion of conditions favoring capitalist property and production; a sharpening of awareness of connections between local conflicts and national power struggles; a concentration of power in a growing, increasingly centralized state. In looking at Dijon's little serenade of 1790, we witness a small reaction to a very large transformation.

If the serenade was clearly part of the revolutionary struggle, it was just as clearly a piece of the eighteenth century. We have already noticed the importance of song to public displays of sentiment in the Lanturelu. But we have not yet noticed the widespread form of action which the 1790 night music most closely resembles. It is the *charivari*—often corrupted into "shivaree" in American English, and often called Rough Music in England.

Charivari Before and After the Revolution

The basic action of the charivari runs like this: assemble in the street outside a house, make a racket with songs, shouts and improvised instruments such as saucepans and washtubs, require a payoff from the people inside the house, then leave if and when the people pay. The words and action are mocking, often obscene. They describe and condemn the misdeeds of the house's residents. In its essential form, the eighteenth-century charivari was the work of a well-defined group which bore some special responsibility for the moral rules which the targets of the action had violated. The best known, and probably most widespread, examples concern familial, sexual and marital motality. One standard case is the noisy public criticism of an old widower who married a young woman. In such a case, the makers of the charivari ordinarily came from the young unmarried men of the community, who often comprised a defined, exclusive association: the youth abbey or its equivalent. In the case of moral offenses the payoff required was not always a simple gift or round of drinks. Sometimes the serenaders demanded the departure from the community of the tainted individual or couple. Sometimes the guilty parties left town.

Like most regions of Europe, Burgundy had its own version of the charivari, linked to a complex of local institutions. In Burgundian villages, the "bachelors' guilds" (*compagnies de garçons*) included all the unmarried men of twenty or more. The local bachelors' guild required a cash payment from young men as they reached the minimum age. It kept an eye on their love affairs and even told them which girls they had a right to court. It defended the village maidens from the attentions of men outside the guild. The bachelors' guild collected a substantial payment, in cash or in the form of a festival, from the young men who married and, especially, from outsiders and otherwise unsuitable men who dared to marry women from the locality. This last category of marriages was a common occasion for charivaris and brawls. In Burgundy, the same bachelors' guild often had responsibility for public bonfires in Lent and at other sacred moments of the year, gathered wood for that purpose, and had the right to collect a contribution from each household in compensation for its efforts. At the local scale, it was thus a significant institution which provided services, bound the young people together and exercised genuine social control. The charivari, for all its apparent quaintness and triviality, had profound roots in the regional culture.

In that light, the observer of Burgundy's political life *after* the Revolution notices some curious reflections of the old regime. Under the July Monarchy Dijon's police archives are jammed with old-fashioned charivaris. For example, in July 1834:

> On the 22d instant, toward 9 o'clock at night, some youngsters gave a charivari to the newlyweds– Baudry, a tailor, and Miss Ody–who did not give a ball; that fact occasioned a rather large gathering on the rue St. Nicolas, but did not produce any disorder, and the *charivariseurs* fled at the sight of the gendarmes (A. D. Côte d'Or 8 M 29).

The charivari's being police business was not entirely new, since even in the eighteenth century the municipal police intervened from time to time when a charivari was too raucous or too long. The intervention of the police nevertheless shows us the opening of a breach between bourgeois law and the law of popular custom.

Beside the usual applications of the charivari to the improperly married, furthermore, we find its use for explicitly political purposes. A police report from 8 September 1833 informs us that:

Yesterday evening the 7th instant, toward nine o'clock, a charivari took place outside the Hotel du Parc on the occasion of the stopping in this city of a deputy named M. Delachaume, coming from Paris on his way to Châlons-sur-Saône, whither he went at four o'clock this morning. The charivari only lasted a few moments. It began on the rue des Bons Enfants, where the organizers, known to be republicans, assumed that M. Delachaume was having supper with one of his friends. But having learned differently, they went to the Hotel du Parc, where a crowd of more than 300 persons gathered at the noise they made. The noise soon stopped at the request of one of them, a certain Garrot, known to be a fiery republican; he raised various cries: *A bas le rogneur de budget, le con de député,* etc. and other indecent words we could not make out. After those cries they left, along with the people whom the scandalous spectacle had attracted. With Mr. Garrot at the head of all these young people, most of them workers and some diguised in work clothes and others in straw hats, the group scattered and later gathered at the Republican Club located at the Place d'Armes over the Thousand Columns cafe (A. D. Côte d'Or 8 M 29).

A charivari? Certainly a transplanted one. The event retains some features of its form, but aims at a political enemy and operates under the guidance of a republican association with its headquarters a private room in a cafe. Those are nineteenth-century devices. Nevertheless, to the eyes of Dijon's captain of gendarmes, it is a charivari.

Another police report ten days later likewise sheds a revealing light on the nineteenth-century version of the charivari:

On the evening of the 18th, it was said that a serenade would be given to M. Petit, deputy royal prosecutor, who had just resigned on refusing to make a search which took place at the offices of the *Patriot,* and also that a charivari would be given to the royal prosecutor, who ordered that search. The gendarme patrol was therefore sent to the homes of M. Petit and the royal prosecutor, but disorder was seen (A. D. Côte d'Or 8 M 29).

This juxtaposition of the serenade and the charivari tells us about another significant feature of these means of action: the existence of gradations of the performance running from very negative to very positive. One could organize a friendly charivari: a serenade. In fact, when the deputy-philosopher Etienne Cabet arrived in Dijon in Novermber 1833, "many young people" immediately gave him a serenade. During the festivities the innkeeper Mortureux was arrested for "seditious cries;" he had shouted "Long live the Republic" (A. D. Côte d'Or 8 M 29).

For another twenty years, the charivari continued to fill the police dossiers of Dijon–and, for that matter, of other French cities. After the revolution of 1848, its irrevocable decline began. If you run through the dossiers of the Third Republic, you encounter plenty of actions of workers and peasants which attract police attention, but almost no trace of that once-flourishing ritual, in either its moral or its political form. So we are dealing with a form of action which did plenty of work for the ordinary people of the old regime, which adapted to different circumstances and to broad social changes, but which went into retirement in the age of unions, associations and political parties.

The existence of that range of applications of a musical sanction raises an interesting series of problems. First of all we notice the paradoxical combination of ritual and flexibility. As in every well-defined, familiar game, the players know how to modify, improvise, elaborate, even innovate while respecting the ground rules. From the Revolution onward, we see the players extending the charivari from its moral base to explicitly political affairs. The charivari is a well-defined means of collective action, parallel in that regard to voting, demonstrating, petitioning and striking. Like every means of collective action, the charivari has its own applications and its particular history. But at a given point in history it belongs to a familiar repertoire of collective actions which are at the disposal of ordinary people. The repertoire of collective actions therefore evolves in two different ways: the set of means available to people changes as a function of social, economic and political transformations, while each individual means of action adapts to new interests and opportunities for action. Tracing that double evolution of the repertoire is a fundamental task for social history.

How the Revolution Mattered

What that trace shows makes quite a difference to our understanding of major political changes. We can, for example, imagine three different roles for the French Revolution in the transformation of collective action: as a hinge, as a milestone or as an episode. If it acted as a *hinge,* the Revolution changed the whole direction in which collective action was evolving. Thus Albert Soboul, despite some concessions to pre-revolutionary changes and to the general drift of history, declares that the Revolution "transformed French existence fundamentally, making it correspond to the views of the bourgeoisie and the owning classes."[4]

Seen as a *milestone,* the Revolution marked but one stage among others in the course of a transformation already well begun, and continuing afterward. Michelet, for example, portrays an acceleration of the march of justice and of the French people under the Revolution. In his view, the acceleration reinforced the continuous movement of history, rather than contradicting, interrupting or even deflecting it.

Finally, if we see the Revolution as an *episode,* we claim that at most it broke the continuity of a set of social conditions which took hold again later as if the Revolution had not taken place. Although he does allow the Revolutionary period some peculiarities of its own, Yves-Marie Bercé's analysis of peasant uprisings from the sixteenth to the nineteenth century concludes that "the peasant risings of 1789–93 do not display any fundamental break with the prior pattern of communal revolts. They were in fact a survival of old forms, and did not mark the appearance of new forms of violence."[5]

The notions of the Revolution as hinge, milestone or episode obviously apply to popular collective action as well as to social organization in general. Our historical promenade in the Dijonnais leads in the direction of the second notion: milestone rather than hinge or episode. The Revolution, that is, marked a stage of a process which was already visible in the eighteenth century and was

still active in the nineteenth. The stage was crucial. The process itself was complex, including the resistance of local interests against the incursions of the state and of capitalism as well as the rise of different types of association as the bases of collective action, the nationalization of power struggles and a sort of politicization of collective action. These conclusions emerge at three different levels: from the study of the occasions of collective action from the mid-eighteenth to the mid-nineteenth century; from the analysis of the repertoire of collective action during the same period; and from reflection on the work of the Revolution itself.

At the level of occasions for collective action, it is remarkable how much the defense of threatened interests outweighed the pursuit of hopes for a happier future. If in France as a whole the seventeenth century was the heroic age of tax rebellions, in the eighteenth and first half of the nineteenth century that collective resistance to fiscal innovations continued, while struggles over food supply and common rights increased. In general, the interests at play were those of small local units, especially peasant communities. The growth of capitalism and the expansion of the state required the "liberation" of resources over which the needs of the local unit had exercised priority. The Revolution played the dialectical role of accelerating the threat while increasing the chances for resistance to it.

At the level of the repertoire of collective action, the century from 1750 to 1850 brought an amplification and elaboration of the means available to people without eliminating any of the principal forms of action already in existence at the beginning of the period. It was the second half of the nineteenth century that brought the disappearance of the charivari, the classic food riot, the armed rebellion against the tax collector, and even the inter-village brawl. During the previous hundred years, in contrast, we see the appearance of the demonstration, the development of the strike, the rise of the deliberately-called meeting as means and context of action. Despite the defensive orientation of an important part of the period's collective actions, the means of offensive collective action were forming. They were forming on an enlarged scale, on the base of new sorts of organizations. The Revolution again played a contradictory role. Although the revolutionary legislation opposed special-interest associations, the experience of popular assemblies, revolutionary associations and national elections provided a model and, to some degree, a guarantee for action organized around a collective interest.

Rural Conflicts Before and After

The experience of Burgundy again gives us some concrete illustrations of these general processes. In rural Burgundy, the collective action of the eighteenth century had a strong anticapitalist orientation. It was, as we have already seen, the golden age of food riots. The crises of 1709, 1758 and 1775 brought their clusters of conflicts, and others appeared in between the great crises. That is the meaning of the 1770 edict of the Parlement of Burgundy which, like so many other edicts of the period, forbade anyone "to gather and stop wagons loaded with wheat or other grain, on roads, in cities, towns or villages, on pain of special prosecution…" (A. D. Côte d'Or C 81). That blockage of grain expressed the demand of ordinary people that the needs of the community have priority over the requirements of the market. The market, and therefore the merchants as well.

The second common form of anticapitalist action was less routine and more ironic. It was local resistance to the landlords' consolidation of lands and of rights in the land. The irony lies in our normal readiness to place the landlords themselves in the anticapitalist camp. As the great regional historian Pierre de Saint-Jacob showed, the Burgundian landlords of the period–including both the "old" nobility and the ennobled officials and merchants– played the capitalist game by seizing the forests, usurping common lands, enclosing fields and insisting on collecting all the use fees to which their manors gave them claim. Rural people fought back. Suits against landlords multiplied, a fact which de Saint-Jacob interprets as evidence not only of seigniorial aggression but also of an increasing liberation of the peasants from traditional respect. (Emmanuel Le Roy Ladurie bids up the argument by writing of a "politicization" of peasant resistance in Burgundy.[6])

Where the lawsuit was impossible or ineffective, peasants resisted the seizure of commons by occupying them, resisted enclosures by breaking the hedges or fences. As Pierre de Saint-Jacob describes it:

> The wardens of Athie were attacked by the people of Viserny for trying to forbid entry to a shepherd. On the lands of Bernard de Fontette, Pierre César du Crest, the lord of Saint-Aubin, organized an unusual expedition. He went with 17 men armed with "guns, stakes and staves" to break down the enclosures. They led in 40 cattle under the protection of two guards "with guns and hunting dogs," and kept the tenants of Bernard de Fontette from bringing in their cattle. In Charmois, at the urging of two women, a band of peasants went to break down a fence set up by the overseer of Grenand who could do nothing but watch and receive the jeers of the crowd. In Panthier, a merchant wanted to enclose his meadow; he got authorization from the local court. People assembled in the square and decided to break the hedges, which was done that night. They led in the horses. The merchant wanted to chase them away, but the young people who were guarding them stopped him, 'saying that they were on their own property, in a public meadow, that they had broken the enclosures and that they would break them again…'[7]

As we can see, the opposition was not directed specifically against the landed nobility, but against the landlords of any class who chewed at the collective rights of the rural community. If in Longecourt in 1764 it was the lord who demanded his own share of the commons, in Darois two years later the Chapter of Sainte-Chapelle, in Dijon, tried to take a share of the communal woods, and in Villy-le-Brûlé in 1769 it was a farmer-notary who enclosed a meadow only to see the ditches filled in by the local people (A. D. Côte D'Or C 509, C 543, C 1552).

What a contrast with rural collective action after the Revolution! Food riots did survive until the middle of the nineteenth century. For example, in April 1829 a crowd in Châtillon forced M. Beaudoin, operator of a flour mill, to sell his wheat at 5 francs and 25 sous per double bushel, when he had posted the price at 5F30 (A. D. Côte d'Or M 8 II 4). At the next market, several brigades of gendarmes were on hand to prevent such "disorders" (A. D. Côte d'Or

8 M 27). Although the food riot continued to flourish, post-revolutionary rural struggles bore hardly a trace of the resistance against the landlords. Instead they concerned the policies, and especially the fiscal policies, of the state.

The active groups of the nineteenth century came especially from the small landholders and the workers of the commercialized, fully capitalist vineyards. Robert Laurent portrays that sort of protest as it took place just after the Revolution of 1830:

> ...in September, the announcement of the resumption of the inventory of wine on the premises of winegrowers started turbulent demonstrations, near-riots, in Beaune. On the 12th of September at the time of the National Guard review 'cries of anger against the Revenue Administration [La Régie] rose from its very ranks.' Told that the residents of the suburbs planned to go to the tax offices in order to burn the registers as they had in 1814, the mayor thought it prudent that evening to call the artillery company to arms and convoke part of the National Guard for 5 o'clock the next morning. On the 13th, toward 8 A.M., 'a huge crowd of winegrowers and workers,' shouting 'down with the wolves, down with excise taxes,' occupied the city hall square. To calm the demonstrators the mayor had to send the National Guard home at once. 'The crowd then dispersed gradually'.[8]

Despite that peaceful dispersal, the authorities had to delay the inventory of wine. In Meursault it was less peaceful: the winegrowers drove out the tax men.

What is more, the anti-tax movement connected directly to political movements. The winegrowing area stood out for its republicanism; that was especially true of the hinterlands of Dijon and Beaune. In fact, we have already had a foretaste of the Burgundian flavor: the search of newspaper offices which incited the serenade and the charivari of September 1833 had to do with the *Patriote de la Côte d'Or*. The newspaper was being prosecuted for promoting resistance to tax collection. Etienne Cabet, deputy of the vineyard region, took up the defense of the newspaper. And during the Cabetian serenade of November 1833, people shouted not only "Long live the Republic" but also "Down with the excise taxes."

What Was Changing?

All things considered, we observe a significant transformation of the repertoire of collective action in Burgundy. As compared with the means of action prevailing before the Revolution, those of the nineteenth century were less tied to a communal base, more attached to national politics. Associations, clubs, societies played an increasing part. Yet there were important continuities: the survival of the charvari, the food riot, the classic anti-tax rebellion; the persistent orientation to the protection of local interests against the claims of the state and the market rather than to the creation of a better future. The old regime repertoire of collective action survived the Revolution. The forms of action themselves altered, adapted to new conditions; among other things, we notice a sort of politicization of all the forms. New forms of collective action arose; so far we have noticed especially the appearance of the demonstration as a distinctive means of action. Later we shall see the strike taking on importance as well. That hundred years spanning the Revolution was a period of transformation and growth of the means of collective action.

What of the Revolution's place in that transformation and growth of the means of collective action? The Revolution brought an extraordinary level of collective action, a politicization of all interests and thus of almost all the means of action, a centralization of power and thus of struggles for power, a frenzy of association and thus of action on the basis of associations, a promotion of the conditions for the development of capitalism and bourgeois hegemony and thus of a mounting threat to non-capitalist, non-bourgeois interests. If that summary is correct, the Revolution acted as a fundamental stage in the course of a transformation far longer, and larger than the Revolution itself. Like the seventeenth-century consolidation of the national state, the changes of the Revolution led to a significant alteration of the prevailing modes of popular collective action.

The evolution of collective action had not ended, however. Although the Dijon winegrowers' demonstrations of the 1830s certainly display many more familiar features than the Lanturelus of the 1630s, they also show their age. Nowadays, the successors of those winegrowers typically assemble outside the departmental capital, grouped around placards and banners identifying their organizations and summarizing their demands. The classic charivari and food riot have vanished, along with a number of other forms of action which persisted into the nineteenth century. Today's large-scale actions are even more heavily concentrated in Dijon, Beaune and other cities than they were in the 1830s. Labor unions and political parties often appear in the action. Although prices and taxes continue to be frequent causes for complaint, such exotic questions as American warmaking in Vietnam and the future of students in sports and physical education exercise many a crowd. As the world has changed, so has its collective action.

The Twentieth Century
In order to find the twentieth-century equivalent of the old Series I of the municipal archives, we have to walk the few blocks to the departmental archives, or even take the three-hour train trip to Paris for an exploration of the national archives. With the Revolution and especially with the building of a national police apparatus under Napoleon, three important changes occurred. First, the surveillance, control and repression of collective action became the business of specialized local representatives of the national government: policemen, prosecutors, spies, and others. Second, the procedures of surveillance, control and repression bureaucratized, routinized, became objects of regular reporting and inspection. Third, *anticipatory* surveillance greatly increased: the authorities watched groups carefully, to see what collective action they might take in the future, and to be ready for it. The user of French archives notices these changes in a significant expansion of the documentation available, and a significant displacement from the files of the many local old-regime authorities which had some jurisdiction over collective action to the files of a relatively small number of agencies of the national government. That is why the departmental and national archives yield so much more of our nineteenth- and twentieth-century evidence.

Bundle SM 3530 of the Côte d'Or departmental archives illustrates all these points. SM 3530 contains reports of *commissaires de police,* regional police officials, from 1914 through 1922. On the whole, SM 3530 is less exotic than its old-regime predecessors. The reports describe nothing so splendid as the 1564 entry into Dijon by Charles IX, when no fewer than twenty-three painters were among the hundreds of people paid for helping prepare the "works and mysteries necessary for the arrival and entry of the King" (A. M. Dijon I 18), or the 1766 city hall concert in honor of the Prince of Condé, which featured the prodigious Mozart children from Salzburg (A. M. Dijon B 400). They do, however, tell us of General Pershing's arrival in 1919 (he and Col. Howlet, the local American commander, dined at the Hôtel de la Cloche; alas, no "works and mysteries" were performed) and of the allegedly antipatriotic performance by music-hall star Montéhus in 1917. (While Dijon's *Le Bien du Peuple* declared that Montéhus had proposed "civil war after the fighting had ended," the five off-duty policemen in the audience who were later interrogated said Montéhus had told the crowd that although he was still a revolutionary socialist, politics would have to wait while there was a war on.) By contrast with the cramped handwritten minutes and elegantly penned proclamations of the seventeenth century, these twentieth-century dossiers contain many typewritten reports, some telegrams, occasional notes of telephone conversations, scattered newspaper clippings and a few standard printed forms. As archeological specimens, they clearly belong to our own era.

Those are only their most superficial ties to the twentieth century. The dossiers of SM 3530 also provide clear traces of the great events of the time: the World War appears in such guises as the antiwar demonstrations of 1914 and the ceremonies, on the Fourth of July 1918, renaming the Place du Peuple as the Place du Président Wilson. The Russian Revolution shows up in 1918 in the form of "Bolshevist propaganda" spread by the detachment of 220 Russian soldiers at Dijon and by a few Russian civilians in the city. The national split of the labor movement into Communist and Socialist branches leaves its mark in the 1922 fractionation of the departmental labor federation. The major events of political history have their immediate counterparts in the stream of collective action gauged by the local police.

The reports of 28 July 1914 give a sense of the twentieth-century tone:

> This evening, toward 6 p.m., a group of about a hundred workers, composed mainly of Spaniards and Italians and also of young people from the city aged 16 to 18, almost all of them workers at the Petit Bernard glassworks, formed spontaneously into a parade at the Place du Peuple and, passing through Chabot Charny and Liberté streets, went to the Place Darcy, shouting 'Down with war! We want peace!' Because the demonstration was growing from moment to moment and because it seemed to be of a kind which would produce disorder in the streets and agitate popular feeling, I immediately took the necessary measures to stop the demonstration and, with the aid of a number of the available police, I managed to disperse the demonstrators at the Place Darcy and on the Boulevard de Sévigné, and by 7:20 calm had returned.

The inspector's helpers had picked up the group's marching orders, which read "Calm. Don't resist the police, disperse. In case of breakup, reform at the corner of *Le Miroir*. If broken up again, reform in front of *Le Progres,* then in front of *Le Bien Public.* No shouts, no singing. In front of *Le Progrès,* only one shout: Vive la paix."

To anyone who has taken part in twentieth-century demonstrations, both sides of the story are wearily familiar. Despite his allusion to "spontaneity," the police inspector recognizes the event as an unauthorized demonstration, and takes the standard steps to check it. The glassworkers, on their side, anticipate the reaction of the police, and make contingency plans. The players know their stage directions, although the script leaves plenty of room for improvisation, and no one is sure how it will end. The demonstrators want to assemble as many people as possible in a visible and symbolically significant public place, and to display their common devotion to a single well-defined program. The event shares some properties with the Lanturelu of 1630, the serenade of 1790, the political charivari of 1830. It bears a much greater resemblance to the winegrowers' tax protest of 1830. It

is the full-fledged demonstration, a variety of collective action which germinated in the nineteenth century and flowered in the twentieth.

Demonstrations, strikes and public meetings dominate the publicly-visible actions reported in SM 3530 over the whole period from 1914 to 1922. By Bastille Day 1921 the themes of peace and internationalism had returned to prominence after their dissolution in World War I. On the morning of that holiday the "communist socialists" of Dijon organized a march to the city's cemetery. 150 to 200 people (including some 20 women) gathered at the Place du Président Wilson. Young people distributed handbills as they paraded. At the head of the procession came three dignitaries from the labor exchange, the editor of the socialist newspaper, a former deputy and a departmental council member. "Next came twenty children carrying flowers and three red flags representing the A.R.A.C., the union federation and the socialist party, then six signs saying WAR AGAINST WAR, WE HATE HATRED, AMNESTY, HANDS ACROSS THE BORDER, THOU SHALT NOT KILL (JESUS), THEY HAVE CLAIMS ON US (CLEMENCEAU)." Leaders of the movement gave speeches at the 1870–71 war monument, and members of the crowd ceremoniously laid out three bouquets–one each for the French, Italian and German dead. "The banners were folded up," the inspector tells us, "and the crowd left the cemetery without incident at 11.30 a.m."

In the midst of this series of reports come periodic appraisals of local "public spirit." *Esprit public* refers especially to the likely intensity and direction of collective action on the part of different parts of the population. The job of the spies, informers and observers employed by the police is to gauge and document those likelihoods. In 1918, we find our inspector reporting to the public prosecutor that

> The world of factory and shop workers is complaining about the cost of living but has not been too hard hit so far by the new controls. In any case, they are willing to do their part...The three groups of railroad workers (trains, roadbed and operations) are holding secret meetings, and talking about occupational questions; they expect a follow-through on the promises made to them; that looks to me like a sore point which could bring on

some agitation in the future if they don't receive satisfaction. In my opinion it would be a good idea to resolve the question of special compensation as soon as possible.

Nothing unusual about all this. That is the point: by 1918, we have a police force routinely scanning the world of workers, students and political activists for any signs of "agitation," any predictors of concerted action. That same police force has developed standard procedures for monitoring, containing and, on occasion, breaking up meetings, demonstrations and strikes when they do occur. Its business is repression.

By comparison with the nineteenth century, these twentieth-century actions are large in scale, strongly tied to formal organizations pursuing defined public programs, closely monitored by the police. Their variety and color appear to have diminished: the charivari and its companion forms of street theater, for example, disappeared from the popular repertoire without replacement. Popular collective action channeled itself into meetings, strikes, demonstrations and a few related types of gathering. These recent changes all continue trends which were clearly visible by the middle of the nineteenth century. The same sorts of changes in interest, organization and opportunity that we have seen in the nineteenth century continued in the twentieth: increasing state control of essential decisions and resources, expanding importance of special-interest associations, growing range of governmental surveillance, and so on. In the perspective of the last three or four centuries, the period since the Revolution of 1848 is definitely of a piece.

Long-Run Changes in Collective Action

The chronology of collective action which emerges from our exploration of Burgundy has some surprises in it. If the Revolution of 1789 was not a hinge but a milestone, the less momentous Revolution of 1848 has some claim to be a hinge: a greater change in the character and direction of collective action occurred in the middle of the nineteenth century than at the end of the eighteenth. To find a comparable transition, we must look back to the middle of the seventeenth century, the period of the Fronde. Then, as in the nineteenth century, a great

expansion and centralization of state power altered the character of contention for power. In Burgundy, as elsewhere, the transition showed up first and most visibly as a series of rebellions against new and expanded taxation. The Lanturelu of 1630 is a case in point. From that time on, Burgundy and most of France moved into two centuries of intermittent popular resistance to the expansion of state power and the growth of capitalist property relations. Anti-conscription movements, food riots, invasions of fields, further tax rebellions started that popular resistance.

People had fought taxes and military service long before 1630. The mid-seventeenth century nevertheless served as a hinge in the history of collective action. Before that point local authorities and regional magnates were often available as allies; in popular rebellion they saw the means of retaining their liberties or expanding their power. The great rebellions of the seventeenth century all built on the complicity or active support of local authorities and regional magnates. Starting with the repression of the Fronde, Louis XIV and his ministers managed to check, coopt, replace or liquidate most of their regional rivals. After swelling in the seventeenth century, with considerable support from authorities and magnates, popular resistance continued on its own for two centuries more. It changed form as interests, organization and opportunity shifted. We have noticed the durable rise of the food riot at the end of the seventeenth century, as the pressure on communities to surrender local grain reserves to the demands of the national market increased, and gained the support of royal officials. We have seen the rise and fall of rural efforts to defend communal rights to glean or pasture against the efforts of landlords to consolidate their holdings and make their property claims exclusive. This sort of resistance to the claims of the state and the demands of capitalism persisted unabated into the nineteenth century.

The nineteenth-century transition brought a great and rapid decline in the two-hundred-year-old resistance to statemaking and capitalism. Although the mobilization and politicization of the 1789 Revolution anticipated some of its effects, the Revolution of 1848 marked—and helped produce—a major swing away from the defense of local interests against the expansion of the state and of capitalism, toward popular efforts to organize around interests on a relatively large scale and to seize some control over the state and over the means of production. We have noticed the virtual disappearance of the food riot and the old style of tax rebellion, the flourishing of the strike, of the demonstration, and of the public meeting as means of collective action.

The incentives for analyzing the history of collective action, instead of contenting ourselves with the collective action of our own time, go beyond the desire to understand the past in its own terms. The past helped create the present; knowledge of the impact of the expanding seventeenth-century state on the interests, hopes and grievances of ordinary Frenchmen will help us identify the durable features of that state and of its impact on collective action. If we are so foolish as to seek generalizations about the influence of statemaking—or of industrialization, or of urbanization, or of the expansion of capitalism—on prevailing patterns of collective action, we have no choice but to look at big blocks of historical experience in which statemaking, industrialization, urbanization or the expansion of capitalism were actually occurring. Just such a foolish, absorbing search brought me to Dijon to leaf through seventeenth-century police reports and watch students march through the streets outside the archives.

NOTES

I am grateful to the National Science Foundation for financial support, to the archivists of the departmental and municipal archives of Dijon for aid, and to Martha Guest for help with bibliography. This is an edited version of Working Paper 128, Center for Research on Social Organization, University of Michigan. © 1977 Charles Tilly.

1. H. Millot, *Le comité permanent de Dijon, juillet 1789–février 1790.* "La Révolution en Côte d'Or," new series, no. 1 (Dijon, 1925), pp. 147–148.
2. Colin Lucas, *The Structure of the Terror: The Example of Javogues and the Loire* (London, 1973).
3. Harvey Mitchell, "The Vendée and Counterrevolution: A Review Essay," *French Historical Studies* 5 (1968), pp. 405–429.
4. Albert Soboul. *Précis d'Histoire de la Révolution Française* (Paris, 1962), p. 520.
5. Yves-Marie Bercé, *Croquants et nu-pieds. Les soulèvements paysans en France du XVIe au XIXe siècle* (Paris, 1974), p. 162.
6. Emmanuel Le Roy Ladurie, "Révoltes et contestations rurales en France de 1675 à 1788," *Annales: Economies, Societes, Civilisations* 29 (1974), pp. 6–22.
7. Pierre de Saint-Jacob, *Les paysans du Bourgogne du Nord* (Paris, 1960), pp. 370–371.
8. Robert Laurent, *Les Vignerons de la 'Côte d'Or' au dix-neuvième siècle* (Paris, 1957), pp. 484–485.

26.
Tactical Innovation and the Pace of Insurgency
DOUG MCADAM

Sociological analysis and theory regarding social movements has tended to focus on the causes of insurgency. By comparison, relatively little attention has been devoted to the dynamics of movement development and decline.[1] This article represents a modest attempt to address this "hole" in the movement literature by analyzing the effect of one factor on the ongoing development of a single movement. It studies the relationship between *tactical interaction* and the pace of black insurgency between 1955 and 1970.

The Significance of Tactics and the Process of Tactical Interaction

The significance of tactics to social movements derives from the unenviable position in which excluded or challenging groups find themselves. According to Gamson (1975:140): "the central

McAdam, Doug. 1983. "Tactical Innovation and the Pace of Insurgency." *Americal Sociological Review* 48: 735–754. Reprinted by permission of American Sociological Association.

difference among political actors is captured by the idea of being inside or outside of the polity... Those who are outside are challengers. They lack the basic prerogative of members—routine access to decisions that affect them." The key challenge confronting insurgents, then, is to devise some way to overcome the basic powerlessness that has confined them to a position of institutionalized political impotence. The solution to this problem is preeminently tactical. Ordinarily insurgents must bypass routine decision-making channels and seek, through use of noninstitutionalized tactics, to force their opponents to deal with them outside the established arenas within which the latter derive so much of their power. In a phrase, they must create "negative inducements" to bargaining (Wilson, 1961).

Negative inducements involve the creation of a situation that disrupts the normal functioning of society and is antithetical to the interests of the group's opponents. In essence, insurgents seek to disrupt their opponent's realization of interests to such an extent that the cessation of the offending tactic becomes a sufficient inducement to grant concessions.

Findings reported by Gamson (1975:72–88) support the efficacy of negative inducements or disruptive tactics for many challenging groups. In summarizing his findings, he concludes that "unruly groups, those that use violence, strikes, and other constraints, have better than average success" (Gamson, 1975:87). Piven and Cloward's (1979) analysis of several "poor people's movements" supports Gamson's conclusion. As they note, "...it is usually when unrest among the lower classes breaks out of the confines of electoral procedures that the poor may have some influence, for the instability and polarization they then threaten to create by their actions in the factories or in the streets may force some response from electoral leaders" (Piven and Cloward, 1979:15).

In most cases, then, the emergence of a social movement attests to at least limited success in the use of disruptive tactics. To survive, however, a movement must be able to sustain the leverage it has achieved through the use of such tactics. To do it must either parlay its initial successes into positions of institutionalized power (as, for

instance, the labor movement did) or continue to experiment with noninstitutional forms of protest. Regarding the latter course of action, even the most successful tactic is likely to be effectively countered by movement opponents if relied upon too long. Barring the attainment of significant institutionalized power, then, the pace of insurgency comes to be crucially influenced by (a) the creativity of insurgents in devising new tactical forms, and (b) the ability of opponents to neutralize these moves through effective tactical counters. These processes may be referred to as *tactical innovation* and *tactical adaptation,* respectively. Together they define an ongoing process of *tactical interaction* in which insurgents and opponents seek, in chess-like fashion, to offset the moves of the other. How well each succeeds at this task crucially affects the pace and outcome of insurgency.

As crucial as this interactive dynamic is, it has received scant empirical attention in the social movement literature.[2] Instead research has tended to focus on the characteristics or resources of either opponents or insurgents rather than the dynamic relationship between the two.

Political Process as a Context for Tactical Innovation

As important as the process of tactical innovation is, it derives much of its significance from the larger political/organizational context in which it occurs. That is, the process only takes on significance in the context of the more general factors that make for a viable social movement in the first place.

Elsewhere (McAdam, 1982) is outlined a *political process* model of social movements that stresses the importance of two structural factors in the emergence of widespread insurgency. The first is the level of indigenous organization within the aggrieved population; the second the alignment of groups within the larger political environment. The first can be conceived of as the degree of organizational "readiness" within the minority community and the second, following Eisinger (1973:11), as the "structure of political opportunities" available to insurgent groups. As necessary, but not sufficient, conditions for social insurgency, both factors are crucial prerequisites for the process of tactical innovation. Indigenous organizations furnish the context in which tactical innovations are devised and subsequently carried out. Such organizations serve to mobilize community resources in support of new tactical forms and to supply leaders to direct their use, participants to carry them out, and communication networks to facilitate their use and dissemination to other insurgent groups.[3] This latter point is especially significant. The simple introduction of a new protest technique in a single locale is not likely to have a measureable effect on the pace of movement activity unless its use can be diffused to other insurgent groups operating in other areas. It is the established communication networks characteristic of existing organizations that ordinarily make this crucial process of diffusion possible.[4]

But the effectiveness of such organizations and the tactical innovations they employ also depend, to a considerable degree, on characteristics of the larger political environment which insurgents confront. Under ordinary circumstances excluded groups or challengers face enormous obstacles in their efforts to advance group interests. They oftentimes face a political establishment united in its opposition to insurgent goals and therefore largely immune to pressure from movement groups. Under such circumstances tactical innovations are apt to be repressed or ignored rather than triggering expanded insurgency. More to the point it is unlikely even that such innovations will be attempted in the face of the widely shared feelings of pessimism and impotence that are likely to prevail under such conditions. Tactical innovations *only* become potent in the context of a political system vulnerable to insurgency. Expanding political opportunities then create a potential for the exercise of political leverage which indigenous organizations seek to exploit. It is the confluence of these two factors that often seems to presage widespread insurgency.

Certainly this was true in the case of the black movement (McAdam, 1982: see especially Chapters 5–7). By mid-century the growing electoral importance of blacks nationwide, the collapse of the southern cotton economy, and the increased salience of third world countries in United States foreign policy had combined to grant blacks a measure of political

leverage they had not enjoyed since Reconstruction. Equally significant was the extraordinary pace of institutional expansion within the southern black community in the period of 1930–1960. Triggered in large measure by the decline in cotton farming and the massive rural to urban migration it set in motion, this process left blacks in a stronger position organizationally than they had ever been in before. In particular, three institutions—the black church, black colleges, and the southern wing of the NAACP—grew apace of this general developmental process. Not surprisingly, these three institutions were to dominate the protest infrastructure out of which the movement was to emerge in the period 1955–1960. It is against this backdrop of expanding political opportunities and growing organizational strength, then, that the emergence of the civil rights movement must be seen.

The confluence of indigenous organization and expanding political opportunities, however, only renders widespread insurgency likely, not inevitable. Insurgents must still define the "time as ripe" for such activity and commit indigenous organizational resources to the struggle. Then, too, they must devise methodologies for pressing their demands. It is only at this point that the process of tactical innovation becomes crucial. For if expanding opportunities and established organizations presage movement emergence, it is the skill of insurgents in devising effective protest tactics *and* their opponents' ability to counter such tactics that largely determine the pace and outcome of insurgency. In the remainder of this article attention will center on this dynamic and its effects on the unfolding of black protest activity in this country between 1955 and 1970.

Institutionalized Powerlessness and the Politics of Protest

By any measure of institutionalized political power blacks were almost totally powerless in the middle decades of this century. Of the nearly eight and three-quarter million voting age blacks in the country in 1950 only an estimated three million were registered to vote (Berger, 1950:26), in contrast to the estimated 81 percent registration rate for whites in 1952 (Danigelis, 1978:762). While no contemporaneous count of black elected officials nationwide is available, the number was certainly very small. At the national level, only two Congressman—Dawson (R–IL) and Powell (D–NY)—held elective office. Institutionalized political impotence was most extreme for southern blacks. Some ten and a quarter million blacks still resided in the South in 1950, with barely 900,000 of them registered to vote (Bullock, 1971:227; Hamilton, 1964:275). No blacks held major elective office in the region and none had served in Congress since 1901 (Ploski and Marr, 1976). Moreover, with blatantly discriminatory electoral practices still commonplace throughout the region—especially in the Deep South—the prospects for changing this state of affairs were bleak. Yet a scant twenty years later significant change had come to the South. An entire system of Jim Crow caste restrictions had been dismantled. Black voter registration rates had risen from less than 20 percent in 1950 to 65 percent in 1970 (Lawson, 1976:331). The number of black elected officials in the region climbed to nearly 1,900 after the 1970 elections (Brooks, 1974:293). And with the election of Andrew Young and Barbara Jordan, black southerners were represented in Congress for the first time since 1901.

The pressure for these changes came from an indigenous movement organized and led primarily by southern blacks. In the face of the institutional political powerlessness of this population it is important to ask how this pressure was generated and sustained. The answer to this question is, of course, complex. However, any complete account of how blacks were able to mount such a successful insurgent campaign must focus squarely on their willingness to bypass "proper channels" in favor of noninstitutionalized forms of protest. Having "humbly petitioned" the South's white power structure for decades with little results, insurgents logically turned to the only option left open to them: the "politics of protest." It was the potential for disruption inherent in their use of noninstitutionalized forms of political action that was to prove decisive.

Methods

To measure the pace of black insurgency over this period all relevant story synopses contained in

the annual *New York Times Index* (for the years, 1955–70) under the two headings, "Negroes–U.S.–General," and "Education–U.S.–Social Integration," were read and content-coded along a variety of dimensions. The decision to restrict coding to these headings was based on a careful examination of the classification system employed in the *Index*, which indicated that the overwhelming majority of events relevant to the topic were listed under these two headings.

To be coded, a story had to satisfy four criteria. It first had to be relevant to the general topic of black civil rights. As a result, a good many other topics were excluded from the analysis, for example, stories reporting the achievements of black athletes or entertainers. Besides this general criterion of relevance, to be coded, synopses also had to be judged unambiguous as to (1) the nature of the event being reported (e.g. riot, sit-in, court decision); (2) the individual(s) or group(s) responsible for its initiation; and (3) geographic location of the event. The former two variables, "type of action" and "initiating unit," figure prominently in the analysis to be reported later.

In all better than 12,000 synopses were coded from a total of about 29,000 read. Coding was carried out by the author and a single research assistant. By way of conventional assurances, intercoder reliability coefficients exceeded .90 for all but one variable. For all variables employed in this article, however, reliability ratings exceeded .95.[5]

Black Insurgency and the Process of Tactical Innovation

To assess the effect of tactical innovation on the pace of black insurgency between 1955 and 1970 requires that we be able to measure both insurgent pace and innovation. Two code categories noted in the previous section enable us to do so. The variable, "initiating unit," provides us with frequency counts of all civil rights-related actions for all parties to the conflict (e.g., federal government, Martin Luther King, Jr., etc.). One major category of initiating unit employed in the study was that of "movement group or actor." The combined total of all actions attributed to movement groups or actors provides a rough measure of the pace of movement-initiated activity over time. Figure 1 shows the frequency of such activity between October 1955 and January 1971.

What relationship, if any, is there between tactical innovation and the ebb and flow of movement activity? By coding the "type of action" involved in each reported event, we can compare the frequency with which various tactics were used to the overall pace of insurgency shown in Figure 1. Figures 2 and 3 show the specific activity frequencies for five novel tactical forms utilized by insurgents during the course of the movement.

As these figures show, peaks in movement activity tend to correspond to the introduction and spread of new protest techniques.[6] The pattern is a consistent one. The pace of insurgency jumps sharply following the introduction of a new tactical form, remains high for a period of time, and then begins to decline until another tactical innovation sets the pattern in motion again. A more systematic view of this dynamic is provided in Table 1.

Table 1 reports the use of five specific tactics as a proportion of all movement-initiated actions

during each of the first twelve months following the introduction of each technique.

As the "Total" column makes clear, the sheer number of actions is highest immediately following the introduction of a new protest form, as is the proportion of all actions attributed to the new technique. Thus, tactical innovation appears to trigger a period of heightened protest activity dominated by the recently introduced protest technique. This is not to suggest that the older tactical forms are rendered obsolete by the introduction of the new technique. Table 1 shows clearly that this is not the case. In only 22 of the 60 months represented in the table did the new tactical form account for better than 50 percent of all movement-initiated actions. On the contrary, tactical innovation seems to stimulate the renewed usage of *all* tactical forms. Thus, for example, the economic boycott, largely abandoned after the bus boycotts, was often revived in the wake of sit-in demonstrations as a means of intensifying the pressure generated by the latter technique (Southern Regional Council, 1961). Then, too,

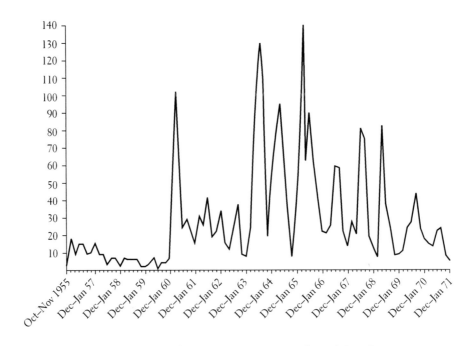

Figure 26.1 Movement-Initiated Actions, Oct–Nov 1955 Through Dec–Jan 1971
Source: *Annual Index* of the *New York Times*, 1955–1971

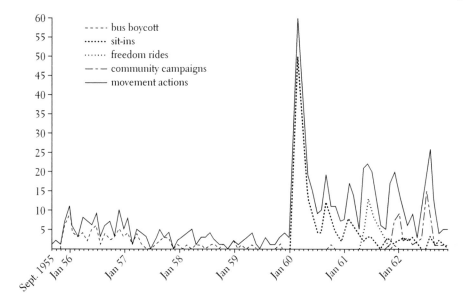

Figure 26.2 Movement-Initiated Actions, September 1955 Through December 1962
Source: *Annual Index* of the *New York Times*, 1955–1962.

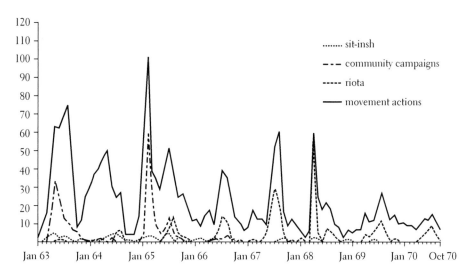

Figure 26.3 Movement-Initiated Actions, January 1963 Through October 1970
Source: *Annual Index* of the *New York Times*, 1963–1970.

Table 1 Tactical Innovations as a Proportion of a Month's Activity by Months Since First Use of Tactical Form

Month Since First Use[a]	Bus Boycott	Sit-in	Freedom Ride	Community Campaign	Riot	Total
0	.86 (6/7)	.57 (24/42)	.19 (4/21)	.06 (1/17)	.14 (7/51)	.30 (42/138)
1	.82 (9/11)	.83 (50/60)	.59 (13/22)	.35 (7/20)	.38 (14/37)	.62 (93/150)
2	.67 (4/6)	.91 (30/33)	.45 (9/20)	.64 (9/14)	.21 (5/24)	.59 (57/97)
3	1.00 (5/5)	.74 (14/19)	.54 (7/13)	.20 (2/10)	.04 (1/26)	.40 (29/73)
4	.50 (4/8)	.53 (8/15)	.83 (5/6)	.50 (3/6)	.00 (0/18)	.38 (20/53)
5	.29 (2/7)	.44 (4/9)	.60 (3/5)	.11 (1/9)	.00 (0/11)	.24 (10/41)
6	.83 (5/6)	.40 (4/10)	.00 (0/17)	***	.00 (0/12)	.23 (11/48)
7	.67 (6/9)	.63 (12/19)	.05 (1/20)	***	.00 (0/8)	.37 (22/60)
8	***	.73 (8/11)	.00 (0/14)	.79 (15/19)	.00 (0/14)	.39 (24/61)
9	.67 (4/6)	.36 (4/11)	.00 (0/10)	.23 (6/26)	.00 (0/17)	.20 (14/70)
10	.29 (2/7)	.29 (2/7)	.00 (0/6)	.08 (1/12)	.11 (1/9)	.15 (6/41)
11	***	.62 (5/8)	.00 (0/9)	***	.29 (6/21)	.33 (15/45)

[a] Listed below are the months of first use for the five tactical forms shown in the table:

Bus Boycott:	December, 1955
Sit-in:	February, 1960
Freedom Ride:	May, 1961
Community Campaign:	December, 1961
Riot:	August, 1965

*** Fewer than 5 movement-initiated actions.

during the community-wide campaign all manner of protest techniques—sit-ins, boycotts, etc.—were employed as part of a varied tactical assault on Jim Crow. This resurgence of the older tactical forms seems to underscore the importance of the process of tactical innovation. The presumption is that in the absence of the heightened movement activity triggered by tactical innovation the older protest forms would not have reappeared. Their use, then, is dependent on the altered protest context created by the introduction of the new technique.

What of the "valleys" in movement activity shown in Figures 2 and 3? A closer analysis suggests that the lulls in insurgency reflect the successful efforts of movement opponents to devise effective tactical counters to the new protest forms. For a fuller understanding of this interactive dynamic, we now turn to a more detailed qualitative examination of the processes of tactical innovation and adaptation surrounding the protest techniques listed in Table 1.

Bus Boycott

The first such technique was the bus boycott. Certainly the most famous and successful of these boycotts was the one organized in Montgomery, Alabama, (1955–56) by the church-based Montgomery Improvement Association (MIA) led by Martin Luther King, Jr. The technique, however, was not original to Montgomery. In 1953 a similar boycott had been organized by the Rev. Theodore Jemison in Baton Rouge, Louisiana.

If not the first, the Montgomery campaign was unique in the measure of success it achieved and the encouragement it afforded others to organize similar efforts elsewhere. In a very real sense the introduction of this technique marks the beginning of what is popularly called the "civil rights movement." From extremely low levels of activism in the early 1950s, the pace of black protest rose sharply in 1956 and 1957.

Consistent with the theme of this article, it is appropriate that we date the beginnings of the movement with a particular tactical, rather than substantive, innovation. After all, the specific issue of discriminatory bus seating had been a source of discontent in the black community for years. Repeated efforts to change such practices had always met with failure until the Montgomery boycott was launched. Why did this tactic succeed where all others had failed? The answer to this question lies in the contrast between the institutional powerlessness of southern blacks at this time and the leverage they were able to mobilize outside "proper channels" by means of the boycott. Outside those channels blacks were able to take advantage of their sizeable numbers to create a significant "negative inducement" to bargaining. That inducement was nothing less than the economic solvency of the bus lines, which depended heavily—70–75% in Montgomery—on their black ridership (Brooks, 1974:110). Such leverage was telling in Montgomery and elsewhere.

The U.S. Supreme Court, on November 13, 1956, declared Montgomery's bus segregation laws unconstitutional. Five weeks later, on December 21, the city's buses were formally desegregated, thereby ending the black community's year-long boycott of the buses. During the boycott an estimated 90–95 percent of the city's black passengers refrained from riding the buses (Walton, 1956).

A similar boycott begun on May 28, 1956, in Tallahassee, Florida, did not result in as clear-cut a victory for insurgents as did the Montgomery campaign. Nonetheless, the boycott once again demonstrated the power of widespread insurgent action by blacks. With blacks comprising 60–70 percent of its total ridership, the city bus company quickly felt the effect of the boycott. Barely five weeks after the start

of the campaign, the bus company was forced to suspend service. With revenues cut by an estimated 60 percent, it simply was no longer feasible to maintain bus service (Smith and Killian, 1958). Several months later bus service was resumed, thanks to several forms of public subsidy devised by city officials. Still the boycott held. Finally, following the Supreme Court's ruling in the Montgomery case, organized efforts to desegregate Tallahassee's buses were instituted. Despite continued harassment, legal desegregation had come to Tallahassee. Finally, the impact of the Tallahassee and Montgomery boycotts (as well as those organized elsewhere) was felt in other locales. Apparently fearing similar disruptive boycotts in their communities, at least a dozen other southern cities quietly desegregated their bus lines during the course of the Tallahassee and Montgomery campaigns.

As effective as the boycott proved to be, it was in time effectively countered by southern segregationists. The adaptation to this tactic took two forms: legal obstruction and extra-legal harassment. The latter consisted of violence or various forms of physical and economic intimidation aimed at members of the black community, especially those prominent in the boycott campaigns. In Montgomery,

> buses were fired upon by white snipers; a teenage girl was beaten by four or five white rowdies as she got off the bus. Four Negro churches were bombed at an estimated damage of $70,000, the homes of Ralph Abernathy and Robert Graetz were dynamited... and someone fired a shotgun blast into the front door of... Martin Luther King's home. (Brooks, 1974:119)

Similar responses were forthcoming in Tallahassee and in other boycott cities (Smith and Killian, 1958:13). These incidents had the effect of increasing the risks of participation in insurgent activity to a level that may well have reduced the likelihood of generating such campaigns elsewhere.

These extra-legal responses were supplemented by various "legal" maneuvers on the part of local officials which were designed to neutralize the effectiveness of the bus boycott as an insurgent tactic. Several examples drawn from the Tallahassee conflict illustrate the type of counter moves that were instituted in many southern communities at this time.[7]

- City police initiated a concerted campaign of harassment and intimidation against car pool participants that included arrests for minor violations and the detention of drivers for questioning in lieu of formal charges.
- The executive committee of the I.C.C., the organization coordinating the boycott, was arrested, tried, and found guilty of operating a transportation system without a license. Each member of the committee received a 60-day jail term and a $500 fine, a sentence that was suspended on condition the defendants engaged in no further illegal activity.
- Following the Supreme Court's desegregation ruling in the Montgomery case, the Tallahassee City Commission met and rescinded the city's bus segregation ordinance replacing it with one directing bus drivers to assign seats on the basis of the "maximum safety" of their passengers. Segregation, of course, was deemed necessary to insure the "maximum safety" of passengers.

Though unable to stem desegregation in the long run, these countermeasures (in combination with the extra-legal techniques reviewed earlier) were initially effective as tactical responses to the bus boycotts.

It wasn't just the short-run effectiveness of these tactical responses, however, that led to the declining pace of black insurgency in the late 1950s (see Figure 2). In point of fact, the bus boycott was a tactic of limited applicability. Its effectiveness was restricted to urban areas with a black population large enough to jeopardize the financial well-being of a municipal bus system. It was also a tactic dependent upon a *well-organized* black community *willing* to break with the unspoken rule against noninstitutionalized forms of political action. This point serves once again to underscore the importance of organization and opportunity in the generation and sustenance of protest activity. Given the necessity for coordinating the actions of large numbers of people over a relatively long period of time, the bus boycott tactic made extensive organization and strong

community consensus a prerequisite for successful implementation. Tactical innovation may have triggered the boycott, but once again it was the confluence of existing organization and system vulnerability—in the form of municipal bus lines dependent on black patrons—that provided the context for successful insurgency. Not surprisingly, these conditions were fairly rare in the South of the mid '50s. Therefore, truly mass protest activity had to await the introduction of a protest tactic available to smaller groups of people. That tactic was the sit-in.

The Sit-in

According to Morris (1981), blacks had initiated sit-ins in at least fifteen cities between 1957 and February 1, 1960. The logical question is why did these sit-ins not set in motion the dramatic expansion in protest activity triggered by the February 1 episode in Greensboro, North Carolina? The answer helps once again to illustrate the importance of organization and opportunity as necessary prerequisites for the dynamic under study here. First, as Morris's analysis reveals, the earlier sit-ins occurred at a time when the diffusion network linking various insurgent groups had not yet developed sufficiently for the tactic to spread beyond its localized origins. Indeed, within a narrow geographical area the expected escalation in protest activity *did* occur. For example, in August, 1958, the local NAACP Youth Council used sit-ins to desegregate a lunch counter in Oklahoma City, Oklahoma. Following this success, the tactic quickly spread, by means of organizational and personal contacts, to groups in the neighboring towns of Enid, Tulsa and Stillwater, Oklahoma, and Kansas City, Kansas, where it was used with varying degrees of success (McAdam, 1982:269; Morris, 1981:750; Oppenheimer, 1963:52).

Secondly, the "structure of political opportunities" confronting southern blacks was hardly as favorable in 1957–58 as it was in 1960. Every one of the pre-Greensboro sit-ins occurred in "progressive" border states (e.g., Missouri, Oklahoma, Kansas). This is hardly surprising in light of the strong supremacist counter-movement that was then sweeping the South (Bartley, 1969; McAdam, 1982). Between 1954 and 1958 southern segregationists mobilized and grew increasingly more active in resisting school desegregation and the organized beginnings of the civil rights movement. White Citizen Councils sprang up throughout the region and came to exercise a powerful influence in both state and local politics (McMillen, 1971). As part of a general regional "flood" of segregationist legislation, several states outlawed the NAACP, forcing the state organization underground and seriously hampering its operation. But the resistance movement was to peak in 1957–58. Total Citizen Council membership rose steadily until 1958, then fell off sharply thereafter. The volume of state segregation legislation followed a similar pattern, peaking in 1956–57 and declining rapidly during the remainder of the decade. By 1960 a noticeable "thaw" was evident in all regions except the "deep South."

Faced, then, with a more conducive political environment and the dense network of organizational ties that make for rapid and extensive diffusion, it is not surprising that the tactic spread as rapidly as it did in the spring of 1960. The events surrounding the Greensboro sit-in are, by now, well known. There on February 1, 1960, four students from North Carolina A and T occupied seats at the local Woolworth's lunch counter. In response, the store's management closed the counter and the students returned to campus without incident. After that, events progressed rapidly. Within a week similar demonstrations had taken place in two other towns in the state. By February 15, the movement had spread to a total of nine cities in North Carolina as well as the neighboring states of Tennessee, Virginia, and South Carolina (McAdam, 1982). By the end of May, 78 southern communities had experienced sit-in demonstrations in which at least 2,000 had been arrested (Meier and Rudwick, 1973:102).

The effect of this tactical innovation on the overall pace of black insurgency is apparent in Figure 2. From low levels of movement activity in the late 1950s, the pace of insurgency increased sharply following the first sit-in in February and remained at fairly high levels throughout the spring of that year. This dramatic rise in movement activity was almost exclusively a function of the introduction and spread of the sit-in as a new tactical form. Not only did local movement groups rush to apply the tactic throughout the South, but these various campaigns soon stimulated supportive forms of movement activity elsewhere. Sympathy demonstrations and the picketing of national chain stores began in the North. At the same time, the existing civil rights organizations rushed to capitalize on the momentum generated by the students by initiating actions of their own (Meier and Rudwick, 1973: 101–104; Zinn, 1965:29).

Why did the introduction of this tactic have the effect it did? Two factors seem to be crucial here. The first is the "accessibility" of the tactic. Even a small group of persons could employ it, as indeed was the case in the initial Greensboro sit-in. Nor was the tactic reserved only for use in large urban areas, as was the case with the bus boycott. In the South nearly all towns of any size had segregated lunch counters, thereby broadening the geographic base of insurgency.

The second factor accounting for the popularity of the tactic was simply that it worked. By late 1961, facilities in 93 cities in ten southern states had been desegregated as a *direct* result of sit-in demonstrations (Bullock, 1970:274). In at least 45 other locales the desire to avoid disruptive sit-ins was enough to occasion the integration of some facilities (Oppenheimer, 1963:273). These figures raise another important question: *why* was the tactic so successful? At first blush the underlying logic of the sit-ins is not immediately apparent. Certainly the logic of the boycott does not apply in the case of segregated facilities. Given that blacks were barred from patronizing such facilities in the first place, they could not very well withdraw their patronage as a means of pressing for change. Instead they sought to create a very different inducement to bargaining. By occupying seats at segregated lunch counters, insurgents sought to disrupt the ordinary operation of business to such an extent that the effected stores would feel compelled to change their racial policies.

The hoped-for disruption of business was only partly a function of the routine closing of the lunch counter that normally accompanied sit-in demonstrations. Obviously, the revenues generated by the lunch counter were only a small fraction of the store's total income and insufficient in themselves to induce the store to negotiate with insurgents. For the tactic to work there had to occur a more generalized store-wide disruption of business. This, in turn, depended upon the emergence, within the community, of a general "crisis definition of the situation." When this occurred, the store became the focal point for racial tensions and violence of sufficient intensity to deter would-be shoppers from patronizing the store. An example will help to illustrate this point. It is drawn from an eye-witness account of the violence that accompanied a 1960 sit-in in Jacksonville, Florida. The account reads:

> Near noon on that day the demonstrators arrived at Grant's store...Grant's then closed its counters after demonstrators sat-in for about five minutes. The sitters then left. As they proceeded toward other stores, a group of about 350 armed white men and boys began running down the street toward the store. Some Negroes broke and ran. The majority, however, proceeded in good order, until four or five members of the Youth Council also panicked and ran. At this point the mob caught up to the demonstrators. A girl was hit with an axe handle. Fighting then began as the demonstrators retreated toward the Negro section of town...A boy was pushed and hit by an automobile...By 12:50 only an hour after the first sit-in that day, Police Inspector Bates reported the downtown situation completely out of hand. A series of individual incidents of mobs catching Negroes and beating them took place at this time. (Oppenheimer, 1963:216)

Clearly, under conditions such as these, shoppers are not likely-to patronize the target store let alone venture downtown. The result is a marked slowdown in retail activity amidst a generalized crisis atmosphere. This state of affairs represents a two-fold tactical advance over that evident during a bus boycott. First, the crisis engendered by a boycott affected fewer people directly and took longer to develop than did a sit-in crisis. Second, as Oberschall (1973:268) notes, "the cost of the boycott fell heavily upon the boycott participants, many of whom walked to work over long distances. Only after months had passed did the loss of income from bus fares create a financial situation worrisome to the municipal administration." By contrast, the financial cost of the sit-in campaign was

felt immediately by the segregationists themselves, making it a much more direct and successful tactic than the boycott.[8]

As is the case with all tactics, however, the impact of the sit-in was relatively short lived. As Figure 2 shows, following the peak in movement activity during the spring of 1960, the pace of insurgency declined sharply in the summer and fall of the year. Part of this decline can, of course, be attributed to the effectiveness of the tactic. Having desegregated facilities in so many cities, there were simply fewer targets left to attack. However, far more important than this in accounting for the diminished use of the tactic was the process of tactical adaptation discussed earlier. Having never encountered the tactic before, segregationists were initially caught off guard and reacted tentatively toward it. Over time, however, they devised tactical counters that proved reasonably effective.

In his thorough analysis of the sit-in movement, Oppenheimer (1963) makes reference to this two-stage phenomenon. He distinguishes between several phases in the development of the typical sit-in. The initial or "incipient state" of the conflict is characterized by "the relatively unplanned reaction to the movement of the police in terms of arrests, by the managers of the stores in terms of unstructured and varying counter-tactics which may vary from day to day..." (Oppenheimer, 1963:168). However, through this process of trial and error, movement opponents were able to devise consistently effective responses to the sit-in tactic (and share them with one another) during what Oppenheimer calls the "reactive phase" of the conflict. These responses included mass arrests by the police, the passage of state or local anti-trespassing ordinances, the permanent closure of the lunch counters, and the establishment of various biracial negotiating bodies to contain or routinize the conflict. The latter adaptation proved especially effective. By defusing the crisis definition of the situation, the disruptive potential of the sit-in was greatly reduced, resulting in a significant decline in the leverage exercised by the insurgents. Indeed, this must be seen as a general aspect of the process of tactical adaptation regardless of the protest technique involved. All protest tactics depend for their effectiveness on the generation of a crisis situation. Yet prolonged use of the tactic necessarily undercuts any definition of crisis that may have obtained initially. James Laue (1971) has termed this process the "neutralization of crisis." He explains: "crisis tolerances change as communities learn to combat direct action and other forms of challenges. In most cities in the early 1960's, sit-ins were enough to stimulate a crisis-definition, but today they are dealt with as a matter of course and are generally ineffective as a change technique" (Laue, 1971:259). And so it was in the South after the initial wave of sit-ins. As a result, the pace of insurgency dropped sharply and civil rights activists resumed their search for potent new tactical forms.

The Freedom Rides

The tactic that revived the movement was the freedom ride. First used by the Fellowship of Reconciliation in 1947 to test compliance with a Supreme Court decision (Morgan v. Virginia, 1946) outlawing segregated seating on vehicles engaged in interstate transportation, the tactic was reintroduced by CORE in May 1961. Prompting its reintroduction was another Supreme Court decision—Boynton v. Virginia—extending the ban against segregation in interstate travel to terminal facilities as well as the means of transportation themselves. To test compliance with the ruling two CORE-organized interracial groups left Washington, D.C., on May 4, bound, by bus, for New Orleans. The buses never reached their destination. Following the burning of one bus near Anniston, Alabama, and a savage mob attack in Birmingham, the riders had to fly to New Orleans to complete their journey. Nevertheless, the ride had more than accomplished its original purpose. Not only had it dramatized continued southern defiance of the Supreme Court's ruling, but it also served, in the words of a contemporary analyst, "as a shot in the arm to civil rights groups just when interest on the part of Southern Negro students seemed to be flagging..." Oppenheimer, 1963:277).

Figure 2 supports Oppenheimer's assessment. Following the initial wave of sit-ins during the spring of 1960, the pace of movement activity foundered badly. Except for a brief flurry of activity in

February–March, 1961, (stimulated, once again, by the introduction of a minor protest technique, the jail-in) the pace of insurgency had dropped to pre–sit-in levels. The initial CORE-sponsored ride changed all this. Inspired by that effort, *and* anxious to capitalize on the momentum it had generated, SNCC activists initiated a second Freedom Ride, which departed from Nashville on May 17. After surviving a mob attack three days later in Montgomery, the second group of riders pressed on to Jackson, Mississippi, where they were arrested and jailed on May 24, on charges of trespassing. Thereafter, the tactic was picked up by groups all over the country. From May to August, separate groups of riders poured into Jackson at the rate of nearly one group a day. By summer's end better than 360 persons had been arrested in connection with the rides (Meier and Rudwick, 1973:140).

In accounting for the impact of the freedom rides one must again point to the ability of insurgents to create a crisis situation of formidable proportions. In this they were helped immeasurably by local segregationists, who responded to the "threat" posed by the rides with a series of highly publicized, violent disruptions of public order. These responses, in turn, prompted a reluctant federal government to intervene in support of the riders. The Justice Department asked a federal district court in Montgomery to enjoin various segregationist groups from interfering with interstate travel; Robert Kennedy ordered 600 marshals to Montgomery to protect the riders; and under administration pressure on September 22, 1961, the Interstate Commerce Commission issued an order barring segregation in interstate travel. Indeed, it seems as if federal intervention had been the goal of insurgents all along. James Farmer, CORE director and chief architect of the rides, described the strategy underlying the campaign: "our intention was to provoke the Southern authorities into arresting us and thereby prod the Justice Department into enforcing the law of the land" (Farmer, 1965:69).

Thus, like the earlier tactics, the rides were used to create a crisis situation. The nature of this crisis, however, was very different from those generated by either the bus boycotts or the sit-ins. In marked the movement's initial use of a protest dynamic whose recognition and conscious exploitation would fuel the heightened pace of insurgency during the period widely regarded as the heyday of the movement. That period begins with the inauguration of John Kennedy as president in January of 1961 and ends with the close of the Selma campaign in May 1965 and the movement's consequent shift to the urban north as a locus of protest activity.

The dynamic in question can be described simply. Impatient with the slow pace of social change achieved through confrontation at the local level, insurgents sought to broaden the conflict by inducing segregationists to disrupt public order to the point where supportive federal intervention was required. This dynamic again emphasizes the crucial importance of political opportunities in setting the context within which the process of tactical innovation operates. With Kennedy's election, the vulnerability of the federal government to this type of pressure increased enormously. Whereas Eisenhower had owed little political debt to black voters or the Democratic South, Kennedy owed much to both groups. The "black vote," in particular, had been widely credited with playing the decisive role in Kennedy's narrow electoral victory over Richard Nixon the previous fall (c.f. Lawson, 1976:256). Kennedy thus came to office with a need to hold his fractious political coalition together and to retain the support of an increasingly important black constituency. This rendered his administration vulnerable to the "politics of protest" in a way Eisenhower's had never been. Recognition of this vulnerability is reflected in the evolution of the movement's tactics. Whereas the earlier tactics had sought to mobilize leverage at the local level through the disruption of commercial activities, the tactics of the next four years aimed instead to provoke segregationist violence as a stimulus to favorable government action. During this period it was the insurgent's skillful manipulation of this dynamic that shaped the unfolding conflict process and keyed the extent and timing of federal involvement and white opposition. Data presented in Figure 4 supports this contention.

The figure clearly reflects the determinant role of movement forces in shaping the unfolding conflict during the early '60s. In their respective patterns of activity, both segregationist forces and the federal government betray a consistent reactive relationship vis-a-vis the movement. With regard to the first of these groups, the pattern of movement stimulus/segregationist response noted earlier is quite evident. In Figure 4 peaks in segregationist activity are clearly shown to follow similar peaks in black insurgency.

The relationship between the federal government and the movement is a bit more complex. Government activity is still responsive to the pace of black insurgency, but as expected, much of this responsiveness derives from the ability of the movement to provoke disruptive segregationist activity. This can be seen more clearly through a logit regression analysis intended to assess the effect of a variety of independent variables on the odds of a federal civil rights-related action.[9] The odds were computed separately for each of six tactical forms—bus boycotts, sit-ins, freedom rides, and three community-wide protest campaigns in Albany, Birmingham and Selma. For each of the first seven weeks following the initial use of the tactic (or beginning of the campaign), the number of movement *actions* that were followed the very next week by federal *events* in the same state was recorded.[10] Likewise the number of movement actions that were *not* followed the next week by government events was also noted. The log odds of a movement action being followed by a federal event constitutes the dependent variable in the analysis.

Nine independent variables were utilized in the analysis. Each of the six "tactics" listed above were treated as independent variables. Five dummy variables were created, with "sit-in" employed as the left-out category. Use of sit-in as the omitted category reflects the fact that it had the least effect of any of the tactics on the dependent variable. In addition to these six tactics, three other independent variables were also entered into the analysis. The first was the number of weeks, ranging from 0–6, since the initial use of the tactic. The second was the total number of movement actions during any given week. The final independent variable was the presence or absence of a segregationist *action* during the week following and in the same state as the initial movement action.

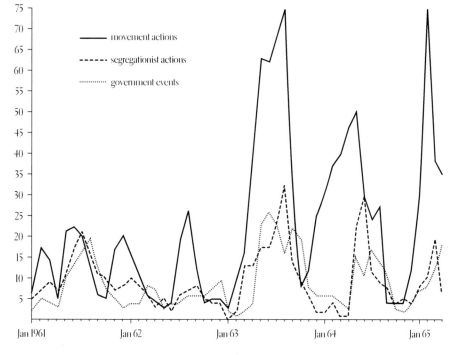

Figure 26.4 Movement Actions, Segregationist Actions and Federal Government Events, January 1961 Through April 1965. (The final eight months of 1965 have been excluded from this figure because they mark the termination of the dynamic under analysis here. In large measure this is due to the shifting northern locus of movement activity.)

Source: *Annual Index* of the *New York Times*. 1961–1965

As reported in Table 2, the results of the logit regression analysis show clearly that not all of the six tactical forms were equally productive of federal action. Indeed, only three of the tactics showed a significant positive relationship with the dependent variable. Not surprisingly, all of these tactics were employed during the Kennedy presidency rather than the "Eisenhower years." As noted earlier, the tactical forms of the "Kennedy years" were designed to prompt favorable federal action by inducing disruptive segregationist violence. Table 2 reflects the operation of this characteristic dynamic.

Both the pace of movement action and the presence or absence of a segregationist response to movement action are significantly related to the odds of federal action. It is the relationship between

segregationist action and the odds of a federal response, however, that is the stronger of the two. Federal activity, then, is still responsive to the overall pace of black insurgency, but as expected, much of this responsiveness appears to derive from the ability of the movement to provoke disruptive segregationist activity. More accurately, then, much of the strength of the relationship between federal and movement activity is indirect, with the stimulus to government involvement supplied by the intervening pattern of segregationist activity.

Returning to Figure 4, we can identify four periods that, in varying degrees, reflect this characteristic three-way dynamic linking black protest activity to federal intervention by way of an intermediate pattern of white resistance. The first of

Table 2 Summary of Logit Regression Analysis
of Odds of Federal Action in Relation to
Various Independent Variables

Tactic	b	β	F
Bus Boycott	−.344	.132	.681
Freedom Rides	.838**	.155	29.084
Community Campaigns			
Albany	.225	.151	2.206
Birmingham	.806**	.113	50.604
Selma	.854**	.102	69.994
Number of Weeks			
Since First Use	−.744**	.187	15.789
Number of Movement			
Actions	.416*	.150	7.654
Segregationist Response	.593**	.752	62.226
Constant	−1.308	.111	138.401

R^2 .67

* Significant at the .10 level.
** Significant at the .01 level.

these periods, as noted earlier, occurred between May–August, 1961, during the peak of activity associated with the freedom rides.

However, even this tactic was not able to sustain high levels of insurgency indefinitely. By August the pace of the rides, and movement activity in general, had declined dramatically. In this decline we can once again see the process of tactical adaptation at work. Following the two violence-marred rides through Alabama, and the federal intervention they precipitated, law enforcement officials in Mississippi worked hard to prevent any reoccurrence of violence in their state. In effect, they had learned to shortcircuit the dynamic discussed above by failing to respond violently to the demonstrators' tactics. Over time the arrival and arrest of a new group of riders in Jackson took on a fairly routine character. The "crisis atmosphere" that had pervaded the initial rides had again been "neutralized." Fortunately, for insurgents the effectiveness of these counter-maneuvers was negated by the

ICC's desegregation order on September 22. The issue of segregation in interstate transportation was dead. Then too, so was the freedom ride tactic and the momentum it had afforded the movement.

Community-wide Protest Campaigns

With the cessation of the freedom rides there again followed a period of diminished movement activity as insurgents groped to develop new protest tactics. The next breakthrough occurred in December 1961 in Albany, Georgia, with the initiation of the first of what might be called the "community-wide protest campaigns." Such campaigns represented a significant tactical escalation over all previous forms of protest. Instead of focusing on a particular lunch counter, bus terminal, etc., insurgents sought to mobilize the local community for a concerted attack on all manifestations of segregation in the target locale. This escalation was a logical response to the routinization of the other protest methodologies discussed previously. Quite simply, the "crisis tolerance" of local segregationists had increased to the point where bus boycotts, sit-ins or freedom rides were no longer sufficient in themselves to generate the leverage required by insurgents. Nothing short of a community-wide crisis would suffice to precipitate the sort of disruption that would grant insurgents increased leverage to press their demands. Indeed, in Albany not even this escalation in tactics was able to achieve significant progress. Yet, over the next three years this tactic was to be refined through a process of trial and error to the point where it was responsible for the most dramatic campaigns of the entire movement.

The Albany campaign took place during the final two months of 1961 and the summer of the following year. Figure 2 again mirrors a rise in movement activity during these two periods. What was absent during the campaign was the pattern of reactive segregationist violence and subsequent federal intervention evident in the freedom rides. Consistent with this view, Table 2 shows only a weak positive relationship between that campaign and subsequent government action. Accounts of the Albany campaign stress the firm control exercised by Police Chief Laurie Pritchett over events there (Watters, 1971:141–229; Zinn, 1962). While systematically denying demonstrators their rights, Pritchett nonetheless did so in such a way as to prevent the type of major disruption that would have prompted federal intervention. To quote Howard Hubbard (1968:5), "the reason...[the movement] failed in Albany was that Chief Pritchett used force rather than violence in controlling the situation, that is, he effectively reciprocated the demonstrator's tactics." Even in "defeat," then, the dynamic is evident. Failing to provoke the public violence necessary to prompt federal intervention, insurgents lacked sufficient leverage themselves to achieve anything more than an inconclusive stand-off with the local segregationist forces in Albany.

The experience of Albany was not without value, however, as the following remarkable passage by Martin Luther King, Jr., attests:

> There were weaknesses in Albany, and a share of the responsibility belongs to each of us who participated. However, none of us was so immodest as to feel himself master of the new theory. Each of us expected that setbacks would be a part of the ongoing effort. There is no tactical theory so neat that a revolutionary struggle for a share of power can be won merely by pressing a row of buttons. Human beings with all their faults and strengths constitute the mechanism of a social movement. They must make mistakes and learn from them, make more mistakes and learn anew. They must taste defeat as well as success, and discover how to live with each. Time and action are the teachers.
>
> When we planned our strategy for Birmingham months later, we spent many hours assessing Albany and trying to learn from its errors. (King, 1963:34–35)

The implication of King's statement is that a fuller understanding of the dynamic under discussion here was born of events in Albany. No doubt a part of this fuller understanding was a growing awareness of the importance of white violence as a stimulus to federal action. As Hubbard (1968) argues, this awareness appears to have influenced the choice of Birmingham as the next major protest site. "King's Birmingham innovation was preeminently strategic. Its essence was not merely more refined tactics, but the selection of a target city which had as its Commissioner of Public Safety,

'Bull' Connor, a notorious racist and hothead who could be depended on not to respond nonviolently" (Hubbard, 1968:5).

The view that King's choice of Birmingham was a conscious strategic one is supported by the fact that Connor was a lame-duck official, having been defeated by a moderate in a run-off election in early April, 1963. Had SCLC waited to launch the protest campaign until after the moderate took office, there likely would have been considerably less violence *and* less leverage with which to press for federal involvement. "The supposition has to be that...SCLC, in a shrewd...strategem, knew a good enemy when they saw him...one that could be counted on in stupidity and natural viciousness to play into their hands, for full exploitation in the press as archfiend and villain" (Watters, 1971:266).

The results of this choice of protest site are well known and clearly visible in Figure 4 and Table 2. The Birmingham campaign of April–May 1963 triggered considerable white resistance in the form of extreme police brutality and numerous instances of segregationist violence. In turn, the federal government was again forced to assume a more supportive stance vis-a-vis the movement. The ultimate result of this shifting posture was administration sponsorship of a civil rights bill that, even in much weaker form, it had earlier described as politically inopportune (Brooks, 1974). Under pressure by insurgents, the bill was ultimately signed into law a year later as the Civil Rights Act of 1964.

Finally there was Selma, the last of the massive community-wide campaigns. It was in this campaign that the characteristic protest dynamic under discussion was most fully realized. To quote Garrow (1978:227):

> ...it is clear that by January 1965 King and the SCLC consciously had decided to attempt to elicit violent behavior from their immediate opponents. Such an intent governed the choice of Selma and Jim Clark [Selma's notoriously racist sheriff], and such an intent governed all of the tactical choices that the SCLC leadership made throughout the campaign....

These choices achieved the desired result. Initiated in January 1965, the campaign reached its peak in February and March, triggering the typical reactive patterns of white resistance and federal involvement (see Figure 4 and Table 2). As regards segregationist violence, the campaign provoked no shortage of celebrated atrocities. On March 9, state troopers attacked and brutally beat some 525 marchers attempting to begin a protest march to Montgomery. Later that same day, the Reverend James Reeb, a march participant, was beaten to death by a group of whites. Finally, on March 25, following the triumphal completion of the twice interrupted Selma-to-Montgomery march, a white volunteer, Mrs. Viola Liuzzo, was shot and killed while transporting marchers back to Selma from the state capital. In response to this consistent breakdown of public order, the federal government was once again pressured to intervene in support of black interests. On March 15, President Johnson addressed a joint session of Congress to deliver his famous "We Shall Overcome" speech. Two days later he submitted to Congress a tough Voting Rights Bill containing several provisions that movement leaders had earlier been told were politically too unpopular to be incorporated into legislative proposals. The bill passed by overwhelming margins in both the Senate and House and was signed into law August 6 of the same year.

However, for all the drama associated with Selma it was to represent the last time insurgents were able successfully to orchestrate a coordinated community-wide protest campaign. Part of the reason for this failure was the growing dissension within the movement. As the earlier consensus regarding goals and tactics gradually collapsed around mid-decade, so too did the ability of insurgents to mount broad-based community campaigns. "The movement—in the special sense of organizations and leaders working together toward agreed goals…fell apart after Selma" (Watters, 1971:330).

But growing internal problems were only part of the reason for the movement's diminished use of this tactic. As was the case with earlier innovations, movement opponents learned to counter the specific tactic and in so doing short-circuit the more general protest dynamic under discussion here. The key to both outcomes lay in the opponents' ability to control the violent excesses of the most rabid segregationists. Through the process of tactical interaction they learned to do exactly that. Von Eschen et al. (1969:229–30) explain:

> The response of the movement's opponents was bound to become less extreme. For one thing, a movement is a school in which both the movement and its opponents learn by trial and error the most appropriate moves. Thus, much of the success of the movement had depended on the untutored, emotional responses of the southern police. In time, however, authorities learned that such responses were counter-productive. In some areas, authorities learned responses sufficiently appropriate to deny the movement its instrument of disorder and to totally disorganize its leadership. In Maryland, for instance, Mayor McKeldin responded to CORE's announcement that Baltimore was to become CORE's target city with a warm welcome and an offer of aid, and the temporary chief of police, Gelston, used highly sophisticated tactics to defuse CORE's strategies.

Finally, the increasing northern locus of movement activity made use of the tactic and the characteristic three-way dynamic on which it depended virtually impossible to sustain. The reason centers on the very different form that white resistance took in the North as opposed to the South.

> One of the functional characteristics of the southern segregationists was that they could be counted on, when sufficiently provoked, to create the violent disruptions of public order needed to produce federal intervention. No such convenient foil was available to the movement outside the south…Without the dramatic instances of overt white oppression, the movement was deprived of both the visible manifestations of racism so valuable as organizing devices and the leverage needed to force supportive government involvement. Having developed an effective mode of tactical interaction vis-a-vis one opponent, insurgents were unable to devise a similarly suitable response to the changed pattern of northern resistance. (McAdam, 1982:214–15)

Urban Rioting

The last of the major tactical innovations of the period was the urban riot of the mid to late 1960s. Though by no means the first use of the tactic, the Watts riot of 1965 seemed to inaugurate an era of unprecedented urban unrest (see Downes, 1970:352). In the three years following the Watts riot "urban disorders" increased steadily. The peaks in riot activity shown in Figure 3 for the summers of 1966–68 reflect the spread of rioting during this period.

That there were differences between the riots and the tactical forms discussed earlier should be obvious. Most importantly, no evidence has ever been produced to indicate that the riots were deliberately planned or carried out by specific insurgent groups, as were the other tactics. There is little question, however, that the riots came to be *used* rhetorically by black leaders as a tactic and widely interpreted as a form of political protest within the black community (Fogelson, 1971:17). Then, too, the often noted selectivity of riot targets suggests that at the very least the rioters were animated, in part, by a limited political definition of their own actions.

In addition to their political use and interpretation, the riots share two other similarities with the other protest techniques discussed above. First, all occasioned a significant breakdown in public order. And, except for the bus boycotts and sit-ins, all served to stimulate directly supportive federal action.[11] Evidence to support this latter contention is drawn from a number of sources. For example, Button (1978) documents a strong (though by no means consistent) pattern of increased federal expenditure for programs benefiting blacks (and poor whites) in 40 American cities following urban riots in those locales. Consistent with the general thrust of Button's work are the data on school desegregation (U.S. Commission of Civil Rights, 1977:18). They suggest a close connection between disruptive insurgency and the pace of federally sponsored school desegregation efforts. Finally, the work of Isaac and Kelly (1981), and Schram and Turbett (1983), among others, argues for a close connection between the riots and the expansion in welfare benefits in the late 1960s.

With use, however, all new tactical forms become less effective, and so it was with the urban riot. After 1965—and especially after 1967—the ameliorative federal response to the riots was increasingly supplanted by a massive control response at all levels of government which was designed to counter the continued threat posed by the disorders. That these efforts had a measurable effect on the actual handling of the riots is suggested by a comparison of data on the 1967 and April 1968 disorders, the latter occurring in the wake of Martin Luther King's assassination.

The first finding of note involves a comparison of the number of law enforcement personnel used in quelling these two sets of disturbances. As shown in Table 3, the force levels used in the 1968 disorders were on the average 50 percent greater than those used the previous year. As Skolnick (1969:173) notes:

> …1968 represented a new level in the massiveness of the official response to racial disorder. In April alone…more National Guard troops were called than in all of 1967…and more federal troops as well…*Never* before in this country has such a massive military response been mounted against racial disorder.

The presence of increased numbers of enforcement personnel facilitated the more thoroughgoing containment efforts desired by those charged with controlling the disorders. As the data in Table 3 indicate, all major indices of official repression, save one, showed increases between 1967 and April 1968. The average number of injuries per disorder in 1968 was nearly 40 percent higher than in 1967. Even more dramatic was the nearly two-fold increase in the average number of arrests between the two years.

In the face of this massive control response, it is hardly surprising that the intensity and pace of movement activity dropped sharply in the final two years of the period under study (Feagin and Hahn, 1973:193–94; Skolnick, 1969:173). Confronted by government forces increasingly willing and able to suppress ghetto disorders with force, and painfully aware of the costs incurred in the earlier rioting, insurgents gradually abandoned the tactic. In effect, the government's massive control efforts had proven an effective tactical adaptation to the riots. Though no doubt sensible, the abandonment of rioting as a form of protest deprived insurgents of the last major tactical innovation of the era. And with the abandonment of the tactic, insurgency once again declined sharply (see Figure 1).

Table 3 Comparative Statistics on Racial Disorders During 1967 and April, 1968[a]

	Year 1967	April 1968	Totals
Number of Disorders	217	167	384
Cities	160	138	298
States	34 (+Wash., D.C.)	36 (+Wash., D.C.)	70 (+Wash., D.C.)
Arrests	18,800	27,000	45,800
Avg. No. of Arrests Per Disorder	87	162	119
Injured	3,400	3,500	6,900
Avg. No. Injured Per Disorder	16	22	18
Killed	82	43	125
Property Damage[b]	$69,000,000	$58,000,000	$127,000,000
National Guard			
Times Used	18	22	40
Number Used	27,700	34,900	62,600
Federal Troops			
Times Used	1	3	4
Number Used	4,800	23,700	28,500

Source: Adapted from Lemberg Center for the Study of Violence, "April Aftermath of the King Assassination," Riot Data Review, Number 2 (August 1968), Brandeis University, p. 60. (Mimeographed).

[a] Excluded from the totals reported in this chart are "equivocal" disorders, so termed by the authors of the study because of sketchy information on the racial aspects of the event.

[b] Property damage refers to physical damage to property or loss of stock (usually through looting), estimated in dollars.

The failure of the insurgents to devise new tactical forms must ultimately be seen as a response to the shifting political and organizational realities of the late 1960s and early 1970s. Just as the earlier innovations had depended upon the confluence of internal organization and external opportunity, the cessation of innovation can be seen, in part, as a function of a certain deterioration in these two factors. Organizationally the movement grew progressively weaker as the '60s wore on. In the face of the collapse of the strong consensus on issues and tactics that had prevailed within the movement during its heyday, insurgents found it increasingly difficult to organize the strong, focused campaigns characteristic of the early 1960s. Instead, by 1970, insurgent activity had taken on a more diffuse quality with a

veritable profusion of small groups addressing a wide range of issues by means of an equally wide range of tactics. Unfortunately, the diversity inherent in this approach was all too often offset by a political impotence born of the absence of the strong protest vehicles that had earlier dominated the movement.

Second, reversing a trend begun during the 1930s, the "structure of political opportunities" available to blacks contracted in the late 1960s in response to a variety of emergent pressures. Chief among these was the mobilization of a strong conservative "backlash" in this country fueled both by the turbulence of the era and the conscious exploitation of "law and order" rhetoric by public officials. When combined with the emergence of other competing issues and the declining salience of the black vote, this "backlash" served to diminish the overall political leverage exercised by insurgents and therefore the prospects for successful insurgency.

Summary

The pace of black insurgency between 1955 and 1970 has been analyzed as a function of an ongoing process of *tactical interaction* between insurgents and their opponents. Even in the face of a conducive political environment and the presence of strong movement organizations, insurgents face a stern tactical challenge. Lacking institutional power, challengers must devise protest techniques that offset their powerlessness. This has been referred to as a process of *tactical innovation.* Such innovations, however, only temporarily afford challengers increased bargaining leverage. In chesslike fashion, movement opponents can be expected, through effective *tactical adaptation,* to neutralize the new tactic, thereby reinstituting the original power disparity between themselves and the challenger. To succeed over time, then, a challenger must continue its search for new and effective tactical forms.

In the specific case of the black movement, insurgents succeeded in doing just that. Between 1955 and 1965 they developed and applied a series of highly effective new tactical forms that, in succession, breathed new life into the movement. For each new innovation, however, movement opponents were eventually able to devise the effective tactical counters that temporarily slowed the momentum generated by the introduction of the technique. With the abandonment of the riots in the late 1960s, insurgents were left without the tactical vehicles needed to sustain the movement. Reflecting the collapse of the movement's centralized organizational core and the general decline in the political system's vulnerability to black insurgency, by decades end the movement had not so much died as been rendered tactically impotent.

NOTES

This research was supported in part by NIMH grant No. 5 RO1 MH20006 04 SSR. The grant supported a larger study of insurgency in the 1960s directed by Charles Perrow, to whom goes my deep appreciation as well as much of the credit for this work. I would also like to thank Al Bergesen, Neil Fligstein, Lois Horton, Michael Hout, John McCarthy, Victoria Nelson-Rader, Michael Sobel and two anonymous reviewers for their extremely helpful comments on various drafts of this paper.

1. I am not alone in noting the relative lack of attention paid to the dynamics of movement development and decline in the sociological literature. Gamson (1975), Piven and Cloward (1977), and Snyder and Kelly (1979) have made similar comments in other contexts. The introduction of resource mobilization and other "rationalistic" theories of social movements, however, has helped focus more attention on the ongoing dynamics of movement development. In the work of such theorists as Tilly (1978). McCarthy and Zald (1973, 1977), and others, one begins to discern the outlines of a systematic framework for analyzing not just the emergence but subsequent development/decline of social movements.

2. Though hardly a major focus of theoretical attention, the dynamic has at least been acknowledged and discussed by a number of movement theorists. Zald and Useem (1982), for example, apply a similar interactive perspective to the study of the ongoing relationship between movements and the counter-movements they give rise to. Such a perspective also informs Tilly's (1978) model of social movements. Finally, elements of an interactive conception of movement development are implied in McPhail and Miller's work (1973) on the "assembling process."

3. In his analysis of the emergence and spread of the sit-in tactic, Morris (1981) offers a richly drawn example of the organizational roots of tactical innovation. In this case it was the indigenous network of southern black churches, colleges and local movement affiliates that supplied the organizational context essential to the successful application and diffusion of the sit-in tactic.

4. A possible exception to the rule involves the urban riots of the mid to late 1960s. In the case of these loosely organized, more diffuse forms of protest, it is likely that the media—particularly television—served as the principal vehicle of diffusion linking rioters in different cities. Within the same city, however, several authors have noted the importance of indigenous associational networks in the spread of the riot (cf. Feagin and Hann, 1973:48–49; Wilson and Orum, 1976:198).

5. For a more complete discussion of the coding procedures employed in this analysis the reader is referred to McAdam, 1982:235–50.

6. In most cases the protest techniques were not really new. Indeed, most had been employed by insurgents previously. What distinguished their use from previous applications was the adoption of the tactic by other insurgent groups. The extensiveness of the adoption is largely attributable to the dense network of communication ties that had developed between insurgents by 1960. Morris (1981) provides a detailed illustration of the crucial importance of formal and informal

ties in the process of tactical diffusion in his analysis of the spread of the sit-in tactic. His analysis merely underscores a fundamental point made earlier: the significance of the process of tactical innovation depends heavily on the organizational resources available to insurgent groups. A well-developed communication network linking insurgents together is perhaps the most critical of these resources.

7. All of the examples are taken from Smith and Killian's (1958) account of the bus boycott in Tallahassee, Florida, and the conflict that stemmed from it.

8. Nor was the cost of the sit-ins for the segregationists merely financial. The symbolic consequences were enormous as well. For southern blacks and whites alike the sit-ins served to shatter certain myths that had served for decades to sustain the racial status quo. Southern blacks who had long felt powerless to effect basic changes in "their" way of life were galvanized by the realization that they were in fact doing just that. For their part many segregationists found it increasingly difficult to maintain their long-held invidious moral distinction between blacks and whites as a result of the glaring symbolic contrast evident in the sit-ins. The dilemma is nicely captured by an editorial that appeared in the prosegregationist *Richmond News Leader* on February 22, 1960, in the wake of sit-ins in that city. In part the editorial read:

> Many a Virginian must have felt a tinge of wry regret at the state of things as they are, in reading of Saturday's "sit-downs" by Negro students in Richmond stores. Here were the colored students, in coats, white shirts, ties, and one of them was reading Goethe and one was taking notes from a biology text. And here on the sidewalk outside, was a gang of white boys come to heckle, a ragtail rabble, slack-jawed, black-jacketed, grinning fit to kill, and some of them, God save the mark, were waving the proud and honored flag of the Southern States in the last war fought by gentlemen. Ehew! It gives one pause. (quoted in Zinn, 1965:27)

In accounting for the sit-ins, then, one must consider the symbolic consequences of the demonstrations, no less than the financial cost to the segregationists.

9. My use of logit regression was motivated primarily by a concern for the likely heteroskedasticity of my data. For an excellent introduction to the technique and its possible uses see Swafford (1980). The unit of analysis in the logit regression was the first seven weeks following the introduction of

each protest tactic. The analysis was based on a total of 84 observations.

10. In coding story synopses a distinction was made between two general types of movement-related activity. *Statements* referred to any written or oral pronouncements related to the topic of civil rights that were issued by a party to the conflict. *Actions* represented a broad category consisting of all other types of activity *except* for statements. The term *event* was used to designate the total of all statements and actions attributed to a particular initiating unit.

This analysis is based on all *events* initiated by the federal government but only the *actions* attributed to movement and segregationist forces. This convention reflects my conception of the dominant conflict dynamic operative during the early 1960s. Movement and segregationist forces tended to engage in a chess-like exchange of strategic *actions* (e.g., marches, court orders, arrests, sit-ins, beatings) within a localized conflict arena. Much of this local maneuvering, however, was played out for the benefit of federal officials, whose *actions* and *statements* came, in turn, to exert a crucial influence over the course of local events.

A second methodological convention should also be clarified at this point. The decision to lag movement actions one month behind both segregationist actions and government events was made *before* the completion of data collection and was based on my reading of many impressionistic accounts of specific movement campaigns. Those accounts invariably stressed the *delayed reaction* of segregationists to movement activity in their community. Thus, for example, we are told that "Birmingham residents of both races were surprised at the restraint of [Bull] Connor's [Birmingham's notorious chief of police] men at the beginning of the campaign" (King, 1963:69). Once mobilized, however, local segregationists could generally be counted on to respond with the flagrant examples of public violence that made a virtually *instantaneous* federal response necessary.

11. This is not to suggest that the bus boycott and sit-ins were unsuccessful. It must be remembered that, unlike the later tactics, the goal of the boycott and sit-ins was not so much to stimulate federal intervention as to mobilize leverage *at the local level* through the creation of negative financial inducements. In this they were largely successful.

27.

Celebration and Suppression: The Strategic Uses of Identity by the Lesbian and Gay Movement

MARY BERNSTEIN

> The organizers of the 1993 lesbian and gay march on Washington] face a dilemma: how to put forward a set of unsettling demands for unconventional people in ways that will not make enemies of potential allies. They do so by playing down their differences before the media and the country while celebrating it in private. (Tarrow 1994, p. 10)

Sidney Tarrow's portrayal of the 1993 lesbian and gay march on Washington highlights a central irony about identity politics and the decline of the Left: Critics of identity politics decry the celebration of difference within contemporary identity movements, charging them with limiting the potential for a "politics of commonality" between oppressed peoples that could have potential for radical social change (Gitlin 1995). On the other hand, the lesbian and gay movement seems largely to have abandoned its emphasis on *difference from* the straight majority in favor of a moderate politics that highlights *similarities to* the straight majority (Seidman 1993).

Over time, "identity" movements shift their emphasis between celebrating and suppressing differences from the majority. For example, the Civil Rights movement underscored similarities to the majority in order to achieve concrete policy reforms. At other times, movements that assert radical racial identities to build communities and challenge hegemonic American culture take center stage. The American feminist movement has alternately emphasized innate gender differences between men and women and denied that such differences exist

or that they are socially relevant. Under what political conditions do activists celebrate or suppress differences from the majority? Why does the stress on difference or similarity change over time?

To answer these questions, this article draws on evidence from several campaigns for lesbian and gay rights ordinances.[1] The lesbian and gay movement was chosen because it is considered the quintessential identity movement (Melucci 1989; Duyvendak 1995; Duyvendak and Giugni 1995). The cultural barriers to acceptance of homosexuality and the challenge of self-acceptance for lesbians and gay men require cultural struggle. However, the lesbian and gay movement has been altered from a movement for cultural transformation through sexual liberation to one that seeks achievement of political rights through a narrow, ethnic-like (Seidman 1993) interest-group politics. This well-documented transition (Altman 1982; Paul 1982; Escoffier 1985; Epstein 1987; Seidman 1993; Gamson 1995; Vaid 1995) has yet to be explained.

This research will show that celebration or suppression of differences within political campaigns depends on the structure of social movement organizations, access to the polity (Tilly 1978), and the type of opposition. By specifying the political conditions that explain variation in strategies within movements, one can better understand differences in forms of collective action across movements.

Identity and Movement Types

Attempts to classify social movements have typically centered around the distinction between "strategy-oriented" and "identity-oriented" movements (Touraine 1981). Abandoning this distinction, Duyvendak and Giugni argue instead that "the real difference is, however, the one between movements pursuing goals in the outside world, for

Bernstein, Mary. 1991. "Celebration and Suppression: The Strategic Uses of identity by the Lesbian and Gay Movement." *American Journal of Sociology* 103: 531–565. Reprinted by permission of The University of Chicago Press. Notes have been renumbered and edited.

which the action is instrumental for goal realization, and identity-oriented movements that realize their goals, at least partly, in their activities" (1995, pp. 277–78). Social movements, then, are classified on "their logic of action," whether they employ an identity or instrumental logic of action, and whether they are internally or externally oriented. Movements such as the lesbian and gay movement are internally oriented and follow an identity logic of action. Instrumental movements, by contrast, engage in instrumental action and are externally oriented (Duyvendak and Giugni 1995, pp. 84–85).

This mechanical bifurcation of movement types, reflected in the division between identity theory on the one hand and resource mobilization and political process theory on the other, has left the literature on contentious politics unable to explain changes in forms of collective action. First, the casual use of the term "identity" obscures fundamental distinctions in meaning (e.g., Gitlin 1995). Second, I argue that theorists must abandon the *essentialist* characterization of social movements as expressive or instrumental because it impairs the study of all social movements. This essentialist characterization stems from the conflation of goals and strategies (i.e., that instrumental strategies are irrelevant to cultural change, while expressions of identity cannot be externally directed) apparent in resource mobilization, political process, and new social movement theories. Finally, attempts to integrate these theories have been unsuccessful.

Subsumed under the rubric of new social movements, "identity movements" have been defined as much by the goals they seek, and the strategies they use, as by the fact that they are based on a shared characteristic such as ethnicity or sex. According to new social movement theorists, identity movements seek to transform dominant cultural patterns, or gain recognition for new social identities, by employing expressive strategies (Touraine 1981; Cohen 1985; Melucci 1985, 1989).

New social movement theory suggests that movements choose political strategies in order to facilitate the creation of organizational forms that encourage participation and empowerment. Thus strategies that privilege the creation of democratic, nonhierarchical organizations would be chosen

over strategies narrowly tailored to produce policy change.

For resource mobilization and political process theorists, identity may play a role in mobilization through solidary incentives (Klandermans 1984, 1988), but once the "free rider" problem is overcome (Olson 1965; Hardin 1982), all other collective action is deemed instrumental, targeted solely at achieving concrete (i.e., measurable) goals. Resource mobilization and political process theorists have neglected the study of identity movements with their seemingly "nonpolitical," cultural goals. Even when culture is recognized as an integral part of sustaining activist communities, changing or challenging mainstream culture is rarely considered a goal of activism. Strategies are seen as rationally chosen to optimize the likelihood of policy success. Outcomes are measured as a combination of policy change ("new advantages") and access to the structure of political bargaining (Jenkins and Perrow 1977; Tilly 1978; McAdam 1982; Gamson 1990). Such a narrow framing of social movement goals can lead to erroneous assumptions about the reasons for collective action and for strategy choice (Turner and Killian 1972; Jenkins 1983). Where goals are cultural and therefore harder to operationalize, theorists assume collective action has no external dimension but is aimed simply at reproducing the identity on which the movement is based (see Duyvendak 1995; Duyvendak and Giugni 1995). This leaves theorists unable to explain social movement action that seems to be working at cross purposes to achieving policy change. Furthermore, it relegates "prefigurative" (Breines 1988; Polletta 1994) politics—a politics that seeks to transform observers through the embodiment of alternative values and organizational forms—to the realm of the irrational.

Although political opportunity or political process (McAdam 1982) models share resource mobilization's assumptions about the relationship between strategies and goals, they provide a more useful starting point for understanding how political strategies are chosen. According to Tilly (1978), forms of collective action will be affected by "political coalitions and…the means of actions built into the existing political organization" (p. 167). These short- and medium-term "volatile" (Gamson and

Meyer 1996) elements of "political opportunity" (Kitschelt 1986; Tarrow 1996; Kriesi and Giugni 1995) include the opening of access to participation, shifts in ruling alignments, the availability of influential allies, and cleavages among elites (Tarrow 1988; Kriesi and Giugni 1995). As the political context changes, strategies should also change. Yet political opportunity models lack specificity in analyzing why or under what political conditions movements choose particular forms of collective action.

Attempts to reconcile the disjuncture between new social movement and resource mobilization or political process theory center on the relationship between forms of collective action and the movement's life cycle. The emergent "new social movements" of the 1960s and 1970s seemed so striking because they utilized innovative, direct action tactics. According to Calhoun (1995):

> As Tarrow (1989) has remarked, this description confuses two senses of *new*: the characteristics of all movements when they are new, and the characteristics of a putatively new sort of movement.
>
> It is indeed generally true that any movement of or on behalf of those excluded from conventional politics starts out with a need to attract attention; movement activity is not just an instrumental attempt to achieve movement goals, but a means of recruitment and continuing mobilization of participants. (P. 193)

In this view, a lack of historical perspective has mistakenly led new social movement theorists to label behavior "distinctive" when it is simply behavior indicative of an emergent social movement.

This criticism of new social movement theory glosses over important empirical and theoretical distinctions. First, not every emergent social movement employs novel or dramatic tactics in order to gain new recruits. Religious right organizations that arose in the 1970s drew on the dense network of conservative churches as well as direct mail lists to mobilize; they did not employ innovative or novel tactics (Diamond 1989). Rather than misattributing certain forms of collective action to the newness of social movements, one should ask what accounts for different forms of mobilization. Furthermore, attributing certain forms of collective action to the

newness of social movements precludes an understanding of why such forms of collective action may emerge at later points in a movement's protest cycle.

Second, the glib dismissal of the sorts of political action attributed to new social movements (Duyvendak 1995; Duyvendak and Giugni 1995) as simply expressive, or unrelated to political structure, ignores the external or instrumental dimensions of seemingly expressive action. If putatively new social movements do challenge dominant cultural patterns, then theorists must take seriously the political nature of such collective action. Social movement theory must examine the challenges all social movements present to dominant cultural patterns.

This research seeks to provide a more complete understanding of the role of identity in collective action. I build in part on political process theory, while incorporating new social movement theory's emphasis on the importance of cultural change to movement activism. I argue that the concept of "identity" has at least three distinct analytic levels, the first two of which have been developed in the social movement literature. First, a shared collective identity is necessary for mobilization of *any* social movement (Morris 1992), including the classic labor movement (Calhoun 1995). Second, identity can be a goal of social movement activism, either gaining acceptance for a hitherto stigmatized identity (Calhoun 1994) or deconstructing categories of identities such as "man," "woman," "gay," "straight" (Gamson 1995), "black," or "white." Finally, this research argues that expressions of identity can be deployed at the collective level as a political strategy, which can be aimed at cultural or instrumental goals. Once the concept of identity is broken down into these three analytic dimensions, then one can explore the political conditions that produce certain identity strategies.

The next section examines analytic uses of the concept "identity" in the social movement literature. Then I present a general model to explain identity strategies. The following sections elaborate the general model by drawing on historical research and interview data to explain diverse identity strategies used in campaigns for lesbian and gay rights ordinances. The essentialist assumptions embedded in new social movement, resource mobilization, and political process perspectives limit their ability to account for these variations. The case studies will show that forms of collective action are the result of specific features of social movement organizations, the type of opposition, and concrete interactions with the state. Finally, I suggest the model's application to the Civil Rights and feminist movements.

Three Analytic Dimensions of Identity

The creation of communities and movement solidarity, which the bulk of research on collective identity examines (Williams 1995), is necessary for mobilization. I define *identity for empowerment* to mean the creation of collective identity and the feeling that political action is feasible (see table 1). In other words, some sort of identity is necessary to translate individual to group interests and individual to collective action. All social movements require such a "political consciousness" (Morris 1992) to create and mobilize a constituency (Taylor and Whittier 1992; Calhoun 1995).

Identity for empowerment is not necessarily a consciously chosen strategy, although it is a precursor to collective action. If a movement constituency has a shared collective identity and the institutions or social networks that provide a cultural space from which to act, then community building and empowerment will be forfeited to "instrumental"

goals of policy attainment. In the absence of visibility or movement organizations, more work must be done to build organizations and recruit activists.

Collective identity can also have an external dimension in mobilization. Beckwith (1995) argues that an actor can use her or his identity to gain "political standing" (i.e., to legitimate participation) in a social movement in which she or he is not directly implicated. So, for example, women involved in coal mining strikes who are not miners can justify participation based on their relations to the miners, such as mother, sister, or wife. The choice of identity (e.g., wife of miner vs. working-class woman) can have implications for future activism.

Identity can also be a goal of collective action (*identity as goal*). Activists may challenge stigmatized identities, seek recognition for new identities, or deconstruct restrictive social categories. New Left organizations of the 1960s, for example, sought not only concrete policy reform, but thought that the creation of alternative cultural forms could foster structural change. Polletta (1994) asserts that "student-organizers of the Student Nonviolent Coordinating Committee (SNCC) saw their task as to mobilize and secure recognition for a new collective identity—poor, 'unqualified' southern blacks—in a way that would transform national and local politics by refashioning criteria of political leadership" (p. 85). Feminists influenced American

Table 1 The Three Analytic Dimensions of "Identity"

Dimension	Description
Identity for empowerment	Activists must draw on an existing identity or construct a new collective identity in order to create and mobilize a constituency. The particular identity chosen will have implications for future activism.
Identity as goal	Activists may challenge stigmatized identities, seek recognition for new identities, or deconstruct restrictive social categories as goals of collective action.
Identity as strategy	Identities may be deployed strategically as a form of collective action. *Identity deployment* is defined as expressing identity such that the terrain of conflict becomes the individual person so that the values, categories, and practices of individuals become subject to debate. *Identity for critique* confronts the values, categories, and practice of the dominant culture. *Identity for education* challenges the dominant culture's perception of the minority or is used strategically to gain legitimacy by playing on uncontroversial themes.

culture by challenging and altering conventional usage of sexist terms in the English language. Gamson (1995) argues that social movement theory must take seriously the goal of contemporary "queer politics" to deconstruct social categories, including "man," "woman," "gay," and "straight." Without a broader understanding of the goals of collective action and their relationship to the structural location of the actors, social movement theory cannot adequately explain strategy choices made by activists.

In addition to influencing motivations and goals of collective action, "cultural resources also have an external, strategic dimension" (Williams 1995, p. 125). I define *identity deployment* to mean expressing identity such that the terrain of conflict becomes the individual person so that the values, categories, and practices of individuals become subject to debate. What does it mean to "deploy identity" strategically? Taylor and Raeburn (1995) view identity deployment as a way to contest stigmatized social identities for the purposes of institutional change. Yet contesting stigma to change institutions is not the only reason for identity deployment. The goal of identity deployment can be to transform mainstream culture, its categories and values (and perhaps by extension its policies and structures), by providing alternative organizational forms. Identity deployment can also transform participants or simply educate legislators or the public.

Identity deployment can be examined at both the individual and collective level along a continuum from education to critique.[2] Activists either dress and act consistently with mainstream culture or behave in a critical way. *Identity for critique* confronts the values, categories, and practices of the dominant culture. *Identity for education* challenges the dominant culture's perception of the minority or is used strategically to gain legitimacy by playing on uncontroversial themes.[3] Although the goals associated with either identity strategy can be moderate or radical, identity for education generally limits the scope of conflict by not problematizing the morality or norms of the dominant culture.

Identity deployment should be understood dramaturgically (Goffman 1959) as the collective portrayal of the group's identity in the political

realm, whether that be in city council hearings or at sit-ins in segregated restaurants. The strategic deployment of identity may differ from the group's (or individuals') private understanding of that identity. In this research, I examine identity deployment at the collective level.

It is important not to conflate the goals of identity deployment with its form (i.e., critical or educational). Both can be part of a project of cultural challenge or a strategy to achieve policy reform. Whether these strategies are associated with organizational forms that encourage participation and empowerment by privileging the creation of democratic, nonhierarchical organizations, as new social movement theory would suggest, or with narrow interest group strategies designed to achieve policy change, as resource mobilization and political process perspectives would suggest, then becomes an empirical question, not an essentialist assumption based on movement types.

Understanding identity as a tool for mobilization, as a goal, and as a strategy will lead to a more comprehensive understanding of social movements. Instead of asking whether identity plays a role in a given movement, we can ask several questions: What role does identity play in mobilization? To what extent is identity a goal of collective action? Why or under what political conditions are identities that celebrate or suppress differences deployed strategically?

General Model

I argue that identity strategies will be determined by the configuration of political access, the structure of social movement organizations, and the type and extent of opposition. In addition to affecting political outcomes (Zald and Ash 1966; Gamson 1990), the characteristics of movement organizations should also influence political strategies. I define *inclusive* movement organizations to be those groups whose strategies, in practice, seek to educate and mobilize a constituency or maximize involvement in political campaigns. *Exclusive* organizations actively discourage popular participation, choosing strategies unlikely to mobilize a movement constituency. Changes in the political context should also influence political strategies (Tilly 1978). I consider that a movement has *access* to the polity if candidates respond to movement inquiries, if elected officials or state agencies support and work toward the movement's goals, or if movement leaders have access to polity members (e.g., through business affiliations, personal contacts, or official positions in political parties). Organized opposition is also an important part of the political context (Meyer and Staggenborg 1996). Most contemporary American social movements eventually face organized opposition to their goals, and this should influence the types of identities deployed. *Routine opposition* will refer to polity insiders (Tilly 1978); that is, those who by virtue of their institutional position (such as a cardinal of the Catholic Church) have the ear of policy makers. *Opposing movements* will refer to groups outside the polity mobilized around the issues of contention (Bernstein 1995; Meyer and Staggenborg 1996).

The role of identity in mobilization will differ across movements, but not because of some abstract essentialism of movement types. For example, identity for empowerment may play a smaller role in mobilizing movements sparked by a "moral shock"—such as the antiwar movement; the antinuclear movement, or the animal rights movement—than in mobilizing movements based on a shared characteristic or identity. But once a movement has emerged, I suggest that the same conditions that determine identity deployment should also apply to movements started by moral shocks.

In order to emerge, a social movement requires a base from which to organize and some sort of collective identity to translate individual into group interests. Movements with access to the structure of political bargaining *or* strong organizational infrastructures that have fostered a shared identity will tend to seek policy change, emphasize sameness rather than difference, and will use identity for education rather than identity for critique (see fig. 1, paths 1, 2a).[4] However, if the movement faces organized opposition from outside the political establishment, and if the movement is led by exclusive, narrowly focused groups uninterested in movement building, the movement may split, with some groups emphasizing differences and community building,

while the exclusive groups continue to emphasize sameness and narrowly focused policy change (a mixed model; see fig. 1, path 2b). In such cases, critical identities may be deployed as much in reaction to movement leadership as to the opposition.

When an emergent movement lacks both political access and an organizational infrastructure or collective identity, then an emphasis on difference will be needed to build solidarity and mobilize a constituency (fig. 1, path 3). Such movements will tend to focus on building community and celebrating difference, as will those sectors of a movement marginalized by exclusive groups encountering nonroutine opposition (fig. 1, path 4b).

Once a movement has been established—with constituency and organizational actors—then movement between the cells in figure 1 may take place as organized opposition emerges or declines, political coalitions shift, and the structures of movement organizations change over time.

After a movement's emergence, the types of identity deployment will be related to the structure of social movement organizations, access to the polity and whether opposition is routine, deriving from polity insiders, or external, arising from organized opposing movements. Changes in short- or medium-term elements of the political context should have a determining effect on forms of collective action such that greater access produces more moderate forms of collective action and identity for education strategies, while closing opportunities will lead to an emphasis on identity for critique. When the polity is relatively open and diverse segments of the activist community are represented in movement organizations or are included in political campaigns, there will be less emphasis on criticizing normative values. Because identity is deployed in the context of concrete interactions, the baseline against which activists define themselves will be influenced by opposing movements. Exclusive social movement organizations, the presence of a strong opposition, and negative interactions with the state will likely result in greater dissension within the community. That dissension will lead to factionalization and will produce moderates who will focus more on education

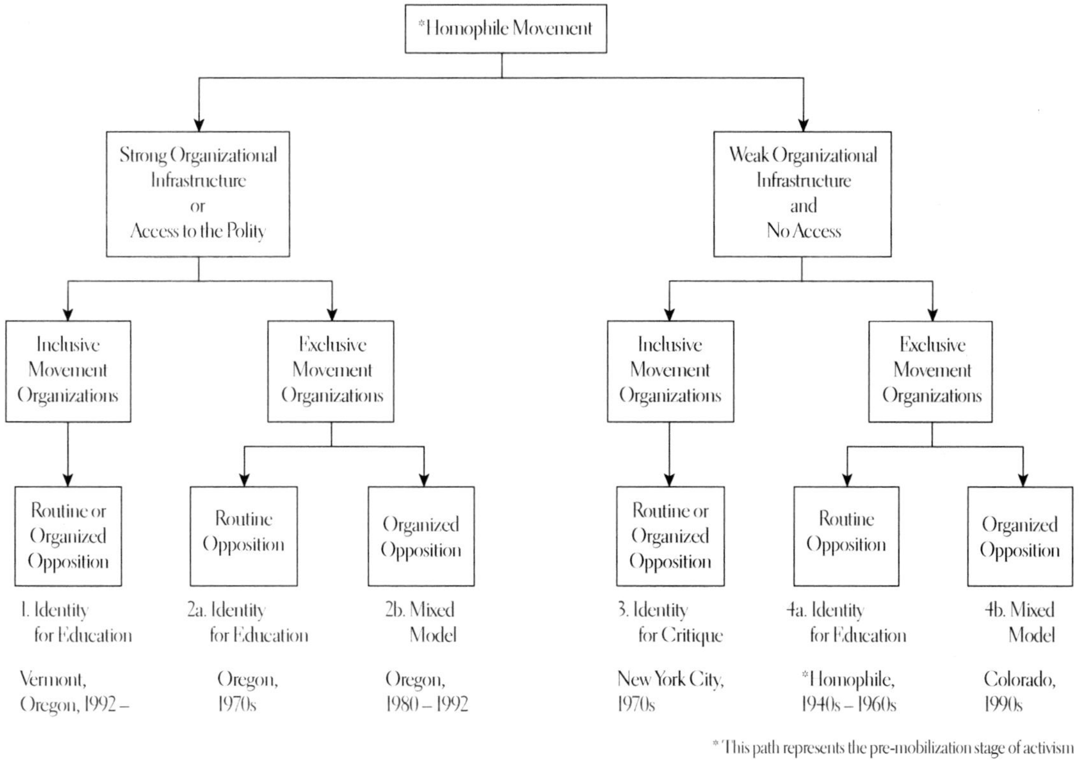

Figure 27.1 Identity deployment in the lesbian and gay movement

and traditional lobbying tactics and radicals who will focus on criticizing dominant values (a "mixed model"). Radicalization in the movement can stem as much from reaction to movement leaders as from reactions to the political context. In short, identity deployment in the political realm will depend on the structure of and relations among movement organizations, the extent of political access, and the type of opposition. The next section draws on evidence from the lesbian and gay movement to suggest more concretely the causal processes that lead to certain types of identity deployment.

The Lesbian and Gay Movement

Detailed historical and qualitative research was employed to understand how political strategies were chosen by activists under distinct political conditions. I conducted field research on city and state campaigns for lesbian and gay rights ordinances in New York City, Vermont, and Oregon. The cases were chosen to vary on the independent variables. Through archival research, I examined movement documents such as press releases and position papers, newspaper accounts from both lesbian and gay and mainstream presses, and transcripts from public hearings. Interviews with selected informants were used to supplement the written material. For each case, I traced the development of state-oriented lesbian and gay organizations, including foundational and position papers that delineate goals, strategies, and guiding principles. For illustrative purposes, I also briefly discuss gay and lesbian responses to antilesbian and antigay legislation in Colorado.

The opposition was investigated through secondary sources.

When lesbians and gay men deploy their identity strategically, debates may center around whether sexual orientation is immutable, what constitutes "homosexual practices," or whether pedophilia is the same as homosexuality. Lesbian and gay lives become the subject of conflict. Nothing about the lesbian and gay movement dictates the strategic use of identity at the collective level. For example, activists could draw attention to discriminatory employment practices, with a universal appeal to everyone's right to a job based on their skills. That is different than disclosing one's sexual orientation to legislators or neighbors, saying "Here I am, know me."

In the case of the lesbian and gay movement, identity for education challenges negative stereotypes about lesbians and gay men, such as having hundreds of sexual partners a year or struggling with uncontrollable sexual urges (Herman 1994), while identity for critique challenges dominant cultural assumptions about the religious or biological "naturalness" of gender roles and the heterosexual nuclear family. Arguably the greatest success of the women's movement has been to break down the division between public and private through challenging traditional notions of gender (Gitlin 1994). Both identity for critique and identity for education can be part of broader projects seeking cultural change or policy reform.

Although many have looked at the relationship between lesbian and gay culture and individual-level identity strategies (Taylor and Whittier 1992; Whittier 1995), few have examined this phenomena empirically, as a collective, consciously chosen political strategy. The rest of this article explores identity strategies along the continuum from critique to education at the collective level. As Seidman (1993, pp. 135–36) argues, we must "relate the politics of representation to institutional dynamics" rather than reducing cultural codes to textual practices abstracted from institutional contexts. The lesbian and gay movement has challenged a variety of institutions in American society, but I will restrict my analysis to interactions with the state because, with the onslaught by the Religious Right, the state has

become one of the central loci of identity deployment. Future research will have to determine the ways diverse institutional dynamics (e.g., the church or psychiatry) influence the creation and deployment of identities.

The Homophile Movement

A collective identity among lesbians and gay men emerged prior to the strategic recruitment of a constituency by organizational actors, as long-term structural changes brought increasing numbers of gay men and lesbians together in urban settings (D'Emilio 1983). The secretive nature of the early homophile organizations (Licata 1980/81; D'Emilio 1983), however, precluded mass mobilization. The only public meeting places for lesbians and gay men—cruising places and Mafia-run bars (Nestle 1987; Chauncey 1994)—were ill-suited for mobilization. Cherry Grove, Fire Island, a visible lesbian and gay summer community, may have provided a more hospitable avenue for mobilization (Newton 1993) but was not linked to a broader organizational infrastructure.

The predominantly underground homophile movement of the 1940s and 1950s has been well documented (Licata 1980/81; D'Emilio 1983). Groups such as the Daughters of Bilitis and the Mattachine Society had exclusive organizational structures,[5] lacked access to the polity, and faced routine opposition from the state (see fig. 1, path 4a). The goals of the homophile movement varied over the years as some sought assimilation while others thought homosexuality was a distinctive and positive trait that should not be subsumed by mainstream culture. Yet both sides agreed on strategies: homophile activists would educate professionals (in particular medical professionals) about the realities of homosexuality; those professionals would in turn advocate for changes in state policies on behalf of homosexuals.

As the social strictures against homosexuality loosened, the lesbian and gay movement became more public through the 1960s (Weeks 1989). Much of the emergent movement's activism appeared to be "expressive," aimed for and at lesbians and gay men. In part, that perception was strengthened by the connection of many activists in post-Stonewall organizations to the New Left (e.g., RadicaLesbians, the Furies, and the Gay Liberation Front [Teal 1971; Marotta 1981; Cruikshank 1992])⁶ who felt that alternative cultural forms would lead to a revolutionary restructuring of society. The visible and outspoken nature of 1960s and 1970s activists accounts for the perception by scholars that the lesbian and gay movement was fundamentally different from other social movements.

But this perception is misguided because it ignores the diversity within the lesbian and gay movement, even around the time of Stonewall. The development of these local movements and the strategies they chose depended on their access to the polity, on their organizational structure, and on the type of opposition they faced. For example, where movement leaders had access to the polity, usually in smaller cities where gay white businessmen had contacts in government (Gay Writers Group 1983) or where earlier movement activities had created political access, as in Washington, D.C. (Johnson 1994–95), expressive action was minimal. In most cases, local movements lacked access to the polity and had to create a constituency. To do so, they had to locate others like themselves. The lack of lesbian and gay institutions, such as churches or bookstores, forced leaders to construct those spaces as well as to launch political campaigns.

When groups lack their own institutions and a political consciousness, they will concentrate on identity for empowerment and community growth. Over time, as institutions and opportunities to act develop, what was once seen as an expressive movement will come to be seen as instrumental as political representation increases and the emphasis on empowerment decreases. Once a movement has been established, forms of collective action will depend on access to decision makers, the extent of opposition, and the degree of inclusiveness of movement organizations.

New York City and Oregon

In 1971, New York City's Gay Activists Alliance (GAA) launched a campaign to add "sexual orientation" to the list of protected categories in the city's human rights ordinance.⁷ Although GAA engaged political authorities in the public realm,

it emphasized identity for critique, seeking to increase publicity and refusing to compromise for the sake of policy change (fig. 1, path 3). Activists borrowed freely from the tactics of other contemporary movements, turning sit-ins into "kiss-ins" at straight bars to protest bans on same-sex displays of affection (*Advocate* 1970a). They held peaceful demonstrations protesting police brutality (Rosen 1980/81) and infiltrated local political clubs to "zap" public officials with questions about police raids on gay bars, entrapment, and support for antidiscrimination policies (Martello 1970b; *Gay Activist* 1972a). Activists consistently refused to dress in accordance with mainstream culture, using their identity to criticize gender roles and heterosexual norms. In short, they used theatrical tactics that increased the scope of the conflict, demanding publicity, regardless of its potentially dilatory effect on achieving policy change. For example, Eleanor Holmes Norton, chair of New York City's Commission on Human Rights, offered GAA members the option of holding private hearings on the ordinance. GAA refused, declaring that it would only participate in open hearings, although that was less likely to achieve policy change. GAA finally secured public hearings after a demonstration—intended to be peaceful—outside General Welfare Committee chair Saul Sharison's apartment building turned bloody when Tactical Police Force officers taunted and then beat demonstrators with their clubs. Despite dissension within GAA, drag queens were ultimately allowed to participate in the hearings. City council members would subsequently exploit the confusion between transvestism and homosexuality to defeat the ordinance (Marotta 1981).

The fight for antidiscrimination legislation in Oregon contrasted sharply with the battle in New York City. Activists in Portland and Eugene in the 1970s—primarily gay white men—had easy access to the polity because of their status as business persons. The Portland Town Council (PTC), an informal coalition of gay-oriented businesses and organizations, was founded in 1970. Due largely to the lack of opposition and the semi-insider status of its members, the PTC won a series of incremental victories culminating in Portland's passage of a law to prohibit discrimination against city employees on the basis of sexual orientation (*Gay Blade* 1975; PTC 1976). In Eugene, activists also capitalized on their insider status by choosing strategies that discouraged mass participation, including secret meetings with council members. In 1977, Eugene passed a lesbian and gay rights ordinance (Gay Writers Group 1983).

The PTC also spearheaded efforts to add sexual orientation to the state's human rights statute. Despite agonizingly narrow defeats of statewide antidiscrimination bills (by one vote in 1975), activists continued to work with state officials. In 1976, at the PTC's request, Oregon Governor Straub created the Ad Hoc Task Force on Sexual Preference to conduct factual research and to make policy recommendations to the Oregon legislature. The PTC served as an advisory board, recommended areas for research, and facilitated interactions between lesbian and gay communities and the task force (PTC 1976; Coleman 1977).

The strategies employed in New York City and Oregon contrasted sharply. When given the choice, New York City activists consistently privileged strategies that challenged dominant cultural values over those that would maximize the likelihood of policy success. By refusing to hold private hearings with the Human Rights Commission, activists increased the scope of conflict. Rather than allaying the fears of legislators and the public by reassuring them of the incremental nature of the policy reform, activists exacerbated those fears by having transvestites testify at public hearings. In Oregon, activists were content to hold secret meetings with lawmakers in order to gain legal change.

What accounts for these diverse approaches to political change? The early stage of New York City's lesbian and gay liberation movement appears to be consistent with a new social movement interpretation. At the time, movement theorists stated explicitly that the battle was over ending oppressive gender roles and the restrictive categories of heterosexuality and homosexuality that inhibited everyone's true bisexual nature (Wittman 1972; Altman 1993; Seidman 1993). Thus activists chose strategies that highlighted differences from the straight majority, seeing themselves as the embodiment of the liberation potential. Uncompromising

strategies that reproduced the identity on which the movement was based and created participatory organizations took priority over goals of achieving policy reform. Creating a sense that gay was good and should be expressed publicly, with pride, would not come through secretive meetings with city officials or concealing drag queens.

In Oregon, on the other hand, little emphasis was placed on creating democratic organizations. The goals in Eugene, Portland, and at the state level were to obtain narrow legal protections. Rather than focus on mobilization, the PTC hired a lobbyist to advocate for the new antidiscrimination legislation (PTC 1976). The comparison of Oregon to New York City suggests that newly emerging social movements will only emphasize differences through expressive tactics to the extent that they lack access to the polity and a strong organizational infrastructure.

Political access and differing resources explain in part the different orientations of the Oregon and New York City activists to cultural and legal change. In New York City, activists faced a closed polity. New York State retained an antisodomy statute, which effectively criminalized the status of being lesbian or gay (Copelon 1990; Cain 1993) and was used to justify police entrapment and bar raids. The New York City police routinely used violence to quell peaceful lesbian and gay demonstrations and were unresponsive to lesbians and gay men who were the victims of violence (*Advocate* 1970b, 1970c; *Gay Activist* 1972b).

Lesbians and gay men needed to become a political minority. To do so, they had to increase visibility at the expense of losing short-term policy battles. Influenced as well by other contemporary movements (e.g., the Civil Rights, New Left, and feminist movements) activists had little to lose and much to gain by radical political action. Although deploying identity for critique may have had long-term political benefits, many saw the goal of a political battle in terms of empowering the lesbian and gay communities. In short, the political battle was an opportunity to create a cultural shift in sensibilities among lesbians and gay men (Marotta 1981).

Despite the importance of the political context, it was in interactions with the state that identities were formed and deployed. Although activists' analysis of the relationship between political and cultural change (Marotta 1981)—either that political campaigns served the purpose of empowering activists or that political reforms would enable cultural change—produced and reinforced critical identities, negative interactions with the state entrenched an oppositional dynamic. The New York City Council's initial refusal to hold public hearings, in addition to the police repression (Rosen 1980/81) that included the attack on demonstrators outside Sharison's building, cemented the antagonistic relationship between activists and the state. Because organizations were inclusive and the lesbian and gay social movement sector was relatively undifferentiated, a cultural critique could only be expressed in the political realm. There was nothing about the movement per se that dictated the deployment of critical identities. Activists' interpretations of the relationship between culture and politics and the types of identities deployed were contingent on interactions with the state.

A second part of the formation of a critical identity was the absence of an organized opposition. Because opposition was routine, lesbians and gay men had only to define themselves against mainstream cultural views in order to criticize the dominant culture. Identities were constructed through interactions with the state, in the absence of organized third parties. In short, inclusive movement organizations, lack of access to the polity, negative interactions with the state, and routine opposition produced critical identities.

Activists in Oregon had greater resources than did activists in New York City, due in part to class and gender differences. The unique access to government officials facilitated by business connections enabled quick passage of local legislation and almost won passage of statewide legislation. Unlike GAA, the PTC had had mostly positive relations with state authorities in Portland, Eugene, and the state capitol. So after narrow losses in the state legislature, rather than respond in a critical way through dramatic demonstrations, the PTC approached Governor Robert Straub for redress (PTC 1976). Had Governor Straub not been responsive to lesbian and gay demands, or, similarly, had

the Eugene City Council initially rebuffed the gay activists, critical identities would have been deployed, as much in reaction to the elite gay leadership as to the state (which is what happened in Oregon more than a decade later).

Critical identities, however, were not deployed in Eugene, and success came easily as a result of political access and the low-key tactics of the gay activists. The elitist attitude and nonparticipatory stance of the gay leadership, however, created antagonisms between different lesbian and gay communities. But because interactions with the state had been positive, as shown by the bill's relatively quick passage, these tensions lay dormant. When newly organized religious right groups placed a referendum to repeal Eugene's lesbian and gay rights ordinance on the ballot, the dissension within the lesbian and gay communities made it difficult for them to present a united front, and the antilesbian and antigay referendum ultimately passed (Gay Writers' Group 1983).

By the end of the 1970s, the lesbian and gay movement had undergone profound internal change.[8] Activists no longer placed the same emphasis on challenging gender roles and the construction of heterosexuality in state-oriented lesbian and gay rights campaigns. As many have observed, an ethnic- or interest-group model that sought achievement of rights replaced the liberation model that sought freedom from constraining gender roles and sexual categories (Altman 1982; Paul 1982; Escoffier 1985; Epstein 1987; Seidman 1993; Gamson 1995). Institutionalized, professionally led organizations often supplanted the grassroots groups of the early 1970s in leading campaigns directed at the state. The gay liberation fronts and the gay activists' alliances had all but disappeared. In addition to internal changes within the lesbian and gay movement, by the end of the 1970s the religious right emerged and worked to oppose all of the changes sought by lesbian and gay activists (Adam 1987).

The next section explains why these changes within the lesbian and gay movement occurred and what accounts for the continued variation in forms of collective action across the United States. Access to political decision makers produced identity for education, as in Vermont (fig. 1, path 1). However, where exclusive groups faced organized opposition, as in Colorado, a mixed model of identity deployment was produced as marginalized groups within the lesbian and gay movement reacted to the lesbian and gay leadership and to the opposition (path 4b). In Oregon, exclusive leadership and intense opposition would later produce a mixed model (path 2b). But as activists realized that sustaining a prolonged campaign against the religious opposition required cooperation among diverse lesbian and gay communities, organizations became more inclusive and an educational model prevailed (path 1).

Vermont

Vermont's lesbian and gay community began organizing more than a decade after the Stonewall riots.[9] Although Vermont had a strong lesbian-feminist community with developed organizational and personal networks, it had not targeted the state about specifically lesbian or gay issues. Motivated by the religious right's attack on lesbian and gay rights, activists decided to work for passage of a statewide bill that would protect lesbians and gay men from discrimination.

Activists quickly obtained official recognition from the governor's office of community-appointed male and female liaisons to the lesbian and gay communities. The liaisons fostered contact with elected officials as well as with the attorney general's office and the Vermont Human Rights Commission. Close collaboration with both offices resulted in the inclusion of protection based on sexual orientation in the state's Hate Crimes Bill (Sussman, see n. 9 above). The Vermont legislature also passed important legislation sought by the AIDS communities (Goslant 1991).

Unlike New York City activists of the early 1970s, the Vermont activists whom I interviewed did not see policy campaigns as a vehicle for staging a cultural critique. In fact, many claimed not to see the issue of gay rights as a cultural battle at all, but as simply a matter of social justice. They took a laissez-faire approach to organizing, and they encouraged participation. They made no attempts to constrain testimony in the public hearings on the lesbian and gay rights bill. Ironically, lesbians and gay men showed up for the hearings conservatively dressed, in clothes many had probably not worn since their first job interviews, choosing in this way not to challenge dominant gender norms. One of the liaisons recounted that she would dress in her "Republican drag" when attending hearings at the statehouse (Perdue, see n. 9).

In the final push for the lesbian and gay rights bill, Vermont activists chose to "put a face on lesbian and gay rights," by fostering personal contact between constituents and their legislators. In addition to telephone campaigns, they activated friendship, organizational, and professional networks to arrange meetings between legislators and their gay and lesbian constituents and other supporters of the bill—what they called "coffee klatches" (Hurlie, see n. 9 above). During these meetings, traditional educational work and identity for education activities took place. Legislators were educated about the scope of the bill, emphasizing that the bill did not endorse a lesbian and gay "lifestyle" but was simply a question of justice. Activists used the meetings to dispel the myth that passing a nondiscrimination law would lead to affirmative action for "queers" (Hurlie, see n. 9) or to certain defeat for legislators who supported the bill. Although fact sheets dispelling myths about, for example, gay men as child molesters, were distributed to each state senator and representative, the meetings capitalized on personal relations (rather than social science studies) to dispel myths about homosexuality (Olsen, see n. 9). By fostering personal contact, activists themselves became the contested terrain. Activists initially targeted the swing votes on the judiciary committee so that the bill could reach the floor, successfully swaying several votes; they then targeted other key legislators. Politicizing the personal also took place among legislators as one closeted gay legislator came out to his colleagues (Hurlie, see n. 9).[10]

New social movement approaches are clearly unable to explain the conservative tactics, the narrow focus on policy reform, and the lack of attention to creating a lesbian and gay constituency in Vermont. The activists I interviewed stated that if a lesbian and gay movement came out of the gay rights campaign, that would be fine, but their goal was to pass the bill. Part of the problem with new social movement theory is its failure to specify the conditions under which collective action is aimed either at strengthening communities and organizations or at changing perceptions of the public and institutional authorities. Activists in Vermont deployed identity for education, but did not seek cultural change through influencing public opinion or creating democratic organizations. In fact, the creation of an ongoing organization was an unintended consequence of the grassroots style of organizing used by activists. The positive interactions with the state and the feeling that victory was possible validated activists' choice of strategies.

The structure of the lesbian and gay organizations running the political campaigns in New York City in the 1970s and in Vermont in the 1980s were similar, yet the two groups adopted vastly different strategies. While New York City activists deployed identity for critique, Vermont activists used identity for education. No formal organizational structure existed in Vermont until after the passage of the statewide lesbian and gay rights bill. Attempts to create a formal structure in Vermont resulted in the demise of the first lesbian and gay political organization, later to be replaced by the Vermont Coalition (see Russell, no. 9 above). In fact New York City's groups may have been somewhat more hierarchically structured, with the Gay Activists Alliance following *Robert's Rules of Order* (Martello 1970a). During the Vermont lesbian and gay rights campaign, there were no official titles (with the exception of the two community-appointed liaisons) or paid positions in the Vermont Coalition. Everyone was encouraged to attend organizational meetings and public hearings and to participate in community events such as the annual pride marches. For example, Holly Perdue (see n. 9), one of the liaisons, recounts that members of the male leather community would be encouraged to serve donuts and coffee at a gay pride rally in an effort to maintain diversity within the movement.

Lesbian and gay activists were able to foster cooperative relationships with polity members in part because of long-term shifts in Vermont politics. Considered a one-party Republican state since the 1950s (Jacob and Vine 1965), by the early 1980s Vermont had a liberal Democratic governor (Madeline Kunin) and a Democratic majority in both houses.

Burlington, one of the state's largest cities, elected self-proclaimed socialist Bernie Sanders mayor.

The insider status of Terje Anderson, an openly gay state and national Democratic Party activist and movement leader, also facilitated access to the polity. Because of his party work, Anderson had access to Governor Kunin who, in 1985, largely at Anderson's request, officially recognized the two liaisons (Hurlie, see n. 9). In 1986, Anderson became chair of the platform committee of the state Democratic Party. Partly as a result of Anderson's efforts, support for lesbian and gay rights was included in the official platform of Vermont's Democratic Party (*Out in the Mountains* 1986). But unlike the early gay rights campaigns of Oregon, where gay men with access to the polity excluded community participation (Gay Writers' Group 1983), Vermont activists encouraged participation in the political process. Furthermore, several state agencies had a tradition of activism, which created more political leverage (Sussman, see n. 9).

A lack of organized opposition also influenced the types of identities deployed. All of the activists I interviewed felt that the emotional outbursts and the lack of decorum characteristic of the mostly church-based religious opposition helped the case for lesbians and gay men. Once again, identities are deployed in the context of real-life interactions in specific social settings. The presence of a religious opposition (no formal, conservative social movement organizations were in evidence) that relied on emotional and religious appeals gave lesbian and gay activists a visible opponent against whom to define themselves. Given that context, it makes sense that activists, of their own accord, would distinguish themselves from the opposition through conservative appearance and professional demeanor.

The interactions between activists and members of the polity and among groups within the activist community produced strategies that emphasized similarities to the straight public and the incremental nature of policy reform. The inclusive nature of the campaign, access to the polity, and the presence of a church-based opposition effectively severed the cultural challenge from the political battle over rights. The next section looks at movements that faced organized opposition.

Oregon

Eugene, Oregon, was among the first cities whose antidiscrimination statute was targeted for repeal. After the repeal, the lesbian and gay community maintained good relations with the state Democratic Party (*Journal* 1977), despite repeated defeats of the statewide antidiscrimination bill. Activists also worked to foster relations with the state's Republican Party. In October 1987, following another defeat of Oregon's statewide lesbian and gay rights bill, Oregon governor Neil Goldschmidt issued an executive order prohibiting discrimination based on sexual orientation by state agencies. The order was payback for lesbian and gay support during his election campaign (Towslee 1987). During that same year, the conservative Oregon Citizens Alliance (OCA) was founded. Early the following year, OCA announced that it would begin a drive to overturn the governor's executive order through a ballot initiative (Towslee 1988b). By November, OCA had achieved its first major victory as Measure 8 was passed and the executive order was repealed (Towslee 1988a).

Bolstered by its success, OCA went on the offensive, seeking to pass a statewide initiative that would condemn homosexuality, nullify existing local ordinances, and prohibit the enactment of future legislation to provide protection from discrimination based on sexual orientation. In 1992 and 1994, OCA gathered enough signatures to place antilesbian and antigay initiatives (Measure 9 and Measure 13, respectively) on the state ballot. OCA also campaigned for a series of local antilesbian and antigay measures, passing such laws in 20 localities by March 1994 (*Lesbian/Gay Law Notes* 1994a).

As the OCA campaigns gained momentum, reported incidents of antilesbian and antigay hate crimes skyrocketed (Egan 1992a). Although neither side was immune from the violence—churches on both sides of the debate were vandalized and OCA leaders received verbal threats (Egan 1992b)—lesbians and gay men experienced the bulk of actual physical assaults (Bull and Gallagher 1996).[11]

What strategies were available to Oregon's lesbians and gay men in the face of such virulent opposition? Activists could have responded to the opposition in a number of ways. They could have used identity for critique to challenge the values and practices of the sex-phobic society by portraying their own sexuality as liberated, free from the debilitating impact of strict gender roles. Additionally, they could have challenged the idea that sexuality is static, fixed throughout a person's entire lifetime, thus decentering heterosexuality as a norm from which homosexuals deviate.

Alternatively, activists could have used identity for education to show that they were just like everyone else. In Vermont, this had taken the form of coming out to legislators, by constituents and by other legislators, as a way to counter myths that homosexuals were sex-obsessed creatures who preyed on innocent children.

Identity strategies were not the only tactics available to lesbian and gay activists in Oregon. Strategies that did not make lesbians and gay men the contested terrain could have been used. Activists could have formed coalitions with ethnic and racial minority groups. They could have focused attention on abstract principles of discrimination and found evidence to support their claims.

The "No on 9" campaign, like Oregonians for Fairness, the group that (unsuccessfully) fought the repeal of Governor Goldschmidt's executive order in 1988 (UPI 1988a), refused to refute the OCA charges point by point (Johnston 1994). Both embarked on slick media campaigns with commercials that never mentioned the words "gay," "lesbian," or "homosexual" (e.g., Richardson 1992). Activists feared making the campaign a referendum on homosexuality. They were afraid that, given a choice, the population might genuinely prefer to discriminate against a minority many despised. There was also concern that addressing OCA's allegations would lend credence to the charges (Johnston 1994).

No on 9's philosophy was to wage and to win a limited campaign. Its goal was not to disrupt dominant notions about homosexuals or to challenge the sex/gender system (Johnston 1994). Nor was its goal to create a long-term organizational infrastructure that could continue to fight OCA initiatives or advocate proactively for legislation. According to Holly Pruett and Julie Davis (1995, p. 7),[12] "The unofficial slogans of CHFO [Campaign for a Hate Free Oregon, which became No on 9] could have been 'campaigns are about getting 50% + 1 on election day—nothing else' and 'a campaign is not a movement.'"

The No on 9 leadership wanted to avoid any type of cultural challenge. Those who deviated most from conservative, heterosexual appearances—that is, those who seemed to fit lesbian and gay stereotypes as "bull dykes" or effeminate men and grassroots activists who wanted to disrupt dominant notions of sexuality—were increasingly distanced from the campaign. According to Bull and Gallagher (1996, p. 53), for example, Metropolitan Community Church pastor Gary Wilson "was asked to pass the word to direct action groups like Queer Nation to keep their activities low-key during the campaign so as not to cause any embarrassment." Fissures in the lesbian and gay communities became more pronounced as the campaign drew on. According to movement leader Julie Davis, Kathleen Saadat, an African-American woman snubbed by the No on 9 leadership, formed the group African-Americans for Human Rights to pursue her own style of organizing (personal communication 1996).

Unlike the New York City activists who embraced the unconventional or the Vermont activists who let each individual present their own case, the No on 9 activists dodged the issue of morality, preferring to focus on abstract principles of discrimination (Johnston 1994). The direct action groups reacted as much to the elitist efforts of the No on 9 leadership as to the opposition. These grassroots, direct action organizations employed more radical tactics, increasing publicity through public demonstrations and civil disobedience (Bull and Gallagher 1996). Spurred by the exclusive leadership and (lack of) response to the organized opposition, the ideological schism embodied in separate organizations became about the relationship between political campaigns and cultural change. The grassroots groups saw the bill as an opportunity to strengthen the lesbian and gay communities and to combat homophobic stereotypes, whereas No on 9 saw the bill as a crucial political goal.

By avoiding identity strategies, specifically by avoiding a defense of homosexuality, Oregon activists exacerbated existing tensions in the lesbian and gay communities. By 1992, the lesbian and gay

movement was split, with one faction focusing on abstract principles of discrimination, underscoring sameness rather than difference (No on 9), while another side became more militant and deployed identity for critique (ACT UP, Queer Nation, Bigot Busters; see Bull and Gallagher 1996). Many lesbians and gay men, including Johnston (1994), resented the fact that homosexuality, itself was avoided by the No on 9 leadership. Avoiding identity strategies necessarily entails a focus on similarities to the majority, and the Oregon campaign was no exception. Had educational strategies been combined with inclusive movement strategies, as in Vermont, the movement would have been strengthened. But by focusing only on winning the immediate campaign, other issues, such as combating negative stereotypes, building a movement, and empowering communities were neglected so the community was divided.

What explains the mixed model of identity deployment that we see in Oregon in the late 1980s and early 1990s? New social movement perspectives help explain the tactics of the radical organizations involved in the rights campaign. The frustration within the lesbian and gay communities over No on 9's failure to dispel myths about homosexuality, and the lack of democratic participation within both the organization and the political campaign, fit with the view that new social movements are about cultural production. However, they are unhelpful in explaining No on 9's strategies.

Activists in Oregon, as in Vermont, brought political experience and professional skills to the rights campaign, yet the structure of the organizations in the two states differed. Although neither stressed public education or community empowerment as a goal, Vermont activists relied on interpersonal networks and grassroots participation, whereas No on 9 limited participation. Unlike the exclusive organizations in Oregon in the 1970s, Oregon activists in the 1980s and early 1990s faced an organized opposition, a circumstance that fostered dissension within the community and led to the deployment of both educational and critical identities (a mixed model, see fig. 1, path 2b).

Political coalitions partly explain No on 9's avoidance of identity strategies and emphasis on sameness in pursuit of instrumental gains, despite the potentially alienating effect on lesbian and gay communities. Those who opposed Measure 9 read like a *Who's Who* of political notables. Current and past Democratic governors as well as Republican gubernatorial hopefuls opposed OCA's measures (UPI 1987, 1988*b*; Raric 1990, 1991). OCA leader Lon Mabon's hard line on an array of social issues, and the hatred his organization seemed to promote, led to a split in the Oregon Republican Party, so that in the end the party stood firmly against the OCA's antilesbian and antigay rights initiatives.[13] In fact, Oregon's entire congressional delegation, including Republican Senators Hatfield and Packwood opposed Measure 9 (Richardson 1992). Community support for lesbian and gay activists also came from newspapers and civil liberterian and religious organizations, including the Oregon Catholic Conference (Baker 1992; *Atlanta Journal and Constitution* 1992; Quindlen 1992).

Measure 9's defeat was a Pyrrhic victory for Oregon's lesbian and gay movement. It became immediately clear that the enemy was not going anywhere. After their loss, the indefatigable OCA members dusted themselves off, got out their clipboards, and began gathering signatures to place Measure 13, a new antilesbian and antigay statewide initiative, on the 1994 ballot. To consolidate its local victories OCA placed numerous antilesbian and antigay charter initiatives on city ballots across Oregon (*Lesbian/Gay Law Notes* 1994*a*, 1994*b*). Lesbian and gay activists needed to recover from the internecine fighting that had worsened schisms within the movement.

In direct response to the exclusive strategies of the No on 9 campaign, which left the lesbian and gay communities badly divided, the "No on 13" leadership sought to build an inclusive campaign that would embark on long-term educational projects and was designed to foster organizations that would last beyond election day (Pruett and Davis 1995) (Path 2b to Path 1). Another group launched a "Speak Out" campaign. In this, quintessential identity for education strategy, 60 people wrote to every radio station, TV network, and chamber of commerce in Oregon, to say that they would present their side of the story. They called to follow up,

sent letters to the editors of local newspapers, and spoke at Kiwanis Clubs, Lions Clubs, and other civic, business, and community groups.

In neighboring Colorado, similar splits handicapped the campaign to defeat Amendment 2, that state's antilesbian and antigay initiative. The main difference between Colorado and Oregon was the extent of state support. Whereas in Oregon the political establishment lined up firmly against the OCA measures, important members of Colorado's Republican Party and key state agencies supported Amendment 2. The Catholic Church remained silent, which was probably construed as tacit endorsement of the measure (Bull and Gallagher 1996, p. 118). Unlike in Oregon where both Measure 9 and Measure 13 were defeated, Amendment 2 passed. Regardless of political access, exclusive movement leadership in the face of organized opposition in both Oregon and Colorado created a mixed model of identity deployment, as diverse segments of the activist communities reacted to both the opposing movement and the lesbian and gay leadership.

Implications

This approach to understanding the strategic deployment of identity has potential applications to other movements based on a shared characteristic. For example, the Southern Civil Rights movement that emerged in the 1950s followed path 1 as shown in figure 2. The complex organizational infrastructure of the South, which included black colleges, black churches, and even beauty parlors, provided a locus from which to organize (Morris 1984). Thus when federal policies began to change, leaders were able to mobilize from an existing base (McAdam 1982; Morris 1984). Emergent, inclusive civil rights organizations underscored sameness rather than difference and sought concrete policy goals.

Over time, the focus on identity for education often gave way to identity for critique as the black power movement gained momentum (fig. 2, path 3). According to Robert Scheer (1970, p. 202), black power, or "black *revolution* [is] the statement of an alternative system of values, the move to acquire power to assert those values, and the express willingness to respond with revolutionary violence to the violence inherent in established power." By fostering an identity based on differences from the majority, black nationalism was a way to challenge dominant cultural values, to build communities, and to create revolutionary change. Leaders hoped that deploying critical identities based on perceived cultural differences would be a crucial step toward economic independence and political power.

I suggest that local variations in political access and organizational infrastructures, as well as the degree of exclusivity of African-American leadership would also account, in part, for the relative stress placed on deploying critical or educational identities. In short, local conditions (political access and the type of opposition) as well as the

relationships among African-American political organizations should help explain the vicissitudes in the deployment of radical racial identities on the one hand and educational identities on the other.

When the feminist movement began to emerge in the 1960s, two activist factions were identified. Older professional women appointed to state governmental commissions on the status of women created formal organizations and began to lobby (Evans 1979; Freeman 1984). What came to be known as the liberal wing of feminism (Eisenstein 1983) stressed similarities to the majority, deployed identity for education (i.e., that there were no socially significant differences between men and women), and focused attention on gaining formal policy

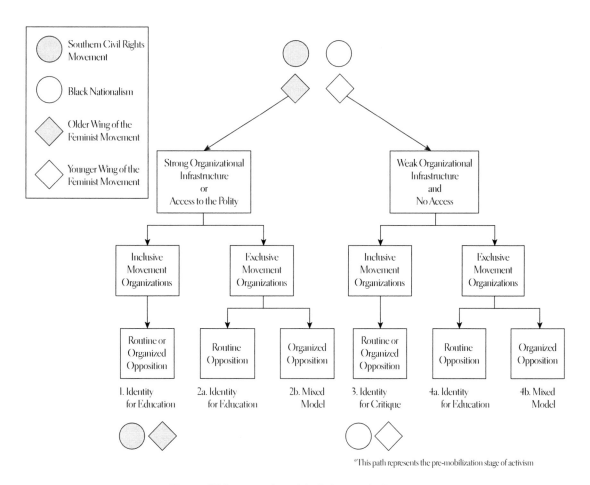

Figure 27.2 General model of identity deployment

reforms (fig. 2, path 1; see Evans 1979; Freeman 1984). Because of their political access, older feminists stressed similarities to men.

The other wing of the emergent feminist movement was dominated by college-age women. Lacking the political access of the older wing, and of course influenced by the New Left, these women stressed identity for critique and their activism followed a dramatically different path from that of the older wing (fig. 2, path 3; see also Evans 1979). The younger wing, which eventually became identified with radical feminism, drew attention to "women's values" deriving from motherhood (Eisenstein 1983) as a positive and distinct characteristic that set women apart from men in socially meaningful ways. Rather than devaluing these traits, critical female identities were deployed to criticize problematic manifestations of male dominance (such as violence [Brownmiller 1975] and nuclear arms [Caldicott 1986]).

Reforming policy and challenging culture was a goal of both strategies. Suppressing differences to denaturalize categories such as "family" challenged the cultural underpinnings of existing policies based on an allegedly natural, gender-based public/private distinction. Stressing differences was also a part of a broader project of normative challenge.[14] Over time, the relative emphasis on stressing similarities or differences changed as local conditions varied.

This brief overview of the feminist and Civil Rights movements broadly suggests how the differing structural locations of the actors, the extent of political access, and the strength of the organizational base from which these movements could mobilize influenced the types of identities deployed. This cursory overview of the movements cannot (and is not meant to) capture their complexity, but only to suggest the importance of understanding identity deployment and *why* certain movements *appear to be* internally or externally directed, and why they seem to seek "instrumental" or "identity" goals.

Conclusion

Essentialist characterizations of social movements as either cultural and expressive or instrumental and political miss the reality that goals and strategies, including identity for education or critique, are related to concrete institutional dynamics and to the structural location of the actors. Collective celebration or suppression of differences in political campaigns is the result of political access, movement interactions with opposing movements and with the state, as well as of interactions among groups within activist communities. Activists' interpretation of the relationship between culture and politics will depend on whom they are being defined against, on prior successes and failures, and on their interactions with polity members.

In New York City during the 1970s, grassroots organizations that emphasized cultural goals faced a closed and hostile polity. Opposition was routine, leaving activists to define their identities in response to state authorities. Negative interactions with the state and the lack of political access led to the deployment of ever more critical identities. By contrast, in Oregon in the 1970s, gay men with insider status by virtue of their race, gender, and class had access to the polity, and local antidiscrimination legislation passed.

In Vermont, democratic movement organizations with easy political access deployed identity for education. The presence of a church-based foe, but lack of organized opposing movements, left activists to construct identities in opposition to the emotional and unprofessional religious opposition. In Oregon in the 1980s, exclusive leadership faced with hostile opposition created dissension among lesbian and gay communities, leading to a mixed model of identity deployment. Responding to the factionalism, new leadership emerged to pursue an inclusive educational strategy. Colorado's lesbian and gay movement also split as a result of infighting, lack of political access, and the exclusive lesbian and gay leadership. Unlike Oregon, however, Amendment 2's passage left the future of Colorado's lesbians and gay men up to the courts.

The tension between political and cultural goals will always be an issue for social movements, not just for the lesbian and gay movement. For example, battles rage over the wisdom of pursuing cultural as opposed to structural and economic change to end poverty among African-Americans in inner cities (West 1993). The interactional framework developed in this paper can be used to explain these tensions.

By understanding the role of identity in social movements, we can move beyond narrow conceptualizations of movements as entities with static goals and strategies in order to understand the relationship between structural location and cultural and political change. Movements employ innovative direct action tactics at various points throughout their life cycle, not just when they are emerging. Such action can be internally or externally directed, depending on the type of movement organizations, level of political access, and the extent of opposition. Instead of asking what is "new" about "new social movements," we should focus on explaining the structural relationship between identity and mobilization, when identity is a goal of collective action, and under what political conditions activists either deploy educational or critical identities or avoid identity strategies altogether.

NOTES

I thank Edwin Amenta, Ellen Benoit, Nancy Cauthen, Kelly Moore, Gilda Zwerman, Yvonne Zylan, and the members of the New York University Politics, Power, and Protest Workshop for comments on earlier drafts of this paper, as well as the *AJS* reviewers for helpful suggestions. I greatly benefited from both discussions with and comments from David Greenberg and Francesca Polletta. I would also like to thank Elizabeth Franqui for her crucial assistance on this paper. This research was supported by a National Science Foundation Dissertation grant (9623937) and by a New York University June Frier Esserman Dissertation Fellowship.

1. Human rights ordinances typically provide protection from discrimination in housing, employment, and public accommodations on the basis of characteristics such as sex, race, and national origin; "lesbian and gay rights bills" typically add "sexual orientation" to this list of protected categories.

2. Individual-level identity-for-critique strategies rooted in oppositional cultures might include feminists not wearing bras or shaving their legs to challenge gender-based appearance norms.

3. Of course justification for political participation can have subversive effects. For example, women in the late 19th century justified their incursions into politics as a natural extension of their role as men's moral caretakers (e.g., Kraditor 1981). Political activism then changed views about women's appropriate roles.

4. Before a movement has emerged publicly, opposition will be routine, because the embryonic movement poses no threat (the apex of fig. 1). Scapegoating would be one exception to this generalization. Movements in this premobilization stage, by definition, lack political access, and if organizational actors exist at all, they are likely to be exclusive, placing little emphasis on mobilization.

5. The homophile organizations did not publicize their meetings for fear of exposing their members as homosexuals (Marotta 1981; D'Emilio 1983).

6. "Stonewall" refers to the 1969 riots that took place in New York City when patrons of the gay afterhours club, the Stonewall Inn, fought back during a police raid. The weekend of rioting that ensued sparked national publicity for the movement, and dozens of new gay liberationist organizations formed (Teal 1971; Marotta 1981; Duberman 1993), accelerating the trend toward radicalism that had begun earlier in the 1960s.

7. In addition to secondary sources, I examined the papers of the National Gay and Lesbian Task Force, from 1973 to 1993, and the collection of veteran gay activist Bruce Voeller, housed at the Cornell University Human Sexuality Collection.

8. I am referring here to the lesbian and gay movement that sought policy change from the state. Much lesbian and gay activism was not oriented toward the state. For example, during the 1970s, lesbian feminists split off from the feminist and gay movements to form separatist institutions and communities (Cruikshank 1992). The political nature of the radical feminist community has been described by others (Taylor and Whittier 1992). Here I refer only to those lesbian or gay organizations that targeted the state.

9. Data for this section come from personal interviews with both lesbian and gay activists and state officials as well as an analysis of *Out in the Mountains* (monthly issues, 1986–92), Vermont's only lesbian and gay newspaper. Interviewees included Keith E. Goslant, liaison to the Vermont governor's office from the lesbian and gay community and member of the Vermont Coalition for Lesbian and Gay Rights (hereafter Vermont Coalition) (personal interview, February 25, 1995); Linda Hollingdale, activist with the Vermont Coalition (personal interview, February 22, 1995); Mary Hurlie, cochair of the Vermont Coalition (personal interview, February 23, 1995); Bill Lippert, activist, and openly gay member of the Vermont State Legislature (personal interview, February 22, 1995); Peggy A. Luhrs, organizer of Vermont's first lesbian and gay pride march, board member of the Vermont Coalition, and director of the Burlington Women's Council (personal interview, February 25, 1995); Paul Olsen, activist; M. Holly Perdue, liaison to the Vermont governor's office from the lesbian and gay community and member of the Vermont Coalition (personal interview, February 24, 1995); Howard Russell, organizer of Vermont's first lesbian and gay pride march and of Vermonters for

Lesbian and Gay Rights, first openly gay candidate for the Vermont State Senate, member Vermont Coalition (personal interview, February 23, 1995); Susan Sussman, director of the Vermont Human Rights Commission (personal interview, February 24, 1995). It should be noted that lesbian publications existed prior to the publication of *Out in the Mountains,* but the lesbian feminist movement did not target the state about specifically lesbian and/or gay issues (Luhrs, personal communication), so those publications are excluded from this analysis.

10. At the time of my interviews, this legislator had still refused to come out publicly (Hurlie, see n. 9 above).

11. Articles appearing between 1988 and 1995, found in an extensive search on Nexis, support this conclusion.

12. Davis and Pruett were the campaign managers in the 1994 "No on 13" campaign.

13. It should be noted that after the 1992 defeat of Measure 9, activists from OCA began a concerted effort to take control of the Oregon Republican Party. At one point the party's leader threatened to create a second Republican Party, in response to the covert takeover mounted by OCA members (Feeney 1993).

14. Even movements not based on a shared characteristic—particularly those mobilized around a moral shock—must decide whether or not to deploy identities strategically. For example, animal rights activists criticize the instrumental rationality of science that privileges human life over animal life to justify animal research. Animal rights activists often deploy critical female identities as moral caretakers to underscore the inhumanity of scientific experiments on animals. At other times, animal rights activists criticize animal experimentation on "rational" scientific grounds as redundant, wasteful, and unneccessary research. In turn, scientists deploy identities by bringing forth pictures of adorable children whose lives were saved as a result of animal research (Jasper and Nelkin 1992; Jasper and Poulsen 1993). In short, scientists combat identity with identity to refute the cultural critique of instrumental rationality.

28.
The Success of the Unruly

WILLIAM A. GAMSON

It is a happy fact that we continue to be shocked by the appearance of violence in social protest. Apparently, frequency is no great cushion against shock for, at least in America, social protest has been liberally speckled with violent episodes. One can exaggerate the frequency—a majority of challenges run their course without any history of violence or arrests. But a very substantial minority—more than 25 percent—have violence in their history. The fact that violence is a common consort of social protest in the United States is not a matter of serious contention.

The consequences of violence are at issue. It is commonly believed to be self-defeating. Evaluating the validity of this belief is made elusive by a tendency that we all have, social scientists and laymen alike, to allow our moral judgments to influence our

Gamson, William A. 1990. "The Success of the Unruly." Pp. 77–88 in *The Strategy of Social Protest.* 2d ed. Belmont, CA: Wadsworth. Reprinted by permission of the author.

strategic judgments and vice versa. Kaplowitz has suggested the following general hypothesis. If strategic rationality does not clearly specify a course of action as desirable but normative criteria do, people will tend to believe that the normatively desirable course of action is also strategically rational.[1]

Violence is relatively unambiguous morally. At most, it is regarded as a necessary evil which may be justified in preventing or overcoming some even greater evil. And for many, the situations in which it is justified are scant to nonexistent. The issue depends on one's image of the society in which violence takes place. In a closed and oppressive political system that offers no nonviolent means for accomplishing change, the morality of violence is not as clear. But when it is believed that effective nonviolent alternatives exist, almost everybody would consider these morally preferable.

In the pluralist image of American society, the political system is relatively open, offering access at many points for effective nonviolent protest and efforts at change. With this premise, the use of violence by groups engaged in efforts at social change seems particularly reprehensible. The above reasoning should apply not only to violence as a means of influence but as a means of social control as well. The use of violence and other extralegal methods for dealing with protestors is also morally reprehensible.

While the moral issues may be clear, the strategic ones are ambiguous. There is no consensus on the set of conditions under which violence is a more or less effective strategy, and the issue has been seriously analyzed only in the international sphere. The Kaplowitz hypothesis, if correct, explains the strong tendency for people to believe that something so immoral as domestic violence is not a very effective strategy in domestic social protest. It also helps us to recognize that the fact that many people regard violence as self-defeating is no evidence that it is actually futile.

The pluralist view, then, acknowledges that collective violence has taken place in the United States with considerable frequency but argues that it is effective neither as a strategy of social influence when used by challenging groups nor as a strategy of repression when it is used by the enemies of such groups. We treat this view here as an hypothesis. It would be comforting to find that moral and strategic imperatives coincide, but the evidence discussed below suggests that they do not.

Violence Users and Recipients

I mean by the term "violence" deliberate physical injury to property or persons. This does not embrace such things as forceful constraint—for example, arrest—unless it is accompanied by beatings or other physical injury. It also excludes bribery, brainwashing, and other nasty techniques. To use the term violence as a catch-all for unpleasant means of influence or social control confuses the issue; other unpopular means need to stand forth on their own for evaluation, and we will explore some of these as well.

Among the 53 groups, there were 15 that engaged in violent interactions with antagonists, agents of social control, or hostile third parties. Eight of these groups were active participants; they themselves

used violence. It is important to emphasize that these "violence users" were not necessarily initiators; in some cases they were attacked and fought back, and in still others the sequence of events is unclear. No assumption is made that the violence users were necessarily the aggressors in the violent interaction that transpired.

Whether they initiate violence or not, all of the violence users accept it, some with reluctance and some with apparent glee. Wallace Stegner (1949, pp. 255–56) describes some of the actions of Father Coughlin's Christian Front against Communism. "In Boston, a *Social Justice* truck went out to distribute the paper without benefit of the mails. When a *Boston Traveler* photographer tried for a picture, the truck driver kicked his camera apart while a friendly cop held the photographer's arms." In another incident in the Boston area, a printer named Levin was approached by Christian Fronters who handed him *Social Justice* and told him, "'Here, you're a Jew, Levin. You ought to read about what your pals have been doing lately. Take a look how your investments in Russia are coming.'…One morning,…Levin came down to his shop to find it broken open and its contents wrecked." In New York, as Stegner describes it (p. 252), Christian Fronters would start fights with passing Jews, would beat up one or two opponents, and then vanish. Another source, Charles Tull (1965. p. 207) writes, that "it was common for the Coughlinite pickets…to be involved in violence with their more vocal critics.…Street brawls involving Christian Fronters and Jews became frequent in New York City.…" Now these accounts are at best unsympathetic to the Christian Front. Some of the clashes may well have been initiated by opponents of the group. For example, Tull points out that the "most notable incident from the standpoint of sheer numbers occurred on April 8, 1939, when a crowd of several thousand people mobbed ten newsboys selling *Social Justice*." Although the Christian Fronters may have been passive recipients of violence in this particular case, on many other occasions they clearly played the role of active participant or more.

The active role is even clearer in the case of the Tobacco Night Riders.…[There was some] violence directed against their constituency, but much of their violence was directed at the tobacco trust as well. "The Tobacco Night Riders were organized in 1906 as a secret, fraternal order, officially called 'The Silent Brigade' or 'The Inner Circle.' Their purpose was to force all growers to join the [Planters Protective] Association...and to force the [tobacco] trust companies to buy tobacco only from the association" (Nall, 1942).

The violence of the Night Riders was the most organized of any group studied. They "made their first show of armed force at Princeton [Kentucky], on the morning of Saturday, December 1, 1906, when shortly after midnight approximately 250 armed and masked men took possession of the city and dynamited and burned two large tobacco factories....Citizens in the business district opened windows and looked out on bodies of masked men hurrying along with guns on their shoulders. They saw other masked and aimed men patrolling the sidewalks and street corners and they heard commands: 'Get back!' And if they did not obey, bullets splattered against the brick walls near by or crashed through the window panes above their heads....Several squads of men had marched in along the Cadiz road and captured the police station, the waterworks plants, the courthouse, and the telephone and telegraph offices. They had disarmed the policemen and put them under guard, shut off the city water supply, and taken the places of the telephone and telegraph operators....Within a few minutes the city was in control of the Riders and all communication with the outside was cut off." With their mission accomplished and the tobacco factories in flames, the men "mounted their horses and rode away singing 'The fire shines bright in my old Kentucky home'" (Nall, 1942, p. 69).

About a year later, the Night Riders struck again at the town of Hopkinsville, Kentucky. It is worth noting, since the argument here views violence as instrumental rather than expressive, that the Hopkinsville raid was twice postponed when it appeared that the town was prepared to resist. "The Night Riders were not cowards," Nall writes, "but their cause and methods of operation did not demand that they face a resistant line of shot and shell to accomplish their purposes." The Night Riders made heavy use of fifth columnists in the town to assure that their raid could be successful without bloodshed. As in the Princeton raid, they carried out the operation with precision, occupying all strategic points. During this raid, they "shot into the...residence of W. Lindsay Mitchell, a buyer for the Imperial Tobacco Company, shattering electric lights and windowpanes. A group entered the house and disarmed him just in time to keep him from shooting into their comrades. He was brought into the street and struck over the head several times with a gun barrel, sustaining painful wounds. The captain of the squad looked on until he considered that Mr. Mitchell had 'had enough' then rescued him and escorted him back to his door" (Nall, p. 78). After the raid, they reassembled out of town for a roll call and marched away singing. The sheriff and local military officer organized a small posse to pursue the raiders and attacked their rear, killing one man and wounding another before the posse was forced to retreat back to Hopkinsville. One might have thought that the Night Riders would have retaliated for the attack made on them by the posse, and, indeed, Nall reports that "some of the Riders considered a second raid to retaliate...but such was not considered by the leaders. They had accomplished their purpose" (p. 82).

The Native American, or American Republican Party, a nativist group of the 1840s, was heavily implicated in less organized violence directed against Catholics. "Traversing the Irish section [of Philadelphia], the [nativist] mob was soon locked in armed conflict with equally riotous foreigners. The Hibernia Hose Company house was stormed and demolished; before midnight, more than thirty houses belonging to Irishmen had been burned to the ground...." A few nights later, roaming the streets, the rioters finally came to Saint Michael's Catholic Church. A rumor that arms were concealed within the building proved sufficient grounds for attack, and while the presiding priest fled in disguise, the torch was applied..." The mob also burned St. Augustine's Church and "throughout the city, priests and nuns trembled for their lives" (Billington, 1963, pp. 225–26). Party leadership repudiated much of this mob action but especially deplored and emphasized the counterattacks: "the killing of natives by foreign mobs." The central involvement of American Republicans was, however, substantial and well-documented.

The other violence users were all labor unions involved in clashes with strikebreakers or police and militia called out to assist and defend the strikebreakers. Among the violence users, then, the challenging group is sometimes the initiator but not always; sometimes the leadership openly defends and advocates the practice but not always. To be classified as a violence user, it is only necessary that the group be an active participant in the violent interactions in which it is involved.

The recipients of violence were passive recipients—they were attacked and either did not or, because they had insufficient means, could not fight back. The International Workingmen's Association, the First International, is one example. In September, 1873, a major financial panic occurred in the United States, resulting in subsequent unemployment and economic dislocation. A mass demonstration was called for January 13, 1874, in the form of a march of the unemployed in New York City. To quote John Commons (1966, p. 220), "It was the original plan of the Committee that the parade should disband after a mass meeting in front of the city hall but this was prohibited by the authorities and Tompkins Square was chosen as the next best place for the purpose. The parade was formed at the appointed hour and by the time it reached Tompkins Square it had swelled to an immense procession. Here they were met by a force of policemen and, immediately after the order to disperse had been given, the police charged with drawn clubs. During the ensuing panic, hundreds of workmen were injured."

Abolitionists were frequent recipients of violence in the form of antiabolitionist riots. The object of the violence was primarily the property and meeting places of abolitionists rather than their persons, although there were frequent threats and some physical abuse as well. The National Female Anti-Slavery Society was victimized on various occasions, although the women themselves were never attacked. Once, when the hall in which they were scheduled to hold a meeting was set on fire by an antiabolitionist mob, the women sought refuge in the home of Lucretia Mott. "As the rioters swarmed through nearby streets, it seemed as if an attack on the Mott house were imminent but a friend of the Motts joined the mob, and crying, 'On to the Motts' led them in the wrong direction" (Lutz, 1968, p. 139). William Lloyd Garrison was attacked at one of the meetings and dragged through the streets. The American Anti-Slavery Society was similarly abused. Eggs and stones were thrown at the audience of several of their meetings. In Cincinnati, rioters attacked the shops and homes of abolitionists, particularly Englishmen. An abolitionist printer in Illinois, Elijah Lovejoy, was killed when he attempted to resist an antiabolitionist mob destroying his shop. Lovejoy's resistance was isolated and provoked a controversy in the fervently nonviolent society. Lovejoy had had his printing presses destroyed three times, "his house was invaded, and his wife was brought to the verge of hysterical collapse. When a fourth new press arrived, Lovejoy determined that he would protect it....When his press was attacked he raised his pistol but was quickly gunned down by one of the mob." Even under such circumstances, "abolitionists in the American Anti-Slavery Society and elsewhere were divided on whether or not to censure Lovejoy's action" (Sorin, 1972, p.91). They did not censure Lovejoy but reasserted their commitment to nonviolent means of achieving the end of slavery.

Members of the National Student League were attacked in the familiar manner of northern civil rights workers going south in the 1960s. In one instance, the cause was the bitter struggle of coal miners in Harlan County, Kentucky. "At Cumberland Gap, the mountain pass into Kentucky, the full impact of Kentucky law and order descended. The road was almost dark when the bus turned the corner over the boundary; out of the approaching night the scowling faces of a mob of more than 200 people greeted the visitors. Cars drove up and surrounded the bus; most of the throng were armed, wearing the badges of deputy sheriffs....There were derisive cat-calls, then the ominous lynch-cry: 'String' 'em up'" (Wechsler, 1935). Students were shoved and some knocked down, but none seriously injured on this occasion.

The recipients of violence, then, unlike the users, played essentially passive roles in the violent episodes in which they were involved. The success or failure of the violence users will enable us to say something about the effectiveness of violence as a means of influence; the success or failure of the violence recipients will help us to evaluate the effectiveness of violence as a means of social control.

The Results

What is the fate of these groups? Are the users of violence crushed by adverse public reaction and the coercive power of the state? Do the recipients of violence rouse the public sympathy with their martyrdom, rallying to their cause important bystanders who are appalled at their victimization and join them in their struggle?

Figure 1 gives the basic results. The violence users, it turns out, have a higher-than-average success rate. Six of the eight won new advantages, and five of these six established a minimal acceptance relationship as well. Of course, some paid their dues in blood in the process as we have seen in the descriptions above. The seven recipients of violence also paid such dues but with little or nothing to show for it in the end. One, The Dairymen's League, established a minimal acceptance relationship with

its antagonist, but none of them were able to gain new advantages for their beneficiary. With respect to violence and success, it appears better to give than receive.

It is worth asking whether the different goals of these groups might account for the difference. The most relevant variable…is whether the displacement of the antagonist is part of the goals. Two of the eight violence users have displacement goals, and two of the seven violence recipients do also. Figure 2 makes the same comparison as Figure 1 but only for those groups that are not attempting to replace their targets. It reveals that every violence user with more limited goals is successful, although the Night Riders were not accepted; every violence recipient was unsuccessful, although the Dairymen's League won minimal acceptance. The earlier result is, if anything, sharpened.

Does Violence Pay?

Am I ready to conclude then that violence basically works? Not quite, or at least not in any simple fashion, and my caution is not due simply to the small number of cases involved and the real possibility of

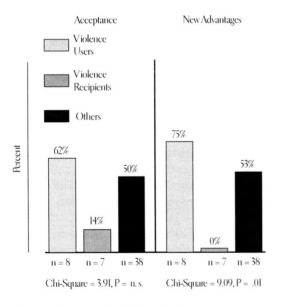

Chi-Square = 3.91, P = n. s. Chi-Square = 9.09, P = .01

* This excludes 12 groups that were involved in violent interactions and experienced arrests.
† This excludes 3 groups that were involved in violent interactions but did not experience arrests.

Figure 28.1 Arrests and Outcome

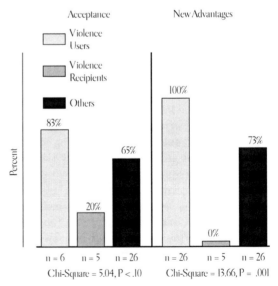

Chi-Square = 5.04, P < .10 Chi-Square = 13.66, P = .001

Figure 28.2 Violence and Outcome Excluding Displacing Groups

sampling error. It is easier to say what these data refute than what they prove.

Specifically, the data undermine the following line of thinking: violence is the product of frustration, desperation, and weakness. It is an act of last resort by those who see no other means of achieving their goals. In this view, the challenging group, frustrated by its inability to attract a significant following and gain some response from its targets of influence, turns to violence in desperation. However, this merely hastens and insures its failure because its actions increase the hostility around it and invite the legitimate action of authorities against it.

When authorities use violence against challenging groups, there are similar dynamics in this argument. Frightened by the growing strength of the challenging group and unable to halt its rising power by legitimate means, tottering on their throne and unwilling to make concessions, the threatened authorities turn to repression. But this attempted repression simply adds fuel to the fire, bringing new allies to the cause of the challenging group and increasing its chances of ultimate success.

However compelling these images may be, they clearly do not fit the data presented here. The interpretation I would suggest is almost the opposite. As Eisinger (1973) puts it in discussing protest behavior in American cities, one hypothesis is that protest is as much a "signal of impatience as frustration." Violence should be viewed as an instrumental act, aimed at furthering the purposes of the group that uses it when they have some reason to think it will help their cause. This is especially likely to be true when the normal condemnation which attends to its use is muted or neutralized in the surrounding community, when it is tacitly condoned by large parts of the audience. In this sense, it grows from an impatience born of confidence and rising efficacy rather than the opposite. It occurs when hostility toward the victim renders it a relatively safe and costless strategy. The users of violence sense that they will be exonerated because they will be seen as more the midwives than the initiators of punishment. The victims are implicitly told, "See how your sins have provoked the wrath of the fanatics and have brought this punishment upon yourselves."

The size of the violence users and recipients supports this interpretation. The violence users tend to be large groups, the recipients small ones. Only one of the eight violence users is under 10,000 (the Night Riders) while five of the seven violence recipients are this small. Such growth seems more likely to breed confidence and impatience, not desperation.

I am arguing, then, that it is not the weakness of the user but the weakness of the target that accounts for violence. This is not to say that the weakness of a target is sufficient to produce violence but that, in making it more likely to be profitable, it makes it more likely to occur. As Figure 2 showed, many challenging groups are able to gain a positive response without resorting to violence, and many collapse without the added push of repression. But groups that are failing for other reasons and authorities that are being forced to respond by rising pressures generally do not turn to violence. This is why, in my interpretation, violence is associated with successful change or successful repression: it grows out of confidence and strength and their attendant impatience with the pace of change. It is, in this sense, as much a symptom of success as a cause.

It is worth noting that, with the exception of the Night Riders, none of the groups that used violence made it a primary tactic. Typically it was incidental to the primary means of influence—strikes, bargaining, propaganda, or other nonviolent means. It is the spice, not the meat and potatoes. And, if one considers the Night Riders as merely the striking arm of the respectable Planters Protective Association, even this exception is no exception.

The groups that receive violence, with one exception, are attacked in an atmosphere of countermobilization of which the physical attacks are the cutting edge. They are attacked not merely because they are regarded as threatening—all challenging groups are threatening to some vested interests. They are threatening *and* vulnerable, and most fail to survive the physical attacks to which they are subjected.

Other Constraints

This argument can be further evaluated by extending it to other constraints in addition to violence.

"Constraints are the addition of new disadvantages to the situation or the threat to do so, regardless of the particular resources used" (Gamson, 1968a). Violence is a special case of constraints but there are many others.

Twenty-one groups (40 percent) made use of constraints as a means of influence in pursuing their challenge. We have already considered eight of them, those that used violence, and we turn now to the other 13. The most common constraints used by these groups were strikes and boycotts, but they also included such things as efforts to discredit and humiliate individual enemies by personal vituperation. Discrediting efforts directed against "the system" or other more abstract targets are not included, but only individualized, ad hominem attacks attempting to injure personal reputation.

Included here, for example, is A. Philip Randolph's March on Washington Committee, designed to push President Roosevelt into a more active role in ending discrimination in employment. A mass march in the spring of 1941 to protest racial discrimination in America would have been a considerable embarrassment to the Roosevelt administration. America was mobilizing for war behind appeals that contrasted democracy with the racism of the Nazi regime. Walter White of the NAACP described "the President's skillful attempts to dissuade us" (quoted in Garfinkel, 1969). The march was, from the standpoint of the administration, something to be avoided, a new disadvantage which the committee was threatening.

William Randolph Hearst's Independence League made liberal use of personal vituperation against opponents. "Most of Hearst's energy was devoted to pointing out the personal inequities of boss Charles F. Murphy. He found himself obliged to go back to the time of Tweed to discover any parallel in political corruption.... 'Murphy is as evil a specimen of a criminal boss as we have had since the days of Tweed'" (Carlson and Bates, 1936, pp. 146–47).

The League of Deliverance made primary use of the boycott weapon, employing it against businesses that hired Chinese labor. They threatened worse. The League's executive committee proposed to notify offenders of their desires and if not complied with, "after the expiration of six days it will be the duty of the Executive Committee to declare the district dangerous....Should the Chinese remain within the proclaimed district after the expiration of...30 days, the general Executive Committee will be required to abate the danger in whatever manner seems best to them" (Cross, 1935). The League, however, never had call to go beyond the boycott tactic.

Among the 13 nonviolent constraint users are three groups that were considered earlier as violence recipients. Including them makes it more difficult to interpret the relationship of success to the use of constraints since this is compounded by physical attacks on the group. Therefore, in Figure 3, we include only those ten groups that employed constraints but were not involved in violent interactions as either user or recipient. The advantage again goes to the unruly. Four-fifths of the constraint users and only two-fifths of the others are successful.

Constraints other than violence can also be used as a means of social control. In particular,

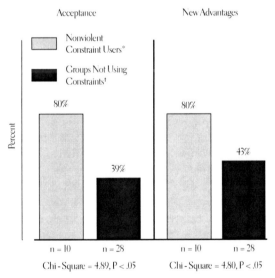

* This includes only those groups making use of constraints as a means of influence that were not involved in violent interactions as either users or recipients.
† This excludes groups that did not use constraints if they were also violence recipients.

Figure 28.3

many groups experience arrest and imprisonment or deportation of members which can be equally as devastating as physical attack, if not more so. Almost two-fifths of the sample (20 groups) had members arrested at some time or another during the period of challenge. These 20 included all eight of the violence users and four of the seven recipients, leaving only eight groups that were not involved in violent interactions but were subjected to arrests.

The Young People's Socialist League had people arrested during both its periods of challenge. "'You're under arrest,'" began an article in *The Challenge,* the YPSL paper. "This was not the first time members of the Young People's Socialist League had heard this pronouncement by officers while they were peacefully demonstrating against injustice." During its period of challenge in the World War I era, the national secretary of the group, William Kruse, was arrested, tried, convicted, and sentenced to 20 years imprisonment but ultimately won on appeal.

The German-American Bund was subject to arrests on a number of occasions. Fritz Kuhn, the group's major leader, was convicted of embezzling Bund funds, income tax evasion, and forgery. Other members were indicted on more political charges such as espionage. Some were tried in New York State under a rarely invoked statute passed in 1923 as a measure against the Ku Klux Klan, but Bundists won on appeal (Rowan, 1939, p. 178).

The American Birth Control League also experienced its share of official harassment. Soon after its organization, Margaret Sanger arrived at Town Hall in New York with her featured speaker, Harold Cox, editor of the *Edinburgh Review.*

She found a crowd gathered outside. One hundred policemen, obviously intending to prevent the meeting, ringed the locked doors of the hall. When the police opened the doors to let people already inside exit, those outside rushed in, carrying Mrs. Sanger and Cox before them. Once inside, Mrs. Sanger tried several times to speak, but policemen forcibly removed her from the platform....Cox managed only to blurt. "I have come across the Atlantic to address you," before two policemen hauled him from the stage. The police arrested

Mrs. Sanger and led her out of the hall while the audience sang. "My Country, 'Tis of Thee."

A few weeks later, with evidence of complicity of the Catholic Church in the raid emerging, Mrs. Juliet Barrett Rublee, a friend of Mrs. Sanger, was arrested "while she was in the act of testifying at an investigation into the charge of church influence behind the [earlier] raid" (Kennedy, 1970, pp. 95–96).

Figure 4 considers the eight groups subjected to arrest, again excluding all groups involved in violent interactions.[2] Only two of the eight groups were successful while nearly 60 percent of the remainder were. The results seem even clearer when we examine the two exceptions. Only two of the eight groups made use of nonviolent constraints—the League of Deliverance used the boycott and the United Brotherhood of Carpenters and Joiners of America used strikes and boycotts. These two groups were the only successes among the eight groups considered in Figure 4. In other words, groups that used neither violence nor any other form of constraint and yet experienced arrest were uniformly unsuccessful. In the absence of offsetting tactics by challenging groups, arrest seems to have the same connection with outcome as receiving violence,

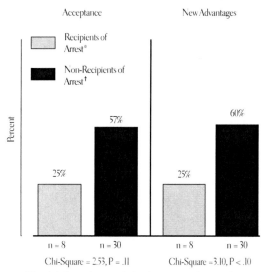

Figure 28.4 Arrests and Outcome

both are associated with failure for the receiving group.

There is another interesting fact about the six groups in Figure 4 that experience both arrests and failure. Five out of the six were attempting to displace antagonists as part of their goals, and three of the six advocated violence in principle even though they never actually employed it. Eisinger points out that "as long as protesters do not manipulate the threat of violence explicitly, they enjoy a slim legality, even, occasionally, legitimacy. Once they employ the threat openly, however, they open the way for authorities to suppress their movement or action" (1973, p. 14).

Groups like the Communist Labor Party, the Revolutionary Workers League, and the German-American Bund put themselves in the position of advocating or accepting violence as a tactic without actually using it. One might call this the strategy of speaking loudly and carrying a small stick. These groups seem to pay the cost of violence without gaining the benefits of employing it. They are both threatening and weak, and their repression becomes a low-cost strategy for those whom they attempt to displace.

Summary

The results on arrests and other constraints seem to parallel those on violence very closely. Unruly groups, those that use violence, strikes, and other constraints, have better than average success. Of the 21 groups that use some form of constraint, fully two-thirds win new advantages and 71 percent win acceptance. Among the ten groups that use no constraints but receive either violence or arrests, none is successful on either criterion. The 22 groups that neither experience nor use constraints fall in the middle, 54 percent (12) win new advantages and half win acceptance.

Virtue, of course, has its own, intrinsic rewards. And a lucky thing it does too, since its instrumental value appears to be dubious. If we cannot say with certainty that violence and other constraints are successful tactics of social influence or social control, we must at least have greater doubt about the proposition that they lead to failure. When used by challenging groups, there is no evidence that they close doors that are open to those who use only inducements and persuasion. When used against challenging groups, there is no evidence that such tactics bring allies and sympathetic third parties to the effective aid of the beleaguered groups, allowing them to gain what would have been impossible acting alone.

Perhaps it is disconcerting to discover that restraint is not rewarded with success. But those who use more unruly tactics escape misfortune because they are clever enough to use these tactics primarily in situations where public sentiment neutralizes the normal deviance of the action, thus reducing the likelihood and effectiveness of counterattack.

NOTES

1. Kaplowitz has explored the interaction between normative and strategic criteria experimentally (1973). He also argues for the complementary hypothesis to the one stated above: If normative criteria do not clearly specify a course of action while strategic criteria do, people will tend to believe that the strategically rational choice is the more normative one.

2. Only three of the 15 groups involved in violent interactions escaped arrests, all violence recipients. The violence in these cases came from hostile third parties—for example, antiabolitionist mobs—and the perpetrators of violence also escaped arrest.

Part 9

Extramovement Dynamics

In Part 8 we focused on the *internal* tactical dynamics of social movements. Only occasionally did we reference the broader interactive dynamics that link movements to other groups in society. But movements do not operate in isolation. Invariably they confront a broader environment populated by a wide array of other actors, each of which has considerable potential to shape the ongoing development and ultimate fate of the movement. In this part we take account of these extramovement dynamics and the ways in which these other parties to the conflict seek to constrain, control, or occasionally aid a given movement.

The sheer variety of these *external* actors complicates our task. It is impossible to touch on all the main ones in a single section, let alone devote readings to each of them. The selections included here highlight the influence of the following five sets of actors: *the media, the general public, law enforcement personnel, other domestic movement groups,* and *transnational SMOs and NGOs.* This excludes two other very important parties to most conflicts: *state actors* (other than law enforcement) and *countermovement groups.* Given the prominence of these two actors, it behooves us to devote a bit of attention to them before offering brief synopses of the articles in this section.

State actors are arguably the single most important external actor shaping the fate of most movements, at least *political* movements. Indeed, the powerful influence of state officials on political movements lies, as we noted in our introduction to Part 2, at the heart of the *political process* model of social movements. According to proponents of this perspective, movements tend to emerge when state authorities are newly vulnerable or receptive to the claims of movement groups (McAdam 1999 [1982];

Tarrow 1998; Tilly 1978). Indeed, some movements are essentially state-initiated. For instance, the Chinese Cultural Revolution was clearly sparked by Mao's call for internal struggle against "bourgeois" and other "reactionary elements" within Chinese society that he feared were compromising the aims and spirit of the 1949 Revolution (Walder 2009). Similarly, the development and long-term impact of a movement is expected to track closely over time changes in the "political opportunity structure." Returning to the above example, Walder's compelling chronicle of the evolution of the Red Guard Movement in Beijing in 1965–67 clearly shows that in certifying "winners" and "losers" among the various movement factions, the Maoist hardliners on the official Cultural Revolution Planning Committee (CRPC) largely determined the trajectory of the overall struggle.

It is more common, however, for political movements to confront divided state authority, with some officials supporting the movement and others opposing. The U.S. civil rights movement affords a classic case of this dynamic, as certain federal officials sought to facilitate the struggle while virtually all southern authorities tried to block or destroy the movement. In this latter effort, state authorities were aided by various *countermovement* groups that developed over the course of the conflict. While movement/countermovement dynamics have been the object of considerable social movement research (Jasper and Poulsen 1993; McAdam 1983, 1999 [1982]; Meyer and Staggenborg 1996; Mottl 1980), it is more common for these three actors—movement, countermovement and state—to be enmeshed in a complex set of relationships reflecting the often contradictory sets of interests that each brings to the conflict. The way these relationships evolve over the life of the conflict is perhaps the single most important factor shaping the ongoing development and ultimate fate of the movement.

The selections in this section, however, focus on other parties to the conflict. The first piece, by Koopmans and Olzak, assesses the impact of media coverage of right-wing violence on "public discourse" regarding the attacks. They are able to empirically link the generally critical tone of this discourse with reductions in actual right-wing violence. At a more general level, then, the article shows how two additional actors, *the media* and *the general public*, can shape the fate of a movement through a common two-step process. In the first step, the media chooses to devote extensive coverage to movement events; in the second, we see the editorial "tone" of that coverage powerfully shaping public opposition or support for the movement. In this case, extensive and critical media coverage of the right-wing violence served to outrage most of the German public, weakening support for a burgeoning neo-Nazi movement.

In the selection by Earl, Soule, and McCarthy, we turn our attention to the role of the police or other social control agents in shaping the dynamics of contention. The goal of the authors is to better understand the factors that explain the presence/absence and behaviors of the police at public protests that took place in New York state between 1968 and 1973. They show that police were far more likely to be present at "threatening events" (e.g., ones that were larger and where protestors used "confrontational" tactics) than nonhreatening ones and that extreme forms of police actions, rather than reflecting some proactive strategy, are more plausibly interpreted as reactions to the "threatening characteristics of events."

The final article focuses on the way external movement groups can ally with and aid the long-term development of a given movement. In their piece, Meyer and CorrigallBrown compare the broader political context in which movement groups sought to forge anti-war coalitions in the first and second Gulf Wars. They conclude that "the political opportunities presented by George W. Bush's administration" encouraged more cooperation and coalition during the second Gulf War than the first.

29.

Discursive Opportunities and the Evolution of Right-Wing Violence in Germany

RUUD KOOPMANS AND SUSAN OLZAK

Since the reunification of Germany in 1990, a wave of radical right violence has killed over 100 persons and wounded thousands (see, e.g., Björgo and Witte 1993; Kurthen, Bergmann, and Erb 1997; Ohlemacher 1994). Immigrants, Jewish synagogues and cemeteries, memorials to World War II and the Holocaust, left-wing groups, handicapped persons, gays, and the homeless were targeted by this violence. Despite this heterogeneity, by the mid-1990s asylum seekers and immigrants predominated as victims. In Germany, the United States, and elsewhere, previous explanations of this type of violence have often emphasized the socioeconomic sources of violence, including unemployment, poverty, and factors increasing ethnic competition between natives and immigrants. These perspectives have not proven wholly satisfactory, because they have received ambiguous empirical support (Wimmer 1997; but see Lubbers and Scheepers 2001) and because they have been unable to explain why some minority groups are targeted more often than others (Olzak 1992; but see Olzak and Shanahan 2003).

In this article, we address these shortcomings by building on existing theories of collective action and media influence to suggest how public discourse provides opportunities for mobilization. Our study explores and tests arguments that public discourse significantly shapes the targets and the temporal and spatial patterns of radical right violence in Germany. A bridge is built between two theoretical perspectives in social movement theory,

political opportunity structure and framing perspectives, and theoretical consequences are drawn from the critical observation that political opportunity structures (hereafter POS) affect movement action only when they are perceived as such by (potential) movement activists (Gamson and Meyer 1996). In contrast, framing theory emphasizes the internal perspective of movements' own meaning-making strategies. Thus, framing theories have difficulty in explaining why some such strategies meet with favorable responses while others do not. Our goal is to push this debate forward by assessing the role of public discourse in producing, amplifying, and dampening rates of ethnic violence.

In the public sphere, movement activists communicate messages to fellow activists and potential adherents, and they thereby gain crucial information about the actions and reactions of authorities, political opponents, allies, and sympathizers. To capture this role of the public sphere, we develop the notion of *discursive opportunities*. We argue that media attention to radical right violence, public reactions by third actors to radical right violence, and public controversies surrounding the targets of such violence can encourage or discourage violent acts in a number of ways. We distinguish three elements of discursive opportunity—differential public visibility, resonance, and legitimacy—that amplify the rate of some types of violence while diminishing or leaving unaffected the rate of other types.

Existing Explanations of Ethnic Violence

Debates on ethnic violence in Germany have long argued that socioeconomic deprivation and disintegration of community ties are primary causes of radical right violence (e.g., Heitmeyer et al. 1992; Krell, Nicklas, and Ostermann 1996; McLaren 1999).[1] This familiar argument holds that under worsening

Koopmans, Ruud and Susan Olzak. 2004. "Discursive Opportunities and the Evolution of Right-Wing Violence in Germany." *American Journal of Sociology* 110: 193–230. Reprinted by permission of The University of Chicago Press. Notes have been renumbered and edited.

economic conditions social groups threatened with marginalization designate specific racial or ethnic minorities as responsible and therefore worthy of exclusion and violence. The socioeconomic situation in Germany after reunification lends credibility to this argument. The merger of East and West Germany has so far failed to produce the "flowering landscapes" promised on the eve of reunification but has instead precipitated severe economic problems. Germany now finds itself below the European Union average on just about any indicator of socioeconomic performance.

However plausible these deprivation accounts are, detailed investigations at the individual level have not provided support for them. For instance, Helmut Willems and his collaborators (1993) found that the perpetrators of radical right violence tended to be fairly average young people from normal family backgrounds who were not significantly more likely to be unemployed than others among their age group. The trajectory of radical right mobilization shows no temporal overlap with trends in socioeconomic development such as economic growth, unemployment, or inflation (Koopmans 2001).

Ethnic competition theorists (e.g., Barth 1969; Olzak 1992; Myers 1997; Nagel 1996) provide an alternative explanation for ethnic conflict, suggesting that competition among racially or ethnically differentiated groups for the same resources releases forces of competitive exclusion, which in turn engenders conflict. Competition theorists have argued that competition need not be objective (Carroll and Hannan 2000). In this view, a high influx of immigrants into a formerly homogeneous region may increase subjective perceptions of increased ethnic competition (even if perceptions are not justified; Bélanger and Pinard 1991; Scheepers et al. 2002). There is scattered research from Germany showing that supporters of the radical right complain that foreigners take away "German" jobs and profit unreasonably from the German social security system, that they are a threat to "German" cultural values, and that—a view especially widespread among the young—"they are after our women" (Willems et al. 1993; Bergmann and Erb 1994). Although perceptions of relative deprivation and ethnic

competition may therefore seem relevant, they have not proven to be sufficient conditions for violent mobilization. Thus, we raise two questions: under what conditions will such feelings and perceptions arise and why is hostility directed against certain outsider groups and not against others? To answer such questions, it is necessary to turn to the political and cultural context in which radical right mobilization occurs.

Political Opportunity Structures

The concept of POS (see, e.g., McAdam 1999, Tarrow 1994; Kriesi et al. 1995) has gained widespread popularity in the literature on social movements and collective action. The basic idea is that the capacity to mobilize depends on opportunities and constraints offered by the political-institutional setting in which collective action takes place. There is little agreement about indicators, but proponents of POS theory often include measures of elite division, electoral competition, electoral instability, the composition of government, and the state's capacity for repression (McAdam 1996).

Gamson and Meyer (1996) observe that political opportunities must be perceived and are subject to interpretation or framing before they can effectively influence movement activists' decisions (see also Goodwin and Jasper 1999). Yet this amendment to POS raises the questions of why certain perceptions and interpretations of political reality spread (while others do not) and why certain actors may effectively succeed in opening new windows of opportunity (when most do not). We suggest that the public sphere mediates between political opportunity structures and movement action. Most people, including most activists, are not full-time political analysts who closely follow and gather independent information on what is going on in the corridors of power, and who have an intimate knowledge of the institutional intricacies of the political system. What most people know about politics comes from the media. POS variables such as electoral instability, elite divisions, or availability of elite allies have no meaning if people do not become aware of them. For most people, such awareness comes from the limited information about political statements, actions, and events that is made public. Just as protests that receive no media coverage at all are, as Gamson and Wolfsfeld (1993, p. 116) call them, "nonevents," regime weaknesses and openings that do not become publicly visible may be considered "nonopportunities," which for all practical intents and purposes might as well not exist at all. In the next section, we develop the notion of "discursive opportunities," to denote those opportunities and constraints that become publicly visible and that can thereby affect mobilization.

How do right-wing activists learn of these opportunities? The perpetrators of radical right violence are young people with generally low levels of interest in institutional politics (Willems et al. 1993). Therefore, it is unrealistic to assume that radical right activists follow developments in politics closely in order to rationally calculate chances of success. Instead we assume that radical right activists learn in a trial-and-error fashion about the efficacy of different mobilization strategies by gauging the public reactions their actions provoke (or fail to provoke). Through the mass media, radical right activists not only learn about their own failures and successes but also gain information about the results of actions undertaken by other activists. In this way, successful strategies are adopted and replicated. Thus, while we do not assume that radical right activists are people who closely read and watch political news, we follow other researchers in assuming that movement activists have a keen interest in following the reactions in the media to their own actions and see media coverage and political response as a measure of success (e.g., Molotch 1979, p. 72; Kielbowicz and Scherer 1986, pp. 84–85; Gitlin 1980).

Discursive Opportunities

Diffusion processes influence ethnic violence, race riots, and protest cycles in general (see, e.g., Tarrow 1989; Koopmans 1993; Myers 2000; Olzak and Shanahan 1996). Yet the theoretical implications of this highly consistent finding have not been sufficiently explored with respect to public discourse in the mass media. For diffusion to occur, channels of communication are necessary, and, at least in modern democracies, the mass media occupy a central role in this regard. The recent rise of protest

event analysis as a methodological tool for social movement studies has sensitized researchers to the dependency of protest on media attention (Mueller 1997; Rucht, Koopmans, and Neidhardt 1999). In the age of mass communication, protests that are completely ignored by the media are unlikely to diffuse to wider constituencies or have an impact on policies.[2]

Only a minority of all attempts at public claim making receive the media attention necessary for widespread recognition. We define *discursive opportunities* as the aspects of the public discourse that determine a message's chances of diffusion in the public sphere (Koopmans and Statham 1999a; see also Ferree 2003). Our argument starts from the assumption that the public sphere is a bounded space for political communication characterized by a high level of competition (see Hilgartner and Bosk [1988] for a similar argument). To be sure, the boundaries of the public sphere are not fixed but expand and contract over time (for instance, consider the increasing numbers of channels of communication such as the Internet or the multiplication of existing ones through cable and satellite television). The scope of media attention may also be affected by short-term trends, such as the media's greater attention to political topics during periods just prior to an election than during times of routine politics.

On a typical day in a medium-sized democratic society, thousands of press statements are issued, hundreds of demonstrations, pickets, and other protests are staged, thousands of individuals write letters to the media or call in on radio and television programs, and dozens of press conferences vie for the attention of the public. The number of channels of communication (newspapers, magazines, radio stations, television networks, and so forth) and the size of their respective news holes (pages, broadcasting time) act as constraints on various inputs. Thus, the media have a finite carrying capacity at any point in time.

Visibility

The discrepancy between the available space in the public sphere and the much larger supply of messages implies that there is competition among groups who aim to get their messages across in the public discourse. To understand these dynamics, we need to distinguish two categories of actors: the *gatekeepers* of the public discourse, on the one hand, and the *claim makers* that appear as speakers in the media, on the other (Neidhardt 1994; Koopmans and Statham 1999b). The gatekeepers of public discourse are the editors and journalists who have the ability to select, shape, amplify, or diminish public messages. The selectivity of coverage and the mechanisms of allocating prominence to covered messages are quite well known for the traditional mass media and include decisions about the size and placement of articles or about the amount and primacy of airing time. The actions of gatekeepers produce the first and most basic type of discursive opportunity that we can distinguish: *visibility*. Visibility depends on the number of communicative channels by which a message is included and the prominence of such inclusion. Visibility is a necessary condition for a message to influence the public discourse, and, other things being equal, the amount of visibility that gatekeepers allocate to a message increases its potential to diffuse further in the public sphere (see Trouillot 1995; Schudson 1995).

From communications and media research we know that "news values" of reporters and editors shape decisions that make a given story newsworthy. For instance, (geographical) proximity, the prominence and prestige of the speaker, and the level of violence and/or conflict, possibilities for dramatization and personalization, and the novelty of a story all influence the likelihood of its being reported in newspaper accounts (Galtung and Ruge 1965; Schulz 1997; McCarthy, McPhail, and Smith 1996; Mueller 1997; Hug and Wisler 1998; Oliver and Myers 1999; Oliver and Maney 2000). Yet, with the partial exception of proximity, news values are not objective in the sense that these characteristics of events, actors, or messages exist outside of and prior to the discursive realm. Notions of who is considered to be prominent and which issues are considered relevant or controversial have emerged from previous rounds of public discourse. They are social products that serve as a lens through which the vast array of events in public and private life are

observed and on the basis of which a small proportion of these events are selected for coverage. Social movement organizers and other public actors anticipate these media selection mechanisms. Thus, many modern protests, including Greenpeace-style professional organizations involved in direct action, are to an important extent scripted and staged to maximize the chances of drawing media attention (Kielbowicz and Scherer 1986; Ryan 1991).

Resonance and Legitimacy

While the relevance of media coverage has been widely acknowledged, less attention has been paid to the fact that the diffusion chances of a given actor's messages also depend on how other, nonmedia claim makers relate to them in the public sphere (but see Ellingson 1995; Steinberg 1999). Other speakers may publicly express support for a movement's actions, or they may react with indignation and rejection to messages that challenge their own position in the public discourse. Sometimes public actors choose to ignore social movement actors in an attempt to deny them the attention crucial for replication. We envision the communication environment of any particular public actor as the source of two further types of discursive opportunity: *resonance* and *legitimacy*. In developing these concepts we have been inspired by the work on collective action frames of David Snow and his colleagues (e.g., Snow et al. 1986; Snow and Benford 1992; see also Gamson and Modigliani 1989). Our focus, however, is on the (often unanticipated) external reactions that radical right mobilization encounters rather than on the framing strategies of movement activists themselves.

Although gaining visibility is a necessary condition for communicative impact, the career of a discursive message is likely to remain stillborn if it does not succeed in provoking reactions from other actors in the public sphere. We refer to this dimension as *resonance*. Resonance has two types of ripple effects. First, resonance enhances reproduction of a message, because, in the eyes of journalists and editors, the message has become more relevant and the actors articulating the message seem more "prominent." Second, messages that resonate travel farther. Through the reactions of other claim makers, the message of the original speaker is at least partially reproduced and may reach new audiences. This happens if established political actors express support for a social movement's actions or demands. This form of supportive resonance we will call *consonance*. However, for movements as for other public actors, even negative resonance, or *dissonance,* is often preferable to no resonance at all (Molotch 1979, p. 72). The rejection of a demand signals its relevance to other actors. Moreover, even a strongly negative public reaction has to reproduce the original message to at least some extent and thereby always runs the risk of providing potential imitators with a model for successful public action (e.g., Holden 1986 for the case of airplane hijackings).

Thus far we have treated consonance and dissonance as having similarly positive effects on the discursive opportunities of a message. Yet it might matter whether there are more negative or positive responses in the public sphere. We define public *legitimacy* as the degree to which, on average, reactions by third actors in the public sphere support an actor's claims more than they reject them. Defined in this way, legitimacy can vary independently of resonance. Highly legitimate messages may have no resonance at all because they are uncontroversial, while highly illegitimate messages may have strong resonance (e.g., for obvious historical reasons, anti-Semitic violence in Germany). The predicted effects of legitimacy on a message's diffusion chances are complicated. All other things being equal, one might expect legitimacy to have a positive effect on diffusion, because it signals agreement with a movement's position. But things will rarely be equal. Ideally, speakers would prefer their messages to have high resonance and high legitimacy, but they usually will have to settle for less. This is because high resonance is often only achieved at the cost of an increase in controversy, which results in a net decrease in legitimacy. Conversely, highly legitimate statements usually provoke few reactions from other claim makers, and the media will not be interested in endlessly repeating messages that are accepted by everybody.[3] This discussion leads us to expect a curvilinear relation between chances of diffusion and legitimacy, with messages whose legitimacy is controversial generally better positioned for replication.

Before moving to the empirical analysis, we wish to clarify that we do not want to be interpreted as presenting a purely mechanical (and unrealistic) argument suggesting that public discourse simply causes ethnic violence. Furthermore, we are aware that our insistence on a connection between public discourse in the mass media and radical right and racist violence is not wholly original (see van Dijk 1993; Jäger and Link 1993). While we share the assumption with earlier scholars that a connection between public discourse and racist violence exists, the mechanisms we offer do not require a direct causal linkage between elite discourses and popular racism. In our view, the public discourse in the mass media affects radical right mobilization not by planting negative stereotypes in activists' heads but by acting as a dynamic selection process that differentially affects the diffusion chances of different types of radical right mobilization. The public visibility and resonance of violence against a particular target group may increase because the position of this group is hotly debated in the public discourse. As a result, the diffusion chances of violence against the target will improve, even if nobody in the public debate refers to the target group by taking an explicitly negative stand.

Data Variables, and Hypotheses

We collected and analyzed information on violence by radical right and xenophobic groups and on public discourse on immigration and ethnic relations from newspaper and official police reports. We include statements on immigration control and legislation, as well as all claims by, against, or on behalf of radical right and ethnic minority groups. The units of analysis are not articles, as is often the case in media content analysis, but are claims made by nonmedia actors. Such claims include public statements, interviews, and press conferences as well as political decisions, judicial actions, demonstrations, and violence.

From our newspaper sources, we gathered information on 11,204 instances of claim making during the period 1990–99. Among these, we identified 930 instances of radical right violent attacks as one of our two measures of right-wing violence (the other is from official police reports). An example of a right-wing violent event is captured with this excerpt "A crowd of 200 local youth shouting 'foreigners out!' and throwing stones last night attacked a hostel for foreign workers in Hoyerswerda." We use reports of public discourse expressing claims on different categories of immigrants or on the radical right to calculate measures of visibility, consonance, dissonance, and legitimacy (discussed below). The following report illustrates a claim that was included in our consonance measure because it expresses a negative opinion toward one of the radical right's target groups: "In a television interview yesterday, Chancellor Kohl said that the strong rise in the numbers of asylum seekers has taken the form of a state crisis." The following is an example of a dissonant claim, which expresses a negative attitude toward the radical right: "Federal President von Weizsäcker condemned the arson attack on the former concentration camp at Sachsenhausen, saying this is an outrageous act that brings shame on Germany."

The data were coded from all Monday, Wednesday, and Friday issues of the national newspaper *Frankfurter Rundschau* between 1990 and 1999.[4] This newspaper was chosen because pretests indicated that it paid more attention to the topics of interest than did alternative sources. For shorter periods of time, samples were drawn from other newspaper sources to check the representativeness of the primary source for the wider media landscape. These other newspapers were the national tabloid newspaper *Bild-Zeitung,* the Turkish immigrant daily *Hürriyel,* as well as three East German local newspapers. Comparisons of these newspapers displayed a consistent pattern. First, in any paired comparison, the *Frankfurter Rundschau* was by far the more inclusive source in terms of the number of claims reported. Second, these quantitative differences had only very small qualitative consequences.[5] For instance, although the *Rundschau* reported more than four times as many claims as *Bild-Zeitung* did, the distributions of claims across actors, issues, and positions with regard to issues were almost the same. This indicates that the *Frankfurter Rundschau* can be considered representative for the wider German media landscape, at least regarding the type of information that we use for our analysis.[6]

We are well aware of the problem of selection bias that affects the use of newspaper data for many research purposes (e.g., McCarthy et al. 1996; Barranco and Wisler 1999; Oliver and Maney 2000). However, in this article we are primarily interested in positive and negative feedback relations between different types of claims *within* the public discourse, as represented in the media. Regarding our dependent variable—radical right violence—we are of course also interested in analyzing to what extent public discourse dynamics affect the rhythm, location, and targets of radical right violence outside the media. Here we are fortunate that the German Federal Office for the Protection of the Constitution (Bundesamt für Verfassungsschutz) publishes statistics on this type of violence that are based on police statistics gathered in the different federal states. The correlation coefficient between radical right violence in our newspaper data and in the official statistics is .53.

The newspaper and police sources did not vary much regarding the distribution of events over time, but they vary substantially across the federal states. These differences are not, as one might have expected, determined by geographical distance: the West-based *Frankfurter Rundschau* reported a larger proportion of Eastern events than did official police statistics. It is difficult to ascertain precisely what causes this difference, but it may be due to a tendency by Eastern police to minimize right-wing violence. Over the 1990s, there were continuous complaints about the lack of attention of Eastern police to radical right violence. To capture some sources of systematic bias, we conduct two separate analyses: first we use data on right-wing violence gathered from police statistics, and, second, we analyze data on events from newspaper sources. For all other measures relevant to economic hardship, competition, and extradiscursive political opportunity structures, we draw on data from the Federal Statistics Office (Statistisches Bundesamt).

Unit of Analysis: Federal States in Germany Across Time

All variables, whether drawn from official statistics or from our newspaper data, are aggregated by year and by federal state to construct a cross-sectional time series data set with 160 cases (16 federal states for the 10-year period 1990–99). Variables thus consist of counts of claims of a specific type (e.g., radical right violence) per year-state combination, year-state averages for variables such as unemployment, or year-state totals as in the case of immigration levels. Thus, we seek to explain variation across states and over time in a panel design.

The choice for this level of analysis was made for a number of reasons. First and importantly, this is the only level for which police statistics on radical right violence are available.[7] Second, below the state level, different official institutions sometimes use different spatial units to gather statistical information. The most often used unit is the *Kreis* (county), but some important data, such as unemployment levels, are gathered on the basis of different spatial units (namely the areas of responsibility of Labor Offices), which only partly coincide with Kreis boundaries. Third, during the 1990s the number of *Kreise* in East Germany was strongly reduced, not only by aggregating existing units but also in many cases by drawing completely new boundaries. As a result, continuous time series at the Kreis level are available for East Germany only from 1994–95 onward, when the reform of Kreis boundaries had been completed. This means effectively that no consistent data are available on the substate level for the region and period in which radical right violence disproportionately occurred, namely East Germany before 1994.

Why not analyze newspaper data (where the locations arc specified) at the local level of analysis? It turns out that there are also difficulties applying information from newspaper sources to a lower level of spatial aggregation. As indicated above, we have 930 cases of radical right violence in our newspaper data. Practically, this means that using an appropriate "at risk" sample of local units (to avoid sample selection bias) would not be feasible, given the enormous number of zero events for the majority of smaller units over most time periods.

Dependent Variable

Our choice of the number of radical right violent events as our dependent variable also requires some clarification. Pragmatically, this choice is dictated

by the police statistics, which do not record numbers of participants in violence and do not provide reliable information on nonviolent events. Because linking media and extramedia data is crucial to our theoretical argument, we prefer to focus on numbers of radical right violent events. As it turns out, violence was by far a favored tactic in the radical right's action repertoire, accounting for 70% of all radical right protests in our newspaper data. Our data suggest that the relevance of the radical right was driven by the frequency and intensity of the violence it produced, rather than by the small numbers of participants at these events.[8]

Techniques for Estimating Event Counts in Panel Data

Our events are arrayed as panel data. We expect that the disturbance process (i.e., error terms that are correlated within states across time) will be correlated across observations due to gradually changing but unobserved characteristics within states. Moreover, we assume that autocorrelation processes will be strongest in adjacent years and less correlated in distant periods. We experimented with several specifications of the correlation matrix of these unobserved correlations and found, consistent with other panel models of collective action, that a first-order autocorrelation specification provided a relatively good fit with the data, when compared with other possible specifications (including random effects models and models of unconstrained correlated errors).

We used an estimation procedure appropriate for analysis of event counts, the method of generalized estimation equations (using the XTGEE routine in STATA, ver. 7). Because variables consist of nonnegative counts with overdispersion, a negative binomial distribution for the dependent variable was modeled, as well as a first-order autoregressive correlation structure, which is typical for time series (King 1989). The first part of our analysis focuses on explaining the volume of radical right violence and uses police statistics to calculate the dependent variable. The second step focuses on explaining the targets of violence, using newspaper data on radical right violence (the police data cannot be differentiated according to the target of violence).

Operationalizations and Hypotheses

The following independent variables—all measured for each year-state combination separately and lagged one year relative to the dependent variable—are used in the analyses.

Measures of socioeconomic deprivation.—We use the state-level gross domestic product on a per capita basis and yearly changes in the state-level unemployment rate.[9] The hypothesis derived from socioeconomic deprivation accounts is that low levels of the gross domestic product and strong increases in the unemployment rate should be associated with high levels of radical right violence.

Measures of ethnic competition.—These are net immigration to a state from outside Germany per 1,000 inhabitants (number of immigrants from abroad minus number of emigrants to other countries) and the interaction term between net immigration and yearly changes in the unemployment rate.[10] The ethnic competition model predicts that immigration and unemployment and their interaction will have strong, positive effects on the level of radical right violence.

Measures of extradiscursive political opportunity structures.—The political complexion of the state government is measured on a right-left scale ranging from "1" (if the right-wing Christian Democrats [CDU] ruled alone) to "6" (for left-wing coalitions of Social Democrats [SPD] and Greens).[11] Years in which a change of government occurred were coded according to the government that was in power for the largest part of the year. We use the absolute difference between the percentage of CDU votes (or Christian Social [CSU] in Bavaria) and SPD votes in state-level elections as a measure of the degree of electoral competition between the two major parties; the scores were then given a negative sign so that high (i.e., close to zero) scores on this variable indicate that both parties capture comparable shares of the vote, which will generally imply a higher level of competition than when one of the two parties clearly dominates.[12]

Studies have shown that the levels of extrainstitutional protest by distinctly political social movements are inversely related to the presence of allies in positions of power within established politics (Kriesi et al. 1995). This is because political allies in

office will be less inclined to support extrainstitutional action, and there is less need for social movements to resort to extrainstitutional pressure when political friends are in power. This implies that we expect the radical right to mobilize less under right-wing governments. Political opportunity theorists further stress the importance of elite conflict and competition, which open up opportunities for social movements to intervene in the political process (Tarrow 1994). Therefore, we expect the level of violence to be higher where the two main political parties are in close competition with one another.

Measures of discursive opportunities.—To measure visibility, we exploit the fact that we have both media data and police data on radical right violence (the police data are more inclusive). In addition, among the newspaper-reported radical right violent events, we can distinguish between those that were reported on the front page and those that were reported less prominently. Combining these, we have two indicators of visibility: (1) front-page violence as a percentage of police-registered violence and (2) front-page violence as a percentage of all newspaper-reported violence. The first measure of visibility will be used in analyses using the police data as the dependent variable, the second in analyses using newspaper-reported violence as the dependent variable.[13] Dissonance is measured by all claims directed against the radical right and xenophobia, including a wide range of forms such as public condemnations and countermobilization, as well as state repression against the radical right. Consonance (with the radical right) is measured by all claims directed against immigrants and minorities, mostly in the form of public statements. In order to keep dependent and independent variables separate, our consonance measure excludes any anti-immigrant claims that were made by radical right organizations, spokespersons, or groups. Finally, legitimacy is measured by the share of consonant claims among all claims on the radical right, immigrants, and minorities. Here, too, we exclude claims made by radical right actors.

In line with the theoretical arguments outlined above, high levels of visibility, consonance, and legitimacy are expected to lead to higher levels of violence. As we have argued, high levels of legitimacy may dampen rates of protest when a movement's claims (or tactics) become seen as uncontroversial and uncontested and thereby fail to gain media attention. However, given the position of the radical right at the margins of the German polity, this argument makes less sense. The expectation with regard to dissonance is less clear: on the one hand, dissonant claims may further contribute to diffusion of violence by the (unintended) publicity that they give it; on the other hand, dissonance also undermines the legitimacy of violence and signals the mobilization of countermovements and popular rejection of the radical right.

Control variables.—The dummy variable East is one control variable. The former regions of East and West Germany are still very different in many respects. This variable measures whether there is a difference in the level of radical right violence between the East and the West that cannot be explained by the other variables in the model. Net of all other explanatory variables, based on its history of ethnic homogeneity and lack of a democratic tradition, we expect a positive effect of Eastern location on the level of radical right violence. The second control variable is the natural logarithm of the state population in the thousands. Since the dependent variable is a count of instances of radical right violence, it is of course likely to depend on the population size of a given state. Finally, we have the dependent variable lagged one year, which captures diffusion processes unexplained by the other variables in the model.

Results

Explaining the Level of Radical Right Violence

Figure 1 compares the total number of radical right violent events from the official police data with the number from newspaper sources for Germany during 1990–99. While the number of events in police reports (on the left-hand scale) is about 10 times higher than the number of newspaper events (using the right-hand scale), the peaks and valleys are strikingly similar. From 1990 to 1992 we see a steep increase in violence, with the police reports numbering nearly 1,500; these then decline until about 1995–96. In the final years of the decade, we see again a slight increase in the number of events

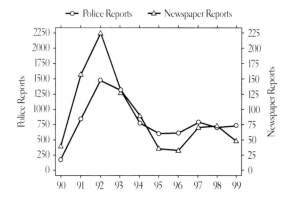

Figure 29.1 Total number of right radical violent events in Germany during 1990–99, newspaper reports compared with police data.

reported, both by the police and by the newspaper. In addition to these fluctuations over time, there was considerable variation among the federal states. In absolute numbers, the highest levels were recorded in Northrhine-Westphalia (an average of 165 yearly events according to the police data) and the lowest in Bremen (six yearly events). Since these also happen to be the most and least populous states, it is more illuminating to compare per capita rates of violence. Per million inhabitants, the average yearly number of radical right violent events ranged from 29 in the Eastern states of Brandenburg and Mecklenburg-Vorpommern to three in Bavaria in the West. Controlling for population size, the rate is clearly higher in the East than in the West. Berlin, in line with its mixed East and West roots, displays an intermediate violence level (15 yearly events per million inhabitants).

To what extent can these temporal and regional differences be explained with traditional theories of ethnic violence? Table 1 compares a baseline model including only past violence levels, population size, and Eastern location to deprivation and ethnic competition models. As the table shows, the deprivation model performs poorly. This finding is consistent with results of many earlier investigations of ethnic violence. In spite of stark differences in economic and social conditions in East and West Germany, the gross domestic product (measured at the state level) has no effect on radical right violence.

Table I Generalized Estimation Equation Effects of Deprivation and Ethnic Competition on Levels of Radical-Right Violence

	BASELINE MODEL		DEPRIVATION MODEL		ETHNIC COMPETITION MODEL	
	B	Z-Score	B	Z-Score	B	Z-Score
Radical right violence[a]	.004***	3.52	.004**	3.05	.005***	3.67
Log population size	.693***	5.82	.686***	5.92	.676***	6.17
Location in East Germany	.669***	4.12	.773**	3.12	1.01***	3.93
Per capita domestic product (in Euros)			.006	.30	.018	1.23
Unemployment rate			−.042	1.11	−.036	0.75
Net immigration/1,000					.029***	3.96
Interaction of unemployment and immigration					−.001	.00
Wald x^2	143***		124***		189***	
N[b]	148		148		148	

Note.—The table refers to Germany in 1990–99. B = unstandardized regression coefficient.

[a] All independent variable (including the lagged dependent variable) are lagged one year.

[b] Missing data left us with 148 state-year combinations with full information.

+ $P < .10$.

* $P < .05$.

** $P < .01$.

*** $P < .001$.

Perhaps most surprisingly (given prior theories), changes in the unemployment level have no impact on violence. The available information for the sub-state level does not indicate a connection between unemployment and radical right violence, either. Well-known hot spots of radical right violence such as Hoyerswerda, Rostock, Cottbus, Greifswald, and Frankfurt (Oder) all had unemployment levels well below the East German average.[14]

In columns 5 and 6 of table 1, we include several measures commonly used to indicate measures of ethnic competition. These do not fare well. In particular, the interaction term between immigration and (changes in) unemployment levels is not significant. However, the level of immigration does have a positive and significant impact on violence in the expected direction. The coefficient of .029 tells us that as the log of net immigration size rises one standard deviation above its mean (from 5.3 to 10.5), the rate of right-wing violence rises about 17%. This is so because $\exp(5.3)^{.029} = 1.16$, compared to the effect of immigration one standard deviation higher, which is $\exp(10.5)^{.029} = 1.36$.[15] While this impact of immigration is substantial, in the absence of a main effect of unemployment and no effect for the interaction term, we interpret this pattern as providing only partial support for previous competition perspectives. Clearly, we must look beyond economic measures for answers to variation in ethnic violence in Germany.

To this end, we investigate the impact on violence of discursive opportunities. In table 2, we retain the variables that were significant in table 1 and add our key measures of discursive opportunities and two measures of extradiscursive political opportunity structures. Taking the first two columns showing

Table 2 Generalized Estimation Equation Effects of Discursive Opportunities on Levels of
Radical Right Violence

	ALL STATES		WESTERN STATES (INCLUDES BERLIN)		EASTERN STATES	
	B	Z-Score	B	Z-Score	B	Z-Score
Radical right violence[a]	.004***	4.59	.004***	3.78	.006**	2.96
Log population size	.638***	6.72	.623***	7.12	.399**	2.54
Eastern location	1.09***	6.44	...	...	...	...
Net immigration/1,000	.021***	3.45	.025**	3.64	−.012	.08
Government coalition (high = left coalition)	.061	1.48	.054	.372	.094+	1.28
Party competition	.019*	2.55	.025**	2.11	.003	.201
Visibility	.980**	2.10	1.96***	6.56	−.315	.322
Anti-immigrant statements (consonance)	.017**	.00	.208***	3.91	.023	.385
Anti-radical right statements (dissonance)	−.008**	.00	−.008+	1.92	−.014***	3.64
Legitimacy	−.015	.21	−.127	.608	.662***	5.60
Wald x^2	782***		2,559***		290***	
N	154		109		45	

Note.—Table refers to Germany, 1990–99. B = unstandardized regression coefficient.

[a] All independent variables (including the lagged dependent variable) are lagged one year.

+ $P < .10$.
* $P < .05$.
** $P < .01$.
*** $P < .001$.

the results for all states, we see that prior violence, population size, and immigration remain important predictors of violence. Of the POS variables, high levels of party competition significantly raise levels of violence. The composition of government does not have a significant effect.

Table 2 shows support for the hypothesis regarding the effect of discursive opportunities. Visibility increases rates of violence in the following year (see also Brosius and Esser 1995). Consonance (measured by the number of negative claims by other actors than the radical right on migrants and minorities) also raises rates of right-wing violence.... [W]e can

calculate that as the number of consonant claims increases by one standard deviation above the mean, the effect of the coefficient for this measure (.017) indicates that the rate of radical right violence in the following year rises by 25%. Conversely, dissonance (measured by claims by other actors against the radical right and xenophobia) significantly decreased the rate of violence. As the number of statements in opposition to the radical right increased by one standard deviation, the rate of right-wing violence subsequently decreased by about 10%, across all states in Germany. When we compare the effect of dissonance between the western and eastern states, we see that the negative effect of anti–radical right statements on the diffusion of radical right violence is especially potent in the East. The inhibiting effect of dissonant claims on violence is interesting, given our argument that dissonance could have either positive or negative effects. The evidence in table 2 suggests that public disapproval dampens subsequent violence. Contrary to the expectations, legitimacy does not play a role in explaining violence (at least not when Eastern and Western states are analyzed together).

In view of the strong differences in history, economics, and immigration patterns between the East and West, it is not surprising that some of the results across this divide diverge. In particular, the net immigration level has no systematic effect on the rate of violence in the East (see the third through sixth columns of table 2). Although violence against immigrants is more widespread in the East, there are fewer immigrants in this part of the country. Moreover, during the period in which anti-immigrant violence rose most dramatically (from 1990 to 1992; see fig. 1 above) the number of foreigners in most parts of East Germany declined because the German government forced many former GDR guestworkers from third-world communist states such as Cuba and Angola to return to their countries of origin. Thus, in large parts of East Germany—including the state of Saxony, where the first big riots occurred—antiforeigner violence escalated at a time when the number of immigrants was small and declining.

The other differences between the East and West are more marginal. Regarding political opportunity structures, the party competition variable is not relevant in the East, but the effect of the composition of government is in the expected direction. This means that in the East radical right violence tended to be somewhat more prevalent when the left was in office in a state. A further difference is that the number of prior consonant claims does not affect rates of radical right violence in the East; however, the effect of legitimacy in the East is highly significant and positive. In addition, we find no effect of visibility in the East, which may be due to the fact that the readership of our newspaper source is concentrated in the West. Despite these regional differences, our general hypothesis regarding the effect of discursive opportunities on the level of radical right violence finds support in both regions.

Explaining the Targets of Radical Right Violence

We now ask if discursive opportunities can also explain the choice of targets of right-wing violence during the 1990s. Table 3 gives an overview of the targets of violence for this decade using the newspaper sources (recall that the police data does not disaggregate violence by target). Right-wing violence had a broad range of variation of targets. The "miscellaneous targets" category includes attacks against homeless persons, disabled persons, tourists, and journalists. One sizable category was that of "unspecific targets," which includes random destruction of property by radical right groups, disturbances at festivals, or attacks where the victims were nonminority Germans in everyday settings (e.g., people leaving a discotheque). We ask, did this distribution represent a relatively fixed rank-ordering of attacks on different groups and targets (Pettigrew 1998, pp. 80–81) or were there significant shifts in targets over time that require explanation?

Table 3 Distribution of Targets of Radical Right Violence

Targets	%
Asylum seekers	36.8
Other immigrant groups/"foreigners" unspecified	31.7
Jewish targets	3.9
Left-wing groups	8.1
Police	1.2
World War II memorials	2.5
Miscellaneous targets	1.2
Unspecific targets	12.8
Total	100.0
No. of events	930

Note.—Table refers to Germany, 1990–99.

Figure 2 suggests that there were indeed important shifts in the radical right's choice of targets. The figure shows the development over time of violence against the categories of asylum seekers, other immigrant groups, and unspecific targets, corresponding to three of the categories in table 3. The category "other targets" combines all the remaining target categories from table 3. The figure shows that the level of violence against "other" and "unspecific targets" remained virtually unchanged across the decade. The trajectory of violence appears to be driven mainly by fluctuation in violence against two particular categories—asylum seekers and other immigrant groups.

The evidence that, initially, immigrants and asylum seekers did not play a predominant role as victims of radical right violence is crucial evidence in support of our public discourse argument. If targets had been constant overtime, then our hypothesis about the amplification role played by the public discourse would be less compelling. In the year 1990, violence against asylum seekers and other immigrants made up only 5% and 15%, respectively, of all radical right violence. A year later, 48% of all violence was directed against asylum seekers and an additional 32% against other immigrants. By 1992, asylum seekers alone accounted for 63% of

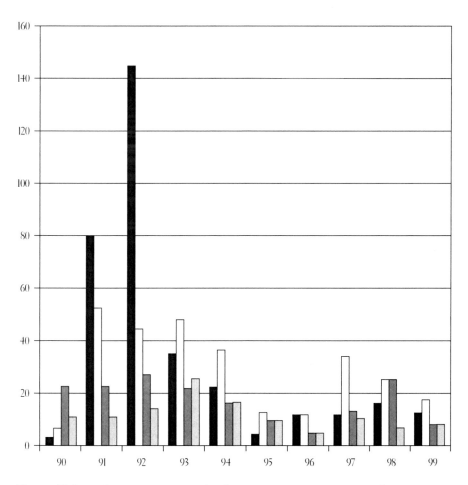

Figure 29.2 Development over time of violence against targets corresponding to categories in table 3; black indicates asylum seekers, white indicates other immigrants, dark gray indicates other targets, light gray indicates unspecific targets.

the radical right's targets. Subsequently, the relative importance of these targets declined again, especially in the case of asylum seekers.

Moreover, the evidence suggests that these shifts across targeted groups were systematically related to the differential discursive opportunities open to the radical right. The first column of table 4 shows for different target groups the average visibility of attacks against these targets, calculated as the fraction of events reported on a newspaper's front page. Attacks against asylum seekers were more likely than any other type of radical right violence to be reported on the front page of the newspaper, with one-quarter of events directed against asylum seekers receiving front-page coverage. Violence against the other two categories of immigrants was slightly less prominently publicized, with 22% of violence against ethnic German *Aussiedler* ("re-settlers") and 20% of violence against other foreigners (mostly former guestworkers such as the Turks) being reported on the front page. Radical right violence that did not target immigrants was least likely to be prominently covered (16% front-page coverage).

Next to visibility, our argument stresses the importance of the degree to which violence resonates with ongoing public debates that refer to particular target groups. In this case, asylum seekers

were a more important focus of public debates than any other potential target group of the radical right. As the second column in table 4 shows, asylum seekers featured prominently in the public debate in the 1990s, with almost 1,400 negative statements on this group over the course of the decade. Survey data from this period show that the Germans considered the asylum issue to be "the most important current political issue in Germany," ranking above issues such as unemployment and the costs and consequences of reunification (Roth 1994). To a lesser (but still important) extent public controversies also raged over other immigrant groups, but, as the second column of table 4 shows, negative statements on other immigrant groups were only half as frequent as those on asylum seekers.

The third group, the Aussiedler, consists of immigrants from Eastern Europe and the former Soviet Union who are officially defined as "ethnic Germans" (*Volksdeutsche*). They are the descendants of (originally) German-speaking groups who (mostly several hundreds of years ago) migrated eastward. According to the German constitution, they have the right to migrate to Germany and to receive German citizenship upon arrival (Bade 1992; Münz, Seifert, and Ulrich 1997). Table 4 shows that there were few negative statements on Aussiedler

Table 4 Visibility and Consonance Indicators for Radical Right Violence against Different Target Groups

	Visibility (%)	Consonance
Asylum seekers	25	1,376
Other immigrant groups/foreigners	20	723
Ethnic German Aussiedler	22	86
Other targets	16	. . .
All targets	21	. . .

Note.—Table refers to Germany, 1990–99. Visibility = percentage of violent actions against target group reported on newspaper front page. Consonance = negative claims on target group by actors other than radical right. We did not collect data on negative claims on nonimmigrant target groups of the radical right, such as homosexuals, the handicapped, or the homeless. During the period under study, none of these groups generated as much political controversy as did the issue of immigration.

compared to those on other immigrant groups. Negative statements on Aussiedler (86) were sixteen times less frequent than those on asylum seekers (1,376). Similarly, the level of violence against this group remained very low. Only 2% of all radical right violence was directed against Aussiedler, that is, 18 times less than the frequency with which asylum seekers were targeted (compare table 3).

Why would the rate of violence and public discourse surrounding this group be so low? At first glance, this finding might be puzzling (especially for competition theories), because the competitive advantage of Aussiedler (in terms of social and political rights) compared to other immigrant groups was substantial during this period. The Aussiedler were the largest immigrant group in the 1990s, surpassing even the already massive influx of asylum seekers (in 1990 alone, 400,000 Aussiedler came to Germany; over the whole decade, they numbered more than 2 million). Unlike other immigrant groups, Aussiedler had immediate access to the same rights and entitlements as native Germans; programs were set up to help Aussiedler find jobs, and they had priority access to housing.[16] In contrast, asylum seekers were prohibited from employment, received only a very low level of social assistance, and were denied access to the regular housing market. Therefore, there can be no doubt with which immigrant group German families and workers were most strongly in competition, namely the Aussiedler. However, unlike all other immigrant groups, the Aussiedler were not designated in the public discourse as ethnically distinct. Thus, even if competition for resources among individuals occurred, it did not adopt an ethnic or racial character (even though they were not necessarily welcomed equally by all Germans; see Pfetsch 1999). As a result of their favored "ethnic Germans" identity, this group experienced little violence, and their status generated little controversy.

In order to further explore the effects of public discourse on the targets of radical right violence, our final step in the empirical analysis compares the effects of public discourse across events with different targets in a multivariate context. Table 5 displays the results of regression analyses with three types of violence as the dependent variables:

against asylum seekers, against other immigrant groups, and against all other targets (this category includes violence against Aussiedler, for which numbers were too low to be analyzed separately). The results in the first two columns of table 5 show that discursive opportunities play a crucial role in explaining violence against asylum seekers, with all four variables attaining significant levels in the expected direction.[17]

Discursive opportunities show weaker effects on violence against other immigrants when compared to violence against asylum seekers. However, we do find significant effects of visibility and legitimacy on violence against other immigrants. Finally, the measures of discursive opportunity do not contribute to the model of violence against all other targets. As we have seen above, public discourse during the 1990s was heavily focused on the issue of asylum seekers and to a lesser extent on other immigrant groups. Our argument predicts that measures of discursive opportunities should favor the diffusion of violence against targets that were the focus of public debate. Conversely, other forms of radical right violence, which do not resonate with ongoing public controversies, should be left unaffected by our public discourse measures. The evidence supports the contention that differential stimuli from the public sphere explain the evolution of the target repertoire of the radical right that we saw in figure 2 above.

Two other findings in table 5 deserve mention. First, the effects of POS measures (measured by government coalitions and party competition) are not significant in any models in table 5. This bolsters our earlier argument that publicly manifest, rather than latent, structural political opportunities are decisive for explaining movement mobilization. Second, the persistence of a strong effect of immigration in all three regressions supports contentions from competition theory that hold that immigration provokes ethnic violence. Rising immigration may provoke violence against a wide range of targets, including nonimmigrant groups. Yet over time, with the growing focus of the public discourse on particular immigrant groups, we see violence concentrating on these publicly resonant targets, which were not necessarily the groups that

Table 5 Generalized Estimation Equation Effects of Discursive Opportunities on Violence against Different Target Groups

	VIOLENCE AGAINST ASYLUM SEEKERS		VIOLENCE AGAINST OTHER IMMIGRANTS		VIOLENCE AGAINST OTHER TARGETS	
	B	Z-Score	B	Z-Score	B	Z-Score
Violence against target group[a]	.055**	2.96	.030	1.29	−.025	.40
Log population size	.567***	3.63	.544**	2.83	.358**	2.10
Eastern location	2.77***	6.62	1.57***	3.20	1.99***	6.39
Net immigration/1,000	.112***	7.68	.570***	3.23	.056***	4.26
Government coalition (high = left coalition)	.095	1.47	−.071	.69	.031	.31
Party competition	−.009	.47	−.016	.91	.004	.23
Visibility	.200**	2.41	.048**	3.07	−.010	.44
Anti-immigrant statements (consonance)[b]	.063**	2.10	−.025	.67	−.002	.91
Anti–radical right statements (dissonance)	−.026+	−1.76	.007	.81	.002	.89
Legitimacy	1.06+	1.66	.567+	.311	−.06	.14
Wald x^2	469***		263		589	
No. cases	138		138		138	

Note.–Table refers to Germany, 1990–99. B = unstandardized regression coefficient.

[a] All independent variables (including the lagged dependent variable) are lagged one year.

[b] Cols. 1 and 2: consonance (with the radical right) includes only negative statements on asylum seekers. For cols. 3 and 4, consonance includes negative statements on other immigrant groups only. For cols. 5 and 6, consonance includes negative statements against all immigrant groups.

+ $P<.10$.

* $P<.05$.

** $P<.01$.

*** $P<.001$.

stood most clearly in socioeconomic competition with the perpetrators of violence.

Discussion and Conclusions

Why have previous explanations—ranging from economic deprivation to ethnic competition models and POS theories—proved unsatisfactory in explaining right-wing violence? The POS perspective offered us a point of departure for answering this research question. Taking up the longstanding criticism that political opportunities can affect movement action only when they are perceived as such, we emphasized that opportunities will influence the trajectory and targets of protest to the extent to which they have become visible in the mass media. We have introduced the notion of "discursive opportunities" to capture these publicly visible opportunities and constraints for movement action.

We have argued that the expansion of the mobilization of the radical right—like any other type of collective action—depends on diffusion processes. The three types of discursive opportunities that we have distinguished, visibility, resonance (with its two variants consonance and dissonance), and legitimacy, act as mechanisms in positive and negative feedback processes that differentially affect the diffusion chances of various types of radical right action. This dynamic, evolutionary approach rests on processes of selection and differential replication of variations of radical-right collective action as a function of if and how journalists report them and third actors react to them in the public sphere.[18] Actions and tactics that are publicized by the mass media offer a model for successful public action to others who share the same goals (or who simply want the same degree of publicity). We further found that acts of violence that provoke more public reactions by third actors (what we have called resonance) have better chances of reproduction. If public reactions by other actors to a particular type of violence are at least partly positive (i.e., it has a certain degree of legitimacy), the likelihood of replication will be further increased. Imitation of violence that becomes visible and resonant in the public sphere need not be considered as unreflexive (or irrational), as sometimes implied by the "contagion" metaphor used to describe diffusion processes. To the contrary, given the fact that most attempts to achieve public attention are unsuccessful, the replication of models of collective action that have high visibility and resonance in the public sphere is demonstrably rational, since their adoption may be expected to confer similar media attention on the imitators.

We believe that our model of the dynamics of the public discourse and the role of discursive opportunities in shaping the evolution of political contention has relevance beyond an explanation of ethnic violence. In principle, the theoretical assumptions of our model apply to interaction in the public sphere, regardless of its form or content. The type of analysis we have presented here can be applied to other issue fields and other types of collective action. For instance, one might study how the public discourse on environmental issues affects the diffusion chances for environmental protest by making some types of protest addressing

certain topics and directed against certain adversaries more visible, resonant, and legitimate, and others less so. Applications of our approach need not be limited to social movements or protest mobilization. The model also seems applicable to the study of the careers of more conventional forms of public action, for instance in explaining the differential success of presidential or legislative candidates' attempts to set the public agenda during election campaigns. We hope to have convinced other researchers working on similar topics of the potential gains of taking into account the discursive context of mobilization and collective action in the public sphere. We also hope that our notion of discursive opportunities may help to bridge the gap between political opportunity structure and framing perspectives in the social movement literature, and that it may suggest some common grounds for a dialogue between the (often juxtaposed) "political" versus "cultural" approaches to collective action.

Finally, our analysis suggests new ways in which newspaper sources can be used to study collective action. So far, event analyses of collective action have captured little of the communicative context in which protest occurs. Our analysis shows that the mass media may be a rich source of information about discursive context variables that may significantly improve our explanations of collective action. There is more to the public sphere than just newspapers, which are only one source of public discourse about collective action and its aims and targets. Television, radio, books, magazines, specialized journals, and Internet Web sites all carry information about events and debates surrounding them that could be coded and used in models of public discourse dynamics. Clearly our work is just a beginning step toward understanding how and why the dynamics of public discourse shape the evolution of collective action.

NOTES

An earlier version of this article was presented by the first author at the annual meeting of the American Sociological Association in Anaheim, California, in August 2001. The authors would like to thank Paul DiMaggio, Jennifer Hochschild, Meindert Fennema, Jack Goldstone, Carol Mueller, Steven Pfaff, Suzanne Shanahan, Marc Steinberg,

Jean Tillie, and the *AJS* reviewers for their useful comments and suggestions.

1. See also Falter, Jaschke, and Winkler (1996) and Kowalsky and Schroeder (1994).

2. Diffusion also happens in the absence of mass media attention, by way of a movement's indigenous channels of communication, e.g., interpersonal networks or movement media. However, we would argue that the scope of interpersonal diffusion is more limited.

3. Social movement research illustrates the point that tactics seen as disruptive, violent, or innovative will raise rates of protest (McAdam 1983), but only up to a point (Olzak and Uhrig 2001).

4. Trained coding assistants used a standardized codebook to identify and code all relevant claim-making activity from newspaper sources (available on request from the first author). Researchers did not rely on a set of keywords but instead reviewed all sections of the papers for relevant articles. Comparisons across six coders yielded $\alpha = .92$.

5. A more specialized audience will naturally shape the type of events addressed by a paper. Thus, *Hürriyet* obviously reported more claims by Turkish organizations, while regional papers reported more claims made in their own region.

6. An additional coding of editorials revealed important qualitative differences. For instance, the *Bild* editorials were more in favor of restricting immigration than those of the *Rundschau*. To minimize the influence of editorial bias, we exclude all editorials and opinion pieces.

7. The Federal Office for the Protection of the Constitution also publishes *monthly* statistics on radical right violence, but these are not differentiated for the 16 states.

8. The total number of participants in all radical right violent events in our data set across the whole 10-year period and all 16 states amounts to only about 17,000 (i.e., slightly more than 30 participants on average per event), but this probably includes sequential participation by the same set of activists. For about 40% of the events, exact numbers of participants are missing, which precludes any systematic analysis of event size.

9. We considered both the rate itself and yearly changes in preliminary analyses, but the results were more robust in the models using yearly changes and so we report these results.

10. In preliminary analyses, we also considered the gross number of immigrants, uncorrected for emigration, which performed less well. Moreover, the net immigration variable more accurately indicates potential competition pressures as a result of migration. In addition, we investigated whether there was any effect from migration flows within Germany, which was not the case. Finally, an alternative measure of immigration, foreigners as a percentage of the population, had no effect.

11. The other codes used were "2" for a government of CDU and the centrist Liberal Democrats (FDP), "3" for coalitions of CDU and SPD, "4" for coalitions of SPD and FDP, and "5" for the SPD ruling alone.

12. For years in between elections, the vote percentages were interpolated.

13. We also aggregated all counts of media-reported violence (front-page or not) as a percentage of police-registered violence for a third measure of visibility. As anticipated, this alternative indicator of visibility had similar but slightly weaker effects.

14. This information is based on data for the year 1994, the first year after the East German Kreis reform. Matching as far as possible the spatial units of unemployment statistics with the Kreis boundaries, we find a negative (but not significant) correlation between unemployment levels in 1994 and levels of violence across the period 1990–99 in the East, whereas in the West the correlation is significantly positive, although rather weak (.19).

15. Because of missing unemployment data, table 1 reports analyses for 148 cases, while we present descriptive statistics in app. table A1 for 154 cases. This did not affect this calculation, though—the effect of immigration is the same.

16. By the end of the 1990s, Germany had gradually moved away from an ethnic conception of citizenship. As a consequence, the privileges of Aussiedler were reduced, and the contrast between the treatment of Aussiedler and other immigrants became less sharply defined.

17. Apart from the consonance variable (see table 5, n. b), none of the discursive variables could be calculated by target group. It would have been ideal—and might have strengthened the results—if legitimacy, visibility, and dissonance could be computed for each target separately. However, this was not possible as there were too many empty cells of state-year combinations with no violence against a target group for which legitimacy and visibility measures are undefined.

18. For a further elaboration of this evolutionary approach to political contention, see Koopmans (2004).

30.

Protest Under Fire? Explaining the Policing of Protest

JENNIFER EARL, SARAH A. SOULE AND JOHN D. McCARTHY

The peak of the cycle of mass protest in the United States in the late 1960s seems to many to showcase both the persistence of protesters in the face of adversity and the brutality of police departments that faced dissent—their behavior standing as an exaggerated example of the "escalated force" doctrine of the policing of public gatherings (McCarthy and McPhail 1998; McPhail, Schweingruber, and McCarthy 1998). For example, the aggressive and perhaps even malevolent behavior of the Chicago police toward protesters during the 1968 National Democratic Convention was interpreted by social scientists at the time as standard police operating procedure (Walker 1968). Skolnick's (1969) examination of the violent reaction of Chicago police to protesters at the convention finds that such reactions were fairly typical of police behavior in Chicago in the 1960s. He concludes: "What happened during the Chicago convention, therefore, is not something totally different from police work *in practice.* Our analysis indicates that the convention violence was unusual more in the fact of its having been documented than in the fact of its having occurred" (p. 248). In a similar vein, Stark (1972) analyzes police responses to protest in the 1960s in a range of cities (Los Angeles, Berkeley, Detroit, and Chicago among others) and concludes that police rioting and violence was to be expected at protest events at the time: "Given the present state of affairs among our police, the fact that they are prone to rioting and violence is to be expected" (p. 8; emphasis removed).

The overt behavior of police toward public protesters during this period was only one form of the social control of dissent by authorities. Policing in

less public venues also contributed to the impression that authorities often overreacted to and overstepped where social movements were concerned. A variety of more covert strategies of policing included extensive undercover surveillance, vigorous disinformation campaigns, and the harassment of activist leaders (Marx 1979). Indeed, as Earl (2003) reports, governments and private entities can use a wide range of repressive strategies. Police presence and action is only one form of protest control.

Nonetheless, the lion's share of academic attention has focused on more public protest policing. Overt repression of protest by police has the virtues of being systematically observable and well-studied, as well as serving as a useful indicator of authorities' general program of social control toward particular dissident groups (della Porta 1995). Thus, as many researchers have before us, we focus on the overt policing of protest with the aim of understanding broader processes of social control by authorities during the peak of this particular cycle of mass protest.

However, we depart from prior work on protest policing in important ways. Several strands of research on protest policing have drawn heavily on notorious instances of police repression from the 1960s and early 1970s as well as on academic arguments that suggest that egregious police response to protest is fairly typical (Ericson and Doyle 1999; Hodgson 2001; Jefferson 1990; Waddington 1998).[1] As such, three chief weaknesses in the study of policing of protest have resulted.

First, researchers continue to focus on instances of extreme repression of protest without paying enough attention to the bulk of protest that, in fact, drew a much less dramatic response from police. Put differently, research on repression has developed a skewed and overly narrow image of police response to protest by largely ignoring the *range* of police responses to protests.

Earl, Jennifer, Sarah A. Soule, and John D. McCarthy. 2003. "Protest Under Fire? Explaining the Policing of Protest. *American Sociological Review* 6: 581–606. Reprinted by Permission of American Sociological Association.

Second, because of this somewhat narrow view of protest policing, little research has examined why some protests drew extreme responses from police, while other protests seemingly went unnoticed. In other words, without a comparative lens that considers heavily repressed protest alongside protest that drew little or no police response, it is difficult to understand what features of protest draw different levels of repression.

Finally, when researchers *have* attempted such explanations, few have tested competing explanations of the variation in police responses to protest. Instead, research has largely tested one or two explanations at a time (Koopmans 1993; White 1999; Wisler and Giugni 1999). Taken together, strong tests of competing explanations of police action during this cycle of mass protest have not been adequately conducted.

We address these three weaknesses here. Drawing on evidence from protest events in New York State that were reported in the *New York Times* between 1968 and 1973, we show that, even during that highly contentious period, severe repression of protest events was relatively rare. More important, we expand upon and evaluate several competing accounts that have been developed to explain the variation in police reaction to protest events. Guided by these competing accounts, we ask two questions. First, what features of a protest event determined whether police attended the event? And, second, if police were present, what actions did they take toward protesters?

Explaining Police Presence and Action at Protest Events

Much of the recent research on the relationship between repression and protest focuses on how repression affects subsequent protest (Churchill 1994; Fantasia 1988; Hirsch 1990; Khawaja 1993; Koopmans 1995; Kriesi et al. 1995; Lichbach 1987; McAdam 1982, 1988; Piven and Cloward 1977). Although this research adds to scholarship on the *effects* of repression, it does not shed light on questions about when and to what extent police repression of protest will occur. Surprisingly, fewer studies consider these important issues even though, in many ways, these questions should precede questions about the effects of repression. Recognizing the importance of answering logically prior questions about variations in police responses to protest, our central concern is to expand and evaluate existing explanations of police presence and their actions at public protest events.

Two strands of research have already set such a course by casting repression as the dependent variable, thereby attempting to explain variation in repression either over time or across groups or countries. The first strand of research has taken the notorious images discussed above as a baseline and examined changes in police responses to protest *over time*. In particular, researchers argue that protest policing has moved away from the norm of "escalated force" that was typical during the cycle of protest that we examine here (e.g., see della Porta and Reiter 1998). A number of Western nations have since replaced the escalated force model with a "negotiated management" model of policing (McCarthy and McPhail 1998; McPhail et al. 1998). Although contributing greatly to an overall understanding of variations in repression and protest policing over time, this work has been largely silent about which protest events or social movements are more likely to be repressed *during the period when escalated force prevailed*.

A second strand of research has examined which protest events or movements are more likely to face police repression at a given time and across time (e.g., Carley 1997; della Porta and Reiter 1998; Loveman 1998; White 1999; Wisler and Giugni 1999). In general, this research falls into four major theoretical camps, which share the assumption that police actions toward protest vary and that scholars must seek to understand the mix of factors that affect the likelihood of different police action at different protest events. In doing so, each camp implicitly rejects the narrow view of police action as ubiquitously egregious and instead acknowledges a range of police actions at protests. However, the four camps vary considerably in terms of the theoretically salient factors they identify in their explanations of the variation in police actions.

The Threat Approach

Some scholars argue for a "threat" based model of repression in which the larger the threat to political elites, the greater and more severe the expected repression. Davenport (2000) argues that the threat model is the most supported model of repression to date. For instance, McAdam (1982) finds that groups using noninstitutional and confrontational tactics face greater repression.[2] Similarly, McAdam (1982) and Bromley and Shupe (1983) argue that groups pursuing revolutionary or radical goals will be repressed more strongly than will moderate groups. This is similar to Tilly's (1978) argument that "accepted groups" with small goals will be repressed less and to Wisler and Giugni's (1999) finding that counter-cultural groups are repressed more often. Finally, research suggests that the larger the size of the protest, the more threatening the event and thus the higher the likelihood of repression (Tilly 1978).

The Weakness Approach

Another strand of work suggests that weakness begets repression. Gamson ([1975] 1990) introduces the idea that repression might be dangerous for power holders because elites risk public ridicule if they fail in their repressive attempts. Thus, he argues that power holders will only repress movements that they think will collapse under pressure.

Because Gamson is largely addressing the question of which *movements* will be repressed, as opposed to which *protest events* or *movement organizations* will be repressed, it is useful to probe more deeply into what Gamson means by weakness. We expand on Gamson's work by suggesting how the weakness of a given protest event might be assessed, and reacted to, by authorities.

The "weakness-from-within" approach highlights the relative (in)ability of protesters to react to undue or severe uses of repressive force. Movements or protest events that are "strong" should be able to react with ease and effectiveness to repressive actions, while "weak" movements and events should lack such a capacity. In this view of weakness, protests composed of politically subordinated groups, such as racial and ethnic minorities, religious minorities, and the poor (Piven and Cloward 1977), are perceived as being less able to resist repression by police or less able to retaliate politically against repressive policing agencies (Stockdill 1996). As well, one could understand weakness from the perspective of resource mobilization: Protests with few or no social movement

organizations (SMOs) present are weaker than protests with more SMOs present because there is no organizational vehicle available for pursuing repression-related grievances.

A "weakness-from-without" understanding is also supported by recent work. This view of weakness suggests it is not just the ability of protesters to politically react to repression that structures police action, but the willingness of outside audiences to monitor and react to repression. Because monitoring police actions often begins with press coverage, it is reasonable to expect that, all else being equal, the more prominent the media coverage, the higher the capacity for outside monitoring. Indeed, Wisler and Giugni (1999) find an inverse relationship between the level of media coverage and repression. That is, prior aggregate media attention is thought to tap the ability of outside actors to monitor authorities and repressive actions, suggesting that protests that are less "protected" by the watchful eye of the media may be "weaker" and thus more prone to repression.

It is important to note that threat and weakness are not always competing explanations. That is, a protest could be "high" on threat and yet be "low" on weakness, and vice versa. For instance, a protest by poor minorities (which would be considered "weak") could advocate Communism and use confrontational tactics (which would be considered threatening). In this scenario, the goals and tactics would be highly threatening even though the protesters would be fairly weak. In fact, there are strong historical examples of this. Pioneer black sit-in participants were weak in the sense considered here; indeed, it was their total lack of political voice in the South to which the civil rights movement directed its attention. Yet, these same protesters popularized an extremely threatening tactic: the sit-in. Although this distinction has not often been considered in the literature, analytically separating these elements in an analysis can contribute to our understanding of protest policing by helping to determine the relative importance of threat and weakness to police response.

An Interactive Approach to Threat and Weakness

Although not clearly developed in the repression literature, a few case studies suggest that severe repression is more likely when a movement or protest event is highly threatening *and* primarily composed of socially marginalized participants (see Gamson [1975] 1990). This approach differs from the prior two in that it suggests that there is an interaction between threat and weakness, which requires researchers to move beyond simply considering the additive effects of threat and weakness. For instance, the premise behind the Freedom Summer campaign was that affluent young whites could more safely engage in threatening protest activities than could blacks in Mississippi (McAdam 1988). That is, the combination of threatening tactics and black protesters most likely would have led to extreme action by the Mississippi police. To the extent that violence was expected in Mississippi, it was also expected that outside authorities would react more strongly to attacks on young whites than to violence against blacks. Similarly, Stockdill (1996) finds in his study of the high-threat HIV/AIDS movement that protest actions predominately undertaken by people of color were more likely to have been repressed, and repressed vigorously, compared with similar protests by whites.

The Police Agency Approach

Finally, some scholars suggest that internal police characteristics affect trends in repression. Because this approach has yet to cohere into a formal approach, we include the major propositions that have been suggested thus far. For instance, Stockdill (1996) argues that police forces that have historically high rates of brutality may be more repressive with respect to social movements and protest events. Other researchers suggest that the state's capacity to repress is decisive in explaining the overall levels of repressive action and also how that action will be allocated across movements and events within a given period (Boudreau 2001). Thus, large police departments with access to more resources will have a greater capacity to repress than will smaller forces with lower budgets and fewer officers.

Despite the renewed interest in repression signaled by these four research approaches, problems remain in this area of scholarship. First, most research on the repression of public protest makes few distinctions among different types of police

action at protests (but see Khawaja 1993). In fact, the literature treats potential differences among police actions at protests quite coarsely: Many simply use the presence or absence of authorities as an indicator of repression (e.g., Koopmans 1993). Scholars who *have* moved beyond a dichotomous approach to repression often only study differences between strikingly different levels of force. For instance, Wisler and Giugni (1999) compare the use of three levels of force: police presence, "legalistic policing," and the use of rubber bullets, while White (1999) examines the internment of social movement activists and the number of weapons seized.

Second, when approaches have attempted to explain which protest events or social movements are more likely to be repressed by police during a given period, these studies usually have developed and tested only one or two central hypotheses. This means that few new approaches have been compared with existing approaches, creating a serious dilemma in the literature. For instance, Koopmans (1993) is largely concerned with the position of the protest event within the protest cycle; White (1999) is largely concerned with the effect of Protestant versus Catholic affiliation on the policing of social movements in Ireland; Wisler and Giugni (1999) are concerned with the effect of media coverage on protest policing. None of these scholars, however, test their accounts against a range of alternatives and the literature is thus unable to adjudicate *among* approaches.

We address these gaps and problems in scholarship on repression by developing new hypotheses that are more sensitive to subtle differences in police response. To test these hypotheses, we use *cross-movement data* on protest events that occurred in New York State from 1968 to 1973. As a result, our analysis allows a more nuanced and complex understanding of the dynamics of police response to protest than has been available previously.

Combining Approaches and Sensitizing Hypotheses to the Level of Police Action

We focus on protest policing at public protest events while recognizing that this particular form of repression is only one of a wide range of repressive strategies from which authorities can choose (Earl 2003). We focus exclusively on protest policing for several reasons. First, protest policing represents the most public and one of the most common forms of repression. Even when covert repression does occur, the vast majority of social movement participants will personally encounter policing only at protest events. Finally, because the police serve as gatekeepers to the judicial system, they are integral to larger systems of repression (Barkan 2000, 2001), and often signal trends in wider systems of social control (della Porta 1995).

Further, following Tilly's (1978) suggestion that repression is in part a result of authority-protester interactions, we conceive of protest policing as a two-stage process in which police must first decide to attend a protest event and then decide what actions to take once they are present. We also recognize that police at a protest event have a wide array of policing options, ranging from continued presence with no further action to the deployment of escalated force (McCarthy and McPhail 1998; McPhail et al. 1998).

Taking these insights together, we argue that the four existing approaches discussed above can be further developed by contextualizing each approach's predictions to the type of police action understudy. That is, while each of the approaches implicitly assumes that police behavior toward protest is variable and that this variability deserves explanation, none of the approaches includes an explicit description of the contours of that variability, nor are hypotheses keyed to varying types of police action. To recognize and make theoretical use of variability in police behavior, we generate several hypotheses.

We begin by considering the relationship of threat and weakness to protest policing. Because authorities have limited resources with which to repress, we argue that they should place a premium on being able, at the very least, to monitor more threatening protests. Thus, we suspect that more threatening protests will be more likely to have the police in attendance. In contrast, we do not expect that weakness will affect police attendance because there is no theoretically informed reason to expect that police will have an interest in monitoring a weak group's protests. Thus, by simply discriminating between police presence and action, we can

more precisely suggest when various explanations may (or may not) be appropriate.

We also expect that authorities, once present at an event, cannot afford to ignore threatening activities, groups, or goals without appearing weak to the public. Authorities are likely to react to highly threatening events because inaction in the face of threat suggests the police are outmaneuvered or are simply overly permissive. Thus, we predict that authorities will respond to high levels of threat with high levels of repressive force no matter how strong or weak the protesters.

Although we expect that the vast majority of highly threatening events will be responded to by authorities, we also expect that situational threats will be particularly salient in predicting severe police action at protest events. That is, we predict that activities that threaten the ability of authorities to control a specific protest event, such as protesters' use of confrontational tactics and/or the presence of large numbers of protesters, will pose a particularly salient public relations challenge to authorities and will be more likely to prompt a severe response by authorities.

Once police are present, the weakness approach suggests that authorities will opportunistically direct repressive activities at weaker groups. However, there is an important cap to the amount of force that can be directed at weaker protesters without increasing the likelihood that external watchdogs or monitors will react in defense. That is, external watchdogs and the public are often willing to overlook moderate amounts of police intervention, but the severe use of force—as the history of southern policing shows (Barkan 1984)—is likely to provoke external critique. Given this, we expect that the weakness of a protest group will predict intermediate uses of repressive force, or "legalistic" policing (Barkan 1984), but that police will not risk using extreme force.

In addition to the first-order threat and weakness hypotheses, we test Stockdill's (1996) suggestion of a threat x weakness interaction. Because the logic of this argument focuses on the most extreme forms of police repression, we expect that the interaction terms will be significant only for severe deployments of force.

Finally, in keeping with research on police organizations and repressive force, we expect that police capacity may affect types of police action that depend on resources and facilities. In particular, we expect that police departments with more resources and policing capacity will be more able to monitor protests while still attending to their routine policing duties. Thus, protests that occur in jurisdictions of high-capacity departments should be more likely to be monitored. Resources and capacity should also affect police actions at protest events. A great deal of training and manpower is required to peacefully police protest events. Thus, we expect that departments with more resources for training and higher staffing levels will be less likely to resort to violence in controlling protest. However, we also acknowledge that prior brutality may beget subsequent brutality. Specifically, we predict that recent allegations of brutality will be associated with uses of major force at subsequent protest events. By joining our conceptualization of protest policing with existing theoretical approaches, then, we develop more specific and nuanced hypotheses about police presence and the conditions under which legalistic and force-based police responses will be used.

Data and Methods

Identifying Protest Events

Our primary source of data is reports on "public collective action events" drawn from daily editions of the *New York Times* (*NYT*) from 1968 to 1973. We focus on the 1968 to 1973 time period for several reasons. First, this period does not merely provide a storehouse of samples: it encapsulates a period when the "escalated force" doctrine of protest policing was dominant in the United States generally, and in New York City and New York State in particular. As such, this period represents a theoretically meaningful period on which to focus (Griffin 1992; 1995; Isaac and Griffin 1989), and a period in which a coherent approach to protest policing is argued to exist (McCarthy and McPhail 1998; McPhail et al. 1998). Second, the four theories of police response we draw upon, for the most part, were developed to account for police behavior during this period. Finally, to provide a strong test of whether egregious police action was exceptional or normative, we have

chosen a period in which many would imagine brutality to have reigned supreme. These six years represent a high-water mark in public protest activity in the United States and also include many of the more notorious instances of police violence. In fact, at the national level, the period is book-ended by the 1968 Democratic National Convention and the exposure of the FBI's COINTELPRO program (Cunningham forthcoming).

Although events during this period that occurred in other areas of the country were coded as part of a larger project, we examine here only the events that occurred in New York State. We do this for several reasons. First, because some hypotheses pertain to local police departments, such as police capacity, we needed to identify a geographic area that allowed extensive variation among police departments. New York State and California each offer this kind of variation as those states are home to the two largest police forces in the country (NYPD and LAPD respectively) as well as many smaller, less well-equipped, and less professional departments.

Second, it was important to identify an area that in many ways represented a microcosm of police-protester and police-public interactions at the height of the period of escalated force. New York State satisfies these criteria. The New York media fostered an impression of the commonness of the repression of dissent early in the period of our study. For example, during the summer of 1969 a group of Black Panthers was arrested in Manhattan and their conspiracy trial subsequently became the object of intense media coverage. The bloody conclusion to the Attica uprising occurred in September of 1972 (Wicker [1975] 1994), and the controversy over civilian review boards that began with their creation in New York City in 1966 (Niederhoffer 1969) was fueled further by the Knapp Commission Report (1973) that was released in 1973.

Finally, to the extent that there is even a possibility of regional or geographic biases in the reporting of events (McCarthy, McPhail, and Smith 1996), we minimize that potential by focusing on New York State exclusively as our data source is the *NYT*.

In addition to the restrictions regarding the time period and state, to be included in our data set an event had to meet three basic criteria. First, there had to have been more than one participant at the event as our concern is with collective action. While it is tempting to include individual acts of protest (e.g., self-immolation), we code only those events that were explicitly collective in nature. Second, the participants must have articulated some claim, either a grievance against some target or an expression of support. Thus, gatherings of people that did not explicitly articulate a claim (e.g., block parties, annual parades, outdoor concerts, etc.) are not coded. Finally, the event must have happened in the public sphere to be included in our data set. Thus, we do not include, for example, private meetings by social movement actors. The major forms and activities of collective action events in our data set include: rallies, demonstrations, marches, vigils, picketing, civil disobedience, sit-ins (and derivatives of sit-ins like "sleep-ins," "shopins," etc.), motorcades, dramaturgical demonstrations, petitioning, tabling, symbolic displays, riots, mob violence, and collective physical and verbal attacks.

Note that events could include conventional kinds of activities as well as nonconventional ones. In our analyses, however, we explicitly exclude events that would not, under normal circumstances, have much likelihood of police presence, such as letter-writing campaigns, lawsuits, and press conferences. We also exclude events that took place in total institutions (Goffman 1961, 1984), such as in prisons, jails, or mental institutions, because the dynamics of protest policing in such institutions are likely to differ significantly from protest policing in less controlled environments. In total, 1,905 events met all of our criteria for inclusion.[3] These events represent the relevant population of events reported in the *NYT* and a sample of events that occurred during the 1968–1973 period in New York State.

Coding Data from the *NYT*

Data collection and coding took place in two separate stages. The first stage involved research assistants reading the daily editions of the *NYT* and photocopying all reported events. The second stage involved research assistants coding the content of these events. At both stages, periodic interassistant reliability checks were performed to assure

consistency. Reliability estimates were consistently at or above 90-percent agreement.

Using newspaper reports on protest events as our source of event data follows a long tradition in the social movements literature (Eisinger 1973; Jenkins and Perrow 1977; Kriesi et al. 1995; McAdam 1982; McAdam, McCarthy, and Zald 1988; Olzak 1989, 1992; Rosenfeld and Ward 1996; Soule 1992, 1995, 1997; Tarrow 1989; Tilly, Tilly, and Tilly 1975). From classic studies (Jenkins and Perrow 1977; Tilly et al. 1975) to more contemporary research (Moore and Shellman 2001: Snow, Soule, and Cress 2001), researchers have demonstrated the usefulness of protest event data gathered from newspaper archives. Newspapers have been a prominent data source because they allow researchers to collect data on historical movements (Tarrow 1996) and cross-national protest (Kubik 1998; Poe et al. 2000; Tarrow 1996).

However, the use of national newspaper reports as a source of protest event data is not without its critics. For instance, critics claim that newspaper reports of collective action are subject to biases stemming from the fact that certain events are less likely to be covered in particular newspapers, specifically *national* newspapers. Critics argue that the more "newsworthy" an event, the more likely it is that the event will be reported in a national newspaper (Hug and Wisler 1998; McCarthy et al. 1996; Oliver and Maney 2000; Oliver and Myers 1999; Swank 2000).

With respect to the most important criterion for the newsworthiness of a protest event—intensity—the critics who claim that less intense events are less likely to be reported by national newspapers have not examined this issue for our period of study. For example, Oliver and Myers (1999) and Oliver and Maney (2000) argue that, in the mid-1990s, less intense and more institutionalized protest was less likely to be covered in newspapers. In contrast, protest in general was far from institutionalized in our period of study (1968–1973), a point that these authors recognize in their own work. Thus, we would expect more extensive coverage of protest events in 1968–1973 by the *NYT*. Also, to the extent to which the proximity of an event to a news source has been found to affect reporting (McCarthy et al.

1996), recall that we limit our focus to only those events reported to have occurred in New York State.

Questions also have been raised about the accuracy of newspaper reports about specific details of protest events. Efforts to validate such reports of what journalists call "hard news" items, however, find high levels of correspondence between news reports and reports by independent information sources. For instance, media reports of the goals of protest organizers and the organizers' own statements of their goals entered on permit applications submitted to authorities in Washington, D.C. before each event show quite high levels of association based on a rather detailed set of goal categories (McCarthy et al. 1998). Further analysis of that data also shows high levels of accuracy of the reporting of the names of sponsoring SMOs. The correspondence between police estimates and those of newspaper reports of the details of protest events in Minsk, Belarus, where the police and journalists are adversaries, also show similarly high rates of agreement about the form of the event, whether arrests had taken place, and whether the event was officially sanctioned (Titarenko et al. 2001). Similarly high levels of correspondence are also evident for estimates of crowd size in both of these studies, despite widespread impressions that are created by the common complaints about such estimates by protest organizers and critics (Parenti 1993).

Because the questions we address have to do specifically with the policing of protest, concerns about the reliability of journalistic reports on aspects of police behavior are relevant. Although scholars have scrutinized many aspects of newspaper-based protest event research, little attention has been paid to the reliability of journalistic reports on police behavior. Nonetheless, we are confident about the reliability of the journalistic accounts for two reasons. First, as Davenport (2001) notes, mainstream and moderate news sources are generally more attentive to the authorities and their agents than are radical and alternative news sources. Hence, we expect that the *NYT* will err on the side of including accurate information about policing. Second, in coding the 1,905 events in New York State (and 4,784 in the United States), articles describing events often

included statements like "police took no action," or "no arrests were made." So even when police were present but did not actually do anything, journalists still were likely to note their presence.

Methods

We test our hypotheses using a series of logistic and multinomial logistic regressions. We argue that protest policing is a two-stage process. The first stage of this process—police attendance at a protest event—is modeled using a series of logistic regressions in which the dependent variable is the log odds of police presence at a protest event. The second stage of the process *limits the sample to events in which police were present* and uses multinomial logistic regressions to model the log odds of *different types of police action*. (See Long [1997] for a thorough discussion of both logistic and multinomial logistic regressions.)

This conceptualization and modeling of the protest policing process moves prior research an important step forward. Most current research on police action has simply examined the presence or absence of police as a measure of repression (Koopmans 1993) or compared grossly different strategies (White 1999; Wisler and Giugni 1999). Regardless, researchers have typically employed logistic regressions when studying the policing of protest events.[4] Such an approach tacitly assumes that authorities make discrete and independent decisions about tactical deployments (e.g., police decide to use tear gas independently of their decision to use a baton charge or to take no action all). Empirically, this method does not match the decision-making process of police agencies and officers; the police must make decisions about which *combinations* of tactics to deploy.[5]

Operationalization of Police Responses to Protests

To more accurately model this combinatorial reality, we create a dependent variable that is based on theoretical groupings of observed combinations of police tactics in New York State in 1968–1973. The following six tactics served as the basis for the groupings: police presence, limited action,[6] the use of barricades, the use of physical force (e.g., hand-to-hand combat), the use of weapons (e.g., tear gas), and the use of arrests. Of the analytically possible combinations of these 6 tactics, only 11 actually occurred in New York in the period of this study. Important theoretical similarities were noted among these 11 combinations, and the combinations were collapsed accordingly; this resulted in a five-category dependent variable.

The five categories are as follows.[7] First, there is the "Do Nothing" approach, in which officers show up at a protest event but take no further action. For example, on April 25, 1968 a group of black students at Long Island University barricaded themselves in the provost's office with a list of demands, including the hiring of more black faculty and increasing the number of scholarships for black students. The *NYT* article describing this event states that the University summoned 25 police officers, but no arrests were made and no other actions were taken (Farber 1968).

Second, in the "Nothing to See Here" approach, officers show up and take only limited action (which excludes the use of arrests or physical coercion). These events often featured police performing minor tasks, such as traffic direction or gathering information from protesters.

Third, there is the "Ounce of Prevention/Legal Eagles" approach, in which officers try to prevent disorder by erecting barricades, reacting to protest by making arrests, or combining the use of barricades and arrests. For instance, on October 1, 1968, teachers and students in Brooklyn staged a walkout to protest the return of 83 teachers accused of misconduct. Police erected barriers and arrested nine people (Buder 1968).

The fourth response, which we call the "Dirty Harry" strategy, is a force-reliant manner of dealing with protesters, in which officers use physical force and sometimes use weapons, such as tear gas.[8] For example, on May 27, 1971, demonstrators from the Progressive Labor Party, a Marxist organization, disrupted a meeting of New York's City Council Finance Committee that was responsible for cutting jobs and city services. Police were described as using "fists and clubs" and as marching "quickly in pairs" to subdue demonstrators (Burks 1968:13).

The final response type is the "Calling All Cars" approach in which officers combine all the tactics they have available: Officers use force, make arrests, and frequently use weapons, such as tear gas. For example, in April of 1968, students at Columbia University took over several buildings on campus to protest the construction of a gymnasium and the University's affiliation with the Institute for Defense Analysis, a government-funded military research entity. The occupation ended in a police raid in which police used violence and arrested 720 protesters (Fox 1968:1).

Figures 1 and 2 display the frequencies of these five types of police responses at New York protest events during the study period. The pie chart indicates the total deployments, by percentage, for each type of response from 1968 to 1973. It reveals overall patterns in the deployment of different police approaches. First, and quite importantly given great speculation about the relative frequency of police actions at protest events, the number of no-shows (i.e., events that the police were not reported to have attended) is overwhelming—69 percent of events occurred without police presence. Thus, the modal police response to protest during this period was to ignore it.[9]

Despite expectations of finding a high incidence of highly repressive police actions in this period (Skolnick 1969; Stark 1972), the descriptive statistics show that preventive and legalistic approaches predominated. Strategies that included force were not as frequent as many would expect. The Dirty Harry strategy, which is entirely force-based, is the least frequent response to protest in this period, representing just under 2 percent of all of the events during this period. This finding serves as an important correction to the popular caricatures of egregious police action.

Figure 2 captures the distribution of police deployments by year, as well as the overall trend in the number of events. For instance, 1969 featured the largest number of protests, while 1973 saw the fewest. Further, although there are slight variations in the relative frequency of different police approaches each year, an amazingly consistent picture of overall police action is depicted. That is, Dirty Harry was not heavily used in one year and

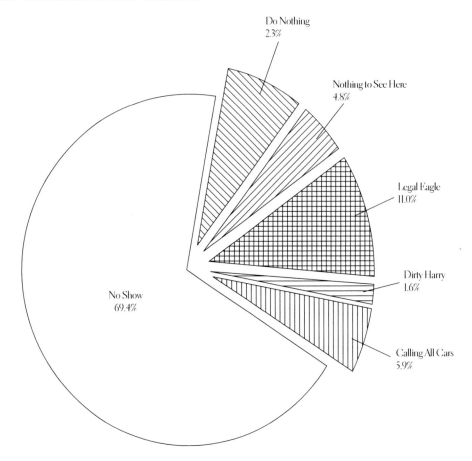

Figure 30.1 Total Police Deployments at Protest Events: New York, 1968 to 1973
(Number of cases = 1,905.)

then absent in the next, nor did other deployments experience noticeable shifts in usage. These findings buttress our assumption of relative stability in police responses to protest events from year to year during this period.

Operationalization of Independent Variables
THREAT. To measure threat, we employ five variables. First, a logged count of the number of protesters reported at the event serves as a measure of protest size (the measure is logged to correct for heteroskedasticity). We predict that police will place a high priority on monitoring large protests, and

hence will attend large protests at a higher rate. We also expect that large protests will more frequently prompt police action because large numbers of people are harder to control, present more opportunities for lawbreaking, and are more threatening to the physical safety of officers present and to the power of political elites as well.

Second, a dummy variable indicating the use of confrontational tactics, such as sit-ins, office takeovers, and meeting disruptions (see Appendix A for a list of confrontational tactics), is included as a second measure of threat.[10] We hypothesize that the use of these confrontational tactics will prompt

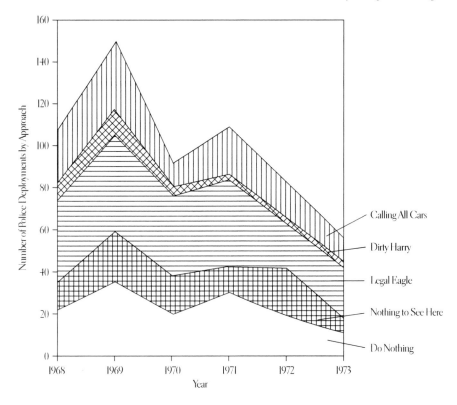

Figure 30.2 Number of Police Deployments at Protest Events, by Year: New York, 1968 to 1973 (Number of cases = 1,905.)

a police presence, either through "calls for service" by concerned citizens or through a police desire to monitor potentially disruptive gatherings.[11] Further, we expect that the use of confrontational tactics will be perceived as threatening to line officers, prompting more repression.

Third, we employ a dummy variable for advocating radical goals that is coded 1 (for claims such as racial and ethnic power, pro-Communism, and pro-gay rights), and 0 otherwise.[12] We hypothesize that protests advocating radical goals are viewed as more threatening by political elites, prompting a high likelihood of police presence and more serious police action.[13]

Finally, the number of protester goals (a measure of the multiplicity of goals) and the number of protest targets (a measure of the multiplicity of

targets) are entered into models. We predict that the more diverse and extensive the goals of a protest (Tilly 1978) or the more targets a protest has, the more threatened political elites are likely to feel.[14] Because the threat model argues that threat is translated into repression, we expect that police will be more likely to attend and more likely to take action at protests with large numbers of goals or targets. All five measures of threat are drawn directly from the *NYT* event data and are constructed as consistently as possible with existing studies of threat.

WEAKNESS. We conceive of weakness resulting from characteristics of protesters (weakness-from-within) and a paucity of external monitoring (weakness-from-without). To capture the weakness-from-within specification we employ four variables. First, we include a dummy variable for the presence of racial and ethnic minorities and other subordinated populations, such as the poor (see Appendix A for a list of groups), with the expectation that subordinate group presence will increase the likelihood of moderate police action.[15] With the same expectation, we employ a dummy variable for the presence of college students. Depending on their age, young people and students either cannot or do not vote in large numbers, which limits their political power. With both variables, the concern is over the extent to which each group could easily seek redress through normal political channels if their protests were policed in a manner they found objectionable. Clearly, wealthy white protesters are more likely to have avenues for political voice and redress than are subordinate group protesters; similarly, adults with voting rights are more likely to have avenues for political voice and redress than are youths without formal political access (i.e., voting rights).[16]

To tap a resource mobilization specification of weakness-from-within, we include a variable indicating that at least one SMO was present at the event.[17] We expect that SMO absence indicates a weak capacity to respond to police actions against protesters and thus raises the likelihood of moderate police action. We also include the number of SMOs present because additional SMOs should increase the avenues of redress available. Low SMO counts are also expected to increase the likelihood of moderate police action.[18]

To measure weakness-from-without, or the ability of outside actors to monitor the political elite and police response to protesters, we focus on prominent media attention. We include a count of the total number of protest events discussed in front-page *NYT* stories from the prior month (one-month lagged count). Front-page stories are much more likely to be read and thus much more likely to serve a real monitoring function. In particular, we predict that low profiles for protest in the prior month will be associated with moderate coercion or legalistic policing. This focus on media attention is supported by work on Swiss protests (Wisler and Giugni 1999).

INTERACTION TERMS. Stockdill (1996) predicts an interaction between threat and weakness. We measure this possibility by introducing three interaction terms: (1) subordinate group presence x use of confrontational tactics; (2) subordinate group presence x advocating radical goals; and (3) subordinate group presence x logged number of protest participants. In each case, the expectation is that a significant interaction term will increase the likelihood of police actions involving force—as represented by the Calling All Cars and Ditty Harry approaches.

POLICE MEASURES. We employ two related police measures. First, we capture the capacity of the police force to impose social control by measuring the per capita dollars spent annually on law enforcement in the county in which the event occurred. Figures were drawn from the Census of Governmental Units, City and County Data Books, and U.S. census data. In those few cases where yearly measures of spending or county population were not available, values were linearly imputed from earlier and later values.[19] We expect that police forces with more resources will be able to monitor more protests, thereby increasing the likelihood of police presence. We also expect that departments with more resources are better able to staff, train, and equip officers so that officers avoid more violent interactions with protesters.

To measure prior brutality, we rely on the number of allegations of police brutality at protest events in a county, as reported by the *NYT,* in the prior six calendar months. Although we would prefer to count actual brutality complaints filed against police agencies, these data vary markedly in quality and are particularly suspect during this period because fights over civilian review made such statistics especially sensitive to politically motivated data collection schemes (Kobler 1975). Here, the expectation is that brutality begets brutality, leading high numbers of recent allegations to be subsequently associated with high rates of police deployments involving force (e.g., the Calling All Cars and the Dirty Harry approaches).[20]

CONTROL VARIABLES. Several control variables are entered in the models, although they are not included in the reported results. First, the percentage of voters in the county where the protest occurred that voted for the Democratic presidential nominee in the most recent presidential election controls for the political climate of the county. Second, a dummy variable for whether or not the protest event was an African American civil rights protest is entered because the literature notes the possibility of disproportionate police hostility toward this movement during this period (Barkan 1984; McAdam 1983; Stark 1972). Third, the logged duration of the protest event in days is entered because long protest events create more opportunities for police presence (i.e., police have less time to learn of and respond to short protests while long protests create ample time for police intelligence and response). Protest duration is logged to reduce heteroskedasticity. Fourth, the logged length of the *NYT* article(s) reporting the event is entered to control for possible effects of the level of detail provided in descriptions of the protest. Finally, fixed effects for the three areas in the New York City metropolitan area are included (Long Island, Westchester County, and the five counties of New York City), and a fixed effect for Albany (the state capital) are also entered into models to reduce spatial autocorrelation and heteroskedasticity.

Results

Police Presence at Protest Events

Table 1 reports the results from the full and reduced logistic regression models. The full model includes all of the variables described above, including control variables (although their coefficients are not reported). The reduced model is trimmed to exclude nonsignificant coefficients (except nonsignificant control variables). We use a two-pronged test for variable removal: The coefficient must be nonsignificant at the $p < .05$ level *and* the group of removed variables must be jointly nonsignificant (which is judged by a -2 log-likelihood comparison of models including and excluding the set of variables). Appendix B contains logistic regression models that test each approach separately so that readers may examine how the results differ when all approaches are compared in isolation instead of simultaneously.[21]

Table 1 suggests that threat is a major predictor of police presence, confirming our hypothesis. Three of the threat variables in the reduced model are significant and in the expected direction: protest size,

the use of confrontational tactics, and advocating radical goals. The impacts of these variables are noteworthy. Events that include confrontational tactics are more than seven times more likely to result in police presence than are events that do not include such tactics.[22] The odds of police presence are 54 percent greater if the size of the protest increases by one standard deviation. Similarly, events that include radical goals are almost twice as likely to result in police presence. Clearly, these variables have strong statistical and substantive effects on the likelihood of police presence.

In contrast, while three weakness variables are ultimately significant in the reduced model—subordinate group presence, college student presence, and SMO presence—two of these work in the opposite direction than expected by weakness arguments. That is, while subordinate group presence increases the likelihood of police presence, as weakness theorists predict, college student presence unexpectedly decreases the likelihood of police presence, and SMO presence unexpectedly increases the likelihood of police presence. The finding for college student presence can be understood in several ways. First, many student protests were held on campuses, which may have preferred to use private security forces instead of local police. Second, college students may have parents who are willing to use their own political connections when their children have interactions with the police.[23] For the unexpected SMO effect, we speculate that SMOs are more likely to have prior relationships with police and to plan their events in advance, allowing police an increased opportunity to attend such protests either proactively or as a result of a call for service.

The coefficient for subordinate group presence is less decisive than weakness theorists would hope: The odds of police presence are only 46 percent higher when subordinated groups participated in events, and this is less substantial than the factor changes produced by the threat comparisons. While weakness scholars may be surprised by these findings, they do confirm our hypothesis.

In addition to the additive tests of threat and weakness, we also included three interaction terms as suggested by Stockdill's (1996) work. None of these terms is significant, however. Although the

Table 1 Logistic Regression Coefficients Predicting Police Presence at Public Protest Events: New York, 1968 to 1973

Independent Variable	FULL MODEL		REDUCED MODEL	
	Coef.	S.E.	Coef.	S.E.
Threat				
Protest size (log)	.192**	(.036)	.221**	(.032)
Confrontational tactics	1.958**	(.150)	1.964**	(.132)
Number of goals	.009	(.074)	—	
Number of targets	−.019	(.101)	—	
Radical goals	.601**	(.157)	.660**	(.132)
Weakness				
Front-page news coverage in prior month's *NYT*	−.008	(.008)	—	
Subordinate group present	−.229	(.476)	.380**	(.130)
College students present	−.624**	(.152)	−.663**	(.148)
SMO presence	.218	(.133)	.270*	(.116)
Number of SMOs present	.039	(.042)	—	
Threat × Weakness Interactions				
Confrontational tactics × Subordinate group presence	.091	(.295)	—	
Radical Goals × Subordinate group presence	.170	(.285)	—	
Protest Size × Subordinate group presence	.107	(.074)	—	
Police Characteristics				
Police force capacity	8.497**	(3.055)	8.224**	(2.874)
Number of prior brutality allegations	.033	(.040)	—	
Constant	−7.332**	(1.023)	−7.506**	(1.006)
−2 log-likelihood	−958.531		−962.168	
McFadden's R^2	.166		.163	
BIC' statistic	−207.937		−260.886	

Note: Standard errors are in parentheses. The number of observations is 1,859 because of missing data. All models were run excluding these cases to increase comparability. Models include all control variables, but results for controls are not reported in the table.

*P < .05   **P < .01 (two-tailed tests)

bivariate correlations between the interaction terms and the main effects are not high enough to be worrisome, we also ran the threat-only model on split samples in models not shown here; one sample included only protests in which subordinate group members were present; the other sample included only protests in which subordinate group members were not present. This produces a simultaneous interaction with all terms in the model and allows us to test for the interaction effects without concerns about multicollinearity produced by the interaction term itself.[24] Comparisons of the results from these models also show no support for importance of the interaction terms.

Finally, the police force variables show mixed results in the models of police presence. In keeping with our prediction regarding the effect of greater police capacity, we find that high police capacity is associated with a greater likelihood of police presence. That is, where increased protest attendance and monitoring by police is concerned, capacity does make a significant difference. In fact, a one standard deviation increase in per capita police expenditures increases the odds of police presence by about 38 percent. However, although Stockdill (1996) suggests that prior brutality should predict later brutality, prior reports of brutality do not affect the likelihood of police presence as shown by the nonsignificant coefficient for prior allegations of brutality.

This examination of the logistic regression coefficients suggests that our hypotheses concerning police presence are fairly well supported. As we expected, the threat model is decisive, although weakness is shown to not play a major role. In keeping with our suspicions about the merit of the weakness approach for explaining police presence, we are also not surprised that the interactive threat and weakness approach offers no real explanatory power. Finally, as we expected, police presence is made more likely as police capacity increases. Our brutality-related prediction focuses largely on police action, not police presence, so those negative findings were expected as well.

Police Action at Protests
In addition to modeling police presence, we also model police action using multinomial logistic

regressions conditioned on police presence. Specifically, we reduce the sample to the set of events at which police were present, and we complete multinomial logistic regressions on the five police responses to protest outlined above (and shown in Figure 1). For each set of independent variables, we ran separate multinomial logistic regressions.... Using those results, and results from a full model that includes all independent and control variables, we trimmed the full model until a final reduced model emerged.[25] In addition to including all control variables, the reduced model includes only theoretically important variables that have significant coefficients.[26] In all, the reduced sample of events with police present and this modeling technique allow us to consider the dynamics of police responses to protest events.[27]

Ultimately, only four theoretically important variables are included in the reduced model: protest size, the use of confrontational tactics, prior major media coverage, and college student presence.[28] None of the other threat and weakness variables, the interaction terms, or the police brutality measures is significant. Thus in terms of the significance of variables, threat and weakness are the only clearly important ones.

However, we are also interested in the magnitude and direction of the coefficients. Thus, Table 2 reports predicted probabilities from our final multinomial logistic regression model. We present the predicted probabilities in lieu of a standard presentation of coefficients for two reasons. First, this presentation allows us to reduce the often cumbersome and confusing results produced by multinomial logistic regressions into fairly straightforward comparisons of probabilities. And it also avoids the lengthy format of the standard presentation.[29]

The base probabilities are the predicted probabilities for each type of police reaction to protest computed with all continuous variables at their means and all dummy variables turned off.[30] Readers can compare the base predicted probabilities with the probabilities produced by changing the value of an independent variable in the model to discern the size and direction of the effect (recalling that all four variables have statistically significant effects). For example, the use of confrontational tactics

Table 2 Predicted Probabilities of Police Strategy Deployment at Protest Events: New York, 1968 to 1973

Protest Characteristic	POLICE STRATEGY/PROBABILITY				
	Do Nothing	Nothing to See Here	Legal Eagle	Dirty Harry	Calling All Cars
Base Probability	14	29	36	1	21
Threat					
Protest size at 10th percentile	11	35	41	a	13
Protest size at 25th percentile	12	33	40	a	15
Protest size at 75th percentile	15	27	33	1	24
Protest size at 90th percentile	17	22	27	1	34
Confrontational tactics	4	21	26	2	49
Weakness					
Front-page news coverage at 10th percentile	18	25	37	a	20
Front-page news coverage at 25th percentile	17	26	37	a	20
Front-page news coverage at 75th percentile	13	31	35	1	21
Front-page news coverage at 90th percentile	9	37	33	1	21
College students present	22	30	37	1	11

Note: Probabilities may not sum to 100 because of rounding error. The base probabilities in Row 1 were calculated with continuous variables set at their means and all dummy variables turned off. The model on which this table is based included the reported independent variables and all control variables. N = 574.
[a] Probability approaches zero.

increases the probability that a Calling All Cars strategy will be used from a base probability of 21 percent to 49 percent. Put differently, only about 1 in 5 protests that did not use confrontational tactics would be met with a Calling All Cars strategy, while almost 1 in 2 protests using confrontational tactics would be met by this police approach.

Where protest size is concerned, the main impact of increased protest size is to decrease the probability that police will employ a Nothing to See Here or a Legal Eagle approach. Consequently, increasing protest size increases the probability that police will either Do Nothing or deploy a strategy that involves force and/or weapons (i.e., Dirty Harry or Calling All Cars). For example, when police respond to small protests (those in the 10th percentile of protest

size), there is a 35-percent chance that they will use a Nothing to See Here strategy, and a 41-percent chance that they will use a Legal Eagle strategy. Together, the odds of one of these approaches being used is an overwhelming 76 percent. As protest size increases to the 90th percentile, these probabilities plummet so that the Nothing to See approach has only a 22-percent probability of use and the Legal Eagle approach has only a 27-percent probability. Meanwhile, increasing protest sizes drive the probability of Calling All Cars from a 13-percent probability for protests in the 10th percentile of protest size to a 34-percent probability for protests in the 90th percentile of protest size.

We speculate that both police inaction and uses of police force become increasingly likely as protest size rises because police may find it difficult to make arrests in large crowds or to interact with large crowds without inciting protesters. That is, police recognize that controlling a large, angry crowd is much more difficult than controlling a small, angry crowd. Because arrests and significant police intervention in protests often incites anger on the part of protesters, police may prefer to avoid making arrests or significantly interacting with the protesters until absolutely necessary. When a protest becomes so out of control that the police feel inaction is no longer possible, it may also be the case that limited action or purely legalistic approaches to protest control are also impossible. Thus, ironically, increasing protest size may encourage police to do nothing up to the point where intervention is so necessary that only serious uses of coercion are seen as possible alternatives.

The use of confrontational tactics increases the probability that police will take some action: The probability of Doing Nothing drops from 14 percent to 4 percent when confrontational tactics are used. In particular, confrontational tactics substantially increase the probabilities of strategies that include force and/or weapons, such as the Calling All Cars and Dirty Harry approaches. Summing the probabilities for using Calling All Cars (49 percent) with the probability for using a Dirty Harry approach (2 percent) indicates that protests that employ confrontational tactics are more likely than not to be met with police violence.

Weakness theorists argue that *more* front-page news coverage increases the likelihood of Doing Nothing, while our hypothesis suggests that *less* front-page news coverage should increase the likelihood of moderate forms of police action. In actuality, neither prediction is supported. A review of the probabilities associated with front-page news coverage reveals that increased coverage decreases the probability of Doing Nothing. However, although statistically significant, the substantive impact of this effect is not very large. Protests that occur in a month after particularly low front-page protest reporting (the 10th percentile) have an 18-percent probability of police Doing Nothing; this probability decreases to only 9 percent for protests that occur in month following high front-page protest

coverage (the 90th percentile). We suspect that this effect is due to public pressure on police to control protest following major protest series. That is, while weakness scholars would expect the public and media to play a watchdog role, the public may be much less tolerant of mass protest than this prediction assumes.

Finally, college student presence reduces the probability of Calling All Cars from a base probability of 21 percent, or roughly 1 in 5 protests, to a 11-percent probability, or about 1 in 10 protests. This result contradicts weakness theorists expectations as college student presence should have indicated weakness-from-within and thus should increase the probability of more severe forms of police action. This result also contradicts our hypothesis suggesting that college student presence should increase the likelihood of limited or legalistic policing. Nonetheless, these results are consistent with the logistic regression results, which indicate that protests including college students are at relatively lower risk for police presence and action than they would be otherwise.

In unreported models we substituted the college student variable for a "youth and students" dummy variable to see whether age or educational status was responsible for the college student effect. The youth and student variable was not significant in the logistic or multinomial logistic regression models, indicating that age was not the explanation for the effect of the college student variable. That is, if other explanations such as the political strength of parents or the unwillingness of police to assault youths were responsible for this student effect, they also should have prompted statistical significance for a "youth and student" dummy variable. As this was not the case, the mechanism should be student specific. Indeed, we argue that this dampening effect is due to the desire of universities to handle student protest internally and without outside police intervention whenever possible.

Across this broad range of multinomial regression results a few central findings are critical. First, the relatively small number of statistically significant variables in the multinomial logistic regression models of police action suggests that while current approaches are able to illuminate factors affecting police presence, these same approaches are less helpful in explaining police action. This finding underscores our central theoretical claim: Researchers must move away from presence/absence formulations of repression and toward more theoretically and methodologically sensitive conceptualizations of police action. Further, we must refine existing theories so that hypotheses can distinguish among the suspected effects of independent variables on different forms of police action.

Second, the differences between the positive multinomial logistic regression results and the positive logistic regression results similarly underscore the importance of modeling police presence and police action separately. We have shown that two different (but perhaps related) processes drive police decisions to attend protests and police decisions regarding the action to take once present at protests. If one process drove both, the results from the logistic and multinomial logistic regressions would have been almost identical. Instead, the results for threat are similar, but other results vary markedly.

Third, of the small number of statistically significant coefficients, threat is again dominant. In fact, both significant threat coefficients are in the expected direction, while both weakness coefficients are in the opposite direction than predicted.

Finally, when the size of probability changes are examined, threat is again the decisive factor. For example, the use of confrontational tactics produced dramatic changes in the predicted probability of deploying a Calling All Cars strategy.

Summary and Conclusions

In a period known in U.S. history for infamous "police riots" and egregious police violence, we found that police usually did not use force to control protests. In fact, police were not reported, on average, to even attend protest events. Despite popular and academic beliefs to the contrary, we have shown that police have varied responses to protest.

Our research took advantage of that variation to theoretically extend, and then test, competing explanations of police repression and protest policing. Although research on repression and protest

policing has greatly advanced our understanding of the factors that affect police action, earlier work was not as sensitive to differences *between* explanatory factors. However, because we simultaneously tested arguments derived from competing theories of repression and protest policing as well as our own original hypotheses, we could empirically compare the explanatory power of the several different research approaches.

In terms of our specific findings, recall our general theoretical expectations: Police presence and actions will be the result of the threat posed by protesting groups, their weakness, or some combination of the two. Our results, in summary, support the importance of threat. Large protests, confrontational protests, and protests that endorsed radical goals were more likely to draw police presence, and event size and the use of confrontational tactics escalated police response once police arrived. The pattern of results suggests that situational threats—like the use of confrontational tactics and protest size—are more important to the police present at the event than other, more diffuse threats, such as advocating radical goals.

Net of threat, other factors also matter: subordinate group presence and SMO presence increase the probability of police presence, while the presence of college students dampens it. Increases in total front-page coverage of protest spurred the police into action instead of providing protective external monitoring. However, these findings are not supportive of the importance of weakness (because they largely run contrary to weakness expectations) or the interaction between threat and weakness.

Overall, our results reveal the importance of theoretical and methodological sensitivity to the types of police action under study. For example, although it is clear from our analyses that the threat approach is the most plausible, it is also clear that threat, like other approaches, does not explain equally well police presence and different types of police action. In fact, our results indicate that complicated relationships exist between the level of repression and various explanatory factors. Research that uses a presence/absence formulation of repression or that makes only a few distinctions among levels of repression misses important nuances in these relationships.

The pattern of results for *police presence* is consistent with broader patterns of social control of dissident groups by Federal authorities during the period of study. For instance, the FBI's COINTELPRO program targeted certain groups with radical goals (e.g., "new left groups") for surveillance and disruption (Marx 1979), but those repressive efforts were not sensitive to the actual level of threat posed by the groups in the community. As Cunningham (forthcoming) shows, for instance, FBI headquarters urged action against local Students for a Democratic Society (SDS) chapters, whether or not they had a sizeable membership or were seen as posing any threat by their local FBI office. In contrast, *police action* at protest events in New York state during the period, reflecting one of the principles of the escalated force doctrine, were influenced toward the increased use of force and/or weapons by the *actual* threats of large events and the use of confrontational tactics by protestors.

Is the pattern of results we have uncovered unique to New York State and the period 1968 to 1973 for which we have evidence? We expect that similar patterns of police presence and action occurred in other U.S. cities during the same period because those cities also likely experienced many public protest events that varied in size and the extent to which protesters used confrontational tactics and, most important, had local police forces operating under the "escalated force" doctrine. And although our concepts and measures of threat (and of weakness) are, to some extent, social constructs that are historically situated (e.g., which goals are radical and which tactics are confrontational), we believe that there was some continuity during the period across communities in what was perceived as threatening by political elites and authorities.

We are not so certain that similar patterns would be found if they were assessed for later periods in cities like San Francisco or Washington, D.C. that eventually adopted a "negotiated management" approach to policing protest events. We expect, for instance, that the importance of confrontational tactics for explaining escalation of force would

be dampened in such instances as police actively sought other solutions (e.g., allowing protesters to disrupt traffic by sitting down in the middle of the street, rather than forcibly removing them or arresting them). On the other hand, the sheer increase in diversity of participants that accompanies large events may affect the likelihood of the use of force and/or weapons regardless of the logic of response on which the police are operating. In any case, we suspect that police response to protest events is not only a function of variation in the nature of the events and the protesters themselves but also of variation in the approaches taken by police. That variation was controlled in this research by our choice of time period. Replication of these analyses for a later period will allow an evaluation of these expectations.

NOTES

This research was supported by grants from the National Science Foundation (SBR-9709337, SBR-9709356, and SES 9874000) and a graduate research fellowship from the National Science Foundation. Funding from the University of Arizona Vice-President for Research Small Grants Program supported data collection. We also thank Doug McAdam and Susan Olzak for their role in collecting the data used for this project; Andrew Martin for supplemental data collection; Ron Breiger, Elisabeth Clemens, Christian Davenport, Clark McPhail, and Calvin Morrill for comments on early drafts; and the *ASR* Editors and anonymous reviewers for their comments.

1. We use "protest policing" and "repression" interchangeably to refer to the social control of public protest by police. Neither use is normatively intended.

2. This is a slight-simplification of McAdam's (1983) work on tactical innovation, which suggests a time delay between the introduction of an innovative confrontational tactic and its subsequent repression. Other work suggests that this finding holds outside of the civil rights movement (Koopmans 1993).

3. Our models use slightly fewer cases because of missing data; N = 1,859 protest events.

4. When researchers have examined repression that occurs outside the confines of particular protest events, such as White's (1999) examination of internment and weapons seizure, other statistical methods have been used.

5. We chose not to use logistic regressions for specific tactical deployments, such as the use of barricades, arrests, and so on, because we believe that such a method inaccurately assumes, by modeling tactical deployments separately, that

the use of barricades is a distinct decision from the use of force. Instead, we argue that the police decide to deploy sets of tactics that in their totality are meant to accomplish the goals that the police have for a specific event. Because multinomial logistic regression allows us to compare these sets of tactics (or, more succinctly, police strategies), we argue this technique better models the actual process of protest policing and police decision-making.

6. Limited action is defined as taking action but not using arrests, force, or any sort of equipment (e.g., barricades) and thus is exemplified by actions such as negotiation with protesters or traffic control.

7. These categories should not be thought of as ordered. For instance, as Barkan's (1984) research shows, legalistic policing is not necessarily less controlling or damaging than violent policing. It would be inaccurate, then, to treat arrests as if they were less repressive than approaches using violence. Thus, we do not use an ordered logit or any other method that might imply some rank-ordering of police approaches along a continuum of repressive action.

8. This strategy is similar to what Klockars (1980) refers to as "Dirty Harry" police behavior, police strategies that prioritize ends over means in controlling crime or disorder. Even though our analysis demonstrates that there are few good predictors of this strategy's use, we employ it in models for two reasons. First, it is a theoretically important category of police action because it most closely captures police lawlessness and police rioting (Stark 1972). Second, including this approach in models allows us to also isolate other categories of action, such as "Calling All Cars," which is the fifth category of police action.

9. These frequencies also imply that if we had relied on police records to generate our data set (as might be suggested by Hug and Wisler 1998; Oliver and Maney 2000; Oliver and Myers 1999), we would have missed the majority of events that took place during this period.

10. We do not distinguish between confrontational and illegal tactics for several reasons. First, the thrust of the threat approach argues that it is not the illegality of confrontational tactics that is threatening but rather their inherent disruptive nature, suggesting that a fair test of the threat approach should consider confrontational tactics generally. Second, recent research has shown that police do not react to many observed instances of lawbreaking: Waddington (1994) suggests that police radically underenforce the law at protest events. This is consistent with a substantial amount of prior policing research demonstrating that police do not react to all instances of lawbreaking (Black and Reiss 1970; Bittner 1967a; Lundman 1974; Peterson 1971; Wilson 1968). Instead, enforcement often relates to other goals or concerns of the officer (Bittner 1967a, 1967b; Pastor 1978; Wilson 1968).

11. Calls for service are calls requesting a police response, like contemporary 911 calls. If police had initially decided not to attend a protest (or did not know that a protest was going to occur), the police may ultimately attend if a call for service is received.

12. To test for sensitivities to different specifications of radical goals, we tested two alternatives: a narrow specification, in which only revolutionary goals such as pro-Communist claims were considered, and a broad specification, in which a wide array of leftist claims were considered. Results for the broad specification were similar to the specification reported in the main text. Results for the narrow specification were not significant, but only a very small number of protests had revolutionary goals.

13. Protesters can articulate more than one goal. For this analysis, any event that articulated at least one radical goal was coded 1, even if a nonradical goal was also articulated.

14. We argue that more targets and goals indicate relatively more calls for change, and thus present a relatively greater threat to the status quo. However, it is also possible that intense focus on a single goal or tactic may be more threatening to political elites. Fortunately, our data can adjudicate between these competing interpretations because this alternative specification would predict a significant negative effect for the number of protest goals and/or targets such that fewer goals and/or targets would increase the likelihood of police presence and action. In the end, our analyses find that a third alternative is more empirically supportable: Neither the number of targets nor the number of goals significantly affects police presence or action, such that neither construction of threat is empirically supported.

15. We also tested two alternative specifications of subordinate group presence: A specification requiring that *only* subordinate group protesters protested, and a specification that focused exclusively on the presence of racial and/or ethnic minorities. Both alternatives were either not significant or behaved similarly to the reported specification of subordinate group presence.

16. Protests in which minorities are present could be more likely to be policed heavily, not because of the identity of the actors but because of the confrontational character of the protest. If this alternative hypothesis were supported, we would expect a nonsignificant coefficient for subordinate group presence and a significant coefficient for confrontational tactics.

17. To determine whether completeness of reporting might have affected our results for these variables, we control for article length in all models.

18. Future research should consider whether the presence of specific SMOs affects policing.

19. We also tested an alternative specification of police capacity: logged dollars spent per year in the county in which the protest occurred. This specification performs similarly to the per capita measure of spending, indicating the robust nature of our results. A per capita measure of police manpower was available for all counties only for 1967. Because we could not capture changes over time, we believe that our time-varying measure of police capacity is the superior indicator.

20. Because we rely on press reports of brutality, an alternative hypothesis is also possible; Police may be *less* likely to engage in brutal actions in the wake of recent publicized accusations of brutality because of public relations concerns. If so, the coefficient for brutality allegations should be negative and significant.

21. We do not present these "single-approach" models in the main text or engage in other analyses because we are interested in the *comparative* merit of different theoretical approaches. Indeed, one of our principle contributions is to move beyond more traditional single-approach tests and toward a more synthetic and comparative analysis.

22. Factor changes are computed using the formula $e^{\beta x \times \Delta x}$ (in this case it equals $e^{1.964 \times 1}$, or 7.13). Interested readers should see Long (1997) for related formulas.

23. This second interpretation is less likely, though, because of the findings related to youth and student presence reported in the discussion below of police action models.

24. These models are available from the first author on request.

25. We report on a reduced model for a number of reasons. First, and perhaps most important, we present the multinomial results in the form of predicted probabilities. Debate exists over the production of such predicted probabilities using models that include nonsignificant variables because all variables in a model (both significant and nonsignificant) could be included in the production of probabilities derived from that model. One way to avoid this difficulty is to produce a reduced model that excludes nonsignificant coefficients, and that is the approach we adopt here. Parsimony

suggests that we should prefer the least complicated model available (and the predicted probabilities it produces). Because model fit scores suggest that the reduced model is a statistically adequate replacement for the much more complicated full model, we report on the reduced model here. Finally, although Table 1 reports both the full and reduced logistic regression models, the lengthy nature of multinomial results precludes a similarly detailed presentation of the full multinomial model here.

26. Because multinomial logistic regressions produce one coefficient for each independent variable per category of the dependent variable (save the omitted, or "base," category), to determine significance we require that the variable affect the overall fit of the model at the $p < .05$ level, using a log-likelihood difference comparison. This procedure allows us to test whether all coefficients related to a single independent variable can be constrained to zero without affecting the model fit, which is a stronger test than simply asking whether any one of the four coefficients per independent variable is significant. Interested readers can consult Long (1997) and Long and Freese (2001).

27. Multinomial logistic regression assumes the "independence of irrelevant alternatives." Statistically, a Hausman test assesses the validity of this assumption. The Hausman scores for our models approach 0 and have associated probabilities that approach 1, indicating that the assumption is met by our model.

28. Although no measure of police capacity warranted inclusion in the final reduced model, the police capacity measure that employed logged dollars spent on law enforcement approached significance, indicating that large police capacity might reduce the likelihood of using a Dirty Harry approach.

29. A printout of full and reduced models is available on request from the first author.

30. We used Long and Freese's (2001) SPost Suite to produce these predicted probabilities.

31.

Coalitions and Political Context: U.S. Movements Against Wars in Iraq

DAVID S. MEYER AND CATHERINE CORRIGALL-BROWN

The months leading up to the recent war in Iraq were marked by unprecedented global protest against the planned attack. On coordinated dates in the middle of each month, from December 2002 to March 2003, millions of people around the world demonstrated, marched, and rallied. The numbers attending each event increased with the perceived imminence of war, as did the volatility of the crowds, which were largest in countries whose governments supported the war. In the United States demonstrators assembled in large cities on the same dates, with more than 500,000 protesters reported in New York City on February 15. Such coordinated and sustained opposition to a war that had not yet started is a new development in protest politics. But how did activists in such disparate settings manage to stage such dramatic opposition?

The mobilization of large-scale protest requires coordination among new and existing organizations, frequently through the development of social movement coalitions, a topic ripe for both empirical research and theory. Here, we recount the story of one demonstration to raise the broader issues of coalitions in social movements. We then consider existing theory on coalitions in social movements, using examples from the recent antiwar movement to illustrate our concerns. We examine the Win Without War coalition, which reflects the diversity of concerns commonly represented in such coalitions. Analyzing statements on participating groups' websites, we assess the importance of antiwar politics in each group's actual priorities. After

the war started, many groups that had joined in the effort to prevent it gradually shifted from active antiwar efforts to focus on their prior commitments, even without formally leaving the antiwar coalition. There are costs and benefits for individual groups associated with joining a coalition and, as the political context changes, so too do the priorities of the individual groups. We conclude by considering the implications of a coalitional approach to social movements, and call for more research on related issues.

One March Against the War

On Saturday, March 15, an estimated 100,000 to 250,000 people[1] stretching more than 30 blocks marched from Times Square to Waverly Place in lower Manhattan, to protest the newly commenced invasion of Iraq (Eaton 2003). This demonstration provides a springboard to discuss fundamental issues in social movement politics. First, protesters represented a range of political perspectives, including radical pacifists, foreign policy isolationists, and internationalists, all having found cause to oppose the Bush administration. They also represented a range of occupations, including students, clergy, well-known actors and enter-tainers, and elected officials. Although the march was overwhelmingly nonviolent, a small group broke off to attempt more aggressive actions on side streets, skirmishing with police and generating nearly fifty arrests.

Second, the demonstration was one of many around the United States, including Washington, DC, Salt Lake City, Chicago, Los Angeles, and San Francisco. The antiwar movement's extensive mobilization, comprising millions in the full range of movement activities well before the war started, and continuing, albeit in different forms and at lower levels, throughout the war and occupation,

Meyer, David S. and Catherine Corrigall-Brown. 2005. "Coalitions and Political Context: U.S. Movements Against wars in Iraq." *Mobilization* 10: 327–344. Reprinted by permission.

raises important questions about the relationship of social movements to political circumstances.

Third, this antiwar movement was not limited to the United States. That same Saturday, demonstrators assembled around the world, with volatile, angry, and disruptive rallies in Arab and Muslim countries, including Indonesia, Yemen, Egypt, Jordan, Bahrain, Lebanon, and the Palestinian territories, and no less large and disruptive rallies across Europe. And the March demonstrations were smaller than those a month earlier, in which millions of people marched around the world, with the largest turnouts in countries whose governments supported the war, more than one million protesters were reported at each of the February 15th demonstrations in Barcelona, Rome, London, and Madrid. Even as the politics of protest varied across contexts, the impending war provided a common focal point for diverse concerns. Although activist efforts to coordinate events transnationally are not new (e.g., Carter 1992; DeBennedetti 1980; Solo 1988; Wittner 1998), their degree of success was.[2] Focusing on why, how, and under what circumstances activists chose to cooperate highlights key issues at the heart of understanding contemporary social movements.

Here, we use the antiwar movement in the United States to examine the nature of social movement coalitions, outlining countervailing pressures on social movement groups to cooperate and to compete. We will argue that the nature of movement coalitions can be best understood by focusing on the external circumstances under which coalitions develop, and suggest that we can discern a pattern of coalition development and decline by looking at the political opportunities surrounding social movements. Taken together, we have a window into the coalition politics that characterize contemporary social movements in liberal polities, and an opportunity to examine cooperation and conflict over issues, goals, and tactics.

Social Movements, Organizations, and Coalitions

Social movements are sustained interactions between challengers and authorities on matters of policy and/or culture, including a range of activity inside and outside mainstream political institutions (following Tarrow 1998; Tilly 1978). At least in liberal polities, social movements are coalition affairs, featuring sometimes loosely negotiated alliances among groups and individuals with different agendas. Indeed, contemporary social movements are often comprised of multiple formal coalitions, competing for predominance and adherents while cooperating—to some extent—on matters of policy. Although it is a grammatical convenience to speak about THE peace movement, THE antiglobalization movement, or THE environ-mental movement, such labels distort the reality of social movements, reifying boundaries and movements that are actually much sloppier affairs. This antiwar mobilization included groups ranging from the Christian pacifists to the International Socialist Organization, both of which offer far broader—and substantially different—agendas for reform than just stopping this war. Marchers at the peace demonstrations after the war began knew that they agreed with those next to them on one key issue. Social movements are always about more than their explicitly articulated claims, and many activists surely agreed on much else (della Porta and Rucht 1995; Meyer and Whittier 1994), but the full range of concerns is much broader, diverse, and contested than what can be gleaned from any one manifestation of activism.

Social movements are comprised of organized groups and individuals cooperating, to some degree, on a set of common issues. Although the research mobilization tradition (e.g. McCarthy and Zald 1977) put social movement organizations at the center of analysis, relatively little work that explicitly considered the dynamics of social movement coalitions followed (but see Gerhards and Rucht 1992; McCammon 2001; McCammon and Campbell 2002; Zald and McCarthy 1987; Staggenborg 1986; Rochon and Meyer 1997; Van Dyke 2003). The growth of a political process approach (Tilly 1978; McAdam 1982; Tarrow 1998; Meyer 2004) generally turned attention toward events (Olzak 1989; Earl et al. 2004), rather than the organizations, activists, and processes that create them.

The "polity model" (Gamson 1990; Tilly 1978) located challengers outside a monolithic state, and thereby obscured important elements of social movements. Early articulations emphasized single challengers as opposed to a range of actors engaged in mounting challenges. Some qualifications of the model are in order. First, in contemporary liberal polities the sharp demarcation between conventional politics and movement politics is hard to find. Elected officials protest, sometimes even engaging in civil disobedience, and activists who protest also vote, lobby, and participate in party politics. As such, movement coalitions straddle the boundaries between institutional and extra-institutional politics (Stearns and Almeida 2004). Second, movements are not unitary actors, but are comprised of groups with a range of interests and concerns. Although Gamson (1990) recognized that allies could improve a single challenger's prospect for success, he focused on individual challenging organizations.

Recognition of the breadth of movement activism and concerns emphasizes the dynamic nature of social change efforts and social protest movements. Activists draw both grievances and resources from more mainstream sources. Further, they use extra-institutional or non-conventional protest as a lever to enhance the political efficacy of allies working within institutions, closer to the formal policymaking process. As they build inroads into political institutions, they alter the grievances, resources, and opportunities available to dissidents, including themselves. Because the different groups enter activism with distinct priorities and longer term goals, a movement's interaction with mainstream politics affects the strength of coordination among its participating organizations. The attractions of protest or mainstream politics vary for each group, as will their commitment to the strongest movement of the moment.

In this regard, it is important to point out that the extent of cooperation within a coalition will vary from coalition to coalition, and among cooperating groups within a coalition. Even when organized groups or their leaders agree on the general direction that policy should move, they may choose not to work together on affecting political mobilization or influence. The extent of cooperation varies over two dimensions, in degree and over time

(Tarrow 2004). In terms of the degree of cooperation, at a base level, groups can endorse the efforts and claims of other groups, but the extent of attention or resources they offer those groups varies tremendously. Joining a coalition may entail no more than agreeing to lend a group's name to a manifesto or website, with no substantial commitment of resources, and input on goals or strategies limited by the threat to withdraw the name. On the other hand, groups can coordinate strategy, formally negotiate a division of labor, and share resources, including staff time. The second dimension of cooperation is temporal; groups can maintain a formal affiliation only for the support of a discrete event or for a coordinated campaign that lasts over a period of years and transcends several political issues. In such cases, the coalition often becomes a distinct organization in its own right, with independent staff, membership, and fundraising.

Because social movements are about more than their expressly articulated aims, each expression of political demands is partial. Activists and organizations generally offer broad analyses of social ills, only a small portion of which can be expressed on a placard or banner, or articulated in a demonstration. A given mobilization can offer the chance to make claims only on the most urgent or promising set of issues. Articulating a fully developed long term agenda runs the risk of alienating potential supporters and invigorating political opposition (Meyer and Staggenborg 1996). On the other hand, articulating an ill-defined set of claims runs the risk of being easily co-opted and demobilized by political authorities. Activists thus face the challenge of developing demands that are clear enough to be significant, and narrow enough to avoid alienating supporters and mobilizing the opposition.

In making decisions about alliances and issues, a social movement organization operates in the service of at least three distinct, but interrelated goals: (1) to pressure government to affect the policy changes it wants; (2) to educate the public and persuade people of the urgency of the problems it addresses and the wisdom of its position; and (3) to sustain a flow of resources that allows it to maintain its existence and efforts (Zald and McCarthy 1987; Wilson 1995). What is useful for achieving one objective is not always helpful in working toward another. As example, the literature on lobbying (e.g. Berry 1999; Schlozman and Tierney 1986) suggests that moderation, credibility, and restraint are keys to influence on Capitol Hill. At the same time, those very qualities are anathema to maintaining a high public profile, and thus publicizing ideas, and may make sustaining a flow of resources for a citizen group more difficult. In contrast, a politics of polemic, characterized by dramatic action, may be very useful in maintaining a public profile, but the action may supersede the analysis (say, for example, a dramatic civil disobedience action, like those staged by Operation Rescue). While satisfying supporters, it may reach few others and can even mobilize the opposition (Meyer and Staggenborg 1996). In the case of groups with foreign policy concerns, transnational connections and alliances, which can heighten the visibility, volatility, and scope of a social movement, might also raise suspicion among policy-makers.[3] Organizations then must balance a profile that contains some mix of these three functions, mindful of maintaining a balance that works for them. We need to see every choice of issue, tactic, and alliance as something that offers advantages and risks along these three dimensions.

For any organization, the initial choice to join a coalition like the one against the war in Iraq immediately necessitates other choices: first, what, if any, alternative policies to offer; second, what means to use in making claims; third, who, if anyone, to work with in making these claims; and fourth, how much effort to direct to the coalition's collective process. For heuristic purposes, *we can think about the process of recruiting social movement organizations to a coalition as being analogous to the process by which individuals are recruited to social movement organizations.* In both of these situations, the choice to participate, carries with it potential costs and benefits, partly dependent upon the nature and extent of participation. On the one hand, cooperation among groups increases the visibility of the movement, increasing its chances at political efficacy. Additionally, because organizations have distinct audiences, a broad coalition affords the prospect of mobilizing a wider range of people, tactics, and entry into a greater number of institutional niches.

Organizations can specialize in terms of issues or tactics, enhancing not only the profile of the movement as a whole, but also its volatility and flexibility (Staggenborg 1986). Tactical diversity and multiple constituencies are assets for a movement in many ways. Radical action can enhance the visibility and credibility of moderates, although it can also discredit them (Haines 1988). Multiple organizations allow a movement to escalate (McAdam 1982) in the face of potential setbacks faced by any single organization.

At the same time, coalition participation carries risks. By cooperating with groups that may appeal to the same finders or member, an organization may obscure its own identity in service of a larger movement, diminishing its visibility in mass media (Rohlinger 2002) or its capacity to recruit members or raise funds. As with individuals, organizations cultivate distinct organizational identities that define them to both members and the outside world (Clemens 1993). Such identities encourage certain alliances, while forestalling others. Alliances can compromise identities, and can visibly associate organizations with unreliable or tainted allies. In addition, social ties and networks, significant factors in the participation of individuals in social movements, are also important predictors of cooperation among groups. In this way, a group will be more likely to cooperate with others with whom they have worked in the past or with whom they share common members (Van Dyke 2003). Each decision then is not independent, but rather is nested in a history of past decisions and existing relationships.

Choices are more obvious for some organizations than others, depending upon the issue. The decision to oppose the war through non-violent action, including civil disobedience, was simple for, say, the War Resister's League (WRL), a small pacifist group nearly 100 years old, whose identity is defined by precisely such actions, and whose relatively small organizational presence is supported by loyal donors committed to the absolute nature of the WRL agenda. In contrast, the decision to participate is more difficult for organizations like the National Association for the Advancement of Colored People (NAACP) or the National Organization for Women

(NOW), as they maintain a profile and base of support largely on other political issues. Undertaking a strict antiwar stance, engaging in particularly contentious tactics, or affiliating with marginal groups entails risks. At once, it threatens access to a set of political insiders, potentially directs attention away from other issues the group sees as critical, and may alienate supporters, members, and allies. In addition to making a statement on issues of vital concern, participation against the war can afford such organizations the opportunity to mobilize, raise the organizational profile and visibility of the group, and perhaps direct more attention to other issues of their concern. That a large portion of the leadership or membership may see the antiwar position as appropriate only sets the stage for a decision, it does not define it.

Coalitions are both a distinct set of organizational forms (Clemens 1993), as well as a structuring mechanism coordinating dissent and protest (McAdam, Tarrow, and Tilly 2001; Tarrow 2004). A coalition includes a range of groups, bringing with them different constituencies, analyses, tactical capabilities, and resources and cooperating on some piece of a political agenda (Rochon and Meyer 1997). The template flyer at any large demonstration in the United States today is comprised of a laundry list of organizations (cf., Gerhards and Rucht 1995). While there are costs and benefits for individual organizations when joining a coalition, for the prospects of advancing a political position, coalition politics are beneficial. Increased visibility aids in the pedagogic goals of movements; they give potential members a place to join in and provide additional access points to government. As a movement grows in power, more groups find incentives to join in, to use the large light of a successful mobilization to bring attention to themselves and their causes. This is what we saw in the extraordinary February 15th and March 15th marches around the world, and in the virtual (internet) march on Washington which, organizers claimed, mobilized more than 2 million people.

More generally, the coalition is a generic form that can include a broad variety of negotiated arrangements of two or more organizations coordinating goals, demands, strategies of influence, and events. Given the organizational imperatives sketched above, negotiating cooperation on any of these matters involves understandable difficulties and requires significant efforts, generally greatest for more extensive coordination. As a result, it is worthwhile to track periods of greater and lesser cooperation among groups and the context in which they take place.

The literature on coalitions effectively lays out the dilemmas inherent in coalition participation, identifying potential conflicts over resources (Zald and Ash 1966; Zald and McCarthy 1987; Wilson 1996; Staggenborg 1986), frames and values (Benford 1993; della Porta and Rucht 1995; Gerhards and Rucht 1995), and the coordination of organizational and political goals with actions (Staggenborg 1986; Hathaway and Meyer 1997). We can understand why, in general, organizations would choose to cooperate, and how they might negotiate workable relationships. At the same time, there is relatively little work that explicitly considers the elements of the political environment that encourage or discourage cooperation among groups, and the dynamic nature of relationships among participating groups.

External circumstances alter the costs and benefits of cooperation, to say nothing of the perceived urgency for collective action (Meyer 2004). Recently, a few scholars have directed attention to the contextual factors that affect the calculus of cooperation. McCammon and Campbell (2002), in an historical study of the suffrage movement, examine alliances between suffragettes and the Women's Christian Temperance Union. They find that alliances are most likely to form in response to political threats, including mobilization and organization of the opposition (in this case, brewers' associations) and the prospects of legislative defeats. Similarly, in a longitudinal study of student activism across a wide range of American campuses, Van Dyke (2003) finds that both proximate (campus-based) and national threats spurred cooperation among a broad range of student activist groups.

This makes sense to us. We contend that coalition dynamics roughly approximate similar decisions that individuals make about participating in a social movement. Building on this insight, we can offer a theory of cooperation among social movement groups that follows the logic of social movement cycles (Tarrow 1989; Meyer and Imig 1993). Groups join coalition efforts when they see their efforts on a particular set of issues and efforts as urgent and potentially efficacious. Like individuals, most groups represent a range of political concerns, and external conditions play a substantial role in organizing their relative priorities. Following McCammon and Campbell (2002) and Van Dyke (2003), threats, defined as unwanted policy initiatives, are likely to spur cooperation. During favorable political circumstances, groups are likely to have less interest in cooperating with others. In other words, threats lead the urgency of cooperation to outweigh the inherent risks. When external circumstances change, altering either the perceived urgency or efficacy of mobilization, organizations return to their core concerns and activities. Importantly, groups generally don't need to exit coalitions in order to refocus their own priorities and activities. Paper coalitions may continue, but the commitment to coordinated collective action dissipates, as does the extent of actual cooperation. We develop these ideas in an analysis of a recent social movement coalition.

Gulf Wars and Peace Movement Coalitions

Two wars against Iraq prosecuted by international coalitions led by the United States and Presidents named George Bush provide an interesting comparison for analyzing the importance of political context in coalition formation. The political contexts surrounding these wars differ significantly on a number of dimensions, including: the justification for war, the action demanded for the "offending" party; the level of international support; and the extent and importance of Congressional debate. By examining these contextual differences, it is possible to begin to explain the differing levels of movement coalition formation against each of these wars.

In the first Gulf War, the United States' call for action followed Iraq's 1990 invasion of Kuwait by about a week. President George Bush demanded that Iraq leave Kuwait, pro-claiming that the occupation would not stand, and announcing that the United States would apply force to achieve its will. He cultivated very broad international support, engaging thirty-six countries in his war coalition, including major allied powers, all supported by a UN resolution. The coalition received endorsements and financial support from Arab countries and other Gulf states, which supported the removal of the Iraqi military from Kuwait. In addition, Kuwait, Saudi Arabia, and other Gulf states donated $36 billion to the campaign. In this political context, committed peace activists had a difficult time engaging a broader public or winning institutional allies. The movement's potential for growth was circumscribed by the extent of international support, and the apparent viability of an institutionally oriented strategy. Indeed, national attention was riveted to a Congressional debate on authorizing the war, which ultimately ended on January 13, days before the war started.[4] Although Congress ultimately authorized the war, this outcome was by no means certain with several notable congressional "hawks" and former military leaders opposing the action. Nevertheless, when the bombing commenced on January 17, this movement essentially disappeared (Swank 1997; Bibliography of Protests 1991).

The second Gulf War provides a dramatic contrast. In this case, the American justification for war was not precipitated by a discrete provocative action, but was instead based on President George W. Bush's evaluation of the Iraqi regime and its president, Saddam Hussein, in the context of generalized concerns about nuclear proliferation, global terrorism, and international weapons-control regimes. Framed as a component of the war on terrorism, Bush criticized Iraq's expulsion of UN inspectors looking for weapons of mass destruction years earlier, and called for regime change. Considerably less successful, perhaps less concerned, with building international support than his father, the administration began a military buildup in the fall of 2002 with the support of 30 countries. Although the number of participating nations was close to that in the coalition organized by the first President Bush, support was in fact, substantially thinner. First, there were many notable absences on the list of coalition members. No Arab states endorsed the military action, not even traditional US allies in the region such as Egypt and Saudi Arabia. In addition, major NATO alliance members, such as Canada, Belgium, Norway, France, and Germany, vigorously opposed the war. Second, the commitments of some nations appeared coerced. The only African countries that endorsed the military action, for example, were Ethiopia and Eritrea, both seeking U.S. backing in a boundary dispute between their countries. The only Latin American countries represented were El Salvador, Nicaragua, and Columbia, all hosting US-funded wars on drugs in their territories. Finally, the second Gulf War was not supported by the UN. Vigorous international criticism led the U.S. to avoid a final vote in the UN even as it, paradoxically, justified the invasion as an effort to enforce international law and United Nations' resolutions.

Americans concerned with the wisdom of war on Iraq had little reason to invest in an institutional strategy for influence. Both Houses of Congress, controlled by the Republican party and on the eve of an election, voted to authorize the President to use force with over-whelming majorities on October 11, 2002, fully five months before the bombing would start.[5] Some opponents of war actually argued that authorizing force would give the President more negotiating leverage and, consequently, reduce the likelihood of war. President Bush was clear at this point that he would not be going back to either the United Nations or Congress, leaving opponents of the war with only movement strategies for influence.

In this context millions of people mobilized against the second Gulf War globally. In the United States, at least six broad coalitions emerged to coordinate antiwar efforts, described in table 1. Membership in these coalitions required vastly different levels of commitment and cooperation. Further, overlapping memberships, the recognition of individual as well as organizational memberships, and the quickly emergent independent organizational identity of some of these coalitions, make it very hard to sort out which group was doing what with whom. What was clear, however, was extensive antiwar organization and mobilization.

We will examine the Win Without War coalition, formed in response to the threat of war, as an example of these coordinated efforts, and as a

means to consider coalitional dynamics. We chose this coalition for illustrative purposes because, as the smallest of the coalitions opposing the war with only organizations as members, it was empirically manageable, yet politically diverse. Long time activists, including representatives from both well-established peace and justice groups, like Women's Action for New Directions, the American Friends Service Committee, and Peace Action, and newer groups concerned with social justice and globalization, met in Washington, DC on October 25, 2002, two weeks after the congressional vote, to devise strategy for the growing anti-war movement. They were critical of the politics of International ANSWER, which was reluctant to criticize Saddam Hussein or discuss human rights, and committed to develop a broader political profile for the antiwar movement. At that time, they sponsored the formation of two broad-based coalitions. One, United for Peace and Justice, would be oriented toward grassroots politics, including large demonstrations and nonviolent action; the other, Win Without War, would be a more formal association of well-established mainstream organizations with the capacity to make decisions more quickly and forge alliances that reached deeper into mainstream institutional politics (Cortright 2004). The double coalition strategy was controversial among the activists, who saw divisions in their efforts, but it reprised the strategy of the antinuclear weapons movement in the 1957 and 1958, which created one coalition for direct action (Committee for Non-Violent Action) and another for mainstream politics and public education (Committee for a Sane Nuclear Policy, or SANE).[6] Both coalitions quickly took on their own organizational identities and commitments (Wittner 1997).

Based on the articulated concerns of each Win Without War group, we assess their efforts on the war after the peak of mobilization had passed. Table 2 lists the groups involved in the Win Without War coalition and their main areas of focus, as judged by their mission statements. It is worth underscoring the variety of reasons activists expressed for opposing this war and that many organizations belonged to more than one coalition.

Win Without War is a coalition of 41 diverse groups opposed to the war in Iraq. Like the other

Table 1 American Anti-Iraq War Coalitions

Coalition	No. of Members	Campaigns	Mission Statement
United for Peace and Justice	Over 650	Iraq Global Justice Nuclear Disarmament	United for Peace is a coalition of more than 650 local and national groups throughout the United States who have joined together to oppose our government's policy of permanent warfare and empire-building.
International ANSWER (Act Now to Stop War and End Racism)	Approx. 150	"Bring the Troops Home Now" (Vote No War) Stop FBI's targeting of Antiwar movement	Founded in the days after September 11, 2001, ANSWER seeks immediate action against the Bush administration's rush to war and the racist attacks against the Arab and Muslim communities in the US.
AWARE (Antiwar, Anti-Racism Effort)	Unlisted	Mutual Aid Pact (to assist people who are persecuted in the "war on terror") Peace-discuss (program to disseminate information about the war)	AWARE is an alliance of groups and individuals working to oppose war and present alternatives. Our common concerns include military build-up, the threat of global de-stabilization, and the reduction of civil liberties. We come together to coordinate our efforts, share resources and ideas, and make large-scale actions possible as we work toward peace and justice.
Not In Our Name	Approx. 100	The War on the World's Detentions, Deportations, Roundups of Immigrants, and Police State Restrictions	The Not In Our Name Project is a national network of individuals and organizations committed to standing with the people of the world. "We believe that as people living in the United States it is our responsibility to resist the injustices done by our government, in our names." Our mission is to build, strengthen and expand resistance to stop the U.S. government's entire course of war and repression being waged in the name of "fighting terrorism."
National Youth and Student Peace Coalition	15 national student and youth organizations	Opposing the War for Economic reasons, environmental reasons, safety reasons, and to protect freedom in the US.	The National Youth and Student Peace Coalition was formed in response to the events of September 11, 2001, and has worked to build strategic, long-term student and youth opposition to war, both abroad with bombs and bullets, and at home with racism, cuts to education, and freedom-limiting "anti-terrorism" policies.

Table 2 Win Without War Coalition Groups

Group Name	Group Type
Council for a Livable World	AW
Fourth Freedom Forum	AW
Peace Action	AW
Veterans for Common Sense	AW
Veterans for Peace	AW
Artists United to Win Without War	AW
Musicians United to Win Without War	AW
Physicians for Social Responsibility	AW/Soc.Just.
True Majority	AW/Intl. Pol.
Greenpeace	Env.
Sierra Club	Env.
American-Arab Anti-Discrimination Committee	Id. Grps.
Feminist Majority	Id. Grps.
NAACP	Id. Grps.
National Gay and Lesbian Task Force	Id. Grps.
National Organization for Women	Id. Grps.
Rainbow/Push Coalition	Id. Grps.
Soulforce	Id. Grps.
Women's Action for New Directions	Id. Grps.
Campaign for UN Reform	Intl. Pol.
Education for Peace in Iraq Center	Intl. Pol.
Global Exchange	Intl. Pol.
Oxfam America	Intl. Pol.
Conference of Major Superiors of Men	Rel.
Leadership Conference of Women Religious	Rel.
National Council of Churches	Rel.
NETWORK—A National Catholic Social Justice Lobby	Rel.

Table 2 (*Continued*)

Group Name	Group Type
Shalom Center	Rel.
Soioumers	Rel.
The Tikkun Community	Rel.
Unitarian Universalist Association of Congregations	Rel.
United Church of Christ	Rel.
United Methodist Church General Board of Church and Society	Rel.
Pax Christi USA	Rel./AW
American Friends Service Committee	Soc. Just./AW
Business Leaders for Sensible Priorities	Soc. Just.
Families USA	Soc. Just.
MoveOn	Soc. Just.
Us Foundation	Soc. Just.
USAction	Soc. Just.
Working Assets	Soc. Just.

Group Types: Id. Grps. = Based on Sexual Orientation, Ethnicity, or Gender indentity; Env. = Environmental Groups; Rel. = Religious Groups; Intl. Pol. = International Policy; AW = Antiwar, Soc. Just = Social Justice
Source: http://www.winwithoutwarus.org/html/coalition. html. Information on the current objective of the coalition groups found on their websites (accessed through the winwithoutwar homepage). Information retrieved December 2003.

coalitions mentioned above, it engaged in a range of activities, including sponsoring demonstrations and issuing statements. The composition of this coalition indicates the breadth of the antiwar movement. Based on the *Encyclopedia of Associations* and organizational web sites, we coded the participant groups by primary purpose (table 3). Groups whose primary identities are directed to issues of war and peace comprised slightly more than a quarter of the coalition, and Win Without War contained many groups whose identities were derived primarily

Table 3 Win Without War Coalition Groups by Type

Group Type	N
Antiwar (AW)	11
Environmental (Env.)	2
Identity Groups (Id. Grps.)	8
International Policy (Intl. Pol.)	5
Religion (Rel.)	11
Social Justice (Soc. Just.)	8
Total	41*

* There were 41 groups in the coalition. 4 groups were coded as two types.
Source: http://www.winwithoutwarus.org/html/coalition.html. Information on the current objective of the coalition groups found on their websites (accessed through the winwithoutwar homepage). Information accessed December 2003.

from other constituencies or causes. The nature of this coalition supports the claims by della Porta and Rucht (1995) and Meyer and Whittier (1994) about families or communities of movements who share concerns not always expressed by the movement of the moment, and move from issue to issue depending upon political circumstances.

We know this new movement included people who had been out protesting in the streets before, including activists against corporate globalization, but this mobilization was much broader. Therefore, we need to understand how the people who had been constantly trying to mobilize opposition against some element of the Bush presidency were able, uncharacteristically, to reach and activate a much broader public. In order to understand this newfound success we must examine how the political context of the first and second Gulf Wars differed with one context providing more fertile soil for mobilization and coalition formation.

First, it is important to note that President George W. Bush offered dramatic moves on several policy fronts, and the explicit articulation of a preemption doctrine represented a new and controversial posture for American foreign policy. Essentially, President Bush (2002) announced that

the United States would wage aggressive wars against countries that might one day represent a threat to American interests, even if they did not do so at the moment. As a result of this sharp doctrinal shift, movement activists found support from dissident experts in the United States, including the editorial pages of most major American newspapers, with the usually liberal *Washington Post* being a notable exception (Getlin 2003). Indeed, the extreme skepticism from national security experts, including both out-of-power experts, and academic analysts, was striking. In September of 2002, for example, journalist Nicholas Lemann (2002) published a provocative piece in *The New Yorker* focusing on opposition to the war on Iraq among "realist" experts supported both the invasion of Afghanistan and the larger war on terror; they viewed the then-planned Iraq episode as a diversion from more important military action against terrorism.[7]

Prominent and visible expert opposition allowed activists to claim credibly that the Bush administration's conduct of policy was both a departure from previous policies and a threat to global peace. Activists took cues about enhanced political opportunities for mobilization, cues that suggested the time was ripe for dissent as well as what issues were available for challenge (Tarrow 1996). At the same time, social movement activism encouraged political leaders, including elected officials to stake out stronger positions against the war. Former Vermont Governor Howard Dean, seeking the Democratic nomination for the presidency in 2004, took a strong antiwar stance and immediately gained political attention from the op-ed pages and financial support from opponents of the war. The strong position brought him credibility among activists and served as a basis for fundraising and differentiating himself from other hopefuls. There is thus a synergistic dynamic in which institutional and extrainstitutional actors can encourage each other in a political spiral of escalation.

Peace activists exploited these opportunities, as organizers saw the war as a powerful issue around which to demonstrate Americans' concerns with democracy, the quality of public life, and political participation. Opposing the war was both intrinsically important, but also an issue that might have provided a leading edge for broader mobilization.

The key to the successful mobilization of this peace movement, and indeed, any movement, is in unifying and mobilizing groups that had previously embraced a wide range of issues, around a clear single demand, in this case: "Don't go to war now." This network of local and national groups, many affiliated with other social institutions such as churches, schools, or other national organizations, was itself a legacy of previous movement mobilizations. President Bush also allowed activists to make connections by pursuing a broad agenda of his own. When the target of opportunity is the President, as in this situation, the enemy of my enemy is my friend. Thus, opponents of conservative activist Miguel Estrada's appointment to a federal appellate court, supporters of stricter standards for car manufacturer's fleet mileage, opponents of cuts in the tax on stock dividends, all found something in common with antiwar activists.

In summary, a few important factors made these broad coalitions possible. First, President Bush offered bold policy initiatives on several fronts simultaneously, and began his administration with tenuous legitimacy and little in the public reservoir of trust. Additionally, the President seemed to lack the political skills of his immediate predecessor, or of his father, who negotiated a very broad international coalition to support of the first Persian Gulf War. The younger Bush provoked opposition from many governments, as well as citizens, of Western Europe. Second, movement organizations had been organizing on a variety of issues on the liberal left end of the political spectrum over the past decade, and these organizations have provided a foundation for antiwar activism. This includes groups like Moveon.org, formed to oppose the impeachment of President Clinton, and the range of anticorporate globalization groups that had challenged Clinton's trade policies. Third, improved global communications, most clearly represented by the internet, facilitated communication and coordination both nationally and internationally (Bennett 2003). Fourth, the Bush administration allowed the movement to unite around a very simple and urgent demand, not to start a war against Iraq immediately.

This demand was minimalist shorthand uniting those who also articulated a "Hands-off Iraq" position with others who articulated support for a broader international military and diplomatic effort to contain—or even oust—the dictator.

It is worthwhile to note that the first groups involved in this campaign, including International ANSWER, espoused a politics substantially out of step with the vast majority of those marching. Indeed, ANSWER had been organizing against economic and trade sanctions on Iraq for years. But activists from other groups were willing to join in ANSWER's events, showing up and trying to redefine them. There appears to be no long term advantages in being the initiator or an early riser (Tarrow 1989) in a movement coalition. Until the bombing started, the public definition of the antiwar movement was deferential to the more mainstream elements of the movement. Indeed, a very sympathetic press has continually portrayed this group of peace activists as not like the usual suspects/activists, but "regular" people. Of course, large demonstrations virtually always include a range of interests and participants, but media can focus on different elements in an event. The "regular folk" emphasis is a mark of supportive media framing (cf., Rojecki 1999; Gitlin 1981).

Efforts in the United States were part of a larger global antiwar mobilization. The feeling of connection, albeit mostly vicarious through the web and television, encouraged action, increasing the sense of urgency and the sense of possibility. The Bush administration's sporadic engagement in world affairs and its failure to build international support for its program contributed to distrust both abroad and domestically. By coming late to the UN, and only in response to the first protests, by rejecting international cooperation on other salient issues, especially the Kyoto protocol, and by failing to do whatever it took to extend its "coalition of the willing," the Bush administration left available a very broad coalition to oppose the war. Internationally, citizenries with other qualms about the Bush agenda could seize on this issue.

The Bush administration's political management of preparations for war made it much easier for activists to build a broad and very diverse antiwar movement comprised of multiple diverse coalitions. The urgency of the proximate war, the growth of international opposition, and the continued increase in the number of troops in the Persian Gulf encouraged groups to de-emphasize or ignore fundamental political differences to unite in opposition to the war. Indeed, criticism of President George W. Bush was often coupled with criticism of the Iraqi regime, and even supporters of the war questioned the claims and competence of the Bush administration. Thus, Timothy Garton Ash (2003) has written that Bush was wrong, but Blair right, even as both supported the war. Thomas Friedman (e.g. 2003), virtually always accompanied his support for the war as a means for democratizing the Middle East with criticism of President Bush's efforts and competence. In the lead up to the war, all of this made the efforts of the antiwar movement easier. Activists did not have to resolve among themselves disputes about the nature of the Iraqi regime or appropriate alternatives to invasion (e.g., Walzer 2003). In effect, by vigorously advancing a policy with elements unpopular among a wide variety of experts and pundits, the Bush administration gave activists a great deal of room in which to work to build a coalition.

Sustaining Coalitions

The very breadth of the movement and its extraordinarily simple platform at peak mobilization ("The world says no to war") were its greatest advantages and its largest vulnerabilities. Differences among coalition groups always provide the soft underbelly of social movements (Benford 1993) that skillful politicians exploit. As with other movements, organizers' efforts are constrained by a constantly shifting field of actual and potential coalitions; the management of potential tensions among the organizations sponsoring a movement campaign is an important factor affecting the processes of social movement growth and decline.

At the same time, the peak of mobilization is always limited, at least partly because political leaders respond. In this case, Bush responded by explicitly rejecting the movement's demands and waging war (although the conduct of the war was influenced by the movement in less visible ways [Arkin 2003]),

an unambiguous defeat for the movement. Changes in policy, political alignments, or even rhetoric, alter the constellation of political opportunities for each organization, leading to a reconsideration of previous political choices and alliances (Meyer 2004). Although the dynamics of coming together and growing apart are mediated by personal relationships and political skill, the critical factor is the relationship of the movement as a whole to external political circumstances, or the structure of political opportunities.

The history of earlier peace movement efforts reflects this process over and over again. For example, in the case of the nuclear freeze, a broad coalition united to oppose the Reagan administration's arms control and nuclear weapons policies during the early 1980s, proffering a policy proposal that participating groups defined differently (Meyer 1990; Rochon and Meyer 1997). At the height of mobilization, it comprised groups that opposed nuclear weapons altogether and advocated unilateral action and others that saw the freeze as a vehicle to use to press the Reagan administration to return to the previous U.S. policy of bilateral arms control negotiations and moderated technical modernization. As the administration responded to movement pressures, by moderating rhetoric, cutting the growth in military spending, and re-establishing arms control negotiations with the Soviet Union, the freeze coalition dissipated. Differences among various freeze organizations emerged more prominently as institutionally oriented politics consumed more activist efforts. Groups that had enlisted in the freeze because they faced closed doors on Capitol Hill left the coalition when those doors opened. As the practical limits of this institutional and instrumental orientation became clearer, however, organizational leaders found it increasingly difficult to cooperate. The more institutional wing saw the prospect of progress, the disarmament wing saw a sellout on the horizon, and the middle saw less to organize around (Meyer 1990, 1993a; Sawyers and Meyer 1999).

This difficulty in sustaining coalitions can also be seen in the Win Without War coalition, albeit in response to a more conspicuous political defeat The selection of issues by groups reflect the material concerns of building and supporting an organization, but also the question of defining and actualizing an identity predicated upon particular kinds of interactions with the outside world. Groups' strategic choices were bounded by their sense of themselves, so some groups could not cooperate in their opposition to war because of other political differences. Although theoretically groups might have a wide range of available options in rhetoric and tactics to respond to changing opportunities, ideology, and history limit the real possibilities. A rational calculus of risks and benefits can only be a starting point in analyzing the actual development of cooperative relationships. When an issue is particularly salient, when mobilization seems particularly urgent, groups have greater incentives to overcome or overlook differences. The prospect for some influence, however, encourages differentiation. (Had the United States endorsed a strong multinational inspections regime, coupled with focused sanctions and continued monitoring of "no-fly" zones in Northern and Southern Iraq, it is unlikely that International ANSWER and, for example, United for Peace and Justice would continue to overlook their own differences.)

Obviously, states have an interest in managing and dissipating dissent, and the United States is founded on institutions designed to do exactly this (Meyer 1993a). In the case of the recent antiwar movement, President Bush responded by explicitly rejecting the movement's claims. At the same time, the war radically changed the context in which activists could try to mobilize opposition. The ongoing aftermath of a relatively brief war and an extended military occupation, oddly, suggests a similar pattern of coalition fragmentation. Although the large demonstrations, again globally, and increased militancy immediately upon the start of war were unprecedented at the early stages of a war that seemed to be going inordinately well, they also exposed potential rifts within the antiwar coalition. These demonstrations were smaller than those before the war started, tailing off rather quickly over time. The evident defeat and neglect of movement concerns, and the pressure to support

troops in the field or make accommodations with a *fait accompli*, made mobilization against the war far more difficult. The Bush administration's initially successful framing of the war as a success, accomplished with relatively few American and British casualties and minimal collateral damage has thus far withstood disturbing revelations and ongoing conflicts. Even as this perception erodes, it's harder to find a common cause on which a broad public can agree. This military "victory" also exacerbated existing rifts in the movement Groups active in the peace movement had already brokered differences; most significantly, many opponents of the war, including presidential hopeful Howard Dean, later opposed a quick U.S. exit from Iraq that others demanded.

Besides ultimate goals, tactical conflicts also divided the movement. Increased civil disobedience after the war exacerbated old debates about tactics, and allowed the government to arrest and to marginalize activists within the more militant wing of the movement (Zernicke 2003; Zemicke and Murphy 2003). The possibility of police action at demonstrations sends some people home right away, as does the increased presence of counterdemonstrators. Prior to the war, while some groups explicitly challenged the entire notion of patriotism, others proclaimed their own dissent as patriotic. Media savvy leaders in this movement, many veterans of earlier campaigns, have pressed a rhetoric of patriotism and sympathy and support for troops, seeking to prevent the Bush administration from using the radical flank to discredit the entire movement (Neuman 2003). But this balance was harder to maintain as the bombing started.

Institutionalizing this dissent means negotiating a routine set of relationships with various groups in the antiwar coalition, and the American political system offers repeated opportunities for institutional political action that can undermine the attraction of political activism outside. If the past is predictor, this will mean marginalization and neglect of some, inclusion, if primarily symbolic of others, while a large set just falls out as the movement coalition fragments (Meyer 1993a). Already, groups have begun to move on to new, more promising issues, as well as other means to make claims about the war. Moveon, for example, fully engaged in the politics of the competition for the Democratic presidential nomination, and then opposed George Bush in the general election. Indeed, during 2004 the presidential campaigns superceded street protest and demonstrations. It is worth noting that Presidential election years have historically meant diminished protest by peace movements, particularly as the election approaches (Meyer 1993b). The NAACP and NOW are less likely to discuss the war, for example, as their own pressing issues remain. Meanwhile, International ANSWER dropped from public attention.

Transnational allies on the war are no longer united with U.S.-based groups no longer looking at foreign policy. In retrospect, the apparent unanimity among demonstrators globally was limited to opposition to the pending war. Surely, most of the activists globally have not disappeared, but like their American counterparts, they have turned their attention to more promising or pressing issues than

the war they could not prevent. The lion's share of such issues is bounded by domestic politics within nation states. The bonds of affiliation in a transnational coalition are necessarily thin (cf., Bandy and Smith 2005).

Again, the case of Win Without War illustrates these processes. Although paper cooperation among the constituent groups remains, less than a third of the groups who committed to antiwar activity before the war list the war in Iraq as a major area of concern by December 2003. Venn diagrams also illustrate the atrophy of bridges and connections among groups based on their identities and causes (see figures 1 and 2 for a comparison of the original coalition and the coalition in December 2003). It is clear that groups with anti-war agendas as central to their core concerns have been more likely to remain in the anti-war coalition. Other groups, for whom the cause is secondary, such as groups focused on identity politics, religion, social justice, and the environment, have been more apt to redirect their focus back to their primary concerns.

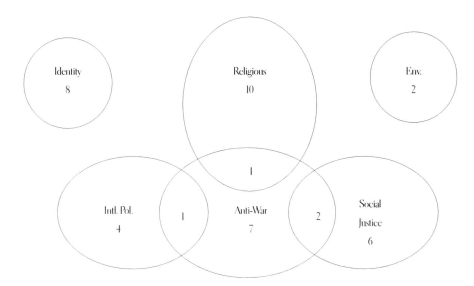

Env. = Environmental; Intl. Pol. = International politics

Figure 31.1 Original Win Without War Coalition Groups by Type

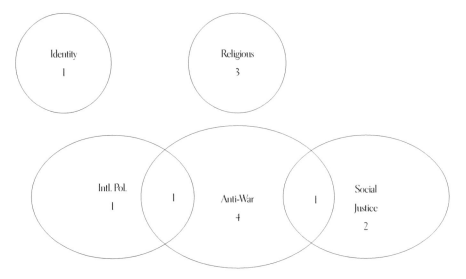

Env. = Environmental; Intl. Pol. = International politics

Figure 31.2 Win Without War Coalition Groups Still Focused on Iraq in Dec. 2003 by Type

Conclusion

In this article, we used the recent case of a large mobilization against war to examine a more general process of social movement politics, particularly as related to the mechanisms of movement coalitions. We mean to suggest that adopting a coalitional approach to analyzing social movements affords both greater empirical validity and theoretical leverage in looking at social movements. It bears reiterating a few key elements of the insights of a coalitional approach to studying social movements suggested here.

First, although it is useful shorthand to speak of a social movement as a unitary actor, movements are comprised of diverse elements cooperating and competing on different issues at a given time. Activists, working in coordination and in groups, make and act upon decisions in a way that movements cannot. In describing movement activists and activities, we take analytical liberties in identifying what we view as the most significant, problematic, or interesting trends within a broad coalition. It is also critical to recall that the actual direction

of a social movement coalition is not determined without political conflicts within that coalition, as activists and organizations compete to actualize their visions of optimal movement politics.

We have suggested certain tendencies in the recent antiwar coalition, and whether these patterns apply to other coalitions is a question begging for empirical examination. Specifically, are coalition efforts most coordinated and least contentious during the middle phases of a social movement campaign, after mobilization has taken off but before it has made obvious inroads or suffered clear defeats? Are the patterns of coalition formation in campaigns about foreign policy or international issues fundamentally different than those on domestic policies, where political culture or federalism may play fragmenting roles?

Second, the decision to join a movement coalition carries with it costs and benefits for individual organizations, just as the decision to join a social movement carries with it costs and benefits for individuals. By joining with others, individual social movements can bring more attention and focus on issues that they consider important. At the same time, coalition politics often takes attention away from the participating organizations' original interests. The costs and benefits of joining a movement will be affected by the political context and, as the context changes, groups may be more or less likely to be willing to absorb the costs and participate in a coalition. Coalitions are difficult to sustain for just this reason. When the political context changes and the threat seems less proximate, less changeable, or less important, individual organizations will be more likely to abandon coalition work, either formally or by focusing their efforts elsewhere. Finally, although the political skills of activists and organizers are important in understanding the growth and decline of coalitions, it is critical to consider the circumstances in which they cooperate, or not. Political leaders have great latitude in shaping their opposition, buying peace on some fronts in order to isolate, cauterize, or neutralize others. Policy threats and political exclusion are likely to do most to cause social movement groups to work together (McCammon and Campbell 2002; Van Dyke 2003). When threats pass, however, the incentives to cooperate are likely to be outweighed by the risks—and the lure of other concerns.

It is important to focus on a coalitional framework for understanding social movements in order to illuminate past mobilizations as well as ways in which movements may be more or less successful in the future. Moreover, the nature of group coordination and cooperation is likely to have cyclic analogues at both larger and smaller scales. At the micro-level, groups are likely to consider the

decisions to cooperate in much the same way that individuals consider whether to join mobilization efforts, mindful of both political circumstances and individual concerns. At a broader level, the patterns of cooperation and differentiation are also likely to parallel cycles of mobilization and demobilization. For this reason, we call for further study of coalitional politics and the role of political context on shaping social movement coalitions.

NOTES

We are grateful for helpful comments from Stephanie DiAlto, Jai Kwan Jung, Ellen Reese, Dieter Rucht, David Snow, Yang Su, Heidi Swarts, Mayer Zald, and *Mobilization's* anonymous reviewers.

1. Journalists now recognize both the difficulty and the politics of estimating the number of participants at a demonstration, and so routinely report broad ranges of numbers.

2. In the early 1980s, intensive efforts for transnational coordination generated many meetings, a series of large conferences, and one round of simultaneous demonstrations (Meyer 1990; Wittner 1997, 2003). Coordination was complicated by different analyses and priorities on opposite sides of the Atlantic (Cortright and Pagnucco 1997).

3. On transnational coalitions, see Bandy and Smith (2005).

4. The House supported the war, 250–183; the Senate margin was tighter, 52–47.

5. Lopsided votes in the House (296–133) and the Senate (77–23) reflected a tense political climate. The attack on the World Trade Center and the Pentagon on September 11th created a climate of fear in the United States and a political "rally around the flag." effect, leading to increased support for the President (see Mueller 1973).

6. This double coalition strategy is an artifact of the Cold War (Coy and Woehrle 1996).

7. Mass market and broadcast media were less critical (Kull, Ramsey, and Lewis 2003).

Part 10

Intramovement Dynamics

In Part 9 we examined "extramovement" dynamics, the ways in which other groups and parties to the conflict, in interaction with movement forces, shape the fate of movements. But the course and character of movements are not determined solely by external influences and pressures. Equally important in understanding the development of movements are the structure and character of their own internal processes. Here we focus on these "intramovement" dynamics.

The importance of internal factors in understanding the development of social movements has been recognized for a long time. In fact, perhaps the oldest theoretical tradition in the study of social movements focuses exclusively on processes internal to the movement. Associated with the work of Max Weber (1963) and Robert Michels (1959), this theory holds that movements inevitably grow more conservative over time through the related internal processes of "oligarchization," "goal displacement," and the "routinization of charisma." Catalyzed by charismatic leaders focused on radical change goals, movements, in this view, inevitably ossify as charismatic authority gives way to bureaucratic and organizational survival and narrow self-interest comes to substitute for the original idealistic aims of the cause. All around us, or so the argument goes, we see the compromised, organizational, remnants of failed movements.

In a classic 1966 article, Mayer Zald and Roberta Ash challenged the inevitability of the Weber/Michel thesis, suggesting that the outcome of internal movement processes was, in fact, developmentally quite variable. Inspired by this more open-ended view of movement development, scholars—organizational no less than movement—have devoted considerable energy over the past 40 years to exploring various intramovement processes.

The four selections in this part reflect the ongoing interest in how various internal dynamics affect the developmental course and character of social movements.

The first selection, another classic article by Verta Taylor, introduced the term abeyance structure to the lexicon of movement scholars. More importantly, it shed light on a heretofore unexplored phase of movement development and a set of internal processes critical to the long-term survival of activist cultures. Drawing on data on women's activism between 1945 and the 1960s, Taylor shows that a feminist culture of struggle did not die following the Suffrage victory in 1920, only to rematerialize in the 1960s. Rather, the culture survived but was in abeyance during most of the period. The term "abeyance" is used to refer to a holding pattern in which movements, or more accurately, activist cultures, survive in a political environment that is nonreceptive or antagonistic. Taylor illuminates how a feminist tradition of struggle was sustained during this period through the active maintenance of a "movement abeyance structure."

The second selection, by Suzanne Staggenborg, examines the consequences of McCarthy and Zald's (1973, 1977) professionalization thesis in relation to social movements by analyzing the impact of three types of leadership (professional, nonprofessional volunteers, and nonprofessional staff) and two types of organizational structure (formal and informal) on the development of the prochoice movement. Using data drawn from case histories of 13 prochoice movement organizations, Staggenborg finds that while professional leaders are not entrepreneurial in the sense of initiating movements and creating new tactics, they do tend to formalize the movement organizations they lead. Additionally, formalized social movement organizations are found to be more adept than informal ones at maintaining themselves, especially during difficult times. These findings can be interpreted as offering partial support to both the Weber/Michels emphasis on the moderating effects of bureaucratization, as well as the resource mobilization emphasis on the importance of professionalization for the long-term survival of movements. As such, they add nuance to our understanding of the complicated and contingent effects that follow from the creation and long-term sustenance of formal social movement organization.

In the third selection, Joel Andreas complicates our understanding of organizational trajectories in contention all the more by way of his compelling case study of the emergence and development of the most prominent rebel organization in Beijing during the Chinese Cultural Revolution. What makes Andreas's account so unique and theoretically important is his insistence that only by turning the Weber/Michels thesis on its head can you understand the Cultural Revolution generally and the meteoric rise of the rebel movement that is the centerpiece of his study. That is, far from charisma always succumbing to bureaucratic authority, the Cultural Revolution represented the triumph of charisma at the expense and destruction of bureaucratic structures throughout Chinese society. Not only did Mao's personal charisma unleash the movement in the first place, but for most of its tumultuous life the Cultural Revolution privileged charismatic leadership over all other forms of authority. At the most general level, Andreas's article should be read as a plea to scholars of social movements and revolution to restore the concept of charisma to its rightful place in the study of contentious politics.

The final selection moves us away from the study of leadership and organization to another internal process—diffusion—critical to the development of social movements. In fact, absent at least some level of diffusion, it is highly unlikely that a movement would ever surface to public attention. While we tend to think of movements as broad national or even transnational struggles, they are never born as such. Instead they begin as highly localized conflicts that, only on rare occasions, spread—or diffuse—widely enough to become the highly visible struggles we know them as. Why do only some conflicts and associated tactics diffuse, and by what means do they do so? Sarah Soule (2004) provides a general synthesis of research addressing these questions, but in a chapter taken from his book, *The New Transnational Activism*, Sidney Tarrow addresses such questions by highlighting the increasing incidence of the transnational diffusion of movement tactics, frames, and organizational forms.

32.

Social Movement Continuity: The Women's Movement in Abeyance

VERTA TAYLOR

Introduction

Scholars of the social movements of the 1960s have by and large held an "immaculate conception" view of their origins. These "new social movements" (Klandermans 1986) seemingly emerged out of nowhere and represented a sudden shift from the quiescent 1940s and 1950s (Flacks 1971; Touraine 1971; McCarthy and Zald 1973; Jenkins 1987). Recent empirical work, however, challenges this view, suggesting that the break between the sixties movements and earlier waves of political activism was not as sharp as previously assumed (e.g., Isserman 1987; McAdam 1988). The overemphasis on movement origins and on new elements in the sixties movements has blinded students of social movements to the "carry-overs and carry-ons" between movements (Gusfield 1981, p. 324). What scholars have taken for "births" were in fact breakthroughs or turning points in movement mobilization.

This paper develops a framework that specifies the processes of movement continuity. The framework is grounded in research on the American women's rights movement from 1945 to the mid-1960s. Most accounts trace its origins to the civil rights movement (Freeman 1975; Evans 1979). Yet the women's movement, like the other movements that blossomed in the 1960s, can also be viewed as a resurgent challenge with roots in an earlier cycle of feminist activism that presumably ended when suffrage was won. My approach relies heavily on the central premises of resource mobilization theory: political opportunities and an indigenous organizational base are major factors in the rise and decline of movements (e.g., Oberschall 1973; McCarthy and

Taylor, Verta. 1989. "Social Movement Continuity: The Women's Movement in Abeyance." *American Sociological Review* 54: 761–775. Reprinted by permission of American Sociological Association.

Zald 1977; McAdam 1982; Jenkins 1983). The paper makes a new contribution by elaborating certain abeyance processes in social movements and by specifying features of social movement abeyance organizations. The term "abeyance" depicts a holding process by which movements sustain themselves in nonreceptive political environments and provide continuity from one stage of mobilization to another.

After discussing data sources, the analysis briefly describes the history of the American women's movement and the persistence of a small band of feminists who, in the 1940s and 1950s, continued to remain faithful to the political vision that had originally drawn them into the suffrage movement nearly a half century earlier. Because the cultural and political climate had changed, these women found that their ideals and commitment to feminism marginalized and isolated them from the mainstream of American women. I argue that their form of activism is best understood as a social movement abeyance structure. Finally, I delineate the features of abeyance structures that were a source of movement continuity by tracing the consequences of postwar activism for the contemporary women's movement. I conclude by exploring the implications of the abeyance hypothesis for understanding the organizational and ideological bridges between earlier activism and the development of other movements of the 1960s.

Abeyance Processes in Social Movements

The term "abeyance" is borrowed from Mizruchi (1983) and is central to a theory of social control. Abeyance structures emerge when society lacks sufficient status vacancies to integrate surpluses of marginal and dissident people. The structures that absorb marginal groups are abeyance organizations. They temporarily retain potential challengers to the status quo, thereby reducing threats to the larger social systems. Abeyance organizations have certain properties that allow them to absorb, control, and expel personnel according to the number of status positions available in the larger society (Mizruchi 1983, p. 17).

Although Mizruchi recognizes the social change potential of abeyance organizations, he does not address this aspect systematically (Kimmel 1984). I both challenge and extend Mizruchi's thesis to hypothesize that social movement abeyance organizations, by providing a measure of continuity for challenging groups, also contribute to social change. I hold that the abeyance process characterizes mass movements that succeed in building a support base and achieving a measure of influence, but are confronted with a nonreceptive political and social environment. A central tenet of resource mobilization theory concerns the role that changing opportunity structures play in the emergence and the attenuation of collective action (McCarthy and Zald 1973; Barkan 1984; Jenkins 1983). As a movement loses support, activists who had been most intensely committed to its aims become increasingly marginal and socially isolated. If insufficient opportunities exist to channel their commitment into routine statuses, then alternative structures emerge to absorb the surplus of people. These structures both restrain them from potentially more disruptive activities and channel them into certain forms of activism. In short, a movement in abeyance becomes a cadre of activists who create or find a niche for themselves. Such groups may have little impact in their own time and may contribute, however unwillingly, to maintenance of the status quo. But, by providing a legitimating base to challenge the status quo, such groups can be sources of protest and change.

The following factors are relevant to the abeyance process. First, certain factors external to a movement create a pool of marginal potential activists. These include *changes in opportunity structures* that support and constrain the movement and an *absence of status vacancies* to absorb dissident and excluded groups. Second, there are internal factors or organizational *dimensions of social movement abeyance structures: temporality, commitment, exclusiveness, centralization,* and *culture.* Since

these dimensions were inductively derived, I elaborate them with the case at hand. The significance of abeyance lies in its linkages between one upsurge in activism and another. I delineate three ways that social movement abeyance structures perform this linkage function: through promoting the survival of *activist networks,* sustaining a repertoire of *goals and tactics,* and promoting a *collective identity* that offers participants a sense of mission and moral purpose.

Data

Most accounts describe the American women's movement as peaking in two periods (Chafe 1972; Freeman 1975; Klein 1984). The first wave, generally referred to as the suffrage movement, grew out of the abolitionist struggle of the 1830s, reached a stage of mass mobilization between 1900 and 1920, and declined after the passage of the suffrage amendment. The second wave emerged in the mid-1960s, reached a stage of mass mobilization around 1970, and continued into the 1980s (Carden 1974; Evans 1979; Ferree and Hess 1985).

Curiosity about what happened to the organizations and networks of women who participated in the suffrage campaign led to the research described here. There are two reasons for focusing on the period from 1945 to the mid-1960s. First, other researchers have explored the period from 1920 to 1940 (Lemons 1973; Becker 1981; Cott 1987). Second, most researchers see the civil rights movement as the major predecessor to the contemporary women's movement (e.g., Freeman 1975; Evans 1979; McAdam 1988). By examining feminist activity in the decades just prior to the resurgence of feminism as a mass movement, I hoped to shed light on the accuracy of this view.

The data for this study come from documentary material in public and private archival collections and interviews with women who were activists from 1945 to the 1960s. Fuller description of the movement in this period and complete documentation are available in Rupp and Taylor (1987).

(1) Archival data included the papers of the National Woman's Party and the League of Women Voters, the two major factions of the suffrage movement, and the papers of the President's Commission on the Status of Women (1961–63), whose activities facilitated the

resurgence of the contemporary women's movement. Other material examined were unofficial and official organizational documents, publications, personal letters, and memos in public and private collections, most of which are housed at the Schlesinger Library at Radcliff College or the Library of Congress. The papers of individual women provided an important source of information; not only about their organizational careers, but also about the activities of diverse women's organizations.

(2) The second source of data was 57 open-ended, semistructured, tape-recorded interviews, conducted between 1979 and 1983, with leaders and core members of the most central groups involved in women's rights activities. Twelve of the women were active at the national level and thirty-three at the local level. Twelve other transcribed interviews conducted by other researchers and available in archival collections were used.

The Women's Movement in the Postsuffrage Decades: The Transformation of Feminist Activism

Feminism activism continued in the years after the suffrage victory but was transformed as a result of organizational success, internal conflict, and social changes that altered women's common interests (Lemons 1973; Becker 1981; Buechler 1986; Cott 1987). Deradicalization and decline of the women's movement left militant feminists limited avenues through which to pursue their political philosophy.

In 1920, with the vote won, the women's movement was left with no unifying goal. Moreover, tactical and ideological differences divided militant from moderate suffragists and those who saw winning the vote as a means from those who viewed it as an end. As a result, the major social movement organizations of the suffrage movement evolved in two opposing directions.

The militant branch of the movement, the National Woman's Party (NWP), launched a relentless campaign to pass an Equal Rights Amendment (ERA) to the constitution. The NWP was never a mass organization but saw itself as a feminist vanguard or elite (Lunardini 1986). Hoping to enlist the support of former suffragists, NWP leader Alice Paul instead alienated both socialists and moderate

feminists by her dictatorial style and the decision to focus on the ERA. The vast majority of suffragists feared that the ERA would eliminate the protective labor legislation that women reformers had earlier struggled to achieve (Balser 1987).

The mainstream branch of the movement, the National American Woman Suffrage Association, formed the nonpartisan League of Women Voters. It spearheaded the opposition to the ERA, educated women for their new citizenship responsibilities, and advocated a broad range of reforms. Other activists in the suffrage campaign channeled their efforts into new or growing organizations that did not have an explicitly feminist agenda but promoted a vast range of specific causes that, in part, grew out of the expanded role options available to women (Cott 1987). Thus, even though the women's movement was rapidly fragmenting, feminist activism continued throughout the 1920s and 1930s. But in the face of increasing hostility between the two camps of the suffrage movement, cooperation developed on only a few issues.

In addition to goal attainment and internal conflict, a third factor contributed to the dissipation of the mass base of the women's movement. Ironically, the role expansion for which the movement had fought fractured the bonds on which the solidarity of the movement had been built. As women's lives grew increasingly diverse, the definition of what would benefit women grew less clear.

As a result, the NWP—which alone continued to claim the title "feminist"—had become increasingly isolated from the mainstream of American women and even from women's organizations. With the demise of the large mass-based organizations that propelled the suffrage movement, the more radical feminists sought out the NWP. When the NWP captured the feminist agenda, however, the broad program of emancipation narrowed to limited goals and tactics pursued by an elite group of women (Cott 1987). This spelled the final demise of feminism as a mass movement.

Feminist Activism from 1945 to the 1960's: the Women's Movement in Abeyance

From 1945 to the 1960s, women's rights activists confronted an inhospitable political and social environment. Women who advocated equality found few outlets for their activism and became increasingly marginal and isolated from the mainstream of American women. Two social processes had this effect: first, advocates of women's rights lacked access to and support from the established political system; and, second, the cultural ideal of "the feminine mystique" that emerged after World War II affirmed the restoration of "normal family life" and discredited women who protested gender inequality.

Changing Opportunity Structure: Nonreceptive Political Elites

Despite an increase in the female labor force and the female student body in institutions of higher education, support for women's rights and opportunities declined sharply following the Second World War. By 1945, the women's movement had further fragmented into three overlapping interest groups, each with a different political agenda (Harrison 1988, p. 7). Because women's issues were not generally salient, the three groups lacked political access and influence. Just as important, when they did gain access to political elites, they often canceled out each other's influence.

One interest group consisted of a coalition of women's organizations associated with the Women's Bureau of the Department of Labor. Throughout the 1940s and 1950s, this coalition sought to improve women's working conditions and defeat the ERA. Despite its governmental status, the Women's Bureau had little political clout, and the coalition used much of its influence to fight supporters of the ERA.

A second group consisted of a network of women in politics, including women active in the women's divisions of both the Democratic and Republican parties. They advocated the election and appointment of women to policy-making positions despite a dramatic decline in women's political opportunities after the Second World War. For the most part, the selection of women for policy-making positions was done by party women without regard for their position on women's issues (Harrison 1988, p. 64). Since women officials generally had no policy role and little influence on women's issues, advocating

token appointments of women diverted attention from major policy questions such as the ERA.

A third group, the National Woman's Party, remained furthest outside the established political order. By 1944, the NWP had begun a major campaign to get Congress to pass the ERA and had managed to garner support from a few women's organizations. Confronted with the establishment of the National Committee to Defeat the Unequal Rights Amendment, spearheaded by the Women's Bureau, the NWP sought the support of both political parties. Presidents Truman and Eisenhower endorsed the ERA, both party platforms advocated it, and Congress considered it in 1946, 1950, and 1953. Yet such support was more a nod to women than a serious political consideration (Freeman 1987).

None of these three groups made much progress in attaining their goals in the 1940s and 1950s. Although women's organizations succeeded in having 236 bills pertaining to women's rights introduced into Congress in the 1950s, only 14 passed (Klein 1984), p. 18. This reflected not only organized women's lack of political access and their conflicts; but also the exaggerated emphasis on sex roles that emerged on the heels of the Second World War.

Status Vacancy and Marginality

Following the war, a variety of social forces helped to reinstitutionalize traditional family life supported by rigid sex role distinctions (Friedan 1963; Breines 1985; May 1988). Women whose roles did not center on the home and family were considered deviant. In 1957, 80 percent of the respondents to a national poll believed that people who chose not to marry were sick, immoral, and neurotic (Klein 1984, p. 71). As a result of the pressure, fewer married women remained childless in the 1950s than in the 1900s—only 6.8 percent compared to 14 percent (Rupp and Taylor 1987, p. 15). Indicative of the tide, in 1945 only 18 percent of a Gallup Poll sample approved of a married woman's working if she had a husband capable of supporting her (Erskine 1971).

In addition to criticizing women who did not conform to the cultural ideal, the media denounced feminism, discredited women who continued to advocate equality, and thus thwarted the mobilization of discontented women (Rupp 1982). The most influential attack came from Ferdinand Lundberg and Marynia Farnham's popular and widely quoted book, *Modern Woman: The Lost Sex* (1947), which denounced feminists as severe neurotics responsible for the problems of American society. In the face of such criticism, only the NWP continued to claim the term "feminist." In fact, the core group of women in the NWP differed in major respects from the cultural ideal. An analysis of the 55 leaders and most active members of the NWP indicates that, by 1950, the majority were white, middle- or upper-class, well educated, employed in professional or semiprofessional occupations (especially law, government, and higher education), unmarried or widowed, and older (in their fifties, sixties, or seventies).[1] Specifically 71 percent of the women were employed: 97 percent were over the age of 50; and 60 percent were unmarried or widowed. In short, the lifestyles of the women, while relatively advantaged, were not normative. Feminists were largely unattached women with time, money, and other resources that facilitated their activism. Yet the retreat of a broad-based women's movement left few outlets to express their views either inside or outside the established political arena.

In summary, as the political and cultural wave that had once carried feminism forward receded, members of the NWP paid for their lifelong commitment with a degree of alienation, marginality, and isolation. Nevertheless, the NWP provided a structure and status capable of absorbing these intensely committed feminists and thus functioned as an abeyance organization.

Dimensions of Social Movement Abeyance Structures

The abeyance process functions through organizations capable of sustaining collective challenges under circumstances unfavorable to mass mobilization. Properties of abeyance organizations help an organizational pattern to retain potentially dissident populations. My analysis of the women's rights movement in the postwar period suggests that the most relevant variables with respect to the abeyance process are: temporality, purposive commitment, exclusiveness, centralization, and culture. Since these variables are derived from a single case,

each dimension is treated as a hypothetical continuum with respect to other cases.

Temporality. By definition, of course, an abeyance structure persists throughout time, but temporality refers to the length of time that a movement organization is able to hold personnel. Activism provides a community that is an alternative source of integration and, thus, can have an enduring effect beyond a particular period in an individual's live (Coser 1974; White 1988).

During the 70-odd years of the first wave of the women's movement, a number of women's rights groups emerged and provided alternative status vacancies for large numbers of mainly white and middle-class women (Flexner 1959; Buechler 1986; Chafetz and Dworkin 1986). Among the 55 leaders and core activists of the NWP, 53 percent had been recruited at least four decades earlier during the suffrage campaign.

For NWP members, early participation in high-risk activism (McAdam 1986), including picketing the White House, engaging in hunger strikes while imprisoned, and burning President Wilson's speeches, kept them involved long after the suffrage victory. Lamenting the passage of that period, Florence Kitchelt asked a fellow suffragist in 1959 whether she ever felt "as I do that the modem woman is missing something very thrilling, uplifting as well as unifying in not being able to take part in a suffrage campaign? Those were the days."[2] Katharine Hepburn, mother of the actress, in a speech to women's rights activists, described her experiences in the suffrage struggle. "That whole period in my life I remember with the greatest delight," she said. "We had no doubts. Life was a great thrill from morning until night."[3] Involvement in the suffrage movement had a powerful and enduring effect on participants, so much so that they continued even into the 1950s to promote women's rights in a society antagonistic to the idea. The strong and lasting effects of participation in high-risk activism is supported by McAdam's (1988) study of participants in the 1964 Freedom Summer project.

By the 1940s and 1950s, a core of women in the NWP had devoted a major portion of their lives to feminist activity. Typical participation patterns are reflected in the comments of two members. In 1952, one woman wrote, "Since 1917 I have devoted all my spare time to feminism."[4] Another woman asked in 1950 for a "cure for giving too much of one's time to one thing," although she still continued to devote herself to passage of the ERA.[5] Not surprisingly, the most striking characteristic of the NWP membership was advanced age. Isserman (1987, p. 24) found a similar age structure in another organization that provided continuity between two stages of mass mobilization, the American Communist Party in the 1940s and 1950s. Constant numbers—even if small—are better for morale than steady turnover, so temporality enhances the likelihood that an organization will continue to endure.

Purposive commitment. Commitment refers to the willingness of people to do what must be done, regardless of personal rewards and sacrifices, to maintain a collective challenge and is essential for holding an organizational pattern alive between stages of mass mobilization. Research on social movement involvement has focused primarily on the types of incentives that induce activists to make an initial commitment to a movement (e.g., Pinard 1971; Fireman and Gamson 1979; Oliver 1983; McAdam 1986). In exploring movement continuity, we must pose a different question: why do individuals maintain radical or unpopular convictions over time?

The few studies that have explored this question suggest that the nature of and incentives for commitment depend on a movement's stage in the mobilization process. Kanter's (1972) research on American communes concludes that groups characterized by high commitment are more likely to retain participants and to endure. Other research suggests that, although individuals may become activists through solidary or material incentives, continued participation depends upon high levels of commitment to group beliefs, goals, and tactics (Hirsch 1986; White 1988).

From its inception, the NWP appealed to women with strong feminist sympathies. By the 1950s, continued participation depended largely on the singleness of members' devotion to the principle of sexual equality embodied in the Equal Rights Amendment. Rejecting all other proposals for a feminist program, NWP leaders insisted that

ideological integrity and the dogged pursuit of legal equality, not membership gain, would guarantee triumph.

A dedicated core of NWP members worked for the ERA by lobbying Congress and the President, seeking endorsements from candidates for political office and from other organizations, establishing coalitions to support the amendment, and educating the public through newspaper and magazine articles, letters to the editor, and radio and television appearances. Commenting on the persistence of feminists' lobbying efforts, one Representative from Connecticut wondered in 1945 "whether or not the Congress meets for any other purpose but to consider the Equal Rights Amendment."[6] Since the NWP depended entirely on the volunteer work of members, commitment was built on sacrifices of time, energy, and financial resources. Recognizing the impact of such high levels of commitment, one new recruit commented that "the secret of the ability of the group to do so much in the face of such odds is that it can attract just such devotion and loyalty."[7]

Commitment, then, contributes to the abeyance process by ensuring that individuals continue to do what is necessary to maintain the group and its purpose even when the odds are against immediate success. Moreover, such intense commitment functions as an obstacle to participation in alternative roles and organizations.

Exclusiveness. Organizations vary according to their openness to members, some having more stringent criteria than others. Mizruchi (1983, p. 44) hypothesizes that the expansion-contraction of an abeyance organization's personnel occurs in response to changes in the larger social system's requirements for absorption, mobility, or expulsion of marginal populations. To absorb large numbers of people who are unattached to other structures requires organizations to be inclusive, as happens during the peak mobilization of social movement organizations. In cycles of decline, however, when challenging groups lack widespread attitudinal support, organizations become exclusive and attempt to expel or hold constant their membership. Zald and Ash (1966) contend that exclusive movement organizations are more likely to endure than inclusive ones.

At the peak of the suffrage struggle, the NWP was inclusive across the class and political spectrum (Cott 1987, pp. 53–55). It attracted wage-earning women from a variety of occupations as well as elite women social activists. Its members had ties to political parties, government, and industry, as well as to the socialist, peace, labor, and antilynching movements. But when the NWP launched its ERA campaign, many bodies organized on occupational, religious, and racial grounds and devoted to other policy issues began to absorb women from mainstream suffrage groups and siphon off NWP members. This left the NWP with a small and relatively homogeneous permanent core of feminists.

By the end of World War II, the NWP had lost most of its members and was not attracting new ones. Compared to its 60,000 members in the last years of the suffrage campaign, the NWP had about 4000 "general" members by 1945 and only 1400 by 1952. More revealing, it listed 627 "active" members in 1947 and 200 by 1952. Although the NWP also lost members as a result of an internal conflict over whether to expand membership in 1947 and again in 1953, the leadership preferred to keep the organization a small elite vanguard. As one member put it, "no mass appeal will ever bring into the Party that type of woman who can best carry forward our particular aims. We are an 'elect body' with a single point of agreement."[8]

Just as important, the membership of the NWP also grew increasingly homogeneous and socially advantaged over the decades. Of 55 core activists, 90 percent of the employed held professional, managerial, or technical positions. Several researchers have noted that intellectuals and other privileged groups are likely to be overrepresented among the leadership and supporters of neo-liberal and communal movements. Some have attributed this to the risks and resources that participation entails (Lenin 1970; McCarthy and Zald 1973; Oberschall 1973, p. 161), while others look to the unique political culture of intellectuals and professionals (Pinard and Hamilton 1988).

Despite the fact that the NWP leaders preferred a small homogeneous membership, they recognized the significance of size and diversity for public impact. In order to give the appearance of a mass constituency, the NWP devised certain strategies. Members maintained multiple memberships in women's organizations in order to win endorsements for the ERA; they established coalitions to give the impression of a large membership; they financed a "front" organization to give the appearance of cooperation between feminists and labor women; and they recruited leaders of the National Association of Colored Women in order to obtain its endorsement of the ERA. Yet, despite attempts to appear inclusive, the NWP did not seriously try to build an indigenous base of support.

Organizational exclusivity is closely related to the commitment variable. Organizations that insist upon high levels of purposive commitment and make stringent demands of time and financial resources cannot absorb large numbers of people. They are, however, good at holding constant those members that they have. Thus, exclusiveness is an important characteristic of abeyance organizations because it ensures a relatively homogeneous cadre of activists suited to the limited activism undertaken.

Centralization. Organizations vary in their centralization of power. Some operate through a "single center of power," whereas decentralized groups distribute power among subunits (Gamson 1975, p. 93). Although centralization contributes to a decline in direct-action tactics (Piven and Cloward 1977; Jenkins and Eckert 1986), it has the advantage of producing the organizational stability, coordination, and technical expertise necessary for movement survival (Gamson 1975; Wehr 1986; Staggenborg 1989).

By the end of World War II, the NWP functioned almost entirely on the national level with a federated structure in which local and state chapters had little control. State branches, which had been active in the 1920s, consisted in most cases of little more than a chairman and served the organization primarily as letterheads to use in lobbying senators and representatives.[9]

A national chairman headed the NWP. The Party's founder and leading light, Alice Paul, however, directed and kept a tight reign on its activities, even though she formally occupied the chair for only a brief period from 1942 to 1945. As one member described it, Paul "gave the chairman all deference. But if you were a wise chairman, you did what Alice Paul wanted, because she knew what was needed."[10] The chairman headed a national council that met periodically at the Washington headquarters. There was also a national advisory council composed of prominent women who lent their names to the group's work.

Paul, reputedly a charismatic leader committed to the point of fanaticism, maintained tight control over the ERA campaign. She decided when it was time to press Congress and when to maintain a low profile and, according to members' reports, worked from six in the morning until midnight. On at least two occasions serious conflict erupted over the lack of democratic procedures in the Party. It focused specifically on Alice Paul's autocratic leadership style and on the refusal of the national leadership to allow state branches to expand membership. A letter, circulated in 1947, contained charges typical of those directed against Paul: "You have made it clear that you consider yourself and the small group around you an elite with superabundant intellect and talents, and consider us, in contrast, the commonfolk."[11] Thus centralization of leadership, like exclusiveness, had the potential to provoke conflict among members. But it also had advantages in a nonreceptive political environment.

Paul used her influence to direct a small group of activists with highly specialized skills—lobbying and researching, testifying, and writing about policy issues—who viewed themselves as an embattled feminist minority. The NWP was able to finance its activities with some invested funds, dues, contributions from members, and revenue from the rental of rooms in its Washington property. As a result, activists did not have to expend energy generating resources to maintain the organization.

This kind of central direction allowed the NWP to sustain the feminist challenge through the years by concentrating on a single strategy that could be carried out by a dedicated band of activists with highly specialized skills. Thus, centralization contributes to the abeyance process by ensuring the maintenance of organization and at least minimal activity during periods when conditions do not favor mass mobilization.

Culture. The culture of a social movement organization is embodied in its collective emotions, beliefs, and actions. Although all social movements create and bear culture, movement organizations vary in the character and complexity of their cultures (Lofland 1985).

The effectiveness of an organization with respect to its abeyance function depends, in part, on its capacity to motivate persons to assume certain positions. As the larger political and cultural atmosphere becomes less hospitable to the social movement, recruitment of personnel becomes difficult. In order to make participation more attractive, organizations must elaborate alternative cultural frameworks to provide security and meaning for those who reject the established order and remain in the group. Previous research suggests that the more highly developed an organization's culture, the more it offers members the satisfaction and other resources necessary for its survival (Kanter 1972; Lofland 1985).

The NWP developed an elaborate and expressive culture through activities at the Alva Belmont House, its national headquarters in Washington, D.C. Belmont House served not only as an office for national council meetings, but also as a center where lobbying efforts were coordinated and where the monthly newsletter was published. It also created the kind of female world essential to the maintenance of feminism (Freedman 1979; Rupp 1985). A few women lived at Belmont House and in two other Party-owned houses, while lobbyists stayed there from a few days to several months. In addition, Belmont House was the site of feminist events and celebrations: teas to honor women politicians or sponsors of the ERA, victory celebrations, and parties on Susan B. Anthony's birthday or on the anniversary of the suffrage victory. The activities and relationships women formed at Belmont House provided both ideological and affective support for participation in women's rights work.

Although NWP members believed in the pervasiveness of discrimination against women, the Party did not develop and advance a well-articulated ideological and theoretical position. Rather, feminism was defined principally through a culture that promoted a feminist worldview. One member expressed her world view, complaining of "Masculinity running rampant *all over the earth!*" and rebelling at the "utter man-mindedness" she saw all around her.[12] Alice Paul characterized women's rights advocates as sharing a "feeling of loyalty to our own sex and an enthusiasm to have every degradation that was put upon our sex removed."[13] Despite occasional conflict over whether men should be brought into the movement, the NWP retained a separatist strategy. To ensure that the Party remain committed to its original vision— collective action by women for women—wealthy benefactor Alva Belmont included a clause in her bequest revoking her legacy if men ever joined or participated in the organization.

In addition to reinforcing feminist beliefs, the culture harbored at Belmont House fulfilled expressive and symbolic functions that contributed to the survival of feminism. Women who lived and worked at the house became, for some, the "Woman's Party family." Many who could not live at the house, because of family, work, and financial constraints, made regular pilgrimages in order to remain a part of the women's community. One member wrote that she was "looking forward with joy to my return home, and *Home* to me now, means the dear Alva Belmont House."[14] In fact, bringing friends to Belmont House was the primary way that women recruited new members.

Personal ties of love and friendship among members were an important cultural ideal. A willingness to shape personal relationships around the cause was, in large measure, what made possible the intense commitment of members. NWP members described their ties as mother-daughter or sororal relationships, and members' letters to one another were filled with expressions of intimacy and friendship. Ties among members took the form of close friendships, intense devotion to Alice Paul, and couple relationships. Having another woman as life partner seemed to facilitate feminist work because these women's personal lives meshed well with their political commitments.

Movement organizations that cultivate and sustain rich symbolic lives, then, enhance the abeyance function by helping to hold members. This finding is consistent with other research that demonstrates

that commitment to peers and to a shared political community promotes sustained involvement in social movements (Rosenthal and Schwartz forthcoming; McAdam 1988; White 1988).

In summary, I have described the NWP in the post-1945 period as an organizational pattern characterized by high longevity of attachment; intense levels of individual commitment to movement goals and tactics; high exclusiveness in terms of membership; high centralization that ensures a relatively advanced level of specialized skills among core activists; and a rich political culture that promotes continued involvement in the movement. This appears to be the ideal combination of factors necessary to hold a movement in abeyance until the external forces make it possible to resume a more mass-based challenge.

Consequences for the Resurgent Women's Movement

However movement success is measured, the women's rights movement from 1945 to the mid-1960s was not successful in its own time. But a more important question is: what consequences, if any, did the actions of feminists in this period have for the revitalized movement for gender equality in the late 1960s? The founding of the National Organization for Women (NOW) in 1966 serves as a useful signpost marking the rise of the contemporary women's movement. NOW brought together labor union activists, government employees, and longtime feminist activists and took leadership of the liberal branch of the movement (Freeman 1975). At about the same time, younger women involved in the civil rights and New Left movement formed the more locally organized radical branch.

Studies have not generally recognized connections between the existing women's rights movement and the resurgent one. My analysis suggests three ways in which the activism of the NWP shaped the feminist challenge that followed. It provided preexisting *activist networks,* an existing repertoire of *goals and tactics,* and a *collective identity* that justified feminist opposition. These elements constitute the most important consequences of abeyance structures for future mobilization around persistent discontents.

Activist Networks

A substantial body of research documents the significance of preexisting links and organizational ties among individuals for the rise of collective action (e.g., Snow, Zurcher, and Ekland-Olson 1980; Freeman 1979, 1983; Rosenthal et al. 1985). The feminist network of the 1940s and 1950s affected the resurgent movement of the 1960s in two ways. First, activism by NWP members played a crucial role in two key events: the establishment of the President's Commission on the Status of Women, convened by President Kennedy in 1961, and the inclusion of sex in Title VII of the Civil Rights Act of 1964, which forbade discrimination in employment. Second, many women who participated in the struggle for women's rights in the 1940s and 1950s became active in the resurgent women's movement, especially the liberal branch. NWP members were among the founders and charter members of NOW. Of the 10 individuals who signed NOW's original Statement of Purpose, 4 were members of the NWP (Friedan 1976). In her account of the early years of NOW, founder Betty Friedan (1976, pp. 110–17) describes an "underground network" of longtime committed feminists who provided crucial resources necessary for the formation of NOW. Even Alice Paul joined NOW, although she criticized NOW members for acting "as if they've discovered the whole idea."[15]

Although less common, a few NWP members established ties to the radical branch. One member met with the women's caucus of the National Conference on New Politics in Chicago in 1967, a conference that helped spark the formation of the radical branch. Another member attended a speech by Kate Millett at Purdue University in the early 1970s and handed out ERA literature to the crowd. Contrasting vividly the feminists of her generation with those of the 1970s, she noted that she was the only one there in a hat and that everyone else, including Millett, had long hair.[16] Thus a committed core of activists helped to provide resources for a resurgent more mass-based movement.

Goals and Tactical Choices

Tilly's (1979) concept of repertoires of collective action provides the greatest insight into the ways

that actions of a challenging group at a given point in time can affect actions of a subsequent group. Thus, the forms of action available to a group are not unlimited but are restricted by time, place, and group characteristics. Movement goals and strategies are learned, and they change slowly. Extending Tilly's hypothesis, the array of collective actions that a movement develops to sustain itself should influence the goals and tactics adopted by the same movement in subsequent mass mobilizations.

This is indeed the case with respect to the American women's rights movement. Although the NWP abandoned disruptive and militant strategies after the suffrage victory, it retained the same goal—a constitutional amendment. Largely as a result of NWP pressure, NOW voted at its second conference in 1967 to endorse the ERA, which became the most unifying goal of the movement by the 1970s (Ferree and Hess 1985; Taylor 1989). Further, NOW adopted many of the NWP's institutionalized tactics, such as lobbying, letter writing, and pressuring the political parties. NOW even made use of the NWP's political connections and its list of ERA sponsors.

The ERA example illustrates the ways that existing repertoires of action can both facilitate and constrain a movement. The final campaign for the ERA in the late 1970s and early 1980s mobilized massive numbers of participants, swelling the ranks of NOW to almost 200,000 and its budget to nearly 3 million dollars (Gelb and Palley 1982; Mueller unpublished). During its early years, with its equal rights emphasis which appealed mainly to white and middle-class women, NOW alienated black and union women (Giddings 1984). Thus, the liberal branch of the contemporary women's movement, by adopting the goals and strategies of earlier feminists, found it difficult to shake the class and race limitations of its predecessors.

For a movement to survive periods of relative hiatus, it must develop a battery of specialized tactics that can be carried out by an activist cadre without the support of a mass base (Oliver and Marwell 1988). These become a part of a group's repertoire of collective action and influence the subsequent range of actions available to future challenges.

Collective Identity

Collective identity is the shared definition of a group that derives from its members common interests and solidarity. Although resource mobilization theorists minimize the importance of group identity and consciousness in the rise of social movements (McCarthy and Zald 1973, 1977; Jenkins and Perrow 1977), these factors are central to theorists of the "new social movements" (e.g., Pizzorno 1978; Cohen 1985; Melucci 1985; Klandermans 1986). They suggest that, by definition, social movements create a collective oppositional consciousness. Mueller's (1987, p. 90) research on the women's movement suggests that changes in consciousness can have long-term significance because they can serve as a resource for future mobilization.

The creation of a shared collective identity requires the group to revise its history and develop symbols to reinforce movement goals and strategies (Gusfield 1970, p. 309–13). For the 1960s women's movement, the NWP, because of its ties to suffrage, became an important symbol of the long history of women's oppression and resistance. As a result of its historical significance and prime location, Belmont House was used throughout the 1970s for celebrations of women's movement history, as a temporary residence for scholars and students engaged in feminist research, and as a place for ERA lobbyists to meet. Moreover, Alice Paul, who earlier had sparked so many conflicts, became the quintessential symbol of feminist commitment. In 1977, NOW sponsored a birthday benefit for her at Belmont House that was attended by members of a wide range of feminist organizations. Even after Paul's death in 1977, the NWP continued to list her as founder on its letterhead and to advertise "Alice Paul Jail Jewelry," a replica of the famous jailhouse door pin proudly worn by imprisoned suffragists.

The significance of the NWP grew as younger and more radical women discovered the legacy of militant feminism. Even in 1981, the NWP's symbolic importance remained great enough to inspire an attempted takeover by a group of younger feminists, led by Sonia Johnson, who claimed the militants who first formed the NWP as their foremothers and even adopted the original name of the Party. Ironically, as the contemporary women's movement grew stronger and more militant, the actual heirs of the early militants grew increasingly isolated and less central in the struggle for women's rights.

In an abeyance phase, a social movement organization uses internally oriented activities to build a structure through which it can maintain its identity, ideals, and political vision. The collective identity that it constructs and maintains within a shared political community can become an important symbolic resource for subsequent mobilizations.

Conclusion

This paper presents new data that challenge the traditional view that no organized feminist challenge survived in the 1940s and 1950s. I have used the NWP case to highlight the processes by which social movements maintain continuity between different cycles of peak activity. I analyze the factors associated with adaptations of Mizruchi's (1983) abeyance process. Abeyance is essentially a holding pattern of a group which continues to mount some type of challenge even in a nonreceptive political environment. Factors that contribute to abeyance are both external and internal to the movement. Externally, a discrepancy between a surplus of activists and a lack of status opportunities for integrating them into the mainstream creates conditions for abeyance. Internally, structures arise that permit organizations to absorb and hold a committed cadre of activists. These abeyance structures, in turn, promote movement continuity and are employed in later rounds of mass mobilization.

Although any theory based on a single case is open to challenge, recent research points to the utility of the abeyance model for understanding other movements of the 1960s, particularly the civil rights (McAdam 1988), New Left (Gittlin 1987; Isserman 1987; Hayden 1988), and gay rights (D'Emilio 1983) movements. But this work has not yet had major impact on revising theory about the sixties movements or on social movement theory in general.

Why have scholars of social movements neglected sources of continuity between cycles of movement activity and, instead, preferred an "immaculate conception" interpretation of social movements? First, scholars generally are more interested in movements undergoing cycles of mass mobilization and have done little research on movements in decline and equilibrium. Second, the limited conceptualization of movement organization in the literature has perpetuated classical conceptions of social movements as numerically large and mass-based. Research on a variety of organizational forms, including becalmed movements (Zald and Ash 1966), professional movements (McCarthy and Zald 1973), movement halfway houses (Morris 1984), elite-sustained movements (Rupp and Taylor 1987), and consensus movements (McCarthy and Wolfson unpublished), is now challenging the classical view by suggesting that these types of movements are capable of sustained activism in nonreceptive political climates (Staggenborg 1988). Third, existing approaches overlook social movement continuity by neglecting to think about outcomes (Gamson 1975). Focusing on sort-term gains ignores the possibility that social reform proceeds in a ratchetlike fashion, where the gains of one struggle become the resources for later challenges by the same aggrieved group (Tarrow 1983).

The research presented above specifies the ways that organizational and ideological bridges span different stages of mobilization. Most movements have thresholds or turning points in mobilization which scholars have taken for "births" and "deaths." This research suggests that movements do not die, but scale down and retrench to adapt to changes in the political climate. Perhaps movements are never really born anew: Rather, they contract and hibernate, sustaining the totally dedicated and devising strategies appropriate to the external environment. If this is the case, our task as sociologists shifts from refining theories of movement emergence to accounting for fluctuations in the nature and scope of omnipresent challenges.

NOTES

This paper is part of a larger collaborative study of the American women's rights movement conducted with Leila J. Rupp. The research was supported by a Basic Research Grant (RO-'0703-81) from the National Endowment for the Humanities and by grants from The Ohio State University. A Radcliffe Research Scholars fellowship awarded to Rupp supported a great deal of the documentary research. I thank Joan Huber, Craig Jenkins, Carol Mueller, Laurel Richardson, Leila Rupp, Mayer Zald, and the *ASR* reviewers for helpful comments on earlier drafts.

1. This analysis of the leadership and core membership is based on a careful reading of archival material, particularly correspondence, as well as research in biographical sources. For 55 women identified as leaders and core members, information was recorded about race, class, education, occupation, age, place of residence, political affiliation, political views, marital status, presence and number of children, living situation, and time of first involvement in the women's movement. In addition, any comments made by participants about the social characteristics of the membership were noted.

2. Florence Kitchelt to Katharine Ludington. August 14, 1950, Florence Kitchelt papers, box 6 (175). Schlesinger Library (SL), Radcliffe College, Cambridge, Massachusetts.

3. Katharine Hepburn, speech to the Connecticut Committee, n.d.[1946], Kitchelt papers, box 6 (153), SL.

4. Betty Gram Swing to Ethel Ernest Murrell, October 3, 1952, National Woman's Party (NWP) papers, reel 99.

5. Mary Kennedy to Agnes Wells, July 12, 1950, NWP papers, reel 97.

6. Joseph E. Talbot to Florence Kitchelt, February 12, 1945, Kitchelt papers, box 8 (234), SL.

7. Mamie Sydney Mizen to Florence Armstrong, October 25, 1948. NWP papers, reel 94.

8. Open letter from Ernestine Bellamy to Ethel Ernest Murrell, May 24, 1953, NWP papers, reel 99.

9. I use the term "chairman" because that was the term used at the time. It seems historically inaccurate to change this usage.

10. Interview no. 2.

11. Laura Berrien and Doris Stevens, "An Open Letter to Miss Alice Paul," Committee on Information, Bulletin No. 4, July 30, 1947, Katharine A. Norris papers, box 2 (7), SL.

12. Rose Arnold Powell, diary entry, Nov. 2, 1960, Powell papers, box 1, v. 8, SL; Rose Arnold Powell to Mary Beard, June 23, 1948, Powell papers, box 2 (27), SL.

13. Alice Paul, "Conversations With Alice Paul: Woman Suffrage and the Equal Rights Amendment," an oral history conducted in 1972 and 1973 by Amelia R. Fry, Regional Oral History Office, University of California, 1976, p. 197.

14. Mary Alice Matthews to Alice Paul, March 24, 1945, NWP papers, reel 85.

15. Interview no. 12.

16. Mary Kennedy to Alice Paul, February 11, 1971, NWP papers, reel 112.

33.

The Consequences of Professionalization and Formalization in the Pro-Choice Movement

SUZANNE STAGGENBORG

As a result of the conceptual work of McCarthy and Zald (1973, 1977), the notion of the "professionalized" social movement is now firmly associated with the "resource mobilization" approach to collective action (cf. Jenkins 1983). They argue that professionalized movements are increasingly common as a result of increases in sources of funding for activists who make careers out of being movement leaders. In contrast to what they term "classical" movement organizations, which rely on the mass mobilization of "beneficiary" constituents as active participants, "professional" social movement organizations (SMOs) rely primarily on paid leaders and "conscience" constituents who contribute money and are paper members rather than active participants. Importantly, this analysis suggests that social movements can be launched with adequate funding. "Entrepreneurs" can mobilize sentiments into movement organizations without the benefit of precipitating events or "suddenly imposed major grievances" (Walsh 1981) and without established constituencies.

McCarthy and Zald's analysis of professional movement organizations recognizes that there are different types of movement participants and different types of SMOs, which require different levels and types of participation. Although few theorists have expanded on the McCarthy-Zald analysis of professional movement organizations (exceptions are Cable 1984; Jenkins and Eckert 1986; Kleidman 1986; and Oliver 1983), such conceptual

Staggenborg, Suzanne. 1988. "The Consequences of Professionalization and Formalization in the Pro-Choice Movement." *American Sociological. Review* 53: 585–606. Reprinted by permission of American Sociological Association.

development is important because different types of organizational structures and participants have consequences for movement goals and activities. Examination of the effects of organizational leadership and structure is relevant to debates over movement outcomes, such as those generated by Piven and Cloward's (1977) thesis that large formal movement organizations diffuse protest.

This paper explores the consequences of professionalization in social movements by analyzing the impact of leadership and organizational structure in the pro-choice movement. My analysis is based on documentary and interview data gathered on the pro-choice movement (Staggenborg 1985) and focuses on a sample of 13 pro-choice movement organizations, including 6 national organizations and 7 state and local organizations from Illinois and Chicago (see Table 1). Documentary data cover the histories of the organizations from their beginnings to 1983.[1]

Fifty individuals were interviewed, including leaders and rank-and-file activists, who were active in the organizations during different periods. I analyze the changes in leadership and internal structures of the SMOs and the impact of these changes on the movement. In particular, I focus on changes in three major periods of the abortion conflict: the years prior to legalization of abortion in 1973; 1973 to 1976, when Congress first passed the Hyde Amendment cutoff of federal funding of abortion; and 1977–1983 following the antiabortion victory on the Hyde Amendment.

I begin by making some conceptual distinctions among three types of movement leaders and two major types of SMOs and then use these distinctions to classify the organizations by structure (see Table 2). Next, I examine the impact of leadership on

Table 1 Sample of National and State/Local Pro-Choice SMOs

	Dates
National Organizations	
National Abortion Rights Action League (NARAL), formerly National Association for the Repeal of Abortion Laws (NARAL) until 1973	1969–
Religion Coalition for Abortion Rights (RCAR)	1973–
Zero Population Growth (ZPG)	1968–
National Organization for Women (NOW)	1966–
National Women's Health Network (NWHN)	1975–
Reproductive Rights National Network (R2N2)	1978–1984
State/Local Organizations	
National Abortion Rights Action League of Illinois (NARAL of Illinois), formerly Illinois Citizens for the Medical Control of Abortion (ICMCA) until 1975 and Abortion Rights Association of Illinois (ARA) until 1978	1966–
Illinois Religious Coalition for Abortion Rights (IRCAR)	1975–
Chicago-area Zero Population Growth (Chicago-area ZPG)	1970–1977
Chicago Women's Liberation Union (CWLU)	1969–1977
Chicago National Organization for Women (Chicago NOW)	1969–
Chicago Women's Health Task Force (CWHTF)	1977–1979
Women Organized for Reproductive Choice (WORC)	1979–

the formation of movement organizations and the formalization of SMOs. Then I examine the impact of formalization on the maintenance of SMOs, their strategies and tactics, and coalition work. Tables 3 through 6 summarize data for each SMO on the pattern of leadership and structural influence. More detailed case material illuminates processes under certain circumstances that may be more generalizable. Finally, I argue that the professionalization of social movements and activists does not necessarily help expand the social movement sector by initiating activities and organizations, but that professionalization and formalization importantly affect the structure and maintenance of social movement organizations, their strategies and tactics, and their participation in coalition work.

Conceptual Distinctions
Types of Leadership in SMOs

With the professionalization of social movements and the availability of funding for staff positions, several types of leaders are found in SMOs (cf. McCarthy and Zald 1977, p. 1227; Oliver 1983, pp. 163–64). *Professional managers* are paid staff who make careers out of movement work. Professional managers are likely to move from one SMO to another and from movement to movement over their careers (see McCarthy and Zald 1973, p. 15). Two types of *nonprofessional leaders* are *volunteer leaders* and *nonprofessional staff leaders*. Volunteer leaders are not paid.[2]

Nonprofessional staff leaders are compensated for some or all of their time, but are not career

Table 2 Organizational Structures of Sample SMOs over Time

SMO	Pre-1973	1973–76	1977–83
National			
NARAL	informal	transition to formalized	formalized
RCAR		formalized	formalized
ZPG	informal	informal	transition to formalized
NOW	informal	transition to formalized	formalized
NWHN		informal	transition to formalized
R2N2			informal
State/Local			
ICMCA/ARA/NARAL	informal	informal	formalized
IRCAR		informal	transition to formalized
Chicago-area ZPG	informal	(inactive)	(inactive)
Chicago NOW	informal	transition to formalized	formalized
CWLU	informal	informal	
CWHTF			informal
WORC			informal

Note: Details on organizational structures of sample SMOs are provided in Tables 3 and 4.

activists. Rather, they serve as SMO staff for a short term and do not regard movement work as a career. As I argue below, there may be significant differences in orientation of leaders within this category based on whether the nonprofessional staff leader is temporarily dependent on the movement income for a living. Those who are dependent on the income may behave like professional managers in some respects, whereas those with other sources of income (or those willing to live at subsistence level) may behave more like volunteers. All three types of leaders are, by definition, involved in organizational decision making. All three are also included in the category of *activists,* as are other nonleader members who are actively involved in the SMO as opposed to being paper members.

Paid leaders, then, may or may not be "professionals" in the sense of making careers out of

movement work and, as Oliver (1983, p. 158) shows, may come from the "same pool" as volunteers. Of course, leaders who do not begin as movement professionals may become career activists. Both professional and nonprofessional leaders learn skills (e.g., public relations skills) that they can easily transfer from one organization to another and from one cause to another. Both professionals and nonprofessionals can serve as *entrepreneurs*—leaders who initiate movements, organizations, and tactics (cf. Kleidman 1986, pp. 191–92). However, as I argue below, nonprofessional leaders are more likely to initiate movements (as opposed to SMOs) and tactics than are professionals.

Types of Movement Organizations

Changes in the structures of SMOs have occurred along with the professionalization of social

Table 3 Organizational Characteristics of Sample SMOs: Informal SMOs

SMO	Decision-making Structure and Division of Labor	Membership Criteria/Records	Connections to Subunits	Leadership
Pre-1973 NARAL	informal control by small group of leaders on executive committee; board of directors representative of state organizations had no power; little division of labor	list of supporters rather than formal members, not formally maintained	loose connections to completely autonomous organizational members	volunteers and one nonprofessional staff director
Pre-1977 ZPG	control by self-appointed board of directors; no participation by rank-and-file membership in national decision making; division of labor between Washington lobbying office and California office	dues-paying membership, but sloppy record keeping, little follow-up on members	loose connections to completely autonomous chapters	volunteers
Pre-1973 NOW	elected board and officers; major decisions made by membership at annual conference; division of labor between administrative office, public information office, and legislative office	dues-paying membership, lack of reliable membership records	very poor communication with chapters, lack of national-local coordination	volunteers
Pre-1977 NWHN	decision making by informally recruited board of directors and five founders; informal division of labor	local organizations signed up by founders, no criteria for active involvement	loose connections to completely autonomous organizational members	volunteers
R2N2	decision making initially done by membership at two annual membership conferences; regionally elected steering committee and annual membership conference; informal division of labor	membership open to any organization sharing principles; no criteria for active involvement	difficulty integrating many organizational members into organization	volunteers and one staff coordinator

	Decision making and division of labor	Membership	Subunits	Staff
ICMCA/ARA	informal decision making by board and executive director; informal division of labor created by director as needed	list of supporters rather than formal members	informal connection to autonomous "chapters" in other parts of state	volunteers and nonprofessional staff director
Pre-1977 IRCAR	Policy Council of informally selected individuals active in member denominations; informal division of labor among small group of activists	religious organizations in agreement with principles; no criteria for active participation	difficulty in involving subunits in organization	volunteer leaders and coordinator
Chicago-area ZPG	informal decision making and division of labor among small number of activists and coordinator	no formal membership or records	loose connections to area chapters until they declined	volunteers
Pre-1973 Chicago NOW	informal decision making by board consisting of most active members; informal creation of committees by interested members	dues-paying membership	committees form and act independently	volunteers
CWLU	decision making by steering committee and in citywide meetings of membership; many experiments with structure, attempts to involve all members	list of supporters, dues initially voluntary, later required but not always collected; anyone active in workgroup or chapter was a "member"	loosely connected workgroups and chapters that were completely autonomous	volunteers and nonprofessional, part-time staff
CWHTF	informal decision making and division of labor by small group of activists	exclusive "membership" of small group of friends	no subunits	volunteers
WORC	changing structure consisting of steering committee and various issue and work committees; attempts to rotate tasks and include all members	list of supporters; members include anyone who participates	typically not large enough for subunits; committees form and dissolve as needed	volunteers and one part-time nonprofessional staff

Table 4 Organizational Characteristics of Sample SMOs: Formalized SMOs (including SMOs in transition to formalized structure)

SMO	Decision-making Structure and Division of Labor	Membership Criteria/Records	Connections to Subunits	Leadership
Post-1973 NARAL	decision making by elected board of directors, executive committee; division of labor by function with paid staff as lobbyists, media experts, fundraisers, etc.	dues-paying membership, professional direct-mail techniques	formalized connections to affiliates; training and funds provided	professional leaders along with volunteer board
RCAR	decision making by board of directors consisting of formal representatives of denominational members; division of labor by function using paid staff	denominations that agree with principles; expectation of active involvement	financial support to affiliates that report activities annually to national organization	professional leaders together with volunteer board members
Post-1977 ZPG	decision making by board of directors and staff; division of labor by function using paid staff	dues-paying membership, professional direct mail; list of active members who participate in letter writing	some financial aid for chapter projects; formal guidelines for chapters developed	professional staff along with volunteer board
Post-1973 NOW	decision making by elected board and officers and delegates at national convention; division of labor by function using paid staff	dues-paying individuals, professional direct mail; chapters	communication with chapters established as national organization expanded staff and increased finances; state and regional organizations created to further coordination	professional leaders

Post-1977 NWHN	decision making by formally elected board of directors; division of labor using paid staff	dues-paying membership, direct mail; attempts to actively involve organizational members	organization of first official chapters	professional staff together with volunteer board
NARAL of Illinois	decision making by board of directors elected on rotating basis; division of labor among committees using paid staff	dues-paying membership plus activists	committees created to perform needed tasks	professional director together with volunteer board
Post-1976 IRCAR	formally elected Policy Council consisting of representatives from member denominations; creation of area units of activists	denominations agreeing with principles; attempts to encourage more active participation	more formalized ties to members and creation of formal area units	paid part-time director and volunteers
Post-1973 Chicago NOW	elected officers and board of directors; committees based on priorities screened by board and voted by membership; division of labor increasingly based on function using paid staff	dues-paying members plus activists	committees tightly integrated into organization, no longer autonomous	professional staff and paid officers

Table 5 Consequences of SMOs: Informal Organizations

SMO	Maintenance/Expansion/Decline	Major Strategies and Tactics	Coalition Work
Pre-1973 NARAL	23 organizational members in states, 500–2,000 individual members, 1–2 staff, budgets of $30–70,000	demonstrations, support for abortion referral services, coordination of state lobbying campaigns, encouragement of litigation	minor participation in short-lived coalitions
Pre-1977 ZPG	high of 400 affiliates, 35,000 members in early 1970s; drop to about 60 affiliates, 8,500 members with budget of $350,000 in mid-70s	demonstrations, abortion referral work, state legislative lobbying, educational activities prior to 1973; Congressional lobbying, educational work after 1973	staff support for Congressional lobbying coalition after 1973
Pre-1973 NOW	initial membership of 1,200 individuals, 14 chapters; budget of $7,000 in 1967	participation in demonstrations on abortion	minor participation in short-lived coalitions
Pre-1977 NWHN	initial participation of about 50 activists	support for local demonstrations	no active participation
R2N2	50–90 affiliates, high budget of $50,000; dissolution in 1984 due to lack of resources	demonstrations; grassroots organizing; petition campaign against Hyde Amendment; educational work	experienced great difficulty in attempts to participate in lobbying coalition, lack of communication with other SMOs in coalition
ICMCA/ARA	active core of 30–35, part-time director, mailing list of about 700 contributors up until about 1976, when organization declined to about 60 paying members	demonstrations, state legislative lobbying, encouragement of litigation, educational activities prior to 1973; continued state legislative lobbying, Congressional letter-writing campaigns, educational work until decline in 1976	minor participation in largely unsuccessful pre-1973 coalition and short-lived 1977 coalition
Pre-1977 IRCAR	small core of activists: initial budget of $2,500, 8 denominational members, volunteer director through 1976	participation in demonstrations; lobbying in state legislature, letter-writing campaigns to Congress, educational activities	no major coalition work

	Membership	Activities	Coalition participation
Chicago-area ZPG	high of about 11 area chapters, low of 3 and small core of activists in early 1970s; largely inactive after 1973 with exception of failed attempt to revive the organization in 1977	participation in ICMCA demonstrations, lobbying activities prior to 1973; inactive after early 1970s	minor participation in largely unsuccessful pre-1973 coalition; endorsement of coalition activities in 1977 prior to dissolving
Pre-1973 Chicago NOW	about 20 active members, a few hundred paying members in early 1970s	participation in demonstrations, support for abortion referral work and support for ICMCA lobbying work by head of abortion committee	participation in short-lived coalitions
CWLU	200–300 active members, numerous chapters and work groups, mailing list of 900 by 1971; greatly reduced active membership and number of chapters and work groups by mid-70s; formally dissolved in 1977	demonstrations, illegal abortion service, educational work prior to 1973; community organizing project to improve access to abortion after legalization, pickets and meetings to pressure providers, formation of Health Evaluation and Referral Service to rate abortion clinics and influence standards of service delivery; decline in activity by 1975–76	participation in largely unsuccessful attempts at coalition work prior to 1973
CWHTF	never more than about 15 active members, dissolved in 1979	demonstrations, educational work to fight Medicaid funding cutoff in 1977	participation in short-lived coalition in 1977 characterized by a great deal of conflict
WORC	high of about 30 active members in late 1970s, decline to about 10 active members in early 1980s; 100–150 paying members	demonstrations, petition campaigns around Medicaid funding cutoffs and closing of public hospital abortion facility, educational work	experienced great difficulty in attempts to participate in Illinois Pro-Choice Alliance, eventually became inactive in coalition

Table 6 Consequences of SMO Structure: Formalized Organizations (including SMOs in transition to formalized structure)

SMO	Maintenance/Expansion/Decline	Major Strategies and Tactics	Coalition Work
Post-1973 NARAL	10,000 members, 4–8 staff, budget reaches $200,000 by 1976; 40 state affiliates, 140,000 members, 25 staff, budget reaches $3 million by 1983	Congressional lobbying, litigation from 1973 on; campaign work, PAC contributions, grassroots organizing beginning in late 1970s	began working in Congressional lobbying coalition in 1973; leadership role in lobbying coalition by mid- to late 1970s
RCAR	began with 24 organizational members, 13 affiliates, several staff, budget of $100,000; 31 organizational members and 28 affiliates, 8–10 staff and budget of $700,000 by 1983	educational work, Congressional lobbying since 1973; increased local organizing in late 1970s	began working in Congressional lobbying coalition in 1973; leadership role in lobbying coalition by mid- to late 1970s
Post-1977 ZPG	about 20 affiliates, 12,000 members, budget of $650,000	Congressional lobbying	cooperation in letter-writing campaigns in response to alerts from coalition leaders
Post-1973 NOW	40,000 members, 700 chapters by 1974; budget of $500,000 by 1976; membership reaches 250,000, budget reaches $6,500,000 by 1983	Congressional lobbying work, educational work after 1973; political campaign work and PAC contributions by late 1970s	participation in Congressional lobbying coalition
Post-1977 NWHN	membership of 300 organizations, 13,000 individuals, budget of $300,000 by 1983	educational work; Congressional testimony	participation in Congressional lobbying coalition
NARAL of Illinois	high of 200 active members, 4,000 paying members, budget of $80,000, full-time director and 3–4 part-time staff in early 1980s	legislative lobbying in late 1970s combined with political campaign work in early 1980s	participation in coalitions in late 1970s; leadership role in Illinois Pro-Choice Alliance
Post-1976 IRCAR	mailing list of 600–15,000, 13 denominational members, part-time paid director; budget high of $10,000	legislative lobbying, educational work; expansion of state organizing efforts in 1980s	participation in coalitions in late 1970s; increased role in 1980s
Post-1973 Chicago NOW	about 500 paying members, budget of $10,000 in mid-1970s; about 50 active members, 3,000 paying members, budget of $175,000 by 1984	legislative lobbying and political campaign work in late 1970s and 1980s	participation in lobbying coalition in late 1970s and 1980s

movement leadership. In contrast to "classical" SMOs, which have mass memberships of beneficiary constituents, McCarthy and Zald (1973, 1977) argue that movement organizations with professional leadership have nonexistent or "paper" memberships and rely heavily on resources from constituents outside of the group(s) that benefit from movement achievements. Professional movement activists are thought to act as entrepreneurs who form such organizations by appealing to conscience constituents. The difficulty with this characterization of the structural changes in SMOs led by professionals is, as Oliver (1983) notes, that many such SMOs have both active and paper memberships. Similarly, organizations may rely on a mix of conscience and beneficiary constituents for resources.

An alternative characterization of structural differences in SMOs is based on differences in operating procedures. *Formalized* SMOs[3] have established procedures or structures that enable them to perform certain tasks routinely and to continue to function with changes in leadership. Formalized SMOs have bureaucratic procedures for decision making, a developed division of labor with positions for various functions, explicit criteria for membership, and rules governing subunits (chapters or committees). For example, the formalized SMO may have a board of directors that meets a set number of times per year to make organizational policy; an executive committee of the board that meets more frequently to make administrative decisions; staff members who are responsible for contacts with the mass media, direct mail campaigns, and so forth; chapters that report to the national organization; and an individual rank-and-file membership. As I argue below, this type of SMO structure is associated with the professionalization of leadership. In contrast, *informal* SMOs[4] have few established procedures, loose membership requirements, and minimal division of labor. Decisions in informal organizations tend to be made in an ad hoc rather than routine manner (cf. Rothschild-Whitt 1979, p. 513). The organizational structure of an informal SMO is frequently adjusted; assignments among personnel and procedures are developed to meet immediate needs. Because informal SMOs lack

established procedures, individual leaders can exert an important influence on the organization: major changes in SMO structure and activities are likely to occur with changes in leadership. Any subunits of informal SMOs, such as work groups or chapters, tend to be autonomous and loosely connected to one another. Informal organizations are dominated by nonprofessional, largely volunteer, leaders.

The SMOs in my sample are classified by structure in Table 2 based on the above criteria; details explaining the classifications are provided in Table 3.[5] The major categories of formalized and informal SMOs are, of course, ideal types. In reality, some SMOs share elements of each type, often because they are in the process of changing structures. When SMOs formalize, they typically do so very gradually. Some SMOs look formalized on paper, but are informal in practice. Important differences also appear among SMOs within each of the two major categories (e.g., some are centralized and others decentralized; cf. Gamson 1975). Nevertheless, the two major types of SMOs do differ from one another in important ways discussed below.

The Impact of Professional Leadership
The Initiation of Social Movements
Because professional movement activists can easily transfer their skills from one movement to another, McCarthy and Zald suggest that professional activists are likely to become entrepreneurs who start new organizations in which to work. If this is the case, an increase in movement careers should help to expand the social movement sector. Grievances can be manufactured by professional activists and SMOs, making the formation of social movements at least partially independent of overt grievances and environmental conditions (cf. Oberschall 1973, p. 158).

The McCarthy-Zald argument has been challenged on grounds of lack of evidence that professional managers and their SMOs originate insurgent challenges, although they may play a role in representing unorganized groups in more established interest group politics (Jenkins and Eckert 1986. p. 812). In the case of the civil rights movement, researchers have shown that informal indigenous SMOs initiated and led the movement

(Morris 1984; Jenkins and Eckert 1986). In the case of the pro-choice movement, all of the SMOs in my sample that were active in the early movement were informal SMOs (see Table 2). The leaders who initiated SMOs that formed in the period prior to legalization were all nonprofessional leaders, mostly volunteers (see Table 3).

Professional managers may act as entrepreneurs in creating SMOs (as opposed to movements and collective action), but my data, together with cases from the literature, suggest that professionals are less likely than nonprofessionals to act as entrepreneurs. When professionals do initiate movement organizations, they are likely to be formalized rather than informal SMOs. Common Cause, for example, was initiated by a professional manager who created a formalized organization (see McFarland 1984). Many community organizations, which are often created by professional leaders, are also formally organized (see Delgado 1986). In my sample only the national Religious Coalition for Abortion Rights (RCAR) was initiated by individuals who might be called professional leaders; they included a staff member of the United Methodist Board of Church and Society. All of the other SMOs in my sample were initially organized by nonprofessional activists as informal SMOs (see Tables 2, 3, and 4). Significantly, RCAR is also distinctive in that it originated as a formalized organization to mobilize existing organizations for institutionalized tactics (e.g., lobbying Congress) in a period when the movement as a whole was becoming more established.[6]

Given the lack of evidence that movement professionals initiate movements and informal SMOs, it is necessary to reconsider the relationship between the roles of movement "professional" and movement "entrepreneur." McCarthy and Zald suggest that, in response to the availability of resources, movement professionals become movement entrepreneurs, initiating movement activities and organizations because they are career activists looking for preferences to mobilize. Although no systematic evidence on the entrepreneurial activities of professional and nonprofessional leaders has been collected, my data indicate that the roles of "entrepreneur" and "professional" are, in some cases, distinct (cf. Roche and Sachs 1965).

An example of a nonprofessional entrepreneur in the abortion movement is Lawrence Lader, a writer and family planning advocate who published a book (Lader 1966) reporting on the large number of abortions being performed by licensed physicians in the U.S. and advocating legal abortion. After his research was published, Lader was inundated with requests for the names of doctors from women seeking abortions. He began to make referrals to women and then announced his referral service publicly as a strategy intended "to stir as much controversy and debate as possible while bringing the facts to the public" (Lader 1973, p. xi). Lader played a role in getting others to employ this strategy, including the clergy who founded the Clergy Consultation Services on Abortion (see Carmen and Moody 1973). He later helped to found NARAL in 1969 and, more recently, founded another organization, the Abortion Rights Mobilization. Although remaining intensely interested in abortion and related family planning issues, Lader has not made a professional career out of his movement work; he continued to pursue his career as a writer while playing an entrepreneurial role in the movement.

Examples of nonentrepreneurial professionals in the pro-choice movement who have moved among established movement and political positions include Karen Mulhauser, an executive director of NARAL who became the executive director of Citizens Against Nuclear War after leaving NARAL in 1981. The NARAL director who succeeded her, Nanette Falkenberg, had previously been involved in union organizing work. In Illinois, the first professional leader of NARAL of Illinois was involved in community organizing work before taking the position of NARAL executive director and became a staff member of a political campaign after leaving NARAL.

These examples suggest that different factors may be responsible for the creation of two distinct roles. Movement entrepreneurs, the initiators of movement organizations and activities, may become paid activists who benefit from the existence of the same resources that support professional managers, but they typically do not make careers out of moving from one cause to another and they may never find paid positions that suit them. Rather, they found movement organizations and initiate tactics for the same reasons that other constituents join them. That is, they have personal experiences and ideological commitments which make them interested in the particular issue(s) of the movement. They are also tied into the social networks and preexisting organizational structures that allow the movement to mobilize and are influenced by environmental developments (e.g., legalization of abortion in 1973) that make movement issues salient and provide opportunities for action (cf. Oliver 1983).

Professional managers, on the other hand, are not likely to be the initiators of social movements. They make careers out of service to SMOs and are often hired to come into SMOs that already have formal structures or are in the process of becoming formalized. Professional leaders are likely to care very much about the cause of the SMO—even if they aren't initially motivated out of particular concern for the issue(s) of the SMO. However, professionals' concerns with the particular causes of SMOs are part of their more general concern for a range of issues—the orientation toward social activism that made them choose a professional reform career.

Professionalization and the Formalization of SMOs

Not only are movement entrepreneur and professional distinct roles, but movement entrepreneurs and other nonprofessionals are likely to differ from professional managers in their organizational structure preferences. While McCarthy and Zald (1977) suggest that movement entrepreneurs create "professional" SMOs, my data support the argument that movement entrepreneurs prefer informal structures and may resist creation of formalized SMOs run by professional leaders. The professionalization of social movements (i.e., the rise of career leadership) is associated with the formalization of SMOs for two reasons: (1) professional managers tend to formalize the organizations that they lead; and (2) the SMOs that have the resources to hire professional managers are those with formalized structures.

Movement entrepreneurs prefer informal structures that enable them to maintain personal control. As the analogy to business entrepreneurs suggests,

movement entrepreneurs are risk-takers (cf. Oliver 1983) who initiate movement organizations without certainty of success, just as capitalist entrepreneurs risk investment in new products. Like capitalist entrepreneurs, movement entrepreneurs are likely to be personally involved in the enterprise, desiring personal control over decision making because they have taken the risks to establish an organization or movement. In contrast to the professional manager who brings skills to an organization and expects to operate within an established structure, movement entrepreneurs may try to prevent the creation of an organizational structure in which decision making is routinized and, therefore, less subject to personal control.

The history of leadership in NARAL, which was founded in 1969 as the National Association for the Repeal of Abortion Laws, reveals that conflict between entrepreneurial leadership and formalization occurs in some circumstances. NARAL founders were not professional movement organizers in the sense of being career movement activists; rather, they were persons who had become dedicated to the cause of legal abortion as a result of their prior experiences, primarily in the family planning and population movements that provided the most important organizational bases for the rise of the single-issue abortion movement (see Staggenborg 1985). Because the decision-making structure was informal (see Table 3), a movement entrepreneur who became chairman of the executive committee exerted a large amount of control over the organization; as he commented in a 1984 interview about his own style of leadership:

> Let's face it....I don't believe in endless meetings, I like to make quick decisions. Maybe I acted unilaterally sometimes, although I was always careful to check with the executive committee. Some people objected to my calling [other members of the executive committee] and getting their approval on the phone. [But] we couldn't meet, we had to move fast, so I polled the exec committee around the country by phone. (Personal interview)

Although there were some disagreements among NARAL executive committee members in the pre-1973 years, the informal decision-making structure seems to have worked fairly well at a time when the movement was very young, abortion was illegal in most states, and it was necessary to act quickly to take advantage of opportunities for action and to meet crises (e.g., the arrests of leaders involved in abortion referral activities).

After legalization, however, conflict over the decision-making structure occurred as NARAL attempted to establish itself as a lobbying force in Washington and to expand by organizing state affiliates. At this point, there was a power struggle within the organization between long-time leaders and entrepreneurs of NARAL and newer activists who objected to "power being concentrated in the hands of a few men in New York City" and who supported having persons "who are doing the work of the field—the State Coordinators" on the board (documents in NARAL of Illinois papers; University of Illinois at Chicago). The latter faction won a critical election in 1974 resulting in a turnover of leadership on the NARAL executive committee. Although the executive committee remained the decision-making body of the organization, practices such as the use of proxy votes and phone calls to make important decisions were discontinued (personal interview with 1974 NARAL executive director), resulting in more formalized decision-making procedures that involved more activists at different levels. Another major change that occurred at this point was that for the first time the executive director and other paid staff became more important than the nonprofessional entrepreneurs as NARAL leaders. It was only with the defeat of movement entrepreneurs as organizational leaders that NARAL began to formalize and eventually grew into a large organization capable of acting in institutionalized arenas.[7]

If movement entrepreneurs interfere with the formalization of SMOs, as this case suggests, professional managers encourage formalization. While informal structures are associated with nonprofessional leadership, all of the organizations in my sample that have moved toward a more formal structure have done so under the leadership of professional managers (see Tables 3 and 4). Although further study of the leadership styles of professional managers compared to nonprofessional SMO leaders is necessary, my data suggest some reasons why

professional managers tend to formalize the SMOs that they lead. Insofar as a bureaucratic or formalized structure is associated with organizational maintenance (Gamson 1975), professional leaders have a strong motivation to promote formalization: ongoing resources are needed to pay the salary of the professional manager. However, the motivation to promote financial stability is also shared by nonprofessional staff who are dependent on their income from the SMO position; moreover, it is possible to secure stable funding by means other than formalization. It is also important that professional managers are interested in using and developing organizing skills and expanding the SMOs they lead because this is what they do for a career. A formalized structure, with its developed division of labor, enables the professional manager to achieve a degree of organizational development not possible in informal SMOs.

The case of the Abortion Rights Association of Illinois (formerly Illinois Citizens for the Medical Control of Abortion and later NARAL of Illinois) reveals the role of professional leadership in the creation of organizational stability and bureaucracy. From 1970 to 1976, ICMCA/ARA was led by a nonprofessional director who was paid a small salary, but who volunteered much of her time and was often not paid on time due to financial problems of the organization. She was extremely effective, but did not create a structure such that others could easily carry on her work. Rather, organizational activities were carried out by force of her personality.[8] Moreover, volunteer efforts were channeled into instrumental tactics like lobbying, and little emphasis was placed on organizational maintenance activities such as fundraising. When she resigned in early 1976, ARA entered a period of severe decline due to inept leadership and neglect of organizational maintenance.

A new director hired in 1978 was the first to develop a stable source of financial resources for the SMO. Although not a professional manager, the new director was highly motivated to secure funding because, unlike the previous directors, she was a graduate student who did not have a husband who made enough money to support her while she volunteered her time. She needed the money from the job and did not intend to work as a volunteer when there was not enough money to pay her salary (about $11,000 a year for part-time work) as had previous directors. Consequently, she set about trying to figure out how to bring a stable income to the organization. She eventually was able to do so by personally convincing the owners of a number of abortion clinics in the city to make monthly financial contributions to NARAL (personal interview with 1978–80 NARAL of Illinois director). Thus, it was important that the leader of Illinois NARAL was someone who, while not a career activist, did need to be paid and was therefore motivated to provide the organization with financial stability. However, the financial stability was based on the personal appeal of the organization's director; the contributions from clinics were received as a result of personal relationships with clinic owners established by the NARAL director. After she left NARAL and a new director replaced her in the fall of 1980, the organization lost these contributions and went through a period of budget tightening.

It was not until the first career professional took over leadership of NARAL of Illinois that the organization became more formalized and less dependent on the personal characteristics of its leaders. The director hired in 1980, who stayed with NARAL until 1983, was a young woman who had previously done community organizing work and who, unlike her predecessor, wanted a career in "organizing." She did not have any experience working on the abortion issue prior to being hired as the director of Illinois NARAL, but saw the job as a good experience for her, a way to develop her own skills and enhance her career objectives. Like other leaders, the professional manager was highly committed to the goals of the movement, both because of pro-choice views formed prior to directing NARAL and because of her experiences in working with NARAL. But the professional director's orientation to her job led her to make important changes in the structure of the organization.

Until Illinois NARAL's first professional manager took over, the board of directors was selected from the same pool of long-time activists, many of whom were highly involved in other organizations like Planned Parenthood and not very active in ARA/

NARAL. Consequently, there was little division of labor in the organization and it was heavily reliant on the abilities of its executive director. When she was hired in 1980, the new director insisted that the board selection procedures be revised so that active new volunteer recruits could serve on the board and so that the terms of service on the board were systematically rotated. This procedure was implemented in 1980, resulting in a board composed of active volunteers along with some old board members who continued to serve on a rotating basis to provide experience to NARAL. The result was that a formal procedure for bringing new and active members into the decision-making structure of the organization was established for the first time. This change was important in making the organization less exclusively dependent on its executive director for leadership. It also made volunteers more available to the executive director for use in organizational maintenance activities, such as the NARAL "house meeting" program,[9] which provided an important source of funds to the SMO in the early 1980s. In Illinois NARAL and in other SMOs (see Table 4), formalization occurred as professional managers took over leadership. Once a formalized structure is in place, SMOs are better able to mobilize resources and continue to hire professional staff (see below).

The Consequences of Formalization
The Maintenance of Social Movement Organizations

While informal movement organizations may be necessary to initiate movements, formalized SMOs do not necessarily defuse protest as Piven and Cloward (1977) argue; rather, they often perform important functions (e.g., lobbying) following victories won by informal SMOs (Jenkins and Eckert 1986, p. 827). And, while informal SMOs may be necessary to create the pressure for elite patronage, formalized SMOs are the usual beneficiaries of foundation funding and other elite contributions (Haines 1984; Jenkins 1985b; Jenkins and Eckert 1986). Consequently, formalized SMOs are able to maintain themselves—and the movement—over a longer period of time than are informal SMOs. This is particularly important in periods such as the one following legalization of abortion, when movement issues are less pressing and mobilization of constituents is more difficult.

Jenkins (1985b, p. 10) argues that one of the reasons that formalized SMOs are able to sustain themselves is that foundations prefer dealing with organizations that have professional leaders and "the fiscal and management devices that foundations have often expected of their clients." In the case of the civil rights movement, foundations "selected the new organizations that became permanent features of the political landscape" through their funding choices (Jenkins 1985b, p. 15). It is important to recognize, however, that this selection process is a two-way street. Formalized SMOs do not just passively receive support from foundations and other elite constituents; they actively solicit these resources. They are able to do so because they have organizational structures and professional staff that facilitate the mobilization of elite resources. Most importantly, professional staff are likely to have the know-how necessary to secure funding (e.g., grant-writing skills and familiarity with procedures for securing tax-exempt status).

The ability of formalized SMOs to obtain foundation funding is part of a broader capacity for organizational maintenance superior to that of informal SMOs. Paid staff and leaders are critical to the maintenance of formalized SMOs because they can be relied on to be present to carry out tasks such as ongoing contact with the press and fundraising in a routine manner. A formalized structure ensures that there will be continuity in the performance of maintenance tasks and that the SMO will be prepared to take advantage of elite preferences and environmental opportunities (cf. Gamson 1975). Of course, volunteers might well have the skills to perform such tasks, and some informal SMOs do maintain themselves for a number of years, even in adverse environmental conditions (cf. Rupp and Taylor 1987). However, it is much more difficult to command the necessary time from volunteer activists on an ongoing basis. When informal SMOs do survive for many years, they are likely to remain small and exclusive, as was the case for the National Women's Party studied by Rupp and Taylor (1987) and Women Organized for Reproductive Choice in my sample (see Table 5).

The superior ability of formalized SMOs to maintain themselves is documented by the experiences of organizations in my sample (see Tables 5 and 6). On the national level, all of the surviving pro-choice organizations have at least moved in the direction of formalization (see Table 2). The one organization that did not do so, the Reproductive Rights National Network, was formed in a period of intense constituent interest in the abortion issue created by events such as passage of the Hyde Amendment cutoff of Medicaid funding of abortion in late 1976 and the election of anti-abortion president Ronald Reagan in 1980, but was unable to maintain itself after this period. On the local level, the movement industry declined in the period after legalization due to the lack of formalized SMOs (see Tables 2 and 5). The exception was Chicago NOW, which was moving toward formalization but which was concentrating its energies on the Equal Rights Amendment rather than on the abortion issue. In the period after the environmental stimulus of the Hyde Amendment, the local pro-choice SMOs that became stable were those that began to formalize. Among informal SMOs, only Women Organized for Reproductive Choice (WORC) has survived and it has remained a small organization. Thus, on both the national and local levels, formalized SMOs have been stable organizations that helped to sustain the movement during lulls in visible movement activity brought about by environmental developments.

Not only do formalized SMOs help keep a movement alive in periods when constituents become complacent, such as that following legalization of abortion, but they are prepared to take advantage of opportunities for mobilization when the environment changes. In the late 1970s, when the anti-abortion movement scored its first major victories, including the cutoff of Medicaid funding for abortions, adherents and constituents were alerted by visible threats to legal abortion, and the ability of the pro-choice movement to mobilize was greatly enhanced. However, it was important not only that the environment was conducive to mobilization but also that the pro-choice movement had formalized organizations that were stable and ready for combat (cf. Gamson 1975). In NARAL, professional leaders were available with the skills and know-how necessary to form a political action committee, launch a highly successful direct-mail drive, create an educational arm, obtain foundation grants, and organize state affiliates.

In contrast to the success of NARAL and other formalized SMOs in mobilizing resources (see Table 6), informal movement organizations were not as prepared to take advantage of constituent concerns in the late 1970s. The Reproductive Rights National Network (known as R2N2), an informal SMO formed in the late 1970s, received a donation of money to undertake a direct-mail campaign during this period, but the attempt to raise money and recruit activists in this manner was unsuccessful because activists in the organization's national office did not have the experience to carry out the program properly (personal interviews with 1980–83 R2N2 coordinator and steering committee member). There might have been local activists in the organization with direct-mail skills who could have directed this campaign, but in this instance, and in others, the informal structure of the organization made access to such skills difficult to obtain. As one steering committee member commented in an interview, R2N2 suffered from "the classic leadership problem"—the difficulty of trying to get people "to do what they are supposed to do" and the problem of "no one being around" to coordinate work—that has long affected the "younger branch" of the women's movement (see Freeman 1975) of which R2N2 was a descendent. Ultimately, this structural problem led to the demise of R2N2 after the period of heightened constituent interest in abortion ended.[10]

Formalized SMOs, then, are able to maintain themselves during periods when it is difficult to mobilize support and are consequently ready to expand when the environment becomes more conducive. An important reason for this is that they have paid leaders who create stability because they can be relied on to perform ongoing tasks necessary to organizational maintenance. However, stability is not simply a matter of having paid activists; it is also important that formalized SMOs have structures that ensure that tasks are performed despite a turnover in personnel. It is the combination of formalized structure and professional leadership that facilitates organizational maintenance in SMOs.

Strategies and Tactics

While Piven and Cloward (1977) appear to be mistaken in their claim that formalized SMOs necessarily hasten the end of mass movements, their argument that formalization leads to a decline in militant direct-action tactics remains important. Formalization does affect the strategic and tactical choices of SMOs. First, formalized SMOs tend to engage in institutionalized tactics and typically do not initiate disruptive direct-action tactics. Second, formalized SMOs are more likely than informal SMOs to engage in activities that help to achieve organizational maintenance and expansion as well as influence on external targets.

Formalization and institutionalized tactics. The association between formalization and institutionalization of strategies and tactics occurs for two reasons: (1) As environmental developments push a movement into institutionalized arenas, SMOs often begin to formalize so they can engage in tactics such as legislative lobbying (cf. Cable 1984). Formalization allows SMOs to maintain the routines necessary for such tactics (e.g., ongoing contacts with legislators) through paid staff and an established division of labor. (2) Once SMOs are formalized, institutionalized tactics are preferred because they are more compatible with a formalized structure and with the schedules of professional activists. For example, institutionalized activities can be approved in advance; the amount and type of resources expended for such efforts can be controlled; and activities can be planned for the normal hours of the professional's working day.

The history of the pro-choice movement clearly reveals that formalization accelerated as environmental events forced the movement into institutionalized arenas. Prior to 1973, the movement to legalize abortion was an outsider to established politics. Although institutionalized tactics were employed in this period, no SMO confined its activities to institutionalized arenas; demonstrations and quasi-legal or illegal abortion-referral activities were common tactics (see Table 5).[11] After legalization in 1973, the arena for the abortion conflict switched to Congress and SMOs like NARAL began to formalize in order to act in that arena. After the Hyde amendment was passed in 1976, the political arena became the primary battlefield for the abortion conflict, and formalization of SMOs within the movement accelerated. Although informal SMOs in my sample did engage in some institutionalized tactics, the organizations that sustained a heavy use of tactics such as legislative lobbying and political campaign work were most commonly formalized SMOs (see Tables 5 and 6). It is possible for informal SMOs to engage in such tactics, but only as long as the leaders of the organization have the necessary know-how and other organizational resources. Formalized organizations are able to maintain such activities, despite changes in leadership, due to their structural division of labor.

Environmental forces and events, including countermovement activities, do place strong constraints on the tactics of SMOs. When environmental events call for nonroutine direct-action tactics, informal movement organizations typically play a critical role in initiating these tactics (Jenkins and Eckert 1986). In the case of the civil rights movement, for example, Morris (1984) shows that the formalized NAACP preferred to focus on legal and educational tactics, while informal SMOs were engaging in direct-action tactics. However, even the NAACP engaged in some direct-action tactics through its youth divisions at a time when it was clear that progress could only be made through tactics such as the sit-ins initiated by informal SMOs.

When formalized SMOs do engage in direct-action tactics, however, they are likely to be nondisruptive, planned versions of the tactics. NARAL's use of the "speak-out" tactic in the period following 1983 provides some evidence on this point. This was a period when the pro-choice movement was beginning to take the offensive in the legislative and political arenas, particularly after anti-abortion forces failed in their attempt to pass a Human Life Bill through Congress in 1982 and the Supreme Court delivered a ruling in 1983 that struck down most of the restrictions on abortion that had been passed by state and local legislatures. The anti-abortion movement responded to these developments by forcing a switch away from the institutionalized arenas, in which pro-choice forces were beginning to gain the upper hand, to public relations tactics such as the film *The Silent Scream*.[12] As a result of media coverage that began to focus on the issue of fetal rights (cf. Kalter 1985), pro-choice organizations such as NARAL were forced to respond. NARAL chose to employ a version of the speak-out tactic originated by women's liberation groups in the late 1960s. Originally, the speak-out was a spontaneous type of public forum at which women spoke out about their experiences as women, relating their own stories about illegal abortions and so forth. NARAL's version of this tactic was a planned one; to focus media and public attention on women rather than on the fetus, NARAL asked women around the country to write letters about their experiences with abortion addressed to President Reagan and other elected officials and send the letters to NARAL and its affiliates. The letters were then read at public forums on a scheduled day. This case suggests that formalized organizations can switch from tactics in institutionalized arenas to other tactics when necessary, but the tactics they choose are likely to be orderly versions of direct-action tactics originated by informal SMOs.

Formalization and organizational maintenance tactics. Not only are the tactics of formalized SMOs typically institutionalized, but they are also frequently geared toward organizational maintenance and expansion, in addition to more instrumental goals. This was certainly the case for NARAL and its affiliates, which embarked on a "grassroots organizing" strategy known as "Impact '80," intended to expand NARAL, and its political influence, in the late 1970s (see, for example, *NARAL News*, November 1978). It was also the case for NOW, which engaged in a number of high-profile tactics around abortion that were used in membership appeals in the 1980s (see, for example, *National NOW Times*, September/October 1979). In Chicago NOW, there was explicit discussion of the membership-expanding potential of the abortion issue in the late 1970s and early 1980s (personal interview with Chicago NOW executive director).

The experiences of organizations in my sample suggest that professional leaders play an important role in influencing organizations to adopt tactics that aid organizational maintenance. In several organizations, professional staff were responsible for undertaking direct-mail campaigns that helped to expand the organization. In NARAL, an experienced director who took over in 1974 began a direct-mail campaign that was later expanded by other professional leaders (personal interviews with 1974–75 and 1975–81 NARAL executive directors). In the NWHN, an executive director succeeded in expanding organizational membership in the late 1970s through direct mail despite the concerns of nonprofessional leaders that direct mail would bring uncommitted members into the organization (personal interviews with NWHN board members). In ZPG, a professional manager was responsible for reversing the decline in individual membership in the organization through direct mail after he finally convinced the nonprofessional leaders on the ZPG board to undertake the campaign (personal interview with 1976–80 ZPG executive director).

The case of Illinois NARAL is particularly valuable in revealing the role of professional leaders in advancing strategies that aid organizational expansion. In the early 1980s, the NARAL affiliate made important changes in its strategies and tactics, switching from an emphasis on legislative lobbying to heavy involvement in political campaign work. This switch was part of the national NARAL Impact '80 program, which began to be implemented by Illinois NARAL in 1979. However, it was not until the early 1980s, after a professional manager took over, that Illinois NARAL really became committed to the new tactics, which included political campaign work and workshops to train volunteers, house meetings to recruit new members, and an "I'm Pro-Choice and I Vote" postcard campaign.

One reason why the switch in mobilization tactics occurred after 1980 was that the national NARAL organization had by this time become much better organized in implementing the grassroots organizing program through training and grants to local affiliates (see Table 4). As the national organization became more formalized, it was able to extend more aid through its bureaucratic structure to affiliates and to exert more influence over their tactics. In fact, NARAL affiliates signed formal contracts in exchange for national funds to carry out programs in the early 1980s. The other reason was that there were important differences in the state of the organization and in the orientations of the Illinois

NARAL directors who served from 1978–1980 and from 1980–1983, which resulted in different strategies and tactics.

Because ARA was in a state of decline when she was hired in 1978 (see Table 5), the new director spent much of her time in administrative tasks; securing funding, renewing contacts with members, and organizing the office. Due to her organizational skills and attractive personal style, she was highly successful at reviving the organization. In doing so, she used the skills of constituents but did not create a formalized organization. NARAL's strategies and tactics were determined solely by the pragmatic and instrumental approach of the 1978–80 executive director. Rather than concentrating on bringing large numbers of activists into the organization, she recruited volunteers with particular skills, including her friends, for specific tasks. Tactics were aimed less at gaining exposure for NARAL than at accomplishing specific objectives. For example, when a Chicago alderman moved to introduce an ordinance in the city council restricting the availability of abortions, the NARAL director worked to have the measure killed through quiet, behind-the-scenes maneuvers. In this instance and in lobbying work in the state legislature, she made use of the skills and influence of seasoned activists.

Due to her success with such tactics and her lack of concern with organizational expansion, the 1978–80 director was not sold on the national NARAL "Impact '80" program, which was intended to expand NARAL and make the organization a visible political force. In accordance with the national organization's wishes, she tried to implement the program, conducting a limited number of house meetings. But she remained unconvinced of their effectiveness, preferring more efficient methods of fundraising and recruitment. She had similar objections to other parts of the national NARAL grassroots organizing program. When I asked her about the political skills workshops, she replied:

> I refused to do those political skills workshops. I didn't have time, I said [to national NARAL], I'm doing the house meetings program—that's enough. I really just didn't think they were necessary— there are enough organizations like the League of Women Voters which do political skills training.

From an organizational point of view, I guess it's good to do your own skills training to show that the organization is really involved. (Personal interview)

Although she recognized the organizational value of such tactics, this director was not primarily concerned with organizational expansion, but with more specific goals, such as defeating particular pieces of anti-abortion legislation. She was accustomed to using individual skills for this work rather than mobilizing large numbers of activists. When asked about campaign work, she replied:

I do think the "I'm Pro-Choice and I Vote" [postcard campaign] was important in getting the message across to legislators and candidates in a public way. I put a lot of emphasis on [abortion] clinics for post cards because there was a ready-made setting for getting people to sign them.... As far as the campaign work, it was clear to me at the time that Reagan was going to be elected. It was too late in 1980 to make a difference. And, on the local level, there are already liberal groups...that almost always support pro-choice candidates anyway.... I'm just not that much on duplicating efforts which I think NARAL is doing with the campaign work. (Personal interview)

As these comments indicate, the 1978–80 Illinois NARAL director preferred instrumental tactics rather than organizing tactics as a result of her background and experiences. She saw the house meetings as an inefficient way to raise money, and, while she recognized that political-skills workshops and campaign work were good for organizational visibility, she was not convinced of their effectiveness for achieving movement goals—her primary concern. She used the "I'm Pro-Choice and I Vote" postcards as a signal to legislators rather than as an organizing tool. Due to her influence, most of Illinois NARAL's activities during her tenure were instrumentally targeted at state legislators.

It was not until an executive director with experience in community organizing work and with ambitions for a movement career was hired in 1980 that the Illinois NARAL affiliate enthusiastically implemented the national NARAL grassroots organizing program. In contrast to her predecessor, who had no interest in organizing *per se*, the new director was anxious to engage in "organizing" work

to expand the local affiliate and eagerly began to develop the house meeting program that was part of the national NARAL organizing strategy. One of the reasons that she was successful in doing so was that, as described above, she created a more formalized organization. Whereas her predecessor had been reluctant to delegate certain tasks, including speaking at house meetings, the new director made heavy use of a division of labor that had not existed in the previously informal SMO. Aided by her past experience with community organizing, she was highly successful at training volunteers to conduct house meetings and, with funds raised from the meetings and some financial aid from national NARAL, was able to hire an organizer to run the house meeting program, thereby increasing the division of labor in the SMO.

The new director's strategic approach was clearly influenced by her professional interest in organizing tactics. She used the NARAL house meeting program to raise money, but also as a means of bringing new activists into the NARAL organization. And just as the house meetings were used as an organizing tool, so were the NARAL postcards. As the NARAL director explained:

The best thing about the postcards was that they gave us new contacts. We would set up tables in different places and people would come up and sign and say things like "I'm really glad someone is doing something about this issue." And then we'd say, "Would you like to get more involved?" and we got a number of activists that way. We also got names for a mailing list....So the postcards were good as a way of making contacts, a means of exposure for the organization. The actual effect of the postcards on legislators was, I think, minimal. I know some of the legislators never even opened the envelope; when we delivered an envelopefull to Springfield, they'd just throw them away. (Personal interview)

Thus, Illinois NARAL employed tactics oriented toward organizational goals after moving toward formalization. This local case history suggests that professional leaders may be more likely than nonprofessional staff and volunteers to influence SMOs to engage in tactics that have organizational maintenance functions rather than strictly instrumental goals because they have organizational skills that they want to use and develop.

Coalition Work

The formalization of social movement organizations also has implications for coalition work within movements. In my sample, formalized SMOs have played the dominant roles in lasting coalitions (see Tables 5 and 6). Coalitions among formalized SMOs are easier to maintain than are coalitions among informal SMOs or between formalized and informal SMOs because formalized SMOs typically have staff persons who are available to act as organizational representatives to the coalition and routinely coordinate the coalition work. Just as paid staff can be relied on to carry out maintenance tasks for SMOs, they can also be relied on to maintain contact with the representatives of other SMOs in a coalition. When all of the SMO representatives are paid staff, coordination is easiest. While volunteers can represent SMOs in coalitions, it is more difficult to keep volunteers in contact with one another and to coordinate their work, particularly in the absence of a formalized coalition organization with paid staff of its own. Thus, paid staff help to maintain coalitions, thereby lessening the organizational problems of coalition work (see Staggenborg 1986, p. 387).

The experiences of the Illinois Pro-Choice Alliance (IPCA), a Chicago-based coalition organization, reveal the impact of organizational structure on coalition work. Formalized movement organizations, including NARAL of Illinois and Chicago NOW, have played a major role in this coalition, while informal organizations, such as Women Organized for Reproductive Choice (WORC), have had a difficult time participating in the coalition. One past director of the Illinois Pro-Choice Alliance recognized this problem, commenting in an interview:

> ...there is a real difference between groups which have paid staff and the grassroots groups which are all volunteers. The groups with paid staff have a lot more opportunity to participate [in the coalition]—even trivial things like meeting times create problems. The groups with paid staff can meet in the Loop at lunch time—it makes it easier. Also...people from the grassroots groups tend to be intimidated by the paid staff, because as

volunteers the grassroots people are less informed about the issue. Whereas for the staff, it's their job to be informed, and they have the resources behind them....I think too that the grassroots people have higher expectations about what can be done. They're volunteers who may have worked all day, then they do this in the evenings; they're cause-oriented and they expect more out of people and projects. Paid staff are the opposite in that they work on the issue during the day and then want to go home to their families or whatever at night and leave it behind. They want to do projects with defined goals and time limits, projections as to the feasibility and all that. Not that paid staff are not committed people. I think it's good to have a balance between the grassroots and staffed groups. Without the grassroots people. I think things would be overstructured; with just the grassroots people, well, there's too much burnout among them. The staffers tend to last a lot longer. (Personal interview)

These perceptions are borne out by the difficulties of Women Organized for Reproductive Choice in trying to participate in the IPCA. WORC members interviewed also spoke of the problems they had attending IPCA meetings at lunchtime in downtown Chicago, a time and place convenient for the staff of formalized SMO members of the coalition but difficult for WORC members, who tended to be women with full-time jobs in various parts of the city. Another reason for the difficulty is that the coalition has focused on institutionalized lobbying activities, tactics for which WORC members have neither the skills nor the ideological inclination. Efforts by WORC to get the coalition to engage in a broader range of tactics, including direct-action tactics, have been unsuccessful. On the national level, the Reproductive Rights National Network had nearly identical problems participating in the Abortion Information Exchange coalition (see Staggenborg 1986). Formalized SMOs play an important role in maintaining coalitions, but they also influence coalitions toward narrower, institutionalized strategies and tactics and make the participation of informal SMOs difficult.

Conclusion

While professionalization of leadership and formalization of SMOs are not inevitable outcomes of social movements, they are important trends in many movements (cf. McCarthy and Zald 1973, 1977; Gamson 1975, p. 91). There is little evidence, however, that professional leaders and formalized SMOs will replace informal SMOs and nonprofessionals as the initiators of social movements and collective action. While systematic research on the influence of different types of movement leaders is needed, my data show that the roles of entrepreneur and professional manager are in some cases distinct. This is because environmental opportunities and preexisting organizational bases are critical determinants of movement mobilization; movement entrepreneurs do not manufacture grievances at will, but are influenced by the same environmental and organizational forces that mobilize other constituents. Contrary to the arguments of McCarthy and Zald (1973, 1977), nonprofessional leaders and informal SMOs remain important in initiating movements and tactics that are critical to the growth of insurgency (cf. McAdam 1983).

Professionalization of leadership has important implications for the maintenance and direction of social movement organizations. My data suggest that professional managers, as career activists, tend to formalize the organizations they lead in order to provide financial stability and the kind of division of labor that allows them to use and develop their organizational skills. Once formalized, SMOs continue to hire professional managers because they have the necessary resources. Contrary to the arguments of Piven and Cloward (1977), formalized SMOs do not diffuse protest but play an important role in maintaining themselves and the movement, particularly in unfavorable environmental conditions when it is difficult to mobilize constituents. Formalized SMOs are better able to maintain themselves than are informal ones, not only because they have paid staff who can be relied on to carry out organizational tasks, but also because a formalized structure ensures continuity despite changes in leadership and environmental conditions. Thus, a movement entrepreneur who prevents formalization by maintaining personal control over an SMO may ultimately cause the organization's demise. A movement that consists solely of informal SMOs is likely to have a shorter lifetime than a movement that includes formalized SMOs. Similarly, a coalition of informal SMOs has less chance of survival than a coalition of formalized SMOs.

While formalization helps to maintain social movements, it is also associated with the institutionalization of collective action. Formalized SMOs engage in fewer disruptive tactics of the sort that pressure government authorities and other elites to make concessions or provide support than do informal SMOs. Formalized SMOs also tend to select strategies and tactics that enhance organizational maintenance. Given the prominent role of professional managers in formalized SMOs, these findings raise the Michels ([1915] 1962) question of whether formalized organizations with professional leaders inevitably become oligarchical and conservative, as Piven and Cloward (1977) argue. Based on my data, I dispute the conclusion that formalized SMOs necessarily become oligarchical. In fact, many seem more democratic than informal SMOs because they follow routinized procedures that make it more difficult for individual leaders to attain disproportionate power. As Freeman (1973) argues, "structureless" SMOs are most subject to domination by individuals.

The tendency of formalized SMOs to engage in more institutionalized strategies and tactics than informal SMOs might be interpreted as a conservative development, given findings that militant direct-action tactics force elite concessions (cf. Jenkins and Eckert 1986). Informal SMOs, with their more flexible structures, are more likely to innovate direct-action tactics. However, the institutionalization of movement tactics by formalized SMOs does not necessarily mean that movement goals become less radical; an alternative interpretation is that movement demands and representatives become incorporated into mainstream politics. For example, the National Organization for Women is now an important representative of women's interests in the political arena. While the longterm implications of this phenomenon for the social movement sector and the political system require further investigation, it is certainly possible for formalized SMOs to exert a progressive influence on the, political system.

Finally, my research raises the question of whether movements inevitably become formalized or institutionalized, as suggested by classical theories of social movements, which argue that movements progress through stages toward institutionalization (see Lang and Lang 1961; Turner and Killian 1957 for discussions of such stage theories). In the case of the prochoice movement, there has clearly been a trend toward formalization. As Gamson (1975, p. 91) notes, there does seem to be a kernel of truth to theories that posit an inevitable trend toward bureaucratization or formalization. However, as Gamson also notes, "the reality is considerably more complex" in that some SMOs begin with bureaucratic or formalized structures and others never develop formalized structures. Although neither Gamson nor I found cases of SMOs that developed informal structures after formalization,[13] such a change is conceivable under certain circumstances (e.g., if nonprofessional staff are hired to replace professional managers, a development most likely at the local level). Classical theories of the "natural history" of a movement focus on the institutionalization of a movement as a whole and ignore variations in the experiences of different SMOs within the movement. My research shows that SMOs vary in the ways in which they deal with internal organizational problems and changes in the environment. Formalization is one important means of solving organizational problems, particularly as SMOs grow larger; however, SMOs can also develop alternative structures. Important variations exist within the two broad categories of SMO structure that I have identified; further empirical research on leadership roles and SMO structures and their impact on organizational goals and activities is necessary.

NOTES

The research for this paper was supported by National Science Foundation Dissertation Grant No. SES-8315574. Frank Dobbin, Carol Mueller, Rod Nelson, and two *ASR* reviewers provided helpful comments on earlier drafts of this paper.

1. Manuscript collections used include the Women's Collection at Northwestern University, which contains newsletters and documents from NARAL, RCAR, ZPG, CWLU, ICMCA/ARA/NARAL of Illinois, and several coalitions; the papers of ICMA/ARA/NARAL and Chicago NOW at the University of Illinois, Chicago; the CWLU papers at the Chicago Historical Society; the Lawrence Lader papers at the New York Public Library; the public portions of the NARAL and NOW papers at the Schlesinger Library of Radcliffe College; and private papers provided by informants.

2. Volunteers may be "professionals" in the sense that they spend many years, perhaps a lifetime, doing movement work. However, they differ from professional managers in that they do not earn a living through movement work.

3. The term *bureaucratic* might be substituted for "formalized" (cf. Gamson 1975). However, I have used the latter because SMOs are never as bureaucratic as more established organizations such as corporations and government agencies (cf. Zald and Ash 1966, p. 329).

4. I have used the term *informal* to describe this type of SMO structure for want of a more positive label. The terminology of the existing literature on organizations and social movements is inadequate. The term *classical* used by McCarthy and Zald (1973, 1977) does not describe the structure of the SMO. The more descriptive term *grass roots* implies a mass membership base that may or may not be present in either "formalized" or "informal" SMOs. The term *collectivist* used by Rothschild-Whitt (1979) refers to a specific type of decision-making structure which is distinguished from "bureaucratic" organization; not all informal SMOs are collectivist. Freeman's (1979, p. 169) term *communal* for "small, local, and functionally undifferentiated" organizations is inappropriate because not all informal SMOs are local organizations.

5. An appendix with further details on sample SMOs is available on request from the author.

6. The distinction between such formalized SMOs and interest groups or lobbies is not a sharp one (cf. Useem and Zald 1982). There is clearly a need for greater conceptual clarification of the differences between formalized SMOs and interest groups based on empirical research.

7. The conflict between entrepreneurial and professional roles also became apparent to me when I interviewed the anti-abortion leader Joseph Scheidler as part of another study. Scheidler helped to form several anti-abortion groups and was fired as executive director from two organizations for engaging in militant direct-action tactics without going through the proper organizational channels (see Roeser 1983). He finally founded his own organization in 1980, the Pro-Life Action League, in which he is unencumbered by bureaucratic decision-making procedures. As he told me in a 1981 interview:

> I don't like boards of directors—you always have to check with them when you want to do something—and I was always getting in trouble with the board. So I resigned, or they fired me, however you want to put it, because

they didn't like my tactics.... The Pro-Life Action League is my organization. I'm the chairman of the board and the other two board members are my wife and my best friend. If I want to do something, I call up my wife and ask her if she thinks it's a good idea. Then I have two-thirds approval of the board! (Personal interview)

Additional examples of such conflict between the entrepreneurial and professional roles in the social movements literature can be cited. In the farm worker movement, there has been conflict over the leadership of Cesar Chavez, who attempted to maintain personal control over the United Farm Workers at a time when others wanted to create a more bureaucratic union structure (see Barr 1985; Jenkins 1985a, pp. 204–6). In the gay rights movement, the "brash" activist Randy Wicker left the New York Mattachine Society to found "the Homosexual League of New York, a one-man organization designed to give him a free hand to pursue his own plans" (D'Emilio 1983, pp. 158–59). In the environmental movement, Friends of the Earth founder David Brower was ousted from the organization after he failed in his attempts to maintain control over the SMO and prevent it from becoming formalized (Rauber 1986). And in Mothers Against Drunk Driving (MADD), there has been conflict over the role of MADD's entrepreneur, Candy Lightner, who has attempted to maintain personal control over a bureaucratizing organization (Reinarman 1985).

8. By all accounts this leader had an extraordinary ability to recruit volunteers for various tasks. As one of my informants explained, "She was really effective at getting people to do things. She would keep after you so that it was easier to do what she wanted rather than have her continue to bug you." Another activist concurred, "There was nothing like having her call you at 7AM and tell you what you were going to do that day!" The problem of reliance on the personal characteristics of this director was later recognized by a board member who commented that the problem with the long-time director was that she kept knowledge about the organization "in HER head" (document in private papers), making it difficult for her successor to assume control.

9. The "house meeting" tactic, which involved holding meetings in the homes of NARAL members or other interested persons, was a recruitment tool developed as part of a national NARAL grassroots organizing program.

10. The delay experienced by Women Organized for Reproductive Choice in obtaining the 501(c)3 tax status that allows a nonprofit organization to obtain tax-deductible contributions also reveals the difficulties that informal SMOs have with organizational maintenance. Although there were several local Chicago foundations willing to fund organizations such as WORC, the SMO was unable to take advantage of these opportunities for some time because it had not obtained the necessary tax status. When I asked WORC's sole part-time, nonprofessional staff leader why the tax status had not been obtained, she replied that the delay occurred because she was the only one who knew how to apply for the status, but that she simply had not had the time to do it yet.

11. Abortion-referral activities were regarded by many activists as a militant means of challenging the system (see Lader 1973). In the case of women's movement projects such as the CWLU Abortion Counseling Service, there was an attempt to create an alternative type of organization as well as to serve the needs of women.

12. *The Silent Scream* attempted to use sonography to make its case that the fetus suffers pain in an abortion. The film was distributed to members of Congress and received a great deal of media attention, helping to shift the debate on abortion to "scientific" issues.

13. Although it never developed a structure that could be called formalized, one SMO in my sample, Women Organized for Reproductive Choice, did become even more informal as it became smaller.

34.

The Structure of Charismatic Mobilization: A Case Study of Rebellion During the Chinese Cultural Revolution

JOEL ANDREAS

Are social movements fated to become more conservative as they become more organized? Weber offered a cogent explanation for why many social movement organizations follow this path. Modern organizations, he argued, inculcate in their members a bureaucratic orientation toward rules and organizational hierarchies; this is especially true of organizational officials, who develop a rational orientation toward the existing order, imprisoning themselves within its rules.[1] Elaborating on Weber's ideas, Michels ([1915] 1959) argued that organizations inherently concentrate power in the hands of officials, and even revolutionary parties abandon radical goals as their leaders accommodate themselves to the status quo and secure a comfortable place within it. These theses, concisely conveyed in Weber's famous description of bureaucracy as an "iron cage" and in Michels's "iron law of oligarchy," have long haunted those of us with an aversion to cages and oligarchies.

Weber's theory of bureaucracy, however, is only one element of a larger cyclical theory of revolutionary change, in which conservative organizations are never immune from radical transformation or eclipse. Charisma, of course, is the agent of upheaval in Weber's cycle. Unfortunately, charisma virtually disappeared from the study of social movements as a result of a dramatic paradigmatic shift in the 1970s. While charismatic authority played a key role in the earlier paradigm, which relied on social-psychological explanations, the new paradigm, which stressed the rational pursuit of interests, had little use for a concept so strongly associated with

Andreas, Joel. 2007. "The Structure of Charismatic, Mobilization: A Case Study of Rebellion During the Chinese Cultural Revolution." American Sociological Review 72: 434–458. Reprinted by permission of American Sociological Association.

irrationality. Consequently, the literature spawned by the new approach almost entirely abandoned the concept of charismatic authority. Yet the absence of charisma in scholarly analysis has not prevented the regular emergence of social movements with charismatic characteristics; this is especially true of radical movements that challenge the existing order. By neglecting charisma, scholars have relinquished a valuable tool with which to analyze these movements and have lost half of a conceptual framework that might profitably be used to understand the twists and turns of all social movements.

In this article, I make a case for bringing charisma back into the study of social movements. I argue that employing the concepts of bureaucracy and charisma in tandem sheds considerable light on issues at the center of longstanding debates about the conservative tendencies of social movement organizations. I use the Chinese Cultural Revolution to illustrate this point. Before delving into the particulars of this episode, however, it is necessary to revisit the issues that led to charisma's banishment from social movements scholarship and to set forth a framework in which charisma can be integrated into the current paradigm.

Bringing Charisma Back into Social Movement Scholarship

In the social-psychological paradigm, which reigned from the 1940s through the 1960s, social movements are caused by traumatic structural changes that produce anxiety in individuals. Charisma plays a critical role in this "structural strain" model, as it provides a link between individual anxiety and sustained collective behavior. Individuals uprooted from traditional institutional arrangements are seen as susceptible to charismatic appeals, which offer new interpretations of the world, suggest targets for the hostility generated by structural strain, and generate powerful emotional bonds between a leader and his or her followers. Talcott Parsons (1947:70–72), who helped introduce Weber's concept to the English-speaking world, outlined how charisma might be integrated into strain theories of collective behavior. Over the next three decades, the most influential general theories of collective behavior depended on charisma as an essential element (Gurr 1970; Kornhauser 1959; Smelser 1962; Turner and Killian 1957), and a number of scholars produced more narrowly defined works on charismatic movements and leaders (Downton 1966; Friedland 1964; Marcus 1961; Wallace 1956).[2]

Many of these scholars viewed disruptive collective behavior with trepidation and attempted to diagnose conditions that caused such behavior and identify effective methods of prevention and control. Advocates of the new paradigm, in contrast, were more sympathetic with social movements, which they saw as potential agents of positive social change. While the old school saw structural disruptions as causes of stress, the new school saw these disruptions as political opportunities; while the old school attributed successful collective action to the psychological attraction of charismatic appeals, the new school attributed this success to the effectiveness of a movement's strategy and its ability to mobilize resources (Gamson 1975; McAdam 1982; McCarthy and Zald 1977; Tilly 1978). Advocates of the new paradigm found two aspects of the charismatic depiction of social movements particularly unappealing: the portrayal of movement actors as irrational and the emphasis on the leader. Much of the previous literature depicted social movements as comprised of a prophet-like figure and an amorphous mass of true believers moved by emotional attachment and irrational beliefs. In the new literature, both leaders and followers were strategic actors pursuing their interests, and the focus shifted to movement organizations rather than leaders (who were now political entrepreneurs, rather than prophets). Weber's concept, therefore, held little attraction for advocates of the new paradigm, who were partial to structural explanations and keen to recover the role of the masses (who had been left out of traditional "great men" accounts of history).

Since its triumph, however, the new paradigm has gradually made room for psychological and cultural factors, some of which recall elements of the old social-psychological paradigm (although they have been shorn of the earlier structural-functional framework and pathological connotations). The original hard-nosed objectivism of the strategic actor approach has slowly softened as scholars have recognized the importance of understanding the subjective meanings that participants attach to their actions and the sources of their commitment. As a result, identity formation, the crafting of collective action frames, and other cognitive and psychological processes have been incorporated into the prevailing paradigm (Klandermans 1984; Snow 2004; Snow and Benford 1992). This has allowed scholars to consider the role of movement leaders in these processes, especially their role in promulgating new conceptions of the world that make the status quo seem unjust and the impossible seem possible (Morris 1984; Morris and Staggenborg 2004).

As Melucci (1996), a leading proponent of the shift toward cultural and psychological approaches, noted, Weber assigned these tasks to charismatic leaders. Scholars in the mainstream paradigm also have suggested that charisma plays a more important role than current theoretical models admit. Morris, who argued that Martin Luther King Jr. and others converted the institutionalized charismatic authority of churches into a force for pursuing movement goals, called on social movement scholars to give more attention to charismatic leadership and the "deep cultural and emotional processes that inspire and produce collective action" (Morris 2000:450–52). Thus, renewed appreciation for psychology and culture may be paving the road for the reintroduction of Weber's concept into the mainstream of social movement theory.

In this article, I integrate charismatic authority into the current paradigm, but not by way of the psychological road. Instead, I extend the discussion of charisma beyond social-psychology and into the realm of political strategy and mobilizing structures. While it is understandable that the social-psychological school dwelt on the psychological aspects of charisma, there is no reason that discussion of charismatic authority should be restricted to the psychological realm. Although the importance of cognitive and emotional factors in social movements cannot be denied, the concept of charismatic authority has much broader application. It is time to free the concept from the confines of social-psychology.

Charisma lost favor among practitioners of the current paradigm because of its association with irrationality, which many erroneously believe makes it incompatible with strategic action. While Weber (1978) characterized charismatic authority as irrational, his meaning was different. "Bureaucratic authority," he wrote, "is specifically rational in the sense of being bound to intellectually analyzable rules, while charismatic authority is specifically irrational in the sense of being foreign to all rules" (p. 244). This definition does not exclude the pursuit of interests. Among Weber's examples of charismatic types, after all, were pirate chiefs and warlords, whose followers were certainly interested in worldly goods. Although many charismatic movements promote asceticism, charisma is not defined by an indifference to material or honorific interests, but rather by an aversion to routine, rule-bound economic activity and the accompanying petty calculus, which distracts from the charismatic mission (Weber 1978:1113). This leaves plenty of room for strategic action. For example, the instrumental concerns that inspire a peasant, in ordinary times, to practice economic diligence and thrift may not be altogether different from those that inspire the same peasant, in extraordinary times, to join an insurrectionary movement that promises land redistribution. In the first instance, interests are pursued by following the rules, while in the second they are pursued by breaking the rules. This is the distinction Weber drew attention to when he contrasted bureaucratic and charismatic authority. It is a critical distinction, and it generates valuable concepts with which to analyze not only the goals of social movements, but also their forms of organization and mobilizing methods.

Charismatic and Bureaucratic Mobilization

Although Weber never expressly defined his concept this way, charisma might also be defined as the ability of a leader to mobilize people without the benefits or constraints of formal organization. Bureaucratic and charismatic authority are antithetical in principal and frequently at odds in practice. Charisma, Weber emphasized, is intrinsically hostile to the institutional hierarchies, regulations, and procedures that characterize bureaucracies. Organization (with its bureaucratic offices and rules) hinders charisma, and charisma (with its contempt for offices and rules) undermines organization. Yet, pragmatic considerations inevitably bring about combinations of the two. Radical movements, in particular, require elements of both: they are inspired by a mission that challenges the legitimacy of the existing order, but they also depend on formal organizational structures and norms that facilitate cohesion and collective action.

Charismatic and bureaucratic authority coexist uneasily within social movements, and the combination is inherently unstable. The advance of bureaucracy portends the extinction of charisma, and charismatic eruptions undercut bureaucratic authority. Weber frequently returned to this theme. He pointed out that political parties often start as charismatic followings, but develop bureaucratic hierarchies based on calculable rules, technical expertise, and a rational orientation to the existing order. This development results in conflict between charismatic leaders, whose power derives from a transcendent mission, and party officials, who favor bureaucratic norms engendered by the party organization. In all types of organizations, bureaucratic routinization diminishes the power of charismatic founders and enhances the power of officials, but official power remains susceptible to new charismatic challenges. Such conflict within organizations is part of a wider cyclical pattern, in which charisma overturns existing structures and routines, only to give way to new structures and routines (Weber 1978:252–54, 1130–56).

Weber's essays present us with two basic propositions regarding the evolution of modern social movements: 1) conservative tendencies in radical organizations typically involve the bureaucratic routinization of charisma, and 2) radical tendencies in conservative organizations typically have charismatic inspiration.[3]

We can also extrapolate from Weber's basic concepts two types of mobilization: charismatic and bureaucratic. Each is characterized by distinctive types of organizational norms and means of producing cohesion. In bureaucratic mobilization, cohesion is produced by a bureaucratic hierarchy of authority with formal decision-making procedures and a clear chain of command. Authority resides in offices and does not depend on the personal characteristics of the individuals who occupy these offices, and promotion is carried out through formal processes based on technical qualifications. In charismatic mobilization, cohesion is produced by a commonly accepted mission defined by charismatic individuals. There is no formal hierarchy of offices, but rather a charismatic hierarchy of authority, in which a central leader is surrounded by disciples chosen because of their devotion to the cause, and local leaders gather their own followers. Each of these leaders becomes an agent of the common mission, borrowing the charismatic authority of the central leader, but also generating his or her own authority. The movement is bound together by informal networks, and decision making and promotion take place without set rules and procedures.[4] These are, of course, only ideal types created for analytical purposes, and actual social movements combine characteristics of both. Indeed, each type might appropriately describe the mobilizing structure of a single organization at different historical moments.

In this article, I employ these two propositions and two conceptual types to help explain the origins and results of the Cultural Revolution, and I use this dramatic episode to illustrate and further elaborate these propositions and concepts.

Reconsidering the Role of Charisma in the Cultural Revolution

The Cultural Revolution was an unusual social movement in that Mao Zedong called on students, workers, and peasants to attack the local officials of his own party. At the time, 17 years after the 1949 Revolution, the Chinese Communist Party (CCP) was at the height of its power. Every school, workplace, and village was organized around a party branch, and the authority of the local party secretary was virtually beyond challenge. The rebel movement Mao called into being had little formal organization and was led by inexperienced youths. Yet within six months, with Mao's support, it completely undermined the authority of the party organization, and young rebels declared they had seized power from party committees in schools and workplaces around the country.

Scholarship about the Cultural Revolution also experienced the paradigmatic shift that transformed the social movements field. The authors of several of the earliest studies, oriented by the then prevailing social-psychological approach, sought to identify the psychological determinants of participants' behavior (Hiniker 1977; Lifton 1968; Pye 1968; Solomon 1971). Lifton, in particular, highlighted the irrationality of participants, portraying an image of young Red Guards—"true believers" blindly devoted to Mao and prone to fanatical, violent behavior in moments of collective excitement—that fit the classic social-psychological model of charismatic movements to a tee.

Subsequent scholars, inspired by the new paradigm, insisted that Cultural Revolution activists were rationally pursuing their own interests, and they attempted to free their explanations as much as possible from the taint of charisma (Chan, Rosen, and Unger 1980; Lee 1978; Wang 1995). In his analysis of factional contention in the industrial city of Wuhan, Wang presented the most theoretically sophisticated defense of the rational orientation of Cultural Revolution activists. Determined to counter the idea that they were blindly following Mao, Wang titled his study *The Failure of Charisma*. He found that although activists considered themselves to be Mao's disciples, they interpreted his messages according to their own interests. Furthermore, even though they said they were fighting for ideological goals (and perhaps believed this themselves), their actions showed they ultimately had more instrumental concerns. Thus, in both the social-psychological and rational actor accounts of the Cultural Revolution, charisma is associated with a type of irrationality that diverts participants from pursuing their own interests. Wang's diligent effort to parse the irrational appeal of charisma from the pursuit of interests is an admirably precise expression of the misconception that is common to both the old and new paradigms: that charisma and strategic action are mutually exclusive phenomena.

Scholars who developed rational actor accounts of the Cultural Revolution were particularly determined to dispel previous accounts that portrayed activists as an undifferentiated mass. They identified differences among contending local organizations, which they explained in terms of group interests. Individuals from disparate disadvantaged groups banded together to form "rebel" factions, which battled "conservative" factions representing privileged groups. In these accounts, Mao's abrupt insistence that authorities desist from suppressing protests created political opportunities for the rebels, and the emergent mass organizations were constantly maneuvering to take advantage of factional struggles in the party. Although these interest group explanations of the Cultural Revolution have been criticized for ignoring political complications (Walder 2002), they have been widely accepted.

I have previously disputed specific aspects of these interest group accounts, while accepting their basic premise (Andreas 2002). Here I turn to a different problem. How can we explain the cohesion and effectiveness of the rebel movement? What convinced individuals, dispersed across a huge country and connected by only feeble organizational ties, to unite around a specific set of political objectives and to act cohesively and decisively at critical moments? How could such fledgling and loosely organized groups overturn the entrenched power of local party organizations? Neither the early social-psychological accounts nor the later rational actor accounts provide satisfactory answers to these questions. On the one hand, the authors of the social-psychological accounts were interested in participants' motivations and the bonds that tied them to their leader and their fellow activists, but they were less concerned with the effectiveness of strategies and organizational forms. On the other hand, although the authors of the interest group accounts turned their attention to strategy and organization, their analyses of interests and political opportunities do not provide an explanation for the rebels' cohesion and effectiveness. Individual interests can as easily divide as unite, common

interests do not automatically generate collective action, and political opportunities are only a passive factor.

In this article, I develop an explanation for the rebel movement's cohesion and effectiveness by using the concept of charisma to analyze the movement's structure. The rebel movement was able to maintain cohesion despite its lack of formal organization because it had a charismatic hierarchy of authority. Moreover, it was highly effective in undermining bureaucratic authority because of its lack of formal organization, which encouraged a rule-breaking spirit. It was the loose organization typical of charismatic mobilization that gave the movement its extraordinary destructive power.

Research Agenda and Data

This article examines in detail a single organization, the Jinggangshan Regiment of Tsinghua University, China's leading school of engineering and technology. In part because of the stature of the university and its proximity to the center of power in Beijing, Jinggangshan became the most famous rebel organization in the country and its leader, a student named Kuai Dafu, came to symbolize the seditious bravado that characterized the movement. I chose to conduct a case study of a single organization to obtain a detailed ground-level understanding of the political aims and organizational characteristics of the movement. Although the prominence of Jinggangshan made it peculiar in some ways, the basic aims and organizational characteristics described below were largely shared by similar organizations across the country.[5]

I conducted this research as part of a larger investigation into the postrevolutionary history of Tsinghua University. Most data was collected during 20 months of field research between 1998 and 2001. Data was obtained from two main types of sources: interviews and contemporary factional publications. I interviewed 76 people who were members of the Tsinghua University community during the factional fighting of the Cultural Revolution, including students, teachers, clerical staff, workers, and school officials. Among those interviewed were leaders and members of both of the main contending factions.[6] I also made use of other retrospective accounts, including personal memoirs and official, semiofficial, and unofficial histories. Contemporary sources include newspapers, pamphlets, and fliers published by the rival university factions.

It was important not only to obtain a wide variety of perspectives, but also to compare contemporary and retrospective accounts, which have complementary strengths and weaknesses. Contemporary newspapers and fliers recorded events from a period perspective, while retrospective interviews provided access to personal experiences and interpretations. While contemporary publications were produced under the political constraints and incentives of the period, memories of past events, motivations, and ideas have undergone a conscious or unconscious metamorphosis as subsequent events and political and ideological changes (official, collective, and personal) make their imprint.

Origins of the Cultural Revolution

Before turning to the student movement at Tsinghua University, it is necessary to explain the origins of the Cultural Revolution. The explanation advanced here, which depends heavily on previous scholarship, describes the upheaval as a product of contradictions between the charismatic and bureaucratic elements that together constituted the CCP. All revolutionary political parties must marry an ideology that requires breaking society's rules with an organizational form that requires adherence to party rules. This combination was epitomized by the Leninist party, a highly successful model adopted by Marxist revolutionaries around the world, including Chinese Marxists. Communist leaders inspired their followers with a millenarian vision, while marshalling their efforts through a highly disciplined party organization. As Schurmann showed in his classic work, *Ideology and Organization* (1968), this was a potent combination that allowed the Chinese communists to mobilize a successful insurrectionary movement, but it also harbored powerful contradictions that became especially acute after the CCP took power.

Contradictions Within Bureaucratic Mobilization

The CCP, like other victorious communist parties, assumed responsibility for administering a society based on class structures it was programmatically committed to destroying. This led to a tumultuous style of governance, as it did in the early decades of the Soviet Union, punctuated by recurring state-led political movements.[7] These movements, including land reform, collectivization, and the Great Leap Forward, were instruments of revolution from above, used by the new regime to attack the old elite classes and tear down institutions on which their power and privileges were based. Brief periods of calm were broken by new class-leveling campaigns that violently overturned elements of the status quo, abrogating existing policies and practices, and creating new ones. These movements invoked transcendent communist goals in an immediate fashion that made existing structures intolerable and radical change imperative. They conjured up visions of a bright communist future, concentrated popular hostility against elements of the prevailing order and existing elites (or already dispossessed and disenfranchised elites), and radically transformed the social order. Although these campaigns were highly disruptive, their methods were essentially bureaucratic, as they relied on mobilizing a vast party organization that extended down to the basic levels of society. Orders were passed down the party's chain of command from the center to regional and local branches, which mobilized subsidiary mass organizations, activating hundreds of millions of people. Thus, even after the communists took power, the recipe that brought them to power, combining a transcendent class-leveling ideology with a bureaucratic organization, had not yet exhausted its revolutionary potential.

Political movements were always initiated by Mao, who had established for himself a position *above* party deliberations, a position Meisner (1982) likened to that of a prophet. Within the central party leadership, there was a widely recognized division of labor, in which others handled day-to-day administrative affairs, while Mao assumed responsibility for keeping alive the communist goal of eliminating class distinctions. The party's transcendent ideological goals and the practical demands of governance became embodied, respectively, in Mao and other party leaders. Like the war chief in a tribe where power is divided between a war chief and a peace chief, Mao's power was ascendant during moments of mass mobilization.

Several scholars have suggested that Leninist parties created political movements in which charisma was not embodied in an individual, but in the party. Lenin's "party of a new type," wrote Jowitt (1983), was conceived of as "an amalgam of bureaucratic discipline and charismatic correctness" that took the "fundamentally conflicting notions of personal heroism and organizational impersonalism and recast them in the form of an organizational hero" (p. 277). Constas (1961) suggested that victorious Leninist parties created a "charismatic bureaucracy," in which expansion of bureaucratic power became the charismatic mission. Each of these interpretations provides insights into the results of the communist combination of charisma and bureaucracy, but by emphasizing the unified product of the merger they direct our attention away from its contradictions.

Some scholars of postrevolutionary China have taken the opposite tack, arguing that the Cultural Revolution was a product of tensions between Mao's charismatic authority and the bureaucratic authority of the party organization.[8] In seeking to explain Mao's motivations, some emphasized personal power, while others stressed ideological goals. These explanations are not contradictory, of course, as Mao's commitment to the communist mission was inseparably tied to his conception of his own role in achieving this mission.

The Cultural Revolution can be seen as a manifestation of tensions that were present in all Leninist parties that came to power by means of indigenous revolutions. Starting with Lenin, communist leaders stridently denounced bureaucrats, and bureaucratic methods and attitudes, for impeding the implementation of the communist program.[9] In his study of postrevolutionary Cuba, Gonzalez (1974) produced an insightful analysis of this type of conflict, highlighting the friction between Fidel Castro's charismatic leadership style and the bureaucratic norms of the party organization. Castro presented this conflict in ideological terms, appealing to the people to fight for "mass methods" as opposed to administrative and technocratic methods, which he criticized as elitist and incompatible with "advancing

the revolutionary process" (pp. 224–25). A communist party's transcendent mission inevitably clashed with the bureaucratic rationality of its organizational form, and this dissonance was frequently exacerbated by conflicts between the paramount leader, whose authority was tied to advancing the communist mission, and the party bureaucracy, which was charged with administering the country.[10] Nowhere, however, were the effects of this clash more pronounced than in China.

Challenging Bureaucratic Authority

In 1966, Mao divorced the communist class-leveling mission from the party organization and used his personal charismatic authority to turn the mission against the organization. He abandoned conventional bureaucratic methods of mobilization and instead appealed directly to students, workers, and peasants (including both party members and nonmembers), calling on them to form rebel organizations that were autonomous of party control and could, therefore, direct their fire at the party organization.

The official rationale for the Cultural Revolution can be found in the thesis that the Soviet Union, China's model, was undergoing a process of "peaceful evolution" from socialism into a form of "state capitalism." According to Mao and a group of radical theorists associated with him, Soviet officials had become an exploiting class without fundamentally changing the social structure. Since China had closely followed the Soviet model, the Chinese social structure was also seen as harboring the seeds of exploitation, and the main danger to the communist project came not from the overthrown propertied classes or from external enemies, but rather from "new bourgeois elements" *inside* the party. To avoid peaceful evolution to state capitalism, Mao and his radical associates proclaimed, it was necessary to carry out a "continuing revolution under the dictatorship of the proletariat." This revolution was to be directed against an emergent exploiting class, which they identified as "those in power in the party who are following the capitalist road," condensed to the shorthand term, "capitalist roaders." Criticism of the capitalist roaders highlighted the problem of "bureaucracy," the essential meaning of which, in the Chinese communist lexicon, was the concentration of power in the hands of officials. In 1965, on the eve of the Cultural Revolution, Mao warned that party officials were becoming an incipient "bureaucratic class." "These people," he wrote, "have become or are in the process of becoming bourgeois elements sucking the blood of the workers." They were, he added, the "main target of the revolution" (Mao [1965] 1969).

Because Mao's target was the party organization, he could not rely on it to mobilize people to participate in this movement. Instead he went outside the party organization to directly mobilize students, workers, and peasants. During the first two months of the Cultural Revolution, there was a dramatic transition from bureaucratic to charismatic mobilization. The watershed event in this transition was Mao's recalling of work teams that had initially been dispatched by party authorities to lead the movement.

Party leaders had long employed work teams to rectify problems in local party organizations and ensure that political campaigns were implemented in the fashion intended by the center. During Land Reform (1946 to 1952), for instance, work teams spent months supervising the implementation of the campaign in villages, making sure local communist cadres were not protecting landlords and rich peasants. Work teams were also charged with investigating cadre corruption and abuses of power, an ongoing effort that culminated in the Socialist Education Movement (1963 to 1966). Work teams temporarily took charge of villages, factories, and schools—setting aside the local party committees— and organized peasants, workers, and students to help investigate and criticize local leaders. They inspired fear among local cadres and were effective in enforcing party discipline and rooting out cadre corruption.[11]

In 1966, therefore, it was quite natural for party leaders to assume work teams would be the appropriate method to carry out Mao's latest initiative. This time, however, Mao was not simply seeking to discipline errant officials; he wanted to challenge the authority of the entire party organization. The work team method was ill-suited for this task because it relied on top-down methods, reinforcing the authority of the party hierarchy. The problem with previous efforts to reform the party, Mao concluded, was that they were directed from above. "In the past we waged struggles in rural areas, in factories, in the cultural field, and we carried out the Socialist Education Movement," he noted. "But all this failed to solve the problem because we did not find a form, a method, to arouse the broad masses to expose our dark aspect openly, in an all-round way and from below."[12]

During the early months of the Cultural Revolution, Mao allowed central party authorities, led by President Liu Shaoqi, to send work teams to schools and workplaces, but he immediately undermined the authority of these teams by commissioning a series of newspaper and radio commentaries that condemned efforts to control the movement and declared that "the masses must educate themselves" and "liberate themselves."[13] This message incited confrontations between students and work teams (as well as between workers and work teams), which led to the emergence of a rebel movement that pledged loyalty to no one but Mao. This process can be observed in the dramatic events at Tsinghua University that led to the creation of the Jinggangshan Regiment.

Transition from Bureaucratic to Charismatic Mobilization

On June 8, 1966, a work team composed of several hundred party officials arrived at Tsinghua. It took charge of the school and suspended all university and department-level cadres. Tsinghua had been in turmoil since the end of May, when a small group of radical teachers at nearby Peking University publicly posted a caustic "big-character poster" denouncing the school's leadership for practicing a "revisionist education line." Mao had endorsed the poster, and Tsinghua students had flocked to the Peking University campus, eager to witness the ensuing controversy. Soon the Tsinghua campus was embroiled in a debate about the school's own leadership. Classes stopped and the walls of campus buildings were covered with contending posters attacking and defending the university administration. The work team, dispatched by central party leaders, authoritatively settled the debate by condemning Tsinghua Party Secretary Jiang Nanxiang and the entire university party committee. They began mobilizing students and teachers to write big-character posters and participate in "criticism and struggle" meetings denouncing the university leadership.

Soon after the work team arrived, Kuai Dafu, a 21-year-old chemical engineering student, wrote a series of big-character posters accusing work team leaders of trying to control the student movement and protecting Jiang and other top university cadres by refusing to bring them before mass meetings. Kuai, whose parents were both members of their village party branch, had been very active in party-led student political activities. He was head of the editorial committee at Tsinghua's broadcasting station when he took this fateful first step on a path that would make him into the party organization's implacable enemy. The work team, headed by Ye Lin, deputy chairman of the State Economic Commission, and populated by other distinguished members including President Liu Shaoqi's wife, Wang Guangmei, had locked the university gates, prohibited contact between students of different departments, and required advance approval of big-character posters. In his unapproved posters, Kuai called for the expulsion of the work team from campus. "I didn't like the work team's methods," Kuai told me. "The newspapers said it should be a students' movement, but the work team wanted to control everything very closely. That's not what Mao Zedong was urging us to do.... Liu Shaoqi...didn't understand Mao's thinking; he thought the universities were very chaotic, so he sent the work teams to try to control the situation. The work team...suppressed the students."

On June 24, the work team convened a campus-wide meeting to criticize Kuai, condemning him as a "counterrevolutionary." An unrepentant Kuai denounced the work team, winning loud applause from perhaps half of the thousands of students crowded into and around the school's main auditorium. A student selected by the work team to help control access to the stage ended up supporting the opposition instead: "I didn't know who was wrong or right, but I felt...the work team didn't let Kuai Dafu express himself, so I stopped...the work team's people [from approaching the stage] and I helped Kuai Dafu. I felt that if it was a debate, then both sides should have the freedom to speak."

Students and teachers, who were accustomed to the tightly controlled political environment at the university before the Cultural Revolution, were astonished by Kuai's defiance. "At that time, you couldn't doubt the leaders, so it became a big deal," explained Ke Ming, a student who supported Kuai and later played an important role in the movement. "That changed during the Cultural Revolution—then you could. That was the impact of Mao Zedong thought. The extraordinary thing about Kuai Dafu was that he saw that back then, and he didn't back down." The campus split into into two incipient factions, one supporting and one opposing the work team. Although the team mobilized students to criticize classmates who had supported Kuai, labeling them "Rightists" and "counterrevolutionaries," it was never able to reimpose the kind of control that had existed before the Cultural Revolution.

In late July, Mao ordered the work teams removed from schools, and a few days later he issued what he called his first big-character poster, titled "Bombard the Headquarters." The poster sharply denounced the methods of the work teams: "In the last fifty days or so, some leading comrades from the central down to the local levels have ... [proceeded] from the reactionary stand of the bourgeoisie, they have enforced a bourgeois dictatorship and struck down the noisy and spectacular Great Proletarian Cultural Revolution movement. They have stood facts on their head, juggled black and white, encircled and suppressed revolutionaries, stifled opinions differing from their own, imposed a white terror, and felt very pleased with themselves" (MacFarquhar and Schoenhals 2006:90).

A veteran teacher described the unprecedented and somewhat bewildering situation that members of the Tsinghua community encountered after the work team was withdrawn: "Before we had learned to obey the party committee; then after the party committee was gone, we listened to the work team because it represented the party. After the work team left, there was no more control, things were freer—if you wanted to, you could follow the students; if you didn't want to, you didn't have to."

Before the work team left, it hastily appointed a Cultural Revolution Preparatory Committee, led by students whose parents were top party officials, to take charge of the movement. Mao, however, encouraged everyone to form their own "fighting groups," and over the following weeks students, teachers, and workers at the university formed many small groups, which coalesced into two contending factions. The self-styled rebel faction condemned the recently departed work team, while their opponents, led by members of the Preparatory Committee, supported it. The underlying question was whether or not the party organization should control the student movement.

Kuai Dafu and several of his classmates established their own fighting group, which they named Jinggangshan after the mountain stronghold in Jiangxi Province from which Mao and others launched their guerrilla strategy in 1927. Kuai, who even while he was under investigation by the work team in July had received visits from leaders close to Mao, was rewarded for his defiance with invitations to participate in Beijing-wide meetings to promote the most radical of the new student organizations. In October, Jinggangshan and its allies at other Beijing schools helped organize a huge rally to condemn the "bourgeois reactionary line" carried out by the party authorities and the work teams, and to denounce the "conservative" student organizations that had come to the party organization's defense.

With public support from close associates of Mao, Jinggangshan soon became the dominant rebel organization at Tsinghua and by the end of the year, after the conservative faction had collapsed, it took complete charge of the campus. In the spring of 1967, however, more moderate students, increasingly dismayed by the radicalism of Kuai Dafu and other Jinggangshan leaders, organized a new coalition dedicated to defending the "good cadres" at the university. After that, students, teachers, and workers at Tsinghua coalesced into two fairly stable contending factions, the "radicals" and the "moderates." The radicals, led by Kuai, attacked the pre-Cultural Revolution status quo and the party establishment, while the moderates defended the status quo and the party establishment.[14] Similar radical and moderate factions emerged in schools and workplaces across China, and conflict between these two camps gripped both Tsinghua and the country for the next 15 months.[15]

The Radicals' Mission

The goal of the Cultural Revolution, Jinggangshan activists declared in their newspaper, was to do away with the existing "hierarchical system, cadre privileges, the slave mentality, the overlord style of work, and the bloated bureaucracy" (*Jinggangshan*, May 13, 1967).[16] Bureaucratism was the radicals' main target and their solution was to implement "mass supervision" over cadres. They took up this task with relish, hauling university officials up on stages to be criticized, and sometimes cruelly humiliated, by their subordinates. The main practical issue that divided the factions at Tsinghua was the rehabilitation of university officials. The moderate faction thought that after cadres had made self-criticisms, most of them should be brought back to work; even if they had made mistakes, they argued, most cadres were basically good. Kuai and the radicals adamantly opposed the rehabilitation of all but a handful of university cadres.

The radicals directed their attacks against both individual party leaders and fundamental features of the underlying political system. They challenged the authority of the party committee and party offices, criticized the party's culture of political dependency, and denounced the system of career advancement based on political loyalty. The greatest gain of the Cultural Revolution, Jinggangshan activists declared, was "destroying the servile thinking" that had been encouraged by the party organization (*Jinggangshan*, April 5, 1967). Radical efforts to condemn the culture of political dependency were given a boost by a campaign Mao launched in the spring of 1967 to criticize Liu Shaoqi's book, *How to Be a Good Communist* ([1939] 1972), which was the principal guide for the conduct of communist cadres and required reading for those aspiring to join the party. In the book, Liu, who was both the country's president and the CCP's organization chief, stressed that party members must submit to the will of the party organization. Mao declared: "Party members in the past were isolated from the masses because of the influence of *How to Be a Good Communist*,

[they] held no independent views, and served as subservient tools of the party organs. The masses in various areas will not welcome too quick a recovery of the structure of the party" (Dittmer 1998:317).

Jinggangshan used the campaign as an opening to attack the modus operandi of Tsinghua's party organization, particularly its recruitment apparatus. They claimed that university party secretary Jiang Nanxiang, like Liu, had encouraged careerism among party members and demanded subservience in exchange for opportunities to climb up the party hierarchy. They denounced Jiang's motto, "Be obedient and productive," and claimed that he had cultivated a particularly servile group of cadres at Tsinghua. In a scathing essay published in the *Jinggangshan* newspaper, a midlevel university cadre wrote that Jiang's main criterion for selecting cadres was "obedience." The author, who described himself as a "pure Tsinghua-brand cadre," displayed a mastery of the criticism/self-criticism style required during the Cultural Revolution: "To be a good cadre, you had to obey 'Comrade Nanxiang' and the 'school party committee.' As long as you were obedient, you could become an official, you were placed in an important position, and you were deeply grateful." As a result of this kind of selection and lengthy training at the university, the author continued, Tsinghua cadres had been particularly damaged by Liu's "self-cultivation" mentality: "They always stick to convention and have a slave mentality; in their work they are only responsible to those above them, and they care more about following the regulations than about right and wrong. While they are subservient yes-men towards those above them, they exercise a bourgeois dictatorship over those below them and suppress divergent opinions" (*Jinggangshan*, April 18, 1967).

The radicals not only criticized university party officials but also enthusiastically attacked higher-level party leaders. "Those taking the capitalist road," an article in Jinggangshan's newspaper declared, "have captured part of the state machinery in China (and it has become capitalist state machinery)." What was required, therefore, was "a great revolution in which one class overthrows another." This was the task of the Cultural Revolution, "an explosion of the long-accumulated class conflict in China" that was essentially the same kind of thoroughgoing political and social revolution as had taken place in 1949 (*Jinggangshan*, July 5, 1968). "Our primary target was those [party leaders] who were taking the capitalist road," Kuai Dafu told me. "We thought they were the main source of capitalist restoration. Those who had already been overthrown—the so-called old Rightists, the old intellectuals, the old Nationalist Party—they were not the main problem. The danger of restoration came from within the Communist Party's own ranks, from some of its own leaders."

Ideology, Interests, and Mobilization

How did the radicals convince people to join them in fighting for this cause? How did they rally people to act as a cohesive and effective force? In answering these questions, social-psychological accounts have stressed ideology, while rational actor accounts have stressed interests, and in both cases paradigmatic predilections have obscured the relationship between the two. This has created different kinds of problems in each of the paradigms.

Hiniker (1978), author of one of the most sophisticated social-psychological explanations, argued that Cultural Revolution activists were motivated by the incongruence between postrevolutionary reality and communist egalitarian ideals. "Successful bureaucratization," he wrote, "engenders cognitive dissonance in those ideologically committed to charismatic leadership" (p. 535). This cognitive dissonance drove the truly committed to strive even harder to bring reality in line with their millenarian vision. Hiniker contrasted this ideological orientation with the pragmatic orientation of others, who were more concerned about material well-being than ideological goals. While the latter responded to the bureaucratic leadership style that prevailed before the Cultural Revolution, the former responded to Mao's appeal for redemption in 1966. Hiniker thus identified two types of "followers" in China: one a pragmatist and the other a true believer.

Although there was a profound difference between the type of activism fostered by Mao's call for rebellion during the Cultural Revolution and that which had been fostered by the party organization before the Cultural Revolution, the difference was not that one was inspired by ideological and the other by instrumental goals. Instead, the difference was whether activists pursued their goals, instrumental or ideological, by following or by breaking the rules. Political activism in postrevolutionary China, whether before or during the Cultural Revolution, always involved a close connection between instrumental and ideological goals. This common feature, along with the differences between the two types of activism, can be seen by comparing the criteria used to evaluate activists during the two periods.

Before the Cultural Revolution, membership in the party and in its training and recruiting arm, the Communist Youth League, was very important in terms of career considerations, and almost all Tsinghua students eventually joined the league. To gain membership, they had to compete with other students in demonstrating their commitment to communist ideology and collectivist ethics, including a willingness to "serve the people," exemplified by hard work, selflessness, and public spirit. Shirk (1982) noted the irony in this competition: to achieve their personal ambitions, students had to prove their selflessness. Nevertheless, she did not find that her informants lacked ideological commitment or a sense of moral duty, only that these were intimately linked with their efforts to get ahead.

The process of joining Jinggangshan and advancing to leadership positions in the organization was much less formal, but rebel activists were also expected to exhibit commitment to communist ideology and collective spirit. The criteria rebels used to evaluate their comrades, however, were different than those used by the youth league and the party in one key respect. Because the youth league and the party were intent on selecting young people who could work effectively in an organizational hierarchy, taking direction from above and giving direction to those under their supervision, compliance with bureaucratic authority was highly prized. In contrast, rebel activists were expected to demonstrate a willingness to challenge bureaucratic authority.

Like activists in the past, Cultural Revolution rebels were keen to demonstrate their commitment to communist ideals and their selflessness, but altruism was now connected with taking risks in thought and action. This is apparent in the way a Jinggangshan activist described himself and his comrades: "Those who thought creatively and had different opinions supported Jinggangshan. I didn't care about the personal cost; if something was wrong—then challenge it." Kuai Dafu, who eventually spent 17 years in prison as a result of his prominent role in the rebel movement, repeated this theme of disregard for personal well-being, adding a sense of historical drama; "We were acutely aware that [the Cultural Revolution] would probably fail and we knew we would be on the losing side and would be suppressed.... Most people opposed the Cultural Revolution—very few really followed Mao....But we felt we were an important minority and that it was our duty to fight for his ideas.... We were fighting for ideals, for a new world."

Some of Kuai's opponents were not so convinced of his altruism. A supporter of the moderate faction described him in a more opportunistic light: "Kuai Dafu saw there was an opportunity to become somebody different....When you come from a very poor back-ground [as he did]...you kind of have the nature of rebelling. When you get an opportunity, those people are brave; they stand up and do something different that eventually may benefit them." It is not easy to arbitrate between altruistic and instrumental interpretations of Cultural Revolution activists' motivations. Kuai was certainly an ambitious young man, and it is likely that personal ambitions were involved in his eagerness to take up the rebel cause. To prove his rebel credentials, however, Kuai had to demonstrate that he was willing to make great sacrifices, even die, for the cause. Ambition and altruism were insolubly linked.

Thus, ideological *and* instrumental goals were important both before and during the Cultural Revolution. Before the Cultural Revolution, however, youth league activists weighed moral and instrumental considerations in an orderly world governed by calculable rules, while during the Cultural Revolution rebel activists weighed moral and instrumental considerations in a world of revolutionary possibilities and dire risks. Both types of activists were ambitious, but youth league activists sought to realize their goals—whether ideological or instrumental—by working within the system, while Cultural Revolution rebels sought to realize their goals by overturning the system.

By presenting Cultural Revolution rebels as true believers indifferent to material interests, Hiniker made the movement impervious to interest-based analysis. In contrast, Lee (1978), whose early analysis of factional contention during the Cultural Revolution remains one of the best of the rational actor accounts, did not believe any Cultural Revolution activists were true believers: "The mass organizations were almost exclusively concerned with narrow group interests, particularly power interests. To them, ideological and policy considerations were mere means to advance their political interests" (p. 5). The movement offered insurgent leaders a chance to gain power. Lee argued, but it also offered rewards to their followers. Individuals who suffered disadvantages under the existing order saw in the rebel movement the possibility of changing the system and improving their lot. Thus, material interests, not ideological convictions, motivated the rebels.

The problem with explanations of radical upheavals that depend so heavily on the unmediated power of interests is that individuals' conceptions of their interests under normal circumstances are largely shaped by existing institutions and rules. As game theory suggests, rules confer interests. To conceive of practical interests that transcend existing institutions requires not only a creative imagination, but a conviction that these institutions can be overturned. Under ordinary conditions, these are not interests, but pipe dreams. The mobilizing success of a radical movement can be measured in terms of its ability to turn such impractical dreams into practical goals. Interests do, indeed, propel people to join insurrectionary movements, but these are not routine everyday interests; they are interests that can only be invoked by visions of radical change. Because pursuing this type of interest requires sacrificing everyday interests, such a pursuit becomes a mission, beyond the realm of everyday rationality. Such missions are fraught with danger and uncertainty, which is one reason they are so often given by God or by History.

Many of the disadvantaged choose not to join rebel movements, and sometimes they even join the forces of order. There are many reasons for this: individuals' understanding of their interests might be so strongly tied to prevailing power relations that they cannot imagine interests that transcend those relations, they might not believe the lofty promises made by rebel leaders about the new order they are fighting to bring into being, or they might not be convinced they will prevail. The Cultural Revolution was no exception—in factories and villages members of the most disadvantaged social groups fought on both sides of the barricades.

In the elite confines of Tsinghua University, it was difficult to distinguish between the radical and moderate camps in terms of their members' social backgrounds, a situation that also prevailed at other universities (Rosen 1982; Walder 2002). There were children of intellectuals, party cadres, peasants, and workers on both sides, and although a contemporary survey recorded that 63 percent of student party members and student cadres supported the moderate faction, at least 27 percent supported the radical faction (Shen 2004:115). Indeed, the radicals were led by students like Kuai, who had unblemished family histories and seemingly bright futures in the political establishment—until they joined the rebel movement. Although Kuai and his confederates had the invaluable backing of China's paramount leader, they were faced with the difficult task of convincing Tsinghua students, a highly select group virtually guaranteed comfortable and prestigious positions in the existing order, that they were interested in tearing down China's elite educational and political institutions to build a still nebulous egalitarian world.[17]

At Tsinghua, as elsewhere, collective action required more than the direct impetus of interests. I am not arguing that interests were not important, but rather that, as Snow (2004) put it, "interpretative processes matter" (p. 383). To understand how social movements mobilize people to accomplish radical aims, it is necessary to study the dynamic relationship between interests and ideology, as well as the mobilizing structures that social movements employ. I tackle the latter problem here, employing the concept of charismatic mobilization to analyze the structure of the radical faction during the Cultural Revolution. Charismatic mobilization is particularly dependent on ideology because this type of movement, which lacks strong organizational forms, is held together largely by commitment to a common mission, and the capacity for coordinated action is generated by a charismatic rather than a bureaucratic hierarchy of authority.

Charismatic Strategy and Organization
Top and Bottom Versus the Middle

While most charismatic movements originate from below, the Cultural Revolution originated from the top—Mao issued his call for rebellion from the very pinnacle of the state apparatus. Although unusual, this can be understood as an instance of a recurring historical pattern described by Weber, in which the power of an elite group is weakened by the concerted action of a central ruler and social groups at lower echelons of the social hierarchy. Such concerted action can take the form of a social movement that is essentially charismatic because it relies on the personal authority of a central ruler who abandons bureaucratic or traditional hierarchies, which normally underpin his authority, and directly appeals to the populace.

In his perceptive analysis of the Cultural Revolution. Lupher (1996) recognizes this pattern, which he calls the "top-and-bottom-versus-the-middle strategy of power restructuring" (p. 13). Mao at the top and his rebel followers at the bottom shared the goal of undermining the power of the officials who staffed the party offices in the middle. Moreover, Mao and the rebels depended on each other. Without the rebels, Mao's crusade against the party bureaucracy would have had little impact, and without Mao's support, the rebels could not have survived. The personality cult surrounding Mao reached its height during the Cultural Revolution. His image, associated with a red sun that conjured up divinity, was ever present and his words were imbued with infallibility. Although Mao expressed discomfort with extreme manifestations of this "individual worship" (Snow 1971:174–75), it certainly reinforced his personal authority while he was challenging the authority of the party organization. The rebels were just as dependent on Mao's infallibility,

which they invoked to justify their existence and ward off recriminations by local authorities.

The dynamics of this top-and-bottom-versus-the-middle strategy were evident in Kuai Dafu's first big-character poster denouncing the work team, in which he wrote: "We will oppose anyone who opposes Mao Zedong thought, no matter how great his authority or who he is" (Kuai 1966:4). Kuai's manifesto was both an unprecedented challenge to the authority of the party hierarchy and an expression of unstinting loyalty to the party's supreme leader (or, more precisely, to the mission expressed in his thought). In fact, Kuai used his loyalty to the supreme leader as a weapon to challenge party officials.

The key difference between bureaucratic and charismatic mobilization in China was that the former entailed following the guidance of the party hierarchy, while the latter entailed following Mao's personal leadership. Mao enjoyed tremendous power and could change the course of events simply by uttering a few words. But Mao was a distant god and his words were few. Once the authority of the party hierarchy had been challenged in the summer of 1966, people gained unprecedented power to think and act independently. Ironically, the extreme concentration of power in the hands of the CCP's top leader provided an opening for people at the bottom to challenge the entrenched power of party cadres. Ke Ming, the Tsinghua student leader, described how the party hierarchy's authority was undermined: "Before the Cultural Revolution, everything came down from above, one level at a time. You had to listen to those right above you. Then suddenly Mao went around the hierarchy and told the masses that the people between him and them had problems; that they should not listen to them.... This was the first time we had room to think for ourselves."

This new freedom was not limited to private thoughts; individuals were encouraged and even expected to criticize university officials. A radical activist at the middle school attached to Tsinghua University compared the Cultural Revolution with the situation today: "The government [today] criticizes the Cultural Revolution for being repressive, but for many of the masses it was a rare opportunity to speak out and criticize the leaders. When else could you get up on stage and openly criticize your leaders and debate? Who would get up on stage and criticize the president of Tsinghua today?"

Tsinghua students enthusiastically took advantage of this situation, covering the campus with provocative big-character posters and engaging in vehement debates. In previous political movements, there had been debates and big-character posters, but except for a six-week period during the 1957 Party Rectification campaign, they had always been closely orchestrated by the university party organization. Now there was no omnipotent organization to oversee and arbitrate the debate. Although acceptable political expression remained sharply limited, students engaged in real debates. "The two factions at Tsinghua were not just following blindly—they thought deeply about these problems," explained student activist Ke Ming, who originally supported Kuai but later became a leader of the moderate faction. "Of course, the thinking was also very limited. They all believed in Mao, but [different groups] had different interpretations of Mao."

Charismatic Hierarchy of Authority

Although Weber noted charismatic movements' aversion to bureaucratic rules and hierarchies, he wrote little about their organizational structure. How can a large, geographically dispersed movement act in a coordinated fashion without a bureaucratic structure? How does such a movement function at the local level, far from the central leader? The Cultural Revolution provides an instructive case because tens of millions of people throughout a huge country were involved, and the movement's antibureaucratic mission made it particularly hostile to bureaucratic organizational norms.

The organizational structure of Cultural Revolution factions bore little resemblance to the bureaucratic machinery of the party. "All organizations during the Cultural Revolution were not very formal," recounted Ke Ming. "They were not like the party, with clear membership and leadership." The discipline, regulations, procedures, and hierarchical structure of the party were replaced by much looser and more haphazard organizational norms. The cohesion of the movement depended on a

hierarchy of authority, but this hierarchy had charismatic rather than bureaucratic characteristics.

To lead the movement, Mao created the Central Cultural Revolution Small Group (CCRSG). As Dittmer (1987) pointed out, the group resembled the "personal staff" of select disciples that, as Weber noted, often surround charismatic leaders. CCRSG members typically shared two characteristics: ideological commitment to Mao's radical program and a lack of bureaucratic power in the party organization. The group was led by Mao's personal secretary, Chen Boda, and Mao's wife, Jiang Qing. Most other members were writers who had demonstrated a devotion to Mao's class-leveling agenda. Although the CCRSG was formally an ad hoc committee attached to the party's political bureau, it answered to no one but Mao. It stood outside the party bureaucracy and led the attack against it.[18]

No formal organizational links existed between the CCRSG and the myriad local rebel organizations. The most important structural feature of the rebel movement was that it was composed of self-organized local groups. This does not mean that the movement arose spontaneously; on the contrary, it arose in response to Mao's call. Moreover, the rise to prominence of specific local leaders and groups was in part the result of intervention by powerful individuals associated with Mao. While rebel groups depended on the support of the CCRSG, the movement was not organized from above. Local rebel leaders nominated themselves and gathered their own followers. Although they appealed to Mao and his lieutenants for recognition, no formal hierarchy of command was ever established.

The local organizations were structured like political coalitions, reflecting their ad hoc origin. Both the radical and moderate factions at Tsinghua were alliances made up of small fighting groups organized by students, teachers, and university workers. After these fighting groups affiliated with one faction or the other, they remained the basic units of the larger organizations. Membership in the fighting groups fluctuated as individuals joined and left and entire groups sometimes quit one coalition to join another.

The leadership structure of the student-led factions reflected their character as coalitions. Both

Jinggangshan and its moderate rival were led by committees that co-opted members from among leaders of the largest and most influential fighting groups that made up their ranks. The fighting groups were expected to adhere to decisions made by the leadership committees, but there was little semblance of a chain of command in either organization. With time, each faction developed a fledgling bureaucratic apparatus, with ad hoc and permanent committees assigned to develop political positions and take responsibility for aspects of the organizations' work. Nevertheless, political activity was still largely the work of the small, fluid fighting groups that made up the larger organizations. Members of these groups discussed the issues of the day and collectively wrote big-character posters. When factional contention turned violent, each group often procured or made its own weapons.

The rival factions at Tsinghua maintained informal ties with organizations around the country. These were based largely on personal relationships established during the Great Link-Up movement in the fall and winter of 1966, when millions of students from Tsinghua and other schools traveled around the country to "link-up" with others and "exchange revolutionary experiences." Mao insisted that local authorities welcome these rebel emissaries and provide them with free transportation, food, and lodging. These agents of rebellion went to other schools, factories, and villages, spurring the formation of local rebel groups. The Great Link-Up was designed to break the power of local party officials and make certain no party committee escaped unchallenged. Mao's proclamations were essential to this effort, but insufficient, as local leaders proved adept at simulating compliance with Cultural Revolution directives without actually relaxing control over their subordinates. Mao encouraged what every political establishment fears most: an opposition movement extending across geographic, institutional, and class boundaries that raises not only local and partial grievances, but focuses on the governance of the country.

During the Great Link-Up, people determined their own itineraries and Tsinghua students fanned out around the country to promote the organization of local rebel movements. Some students stayed in other provinces, where, due to the prestige of the Tsinghua Jinggangshan organization, they often played leading roles in local rebel organizations. Although these students represented themselves as emissaries from the Tsinghua organization, their ties to Beijing were informal and they operated with wide latitude.

Because Kuai and other Jinggangshan leaders enjoyed direct personal ties with members of the CCRSG, the Tsinghua organization became an important node in an amorphous radical network that extended to all comers of the country. It acted as an informal link between local organizations and the central group, relaying messages in both directions. Nevertheless, this was an unruly network. Jinggangshan leaders were particularly feisty, joining abortive campaigns against some of their powerful patrons in the CCRSG, including Kang Sheng, Xie Fuzhi, and Zhang Chunqiao, none of whom were men to cross lightly.[19]

Despite the informality of these factional networks, their capacity for coordination was in some ways very impressive. The daily newspapers published by Jinggangshan and its moderate rival were distributed across China through informal activist networks. During the height of the factional contention, Jinggangshan's newspaper had a greater circulation than any other newspaper in China, with the exception of the CCP's flagship. *People's Daily* (Dittmer 1998:247).

The charismatic hierarchy of authority that held together the rebel movement was much more fluid and volatile than the party's bureaucratic hierarchy. It was not based on the "charisma of office" Weber described in his discussion of the bureaucratic routinization of charisma, but rather a charisma more true to his ideal type. Charismatic authority was diffused through the entire movement, from top to bottom. Local leaders, such as Kuai Dafu, never had Mao's celestial status, but they all nominated themselves, gathered their own followers, and established their own charismatic credentials. They shared the authority emanating from Mao's mission, but they also bad to demonstrate their own seditious mettle and mobilizing ability. Moreover, this was true not only of the leaders of local factions, but also of the students, teachers, and workers who led the small fighting groups that made up these organizations. Although Mao provided the general orientation, his followers were all qualified to interpret the mission and determine the local road forward. This amorphous structure made the rebel movement susceptible to violent schisms, but it also fostered an insubordinate temperament that gave the movement devastating force.

"Rebel Spirit" and the Impact of the Rebel Movement

Mao's phrase, "It's right to rebel," became the motto of Cultural Revolution activists. Members of Jinggangshan took pride in their "rebel spirit"— their independent thinking and willingness to challenge authority. Kuai Dafu, who owed his leadership position to his defiance of the work team, was fond of citing the traditional insurgent maxim that was also a favorite of Mao's: "He who does not fear death by one thousand cuts dares to pull the emperor from his horse." The chaos of the Cultural Revolution promoted a type of activist who thrived in conditions of political upheaval. This was true both of Jinggangshan and the moderate faction. Even defense of the status quo fell to activists who shared with their radical adversaries a proclivity for ideological polemics, political battles, and historical drama.

The impact of the rebel movement was extraordinary. The authority of the party organization, which before the Cultural Revolution could not be challenged, was shattered. This outcome required the combined efforts of Mao at the top and rebel organizations at the bottom. Mao depended on millions of rebel activists to challenge the authority of local party organizations, and the rebels depended on Mao's personal authority to protect and legitimate their movement.

The Cultural Revolution redistributed power, benefiting the top and the bottom at the expense of the middle. On the one hand, the rebel assault on the party organization further concentrated power in the hands of Mao. Ke Ming expressed this in a cogent metaphor: "During the Cultural Revolution all power went to Mao Zedong. All the small gods were overthrown—there was only one big god Before, the party committee secretary had been a small god; not anymore." On the other hand; the movement dispersed power at the bottom. Power passed from local party officials to fledgling mass organizations, all of which were competing for mass support. Students, workers, and peasants gained unprecedented power to exercise "mass supervision" over the officials who previously had tremendous control over their lives. The fate of individual cadres in schools, workplaces, and villages was debated at mass meetings in which the participants evaluated their self-criticisms and discussed who among them should be restored to leadership positions.

In the summer of 1968, after contention between radical and moderate factions had degenerated into increasingly violent confrontations that brought China to the brink of civil war, Mao countenanced the suppression of factional activity. The contending factions were disbanded and the party organization was gradually rebuilt.[20] The extraordinary authority that party officials had enjoyed before the Cultural Revolution, however, was never completely restored. Mai Qingwen, a senior official at Tsinghua, explained that rebel attacks on party cadres had permanently damaged the party's *weixin,* a term that can be translated as prestige, popular trust, or authority. "All the leading cadres were criticized, and whether or not the criticisms were correct, the conclusion was that they were all bad," he told me. "So the *weixin* of the party fell."

In China today, the years before the Cultural Revolution are widely remembered as a period when the CCP enjoyed tremendous prestige and local cadres had unchallenged authority. Many people I interviewed remembered this highly effective system of political control with nostalgia, while others felt deep antipathy. Most, including Mai, were ambivalent, expressing both nostalgia and antipathy. Whatever their feelings, there was general agreement that the authority of the party organization was never the same after Mao let loose a tide of popular criticism against communist officials in 1966.

The destructive antibureaucratic power of the Cultural Revolution was made possible by its charismatic structure. This loose structure not only had room for rebels, but it cultivated and rewarded their subversive inclinations. The "rebel spirit" celebrated by Cultural Revolution activists could not have survived long if their own organizations had been governed by formal rules and hierarchies of authority. In elaborating this explanation, I hope to have convinced readers that the concept of charisma can be employed to answer questions posed by the current social movements paradigm about the efficacy of mobilizing structures without undermining the paradigm's theoretical premises.

Discussion

Charisma and the Efficacy of Informal Organization

In their seminal book, *Poor People's Movements* (1977), Piven and Cloward advanced the controversial thesis that informally organized movements can be more effective than formally organized movements in accomplishing radical goals.[21] Echoing Weber and Michels, they argued that formal organization is inherently conservative because it concentrates power in the hands of officeholders, who tend to favor accommodation with the existing order (in terms of both methods and goals) to preserve the organization and their own positions in it. Highly structured movement organizations, therefore, often stifle the element that makes radical mass movements effective—their capacity to disrupt the status quo. In those critical and transitory moments when large numbers of people are suddenly willing to break the rules and disrupt the established order, mass collective action does not require formal membership, bylaws, or elaborate organizational hierarchies, and it is often better off without them.

This article lends support to Piven and Cloward's thesis. The rebel movement during the Cultural Revolution was effective because of its amorphous organizational principles. The rebels were only able to break the entrenched power of the party organization because of their visceral antipathy toward bureaucratic authority and their enthusiasm for breaking the rules—a "rebel spirit" fostered by the loose organizational norms of charismatic mobilization. At the same time, this article addresses a concern that has long troubled Piven and Cloward's critics: Without formal organization, how can

movement participants act in a coordinated fashion? In the case of the Cultural Revolution, the rebels acted cohesively and decisively at key moments despite their lack of formal decision-making procedures and organizational hierarchies. Their cohesion was produced by a hierarchy of authority, but one that was not based on a formal chain of command. It was based, instead, on commitment to a common mission proclaimed by a charismatic leader, and charismatic authority was diffused from the top to the bottom of the movement.

Charismatic authority, I would suggest, is often a critical element in the type of informally organized radical movements to which Piven and Cloward called attention. At the height of these movements, when ordinarily quiescent people are swept up in a quest for denied rights that suddenly seem not only just but also attainable, a multitude of charismatic leaders and fledgling organizations spring forth to champion the cause. The African American movement of the 1960s, for instance, was led by many individuals with this kind of inspiration, including Elijah Muhammad, Martin Luther King Jr., Malcolm X, James Farmer, Stokely Carmichael, Gloria Richardson, Huey P. Newton, and many others. No single figure dominated the entire movement, but this is true of many charismatic movements.[22] The power and resiliency of the movement, Gerlach and Hine (1970) argued, was due in large part to its charismatic character and decentralized structure. In using charisma to analyze the structure of social movements, Gerlach and Hine explored the territory this article has begun to chart. Their investigation into the effectiveness of mobilizing structures made them pioneers in the new social movements paradigm, but their interest in charisma unfortunately found little echo among their colleagues.

While Piven and Cloward's thesis about the disruptive power of informal organization is sound, there is reason to doubt their thesis if it is rendered absolute—that *only* informally organized movements can accomplish radical goals. History is replete with examples of formally organized insurgent movements that have profoundly changed society. The Chinese communists, for example, could not have sustained decades of rural insurrection without building a disciplined party organization, and ultimately they were able to use bureaucratic methods of mobilization to overturn and fundamentally transform the existing order. Gamson (1975) and McAdam (1982) had reason to argue that even the most radical challengers must develop formal organizational structures to sustain their movements. Indeed, most movements create some bureaucratic form of coordination, and to the extent they do, they move toward bureaucratic methods of mobilization.

Both charismatic and bureaucratic mobilization can accomplish radical goals, but they each have distinct structural characteristics, which give them different types of disruptive capacities. Despite its martial name, the Jinggangshan Regiment could not have carried out the protracted rural warfare that brought the CCP to power; nor could the CCP have generated the type of rebel spirit that enabled Jinggangshan to rouse the masses against it.

The concept of charismatic mobilization is designed to capture common structural characteristics of an extremely varied set of actual social movements. Although I have used the rebel movement during the Cultural Revolution as an example, no single case can serve as a definitive template for charismatic mobilization. The Cultural Revolution can certainly be disqualified from such an assignment because of its peculiarity. The movement's top-and-bottom-versus-the-middle strategy sets it apart from most charismatic movements, which emerge from below. Moreover, China at that time was governed by a revolutionary regime in which bureaucratic institutions were still infused with elements of charisma, enhancing the potential for charismatic mobilization and weakening the bureaucracy's capacity to resist.

Nevertheless, the rebel movement during the Cultural Revolution shared certain essential features with other instances of charismatic mobilization. Even when a single leader enjoys tremendous authority within such a movement, formal organization is only weakly developed and local groups are largely self-organized. Without formal organization, the movement's cohesion depends on self-nominated local leaders who embrace the paramount leader's mission and become its local interpreters. The

movement is united by a common mission, rather than by formal hierarchies and organizational discipline. This type of structure, which fosters disregard for established authority, engenders the distinctive power of charismatic mobilization. If successful, a movement of this kind can effectively challenge the legitimacy of the existing order and, on this basis, mobilize huge numbers of people and generate intense commitment and energy. Although such moments are often brief, their impact can be profound.

The Cultural Revolution rebel movement provides a dramatic example of how this kind of loose, mission-driven structure facilitates the rebellious, rule-breaking power of charismatic mobilization. At the same time, the movement also manifested some of the characteristic flaws and limitations of this type of mobilization. Although the rebels were united in their determination to challenge the party organization's authority, they were hardly a unified movement. The profusion of local charismatic figures did not always facilitate cooperation, and rebels fought with other rebels, as well as with moderate defenders of the establishment. The movement was resistant to mundane notions of rationality, it tended to see the world in Manichean polarities, and it imbued its top leader with extraordinary personal powers. It was short-lived, unstable, and convulsive—more fit for destruction than construction.

The fact that charisma has unattractive features, however, is no reason to banish the concept from social movement scholarship. Its purpose is analytical, and its utility should be determined by its ability to accurately describe and predict actual phenomena, whether or not these are entirely pleasing to the observer. Once we make charismatic mobilization a topic of serious inquiry, we can begin to analytically address the causes and consequences of its less attractive features, as well as evaluate methods of mitigation (in the same manner as many have discussed the unattractive features of bureaucracy).

The Conservative Tendency of Social Movement Organizations and the Weberian Cycle
In the long-standing debate about why social movement organizations tend to become conservative,

many scholars have begun their contributions by identifying Weber (or Michels) as the author of a theory that predicts movement bureaucratization, and have then proceeded to identify means of avoiding this fate.[23] For the last three decades, Weber's twin concept of charisma has been largely absent from this discussion. In this article, I have suggested that we can better understand the twists and turns of social movement organizations by using these concepts in tandem; while radical movements that take advantage of the bureaucratic efficiencies of formal organization tend to become more conservative, all bureaucratic organizations are susceptible to charismatic upheavals. In the Weberian cycle, bureaucratic structures are built only to be torn down again.[24]

Weber's famous "iron cage" analogy was based on the following insight: it is ultimately impossible to counter the conservative tendencies of bureaucratic organization by means of institutional arrangements because the effectiveness of such arrangements, no matter how well-intentioned and intelligently designed, is circumscribed by their innate respect for the specific rationality that underpins the existing hierarchies of authority. This thesis has long been considered pessimistic. In the long run, however, it is only pessimistic if it is combined (as Weber did in his darker moments) with a prediction that bureaucratic rationality is destined to overcome the threat of charismatic challenges once and for all. Is there persuasive evidence for such a prediction?

Despite the virtual absence of charisma from mainstream social movement scholarship for the past three decades, the world today is hardly lacking in movements that Weber would have described as charismatic. Recent events in Mexico, Bolivia, Georgia, Lebanon, Iraq, Nepal, and elsewhere continue to demonstrate the power of charismatic appeals. Some of these movements have religious inspiration, while others are adamantly atheist; some reject any association with existing states, while others have captured the commanding heights of state power; some have been created from scratch, while others have converted established organizations into vehicles for pursuing new charismatic missions; some rally the poor, while others champion a disenfranchised middle class; and some require a vow of poverty, while others mobilize their followers with promises of material rewards. What they all share is a determination to accomplish their goals by breaking the rules.

Bureaucracy and charisma are most valuable when used in tandem, not only because they define each other by contrast and are constituent elements of a single cycle, but also because they are bound together in practical combinations and by their intrinsic opposition. As I have noted, all radical movements inherently contain elements of both, and the tension between them is played out dramatically as these movements rise and fall. In China, the contradictions created by the CCP's marriage of charisma and bureaucracy ultimately gave rise to the Cultural Revolution, a charismatic challenge to bureaucratic conservatism. Such a challenge might come from the top of an organization, as it did in China, or it might come from the middle or the bottom. Martin Luther, John L. Lewis, Ruhollah Khomeini, and Hugo Chavez come to mind when thinking of individuals who launched charismatic movements from positions of authority within conservative organizations, In each case, the challengers reached back to the charismatic origins of their organizations (whether in the immediate or the distant past) to find language with which to question the legitimacy of prevailing institutional accommodations. Charismatic challenges to conservative institutions can come from within as well as from without, and the Cultural Revolution is a prominent example of the former.

NOTES

Research for this article was supported by Fulbright- Hays, Spencer Foundation, and Peking University fellowships, and was facilitated by the Tsinghua University Education Research Institute. I also thank the many people connected with the university who graciously told me their stories. Rogers Brubaker, Michael Mann, Shaojie Tang, Xiaoping Cong, Chaohua Wang, Paul Pickowicz, Xiaowei Zheng, Andrew Walder, Yang Su, Margaret Kuo, Steven Day, Shengoing Wu, Eileen Cheng, Elizabeth Vander Ven, Peter Andreas, William Rowe, Marta Hanson, Tobie Meyer-Fong, Giovanni Arrighi, Beverly Silver, Melvin Kohn, Dingxin Zhao, Lili Wu, Jonathan Unger, Jerry Jacobs, Vincent Roscigno, Randy Hodson, and several anonymous readers gave me helpful advice and comments.

1. A compilation of Weber's essays on bureaucracy and charisma can be found in Weber (1978). Insightful interpretations can be found in Bendix (1960) and in Gerth and Mills's (1946) introduction to their collection of Weber's works.

2. A number of scholars, often continuing to work explicitly within the structural strain paradigm, have produced more recent studies that explore the nature of charismatic movements (e.g., Madsen and Snow 1991; Rinehart 1997; Schweitzer 1984; Willner 1984), but their work has largely been done in isolation from the now dominant paradigm.

3. In Weber's revolutionary cycle, charisma always plays the disruptive role, but normal routines can rely on either bureaucratic or traditional authority (or a combination of the two). To make full use of Weber's trilateral framework it would be necessary to also consider the role of tradition. I have nevertheless chosen to focus on the simpler bilateral relationship between charismatic and bureaucratic authority because such a focus allows for greater clarity of theoretical exposition. This focus is warranted on both general and specific grounds. Although traditional authority continues to be important, its role has declined as bureaucratic norms have displaced traditional norms in modern political organizations (both conservative and insurgent). In the case under consideration here, the Chinese Communist Party's bureaucratic hierarchy was, indeed, infused with traditional-type relationships, and these were reflected in the factional conflicts of the Cultural Revolution (Walder 1986). But these relationships, which had been cultivated by party officials over a long period of time, were most important in the conservative factions that defended the local party establishment, The rebels did have powerful patrons (including Mao and his disciples in the center), but these were typically new relationships that grew out of the extraordinary conditions of the Cultural Revolution, and their character was essentially charismatic.

4. For a discussion of the organizational principles characteristic of charismatic authority, see Weber (1978:242–46, 1112–19). For a worthy effort to further elaborate these principles, see Panebianco (1988:65–67, 143–62). Both Weber and Panebianco stressed the role of the central leader and neglected the fact that movements lacking bureaucratic organization also require local leaders who gather their own charismatic followings.

5. Song and Sun (1996) and Tang (1996) described Jinggangshan as typical of organizations in the radical camp across China.

6. The interviews took place between 1998 and 2006. Most were conducted in-person and were tape recorded. Many people graciously spoke with me on multiple occasions for many hours. With the exception of Kuai Dafu, I have not used the individuals' real names.

7. Tucker (1961) and Lowenthal (1970) endeavored to theoretically describe this type of revolutionary regime.

8. Dittmer (1987) presented this thesis in the most elaborate fashion, and Ahn (1974), Whyte (1974), and Hiniker (1978) made similar arguments. Schwartz (1968), Schapiro and Lewis (1969), Tsou (1969). Lee (1978), and Moisner (1982) highlighted similar dynamics in the conflict between Mao and the party organization, although they did not use the language of charisma versus bureaucracy.

9. See, for instance, Lenin ([1923] 1975).

10. Although the Leninist model stressed the importance of the organization, the prominence of individual leaders—for example, V. I. Lenin, Ho Chi Minh, Joslp Tito, Enver Hoxha, Fidel Castro, and Amilcar Cabral—in successful communist revolutions suggests that the role of personal charisma remained important. Tucker (1968) argued that Lenin transformed the Russian Marxist movement into a charismatic one.

11. For accounts of work team methods during Land Reform and the Socialist Education Movement, see Hinton (1966), Friedman, Pickowicz, and Selden (1991), and Chan, Madsen, and Unger (1984).

12. Excerpt from a talk delivered by Mao in February 1967, cited in Lin ([1969] 1972:447).

13. These slogans, which had frequently appeared in the press, were officially consecrated in Central Committee of the Chinese Communist Party ([1966] 1972).

14. Both factions emerged out of a split in Jinggangshan and each insisted on keeping the organization's name; the radical faction was popularly known as the "Regiment," and the moderate faction was known as "April 14th" (the date of its founding rally). I use "Jinggangshan" to refer to the radical faction so as not to unduly burden the reader with organizational names. Narratives by Hinton (1972). Tang (2003), and Zheng (2006) recount the twists and turns of the factional conflict at Tsinghua.

15. I use the term "rebels" to refer more broadly to the antibureaucratic movement during the Cultural Revolution and "radicals" to refer more narrowly to the camp that opposed the moderates after the spring of 1967.

16. A collection of *Jinggangshan,* the daily newspaper published by the Jinggangshan Regiment at Tsinghua University between December 1966 and August 1968, has been reproduced in Zhou (1999).

17. For detailed analyses of the interests at stake and the factional divisions at Tsinghua, see Andreas (2002) and Tang (2003).

18. For analyses of the CCRSG and its members, see Lee (1978). Dittmer (1987), and MacFarquhar and Schoenhals (2006).

19. See Tang (1996:52), Hunter (1969:230), Hinton (1972:284), and *Jinggangshan* (August 26, 1967).

20 I have previously analyzed Mao's efforts to institutionalize the antibureaucratic program of the Cultural Revolution during the last years of his life, which included fostering a

system of factional contention within the party and creating institutionalized mechanisms of "mass supervision" over cadres. See Andreas (2006).

21. Piven and Cloward (1977) stirred an ongoing debate. See, for instance, McAdam (1982), Gamson and Schmeidler (1984), Cress and Snow (1996), and Barker (2001).

22. Movements that coalesce around a central charismatic figure are often the result of one leader rising above a field of charismatic rivals. In his investigation of Melanesian cargo cults, Worsley (1974) found both centralized and decentralized movements. The common image of charismatic movements, in which everyone follows a single leader, is probably an artifact of teleological selection (because unified movements usually have greater impact).

23. For recent contributions to this discussion, see Rucht (1999), Voss and Sherman (2000). Barker (2001), and Clemens and Minkoff (2004).

24. Michels's "iron law of oligarchy" is also a theory of revolutionary cycles, and, as Gouldner (1955) pointed out, it might just as well be called an "iron law of democracy."

35.
Diffusion and Modularity

SIDNEY TARROW

The destruction of the World Trade Center by two suicide airplane-bombs on September 11, 2001, left most Americans dazed, humiliated, and enraged. Many would probably have been surprised to learn that the killings on September 11, 2001, compared in number—if not in spatial concentration—with the long record of suicide bombings since the early 1980s, in Beirut in the early 1980s, South Asia in the early 1990s, Israel/Palestine throughout that decade, and in Iraq against the American occupiers and their local allies in 2003–4.

In fact, when Eli Berman and David Laitin examined the number of victims of suicide bombers before and after September 11th, they found that 420 were killed in 1983, 400 in 1998, and more than 200 each in 1985, 1995, and 1996 (Berman and Laitin 2005: table A2), with probably much higher numbers after the Iraq war.[1] Figure 1, calculated from their careful reconstruction and tracing a three-year moving average of the number of suicide attacks around the world from 1983 to 2002, shows that suicide bombings grew steadily before September 11, 2001.

Before it became the privileged tool of Islamist martyrs, suicide bombing was part of a much broader range of actions. As the bloody 1980s gave way to the even bloodier 1990s, the tactic became "modular"—that is, like the demonstration and the strike in the past history of contentious politics, it was employed in a wide range of causes in a number of different places (Tarrow 1998: ch. 3). From the Lebanese Civil War in the early 1980s and Sri Lanka in the early 1990s, it spread to the "Second Intifada" in Palestine/Israel and then to the transnational Islamist movement. From a form that was employed only where more conventional forms of contention were too risky, suicide bombing became a routine part of the coordinated strategies of transnational political Islamism.

Much of the research on suicide bombers since September 11 has focused on the motives and the character of those who choose to end their lives in this way.[2] Less attention has been given to the processes that diffused this new and ruthless form of attack and made it part of the twenty-first century's repertoire of contention. There have been two unfortunate outcomes of this understandable focus on the actors: first, it distracted analysts from the varieties of its modes of diffusion (but see Sageman 2004); second, its almost unique horror diverted attention from comparing its diffusion with that of other, less lethal forms of contentious politics. When we do so, we will see that it has diffused across borders in ways that are remarkably similar to less lethal forms of contention.

Tarrow, Sidney. 2005. "Diffusion and Modularity." Pp. 99–119 in *The New Transnational Activism*. New York: Cambridge University Press, Reprinted by permission.

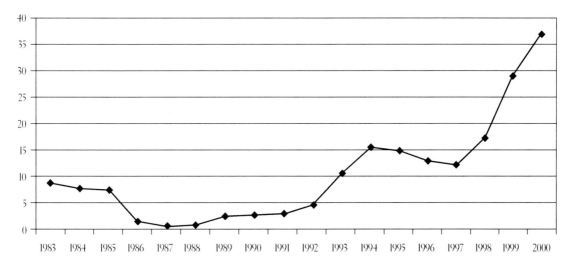

Figure 35.1 Three-Year Moving Average of Number of Suicide Bombing Attacks, 1983–2002. *Source:* Berman and Laitin 2005, table A2.

In this chapter I focus both on the variety of processes of transnational diffusion and on diffusion among very different forms of collective action. As examples, I use evidence from two movements in different parts of the world: the diffusion of non-violent resistance from India to the United States and then to former socialist countries; and the diffusion of the Zapatista solidarity network from Chiapas to North America. In both cases—as in the case of the suicide bombing—diffusion travels through well-connected trust networks ("relational diffusion"), through the media and the internet ("nonrelational diffusion"), and through movement brokers ("mediated diffusion"). Among them, these processes produce the emulation of local forms of collective action in other places and contribute to the spread of contentious politics across the globe.

Constraints and Inducements

How does a new form of collective action or a social movement spread? In his studies of what has come to be called "the repertoire of contention," Charles Tilly (1986:10) writes that the existing repertoire grows out of three kinds of factors: a population's daily routines and internal organization, the prevailing standards of rights and justice, and the population's accumulated experience with collective action. But he also emphasizes learning: what people *know* about how to contend in various places and at different periods of history constrains change in the repertoire. If this is true, then there are both inducements and constraints on the spread of a new form of contention from one country to another.

Both the inducements and the constraints can be seen historically, as state building and capitalism triggered the invention of new forms of contention. As the early modern state consolidated, people resisted with tax revolts, conscription riots, and petitions; and as market capitalism took hold, grain seizures, strikes, and turnouts were used to resist its pressures. If there was no state trying to extract a surplus or build an army, there would be no tax revolts or conscription riots; and if there were no capitalists attempting to assemble workers in factories and exploit their labor, there would have been no strikes. Capitalism and state building were the major macroprocesses triggering the development of the modern repertoire of contention (Tilly 1995b).

But once invented in response to structural change, new forms of contention could be imitated and modified far beyond their origins and outside the structural relations that had produced them. For example, once its efficacy was demonstrated, the strike spread from industry to services; petitions that had proved useful against individual state officials could be employed as a political tactic against slavery; turnouts against local capitalists transformed into demonstrations against all manner of antagonists; protesters refusing to leave a particular official's office transmuted into the sit-in. Countering the specificity and locality of the repertoire of contention was its modularity and transferability across space and into different sectors of movement activity (Tarrow 1998: ch. 3). With globalization and internationalization, both the speed and the modularity of diffusion of forms of contention have increased.

This duality in the repertoire is the source of our central question for transnational contention: *How do forms of collective action that arise out of specific national configurations of conflict spread to other venues?* And, in particular, how do internationalization and globalization affect the speed and facility with which these forms diffuse? Determined activists have always been able to adapt new forms of contention across borders. But with the growth of internationalization and global communication, diffusion has both increased and accelerated. For example, while it took a half-century for antislavery agitation to spread from England to the European continent and across the Atlantic (Drescher 1987), suicide bombing diffused across Asia and the Middle East within a decade of its first use in Lebanon. What kinds of processes have speeded the diffusion of new forms of contention?

Pathways of Transnational Diffusion

Internationalization and communication are the large impersonal processes that lie in the background of all forms of transnational diffusion. Internationalization creates regular channels for communication and awareness of institutional similarities and differences among actors in different places. That information has to spread for diffusion to occur is true by definition, but what seems to be new in today's world is the rapidity and ease of information transfer. New forms of communication, such as text messaging and the internet, make it easier for activists to communicate with one another at great distances and even in the midst of an episode of contention (Danitz and Strobel 2001; Rheingold 2002; Tilly 2004b: ch. 5).

But *how* does a new form of contention spread, and what lessons does this have for transnational contention in general? From his study of the spread of the Salafist Jihad, Sageman allows us to identify three main pathways of diffusion: relational, nonrelational, and mediated diffusion.

As in any form of collective action, social bonds and personal networks were important in the spread of the Islamist network (Sageman 2004: ch. 5). Not only did Islam and Arabic provide a universal faith and a common language; interpersonal trust, family ties, and common local origins helped to create "small world networks" among people who identified with one another and were prepared to emulate one another's actions (p. 139). This is what I call *relational diffusion*. It transfers information along established lines of interaction through the attribution of similarity and the networks of trust that it produces (Lee and Strang 2003).

The Islamist movement also spread through *nonrelational diffusion*. By this term I mean diffusion among people who have few or no social ties. Although this can occur by word of mouth, many of today's movements spread through the mass media and electronic communication. By historical accident, the Islamist movement's growth coincided with the coming of the internet, "making possible a new type of relationship between an individual and a virtual community" (Sageman 2004: 160–3). This not only sped the diffusion of the movement but favored its "theorization": a kind of "folk theory" that defines some thing or activity in abstract terms and locates it within a cause-effect or functional scheme.[3] Theorization can be highly abstract and complex, like the role of "class struggle" in the Marxist ontology, or it can be reduced to a few symbols and guides to action. The media and especially the Internet encouraged the diffusion of an extremely one-sided reading of Islam, reducing the level of discourse to the lowest common denominator and identifying the suicide bombing as a tool that would bring glory to the martyr and success to the cause (p. 162).

Third is what I call *mediated diffusion*. In the jihadi networks he studied, Sageman (2004: 169ff.)

identified a number of movement "nodes" comprising individuals within a geographic cluster, with various clusters interrelated by a small number of weak links. What kept these weak links alive is brokerage, the connection of two unconnected sites by a third, which works through movement "halfway houses," immigrants, or institutions. Brokers may never participate in contentious politics, but their key position in between otherwise unconnected sites can influence the content of the information that is communicated.

The general tendency of students of social movements has been to focus on the first process, relational diffusion, in which innovations travel along established lines of interaction to be emulated and adopted elsewhere.[4] Like the spread of hybrid corn or the adoption of new medical practices, the adoption of new forms of collective action often follows the segmented lines of interpersonal interaction among people who know one another or are parts of networks of trust. But in an age of massive immigration and cheap and easy transportation, information about collective action can spread through third parties, or brokers, who connect people who would otherwise have no contact with one another.

Figure 2 offers a simple descriptive model of these three processes of transnational diffusion, with the key mechanism in the first path the attribution of similarity, in the second the theorization of political Islamism through impersonal media, and, in the third, brokerage. Each of the pathways in Figure 2 is familiar from the history of both cultural movements and contentious politics in Europe and America:

- *Relational diffusion in Norman England.* When the new style of Gothic cathedral building, which began in the Abbey of St. Denis outside of Paris in 1137, crossed the Channel to England, this was an example of relational diffusion—the Normans, after all, had invaded England from France in 1066. It was transferred by two contemporary connections: the numerous French clergy who served in England and the many English priests who had studied at the great cathedral schools of Chartres and Notre Dame (Scott 2003: 14).
- *Nonrelational diffusion in America.* The diffusion of rebellion through England's North American colonies had many relational sources (e.g., the famous Committees of Correspondence), but one of the most important was nonrelational: the availability of a plethora of printed pamphlets and books, of which Tom Paine's *Common Sense* was the most famous and the most durable. Bernard Bailyn (1967) points out that America in the 1770s was virtually flooded with newspapers and pamphlets. Paine's book, which "theorized" revolution for the American public, sold thousands of copies, many of them read aloud by purchasers to groups of listeners in village squares.
- *Mediated diffusion through movement missionaries.* Through individual missionaries and movement organizations, people who might otherwise have remained ignorant of one another's claims are brought together. Both the

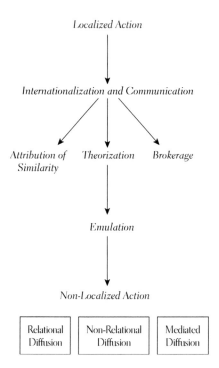

Figure 35.2 Alternative Pathways of Transnational Diffusion

Protestant "saints" who smuggled Protestant tracts across Europe during the Reformation and the anarchists who brought their faith to southern Italy, Spain, and Latin America were "brokers" in the spread of revolutionary movements (Walzer 1971; Joll 1964).

Diffusing Nonviolence

Modern social movements have direct access to a variety of networked relational ties (Arquilla and Ronfeldt 2001; Keck and Sikkink 1998). In addition, autonomous channels of communication transmit information about new movements or forms of action. And various of institutions and "rooted cosmopolitans" are available to act as movement brokers. All three forms of diffusion combined in the transnational diffusion of one of the most successful innovations in contentious politics in the twentieth century: the strategy of nonviolent resistance.

The Gandhian Origins of Nonviolence[5]

"As the days unfolded," wrote Martin Luther King Jr. (1958: 84–5) of the early days of the American civil rights movement,

> the inspiration of Mahatma Gandhi began to exert its influence. I had come to see early that the Christian doctrine of love operating through the Gandhian method of nonviolence was one of the most potent weapons available to the Negro in his struggle for freedom.... Nonviolent resistance had emerged as the technique of the movement, while love stood as the regulating ideal. In other words, Christ furnished the spirit and motivation, while Gandhi furnished the method.

Dr. King was not the first African American to try to bring the theory of nonviolence from India to the United States. Sean Chabot (2003: 3) writes: "King was certainly not the first—and arguably not even the most creative—actor involved in the Gandhian repertoire's transnational diffusion." From the 1930s onward, men like Howard Thurman, Benjamin Mays, James Farmer, and George Houser had visited India to meet with Gandhi and returned to the United States inspired by the doctrine of nonviolence. But King and others in the 1960s succeeded

as domesticators of the practice of nonviolence in America.

The theory of nonviolence has sometimes been defined quite broadly as a moral preference for any form of contention that is not violent (Schell 2003) and sometimes very narrowly to refer to the specific forms of collective action that Mohandas Gandhi developed in South Africa and brought to preindependence India (Bondurant 1958). But at the heart of nonviolence is a strategic theory: "aggressive measures to constrain or punish opponents and to win concessions through disruptive but not violent means" (Ackerman and DuVall 2000: 2). It was the successful transference of this strategy by movement brokers—and not the specific forms that Gandhi developed—that would explain its success in places as far removed from India as the United States in the 1960s and Serbia and Georgia after the fall of communism.

Of course, Gandhi developed the practice of nonviolence to resonate within the specific context of Indian civilization (Bondurant 1958: ch. 4). "The tendency of the Indian civilization," he wrote, "is to elevate the moral being" (quoted in Schell 2003: 123). This, in effect, *domesticated* the principle of nonviolence (p. 126). To this theoretical core, Gandhi added his own aesthetic and communitarian beliefs. Bondurant (1958: 105) writes: "Gandhi used the traditional to promote the novel; he reinterpreted tradition in such a way that revolutionary ideas, clothed in familiar expression, were readily adopted and employed towards revolutionary ends." The resulting amalgam was the doctrine and practice of *satyagraha* (ch. 3).

From India to America

To be successful in the United States, the strategy of nonviolence would need to be dislocated and relocated in very different conditions. True, both colonial India and the American South were repressive societies with a patina of Anglo-American rule of law. But the American South was a Christian, not a Hindu-Muslim society, and one in which a single racial divide replaced a society of many castes and where, in place of the naked domination of colonialism, a fiction of democracy overlay the reality of racial oppression.

All three of our pathways can be observed in the transfer of nonviolence from its Gandhian origins to the American civil rights movement:

- *Relational diffusion.* Indian exiles, religious pacifists, and African American theologians, and organizations like the Congress of Racial Equality (CORE) and the March on Washington Movement (MOWM) brought the movement directly to America.
- *Nonrelational diffusion.* The movement was promoted in the African American press and in writings of authors like Joan Bondurant (1958), who first went to India as an American intelligence agent during the war, became fascinated by Gandhi, and returned to study the movement and publicize it in the West. Through these impersonal agents, the movement was reduced in form and "relocated" in the United States (Chabot 2003: 7; R. Fox 1997: 75–80).
- *Mediated diffusion.* "Movement halfway houses," such as the Highlander Folk School, taught the methods of nonviolence to a range of future activists (Horton 1989).

The federal government served as a facilitator of nonviolence too. As beefy sheriff's deputies unleashed police dogs and aimed water cannon at peaceful demonstrators in the glare of national television, it was difficult for the federal government to avoid intervening on their behalf (Tarrow 1992). As the once-solid South shifted to the Republicans and African Americans began to appear as a significant electoral force, for the Democrats in power to acquiesce in the repression of civil rights demonstrators would have been political suicide (Piven and Cloward 1977: ch. 4; McAdam 1983). Washington's intervention was also fed by the country's foreign policy posture. It would have been hypocritical for a country that claimed to lead the free world to be seen to condone the brutalization of people demanding nothing more than the right to vote.

If relational, nonrelational, and mediated diffusion facilitated the diffusion of nonviolence to the United States, how would the strategy fare in settings in which communication is suppressed and political change is opposed by a brutal dictatorship?

In this age of internationalization and electronic communication, and in the presence of transnational agents who assisted in its transfer, the constraints against diffusion of nonviolence are much weaker, and the strategy of nonviolence could travel quite far indeed, as the following examples show.

Postsocialist Nonviolence[6]

The brutal nationalist regime of Slobodan Milosevic would seem like the least likely venue to welcome the practices of Gandhi and King. A wily Leninist who was quick to scent the winds of change in the Balkans well before 1989, Milosevic undermined what was left of Yugoslav unity in the early 1990s by fomenting a war with Croatia and encouraging the Bosnian Serbs to attack Bosnia-Herzegovina. When the horrors of genocide in Bosnia led to a reaction from the West, Milosevic made a deal with the Americans and West Europeans that left his Bosnian henchmen adrift. When he invaded Kosovo, which the Serbs claimed as a Serbian province, NATO bombing forced him to withdraw.

Politically unassailable as long as he controlled his army and police, Milosevic's position weakened in the mid-1990s as his regime's economic ineptitude and corruption and the costs of his wars began to sink in. As his country's isolation tightened, inflation raged, and unemployment grew, his popularity eroded. Ruthless cunning, control of the press, and support from the remnant of the Communist *apparat* helped Milosevic hold onto power until November 1996, when the formerly divided opposition parties mounted a coalition, Zajedno (Together), to challenge Milosevic in the local elections. When they won fourteen of the country's municipal governments, including Belgrade, the government blithely declared the results illegal.

Such a tactic could only work if three things were true: if the move was backed by a credible show of force, the media remained under state control, and no one from outside the country was watching. But by mid-1996 these conditions no longer held. Still smarting from the retreat from Kosovo, the army stayed on the sidelines, foreign media substituted for the repressed local press and television, and the Organization for Security and Cooperation in

Europe (OSCE) investigated the electoral outcomes and validated Zajedno's success. That was the background for the wave of contention that began with the stolen elections of November 1996 and lasted until Milosevic was overthrown in 2000.

Would the Balkans once again explode into violence? When protesters pelted state media with eggs for refusing to cover their activities, the police responded with violence to drive them off the streets. But from the beginning of the campaign against the stolen elections, the centerpiece of the protests was a series of nightly marches through the center of Belgrade organized by an opposition using nonviolent sanctions. For nearly two months, demonstrators marched, sang, blew whistles, listened to speeches, alternately heckled and fraternized with the police, and went to court to keep the pressure on Milosevic. As one observer wrote, "The regime was fired at with eggs, blown at with whistles, banged with pots and pans, and ridiculed by clowns" (Vejvoda 1997: 2).

That was only the first stage of a widespread campaign of civil disobedience that culminated in 2000. Encouraged by the opposition's ability to turn around the stolen elections, a student movement called Otpor (Resistance) developed to challenge Milosevic's attempt to control the universities. From the beginning, Otpor's strategy was deliberately nonviolent. In the words of one activist, "We knew what had happened in Tiananmen, where the army plowed over students with tanks. So violence wouldn't work—and besides, it was the trademark of Milosevic, and Otpor had to stand for something different."[7] Otpor developed a sophisticated strategy of targeting Milosevic personally for all the country's ills, adopting slogans that implied the movement was spreading, and using antics and theatrical tactics instead of mass demonstrations that could be targeted by the police.

Brokerage in the Balkans

Otpor's understanding of how to use nonviolent sanctions was in part the result of diffusion from the United States. Miljenko Dereta, the director of a private group called Civic Initiatives, got funding from Freedom House to print and distribute five thousand copies of Gene Sharp's book on nonviolence, *From Dictatorship to Democracy* (1993). Otpor also translated sections of Sharp's three-volume work, *The Politics of Nonviolent Action* (1973), into a Serbian-language notebook they called the "Otpor User Manual." The activists also received advice from the Balkans' director of the U.S. Institute for Peace, from the National Endowment for Democracy, and from Colonal Robert Helvey, who had studied with Sharp and worked as an independent consultant organizing nonviolent trainings in Budapest for the International Republican Institute.[8]

Of course, the embrace of nonviolence was not the only reason for Otpor's success. The regime's failure to hold onto Kosovo, the bombings of Serbian cities, and the country's growing isolation and economic decline were important factors, too. So was the spreading belief among Serbs that the European Union and the United States had had enough of Milosevic. But the nonviolent protest campaign organized by Otpor and backed by its international allies was a major efficient cause of Milosevic's overthrow.

From Belgrade to Tbilisi

Nonviolent sanctions played a crucial role in the diffusion of the Otpor model from the Balkans to the Caucasus. In November 2003 President Eduard Shevardnadze, one-time Soviet foreign minister turned Georgian patriot, rigged a parliamentary election to provide a sure victory to the parties that supported him. Since declaring independence from the Soviet Union, Georgia had drifted into a situation of corruption, economic decline, and ethnic separatism from three border areas, encouraged semicovertly by Russia. As the country sank into instability, its strategic importance grew because of the pipeline that American interests wanted to construct through its territory from recently opened oil fields in Azerbaijan. American political interests were also present in U.S. government support for political parties and civil society groups hoping to build democratic institutions (*Washington Post,* Nov. 25, 2003, A22).

Shevardnadze was no Milosevic. But as in Serbia, it was his attempt to foil the electoral process that brought down his government. Three weeks of peaceful street protests culminated in a "March of the Angry Voters," led by Mikheil Saakashvili, leader of the opposition coalition and the country's president after Shevardnadze was forced to step down. For months, activists led by the student group Kmara had engaged in graffiti, leaflet, and poster campaigns against corruption and police brutality, and for university reform and media freedom. This was no spontaneous demonstration but "a coordinated plan…for tens of thousands of citizens to converge by buses, cars and trucks on the capital, Tbilisi."[9]

Where had the opposition learned these tactics? Although the deft hand of U.S. advisers could be read between the lines, this was no CIA-engineered plot. In the months before the election, Saakashvili had traveled to Serbia to contact the former organizers of the anti-Milosevic movement. He returned with a plan for nonviolent action modeled closely on the success of Otpor. This was followed by ex-Otpor activists traveling to Georgia to conduct trainings in strategic nonviolent struggle for Georgian reformists, civil society activists, students, and members of the political opposition, who, in turn, trained a cadre of grass-roots activists.

If electronic communication played an important role in Serbia, in Georgia it was crucial. An important tool in the campaign in Tbilisi, according to the *Washington Post* report, was the American-made documentary on the fall of Milosevic, *Bringing Down a Dictator,* supported by the Washington-based International Center for Nonviolent Conflict. The film was both used as a teaching tool at the Georgian trainings and shown on the independent national television station. "Most important was the film," said Ivane Merabishvili, general secretary of the National Movement party that led the revolt. "All the demonstrators knew the tactics of the revolution in Belgrade by heart because they showed…the film on their revolution. Everyone knew what to do. This was a copy of that revolution, only louder" (*Washington Post,* Nov. 25, 2003, A22).

The successful diffusion of nonviolence from India to the United States and then to the Balkans and the Caucasus does not mean that nonviolence is a panacea for defeating dictators or rolling back racism. After all, following Gandhi's death and the establishment of an Indian democracy, religious violence ran rampant across India. And following the successes of the civil rights movement, new forms of racial segregation developed in the American South (Andrews 2002, 2004). As for Serbia and Georgia, the future of those countries is still in doubt. But these examples show that innovations in the repertoire of contention can cross broad cultural and spatial divides even where established lines of interaction are weak. A second example—the diffusion of the Zapatista solidarity network—shows how important nonrelational and mediated diffusion have become in today's connected world.

Diffusion from Chiapas[10]

On January 1, 1994, a hitherto unknown guerrilla group in the southern Mexican state of Chiapas attacked police barracks in the city of San Cristóbal de las Casas and in surrounding towns. The rebellion broke out on the same day as the North American Free Trade Agreement treaty (NAFTA) came into effect among Canada, Mexico, and the United States. In committing Mexico to open its borders to trade with its more-powerful northern neighbors, NAFTA promised a boon for commercial agriculture but threatened the survival of poor dirt farmers in the South.

The coincidence of the rebellion with the start of NAFTA gave the Zapatista movement an international allure from the start, although its "spokesperson," who called himself Subcomandante Marcos, was soon at pains to emphasize its roots in the historical oppression of Mexico's indigenous peoples. Although its guerrilla actions failed to spread to other regions of Mexico, the EZLN received instant support from both within and outside the country. In Mexico City, where hundreds of thousands of people demonstrated in favor of the insurgents, the progressive newspaper, *La Jornada,* emerged as an unofficial press agency for the rebels. In Rome, the left-wing newspaper, *Il Manifesto,* taking much of its coverage from *La Jornada,* spread word about the rebellion to an Italian public during a period in which the traditional left was in disarray. Soon, hundreds of activists from Europe and North America arrived in Chiapas to support the rebels and, by their presence, helped to hold off the threat of military repression (Bob 2005).

Meanwhile, in Austin, Texas, an important sympathizer, Harry Cleaver, began to filter e-mail messages about the insurgency to progressive groups around the United States, and soon a number of listservs and websites appeared that were dedicated to the insurgency.[11] The wave of solidarity produced what some excited spirits called a global "Netwar," the first cycle of protest to be fueled by the internet. That claim turned out to be exaggerated, but the diffusion of the movement's message from a backward state in southern Mexico to international public opinion was probably a factor in preventing the insurgents' repression. Ultimately, it created what Thomas Olesen (2005) has called an "international solidarity network."

As the movement developed and word about it spread, traditional borders of space and culture appeared to collapse. As Olesen (2005: 2) observes: "Notwithstanding the obvious distance in both physical, social, and cultural terms" between the core insurgents and their supporters, "the movement won a great deal of solidarity, mainly from Western Europe and North America." In fact, "the interest and attraction generated by the EZLN beyond its national borders is matched by no other movement in the post–Cold War period." All three of our processes of diffusion helped to spread word of the movement and create this movement of solidarity.

Relational and Nonrelational Diffusion

With a long *indigenista* tradition, Mexicans were prepared to interpret the insurrection in culturally resonant terms. In a country in which between 12 and 14 percent of the population are *indios*,[12] solidarity with the EZLN found its first basis among existing supporters of indigenous rights. Following the initial attacks in San Cristóbal, there were massive demonstrations of solidarity in Mexico City and elsewhere; in various parts of the country, representatives of other indigenous groups expressed solidarity with the EZLN. Recent events, like the repeal of Article 27 of the Mexican constitution, also made peasants fear that their land would be bought up by big agricultural interests.

But relational diffusion was not the only channel for the movement's diffusion; nonrelational diffusion played an important role too. Until the 1990s, press freedom in Mexico was extremely constrained by the government and the ruling party. Not only were newsprint and advertising revenue controlled by the government, but independent journalists would often fall prey to mysterious "accidents" and disappearances. Yet diffusion of news of the rebellion through the press was extremely important, both in spotlighting and limiting government repression in Chiapas and in the creation of the EZLN solidarity network.

There were several reasons for this. First, the EZLN emerged at a particularly conflictual period of Mexican politics, in which the press and the electronic media were beginning to escape the heavy hand of PRI control. Three major dailies signaled their independence from the government by publishing critical articles.[13] Second, information about the rebellion was transmitted to a specialized public of related groups and sympathizers through websites sponsored by the Zapatistas. It was also generated to a broader public through websites unrelated to the Zapatistas and through independent e-mail traffic and the press.

Taking control of San Cristóbal, and "distributing written statements, granting lengthy interviews, and posing for photographs by the city's gathered media" (Bob 2005: 128), the group developed a skillful media strategy from the beginning. Clifford Bob points out that gaining media coverage was one of the "primary objectives" of the movement, one that was actually facilitated by the government, which at first allowed news of the insurrection to get out, then banned reporters from the region, and finally relented from armed repression under broad international and domestic pressure.

As the mainstream press "corroborated Chiapas' long history of poverty and political repression" (Bob 2005: 165), reporting on the government's heavy-handed military reaction, it began to frame the movement as "an army of innocents" in danger of falling victim to vengeful forces, rather than as a guerrilla group that had taken over a major town (p. 145). Days after the cease-fire, Zapatista communiqués began reaching receptive journalists. Mainly the product of Marcos's "prolific, pointed and playful pen, these writings spanned hard-hitting communiqués and manifestoes, tendentious fables (told by a beetle), a fanciful children's story, and inexplicable, almost hallucinatory ravings" (p. 142).

Although it is never easy to measure the success of a media strategy, the press was important to the Zapatista rebellion in two important ways. First, it played a major role in framing the movement in a sympathetic light, thereby producing a positive reaction in Mexican public opinion. Polls showed a 61 percent approval rating for the zapatistas right after the uprising and 75 percent a month later (Bob 2005: 136). Second, the Mexican army was diverted from its original use of overwhelming force, in large part by the pressure of public opinion that was mobilized through the press (Arquilla and Ronfeldt 2001). Nonrelational diffusion was an important process in legitimating the rebels and preventing their immediate repression.

Mediated Diffusion

Much of the information that led to the formation of an international Zapatista solidarity network passed through a set of linked brokerage ties reaching into North American and Western European society. Olesen charts five different levels in what he calls transnational zapatismo's "information circuit": first there were the indigenous communities of Chiapas; then a range of Mexican and Chiapas-based organizations that functioned mainly as information gatherers and information condensers; next actors who passed the information beyond the borders of Chiapas and Mexico through the internet and other links; then a circle of "periphery actors" who were dependent on core actors for their information but still devoted a significant part of their time and resources to these issues; and, finally, people who had irregular and transitory ties to people closer to the core but devoted little time to the issue of Chiapas and the EZLN (summarized from Olesen 2005: 67–78).

The most central broker was, of course, the man who calls himself Subcomandante Marcos. Coming from a traditional urban leftist intellectual background, Marcos was a classical rooted cosmopolitan, embedding himself deeply within the Lancandòn rain forest for a long period of time before the insurgency broke out. His words,

according to Higgins, became "bridges between the Indian world of the southeast and the even-more-pervasive world of global politics" (2000: 360, quoted in Olesen 2005: 10). "With a well developed sense of public relations…he is a mediator," writes Olesen (p. 10), "translating the EZLN indigenous struggle into a language that is understandable to a non-Mexican audience."

The media image of Marcos carrying his laptop through the jungle and uploading communiqués via a cell phone assigned too much importance to this central node of the network. Much of the information about the insurgency came from second-level brokers, like *La Jornada,* which one Chiapenecan activist jokingly described as *"The Chiapas Gazette"* (quoted in Hellman 1999: 175). *La Jornada,* in turn, was the main source of information for sympathetic foreign journalists whose access to and information about Chiapas was rudimentary. Other second-level nodes were listservs like Chiapas 95 and Chiapas-L, and the *Ya Basta!* website established in March 1994 by Justin Paulson (Olesen 2005: ch. 3; Paulson 2000: 283). These sites were mainly responsible—far more than Marcos himself—for the construction of what Judy Hellman (1999) has called a "virtual Chiapas." In the process the complexity of the message was reduced, to the point at which many in the United States and Western Europe had only the vaguest idea of the ethnic heterogeneity and political cleavages within the region.

Conclusions

From this rapid survey of the diffusion of suicide bombing, nonviolent sanctions, and the spread of the Zapatista solidarity network, what can we infer for the broader question of when and how new forms of contention, new movements, and international solidarity will be diffused across borders?

First, a disclaimer. My account does not tell us why thousands of African American teenagers were willing to face the truncheons and police dogs of sheriff's deputies or why "thousands of people around the world would take notice of a group of less than one thousand mostly unarmed, barefoot peasants carrying out brief takeovers of seven minor municipalities in a backwater state in Mexico."[14] Transnational diffusion does not guarantee either the success of a new form of contention or its popularity among people far from the field of struggle. Had the civil rights movement not coincided with the foreign policy and electoral incentives of the Kennedy administration, Jim Crow might have survived longer in the American South. Had nonviolence been employed in more efficiently authoritarian regimes than Serbia or Georgia, it might not have led to movement success. And had the Mexican government not already been under pressure to democratize, Marcos's amateur guerrillas might have been smashed. The mechanisms we have adduced produced three complementary processes of diffusion, but these processes did not guarantee success.

Three main conclusions do emerge from these analyses. First, as in Tilly's concept of the repertoire of contention, new forms of collective action emerge from the structural development of the societies in which they are invented and are sustained by people's understandings about how to contend, where to contend, and which forms of contention are legitimate. Islamist suicide bombers drew on the concept of jihad and on the image of the heavenly paradise they thought they would enter if they sacrificed their lives to the resurgence of Islam. *Satyagraha* and its associated cultural forms grew out of and were adapted to the Indian subcontinent and would have been exotic had they been transferred literally to the American South, Serbia, or Georgia. The EZLN drew on the heritage of Emiliano Zapata, and on the historical land hunger and ethnic identity of Chiapanecan Indians.

But, second, as we have seen, new forms of collective action diffuse to places in which they are not native. Facilitated by internationalization and global communication and through diffusion processes that detach it from its origins and domesticate it in new settings, direct ties between originators and adopters, nonrelational transmission through the media, and mediated diffusion through brokerage help to bridge cultural and geographic divides and diffuse new forms of collective action across borders.

Third, although we cannot.predict outcomes from processes, we can hypothesize that these processes will vary in their effects according to their major driving mechanisms. In relational diffusion, the attribution of similarity facilitates trust, but its dependency on segmented networks limits its range. In nonrelational diffusion, "theorization" makes it possible to transport a message to a new venue, but the need to reduce it to a form of "folk wisdom", reduces its complexity and can produce a simplistic version that receivers can interpret as they like.[15] In the third process, brokerage through movement halfway houses and third parties speeds the transfer of information but gives intermediaries great importance in reshaping the message.

This takes us to the major question that emerges from these analyses: what are the global consequences of the three variants of diffusion? All three of the processes I have examined produced horizontal—and not vertical—patterns of diffusion. Although adherents of both jihadist Islamism and the faith of nonviolence see them as universally applicable, and many supporters of the Zapata rebellion saw it as the harbinger of a global movement, both universality and the formation of a global movement require a *vertical* shift in scale, and that cannot occur without the coordination of collective action at a higher level.

In earlier chapters, I argued that internationalism provides a setting in which, by using international regimes, institutions, and encounters as focal points, nonstate actors encounter one another in international venues. But meeting and recognizing others with similar claims is not sufficient to build a transnational movement. For that to happen requires sustained work at an international level, the formation of broader networks of trust, and the coordination of collective action beyond the national state. The next chapter examines this process in greater depth as I investigate the potential for "scale shift" of contentious politics.

NOTES

This [work grew] out of two earlier joint efforts with my collaborators, Doug McAdam and Charles Tilly. See McAdam, Tarrow, and Tilly 2001: ch. 11, and Tarrow and McAdam 2005. I thank them both for their help and their collaboration.

1. I use the conditional "probably" because there are unsolved problems of coding actual—as opposed to media reports of—suicide bombings against the American occupation of

Iraq. Both the occupying forces' and reporters' motives in reporting attacks as "suicide bombings" may be suspect. I am grateful for this observation to David Laitin as well as for permission to draw from his and Eli Berman's unpublished paper.

2. Interpretations of the motives of suicide bombers have ranged from journalists' images of crazed fanatics attempting to enter paradise, to more detached statistical analyses by economists (Krueger and Maleckova 2003), to realist and rational choice models of collective action by political scientists (Pape 2003; Berman and Laitin 2005). Microanalysis shows that the tactic cannot be reduced to a reflex of economic distress (Krueger and Maleckova 2003) and is most likely to be employed by members of one religious or ethnic group against another (Berman and Laitin 2005; Bloom 2004: 6). Geographic analysis shows that—with the exception of Sri Lanka, where seventy-five of these attacks took place- organizations that mounted suicide bombings mainly come from the Middle East (Berman and Laitin 2005; table 1). Leadership analysis points to a combination of psychological and relational factors (Sprinzak 2000; also see Bloom 2004).

3. I thank David Strang for offering this definition, drawn from his work with John Meyer. See Strang and Meyer 1993.

4. See the discussions in Jackson et al. 1960; McAdam 1999; McAdam and Rucht 1993; Pinard 1971; Rogers 1983; Strang and Meyer 1993; and Soule 1997.

5. This section is much in debt to the original doctoral dissertation of Sean Chabot (2003). Also see Chabot 2002.

6. I am grateful to Jack DuVall for his advice in the preparation of this section. With Peter Ackerman, DuVall has followed closely and helped to advance the cause of nonviolence as producers of documentary films, one of which, *Bringing Down a Dictator,* had important effects in the diffusion of nonviolence to the Caucasus. For information on their International Center for Nonviolent Conflict, go to http://www.nonviolent-conflict.org/resources.shtml.

7. Interview with Srdja Popovic, from a videotaped interview by Steve York, Belgrade, Yugoslavia, November 13, 2000, for the York-Zimmerman-directed PBS documentary, *Bringing Down a Dictator* at http://www.pbs.org/weta/dictator/otpor/nonviolence.html.

8. In an interview for the PBS documentary, *Bringing Down a Dictator,* Helvey recalled, "You know, they [Otpor] had done very, very effective work in mobilizing individual groups.

But there was something missing to take them beyond protest into actually mobilizing to overthrow the regime. I just felt that something was lacking. They were doing something very, very well, but there seemed to be an invisible wall here that they needed to get over. So we started with the basics of strategic nonviolent struggle theory. And I did it sort of as a review because apparently they were doing many things right so there must have been some basic understanding. But sometimes you miss some of the dynamics of it if you don't understand the theory." See the transcript of Helvey's interview for *Bringing Down a Dictator* at http://www.pbs.org/weta/dictator/otpor/ownwords/helvey.html.

9. The source of this report is a press release from the International Center on Nonviolent Conflict, "Georgia's Nonviolent Resistance: Briefing Sheet." I am grateful to Shaazka Beyerle, associate director of the center (sbeyerle@nonviolent-conflict.org), for help in preparing this narrative.

10. More than usual, this section is dependent on the observations of other scholars, graciously shared with me. In the case of the Zapatista movement, I was helped by the advice of Clifford Bob, Judy Hellman, Thomas Olesen, and Heather Williams.

11. Cleaver's role can be found at http://www.eco.utexas.edu/faculty/Cleaver.

12. Data from Wilkie 2001: table 532: 104. Also see Yashar 2005.

13. Heather Williams, in a personal communication, points out that one of these three, *La Riforma,* was almost closed down for its independent views in the year before the rebellion and might not have survived without it.

14. Quoted from a personal communication to the author by Heather Williams.

15. Judy Hellman reports that part of the appeal of Subcomandante Marcos's writings for European and North American Zapatistas was the possibility of interpreting his words to fit local realities. In interviews with Zapatista activists in Italy, one of them solemnly told her that "'The thought of Subcomandante Marcos teaches us that it is appropriate for us here in Padua to put forward a slate of candidates for the forthcoming municipal elections.' This at the very moment when Marcos was calling upon the Chiapanecan sympathizers to boycott the 2000 presidential elections in Chiapas." In a personal communication to the author.

Unit

IV

Do Movements Matter?

Part II

Outcomes and Impacts

In this final section of the book we take up the issue of movement outcomes. Presumably the ultimate justification for studying social movements lies in their capacity to bring about various kinds of social change. Those involved in social movements certainly assume the potential significance of movements as vehicles of social change. So it is somewhat surprising that movement scholars were slow to devote systematic empirical attention to the crucial issue of "outcomes and impacts." In our introduction to this section of the first edition of this reader, we lamented the relative absence of work on this topic. Happily, in the intervening period, movement scholars have devoted much more attention to the issue. The selections included here represent the fruits of some of that labor.

Why were scholars slow off the mark in addressing the topic? Elsewhere we have speculated that perhaps their own political values led them to assume the social change significance of movements (McAdam and Su 2002). But we also suspect that the daunting methodological challenges one faces in trying to assess impact also discouraged work on the topic. An example will help to illustrate these challenges. Take the case of the women's movement in the United States. One could easily generate a list of changes in American society since, say, 1975, that could plausibly be attributed to the women's movement. Examples include: the expansion of abortion rights occasioned by *Roe v. Wade*; the increase in the number of female elected officials; higher rates of conviction and stiffer sentences for rape; the spread of gender-neutral language; and the entrance of large numbers of women into previously male occupational domains (e.g., law, medicine, academia). But generating such a list is hardly the same as proving the connection between the movement and any of these changes.

To move beyond the realm of the plausible, the researcher must confront two daunting challenges. First, one must show that the relationship between the movement and the presumed outcomes is not *spurious*. A spurious relationship occurs when two phenomena are themselves a product of a third phenomenon that causally prrecedes the other two. Let us illustrate the concept with an example that bears directly on the role of the women's movement as a force for social change.

Women's movements are now an established force in most countries around the globe. Given this fact, it would seem reasonable to attribute all manner of pro-feminist policy changes in these countries to these domestic movements. But sociologist John Meyer has long argued that these movements *and* the policy changes that appear to flow from them are, in fact, the products of a broader and temporally prior change process. Meyer and colleagues contend that over the past century or so, and accelerating since World War II, we have seen the spread of Western "civic" norms around the globe (Boli and Thomas 1997; Meyer et al. 1997a, 1997b). As a result of this diffusion process, policies that emphasize human rights, environmentalism, and, most important for our example, women's rights are now among the central normative "requirements" for standing among nations in the current global order. From this perspective, the women's movements we see around the globe are more an expression of the broader diffusion process than a force for change in their own right. We might counter by asking where these normative requirements came from if not from the feminist movements that developed in the democratic West in the 1960s and 1970s. We cannot hope to resolve the matter here; we raise it simply to underscore just how difficult it is to prove the causal potency of movements relative to other change processes.

Even if we could empirically rule out other prior causes, we would still have to contend with a second difficult issue, the matter of *mechanisms*. By mechanisms we mean those specific processes that account for the causal impact of social movements. Sticking with the prior example, take any given change plausibly attributed to the women's movement and ask yourself the "mechanisms question." Can we specify the means by which the movement achieved this outcome? In some cases, such as the passage of a bill advocated by feminists, the means or mechanism would seem to be clear. In this case, the assertion of a tight causal link between the movement and the outcome in question would seem to be justified. But with other possible outcomes—a rise in the divorce rate, for instance—it would be a good bit harder to specify, let alone test for, specific causal mechanisms linking the movement to the change in question. In such cases, a final judgment regarding the impact of the movement may prove elusive. As you read these selections, you might want to reflect on these tough conceptual and methodological issues, asking yourself how well you think the author(s) handled them.

Setting aside these issues, we also want to use this introduction to distinguish various general categories of outcomes that might be reasonably ascribed to a given movement. At the most basic level, movements strive to achieve fairly specific, direct outcomes. In the case of 15 U.S. homeless movement organizations studied by Cress and Snow (2000), for example, they found that movements tried to attain one or more of four types of outcomes: representation on city task forces and service provider boards; resources such as office space and supplies; rights such as eliminating police harassment and merchant and service provider discrimination; and relief from the trials of street life, such as better accommodative facilities (e.g., shelters and showers) In addition to such specific goals, it is important to note that the effects movements ultimately attain may be much broader and quite often unintended. Consider the civil rights movement in the United States. Most obviously, the movement helped to achieve a great deal of consequential *state action*. This would include such landmark pieces of federal legislation as the Civil Rights Act of 1964, the 1965

Voting Rights Act, as well as countless other executive, legislative, and judicial decisions at all levels of government.

Of more general political significance were the *electoral changes* brought about by the movement. Three major changes can be identified in this regard. First, the restoration of voting rights to African Americans in the South paved the way for a rapid expansion in black political representation in the region. Second, blacks took advantage of the momentum generated by the movement to become a major force in urban politics throughout the country. But the most consequential electoral shift was unintended. As newly registered black voters moved into Democratic Party politics in the South, white "Dixiecrats" fled the party in large numbers, establishing, for the first time, viable Republican Party organizations throughout the region. The once "solid" Democratic South quickly became the most dependably Republican region in the country. The first to recognize the significance of this shift was Richard Nixon. Running on what he called his "southern strategy," Nixon was elected to the White House in 1968, establishing an enduring "electoral regime" that has kept the White House in mostly Republican hands for the past 40 years.

Leaving the realm of institutionalized politics, the civil rights struggle may also be plausibly implicated in any number of broad *social/cultural changes* to take place in the United States. over the past 35 years. The striking gains in attitudinal support for integration and nondiscriminatory practices is but one example. Another would be the dramatic increase in interracial marriage (Rosenfeld 2005). Then there is the movement's crucial *impact on other movements*. As several studies have shown, many of the other New Left movements of the 1960s and 1970s were inspired by the ideological, organizational, and tactical "lessons" of the civil rights struggle (Evans 1980; McAdam 1988).

Finally, movements—as a number of researchers have shown—also have the potential to dramatically alter the *life-course outcomes* of those engaged in the struggle (Fendrich 1993; McAdam 1988, 1989, 1999). Thus movements can be vehicles of personal as well as broader political and social change. Indeed, the first selection in this section illustrates this potential among what, at first blush, might seem like an unlikely population. Frances Hasso documents the existence of a "feminist generation" of working class Palestinian women whose involvement in women's organizations in the late 1980s and 1990s led to an enduring commitment to a "gender-egalitarian ideology" and a sustained sense of "self-efficacy."

The second selection, by McCammon et al., also focuses on the impact of feminist activism, though in a very different time and place from the first selection. It looks at the efforts of activists in the U.S. Women's Jury Movement in the first half of the twentieth century to broaden laws to give women the opportunity to serve on juries. This success, as the authors show, varied considerably over time and across states. Empirically, they link this variability to (a) the different frames used by the state-level movements and (b) the cultural context—or "discursive opportunity structure"—in which these frames were deployed.

The third and fourth selections are by two scholars who have contributed as much as anyone to our understanding of the long-term political effects of movements. In the first of these pieces, Edwin Amenta and two colleagues propose and test a "political mediation" theory to account for state-level variation in Old Age Assistance payments. They show statistically that the state-level strength of the old-age pension movement is significantly related to the size of Assistance payments, offering evidence not only in support of the theory but the general proposition that movement mobilization can powerfully affect policy outcomes.

In the fourth selection, Kenneth Andrews drops down a level of analysis from Amenta et al. and looks, within Mississippi, at county-level variation in the size of poverty programs as a function of the strength of the civil rights movement in those locales. Consistent with the exemplary body of work he has published on the general topic (1997, 2004), Andrews shows, in this article, that "counties with strong movement infrastructures generated greater funding for Community Action Programs." Adding complexity to his analysis, the author also takes account of the strength of the "white resistance" movement at the county level, documenting the very complex interactions between civil rights forces, segregationists, local powerholders, and federal agencies that shaped the outcomes across all counties.

36.

Feminist Generations? The Long-Term Impact of Social Movement Involvement on Palestinian Women's Lives

FRANCES S. HASSO

Introduction and Theoretical Framework

There is a rich and now extensive literature on women's social movement involvement (Basu 1995; Blee 1998; Jaquette 1994; West and Blumberg 1990; Badran 1995; Hart 1996; Ray 1999; Robnett 1997; Taylor 1996; Whittier 1995). This literature has focused on the various identities that mobilize women; gendered discourses and differences in movements; the effectiveness of movements in terms of macroinstitutional and ideological outcomes; the mobilizational narratives or "frames" of social movements; the persistence, albeit shifting nature of, feminist involvement over time; and identity formation among social movement participants. There is very little research, however, addressing the impact of such participation on individual women after involvement in a social movement ends.

In addition, most of the gender and social movement research, particularly in U.S. sociology, continues to empirically focus on women and gender in the United States and Western European countries (see Basu 1995; Moghadam 2000; Ray and Korteweg 1999). This is probably related to the genealogy of the discipline and the usually unaddressed geographic division of labor, at least in the United States, between sociology and anthropology. This division is more difficult to sustain in an era of interdisciplinary research and for sociologists whose backgrounds are non-Western or whose intellectual interests are broader. The most serious implications of the U.S. and Western European focus of sociological social movement theory, however, is related

to the frequently universalistic theorizing that too often takes for granted the particularistic empirical bases (economic, political, and cultural) of this theorization.

This article explores the individual impact of social movement participation using longitudinal qualitative research with Palestinian women from the Occupied Palestinian Territories. I argue that there exists among these former participants a "feminist generation" that is differentiated by its egalitarian gender ideology and sense of self-efficacy. I avoid "the dilemma of particularism versus universalism" (Ray and Korteweg 1999, p. 48), whereby Third World women (and people outside the "West") are seen as either intrinsically different from or fundamentally similar to non–Third World women. Also important is resisting the problematic dichotomy of Third World women as either victims (Mohanty 1991) or heroes (Carr 1994, p. 154). As Robert Carr and Leela Fernandes have noted, both sides of this dichotomy are dehistoricized, deterritorialized, and simplistic in their constructions of wholly agentic or overly passive subjects (Carr 1994, p. 155; Fernandes 1999, p. 148).

Karl Mannheim has argued that "similarly located contemporaries" who share an affinity in their collective response to the events of tumultuous historical moments constitute a "political generation" (Mannheim 1952, pp. 303–4). Generation as a temporal, biological, historical "location," he argued, is transformed into generation as "actuality" when individuals "participate in the process of social transformation" during turbulent periods (pp. 303–4). The members of a political generation appear to be bound together and differentiated from the larger population in ways that are important and persistent even after the passage of turbulent historical periods (pp. 299–310). Most empirical

Hasso, Frances S. 2001. "Feminist Generations? The Long-Term Impact of Social Movement Involvement on Palestinian Women's Lives." *American Journal of Sociology* 107: 586–611. Reprinted by permission of The University of Chicago Press.

studies addressing the long-term impact of social movement involvement on individual lives largely substantiate Mannheim's argument (Fendrich and Tarleau 1973; Fendrich 1974; Fendrich and Krauss 1978; Jennings and Niemi 1981; Jennings 1987; McAdam 1989). The more intense the participation, the more significant and enduring is the impact on individual lives, particularly when there are social ties and structural supports to facilitate ideological maintenance (Jennings and Niemi 1981, pp. 364, 377; Abramowitz and Nassi 1981; Whalen and Flacks 1980, p. 231; Marwell, Aiken, and Demerath 1987; McAdam 1989; also see Newcomb 1943; Newcomb et al. 1967; Alwin, Cohen, and Newcomb 1991; Cohen and Alwin 1993).

This article is based on a two-wave panel study, the first conducted in 1989 and the second in 1995, with Palestinian women who in 1989 were employed in income-generating projects and preschools sponsored by the Palestinian Federation of Women's Action Committees (PFWAC). The PFWAC was a nationalist-feminist organization created in the Occupied Palestinian Territories in 1978 by women who were also leaders of the Democratic Front for the Liberation of Palestine (DFLP), one of the four primary constituent parties of the Palestine Liberation Organization (PLO). I argue that deep PFWAC involvement beyond employment helped to produce a feminist generation that persisted years after the end of the PFWAC.

The existing research on former social movement activists indicates that the impact of political participation is to some extent independent of the biographical criteria that lead some and not others to participate in such historical moments of opportunity in the first place. That is, self-selection appears to be important in explaining what categories of people are likely to participate in and be influenced by such political and intellectual currents (Jennings and Niemi 1981, pp. 339, 378–79) but does not fully explain the attitudinal and behavioral differences that occur after such participation. The PFWAC findings similarly demonstrate that while most of the women who compose this feminist generation were comparatively more independent-minded before their PFWAC involvement, they had not necessarily been feminist in their orientations.

Deep political engagement, not surprisingly, pushed them in new ideological and personal directions.

Exploring whether and to what extent PFWAC involvement produced a feminist generation would seem to require a definition of *feminism,* which, as many feminist scholars have noted, is contested and best defined plurally and in a contextualized, historicized manner.[1] In any given context, women will have multiple and imbricated locations and identities and various sources of support and subordination. Because not all sources of subordination are simply based on gender, and because women themselves are often different and unequal from each other along nongender axes, their feminist visions of the future can often differ fundamentally.[2] The feminisms of Third World women (like those of poor women, U.S. women of color, or "minority" women in other countries) usually assume that "gender discrimination is neither the sole nor perhaps the primary locus of oppression" (Johnson-Odim 1991, p. 315).

Women's responses to inequality or subordination are always structured by, and occur in negotiation with, past and present cultural, political, material, and discursive circumstances. Sometimes women will *accommodate* to the gender order, as did lower-middle-class women in Cairo, who Arlene Macleod argued were caught in crosscutting, overlapping subordinate interactions in which it was not clear which hierarchy—gender, class, or global inequities—was the most important source of their problems (1991, p. 145).

In contrast to either accommodating or taking dramatic resistant action that they are unlikely to win, several researchers have argued that subalterns are likely to engage in lower-scale, nonconfrontational responses to oppressive conditions (Scott 1986). These responses will usually draw on, and sometimes rearticulate, existing cultural and social repertoires. The Malaysian women electronic workers studied by Aihwa Ong (1987), for example, sometimes responded to their exploitation, loss of dignity and autonomy, and poor working conditions with "spiritual possessions" on the factory floor. Lila Abu-Lughod (1986, 1990) found a variety of expressive resistance strategies, most of them nonconfrontational but culturally important, among the Egyptian Bedouin women she studied (also see Reissman 2000). It is difficult to define such responses as *either* resistance or accommodation; they can be, and probably are, both.

Patricia Hill Collins has argued for the importance of seeing as feminist the everyday, individual acts whose focus is creating or maintaining dignity, self-definition, self-reliance, and independence (1991). Sherna Berger Gluck demonstrated that for working-class women in particular, "changes in consciousness are not *necessarily* or *immediately* reflected in dramatic alterations in the public world" (1987, p. x). Many of the most important changes for white, Mexican-American, and black former "Rosie the Riveters" were private and individual (Gluck 1987, p. 269).

I also found former PFWAC employees' feminism to exist at individual levels:[3] relatively gender-egalitarian social and political attitudes and a high sense of self-efficacy influenced their decisions in a number of areas. The women often indicated that this sense of self-efficacy was at least partly the result of PFWAC experience and socialization.

While members of the PFWAC feminist generation (and even many of the women who were influenced less dramatically) sometimes challenged and changed the status quo in their social worlds in a range of ways, it is important to recognize that the nonexistence of local and national feminist institutional support and a stable, sovereign state with at least some accountability to women considerably limited the range of feminist possibilities for these women.

Some gender scholars, in contrast, have argued that the fluidity that occurs in periods of state crisis, instability, or regime transition sometimes provided *more* opportunities for women and women's movements in the Middle East and North Africa (MENA) to gain significant political and economic influence. Moreover, MENA and other states often limit feminist possibilities through the control and co-optation that occurs with the establishment of state feminism (Brand 1998, pp. 8–12). While it is true that states are often relatively less accountable (and contradictory in terms of legislation and policy) to women, the poor, and "minority" constituents, they nevertheless have the potential to provide crucial safeguards for these groups if they are at least premised on ideals of democratic accountability. Clearly, however, the possibilities for realizing this state protection and accountability depend to some extent on the existence of strong advocacy movements, in this case feminist organizations, that are independent of the state and representative of a significant constituency.

PFWAC and DFLP: Feminism, Nationalism, and Crisis

The PFWAC was committed to the mass mobilization of women in the Occupied Palestinian Territories for the dual purposes of gaining national liberation and improving women's gender status—the organization had an explicitly nationalist-feminist agenda. This agenda placed significant importance on women's attainment of equal rights with men in "public sphere" matters—wages, job opportunities, education, and political participation. PFWAC leaders assumed that employment would give women the economic leverage to alter their home environments, and political activity would expose the contradictions of their own exploitation as women in their homes, leading them to take action that transformed their lives (Hasso 1998).

While the establishment of PFWAC preschools and income-generating projects was consistent with this ideological agenda, there were pragmatic political purposes as well. The preschools facilitated the mobilization of working-class women into the PFWAC and the Democratic Front for the Liberation of Palestine (DFLP) by providing needed day care to three categories of women: politically uninvolved "housewives" (*rabaat buyut*), employed married women with children, and politically active married women with children. PFWAC employment in the income-generating projects and preschools was also an avenue for mobilizing these women (and their family members) into the PFWAC because it provided needed money, it occurred in a unisex associational space that did not require supervision from male bosses (the situation that existed in most textile factories in the territories), and the work was with a politically and socially respected organization. This was important for the women employees themselves, their often socially conservative families, and the communities in which these projects existed.

Because the DFLP, like all PLO parties, was illegal in the territories under Israeli military law, its *formal* political, organizational, and financial bodies existed outside the territories (in Jordan, Syria, Tunisia, and Lebanon), where major party decisions were usually made and communicated to cadres inside. The possibility of eventual conflict between what Palestinians call "the inside" (*al-dakhil*) and "the outside" (*al-kharij*) was overdetermined by this geographic dispersal of the resistance movement and different regional-political conditions in the Arab world. The geographic dispersal did not become a serious issue of contention in the DFLP (ironically, these differences emerged among members of the Political Office *outside* the territories) until mid-1988, approximately seven months into the Palestinian uprising (*intifada*), when it appeared that a political resolution to the Arab-Israeli conflict might be on the horizon. By September 1990, the DFLP and the PFWAC in the territories each had informally split into two organizations, ostensibly over the unequal distribution of "inside/outside" power and disagreement over the nature of a resolution with Israel (Hasso 1997, chap. 4). During and after the split, the DFLP, the PFWAC, and their offshoots lost most of the popular support built over many years in the Occupied Palestinian Territories.

By splitting over the same issues that divided the party, as opposed to differences over gender ideology or program, the PFWAC contradicted one of its foundational arguments: that gender and national liberation were equally important. On another level, however, the PFWAC split indicates the impossibility of excising "politics," in this case nationalist politics, from feminist subjectivity. During this period, DFLP party women were systematically disenfranchised from extraordinary political power in the territories by party men in both DFLP factions. All of this, combined with a general demobilization of the population in the territories that came with the (unsuccessful) Madrid negotiations and Oslo Accords,[4] ended the PFWAC as it had historically been constituted in the Occupied Palestinian Territories.

Method, Demographics, and the Politics of Research

In 1989, when I was an unpaid PFWAC intern, I conducted semistructured interviews with 63 women who were employed by the PFWAC; these included all the nonmanagerial workers in the five major income-generating projects and 35 teachers in six selected PFWAC day care centers and nurseries throughout the territories.[5] I reinterviewed 56 of these women in late 1995,[6] approximately five years after the demise of the PFWAC.[7] The findings discussed in this article are limited to the 56 women who were interviewed in both time periods. I conducted all of the interviews in Arabic. In 1989, security considerations did not allow for audio recording, so I relied on note taking (with immediate longhand translations into English); in 1995, I audiotaped and fully translated and transcribed all but two of the reinterviews.

The 1989 interviews, which took one to two hours each, focused on women's everyday lives: what they did the previous day from morning until evening, why they worked, how the money they earned was spent, their family relationships, gender relations in the household, political attitudes, and their views on gender relations, marriage, family planning, and child rearing. In 1995, I was similarly interested in women's gender ideologies and practices, in addition to their personal choices in the intervening six years, their attitudes toward the PFWAC, their assessment of their PFWAC experience, and their situations at home, especially given the dissolution of the PFWAC and the overall political demobilization that had occurred with the end of the intifada.[8]

The 56 women who were interviewed and reinterviewed six years later had been affiliated with the PFWAC for a mean of 2.26 years in 1989.[9] The mean and median age of these women was 24 years. Of the 56, 50% were West Bankers, 27% were Gazans, and 23% were from East Jerusalem; 50% were villagers, 45% were town residents, and 5% lived in refugee camps.[10] In 1989, 80% were single. Of the 56 reinterviewed women, 18 had married between 1989 and 1995, 27 had remained single, and one woman was engaged to be married.

Based on the economic standards of the territories, in 1989, 20% of the women were very poor,

64% were average low income, and 16% were in households that were, relatively speaking, comfortable economically.[11] Between 1989 and 1995, the economic position of seven of the 56 women had deteriorated from average low-income to very poor, four previously very poor women became either average low-income or comfortable, and 10 formerly average low-income women became relatively comfortable. Overall, the number of women in the relatively comfortable category almost doubled, to 30%, despite an overall deterioration in the economic situation for Palestinians in the territories. (The implications of this are discussed later.) The largest proportion of women, 53%, remained in the average low-income category.

It is important to attend to the political context in which the 1995 reinterviews occurred. Asking women about anything having to do with the PFWAC was a sensitive endeavor and was invariably colored by the events that culminated in the splits of both the DFLP and the PFWAC. The norm during the PFWAC division was personalized attacks, particularly through the spreading of rumors about collaboration with the Israeli military government, sexual promiscuity, and corruption, which had the almost immediate effect of alienating most women from the PFWAC and the DFLP.

The women interviewed had other reasons to be unhappy with the PFWAC and its former leadership. From 1990 through 1992—when it was unclear which faction would control the preschools and income generating projects, whether these projects would be terminated, or how they would be financed—most women continued to run the projects without pay, some for as long as a year.[12] Bills for utilities, food (for preschool children), and other project expenses mounted during this period, and many women gave me tallies of money they were owed and asked me to appeal to the former PFWAC leaders to pay them. Others either harassed former PFWAC leaders or found young men in the neighborhood to pressure the leaders to pay them.

Trying to assess which women had been very active in the PFWAC (or the DFLP) beyond their PFWAC employment, an issue that was too politically dangerous to raise in 1989, was complicated by this history. In 1995, five women denied being active

with the PFWAC, although I had strong evidence indicating they had been somewhat or very active with the organization or the DFLP. For example, when I asked a 25-year-old Ramallah-area woman in 1989 how her family had reacted to her decision to work in the PFWAC project, she had replied, "My family was very difficult at first. I was the first girl to leave to work. [They believe] girls shouldn't go out and work. It took a long time, three months, to convince them to allow me to work [in the PFWAC preschool]. People from the *lijan* [PFWAC] came to convince my mother to let me work." When asked, "If it weren't economically necessary, would you still work outside the home?" she replied, "I would continue only if it was internal to the *lijan*. I've been a [PFWAC] member for *seven* years" (respondent 30, 1989; emphasis added).

In 1995, in contrast, when I asked her to evaluate the PFWAC, she responded, "I didn't work with the *lijan*." When I asked, "In general, how do you feel about your work with the [PFWAC] preschool? Do you feel it has had any significant effect on your life?" She responded, "No, it did not affect my life, my life was that I was only a worker there and then I would go home. I didn't use to get involved in their work; no, no, no" (respondent 30, 1995).[13] Most women felt, as did a respondent from Hebron, that "in the end, the [PFWAC] political goals turned out to be more important than the social goals. That's my opinion" (respondent 63, 1995).

I usually had to overcome strong suspicions before I could reinterview women in 1995, whom I often had to reassure that I was not affiliated with the DFLP or the faction that separated from it, Fida. Most PFWAC women were bitter and felt betrayed by the PFWAC, the DFLP, and Fida. Others wondered whether I was attempting to gather information for the Palestinian National Authority, which they generally distrusted. Two women were nervous enough not to allow me to audiotape the reinterviews.

The sense of betrayal is captured in the words of one former activist from Gaza:

It is difficult for a person to bear the things that happened....I quit, but I didn't want to quit. I feel like I'm like the other women [now], women who couldn't wait until they married and stayed at home. This is not a good thing—the amount of exhaustion that a female person [*al-wahda*] put in, the amount of struggle she gave, and in the end, it is over. No. I'm thinking, for example, even though I am home [right now], that I will sit for a specific period with the children at home, until they enter school....I would organize myself and my situation and then I would start thinking about a project that would be for everybody or to enter an appropriate women's organization. (Respondent 10, 1995)

Gatekeepers, who were usually not an issue in 1989 because most interviews were conducted at a PFWAC workplace, were a major problem in 1995, when I usually arranged to meet with women in their homes. In some situations, these gatekeepers made it difficult for me to speak directly to the woman I was trying to locate. More often, interviews were interrupted by husbands, in-laws, mothers, or brothers who were either suspicious of my intentions or, after confirming my neutrality, assumed that I had the power to get them resources they really needed (e.g., U.S. citizenship, money, or a job). One mother, whose unmarried daughter's reputation was seriously hurt by false rumors spread during the PFWAC and DFLP splits, refused to leave the room during an interview (nudging her daughter's leg to censor her responses to certain questions). My repeated attempts in the following few weeks to speak to the daughter privately, especially after she slipped me a note giving me her phone number and asking me to contact her, failed because she was rarely allowed to leave her home, and I could never be sure whether her mother was listening to our phone conversations. The respondent eventually filled out a blank questionnaire that I delivered and picked up.

Rather than romanticizing their PFWAC past or providing what they may have believed were socially desirable answers about the impact of the PFWAC on their lives (given my 1989 volunteer affiliation with the organization), women veered in the opposite direction. Sometimes they denied and other times they understated their PFWAC involvement and its impact on their lives.

PFWAC Affiliates and the Nature of Their Involvement

PFWAC women employees moved from their homes into a new socializing environment that expected them to engage with the national and gender issues of the day. However, not all the women made the move from employee to activist. I divided PFWAC affiliates into three categories of involvement. Of the 56 reinterviewed women, 16 (29%) were strictly employees, not participating in PFWAC activities beyond coming to work and establishing friendships there. Another 15 women (27%) were active in some limited PFWAC activities beyond employment. These women occasionally attended demonstrations, sit-ins, and political seminars, and often participated in educational seminars or courses. This second group rarely crossed over into DFLP activity, which was always composed of both men and women. Finally, 25 women (45%) had been *very* active in the PFWAC, and sometimes also the DFLP, in addition to employment in a PFWAC project. Very active women not only regularly attended events like educational and political seminars, demonstrations, funerals, and prison visits (particularly during the intifada), but they organized, coordinated, and mobilized for women's health seminars, literacy projects, demonstrations, and graffiti writing for the PFWAC or the DFLP.

I asked all the PFWAC women reinterviewed in 1995 to compare themselves retrospectively to their friends and relatives previous to their PFWAC affiliation: Were they more "timid," "the same," or "more independent minded" in comparison to other women? While recall bias is important, women's retrospective reports in 1995 were largely consistent with information in their 1989 interviews.[14] Of the 56 women, 29% described themselves as previously "more timid," 41% described themselves as "the same" as other women, and 30% described themselves as relatively more "independent minded." In this respect, it appears that PFWAC *employment* attracted a broad range of women in terms of personal disposition.

Political activity beyond PFWAC employment, not surprisingly, was most attractive to the women who reported being more independent minded compared to their neighbors and relatives: 12 of these 17 women (71%) were in the most active category of PFWAC affiliates. The 16 women who reported pre-PFWAC timidity and the 23 who reported that they were the same as others did not differ in the level of their PFWAC involvement: they were about evenly distributed among the three levels of activity, indicating little relationship between self-reported predisposition and level of PFWAC involvement among these two groups of women.

Resistance and Accommodation: The Impact of the PFWAC on Community, Worldviews, and Self-Efficacy

In the remainder of the article, I use women's narratives to address the importance of the PFWAC's existence (and disappearance) as a nationalist-feminist institution in their communities. Second, I address the impact of PFWAC affiliation and socialization on their political and social attitudes and worldviews. Finally, I explore women's decisions in relation to employment, education, and marriage to argue that the women who were most deeply influenced by their PFWAC experience were the most likely to have a gender egalitarian sensibility and a high sense of self-efficacy that improved their individual situations.

Feminist Community Power

The generation of more empowering life options depends in part on an individual's ability to denaturalize her existing circumstances and imagine alternative possibilites. As indicated below, such imaginings are fostered, and turned into potentially transformative action(s), by an environment that provides discursive, social, and institutional support.

> It's not right to say that things changed when I began working. It's more accurate to say that things changed when I joined the PFWAC. Now, if I want to leave, I don't give them [family] reports or have to tell them. They never allowed me to leave the house before. Now I can go on visits, trips, to the PFWAC offices, wherever I want to go. I used to expect that my parents would say "no" to anything. I recently asked my father if I could travel to Jordan and he just said "yes." (Respondent 47, 1989)

An important part of the PFWAC legacy was its institutional support for girls and women in the communities in which it had branches. Such support operated on a number of levels. On one level was the idiomatic or ideological importance of an

organization run by women with a gender-egalitarian ideology. It is not surprising that in a gender-conservative environment legitimated by religious, nationalist, or other ideologies, alternative, more egalitarian idioms bolster girls and women who challenge or resist the status quo. On another level was the importance of the institutional support (composed of PFWAC cadres and leaders) that could be, and often was, mobilized to defend or "convince" family members to ease restrictions that limited a girl or woman's ability to work, travel, or become politically active. A girl or young woman arguing with a brother, father, uncle, mother, or husband about a gender-related restriction knew that a feminist-nationalist organization seen to be part of the community, but also larger than that community (with branches throughout the country), existed to intervene, if necessary, on her behalf. The importance of this community institutional support, and the implications of its collapse, came up regularly in the 1995 reinterviews with former PFWAC affiliates.

One 27-year-old Gazan, who had worked in the PFWAC biscuit project, had been very active and indicated that her life had been transformed by her involvement. She stated, "The period of the *lijan* [PFWAC] was a very, very good period for women. You know, in fact, you could not imagine the personal freedom. And the *lijan* opened many things for women, without the... women themselves knowing that these things were beneficial until she did not have them anymore" (respondent 9, 1995).

Many women, especially those who had few opportunities to leave their homes, missed the PFWAC days and the social space afforded by the organization in an almost physical way. These women were still devastated by what had happened, both to the PFWAC and to themselves since its demise, as indicated by a Jerusalem villager:

> When I sit by myself and go back and think about what we used to do; we used to go to the Old City; we used to go to demonstrations; we would go to the hospital. Daily, daily, we had something to do. To get cut off all at once like this—they [the PFWAC and the DFLP] don't even have a presence [anymore]. When people from Fateh [the largest political movement] ask, "Where did you

all go? What are you all doing? Why are you sitting at home doing nothing?" Me, psychologically,
when I hear this, I get exhausted. Even though I've
left them for a while,...because of the level of my
love for the *lijan* even until now I don't hate them.
(Respondent 2, 1995)

A Ramallah respondent who believed she was
trapped in her village noted that nonconforming
action was difficult for women to take without
some cultural and institutional support. She said,
"When [an unemployed girl]...every day or every
other day goes out, the people start talking." I
asked, "How do you feel when people start talking?"
She responded, "I begin to not want to do anything.
People here are all like each other. But if there were
people, for example, one or two people to help, one
would begin to take risks. But I'm all by myself and
I can't, I can't violate all the laws of this village; this
is a small town" (respondent 38, 1995).

These narratives demonstrate the limits of individual challenges and the importance of local,
institutional feminist support for women attempting to challenge the gender status quo. While there
are many Palestinian feminist organizations in the
post-intifada period, they are largely concentrated
in urban areas and focus on organizing externally
funded workshops, participating in international
conferences, and extracting gender concessions
from a Palestinian rentier parastate, whose powers
are largely limited (by the Oslo Accords) to providing municipal services and policing the local
population. While these feminist organizational
foci are important, they have little impact on most
Palestinian women's lives. A more decentralized
presence of Palestinian feminist organizations
would likely bolster their agendas and help ensure
that they are attuned and responsive to various
women's needs.

Social and Political Worldviews: "The Daughters of the Committees"

For many women, engagement with the PFWAC
dramatically reconstituted their gender ideologies,
political worldviews, sense of the possible, and self-
definitions. For these women, involvement also
produced a strong sense of cohort or generational
consciousness—a feeling that their individual

potential was redefined as a result of their collective
existence and power.

> Socially and educationally, we advanced very,
> very much. When I was sitting at home, I was
> nothing—it was as if I didn't exist. After I left and
> joined the PFWAC—I give them a thousand thanks
> for this—first, it provided me the opportunity to
> become economically independent. Also, we didn't
> used to do courses and things like that. These
> courses increased our awareness and allowed us
> to increase other women's awareness. When any
> issue came up we used to meet about it....The
> *lijan*...developed my own person and my personal-
> ity. (Respondent 2, 1995)

This was a Jerusalem villager's response to the question of whether she was different from women who
had not joined the PFWAC. When reinterviewed
in 1995, she was pregnant, secretly smoked, and
often argued with her husband, particularly about
his expectation that her political opinions should
parallel his ("like a parrot"). She was among the 18
women for whom PFWAC involvement appeared to
be extremely important, probably the most important thing they had done in their lives at the time
of involvement. These women reported or indicated
that their lives and worldviews were transformed as
a result of their involvement.[15] They often referred
to themselves as "the daughters of the [Palestinian
Federation of Women's Action] committees" (*banaat
al-lijan*) and believed that they were very different
from other women who had not been active in the
PFWAC. According to a Gazan who had said that
joining the PFWAC was the most significant event
in her life: "When I entered the federation, I felt that
I became an active person who had entered another
world. The woman who did not enter the federation
and did not participate and did not make the effort,
I feel that she does not know anything; I feel that
she is in one world and I am in another" (respondent 10, 1995).

For an additional 31 of the women reinterviewed
(these women were almost evenly split in terms of
their level of PFWAC activity), PFWAC involvement
had expanded their social world and their worldviews—widening their social relations; increasing
their self-confidence, especially outside the home;
making them more aware of gender issues; and

increasing their knowledge of and engagement with nationalist issues. As one Gazan put it, "Before the *lijan* [PFWAC], a person did not go out, did not mix with other people. When the PFWAC happened, one started to mix with people, to mix with other women, to mix with men. This changed one's situation" (respondent 18, 1995).

The reports of seven women indicated that PFWAC involvement was insignificant or unimportant in their lives. Five of these women had limited their PFWAC affiliation to employment.

It appears that while most women were influenced by PFWAC affiliation, the previously independent minded were the most likely to be transformed by this involvement: 13 of the 18 transformed women reported being comparatively independent minded before PFWAC involvement. This is consistent with Mannheim's argument that self-selection to some extent explains which members of a biological and geographic generation are likely to become members of a "political generation."

In terms of religiosity,[16] PFWAC women were almost twice as likely as Palestinian women in their age group to be nonreligious in 1995. Whereas a 1992 study indicates that about 32% of women 20–39 years old in the territories were not religiously observant (Heiberg 1993*b*, p. 262, fig. 9.9), 57% of PFWAC women were not observant. In terms of religious dress, PFWAC women were about as likely as other Palestinian women to wear the head scarf, but less likely to wear "strict Islamic dress" (both head scarf and robe) (Heiberg 1993*b*, p. 256, table 9.3).[17]

Given the rapidly changing political situation in the Occupied Palestinian Territories and increased pressures on women to don Islamic dress during the intifada, at the end of each interview in 1989, I asked women to respond to the following question: "Let's say that five years from now there was a Palestinian state. What if the state legislated a law mandating Islamic dress [*al-libas al-shar'i*] for all women? What do you think about this?" About 75% of the women did not support the idea of such a dress code being imposed by the future Palestinian state, including 88% of nonreligious women and 59% of religious women. As these numbers indicate, while most women opposed such a law, religious women were much more likely to support it.

Many women were not supportive of such a law but could not see themselves publicly confronting or challenging it. A 23-year-old woman from the town of al-Bireh stressed the difficulty of acting alone in a cultural context that often collectively punishes individual deviation, and she made a distinction, as did many respondents, between personal religious conviction (*iqtinaa'*) and dictated norms: "I feel that if everyone dressed this way, I would have to, even if I weren't convinced, because I would feel ashamed" (respondent 28, 1989).

When reasked the question of whether they supported a Palestinian state that imposed such dress on women by law, women's 1995 responses remained relatively consistent, with 80% opposing the imposition of such dress, including two-thirds of religiously observant women.

While the 25 formerly very active and 15 intermediately active women were proportionally very similar in their opposition to the law (approximately 87%), the 16 women who limited their PFWAC affiliation to employment opposed the fictional mandatory dress law by only 63%.

Similarly, while the women who reported becoming more aware of women's issues or being transformed as a result of PFWAC involvement appeared similar to each other in their opposition to the law (83% and 89%, respectively), they were dramatically different from the women who reported being unaffected by PFWAC involvement. Only three (43%) of these seven women opposed the law. There is no national data that allows for comparison of PFWAC women's responses to women in the larger Palestinian population, although the within-group comparison indicates that PFWAC involvement beyond employment appears to have influenced women's ideas in these areas.

Self-Efficacy

The influence of PFWAC participation for many women went beyond the attitudinal and ideological. The self-efficacy that was fostered contributed to women making various individual decisions that increased their power and improved their lives despite the demise of the PFWAC.

> I cannot say, one way or the another, that I haven't achieved anything from being with the *lijan*

[PFWAC]. No, I learned a lot from being with the *lijan*. I learned how to be conscious, more conscious about my issues as a woman. I learned also how to be independent from them [the PFWAC]. I learned how to go places from them. I got more strong with them. I cannot say that I didn't achieve anything from being with them. And I guess also that being independent now, it's also part of having been with the *lijan*. (Respondent 58, 1995).

Ironically, women, such as this Gazan, who reported that the PFWAC had increased their gender awareness or transformed their lives were the most likely to use the self-confidence and critical skills they had learned to challenge the organization during the intifada. Such women left when they believed the PFWAC had breached its stated commitment to a combined national/feminist project, democratic process, and internal assessment. In the remainder of the article, I explore the ways in which PFWAC involvement influenced women's attitudes and decisions regarding employment, educational attainment, and marriage.

Consistent with PFWAC ideology, most of the women reinterviewed in 1995 viewed paid employment as a source of economic and social independence from family and an opening that allowed them to travel into town and be in public without commentary. This issue became particularly important with the contraction of the PFWAC and women's demobilization. Overall, in 1995 only 24 (43%) of the 56 women were employed.[18] Among the women who had been inactive beyond PFWAC employment and intermediately active, 31% and 33%, respectively, were employed in 1995. Among the formerly very active, in contrast, 56% were employed. The differences are more dramatic among women who reported that PFWAC affiliation had transformed their lives, 11 of these 18 (61%) women were employed. In comparison, 13 of the 31 (42%) women reporting increased awareness of women's issues were employed, and none of the seven who reported being unaffected by PFWAC affiliation were employed.

PFWAC involvement also appears to have strongly influenced women's educational attainment between 1989 and 1995. The PFWAC program was particularly appealing to and often mobilized the most educated among working-class and village women—school teachers, high school graduates, and college students. The PFWAC focused on these women when first entering a new neighborhood because it (accurately) assumed that they would be more effective at mobilizing other women given the respect they usually commanded in their communities (Hasso 1998, p. 461n4). As evidence of this strategy, the 63 PFWAC women in the first wave of this study were better-educated in comparison to the general population in the territories, averaging 11.4 years of education in 1989, while other Palestinian women in their age group averaged about nine years of schooling (Heiberg 1993a, p. 136).[19]

By the time women were reinterviewed in 1995, many had increased their educational attainment even more. One woman who in 1989 had not completed secondary school and three women who had only completed twelfth grade were in college. Two more women were preparing to enter or reenter university in the following academic year. Two women had completed B.A. degrees; one of these women had also received a law degree (apparently the only Palestinian woman attorney in Gaza at that time), and the other was preparing to enter graduate school abroad.

Having a less restrictive family was a necessary but not sufficient condition for educational attainment between 1989 and 1995 since there was no mobility among women in very restrictive families. The relationship between educational mobility and economic situation in 1995 was counterintuitive from a social reproduction (Bourdieu 1977, pp. 72–95) perspective: proportionally, most educational mobility occurred among women who had been "very poor" in 1989; those who had been "average low-income" or "relatively comfortable" were about even in their mobility.

With the exception of one not very active woman who had enrolled in an extra training course since 1989, there was *no* educational mobility among the women who were intermediately active in the PFWAC or inactive beyond employment. Almost all educational mobility between 1989 and 1995 occurred among women who had been very active in the PFWAC, indicating a high sense of self-efficacy that can at least partly be attributed to

PFWAC socialization. Similarly, there was little educational attainment among women for whom PFWAC affiliation had been unimportant, but there was significant mobility among those who had become more aware of women's issues and even more among those who reported that their lives had been transformed by their involvement.

Although it is difficult to disaggregate how much educational attainment would have occurred independently of PFWAC activity, the results indicate that deep engagement with the PFWAC influenced women's ideas about education and their educational attainment. The PFWAC strongly encouraged women's independence and "self-improvement," particularly through employment and education. Consistently, most of the former PFWAC women interviewed, including those who had not increased their educational attainment, saw education as a means by which they could "make" themselves by increasing their social and economic independence. The findings indicate, however, that it was the women who had been very active or reported that the PFWAC had increased their gender awareness or transformed them who were the most likely to act on these ideas despite economic and social constraints.

Marital attitudes and decisions also appear to have been influenced by PFWAC involvement, although this was one area where women often distinguished between their beliefs and desires and what they believed was possible, given cultural and economic constraints. Singlehood, which is stigmatized in most societies, is particularly so in Arab societies, which are highly kin oriented. With one exception, the 18 women who had married between 1989 and 1995 discussed the social coercion compelling marriage and the psychological and other costs of remaining unmarried. As a 29-year-old happily married Ramallah villager who had been very active in the PFWAC stated,

> Marriage is the summit of life.... And in our society...people start asking, "Why is she unwilling to get married?" Not when she reaches 28 or 29, from when she hits 18 years, they say, "Why don't you want to get married? So-and-so got married, why not you?" Until a certain period, I kept saying, "I do not want to get married; right now I want to study;

> right now I want to work." Afterwards, it became an appropriate time for me.... The society constantly comments, even if a woman reaches death, they continue to comment [on her unwed state]. (Respondent 39, 1995)

Seven of the 18 recently married women had discussed and agreed to the terms of marriage with their future husbands before he or his family approached her family to formally request marriage. All seven had been very active in the PFWAC *and* reported that they had been transformed by their PFWAC involvement, indicating a relationship between the intensity and significance of PFWAC involvement, on the one hand, and willingness to violate cultural norms that are particularly salient among village and working-class women, on the other hand.

Women who had been very active or transformed by their PFWAC experience also had more egalitarian relationships with their spouses and in-laws and thus higher rates of marital satisfaction. This appeared to be related to their willingness to set ground rules safeguarding their freedoms both before they chose their spouses and after they married. One woman, a Gazan who had been very active in the PFWAC and reported being transformed by this involvement, had it written in her Sunni Muslim marriage contract that her husband could not compel her to wear full Islamic dress after marriage (respondent 9, 1995).

Of the 56 women reinterviewed in 1995, 46 had been single in 1989. Given the strong cultural pressure on women to marry, a surprising proportion of them, 59%, not including one engaged woman, had remained single in 1995 (their mean age was 30.7 years). In comparison to data gathered in a 1992 survey of the territories, PFWAC women were almost three times more likely to be single than women of similar age in the larger population (see Hammami 1993, p. 291, table 10.4).

As would be expected, the women who had remained single stressed the psychological and social costs of remaining unmarried. With one exception, however, all had declined a number of opportunities to marry because the men were "inappropriate" for them (*mish munasib ili*). Moreover, 70% of the 27 single women were unwilling to marry unless they were sure it was "Mr. Right." When asked whether

her life would improve, stay the same, or worsen if she married, a 34-year-old Jenin-area resident who ran her own preschool (she had been very involved beyond PFWAC employment and reported becoming more aware of gender issues) replied, "It depends on the conditions that I impose [laughs]!" When asked, "So what are the conditions you are going to lay down?" (both laughing), she replied, "I have to stay the way I am, having my freedom. If he agrees, he agrees. If he does not, no." When I said, "So your conditions are that you maintain your freedoms," she agreed, saying, "That I can go wherever I want, that I continue working" (respondent 56, 1995).

A Ramallah-area woman, also employed, said that she remained unmarried (and had recently declined an offer) because "he either has to be the appropriate person or forget it." She also suggested that she would leave a man she married if she was unhappy with him (respondent 37, 1995). She had been intermediately involved beyond PFWAC employment and had reported becoming more aware of gender issues as a result.

An additional two women had decided to forswear marriage. One of these, a Ramallah-area woman who had been intermediately involved in the PFWAC beyond employment and reported being transformed, had decided not to wed after watching her three sisters (one younger) suffer through unhappy marriages. She refused family and community pressure to marry and was the only daughter who completed high school and passed her high school matriculation exams. Like many of the women interviewed, she feared losing freedom and independence with marriage. "I like living freely; for no one to pressure me. I don't know what kind of man will come along. And of course, married life is not an experiment. So in order not to face these problems, I felt this way" (respondent 33, 1995).

My findings indicate that, more than anything else, some economic security facilitated women's decisions to remain single. Indeed, 22 of the 27 single women were either in the average low-income or relatively comfortable economic categories. The relatively comfortable single women were those who had been intermediately or very active in the PFWAC and had dramatically advanced in terms of educational attainment in the previous six

years, contrary to what their originating class backgrounds would lead one to expect. While self-selection in terms of personality, and, in some cases, other variables such as supportive families, cannot be ruled out as partial explanations for women's feminist ideas or their ability to translate these into actions regarding marriage, their own reports and my extensive research on PFWAC history point to the importance of their PFWAC socialization and experiences.

Conclusion

Lila Abu-Lughod has argued for the importance of looking at resistance (and, I would argue, accommodation) as "diagnostic of power" (1990, p. 42). Rather than reading "all forms of resistance as signs of the ineffectiveness of systems of power and of the resilience and creativity of the human spirit" (p. 42), we should focus more deeply on what different types of resistance, and, again, accommodation, tell us about the genealogies, forms, and (institutional, individual, and cultural) sources of power in any given context. As the Palestinian women I reinterviewed often made clear, their choices in the intervening six years had occurred in negotiation with economic, political, and cultural constraints, including high unemployment rates, poverty, and economic instability; Israeli military occupation; statelessness; personal status laws that codified women's second-class citizenship in certain areas; a weak public transportation system that limited particularly village women's physical mobility; gendered norms that limited women's options; and a cultural context where kinship, community bonds, and what Suad Joseph calls "connectivity" were robust and highly valued by all (Joseph 1993). For the women interviewed, the constraints also included the demise of the PFWAC itself, which had been a source of feminist institutional, ideological, and cultural support.

Because the state cannot be relied on to supersede family authority, most women's options were ultimately dependent on their individual family situations and their willingness and ability to "bargain with patriarchy" (Kandiyoti 1988) in their families and communities. This makes it particularly difficult to act radically in individual or collective contexts.

Although one could view the PFWAC as having "failed" in the feminist component of its agenda, the findings indicate that the organization had succeeded for many of its former participants and activists. The PFWAC experience produced a feminist generation that remained distinctive approximately five years after the demise of the organization. While acts that challenge gender norms at the individual level are necessary, however, they are not sufficient for systematically transforming the gender order, and they leave most women with little cultural or institutional support when they take such risks. Mass-based, accountable feminist movements that recognize the diverse needs of women and advocate on their behalf in a range of arenas continue to be particularly important for the well-being of many Palestinian women.

NOTES

An earlier formulation of the material in this article appeared in the author's dissertation (Hasso 1997). Talks based on previous versions of this article were presented at the University of Kentucky, Oberlin College, Antioch College, and the American Sociological Association meetings in 1999 and 2000. James House, Lynn Warner, Barbara Risman, and Jeffrey Dillman read earlier versions of this article and provided very helpful suggestions. Ellen Riggle, Tyrone Forman, and Suparna Bhaskaran contributed valuable additional methodological perspectives. I also appreciate the useful comments of the *AJS* reviewers. This article is dedicated to the Palestinian women interviewed, who graciously allowed me into their lives. I am also grateful to the PFWAC's generosity and openness to me during difficult times for the organization. Research for this article was funded by a 1995 dissertation grant from the Social Science Research Council and the American Council of Learned Societies, a 1996 Woodrow Wilson Women's Studies Dissertation Fellowship, a 1996 Robin I. Thevnet Summer Research Grant from the University of Michigan Women's Studies Program, and a 1996 one-term dissertation fellowship from the Rackham School of Graduate Studies at the University of Michigan, Ann Arbor.

1. At its core, I would argue, a feminist consciousness requires a commitment to sexual egalitarianism (an idea with diverse implications and meanings in different historical and cultural contexts) and a recognition that subordination based on sex/gender is socially rather than "naturally" determined (for other definitions, see Evans [1979, pp. 219–20], Offen [1988] and Johnson-Odim [1991]).

2. And there is always the possibility of nonfeminist visions and feminist visions that resist addressing or reproduce racial, sexual, economic, international, or other inequalities.

3. The equivalent Arabic term for "feminism" is *wa'i nisaai,* or "women's awareness."

4. On October 28, 1991, a Palestinian delegation from the territories met in Madrid with a delegation from the Israeli government for the first of 11 rounds of unsuccessful negotiations that continued through September 1993. Between January and September 1993, PLO Chairman Yasir Arafat and a team of Fateh officials secretly negotiated with Prime Minister Yitzhak Rabin and a team of Israeli government officials under the sponsorship of the Norwegian government. These negotiations culminated in mutual recognition between the PLO and the Israeli government on September 9, 1993, followed by the signing of the Israeli-PLO "Declaration of Principles" (DOP), also known as the Oslo Accords, in Washington, D.C., on September 13, 1993.

5. The five income-generating projects were a dry baby food project, a ceramics and embroidery project, a sewing project, a biscuit project, and a dairy project.

6. Of the seven women not reinterviewed, one Ramallah-area woman (respondent 31), whom I was only able to reach by phone, refused with no explanation; one Gazan and one Jenin-area resident (respondents 57 and 59) had relocated to Gulf states with their husbands; I could not find a Ramallah-area woman (respondent 26) who had married; one woman, a Hebronite (respondent 64), was out of the country with her husband receiving medical treatment; and another two women (respondents 60 and 49), one from Bureij refugee camp (in Gaza) and another from a Jerusalem-area village, were not interviewed because they had moved and I was unable to locate them. All seven women not reinterviewed were married; four of these had married since 1989.

7. I conducted the first wave of this research during a 1989 six-month internship with the PFWAC Production Committee, while I was an M.A. student in Arab studies (with a concentration in economic development) at Georgetown University. I was kindly granted permission to do so by PFWAC leaders Zahira Kamal and Sama 'Aweidah. I came to know most of the project employees through my occasional site visits and their attendance at periodic meetings in the PFWAC central office in Beit Hanina, Jerusalem, where I was based. Similarly, teachers came to the Beit Hanina offices for regular training sessions and were familiar with me on that basis. I was also known to the teachers at the largest PFWAC day care center, which was also in Beit Hanina, because for three months I lived in a small apartment attached to that center and a PFWAC-sponsored medical clinic. In 1995, I returned to Palestine as a University of Michigan sociology graduate student conducting dissertation research.

8. Members of my dissertation committee—Salim Tamari, James House, Janet Hart, and Sonya Rose—provided crucial advice, on the construction of the 1995 interview protocol. Salim Tamari assisted with the 1989 protocol as well.

9. I do not address number of years affiliated or employed with the PFWAC in any of these analyses since I found that

the nature and intensity of affiliation was far more important than length of affiliation or employment.

10. In total, 60% of the population in the territories (80% of Gazans and 40% of West Bankers) live in urban areas. Urban areas include many refugee camps (Abu Libdeh, Ovensen, and Brunborg 1993, p. 41). Thus, the PFWAC women interviewed were more likely to be from villages in comparison to the larger population.

11. For very poor families, buying food was often a problem, they did not have telephones, almost two-thirds had no washing machine, and few had an automobile (most had access to a shared refrigerator). Average low-income families usually did not own a phone or a car, often owned the (very modest) roof over their heads, usually had a television set and a washing machine (that sometimes were not working properly), often supplemented their food stocks through small-scale cultivation, and usually avoided nonessential public transportation because it was expensive. Women who were *relatively* comfortable (possibly equivalent to the U.S. "lower-middle-class") worried less about food, housing, and health care, although they usually contributed at least part of their pay to their households because men (brothers, fathers, or husbands) were often unemployed, intermittently employed, or underemployed. These women lived in households with refrigerators, televisions, and sometimes automobiles as well. (Only one or two women in the latter category had access to a car in 1989; in 1995, a number of women had attained licenses or had bought cars).

12. Some women continued working without pay until they realized that the PFWAC had indeed fallen apart or the new parties were closing most of the projects and demobilizing the rank and file.

13. When I returned to the United States and first compared this Ramallah-area respondent's 1989 information with her very different 1995 responses, I thought I had reinterviewed the wrong person. A friend in Palestine, however, visited the woman interviewed in 1995, and the respondent confirmed that she was interviewed by me in 1989.

14. I compared these 1995 self-reports with women's responses to 1989 questions about why they wanted to work with the PFWAC, how family members had responded to this desire,

and strategies they used to counter family resistance. As I had not interviewed women prior to their PFWAC involvement, I had no other source of information regarding their pre-PFWAC subjectivities.

15. Of the 18 women who reported or indicated that their lives were transformed by their involvement, 15 had also been very active in the PFWAC.

16. Women were coded as religious/not religious based on the presence/absence of statements in their interviews indicating that they prayed at least once a day, read religious literature, watched religious programming, wanted the man they married or their husband to pray or fast, or wanted an Islamic state. In 1989, I coded 46% of the women as religious and 54% as nonreligious. Religiosity largely remained constant between 1989 and 1995, with 75% of the women continuing to be religious or non-religious, and the remainder about evenly split between those who became more religious and those who became less religious.

17. Although I use the term "Islamic dress" in this article to denote the wearing of a specific style of headscarf and robe, it is important to recognize that what that means and looks like (the sartorial practice and garments) varies in historical moment and location. Moreover, even with its dominant or hegemonic meaning in a given time and place, it has invariably been subject to either individual violations or systematic challenge by Muslim and secular feminists. As with other gender-related debates, Muslim feminists who have engaged in such contestation have largely done so by challenging the contemporary relevance of conservative gender discourses and interpretations of sacred legal texts.

18. Almost all the working women were in preschool and other teaching positions. Four taught in and ran their own preschools. The entrepreneurs were all single and West Bankers (three of four in villages). One of these women also ran a small store largely catering to village children. Of the 32 unemployed women, 20 were eager to work but either could not find socially appropriate employment or were not allowed to work by their families.

19. Those with higher educational levels in 1989 were more likely to report that they were transformed by their PFWAC experience.

37.

Movement Framing and Discursive Opportunity Structures: The Political Successes of the U.S. Women's Jury Movements

HOLLY J. McCAMMON, COURTNEY SANDERS MUSE, HARMONY D. NEWMAN, AND TERESA M. TERRELL

Social movement participants often concentrate their efforts on bringing about changes in law or public policy. Although they do not always pursue political goals (Van Dyke, Soule, and Taylor 2004), when movement activists do seek such outcomes, they typically must persuade lawmakers or other public officials that a change in policy is the appropriate course of action. For some time now, social movement scholars have investigated how and under what circumstances movement groups are able to bring about significant political changes (Amenta and Caren 2004). Such studies provide evidence that a variety of factors aid collective actors in achieving their political goals. For example, activists' degree of mobilization, a favorable political climate, and positive public opinion have all been shown to help activists achieve political goals (Burstein and Linton 2002; Soule and Olzak 2004).

Yet, most key empirical investigations of the political effectiveness of movements overlook the role of *framing* in winning changes in law (see, e.g., Amenta, Olasky, and Caren 2005; Andrews 2001; Soule and Olzak 2004). Snow, Benford, and their colleagues (Snow and Benford 1988; Snow et al. 1986) show that movement framing takes place when collective actors articulate their interpretations of the social or political problem at hand, its solution, and the reasons why others should support efforts to ameliorate the condition. It may seem an obvious point to state that lawmakers

decide to revise laws in part because they are convinced by activists' arguments. But scholars have conducted little systematic empirical research on the effects of collective action framing in convincing political leaders to change laws (Benford and Snow 2000:632; Snow 2004:391–92). Cress and Snow (2000) and McCammon and colleagues (2001) offer two systematic empirical studies that compare activist frames to discern which frames are effective in gaining political reforms and which are not. We discuss their work in detail below, but note here that both studies fail for the most part to situate the framing efforts of movement actors in the larger cultural context in which the framing occurs.

In this article, we explore movements' capacity to produce political change through framing. We argue that to understand fully why certain frames succeed in persuading lawmakers to redefine the law, one must consider not only the content of the frames but also the broader circumstances in which framing takes place. We argue—and provide evidence—that movement frames and the political and cultural environment in which they are expressed *work in combination* to produce a movement's desired political outcome. To heighten a movement's chances of convincing lawmakers to change the law, movement actors must incorporate or respond to critical discursive elements in the broader cultural environment. For instance, if movement participants offer frames that tap into a hegemonic discourse, they are more likely to be politically effective (Koopmans and Statham 1999). When cultural milieus are "unsettled" (Swidler 1986), collective actors are likely to achieve their political goals if they frame their arguments in themes, narratives, or even contradictions that surface at such unsettled junctures (McAdam 1994). Moreover, opposition claims can present cogent

McCammon, Holly J., Courtney Sanders Muse, Harmony D. Newman, and Teresa M. Terrell. 2007. "Movement Framing and Discursive Opportunity Structures: The Political Successes of the U.S. Women's Jury Movements." *American Sociological Review* 72: 725–729. Reprinted by permission of American Sociological Association.

ideational elements that, if not responded to by a movement, can undermine efforts to convince lawmakers and forestall success. In short, if activists frame their grievances without regard to dynamics in the broader cultural context, their messages are far less likely to be politically effective.

We develop our theoretical hypotheses on the combined effects of framing and the cultural and structural contexts in detail below. To explore this idea empirically, we examine the U.S. women's jury movements. In roughly the first half of the twentieth century, following ratification of the Nineteenth Amendment giving women voting rights, a number of women's groups mobilized to attain another legal right for women, the right to sit on juries. While this mobilization was not as large and did not receive the same publicity as the suffrage movement, it nonetheless was a pronounced and sustained effort by organized women to broaden their roles in the larger public and civil arenas. Variation in the types of frames these activists used, as well as the contexts in which they used them, provide an opportunity to systematically explore the combinations of frames and contexts most effective in convincing lawmakers to alter jury law.

The Women's Jury Movements: Framing Efforts and Victories

Although one contemporary observer states that "since the enfranchisement of women, one of the most interesting movements among the various women's groups has been this very struggle for jury service" (Corkell 1930:84), few have written about women's efforts to sit on juries in the United States. This phase of women's activism has largely been ignored in both women's history (although see Kerber 1998) and in sociological studies of the women's movement (for a rare exception, see Taylor 1989). Not surprisingly, scholars have paid far more attention to the larger "first" and "second" waves of feminism—the suffrage movement and the ERA campaigns in the 1970s and 1980s. Yet, the history of the jury movements reveals that the decades between these surges in activism were years of continued organized agitation on the part of women for full civil rights, with much of the activity taking place at the state rather than federal level. A small

number of secondary historical accounts of these state movements exist, most focusing on events in a single state (e.g., Perry 2001). Other work considers the development of both federal and state judicial decisions on woman jurors (e.g., Ritter 2002). Such studies, though, typically miss both organized women's efforts to change the law and the critical decisions made by state legislatures to expand jury panels. Our data show that activists considered state legislatures to be the crucial decision-making body on the issue. Yet no investigation of the jury movements thus far offers a detailed comparison of these state-level efforts, and no investigation focuses on the critical developments in legislative law.

Time and again, in the first half of the twentieth century, jury activists in state-level League of Women Voter organizations (LWV), Business and Professional Women's Clubs (BPW), branches of the National Woman's Party (NWP), and the Federation of Women's Clubs (FWC) lobbied state lawmakers, held rallies or automobile tours designed to mobilize support for jury bills, and used the local media to bring about favorable public opinion. Their efforts met with varying levels of success. Table 1 provides the years, by state, in which women won the right to sit on juries. In a handful of states, this happened prior to ratification of the 1920 federal suffrage amendment (although in each case women had already secured voting rights in the particular state). A number of states, such as Delaware, Indiana, and Iowa, gave women the right to sit on juries along with the ballot. In some of the states that gave jury rights a year later in 1921, women's organizations lobbied heavily for the change (Lemons 1973:69–70). Aside from the states that granted women a place on juries automatically with suffrage, concerted campaigns took place to change jury laws in the vast majority of the remaining states. In New York and Texas, for instance, the state LWVs began their work immediately after voting rights were secured and continued almost nonstop until women could serve on juries in those states.

We uncovered a diversity of frames that movement participants used to argue that women should join men in the jury box and help in the shaping of justice. (We discuss data sources below). The women's

Table 1 Years in which Women Won the Right to Participate on State Juries

1911	Washington[a]
1912	Kansas, Oregon
1917	California
1918	Michigan, Nevada
1920	Delaware, Indiana, Iowa, Kentucky, Ohio
1921	Maine, Minnesota, New Jersey, North Dakota, Pennsylvania, Wisconsin
1923	Alaska[b]
1924	Louisiana
1927	Rhode Island
c. 1930s	Utah[c]
1937	Connecticut, New York
1939	Illinois, Montana
1942	Vermont
1943	Idaho, Nebraska
1945	Arizona, Colorado, Missouri
1947	Maryland, New Hampshire, North Carolina, South Dakota
1949	Florida, Massachusetts, Wyoming[c]
c. 1950s	Arkansas[d]
1950	Virginia
1951	New Mexico, Tennessee
1952	Hawaii[b], Oklahoma
1953	Georgia
1954	Texas
1956	West Virginia
1966	Alabama, Mississippi
1967	South Carolina[e]

[a] Washington and Wyoming both granted women jury rights prior to this, but the right was rescinded in both cases. A few judges in Colorado and Idaho allowed women to sit on juries

Table 1 (*Continued*)

prior to 1911, but women only rarely did so in these states (*New York Times* 1902, 1912).

[b] Alaska and Hawaii granted women jury rights prior to statehood.

[c] An 1898 Utah law enabled women to sit on juries but then expressly exempted them. There is little evidence women sat on juries in any number until the 1930s (Matthews 1929; Utah State Courts 2006).

[d] Although Arkansas passed a statute permitting women on juries in 1921, there is little indication that women served on juries until the 1950s. See *Balley v. States of Arkansas* (1949).

[e] In our analysis we use 1966 as the year in which women in South Carolina won jury rights because in that year both a legislative vote and a referendum gave women a place on juries. In 1967, the legislature simply enacted enabling legislation.

groups attempting to change jury laws, as well as the groups opposing them, used frames to persuade potential followers, the public, and those with political power to support their side of the debate. Such frames are strategic frames, or frames "developed and deployed to achieve a specific purpose" (Benford and Snow 2000:624). The frames jury activists typically relied on combined diagnostic and motivational elements (Snow and Benford 1988:200–04). The diagnostic elements allowed movement actors to define the problem at hand along with its causes. The motivational component, as we discuss below, was critical in providing rationales for potential political supporters to side with the jury activists and thus helped persuade and convince political backers of the activists' point of view.

At a superficial level, the problem or diagnosis for jury proponents was simply women's exclusion from jury panels, and the cause was outdated and discriminatory jury laws. At a deeper level, however, supporters of women on juries provided two general types of interpretations, or frames, of the problem, what we call similarity and difference master frames. Difference and similarity (or equality) themes are apparent throughout the history of the women's movement (Cott 1987; Mathews and De Hart 1990). Because these frames reflect the rhetorical strategies of numerous social movement organizations over time, following Snow and Benford (1992:138), we refer to them as master frames.

In the first of these master frames, the similarity frame, activists emphasized the *similarities between women and men* and the need to treat men and women equally. Jury activists diagnosed the problem—women's exclusion from juries—as an injustice to women who, under more just laws, would be permitted participation on juries. The rationale or motivation for supporting jury rights for women in this frame was that; if women and men were similar, then it was unfair to exclude women from the jury bench while men were welcomed.

Activists put forward a number of specific formulations of the similarity master frame. Proponents frequently argued that women were just as *competent* as men in their intellectual ability to digest the facts of cases and render a verdict on the guilt or innocence of a defendant (see Table 2 for percentages of the overall number of frames represented by each subframe). An activist in Maryland, for example, argued that "women can measure up with men intellectually" (*Washington Post* 1947). Champions of women on juries also argued that women were citizens just as men were, and thus women should

perform the *duties* of citizenship just as men did, Woman-juror supporters in Colorado widely distributed a National League of Women Voters' pamphlet stating, "Jury service is a form of participation in the process of government, a social responsibility that should be shared by all citizens—men and women alike" (CO LWV Collection 1939). In a third formulation of the similarity master frame, activists maintained that women had a *right* to participate in the administration of justice in their communities, just as men did, and excluding women from juries prevented them from exercising their voice in the judicial system. A member of the Massachusetts jury movement illustrated this claim by arguing that "a woman has just as much right as a man to serve on a jury" (Siegel 1981). Finally, the similarity frame took a fourth form as activists emphasized women's similarity to men by arguing that women were increasingly moving into *roles* previously held strictly by men. Women's broader participation in society—as lawyers, judges, and business leaders, for example—should therefore qualify them for a place on juries. Because of these extended roles, activists argued, women's experiences and knowledge of the world were broader, just as men's were, and thus, again, it was unfair to exclude them from this civil participation.

The second master frame supporters of women jurors relied on emphasized the *differences* between women and men, thus providing a different diagnosis of the problem. In this frame, the problem was not unfairness to women (as was the case with the similarity frame) but rather the damage done to the courts and to justice itself by women's exclusion. Activists argued that men and women were different, and excluding women from juries meant excluding an important non-male perspective from jury deliberations. The motivation for supporting the cause offered by the difference frame was an understanding that women's unique perspective, as homemakers and nurturers, would enhance jury deliberations, allowing juries to render more impartial and just verdicts.

Two subthemes are prominent in the difference master frame. In the first, jury activists used the basic argument that preventing women from serving on juries withheld an important and needed

Table 2 Fremes Used by Proponents of Women on Juries

Name of Frame	Percent of Overall Number of Frames
Similarity Master Frame:	40
Competent Frame	15
Duty Frame	12
Rights Frame	6
Roles Frame	7
Difference Master Frame:	24
Women's View Frame	19
Peers Frame	5
War Frame:	1[a]
Shortage Frame	.50
Equality Frame	.30
Total:	65[b]

[a] The percentage of frames referencing war is small, but these frames were used only in the handful of war years.

[b] The overall number of frames in favor of women on juries is 1,984.

women's view from court deliberations. In using this frame, activists argued that women offered a view of society and its inhabitants that was typically distinct from that of men, and because of this, the exclusion of women impeded justice in the courts. For instance, a jury proponent quoted in Georgia's *Atlanta Constitution* stated that "women living at home are more able to keep the warm, human approach to problems, which I believe could well be used in the court of justice" (McKinley 1948). Some emphasized the importance of women jurors in specific types of legal cases, as did this activist in Texas when she stated, "It is in crimes against women and children where women on juries render the greatest service" (Jane McCallum Papers 1939).

A second formulation of the difference frame was the *peers* frame. Activists using this frame held that the courts were harmed by women's absence, but they specifically took the perspective of female defendants and drew on constitutional provisions in the Sixth and Seventh Amendments stating that U.S. citizens were guaranteed an impartial trial by jury. According to this frame, preventing women from serving on juries denied a woman on trial this legally protected right and thus interfered with justice in the court system. An article in the Nebraska League of Women Voters newsletter illustrated this view: "The United States has inherited the jury system from England, where it was recognized by the Magna Carta which provided that none should forfeit life or lose his freedom or his estate, without a trial by his peers" (*The Intelligent Voter* 1925). This frame assumed that men were not women's peers; only women, with their different ways of understanding the world, could fill this role, making women a necessary component of juries.

Table 2 shows that 'women juror activists relied more often, on arguments emphasizing men's and women's similarities rather than their differences. The similarity frame accounts for 40 percent of all the frames we uncovered, while the difference frame makes up 24 percent. Determining the reasons for this imbalance is beyond the scope of our present research, but it is not entirely surprising that—in an era in which women recently won a major political victory (the vote) and the gendered culture was slowly, with fits and starts, becoming

more egalitarian in multiple spheres of social life (Rosen 2000)—those seeking greater legal rights for women frequently drew on egalitarian beliefs to stake their claim.

Together the similarity and difference frames account for nearly two-thirds (64 percent) of the arguments we gathered from the jury supporters. The remaining third includes a number of other arguments, none of which occur in greater frequency than the frames discussed thus far. We highlight one of these remaining frames, a *war* frame, given its frequent (and, as we show below, effective) use during wartime. A number of the state jury movements continued their agitation for changes in law during World Wars I and II. Some incorporated the war into their jury rhetoric. These arguments tended to take one of two forms. The first and more common was the *war shortage* subframe. The reasoning used in a flyer by the Colorado Citizens' Joint Legislative Committee (a CO LWV organization formed to work on a statewide jury campaign) illustrates this frame well: "Due to the War Emergency, the number of men available for jury service has become so curtailed that it has hampered the trial of jury cases. Women jurors can relieve this situation" (Business and Professional Women's Club of Denver 1943).

A second war frame, used infrequently, is what we call a *war equality* subframe. As a proponent of jury rights in Vermont argued, "Equality and justice under the Stars and Stripes is the principle for which we are waging this war.... [E]lection day gives the voters here at home an opportunity to express themselves...in order that our talk of equal rights and freedom may not be simply an empty boast" (Beebe 1942). This subframe drew on themes in the similarity master frame, but it was distinct in that, like the war shortage subframe, it linked women's equality to the war. In the two war subframes, jury activists formulated their assertions in ways they hoped would resonate with the country's backing of the war effort, making support for women's jury rights a way of supporting U.S. soldiers fighting overseas.

Theorizing Framing's Political Effects
Little systematic empirical research has been done on the successes and failures of framing efforts by

movement actors as they work to change the law. In their review of the literature, Benford and Snow (2000:632) find only one investigation in which researchers systematically compare the political impacts of different types of frames in order to discern which frames are more persuasive and thus more effective in attaining movement political goals (see also Snow 2004:391–92). They cite Cress and Snow's (2000) Qualitative Comparative Analysis of discursive advocacy for the homeless. Cress and Snow conclude that more articulate or detailed diagnostic and prognostic frames help homeless advocacy groups succeed politically. They say little, however, about the broader cultural environment in which collective action framing takes place, instead making the case that framing has a direct effect on changes in policy.

Since Benford and Snow's assessment, McCammon and colleagues (2001) have offered a quantitative (event history) investigation of the state-level successes of the woman suffrage movements in changing voting rights laws. They find that when suffragists used arguments high-lighting women's traditional roles as mothers and homemakers—for example, women would use the vote to protect children and the home—suffragists were more successful in convincing lawmakers to give women voting rights because such arguments tapped into beliefs widely accepted at the time. While this suggests that politically successful frames are those that align well with popular beliefs, the authors do not develop the argument further. Other researchers explore the effectiveness of particular frames in convincing political leaders to alter policy, but they do not base their conclusions on a systematic comparison of successful and unsuccessful frames (e.g., Reese 1996). Such findings, though, also suggest that politically successful frames are those that articulate commonly held beliefs and values. Overall, empirical investigations of how movement framing succeeds in winning legal change remain quite limited, and few researchers consider in any depth how framing and the cultural and political context combine to produce change.

Nonetheless, we draw on this small empirical literature, as well as a few investigations of frames that succeeded in mobilizing new movement recruits

(Diani 1996; McVeigh, Myers, and Sikkink 2004) and various theoretical statements on framing's effects, to generate a series of hypotheses concerning the likely political effects of movement discursive tactics. We expect that circumstances in the broader context will shape the political impact of movement framing. That is, *we theorize that specific discursive elements and structural circumstances in the broader cultural and political context will moderate the capacity of a collective action frame to win the support of lawmakers.* While, as Cress and Snow's (2000) results show, movement frames can have a direct and unmoderated effect on policy change—and with this we do not disagree—we argue that framing's influence also takes place through a more complex process. Though they do not consider framing, various social movement scholars point out that the circumstances shaping whether movements achieve their political goals often work in conjunction with one another. For instance, Amenta and colleagues (2005), in developing and testing the political mediation model, provide evidence that collective actors have the greatest likelihood of achieving political success when they are well mobilized *and* when political opportunities exist. We build on this *conjunctural* or *interactive* thinking to argue that circumstances in the broader cultural and political context will moderate the influence of collective action frames on political outcomes.

As Snow and colleagues (1986) tell us, a critical step in persuading others is to diagnose the problem in ways that emphasize salient values and beliefs of the recipients of the message. Quite simply, if activists shape their frames not only to align with their own core beliefs and goals but also to highlight principles important to the recipients of their framing efforts ("frame bridging," as Snow and colleagues refer to it), their claims are more likely to *resonate* and thus, importantly, to *persuade* target populations. While a number of researchers consider the role of cultural resonance in recruiting new members to social movement organizations (e.g., McCammon 2001), we argue that a similar dynamic should apply to policymakers, those whom activists must convince in order to bring about legal change. Similar to McCammon and colleagues' (2001) work on the suffragists, we argue that politically success-ful frames will resonate with ideas widely accepted in broader society, including among lawmakers.

To theorize *which frames will resonate or per-suade,* however, a researcher must have a sense of the salient beliefs, values, and ideologies in the larger cultural milieu (Gamson 1988). As Oliver and Johnston (2000) point out, frames are distinct from the "larger system of meaning" that constitutes ide-ology. Movement actors, however, can tap into this larger system of meaning by articulating frames that echo, amplify, and even extend specific aspects of ideological orientations (Snow and Benford 2000:58–59). Steinberg (1999) refers to this broader cultural milieu as a "discursive field" within which certain hegemonic discourses (or salient beliefs and values) reign. We draw on these conceptualizations to argue that movement frames that tap into key elements in the discursive field are more likely to be politically successful. Koopmans and Statham (1999:228) introduce the term "discursive oppor-tunity structure" to identify ideas in the larger political culture that are believed to be "sensible," "realistic," and "legitimate" and that facilitate the reception of certain movement frames. While the concept of discursive opportunity structure pro-vides an important tool for understanding which frames will be politically persuasive, the concept itself remains underdeveloped in the literature. We develop three aspects of discursive opportunity structures that help explain more fully why some collective action frames are successful in convinc-ing lawmakers to implement new laws, while others are not.

First, as Gamson and Meyer (1996) point out in discussing political and cultural opportunities, some opportunity structures for movement success can be quite *stable* while others are far more *vola-tile.* This conceptualization can also be applied to the discursive context in which movements frame their arguments. Discursive opportunity structures themselves, on one hand, can be highly stable struc-tures. That is, opportunities for politically effective collective action framing can stem from discourses that are long-lived and deeply embedded in the surrounding culture. Steinberg's (1999:745–46) hegemonic discourses and Oliver and Johnston's

(2000) extant ideologies are key examples of more stable discursive opportunity structures. On the other hand, the social context can produce far more volatile discursive opportunities—opportunities for successful movement framing that derive from relatively short-lived or relatively new ideational elements. These can still be critical or highly salient elements, but they are beliefs or values that are cul-turally significant for a shorter period of time or that are deemed important but are just emerging. These discursive elements provide a shifting ter-rain for movement activism. To understand the ori-gin of emergent discursive opportunity structures, we borrow from the political process model. More volatile discursive opportunities result when a shift in political or social circumstances alters "the cal-culations and assumptions on which the political establishment is structured" (McAdam 1999:41), resulting in a more sympathetic political climate for movement demands, often through changed attitudes of political decision-makers or through an increase in movement allies in positions of politi-cal power (Soule and Olzak 2004). These emergent discursive opportunities can stem from emergent political (or, as we discuss below for the jury activ-ists, gendered political) opportunities. It is quite possible that both stable and changing elements in the broader discursive context occur simultane-ously, for cultural contexts almost never contain just one discursive opportunity structure but rather are made up of numerous, overlapping discourses, some more stable and some more changing.

Second, Ferree (2003:306) tells us that "all dis-cursive opportunity structures are inherently selec-tive," meaning that some movement frames resonate with critical elements in the larger discursive field, while others do not, because the resonant frames tap into the vocabulary, underlying principles, and narratives of salient discourses in the broader cul-tural environment. Wuthnow (1987:163) also speaks of the "selective relationships between ideological forms and social environments." Inglehart's (1977) description of a shift from materialist to postmate-rialist values suggests how changes in the discursive landscape may result in certain movement frames being successful in one period while other frames are successful in another period. We develop this selective effect further by pointing out that some discursive opportunity structures provide fertile ground for only *a narrow range of collective action frames,* perhaps even just one type of frame, while other discursive opportunities select *a wider range of frames* as persuasive. In the latter case, a discursive opportunity may provide a circumstance in which political elites are more receptive generally to the claims—made in a myriad of frames—of movement activists. This type of discursive opportunity structure provides a more receptive environment for movement framing as a whole, unlike the narrower opening provided by a more selective discursive opportunity structure where only one or two specific frames may gain a rhetorical advantage.

The final theme to orient our thinking about discursive opportunity structures is that while they are, in varying ways, apparent in the broader culture, in the end *movement actors are agents who make decisions about how to respond to such opportunities,* discursive and otherwise (Ferree 2003; Gamson and Meyer 1996). To a significant extent, such opportunities are socially constructed. Even when activists recognize opportunities, they may or may not take advantage of them, regardless of whether the opportunity is stable or dynamic or narrow or broad. Activists may articulate frames tailored to the cultural context; but on other occasions or among other activist groups, movement actors, for a variety of reasons, may not seize the opportunity and may not align their framing with the broader environment. As we develop our specific hypotheses below, we theorize that groups responding to discursive opportunities, that is, collective actors who articulate frames to "fit" with critical elements in the broader discursive context, are more likely to be politically effective. Movement framing that succeeds in persuading lawmakers to change the law is thus the result of the combined effect of a discursive opportunity structure *and* movement actors who deploy frames in ways that align or fit with this discursive opportunity structure.

Below we develop six hypotheses describing how discursive opportunity structures influenced the political impact of movement framing for the jury activists. These discussions, as well as our quantitative analyses, further elaborate our claims about the stability or volatility and narrowness or broadness

of discursive opportunities. They also reveal how changing discursive opportunities can be the result of emerging gendered political opportunities and how movement actors must perceive and act upon a discursive opportunity in order to frame effectively.

A Legal Discursive Opportunity Structure

Ferree (2003) takes the notion of discursive opportunity structure in a specific direction by emphasizing the ways in which key legal institutions and their actors and texts define, develop, and maintain hegemonic ideas. She points specifically to court decisions, constitutional texts, and statutory law as the venues in which hegemonic ideas are articulated and disseminated. To the degree that collective action frames draw upon critical concepts emphasized in the legal domain, activists' claims are more likely to resonate and, thus, to persuade potential supporters—including, we argue, lawmakers.

Some of the frames employed by jury proponents drew heavily on a hegemonic and long-lived legal discourse in the United States, particularly on the language of the rights and responsibilities of citizenship. The rights and duties frames (both subtypes of the similarity master frame) and the peers frame (a subtype of the difference frame) each articulate ideas prominent since the founding of U.S. law. The first 10 amendments to the Constitution are the core embodiment of the rights-based culture of U.S. law, setting forth citizens' rights such as freedom of speech, assembly, and religion. With constitutionally protected rights come citizenship responsibilities as well. Citizenship duties are also spelled out in core legal texts, such as the duty to obey the law, which is defined in the civil code and in felony and misdemeanor criminal law. Along with citizenship rights and duties, the notion of a jury of one's peers is also distinctly stated in U.S. law. The Sixth Amendment guarantees the right to a trial by an impartial jury in criminal cases, and the Seventh Amendment grants trial by jury in civil cases. In utilizing the rights, duty, and peers frames, jury activists thus appealed to conspicuous themes in U.S. law and tapped into a stable and hegemonic legal discursive opportunity structure. The discursive opportunity provided by these key legal texts is, however, highly selective in nature. We do not expect that all jury activist frames will be more persuasive given this legal discursive opportunity. Rather, those frames that tap into core legal principles should be more persuasive with lawmakers. This leads us to the following hypothesis:

> *Hypothesis 1:* The rights, duty, and peers frames should be effective in inducing lawmakers to expand jury laws to include women because these frames align with a hegemonic legal discourse.

A Traditional Gendered Discursive Opportunity Structure

It is possible and, in fact, highly likely that within a single society more than one hegemonic discourse holds sway. This is precisely what occurred for the jury activists. As they formulated their frames, advocates incorporated ideational elements from both a hegemonic legal discourse and from a hegemonic (yet, as we discuss below, increasingly contested) traditional gendered discourse.

In the male-dominated political environment of the first half of the twentieth century, traditional gendered assumptions about women's and men's appropriate roles continued to have a firm hold, even in the face of important challenges and new developments (such as the suffrage movement and women's voting rights) (Reese 1996; Ritter 2002). Many believed that women were men's political inferiors. Gender differences were believed to be natural, even divinely ordained. A separate spheres ideology, specifying that men and women were different and thus should fulfill different roles in society with men in the public (and judicial) sphere and women in the private or domestic realm, was commonly espoused.

These traditional assumptions provided a discursive opportunity for the jury activists, though, and some proponents of women on juries formulated frames that adopted key themes of this gendered discourse. The women's view and peers frames, both subtypes of the difference master frame, agreed that women and men were indeed different. In using these frames, jury advocates argued that women understood the female mind, its motivations, and the circumstances in which women could find themselves, and they understood,

far better than men, the domestic sphere and its complications. Differences in women's and men's conceptualizations of the world around them, jury activists urged, meant that women were needed on juries, just as were men. While the women's view frame drew solely on the traditional gender roles discourse, the peers frames, as discussed above, also drew on a legal discourse and combined the two discourses. In both the women's view and peers frames, by adopting the idea of gender difference, jury proponents aligned their claim for parity in the jury box with dominant gender difference beliefs.

We expand Ferree's (2003) understanding of discursive opportunity structures as being rooted in only legal institutions by arguing that they can also derive from gender as an institution. As Acker (1992) argues, not only are institutions gendered, but gender, with its regular and long-lived patterns of inequality, is itself an institution, and gender as an institution carries with it a belief system, historically saturated with assumptions of gender difference and inequality. Although historically hegemonic, in the first half of the twentieth century these ideas were increasingly challenges, primarily by activists seeking to broaden wonen's legal rights and introduce greater social and political equality between women and men. The discursive opportunity structure provided by traditional gender beliefs was not nearly as stable a set of ideas as that of the hegemonic legal discourse concerning the rights and duties of citizenship.[1] Like the legal opportunity structure, however, the traditional gendered discursive opportunity structure was narrowly focused in that it, too, selected specific frames—the women's view and peers frames—as more persuasive frames. The presence of a traditional gender discourse suggests an additional hypothesis:

> *Hypothesis 2:* The women's view and peers subframes should be effective in persuading legislators to pass women's jury bills because they tap into a prominent discourse of gender difference.

Women in the Legal Profession as a Discursive Opportunity Structure

McCammon and colleagues (2001; see also Taylor 1999: 13–16) show that gendered political opportunities for policy reform occur when changes in gender relations—such as women's inroads into previously male spheres of activity in the professions, higher education, and politics—begin to alter beliefs and attitudes toward women's public activities, making greater numbers of citizens and lawmakers receptive to broadening women's legal rights. We argue that such a gendered political opportunity provided an emerging discursive opportunity for jury activists, one quite different than the traditional gender discursive opportunity just discussed.

In the first part of the twentieth century, state legislators' willingness to expand jury service to women was likely influenced by women's movement into the legal profession as lawyers and judges. Their presence in the courtroom in a professional capacity may have introduced increasing doubts about excluding women from juries. Quite simply, policymakers might have been prompted to ask, if women were lawyers and judges, why shouldn't they also be jurors? These questions should have made legislators more open to activists' arguments on why women should be jurors and thus would provide a broad discursive opportunity for activist framing.

We do not hypothesize selective or narrow moderating effects because the historical record does not suggest such a pattern. For instance, some lawmakers, when confronted with greater numbers of women lawyers and judges, seem to have been persuaded by similarity arguments, others by difference arguments. In Massachusetts, New York, and Vermont, states with proportionately the highest numbers of women lawyers (U.S. Bureau of the Census, various years), politicians can be found restating both the jury activists' similarity *and* difference frames. For instance, in New York in 1930, in a legislative debate over jury rights for women, lawmakers stated that, like men, women should have the right to sit on juries (a similarity frame), while at the same time they argued that women's different views would significantly improve jury proceedings (a difference frame) (*New York Times* 1930).

> *Hypothesis 3:* We hypothesize that women's movement into the legal profession will enhance the overall potency of pro-jury framing.

Women in the State Legislatures as a Discursive Opportunity Structure

Another gendered political opportunity that surfaced during the period of jury rights activism was an increase in women holding elected offices in state legislatures (Cox 1996). The historical record shows that a primary source of political support for women's jury rights came from female legislators. Although their numbers were not large in the first half of the twentieth century, and not all female legislators supported jury rights (e.g., Jennie Loitman Barron Papers 1923), in some states during some years, women lawmakers worked vigorously in support of women's jury bills, plotting legislative strategy with activists and attempting to convince their male colleagues to support jury rights. For example, in Massachusetts in 1941 all four female members of the House worked together to introduce a jury bill (LWV of Northampton 1941).

Where such political support was present, a gendered political opportunity for jury reform existed, and this in itself should have increased the likelihood for legal reform (McCammon et al. 2001; Soule and Olzak 2004). Importantly, though, we argue that the presence of a gendered political opportunity for reform produced a discursive opportunity for jury movement framing. Where female lawmakers worked in favor of jury rights reform, we expect that the effects of movement actors' framing efforts will be enhanced—that is, a combined effect of framing and gendered political opportunity will occur. Where supportive lawmakers exist, activists' frames are more likely to fall on sympathetic ears and be reiterated by these lawmakers as they interact with their colleagues in legislative debates, closed-door sessions, and informal conversations. We thus theorize that a broad rather than narrow or selective discursive opportunity structure for activists results from there being supportive women in legislative office. Female lawmakers, in fact, can be found espousing both similarity and difference arguments (e.g., *Atlanta Journal* 1953).

> *Hypothesis 4:* We hypothesize that supportive female lawmakers will enhance the political effectiveness of movement collective action framing.[2]

Opposition Framing as a Discursive Opportunity Structure

Benford (1987) draws our attention to another critical component in the process of movement persuasion, counterframing. More often than not, movement actors confront opposition to their cause, opposition that falls somewhere along a continuum of highly organized and well-funded to sporadic and individually-based "public opinion" and that can exist both inside and outside formal political forums. In any case, if policy decision-makers (some of whom may comprise the opposition) hear the opposition's voice, movements run the risk of losing ground in their discursive struggles, particularly if they do not effectively respond to their opponents' claims. Benford (1987:75) tells us that counterframing is "an attempt to rebut, undermine, or neutralize a person's or groups myths, versions of reality, or interpretive framework." To succeed politically, movements confronted with opposition, we argue, must effectively counterframe their opponents' claims. That is, they must broadcast frames that directly and effectively neutralize contrary assertions made by those opposing the movement's goals (Hewitt and McCammon 2004). Opposition framing presents another discursive opportunity for movement activists, albeit one that is highly dynamic, changing as the opposition's claims shift. Opposition frames also define specific and narrow framing responses movement actors will, in all likelihood, need to supply to rebut or neutralize their opponents' claims.

Jury activists frequently confronted individuals and groups who opposed women jurors. In Vermont, for instance, in the late 1930s and early 1940s, groups of "average women" showed up at legislative hearings stating that they did not want to serve on juries (*Burlington Free Press and Times* 1941; *Rutland Daily Herald* 1939). In Maryland, members of the Southern MD Society of the Colonial Dames of America turned out at legislative hearings to oppose jury duty for women (*Baltimore Sun* 1947). Data we gathered on statements by opponents of women on juries show that they most frequently diagnosed the problem as women on juries *harming the courts*. Those opposed argued that harm would occur in a variety of ways: women

were unfit for jury service (e.g., they were too emotional, uninterested, and intellectually unprepared) and this would hinder the course of justice; courthouses were not equipped to handle female jurors (e.g., courthouses lacked proper overnight and toilet facilities for women) and this would impede the proper execution of trials; and women would be invading the male space of the courtroom and (male) lawyers and judges would have to behave differently given women's presence on juries. As is frequently the case among opponents of expanded rights for women (Jaggar 1990), all of these arguments emphasize women's and men's differences.

Proponents of women on juries sometimes responded directly to opponents' claims, using frames that rebutted or neutralized their opponents' assertions. For example, proponents often relied on the pro-jury competent frame (see Table 2) to respond to opponents' claims that women were unfit for jury duty. Jury supporters argued that women were indeed fit, and they employed the competent frame to extol women's intellectual and deliberative abilities. Those supporting women on juries also used what we refer to as a *courthouse* frame to neutralize their opponents' allegations that courthouse facilities were inadequate for female jurors. Jury supporters responded that courthouses employed female bailiffs and court reporters, and female lawyers were not uncommon. Toilet facilities existed for these court employees and professionals, and women jurors would simply make use of the same lavatories. Hotels were a solution to a lack of overnight accommodations, and costs associated with improvements to courthouses or the use of hotels would not be high. They also simply pointed out that few trials involved overnight stays.

Hypothesis 5: We hypothesize that where opponents claim that women will harm the court system and where proponents respond with neutralizing counterframing (that women are competent to serve and that courthouse facilities are adequate), jury activists will succeed in changing jury laws.

A Wartime Discursive Opportunity Structure

Finally, wartime presented a relatively short-lived discursive opportunity structure that also resulted in certain frames being more politically successful than others. During World Wars I and II, a discourse of heightened patriotism, democratic ideals, support for the troops, and aid for the war effort spread rapidly. We argue that jury activists who incorporated the war into their pro-jury frames were more likely to succeed politically. Some did so by arguing that women could support the war effort by serving on juries. Male jurors were in short supply due to the draft, and women could ameliorate this problem. Other activists argued that a war for democracy in Europe should be supported by equal political and civil rights, including jury rights, for women at home. These frames invoked the war as a reason for opening jury boxes to women and allowed activists to tap into the wartime discourse. The wars shifted the political and cultural terrain (akin to the gendered political opportunities we discuss above) and provided a discursive opportunity, one that was quite narrow, selective, and relatively short-lived,

> *Hypothesis 6:* We hypothesize that the use of war frames during wartime should increase the likelihood of a state legislature granting women a place on juries.

Additional Factors Influencing Movement Political Outcomes

Burstein and Linton (2002) rightly argue that *public opinion* plays an important role in democracies in determining whether legal reform will occur. If citizens in general oppose a piece of proposed legislation, then lawmakers, who in time will face reelection, are unlikely to ignore this public resistance, and thus public opposition should reduce the chances of the bill being passed. We include an indicator of public opposition to jury service for women in our analyses.

A number of researchers (e.g., Andrews 2001) provide evidence that *an organized movement—* one in which one or more social movement organizations are actively pressing for change—is more likely to secure a sought-after policy. While all the jury movements had an organizational presence (e.g., via the LWV or NWP), some formed a separate group to coordinate jury work among multiple state organizations. For example, in Illinois the IL Committee for Women on Juries formed in 1927, six years after the IL LWV and Women's Bar Association of IL began their work for jury rights. It may be that in states with a movement organization devoted solely to women's jury rights, a women's jury law is more likely to be passed. We examine such a measure in our analyses below.

Amenta and colleagues (2005) move beyond a simple organizational presence argument and explore whether *the activity level* of movement organizations heightens their effectiveness in winning reforms. They ask whether movements that are more active are also politically effective movements. We follow Amenta and his colleagues' lead and include an indicator of the number of types of activities (excluding framing) engaged in by groups working for a change in jury law.

Finally, McCammon and colleagues (2007) find that movements engaged in *strategic adaptation* are more likely to succeed in reaching their political goals. Strategic adaptation is a four-step process in which collective actors: (a) perceive signals from the broader environment, often from political elites, particularly concerning reasons for the movement's lack of success, (b) evaluate their current tactics in light of these signals to determine whether existing actions are effective, (c) reformulate tactics in light of the signals and their evaluation, choosing tactics that movement actors perceive to be a better approach to achieving their goals, and (d) develop and utilize the new tactics. Some of the jury movements (e.g., California and New York) were quite strategic, regularly engaging in this adaptive behavior. Other state movements rarely, if ever, engaged in reflective, self-evaluation and simply employed the same tactics year after year (e.g., Massachusetts and Nebraska). According to this argument, more strategic movements are more likely to win a change in jury law. We consider this in our analyses as well.

Data and Methods

We use logistic regression to explore whether the political influence of activist framing is moderated by discursive opportunity structures. Our data are annual, state-level measures. We include 15 states in our analysis: CA, CO, GA, IL, MD, MA, MO, MT,

NE, NY, SC, TN, TX, VT, and WI. Because so few secondary accounts of the state jury movements exist, collection of primary data involving trips to each state and a total of more than 50 archives was necessary; thus inclusion of all states was not feasible. Our states, however, provide important variation in the timing of the various legal victories. California, for example, is an early state, while South Carolina passed jury rights much later. Texas had a long-lived campaign, while Wisconsin's took only one year. Our states also provide regional diversity along with variation in their political and cultural climates. States in the South, for instance, tended to be more conservative about women's roles (Scott 1970), while some argue that states in the West were more progressive (McCammon and Campbell 2001). The tactics of our state movements vary as well. In Nebraska, for instance, the activists remained fairly staid in their approach, simply lobbying lawmakers at each legislative session, while in Maryland in the early 1930s activists used a variety of tactics, including staging protests in front of the state legislature with signs demanding that lawmakers broaden women's legal rights (Kennard 1931). Some of the state movements were strategically adaptive in their approach to winning jury service (McCammon et al. 2007). In Illinois, for example, movement leaders regularly recalibrated their tactics to respond to resistance from opponents. In Montana, a state on the other end of the strategic continuum, we find little evidence of such adaptation; instead, movement leaders relied on the same tactics year after year, much like in Nebraska. Our measures span the years 1913 to 1966: Some of the earliest campaigns by women's groups to change jury laws took place in the 1910s, with Colorado women beginning their efforts in 1913. South Carolina was the last state to grant jury service to women, not doing so until 1967 (see Table 1, including note e).

We construct our quantitative data set from a content analysis of extensive historical records collected from archives for our 15 states. The primary records we use are quite rich and come from archives as varied as the California Historical Society, the University of Illinois at Chicago Daley Library Special Collections, and the Lincoln, Nebraska League of Women Voters Office Archive. We use a large variety of manuscript collections, particularly those of women's organizations spearheading the campaigns and the personal papers of activists and politicians. We combine these with the often extensive local newspaper coverage, articles from women's periodicals (e.g., *Equal Rights* and *Independent Woman*), legal and political documents (courts decisions, briefs, legislative journals, and statutes), and a small number of secondary sources (e.g., Perry 2001). Unless noted otherwise, our measures come from these sources.

Our dependent variable is a dichotomous measure of the passage of a state jury law, coded "0" for years prior to the enactment of jury rights in a state and "1" for the year in which women's jury rights were granted. A state drops out of the analysis once jury rights are granted because it is no longer "at risk" of enacting jury service for women.

Our measures of activist frames (as well as those of the opposition) derive from our content analysis of the historical sources. All of the authors, along with two additional research assistants, participated in collecting these data. Each coder read a subset of the historical documents and recorded any instance of pro- or anti-jury framing. We recorded the content of the frame and then tallied the number of times annually that activists in a state used each type of frame (e.g., the duty or peers argument). We use the annual tallies in our analysis. In reading the historical sources, the coders decided independently of one another whether a diagnostic/motivational frame (or frames) was being put forward by jury activists. Such frames take the form of arguments in favor of (or against) women on juries. Because all coders did not read all sources, we assessed interrater reliability on a small subset of sources for determining if and where a diagnostic frame existed in the text. Krippendorff's alpha for interrater reliability is .84 (Krippendorff 1980). One coder (the lead author), in consultation with the other coders, then determined in which category (e.g., the competent frame or the rights frame) each frame belonged, and thus no interrater reliability measure is needed for this step.

We draw the activist frames from activist speeches, articles or letters in newspapers (written by activists or in which activists were quoted), their pamphlets or flyers, organizational documents outlining topics for pubic speeches, minutes of legislative hearings at which activists spoke, letters to lawmakers, and radio interviews to capture what Kubal (1998:543) refers to as public or "front region" claims. Documents in the archival collections and our review of local newspapers provide these materials. While some state movements relied more heavily on certain types of frames (e.g., the war frames were more common in Colorado, Missouri, and Nebraska, and the rights frame was used most frequently in Wisconsin), the small secondary literature that considers the rhetoric of the jury activists does not suggest that our data collection overlooks frequently relied-upon arguments (Perry 2001; Ritter 2002). An activist is defined as anyone working to bring about jury service for women. Almost all were associated with one or more of the organizations working for jury rights (e.g., the LWV or NWP). Politicians' framing efforts are excluded from our framing measures, because our analysis attempts to discern the impact of movement framing on the willingness of lawmakers to pass new jury laws.

All of our framing measures are a count of the number of times in a given year the movement used a particular type of frame with one exception. To operationalize the neutralization or rebuttal of opposition framing by movement actors, we use an indicator of years in which opposition claims that jury rights for women would harm court proceedings were met with supporters' claims that women on juries would not impair courtroom deliberations. This measure equals "1" for years in which both the opposition's assertions and the movement's response were present and "0" otherwise.

In addition to our framing measures, we include various other measures in our analysis that may (a) directly influence movement political success and/or (b) moderate movement framings influence on legal change. We include two measures of *gendered political opportunities* to indicate the discursive opportunities they create. The first is measured with the percentage of all lawyers in a state who are female (US. Bureau of the Census, various years). These data are available only for decennial census years and are linearly interpolated for the interim

years.[3] The second gendered political opportunity is a measure of female lawmakers actively working for jury reform (equal to "1" if female lawmakers made prominent public statements in favor of a jury bill, introduced a jury bill, or worked closely with the jury organizations). We include interaction terms in our models, constructed by multiplying our framing measures by the gendered political opportunity measures, to gauge the degree to which the influence of framing on movement political outcomes is moderated by the discursive opportunities provided by these gendered political opportunities.

Our measure of *wartime* is a dichotomous indicator equal to "1" for 1917 to 1918 and 1942 to 1945, the years of U.S. involvement in World Wars I and II respectively (and "0" otherwise).

Our indicator of *public opposition* to jury service for women is a measure summed across various dimensions of public opposition. Each dimension is coded dichotomously (equal to "1" if present in a given year and "0" otherwise) and then summed to create an opposition measure. The various dimensions of opposition are: the presence of individuals or groups (or non-lawmakers) speaking publicly against jury rights for women, newspaper articles or editorials written in opposition, legislators reporting that their constituents do not support women on juries, and jury activists revealing their difficulties in recruiting supporters.

We include three measures to gauge the impact of movement mobilization on passage of the jury laws. The first is a measure of whether the activists formed *an organization specifically to work on broadening jury laws,* coded "1" for years in which such an organization exists and "0" otherwise. The second measure is an indicator of *the number of types of activities* engaged in by groups working for a change in jury law. These activities range from coordinated letter-writing campaigns directed at lawmakers to fundraising efforts, auto tours, public speeches, and lobbying. We do not include framing efforts in our measure to avoid redundancy with our framing measures. Each activity is coded "1" if it occurs in a given year for a state movement (and "0" otherwise). The individual measures are then summed to produce an aggregate activity measure. Finally, our measure of *strategic adaptation* is a count in any given year of the number of strategic steps taken by a state jury movement. Such strategic steps include: (a) perceiving signals from the broader environment, often from political elites, particularly concerning reasons for a lack of success on the part of movement actors, (b) evaluating the movement's current tactics in light of these signals to determine whether existing actions are effective in advancing the movement toward its goal, (c) reformulating tactics in light of the signals and their evaluation, as well as choosing tactics that movement actors perceive to be a better approach to achieving their goals, and (d) developing and utilizing the new tactics.[4]

Results

Tables 3 to 5 present the results of our logistic regression analyses. The results in Table 3 address Hypotheses 1 and 2 concerning legal and traditional gender discursive opportunity structures as well as Hypotheses 5 and 6 on counterframing and wartime framing. The results in Table 4 address Hypothesis 3 on women in the legal profession, and those in Table 5 correspond to Hypothesis 4 on women lawmakers working for jury reform. There is substantial evidence in the findings that the context in which movement framing takes place moderates the political effectiveness of discursive tactics. Not all contexts, however, are shown to influence the effects of movement framing.

Models 1 and 2 in Table 3 reveal that the jury rights and duty frames have a significant positive effect on the passage of jury laws, suggesting that the discursive opportunity structure rooted in a hegemonic legal discourse of citizenship rights and duties gives these frames persuasive power. We thus find support for Hypothesis 1 in these results. When activists argued that women should sit on juries because it was their right or duty as citizens to do so, as activists did in Texas and Wisconsin in the years they won jury service, they were more likely to convince lawmakers to make jury laws more inclusive. The TX LWV, in fact, highlighted the duty frame in the "kit" it sent its members, telling them to emphasize such arguments in radio interviews and speeches (Texas LWV Records 1954). The other similarity subframes, the competence

and roles frames, are not statistically significant, as expected (see Models 3 and 4). They do not tap into the hegemonic legal discourse (or another theorized discursive opportunity structure) and are thus less effective in convincing lawmakers to broaden the law to include women.

The results in Models 5 and 6 show that neither activists' use of the women's view frame nor the peers frame increased the likelihood that lawmakers would change the law to include women on juries. Neither coefficient is statistically significant. This indicates that when jury proponents framed their rationale for including women on juries in terms of differences between women and men, tapping into a separate spheres ideology (or, in the case of the peers argument, the legal discourse of a jury of one's peers), such arguments did not convince lawmakers to put women on juries. It may be that the separate spheres ideology was losing its foothold in the broader culture, at least in terms of making the case that women should participate more broadly in democratic institutions. Women's unique contributions appear to be a less persuasive frame than arguments based on principles of legal equality. The results do not support Hypothesis 2, the argument that a discursive opportunity structure anchored in traditional views about men's and women's roles will enhance the persuasive impact of these frames (although we reconsider the results for the peers frame; see Table 4).

In Model 7 of Table 3, we see that when proponents of jury rights took discursive steps to neutralize or rebut their opponents' claims (embedded in this framing measure is the concurrent incidence of the opponent's assertion *and* its rebuttal by jury proponents), jury movements significantly increased their likelihood of bringing about a reform in jury law (Hypothesis 3). For instance, where activists countered claims by opponents that women were not competent to serve and that women's presence on juries would harm the court system with assertions that women were indeed competent and would not harm court proceedings, jury activists were more likely to succeed. South Carolina jury proponents did precisely this in the final stages of their campaign, on occasion even presenting their opponents' arguments first and then rebutting

Table 3 Maximum Likelihood Coefficients from a Logit Analysis of Factors Influencing Passage of State Women Jurors Laws, 1913 to 1966

	Model 1	Model 2	Model 3	Model 4	Model 5	Model 6	Model 7	Model 8
Women Lawmakers Active	2.650*	2.673*	2.709*	2.754*	2.672*	2.668*	2.563*	2.797*
	(.985)	(1.012)	(.967)	(.969)	(.966)	(.984)	(.989)	(1.026)
Percent Lawyers Female	−.162	−.247	−.074	−.119	−.085	−.048	−.101	−.006
	(.375)	(.402)	(.357)	(.363)	(.359)	(.358)	(.388)	(.372)
War Years	3.500*	3.431*	3.135*	3.292*	3.208*	3.060*	3.447*	2.223*
	(1.177)	(1.142)	(1.092)	(1.127)	(1.121)	(1.054)	(1.170)	(1.245)
Public Opposition	.412	.212	.349	.359	.345	.342	.160	.338
	(.474)	(.499)	(.455)	(.452)	(.456)	(.482)	(.467)	(.467)
Jury Organization	.788	.817	.375	.334	.491	.316	.150	.395
	(.951)	(.954)	(.912)	(.888)	(.947)	(.895)	(.979)	(.911)
Movement Activities	.380*	.382*	.452*	.449*	.440*	.465*	.484*	.467*
	(.158)	(.156)	(.152)	(.149)	(.155)	(.147)	(.155)	(.155)
Movement Strategic Campaigning	.614*	.611*	.491*	.535*	.509*	.501*	.477*	.570*
	(.265)	(.269)	(.249)	(.252)	(.250)	(.252)	(.264)	(.255)
Rights Frame	.404*	—	—	—	—	—	—	—
	(.219)							
Duty Frame	—	.235*	—	—	—	—	—	—
		(.133)						
Competent Frame	—	—	.053	—	—	—	—	—
			(.133)					
Roles Frame	—	—	—	.191	—	—	—	—
				(.171)				
Women's View Frame	—	—	—	—	.063	—	—	—
					(.108)			
Peers Frame	—	—	—	—	—	.048	—	—
						(.303)		
Neutralization/ Rebuttal Frame	—	—	—	—	—	—	1.485*	—
							(.793)	
War Shortage or Equality Frame	—	—	—	—	—	—	—	1.829*
								(.814)
Constant	−6.99*	−6.70*	−6.84*	−6.91*	−6.86*	−6.84*	−7.13*	−7.18*
Likelihood-ratio Chi-square	65.23*	65.02*	62.00*	62.90*	62.18*	61.88*	65.47*	70.50*

Note: N = 464. Numbers in parentheses are standard errors.

* $p \leq .05$ (one-tailed test).

Table 4 Maximum Likelihood Coefficients from a Logit Analysis of Factors Influencing Passage of State Women Jurors Laws, 1913 to 1966

	Model 1	Model 2	Model 3	Model 4	Model 5	Model 6
Women Lawmakers Active	2.66*	2.833*	2.967*	3.120*	2.85*	3.657*
	(.993)	(1.153)	(1.091)	(1.122)	(1.071)	(1.305)
Percent Lawyers Female	−.236	−.501	−.466	−.544	−.436	.097
	(.422)	(.456)	(.469)	(.461)	(.456)	(.405)
War Years	3.458*	3.370*	3.333*	3.578*	3.248*	4.116*
	(1.168)	(1.148)	(1.141)	(1.202)	(1.128)	(1.418)
Public Opposition	.404	.040	.307	.254	.278	−.022
	(.479)	(.515)	(.485)	(.477)	(.491)	(.535)
Jury Organization	.793	.817	.512	.677	.679	.972
	(.953)	(1.017)	(.959)	(.949)	(.986)	(1.017)
Movement Activities	.380*	.456*	.440*	.445*	.432*	.629*
	(.158)	(.182)	(.159)	(.158)	(.161)	(.178)
Movement Strategic Campaigning	.635*	.622*	.553*	.654*	.588*	.878*
	(.270)	(.283)	(.260)	(.269)	(.264)	(.309)
Rights Frame	.337	—	—	—	—	—
	(.281)					
Rights × Female Lawyers	.059	—	—	—	—	—
	(.152)					
Duty Frame	—	−.330	—	—	—	—
		(.465)				
Duty × Female Lawyers	—	.547	—	—	—	—
		(.457)				
Competent Frame	—	—	−.150	—	—	—
			(.244)			
Competent × Female Lawyers	—	—	.276	—	—	—
			(.185)			
Roles Frame	—	—	—	−.246	—	—
				(.486)		
Roles × Female Lawyers	—	—	—	.584	—	—
				(.466)		
Women's View Frame	—	—	—	—	−.085	—
					(.182)	
Women's View × Female Lawyers	—	—	—	—	.156	—
					(.122)	

Table 4 (*Continued*)

	Model 1	Model 2	Model 3	Model 4	Model 5	Model 6
Peers Frame	—	—	—	—	—	−1.665*
						(.713)
Peers × Female Lawyers	—	—	—	—	—	1.783*
						(.603)
Constant	−7.159*	−7.232*	−7.168*	−7.448*	−7.041*	−9.356*
Likelihood-ratio Chi-square	65.40*	68.32*	65.05*	66.91*	64.92*	11.38*ᵃ

Note: N = 464. Numbers in parentheses are standard errors.

ᵃ The likelihood ratio test conveys that the model with the peers interaction term is a significant improvement in overall fit compared to a model without the interaction term (comparison of Model 6, Table 3 and Model 6, Table 4).

* $P \leq .05$ (one-tailed test).

them (LWV of South Carolina 1966). Our results show that it is important for movement actors to respond to counter claims made by opponents. Not engaging the discursive opportunity provided by opposition framing may well be detrimental for a movement.

We also find that, during wartime, activists who used wartime shortage and equality frames were more likely to win jury rights (Table 3, Model 8; Hypothesis 4). The CO LWV, in its final push for jury rights, performed a skit on a number of radio stations in which a "judge" would ask about the attendance of a particular juror, and the "juror's wife" would answer that her husband was "somewhere in Normandy" or "at sea on a destroyer" and he would not be able to serve on the jury (CO LWV Collection 1944). Our results suggest that this kind of public message, broadcast widely in the state during World War II, contributed significantly to women's victory in winning jury rights during the war. Not all jury activists took advantage of wartime. We find no evidence of wartime framing in Tennessee, for instance, and jury activists were not successful in that state until 1951. Where activists used the discursive opportunity of wartime, however, they were more effective in winning changes in jury law during the war years.[5]

Tables 4 and 5 report results for models containing interaction terms between (a) either women lawyers (Table 4) or women lawmakers (Table 5) and

(b) our framing measures to test Hypotheses 5 and 6. In neither case do the discursive opportunities provided by these gendered political opportunities bolster the effects of movement framing generally. That is, the results do not show that all or most of the framing measures are statistically significant in the presence of larger proportions of female lawyers (Table 4) or where female lawmakers worked for passage of a jury bill (Table 5). There is one exception, however. The results in Table 4 show that the changed gender attitudes fostered by a higher percentage of female lawyers in a state strengthens the influence of the peers frame (see Model 6). The peers frame has no independent effect in Table 3 (see Model 6), but the results in Table 4 show that where women made greater inroads into the legal profession, lawmakers were more willing to reform jury laws when activists used the claim that women ought to be tried by a jury of their peers. Massachusetts and Vermont illustrate this effect. Both states had higher than average proportions of female attorneys, and in the years in which women won a place on juries, jury activists successfully used jury-of-one's-peers arguments.

The gendered political opportunity of more women lawyers, these results suggest, could provide a discursive opportunity for effective movement framing, specifically when activists used the peers frame. Hypothesis 5, then, receives a bit of support. Hypothesis 6, that supportive female

Table 5 Maximum Likelihood Coefficients from a Logit Analysis of Factors Influencing Passage of State
Women Jurors Laws, 1913 to 1966

	Model 1	Model 2	Model 3	Model 4	Model 5	Model 6
Women Lawmakers Active	2.953*	2.228*	2.383*	6.058*	2.392*	11.813*
	(1.178)	(1.108)	(1.069)	(951.061)	(1.126)	(2716.146)
Percent Lawyers Female	−.154	−.222	−.057	−.058	−.074	−.020
	(.371)	(.410)	(.360)	(.375)	(.360)	(.361)
War Years	3.683*	3.124*	2.921*	2.953*	3.015*	3.005*
	(1.273)	(1.126)	(1.102)	(1.103)	(1.168)	(1.064)
Public Opposition	.382	.189	.355	.402	.358	.340
	(.481)	(.508)	(.458)	(.457)	(.457)	(.483)
Jury Organization	.708	.892	.473	.614	.583	.393
	(.953)	(1.01)	(.943)	(.942)	(.985)	(.920)
Movement Activities	.372*	.449*	.459*	.458*	.445*	.464*
	(.159)	(.173)	(.155)	(.151)	(.156)	(.146)
Movement Strategic Campaigning	.619*	.602*	.494*	.572*	.520*	.500*
	(.267)	(.270)	(.252)	(.254)	(.253)	(.255)
Rights Frame	.547*	—	—	—	—	—
	(.335)					
Rights × Female Legislators	−.233	—	—	—	—	—
	(.433)					
Duty Frame	—	−.482	—	—	—	—
		(.853)				
Duty × Female Legislators	—	.856	—	—	—	—
		(.969)				
Competent Frame	—	—	−.113	—	—	—
			(.383)			
Competent × Female Legislators	—	—	.256	—	—	—
			(.449)			
Roles Frame	—	—	—	−13.818	—	—
				(3244.36)		
Roles × Female Legislators	—	—	—	16.186	—	—
				(3707.84)		
Women's View Frame	—	—	—	—	−.045	—
					(.305)	
Women's View × Female Legislators	—	—	—	—	.148	—
					(.355)	

Table 5 (*Continued*)

	Model 1	Model 2	Model 3	Model 4	Model 5	Model 6
Peers Frame	—	—	—	—	—	−13.718
						(3995.676)
Peers × Female Legislators	—	—	—	—	—	15.793
						(4566.487)
Constant	−6.703*	−6.302*	−6.405*	−9.969	−6.411*	−14.606
Likelihood-ratio Chi-square	65.51*	66.49*	62.51*	65.13*	62.41*	62.74*

Notes: N = 464. Numbers in parentheses are standard errors. Deviation scores are used for the components of the interaction terms to reduce the influence of collinearity.

* $p \le .05$ (one-tailed test).

lawmakers would heighten the impact of collective action frames, is not supported at all. None of the framing measures are significant where female lawmakers were actively working for more inclusive jury laws.

More importantly, though, the finding in Table 4 for the peers argument, combined with those in Table 3 for the rights and duties frames, point to the pivotal role of the broad legal discourse in shaping the effectiveness of movement frames. The peers frame, like the rights and duty frames, draws on widely held legal constructs. The results for the peers frame, now combined with those for the rights and duty frames, further strengthen our claim that politically effective frames are those that tap key legal principles (Hypothesis 1). The law thus provides powerful discursive opportunities for compelling activist framing.

Other factors, in addition to movement framing, influence when jury laws were passed (see results in Tables 3 to 5). The gendered political opportunity provided by women lawmakers actively working for passage of a more inclusive jury law had a direct effect on the passage of such a law. Where female lawmakers pushed for legal recognition of women jurors, such laws were more likely to be enacted. A higher percentage of female attorneys, however, did not have an independent effect on the passage of women's jury laws. Its only influence is in the form of a moderating effect, broadening the type of framing effective in winning a change

in law. Also, women were more likely to gain jury service during wartime, even when they did not use wartime frames. Contrary to Burstein and Linton's (2002) expectations about the importance of public opinion, public opposition to the expansion of jury rights to women did not impede enactment of the laws. Perhaps opposition was simply not widespread enough to have an impact. A 1937 poll conducted by the Institute of Public Opinion found that in most states the majority supported women's presence on juries (*Washington Post* 1937). It may be, as Burstein and Linton argue, that because of generally favorable public opinion, at least by 1937, the state jury movements were able to influence the law.

While movement framing played a role in determining when state jury laws changed to include women, other aspects of the jury movements also influenced the passage of the laws. Both the activity and strategic adaptation measures are consistently statistically significant across our models. Jury movements that were more active and strategic in adapting their tactics to their political environments were more likely to succeed. This adds support to Amenta and colleagues' (2005) and McCammon and colleagues' (2007) claims about the importance of these aspects of movement mobilization. Jury movements that organized a separate group to tackle the jury issue, however, were no more likely to win a change in law than those in which women worked on the issue via their existing organizations (such as the LWV or FWC).[6]

Discussion and Conclusions

Scholars have paid only limited attention to the role of social movement discursive tactics in aiding activists as they seek political reform. This article addresses this empirical gap, providing an analysis of the policy impact of collective action framing by women's jury rights activists in the first half of the twentieth century.

The article's theoretical argument is that discursive elements in the broader culture moderate the political influence of movement framing. *The results are clear: in a number of ways discursive opportunity structures in the broader environment increase the effectiveness of specific movement frames.* Our findings show that understanding how a social movement succeeds in gaining policy reform entails careful consideration of its framing efforts, especially the ways in which framing's effectiveness is influenced by the discursive and political contexts. Thus, the conjunctural or interactive theorizing espoused by researchers such as Amenta and colleagues (2005) is important to examine in the study of movement framing's impact. We expand arguments of conjunctual causation beyond a focus solely on political opportunities to consider that cultural and discursive opportunities matter. Not only do political opportunities interact with movement mobilization to enhance the chances that collective actors will succeed in winning a change in law, but cultural opportunities in the broader context do so as well.

The article also reveals the complex ways in which *stable and changing discourses* can shape the impact of movement framing efforts. In the case of the jury activists, a highly stable and hegemonic legal discourse, centered on the legal rights and duties of citizenship, provided a discursive opportunity for politically effective framing. Activists who used the language of citizen rights and duties as a rationale for including women on juries were able to persuade law-makers to reform jury laws. A few law and society scholars have begun to consider how legal arguments shape movement mobilization and collective identity and how such legal rhetoric might contribute to a movement's success in winning legal change (e.g., McCann 1998). Our work contributes to this scholarship by providing

systematic evidence that legal framing can be a potent symbolic tool for activists as they seek changes in law. Opposition framing and wartime, however, both provided discursive opportunity structures that were far less stable, and, in the case of opposition frames, perhaps less hegemonic.

Since opposition claims and wartime served up discursive themes that were often salient for only a short while, these were more dynamic discursive opportunities for movement participants. In the case of opposition framing, if jury activists countered with claims that neutralized or rebutted the opposition's position, activists were more likely to succeed in convincing law-makers to give women a place on juries. During wartime, if those agitating for change articulated frames linking the jury cause to an emerging discourse centered on supporting the war effort, they again were more likely to prompt lawmakers to alter jury laws. We find that discursive opportunity structures can be defined by a stable and hegemonic legal discourse or by far more volatile elements in the discursive field.

Our results also show that the broader culture has a *selective effect* on which frames will be most persuasive among political leaders. We do not find a more generalized effect where a discursive opportunity enhances the impact of movement framing across the board. Discursive opportunities appear to be narrower in their results, providing fertile ground for specific frames but not all movement rhetoric at once. Our measures of gendered political opportunity structures—women's presence in the legal profession and as supporters of broadened jury laws in state legislatures—and the discursive opportunities they fostered do not have the expected effects. They did not result in a greater receptiveness for the jury movements' arguments. As researchers explore how movement framing works in combination with the broader cultural context, our results suggest paying careful attention to the selective qualities of opportunity structures.

But while discursive opportunities exist in the broader context, it remains *in the hands of activists* to perceive and take advantage of such opportunities. The choices movement actors made concerning their public framing of jury service for women, our results show, mattered. For instance, Wisconsin, one of the earliest states to gain a place in the jury box for women, had activists who utilized the rights frame—a frame that taps into a hegemonic legal discourse—more frequently than any other frame. This likely produced the Wisconsin movement's early success. Moreover, state movements that used war framing were more likely to gain jury rights during the war. Agency matters. Movement actors who tailor their framing to tap into discursive opportunities are more likely to succeed politically.

We end our discussion with a caveat. While our dependent variable allows us to explore the circumstances giving rise to a change in the law governing women's right to sit on juries, this measure does not necessarily indicate changes in practice. That is, our dependent variable does not measure the precise number of women sitting on juries. The historical record suggests that in some states women continued to be excluded from jury work after the law changed. For instance, in New York, a study as late as 1973 found that women were underrepresented on juries due to discrimination against women in the selection of jury panels (Schweber 1979). Moreover, in some states, the impact of a new jury law was tempered because other new laws provided exemptions for women if they chose to use them. As movement outcome scholars (e.g., Amenta and Caren 2004) note, political effectiveness not only lies in the enactment of new law but also in a law's specific provisions, its implementation, and its behavioral consequences.

The ways in which the context influences framing's effectiveness are complex, but this need not drive us, in our investigations of movement framing's political impact, away from exploring these richly textured processes. An overarching theme found in the interplay between movement framing and the broader context is that *to be politically effective, a movement must respond and interact with its environment as it frames its arguments.* Whether in rebutting the opposition, taking advantage of changed rhetorical circumstances such as wartime, or tapping into a hegemonic legal discourse, to succeed politically, movements should adapt their framing to the broader cultural context.

NOTES

This work was funded by a National Science Foundation grant (SES 0350400) and a Vanderbilt Research Scholar grant to the first author. We thank Soma Chaudhuri, Claire Dawson, Lyndi Hewitt, Carrie Smith, and Terrie Spetalnick for help with data collection, and Mike Ezell for statistical assistance. Anonymous *ASR* reviewers provided helpful comments.

1. Beliefs concerning citizenship rights and duties were also contested, but these challenges were not as fundamental as the challenges to the separate sphere ideology. Activists' efforts to broaden jury laws to include women contested legal definitions of citizenship rights and duties. The challenges, however, did not dispute the very existence of citizenship rights and duties, whereas challenges of the separate spheres ideology often did question the need for the belief itself.

2. We examined other measures of political opportunity: male lawmaker support, female lawmakers in the state legislature, Democrats or Republicans in legislative office, support from nonlegislative political actors (e.g., the governor, attorney general), and levels of party competition. None are statistically significant (analyses not shown). We also examined the combined effect of higher levels of mobilization (using our movement measures) and our measure of political opportunity (female lawmakers acting in support of a jury bill) to explore a political mediation effect, but we find no statistically significant results (analyses not shown).

3. Data on female state judges are not available for the years under study. We examined two other measures indicating a gendered political opportunity for broadening jury laws: whether a state enacted women's suffrage before ratification of the federal amendment and whether the state is a Western state. Neither measure is significant in our models (not shown).

4. We present the results below without corrections for temporal and regional dependence. Inclusion of year and regional dummy variables as suggested by Beck, Katz, and Tucker (1998) do not alter our findings (analyses not shown). We also tested for differences in the residual variances across groups for our interaction models (Allison 1999). Unobserved heterogeneity in logit models can corrupt model coefficients. We find no such differences across groups, where groups are defined as units (a) with/without higher percentages of female lawyers and (b) with/without female lawmakers working for jury rights (analyses not shown), and thus do not employ corrections for group differences in the results shown.

5. Because the wartime frames were used only during wartime, we do not construct a multiplicative interaction term to assess the effect of the war frames; we examine simply the main effect of the wartime framing variable. We also run our wartime framing model without the war years variable, although collinearity between the measures is not a problem.

The war framing measure is significant and positive without the war years measure (results not shown).

6. In models not shown, we included a control variable for years in which a jury law or referendum was more likely to pass, that is, a dichotomous measure of the year in which the state legislature met or in which a jury referendum was voted upon. The measure is not significant in our models, suggesting that our other measures (the framing and opportunity variables, for instance) are doing a reasonable job of explaining why, during legislative session and referendum years, jury laws were more likely to pass. We do not include the control measure in the models we present because of perfect prediction problems in some of the models.

38.
Age for Leisure? Political Mediation and the Impact of the Pension Movement on U.S. Old-Age Policy

EDWIN AMENTA, NEAL CAREN, AND SHEERA JOY OLASKY

Scholars have increasingly turned their attention to the consequences of social movements (cf. McAdam, McCarthy, and Zald 1988 and Amenta and Caren 2004). Much of this work has focused on the external consequences of movements, especially those relating to states and struggles over legislation. Despite this work, one reviewer (Giugni 2004) recently argued that our knowledge accumulation on the subject has thus far been minor. Others (McAdam 1999; Zald 2000) argue that the political process and resource mobilization models do not help to explain the consequences of these movements. Other reviewers (Burstein and Linton 2002) claim that quantitative analyses in this area have frequently been misspecified and that when public opinion is taken into account challengers are found to have little direct influence on state-related outcomes.

In this paper, we seek to contribute to this debate by elaborating and appraising a political mediation theory of social movement consequences (Piven and Cloward 1977; Amenta, Carruthers, and Zylan 1992; Skocpol 1992; Amenta, Bernstein, and Dunleavy 1994; Fording 1997; Amenta, Halfmann,

Amenta Edwin, Neal Caren, and Sheera Joy Olasky. 2005 "Age for Leisure? Political Mediation and the Impact of the Pension Movement on U.S. Old-Age Policy." *American Sociological Review* 70: 516–538. Reprinted by permission of American Sociological Association.

and Young 1999; Lipset and Marks 2000). Instead of asking whether movements are generally influential or whether certain aspects of movements are always influential, as others have done, we ask under what conditions are social movements likely to be influential. Our political mediation theory holds that political contexts mediate the influence of challengers' mobilization and strategies. We argue that in some favorable contexts mobilization may be enough in itself for a challenger to exert influence and that under more difficult political circumstances more assertive strategies are needed. In yet more difficult political contexts (which we specify), a movement may not be able to exert any influence. Moreover, we argue that it takes a combination of favorable political contexts, mobilization, and assertive actions to bring about far-reaching state outcomes. We specify what constitutes long- and short-term favorable and unfavorable political contexts, as demanded by critics of previous social movement research (Goodwin and Jasper 1999); these differ from the standard four of the political opportunity model (McAdam 1996; Tarrow 1996). We also reconceptualize what counts as an assertive strategy (cf. McAdam 1999; Kitschelt 1986), as previous definitions have been too broad to address different means employed by state-oriented challengers.

We appraise the model and some alternatives by analyzing the impact of the U.S. old-age pension movement on old-age policy in its formative years. Though largely forgotten today, the old-age pension movement was a major political phenomenon. The Townsend Plan,[1] the largest mass pension organization, was formed in 1934 and in less than two years had organized two million older Americans into Townsend clubs behind the slogan "Youth for Work—Age for Leisure." Townsend Plan supporters made up one of only about thirty social movement organizations ever to attract I percent or more of the U.S. adult population (Skocpol 2003). In 1936, the Townsend Plan was the subject of more than 400 articles in the *New York Times,* placing seventh among all twentieth-century social movement organizations (see Table 1) in number of mentions in their peak year. In addition to the Townsend Plan, many notable state-level pension organizations demanded generous support for the aged—senior citizens' pensions—rather than the subsistence-level assistance or restricted, wage-related annuities provided or promised by the 1935 Social Security Act. The old-age pension movement case is a useful one to appraise political mediation theory as the movement varied greatly in its mobilization and actions and operated in multiple political contexts, across states and times.

In addition, because the theory has implications for different outcomes, we employ a variety of data on outcomes. The first data set concerns state-level Old Age Assistance (OAA) programs, which were the main support for the aged from 1936 through 1950. We examine the generosity of OAA stipends and the program's coverage among the aged population. These two outcomes add leverage to our analysis, because the pension movement's claims and strategies largely focused on the amount of benefit, rather than extent of coverage, and thus we would expect that the presence and activity of pension organizations would influence the amount of benefit more than the coverage. We also examine which senators voted for a 1939 measure aiming to transform U.S. old-age policy into generous senior citizens' pensions for most adults over 60 years. The political mediation model holds that effecting radical change requires more extensive determinants than does influencing more moderate programs, and the voting data address these claims.

We use two methods to appraise arguments: multiple regression analysis and fuzzy set qualitative comparative analysis (FSQCA), the latter of which facilitates the examination of complex and multiple causal arguments (Ragin 1987, 2000), such as those of the political mediation model. Each type of analysis supports our claims.

The State-Related Consequences of Social Movements and Political Mediation Theory
Moderate and Radical Influence

A first step for scholars who seek to study state-related consequences of social movements is to define "success" or "influence" for challengers making state-related claims. We follow in the footsteps of most state-related research, focusing on new advantages (see Gamson [1975] 1990; Amenta and Caren 2004; Meyer 2005). But we reject Gamson's ([1975] 1990) definition of "success"—whether a challenger's claims were mainly acted on—because of its limitations. Challengers differ in how far-reaching their goals are, and thus a challenger may fail to achieve its stated program, but still win substantial new advantages for its constituents (Amenta and Young 1999). There are also the possibilities of negligible "successes," such as a program that did not realize its intended effects, and negative consequences, such as repression or restrictions on movements (Piven and Cloward 1977; McCarthy and McPhail 1998).

For these reasons, we employ a wider concept of influence based on collective goods, or group-wise advantages or disadvantages from which nonparticipants in a challenge cannot be easily excluded (Hardin 1982). Collective goods can be material, such as categorical social spending programs, but they can also be less tangible, such as new ways to refer to members of a group. Most state-related collective action in democratic political systems is aimed at major changes in policy and the bureaucratic enforcement and implementation of that policy (Amenta and Caren 2004). State social policies are institutionalized benefits that provide collective goods routinely to those meeting specified requirements (Skocpol and Amenta 1986). Once enacted and enforced with bureaucratic means, categorical social spending programs provide beneficiaries

Table 1 Top 25 U.S. Social Movement Organizations in the 20th Century, by Mentions in Articles in Peak Year, in the New York Times and the Washington Post

Organization (Peak Year)	New York Times Articles	New York Times Front Page	Washington Post Articles
1. American Federation of Labor (1937)	1,050	205	476
2. Black Panthers (1970)	1,028	111	617
3. CIO (1937)	786	186	325
4. NAACP (1963)	762	128	446
5. Ku Klux Klan (1924)	672	180	339
6. Anti-Saloon League (1930)	409	99	91
7. Townsend Plan (1936)	402	68	118
8. Students for a Democratic Society (1969)	381	90	174
9. Congress of Racial Equality (1963)	369	32	86
10. America First Committee (1941)	280	24	121
11. American Legion (1937)	263	70	200
12. John Birch Society (1964)	255	32	128
13. League of Women Voters (1937)	246	4	117
14. American Civil Liberties Union (1977)	231	24	102
15. Moral Majority (1981)	221	10	268
16. Southern Christian Leadership Conference (1968)	215	36	142
17. German American Bund (1939)	200	32	71
18. Student Nonviolent Coordinating Committee (1966)	195	47	76
19. Veterans of Foreign Wars (1950)	180	22	104
20. American Liberty League (1936)	174	53	136
21. Christian Coalition (1996)	170	52	253
22. Association Against the Prohibition Amendment (1930)	168	56	37
23. Weathermen (1970)	159	22	92
24. Symbionese Liberation Army (1974)	157	23	97
25. Jewish Defense League (1971)	145	31	91

Note: CIO = Congress of Industrial Organizations; NAACP = National Association for the Advancement of Colored People.

rights of entitlement. With bureaucratic reinforcement, an issue can become privileged in politics, biasing the political system in favor of the group. Benefits through legislation can range from structural benefits that extend the political leverage of a group, such as enhanced voting, associational, or civil rights, to one-shot pecuniary benefits, such as summer jobs, extensions of unemployment insurance, housing vouchers, or bonus payments. We argue that effecting more radical changes requires more extensive favorable conditions, both internal and external.

The old-age pension movement demanded generous and unrestricted grants to all nonemployed Americans over the age of 60 for their lifelong service to the country—or what it called "pensions" for "senior citizens." Pension proponents in individual states demanded that OAA programs be converted into pension programs. Their demands were not met. Our focus, however, is on whether these groups had an impact on OAA, which permanently changed the relationship between the state and the aged. We also address whether the movement affected a Senate vote for a pension alternative to existing old-age programs. Finally, we estimate the conditions under which such radical action may have been possible.

Political Mediation Theory

Many scholars have developed (Piven and Cloward 1977; Amenta et al. 1992; Skocpol 1992; Amenta et al. 1994; Fording 1997; Amenta et al. 1999; Lipset and Marks 2000) or tested (Cress and Snow 2000; Soule and Olzak 2004; Giugni 2004) political mediation models of social movement consequences. The basic idea is that challengers must engage in collective action that changes the calculations of relevant institutional political actors and thus mobilize and adopt strategies in ways that fit political circumstances. State actors must in turn see a challenger as potentially facilitating or disrupting their own goals—for example, augmenting or cementing electoral coalitions, gaining in public opinion, or increasing support for the mission of governmental bureaus. Political mediation theory rejects the idea that individual organizational forms, strategies, or political contexts will *always* influence challengers,

as is generally argued (see Amenta and Caren 2004 for review). Instead, the theory posits that different mobilizations and collective action strategies will be more productive in some political contexts than in others.

The most extensive versions of the political mediation theory (Amenta et al. 1999; Amenta forthcoming) build upon arguments that resource mobilization, strategies, and political context influence the consequences of movements. These versions argue that mobilizing relatively large numbers of committed people is probably necessary to winning new collective benefits for those otherwise underrepresented in politics (Rucht 1998; Skocpol 2003; see review in McCarthy and Zald 2002). In addition, making claims regarding the worthiness of the group (Tilly 1999b) and the plausibility of its program (Cress and Snow 2000; Ferree et al. 2002) is also necessary. Favorable political contexts, both long- and short-term, are also helpful (Jenkins and Perrow 1977; Kitschelt 1986; Kriesi 1995; Almeida and Stearns 1998; Meyer and Minkoff 2004). The political mediation model, however, helps to explain the impact of social movements by examining mobilization and strategies in combination with different sorts of political contexts. In highly favorable political contexts, all that should be required is a certain threshold of resource mobilization and minimally plausible and directed framing and claims-making. In less favorable political contexts, more assertive strategies of collective action would be required for a social movement to have influence. In yet other political contexts, where powerful systemic conditions work against challengers, it may be impossible for the challengers to exert much influence. In short, the context must be extremely favorable and the mobilization and action extensive for challengers to achieve the most radical goals.

Elaborating the Theory

According to political mediation theory, the ability of a challenger to win collective benefits depends partly on conditions it can control, including its ability to mobilize, its goals and program, its form of organization, and its strategies for collective action, including issue framing and other claims-making. However, the impact of even well-mobilized challengers also depends on political context. Political mediation theory holds that political conditions influence the *relationship* between a challenger's mobilization and collective action on the one hand, and policy outcomes on the other. It holds that mobilization and collective action alone are often insufficient to effect changes in public policy that would benefit a challenger's constituency. The model posits relationships between mobilization and strategies and structural and short-term political contexts. The argument focuses on specific political contexts, taking into account criticisms that political opportunity models are often conceptualized at too broad a level to be empirically tested (Goodwin and Jasper 1999; cf. Meyer and Minkoff 2004). Our political mediation argument also differs from political opportunity structure arguments (McAdam 1996; Tarrow 1996) in that the latter tend to address the mobilization of challengers than their political consequences (Zald 2000). Also, our understanding of political contexts is based not on standard political opportunity factors, but on contexts found influential in altering social policy (Mayhew 1986; Skocpol 1992; Amenta 1998; Hicks 1999; Huber and Stephens 2001).

The political mediation theory holds that specific long-term aspects of political and party systems influence the productivity of challengers' action. First, the degree to which formally democratic institutions are bound by democratic practices is key (Amenta 1998; Tilly 1999a). An extension of democratic rights entails lowering the legal restrictions on institutional political participation for the common citizens, including their ability to assemble and discuss issues. A highly democratized polity is also characterized by meaningful choices among parties or factions. By contrast, an underdemocratized polity is one in which political leaders are chosen by way of elections, but in which there are great restrictions on political participation, political assembly and discussion, voting, and choices among leadership groups. An underdemocratized political system greatly dampens the impact of the collective action of challengers, assuming they are able to arise in these polities. Underdemocratized political systems are characterized by noncompetitive elections and formal and informal restrictions on voting, such as poll taxes, extensive eligibility tests, harassment, and violence. The United States, especially the South, included many underdemocratized polities, as franchise barriers were erected at the end of the nineteenth century and persisted through most of the twentieth century (Burnham 1974).

Second, patronage-oriented political parties—that is, autonomous, long-lasting, hierarchical organizations that seek to nominate candidates for a wide range of public offices and rely substantially on material incentives (Katznelson 1981; Mayhew 1986)—tend to deflect claims for collective benefits sought by pro-social spending challengers. Granting automatic and long-term entitlement claims to groups of citizens limits the sort of discretionary spending, such as for government jobs and contracts, that maintains a patronage-oriented political organization. For these reasons patronage-oriented parties regard social movement organizations as a menace and consider programmatic spending policies a threat to the individualistic rewards on which such parties thrive. Although it is not impossible for movements to exert influence under these circumstances, these structural impediments make it difficult, and also often thwart the efforts of state actors and insurgents in the party system to enact or enhance programmatic public spending policies in favor of challenging groups. The United States, especially in the Northeast and Midwest, was characterized by many patronage-oriented party systems for most of the twentieth century (Mayhew 1986).

Medium-range and short-term political contexts also influence the prospects of mobilized groups that hope to gain leverage in political systems that are mainly democratized and are not dominated by patronage-oriented parties. Domestic bureaucrats are key actors here. Bureaucrats whose mission is consistent with that of a challenger—assuming they have initiative, talent, and power—may provide administrative rulings, enforce laws, or propose new legislation that aids a challenger's constituency, even within the context of an otherwise indifferent or opposed state (Skocpol 1992). These domestic bureaucrats may advance such legislation further than they had intended if a challenger summons a show of strength. These arguments are similar to Kitschelt's (1986) about the role of implementation capacities. But our arguments are both wider, in considering the different ways in which domestic bureaucracies might amplify the impact of challengers' collective action, and more localized, as the relevant bureaucracies will differ according to the challenger and its constituency. Bureaucracies centrally concerned with social and labor issues were inaugurated largely in the 1910s in the United States; they varied widely in their orientation and power in the 1930s, and continue to do so today.

Another crucial factor is the partisanship of the regime in power. A new political regime or government, hoping to add to its coalition, may aid the constituency of social movements by proposing spending or other legislation that favors a certain group. A regime that is favorable or open to the possibility of increased social spending would be expected to amplify the impact of a challenger's mobilization and collective action, while a regime opposed to social spending would dampen it. Often parties have long-standing commitments to ideological positions or groups whose interests and goals may conflict with those of challengers (Klandermans and Oegema 1987). For state-oriented challengers who seek collective benefits through sustained public spending, the position of the regime on higher taxation is crucial. Since the 1930s the U.S. Republican party and its representatives have tended to oppose automatic, programmatic spending claims because they imply higher taxation, whereas the national Democratic party and Democrats outside the South have tended to be "reform-oriented"—more open to policy claims requiring taxation (Amenta 1998; Hicks 1999). Regime conditions varied widely across the United States in the 1930s, as some northern states followed the national trend to elect pro–New Deal Democrats and others did not. Partisanship variations have persisted to this day, with the South having largely turned reliably Republican in the decades after the Civil Rights and Voting Rights Acts of the 1960s.

The mediation model expects these contexts to affect the influence of movement activity. If the political regime is open to the claims of challengers and the domestic bureaucrats are professionalized and favorably disposed to the challenger's constituency, limited activity on the part of the challenger, even simply providing evidence of mobilization, is likely to be sufficient to produce increased collective benefits. The challenger needs mainly to demonstrate that it has support, such as through writing letters, holding rallies, petitioning, initiating public awareness campaigns, staging limited protest, or even engaging in visible internal events. Members of a reform-oriented regime are likely to use such evidence of mobilization as a confirmation of the beneficiary group's relative importance in an electoral coalition. If a reform-oriented regime has many issues on its agenda, it is more likely to address first the issues being pressed by mobilized groups. Domestic bureaucrats are likely to portray the mobilization as indicating the need for the augmentation or greater enforcement of its programs. If the regime hopes to add to its coalition or if domestic bureaucrats have a mission that is not yet realized, the best-mobilized groups are likely to win the greatest benefits in public policy for their constituencies.

By contrast, achieving collective benefits through public policy is likely to be more difficult if neither an open regime nor administrative authority exists. When the regime is opposed to the challenger or sees no benefit in adding the challenger's beneficiary group to its coalition and when state bureaucracies in the area are hostile, the sorts of limited protest listed above are likely to be ignored or to have a negligible effect. In the face of more difficult political circumstances, more assertive or bolder collective action is required to produce collective benefits. Here we drop the standard distinction between "disruptive" and "assimilative" (Kitschelt 1986) and "noninstitutional" and "institutional" (McAdam 1999) strategies, instead focusing on variations in assertiveness of action, with "assertive" meaning the use of increasingly strong political sanctions—those that threaten to increase or decrease the likelihood of political actors gaining or keeping something they see as valuable (their positions, acting in accordance with their beliefs) or to take over their functions or prerogatives. Sustained political action to unseat a representative, for example, would be more threatening than, say, dispatching protesters to picket or to occupy the representative's office. The institutional collective action of challengers works largely by mobilizing large numbers of people behind a course of action, often one with electoral implications. This collective action may be designed to convince the general public of the justice of the cause and influence elected and appointed officials in that manner, but it can also demonstrate to these officials that a large segment of the electorate is willing to vote or engage in other political activity on the basis of a single key issue.

If the political regime is not supportive of the challenger's constituency or issue, collective action will be most productive if it focuses on elected officials. Such action might neutralize those who would otherwise be hostile to legislation and win the support of those who would be indifferent. Assertive action might include contesting elections, such as endorsing and supporting the opponents of hostile incumbents or winning promises from them and then providing support. Newcomers elected with a challenger's endorsement and support would be especially likely to support its program or other programs benefiting its constituents. Other assertive action would include attempting to override legislative authority, as through direct democratic devices such as the initiative, referendum, and recall. Such displays of influence might alter the views of legislators in whose states the mobilizations took place, even when the actions fail. In the face of strong electoral sanctions, legislators previously opposed may come to support moderate measures that benefit the group represented by the challenger.[2]

The mediation argument also addresses the characteristics of outcomes and legislation at issue. The more radical and far-reaching the outcome, the greater the favorable conditions required and the more the movement may have to do to influence it. Thus for some outcomes, such as improving existing programs, merely mobilizing under favorable contexts would be enough to exert influence. Similarly, employing assertive sanctions when conditions are structurally favorable but the short-term context is unfavorable may be enough. Fundamentally altering policy, however, is likely to take both strong mobilization and extensive assertive shows of strength.

Even these may not be enough to create sweeping changes in policy; more favorable political conditions may also be necessary. The same is likely to be true for bids to transform the structural position of groups, such as through new voting or civil rights.

To summarize, political mediation theory holds that the influence of mobilization and strategies of action are conditional on specific political contexts. Some systemic political contexts—an underdemocratized polity and a patronage-oriented party system—will deaden the influence of challengers. Medium-range and localized political contexts will have a more variegated effect on the relationship between a challenger's collective action and state-related results. Regimes and bureaucracies open to challengers' claims will tend to repay the challengers' mobilization. Even in democratized polities and non-patronage-oriented party systems, however, regimes and bureaucracies may still be unfavorable. In these circumstances social movements would need to engage in assertive collective action in order to win new benefits. Before we employ quantitative analyses to appraise the individual influence of various factors, and formal qualitative analyses to address the multiple theoretical interactions and causal pathways, we briefly introduce the old-age pension movement and U.S. old-age policy.

The Old-Age Pension Movement, U.S. Old-Age Policy, and our Analyses
The Townsend Plan and the Old-Age Pension Movement

The Townsend Plan was founded in January 1934 by Dr. Francis E. Townsend, a laid-off, 66-year-old Long Beach medical assistant, and Robert Earl Clements, a 39-year-old real estate broker (Holtzman 1963; Mitchell 2000; Amenta forthcoming). The purpose of the organization was to promote the enactment of the pension-recovery program Townsend had first outlined in letters to the editor of the *Long Beach Press Telegram* in September 1933. The plan called for $200 monthly pensions to all nonemployed citizens over 60 years, excluding criminals, and was designed to end the Depression and ensure prosperity through the mandatory spending of these pensions, as well as to end poverty among the elderly. Clements assembled a hierarchical organizing staff paid by commission, and Townsend was the organization's symbol and spokesman, akin to the role that Colonel Sanders played for Kentucky Fried Chicken. To maintain enthusiasm and mobilize resources, Clements and Townsend inaugurated Townsend "clubs"—local affiliates with no formal decision-making powers, but that met regularly to hear speakers, collect donations, and act in political campaigns. The Townsend Plan grabbed national attention in late 1935 when it was organizing clubs at the rate of one every two hours. At that point, legislation it had endorsed would have provided almost all senior citizens with about $60 per month, less than $200 but far more than what was promised by the Social Security Act.

Although Townsend clubs and their members remained the backbone of the old-age pension movement, they were joined by a number of pension organizations later in the 1930s. A group known as Ham and Eggs won national attention in 1938 with its program to provide $30 every Thursday to aged Californians. Other notable state-level pension organizations included the National Annuity League of Colorado and the Old Age Pension Union of Washington. In different states many coalitions formed briefly around specific initiatives, especially in 1938, when eight pension initiatives were placed on state ballots. For the most part, these initiatives concentrated on providing more generous benefits than existing programs, although the movement also stood for a wider extension of benefits to the aged. The pension movement existed for almost two decades under diverse national political circumstances and across state-level polities. The Townsend Plan chose to ignore the state level in the 1930s, arguing that improving OAA programs in individual states would hinder efforts to enact pensions at the national level. But the Townsend Plan, too, eventually began to demand changes in state old-age laws, placing propositions for $60-per-month pensions on the ballots of a few western states in 1943. These efforts failed, and by 1950 the Townsend Plan had lost most of its membership.

U.S. Old-Age Policy and the Present Research

The 1935 Social Security Act created two old-age programs. One was a national, proto-old-age

insurance program, which was not scheduled to make any payments until 1942. The second was a federal-state matching program called Old Age Assistance, which immediately provided benefits to the aged in individual states. OAA was the workhorse of old-age protection during the Depression, the Second World War, and immediately afterward. It was upgraded in 1939 and was not eclipsed by Old Age and Survivors Insurance (known now as "Social Security") until the 1950s. We ascertain first whether the old-age pension movement influenced OAA programs and, if so, in what ways and why. OAA programs are useful in a test of our arguments because the various state programs did not converge in their generosity and coverage, and the pension movement sought to convert them into pension-like programs with more generous benefits, often through initiatives. We would expect the pension movement to have greater influence on the generosity of programs than on the extension of programs.

We also seek to determine whether the pension movement induced senators to vote for a measure to replace the two programs with a senior citizens' pension and, if so, what types of activities were effective, by analyzing roll-call votes (McAdam and Su 2002; Soule et al. 1999) through multiple regression analyses. We focus on 1939, the year that the Social Security Act was amended and the only year that there were votes on senior citizens' pensions. The so-called Lee amendment (S76–1061), though not specifically a vote on authorized Townsend Plan legislation, would have created a widespread and generous $40 per month benefit, twice as large as the average OAA payment. The $40 figure was also the median amount that public opinion polls indicated that the government should pay in monthly old-age benefits (Gallup 1936, 1939). Although the amendment failed, by a vote of 17 to 56, putting on the Congressional agenda a radical alternative and lining up votes behind it (Kingdon 1984) is one way for a challenger to influence the political process and public policy, as it can induce opponents to accept more moderate legislation. Indeed, observers suggest that this is what happened in 1939 in the case of the pension movement (Huston 1939). The Lee amendment vote also gives us an opportunity to compare the determinants of influencing existing programs with those of altering policy in a more fundamental way. Because the Townsend Plan was mainly engaged at the national level and made plausible claims about pensions at the time, we expect it should be influential.

These state and national policy outcomes provide a large number of cases, making it possible to control for other variables that might also have influenced old-age policy-variables that are often ignored in studies of the impact of social movements (Earl 2000). Scholars of social policy argue that democratized political systems, left-wing regimes, powerful domestic bureaucracies, favorable public opinion, and economic and demographic developments might all influence the policy changes that others might attribute to the presence or activity of a social movement (Amenta, Bonastia, and Caren 2001; Skrentny 2002). Worse, some of these conditions, such as an increase in the aged or the rise to power of the Democratic party, may have spurred both the pension movement and political action on old-age benefits (Amenta and Young 1999). Our analyses address these issues.

Explaining Old-Age Assistance in Its Formative Years
Dependent Measures

We examine two basic components of Old Age Assistance programs, their generosity and their coverage, from their first year in operation in 1936 through 1950, when the Social Security Act was amended to upgrade old-age insurance. The first dependent measure is the *average size of the OAA benefit,* an indication of the relative generosity of states. . . . In addition, we examine each state's *OAA coverage*—the state's commitment to providing assistance broadly to elderly residents. State legislation generally set the parameters controlling these programs. Benefit levels and coverage varied dramatically from state to state.

Independent Measures And Expectations

We appraise the main social movement and political mediation arguments through a series of independent measures. Three capture different facets of the political institutional aspects of the mediation

theory, and they vary little over time. As an indicator of voting rights and polity democratization, we consider the *poll tax,* a key, though far from the only, means to restrict the franchise. Nine states had poll taxes at the start of the period, but Florida and Georgia dropped theirs. We expect that under-democratized political systems, characterized by restrictions on the franchise, would discourage movements for generous public spending programs as well as OAA benefits and coverage. We also include a measure of *patronage party organizational strength,* with the expectation that such party organizations would discourage categorical public spending, resulting in less generous benefits and restricted coverage. We also include *administrative strength,* a measure of the strength and structure of the state labor commissions. Although they did not typically control OAA, their existence indicates overall domestic bureaucratic development and power, and we would expect them to have a positive influence on OAA outcomes.

Two measures address medium-term political and administrative conditions. We would expect that control of the state government by a pro-spending party would lead to higher quality OAA programs. We model *democratized Democratic control* by including a measure for control of the governor's mansion and both houses of the state legislature by the Democratic party in states without poll taxes. Additionally, we include a measure of *OAA county funding.* We expect that higher county contributions to OAA would negatively influence OAA outcomes, as counties had fewer and more contentious taxing opportunities, mainly real estate levies.

We also employ several control measures. *Per capita income* addresses how much social spending states could afford; we expect that higher per capita income would positively influence OAA (Wilensky 1975). We also include *percentage black* to take into account the potentially dampening impact of race on OAA benefits (Quadagno 1988; Lieberman 1998). *Percentage aged* in each state is likely to spur demands for old-age benefits (Mitchell 2000). We also include measures of *pro-old-age public opinion.* Public opinion is sometimes argued to be the only direct influence on public policy (Burstein 1999) and often is absent in empirical studies of movement consequences, possibly resulting in their models being misspecified and their conclusions faulty (Burstein and Linton 2002). We analyze two 1938 Gallup polls, the earliest polling efforts on old age that survive in forms suitable for state-level analyses. We focus on the question "How much per month should be paid to a single person?" in our analyses of OAA generosity. The median choice was $40. For OAA coverage, we examine the question "Do you think pensions should be given to all old people, or only to old people who are in need?" About 20 percent chose "all." Responses are aggregated to the state level. Although there is no systematic information on the saliency of the issue, it is likely that old age was a prominent issue through 1941, when the Second World War began. We therefore include control measures for the war and postwar time periods.[3]

Finally, we consider three pension movement measures, Townsend club activity, change in club activity, and electoral initiatives. First, we operationalize *Townsend club activity*[4] in two ways. Given the expectation that high mobilization will have a lasting influence (McCarthy and Zald 2002), we measure club activity at its *peak value* for a state. Second, we measure the *change in activity*, which has been argued to be more likely than the overall mobilization level to influence politicians who are seeking information relevant to their reelections (Burstein and Linton 2002). We also include a measure for the most assertive movement strategy to influence state legislators—the placing of *pension propositions* on the ballot. These propositions were usually designed to make OAA more generous, and less frequently to relax eligibility requirements. While the vast majority of these efforts failed, and the successes were countered by subsequent legislation, we expect that propositions would have a positive impact on OAA generosity. Propositions usually involve a political show of force: their proponents petition, dramatize an issue, and insert it onto the political agenda. In this instance, we expect that they would pressure politicians to prove their commitment to their aged constituents.

Although it is not possible to test all the interactions in the political mediation argument with multiple regression, the model does provide different expectations across the independent measures and across time. First, we expect the long-term institutional factors to influence both aspects of OAA, as these are general influences on social policy. But we also expect the social movement measures to have a greater influence on the average benefit than in coverage, because the claims and demands of the pension movement were largely focused on higher benefits.

Multiple Regression Results

Our cross-sectional panel data set includes information on the 48 states, each over a period of 14 years. Under these circumstances, with multiple cases from the same state and multiple cases from the same year, we expect that the error terms would not be independent and identically distributed, making pooled OLS regression inappropriate. Moreover, our data set is case dominated, with many more cross-sectional cases than years, rather than temporarily dominated, as is typical in time-series cross-sectional research (Beck 2001). For these reasons we employ a GLS random-effects model, which allows for both time-varying and time-invariant variables (Western and Beckett 1999; Kenworthy 2002; Beckfield 2003). Additionally, we expect that spending by a state in a given year will be related to its spending in the previous year, potentially producing serially correlated errors. The Wooldridge (2002) test for autocorrelation in panel data reports significant evidence of first-order autocorrelation in our models, and we employ the Baltagi-Wu (1999) estimator to remove this disturbance. For the average size of OAA benefits and coverage, we report an initial model estimating the effects of political contextual factors and control measures, and then a full model that adds social movement measures in order to ascertain whether they add to the explanation.[5]

Table 2 presents the results for the average size of OAA benefit. The initial model, Model 1, yields significant coefficients at the .05 level or better for the political context measures, with the exception of democratized Democratic control. All the control measures, except for the war period, are significant. The full model, Model 2, which accounts for almost 70 percent of the overall variance, yields

Table 2 Average Size of the Old Age Assistance Benefit and OAA Coverage on Selected Independent Measures

	BENEFIT SIZE		COVERAGE	
	Model 1	Model 2	Model 3	Model 4
Institutional Measures				
Poll Tax	−4.584*	−3.897	−3.183	−3.100
	(1.88)	(1.61)	(1.18)	(1.14)
Patronage Party Strength	−1.220**	−0.871*	−2.880**	−2.858**
	(2.50)	(1.74)	(4.65)	(4.45)
Administrative Strength	3.918*	3.879*	−0.941	−0.974
	(2.15)	(2.19)	(0.44)	(0.46)
Democratized Dem. Control	−0.067	0.299	3.265**	3.315**
	(0.07)	(0.30)	(3.34)	(3.33)
OAA County Funding	−0.104*	−0.090*	−0.123**	−0.123**
	(1.96)	(1.70)	(2.34)	(2.33)
Movement Measures				
Townsend Club Activity	—	1.229*	—	0.075
	—	(2.15)	—	(0.12)
Pension Proposition	—	1.374	—	0.625
	—	(1.44)	—	(0.74)
Control Measures				
Pro-Old-Age Public Opinion	0.306**	0.300**	0.100	0.097
	(3.81)	(3.83)	(1.32)	(1.27)
Per Capita Income	0.007**	0.007**	0.001	0.001
	(4.86)	(5.10)	(0.66)	(0.71)
Percentage Aged	1.347**	1.323**	−0.957*	−0.946*
	(3.70)	(3.66)	(2.46)	(2.42)
Percentage Black	−0.188*	−0.119	−0.067	−0.061
	(2.11)	(1.29)	(0.65)	(0.55)
War Period	0.971	0.557	2.262**	2.219**
	(1.30)	(0.73)	(3.16)	(3.03)
Postwar Period	4.862**	4.354**	1.870	1.788
	(4.93)	(4.35)	(1.94)	(1.82)
Constant	5.184	−0.781	32.778**	32.288**
	(1.08)	(0.14)	(7.97)	(6.54)
Observations	672	672	672	672
Number of states	48	48	48	48

Table 2 (*Continued*)

	BENEFIT SIZE		COVERAGE	
	Model I	Model 2	Model 3	Model 4
R^2	0.69	0.70	0.30	0.31
x^2	410.83**	427.25**	59.51**	60.14**
Df	12	14	12	14

Notes: Data shown are unstandardized coefficients from random effects regressions. The absolute values of z statistics are in parentheses. For definitions of measures, see text and Appendix.

* $P < .05$; ** $P < .01$ (one-tailed; except for percent aged, war period, and postwar period).

positive and significant coefficients for Townsend club peak-level measure at the .05 level and the proposition measure at the. 10 level. Moving up a level in Townsend club mobilization is worth $1.23 per month, and placing a proposition on the ballot is worth about $1.37 per month. Both are substantial gains since the average payment in 1950 dollars across the entire period was about $37 per month. In Model 2, moreover, administrative strength and OAA county funding remain significant at the .05 level, and the poll tax measure is significant at the .10 level. States with a poll tax spent approximately $3.90 less per month on OAA, while those with a tradition of domestic administrative development spent about $3.88 more per month, after controlling for other factors. The public opinion measure also remains significant and substantial. A declaration of an additional dollar for the appropriate amount of stipend was worth 30 cents. However, when we substitute the measure of change in Townsend activity for the peak value of Townsend activity, the measure is insignificant. This suggests that policymakers are not responding to new information about the challenger. In addition, the coefficient for the World War II period was positive, which is counter to expectations given the drop in attention to domestic issues, though it falls short of significance.

Table 2 also presents the results for an initial and full model on OAA coverage in Models 3 and 4, respectively. Patronage party strength, democratized Democratic control, and OAA county funding are significant at the .01 level in Model 3. States

with Democratic control cover approximately 3.3 percentage points more of their elderly population, and moving up one level in Mayhew's five-level measure of patronage party strength diminishes coverage by 2.9 percentage points. Moving up 10 percentage points in public opinion to cover all the aged meant an increase of one percentage point in coverage. These were substantial influences, as the average coverage across all states and time periods was about 22 percent. Among the other control measures, the coefficient for percentage aged is significant and negative, whereas the war and postwar period coefficients are both significant and positive. The war did not lead to the reduction of coverage—just the opposite. The coefficients for race and income are in the expected directions, but insignificant. Model 4 explains 30 percent of the overall variance. However, neither of the social movement measures, when added, has a significant impact on spending coverage.

In summary, structural and short-term political contextual factors strongly affected both OAA measures, and in the predicted directions, although each measure was not significant in all models. Among the control measures, public opinion influenced both outcomes. The findings for the social movement measures were mixed. Townsend club activity and propositions significantly and substantively influenced the average monthly old-age stipend, but they did not influence coverage under OAA. These results, however, fit with political mediation expectations, as the pension movement's claims and collective action were focused largely on the size of the benefit rather than coverage, and thus we would expect a differential influence.

Qualitative Comparative Analyses

The expectations of the political mediation model are combinational, and these sorts of arguments can often be better assessed using FSQCA, for which multicollinearity is not problematic (see Ragin 1987, 2000). Here we employ crisp rather than fuzzy sets, as most of the independent measures are nominal. We located 13 states with GENEROUS OAA benefits.[6] (In FSQCA notation, a measure written with all capital letters denotes its presence, while one written in all lowercase denotes its absence.) Two of the institutional political measures are nominal. States that employed a poll tax during this period are designated POLLTAX. Those where the state's labor commissioner had rule-making authority over safety laws throughout the period are labeled ADMIN. States that were largely controlled by PATRONAGE party organizations are those that score either of the top two values on Mayhew's (1986) scale. States where the Democratic party controlled the governor's mansion and both houses of the legislature for at least 40 percent of the time are considered DEMOCRATIC. As for social movement measures, states that had reached the highest level of Townsend club presence at any time are considered highly MOBILIZED, and states where the pension movement placed one or more proposition on the ballot are said to have had ASSERTIVE collective action.

We begin by comparing the theoretical expectations of the political mediation model with those configurations standard in the social policy literature. The configurational theoretical expectations from the institutional politics model of social policy (Amenta and Halfmann 2000) for generous old-age spending, net of economic controls, are as follows:

$$\text{polltax}^{\cdot}\ \text{patronage}^{\cdot}\ \text{ADMIN}^{\cdot}\ \text{DEMOCRAT}.$$

(In FSQCA notation, an asterisk (·) indicates the logical operator *and*; a plus sign (+) indicates the logical operator *or*.) This expression reads as follows: States without poll taxes and without patronage-oriented parties and with strong administrative powers and with Democratic party regimes are expected to produce generous social programs. By contrast, the political mediation argument suggests that the mobilization and collective action of challengers can also spur policy, according to the following expression:

$$\text{polltax}^{\cdot}\ \text{patronage}^{\cdot}\ (\text{MOBILIZED}^{\cdot}$$
$$(\text{DEMOCRAT+ADMIN}) + \text{ASSERTIVE}).$$

This means that in structurally conducive and politically favorable short-term situations, only challenger mobilization is needed to produce collective benefits. When short-term political conditions are less favorable, more assertive action is the best strategy. This type of activity is sufficient to bring results.

While there are 64 theoretically possible combinations of the six dichotomous independent variables, only 21 combinations describe the experiences of the 48 states during this period. The results indicate that six of the combinations consist of states that always exhibited generous stipends.[7] (See Table 3.) The six expressions in Table 3 account for 11 of the 13 positive cases. These reduce to three that encompass each of the successful cases and can be combined in one expression (see Table 3). Necessary conditions for high OAA benefits were the absence of poll taxes and patronage parties. However, other conditions also had to be present to account for high OAA benefits: administrative powers and Democratic party control; Democratic party control and mobilization; or assertive collective action alone.

These results have implications for both the standard institutional political model and the political mediation model. First, as expected by both models, democratic rights and the absence of dominant patronage parties are necessary for high OAA spending. This suggests that under some structural, systemic conditions the activity of both institutional political actors and social movements are likely to be thwarted. In political situations where it is possible to promote policy, the predictions of the standard institutional model and the political mediation model are all borne out. The standard institutional model holds that in favorable systemic political circumstances, a favorable regime and administrative powers would be likely to produce generous social policy. One of the reduced combinations indicates precisely that.

Table 3 Six-Measure FSQCA Results for Generous OAA Benefits

Individual Configurations (and numbers of states)

   polltax * patronage * ADMIN * democrat * MOBILIZATION * ASSERTIVE (5) +

   polltax * patronage * ADMIN * DEMOCRAT * MOBILIZATION * ASSERTIVE (2) +

   polltax * patronage * admin * DEMOCRAT * MOBILIZATION * assertive (1) +

   polltax * patronage * ADMIN * DEMOCRAT * mobilization * assertive (1) +

   polltax * patronage * ADMIN * democrat * mobilization * ASSERTIVE (1) +

   polltax * patronage * admin * DEMOCRAT * mobilization * ASSERTIVE (1)

Reduced Forms of Configurations

   polltax * patronage * ADMIN * DEMOCRAT +

   polltax * patronage DEMOCRAT * MOBILIZATION +

   polltax * patronage * ASSERTIVE

   polltax * patronage * (DEMOCRAT * (ADMIN + MOBILIZATION) + ASSERTIVE)

Note: For FSQCA notation and definitions of measures, see text.

The results also provide strong support for the mediation model. Two of the hypothesized combinations expected to lead to generous OAA benefits are present. As before, only under some long-term political contextual conditions is movement influence possible. Necessary conditions for influence include the absence of both poll taxes and dominant patronage parties. Under these circumstances and a favorable short-term political circumstance, the Democratic party holding power, only extensive movement mobilization is necessary to bring about high OAA benefits, and together they are sufficient. When there are no medium- or short-term conditions in favor, neither a long-standing domestic administrative tradition nor a Democratic regime in power, assertive action is sufficient to produce high OAA benefits.

Who Voted for Senior Citizens' Pensions in 1939?

Next we turn to the Senate vote on an old-age pension measure, the proposed Lee amendment to the Social Security Act Amendments of 1939. Lee's amendment would have provided pensions of $40 per month to all aged Americans and would have replaced existing old-age programs. Though not specifically a vote on Townsend Plan-sponsored legislation, the Lee amendment would have provided a generous, widespread, nationally financed pension, which was the hallmark of Townsend's

proposal. Funding these pensions was a more radical outcome and one demanded by the pension movement. The amendment failed, 17–56. But forming a coalition behind a radical alternative is a way to induce legislators to support more moderate legislation that they might not otherwise have favored. We analyze the vote for the Lee amendment both by logistic regression and FSQCA techniques. The latter are important because the mediation theory expects that many favorable circumstances are necessary to influence this sort of radical outcome.

For the regression analyses, we use many of the previous independent measures, adjusted for the year. For partisanship, however, we employ the party affiliation of the senator, noting whether he or she was a non-poll tax Democrat or a member of a radical third party. Public opinion in these models is measured by the state-level support expressed in a December 1938 Gallup poll for the so-called Lodge bill. That proposal would have provided for $60 monthly pensions for almost all aged Americans, with $40 being provided by the federal government. About 65 percent of those expressing an opinion were in favor. We also employ a measure of whether the senator was endorsed by the Townsend Plan, which urged clubs to support those whom it endorsed. The pension measure may be more valid than the endorsement measure, as only a third of the senators came up for election in 1938. Because of the smaller number and the different nature of the cases, we use a modified version of the model to explain OAA outcomes. In the first model, we include the poll tax and patronage party measures, as well as the partisanship measure. We also include the control measures for income, percentage aged, and public opinion.[8] In a second model, we add the three movement measures to see if they add anything to the explanation.

Table 4 shows two logistical regression models of the vote in favor of the radical Lee amendment. Model 1, including all the non-movement-related measures, explains about 20 percent of the variance and correctly predicts about 78 percent of the cases. Two of the political contextual measures are significant and in the proper direction, with a negative influence of dominant patronage parties and a positive influence of democratized Democratic or third party affiliation on the odds of voting for senior citizens' pensions. The control measure public opinion in favor of the Lodge bill has a positive effect, significant at the .10 level, whereas the control percent aged has a negative effect.

Model 2 provides a significant improvement of fit. The pseudo R-squared jumps from about .20 to about .40, and the increase in predictive power is from about 78 percent to about 84 percent, which is a shift from predicting 57 of 73 cases correctly to 61—or a quarter of the remaining cases. Townsend club strength significantly increases the likelihood of a senator's voting for the bill. So does a pension initiative, though at only the .10 level. Having a pension initiative in a state makes a senator almost three times more likely to vote for the Lee amendment, from about 9 percent to about 25 percent. The Townsend endorsement has a positive, but insignificant, effect, possibly because only one third of senators were subject to being endorsed. The measure of patronage party strength becomes insignificant, perhaps because it was exerting influence by dampening the pension movement. Also, in the final model the measure of public opinion is significant at the .05 level and substantively important. A movement from 60 percent of the public supporting the Lodge bill to 80 percent would increase a senator's chance of voting for the Lee amendment from about 7 percent to about 25 percent.[9]

We now turn to examining combinations of conditions leading to positive votes through FSQCA. Again, because most of the independent measures are categorical, as is the dependent measure, we employ crisp-set analyses. We score those in favor as one, and those opposed as zero, and begin our analyses with the same independent measures as before, though this time we include whether the senator had a Democratic or radical third party affiliation (DEM/THIRD) and omit the administrative variable, which is not applicable nationally. Although the mobilization measure is the same, we combine the measure of initiatives and endorsements (ASSERTIVE), treating these statewide assertive activities as functionally equivalent, to reduce the complexity in the results. Our expectations here are that it may take both high mobilization and assertive action in the most favorable possible contexts to reach this more radical result. Because of the low percentage of positive votes, almost all truth table combinations that include positive votes are "contradictory," including one or more negative votes. Because we are interested in understanding the conditions under which it is reasonably likely for a senator to vote for a radical program, we reduce combinations in which at least half of the senators supported the pension amendment.

Three combinations provide the greatest support for the amendment:

polltax*patronage*DEM/THIRD·
MOBILIZATION*ASSERTIVE +
polltax*PATRONAGE*DEM/THIRD·
MOBILIZATION*assertive +
polltax*patronage*dem/third·
mobilization*ASSERTIVE

As before, a lack of voting restrictions is a necessary condition. The first combination, which provides the most positive votes, six, is also the one closely associated with political mediation thinking. It includes all possible favorable conditions: a Democratic or third party affiliation, a strongly mobilized pension movement, and assertive action. The second combination suggests that high mobilization alone in an already favorable political context can be influential.

Table 4 Voting for the Radical Lee Pension Amendment on Selected Independent Measures

	Model 1	Model 2
Institutional Measures		
Poll Tax	0.196	4.602
	(0.13)	(1.85)
Patronage Party Strength	−0.477*	0.212
	(1.92)	(0.57)
Non–Poll–Tax Democrat or Third Party Member	1.464	3.220*
	(1.56)	(2.11)
Movement Measures		
Townsend Club Activity	—	1.279*
		(2.28)
Pension Proposition	—	2.018
		(1.64)
Townsend Endorsement	—	1.035
		(0.83)
Control Measures		
Pro-Old-Age Public Opinion	0.045	0.079*
	(1.61)	(2.09)
Per Capita Income	−0.001	−0.001
	(0.37)	(0.41)
Percentage Aged	−0.428	−1.255*
	(1.69)	(2.48)
Constant	−1.606	−7.966
	(0.54)	(1.92)
Observations	73	73
Pseudo R^2	0.20	0.41
x^2	15.97*	32.24**
Df	6	9

Notes: Data shown are unstandardized coefficients from logistical regressions. The absolute values of z statistics are in parentheses. For definitions of measures, see text and Appendix.
* $P < .05$; ** $P < .01$ (one-tailed; except for percent aged).

The third indicates that assertive action will provide an alternative means of exerting influence in less favorable situations. However, the last two combinations help to identify only three additional senators voting for pensions. The results support political mediation thinking, but also suggest that yet other factors than those in this version of the model may be needed to identify legislators most willing to support the programs of state-oriented movements.

Conclusion

To summarize, our main claim is that the collective action of state-oriented challengers and their influence on public policy is politically mediated in specific ways. Challengers control their strategies and, to be effective, must be able to alter them according to political contexts. Under certain political institutional conditions, notably restrictions on democratic practices and the entrenchment of patronage-oriented political parties, the impact of state-oriented challengers is likely to be greatly dampened. In the first half of the twentieth century, only about half of the state-level U.S. polities were structurally open to influence. Under these open conditions and more favorable conditions over the medium and short term, little more than mobilization is needed for social movements to have influence, whereas in less short-term politically favorable conditions more assertive action is necessary. Like scholars of framing, we argue that the influence of a challenger is likely to be confined to the issues that it plausibly engages. To achieve radical results, the most favorable conditions, mobilization, and assertive action are required.

The results on the development of Old Age Assistance and on the Senate vote bear out these claims. All sets of results also provide some support for the views that high mobilization is a key to influence and that strategies matter. In addition, Townsend club activity seemed to have a continuing influence on OAA generosity, whereas changes in activity did not seem to influence policy-makers similarly. This suggests that organization and mobilization may pay longer-term dividends for challengers, though perhaps only so long as the movement as a whole remains viable. Assertive strategies also influenced old-age policy. Pension initiatives had a significant influence on OAA stipends. The results also suggest that the standard distinction between institutional and non-institutional and disruptive and assimilative action is too broad to address the sorts of collective action that matter in political processes. Also, the fact that the pension movement largely concerned itself with high benefits led to a differential influence on OAA generosity and coverage, with the movement spurring benefit levels, but not coverage. These results suggest that movement claims-making can limit the influence of challengers and that being flexible in this area may make wider benefits possible for a movement's constituency.

The formal qualitative results also support the mediation idea: that challengers need to match collective action strategies to political contexts. Combinations of conditions associated with high OAA pensions were as expected by the political mediation model. One of three combinations included a Democratic regime and Townsend club mobilization, suggesting that under short-term favorable circumstances, mobilization was sufficient to bring gains in OAA spending. Another combination indicated that when short-term political conditions were not necessarily favorable, the aggressive strategy of initiatives proved sufficient to bring about high OAA benefits. On the vote to transform old-age policy, movement mobilization and assertive action under favorable conditions brought positive results.

Our research should not be interpreted to mean that this or that variable should be expected always to bring influence for challengers or to mean that social movements are usually likely to produce policy results. Our point is simply that social movements can be influential under certain conditions. It seems likely that most movement organizations are not likely to be highly influential, given that challengers start from a position of relative disadvantage in political power. The pension movement included a fairly powerfully organized and mobilized set of challengers with widespread support, and the old-age issue was a prominent one in the 1930s and 1940s. The results we report here may pertain only to the most significant and highly publicized movements. That said, there is no reason to believe that policy results of the sort that we find would be confined to a movement based significantly on one large challenging organization like the Townsend Plan. Decentralized challengers and coalition-based movements combining the same characteristics might achieve similar sorts of results.

The results also support the view that public opinion influences public policy and movements can have a further indirect impact on policy by influencing the general public about its mission, program, or constituency. However, the strong version of the public opinion argument finds little support. Adding public opinion measures did not mean that other causes faded into insignificance. Although data limitations made it impossible to appraise directly the influence of the relative saliency of public opinion, the old-age issue had a high profile in the late 1930s, and its saliency was due at least in part to the pension movement. The Gallup polls taken in late 1935 and early 1936 were largely a result of the rise of the Townsend Plan, and the polls taken in 1938 and 1939 were in a response to a resurgent pension movement (Amenta forthcoming). The results here also line up with the idea that the influence of opinion polls on political actors may be historically variable and requires explanation in itself. We hope that promising ideas about the contingent impact of public opinion on policy (Jacobs and Shapiro 2000; Burstein and Linton 2002; Manza and Cook 2002) are set out more explicitly and empirically examined. Scholars of the impact of social movements may need to model the influence of challengers on opinion and from there on state outcomes.

As the results show, the political mediation model, as currently constructed, seems only partially adequate to understanding the more radical and difficult-to-achieve outcomes for social movements. Favorable shifts in public opinion (Burstein 1999; Giugni 2004) or innovative framing (Cress and Snow 2000) or gaining ground in discursive struggles through the mass media (Ferree et al. 2002) may be required in addition to factors identified by the political mediation theory to achieve fundamental changes demanded by challengers.

Also, as studies mount, both from social movement scholars and political sociologists examining state policy, the impact of movements on policy seems to be understood at least as well as the determinants of mobilization, which seem considerably more controversial (cf. Goodwin and Jasper 1999; McAdam 1999; Ferree and Merrill 2004; Meyer 2004). It is no longer enough for students of the policy consequences of movements to justify their research as being on a novel subject. What we need are theoretical refinements and advancements of more complex ideas and the types of investigations, whether quantitative, formal qualitative, or historical, that can enable us to appraise theory and further our understanding of the influence of movements on political outcomes. We also need to address whether political mediation ideas are applicable or whether completely new theorizing is needed to understand the many attempts at influence by movements that are not mainly directed at the state (Amenta and Young 1999; Earl 2004).

NOTES

For helpful comments and criticism on a previous version of this paper, the authors thank Laure Bereni, Jennifer Earl, Jeff Goodwin, David F. Greenberg, LaDawn Hagland, Mildred A. Schwartz, the NYU Politics, Power, and Protest Workshop, three anonymous ASR reviewers, and the ASR editor.

1. Although most scholars, following Holtzman (1963), refer to this organization and phenomenon as the "Townsend movement," we call it the Townsend Plan first and foremost for historical accuracy. Robert Earl Clements, the organization's initial leader, thought "Townsend Plan" was appealing and used that name. The newspapers did likewise. The New York Times index accordingly refers to the Townsend Plan and searching ProQuest for "Townsend movement" misses most articles on the Townsend Plan. Also, the Townsend Plan was a social movement organization rather than a movement. In addition, "Townsend Plan" later became the official name of the organization.

2. Assertive action directed at unfavorable bureaucracies is also expected to be more productive than mobilization and limited protest. Unfortunately, we were unable to gain systematic information across states regarding this sort of protest and so cannot test that part of the argument here.

3. The first Gallup poll on old-age benefits was taken in 1935, but the data do not survive. Other data are often not usable, because Gallup's questions were often poorly worded. From the first poll forward Gallup found that overwhelming percentages of Americans were in favor of government provided old-age "pensions," a word used indiscriminately at the time to refer to all manner of aid to the aged (Schiltz 1971: chapter

2). Gallup occasionally asked respondents about the saliency of issues, but they were usually asked to volunteer answers, resulting in numbers too small to aggregate to the state level (see Weakliem 2003) even if they had survived. For comprehensive listings of the results of polls on old age, see Cantril and Strunk (1951:541–46) and Schiltz (1971).

4. Note that we cannot, unfortunately, appraise arguments about the strategic capacities (Ganz 2000) and movement infrastructures of challengers (Andrews 2001), as these did not vary greatly for the Townsend Plan, and it is difficult to get information by state and year for other old-age campaigns. For the most part, the Townsend Plan would have to be considered high on strategic capacities and infrastructural resources. It also had an innovative form of organization, combining aspects of real estate sales organizations and fraternal organizations in a social movement organization. To the extent that the Townsend Plan mobilization influenced policy it can be considered a supportive result for these perspectives.

5. For the full models, the Hausman specification test indicated that the efficient random effects model was not significantly different from the consistent fixed effects model, and we performed a Ramsey regression specification error test (RESET) for omitted variables for each year. The results (not shown, but available on request) were significant for only one year, which is additional evidence for the suitability of the random effects model.

6. To determine which states provided generous OAA benefits, we average the residuals of a baseline modeling, including only per capita income and percentage aged for each state across our entire time period. We designate the 13 states that had an observed value that was 10 percent larger than the predicted value, where there was a large break in the data, as generous spenders. The 10 states where the observed value is greater than predicted but less than 10 percent higher are coded as intermediate or "don't care" cases, and the 25 remaining states are coded as zeros.

7. Contradictory combinations mainly consisted of failures and are treated as such.

8. We also included a control for, union density—union members in 1939 as a share of the nonagricultural employed (see Amenta and Halfmann 2000)—because it is often argued that unions spur old-age programs. This measure proved to be insignificant in our model (results not shown, but available on request), and we omitted it.

9. We also engaged in a similar logistical regression analysis of voting for the Townsend Plan bill, HR 6466, in the House of Representatives that year. HR 6466 also called for senior citizens' pensions for the nonemployed who were over 60 years old, based on a transactions (sales) tax and other taxes, and was expected to produce initial benefits of about $60 per month. The bill failed, 306–101. We did not report these results (available upon request) mainly because they largely replicate the Senate results.

39.

Social Movements and Policy Implementation: The Mississippi Civil Rights Movement and The War on Poverty, 1965 to 1971

KENNETH T. ANDREWS

Social movement scholars agree that the question of a social movement's impact on political change is important and understudied. Over the past four decades, leading scholars have reviewed the relevant literature on social movements and have noted the limited amount of systematic research on outcomes (Diani 1997; Eckstein 1965; Giugni 1998; Marx and Woods 1975; McAdam, McCarthy, and Zald 1988; Tarrow 1998). Burstein, Einwohner, and Hollander (1995) observe that, "the field of social movements grew tremendously in the 1970s and 1980s, but the study of movement outcomes did not.... [The result is] that we still know very little about the impact of social movements on social change" (p. 276). Furthermore, the question of movement impact addresses one of the most important concerns of movement participants—the efficacy of social movements.

I have two major objectives in this paper. First, I provide a conceptual framework for analyzing movement outcomes. Most discussions focus on the analytic problems of establishing whether movements create change, but how movements generate political change must also be examined. I identify and compare the major theoretical models used to explain the relationship between movements and political change. I argue that our understanding of the influence of social movements will be greatly improved by delineating models that specify how movements generate institutional change (McAdam and Snow 1997). I propose a "movement infrastructure" model that focuses on the organizational

structure, resources, and leadership of a movement to explain its impact on the political process. Second, I present an extensive analysis of the effects of the civil rights movement in Mississippi on the implementation of poverty programs at the local level. I investigate whether local movements directly and indirectly shaped the implementation of federal policy in Mississippi. First, a quantitative analysis of poverty program funding examines the impact of movement organization, white counter-mobilization, social, political, and economic factors on funding from 1965 to 1971. Two case studies follow that assess the impact of local civil rights movements on the form and content of poverty programs in their communities.

Conceptualizing Movement Outcomes
Outcomes as Changes in Political Institutions
I focus on outcomes rather than success. Recent research has identified methodological and theoretical problems with studying success (Amenta and Young 1999; Giugni 1998). Success implies the attainment of specific, widely shared goals, but the goals of most social movements are contested by participants and observers. Goals also change over the course of a movement. Studying outcomes avoids these problems and allows scholars to focus on unintended and negative consequences as well as successes.

The analysis here pertains to *political* movements and *institutional* outcomes in the political arena. Political movements involve a sustained challenge to existing power relations, and they employ disruptive, nonroutine tactics that publicly challenge the distribution and uses of power in the broader society (Gamson 1990; McAdam 1982; Schwartz 1976; Tilly 1978). This focus excludes movements focused on changes internal to a group

Andrews, Kenneth T. 2001. "Social Movements and Policy Implementation: The Mississippi Civil Rights Movement and the War on Poverty, 1965 to 1971." *American Sociological Review* 66: 71–95. Reprented by permission of American Sociological Association.

and its members. Because political movements also directly or indirectly make claims on the state, I focus on institutional outcomes. Typically, political movements attempt to build organizations and change the culture and consciousness of their members or the broader public. In fact, a movement's impact on institutions often depends on its ability to build organizations and shape collective identities (Mueller 1987). These movements, however, seek change in political institutions, and those changes may take a variety of forms such as: (1) gaining access to the decision-making process, (2) altering an institution's goals and priorities, (3) securing favorable policies, (4) insuring that those policies are implemented, or (5) shifting the distribution of institutional resources to benefit the movement's constituents (Burstein et al. 1995; Gamson 1990; Kreisi et al. 1995; Schumaker 1975).[1] Overall, a focus on institutional outcomes makes sense because it encompasses the long-term goals of many social movements. In addition, a focus on institutional outcomes has a methodological advantage because in many cases these outcomes are more easily measured than cultural, attitudinal, and psychological outcomes. Political outcomes provide an important indicator of "the results of [the civil rights] movement in the lives of black southerners" (Button 1989:4).

Opportunity Structures, Institutional Arenas, and Key Actors

Political process theories note that the emergence of social movements is patterned by broad changes in the "political opportunity structure" (McAdam 1982). This observation points to one of the methodological challenges for research on movement outcomes: If changes in the opportunity structure facilitate the emergence of a social movement, then those same changes may account for the apparent impact of a movement (Amenta, Dunleavy, and Bernstein 1994). The importance of opportunity structures has been established, but few scholars would argue that they have a singular and deterministic effect on social movements (Goldstone 1980; Kitschelt 1986). Rather, the emergence and maintenance of a social movement is in part attributable to the internal dynamics of the movement

itself. In addition, some scholars argue that the impacts of movements on opportunity structures should be studied. For example, McAdam (1996) notes that "our collective failure to undertake any serious accounting of the effect of past movements on…political opportunities is as puzzling as it is lamentable" (p. 36).

Any analysis of movement outcomes must examine the structure and strategies of the relevant exogenous political actors and institutions. Movements make claims that directly or indirectly impinge on other groups. Thus, movements have complex and sometimes unexpected relationships with other groups that become allies or opponents. They also mobilize within institutional settings that structure conflict and possible outcomes. For example, federal agencies are constrained by their relationship to Congress and public opinion (Burstein 1999). These rules and resources shape the possible responses of state actors to social movements.

Measuring Outcomes Over Time

For methodological and conceptual reasons, I need to measure multiple outcomes and to measure outcomes over time (Andrews 1997; Banaszak 1996; Button 1989; Snyder and Kelly 1979). Movement outcomes over time must be measured because movements change their tactics and goals. For example, Katzenstein (1990) finds that feminist activists in 1973 organized around the issue of ordination, but by 1983 the movement had broadened its analysis and goals to include "running shelters for homeless women; doing prison work; organizing in the sanctuary movement; joining in protests against US intervention in Central America; running empowerment workshops, lesbian retreats, and conferences to build bridges between women religious and laywomen" (p. 41; also see Katzenstein 1998). Another reason for measuring outcomes over time is that the form and degree of influence may vary over time (Andrews 1997). By focusing on a movement's immediate impact the movement's influence could be over- or underestimated.

In sum, analyzing movement outcomes involves: (1) examining different forms of political change (e.g., access, policy enactment, implementation), (2) analyzing opportunity structures, institutional arenas and key actors that shape movement dynamics, (3) incorporating temporal processes by measuring outcomes over time.

Four Divergent Views on Movements and Outcomes

Studies of the impact of social movements have typically focused on the question of whether movements exert influence. In those cases for which one can identify the influence of movements on institutional change independent of other nonmovement factors, a second set of questions must be answered. First, the causal argument must be specified. What characteristics of a movement or movement activity account for the impact? Second, the mechanisms of influence must be revealed. What is the process or mechanism by which a movement influences a political institution? There are several prominent answers to these questions.

Analyses of movement outcomes will be improved by systematically comparing and elaborating these contending models. In my view, no single model can account for the ways movements generate change. This view stems from the variety of cases and political contexts that have been studied as "social movements." Nevertheless, there is a relatively limited set of possibilities, and our understanding of movement impacts will be improved by specifying those models as "ideal types." Scholars often operate with an implicit model that remains undertheorized. Elaborating these models allows researchers to ask how particular cases diverge from the theoretical models. Most important, comparing different models can direct scholarship toward broader questions about variation across movements and political contexts.[2]

I delineate four major approaches to the relationship between movements and outcomes.[3] Each model singles out key elements that account for a movement's impact, and each implies different mechanisms through which movements can exert influence. These distinct ways of thinking about movement impact are rarely made explicit or contrasted with one another in sociological research. By explicating each, I aim to clarify the lines of debate in the field and place my research within that debate.

Action-Reaction Models: Disruption or Persuasion

In the first two models, which I call "action-reaction" models, mobilization has the momentary potential to leverage change through its impact on political elites, electoral coalitions, or public opinion. Within the action-reaction approach, theorists describe two possible routes whereby movements are influential.

In one route, movements are dramatic, disruptive and threatening to elites, which prompts a rapid response—typically either concessions and/or repression. Piven and Cloward (1977) have been the primary proponents of this view arguing that "the most useful way to think about the effectiveness of protest is to examine the disruptive effects on institutions of different forms of mass defiance, and then to examine the political reverberations of those disruptions" (p. 24). For Piven and Cloward (1977), it is not clear that protest has an independent impact because it "wells up in response to momentous changes in the institutional order. It is not created by organizers and leaders" (p. 36). Protest is one link in a sequence, and once the sequence is initiated protesters have little control over the policy response. The authors conclude that "whatever influence lower-class groups occasionally exert in American politics does not result from organization, but from mass protest and the disruptive consequences of protest" (Piven and Cloward 1977:36).

Organizations, particularly mass-based membership organizations, are doomed to failure because powerless groups can never mobilize as effectively as dominant groups in a society. As a result, organization can only lessen the disruptive capacity and efficacy of protest (Piven and Cloward 1984, 1992; also see Gamson and Schmeidler 1984; Morris 1984). Elite reaction is ultimately focused in a self-interested way on ending protest. Analyzing urban policy changes in the 1960s, Katznelson (1981) argues that "the targets of these public policies were not objects of compassion, but of fear born of uncertainty" (p. 3). Policymakers caught off guard by protest, attempt to quickly assemble a strategy of repression, concessions, or a combination of the two that will end the protest wave (Tarrow 1993). Disruption models focus on the limitations of protest on policymaking beyond the agenda-setting stage.

In the second version of the action-reaction model, movements are dramatic and generate support from sympathetic third parties that take up the cause of the movement. The intervening role of "third parties," "bystander publics," or "conscience constituents" is critical. In a classic essay, Lipsky (1968) argues that "the 'problem of the powerless' in protest activity is to activate 'third parties' to enter the implicit or explicit bargaining arena in ways favorable to protesters" (p. 1145). Lipsky claims that "if protest tactics are not considered significant by the media…protest organizations will not succeed. Like the tree falling unheard in the forest, there is no protest unless protest is perceived and projected" (p. 1151; also see Benford and Hunt 1992).[4]

Garrow (1978) argues that civil rights campaigns, especially in Selma, Alabama, generated momentum for the 1965 Voting Rights Act. For some theorists, repression is an intervening link. For example, Garrow argues that attacks by southern officials on civil rights activists further solidified the support of bystanders. Burstein (1985) shows that the movement did not reverse the direction of public opinion arguing that movements are probably unable to have such a substantial impact on opinion. Rather, protest increased the salience of the civil rights issue, and political representatives were able to act on those louder and clearer signals (Burstein 1999). In this view protest is a form of communication, and persuasion is the major way that movements influence policy (Mansbridge 1994).

These two versions of the action-reaction model differ: The first emphasizes disruptive and often violent action forcing a response from political elites; the second proposes that protest can mobilize sympathetic third parties that advance the movement's agenda by exerting influence on political elites. But both versions of the action-reaction model share the assumption that (1) large-scale dramatic events shape the process of change by, (2) mobilizing more powerful actors to advance the movement's cause, and (3) that (implicitly) movements have little or no direct influence beyond this initial point. In both versions, the primary focus is on public protest events rather than on organizations.

Access-Influence Model: Routinization of Protest

The third major approach argues that the determinant of movement efficacy is the acquisition of routine access to the polity through institutionalized tactics. This approach typically describes a drift toward less disruptive tactics such as electoral politics, coalitions, lobbying and litigation. Organization and leadership figure prominently in this model. Organizational changes parallel the tactical shift including increasing centralization and bureaucratization of movement organizations. In short, social movement organizations evolve into interest groups. In the "access-influence" model, the organizational and tactical shifts are accompanied by an increase in influence over relevant policy arenas. In contrast, the action-reaction model would predict that movement influence declines as tactics become routinized and organizations become incorporated. Most important, the access-influence model argues that disruptive tactics have little independent impact on institutional change. In their study of the impacts of black and Hispanic political mobilization on a variety of policy outcomes, Browning, Marshall, and Tabb (1984) argue that protest and electoral strategies were used together effectively, but "demand-protest strategies by themselves produced limited results in most cities" (p. 246).

Access-influence models also assert that securing insider status is more consequential than pursuing a single, specific policy objective. Rochon and Mazmanian (1993) argue that the antinuclear movement, by advocating a single piece of legislation, was unsuccessful. In contrast, the environmental movement, especially antitoxic groups, attempted to become a legitimate participant in the regulatory process. By gaining access, the movement has been able to have a substantial, long-term impact on policy (also see Costain 1981; Sabatier 1975).

The access-influence model has fewer proponents within the movement literature than the action-reaction models. However, the notion that "routine" tactics are most efficacious is consistent with pluralist theories of democracy that view the political system as relatively open to citizen influence. In this model, organization-building (especially professionalization, bureaucratization, and centralization) provides movements with the necessary tools to operate in the interest group system where bargaining is the key mechanism of influence.

The Movement Infrastructure Model

Finally, I propose a "movement infrastructure" model. Three components of a movement's infrastructure must be examined to explain its influence on the policy process: leadership, organizational structure, and resources. Infrastructures that allow the movement to employ multiple mechanisms of influence (including disruption, persuasion, and bargaining) will have the greatest impact on policy implementation. At a general level, the autonomy and continuity of the infrastructure are key factors explaining the long-term viability and impact of the movement, sustaining a movement through shifts in the broader political environment (Andrews 1997; Rupp and Taylor 1990). A strong movement infrastructure can spur political elites to initiate policy concessions in response to the perceived threat of the movement. That threat rests on the belief that a movement has the capacity to institute more substantial change through parallel, autonomous institutions.

Leaders and organizations must be embedded in indigenous, informal networks. Such links make leaders more responsive to their constituency and less easily co-opted (Morris 1984). Robnett (1996) distinguishes between formal leaders (e.g., ministers) and an intermediate layer of "bridge leaders," who stand at nodal points within the informal networks of a community. This type of leadership structure can generate ongoing tension within a movement. However, it also can provide advantages, such as innovation (Stepan-Norris and Zeitlin 1995). A differentiated leadership structure allows for communication to various audiences including participants, potential recruits, opponents, and state actors (Klandermans 1997). A leadership structure with a diversity of skills and experiences will be better able to use mass-based tactics as well as routine negotiation with outside groups (Ganz 2000; Gerlach and Hine 1970).

The critical role of preexisting organization and resources has been established in the emergence of

social movements. To persist over time, movements must forge new organizational forms and establish independent resource flows (McAdam 1982; Schwartz 1976). In the mobilization process, the informal structure of relationships among activists and organizations must be expansive across communities and subgroups. In the policymaking process, formal organizations become a necessary vehicle for advancing a group's claims. Organizational structures can alter the routine operation of the political process when they are perceived as legitimate and/or threatening by established political actors (Clemens 1997; Gamson 1990).

Movements that rely primarily on the "mobilization of people" rather than on financial resources are more likely to continue using protest tactics (Schwartz and Paul 1992). As a result, their strategic and tactical options are broader (Ganz 2000). Ultimately, movements require substantial contributions of volunteer labor to maintain organizations and launch protest campaigns. This is seen most clearly at the local level where movement organizations are less likely to maintain a paid, professional staff.

In the movement infrastructure model, strategy and tactics depend on a movement's leadership, organization, and resources. This contrasts with the action-reaction model that either views protest and organization in conflict with one another or pays little attention to organization. Strategy and tactics are conceptualized broadly in the infrastructure model and range from protest to the building of counter-institutions.

In sum, strong movement infrastructures have diverse leaders and a complex leadership structure, multiple organizations, informal ties that cross geographic and social boundaries, and a resource base that draws substantially on contributions from their members for both labor and money. These characteristics provide movements with greater flexibility that allows them to influence the policy process through multiple mechanisms.

Comparing the Models

The movement infrastructure model builds on the insights of the prior three models. First, it assumes, like the action-reaction models, that there are key moments when movements can be especially effi-cacious. Further, it assumes that disruptive tactics are important for movements to have an impact, especially when disruptive tactics are creatively injected into routine political processes. The move-ment infrastructure model differs from the others because it emphasizes the building and sustaining of movement infrastructures as an important deter-minant of the long-term impact of these movements (in contrast to short-term impacts, like agenda-setting). Furthermore, unlike the access-influence model, these organizations have the greatest impact when they maintain their ability to use both "out-sider" and "insider" tactics. Litigation, lobbying, and electoral politics can be effectively employed by social movements. However, movements lose key opportunities for leverage in the political pro-cess when they quickly adopt the tactics of "interest groups" and abandon "insurgent" tactics.

Movements must be able to create leverage through multiple mechanisms. The prior three models focus on a single mechanism as the primary means by which movements create change (e.g., disruption, persuasion, or negotiation). The move-ment infrastructure model accounts for the ability of movements to impact political change through multiple mechanisms, and this change can occur when a movement's leadership and organization allow for strategic flexibility.

The pattern of outcomes for a movement may depend on processes described by each of these models. For example, both action-reaction models focus on agenda-setting as the primary outcome that movements can influence. In contrast, access-influence and movement infrastructure models examine later stages in the policymaking process. Ultimately, researchers should use these models to compare across different types of social movements and political contexts. The analysis I present here demonstrates the utility of the movement infra-structure model as applied to the Mississippi case.

Research Design
The War on Poverty as an Outcome
The War on Poverty created a new set of opportuni-ties and constraints for the civil rights movement. These programs brought substantial resources into impoverished communities, providing opportuni-ties for blacks to influence the shape and direction of policy. At first glance, it is surprising how thor-oughly local movements became involved in the War on Poverty. After all, the publicly stated goal of the movement in the early 1960s was gaining access to electoral politics. However, an underlying objec-tive of the movement in Mississippi was building local movements that could define and pursue their own goals (Payne 1995). The early movement orga-nizations were not directly involved in the War on Poverty. Nevertheless, local movements continued to operate in the post-1965 period and attempted to shape the local implementation of poverty pro-grams. Many local activists defined economic empowerment as a natural outgrowth of the politi-cal empowerment pursued through voter registra-tion. In fact, many believed that political power would be meaningless unless black communities could generate viable economic programs (Dorsey 1977).

There were several obstacles to movement influ-ence. First, the objectives of federal agencies con-strained the ability of local movements to direct the War on Poverty. The "professionalization of reform" could reduce the participation and influence of the poor to a primarily symbolic role (Helfgot 1974; also see Friedland 1976). In addition, the adminis-tration of poverty programs required negotiations with many community groups, some of which were potential allies or opponents of civil rights activists. While movement mobilization shaped the distribu-tion and development of antipoverty programs in Mississippi, these programs also shaped the direc-tion of local movements.[5] Once the War on Poverty was initiated, local movements in Mississippi and across the country attempted to secure resources and shape programs (Patterson 1994: 146). Quadagno (1994) notes that a "crucial linkage...unquestion-ably did develop between the civil rights movement and the War on Poverty" (p. 28).

The poverty programs in Mississippi can be examined as an outcome of the civil rights move-ment for four main reasons: (1) the poverty pro-grams and the civil rights movement both targeted an overlapping arena of activity, (2) there was substantial and ongoing interactions between civil rights activists and the Office of Economic Opportunity, (3) the programs provided benefits to the movement's primary constituency (blacks in the South), and (4) there is significant variation across states and counties in local actors' influence on the programs.

Study Design: Quantitative and Qualitative Analyses

Mississippi is an important case for examining the long-term impacts of the civil rights movement. The state is widely known for its institutionalization of the "tripartite system of domination"—a term Morris (1984) has used to describe the political, economic, and personal bases of racial inequality in the U.S. South. On one hand, Mississippi can be viewed as a test case where the movement met its most intense resistance. At the same time, there is substantial variation within the state across key variables: movement mobilization, countermovement, structural characteristics, and the implementation of poverty programs.

Follow Amenta's (1991) suggestion of analyzing subunits, I use counties as the unit of analysis to strengthen the theoretical value of the study. This focus has substantive merit because the Mississippi movement targeted counties as areas within which to organize. In addition, counties are the most important local political unit in the South (Krane and Shaffer 1992). Finally, poverty programs were instituted in Mississippi across counties rather than across municipalities.

The research here combines two complementary strategies: (1) a quantitative analysis of Mississippi counties that allows for precise estimates of the distribution of programs and funding, and (2) qualitative evidence from case studies using interview and archival data. Most previous research on the War on Poverty has focused on urban areas, riots, and the distribution of poverty programs (Button 1978; Fording 1997). Beyond single case studies, few scholars have examined the impacts of social movement processes on poverty programs. In my quantitative analysis, I ask whether movements had an impact on poverty programs independent of other relevant factors.[6] After establishing that movements did have an impact on poverty program funding, I use case studies to examine the *processes and form* of conflict at the local level (i.e., the mechanisms through which local movement organizations shaped the development of poverty programs).

The primary sources are the records of movement organizations and information from the Office of Economic Opportunity. These sources provide data on the key actors, their activities, and their analyses of the political landscape. For the case studies, written records are supplemented with participant interviews from published and unpublished collections.

The Civil Rights Movement and the War on Poverty: National and State Contexts
The National Context of the War on Poverty[7]

On August 20, 1964, President Lyndon Johnson signed the Economic Opportunity Act, a key component of his Great Society agenda. The initiation of the War on Poverty coincided with a set of national policy initiatives of the early 1960s, including the 1964 Civil Rights Act and the 1965 Voting Rights Act—legislation that altered the political context of the civil rights movement. The War on Poverty included a cluster of programs administered primarily through the newly formed Office of Economic Opportunity (OEO). (Table 1 provides a list of acronyms used throughout this paper.) The War on Poverty lacked a unified approach conceptually and administratively. For example, the 1964 legislation included plans for Neighborhood Youth Corps, Community Action Programs, Head Start, Volunteers in Service to America (VISTA), and the college work-study program (Patterson 1994). Through the 1960s, OEO administered the majority of these programs, allowing them to bypass old-line agencies like the Department of Labor and local or state agencies. Over time, however, the major poverty programs were phased out or shifted over to the more conservative agencies, and in 1973 OEO was eliminated (Quadagno 1994).

Among the various poverty programs, the Community Action Program (CAP) received the greatest attention and became almost synonymous with the War on Poverty. Policymakers pushing "community action hoped to stimulate better coordination among the melange of public and private

Table 1 List of Acronyms and Organizations

Acronym	Organization
ACBC	Associated Communities of Bolivar County
CAP	Community Action Program
CDGM	Child Development Group of Mississippi
CMI	Central Mississippi, Inc.
COFO	Council of Federated Organizations
CORE	Congress of Racial Equality
MFDP	Mississippi Freedom Democratic Party
NAACP	National Association for the Advancement of Colored People
OEO	Office of Economic Opportunity
SNCC	Student Nonviolent Coordinating Committee

agencies delivering social services" (Peterson and Greenstone 1977:241). This objective, however, was abandoned in favor of "citizen participation." OEO and local CAPs had little impact on the established agencies providing services to poor communities. As a result, CAPs administered many of the new antipoverty programs. CAPs were coordinated at the local level through a CAP Board that served as the overarching administrative body and provided a point of potential access for local movements. This opening paved the way for intense conflicts between local groups attempting to gain access to CAP boards in order to influence the flow of OEO funds.

The Mississippi Civil Rights Movement

In Mississippi, the Student Nonviolent Coordinating Committee (SNCC) began developing community projects in the early 1960s around voter registration (Carson 1981; Dittmer 1994; Payne 1995). These early projects linked the small network of indigenous NAACP leaders and an emerging group of grassroots leaders exemplified by Annie Devine, Fannie Lou Hamer, and Victoria Gray (Payne 1995). Civil rights projects met intense repression across the

state from local law enforcement and local whites. SNCC's early efforts were expanded during the 1964 Freedom Summer project that brought college students from across the country into the local movements. Two features of this early period stand out: (1) the intensity of white resistance and (2) the focus on building local community organizations and leaders.

Following Freedom Summer, the newly formed Mississippi Freedom Democratic Party (MFDP) challenged the all-white Mississippi delegation to the Democratic National Convention in Atlantic City. This is often portrayed as the final chapter of the Mississippi movement as national attention shifted away from the southern movement following passage of the 1965 Voting Rights Act. However, key struggles took place at the state and local levels concerning the implementation of voting rights and social policies. Both the NAACP and MFDP continued to pursue a civil rights agenda after 1965 in Mississippi. The period following the Atlantic City convention was marked by increasing conflict between the two dominant organizations. In the electoral arena, both organizations supported candidates in local and state elections. Local branches of both organizations pursued school desegregation, organized boycotts and demonstrations, and pushed for expanded poverty programs in their communities (McLemore 1971; Parker 1990).

The Child Development Group of Mississippi: Early Involvement in the War on Poverty

From their origins, poverty programs in Mississippi were closely tied to the dynamics of the civil rights movement. One of the earliest and most celebrated programs, the Child Development Group of Mississippi (CDGM), administered Head Start centers across the state building directly on the movement's base of Freedom Schools and community centers. CDGM provided an entry point for activists into the War on Poverty (Greenberg 1969).

CDGM was formed by a small group of policymakers and psychologists with loose connections to the Mississippi movement. For example, Tom Levin, the first director of the program, had participated in Freedom Summer through the Medical Committee for Human Rights, a group providing medical assistance to local projects. Despite these ties, when proposals for CDGM were circulated in early 1965, the response from SNCC and MFDP's state-level leadership was one of skepticism and opposition (Payne 1995). Many movement leaders were suspicious of the federal government and the initiatives of white liberals following the challenge at Atlantic City (Dittmer 1994). Thus, the state-level civil rights organizations made little effort to support CDGM.

Nevertheless, CDGM quickly diffused through the local movement infrastructure. In April 1965, CDGM held its first statewide meeting to begin developing the organization for the upcoming summer. At the first meeting, representatives from 20 communities attended. By the second meeting in the middle of April, that number had increased to 64 (Greenberg 1969:18, 22). For the first summer, Payne (1995) reports that "on opening day of the eight-week session, eighty-four centers opened across the state, serving fifty-six hundred children" (p. 329). Greenberg (1969), the OEO staff person responsible for CDGM, claims that "CDGM stood on the shoulders of COFO and its companion projects which were active the preceding summer" (p. 28).

Holmes County illustrates the relationship that developed between the civil rights movement and CDGM at the local level. An inspection during the second year of the program found that 102 of the 108 staff members in Holmes County were active members of MFDP. Reflecting the strength of the local movement, the investigation found that "many of the Negroes in the communities around the centers have donated money and time to build buildings for the centers and work with the programs" (NA, RG 381, Box 108, July 30, 1966).[8] Bernice Johnson, who worked with CDGM in Holmes County, recalled that community centers were used in the daytime for Head Start and at night for the MFDP (Bernice Johnson, interviewed by author, June 20, 1996). The same core groups of activists participated in both activities. Investigations across the state showed that CDGM staff were affiliated with COFO, SNCC, CORE, NAACP, the Urban League, the Delta Ministry, and MFDP (NA, RG 381, Box 108, July 5, 1966).

The strong relationship between local movements and CDGM made the Head Start program a target of opposition, including violence. The primary resistance came from influential Mississippi politicians, including Senator James Eastland, who chaired the Judiciary Committee, and Senator John Stennis, who chaired the Appropriations Committee. The opposition to CDGM resonated with growing fear from around the country that the War on Poverty was funding black insurgency (Quadagno 1994).

CDGM acquired its second grant for the 1966 summer after a massive mobilization including a demonstration in which "forty-eight black children and their teachers turned the hearing room of the House Education and Labor Committee into a kindergarten" (Dittmer 1994:375). After this, CDGM was funded at 5.6 million dollars. In response,

> Governor Johnson and his allies came to see that by setting up CAP agencies in Mississippi communities, local whites could prevent the flow of federal dollars into programs like CDGM. Under continuing attack from segregationists, OEO was eager to recognize any CAP agency in Mississippi, regardless of its composition. (Dittmer 1994: 375)

This tactical shift is remarkable—that Mississippi politicians opposed to federal antipoverty programs would come to embrace them must be attributed to the threat posed by the Mississippi civil rights movement.[9]

OEO undermined the viability of CDGM by stipulating that in counties with a CAP, Head Start must be administered through the local CAP agency rather than a specialized, statewide program like CDGM. Turning Head Start over to CAPs gave local agencies a high profile in the community. The policy also undermined the movement's control of Head Start in Mississippi. OEO realized that this would shift the attention of movement activists toward local CAPs. In November 1966, OEO's southeast regional director wrote to OEO director Sargent Shriver explaining that "CDGM...had a large number of local poor people involved or hired. These same people can be expected to become involved in local CA[P] activities as their concern or experience warrants" (NA, RG 381, Box 2, November 8, 1966). This became the main battleground as activists attempted to shape Community Action Programs in Mississippi.

Measures and Models: the Formation and Funding of CAPS

Community Action Programs became the central component of the War on Poverty. Did local movements in Mississippi shape the formation and funding of CAPs? If so, in what ways did they influence CAPs? I analyze the funding of Community Action Programs during two phases, the initial development phase from 1965 to 1968 and the later phase of declining resources from 1969 to 1971.[10] The *dependent variable is the amount of CAP funding* for each period. The independent variables include measures of the civil rights movement (*black mobilization*), white resistance to the movement (*countermobilization*), and local characteristics of the county (*political and socioeconomic variables*)....

Black mobilization is measured by three variables. MFDP staff in 1965 and NAACP membership in 1963 distinguishes between the effects of the militant (MFDP) and moderate (NAACP) wings of the Mississippi civil rights movement. I measure black electoral mobilization by the number of black candidates running for office in 1967. Few black candidates won in these initial elections following the Voting Rights Act. However, the variable indicates the early consolidation of organizations and networks focused on electoral politics.

Countermobilization by whites is measured by three variables: incidents of violent resistance during Freedom Summer, the presence of a Citizens' Council organization, and the presence of a Ku Klux Klan organization in the county.[11] The formation of a Community Action Program required some support and participation from local whites, typically from the County Board of Supervisors. Hence, the areas that had most strongly resisted the civil rights movement should be the least likely to seek out or support federal programs. In some counties, for example, local whites became targets of repression if they met with civil rights groups (Dittmer 1994; Harris 1982).

Political characteristics of the county are examined in terms of the political orientation of the electorate and the organizational capacity of the local government. The partisan loyalty of a county's electorate is measured by the percentage of votes cast for Lyndon Johnson in 1964. Higher levels of Democratic loyalty may have been rewarded with higher levels of funding. In addition, I examine the possible influence of local political institutions on program implementation by including the proportion of the labor force employed in local government in 1964. I expect that counties with large political institutions will be more likely to seek out poverty program funding because of their greater organizational capacity (Mazmanian and Sabatier 1983).

Socioeconomic characteristics that might influence the formation and funding of CAPs include the local class structure, the level of poverty, and the population size. I examine the local class structure using three different indicators: (1) the proportion of the labor force employed in manufacturing, (2) the proportion of the labor force employed as professionals, and (3) landowner concentration for commercial farms. Measures of class structure are often used in studies of the policy process. James (1988) finds that manufacturing is a key component of the southern class structure that influences the level of racial inequality in political participation. Hence, I expect manufacturing to have a negative impact on poverty program funding. Professionals were potential supporters of poverty programs, so I expect the proportion employed as professionals to have a positive impact on CAP funding. The measure of landholding concentration estimates the predominance of the traditional plantation economy. Roscigno and Tomaskovic-Devey (1994) find that a similar indicator is an important determinant of local political outcomes in North Carolina. The expected direction of the relationship with this variable is unclear: While southern planters historically had opposed extensions of the welfare state system into the local economy, the mechanization of farming coincided with the rise of the civil rights movement and the initiation of the War on Poverty. This left many farm laborers unemployed, and poverty programs could have been viewed as a viable strategy for addressing the social and economic consequences of technological change (Cobb 1990).

To measure poverty, I use the proportion of households with incomes below $3,000 per year. In these models, using households or individuals produces similar results because they are highly correlated ($r = .994$). I also include a variable measuring the total number of households. To measure poverty and the number of households, I use data from the 1960 census (rather than 1970) because OEO would have used these data at the time. (Analyses using the 1970 data provide similar results.)[12]

The initial models were estimated using OLS regression. However, in the final models I conduct an additional test using a "spatial error" model, which tests for spatial dependence in the model that can result from the geographic proximity of the units of analysis (see Amenta et al. 1994; Gould 1991). The presence of spatial dependence can lead to inflated significance tests (Anselin 1992; Doreian 1980). The autocorrelation term in both models is statistically significant. However, the profile of results for the remaining independent variables is similar to that in the OLS models.[13]

Results

Black Mobilization and Community Action Programs

Table 2 shows that the measures of black mobilization play an important role in the funding of Community Action Programs during both periods: The MFDP has a statistically significant effect in both periods, the NAACP variable is significant for 1965–1968 but not for 1969–1971, and the measure of black electoral organization is positive and statistically significant for 1969–1971.[14]

The models underscore the influence at the local level of the more militant organizations. Quadagno (1994) argues that "OEO promoted black moderates at the expense of more militant civil rights activists" (p. 43). Certainly, OEO attempted to do this. But these analyses show that local movements, especially militant groups, promoted the expansion of OEO programs.

Next I discuss the remaining variables in the CAP models. Then I provide an extended discussion of movement influence. I argue that we must look further to determine whether movement activists, moderate or militant, played a direct role in the administration of CAPs. I draw on two case studies of Mississippi counties to examine *how* movements shaped poverty program formation and funding.

Countermobilization: Repression and Poverty Programs

The negative coefficients for violent resistance during Freedom Summer are statistically significant in both models. Less CAP funding went to those locales that had been sites of the most militant resistance to the civil rights movement. One white leader in Coahoma County articulated the common view that "if the white leaders did not become involved then the alternative was more Federal intervention with the county's antipoverty program being turned over to the Negroes" (Mosley and Williams 1967:8). Most counties had some white leaders who shared this view, but they did not prevail in counties that had high levels of violent repression. Local white moderates were the targets of white violence in some counties, but in counties that were relatively less repressive, moderate white leaders stepped forward to form poverty programs.

This interpretation is supported by evidence from the case studies and broader historical material on the civil rights movement (see Cunnigen 1987; Jacoway and Colburn 1982). In those cases in which local whites supported the civil rights movement, they were often singled out for repression. For example, during Freedom Summer, the Heffners, a white couple, met with civil rights activists in their home in McComb. After this meeting, the Heffners were intimidated until they left the state (Dittmer 1994; Harris 1982). This type of repression was not limited to Freedom Summer. In 1966, for example, a white Head Start teacher in Panola County "received threatening phone calls. On July 16, a letter was distributed around the city of Batesville. It was signed KKK, listed some of the white teachers and aides working in the program and said they would be given just one more opportunity to get out on their own.... As a result of the threat, four white aides left the Head Start program" (NA, RG 381, Box 110, July 17, 1966). OEO field reports and CDGM records document similar efforts to limit white support for the movement and the poverty programs.

Movement scholars often argue that repression has a negative impact on a movement's ability to achieve its objectives (Gamson 1990).[15] This can occur when repression undermines the organizational capacity of the movement, but in this case, I

Table 2 Unstandaradized Coefficients from the Maximum-Likelihood Regression of Community Action Program Funding (in $100,000s) on Selected Independent Variables: Mississippi Counties, 1965–1968 and 1969–1971

Independent Variables	CAP Grants 1965–1968	(S.E.)	CAP Grants 1969–1971	(S.E.)
Black Mobilization				
MFDP membership. 1965	1.942***	(.506)	1.109***	(.243)
NAACP membership, 1963 (logged)	1.646**	(.715)	.451	(.350)
Number of black candidates, 1967	—		.566**	(.211)
Countermobilization				
Violent resistance during Freedom Summer	−1.96***	(.577)	−1.240***	(.283)
Citizens' Council organization in county, 1956	−1.657	(2.401)	−.657	(1.105)
Ku Klux Klan organization in county, 1964	−2.622	(2.324)	−1.707	(1.116)
Political Characteristics				
Percentage voting for Lyndon Johnson, 1964	−.011	(.199)	—	
Proportion employed in local government, 1964	690.229*	(327.970)	415.988**	(156.610)
Socioeconomic Characteristics				
Proportion employed in manufacturing	−.025	(.205)	−.090	(.093)
Proportion professionals	.431	(.374)	.131	(.176)
Landowner concentration	5.251	(7.432)	.107	(3.357)
Poverty, 1959 (proportion of households earning less than $3,000)	43.769*	(25.408)	11.447	(12.129)
Total number of households, 1960 (in 1,000s)	.907*	(.424)	.760***	(.206)
Spatial autocorrelation (λ)	.551***	(.114)	.383**	(.136)
Constant	−53.083*	(26.425)	−18.618	(12.416)
Fit	.422		.562	
Maximized log-likelihood (LIK)	−1,226.3		−1,165.3	
Akaike Information Criterion (AIC)	2,478.6		2,356.6	

Note: Numbers in parentheses are standard errors. "Fit" measures the squared correlation between the predicted and observed values (Anselin 1992). Number of counties = 81.

*$P < .05$
**$P < .01$
***$P < .001$ (one-tailed tests [except landowner concentration; see text])

argue that a different process is operating—repression diminished CAP funding by suppressing the mobilization of other groups.[16]

The Local Context: Political Variables and Poverty

The pattern reported in Table 2 indicates that poverty was significantly associated with high levels of CAP funding during the first period only. County size (measured by the number of households) also has a positive effect in both models. The proportion employed in local government has a positive and statistically significant relationship to poverty program funding in both periods. Partisanship and social class measures do not show statistically significant effects on poverty program funding.

Most CAPs were initiated in the early years following the 1964 legislation. As budget cuts were made through the late 1960s, the funding of new grants was minimal. OEO's broad guideline was to make reductions of "approximately equal percentage" while allowing room for administrative discretion (NA, RG 381, Box 2, October 14, 1966). However, Table 2 reveals some important shifts, including the declining role of poverty and the increasing role of county size (measured by number of households). Overall, the results reported in Table 2 indicate that there was some continuity in the funding of CAPs.

Local Movements and Community Action Programs

The key finding from the regression models, then, is the significant positive impact of black mobilization on the funding of CAPs. However, this finding is consistent with different interpretations. One possibility is that local movements were directly involved in the formation of CAPs. However, another possibility is that movements posed a threat that mobilized other groups in the county to develop poverty programs. These scenarios correspond to Gamson's (1990) concepts of success and preemption: Success occurs when movements gain access to the policymaking process and generate substantive gains; movements are preempted when substantive gains are achieved without access to the policymaking process.[17]

The regression equations do not indicate which of the two interpretations apply in Mississippi. The case studies show that the pattern was more complex. Initially movements were preempted, and this was followed by long struggles with varying degrees of success to achieve access to the policymaking process. Movements gained influence by employing multiple strategies such as disruptive protest, negotiation with OEO officials, and administering independent poverty programs. In short, the movement infrastructure in the community shaped the extent and form of influence that was ultimately achieved.

In 1965 and 1966, Community Action Programs were formed without substantial participation from movement activists. Black participation often involved traditional leaders not affiliated with the civil rights movements (neither the moderate NAACP nor the more militant MFDP representatives), such as ministers and teachers. OEO was, in fact, aware of what it called the "Tom" problem. In early 1966, the southeast regional manager of CAP reported that in Mississippi

> ...the most frequent problem and the one which requires the most time in its solution is representation. Boards on original submission are almost always hand picked and packed in favor of the Governor. Negro representation is always 'Tom.'...Protests almost always follow the selection of such initial Boards and resolution generally takes from 3 to 4 months. (NA, RG 381, Box 2, February 24, 1966)[18]

Even though they were aware of the problem, OEO's grant administrators often did not have detailed information about the local situation and lacked "the technical competence necessary to help with Board problems" (NA, RG 381, Box 2, February 24, 1966). This problem was particularly acute in the early years. During this period, OEO depended on local movements to act as "whistle-blowers."

The Case Studies

The Community Action Programs in Holmes and Bolivar Counties were formed with little direct involvement from activists. However, this changed as each movement attempted to influence local CAPs. The cases differ with regard to the specific strategies deployed by local movements and the way that local elites responded to those efforts. In Holmes County, activists were able to secure positions and influence within the CAP administration and staff. In Bolivar County, activists used a variety of tactics to establish an independent poverty program that operated alongside the local CAP.

Holmes County

In the early 1960s, Holmes County developed one of the most successful local civil rights movements in Mississippi (MacLeod 1991; Payne 1995). The movement developed an infrastructure with broad leadership, multiple organizations, indigenous resources, and strategic flexibility. A core group of activists emerged in the small community of Mileston. Bernice Johnson, one of the first activists from the eastern part of the county, remembers the diffusion process as follows:

> Well, they were constantly trying to get new members. I remember when I first started going to Mileston, I encouraged the people in the community where I lived (which was Sunny Mount) to start having a meeting.... We were constantly going from community to community, from church to church, asking people to allow us to come into your church.... "Set up a community meeting. Elect you some officers—a president, a secretary, a treasurer or what have you—designate a certain time for your community meeting." (Rural Organizing and Cultural Center 1991, p. 70)

By 1964, most of the small communities in the county had held meetings sponsored by the MFDP that culminated in a monthly countywide meeting (Mississippi Department of Archives and History, MFDP Records, Reel 3, n.d.). Sue Lorenzi, a community organizer, reported weekly meetings in 15 different communities in 1966 (State Historical Society of Wisconsin [SHSW], Alvin Oderman Papers, August 27, 1966).

The movement infrastructure included multiple venues for leadership development. Salamon (1971:440), who conducted field research in Holmes County in 1969, estimated that there were approximately 800 formal leadership positions in movement organizations held by 600 different individuals.[19]

Financial resources were modest. However, they were derived from local activities including collections at monthly meetings, plate dinners, and set donations from churches of, for example, $100 a year. The FDP office was sustained by local collections—in 1966, "over $500 was raised ... for its phone, rent, lights, some supplies" (SHSW, Alvin Oderman Papers, August 27, 1966). While the vast majority of resources were generated internally in the form of labor, the movement periodically employed outside help from sources like legal aid organizations or national civil rights organizations.

Ed Brown, one of the early SNCC workers in Holmes County, described the local movement

> ... as opposed to placing the emphasis on confrontational politics we had placed the emphasis on organizing so that in the instances where there were confrontations there was sufficient organizational

strength behind it to make the whites think, you know, twice before doing anything. (Tougaloo College, Tom Dent Collection, July 2, 1979)

The Holmes County movement was a loosely coordinated confederation of movements across the county that expanded the repertoire of skills at the local level and brought local activists into contact with state and national politics.

Initial efforts to form a CAP in Holmes County bypassed the strong movement infrastructure. In the fall of 1965, a committee appointed by the Board of Supervisors began plans to join Central Mississippi, Inc. (CMI), a multicounty CAP. OEO's Southeast Regional Office was skeptical of CMI's initial proposal. Bob Westgate, an OEO staff member, noted that

> ...although there are three Negroes on each of the [five], seven member county boards, I have my doubts of their real value to their people, whether they were really "elected" by their people, and suggest that they should be checked by someone from this office. At least eight of the 15 Negro members are dependent upon the white power structure for their jobs or welfare pension payments (five principals or teachers, two on welfare and one maid). (NA, RG 381, Box 5, December 11, 1965)

Westgate sought information through CORE and NAACP contacts, but neither organization could provide contacts because they did not have organizations in the counties. Originally, CMI had submitted a proposal reporting that 25 percent of the population was black, but OEO required an increase in the number of "minority representatives" when it discovered that the population in the six counties was actually 58 percent black (NA, RG 381, Box 5, December 11, 1965).

OEO was also concerned that "eight of the 20 white board members are 'Johnson colonels'— men who contributed funds and support during Governor Johnson's campaign" (NA, RG 381, Box 5, December 11, 1965). The governor exercised considerable power over CAPs because he had to sign off on grants and the organization's charter. With CMI, Johnson "allegedly held up the signing of the charter until these eight [supporters] were appointed on the board." The president and vice president of the CMI board were Johnson loyalists, and they had strong ties to the local political structure. For example, Ringold, the president, was the attorney for the Board of Supervisors (the most powerful local political body in Mississippi) in Montgomery County (NA, RG 381, Box 5, December 11, 1965).

Because the formation of CMI occurred outside the public arena, it could not be contested by local activists. Daisy Lewis, director of the Holmes County Community Center, observed that "CAP came into Holmes County unexpected before the poor Negro and poor white had the chance to take part in it or decide if it would help our county or not…" (Tougaloo College, Ed King Papers, Box 11, 1966). A group of approximately 40 white leaders held a planning meeting in February 1966 to coordinate efforts. The *Lexington Advertiser* reported that "leaders were told that they have a choice of the county conducting it's own anti-poverty program and 'taking the Negroes along with us' or not acting and have the 'Negroes and civil rights workers' take over" ("Anti-Poverty Program Discussed," February 24, 1966, p. 1). Despite being caught off guard, the movement quickly mobilized to participate in the program. On March 7, a public meeting was held with approximately 500 blacks and 30 whites in attendance (*Lexington Advertiser,* "Holmes CAP Advisory Group," March 10, 1966, p. 1). Activists brought a series of demands including the dissolution of the existing board. A compromise was reached in which six additional members were elected to a temporary advisory committee. Other changes were made, including the election of a 31-member permanent advisory committee that would elect a six-member Board of Directors. In addition, each Head Start center would elect a separate advisory committee. Because the small communities throughout the county were already organized, the movement could elect a majority to the advisory committee and influence key policy decisions of the Community Action Program (Salamon 1971).

The Holmes County movement thus restructured the organization of poverty programs during the course of a single meeting. These policies ensured a high level of movement participation in future program implementation. By securing access to the administration of CAP, the civil rights movement was able to maintain control of Head Start centers through an independent, delegate agency. In addition, CAP initiated several projects that went beyond job training to address rural poverty in Holmes County. While the poverty programs provided services, they also provided jobs—the programs constituted the single largest employer in Holmes County (Salamon 1971).

Bolivar County

In the mid-1960s, the Bolivar County movement was weaker than that in Holmes County. Community organizers had begun campaigns in some towns (e.g., Shaw), but several communities had no movement activity. The movement was held together by a loose network of activists, but it did not have the regular meetings, diverse organizations, or comprehensive presence that Holmes County did. Nevertheless, civil rights activists mobilized a successful, widespread campaign to secure an independent, parallel program. This campaign became a major vehicle for building a movement infrastructure in Bolivar County.

As in Holmes County, the initial plans for a CAP occurred without movement participation. The Bolivar County Community Action Committee was formed in 1965 with key support from local elites including the Board of Supervisors and the Chamber of Commerce. As editor of the *Bolivar-Commercial* and President of the Chamber of Commerce, Cliff Langford provided considerable support for the program. From its beginning, local activists criticized the program for excluding movement participation and appointing conservative blacks to the CAP board. As was the case in many CDGM counties, mobilization crystallized in early 1966 when local leaders in Bolivar County learned that Head Start could no longer be administered through CDGM. Consistent with its new policy, OEO recommended that the Head Start program be shifted to the local CAP. The CDGM group formed a local organization called the Associated Communities of Bolivar County (ACBC). A campaign was launched that simultaneously attacked the local CAP for excluding movement activists and demanded the continuation of Head Start through the established CDGM program. A similar strategy was used in Sunflower County (Mills 1993). Black members of the CAP board were singled out as "Toms" appointed by the "power structure." The CDGM group was outraged that one of the black ministers appointed to the CAP board had denied CDGM access to several churches in 1965 (SHSW, Amzie Moore Papers, Box 2, n.d.b and Box 3, n.d.).

The primary leader of the challenge was Amzie Moore, one of the early NAACP leaders in Mississippi. However, the leadership included a large number of local ministers (from churches in which Head Start centers operated) and the staff from Head Start programs throughout the county. These efforts also received support from the Delta Ministry and MFDP. The challenge could quickly mobilize throughout the organizational infrastructure that had been used to operate Head Start. The local movement, calling itself the "Committee of the Poor in Bolivar County," held mass meetings, circulated a petition, and operated the CDGM centers for approximately 1,200 children on a volunteer basis through the spring of 1966 (NA, RG 381, Box 40, March 17, 1966; SHSW, Amzie Moore Papers, Box 2, January 19, 1966). The volunteer programs demonstrated the commitment of the local movement and posed an ongoing challenge to the legitimacy of the funded project in the county. One OEO investigator noted that the petition "is a forceful and dramatic expression of the feelings of these people of Bolivar County. It does show that there is a good deal of organization at the grass roots level" (NA, RG 381, Box 40, March 3, 1966). In addition to the local activities, leaders went to Washington, D.C. to lobby OEO to maintain the CDGM-based program in Bolivar County.[20]

The Bolivar County CAP tried to respond to charges that its board was unrepresentative by holding open meetings at the local level to discuss program objectives and consolidate support. These meetings provided an opportunity for representatives of the CDGM-based group to publicly criticize the CAP board and build support for their challenge (SHSW, Amzie Moore Papers, Box 2, n.d.a; SHSW, Amzie Moore Papers, Box 2, March 13, 1966). These events culminated in a meeting between CAP and the CDGM group in March at which the Bolivar CAP voted down a proposal to transfer funds to the CDGM group and allow it to administer an independent program. This forced OEO to make a decision regarding the two groups (SHSW, Amzie Moore Papers, Box 2, 1966; SHSW, Amzie Moore Papers, Box 2, March 22, 1966).

OEO was initially opposed to having parallel organizations and favored a reorganization of the existing CAP board. Summarizing an extensive investigation, an OEO report emphasized that "it is *crucially* important that the Bolivar County Community Action Committee be given every consideration for funding" (NA, RG 381, Box 40, 1965). Despite initial support of the local CAP, Bill Seward concluded his investigation for OEO that

> ...although representing less than a third of the Negro population, [the CDGM group] is a potent and vocal force that must be recognized and included in any further OEO programs.... [F]urther postponement [of funding] will raise the level of emotional discontent of the Negro/poor from one of frustration, channeled into constructive effort, to one of frustration resulting in overt demonstration. In other words, there had better be a Head Start and quick *before* the lid blows. (NA. RG 381, Box 40, March 17, 1966)

This analysis led Seward to recommend dividing the funds evenly between CDGM and the local CAP (NA, RG 381, Box 40, March 31, 1966; U.S.-Senate 1967). In April, this was the compromise that OEO reached in Bolivar County—two separate Head Start programs with separate staffs and administrations were funded (SHSW, Amzie Moore Papers, Box 3, April 14, 1966).

Despite initial opposition, support within OEO increased for the movement-based program which had applied for funding as the Associated Communities of Bolivar County (ACBC). A 1967 report noted that "preliminary evaluations indicate that the ACBC programs are probably better than the CA[P]'s." Even though the Bolivar County CAP was making efforts to subsume ACBC within its program. OEO representatives in Mississippi stated that "our position will be to support and maintain ACBC as a separate entity" (NA, RG 381, Box 5, January 13, 1967). The Bolivar County movement leveraged a response from OEO because of its sustained mobilization using conventional and disruptive tactics. In the 1966 year-end report, the southeast regional director singled out Bolivar County because of the "lessening of over-all community tensions" (NA, RG 381, Box 2, December 30, 1966).

The Bolivar County movement was able to use sustained protest to secure an autonomous poverty program. Despite initial opposition, OEO officials came to see the duplication of administrative staff and costs as preferable to an ongoing challenge to their legitimacy in Bolivar County. The movement's challenge depended on an expansive network of activists that could run Head Start centers, coordinate mass meetings, and negotiate the grant-writing process with OEO.

Movements in Holmes County and Bolivar County were successful at maintaining movement-controlled Head Start centers. In addition, both movements posed a credible threat that compelled local political elites to establish well-funded Community Action Programs. However, the counties differed in important respects. In Holmes County, activists achieved greater impact on the structure of CAP by capitalizing on a strong movement infrastructure. In Bolivar County, activists protected movement-affiliated Head Start programs but ceded control to the broader CAP program. This outcome resulted from the relatively greater opposition and the less developed infrastructure in Bolivar County compared with Holmes County.

Conclusion

A striking finding of this study is the extent to which movements shaped the implementation of local poverty programs. While this influence was certainly less than local activists would have desired, it was nonetheless considerable. The quantitative analysis shows that local movements had a positive impact on the amount of CAP funding in Mississippi counties. The case studies support my interpretation of the quantitative evidence and show how movements influenced the formation of Community Action Programs by carving out areas of administrative control.

I propose that researchers specify more precisely *how* movements shape social policy. Even in this small case study, I demonstrate several ways that

local movements influenced policy implementation in Mississippi, including the disruption of program operations, negotiation with agency officials, and symbolic and persuasive protest activities. The greatest influence may have occurred indirectly when movements prompted local white politicians to actively pursue grants for poverty programs.

In terms of the movement-outcome models, the evidence indicates that the impacts of the movement were cumulative, rather than momentary as suggested by the action-reaction models. The movement posed a threat, but the threat was based on the ability of the movement to distribute federal programs independent of local agencies. Local movements used a variety of conventional tactics, but they did not abandon the politics of protest—marches and boycotts were organized in local communities throughout the late 1960s. Rather, movements were most influential when they built local organizations that allowed for an oscillation between mass-based tactics and routine negotiation with agency officials.

The action-reaction models cannot account for the sustained interactions between local movements and OEO officials during the implementation of poverty programs. During much of this period, local activists and program officials collaborated to establish poverty programs. The access-influence model would suggest a drift toward greater professionalization of the movement and the abandonment of protest tactics, but this did not occur as the Bolivar County case illustrates.

The movement infrastructure model shows how movements exert influence through multiple causal mechanisms. The three most crucial mechanisms observed in this study are (1) direct implementation of poverty programs, (2) indirect influence by challenging the political authority of local elites, and (3) disruptive and persuasive protest that compelled OEO to act on behalf of the movement. These forms of influence all derive from the organizational capacity of local movements. Direct program implementation required an extensive leadership cadre that could maintain ongoing ties to OEO officials, other programs throughout the state, and community members. In Bolivar County, activists secured independent programs over the initial opposition of

OEO administrators and the local CAP. The movement-affiliated centers (formerly CDGM) continued to operate Head Start programs in 1966 without funding, illustrating the underlying strength of the local organization. The second form of influence flowed from the first. Because local movements were capable of operating poverty programs independently, they undermined the authority of local officials who had historically administered social programs. Finally, local movements used protest, including disruptive protest in Bolivar County, to bring additional pressure to bear on OEO and to mobilize national support. OEO officials came to see this as an inevitable part of the implementation process in Mississippi with civil rights groups acting as whistle-blowers.

As an analytic strategy, I have addressed the long-standing problems of studying movement outcomes, opening questions about the variation in movement infrastructures and the ability of movements to influence policy. The strategy employed is less generalizable than studies based on a representative sample of social movement organizations or campaigns (e.g., Gamson 1990), yet it avoids some of the problems inherent in studies analyzing multiple movements, such as limited measures of movement impact. While the Mississippi movement is exceptional in some respects, the movement employed organizational forms and strategies that are comparable to those of many other social movements, including labor movements (Fantasia 1989; Ganz 2000), the environmental justice movement (Bullard 1990), and many women's movements (Ferree and Martin 1995; Whittier 1995).

One might reasonably ask whether there were distinctive aspects of the War on Poverty in Mississippi that make this instance of policy implementation and the findings presented here unique? First, the high degree of public participation required by the poverty programs facilitated the movement's access to the programs while bringing the movement's opponents into the implementation process. Second, the high level of local autonomy permitted in the formation and management of projects allowed the movement to pursue local efforts to influence poverty programs rather than pursue a national struggle in which the movement

would have had to target federal actors, especially Congress and the Presidency. Local variation in policy implementation is common for social policies in the United States (Amenta et al. 1994; Banaszak 1996; Clemens 1997), but the model might require modification to accommodate variation in political context (Amenta, Halfmann, and Young 1999). Third, the central role of racial politics in the development of the War on Poverty is seen, for example, in the ongoing efforts of OEO to showcase racial integration in its programs (Quadagno 1994). However, this conflict reveals dynamics of a more general nature in that the long-term goals of program administrators and movement activists often conflict. To address these concerns in a more meaningful way requires similar analyses of other social movements across a variety of policy arenas.

The growing body of research on movement outcomes calls for more explicit development of the causal arguments concerning movement impact. I provide a preliminary map of these arguments that allows for more systematic, comparative research: Future studies of outcomes can address these issues by (1) using quantitative analysis of outcomes across time and policy arenas, (2) giving greater attention to the process and mechanisms of impact through case studies, and (3) synthesizing across specific findings to explain variation across movements and political contexts.

NOTES

I have benefited from comments and criticisms by Michael Biggs, Marshall Ganz, Peter Marsden, Ziad Munson, Shuva Paul, Gerald Platt, Michael Schwartz, Alex Trillo, Mary Vogel, Charlie Zicari, and Bob Zussman. Some of the data collection was supported by an NSF Doctoral Dissertation Improvement Grant (9625597).

1. Movements can also influence "reactive" outcomes such as preventing a policy that would damage the movement or its constituents (Kriesi et al. 1995).

2. For example, Piven and Cloward's (1977) explicit focus on "poor people's movements" suggests that class composition is a key variable (also see Ragin 1989).

3. I focus on theories that explicitly examine the movement/outcome relationship. Other than my brief discussion of political opportunity structure, I do not focus on theories of political-institutional change including (1) pluralist or interest group theories, (2) state-centric theories, or (3) elite theories. Some scholars have contrasted these theories with

"movement theories" of political change (Amenta, Caruthers, and Zylan 1992; Quadagno 1992).

4. These models of movement influence are connected to methodological strategies. For example, Rucht and Neidhardt (1998) argue that media reported protest is a meaningful barometer of all protest: "Insofar as we are interested in those protests which are an input for the political system, media reported protests have a higher validity than the whole range of actual protests" (p. 76).

5. I do not analyze the impacts of poverty programs on the civil rights movement, e.g., whether the programs co-opted the movement (see Eisinger 1979).

6. The data set is drawn from a larger study that includes measures of the civil rights movement, local countermobilization, contextual variables, federal intervention, and other outcomes. This data set includes all Mississippi counties except Hinds County, which includes Jackson, the capitol of Mississippi. The large size of Hinds County makes it an outlier in some analyses. In addition, Jackson served as the organizational center for state-level activities. My interest is in the local forms of mobilization, and in Hinds County these cannot be distinguished from state-level mobilization.

7. For overviews see Friedman (1977), Patterson (1994), Piven and Cloward (1993), and Quadagno (1994).

8. Complete citations for archival material are listed in the bibliography under Archival Sources. "NA" indicates the National Archives and Records Administration, and "RG indicates the Record Group.

9. This opposition to federal intervention was specific to programs that would benefit black Mississippians. Cobb (1990) notes that "Delta planters were skilled in the pursuit and manipulation of federal assistance long before the New Deal," including flood control programs and crop-reduction subsidies (p. 914).

10. The two dependent variables are the total CAP grants for 1965–1968 and 1969–1971 (NA, RG 381, Box 14, n.d.). There were 18 CAPs in Mississippi from 1965 to 1971 of which 8 were multicounty agencies. I used two different strategies for estimating county-level expenditures for multicounty agencies. First, I divided the budget evenly among the counties covered by the CAP. For the second estimation, I divided the budget among the counties proportional to the number of households in each county with an income below $3,000 per year. The two estimates produced similar results; I report the analysis using the "proportional" estimates. Because participation in programs was based on economic eligibility, this strategy is a better, if not perfect, approximation of the distribution.

11. These three variables are not highly correlated, and thus I treat them as distinct modalities of resistance.

12. Similarly, I tested several measures of poverty, such as the number of households with income below $2,000 and $1,000

in these models. Each indicator produced comparable results. The chosen indicator, households earning less than $3,000, is the closest approximation of the federal poverty line. CAP grant applications required that applicants list the percentage of households earning below $3,000. When OEO investigated the composition of CAP boards or program employees to determine whether there was sufficient representation of "the poor," this was the indicator they used. The indicator became so widely used that the movement employed it, and in 1966, MFDP sent out a call for a statewide meeting of all persons earning below $3,000. Studies by political scientists and sociologists measuring poverty with 1960 data have also employed this same indicator (e.g., Colby 1985; Cowart 1969; Friedland 1976).

13. The independent variables that were significant in the OLS models remain significant, with the exception of the presence of Ku Klux Klan organizations.

14. The black candidate variable does not account for the declining importance of NAACP membership. Models omitting the black candidate variable show a similar profile of coefficients, and the NAACP variable remains nonsignificant.

15. The relationship between repression and protest has received considerable attention in recent years and has been strongly influenced by Tilly's (1978) early analysis (Koopmans 1997; Lichbach 1987; Rasler 1996). In contrast, little is known about the impact of repression on outcomes.

16. I conducted a third case study that sheds light on this process. In Madison County, violent repression endured longer than it did in most of Mississippi. Only one effort was made to establish a CAP, and it was unsuccessful (*Madison County Herald,* "CAP Meeting Saturday," April 27, 1967, p. 1).

17. There were some rare cases in which NAACP leaders and liberal whites formed coalitions at the local level—this occurred, for example, in Coahoma County. However, these coalitions were stronger in state-level organizations like the Loyalist Democrats (Dittmer 1994; Simpson 1982).

18. Governors could veto poverty programs unless they were administered through a college or university. Some programs, such as CDGM, were administered through historically black colleges to avoid the veto. Other programs were sponsored by universities outside the South, such as the Tufts Delta Health Center in Bolivar County.

19. The 1960 census reports 19,488 black persons (71.9 percent of the total population) living in Holmes County (U.S. Bureau of the Census 1963).

20. Although there is no precise estimate of the movement's size, the "Outline of Important Events" cited above reports "approximately 7,000 signatures" on the petition (SHSW, Amzie Moore Papers, Box 2, n.d.b; for a copy of the petition see SHSW, Amzie Moore Papers, Box 2, n.d.c).

References

Abanes, Richard. 1996. *American Militias: Rebellion, Racism, and Religion.* Downers Grove, IL: InterVarsity Press.

Abbott, Andrew. 1992. "From Causes to Events: Notes on Narrative Positivism." *Sociological Methods and Research* 20: 428–55.

Abeles, Ronald P. 1976. "Relative Deprivation, Rising Expectations, and Black Militancy." *Journal of Social Issues* 32 (2): 119–37.

Aberle, David. 1965. "A note on relative deprivation theory as applied to Millenarian and other cult movements." Pp. 537–41 in *Reader in Comparative Religion: An Anthropological Approach,* edited by W. Lessa and E. Vogt. New York: Harper & Row.

———. 1966. *The Peyote Religion Among the Navaho.* Chicago: Aldine.

Abrahamian, E. 1980. "Structural Causes of the Iran Revolution." *MERIP Reports* 87: 21–26.

Abramowitz, Stephen I., and Alberta J. Nassi. 1981. "Keeping the Faith: Psychosocial Correlates of Activism Persistence into Middle Adulthood." *Journal of Youth and Adolescence* 10: 507–23.

Abu Libdeh, Hasan, Geir Ovensen, and Helge Brunborg. 1993. "Population Characteristics and Trends." Pp. 35–80 in *Palestinian Society in Gaza, West Bank and Arab Jerusalem: A Survey of Living Conditions,* edited by Marianne Heiberg and Geir Ovensen. Oslo: FAFO.

Abu-Lughod, Lila. 1986. *Veiled Sentiments: Honor and Poetry in a Bedouin Society.* Berkeley and Los Angeles: University of California Press.

———. 1990. "The Romance of Resistance: Tracing Transformations of Power through Bedouin Women." *American Ethnologist* 17: 41–55.

Acker, Joan. 1992. "Gendered Institutions: From Sex Roles to Gendered Institutions." *Contemporary Sociology* 21: 565–69.

Ackerman, Peter, and Jack DuVall. 2000. *A Force More Powerful.* New York: St. Martin's Press.

———. 1970b. "New York Controversy Continues over Snake Pit Mass Arrest." May 13–26, p. 2.

Ackerman, Peter. 1970c. "1,000 Gays Riot in New York." September 30–October 13, pp. 1, 10.

Adam, Barry D. 1987. *The Rise of a Gay and Lesbian Movement.* Boston: Twayne. *Advocate.* 1970a. "Bar in N.Y. 'Liberated' by Gay Kiss-in." November 11–24, p. 3.

Adorno, T. W., E. Frenkel-Brunswick, D. J. Levinson, and R. N. Sanford. 1950. *The Authoritarian Personality.* New York: Harper.

Ahn, Byung-joon. 1974. "The Cultural Revolution and China's Search for Political Order." *The China Quarterly* 58: 249–85.

Aho, James A. 1990. *The Politics of Righteousness: Idaho Christian Patriotism.* Seattle: University of Washington Press.

———. 1993. "The Recent Ethnogenesis of White Man." *Left Bank* 5: 55–63.

———. 1999. "White Man as a Social Construct." *The European Legacy* 4: 62–72.

———. 1994. *This Thing of Darkness: A Sociology of the Enemy.* Seattle: University of Washington Press.

Ainsztein, Reuben. 1979. *The Warsaw Ghetto Revolt.* New York: Holocaust Library.

Alas, Higinio. 1982. *El Salvador, por que la insurrección?* San Jose: Secretariado Permanente de la Comisión para la Defensa de los Derechos Humanos en Centroamerica.

Albuquerque Journal. 1985. "Debate: building the road to change." February 3, Section B, p. 4.

Alexander, Robin. 1999. "Experience and Reflections on the Use of the NAALC." *Memorias: Encuentro Trinacional de Laboralistas Democráticos.* México, D.F.: Universidad Nacional Autónoma de México.

Allen, Nathalie J. and John P. Meyer. 1990. "The Measurement and Antecedents of Affective, Continuance, and Normative Commitment to Organization." *Journal of Occupational Psychology* 63: 1–18.

Allievi, Stefano. 1992. *Le Parole della Lega* (The League's Words). Milan, Italy: Garzanti.

Allison, Paul. 1984. *Event History Analysis.* Thousand Oaks, Calif.: Sage.

Allison, Paul D. 1999. "Comparing Logit and Probit Coefficients Across Groups." *Sociological Methods and Research* 28: 186–208.

Almeida, Paul D. 2002. "Los movimientos populares contra la austeridad económica en América Latina entre 1996 y 2001." *Realidad: Revista de Ciencias Sociales y Humanidades* 86 (Marzo-Abril): 177–89.

Almeida, Paul D. 2003. "Opportunity Organizations and Threat-Induced Contention: Protest Waves in Authoritarian Settings." *American Journal of Sociology* 109: 345–400.

Almeida, Paul D., and Linda Brewster Stearns. 1998. "Political Opportunities and Local Grassroots Environmental Movements: The Case of Minamata." *Social Problems* 45 (1): 37–60.

Altman, Dennis. 1982. "The Gay Movement Ten Years Later." *Nation* (November 13), pp. 494–96.

———. 1993. *Homosexual: Oppression and Liberation.* New York: New York University Press.

Alvarado López, Napoleón, and Jesus Octavio Cruz Olmedo. 1978. *Conciencia y Cambio Social en la Hacienda Tres Ceibas (El Salvador): 1955–1976.* Tesis de Licenciado. University of Costa Rica, Faculty of Social Sciences.

Alwin, Duane F., Ronald L. Cohen, and Theodore M. Newcomb. 1991. *Political Attitudes over the Life Span: The Bennington Women after Fifty Years.* Madison: University of Wisconsin Press.

Amenta, Edwin. 1991. "Making the Most of a Case Study." *International Journal of Comparative Sociology* 32: 172–94.

———. 1998. *Bold Relief: Institutional Politics and the Origins of Modern American Social Policy.* Princeton, NJ: Princeton University Press.

———. 2006. *When Movements Matter: The Townsend Plan and the Rise of Social Security.* Princeton, NJ: Princeton University Press.

Amenta, Edwin, Chris Bonastia, and Neal Caren. 2001. "US Social Policy in Comparative and Historical Perspective: Concepts, Images, Arguments, and Research Strategies." *Annual Review of Sociology* 27: 213–34.

Amenta, Edwin and Neal Caren. 2004. "The Legislative, Organizational, and Beneficiary Consequences of State-Oriented Challengers." Pp. 461–88 in *The Blackwell Companion to Social Movements,* edited by David A. Snow, Sarah A. Soule, and Hanspeter Kriesi. Malden, MA: Blackwell Publishing.

Amenta, Edwin, Bruce G. Carruthers, and Yvonne Zylan. 1992. "A Hero for the Aged? The Townsend Movement, the Political Mediation Model, and U.S. Old-Age Policy, 1934–50." *American Journal of Sociology* 98: 308–39.

Amenta, Edwin, Kathleen Dunleavy, and Mary Bernstein. 1994. "Stolen Thunder? Huey Long's 'Share Our Wealth,' Political Mediation, and the Second New Deal." *American Sociological Review* 59: 678–702.

Amenta, Edwin and Drew Halfmann. 2000. "Wage Wars: Institutional politics, WPA Wages, and the Struggle for U.S. Social Policy." *American Sociological Review* 65: 506–28.

Amenta, Edwin, Drew Halfmann, and Michael P. Young. 1999. "The Strategies and Contexts of Social Protest: Political Mediation and the Impact of the Townsend Movement." *Mobilization* 56: 1–25.

Amenta, Edwin, Sheera Joy Olasky, and Neal Caren. 2005. "Age for Leisure? Political Mediation and the Impact of the Pension Movement on U.S. Old-Age Policy." *American Sociological Review* 70: 516–39.

Amenta, Edwin and Jane D. Poulsen. 1994. "Where to Begin: A Survey of Five Approaches to Selecting Independent Variables for Qualitative Comparative Analysis." Sociological Methods and *Research* 23: 22–53.

Amenta, Edwin, and Michael Young. 1999a. "Democratic States and Social Movements: Theoretical Arguments and Hypotheses." *Social Problems* 46 (2): 153–68.

———. 1999b. "Making an Impact." Pp. 22–41 in *How Social Movements Matter,* edited by M. Giugni, D. McAdam, and C. Tilly. Minneapolis, MN: University of Minnesota Press.

America Votes. 1994. Washington, DC: Elections Research Center, Congressional Quarterly.

American Institute of Public Opinion. 1938a. "Gallup Poll no. 130." Princeton, NJ: American Institute of Public Opinion [producer]. New Haven, CT: Roper Center for Public Opinion Research [distributor].

———. 1938b. "Gallup Poll no. 140." Princeton, NJ: American Institute of Public Opinion [producer]. New Haven, CT: Roper Center for Public Opinion Research [distributor].

Anaya Montes, Melida. 1972. *La segunda gran batalla de ANDES.* San Salvador: Editorial Universitaria.

Anderson, Thomas. 1970. *La Matanza.* Lincoln: University of Nebraska Press.

ANDES-21 de Junio. 1974. "Informe del consejo Ejecutivo a la X asamblea general ordinaria de la labor de ANDES 21 de Junio durante el año 1974." San Salvador: ANDES-21 de Junio (December).

Andreas, Joel. 2002. "Battling Over Political and Cultural Power During the Chinese Cultural Revolution." *Theory and Society* 31: 463–519.

———. 2006. "Institutionalized Rebollion: Governing Tsinghua University During the Late Years of the Chinese Cultural Revolution." *The China Journal* 55: 1–28.

Andrews, Kenneth T. 1997. "The Impacts of Social Movements on the Political Process: A Study of the Civil Rights Movement and Black Electoral Politics in Mississippi." *American Sociological Review* 62: 800–819.

———. 2001. "Social Movements and Policy Implementation: The Mississippi Civil Rights Movement and the War on Poverty, 1965–71." *American Sociological Review* 66: 71–95.

———. 2002. "Movement-Countermovement Dynamics and the Emergence of New Institutions: The Case of 'White Flight' Schools in Mississippi." *Social Forces* 80: 911–36.

———. 2004. *Freedom Is a Constant Struggle.* Chicago: University of Chicago Press.

Andrews, Kevin. 2001. "Social Movements and Policy Implementation." *American Sociological Review* 66: 71–95.

Anner, Mark. 1996. "¿Hacia la sindicalización de los sindicatos?" *Estudios Centroamericanos,* nos. 573–74, 599–614.

Anner, Mark S. 2002. "Local and Transnational Campaigns to End Sweatshop Practices." In *Transnational Cooperation among Labor Unions,* edited by Michael E. Gordon and Lowell Turner. Ithaca, N.Y.: Cornell University Press.

Anselin, Luc. 1992. *SpaceStat Tutorial.* Urbana, IL: University of Illinois.

Ansell, Christopher K. 1997. "Symbolic Networks: The Realignment of the French Working Class, 1887–1894." *American Journal of Sociology* 103 (2): 359–90.

Anti-Defamation League. 1998. "Explosion of Hate: The Danger of the National Alliance." New York: ADI.

Anti-Defamation League. 2002. "The Consequences of Right-Wing Extremism on the Internet." Retrieved February 5, 2002 (www.adl.org/internet/extremism %5Frw/cord_rock.asp).

Arditti, Rita. 1999. *Searching for Life: The Grandmothers of the Plaza de Mayo and the Disappeared Children of Argentina.* Berkeley: University of California Press.

Argueta Antillón, Luis. 1983. "Crecimiento, empleo y necesidades básicas: elementos de análisis." *Boletín de Ciencias Económicas y Sociales* 6 (4): 241–63.

Arjomand, Said Amir. 1989. "The Emergence of Islamic Political Ideologies." Pp. 107–23 in *The Changing Face of Religion,* edited by James A. Beckford and Thomas Luckmann. Newbury Park, CA: Sage.

Arkin, William M. 2003. "The Dividends of Delay." *Los Angeles Times,* February 23.

Armbruster, Ralph. 1995. "Cross National Labor Organizing Strategies." *Critical Sociology* 21 (2): 75–89.

———. 1998a. "Cross Border Labor Organizing in the Garment and Automobile Industries: The Phillips Van Heusen and Ford Cuautitlán Cases." *Journal of World Systems Research* 4 (1): 20–51.

———. 1998b. *Globalization and Cross Border Labor Organizing in the Garment and Automobile Industries.* Ph.D. dissertation. University of California, Riverside.

Armstrong, Elizabeth A. 2002a. "Crisis, Collective Creativity, and the Generation of New Organizational Forms: The Transformation of Lesbian/Gay Organizations in San Francisco." In *Research in the Sociology of Organizations,* edited by Michael Lounsbury and Marc Ventresca, vol. 19. Oxford: JAI Press, 361–95.

———. 2002b. *Forging Gay Identities: Organizing Sexuality in San Francisco, 1950–94.* Chicago: University of Chicago Press.

Arquilla, John, and David Ronfeldt, eds. 2001. *Networks and Netwars: The Future of Terror, Crime and Militancy.* Santa Monica, CA: Rand Corporation.

Arriola Palomares, Joaquín, and José Antonio Candray Alvarado. 1994. *Derechos Prohibidos: Negociación Colectiva y Sindicatos en El Salvador.* Serie documentos de investigación no. 1. San Salvador. UCA Editores.

Arroyo, Alberto P., and Mario B. Monroy. 1996. *Red Mexicana de Acción Frente al Libre Comercio: Cinco años de lucha (1991–1996)*. Mexico: Red Mexicana de Acción Frente al Libre Comercio.

Arthur, Linda Boynton. 1997. "Role Salience, Role Embracement, and the Symbolic Self-Completion of Sorority Pledges." *Sociological Inquiry* 67: 364–79.

Ascoli, Ugo, ed. 1985. *Welfare State all'Italiana* (Welfare State Italian-Style). Bari-Rome, Italy: Laterza.

Ash, Timothy Garton. 2003. "The War After War with Iraq." *New York Times,* March 20.

Ashenfelter, Orley, and George E. Johnson. 1969. "Bargaining Theory, Trade Unions and Industrial Strike Activity." *American Economic Review* 59: 35–49.

Atkinson, Michael. 1986. "The Perception of Social Categories: Implications for the Social Comparison Process." Pp. 117–34 in *Relative Deprivation and Social Comparison,* edited by James M. Olson, C. Peter Herman, and Mark P. Zanna. Hillsdale, NJ: Erlbaum.

Atlanta Journal and Constitution. 1992. "Democrats Slipping in Senate Contests." November 1, C8.

Atlanta Journal. 1953. "Woman's Place in Home, WSB-TV Told." February 5.

Auyero, Javier. 2002. *La Protesta: Retratos de la Beligerancia Popular en la Argentina Democratica.* Buenos Aires: Libros del Rojas.

Axelrod, Robert M. 1984. *The Evolution of Cooperation.* New York: Basic.

Ayres, Jeffrey M. 1998. *Defying Conventional Wisdom: Political Movements and Popular Contention Against North American Free Trade.* Toronto: University of Toronto Press.

Azzam, Maha. 2003. "Al-Qaeda: The Misunderstood Wahhabi Connection and the Ideology of Violence." London: Chatham House. Retrieved August 4, 2006 (http://www.chathamhouse.org.uk/viewdocument.php?documentid=3909)

Babb, Sarah. 1996. "'A True American System of Finance': Frame Resonance in the U.S. Labor Movement, 1866 to 1886." *American Sociological Review* 61 (6): 1033–52.

Babbie, Earl R. 1965. "The third civilization: An examination of Sokagakkai." *Review of Religious Research* 7: 101–21.

Baccetti, Carlo and Mario Caciagli. 1992. "Dopo il PCI e dopo l'URSS" (After PCI and USSR). *Polis* 6: 537–68.

Back, Les, Michael Keith, and John Solomos. 1998. "Racism on the Internet: Mapping the Neo-Fascist Subcultures in 'Cyberspace.'" Pp. 73–101 in *Nation and Race: The Developing Euro-American Racist Subculture,* edited by J. Kaplan and T. Bjorgo Boston, MA: Northeastern University Press.

Bade, Klaus J. 1992. *Ausländer, Aussiedler, Asyl in der Bundesrepublik Deutschland.* Hannover: Landeszentrale für politische Bildung.

Badgett, M. V. Lee. 1993a. "Employment and sexual orientation: Disclosure and discrimination in the workplace." Unpublished manuscript.

———. 1993b. "Economic evidence of sexual orientation discrimination." Unpublished manuscript.

Badie, B. and P. Birnbaum. 1979. *Sociologie de l'Etat.* Paris: Grasset.

Badran, Margot. 1995. *Feminists, Islam, and Nation: Gender and the Making of Modern Egypt.* Princeton, N.J.: Princeton University Press.

Bailey v. State of Arkansas 215 Ark 53, 219 S.W. 2d 424 (1949).

Bailyn, Bernard. 1967. *The Ideological Origins of the American Revolution.* Cambridge, MA: Harvard University Press.

Baker, Ella. 1978. *Interview.* New York, New York.

Baker, Nena. 1992. "Antigay Ballot Stirs Strife in Oregon." *Newsday,* October 18, p. 17.

Bakhtin, Mikhail. 1981. *The Dialogic Imagination: Four Essays,* edited by Michael Holquist. Translated by Caryl Emerson and Michael Holquist. Austin: University of Texas Press.

Balch, Robert W. and David, Taylor. 1978. "Seekers and Saucers: The Role of the Cultic Milieu in Joining a UFO Cult." Pp. 43–65 in *Conversion Careers,* edited by J. Richardson. Beverly Hills, CA: Sage.

Baldassare, Mark. 1975. "The Effects of Density on Social Behavior and Attitudes." *American Behavioral Science* 18: 15–25.

———. 1977. "Residential Density, Household Crowding, and Social Networks." Pp. 101–15 in *Networks and Places,* edited by Claude S. Fischer. New York: Free Press.

Ball, Patrick. 2000. "The Salvadoran Human Rights Commission: Data Processing, Data Representation, and Generating Analytical Records." Pp. 15–25 in *Making the Case: Investigating Large-Scale Human Rights Violations Using Information Systems and Data Analysis,* edited by P. Ball, H. F. Spirer, and

L. Spirer. Washington, D.C.: American Association for the Advancement of Science.

Baloyra, Enrique. 1982. *El Salvador in Transition.* Chapel Hill: University of North Carolina.

Balser, Diane. 1987. *Sisterhood and Solidarity: Feminism and Labor in Modern Times.* Boston: South End.

Baltagi, Badi H. and Ping X. Wu. 1999. "Unequally Spaced Panel Data Regressions with AR(I) Disturbances." *Econometric Theory* 15: 814–23.

Baltimore Sun. 1947. "Jury Service? Positively No Says Colonial Dames Leader." February 3, p. 30.

Banaszak, Lee Ann. 1996. *Why Movements Succeed or Fail.* Princeton, NJ: Princeton University Press.

Bandy, Joe, and Jackie Smith, eds. 2005a. *Coalitions Across Borders: Transnational Protest and the Neoliberal Order.* Lanham, MD: Rowman and Littlefield.

Bandy, Joe, and Jackie Smith. 2005b. "Conclusions: What Have We Learned?" in *Coalitions Across Borders: Transnational Protest and the Neoliberal Order.* Boulder, CO: Rowman and Littlefield.

Bankston, Carl L., III, and Min Zhou. 1996 "The Ethnic Church, Ethnic Identification, and the Social Adjustment of Vietnamese Adolescents." *Review of Religious Research* 38 (1): 18–37.

Barkan, Steven E. 1979. "Strategic, Tactical and Organizational Dilemmas of the Protest Movement against Nuclear Power." *Social Problems* 27: 19–37.

Barkan, Steven E. 1980a. "Criminal Courts and Political Protest: Mobilization and Control in the Southern Civil Rights and Vietnam Antiwar Movement." Unpublished Ph.D. dissertation, Department of Sociology, State University of New York at Stony Brook.

Barkan, Steven E. 1980b. "Criminal Prosecutions in the Southern Civil Rights and Vietnam Antiwar Movements: Repression and Dissent in Political Trials." Pp. 279–99 in *Research in Law and Sociology,* edited by Steven Spitzer. Volume 3. New York: JAI Press.

Barkan, Steve. 1984. "Legal Control of the Civil Rights Movement." *American Sociological Review* 49: 552–65.

———. 2000. "Law as a Vehicle and Obstacle for U.S. Social Movements." Paper presented at the annual meeting of the Society for the Study of Social Problems. August, Washington, D.C.

———. 2001. "Legal Repression and Social Movements." Presented at the annual meeting of the American Sociological Association, August 20, Anaheim, CA.

Barkan, Steven E., Steven F. Cohn, and William H. Whitaker. 1993. "Commitment Across the Miles: Ideological and Microstructural Sources of Membership Support in a National Antihunger Organization." *Social Problems* 40: 362–73.

Barkan, Steven E., Steven F. Cohn, and William H. Whitaker. 1995. "Beyond Recruitment: Predictors of Differential Participation in a National Antihunger Organization." *Sociological Forum* 10: 113–34.

Barker, Colin. 2001. "Robert Michels and the 'Cruel Game.'" Pp. 24–43 in *Leadership and Social Movements,* edited by C. Barker, A. Johnson, and M. Lavalette. Manchester, England: Manchester University Press.

Barker, Roger G. 1968. *Ecological Psychology.* Stanford, Calif.: Stanford University Press.

Barkun, Michael 1994. *Religion and the Racist Right: The Origins of the Christian Identity Movement.* Chapel Hill: University of North Carolina Press.

Barnes, Samuel H. and Max Kaase. 1979. *Political Action: Mass Participation in Five Western Democracies.* London: Sage.

Baron, Ava, ed. 1991. *Work Engendered: Toward a New History of American Labor.* Ithaca, N.Y.: Cornell University Press.

Barr, Evan T. 1985. "Sour Grapes." *The New Republic* 193: 20–23.

Barranco, José, and Dominique Wisler. 1999. "Validity and Systematicity of Newspaper Data in Event Analysis." *European Sociological Review* 15 (3): 301–22.

Barret, Stanley R. 1987. *Is God Racist? The Right Wing in Canada.* Toronto: University of Toronto Press.

Barron, David N. 1992. "The analysis of count data: Overdispersion and autocorrelation." *Sociological Methodology* 179–220.

Barry, Kathleen. 1979. *Female Sexual Slavery.* Englewood Cliffs, N.J.: Prentice-Hall.

Barth, Fredrik. 1969. *Ethnic Groups and Boundaries.* Boston: Little, Brown.

Bartholomew, Amy and Margit Mayer. 1992. "Nomads of the Present: Melucci's Contribution to "New Social Movement' Theory." *Theory, Culture and Society* 9: 141–59.

Bartley, Numan. 1969. *The Rise of Massive Resistance: Race and Politics in the South During the 1950s.* Baton Rouge: Louisiana State University Press.

Bastian, Jean Pierre. 1994. *Protestantismos y modernidad latinoamericana: Historia de unas minorías religiosas activas en América Latina.* Mexico: Fondo de Cultura Economica.

Basu, Amrita 1995. "Introduction." Pp. 1–21 in *The Challenge of Local Feminisms: Women's Movements in Global Perspective,* edited by Amrita Basu. Boulder, Colo.: Westview Press.

Batch, R. and J. Cohig. 1985. "The Magic Kingdom: A Story of Armageddon in Utopia." Presented at the annual meetings of the Society for the Scientific Study of Religion, Savannah, GA.

Bates, Robert H., Avner Greif, Margaret Levi, Jean-Laurent Rosenthal, and Barry R. Weingast. 1998. *Analytic Narratives.* Princeton, N.J.: Princeton University Press.

Bauer, Yehuda. 1989. "Forms of Jewish Resistance During the Holocaust." Pp. 34–48 in *The Nazi Holocaust, Vol. 7: Jewish Resistance to the Holocaust,* edited by M. R. Marrus. Westport, CT: Meckler Corporation.

———. 2001. *Rethinking the Holocaust.* New Haven: Yale University Press.

Baumgartner, M. P. 1984. "Social Control from Below." Pp. 303–45 in *Toward a General Theory of Social Control. Vol. 1: Fundamentals,* edited by Donald Black. New York: Academic Press.

BBC, 2005. "Full Text: Blair Speech on Terror: Response to the London Bus Bombings." London: British Broadcasting Corporation Retrieved on October 22, 2006 (http: //news.bbc.co.uk/1/hi/uk/4689363.stm)

———, 2006. "Excerpts: Al-Zawahiri video comments Thursday, 27 July 2006." London: British Broadcasting Corporation. Retrieved on October 22. 2006 (http: //news.bbc.co.uk/l/hi/world/middle_east/5220204.stm)

Beck, E. M. 2000. "Guess who's coming to town: White supremacy, ethnic competition and social change." *Sociological Focus* 33(2): 153–74.

Beck, E. M., and Stewart E. Tolnay. 1995. "Analyzing historical count data: Poisson and negative binomial regression models." *Historical Methods* 28(3): 125–31.

Beck, Nathaniel. 2001. "Time-Series-Cross-Section Data: What Have We Learned in the Past Few Years?" *Annual Review of Political Science* 4: 271–93.

Beck, Nathaniel, Jonathan N. Katz, and Richard Tucker. 1998. "Taking Time Seriously: Time-Series-Cross-Sectional Analysis with a Binary Dependent Variable." *American Journal of Political Science* 42: 1260–88.

Becker, Howard S. 1953. "Becoming a Marihuana User." *American Journal of Sociology* 59: 235–42.

Becker, Howard S. 1960. "Notes on the Concept of Commitment." *American Journal of Sociology* 66 (July): 32–40.

Becker, Penny Edgell, and Pawan H. Dhingra. 2001. "Religious Involvement and Volunteering: Implications for Civil Society." *Sociology of Religion* 62: 315–35.

Becker, Susan. 1981. *The Origins of the Equal Rights Amendment: American Feminism between the Wars.* Westport, CT: Greenwood.

Beckfield, Jason. 2003. "Inequality in the World Polity: The Structure of International Organization." *American Sociological Review* 68: 401–24.

Beckford, J. and J. Richardson. 1983. "A Bibliography of Social Scientific Studies of New Religious Movements." *Social Compass* 30: 111–35.

Beckham, Barry. 1973. "Some Temporal and Spatial Aspects of Interurban Industrial Differentiation." *Social Forces* 51: 462–70.

Beckwith, Karen. 1995. "Women's Movements and Women in Movements: Political Opportunity in Context." Paper presented at the meetings of the American Political Science Association, August 31–September 3, Chicago.

Beebe, Florence. 1942. "Letters from the People: Eliminate Class Discrimination." *Burlington Free Press and Times,* November 2, p. 4.

Beirne, Charles. 1996. *Jesuit Education and Social Change in El Salvador.* New York: Garland.

Beissinger, Mark. 2001. *Nationalist Mobilization and the Collapse of the Soviet State: A Tidal Approach to the Study of Nationalism.* Cambridge: Cambridge University Press.

Bélanger, Sarah, and Maurice Pinard. 1991. "Ethnic Movements and the Competition Model: Some Missing Links." *American Sociological Review* 56: 446–57.

Bell, Daniel. 1963. "The dispossessed—1962." Pp. 1–38 in *The Radical Right,* edited by Daniel Bell. Garden City, New York: Doubleday and Co.

Bell, Derrick 1992 *Faces At the Bottom of the Well.* New York: Basic Books.

Bell, W. and M. T. Force. 1956. "Urban Neighborhood Types and Participation in Formal Associations." *American Sociological Review* 21: 25–34.

Bendix, Reinhard. 1960. *Max Weber: An Intellectual Portrait.* New York: Doubleday.

Benford, Robert D. 1987. "Framing Activity, Meaning, and Social Movement Participation: The Nuclear Disarmament Movement." Ph.D. dissertation, Department of Sociology, University of Texas, Austin.

Benford, Robert D. 1993a. "Frame Disputes Within the Nuclear Disarmament Movement" *Social Forces* 71: 677–701.

———. 1993b. "'You could be the hundredth monkey': Collective action frames and vocabularies of motive within the nuclear disarmament movement." *Sociological Quarterly* 34: 195–216.

———. 1997. "An Insider's Critique of the Social Movement Framing Perspective." *Sociological Inquiry* 67: 409–30.

Benford, Robert, and Scott Hunt. 1992. "Dramaturgy and social movements: The social construction and communication of power." *Sociological Inquiry* 62: 36–55.

Benford, Robert D. and David A. Snow. 2000. "Framing Processes and Social Movements: An Overview and Assessment." *Annual Review of Sociology* 26: 611–39.

Bennet, David H. 1995. *The Party of Fear.* New York: Vintage-Random.

Bennett, Lerone, Jr. 1960. "What sit-downs mean to America." *Ebony* 15: 35–43.

Bennett, W. Lance. 2003. "Communicating Global Activism: Strengths and Vulnerabilities of Networked Politics." *Information, Communication, and Society* 6: 143–68.

Berbrier, Mitch. 1998. "Half the Battle: Cultural Resonance, Framing Processes, and Ethnic Affectations in Contemporary White Separatist Rhetoric." *Social Problems* 45: 432–50.

Berejikian, Jeffrey. 1992. "Revolutionary Collective Action and the Agent-Structure Problem." *American Political Science Review* 86: 647–57.

Berford, Robert D. 1992. "Social Movements." Pp. 1880–87 in *Encyclopedia of Sociology,* edited by E. Borgatta and M. Borgatta. Vol. 4. New York: Macmillan Publishing Company.

Berger, Morroe. 1950. *Equality by Statute.* New York: Columbia University Press.

Berger, Peter. 1969. *A Rumor of Angels.* Garden City, NY: Doubleday.

Berger, Peter L., and Thomas Luckmann, 1966. *The Social Construction of Reality,* Garden City, NY: Doubleday.

Berger, Ronald J. 1995. "Agency, Structure, and Jewish Survival of the Holocaust: A Life History Study." *The Sociological Quarterly* 36: 15–36.

———. 2002. *Fathoming the Holocaust: A Social Problems Approach.* New York: Aldine de Gruyter.

———. Charles S. Green III, and Kristen E. Krieser. 1998. "Altruism Amidst the Holocaust: An Integrated Social Theory." *Perspectives on Social Problems* 10: 267–91.

Bergesen, Albert J., and Omar Lizardo. 2004. "International Terrorism and the World System." *Sociological Theory* 22: 1.

Berghahn, Sabine. 1995. "Gender in the Legal Discourse of Post-Unification Germany: Old and New Lines of Conflict." *Social Politics* 2 (1): 37–50.

Bergmann, Werner, and Rainer Erb. 1994. *Neonazismus und rechte Subkultur.* Berlin: Metropol.

Berk, Richard A. 1974. "A Gaming Approach to Crowd Behavior." *American Sociological Review* 39: 355–73.

Berlet, Chip, and Matthew N. Lyons. 2000. *Right-Wing Populism in America.* New York, The Guilford Press.

Berman, Eli, and David D. Laitin. 2005. "Hard Targets: Theory and Evidence on Suicide Attacks." http:// dss.ucsd.edu/~elib/RatMartyrs.pdf.

Bernstein, Mary. 1995. "Countermovements and the Fate of Two Morality Policies: Consensual Sex Statutes and Lesbian and Gay Rights Ordinances." Paper presented at the meetings of the American Political Science Association, Chicago, August 31–September 3.

———. 1997. "Celebration and Suppression: The Strategic Uses of Identity by the Lesbian and Gay Movement." *American Journal of Sociology* 103: 531–65.

———. 2002. "Identities and Politics: Toward an Historical Understanding of the Lesbian and Gay Movement." *Social Science History* 26: 531–81.

———. 2005. "Identity Politics." *Annual Review of Sociology* 31: 47–74.

Berrigan, Philip. 1996. *Fighting the Lamb's War: Skirmishes with the American Empire*. Monroe, ME: Common Courage Press.

Berrigan, Philip and Elizabeth McAlister. 1989. *The Time's Discipline: The Beatitudes and Nuclear Resistance*. Baltimore, MD: Fortkamp Publishing Company.

Berry, Jeffrey M. 1999. *The New Liberalism*. Washington, DC: Brookings.

Berryman, Philip. 1987. *Religious Roots of Rebellion*. New York: Orbis.

Best, Joel, ed. 1989. *Images of Issues*. New York: Aldine de Gruyter.

Betz, Hans-Georg. 1993. "The New Politics of Resentment." *Comparative Politics* 25: 413–27.

Betz, Hans-Georg. 1994. *Radical Right-Wing Populism in Western Europe*. New York: St. Martin's Press.

Bevan, John. 1981. *El Salvador: Education and Repression*. London: El Salvador Solidarity Committee.

Bevel, Diane Nash. 1978. *Interview*. Chicago. Illinois. December 14.

Bevel, James. 1978. *Interview*. New York, New York. December 27.

Bhagwati, Jagdish. 2000. "Why Nike is on the Right Track." *The Financial Times*. May 1.

Bibby, Reginald W. and Merlin B. Brinkerhoff. 1974. "When Proselytizing Fails: An Organizational Analysis." *Sociological Analysis* 35: 189–200.

Bibliography of Protests Against Gulf War 1, 1991. www.geocities.com/gulfprotestsbib/ index.html

Bill, James A. 1984. "Resurgent Islam in the Persian Gulf." *Foreign Affairs,* Fall: 108–27.

Billig, Michael. 2001. "Humour and Hatred: The Racist Jokes of the Ku Klux Klan." *Discourse and Society*. 267–88.

Billings, Dwight. 1990. "Religion as Opposition: A Gramscian Analysis." *American Journal of Sociology* 96: 1–31.

Billington, Ray Allen. 1963. *The Protestant Crusade, 1800-60*. Gloucester, MA: P. Smith.

———. 1998. "Osama bin Laden World Islamic Front Statement Against Jews and Crusaders." February 23. Retrieved April 19, 2007 (http: //www.fas.org/ irp/world/para/docs/980223-fatwa.htm)

Bin Laden, Osama. 2002. "Osama Bin Laden V. The U.S.: Edicts and Statements." Retrieved April 19, 2007 (http: //www.pbs.org/wgbh/pages/frontline/ shows/binladen/who/edicts.html).

Binford, Leigh. 1999. "Hegemony in the Interior of the Salvadoran Revolution: The ERP in Northern Morazán." *Journal of Latin American Anthropology* 4 (1): 2–45.

Biorcio, Roberto. 1991. "La Lega come Attore Politico: Dal Federalismo al Populismo Regionalista" (The League as a Politieal Actor: From Federalism to Regional Populism). Pp. 34–82 in *La Lega Lombarda* (The Lombard League), edited by R. Mannheimer, R. Biorcio, I. Diamanti, and P. Natale. Milan, Italy: Feltrinelli.

———. 1992. "The Rebirth of Populism in Italy and France." *Telos* 90: 43–56.

———. 1994. "Elezioni a Milano: Nuove Regole e Nuovi Comportamenti Elettorali" (Elections in Milan: New Electoral Rules and New Voting Behaviors). *Polis* 8: 59–80.

Biorcio, Roberto and Mario Diani. 1993. *Primo Rapporto sull'Associazionismo in Lombardia* (First Report on Voluntary Associations in Lombardy). Milan, Italy: Regione Lombardia-Iref.

Bittner, Egon. 1967a. "The Police on Skid-Row: A Study of Peace Keeping." *American Sociological Review* 32: 699–715.

———. 1967b. "Police Discretion in the Emergency Apprehension of Mentally Ill Persons." *Social Problems* 14: 278–92.

Björgo, Tore. 1998. "Entry, Bridge-Burning, and Exit Options: What Happens to Young People Who Join Racist Groups—and Want to Leave." Pp. 231–58 in *Nation and Race: The Developing Euro-American Racist Subculture*, edited by J. Kaplan and T. Bjorgo. Boston, MA: Northeastern University Press.

Björgo, Tore, and Rob Witte, eds. 1993. *Racist Violence in Europe*. New York: St. Martin's Press.

Black, Donald, 1984. "Crime as Social Control." Pp. 1–27 in *Toward a General Theory of Social Control*. Volume 2: *Selected Problems*, edited by Donald Black. New York: Academic Press.

Black, Donald and Albert J. Reiss. 1970. "Police Control of Juveniles." *American Sociological Review* 35: 63–77.

Blalock, Hubert M. 1967. *Toward a Theory of Minority Group Relations*. New York: Wiley.

Blasius, Mark, and Shane Phelan, eds. 1997. *We Are Everywhere: A Historical Source-book of Gay and Lesbian Politics*. New York: Routledge.

Blau, Peter. 1964. *Exchange and Power in Social Life*. New York: Wiley.

Blau, Peter M. 1977. *Inequality and Heterogeneity.* New York: Free Press.

Blee, Kathleen. 1996. "Becoming a racist: Women in Contemporary Ku Klux Klan and Neo-Nazi Groups." *Gender and Society* 10: 680–702.

Blee, Kathleen M., ed. 1998. *No Middle Ground: Women and Radical Protest.* New York: New York University Press.

———. 2002. *Inside Organized Racism: Women in the Hate Movement.* Berkeley: University of California Press.

Bloom, Mia. 2004. *Devising a Theory of Suicide Terror.* ISERP Workshop on Contentious Politics. New York: Columbia University Press.

———. 2005. *The Marketing of Rebellion: Insurgents, Media and Transnational Support.* Cambridge: Cambridge University Press.

Blumberg, Rhoda L. 1984. "Civil Rights: The 1960's Freedom Struggle". Boston, Massachusetts: Twayne.

Blumer, Herbert. [1946, 1951] 1969. "Collective behavior." Pp. 165–220 in *Principles of Sociology*, edited by A. M. Lee. New York: Barnes and Noble.

Bobbio, Luigi. 1990. *Storia di Lotta Continua* (History of Lotta Continua). Milan, Italy: Feltrinelli.

Bolduc, Vincent L. 1980. "Representation and Legitimacy in Neighborhood Organizations: A Case Study." *Journal of Voluntary Action Research* 9: 165–78.

Boles, Janet. 1991. "Form Follows Function: The Evolution of Feminist Strategies." *Annals of the American Academy of Political Science* 515: 38–49.

Boli, John and George M. Thomas. 1997. "World Culture in the World Polity: A Century of International Non-Governmental Organizations." *American Sociological Review* 62: 171–90.

Boli, John, and George M. Thomas. 1999. "INGOs and the Organization of World Culture." In *Constructing World Culture: International Nongovernmental Organizations Since 1865*, edited by J. Boli and G. M. Thomas. Stanford: Stanford University Press, 13–48.

Bollinger, William. 1987. "El Salvador." Pp. 307–88, in *Latin American Labor Organizations,* edited by G. M. Greenfield and S. L. Maram. New York: Greenwood Press.

Bolton, Charles D. 1972. "Alienation and Action: A Study of Peace Group Members." *American Journal of Sociology* 78: 537–61.

Bond, Julian. 1980. *Interview.* Ann Arbor, Michigan. October 19.

Bonder, Gloria. 1983. "The Study of Politics from the Standpoint of Women." *International Social Science Journal* 35: 569–84.

Bondurant, Joan. 1958. *Conquest of Violence: The Gandhian Philosophy of Conflict.* Princeton: Princeton University Press.

Boor, Myron. 1981. "Effects of United States Presidential Elections on Suicide and Other Causes of Death." *American Sociological Review* 46: 616–18.

Booth, John. 1991. "Socioeconomic and Political Roots of National Revolts in Central America." *Latin American Research Review* 26 (1): 33–73.

Bordo, Susan. 1993. "Are Mothers Persons? Reproductive Rights and the Politics of Subject-ivity." Pp. 71–97 in *Unbearable Weight: Feminism, Western Culture, and the Body.* Berkeley and Los Angeles: University of California Press.

Bordogna, Lorenzo, and Giancarlo Provasi. 1979. "Ilmovimento degli scioperi in Italia, 1881–73." In *Il movimento degli sciopero del XX secolo*, edited by Gian Primo Cella. Bologna: Il Mulino: 169–304.

Borzykowski, Tuvis. 1976. *Between Tumbling Walls.* Belt Lohamei Hagettaot and Hakibbutz Hameuchad Publishing House.

Bossi, Umberto and Daniele Vimercati. 1992. *Vento dal Nord: La Mia Lega, la Mia Vita* (Wind From the North: My League, My Life). Milan, Italy: Sperling and Kupfer.

Boswell, Terry, and William Dixon. 1990. "Dependency and Rebellion: A Cross-National Analysis." *American Sociological Review* 55 (4): 540–59.

Boswell, Terry, and Dimitris Stevis. 1997. "Globalization and International Labor Organizing: A World-System Perspective." *Work and Occupations* 24 (3): 288–308.

Boudreau, Vince. 2001. "Contentious Interactions and State Repression: Toward an Interpretive Framework." Paper presented at the Conference on Mobilization and Repression: What We Know and Where We Should Go From Here? June 22, University of Maryland, College Park, MD.

Bourdieu, Pierre. 1977. *Outline of a Theory of Practice,* translated by Richard Nice. New York: Cambridge University Press.

———. 1977. *Outline of a Theory of Practice.* Cambridge: Cambridge University Press.

Bouzas Ortiz, Jose Alfonso. 1999. "La Experiencia Normativa del Trabajo en la Comunidad Economica

Europea." *Memorias: Encuentro Trinacional de Lab-oralistas Democráticos.* México, D.F.: Universidad Nacional Autónoma de México.

Boyte, Harry C. 1980. *The Backyard Revolution.* Philadelphia, PA: Temple University Press.

Branch, Taylor. 1988. *Parting the Waters: America in the King Years, 1954–63.* New York: Simon & Schuster.

Brand, L.W. 1985. "Vergleichendes Resümee." Pp. 306–34 in *Neue soziale Bewegungen in Westeuropa und den USA,* edited by K.W. Brand. Frankfurt: Campus.

Brand, Laurie A. 1998. *Women, the State, and Political Liberalization: Middle Eastern and North African Experiences.* New York: Columbia University Press.

Brandeis, Elizabeth. 1935. "Labor Legislation." Pp. 399–700 in *History of Labor in the United States, 1896–32,* edited by John R. Commons. New York: Macmillan.

Brauer, Carl. 1983. "Women Activists, Southern Conservatives, and the Prohibition of Sex Discrimination in Title VII of the 1964 Civil Rights Act." *Journal of Southern History* 49: 37–56.

Breines, Wini. 1985. "Domineering others in the 1950s: Image and Reality." *Women's Studies International Forum* 8: 601–8.

Breines, Wini. 1988. "Whose New Left?" *Journal of American History* 75 (2): 528–45.

Breines, Wini. 1989. *Community and Organization in the New Left, 1962–1968: The Great Refusal.* New Brunswick, NJ: Rutgers University Press.

Brekhus, Wayne H. 2003. *Peacocks, Chameleons, and Centaurs: Gay Suburbia and the Grammar of Social Identity.* Chicago: University of Chicago Press.

Briët, Martien, Bert Klandermans, and Frederike Kroon. 1987. "How Women Become Involved in the Women's Movement of the Netherlands." In *The Women's Movements of the United States and Western Europe: Consciousness, Political Opportunities, and Public Policy,* edited by Mary Fainsod Katzenstein and Carol McClurg Mueller. Philadelphia: Temple University Press.

Brigham, John. 1988. "Rights, Rage, and Remedy: Forms of Law in Political Discourse." *Studies in American Political Development* 2: 303–16.

Brint, Steven, and Jerome Karabel. 1991. "Institutional Origins and Transformations: The Case of American Community Colleges." In *The New Institutionalism in Organizational Analysis,* edited by Walter W.

Powell and Paul DiMaggio. Chicago: University of Chicago Press, 337–60.

Brockett, Charles. 1993. "A Protest-Cycle Resolution of the Repression/Popular-Protest Paradox." *Social Science History* 7 (3): 457–84.

Brockett, Charles D. 2005. *Political Movements and Violence in Central America.* Cambridge, UK: Cambridge University Press.

Bromley, David A. and Anson D. Shupe, Jr. 1979. "Just a Few Years Seem Like a Lifetime: A Role Theory Approach to Participation in Religious Movements." Pp. 159–85 in *Research in Social Movements, Conflict, and Change,* edited by L. Kriesberg. Greenwich: JAI Press.

Bromley, David A. and Anson D. Shupe. 1983. "Repression and the Decline of Social Movements: The Case of New Religions." Pp. 335–47 in *Social Movements of the Sixties and Seventies,* edited by J. Freeman. New York: Longman.

Bromley, David A. and Anson D. Shupe, Jr. 1986. "Affiliation and Disaffiliation: A Role Theory Interpretation of Joining and Leaving New Religious Movements." Presented at the Annual Meetings of the Association for the Study of Religion, San Antonio. TX.

Bronfrenbrenner, Kate. 1997. "Final Report: The Effects of Plant Closing or Threat of Plant Closing on the Right of Workers to Organize." Dallas, Tex.: Secretariat of the Commission for Labor Cooperation.

Brooks, Thomas R. 1974. *Walls Come Tumbling Down: A History of the Civil Rights Movement, 1940–1970.* Englewood Cliffs, NJ: Prentice-Hall.

Broshears, Ray. 1971. "S.I.R., the Society for Individual Rights, Conducts Fantastic 'Work-In' at Federal Building." *Gay Activists Alliance Lifeline:* 1.

Brosius, Hans-Bernd, and Frank Esser. 1995. *Eskalation durch Berichterstattung? Massenmedien und fremdenfeindliche Gewalt.* Opladen: Westdeutscher Verlag.

Brown, Cliff, and Terry Boswell. 1995. "Strikebreaking or Solidarity in the Great Steel Strike of 1919: A Split Labor Market, Game Theoretic, and QCA Analysis." *American Journal of Sociology* 100: 1479–1519.

Brown, Lawrence D., and Jonathan A. Fox. 1998. "Accountability Within Transnational Coalitions." In *The Struggle for Accountability: The World Bank,*

NGOs, and Grassroots Movements, edited by J. A. Fox and L. D. Brown. Cambridge: MIT Press, 439–84.

Brown, Roger. 1965. *Social Psychology.* New York: Free Press.

Browning, Rufus, Dale Marshall, and David Tabb. 1984. *Protest Is Not Enough: The Struggle of Blacks and Hispanics for Equality in Urban Politics.* Berkeley, CA: University of California Press.

Brownmiller, Susan. 1975. *Against Our Will: Men, Women and Rape.* New York: Simon & Schuster.

Brubaker. E. R. 1975. "Free Ride, Free Revolution, or Golden Rule?" *Journal of Law and Economics* 18: 147–61.

Bruner, Jerome. 1986. *Actual Minds, Possible Worlds.* Cambridge, Massachusetts: Harvard University Press.

———. 1991. "The narrative construction of reality." *Critical Inquiry* 18: 1–21.

Brusco, Elizabeth. 1995. *The Reformation of Machismo.* Austin: University of Texas Press.

Bryan, Marguente. 1979. "Social Psychology of Riot Participation." *Research in Race and Ethnic Relations* 1: 169–87.

Brysk, Alison. 1996. "Turning Weakness into Strength: The Internationalization of Indian Rights." *Latin American Perspectives* 23: 38–58.

———. 2000. *From Tribal Village to Global Village: Indigenous Peoples' Struggles in Latin America.* Stanford: Stanford University Press.

Bucher, Rue. 1957. "Blame and Hostility in Disasters." *American Journal of Sociology* 62: 467–475.

Buder, Leonard. 1968. "School Clashes Draw Warning of a New Strike." *New York Times,* October 2, p. 1.

Buechler, Steven M. 1986. *The Transformation of the Woman Suffrage Movement: The Case of Illinois, 1850-1920.* New Brunswick, NJ: Rutgers University Press.

———. 1990. *Women's Movements in the United States.* New Brunswick, NJ: Rutgers University Press.

———. 1993. "Beyond Resource Mobilization: Emerging Trends in Social Movement Theory." *Sociological Quarterly* 34: 217–35.

———. 2000. *Social Movements in Advanced Capitalism: The Political Economy and Cultural Construction of Social Activism.* New York: Oxford University Press.

Buechler, Steven M. 2004. "The Strange Career of Strain and Breakdown Theories of Collective Action."

Pp. 47–66 in *The Blackwell Companion to Social Movements,* edited by David A. Snow, Sarah A. Soule, and Hanspeter Kreisi. Malden, MA: Blackwell.

Buerklin, Wilhelm. 1987. "Why Study Political Cycles: An Introduction." *European Journal of Political Research* 15: 131–43.

Bull, Chris, and John Gallagher. 1996. *Perfect Enemies: The Religious Right, the Gay Movement, and the Politics of the 1990s.* New York: Crown.

Bullard, Robert. 1990. *Dumping in Dixie.* Boulder, CO: Westview.

Bullock, Henry Allen. 1970. "Education: parallel inequality." Pp. 269–79 in *The Segregation Era 1863-1954,* edited by Allen Weinstein and Frank Otto Gatell. New York: Oxford University Press.

Bullock, Henry Allen. 1971. "Urbanism and Race Relations." Pp. 207–29 in *The Urban South,* edited by Rupert B. Vance and Nicholas J. Demerath. Freeport, NY: Books for Libraries Press.

Bumiller, Kristen. 1988. *The Civil Rights Society: The Social Construction of Victims.* Baltimore: Johns Hopkins University Press.

Bunce, Valerie. 1999. *Subversive Institutions: The Design and the Destruction of Socialism and the State.* Cambridge: Cambridge University Press.

Bunis, William K., Angela Yancik, and David A. Snow. 1996. "The Cultural Patterning of Sympathy toward the Homeless and Other Victims of Misfortune." *Social Problems* 43: 301–17.

Bunster Burotto, Ximena. 1986. "Surviving Beyond Fear: Women and Torture in Latin America." Pp. 297–325 in *Women and Change in Latin America,* edited by June Nash and Helen I. Safa. South Hadley, MA: Bergin and Garvey.

Bunster Burotto, Ximena. 1988. "Watch Out for The Little Nazi Man that All of Us Have Inside: The Mobilization and Demobilization of Women in Militarized Chile." *Women's Studies International Forum* 11: 485–91.

Burawoy, Michael. 1979. *Manufacturing Consent: Changes in the Labor Process under Monopoly Capitalism.* Chicago: University of Chicago Press.

Burawoy, Michael. 1991. *Ethnography Unbound: Power and Resistance in the Modern Metropolis.* Berkeley, CA: University of California Press.

Burdick, John. 1993. *Looking for God in Brazil.* Berkeley and Los Angeles: University of California Press.

Bureau of Alcohol, Tobacco, and Firearms. 1989. *State Laws and Published Ordinances—Firearms. 19th ed.* Washington, DC: Department of the Treasury.

Bureau of Labor Statistics. 2002. "Major Work Stoppages in 2001." News release, February 17.

Burek, Deborah M., 1994. *Encyclopedia of Associations.* Detroit, MI: Gale Research Inc.

Burgess, Ernest W. 1925. "The Growth of the City: An Introduction to a Research Project." Pp. 47–62 in *The City,* edited by Robert E. Park, Ernest W. Burgess, and Roderick D. McKenzie. Chicago: University of Chicago Press.

Burgess, M. Elaine. 1965. "Race Relations and Social Change." Pp. 337–58 in *The South in Continuity and Change,* edited by John C. McKinney and Edgar T. Thompson. Durham, NC: Duke University Press.

Burghart. Devon. 1996. "Cyberh@te: A Reappraisal." *Dignity Report* 3: 12–16.

Burke, Kenneth. 1989: *On Symbols and Society,* translated by Joseph R. Gusfield. Chicago: University of Chicago Press.

Burks, Edward C. 1968. "Protest Mars Start of Final City Hall Budget Hearing." *New York Times,* May 28, p. 13.

Burlington Free Press and Times. 1941. "Air Bill Permitting Jury Service for Women." February 6, p. 3.

Burnham, Walter Dean. 1974. "Theory and Voting Research: Some Reflections on Converse's 'Change in the American Electorate.'" *American Political Science Review* 68: 1002–23.

——. 1992. "Partisan Division of American State Governments, 1834–1985." [Computer File] Ann Arbor, MI: Inter-university Consortium for Political and Social Research.

Burns, John F. 2000. "In Islam's State, an Islamic Cry for Change." *New York Times,* January 30: Sec 4, 1 and 4.

Burns, Tom. 1992. *Erving Coffman.* New York: Routledge.

Burris, Val. Emory Smith, and Ann Strahm. 2000. "White Supremacist Networks on the Internet." *Sociological Focus* 33: 215–34.

Burstein, Paul. 1979. "Public Opinion, Demonstrations, and the Passage of Anti-Discrimination Legislation." *Public Opinion Quarterly* 43(2): 157–62.

——. 1985. *Discrimination, Jobs, and Politics.* Chicago, IL: University of Chicago Press.

——. 1991. "Legal Mobilization as a Social Movement Tactic: The Struggle for Equal Employment Opportunity." *American Journal of Sociology* 96: 1201–25.

——. 1999. "Social Movements and Public Policy." p. 3–21 in *How Social Movements Matter,* edited by Marco Giugni, Doug McAdam, and Charles Tilly. Minneapolis, MN: University of Minnesota Press.

Burstein, Paul, Rachel Einwohner, and Jocellyn Hollander. 1995. "The Success of Social Movements: A Bargaining Perspective." Pp. 275–95 in *The Politics of Social Protest,* edited by J. C. Jenkins and B. Klandermans. Minneapolis, MN: University of Minnesota Press.

Burstein, Paul and April Linton. 2002. "The Impact of Political Parties, Interest Groups, and Social Movement Organizations on Public Policy: Some Recent Evidence and Theoretical Concerns." *Social Forces* 81: 380–408.

Burstein, Paul, and Kathleen Monaghan. 1986. "Equal Employment Opportunity and the Mobilization of Law." *Law and Society Review* 20: 355–88.

Burt, Martha R. 1992. *Over the Edge: The Growth of Homelessness in the 1980s.* New York: Russell Sage Foundation.

Burt, Ronald S. 1986. "Comment." Pp. 105–7 in *Approaches to Social Theory,* edited by Siegwart Lindenberg, James S. Coleman, and Stefan Nowak. New York: Russell Sage.

Burt, Ronald. 1992. *Structural Holes: The Social Structure of Competition.* Cambridge, Mass.: Harvard University Press.

Bush, George W. 2002. The National Security of the United States, September 2002. Washington, DC: Office of the President.

Business and Professional Women's Club of Denver. 1943. Scrapbook, Flyer of the Citizens' Joint Legislative Committee. Denver Public Library.

Bustamante, Jorge A. 1972. "The 'Wetback' as Deviant: An Application of Labeling Theory." *American Journal of Sociology* 4: 706–18.

Buthe, Tim. 2002. "Taking Temporality Seriously: Modeling History and the Use of Narratives as Evidence." *American Political Science Review* 96: 481–93.

Button, James W. 1978. *Black Violence.* Princeton, NJ: Princeton University Press.

Button, James. 1989. *Blacks and Social Change.* Princeton, N.J.: Princeton University Press.

Cabarrús, Carlos Rafael. 1983. *Génesis de una revolución.* Mexico City: La Casa Chata.

Cable, Sherry. 1984. "Professionalization in Social Movement Organization: A Case Study of

Pennsylvanians for Biblical Morality." *Sociological Focus* 17: 287–304.

Cáceres Prendes, Jorge. 1989. "Political Radicalization and Popular Pastoral Practices in El Salvador, 1969–1985." Pp. 103–48 in *The Progressive Church in Latin America,* edited by S. Mainwaring and A. Wilde. Notre Dame, Ind.: University of Notre Dame Press.

CACSW (Citizens' Advisory Council on the Status of Women). N.d. "Women and the Equal Employment Provisions of the Civil Rights Act" RG 220, box 58, folder "ICSW Meeting Summary Feb. 23, 1965." National Archives, College Park, Md.

Cain, Patricia A. 1993. "Litigating for Lesbian and Gay Rights: A Legal History." *Virginia Law Review* 79: 1551–1641.

Calavita, Kitty. 2001. "Blue Jeans, Rape, and the 'De-Constitutive' Power of Law." *Law and Society Review* 35: 89–115.

Caldicott, Helen. 1986. *Missile Envy: The Arms Race and Nuclear War.* Toronto: Bantam.

Calhoun, Craig. 1982. *The Question of Class Struggle: Social Foundations of Popular Radicalism during the Industrial Revolution.* Chicago: University of Chicago Press.

Calhoun, Craig J. 1991. "The Problem of Identity in Collective Action." Pp. 51–75 in *Macro-Micro Linkages in Sociology,* edited by Joan Huber. Newbury Park, Calif.: Sage.

Calhoun, Charles. 1993. "Nationalism and Identity." *Annual Review of Sociology* 19: 211–39.

———. 1994a. *Neither Gods nor Emperors: Students and the Struggle for Democracy in China.* Berkeley and Los Angeles: University of California Press.

———. 1994b. "Social Theory and the Politics of Identity." Pp. 9–36 in *Social Theory and the Politics of Identity,* edited by Craig Calhoun. Cambridge, Mass.: Blackwell.

———. 1995. "'New Social Movements' of the Early Nineteenth Century." Pp. 173–215 in *Repertoires and Cycles of Collective Action,* edited by Mark Traugott. Durham, N.C.: Duke University Press.

Cameron, A. Colin, and Pravin Triviedi. 1998. *Regression Analysis of Count Data.* New York: Cambridge University Press.

Canadian Steelworkers. N.d. "Steelworkers Humanity Fund's Programme."

Cantor, Daniel, and Juliet Schor. 1987. *Tunnel Vision: Labor, the World Economy, and Central America.* Boston: South End Press.

Cantril, Hadley and Mildred Strunk. 1951. *Public Opinion, 1935–1946.* Princeton, NJ: Princeton University Press.

Čapek, Stella. 1993. "The 'Environmental Justice' Frame: A Conceptual Discussion and an Application." *Social Problems* 40 (1): 5–24.

Caplan, Nathan S. and Jeffrey M. Paige. 1968. "A Study of Ghetto Rioters." *Scientific American* 219: 15–20.

Carden, Maren Lockwood. 1974. *The New Feminist Movement.* New York: Russell Sage.

Cardenal, Rodolfo. 1987. *Historia de una esperanza: Vida de Rutilio Grande.* San Salvador: UCA Editores.

Carey, Gordon. 1959. *Report to CORE National Council.* February 21–22.

———. 1978. *Interview. Soul City,* North Carolina. November 18 (Follow-up telephone interview November 1, 1979).

Carley, Michael. 1997. "Defining Forms of Successful State Repression of Social Movement Organizations: A Case Study of the FBI's COINTELPRO and the American Indian Movement." *Research in Social Movements, Conflicts and Change* 20: 151–76.

Carlson, Oliver and Ernest S. Bates. 1936. *Hearst, Lord of San Simeon.* New York: Viking Press.

Carmen, Arlene and Howard Moody. 1973. *Abortion Counseling and Social Change.* Valley Forge, PA: Judson Press.

Carpio, Salvador Cayetano. 1980. *La huelga general obrera de Abril.* San Salvador: Editorial Farabundo Marti.

———. 1982. *An Interview with Salvador Cayetano Carpio, "Martial" of the General Command of the FMLN.* San Francisco: Solidarity Publications.

Carr, Barry 1999. "Globalization from Below: Labour Internationalism under NAFTA." *International Social Science Journal* 51 (March): 49–59.

Carr, David. 1997. "Narrative and the real world: An argument for continuity." In *Memory, Identity, Community: The Idea of Narrative in the Human Sciences,* edited by Lewis P. Hinchman and Sandra K. Hinchman, 7–25. Albany: State University of New York.

Carr, Robert. 1994. "Crossing the First World/ Third World Divides: Testimonial, Transnational

Feminisms, and the Postmodern Condition." Pp. 153–72 in *Scattered Hegemonies: Postmodernity and Transnational Feminist Practices,* edited by Inderpal Grewal and Caren Kaplan. Minneapolis: University of Minnesota Press.

Carroll, Glenn R., and Michael T. Hannan. 2000. *The Demography of Corporations and Industries.* Princeton, N.J.: Princeton University Press.

Carruthers, Bruce G., and Sarah Babb. 1996. "The Color of Money and the Nature of Value: Greenbacks and Gold in Postbellum America." *American Journal of Sociology* 101: 1556–91.

Carson, Clayborne. 1981. *In Struggle: SNCC and the Black Awakening of the 1960's.* Cambridge, MA: Harvard University Press.

Carson Claybome, ed. 1990. *The Student Voice.* Westport, Conn.: Meckler.

Carter, April. 1992. *Peace Movements: International Protest and World Politics since 1945.* London, New York: Longman.

Cartocci, Roberto. 1994. *Fra Lega e Chiesa* (Between League and Church). Bologna, Italy: il Mulino.

Case, F. Duncan. 1981. "Dormitory Architecture Influences." *Environment and Behavior* 13: 23–41.

Castellanos, Juan Mario. 2001. *El Salvador, 1930–1960: Anlecedentes históricos de la guerra civil.* San Salvador: Concultura.

Castells, Manuel. 1978. *City, Class, and Power.* New York: St. Martin's Press.

———. 1997. *The Power of Identity.* Oxford, UK: Blackwell Publishers.

Cattarinich, Xavier Germain Michel. 1998. "The challenge of militant right-wing extremism to contemporary social movement theory." Master's Thesis. University of Alberta, Canada.

Center for New Community. No date. "Soundtracks to the White Revolution: White Supremacists Assaults on Youth Music Subcultures." Retrieved February 13, 2003 (www.turnitdown.com).

Central Committee of the Chinese Communist Party. [1966] 1972. "Decision Concerning the Great Proletarian Cultural Revolution." Pp. 403–16 in *Essential Works of Chinese Communism,* 2d ed., edited by W. Chai. New York: Bantam Books.

Chabot, Sean. 2002. "Transnational Diffusion and the African-American Reinvention of the Gandhian Repertoire." In *Globalization and Resistance:* *Transnational Dimensions of Social Movements,* edited by Jackie Smith and Hank Johnston. Lanham, MD: Rowman and Littlefield.

———. 2003. "Crossing the Great Divide: The Gandhian Repertoire's Transnational Diffusion to the American Civil Rights Movement." Ph. D. diss., University of Amsterdam.

Chafe, William H. 1972. *The American Woman: Her Changing Social, Economic, and Political Roles, 1920–1970.* New York: Oxford University Press.

———. 1980. Civilities and Civil Rights: Greensboro, North Carolina, and the Black Struggle for Freedom. New York: Oxford University Press.

Chafetz, Janet Saltzman and Anthony Gary Dworkin. 1986. *Female Revolt: Women's Movements in World and Historical Perspective.* Totowa, NJ: Rowan and Allanheld.

Chalmers, David. 1987. *Hooded Americanism: The History of the Ku Klux Klan.* Durham, NC: Duke University Press.

Chan, Anita, Richard Madsen, and Jonathan Unger, 1984. *Chen Village: The Recent History of a Peasant Community in Mao's China.* Berkeley, CA: University of California Press.

Chan, Anita, Stanley Rosen, and Jonathan Unger. 1980. "Students and Class Warfare: The Roots of the Red Guard Conflict in Guangzhou." *The China Quarterly* 3: 397–446.

Chatfield, Charles. 1996. "The Catholic Worker in the United States Peace Tradition." Pp. 1–14 in *American Catholic Pacifism,* edited by A. Klejment and N. Roberts. Westport, CT: Praeger.

Chauncey, George. 1994. *Gay New York: Gender, Urban Culture, and the Making of the Gay Male World, 1890–1940.* New York: Basic.

Chavez, Cesar. 1966. "The Organizer's Tale." Pp. 138–47 in *American Labor Radicalism,* edited by Staughton Lynd. New York: Wiley.

Chestnut, Andrew R. 1997. *Born Again in Brazil: The Evangelical Boom and the Pathogens of Poverty.* New Brunswick, N.J.: Rutgers University Press.

Chow, Tse-tsung. 1967. *The May Fourth Movement: Intellectual Revolution in Modern China.* Stanford, Calif.: Stanford University Press.

Chuchryk, Patricia. 1989. "Subversive mothers: The Women's Opposition to the Military Regime in Chile." Pp. 130–51 in *Women, the State, and Development,* edited by Sue Ellen Chariton, Jana Everett, and Kathleen Staudt. Albany: SUNY Press.

Chuchryk, Patricia. 1991. "Feminist Anti-Authoritarian politics: The Role of Women's Organizations in the Chilean Transition to Democracy." Pp. 149–84 in *The Women's Movement in Latin America: Feminism and the Transition to Democracy,* edited by Jane Jaquette. Boulder, CO: Westview Press.

Churchill, Ward. 1994. "The Bloody Wake of Alcatraz: Political Repression of the American Indian Movement during the 1970s." *American Indian Culture and Research Journal* 18: 253–300.

Cienfuegos, Fermán. 1993. *Veredas de audacia.* San Salvador: Arcoiris.

Citizens' Councils of America. 1956. "Mississippi Citizens' Council Map." *The Citizens' Council,* June, p. 6.

Clark, B. D. 1972. "Iran: Changing Population Patterns." Pp. 68–96 in *Populations of the Middle East and North Africa: A Geographical Approach,* edited by J. L. Clark and W. B. Fisher. London: University of London Press.

Clawson, Dan, and Mary Clawson. 1999. "What Has Happened to the U.S. Labor Movement? Union Decline and Renewal." *Annual Review of Sociology* 25: 95–119.

Cleghorn, Reese 1963. "Epilogue in Albany: Were the Mass Marches Worthwhile?" *The New Republic* (July 20): 15–18.

———. 1970. "Crowned with Crises." Pp. 113–27 in *Martin Luther King, Jr.: A Profile,* edited by C. Eric Lincoln. New York: Hill & Wang.

Clemens, Elisabeth S. 1993. "Organizational Repertoires and Institutional Change: Women's Groups and the Transformation of U.S. Politics." *American Journal of Sociology* 98 (4): 755–98.

———. 1997. *The People's Lobby: Organizational Innovation and the Rise of Interest Group Politics in the United States, 1890-1925.* Chicago: University of Chicago Press.

———. 1999. "Continuity and Coherence: Periodization and the Problem of Institutional Change." In *Social Time and Social Change: Perspectives on Sociology and History,* edited by F. Engelstad and R. Kalleberg. Oslo: Scandinavian University Press, 62–83.

Clemens, Elisabeth S., and James Cook. 1999. "Politics and Institutionalism: Explaining Durability and Change." *Annual Review of Sociology* 25: 441–66.

Clemens, Elisabeth and Debra Minkoff. 2004. "Beyond the Iron Law: Rethinking the Place of Organizations in Social Movement Research." Pp. 157–70 in *The Blackwell Companion to Social Movements,* edited by D. Snow, S. Soule, and H. Kriesi. Malden, MA: Blackwell Publishing.

Clift, Virgil A. 1966. "Educating the American Negro." Pp. 360–95 in *The American Negro Reference Book,* edited by John P. Davis. Englewood Cliffs, N.J: Prentice-Hall.

Cloward, Richard A. and Francis Fox Piven. 1984. "Disruption and Organization: A Rejoinder." *Theory and Society* 13: 587–99.

CNN. 2006a. "Bush: A War Unlike Any We Have Fought Before: Transcript of Presidential Speech Delivered on September 11, 2006." New York, NY: Cable News Network. Retrieved on October 22 (http: //www. cnn.com/2006/POLITICS/09/11/bush.transcript/index.html)

CNN. 2006b. "John Roberts interview with Doron Spielman conducted on July 24 2006." New York, NY, Retrieved on July 25, 2006 (http: //www.cnn.com/2006/WORLD/meast/07/25/mideast.main/index.html)

Cobb, James. 1990. " 'Somebody Done Nailed Us on the Cross': Federal Farm and Welfare Policy and the Civil Rights Movement in the Mississippi Delta." *Journal of American History* 77: 912–36.

Cochavi, Yehoyakim. 1995. "The Motif of 'Honor' in the Call to Rebellion in the Ghetto," Pp. 245–54 in *Zionist Youth Movements During the Shoah,* edited by A. Cohen and Y. Cochavi. New York: Peter Lang.

Cohen, Jean L. 1985. "Strategy or Identity. New Theoretical Paradigms and Contemporary Social Movements." *Social Research* 52: 663–716.

Cohen, Larry, and Steve Early. 1998. "Defending Workers' Rights in the New Global Economy: The CWA Experience." In *Which Direction for Organized Labor? Essays on Organizing, Outreach, and Internal Transformations,* edited by Bruce Nissen. Detroit, Mich.: Wayne State University Press.

Cohen, Ronald L., and Duane F. Alwin. 1993. "Bennington Women of the 1930s: Political Attitudes over the Life Course." Pp. 117–39 in *Women's Lives through Time: Educated American Women of the 20th Century,* edited by Kathleen Day Hulbert and Diane T. Schuster. San Francisco: Jossey-Bass.

Cohn, Jules. 1970. "Is Business Meeting the Challenge of Urban Affairs?" *Harvard Business Review* 48(2): 68–82.

Cohn, Norman. 1961. *The Pursuit of the Millennium.* New York: Harper & Row.

Colby, David. 1985. "Black Power, White Resistance, and Public Policy: Political Power and Poverty Program Grants in Mississippi." *Journal of Politics* 47: 579–95.

Coleman, James S. 1971. *Community Conflict.* New York: Free Press.

Coleman, James S., Elihu Katz, and Herbert Menzel 1957. "The diffusion of an innovation among physicians." Sociometry 20: 253–70.

Coleman, Thomas F. 1977. "Report to Oregon Legislature." *SexuaLawReporter* 4: 41.

Colker, Ruth. 1992. *Abortion and Dialogue: Pro-Choice, Pro-Life and American Law.* Bloomington: Indiana University Press.

Collections Claybome Carson Collection, Martin Luther King, Jr. Papers Project, Stanford University. Stanford, California.

Collections Forman Collection of Audio Tapes. Martin Luther King, Jr. Center for Nonviolent Social Change, Atlanta.

Collections Student Nonviolent Coordinating Committee Papers Microfilm, 1959–72. 1982. Sanford, N.C.: Microfilming Corporation of America.

Collins, Patricia Hill. 1991. *Black Feminist Thought: Knowledge, Consciousness, and the Politics of Empowerment.* New York: Routledge.

Colorado League of Women Voters Collection. 1939, April 7. NLWV's "Women on Juries" Pamphlet. Box 36, Folder 7. University of Colorado, Boulder.

———. 1944, August. "Radio Script: Jury Service by Women." Box 39, Folder 7. University of Colorado, Boulder.

Comaroff, Jean, and John L. Comaroff. 1991. *Of Revelation and Revolution: Chirstianity, Colonialism, and Consciousness in South Africa.* Chicago: University of Chicago Press.

Commission for Labor Cooperation. 2000. *Labor Relations Law in North America.* Washington, D.C.: Secretariat of the Commission for Labor Cooperation.

Commons, John R., et al. *History of Labor in the United States,* Vol. II. New York: A. M. Kelley, 1966.

Compa, Lance. 1999. "The North American Agreement on Labor Cooperation and International Labor Solidarity." *Memorias: Encuentro Trinacional de Laboralistas Democráticos.* México, D.F.: Universidad Nacional Autónoma de México.

Condit, Celeste Michelle. 1990. *Decoding Abortion Rhetoric: Communicating Social Change.* Urbana: University of Illinois Press.

Confalonieri, Maria Antonietta. 1990. "S'Avanza Uno Strano Guerriero" (A Strange Warrior Is Coming Forward). *Ulisse* 3: 3–7.

Congressional Quarterly. 1947–78. *Congressional Quarterly Almanac.* Washington, D.C.: Congressional Quarterly Press.

Connell, R.W. 1992. "A Very Straight Gay: Masculinity, Homosexual Experience, and Gender." *American Sociological Review* 57: 735–51.

Constas, Helen, 1961. "The U.S.S.R.—From Charismatic Sect to Bureaucratic Society." *Administrative Science Quarterly* 6: 282–98.

Converse, Phillip E. 1964. The Nature of Belief Systems in Mass Publics." Pp. 206–61 in *Ideology and Discontent,* edited by David Apter. New York: Free Press.

Cook, Karen, and Joel Whitmeyer. 1992. "Two Approaches to Social Structure: Exchange Theory and Network Analysis." *Annual Review of Sociology* 18: 109–27.

Cook, Maria Lorena. 1996. *Organizing Dissent: Unions, the State, and the Democratic Teachers' Movement in Mexico.* University Park: Pennsylvania State University Press.

Cook, Maria Lorena. 1997. "Regional Integration and Transnational Politics: Popular Sector Strategies in the NAFTA Era." In *The New Politics of Inequality in Latin America,* edited by Douglas A. Chalmers et al. Oxford: Oxford University Press.

Copelon, Rhonda. 1990a. "A Crime Not Fit to Be Named: Sex, Lies, and the Constitution." Pp. 177–194 *The Politics of Law: A Progressive Critique,* rev. ed. Edited by David Kairys. New York: Pantheon Books.

———. 1990b. "From Privacy to Autonomy: The Conditions for Sexual and Reproductive Freedom." Pp. 27–43 in *From Abortion to Reproductive Freedom,* edited by Marlene Fried. Boston: South End Press.

Corbetta, Piergiorgio. 1993. "La Lega e lo Sfaldamento del Sistema" (The League and the System Breakdown). *Polis* 7: 229–52.

Corkell, Genevieve. 1930. "The Feminist Demand for Absolute Civic Equality." *The Federation News,* August 30, p. 84.

Cornell, Stephen. 1996. "Ethnicity as narrative." *Unpublished paper*. Department of Sociology, University of California, San Diego.

Cornfield, Daniel B. 1985. "Economic Segmentation and Expression of Labor Unrest: Striking versus Quitting in the Manufacturing Sector." *Social Science Quarterly* 66: 247–65.

———. 1989. *Becoming a Mighty Voice: Conflict and Change in the United Furniture Workers of America.* New York: Russell Sage.

Cornfield, Daniel B., and Bill Fletcher. 1998. "Institutional Constraints on Social Movement 'Frame Extension': Shifts in the Legislative Agenda of the American Federation of Labor, 1881–1955." *Social Forces* 76: 1305–21.

———. 2001. "The U.S. Labor Movement: Toward a Sociology of Labor Revitalization." Pp. 61–82 in *Sourcebook of Labor Markets: Evolving Structures and Processes,* edited by Ivar Berg and Arne L. Kalleberg. New York: Plenum.

Cornfield, Daniel B., and Hyunhee Kim. 1994. "Socioeconomic Status and Unionization Attitudes in the United States." *Social Forces* 73: 521–32.

Coroi, Gustavo. 2002. *Hitler's Ghettos: Voices from a Beleaguered Society, 1939–1944.* London: Arnold.

Cortright, David. 2004. *A Peaceful Superpower: The Movement Against War in Iraq.* Goshen, IN: Fourth Freedom Foundation.

Cortright, David and Ron Pagnucco. 1997. "Transnational Activism in the Nuclear Weapons Freeze Campaign." Pp. 81–94 in *Coalitions and Political Movements: The Lessons of the Nuclear Freeze,* Thomas R. Rochon and David S. Meyer, eds. Boulder, CO: Lynne-Rienner.

Coser, Lewis A. 1967. "Greedy Organizations. *Archives Europeenes de Sociologie* 8: 196–215.

Coser, Lewis. 1974. *Greedy Institutions.* New York: Free Press.

Costain, Anne. 1981. "Representing Women." *Western Political Quarterly* 34: 100–113.

Costain, Anne N. 1988. "Women's Claims as a Special Interest." Pp. 150–72 in *The Politics of the Gender Gap,* edited by Carol M. Mueller. Beverly Hills: Sage.

Costain, Anne W. 1992. *Inviting Women's Rebellion: A Political Process Interpretation of the Women's Movement.* Baltimore: Johns Hopkins Press.

Cott, Nancy F. 1987. *The Grounding of Modern Feminism.* New Haven, CT: Yale University Press.

County and City Extra. 1992. Lanham, MD: Bernan Press.

———. 1994. Lanham, MD: Bernan Press.

———. 1995. Lanham, MD: Bernan Press.

———. 1996. Lanham, MD: Bernan Press.

Couto, Richard A. 1993. "Narrative, Free Space, and Political Leadership in Social Movements." *Journal of Politics* 55: 57–79.

Cowart, Andrew. 1969. "Anti-Poverty Expenditures in the American States." *Midwest Journal of Political Science* 13: 219–36.

Cox, Elizabeth M. 1996. *Women State and Territorial Legislators, 1895–1995: A State-by-State Analysis, with Rosters of 6,000 Women.* Jefferson, NC: McFarland.

Coy, Patrick G., and Lynne M. Woehrle. 1996. "Constructing Identity and Oppositional Knowledge: The Framing Practices of Peace Movement Organizations during the Persian Gulf War." *Sociological Spectrum* 16 (3): 287–327.

Craig, Steven. 1979. "Efficacy, Trust and Political Behavior." *American Politics Quarterly* 7(2): 225–39.

Cramer, J. 1989. *De Groene Golf. Geschiedenisen Toekomst van de Milieubeweging.* Utrecht: Jan van Arkel.

Craven, Paul and Barry Wellman. 1974a. "The Network City." Pp. 57–88 in *The Community: Approaches and Applications,* edited by M. Effrat. New York: Free Press.

———. 1974b. "Social Movements: An Analytical Exploration of Organizational Forms." *Social Problems* 21: 356–70.

Crawford, Robert, and Devin Burghart. 1997. "Guns and gavels: Common law courts, militias and white supremacy." in *The Second Revolution: States Rights, Sovereignty, and Power of the County,* edited by Eric Ward. Seattle: Peanut Butter Publishing.

Cress, Daniel, J. Miller McPherson, and Thomas Rotolo. 1997. "Competition and Commitment in Voluntary Memberships: The Paradox of Persistence and Participation." *Sociological Perspectives* 40: 61–79.

Cress, Daniel M., and David A. Snow. 1996. "Mobilization on the Margins: Resources. Benefactors, and the Viability of Homeless SMOs." *American Sociological Review* 61: 1089–109.

Cress, Daniel M. and David A. Snow. 2000. "The Outcomes of Homeless Mobilization: The Influence of Organization, Disruption, Political Mediation, and Framing." *American Journal of Sociology* 105: 1063–1104.

Crosby, Faye. 1982. *Relative Deprivation and the Working Woman*. New York: Oxford University Press.

Cross, Ira B. 1935. *A History of the Labor Movement in California*. Berkeley, CA: University of California Press.

Cruikshank, Margaret. 1992. *The Gay and Lesbian Liberation Movement*. Routledge: New York.

Csordas, Thomas. 1994. *The Sacred Self: A Cultural Phenomenology of Charismatic Healing*. Berkeley and Los Angeles: University of California Press.

Cullen, Pauline. 2003. "European NGOs and EU-Level Mobilization for Social Rights." Ph.D. Dissertation, State University of New York at Stony Brook.

Cuminetti, Mario. 1983. *Il Dissenso Cattolico in Italia* (Catholic Dissenters in Italy). Milan, Italy: Rizzoli.

Cunnigen, Donald. 1987. "Men and Women of Goodwill: Mississippi's White Liberals." Ph.D. dissertation, Department of Sociology, Harvard University, Cambridge, MA.

Cunningham, David. 2003. "The Patterning of Repression: FBI Counterintelligence and the New Left." *Social Forces*.

Curtis, Russell L., and Louis A. Zurcher, Jr. 1973. "Stable Resources of Protest Movement: The Multiorganizational Field." *Social Forces* 52: 53–60.

Cutler, Marvin. 1956. *Homosexuals Today: A Handbook of Organizations and Publications*. Los Angeles: ONE.

D'Emilio, John. 1983. *Sexual Politics, Sexual Communities: The Making of a Homosexual Minority in the United States, 1940–1970*. Chicago: University of Chicago Press.

———. 1992a. [1972]. "Foreword." In *Out of the Closest: Voices of Gay Liberation*, edited by Karla Jay and Allen Young. New York and London: New York University Press, xi–xxix.

———. 1992b. *Making Trouble: Essays on Gay History, Politics, and the University*. New York: Routledge.

Dalfiume, Richard M. 1970. "Stirrings of Revolt." Pp. 235–47 in *The Segregation Era, 1863–1954*, edited by Allen Weinstein and Frank Otto Gatell. New York: Oxford University Press.

Dalton, Russell J. 1994. *The Green Rainbow*. New Haven, CT: Yale University Press.

Dalton, Russell J. and Manfred Kuechler, eds. 1990. *Challenging the Political Order*. Cambridge, England: Polity Press.

Daly, Herman. 2002. "Globalization Versus Internationalization, and Four Economic Arguments for Why Internationalization Is a Better Model for World Community." Paper presented at the Conference on Globalization and Social Change, College Park, MD.

Damgaard, Bodil. 1999a. "Cooperación Laboral Transnacional en América del Norte a Finales de los Noventa." *El Cotidiano* 94 (March–April): 23–37.

———. 1999b. "ACLAN: Experiencias y Tendencias Después de Cinco Años." *Memorias: Encuentro Trinacional de Laboralistas Democráticos*. México, D.F.: Universidad Nacional Autónoma de México.

Danigelis, Nicholas L. 1978. "Black Political Participation in the United States: Some Recent Evidence." *American Sociological Review* 43: 756–71.

Danitz, Tiffany, and Warren P. Strobel. 2001. "Networking Dissent: Cyber Activists Use the Internet to Promote Democracy in Burma." In *The Advent of Netwar Revisited*, edited by John Arquilla and David Ronfeldt. Santa Monica, CA: Rand Corporation.

Darley, John M. and C. Daniel Batson. 1973. "From Jerusalem to Jericho: A Study of Situational and Dispositional Variables in Helping Behavior." *Journal of Personality and Social Psychology* 27: 100–8.

Davenport, Christian. 2000. "Introduction." Pp. 1–24 in *Paths to State Repression*, edited by C. Davenport. Lanham, MD: Rowman and Littlefield.

———. 2001. "The Devil Is In the Details: Media Attentiveness, News Production and Unexplored Micro-Foundations of Conflict Event Data." Presented at the Conference on Mobilization and Repression: What We Know and Where We Should Go From Here? June 23, University of Maryland, College Park, MD.

Davenport, Christian, and Marci Eads. 2001. "Cued to Coerce or Coercing Cues? An Exploration of Dissident Rhetoric and Its Relationship to Political Repression." *Mobilization* 6 (2): 151–71.

Davidson, Kenneth, Ruth Ginsburg, and Herma Kay. 1974. *Sex-Based Discrimination: Text, Cases, and Materials*. St Paul, Minn.: West.

Davies, J. 1962. "Towards a Theory of Revolution." *American Sociological Review,* 27: 5–19.

Davies, J. 1969. "The J-Curve of Rising and Declining Satisfactions as a Cause of Some Great Revolutions and a Contained Rebellion." Pp. 671–709 in *Violence in America: Historical and Comparative Perspectives*, edited by Hugh Davis Graham and Ted Robert Gurr. New York: Signet Books.

Davis, Nancy J., and Robert V. Robinson. 1996. "Are the Rumors of the War Exaggerated? Religious Orthodoxy and Moral Progressivism in America." *American Journal of Sociology* 102: 756–87.

de Buen, Néstor. 1999. "El Acuerdo de Cooperación Laboral de América del Norte." *El Cotidiano* 94 (March–April): 5–12.

Decre, Carmen Diana. 1986. "Rural women and agrarian reform in Peru, Chile, and Cuba." Pp. 189–207 in *Women and Change in Latin America*, edited by June Nash and Helen I. Safa. South Hadley, MA: Bergin and Garvey.

Dees, Morris with James Corcoran. 1996. *Gathering Storm: America's Militia Threat*. New York: Harper-Collins Publishers, Inc.

Degler, Carl. 1967. "Revolution without Ideology: The Changing Place of Women in America." Pp. 193–210 in *The Woman in America*, edited by Robert Jay Lifton. Boston: Beacon Press.

Delgado, Gary. 1986. *Organizing the Movement: The Roots and Growth of ACORN*. Philadelphia: Temple University Press.

Delgado Tobar, Juan Alfonso, and Hena Flora Peña Rosales. 1989. *La práctica política del movimiento sindical revolucionario en la coyuntara 1979-1984*. Bachelor's thesis. University of El Salvador, Department of Sociology.

Della Porta, Donatella. 1992. *Social Movements and Violence: Participation in Underground Organizations*. Greenwich, CT: JAI-Press.

———. 1995. *Political Movements, Political Violence, and the State*. New York: Cambridge University Press.

Della Porta, Donatella, and Mario Diani. 1999. *Social Movements: An Introduction*. Malden, Mass.: Blackwell Publishers.

Della Porta, Donatella and Herbert Reiter. 1998. *Policing Protest: The Control of Mass Demonstrations in Western Democracies*. Minneapolis, MN: University of Minnesota Press.

Della Porta, Donatella, and Dieter Rucht. 1995. "Left-libertarian Movements in Context: A Comparison of Italy and West Germany, 1965–1990." Pp. 229–272 in *The Politics of Social Protest*, J. Craig Jenkins and Bert Klandermans, eds. Minneapolis: University of Minnesota Press.

DeMan, Paul. 1979. "Allegories of Reading: Figural Language in Rousseau". Nietzche, Rilke, and Proust. New Haven, Connecticut: Yale.

Denzin, Norman. 1978. *The Research Act: A Theoretical Introduction to Sociological Methods*. New York: McGraw-Hill Book Company.

———. 1987. *The Alcoholic Self. Philadelphia*. Pennsylvania: Temple.

———. 1989. *Interpretive Biography*. Newbury Park, Calif.: Sage.

Deseran, Forrest A. 1989. "Part-time farming and commuting." *Research in Rural Sociology and Development* 4: 171–88.

Devault, George. 1975. "CWA Strike Vote at Ohio State Spurs Word Exchange by Unions." *Columbus Dispatch,* December 6, p. 2C.

Di Palma, Giuseppe. 1991. "Legitimation from the Top to Civil Society." *World Politics* 44: 49–80.

Diamanti, Ilvo. 1992. "La Mia Patria è il Veneto" (Veneto Is My Country). *Polis* 6: 225–55.

———. 1993. *La Lega* (The League). Rome, Italy: Donzelli.

Diamanti, Ilvo and Renato Mannheimer, eds. 1994. *Milano a Roma* (Milan to Rome). Rome, Italy: Donzelli.

Diamond, Sara. 1989. *Spiritual Warfare: The Politics of the Christian Right*. Boston: South End Press.

———. 1995. *Roads to Dominion: Right-wing Movements and Political Power in the United States*. New York: Guilford Press.

Diani, Mario. 1992. "The Concept of Social Movement." *The Sociological Review* 40: 1–25.

———. 1995. *Green Networks. A Structural Analysis of the Italian Environmental Movement*. Edinburgh, Scotland: Edinburgh University Press.

———. 1996. "Linking Mobilization Frames and Political Opportunities: Insights from Regional Populism in Italy." *American Sociological Review* 61: 1053–69.

———. 1997. "Social Movements and Social Capital." *Mobilization* 2: 129–47.

———. 2002. "Network Analysis" Pp. 173–200 in *Methods of Social Movement Research*. Minneapolis: University of Minnesota Press.

———. 2003. "Introduction: Social Movements, Contentious Actions, and Social Networks: 'From Metaphor to Substance.' " Pp. 1–18 in *Social Movement*

Networks: Relational Approaches to Collective Action, edited by Mario Diani and Doug McAdam. New York: Oxford University Press.

Diani, Mario. 2004. "Networks and Participation." Pp. 339–359 in *The Blackwell Companion to Social Movements,* edited by David A. Snow, Sarah A. Soule, and Hanspeter Kriesi. London: Blackwell.

Diani, Mario and Doug McAdam eds. 2003. *Social Movements and Networks: Relational Approaches to Collective Action.* New York: Oxford University Press.

DiBenedetti, Charles. 1980. *The Peace Reform in American History.* Bloomington: Indiana University Press.

DiMaggio, Paul J. 1983. "State Expansion and Organizational Fields." In *Organizational Theory and Public Policy,* edited by Richard H. Hall and Robert E. Quinn. Beverly Hills: Sage, 147–61.

———. 1986. "Structural Analysis of Organizational Fields." *Research in Organizational Behavior* 8: 335–69.

———. 1988. "Interest and Agency in Institutional Theory." In *Institutional Patterns and Organizations: Culture and Environment,* edited by Lynne Zucker. Cambridge: Ballinger, 3–22.

———. 1991. "Constructing an Organizational Field as a Professional Project: U.S. Art Museums, 1920–1940." In *The New Institutionalism in Organizational Analysis,* edited by Walter W. Powell and Paul J. DiMaggio. Chicago: University of Chicago Press, 267–92.

———. 1997. "Culture and Cognition." *Annual Review of Sociology* 23: 263–87.

DiMaggio, Paul, John Evans, and Bethany Brown. 1996. "Have Americans' Attitudes Become More Polarized?" *American Journal of Sociology* 102: 690–755.

DiMaggio, Paul J. and Walter W. Powell. 1983. "The Iron Cage Revisited: Institutional Isomorphism and Collective Rationality in Organizational Fields." *American Sociological Review* 48: 147–60.

———. 1991. *The New Institutionalism in Organizational Analysis.* Chicago: University of Chicago Press.

Dittmer, John. 1994. *Local People: The Struggle for Civil Rights in Mississippi.* Urbana, IL: University of Illinois Press.

Dittmer, Lowell. 1987. *China's Continuous Revolution: The Post-Liberation Epoch, 1949–1981.* Berkeley, CA: University of California Press.

———. 1998. *Liu Shaoqi and the Chinese Cultural Revolution: The Politics of Mass Criticism.* Berkeley, CA: University of California Press.

Dobbin, Frank, and John Sutton. 1998. "The Strength of a Weak State: The Rights Revolution and the Rise of Human Resource Management Divisions." *American Journal of Sociology* 104: 441–76.

Dobratz, Betty A. 2001. "The Role of Religion in the Collective Identity of the White Racialist Movement." *Journal for the Scientific Study of Religion* 40: 287–301.

Dobratz, Betty A. and Stephanie L. Shanks-Meile. 1997. *White Power, White Pride!: The White Separatist Movement in the United States.* New York: Twayne Publishers.

Dollard, John, Leonard Doob, Neal Miller, Herbert Mower, and Robert Sears. 1939. *Frustration and Aggression.* New Haven, CT: Yale University Press.

Donati, Paolo R. 1992. "Political Discourse Analysis." Pp. 136–167 in *Studying Collective Action,* edited by Mario Diani and Ron Eyerman. London: Sage.

Dong, Arthur. 1995. *The Question of Equality: Part One, Out Rage'69.* New York: A Production of Testing the Limits for the Independent Television Service.

Doreian, Patrick. 1980. "Linear Models with Spatially Distributed Data." *Sociological Methods and Research* 9: 29–60.

Dorsey, L. C. 1977. *Freedom Came to Mississippi.* New York: Field Foundation.

Doulin, Tim. 1990. "Possible OSU Strike Illegal, Official Says." *Columbus Dispatch,* September 12, p. 1B.

Downes, Bryan T. 1970. "A Critical Reexamination of Social and Political Characteristics of Riot Cities." *Social Science Quarterly* 51: 349–60.

Downton, James. 1973. *Rebel Leadership: Commitment. Charisma, and the Revolutionary Process.* New York: Free Press.

Downton, James and Paul Wehr. 1991. "Peace Movements: The Role of Commitment and Community in Sustaining Member Participation." *Research in Social Movements, Conflict and Change* 13: 113–34.

———. 1997. *The Persistent Activist: How Peace Commitment Develops and Survives.* Boulder, CO: Westview Press.

Drabek, Thomas, and Enrico Quarantelli. 1967. "Scapegoats. Villains, and Disaster." *Transaction* 4: 12–17.

Dreiling, Michael C. 2001. *Solidarity and Contention: The Politics of Security and Sustainability in the NAFTA Conflict.* New York: Garland.

Drescher, Seymour. 1987. *Capitalism and Antislavery: British Mobilization in Comparative Perspective.* New York: Oxford University Press.

Du, Ruiqing. 1992. *Chinese Higher Education: A Decade of Reform and Development, 1978–1988.* New York: St. Martin's Press.

Duberman, Martin. 1993. *Stonewall.* New York: Dutton.

Dubois, Pierre. 1978. "New Forms of Industrial Conflict, 1960–74." Pp. 1–34 in *The Resurgence of Class Conflict in Europe Since 1968,* edited by Colin Crouch and Alessandro Pizzorno. Vol. 2: London: Macmillan.

Dudziak, Mary L. 2000. *Cold War Civil Rights.* Princeton, NJ: Princeton University Press.

Duerst-Lahti, Georgia. 1989. "The Government's Role in Building the Women's Movement." *Political Science Quarterly* 104: 249–68.

Duff, Robert W. and William T. Liu. 1972. "The Strength in Weak Ties." *Public Opinion Quarterly* 36: 361–66.

Dugan, Kimberly B. 2003. "The Christian Right and Homosexuality: Identity Work in Anti-Gay Organizing." Paper presented at the annual meetings of the Midwest Sociological Society, Chicago, IL.

Duncan, Otis Dudley, and Beverly Duncan. 1955. "Residential Distribution and Occupational Stratification." *American Journal of Sociology* 60: 493–503.

Dunkerley, James. 1982. *The Long War: Dictatorship and Revolution in El Salvador.* London: Verso.

Durham, William. 1979. *Scarcity and Survival in Central America: Ecological Origins of the Soccer War.* Stanford, Calif.: Stanford University Press.

Durkheim, Emile. [1893] 1964. *The Division of Labor in Society.* New York: Free Press.

Durkheim, Émile. 1951. *Suicide: A Study in Sociology,* translated by John A Spaulding and George Simpson. New York: Free Press.

Duyvendak, Jan Willam. 1990a. "The Development of the French Gay Movement, 1975–89." Unpublished paper, Universiteit van Amsterdam.

———. 1990b. "Profiles and trajectories of five social movements." Unpublished paper. University of Amsterdam: PdIS.

———. 1995. "Gay Subcultures between Movement and Market." Pp. 165–80 in *New Social Movements in Western Europe: A Comparative Analysis,* edited by Hanspeter Kriesi, Ruud Koopmans, Jan Willem Duyvendak, and Marco G. Giugni. Minneapolis: University of Minnesota Press.

Duyvendak, Jan Willem, and Marco G. Giugni. 1995. "Social Movement Types and Policy Domains." Pp. 82–110 in *New Social Movements in Western Europe: A Comparative Analysis,* edited by Hanspeter Kriesi, Ruud Koopmans, Jan Willem Duyvendak, and Marco G. Giugni. Minneapolis: University of Minnesota Press.

Dworkin, Andrea. 1989. *Pornography: Men Possessing Women.* New York: Penguin.

Dyer, Joel. 1997. *Harvest of Rage.* Boulder, CO: Westview Press.

Dykeman, Wilma. and James Stokely. 1960. "Sit down chiliun, sit downl" *Progressive* (June 24): 8–13.

Earl, Jennifer. 2000. "Methods, Movements and Outcomes: Methodological Difficulties in the Study of Extra-Movement Outcomes." *Research in Social Movements, Conflicts, and Change* 22: 3–25.

———. 2003. "Tanks, Tear Gas, and Taxes: Toward a Theory of Movement Repression." *Sociological Theory:* 21: 44–68.

———. 2004. "The Cultural Consequences of Social Movements." Pp. 508–30 in *The Blackwell Companion to Social Movements,* edited by David A. Snow, Sarah A. Soule, and Hanspeter Kriesi. Malden, MA: Blackwell Publishing.

Earl, Jennifer, Andrew Martin, John D. McCarthy, and Sarah A. Soule. 2004. "The Use of Newspaper Data in the Study of Collective Action." *Annual Review of Sociology* 30: 65–80.

Earl, Jennifer, and Sarah A. Soule. 2001. "The differential protection of minority groups: The inclusion of sexual orientation, gender and disability in state hate crime laws, 1976–1995." *The Politics of Social Inequality* 9: 3–34.

Eastwood, Mary, and Pauli Murray. 1965. "Jane Crow and the Law: Sex Discrimination and Title VII." *George Washington Law Review* 34: 232–56.

Eaton, Leslie. 2003. "Thousands March in Manhattan Against War." *New York Times* March 22.

Ebaugh, Helen Rose, and Paula Pipes. 2001. "Immigrant Congregations as Social Service Providers: Are They Safety Nets for Welfare Reform?" Pp. 95–110 in *Religion and Social Policy,* edited by Paula Nesbitt. Walnut Creek, Calif.: AltaMira.

Echols, Alice. 1989. *Daring to Be BAD: Radical Feminism in America, 1967–1975.* Minneapolis: University of Minnesota Press.

———. 1992. "'We Gotta Get Out of This Place: ' Notes Toward a Remapping of the Sixties." *Socialist Review* 22: 9–33.

Eckstein, Harry. 1965. "On the Etiology of Internal Wars." *History and Theory* 4: 133–63.

Edelman, Lauren B. 1992. "Legal Ambiguity and Symbolic Structures: Organizational Mediation of Civil Rights Law." *American Journal of Sociology* 97: 1531–76.

Edelman, Lauren B., and Mark Suchman. 1997. "The Legal Environment of Organizations." *Annual Review of Sociology* 23: 479–515.

Edsall, Thomas B., and Mary D. Edsall. 1991. *Chain Reaction.* New York: Norton.

Educational Statistics Yearbook of China. 1989. Beijing: Renmin Chubanshe (People's Publishing House).

Edwards, Bob and Sam Marullo. 1995. "Organizational Mortality in Declining Social Movements: The Demise of Peace Movement Organizations in the End of the Cold War Era." *American Sociological Review* 60: 908–27.

EEOC (Equal Employment Opportunity Commission). 1965a. Press release. September 22. Washington, D.C., EEOC Library.

———. 1965b. *White House Conference on Equal Employment Opportunity.* Transcript of panel 3, "Discrimination Because of Sex." August 19–20. EEOC Library, Washington, D.C.

———. 1966a. Commissioners' meeting no. 84. March 24. EEOC Library, Washington, D.C.

———. 1966b. Commissioners' meeting no. 85. March 29. EEOC Library, Washington, D.C.

———. 1966c. Office of General Counsel. *First Annual Digest of Legal Interpretations July 2, 1965 through July 1, 1966.* EEOC Library, Washington, D.C.

———. 1966d. Press release. April 27. EEOC Library, Washington, D.C.

———. 1966e. "Rule of Reason to Guide EEOC on Sex Discrimination Cases." *Newsletter,* December 1965–January 1966. EEOC Library, Washington, D.C.

———. 1967a. Commissioners' meeting no. 148. March 22. EEOC Library, Washington, D.C.

———. 1967b. "Public Hearings Scheduled on Sex Discrimination in Employment." Press release. April 13. EEOC Library, Washington, D.C.

———. 1968a. Commissioners' meeting no. 180. February 13. EEOC Library, Washington, D.C.

———. 1968b. "The Equal Employment Opportunity Commission during the Administration of Lyndon B. Johnson, November 1963–January 1969." Vol. 1, "Administrative History." November 1. Lyndon Baines Johnson Library, Austin.

———. 1968c. Press release. February 23. EEOC Library, Washington, D.C.

———. 1969. *Third Annual Report.* EEOC Library, Washington, D.C.

———. 1970. *Fourth Annual Report.* EEOC Library, Washington, D.C.

Egan, Timothy. 1992a. "Oregon Measure Asks State to Repress Homosexuality." *New York Times,* August 16, sec. 1, p. 1.

———. 1992b. "Violent Backdrop for Anti-Gay Measure." *New York Times,* November 1, sec. 1, p. 40.

Einwohner, Rachel L. 1999. "Gender, Class, and Social Movement Outcomes: Identity and Effectiveness in Two Animal Rights Campaigns." *Gender & Society* 13: 56–76.

———. 2002. "Motivational Framing and Efficacy Maintenance: Animal Rights Activists' Use of Four Fortifying Strategies." *The Sociological Quarterly* 43: 509–26.

———. 2003. "Opportunity, Honor, and Action in the Warsaw Ghetto Uprising of 1943." *American Journal of Sociology* 109: 650–75.

Einwohner, Rachel L., Jo Reger, and Daniel J. Myers. Unpublished manuscript. "Identity Work, Sameness, and Difference in social Movements."

Eisenstadt, Shmuel N., ed. 1968. *The Protestant Ethic and Modernization: A Comparative View.* New York: Basic Books.

Eisenstein, Hester. 1983. *Contemporary Feminist Thought.* Boston: G. K. Hall.

Eisinger, Peter K. 1973. "The Conditions of Protest Behavior in American Cities." *American Political Science Review* 67: 11–28.

Eisinger, Peter. 1979. "The Community Action Program and the Development of Black Leadership." Pp. 127–44 in *Urban Policy Making,* edited by D. R. Marshall. Beverly Hills, CA: Sage.

Elinson, Howard. 1966. "Radicalism and the Negro Movement." Pp. 355–75 in *Problems and Prospects of the Negro Movement,* edited by Raymond J. Murphy and Howard Elinson. Belmont, CA: Wadsworth.

Ellingson, Stephen J. 1995. "Understanding the Dialectic of Discourse and Collective Action: Public Debate and Rioting in Antebellum Cincinnati." *American Journal of Sociology* 101 (1): 100–144.

Ellison, Christopher G. 1997. "Religious Involvement and the Subjective Quality of Family Life among African Americans." Pp. 117–31 in *Family Life in Black America,* edited by Robert J. Taylor, James S. Jackson, and Linda Chatters. Thousand Oaks, Calif.: Sage.

Emerson, Joan P. 1970. "Nothing Unusual is Happening." Pp. 208–22 in *Human Nature and Collective Behavior.* T. Shibuteni, ed. Englewood Cliffs. NJ: Prentice-Hall.

Emirbayer, Mustafa. 1997. "Manifesto for a Relational Sociology." *American Journal of Sociology* 103: 281–317.

Emirbayer, Mustafa, and Jeff Goodwin. 1994. "Network Analysis, Culture, and the Problem of Agency." *American Journal of Sociology* 99 (6): 1411–54.

Emirbayer, Mustafa, and Ann Mische. 1998. "What Is Agency?" *American Journal of Sociology* 103: 962–1023.

Engelking, Barbara. 2001. *Holocaust and Memory.* London: Leicester University Press.

Epstein, Barbara. 1988. "The Politics of Prefigurative Community: The Non-violent Direct Action Movement." Pp. 63–92 in *Reshaping the U.S. Left: Popular Struggles In the 1980s,* edited by Mike Davis and Michael Sprinker. London: Verso.

Epstein, Steven. 1987. "Gay Politics, Ethnic Identity: The Limits of Social Constructionism." *Socialist Review* 93/94: 9–56.

———. 1999. "Gay and Lesbian Movements in the United States: Dilemmas of Identity, Diversity, and Political Strategy." In *The Global Emergence of Gay and Lesbian Politics,* edited by Barry D. Adam, Jan Willem Duyvendak, and Andre Krouwel. Philadelphia: Temple University Press, 30–90.

Erickson, Kai. 1976. *Everything in Its Path: Destruction of Community in the Buffalo Creek Flood.* New York: Simon and Schuster.

———. 1994. *A New Species of Trouble: Explorations in Disaster, Trauma, and Community.* New York: Norton.

Ericson, Richard and Aaron Doyle. 1999. "Globalization and the Policing of Protest: The Case of APEC 1997." *British Journal of Sociology* 50: 589–608.

Erskine, Hazel. 1971. "The Polls: Women's Role." *Public Opinion Quarterly* 35: 282–87.

Escoffier, Jeffrey. 1985. "Sexual Revolution and the Politics of Gay Identity." *Socialist Review* 81/82: 119–54.

Esseveld, Johanna and Ron Eyerman. 1992. "Which Side Are You On? Reflections on Methodological Issues in the Study of 'Distasteful' Social Movements." Pp. 216–37 in *Studying Collective Action,* edited by M. Diani and R. Eyerman. London: Sage.

Etzioni, Amitai. 1964. *Modern Organizations.* Englewood Cliffs, N.J.: Prentice-Hall.

Evans, Glenn V. 1977. "Interview with Glenn V. Evans." Pp. 187–96 in *My Soul is Rested,* edited by Howell Raines. New York: Bantam.

Evans, John. 1997. "Multi-organizational Fields and Social Movement Organization Frame Content: The Religious Pro-Choice Movement." *Sociological Inquiry* 67: 451–69.

Evans, Peter. 2000. "Fighting Marginalization with Transnational Networks: Counter-Hegemonic Globalization." *Contemporary Sociology* 29 (1): 230–41.

———. 2005. "Counter-Hegemonic Globalization: Transnational Social Movements in the Contemporary Global Political Economy." In *The Handbook of Political Sociology: States, Civil Societies, and Globalization,* edited by Thomas Janoski, Alexander M. Hicks, and Mildred Schwartz. Cambridge: Cambridge University Press.

Evans, Rhonda. 2002. "The Rise of Ethical Trade Advocacy: NAFTA and the New Politics of Trade." Ph.D. dissertation. University of California, Berkeley, Department of Sociology.

Evans, Sara. 1979. *Personal Politics: The Roots of Women's Liberation in the Civil Rights Movement and the New Left.* New York: Knopf.

Evans, Sarah. 1980. *Personal Politics.* New York: Vintage Books.

Evans, Sara M. and Harry C. Boyte. 1986. *Free Spaces: The Sources of Democratic Change in America.* New York: Harper & Row.

Ewick, Patricia, and Susan S. Silbey. 1995. "Subversive stories and hegemonic tales: Toward a sociology of narrative." *Law and Society Review* 29: 197–226.

———. 1998. *The Common Place of Law: Stories from Everyday Life.* Chicago: University of Chicago Press.

Eyerman, Ron and Andrew Jamison. 1991. *Social Movements: A Cognitive Approach.* Cambridge, England: Polity Press.

Ezekiel, Raphael S. 1995. *The Racist Mind: Portraits of American Neo-Nazis and Klansmen.* New York: Viking.

Falter, Jürgen W., Hans-Gerd Jaschke, and Jürgen R. Winkler, eds. 1996. *Rechtsextremismus. Ergebnisse und Perspektiven der Forschung.* Special issue no. 27 of *Politische Vierteljahresschrift.* Opladen: Westdeutscher Verlag.

Fantasia, Rick. 1988. *Cultures of Solidarity.* Berkeley: University of California Press.

Fantasia, Rick and Eric L. Hirsch. 1995. "Culture in Rebellion: The Appropriation and Transformation of the Veil in the Algerian Revolution." Pp. 144–62 in *Social Movements and Culture,* edited by H. Johnston and B. Klandermans. Minneapolis: University of Minnesota Press.

FAPU (Frente de Acción Popular Unificado). 1976. *Mensaje al pueblo salvadoreño.* January 24.

Farber, A. M. 1968. "All-Day Revolt at LIU Ends After Negroes Win 6 of 7 Demands." *New York Times,* April 26, p. 49.

Farmer, James. 1965. *Freedom—When?* New York: Random House.

Farro, Antimo. 1991. *La Lente Verde* (The Green Lens). Milan, Italy: Angeli.

Feagin, Joe R. and Stella M. Capek. 1991. "Grassroots Movements in a Class Perspective." Pp. 27–53 in *Research in Political Sociology,* vol. 5, edited by P. C. Wasburn. Greenwich, CT: JAI Press.

Feagin, Joe R., and Harlan Hahn. 1973. *Ghetto Revolts: The Politics of Violence in American Cities.* New York: Macmillan.

Feagin, Joe R., Anthony M. Orum, and Gideon Sjoberg, eds. 1991. *A Case for the Case Study.* Chapel Hill, NC: University of North Carolina Press.

Feagin, Joe and Heman Vera. 1995. *White Racism: The Basics.* New York: Routledge.

Federal Register. 1967. "Equal Employment Opportunity Commission, Guidelines on Discrimination Because of Sex, Proposed Interpretive Rules." April 14. Vol. 32, pt. 1604.

———. 1969. "Equal Employment Opportunity Commission, Guidelines on Discrimination Because of Sex." August 19. Vol. 34, pt. 1604.

Feeney, Susan. 1993. "Religious Right's Gains Upset Some in GOP Moderates in Party Fight Back Despite Chairman's Call for Unity." *Dallas Morning Star,* September 5, sec. 1A.

Feijoó, Maria del Carmen. 1991. "The challenge of constructing civilian peace: Women and democracy in Argentina." Pp. 72–94 in *The Women's Movement in Latin America: Feminism and the Transition to Democracy,* edited by Jane Jaquette. Boulder, CO: Westview Press.

Fendrich, James M. 1974. "Activists Ten Years Later. A Test of Generational Unit Continuity." *Journal of Social Issues* 30: 95–118.

———. 1993. *Ideal Citizens.* Albany, NY: State University of New York Press.

Fendrich, James M., and Ellis S. Krauss. 1978. "Student Activism and Adult Left-Wing Politics: A Causal Model of Political Socialization for Black, White and Japanese Students of the 1960s Generation." *Research in Social Movements, Conflicts and Change* 1: 231–55.

Fendrich, James, and Kenneth L. Lovoy. 1988. "Back to the future: Adult political behavior of former student activists." *American Sociological Review* 53: 780–84.

Fendrich, James M., and Alison T. Tarleau. 1973. "Marching to a Different Drummer: Occupational and Political Correlates of Former Student Activists." *Social Forces* 52: 245–53.

Ferber, Abby. 1998. *White Man Falling: Race, Gender, and White Supremacy.* Lanham, MD: Rowman & Littlefield.

Fernandes, Leela. 1999. "Reading 'India's Bandit Queen': A Trans/national Feminist Perspective on the Discrepancies of Representation." *Signs* 25 (1): 123–52.

Fernández Moores, Lucio. 2002. "Fue masivo y sin incidentes el acto de repudio a la represión." *Clarín* (Argentine national newspaper), July 4.

Fernandez, Roberto. 1988. "Social Networks and Social Movements: Multiorganizational Fields and Recruitment to Mississippi Freedom Summer." *Sociological Forum* 3: 357–82.

Fernandez, Roberto, and Doug McAdam. 1989. "Multiorganizational Fields and Recruitment to Social Movements." Pp. 315–43 in *Organizing for Change: Social Movement Organizations in Europe and the United States,* edited by Bert Klandermans. Greenwich, Conn.: JAI Press.

Ferree, Myra Marx. 1987. "Equality and Autonomy: Feminist Politics in the United States and West Germany." Pp. 172–95 in *The Women's Movements* of Western Europe and the United States, edited by Mary Katzenstein and Carol McClurg Mueller. Philadelphia: Temple University Press.

Ferree, Myra Marx. 2003. "Resonance and Radicalism: Feminist Framing in the Abortion Debates of the United States and Germany." *American Journal of Sociology* 109: 304–44.

Ferree, Myra Marx, William A. Gamson, Jürgen Gerhards and Dieter Rucht. 2002. *Shaping Abortion Discourse: Democracy and the Public Sphere in Germany and the United States.* New York: Cambridge University Press.

Ferree, Myra Marx and Beth B. Hess. 1985. *Controversy and Coalition: The New Feminist Movement.* Boston: Twayne.

———. 2000. *Controversy and Coalition: The New Feminist Movement Across Four Decades of Change,* third edition. New York: Routledge.

Ferree, Myra Marx and Patricia Martin. 1995. "Doing the Work of the Movement: Feminist Organizations." Pp. 3–23 in *Feminist Organizations,* edited by M. M. Ferree and P. Y. Martin. Philadelphia, PA: Temple University Press.

Ferree, Myra Marx and David Merrill. 2004. "Hot Movements, Cold Cognition: Thinking about Social Movements in Gendered Frames." Pp. 247–61 in *Rethinking Social Movements: Structure Meaning and Emotion,* edited by Jeff Goodwin and James M. Jasper. Lanham, MD: Rowan and Littlefield.

Festinger, Leon. 1962. *A Theory of Cognitive Dissonance.* Stanford, Calif.: Stanford University Press.

Festinger, Leon, Henry W. Riecken, and Stanley Schachter. 1956. *When Prophecy Fails.* Minneapolis: University of Minnesota Press.

Festinger, Leon, Stanley Schachter, and Kurt Back. 1950. *Social Pressures in Informal Groups.* Stanford, Calif.: Stanford University Press.

Feuer, Lewis. 1969. *The Conflict of Generations.* New York: Basic Books.

Fine, Gary Alan. 1995. "Public narration and group culture: Discerning discourse in social movements." In *Social Movements and Culture,* edited by Hank Johnston and Bert Klandermans, 127–143. Minneapolis: University of Minnesota Press.

Fine, Gary Alan, and Kent Sandstrom. 1993. "Ideology in Action: A Pragmatic Approach to a Contested Concept" *Sociological Theory* 11: 21–38.

Fink, Leon. 1985. *Workingmen's Democracy: The Knights of Labor and American Politics.* Urbana: University of Illinois Press.

Finkel, Steven. 1985. "Reciprocal Effects of Participation and Political Efficacy: A Panel Analysis." *American Journal of Political Science* 29 (4): 891–913.

Finkel, Steven E., and James B. Rule. 1986. "Relative Deprivation and Related Psychological Theories of Civil Violence: A Critical Review." Pp. 47–69 in *Social Movements, Social Conflicts, and Change.* V. 9. K. Lang and G. Lang, eds. Greenwich, CT: JAI Press.

Fiorina, Morris P., Samuel J. Abrams, and Jeremy C. Pope. 2006. *Culture War? The Myth of a Polarized America.* New York: Pearson Longman.

Fireman, Bruce and William A. Gamson. 1979. "Utilitarian Logic in the Resource Mobilization Perspective." Pp. 8–44 in *The Dynamics of Social Movements,* edited by M. Zald and J. McCarthy. Cambridge. MA: Winthrop.

Fischer, Claude S. 1977. *Networks and Places: Social Relations in the Urban Setting.* New York: Free Press.

Fisher, Jo. 1989. *Mothers of the Disappeared.* Boston, MA: South End Press.

Fisher, Julie. 1993. *The Road from Rio: Sustainable Development and the Nongovernmental Movement in the Third World.* Westport, CT: Praeger.

FitzGerald, Frances. 1986 [1981]. *Cities on a Hill: A Journey Through Contemporary American Cultures.* New York: Simon and Schuster.

Flacks, Richard. 1971. *Youth and Social Change.* Chicago, Illinois: Markham.

Flacks, Richard. 1988. *Making History: The American Left and the American Mind.* New York: Columbia University Press.

Flexner, Eleanor. 1959. *Century of Struggle.* Cambridge: Harvard University Press.

Fligstein, Neil. 1985. "The Spread of the Multidivisional Form among Large Firms, 1919–79." *American Sociological Review* 50: 377–91.

———. 1990. *The Transformation of Corporate Control.* Cambridge: Harvard University Press.

———. 1991. "The Structural Transformation of American Industry: An Institutional Account of the Causes of Diversification in the Largest Firms, 1919–79." Pp. 311–36 in *The New Institutionalisms in Organizational Analysis,* edited by Walter Powell and Paul DiMaggio. Chicago: University of Chicago Press.

Fligstein, Neil. 1997a. "Fields, Power, and Social Skill: A Critical Analysis of the New Institutionalisms." Unpublished manuscript. Department of Sociology, University of California, Berkeley.

———. 1997b. "Social Skill and Institutional Theory." *American Behavioral Scientist* 40: 397–505.

———. 1998. "Fields, Power, and Social Skill: A Critical Analysis of the New Intuitionalism." Working paper. University of California, Berkeley, Center for Culture, Organizations, and Politics.

———. 2001a. *The Architecture of Markets: An Economic Sociology of Twenty-First Century Capitalist Societies.* Princeton: Princeton University Press.

———. 2001b. "Social Skill and the Theory of Fields." *Sociological Theory* 19(2): 105–25.

Fligstein, Neil, and Doug McAdam. 1995. "A Political-Cultural Approach to the Problem of Strategic Action." Unpublished paper. Department of Sociology, University of California, Berkeley.

Flood, Maureen. 1994. "OSU Employees May Be Striking." *Ohio State Lantern,* April 21, p. 1.

Florer, John Harmon. 1973. "NOW: The Formative Years. National Effort to Acquire Action on Equal Employment." Manuscript. John F. Kennedy Presidential Library, Boston.

Fogelson, Robert M. 1971. *Violence as Protest.* Garden City. NY: Doubleday.

Foley, Michael W., John D. McCarthy, and Mark Chaves. 2001. "Social Capital, Religious Institutions, and Poor Communities." Pp. 215–45 in *Social Capital and Poor Communities,* edited by Susan Saegert, Phillip J. Thompson, and Mark R. Warren. New York: Russell Sage.

Folger, Robert. 1987. "Reformulating the Preconditions of Resentment: A Referent Cognitions Model." Pp. 183–215 in *Social Comparison, Social Justice, and Relative Deprivation,* edited by J.C Masters and W.P Smith Hillsdale, NJ: Lawrence Erlbaum.

Fording, Richard C. 1997. "The Conditional Effect of Violence as a Political Tactic: Mass Insurgency, Welfare Generosity, and Electoral Context in the American States." *American Journal of Political Science* 41: 1–29.

Forest, Jim. 1997. *Love is the Measure: A Biography of Dorothy Day.* Maryknoll, NY: Orbis.

Form, William. 1985. *Divided We Stand: Working-Class Stratification in America.* Urbana: University of Illinois Press.

———. 1995. *Segmented Labor, Fractured Politics: Labor Politics in American Life.* New York: Plenum Press.

Fort, Vincent D. 1989. "The Atlanta Sit-In Movement, 1960–61, an oral study." In *Atlanta, Georgia, 1960–61: Sit-Ins and Student Activism,* edited by David J. Garrow, 113–82. Brooklyn, New York: Carlson.

Foucault, Michel. 1983. "Afterword: The Subject and Power." Pp. 208–226 in *Michel Foucault: Beyond Structuralism and Hermeneutics,* by Hubert Dreyfus and Paul Robinow. Chicago: University of Chicago Press.

Fox, Jonathan. 2002. "Assessing Binational Civil Society Coalitions: Lessons from the Mexico-U.S. Experience." Pp. 341–417 in *Cross-Border Dialogues: U.S.-Mexico Social Movement Networking,* edited by D. Brooks and J. Fox. La Jolla: Center for U.S.-Mexican Studies, University of California-San Diego.

Fox, Jonathan, and L. David Brown. 1998. *The Struggle for Accountability: The World Bank, NGOs, and Grassroots Movements.* Cambridge: MIT Press.

Fox, Richard G. 1997. "Passage from India." In *Between Resistance and Revolution: Cultural Politics and Social Protest,* edited by Richard G. Fox and Orin Starn. New Brunswick: Rutgers University Press.

Fox, Sylvan. 1968. "Faculty Is Split: Some Endorse Strike Called by Students After Police Raid." *New York Times,* May 1, p. 1.

Francisco, Ronald. 1995. "The Relationship between Coercion and Protest: An Empirical Evaluation in Three Coercive States." *Journal of Conflict Resolution* 39: 263–81.

Frank, Dana. 1999. *Buy American: The Untold Story of Economic Nationalism.* Boston: Beacon Press.

Franzosi, Roberto. 1995. *The Puzzle of Strikes.* New York: Cambridge University Press.

Fraser, Lyndon. 2002. "To Tara via Holyhead: The Emergence of Irish Catholic Ethnicity in Nineteenth-Century Christchurch, New Zealand." *Journal of Social History* 36 (2): 431–58.

Frazier, E. Franklin. 1963. *The Negro Church in America.* New York: Schocken Books.

Freedman, Deborah, Arland Thornton, Donald Cambum, Duane Alwin, and Linda Young-Marco. 1988. "The Life History Calendar: A Technique for Collecting Retrospective Data." *Sociological Methodology* 18: 37–68.

Freedman, Estelle. 1979. "Separatism as Strategy: Female Institution Building and American Feminism, 1870–1930." *Feminist Studies,* 5: 512–29.

Freeman, Jo 1973a. "The Origins of the Women's Liberation Movement." *American Journal of Sociology* 78: 792–811.

———. 1973b. "The Tyranny of Structurelessness." *Ms.* 2: 76–78, 86–89.

———. 1975. *The Politics of Women's Liberation.* New York: David McKay.

———. 1979. "Resource Mobilization and Strategy. A Model for Analyzing Social Movement Organization Actions." Pp. 167–89 in *The Dynamics of Social Movements,* edited by Mayer N. Zald and John D. McCarthy. Cambridge, MA: Winthrop.

———. 1983. *Social Movements of the Sixties and Seventies,* New York: Longman.

———. 1984. "The Women's Liberation Movement: Its Origins, Structure, Activities, and Ideas." Pp. 543–56 in *Women: A Feminist Perspective,* edited by Jo Freeman. Palo Alto, Calif.: Mayfield.

———. 1987. "Whom You Know versus Whom You Represent: Feminist Influence in the Democratic and Republican Parties." Pp. 215–44 in *The Women's Movements of the United States and Western Europe,* edited by M. Katzenstein and C. Mueller. Philadelphia: Temple University Press.

———. 1991. "How Sex Got into Title VII: Persistent Opportunism as a Maker of Public Policy." *Law and Inequality* 9: 163–84.

Freston, Paul. 2001. *Evangelicals and Politics in Asia, Africa and Latin America.* Cambridge: Cambridge University Press.

Freudenberg, William R. 1993. "Risk and recreancy: Weber, the division of labor, and the rationality of risk perceptions." *Social Forces* 71: 909–32.

Fried, Marlene Gerber, ed. 1990. *From Abortion to Reproductive Freedom: Transforming a Movement.* Boston: South End Press.

Friedan, Betty. 1963. *The Feminine Mystique.* New York: Dell.

———. 1976. *It Changed My Life.* New York: Dell.

———. 1991. *It Changed My Life: Writings on the Women's Movement.* New York: Laurel.

Friedland, Roger. 1976. "Class Power and Social Control: The War on Poverty." *Politics and Society* 6: 459–89.

Friedland, William. 1964. "For a Sociological Concept of Charisma." *Social Forces* 43: 18–26.

Friedman, Debra and Doug McAdam. 1992. "Collective Identity and Activism: Networks, Choices, and the Life of a Social Movement." Pp. 156–73 in *Frontiers of Social Movement Theory,* edited by A. Morris and C. McClurg Mueller, New Haven. CT: Yale University Press.

Friedman, Edward, Paul Pickowicz, and Mark Selden. 1991. *Chinese Village, Socialist State.* New Haven, CT: Yale University Press.

Friedman, Lawrence. 1977. "The Social and Political Context of the War on Poverty." Pp. 21–47 in *A Decade of Federal Antipoverty Programs,* edited by R. H. Haveman. New York: Academic.

Friedman, Thomas. 2003. "Chicken a la Iraq." *New York Times.* March 5.

Frisbee, Parker. 1975. "Illegal migration from Mexico to the United States: a longitudinal analysis." *International Migration Review* 9: 3–14.

Fuller, Helen. 1960. "'We are all so very happy'." *New Republic* (April 25): 13–16.

Gabin, Nancy. 1990. *Feminism in the Labor Movement: Women and the United Auto Workers, 1935–1975.* Ithaca, N.Y.: Cornell University Press.

Gale Research. 1984–98. *The Encyclopedia of Associations.* Detroit, Mich.: Gale Research.

Gallagher, Charles A. 1994. "White reconstruction in the university." *Socialist Review* 24: 165–187.

Gallant, Mary J. and Jay E. Cross. 1992. "Surviving Destruction of the Self: Challenged Identity in the Holocaust." *Studies in Symbolic Interaction* 13: 221–46.

Gallic, D. 1983. *Social Inequality and Class Radicalism in France and Britain.* Cambridge: Cambridge University Press.

Gallup, George. 1935. "Americans Reveal Their Hopes and Fears in Nation-Wide Poll." *Washington Post,* December 15, p. B1.

———. 1936. "Nation 9 to 1 for Old Age Pensions; Against Townsend Plan." *Washington Post,* January 12, p. B1.

———. 1939. "Political Strength of Pension Movements Growing, Survey Shows." *Washington Post,* February 26, pp. B2–3.

Galtung, Johan, and Marie Homboe Ruge. 1965. "The Structure of Foreign News: The Presentation of the Congo, Cuba and Cyprus Crises in Four Norwegian Newspapers." *Journal of Peace Research* 2: 64–91.

Gamson, Joshua. 1995. "Must Identity Movements Self Destruct? A Queer Dilemma." *Social Problems* 42 (3): 390–407.

———. 1996. "The Organizational Shaping of Collective Identity: The Case of Lesbian and Gay Film Festivals in New York." *Sociological Forum* 11: 231–61.

———. 1998. "Must Identity Movements Self-Destruct? A Queer Dilemma." Pp. 589–604 in *Social Perspectives in Lesbian and Gay Studies: A Reader,* edited by Peter M. Nardi and Beth E. Schneider. London: Routledge.

Gamson, William A. [1975] 1990. *The Strategy of Social Protest.* 2d ed. Belmont, CA: Wadsworth.

———. 1988. "Political Discourse and Collective Action." *International Social Movement Research* 1: 219–44.

———. 1991. "Commitment and agency In social movements." *Sociological Forum* 6: 27–50.

———. 1992a. *Talking Politics.* New York: Cambridge University Press.

———. 1992b. "The Social Psychology of Collective Action." Pp. 53–76 in *Frontiers in Social Movement Theory,* edited by Aldon Morris and Carol Mueller. New Haven, Conn.: Yale University Press.

———. 1995. "Constructing Social Protest" Pp. 85–106 in *Social Movements and Culture,* edited by Hank Johnston and Bert Klandermans. Minneapolis: University of Minnesota Press.

———. 1996. "Safe Spaces and Social Movements." *Perspectives on Social Problems* 8: 27–38.

Gamson, William A., Bruce Fireman, and Steven Rytina. 1982. *Encounters with Unjust Authority.* Homewood, IL: Dorsey Press.

Gamson, William A. and David S. Meyer. 1996. "Framing Political Opportunity." Pp. 275–90 in *Comparative Perspectives on Social Movements: Political Opportunities, Mobilizing Structures, and Cultural Framings,* edited by D. McAdam, J. D. McCarthy, and M. N. Zald. Cambridge, UK: Cambridge University Press.

Gamson, William A., and Andre Modigliani. 1989. "Media Discourse and Public Opinion on Nuclear Power: A Constructionist Approach." *American Journal of Sociology* 95 (1): 1–37.

Gamson, William A. and Emile Schmeidler. 1984. "Organizing the Poor." *Theory and Society* 13: 567–85.

Gamson, William A., and Gadi Wolfsfeld. 1993. "Movements and Media as Interacting Systems." *Annals of the American Academy of Political Science* 528: 114–25.

Gans, Herbert J. 1967. *The Levitowners: Ways of Life and Politics in a New Suburban Community.* New York: Pantheon Books.

Ganz, Marshall. 2000. "Resources and Resourcefulness: Strategic Capacity in the Unionization of California Agriculture, 1959–66." *American Journal of Sociology* 105: 1003–62.

Gardner, John and William Cohen. 1992. "Demographic Characteristics of the Population of the United States, 1930–1950." [Computer File] Ann Arbor, MI: Inter-university Consortium for Political and Social Research.

Garfinkel, Herbert 1969. *When Negroes March.* New York: Atheneum.

Garling, Tommy, and Gary W. Evans. 1991. *Environment, Cognition and Action.* New York: Oxford University Press.

Garner, Roberta. 1996. *Contemporary Movements and Ideologies.* New York: McGraw-Hill.

———. 1997. "50 years of social movement theory." in *Social Movement Theory and Research, an Annotated Bibliography.* Magill Bibliographies: Salem/Scarecrow Press.

Garrow, David J. 1978. *Protest at Selma.* New Haven, Conn.: Yale University Press.

Garth, Bryant G., and Austin Sarat, eds. 1998. *How Does Law Matter?* Evanston, Ill.: Northwestern University Press.

Gay Activist. 1972a. "State and Federal." April. Collection 7301 (National Gay and Lesbian Task Force), box 51, folder "GAA." Cornell University Library.

———. 1972b. "The Inner Circle Affair." May–June. Collection 7301 (National Gay and Lesbian Task Force), box 51, folder "GAA." Cornell University Library.

Gay Blade. 1975. "Hot Flashes." April, p. 3. Lesbian Herstory Archives, New York.

Gay Writer's Group. 1983. *It Could Happen to You: An Account of the Gay Civil Rights Campaign in Eugene, Oregon.* Boston: Alyson.

Geertz, Clifford. 1973. "Ideology as a Cultural System." Pp. 193–233 in *The Interpretation of Cultures.* New York: Basic Books.

Gelb, Joyce and Marian Lief Palley. 1982. *Women and Public Policy.* Princeton: Princeton University Press.

Gellner, E. 1983. *Nations and Nationalism.* Oxford: Basil Blackwell.

Gergen, Kenneth J., and Mary M. Gergen. 1997. "Narratives of the self." In *Memory, Identity, Community: The Idea of Narrative in the Human Sciences*, edited by Lewis P. Hinchman and Sandra K. Hinchman. 161–184. Albany: State University of New York.

Gerhards, Jürgen, and Dieter Rucht. 1992. "Meso-mobilization: Organizing and Framing in Two Protest Campaigns in West Germany." *American Journal of Sociology* 98: 555–596.

Gerlach, Luther P., and Virginia H. Hine. 1970. *People, Power, and Change: Movements of Social Transformation.* Indianapolis: Bobbs-Merrill.

Gerson, Judith. 2001. "'In Cuba I Was a German Shepherd': Questions of Comparison and Generalizability in Holocaust Memoirs." Paper presented at the Conference on Sociological Perspectives on the Holocaust and Post-Holocaust Life, Rutgers University.

Gerth, Hans and C. Wright Mills. 1946. "Introduction." Pp. 3–70 in *From Max Weber: Essays in Sociology,* edited by H. Gerth and C. W. Mills. New York: Oxford University Press.

Geschwender, James. 1964. "Social Structure and the Negro Revolt." *Social Forces* 43: 248–56.

———. 1971. *The Black Revolt: The Civil Rights Movement, Ghetto Uprisings, and Separatism.* Englewood Cliffs, N.J.: Prentice-Hall.

———. 1973. "Relative Deprivation and Participation in the Civil Rights Movement." *Social Science Quarterly* 54 (2): 403–41.

Getlin, Josh. 2003. "Editorials Reflect Public Ambivalence About War." *Los Angeles Times.* March 18.

Giddens, Anthony. 1976. *New Rules of Sociological Method: A Positive Critique of Interpretative Sociologies.* New York: Basic Books.

———. 1979. *Central Problems in Social Theory.* Berkeley and Los Angeles: University of California Press.

Giddings, Paula. 1984. *When and Where I Enter: The Impact of Black Women on Race and Sex in America.* New York: Bantam.

Giglioli, Pier Paolo and Gianpietro Mazzoleni. 1992. "Processi di Concentrazione Editoriale e Sistema dei Media" (Publishers Mergers and Media System). Pp. 191–209 in *Politica in Italia: 1990,* edited by R. Catanzaro and F. Sabetti. Bologna, Italy: il Mulino. (English translation in *Italian Politics Yearbook: 1990.* London, England: Pinter.)

Giles, Michael. 1977. "Percent black and racial hostility: An old assumption reexamined." *Social Science Quarterly* 58: 412–417.

Giles, Michael, and Arthur Evans. 1985. "External threat, perceived threat, and group identity." *Social Science Quarterly* 66: 55–66.

Gilroy, P. 1991. *There Ain't No Black in the Union Jack: The Cultural Politics of Race and Nation.* Chicago: University of Chicago Press.

Ginsberg, Faye. 1990. *Contested Lives: The Abortion Debate in an American Community.* Berkeley and Los Angeles: University of California Press.

Ginsborg, Paul. 1990. *Italy Since 1943.* London, England: Penguin.

———. ed. 1994. *Stato dell'Italia* (State of Italy). Milan, Italy: il Saggiatore-Bruno Mondadori.

Githens, Marianne, and Dorothy McBride Stetson. 1996. *Abortion Politics: Public Policy in Cross-Cultural Perspective.* New York: Routledge.

Gitlin, Todd. 1980. *The Whole World Is Watching.* Berkeley: University of California Press.

———. 1987. *The Sixties: Years of Hope, Days of Rage.* New York: Bantam Books.

———. 1994. "From Universality to Difference: Notes on the Fragmentation of the Idea of the Left." Pp. 150–74 in *Social Theory and the Politics of Identity,* edited by Craig Calhoun. Cambridge, Mass.: Blackwell.

———. 1995. *The Twilight of Common Dreams: Why America Is Wracked by Culture Wars.* New York: Metropolitan Books.

Giugni, Marcc G. 1992. "The role of diffusion processes in new social movements: Some conceptual clarifications." New School for Social Research, Center for Studies of Social Change Working Paper (No. 143), July.

Giugni, Marco. 1998. "Was It Worth the Effort? The Outcomes and Consequences of Social Movements." *Annual Review of Sociology* 24: 371–93.

———. 2004. *Social Protest and Policy Change: Ecology, Antinuclear, and Peace Movements in Comparative Perspective.* Lanham, MD: Rowan and Littlefield.

Giugni, Marco, Charles Tilly, and Doug McAdam, eds. 1999. *How Social Movements Matter.* Minneapolis: University of Minnesota Press.

Glaser, Barney G. and Anselm L. Strauss. 1967. *The Discovery of Grounded Theory.* Chicago, IL: Aldine Publishing.

Glock, Charles Y. 1964. "The role of deprivation in the origin and evolution of religious groups." Pp. 24–36 in *Religion and Social Conflict,* edited by R. Lee and M. Marty. New York: Oxford University Press.

Gluck, Sherna Berger. 1987. *Rosie the Riveter Revisited: Women, the War, and Social Change.* Boston: Twayne Publishers.

Goffman, Erving. 1959. *The Presentation of Self in Everyday Life.* Garden City, New York: Doubleday.

Goffman, Erving. 1959. *The Presentation of Self in Everyday Life.* New York: Doubleday.

———. 1961. *Asylums.* New York: Anchor.

———. 1971. *Relations in Public: Microstudies of the Public Order.* New York: Harper Colophon Books.

Goffman, Erving. 1974. *Frame Analysis: An Essay on the Organization of Experience.* New York: Happer Colophon.

———. 1984. "Characteristics of Total Institutions." Pp. 464–77 in *Deviant Behavior,* edited by D. Kelly. New York: St. Martin's.

Gold, Hohn R. 1980. *An Introduction to Behavioral Geography.* New York: Oxford University Press.

Golden, Mariam 1986. "Interest representation, party systems, and the State." *Comparative Politics* April: 279–302.

Goldfield, Michael. 1997. "Race and Labor in the United States." *Monthly Review* 49: 80–97.

Goldstone, Jack. 1980. "The Weakness of Organization: A New Look at Gamson's *The Strategy of Social Protest.*" *American Journal of Sociology* 85: 1017–42.

Goldstone, Jack. 1986. "Introduction: The Comparative and Historical Study of Revolutions." Pp. 1–17 in *Revolutions: Theoretical, Comparative, and Historical Studies,* edited by J. Goldstone. San Diego, Calif.: Harcourt Brace Jovanich.

Goldstone. Jack A. 1991. *Revolution and Rebellion in the Early Modern World.* Berkeley: University of California Press.

Goldstone, Jack. 1998. "Initial Conditions, General Laws, Path Dependence, and Explanation in Historical Sociology." *American Journal of Sociology* 104: 829–45.

Goldstone, Jack A. and Charles Tilly. 2001. "Threat (and opportunity): Popular Action and State Response in the Dynamics of Contentious Action." Pp. 179–194 in *Silence and Voice in Contentious Politics*, Ron Aminzade, Jack A. Goldstone, Doug McAdam, Elizabeth Perry, William Sewell, Jr., Sidney Tarrow, and Charles Tilly. Cambridge, U.K.: Cambridge University Press.

Gollege, Reginald G., and Harry Timmermans. 1988. *Behavioral Modelling in Geography and Planning.* London: Croom Helm.

Gonos, G. 1977. "'Situation' versus 'frame': The 'interactionist' and the 'structuralist' analyses of everyday life." *American Sociological Review* 42: 854–67.

Gonzalez, Edward. 1974. *Cuba Under Castro: The Limits of Charisma,* Boston, MA: Houghton-Mifflin Company.

Goodwin, Jeff. 1997a. "State-Centered Approaches to Social Revolution." Pp. 11–37 in *Theorizing Revolutions,* edited by J. Foran. New York: Routledge.

———. 1997b. "The Libidinal Constitution of a High-Risk Social Movement: Affectual Ties and Solidarity in the Huk Rebellion, 1946–54." *American Sociological Review* 62: 53–69.

———. 2000. *No Other Way Out: States and Revolutionary Movements, 1945–91.* New York: Cambridge University Press.

Goodwin, Jeff and James M. Jasper. 1999. "Caught in a Winding, Snarling Vine: The Structural Bias of Political Process Theory." *Sociological Forum* 14: 27–54.

———. 2004. *Rethinking Social Movements: Structure, Meaning, and Emotion.* New York: Rowman & Littlefield.

Goodwin, Jeffrey, James Jasper, and Francesca Polletta. 2000. "The Return of the Repressed: The Fall and Rise of Emotions in Social Movement Theory." *Mobilization* 5: 65–84.

———. 2001a. *Passionate Politics: Emotions in Social Movements.* Chicago: University of Chicago Press.

———. 2001b. "Why Emotions Matter." Pp. 1–24 in *Passionate Politics: Emotions and Social Movements,* edited by J. Goodwin, J. Jasper, and F. Polletta. Chicago: University of Chicago Press.

Goodwin, Jeff and Steven Pfaff. 2001. "Emotion Work in High-Risk Social Movements: Managing Fear in the U.S. and East German Civil Rights Movements." Pp. 282–302 in *Passionate Politics,* edited by J. Goodwin,

J. M. Jasper, and F. Polletta, Chicago: The University of Chicago Press.

Gordon, David M., Richard Edwards, and Michael Reich. 1982. *Segmented Work, Divided Workers: The Historical Transformation of Labor in the United States.* Cambridge: Cambridge University Press.

Gordon, Linda. 1990. *Woman's Body, Woman's Right: A Social History of Birth Control in America,* rev. ed. New York: Penguin.

Gordon, Sara. 1989. *La guerra política en El Salvador.* Mexico City: Siglo Veintiuno.

Goslant, Keith. 1991. "Madeleine Kunin: A Fond Farewell." *Out in the Mountains* 5, no. 9 (January): 1.

Gould, Roger V. 1990. *Social Structure and Insurgency in the Paris Commune, 1871.* Ph.D. dissertation. Harvard University, Department of Sociology.

———. 1991. "Multiple Networks and Mobilization in the Paris Commune, 1871." *American Sociological Review* 56: 716–29.

———. 1993. "Collective Action and Network Structure." *American Sociological Review* 58: 182–96.

———. 1995. *Insurgent Identities: Class, Community, and Protest in Paris from 1848 to the Commune.* Chicago: University of Chicago Press.

———. 2003. "Why Do Networks Matter? Rationalist and Structuralist Interpretations." Pp. 233–57 in *Social Movement Networks: Relational Approaches to Collective Action,* edited by Mario Diani and Doug McAdam. New York: Oxford University Press.

Gouldner, Alvin. 1955. "Metaphysical Pathos and the Theory of Bureaucracy." *American Political Science Review* 49: 496–507.

Gouldner, Alvin W. 1976. *The Dialectic of Ideology and Technology: The Origins, Grammar, and Future of Ideology.* New York: Seabury Press.

Graham, Hugh Davis. 1990. *The Civil Rights Era: Origins and Development of National Policy 1960–1972.* New York: Oxford University Press.

Gramsci, Antonio. [1935] 1971. *Selections from the Prison Notebooks.* Edited by Q. Hoare and G. N. Smith. New York: International Publishers.

Granberg, Donald. 1982. "Comparison of Pro-Choice and Pro-Life Activists—Their Values, Attitudes, and Beliefs." *Population and Environment* 5 (2): 75–94.

———. 1991. "Conformity to Religious Norms Regarding Abortion." *Sociological Quarterly* 32 (2): 267–75.

Granovetter, Mark S. 1973. "The Strength of Weak Ties." *American Journal of Sociology* 78: 1360–80.

———. 1978. "Threshold Models of Collective Behavior." *American Journal of Sociology* 83: 1420–43.

———. 1982. "The strength of weak ties: a network theory revisited." Pp. 105–30 in *Social Structure and Network Analysis,* edited by Peter V. Marsden and Nan Lin. Beverly Hills. CA: Sage.

Grattet, Ryken, Valerie Jenness, and Theodore R. Curry. 1998. "The homogenization and differentiation of hate crime law in the United States, 1978 to 1995: Innovation and diffusion in the criminalization of bigotry." *American Sociological Review* 63(2): 286–307.

Gray, Andrew. 1998. "Development Policy, Development Protest: The World Bank, Indigenous Peoples, and NGOs." Pp. 267–301 in *The Struggle for Accountability: The World Bank, NGOs, and Grassroots Movements,* edited by J. A. Fox and L. D. Brown. Cambridge: MIT Press.

Grayson, George. 1995. *The North American Free Trade Agreement: Regional Community and the New World Order.* Lanham, Md.: University Press of America.

Green, J.D. 1986. "Counter-mobilization in the Iranian Revolution." Pp. 127–38 in *Revolutions: Theoretical, Comparative, and Historical Studies,* edited by J.A. Goldstone. San Diego: Harcourt Brace Jovanovich.

Greenberg, Polly. 1969. *The Devil Has Slippery Shoes: A Biased Biography of the Child Development Group in Mississippi.* London, England: Macmillan.

Grenier, Yvon. 1999. *The Emergence of Insurgency in El Salvador: Ideology and Political Will.* Pittsburgh: University of Pittsburgh Press.

Griffin, Larry J. 1992. "Temporality, Events, and Explanation in Historical Sociology: An Introduction." *Sociological Methods and Research* 20: 403–27.

———. 1995. "How Is Sociology Informed by History?" *Social Forces* 73: 1245–54.

Griffith, Kati, and Luis Armando Gonzàlez. 2002. "Notas sobre la 'autonomía del Estado: El caso de El Salvador." Pp. 56–77 in *El Salvador: La transición y sus problemas,* edited by R. Cardenal and L. A. Gonzàlez. San Salvador: UCA Editores.

Gross, Michael L. 1994. "Jewish Rescue in Holland and France during the Second World War: Moral Cognition and Collective Action." *Social Forces* 73: 463–96.

Groves, Julian McAllister. 1997. *Hearts and Minds: The Controversy over Laboratory Animals.* Philadelphia: Temple University Press.

Grubsztein, Meir, ed. 1971. *Jewish Resistance during the Holocaust: Proceedings of the Conference on Manifestations of Jewish Resistance.* Jerusalem: Yad Vashem.

Grusky, David, and Jesper B. Sørensen. 1998. "Can Class Analysis Be Salvaged?" *American Journal of Sociology* 103: 1187–1234.

Grynberg, Michal, ed. 2002. *Words to Outlive Us: Voices from the Warsaw Ghetto.* New York: Henry Holt and Company.

Guerra Calderon, Walter. 1976. "Asociaciones comunitarias en el area rural de El Salvador en la decada 1960–1970: Análisis de las condiciones que enmarcan su desarrollo." San José, Costa Rica: CSUCA, Programa Centroamericano de Ciencias Sociales.

Guidos Véjar, Rafael. 1979. "La Crisis Política en El Salvador (1976–1979)." *Estudios Centroamericanos,* no. 369–70 (Julio–Agosto): 507–26.

——. 1980. *El acenso del militarismo en El Salvador.* San Salvador: UCA Editores.

——. 1990. "El movimiento sindical después de la segunda guerra mundial en El Salvador." *Estudios Centroamericanos,* no. 504 (Octubre): 871–92.

Gurney, Joan Neff, and Kathleen J. Tierney. 1982. "Relative Deprivation and Social Movements: A Critical Look at Twenty Years of Theory and Research." *Sociological Quarterly* 23: 33–47.

Gurr, Robert. 1970. *Why Men Rebel.* Princeton, NJ: Princeton University Press.

Gusfield, Joseph R. 1963. *Symbolic Crusade.* Urbana, IL: University of Illinois Press.

——. 1970. *Protest. Reform, and Revolt.* New York: Wiley.

——. 1981. "Social Movements and Social Change: Perspectives of Linearity and Fluidity. "Pp. 317–39 in *Research in Social Movements, Conflict and Change.* Vol. 4, edited by Louis Kriesberg. Greenwich. CT: JAI Press.

Gutman, Yisrael. 1982. *The Jews of Warsaw, 1939–1943.* Bloomington: Indiana University Press.

——. 1994. *Resistance: The Warsaw Ghetto Uprising.* Boston: Houghton Mifflin Company.

Haber, Robert A. 1966. "From protest to radicalism: an appraisal of the student struggle 1960." Pp. 41–9 in *The New Student Left,* edited by Mitchell Cohen and Dennis Hale. Boston: Dorsey.

Haines, Herbert H. 1984. "Black Radicalization and the Funding of Civil Rights: 1957–1970." *Social Problems* 32: 31–43.

——. 1988. *Black Radicals and the Civil Rights Mainstream, 1954–1970.* Knoxville: University of Tennessee Press.

Haines, Valerie A., Jeanne S. Hurlbert, and John J. Betts. 1996. "Exploring the Determinants of Support Provision: Provider Characteristics, Personal Networks, Community Contexts, and Support following Life Events." *Journal of Health and Social Behavior* 37 (3): 252–64.

Halévy, Ellie. 1924. *A History of the English People in 1815.* London: T. Fisher Unwin.

Hamilton, C. Horace. 1964. "The Negro leaves the South." *Demography* 1: 273–95.

Hamilton, Neil A. 1996. *Militias in America: A Reference Handbook.* Santa Barbara, CA: ABC-CLIO Inc.

Hamm, Mark S. 1993. *American Skinheads.* Boston, MA: Northeastern University Press.

——. 2002. *In Bad Company: America's Terrorist Underground.* Boston, MA: Northeastern University Press.

Hammami, Rema. 1993. "Women in Palestinian Society." Pp. 283–311 in *Palestinian Society in Gaza, West Bank and Arab Jerusalem: A Survey of Living Conditions,* edited by Marianne Heiberg and Geir Ovensen. Oslo: FAFO.

Hammond, John. 1998. *Fighting to Learn: Popular Education and Guerrilla War in El Salvador.* New Brunswick, N.J.: Rutgers University Press.

Handler, Joel. 1978. *Social Movements and the Legal System: A Theory of Law Reform and Social Change.* New York: Academic Press.

Hannan, Michael T. and John Freeman. 1989. *Organizational Ecology.* Cambridge, MA: Harvard University Press.

Hardin, Russell. 1982. *Collective Action.* Baltimore, MD: Johns Hopkins University Press.

Hardin, Russell. 1995. *One for All: the Logic of Group Conflict.* Princeton, N.J.: Princeton University Press.

Harnecker, Marta. 1993. *Con la mirada en alto: historia de las FPL Farabundo Marlí a través de sus dirigentes.* San Salvador: UCA Editores.

Harper, Douglas. 1992. "Small N's and Community Case Studies." Pp. 139–58 in *What Is a Case?*

Exploring the Foundations of Social Inquiry, edited by Charles C. Ragin and Howard S. Becker. New York: Cambridge University Press.

Harris, David. 1982. *Dreams Die Hard.* New York: St. Martin's.

Harrison, Cynthia. 1980. "A 'New Frontier' for Women: The Public Policy of the Kennedy Administration." *Journal of American History* 67: 630–46.

Harrison, Cynthia. 1988. *On Account of Sex.* Berkeley: University of California Press.

Hart, Janet. 1992. "Cracking the code: Narrative and political mobilization in the Greek resistance." *Social Science History* 16: 630–668.

———. 1996. *New Voices in the Nation: Women and the Greek Resistance, 1941–1964.* Ithaca, N.Y.: Cornell University Press.

Harvey, David. 1985. *Consciousness and the Urban Experience.* Baltimore: Johns Hopkins University Press.

Hassan, Nasra. 2001. "An Arsenal of Believers: Talking to 'Human Bombs.'" *The New Yorker* November 19: 36–41.

Hasso, Frances S. 1997. "Paradoxes of Gender/Politics: Nationalism, Feminism, and Modernity in Contemporary Palestine." Ph.D. dissertation. University of Michigan, Department of Sociology.

———. 1998. "The 'Women's Front': Nationalism, Feminism, and Modernity in Palestine." *Gender and Society* 12: 441–65.

Hathaway, Dale. 2000. *Allies across the Border: Mexico's "Authentic Labor Front" and Global Solidarity.* Cambridge: South End Press.

Hathaway, Will and David S. Meyer. 1997. "Competition and Cooperation in Social Movement Coalitions: Lobbying for Peace in the 1980s." Pp. 61–79 in *Coalitions and Political Movements: The Lessons of the Nuclear Freeze,* Thomas R. Rochon and David S. Meyer, eds. Boulder: Colorado: Lynne Rienner Publishers.

Hayden, Tom. 1988. *Reunion.* New York: Random House.

Hebdige, Dick. 1979. *Subculture, the Meaning of Style.* London: Methuen.

Heckathorn, Douglas D. 1997 "Respondent-Driven Sampling: A New Approach to the Study of Hidden Populations." *Social Problems* 44: 174–99.

———. 2002. "Respondent-Driven Sampling II: Deriving Valid Population Estimates from Chain Referral Samples of Hidden Populations." *Social Problems* 49: 11–34.

Hegtvedt, Karen A. and Barry Markovsky. 1995. "Justice and Injustice." Pp. 257–80 in *Sociological Perspectives in Social Psychology,* edited by Karen S. Cook, Garry A. Fine, and James S. House. Boston: Allyn and Bacon.

Heiberg, Marianne. 1993a. "Education." Pp. 131–54 in *Palestinian Society in Gaza, West Bank and Arab Jerusalem: A Survey of Living Conditions,* edited by Marianne Heiberg and Geir Ovensen. Oslo: FAFO.

———. 1993b. "Opinions and Attitudes." Pp. 249–82 in *Palestinian Society in Gaza, West Bank and Arab Jerusalem: A Survey of Living Conditions,* edited by Marianne Heiberg and Geir Ovensen. Oslo: FAFO.

Heirich, Max. 1971. *The Spiral of Conflict: Berkeley 1964.* New York: Columbia University Press.

———. 1977. "Changes of Heart: A Test of Some Widely Held Theories of Religious Conversion." *American Journal of Sociology* 83: 653–80.

Heitmeyer, Wilhelm, Heike Buhse, Joachim Liebe-Freund, Kurt Möller, Joachim Müller, Helmut Ritz, Gertrud Siller, and Johannes Vossen. 1992. *Die Bielefelder Rechtsextremismus-Studie: Erste Langzeituntersuchung zur politischen Sozialisation männlicher Jugendlicher.* Weinheim: Juventa.

Helfgot, Joseph. 1974. "Professional Reform Organizations and the Symbolic Representation of the Poor." *American Sociological Review* 39: 475–91.

Hellman, Judith. 1999. "Real and Virtual Chiapas: Magic Realism and the Left." In *Socialist Register, 2000: Necessary and Unnecessary Utopias,* edited by Leo Panitch and Colin Leys. London: Merlin Press.

Hellmich, Christina. 2005. "Al-Qaeda: Terrorists, Hypocrites, Fundamentalists? The View from Within." *Third World Quarterly* 26: 39–54.

Helsel, Rebecca. 1988. "Union to Strike If Talks Fail." *Ohio State Lantern,* March 31, p. 1.

Henriquez, Pedro. 1988. *El Salvador: Iglesia profética y cambio social.* San José, Costa Rica: Editorial DEI.

Herman, Didi. 1994. *Rights of Passage: Struggles for Lesbian and Gay Legal Equality.* Toronto: University of Toronto Press.

Hernandez Pico, Juan, et al. 1973. *El Salvador, año político 1971–72.* San Salvador: Universidad Centroamericana Jose Simeón Cañas.

Herod, Andrew, 1997. "Labor as an Agent of Globalization and as a Global Agent." In *Spaces of Globalization: Reasserting the Power of the Local,* edited by Kevin R. Cox. New York: Guilford Press.

Hewitt, Lyndi N. and Holly J. McCammon. 2004. "Explaining Suffrage Mobilization: Balance, Neutralization, and Range in Collective Action Frames." *Mobilization: An International Journal* 9: 149–66.

Hibbs, Douglas, Jr. 1976. "Industrial Strike Activity in Advanced Industrial Societies." *American Political Science Review* 70: 1033–58.

Hicks, Alexander M. 1999. *Social Democracy and Welfare Capitalism: A Century of Income Security Politics.* Ithaca, NY: Cornell University Press.

Higginbotham, Evelyn Brooks. 1992. "African-American Women's History and the Metalanguage of Race." *Signs* 17: 251–74.

Hilberg, Raul. 1979. *The Destruction of the European Jews.* New York: Harper & Row.

Hilgartner, Stephen and Charles L. Bosk. 1988. "The Rise and Fall of Social Problems: A Public Arenas Model." *American Journal of Sociology* 94: 53–78.

Hinchman, Lewis P., and Sandra K. Hinchman. 1997. *Memory. Identity, Community: The Idea of Narrative in the Human Sciences.* Albany: State University of New York.

Hiniker, Paul. 1977. *Revolutionary Ideology and Chinese Reality: Dissonance Under Mao.* Beverly Hills, CA; Sage Publications.

———. 1978. "Alternation of Charismatic and Bureaucratic Styles of Leadership in Post-Revolutionary China." *Comparative Political Studies* 10: 529–54.

Hinojosa-Ojeda, Raúl. 2002. "Integration Policy from the Grassroots Up: Transnational Implications of Latino, Labor, and Environmental NGO Strategies." In *Cross-Border Dialogues: U.S.-Mexico Social Movement Networking,* edited by David Brooks and Jonathan Fox. La Jolla: University of California, San Diego, Center for U.S.-Mexican Studies.

Hinton, William. 1966. *Fanshen: A Documentary of Revolution in a Chinese Village.* New York: Vintage Books.

———. 1972. *Hundred Day War: The Cultural Revolution at Tsinghua University,* New York: Monthly Review Press.

Hipsher, Patricia. 1998. "Democratic Transitions as Protest Cycles: Social Movement Dynamics in Democratizing Latin America." In *The Social Movement Society,* edited by D. Meyer and S. Tarrow. Lanham, Md.: Rowman & Littlefield Publishers.

Hirsch, Barry T., and David A. Macpherson. 2000. *Union Membership and Earnings Data Book: Compilations from the Current Population Survey.* Washington, D.C.: Bureau of National Affairs.

Hirsch, Eric L. 1986. "The Creation of Political Solidarity in Social Movement Organizations." *Sociological Quarterly* 27: 373–87.

———. 1990a. "Sacrifice for the Cause: Group Processes, Recruitment, and Commitment in a Student Social Movement." *American Sociological Review* 55: 243–54.

———. 1990b. *Urban Revolt: Ethnic Politics in the Nineteenth Century Labor Movement.* Berkeley: University of California Press.

———. 1998. "Social Movements or Revolutions? On the Evolution and Outcomes of Collective Action." Pp. 125–45 in *From Contention to Democracy,* edited by M. Giugni, D. McAdam, and C. Tilly. Lanham, Md.: Rowman & Littlefield.

———. 2001. "Toward a Fourth Generation of Revolutionary Theory." *Annual Review of Political Science* 4: 139–87.

Hobbes, Thomas. 1962. *Leviathan,* edited by Richard S. Peters. New York: Collier Books.

Hobsbawm, Eric. 1984. "Should Poor People Organize?" Pp. 282–96 in *Workers: Worlds of Labor,* edited by E. Hobsbawm. New York: Pantheon Books.

Hochschild, Arlie Russell. 1979. "Emotion Work, Feeling Rules, and Social Structure." *American Journal of Sociology* 85: 551–75.

———. 1983. *The Managed Heart.* Berkeley: University of California Press.

Hodgson, J. F. 2001. "Police Violence in Canada and the USA: Analysis and Management." *Policing* 24: 520–49.

Hodson, Randy. 1996. "Dignity in the Workplace under Participative Management: Alienation and Freedom Revisited." *American Sociological Review* 61: 719–38.

———. 2001. "Disorganized, Unilateral, and Participative Organizations: New Insights from the Ethnographic Literature." *Industrial Relations* 40: 204–30.

Hodson, Randy, Deborah Ziegler, and Barbara Bump. 1987. "Who Crosses the Picket Line? An Analysis of the CWA Strike of 1983." *Labor Studies Journal* 12: 19–37.

Hoffman, David S. 1996. *The Web of Hate: Extremists Exploit the Internet.* New York: Anti-Defamation League.

Hofstadter Richard. 1955. *The Age of Reform.* New York: Knopf.

Hoge, Dean R., Benton Johnson, and Donald A. Luidens. 1995. "Types of Denominational Switching among Protestant Young Adults." *Journal for the Scientific Study of Religion* 34 (2): 253–58.

Holden, Robert T. 1986. "The Contagiousness of Aircraft Hijacking." *American Journal of Sociology* 91: 874–904.

Hollander, Jocelyn A. 1997. "Discourses of Danger: The Construction and Performance of Gender Through Talk About Violence." Ph.D. dissertation, Department of Sociology, University of Washington, Seattle, WA.

———. 2001. "Vulnerability and Dangerousness: The Construction of Gender Through Conversation About Violence." *Gender & Society* 15: 83–109.

Holt, Len. 1965. *The Summer That Didn't End.* New York: Morrow.

Holtzman, Abraham. 1963. *The Townsend Movement: A Political Study.* New York: Bookman Associates.

Homans, George C. 1961. *Social Behavior.* New York: Harcourt.

Horton, Aimee Isgrig. 1989. *The Highlander Folk School: A History of Its Major Programs, 1932–61.* Brooklyn: Carlson Publishing.

Hosteller, Shari. 1986. "The Demise of St. Martin's." *Seeds* October: 15–19.

Howard, Andrew. 1995. "Global Capital and Labor Internationalism in Comparative Historical Perspective: A Marxist Analysis." *Sociological Inquiry* 65 (3/4): 365–94.

Huan, Guocang. 1989. "The Roots of the Political Crisis." *World Policy Journal* 6: 609–20.

Hubbard, Howard 1968 "Five long hot summers and how they grew." *Public Interest* 12: 3–24.

Huber, Evelyne and John D. Stephens. 2001. *Development and Crisis of the Welfare State: Parties and Policies in Global Markets.* Chicago, IL: University of Chicago Press.

Huber, Joan. 1997. "Rational Choice Models in Sociology." *American Sociologist* 28 (Summer): 42–53.

Hug, Simon, and Dominique Wisler. 1998. "Correcting for Selection Bias in Social Movement Research." *Mobilization* 3: 141–61.

Hull, Kathleen E. 1997. "The Political Limits of the Rights Frame: The Case of Same-Sex Marriage in Hawaii." *Sociological Perspectives* 44: 207–32.

Humphreys, Laud. 1972. *Out of the Closets: The Sociology of Homosexual Liberation.* Englewood Cliffs, NJ: Prentice-Hall.

Hunt, Alan. 1990. "Rights and Social Movements: Counter-Hegemonic Strategies." *Journal of Law and Society* 17: 309–28.

Hunt, Scott A. and Robert D. Benford, 1994. "Identity Talk in the Peace and Justice Movement." *Journal of Contemporary Ethnography* 22: 488–517.

Hunt, Scott, and Robert Benford. 1994. "Identity talk in the peace and justice movements." *Journal of Contemporary Ethnography* 22: 488–517.

Hunt, Scott, Robert D. Benford, and David A. Snow. 1994. "Identity Fields: Framing Processes and the Social Construction of Movement Identities." Pp. 185–208 in *New Social Movements: From Ideology to Identity*, edited by E. Laraña, H. Johnson, and J. R. Gusfield. Philadelphia: Temple University Press.

Hunter, Neale. 1969. *Shanghai Journal: An Eyewitness Account of the Cultural Revolution.* Boston, MA: Beacon Press.

Huston, Luther A. 1939. "Congress Wind-Up on or Near July 15 Again Is Predicted." *New York Times.* July 3, p. 1.

Huus, Kari. 2003. "Aryan Nations Plots a Comeback at Idaho Campout." Retrieved June, 24, 2003 (http://www.msnbc.com/news/927968.asp).

Ibrahim, Youssef M. 1979. "Inside Iran's Cultural Revolution." *New York Times* October 14: Sec. 6, 36.

IDHUCA (Instituto de Derechos Humanos Universidad Centroamericana). 1997. "Resumen de los cuadros y gráficos de las violaciones a los derechos humanos ocurridas entre 1975 y 1994. Manuscript. Universidad Centroamericana José Simeón Cañas.

Ignazi, Piero. 1994. *Postfascisti* (Postfascists). Bologna, Italy: il Mulino.

Incisa, Lodovico. 1983. "Populismo" (Populism). Pp. 859–64 in *Dizionario di Politica* (Dictionary of Politics), edited by N. Bobbio, N. Matteucci, and G. Pasquino. Turin, Italy: UTET.

Inglehart, Ronald. 1977. *The Silent Revolution: Changing Values and Political Styles Among Western Publics.* Princeton, NJ: Princeton University Press.

Irkin, Michael Francis. 1969. "The Homosexual Liberation Movement: What Direction?" *San Francisco Free Press*: 8–9.

Irvine, Leslie. 1999. *Codependent Forevermore: The Invention of Self in a Twelve-Step Group.* Chicago: University of Chicago Press.

Isaac, Larry, and Lars Christiansen. 2002. "How the Civil Rights Movement Revitalized Labor Militancy." *American Sociological Review* 67: 722–46.

Isaac, Larry W. and Larry J. Griffin. 1989. "A historicism in Time-Series Analyses of Historical Process: Critique, Redirection, and Illustrations from U.S. Labor History." *American Sociological Review* 54: 873–90.

Isaac, Larry and William R. Kelly. 1981. "Racial insurgency, the state, and welfare expansion: local and national level evidence from the postwar United States." *American Journal of Sociology* 86: 1348–86.

Iser, Wolfgang. 1972. "The reading process: A phenomenological approach." *New Literary History* 3: 279–299.

Isserman, Maurice. 1987. *If I Had a Hammer: The Death of the Old Left and the Birth of the New Left.* New York: Basic.

Istat. 1993a. *Le Regioni in Cifre* (Regional Statistics). Rome, Italy: Istituto Nazionale di Statistica.

———. 1993b. *Compendio Statistico Italiano 1993* (Italy: A Statistical Profile 1993). Rome, Italy: Istituto Nazionale di Statistica.

Jackson, Maurice, Eleanora Peterson, James Bull, Sverre Monsen, and Patricia Richmond. 1960. "The Failure of an Incipient Social Movement." *Pacific Sociological Review* 3: 35–40.

Jacob, Herbert, and Kenneth Vines. 1965. *Politics in the American States: A Comparative Analysis.* Boston: Little, Brown.

Jacobs, David, and Ronald Helms. 2001. "Racial Politics and Redistribution: Isolating the Contingent Influence of Civil Rights, Riots, and Crime on Tax Progressivity." *Social Forces* 80: 91–121.

Jacobs, David, and Katherine Wood. 1999. "Interracial conflict and interracial homicide: Do political and economic rivalries explain white killings of blacks or black killings of whites?" *American Journal of Sociology* 105: 157–190.

Jacobs, Lawrence R. and Robert Y. Shapiro. 2000. *Politicians Don't Pander: Political Manipulation and the Loss of Democratic Responsiveness.* Chicago, IL: University of Chicago Press.

Jacobs, Ronald N. 1996. "Civil Society and Crisis: Culture, Discourse, and the Rodney King Beating." *American Journal of Sociology* 101: 1238–72.

Jacoway, Elizabeth and David Colburn, eds. 1982. *Southern Businessmen and Desegregation.* Baton Rouge, LA: Louisiana State University Press.

Jacquet, Constant H. 1987–98. *Yearbook of American and Canadian Churches.* Nashville: Abingdon.

Jäger, Siegfried, and Jürgen Link, eds. 1993. *Die vierte Gewali: Rassismus und die Medien.* Duisburg: DISS.

Jaggar, Alison M. 1990. "Sexual Difference and Sexual Equality." Pp. 239–54 in *Theoretical Perspectives on Sexual Difference,* edited by D. L. Rhode. New Haven, CT: Yale University Press.

James, David. 1988. "The Transformation of the Southern Racial State." *American Sociological Review* 53: 191–208.

Jane McCallum Papers. 1939, February 27. "Account of Committee on Constitutional Amendments." Box 429, Folder PI. Austin History Center.

Jansen, G. H. 1979. *Militant Islam.* New York: Harper & Row.

Jaquette, Jane S., ed. 1994. *The Women's Movement in Latin America: Participation and Democracy,* 2d ed. Boulder, Colo.: Westview Press.

Jasper, James M. 1997. *The Art of Moral Protest.* Chicago: University of Chicago Press.

———. 1998. "The Emotions of Protest: Affective and Reactive Emotions in and Around Social Movements." *Sociological Forum* 13: 397–424.

———. 2004. "A Strategic Approach to Collective Action: Looking for Agency in Social Movement Choices." *Mobilization* 9: 1–16.

Jasper, James M., and Dorothy Nelkin. 1992. *The Animal Rights Crusade: The Growth of a Moral Protest.* New York: Free Press.

Jasper, James M., and Jane D. Poulsen. 1993. "Fighting Back: Vulnerabilities, Blunders and Countermobilization by the Targets of Three Animal Rights Campaigns." *Sociological Forum* 8: 639–57.

Jay, Karla, and Allen Young, eds. 1992 [1972]. *Out of the Closets: Voices of Gay Liberation.* New York and London: New York University Press.

Jaynes, Gerald, and Robin Williams, Jr. 1989. *A Common Destiny: Blacks and American Society.* Washington, D.C.: National Academy Press.

Jefferson, Tony. 1990. *The Case Against Paramilitary Policing.* Milton Keynes, Buckingham, England: Open University Press.

Jemison, Rev. T. J. 1978. *Interview.* Baton Rouge, Louisiana. October 16.

Jencks, Christopher. 1994. *The Homeless.* Cambridge, MA: Harvard University Press.

Jenkins, J. Craig. 1981. "Sociopolitical Movements." Pp. 81–153 in *Handbook of Political Behavior,* edited by Samuel Long. Vol. 4. New York: Plenum.

———. 1983a. "Resource Mobilization Theory and the Study of Social Movements." *Annual Review of Sociology* 10: 527–53.

———. 1983b. "The Transformation of a Constituency Into a Movement: Farmworker Organizing in California." Pp. 52–70 in *The Social Movements of the 1960s and 1970s,* edited by J. Freeman. New York: Longman.

———. 1985a. *The Politics of Insurgency: The Farm Worker Movement in the 1960s.* New York: Columbia University Press.

———. 1985b. "Foundation Funding of Progressive Social Movements." Pp. 7–17 in *Grant Seekers Guide: Funding Sourcebook,* edited by Jill R. Shellow. Mt. Kisco, NY: Moyer Bell Ltd.

———. 1987a. "Interpreting the Stormy 1960s: Three Theories in Search of a Political Age." *Research in Political Sociology* 3: 269–303.

———. 1987b. "Nonprofit Organizations and Policy Advocacy." Pp. 296–318 in *The Nonprofit Sector,* edited by W. W. Powell. New Haven: Yale University Press.

———. 1995. "Social Movements, Political Representation, and the State: An Agenda and Comparative Framework." Pp. 14–35 in *The Politics of Social Protest: Comparative Perspectives on States and Social Movements,* edited by J. C. Jenkins and Bert Klandermans. Minneapolis: University of Minnesota Press.

Jenkins, J. Craig, and Doug Bond. 2001. "Conflict-Carrying Capacity, Political Crisis, and Reconstruction: A Framework for the Early Warning of Political System Vulnerability." *Journal of Conflict Resolution* 45 (1): 3–31.

Jenkins, J. Craig and Craig M. Eckert. 1986. "Channeling Black Insurgency: Elite Patronage and Professional Social Movement Organizations in the Development of the Black Movement." *American Sociological Review* 51: 812–29.

Jenkins, J. Craig, and William Form. 2005. "Social Movements and Social Change." Pp. 331–49 in *The Handbook of Political Sociology,* edited by Thomas Janoski, Robert Alford, Alexander Hicks, and Mildred Schwartz. New York: Cambridge University Press.

Jenkins, J. Craig, David Jacobs, and Jon Agnone. 2003. "Political Opportunities and African-American Protest, 1948–1997." *American Journal of Sociology* 109: 277–303.

Jenkins, J. Craig, and Bert Klandermans. 1995. "The Politics of Social Protest." Pp. 3–13 in *The Politics of Social Protest: Comparative Perspectives on States and Social Movements,* edited by J. C. Jenkins and Bert Klandermans. Minneapolis: University of Minnesota Press.

Jenkins, J. Craig and Charles Perrow. 1977. "Insurgency of the Powerless: Farm Workers' Movements (1946–1972)." *American Sociological Review* 42: 249–68.

———. 1977. "Insurgency of the Powerless." *American Sociological Review* 42: 249–68.

Jennie Loitman Barron Papers. 1923, February: "Legislative Bulletin: Jury Service for Women." Box 3, Folder 50. Schlesinger Library, Radcliffe College, Harvard University.

Jennings, Kent M. 1987. "Residues of a Movement: The Aging of the American Protest Generation." *American Political Science Review* 81: 368–82.

Jennings, Kent M., and Richard G. Niemi. 1981. *Generations and Politics: A Panel Study of Young Adults and Their Parents.* Princeton, N.J.: Princeton University Press.

Jepperson, Ronald L. 1991. "Institutions, Institutional Effects, and Institutionalism." Pp. 143–63 in *The New Institutionalism in Organizational Analysis,* edited by Walter W. Powell and Paul J. DiMaggio. Chicago: University of Chicago Press.

Jessup, David, and Michael E. Gordon. 2002. "Organizing in Export Processing Zones: The Bibong Experience in the Dominican Republic." In *Transnational Cooperation among Labor Unions,* edited by Michael E. Gordon and Lowell Turner. Ithaca, N.Y.: Cornell University Press.

Johnson, D.G., and R.D. Lee (eds.). 1987. *Population Growth and Economic: Development: Issues and Evidence.* Madison: University of Wisconsin Press.

Johnson, David K. 1994–95. "'Homosexual Citizens': Washington's Gay Community Confronts the Civil Service." *Washington History* 6, no. 2 (Fall/Winter): 45–63.

Johnson-Odim, Cheryl. 1991. "Common Themes, Different Contexts: Third World Women and Feminism." Pp. 314–27 in *Third World Women and the Politics of Feminism,* edited by Chandra Talpade Mohanty, Ann Russo, and Lourdes Torres. Bloomington: Indiana University Press.

Johnston, Hank. 1991. *Tales of Nationalism.* New Brunswick, NJ: Rutgers University Press.

———. 1994. "New Social Movements and Old Regional Nationalisms." Pp. 267–86 in *New Social Movements: From Ideology to Identity,* edited by E. Laraña, H. Johnston, and J. R. Gusfield. Philadelphia, PA: Temple University Press.

Johnston, Hank, and Bert Klandermans, eds. 1995. *Social Movements and Culture.* Minneapolis: University of Minnesota Press.

Johnston, Hank, Enrique Larana, and Joseph R. Gusfield. 1994. "Identities, grievances and new social movements." In *New Social Movements: From Ideology to Identity*, edited by Larana. Johnston and Gusfield, 3–35. Philadelphia, Pennsylvania: Temple University Press.

Johnston, Hank and David A. Snow. 1998. "Subcultures and the Emergence of the Estonian Nationalist Opposition 1945–1990." *Sociological Perspectives* 41: 473–97.

Johnston, Paul. 1994. *Success While Others Fail: Social Movement Unionism and the Public Workplace.* Ithaca, N.Y.: ILR Press.

———. 2001. "Organize for What? The Resurgence of Labor as a Citizenship Movement." Pp. 27–59 in *Rekindling the Movement: Labor's Quest for Relevance in the Twenty-First Century,* edited by Lowell Turner, Harry C. Katz, and Richard W. Hurd. Ithaca, N.Y.: ILR Press.

Johnston, Susan 1994. "On the Fire Brigade: Why Liberalism Won't Stop the Anti-Gay Campaigning of the Right" *Critical Sociology* 20 (3): 3–19.

Joll, James. 1964. *The Anarchists.* Boston: Little Brown.

Joseph, Suad. 1993. "Gender and Relationality among Arab Families in Lebanon." *Feminist Studies* 19: 465–86.

Journal. 1977. "Recall of Portland Mayor Ends in Failure." October 19. Collection 7301 (National Gay and Lesbian Task Force), box 99, folder "Oregon." Cornell University Library.

Jowitt, Kenneth, 1983. "Soviet Neo-traditionalism; The Political Corruption of a Leninist Regime." *American Political Science Review* 35: 275–97.

Juergensmeyer, Mark. 2000: *Terror in the Mind of God: The Global Rise of Religious Violence.* Berkeley: University of California Press.

Kahneman, Daniel, and Amos Tversky. 1979. "Prospect Theory: An Analysis of Decision Under Risk." *Econometrica* 47: 263–291.

Kalter, Joanmarie. 1985. "Abortion Bias: How Network Coverage Has Tilted to the Pro-Lifers." *TV Guide* 33: 7–17.

Kandiyoti, Deniz. 1988. "Bargaining with Patriarchy." *Gender and Society* 2 (3): 274–90.

Kanter, Rosabeth Moss. 1968. "Commitment and Social Organization: A Study of Commitment Mechanisms in Utopian Communities." *American Sociological Review* 33: 499–517.

———. 1972. *Commitment and Community.* Cambridge. MA: Harvard University Press.

Kaplan, Jeffrey. 1995. "Right-Wing Violence in North America." Pp. 44–95 in *Terror from the Extreme Right,* edited by T. Bjorgo. London: Frank Cass.

Kaplan, Jeffrey and Leonard Weinberg. 1998. *The Emergence of a Euro-American Radical Right.* New Brunswick, NJ: Rutgers University Press.

Kaplowitz, Stan. 1973. "An Experimental Test of a Rationalistic Theory of Deterrence." *Journal of Conflict Resolution,* September, 17: 535–72.

Karstedt-Henke, Sabine. 1980. "Theorien zur Erklärung terroristischer Bewegungen" (Theories for the Explanation of Terrorist Movements). Pp. 198–234 in *Politik der inneren Sicherheit* (The Politics of Internal Security), edited by E. Blankenberg. Frankfurt, Germany: Suhrkamp.

Kassow, Samuel D. 1989. *Students, Professors, and the State in Tsarist Russia.* Berkeley and Los Angeles: University of California Press.

Katzenstein, Mary. 1990. "Feminism within American Institutions." *Signs* 16: 27–54.

Katzenstein, Mary Fainsod. 1998. *Faithful and Fearless: Moving Feminist Protest inside the Church and Military.* Princeton, N. J.: Princeton University Press.

Katzenstein, Mary, and Carol Mueller. 1987. *The Women's Movements of the United States and Western Europe.* Philadelphia: Temple University Press.

Katzenstein, P.J. 1987. *Policy and Politics in West Germany: The Growth of a Semisovereign State.* Philadelphia: Temple University Press.

Katznelson, Ira. 1981. *City Trenches.* Chicago, IL: University of Chicago Press.

Kay, Tamara. 2000. "A Conceptual Framework for Analyzing Labor Relations in a Post-NAFTA Era: The Impact of NAFTA on Transnational Labor Cooperation and Collaboration in North America." Paper presented at the annual meetings of the Latin American Studies Association, Miami, March.

——. 2003*a*. "Bypassing the State: The Effects of Legal and Political Contexts on Union Organizing Strategies." Paper presented at the annual meetings of the American Sociological Association, Atlanta, August.

——. 2003*b*. "Even Labor Unions Can Gain from Free Trade." *Yale Global Online,* December 23.

——. 2004*a*. "From Wetback to Compañero: How Regional Economic Integration Helped Undermine Union Racism in North America." Paper presented at the annual meetings of the American Sociological Association, San Francisco, August.

——. 2004*b*. "NAFTA and the Politics of Labor Transnationalism." Ph.D. dissertation. University of California, Berkeley, Department of Sociology.

Kazimi, Nibras. 2006. "Zarqawi's Anti-Shia Legacy: Original or Borrowed?" D.C: Hudson Institute, Retrieved August 2, 2006 (http: //www.futureofmuslimworld.com/research/pubID.50/pub_detail.asp).

Keck, Margaret, and Kathryn Sikkink. 1998. *Activists Beyond Borders: Transnational Advocacy Networks in International Politics.* Ithaca, NY: Cornell University Press.

Keddie, Nikki R. 1981. *Roots of Revolution: An Interpretive History of Modern Iran.* New Haven, CT: Yale University Press.

Kendall, Patricia L. and Katherine M. Wolf. 1941. "The two purposes of deviant case analysis." Pp. 167–70 in *The Language of Social Research,* edited by Paul F. Lazarsfeld and Morris Rosenberg. New York: Free Press.

Kennard, Florence Elizabeth, 1931, "Maryland Women Demand Jury Service," *Equal Rights* 16: 36–7.

Kennedy, David M. 1970. *Birth Control in America.* New Haven: Yale University Press, 1970.

Kenworthy, Lane. 2002. "Corporatism and Unemployment in the 1980s and 1990s." *American Sociological Review* 67: 367–88.

Kepel, Gilles. 2002. *Jihad: The Trail of Political Islam.* Translated by Anthony F. Roberts. Cambridge, MA: Harvard University Press.

Kerber, Linda K. 1998. *No Constitutional Right to Be Ladies: Women and the Obligations of Citizenship.* New York: Hill and Wang.

Kermish, Joseph, ed. 1986. *To Live With Honor and Die With Honor: Selected Documents from the Warsaw Ghetto Underground Archives "O.S." [Oneg Shabbath].* Jerusalem: Yad Vashem.

Kerr, Clark, and Abraham Siegel. 1954. "The Interindustry Propensity to Strike—an International Comparison." Pp. 189–212 in *Industrial Conflict,* edited by Arthur Kornhauser, Robert Dubin, and Arthur Ross. New York: McGraw-Hill.

Khagram, Sanjeev. 2004. *Dams and Development: Transnational Struggles for Water and Power.* Ithaca, N.Y.: Cornell University Press.

Khagram, Sanjeev, James V. Riker, and Kathryn Sikkink. 2002a. *Restructuring World Politics: Transnational Social Movements, Networks, and Norms.* Minneapolis: University of Minnesota Press.

——. 2002b. "From Santiago to Seattle: Transnational Advocacy Groups Restructuring World Politics." In *Restructuring World Politics: Transnational Social Movements, Networks, and Norms,* edited by Sanjeev Khagram, James V. Riker, and Kathryn Sikkink. Minneapolis: University of Minnesota Press.

Khawaja, Marwan. 1993. "Repression and Popular Collective Action: Evidence from the West Bank." *Sociological Forum* 8: 47–71.

Kidder, Thalia G. 2002. "Networks in Transnational Labor Organizing." In *Restructuring World Politics: Transnational Social Movements, Networks, and Norms,* edited by Sanjeev Khagram, James V. Riker, and Kathryn Sikkink. Minneapolis: University of Minnesota Press.

Kielbowicz, Richard B., and Clifford Scherer. 1986. "The Role of the Press in the Dynamics of Social Movements." *Research in Social Movements, Conflicts, and Change* 4: 71–96.

Kilbourne, Barbara, Paula England, and Kurt Beron. 1994. "Effects of Individual, Occupational, and Industrial Characteristics on Earnings: Intersections of Race and Gender." *Social Forces* 72: 1149–76.

Killian, Lewis M. 1964. "Social Movements." Pp. 426–55 in *Handbook of Modern Sociology,* edited by Robert E.L. Faris. Chicago: Rand McNally.

——. 1968. The Impossible Revolution? New York: Random House.

Killian, Lewis M. 1984. "Organization, rationality and spontaneity in the civil rights movement." *American Sociological Review* 49: 770–83.

Kim, Hyojoung, and Peter S. Bearman. 1997. "The Structure and Dynamics of Movement Participation." *American Sociological Review* 62: 70–93.

Kimeldorf, Howard. 1985. "Working Class Culture, Occupational Recruitment, and Union Politics." *Social Forces* 64: 359–76.

——. 1999. *Battling for American Labor: Wobblies, Craft Workers, and the Making of the Union Movement.* Berkeley and Los Angeles: University of California Press.

Kimeldorf, Howard, and Judith Stepan-Norris. 1992. "Historical Studies of Labor Movements in the United States." *Annual Review of Sociology* 18: 495–517.

Kimmel, Michael. 1984. Review of *Regulating Society* by Ephraim H. Mizruchi. *Society,* July/August: 90–92.

Kimmel, Michael, and Abby Perber. 2000. " 'White men are this nation': Right wing militias and the restoration of rural American masculinity." *Rural Sociology* 65(4): 582–604.

King, Debra, 2004. "Operationalizing Meluccl: Metamorphosis and Passion in the Negotiation of Activists' Multiple Identities." *Mobilization* 9: 73–92.

King, Gary. 1989. *Unifying Political Methodology: The Likelihood Theory of Statistical Inference.* Cambridge: Cambridge University Press.

King, Katie. 1986. "The situation of lesbianism as feminism's magic sign: Contests for meaning and the U.S. Women's Movement, 1968–1972." *Communication* 9: 65–91.

King, Martin Luther, Jr. 1958. *Stride toward Freedom: The Montgomery Story.* New York: Harper.

——. 1963. *Why We Can't Wait.* New York: Harper & Row.

Kingdon, John W. 1984. *Agendas, Alternatives, and Public Policies.* Boston, MA: Little, Brown.

Kirby, Robert Gerald. 1992. *Agrarian Politics in El Salvador: 1950–1984.* Ph.D. diss., University of Pennsylvania, Department of Political Science.

Kiser, Edgar. 1996. "The Revival of Narrative in Historical Sociology: What Rational Choice Theory Can Contribute." *Politics and Society* 24: 249–71.

Kissack, Terence. 1995. "Freaking Fag Revolutionaries: New York's Gay Liberation Front, 1969–1971." *Radical History Review* 62: 104–34.

Kitschelt, Herbert P. 1986. "Political Opportunity Structures and Political Protest: Anti-Nuclear Movements in Four Democracies." *British Journal of Political Science* 16: 57–85.

——. 1993. "Social Movements, Political Parties, and Democratic Theory." *The Annals of the AAPSS* 528: 13–29.

——. 1995. *The Radical Right in Western Europe: A Comparative Analysis.* Ann Arbor: The University of Michigan Press.

Klandermans, Bert, 1984. "Mobilization and Participation: Social Psychological Expansions of Resource Mobilization Theory." *American Sociological Review* 49: 583–600.

——. 1986. "New Social Movements and Resource Mobilization: The European and the American Approach." *Mass Emergencies and Disasters* 4: 13–38.

——. 1988. "The Formation and Mobilization of Consensus." *International Social Movement Research* 1: 173–96.

——. 1990a. "Linking the 'old' and the 'new': Movement networks in the Netherlands." Pp. 122–36 in *Challenging the Political Order,* edited by Russell Dalton and Manfred Kuechler. New York: Oxford University Press.

——. 1992. "The Social Construction of Protest and Multiorganizational Fields." Pp. 77–103 in *Frontiers in Social Movement Theory,* edited by A. D. Morris and C. M. Mueller. New Haven. CT: Yale University Press.

——. 1994. "Transient Identities? Membership Patterns in the Dutch Peace Movement." Pp. 168–84 in *New Social Movements: From Ideology to Identity,* edited by E. Larana, H. Johnston, and J. R. Gusfield. Philadelphia, PA: Temple University Press.

——. 1997. *The Social Psychology of Protest.* Oxford, U.K. and Cambridge. Massachusetts: Blackwell.

Klandermans, Bert, and Marga de Weerd. 2000. "Group Identification and Political Protest" Pp. 68–90 in *Self, Identity, and Social Movements,* edited by Sheldon Stryker, Timothy J. Owens, and Robert W. White. Minneapolis: University of Minnesota Press.

Klandermans, Bert and Dirk Oegema. 1987a. "Campaigning for a Nuclear Freeze: Grass-Roots Strategies and Local Governments in the Netherlands." *Research in Political Sociology* 3: 305–37.

——. 1987b. "Potentials, Networks, Motivation, and Barriers: Steps Toward Participation in Social Movements." *American Sociological Review* 52: 519–31.

Klandermans, Bert, and Sidney Tarrow. 1988. "Mobilization into Social Movements: Synthesizing European and American Approaches." In Pp. 1–38 *From Structure to Action: Comparing Social Movement Research Across Cultures,* edited by Bert Klandermans, Hanspeter Kriesi, and Sidney Tarrow. Vol. I of *International Social Movement Research.* Greenwich, CT: JAI Press.

Kleidman, Robert. 1986. "Opposing 'The Good War': Mobilization and Professionalization in the Emergency Peace Campaign." *Research in Social Movements. Conflicts and Change* 9: 177–200.

Klein, Ethel. 1984. *Gender Politics: From Consciousness to Mass Politics.* Cambridge, MA: Harvard University Press.

Klejment, Anne and Nancy Roberts. 1996. "The Catholic Worker and the Vietnam War." Pp. 153–70 in *American Catholic Pacifism,* edited by A. Klejment and N. Roberts. Westport, CT: Praeger.

Klejment. Anne. 1996. "The Radical Origins of Catholic Pacifism: Dorothy Day and the Lyrical Left during World War II." Pp. 15–32 in *American Catholic Pacifism,* edited by A. Klejment and N. Roberts. Westport, CT: Praeger.

Klocklars, Carl B. 1980. "The Dirty Harry Problem." *Annals of The American Academy of Political and Social Science* 452: 33–47.

Knapp Commission. 1973. *The Knapp Commission Report on Police Corruption.* New York: George Braziller.

Kniss, Fred. 1997. "Culture Wars (?): Remapping the Battleground." Pp. 259–80 in *Cultural Wars in American Politics: Critical Reviews of a Popular Myth,* edited by Rhys H. Williams. New York: Aldine De Gruyter.

Kobler, Arthur. 1975. "Police Homicide in a Democracy." *Journal of Social Issues* 31: 163–84.

Konhauser, William. 1959. *The Politics of Mass Society.* New York: The Free Press.

Koopmans, Rudd, 1990a. "Bridging the Gap: The Missing Link Between Political Opportunity Structure and Movement Action." Paper presented at the ISA Congress, Jul. 7–10, Madrid, Spain.

———. 1990b. "Patterns of Unruliness: The Interactive Dynamics of Protest Waves. Unpublished paper, University of Amsterdam: PDIS.

———. 1991. "Demokratie von unten: Neue soziale Bewegungen und politisches System in der Bundersrepublik Deutschland in internationalen Vergleich."
In *Neue soziale Bewegungen in der Bundesrepublik Deutschland,* 2nd edition, edited by R. Roth and Rucht D. Bonn: Bundeszentrale für politische Bildung.

———. 1993. "The Dynamics of Protest Waves: West Germany, 1965–1989." *American Sociological Review* 58 (5): 637–58.

———. 1995. *Democracy from Below: New Social Movements and the Political System in West Germany.* Boulder, CO: Westview.

———. 1996. "Explaining the rise of racist and extreme right violence in western Europe: Grievances or opportunities?" *European Journal of Political Research* 30: 185–216.

———. 1997. "Dynamics of Repression and Mobilization: The German Extreme Right in the 1990s." *Mobilization* 2: 149–65.

———. 2001. "Alter Rechtsextremismus und neue Fremdenfeindlichkeit: Mobilisierung am rechten Rand im Wandel." Pp. 103–42 in *Protest in der Bundesrepublik: Strukluren und Entwicklungen,* edited by Dieter Rucht Frankfurt: Campus.

———. 2004. "Protest in Time and Space: The Evolution of Waves of Contention." Pp. 19–46 in *The Blackwell Companion to Social Movements,* edited by David A. Snow, Sarah A. Soule, and Hanspeter Kriesi. Oxford: Blackwell.

Koopmans, Ruud and Jan-Willem Duyvendak. 1995. "The Political Construction of the Nuclear Energy Issue and Its Impact on the Mobilization of AntiNuclear Movements in Western Europe." *Social Problems* 42: 201–18.

Koopmans, Ruud, and Susan Olzack. 2002. "Right-Wing Violence and the Public Sphere in Germany: The Dynamics of Discursive Opportunities." Paper presented at "Conflict, Culture, and Contention" conference, Princeton University Center for Arts and Cultural Policy Studies, October.

Koopmans, Ruud, and Dieter Rucht. 1995. "Social Movement Mobilization under Right and Left Governments." Discussion paper. Wissenschafszentrum Berlin.

Koopmans, Ruud, and Paul Statham. 1999a. "Ethnic and Civic Conceptions of Nationhood and the Differential Success of the Extreme Right in Germany and Italy." Pp. 225–51 in *How Social Movements Matter,* edited by Marco Giugni, Doug McAdam, and Charles Tilly. Minneapolis: University of Minnesota Press.

Koopmans, Ruud, and Paul Statham. 1999*b*. "Political Claims Analysis: Integrating Protest Event and Public Discourse Approaches." *Mobilization* 4: 203–22.

Kowalsky, Wolfgang, and Wolfgang Schroeder. 1994. *Rechtsextremismus: Einführung und Forschungsbilanz*. Opladen: Westdeutscher Verlag.

Kraditor, Aileen S. 1981. *The Ideas of the Woman Suffrage Movement, 1890–1920*. New York: W. W. Norton.

Krane, Dale and Stephen Shaffer, 1992. *Mississippi Government and Politics*. Lincoln, NE: University of Nebraska Press.

Krasner, Stephen. 1983. *International Regimes*. Ithaca, N.Y.: Cornell University Press.

Krell, Gert, Hans Nicklas, and Änne Ostermann. 1996. "Immigration, Asylum, and Anti-Foreigner Violence in Germany." *Journal of Peace Research* 33: 153–70.

Kriesi, Hanspeter. 1989a. Politische Randbedingungen der Entwicklung neuer sozialer Bewegungen. Pp. 104–21, in *Westliche Demokratie und Interessenvermitlung. Beitrage zur aktuellen Entwicklung nationaler Parteien-und Verbandssysteme*. edited by R. Kleinfeld und W. Luthando. Hagen: Femuniversität-Geamthochschule.

———. 1989b. "The Political Opportunity Structure of the Dutch Peace Movement." *West European Politics* 12: 295–312.

———. 1990. "Federalism and Pillarization: the Netherlands and Switzerland Compared." *Acta Politica* 25: 433–50.

———. 1991. *The Political Opportunity Structure of New Social Movements: Its Impact on Their Mobilization*. Wissenschaftszentrum Berlin für Sozialforschung, FS III 91–103.

———. 1995. "The Political Opportunity Structure of New Social Movements: Its Impact on Their Mobilization." Pp. 167–98 in *The Politics of Social Protest: Comparative Perspectives on States and Social Movements*, edited by J. Craig Jenkins and Bert Klandermans. Minneapolis, MN: University of Minnesota Press.

———. 1996. "The Organizational Structure of New Social Movements in a Political Context." Pp. 152–84 in *Comparative Perspectives on Social Movements*, edited by Doug McAdam, John D. McCarthy, and Mayer N. Zald. Cambridge: Cambridge University Press.

———. 2004. "Political Context and Opportunity." Pp. 67–90 in *The Blackwell Companion to Social Movements*, edited by David A. Snow, Sarah A. Soule, and Hanspeter Kriesi. Malden, Mass.: Blackwell.

Kriesi, Hanspeter, and Marco G. Giugni. 1995. Introduction to *New Social Movements in Western Europe: A Comparative Analysis*, edited by Hanspeter Kriesi, Ruud Koopmans, Jan Willem Duyvendak, and Marco G. Giugni, Minneapolis: University of Minnesota Press.

Kriesi, Hanspeter, Ruud Koopmans, Jan Willem Duyvendak, and Marco G. Giugni. 1995. *New Social Movements in Western Europe: A Comparative Analysis*. Minneapolis: University of Minnesota Press.

Kriesi, H., R. Levy, G. Ganguillet, and H. Zwicky. 1981. *Politische Aktivierung in der Schweiz. 1945–78*. Diessenhofen: Ruagger.

Kriesi, Hanspeter, and Philip van Praag Jr. 1987. "Old and New Politics: The Dutch Peace Movement and the Traditional Political Organizations. *European Journal of Political Science* 15: 319–46.

Krippendorff, Klaus. 1980. *Content Analysis: An Introduction to Its Methodology*. Thousand Oaks, CA: Sage Publications.

Krueger, Alan, and Jill Maleckova. 2003. "Education, Poverty, and Terrorism: Is There a Causal Connection?" *Journal of Economic Perspectives* 17: 119–44.

Krupat, Edward. 1985. *People in Cities: The Urban Environment and Its Effects*. Cambridge: Cambridge University Press.

Kuai, Dafu. 1966. *Qinghua Daxue dazibao* (Tsinghua University Big-Character Posters). Beijing: Tsinghua University Jinggangshan Red Guard Propaganda Team.

Kubal, Timothy J. 1998. "The Presentation of Political Self: Cultural Resonance and the Construction of Collective Action Frames." *The Sociological Quarterly* 39: 539–54.

Kubik, Jan. 1998. "Institutionalization of Protest during Democratic Consolidation in Central Europe." Pp. 131–52 in *The Social Movement Society*, edited by D. S. Meyer and S. Tarrow. Boulder. CO: Rowman and Littlefield.

Kull, Steven, Clay Ramsay, and Evan Lewis. 2003. "Misperceptions, the Media and the Iraq War." *Political Science Quarterly* 118: 569–90.

Kurthen, Hermann, Werner Bergmann, and Rainer Erb, eds. 1997. *Antisemitism and Xenophobia in Germany after Unification*. New York: Oxford University Press.

Kurzman, Charles. 1992. *Structure and Agency in the Iranian Revolution of 1979*. Ph.D. dissertation. Department of Sociology, University of California, Berkeley, CA.

Kurzman, Charles. 1996. "Structural Opportunity and Perceived Opportunity in Social-Movement Theory: The Iranian Revolution of 1979." *American Sociological Review* 61: 153–70.

Kurzman, Dan, 1993. *The Bravest Battle: The Twenty-eight Days of the Warsaw Ghetto Uprising*. New York: Da Capo Press, Inc.

Laba, Roman. 1991. *The Roots of Solidarity*. Princeton, N.J.: Princeton University Press.

Lader, Lawrence. 1966. *Abortion*. Boston: Beacon Press.

———. 1973. *Abortion II: Making the Revolution*. Boston: Beacon Press.

Ladrech, R. 1989. "Social Movements and Party Systems: The French Socialist Party and New Social Movements." *West European Politics* 12: 262–79.

Laffin, Arthur and Anne Montgomery. 1987. *Swords into Plowshares: Nonviolent Direct Action for Disarmament*. San Francisco. CA: Harper and Row.

Lamy, Philip. 1996. *Millennium Rage*. New York: Plenum Press.

Land, Kenneth C., Patricia L. McCall, and Daniel S. Nagin. 1996. "A comparison of Poisson, negative binomial, and semi-parametric mixed Poisson regression models." *Sociological Methods & Research* 24(4): 387–442.

Landino, Rita. and Lynne B. Welch. 1990. "Supporting women in the university environment through collaboration and networking." Pp. 12–19 in *Women and Higher Education: Changes and Challenges*, edited by Lynne B. Welch. New York: Praeger Publishers.

Lang, Kurt and Gladys E. Lang. 1961. *Collective Dynamics*. New York: Thomas Y. Crowell.

Laraña, Enrique. Hank Johnston, and Joseph R. Gusfield, eds. 1994. *New Social Movements: From Ideology to Identity*. Philadelphia: Temple University Press.

Larín, Augusto A. 1972. *La sindicalización de los trabajadores del campo*. San Salvador: Universidad de El Salvador, Facultad de Jurisprudencia y Ciencias Sociales.

Latin American Bureau. 1977. *Violence and Fraud in El Salvador: A Report on Current Political Events in El Salvador*. London: Latin American Bureau.

Laue, James H. 1971. "A model for civil rights change through conflict." Pp. 256–62 in *Racial Conflict*, edited by Gary T. Marx. Boston: Little, Brown.

———. 1989. *Direct Action and Desegregation, 1960–62*. Brooklyn, New York: Carlson.

Laumann, Edward O., and David Knoke. 1987. *The Organizational State: Social Choice in National Policy Domains*. Madison: University of Wisconsin Press.

Laumann, Edward O., and Franz U. Pappi. 1976. *Networks of Collective Action: A Perspective on Community Influence Systems*. New York: Academic Press.

Lawson, James. 1978. *Interview*. Los Angeles, California. October 2 and 6.

Lawson, Steven F. 1976. *Black Ballots*. New York: Columbia University Press.

Layton, Azza Salama. 2000. *International Politics and Civil Rights Policies in the United States, 1941–1960*. New York: Cambridge University Press.

Lazarus-Black, Mindie, and Susan F. Hirsch, eds. 1994. *Contested States: Law, Hegemony, and Resistance*. New York: Routledge.

League of Women Voters of Northampton. 1941, March. "Massachusetts League of Women Voters Bulletin: Meet Our Women Legislators." Box 6, Folder 34, Smith College.

League of Women Voters of South Carolina Papers. 1966, October. "The Roundtable: Women Should be on State Juries." Box 31. Folder "Gov't, Jud., Jury, 60–67." University of South Carolina.

Leahy, Peter J. 1975. *The anti-abortion movement: testing a theory of the rise and fail of social movements*. Ph.D. dissertation. Department of Sociology, Syracuse University.

Lee, Chang Kil, and David Strang. 2003. "The International Diffusion of Public Sector Downsizing." Unpublished paper, Cornell University, Department of Sociology.

Lee, Hong Yung, 1978. *The Politics of the Chinese Cultural Revolution: A Case Study*. Berkeley, CA: University of California Press.

Lefebvre, Henri. 1971. *Everyday Life in the Modern World*. New York: Harper Torchbooks.

Legal Citations *Brown v. Board of Education*. 347 U.S. 483 (1954).

Leicht, Kevin T., and J. Craig Jenkins. 1998. "Political resources and direct state intervention: The adoption of public venture capital programs in the American states, 1974–1990." *Social Forces* 76: 1323–1346.

Leitch, Thomas M. 1986. *What Stories Are: Narrative Theory and Interpretation.* University Park: Pennsylvania State University Press.

Lelyveld, Joseph. 2001. "All Suicide Bombers are Not Alike." *New York Times Magazine* October 28 49–53, 62, 78–79.

Lemann, Nicholas. 2002. "The War on What? The White House and the Debate About Whom to Fight Next" *The New Yorker* September 16, p. 36+.

Lemberg Center for the Study of Violence. 1968. "April aftermath of the King Assassination." Riot Data Review 2 (August), Waltham, MA: Lemberg Center for the Study of Violence, Brandeis University.

Lemons, J. Stanley. 1973. *The Woman Citizen: Social Feminism in the 1920s.* Urbana: University of Illinois Press.

Lemons, J. Stanley. 1973. *The Woman Citizen: Social Feminism in the 1920s.* Champaign, IL: University of Illinois Press.

Lenin, V. I. 1929. *What Is To Be Done? Burning Questions of Our Movement.* New York: International Publishers.

——. 1970. "What is to be Done?" Pp. 458–72 in *Protest, Reform, and Revolt,* edited by Joseph R. Gusfield. New York: Wiley.

——. [1923] 1975. "Better Fewer, But Better." Pp. 734–46 in *The Lenin Anthology,* edited by R. Tucker, New York: Norton and Company.

Leonardi, Robert and Monique Kowacs. 1993. "L'Irresistibile Ascesa della Lega Nord" (The Irresistible Rise of the Northern League). Pp. 123–42 in *Politica in Italia: 1993,* edited by S. Hellman and G. Pasquino. Bologna, Italy: il Mulino. (English translation in *Italian Politics Yearbook: 1993.* London, England: Pinter.)

Lerner, M.J. 1980. *The Belief in a Just World: A Fundamental Delusion.* New York: Plenum.

Lesbian/Gay Law Notes. 1994a. "Florida Supreme Court Dumps Anti-Gay Ballot Measure: Other Ballot Measure News," p. 37.

——. 1994b. "News of Other Initiatives and Referenda," p. 1.

Letwin, Daniel. 1998. *The Challenge of Interracial Unionism: Alabama Coal Miners, 1878–1921.* Chapel Hill: University of North Carolina Press.

Levine, Martin P. 1992. "The status of gay men in the workplace." Pp. 251–66 in *Men's Lives,* edited by Michael S. Kimmel and A. Messner. New York: Macmillan Publishing.

Levitt, Peggy, and Nina Glick Schiller. 2003. "Transnational Perspectives on Migration: Conceptualizing Simultaneity." Center for Migration and Development Working Paper no. 3–09J. Princeton University.

Lewis, Bernard. 2002. *What Went Wrong? Western Impact and Middle Eastern Response.* New York: Oxford University Press.

Lewis, Chester. 1981. *Interview.* Wichita, Kansas. February 3.

Lewis, David L. 1978. *King: A Biography,* 2d ed. Urbana: University of Illinois Press.

Lewis, John. 1978. *Interview.* Washington, D.C. November 9.

Lewis, Michael and Jacqueline Serbu. 1999. "Kommemorating the Ku Klux Klan." *Sociological Quarterly* 40: 139–158.

Lewis, S.C. and S. Sferza. 1987. "Les socialistes français entre l'Etal et la Société: de la construction du parti à la conquête du pouvoir." Pp. 132–51, in *L'Expérience Mitterrand,* edited by S. Hoffman and G. Ross. Paris: PUF.

Lewis, Tammy L. 2002. "Transnational Conservation Movement Organizations: Shaping the Protected Area Systems of Less Developed Countries." Pp. 65–84 in *Globalization and Resistance: Transnational Dimensions of Social Movements,* edited by J. Smith and H. Johnston. Boulder, CO: Rowman and Littlefield.

Li, Jinmin. 1988. "Daxuesheng zhong de Nicaire jiqi jiexi" (An analysis on the Nietzsche fever among university students). *Qingnian yanjiu* (Youth research), no. 12, pp. 30–35.

Licata, Salvatore J. 1981. "The Homosexual Rights Movement in the United States: A Traditionally Overlooked Area of American History." *Journal of Homosexuality* 6: 161–89.

Lichbach, Mark. 1987. "Deterrence of Escalation? The Puzzle of Aggregate Studies of Repression and Dissent." *Journal of Conflict Resolution* 31: 266–97.

Lichtenstein, Nelson. 1980. "Auto Worker Militancy and the Structure of Factory Life, 1937–1955." *Journal of American History* 67: 335–53.

Lichterman, Paul. 1996. *The Search for Political Community: American Activists Reinventing Commitment.* New York: Cambridge University Press.

———. 1999. "Talking Identity in the Public Sphere: Broad Visions and Small Spaces in Sexual Identity Politics." *Theory and Society* 28: 101–41.

Lieberman, Robert C. 1998. *Shifting the Color Line: Race and the American Welfare State.* Cambridge, MA: Harvard University Press.

Lifton, Robert. 1968. *Revolutionary Immortality: Mao Tse-tung and the Chinese Cultural Revolution.* New York: W. W. Norton.

Lin, Piao. [1969] 1972. "Report to the Ninth National Congress of the Communist Party of China." Pp. 437–77 in *Essential Works of Chinese Communism,* 2d ed., edited by W. Chai. New York: Bantam Books.

Lincoln, James R. 1978. "Community Structure and Industrial Conflict: An Analysis of Strike Activity in SMSAs." *American Sociological Review* 43: 199–220.

Linneman, Thomas J. 2003. *Weathering Change: Gays and Lesbians, Christian Conservatives, and Everyday Hostilities.* New York: New York University Press.

Linz, Juan J. 1978. "Crisis, breakdown, and reequilibriation." Pp. 1–124 in *The Breakdown of Democratic Regimes,* edited by Juan J. Linz and Alfred Stepan. Baltimore: Johns Hopkins University Press.

Linz, Juan J., and Alfred Stepan. 1996. *Problems of Democratic Transition and Consolidation.* Baltimore: Johns Hopkins University Press.

Lionberger, H. F. 1960. Adoption of New Ideas and Practices. Ames: The Iowa State University Press.

Lipset, Seymour Martin. 1963. "The sources of the 'radical right'—1955." Pp. 259–312 in *The Radical Right,* edited by Daniel Bell.. Garden City, NY: Doubleday and Co.

Lipset, Seymour Martin and Gary Wolfe Marks. 2000. *It Didn't Happen Here: Why Socialism Failed in the United States.* New York: W. W. Norton and Co.

Lipset, S.M. and S. Rokkan. 1967. "Cleavage Structures, Party Systems, and Voter Alignments." Reprinted in *Consensus and Conflict: Essays in Political Sociology,* edited by S.M. Lipset. New Brunswick, NJ: Transaction Books, 1985: 113–85.

Lipset, Seymour Martin, Martin A. Trow, and James S. Coleman. 1956. *Union Democracy.* Glencoe, Ill.: Free Press.

Lipset, Seymour Martin and Sheldon S. Wolin. 1965. *The Berkeley Student Revolt.* Garden City, New York: Doubleday.

Lipsky, Michael. 1968. "Protest as a Political Resource." *American Political Science Review* 62: 1144–58.

Lipsky, Michael. 1970. *Protest in City Politics.* Chicago: Rand McNally.

Liu, Dehuan, and Dongyou Huang. 1989. "1986 niandi de xuechao yuanyin tanxi" (An analysis on the causes of the student uprising at the end of 1986). *Qingnian yanjiu* (Youth research), no. 5, pp. 27–32.

Liu, Qinglong. 1990. "Shehui yingxiang yu xuexiao sixiang zhengzhi jiaoyu diaocha yu shiyian de sikao" (My investigation and thoughts on social influence and university political education). Pp. 52–61 in *Dui bashi niandai shoudu daxuesheng zongxian yanjiu* (Longitudinal studies on university students in Beijing during the eighties), edited by Lixin Cang. Beijing: Beijing Shifan Xueyuan Chubanshe.

Liu, Shao-chi. [1939] 1972. "How To Be a Good Communist." Pp. 133–51 in *Essential Works of Chinese Communism,* 2d ed., edited by W. Chai. New York: Bantam Books.

Lo, Clarence Y. H. 1990. *Small Property, Big Government.* Berkeley, CA: University of California Press.

Lobao, Linda, and Paul Lasley. 1995. "Farm restructuring and crisis in the heartland: An introduction." Pp. 1–28 in *Beyond Amber Waves of Grain: An Examination of Social and Economic Restructuring in the Heartland,* edited by Paul Lasley, Larry Reistaitz, Linda Lobao, and Katherine Meyer. Boulder, CO: Westview Press.

Lofland, John. 1968. "The Youth Ghetto: Age Segregation and Conflict in the American Sixties." *Journal of Higher Education* 39: 121–143.

———. 1970. "The Youth Ghetto." Pp. 756–78 in *The Logic of Social Hierarchies,* edited by Edward Laumann, Paul M. Siegel, and Robert W. Hodge. Chicago: Marrham.

———. 1978. "Becoming a world-saver revisited." Pp. 10–23 in *Conversion Careers,* edited by J. Richardson. Beverly Hills, CA: Sage.

———. 1985a. "Social Movement Culture." Pp. 219–39 in *Protest: Studies of Collective Behavior and Social Movements,* edited by John Lofland. New Brunswick, NJ: Transaction.

———. 1985b. *Protest: Studies of Collective Behavior and Social Movements.* New Brunswick, NJ: Transaction Books.

Lofland, John. 1993a. "Theory-bashing and Answer-improving in the Study of Social Movements." *The American Sociologist* 24: 37–58.

———. 1993b. *Polite Protestors: The American Peace Movement of the 1980s.* Syracuse, NY: Syracuse University Press.

Lofland, John, and Rodney Stark. 1965. "Becoming a World-Saver: A Theory of Conversion to a Daivant Perspective." *American Journal of Sociology* 30: 862–74.

Lofland, Lyn H. 1973. *A World of Strangers: Order and Action in Urban Public Space.* New York: Basic.

Lofland, Lyn H. 1990. "Is Peace Possible?: An Analysis of Sociology." *Sociological Perspectives* 33: 313–325.

Lomax, Louis E. 1960. "The Negro revolt against 'the Negro leaders'." (June): 41–8.

Lomax, Louis E. 1962. "The Negro Revolt." New York: New American Library.

Long, J. Scott. 1997. *Regression Models for Categorical and Limited Dependent Variables.* Thousand Oaks. CA: Sage.

Long, J. Scott and Jeremy Freese. 2001. *Regression Models for Categorical Dependent Variables using Stata.* College Station, TX: Stata.

Loo, C. 1972. "The Effects of Spatial Density on the Social Behavior of Children." *Journal of Applied Social Psychology* 2: 372–81.

López, Carlos Roberto. 1983. *Industrialización y urbanización en El Salvador, 1969-1979.* San Salvador: UCA Editores.

Lorber, Judith. 2001. *Gender Inequality: Feminist Theories and Politics,* 2d ed. Los Angeles: Roxbury Publishers.

Loveman, Mara. 1998. "High-Risk Collective Action: Defending Human Rights in Chile, Uruguay, and Argentina." *American Journal of Sociology* 104 (2): 477–525.

Lovenduski, Joni, and Joyce Outshoorn. 1986. *The New Politics of Abortion.* London: Sage.

Lowenthal, Richard. 1970. "Development vs. Utopia in Communist Policy." Pp. 33–116 in *Change in Communist Systems,* edited by C. Johnson. Stanford, CA: Stanford University Press.

Lubbers, Marcel, and Peer Scheepers. 2001. "Explaining the Trend in Extreme Right Wing Voting in Germany, 1989-1998." *European Sociological Review* 17: 431–49.

Lubetkin, Zivia. 1981. *In the Days of Destruction and Revolt.* Beit Lohamei Hagettaot and Hakibbutz Hameuchad Publishing House.

Luján, Bertha E. 1999. "Estándares Laborales y Globalización: El Caso del ACLAN." In *El Cotidiano* 94 (March–April): 13–22.

Luker, Kristen. 1984. *Abortion and the Politics of Motherhood.* Berkeley and Los Angeles: University of California Press.

Lumley, Robert. 1990. *States of Emergency.* London, England: Verso.

Lunardini, Christine A. 1986. *From Equal Suffrage to Equal Rights.* New York: New York University Press.

Lundberg, Ferdinand and Marynia F. Farnham. 1947. *Modern Woman: The Lost Sex.* New York: Harper.

Lundman, Richard J. 1974. "Routine Police Arrest Practices: A Commonweal Perspective." *Social Problems* 22: 127–41.

Lungo, Mario. 1987. *La lucha de las masas.* San Salvador: UCA Editores.

Luper, Clara. 1979. "Behold the Walls." Jim Wire.

———. 1980. "Interview." Oklahoma City, Oklahoma. (Follow-up interview. January 1981).

Lupher, Mark. 1996. *Power Restructuring in China and Russia.* Boulder. CO: Westview Press.

Lutz, Alma. 1968. *Crusade for Freedom—Women of the Antislavery Movement.* Boston: Beacon Press.

MacFarquhar, Roderick and Michael Schoenhals, 2006. *Mao's Last Revolution.* Cambridge, MA: Harvard University Press.

Machiavelli, Niccolo. 1950. *The Prince and the Discourses,* translated by Luigi Ricci and Christian E. Detmold. New York: Random House.

MacKinnon, Catharine, and Andrea Dworkin. 1997. *In Harm's Way: The Pornography Civil Rights Hearings.* Cambridge, Mass.: Harvard University Press.

MacLean, Nancy. 1994. *Behind the Mask of Chivalry: The Making of the Second Ku Klux Klan.* New York: Oxford University Press.

Macleod, Arlene. 1991. *Accommodating Protest: Working Women, the New Veiling, and Change in Cairo.* New York: Colombia University Press.

MacLeod, Jay. 1991. "Introduction: Racism, Resistance, and the Origins of the Holmes County Movement." Pp. 1–20 in *Minds Stayed on Freedom.* Boulder, CO: Westview.

Macpherson, W. J. 1987. *The Economic Development of Japan, C. 1868-1914.* New York: Macmillan.

Madsen, Douglas and Peter Snow. 1991. *The Charismatic Bond: Political Behavior in Time of Crisis.* Cambridge, MA: Harvard University Press.

Maguire, Diarmuid. 1995. "Opposition Movements and Opposition Parties." Pp. 199–298 in *The Politics of Social Protest,* edited by J. Craig Jenkins and Bert Klandermans. Minneapolis: University of Minnesota Press.

Mahoney, James. 2001. "Radical, Reformist and Aborted Liberalism: Origins of National Regimes in Central America." *Journal of Latin American Studies* 33 (2): 221–56.

Major, Brenda. 1994. "From Social Inequality to Personal Entitlement: The Role of Social Comparisons, Legitimacy Appraisals, and Group Membership." *Advances in Experimental Social Psychology* 26: 293–355.

Makofsky, Abraham. 1978. "Voluntary Associations in a Climate of Repression: Union Activists in El Salvador." *Human Organization* 37 (1): 57–63.

Maleck-Lewy, Eva, and Myra Marx Ferree. 2000. "Talking about Women and Wombs: Discourse about Abortion and Reproductive Rights in the GDR during and after the 'Wende.' " Pp. 92–117 in *Reproducing Gender: Politics, Publics and Everyday Life after Socialism,* edited by Susal Gal and Gail Kligman. Princeton, N.J.: Princeton University Press.

Mallows, C. 1986. "Augmented Partial Residuals." *Technometrics* 28: 313–19.

Mann, Michael. 1993. *The Sources of Social Power.* Vol. 2, *The Rise of Classes and Nation-States, 1760–1914.* Cambridge: Cambridge University Press.

Mannheim, Karl. 1952. "The Problem of Generations." Pp. 276–320 in *Essays on the Sociology of Knowledge,* edited by Paul Kecskemeti. London: Routledge & Kegan Paul.

———. 1985. *Ideology and Utopia: An Introduction to the Sociology of Knowledge.* San Diego, CA: Harcourt Brace Jovanovich.

Mannheimer, Renato, Roberto Biorcio, Ilvo Diamanti, and Paolo Natale. 1991. *La Lega Lombarda* (The Lombard League). Milan, Italy: Feltrinelli.

Mannheimer, Renato and Giacomo Sani. 1994. *La Rivoluzione Elettorale* (The Electoral Revolution). Milan, Italy: Anabasi.

Mansbridge, Jane. 1994. "Politics of Persuasion." Pp. 298–310 in *The Dynamics of American Politics,* edited by L. C. Dodd and C. Jillison. Boulder, CO: Westview.

Manza, Jeff and Fay Lomax Cook. 2002. "The Impact of Public Opinion on Public Policy: The State of the Debate." Pp. 17–32 in *Navigating Public Opinion: Polls, Policy, and the Future of American Democracy,* edited by Jeff Manza, Fay Lomax Cook, and Benjamin I. Page. New York: Oxford University Press.

Mao, Zedong. [1965] 1969. "Comment on Comrade Ch'en Cheng-jen's Report on Stay at a Selected Spot." Translated in *Current Background* 891: 49.

Marais, Hein. 1998. *South Africa. Limits to Change. The Political Economy of Transition.* Cape Town: University of Capetown Press.

March, James, and Johan P. Olsen. 1976. "Organization, choice under ambiguity." In *Ambiguity and Choice in Organizations,* edited by James G. March and Johan P. Olsen, 10–23. Bergen, Norway: Universitetsforlaget.

Marchant-Shapiro, Andrew. 1990. "Rehabilitating Kornhauser? Mass Society, Networks, and Social Movements." Unpublished paper. Union College. Department of Sociology.

Marcus, John. 1961. "Transcendence and Charisma." *The Western Political Quarterly* 14: 236–41.

Marini, Margaret. 1992. "The Role of Models of Purposive Action in Sociology." Pp. 21–48 in *Rational Choice Theory,* edited by J. S. Coleman and T. Fararo. Newbury Park, Calif.: Sage.

Mariz, Cecilia. 1994. *Coping with Poverty.* Philadelphia: Temple Univeristy Press.

Markoff, John. 1996. *Waves of Democracy: Social Movements and Political Change.* Thousand Oaks, Calif.: Pine Forge Press.

Marks, Gary and Doug McAdam. 1996. "Social Movements and the Changing Structure of Political Opportunities in the European Union." *Journal of West European Politics* 19: 249–78.

Marotta, Toby. 1981. *The Politics of Homosexuality.* Boston: Houghton Mifflin.

Marrs, Texe. 1993. *Big Sister is Watching You: Hillary Clinton and the White House Feminists Who Now Control America—and Tell the President What To Do.* Austin, TX: Living Truth Publishers.

Marrus, Michael R., ed. 1989. *The Nazi Holocaust, Vol. 7: Jewish Resistance to the Holocaust.* Westport, CT: Meckler Corporation.

Marsden, Peter V., and Noah E. Friedkin. 1994. "Network Studies of Social Influence." Pp. 3–25 in *Advances in Social Network Analysis: Research in the Social and Behavioral Sciences,* edited by Stanley Wasserman and Joseph Galaskiewicz. Thousand Oaks, Calif.: Sage.

Marshall, Anna-Maria. 2003. "Injustice Frames, Legality and the Everyday Construction of Sexual Harassment." *Law and Social Inquiry* 28: 659–89.

Martello, Leo Louis. 1970a. "Gay Activists Alliance Forms in New York City." *Los Angeles Advocate,* March, pp. 1, 15.

———. 1970b. "N.Y. Primary a Victory for Gays." *Advocate,* August 5–18, p. 2.

Martin, David. 1990. *Tongues of Fire: The Explosion of Protestantism in Latin America.* Oxford: Basil Blackwell.

Martin, Del. 1970. "Del Martin: Columnist Resigns, Blasts Male Chauvinism." *Vector* (October): 35–7.

Martin, Del, and Phyllis Lyon. 1991. *Lesbian/Woman.* Volcano, CA: Volcano Press.

Martin, Joanne. 1986. "The Tolerance of Injustice." Pp. 217–42 in *Relative Deprivation and Social Comparison: The Ontario Symposium,* vol 4, edited by James M. Olson, C. Peter Herman, and Mark P. Zanna. Hillsdale, NJ: Erlbaum.

Martin, Yancey. 1977. "Interview with Yancey Martin." Pp. 52–56 in *My Soul Is Rested,* edited by Howell Raines. New York: Bantam.

Martinez, Luis. 2000. *The Algerian Civil War, 1990–1998.* New York: Columbia University Press.

Martinotti, Guido and Sonia Stefanizzi. 1994. "Basic Instincts. Le Tendenze Nascoste dell'Elettorato Italiano" (The Hidden Inclinations of Italian Electors). *Reset* 5: 4–6.

Marwell, Gerald, Michael T. Aiken, and N. J. Demerath III. 1987. "The Persistence of Political Attitudes among 1960s Civil Rights Activists." *Public Opinion Quarterly* 51: 359–75.

Marwell, Gerald, Pamela E. Oliver, and Ralph Prahl. 1988. "Social Networks and Collective Action: A Theory of the Critical Mass. III." *American Journal of Sociology* 94: 502–34.

Marwell, Gerald, and Pamela Oliver. 1993. *The Critical Mass in Collective Action: A Micro-Social Theory.* Cambridge: Cambridge University Press.

Marx, Anthony W. 1998. *Making Race and Nation: a Comparison of the United States, South Africa, and Brazil.* Cambridge, UK: Cambridge University Press.

Marx, Gary T. 1979. "External Efforts to Damage or Facilitate Social Movements: Some Patterns, Explanations, Outcomes, and Complications." Pp. 94–125 in *The Dynamics of Social Movements,* edited by M. N. Zald and J. D. McCarthy. Cambridge, MA: Winthrop.

Marx, Gary T. and Michael Useem. 1971. "Majority involvement in minority movements: civil rights, abolition, untouchability." Journal of Social Issues 27: 81–104.

Marx, Gary T., and James L. Wood. 1975. "Strands of Theory and Research in Collective Behavior." *Annual Review of Sociology* 1: 363–428.

Marx, Karl. 1985a. *The Communist Manifesto.* Pp. 221–47 in *Karl Marx, Selected Writings,* edited by David McLellan. New York Oxford University Press.

———. 1985b. *The Eighteenth Brumaire of Louis Bonaparte.* Pp. 300–325 in *Karl Marx: Selected Writings,* edited by David McLellan. New York: Oxford University Press.

Marx, Karl, and Frederick Engels. 1989. *The German Ideology.* Edited by CJ. Arthur. New York: Individual Publishers.

Marx, Mathew. 2000. "OSU Union Overwhelmingly Approves Three-Year Contract." *Columbus Dispatch,* May 26, p. 11E.

Marx, Matthew, and Alice Thomas. 2000. "OSU Workers: No Deal Strike to Go On; University Might Hire More Temps." *Columbus Dispatch,* May 6, p. 1A.

Masters, John C. and William P. Smith. 1987. *Social Comparison, Social Justice, and Relative Deprivation: Theoretical, Empirical and Policy Perspectives.* Hillsdale, NJ: Erlbaum.

Mathews, Donald G. and Jane Sherron De Hart. 1990, *Sex, Gender, and the Politics of ERA.* New York: Oxford University Press.

Matthews, Burnita Shelton. 1929. "The Woman Juror." *Equal Rights* 14: 395–96.

Matthews, Donald and James Prothro. 1966. *Negroes and the New Southern Politics.* New York: Harcourt, Brace, and World.

Mathews, J. D. 1982. "The New Feminism and the Dynamics of Social Change." Pp. 397–425 in *Women's America: Refocusing the Past,* edited by L. K. Kerber and J. D. Mathews. New York: Oxford University Press.

May, Elaine Tyler. 1988. *Homeward Bound: American Families in the Cold War Era.* New York: Basic.

Mayhew, David R. 1986. *Placing Parties in American Politics: Organization, Electoral Settings, and*

Government Activity in the Twentieth Century. Princeton, NJ: Princeton University Press.

Mays, Benjamin and Joseph W. Nicholson. 1933. *The Negro's Church.* New York: Arno Press and the New York Times.

Mazmanian, Daniel and Paul Sabatier. 1983. *Implementation and Public Policy.* Glenview, IL: Scott, Foresman and Company.

McAdam, Doug. 1979. *Political Process and the Civil Rights Movement 1948–1962.* Ph.D. dissertation, Department of Sociology. State University of New York at Stony Brook.

———. 1982. *Political Process and the Development of Black Insurgency, 1930–1970.* Chicago: University of Chicago Press.

———. 1983. "Tactical Innovation and the Pace of Insurgency." *American Sociological Review* 48: 735–54.

———. 1986. "Recruitment to High-Risk Activism: The Case of Freedom Summer." *American Journal of Sociology* 92: 64–90.

McAdam, Doug, John D. McCarthy, and Mayer N. Zald. 1988. *Freedom Summer.* New York: Oxford University Press.

———. 1989. "The Biographical Consequences of Activism." *American Sociological Review* 54: 744–60.

———. 1994. "Culture and Social Movements." Pp. 36–57 in *New Social Movements: From Ideology to Identity,* edited by E. Laraña, H. Johnston, and J. R. Gusfield. Philadelphia, PA: Temple University Press.

———. 1995. "'Initiator' and 'Spin-Off' Movements: Diffusion Processes in Protest Cycles." Pp. 217–39 in *Repertoires and Cycles of Collective Action.* Durham, N.C.: Duke University Press.

———. 1996a. "Conceptual Origins, Current Problems, Future Directions." Pp. 23–40 in *Comparative Perspectives on Social Movements: Political Opportunities, Mobilizing Structures, and Cultural Framings,* edited by Doug McAdam, John D. McCarthy, and Mayer N. Zald. Cambridge: Cambridge University Press.

———. 1996b. "Introduction: Opportunities, Mobilizing Structures, and Framing Processes—Toward a Synthetic, Comparative Perspective on Social Movements." Pp. 1–22 in *Comparative Perspectives on Social Movements: Political Opportunities, Mobilizing Structures, and Cultural Framings,* edited by Doug McAdam, John D. McCarthy, and Mayer N. Zald. New York: Cambridge University Press.

———. 1999b. *Political Process and the Development of Black Insurgency, 1930–70,* 2d ed. Chicago: University of Chicago Press.

———. 1999b. "The Biographical Impact of Activism." Pp. 119–146 in *How Movements Matter,* edited by Marco Giugni, Doug McAdam and Charles Tilly. Minneapolis: University of Minnesota Press.

———. 2003a. "'Eehh, What's Up (with) *DOC*': Clarifying the Program." *Mobilization* 8(1): 126–34.

———. 2003b. "Beyond Structural Analysis: Toward a More Dynamic Understanding of Social Movements." Pp. 281–98 in *Social Movement Networks: Relational Approaches to Collective Action,* edited by Mario Diani and Doug McAdam. New York: Oxford University Press.

———. 1988. "Social Movements." Pp. 695–737 in *Handbook of Sociology,* edited by N. Smelser. Newbury Park, CA: Sage.

———. 1996. *Comparative Perspectives on Social Movements: Political Opportunities, Mobilizing Structures, and Cultural Framings.* Cambridge: Cambridge University Press.

McAdam, Doug, and Ronnelle Paulsen. 1993. "Specifying the Relationship between Social Ties and Activism." *American Journal of Sociology* 99: 640–67.

McAdam, Doug, and Dieter Rucht. 1993. "Cross-National Diffusion of Movement Ideas." *Annals of the American Academy of the Political and Social Sciences* 528: 56–74.

McAdam, Doug, and William H. Sewell, Jr. 2001. "It's About Time: Temporality in the Study of Social Movements and Revolutions." Pp. 89–125 in *Silence and Voice in the Study of Contentious Politics,* Ronald R. Aminzade, Jack A. Goldstone, Doug McAdam, Elizabeth J. Perry, William H. Sewell, Jr., Sidney Tarrow, and Charles Tilly. Cambridge: Cambridge University Press.

McAdam, Doug and David Snow. 1997. *Social Movements.* Los Angeles, CA: Roxbury.

McAdam, Doug and Yang Su. 2002. "The War at Home: Antiwar Protests and Congressional Voting, 1965–1973." *American Sociological Review* 67: 696–721.

McAdam, Doug, Sidney Tarrow, and Charles Tilly. 1996. "To Map Contentious Politics." *Mobilization* 1 (1): 17–34.

McAdam, Doug, Sidney Tarrow, and Charles Tilly, 2001. *Dynamics of Contention.* Cambridge: Cambridge University Press.

McAuley, Dennis. 2005. "The Ideology of Osama Bin Laden: Nation, Tribe and World Economy." *Journal of Political Ideologies* 10: 269–87.

McCain, James. 1978. *Interview.* Sumter. South Carolina. November 18.

McCall, G. J., and J. L. Simmons. 1978. *Identities and Interactions,* 2d ed. New York: Free Press.

McCammon, Holly J. 2001. "Stirring Up Suffrage Sentiment: The Formation of the State Woman Suffrage Organizations, 1866–1914." *Social Forces* 80: 449–80.

———. 2002. "Allies on the Road to Victory: Coalition Formation between the Suffragists and the Woman's Christian Temperance Union." *Mobilization: An International Journal* 7: 231–51.

McCammon, Holly J., Karen E. Campbell, Ellen M. Granberg, and Christine Mowery. 2001. "How movements win: Gendered opportunity structures and U.S. women's suffrage movements, 1866 to 1919." *American Sociological Review* 66: 49–70.

McCammon, Holly J., Soma Chaudhuri, Lyndi Hewitt, Harmony D. Newman, Courtney Sanders Muse, Carrie Lee Smith, and Teresa A. Terrell. 2007. "Becoming Full Citizens: The U.S. Women's Jury Rights Campaigns, the Pace of Reform, and Strategic Adaptation." Department of Sociology, Vanderbilt University, Nashville, TN. Unpublished manuscript.

McCann, Michael, 1998. "How Does Law Matter for Social Movements?" Pp. 76–108 in *How Does Law Matter?* edited by B. G. Garth and A. Sarat. Evanston, IL: Northwestern University Press. .

———. 1994. *Rights at Work: Pay Equity Reform and the Politics of Legal Mobilization.* Chicago: University of Chicago Press.

———. 1998. *Power in Movement,* 2d ed. New York: Cambridge University Press.

McCarthy, Dennis, and Susan Saegert. 1978. "Residential Density, Social Overload, and Social Withdrawal." *Human Ecology* 6: 253–72.

McCarthy, John D. 1987. "Pro-Life and Pro-Choice Mobilization: Infrastructure Deficits and New Technologies." Pp. 49–66 in *Social Movements in an Organizational Society,* edited by Mayer N. Zald and John D. McCarthy. New Brunswick, N.J.: Transaction.

———. 1994. "Activists, Authorities, and Media Framing and Drunk Driving." Pp. 134–167 in *New Social Movements: From Ideology to Identity.* Enrique Larana, Hank Johnston, and Joseph R. Gusfield, eds. Philadelphia: Temple University Press.

———. 1996. "Mobilizing Structures: Constraints and Opportunities in Adopting, Adapting and Inventing." In *Comparative Perspectives on Social Movements: Political Opportunities, Mobilizing Structures and Cultural Framings,* edited by Douglas McAdam, John D. McCarthy, and Mayer N. Zald. Cambridge: Cambridge University Press.

McCarthy, John D., David W. Britt, and Mark Wolfson. 1991. "The Institutional Channeling of Social Movements in the Modern State." *Research in Social Movements, Conflict and Change* 13: 45–76.

McCarthy, John, and Mayer Zald. 1977. "Resource Mobilization and Social Movements." *American Journal of Sociology* 82: 1212–41.

McCarthy, John D. and Clark McPhail. 1998. "The Institutionalization of Protest in the United States." Pp. 83–110 in *The Social Movement Society: Contentious Politics for a New Century,* edited by David S. Meyer and Sidney G. Tarrow. Lanham, MD: Rowan and Littlefield.

McCarthy, John D., Clark McPhail, and Jackie Smith. 1996. "Images of Protest: Estimating Selection Bias in Media Coverage of Washington Demonstrations, 1982, 1991." *American Sociological Review* 61: 478–99.

McCarthy, John D., Clark McPhail, Jackie Smith, and Louis J. Crishock. 1998. "Electronic and Print Media Representations of Washington, D.C. Demonstrations. 1982 and 1991: A Demography of Description Bias." Pp. 113–30 in *Acts of Dissent: New Developments in the Study of Protest.* Berlin, Germany: Sigma.

McCarthy, John D. and Mayer N. Zald. 1973. *The Trend of Social Movements in America: Professionalization and Resource Mobilization.* Morristown, NJ: General Learning Press.

———. 1977. "Resource Mobilization and Social Movements: A Partial Theory." *American Journal of Sociology* 82: 1212–41.

———. 2002. "The Enduring Vitality of the Resource Mobilization Theory of Social Movements." Pp. 533–65 in *Handbook of Sociological Theory,* edited by Jonathon H. Turner. New York: Kluwer Academic/Plenum Publishers.

McCarthy, John D. and Mark Wolfson. Unpublished. "Exploring Sources of Rapid Social Movement Growth: The Role of Organizational Form, Consensus Support, and Elements of the American State." Paper presented at the Workshop on Frontiers in Social Movement Theory, June 1988, Ann Arbor, MI.

McClintock, Cynthia. 1998. *Revolutionary Movements in Latin America: El Salvador's FMLN and Peru's Shining Path.* Washington, D.C.: United States Institute for Peace.

McCollom, Rev. Matthew. 1979. *Interview.* Orangeburg, South Carolina. October 31.

McDew, Charles. 1967. "Spiritual and moral aspects of the student nonviolent struggle in the South." In *The New Student Left, eds. Mitchell Cohen and Dennis Hale,* 51–7. Boston, Massachusetts: Beacon.

McDonagh, Eileen. 1996. *Breaking the Abortion Deadlock: From Choice to Consent.* New York: Oxford University Press.

McDonald, Andrew [William Pierce]. 1989. *Hunter,* Arlington, VA: National Vanguard Books.

McDonald, Ronald. 1969. "Electoral Behavior and Political Development in El Salvador." *Journal of Politics* 31 (2): 397–419.

McFarland, Andrew S. 1984. *Common Cause.* Chatham, NJ: Chatham House.

McIntyre, Lisa. 1994. *Law in the Sociological Enterprise: A Reconstruction.* Boulder, Colo.: Westview.

McKenzie, Roderick D. 1924. "The Ecological Approach to the Study of the Human Community." *American Journal of Sociology* 30: 287–301.

McKinley, Lenna. 1948. "Womanless Juries in Georgia Challenged as No Trial by Peers." *Atlanta Constitution,* February 25, p. 14.

McKinney, Erin Marie. 2000. "OSU Talks Continue: School Officials, Union Extend Strike Deadline at Eleventh Hour." *Columbus Dispatch,* May 1, p. IA.

McKissick, Floyd. 1978. *Interview.* Soul City, North Carolina. November 18 (Follow-up telephone interview November 2. 1979).

McLaren, Lauren. 1999. "Explaining Right-Wing Violence in Germany: A Time Series Analysis." *Social Science Quarterly* 80: 166–80.

McLean, Paul D. 1998. "A Frame Analysis of Favor Seeking in the Renaissance: Agency, Networks, and Political Culture." *American Journal of Sociology* 104 (1): 51–91.

McLemore, Leslie. 1971. "The Mississippi Freedom Democratic Party: A Case History of Grass-Roots Politics." Ph.D. dissertation, Department of Political Science, University of Massachusetts, Amherst, MA.

McMillen, Neil R. 1971. *The Citizens' Council, Organized Resistance to the Second Reconstruction, 1954–1964.* Urbana: University of Illinois Press.

McNall, Scott G. 1988. *The Road to Rebellion: Class Formation and Kansas Populism, 1865-1900.* Chicago: The University of Chicago Press.

McNeal, Patricia. 1992. *Harder Than War: Catholic Peacemaking in Twentieth Century America.* New Brunswick. NJ: Rutgers University Press.

McPhail, Clark. 1971. "Civil Disorder Participation: A Critical Examination of Recent Research." *American Sociological Review* 36: 1058–73.

——. 1973. "The assembling process: a theoretical and empirical examination." *American Sociological Review* 38: 721–35.

McPhail, Clark and David Miller. 1973. "The assembling process: a theoretical and empirical examination." *American Sociological Review* 38: 721–35.

McPhail, Clark, David Schweingruber, and John D. McCarthy. 1998. "Protest Policing in the United States, 1960–1995." Pp. 49–69 in *Policing Protest: The Control of Mass Demonstrations in Western Democracies,* edited by D. della Porta and H. Reiter. Minneapolis, MN: University of Minnesota Press.

McVeigh, Rory. 1999. "Structural incentives for conservative mobilization: Power devaluation and the rise of the Ku Klux Klan, 1915–25." *Social Forces* 77(4): 1461–96.

McVeigh, Rory, Daniel J. Myers, and David Sikkink. 2004. "Corn, Klansmen, and Coolidge: Structure and Framing in Social Movements." *Social Forces* 83: 653–90.

Mead, George Herbert. 1938. *The Philosophy of the Act.* Chicago: University of Chicago Press.

Mears, Daniel P., and Christopher G. Ellison. 2000. "Who Buys New Age Materials? Exploring Sociodemographic, Religious, Network, and Contextual Correlates of New Age Consumption." *Sociology of Religion* 61 (3): 289–313.

Meatto, Keith. 2000. "Real Reformers, Real Results: Our Seventh Annual Roundup of Student Protest" *Mother Jones,* September/October, 20–22.

Meed, Vladka. 1979. *On Both Sides of the Wall: Memoirs from the Warsaw Ghetto.* New York: Holocaust Library.

Meier, August and Elliot Rudwick. 1966. *From Planta-tion to Ghetto.* New York: Hill and Wang.

———. 1973. *CORE, A Study in the Civil Rights Move-ment, 1942-1968.* New York: Oxford University Press.

———. 1976. *Along the Color Line.* University of Illinois Press.

Meisner, Maurice. 1982. *Marxism, Maoism, and Uto-pianism: Eight Essays.* Madison, WI: University of Wisconsin Press.

Melson, Robert P. 1992. *Revolution and Genocide.* Chicago: University of Chicago Press.

Melucci, Alberto. 1985. "The Symbolic Challenge of Contemporary Movements." *Social Research* 52: 789-816.

———. 1989. *Nomads of the Present: Social Movements and Individual Needs in Contemporary Society.* Philadelphia, PA: Temple University Press.

———. 1995. The Process of Collective Identity. Pp. 41-63 in *Social Movements and Culture,* edited by Hank Johnston and Bert Klandermans. Minneapolis: University of Minnesota Press.

Melucci, Alberto. 1996. *Challenging Codes: Collective Action in the Information Age.* Cambridge, England: Cambridge University Press.

Menjívar, Rafael. 1982. *Formacion y lucha del prole-tariado industrial salvadoreño.* San José, Costa Rica: EDUCA.

Merry, Sally Engle. 1990. *Getting Justice and Getting Even: Legal Consciousness among Working-Class Americans.* Chicago: University of Chicago Press.

Meyer, David S. 1990. *A Winter of Discontent: The Nuclear Freeze and American Politics.* New York: Praeger.

———. 1993a. "Institutionalizing Dissent: The United States Structure of Political Opportunity and the End of the Nuclear Freeze." *Sociological Forum* 8: 157-179.

Meyer, David S. 1993b. "Protest Cycles and Politi-cal Process: American Peace Movements in the Nuclear Age." *Political Research Quarterly* 47: 451-79.

Meyer, David S. 1999. "Tending the Vineyard: Cultivat-ing Political Process Research." *Sociological Forum* 14: 79-92.

Meyer, David S. 2002. "Opportunities and Identities: Bridge-Building in the Study of Social Movements."

Pp. 3-21 in *Social Movements, Identity, Culture, and the State,* edited by D. S. Meyer, N. Whittier, and B. Robnett. Oxford: Oxford University Press.

Meyer, David S. 2004. "Protest and Political Opportu-nities." *Annual Review of Sociology* 30: 125-45.

Meyer, David S. 2005. "Social Movements and Public Policy: Eggs, Chicken, and Theory." Chapter 1 in *Routing the Opposition: Social Movements, Public Policy, and Democracy,* edited by David S. Meyer, Valerie Jenness, and Helen M. Ingram. Minneapolis, MN: University of Minnesota Press.

Meyer, David S., and Douglas R. Imig. 1993. "Political Opportunity and the Rise and Decline of Interest Group Sectors." *Social Science Journal* 30: 253-70.

Meyer, David S. and Debra C. Minkoff. 2004. "Concep-tualizing Political Opportunity." *Social Forces* 82: 1457-92.

Meyer, David S. and Suzanne Staggenborg. 1996. "Movements, Countermovements, and the Struc-ture of Political Opportunity." *American Journal of Sociology* 101: 1628-1660.

Meyer, David S. and Sidney Tarrow, eds. 1998. *The Social Movement Society.* Lanham, Maryland: Row-man and Littlefield.

Meyer, David S., and Nancy Whittier 1994. "Social Movement Spillover." *Social Problems* 41: 277-298.

Meyer, John P. and Nathalie J. Allen. 1991. "A Three Component Conceptualization of Organizational Commitment." *Human Resource Management Review* 1: 61-89.

Meyer, John P., Nathalie J. Allen, and Ian R. Gellatly. 1993. "Affective and Continuance Commitment to the Organization: Evaluation of Measures and Analysis of Concurrent and Time-lagged Relations." *Journal of Applied Psychology* 75: 710-20.

Meyer, John W., John Boli, George Thomas, and Fran-cisco O. Ramirez. 1997a. "World Society and the Nation State." *American Journal of Sociology* 103: 1444-1481.

Meyer, John W., David John Frank, Ann Hironaka, Evan Schofer, and Nancy Tuma. 1997b. "The Structuring of a World Environmental Regime, 1870-1990." *International Organization* 51: 623-51.

Meyer, John W., and Brian Rowan. 1977. "Institution-alized Organizations: Formal Structure as Myth and Ceremony." *American Journal of Sociology* 83: 340-63.

Michels, Robert. [1915] 1959. *Political Parties: A Sociological Study of the Oligarchical Tendencies of Modern Democracy.* Translated by E. Paul and C. Paul. New York: Dover Publications.

Michelson, William H. 1976. *Man and His Urban Environment: A Sociological Approach.* Reading, Mass.: Addison-Wesley.

Michotte, Albert E. 1963. *The Perception of Causality.* Trans. T. R. Miles. London: Methuen.

Milkman, Ruth, ed. 2000. *Organizing Immigrants: The Challenge for Unions in Contemporary California.* Ithaca, N.Y.: ILR Press.

Miller, David L. 1973. *George Herbert Mead: Self, Language, and the World.* Austin: University of Texas Press.

Miller, Robert Stevens, Jr. 1967. "Sex Discrimination and Title VII of the Civil Rights Act of 1964." *Minnesota Law Review* 51: 877–97.

Miller. J. Hillis. 1990. "Narrative." In *Critical Terms for Literary Study*, edited by Frank Lentricchia and Thomas McLaughlin. 66–79. Illinois: University of Chicago Press.

Mills, C. Wright 1940. "Situated Actions and Vocabularies of Motive." *American Sociological Review* 5: 904–13.

Mills, Kay. 1993. *This Little Light of Mine: The Life of Fannie Lou Hamer.* New York: Dutton.

Ministerio de Economia. 1978. *Anuario estadistico 1977, Tomo VII: Situación Económica.* San Salvador: Dirección General Estadistica y Censos.

——. 1981. *Anuario estadistico 1979, Tomo X: Situación Cultural.* San Salvador: Dirección General Estadistica y Censos.

Minkoff, Debra C. 1993. "The Organization of Survival: Women's and Racial-Ethnic Voluntarist and Activist Organizations, 1955–1985." *Social Forces* 71: 887–908.

——. 1995. *Organizing for Equality: The Evolution of Women's and Racial-Ethnic Organizations in America, 1955–1985.* New Brunswick, NJ: Rutgers University Press.

Minkoff, Debra. 1997. "The Sequencing of Social Movements." *American Sociological Review* 62: 779–99.

Minkoff, Debra C. 1999. "Bending with the Wind: Strategic Change and Adaptation by Women's and Racial Minority Organizations." *American Journal of Sociology* 104: 1666–703.

Mische, Ann. 2003. "Cross-talk in Movements: Reconceiving the Culture-Network Link." Pp. 258–80 in *Social Movement Networks: Relational Approaches to Collective Action,* edited by Mario Diani and Doug McAdam. New York: Oxford University Press.

Mische, Ann, and Harrison White. 1998. "Between Conversation and Situation: Public Switching Dynamics across Network Domains." *Social Research* 65 (3): 295–324.

Mitchell, Daniel J. B. 2000. *Pensions, Politics, and the Elderly: Historic Social Movements and Their Lessons for Our Aging Society.* Armonk, NY: M. E. Sharpe.

Mitchell, Robert Edward. 1971. "Some Social Implications of High Density Housing." *American Sociological Review* 36: 18–29.

Mizruchi, Ephraim H. 1983. *Regulating Society.* New York: Free Press.

Moaddel, Mansoor. 1992. "Ideology as Episodic Discourse: The Case of the Iranian Revolution." *American Sociological Review* 57: 353–79.

——. 2005. *Islamic Modernism, Nationalism, and Fundamentalism: Episode and Discourse.* Chicago: University of Chicago Press.

Moeller, Robert. 1993. *Protecting Motherhood: Women and the Family in the Politics of Postwar West Germany.* Berkeley and Los Angeles: University of California Press.

Moghadam, Valentine M. 2000. "Transnational Feminist Networks: Collective Action in an Era of Globalization." *International Sociology* 15 (1): 57–85.

Mohanty, Chandra Talpade. 1991. "Under Western Eyes: Feminist Scholarship and Colonial Discourses." Pp. 51–80 in *Third World Women and the Politics of Feminism,* edited by Chandra Talpade Mohanty, Ann Russo, and Lourdes Torres. Bloomington: Indiana University Press.

Mohr, John. 1992. "Community, Bureaucracy and Social Relief: An Institutional Analysis of Organizational Forms in New York City, 1888–1917." Ph.D. dissertation, Department of Sociology, Yale University.

Molina Arévalo, José Ernesto. 1988. *La respuesta sindical ante la crisis en El Salvador, 1944-87.* Maestría en Ciencias Sociales. Mexico City: Facultad Latinoamericana de Ciencias Sociales (FLACSO).

Molotch, Harvey. 1979a. "Capital and Neighborhood in the United States." *Urban Affairs Quarterly* 14: 289–312.

Molotch, Harvey. 1979b. "Media and Movements." Pp. 71–93 in *The Dynamics of Social Movements,* edited by Mayer N. Zald and John D. McCarthy. Cambridge, Mass.: Winthrop.

Monteforte Toledo, Mario. 1972. *Centro America: Subdesarrollo y dependencia.* Mexico City: Universidad Nacional Autonoma de Mexico, Instituto de Investigaciones Sociales.

Montgomery, Tommie Sue. 1982. *Revolution in El Salvador.* Boulder, Colo.: Westview Press.

Montini, Theresa. 1996. "Gender and Emotion in the Advocacy for Breast Cancer Informed Consent Legislation." *Gender & Society* 10: 9–23.

Moore, Barrington, Jr. 1966. *Social Origins of Dictatorship and Democracy: Lord and Peasant in the Making of the Modern World.* Boston: Beacon Press.

Moore, Douglas. 1960. *Journal and Guide.* Vol. LX, March 5, 1960.

Moore, Jack B. 1993. *Skinheads Shaved for Battle: A Cultural History of American Skinheads.* Bowling Green, OH: Bowling Green State University Popular Press.

Moore, Leonard. 1991. *Citizen Klansmen.* Chapel Hill, NC: University of North Carolina Press.

Moore, Will H. 2000. "The Repression of Dissent: A Substitution Model of Government Coercion." *Journal of Conflict Resolution* 44 (1): 107–28.

Moore, Will and Stephen Shellman. 2001. "Does Aggregation Matter? Moves & Turns vs. Time." Paper presented at the Conference on Mobilization and Repression: What We Know and Where We Should Go From Here? June 22, University of Maryland, College Park, MD.

Morales Velado, Oscar, et al. 1988. *La resistencia no violenta ante los regimenes salvadoreños que han utilizado el terror institucionalizado en el periodo 1972-1987.* San Salvador: Universidad Centroamericana Jose Simeon Cañas.

Morgan, William R., and Terry N. Clark. 1973. "The Causes of Racial Disorders: A Grievance-Level Explanation." *American Sociological Review* 38 (5): 611–24.

Morrill, Calvin. 1991. "Conflict Management, Honor, and Organizational Change." *American Journal of Sociology* 97: 585–621.

Morris, Aldon and Carol McClurg Mueller, eds. 1992. *Frontiers in Social Movement Theory.* New Haven, CT: Yale University Press.

Morris, Aldon. 1980. "The origins of the civil rights movement: an indigenous perspective." Ph.D. dissertation, Department of Sociology, State University of New York at Stony Brook.

Morris, Aldon. 1981. "Black southern student sit-in movement: an analysis of internal organization." *American Sociological Review* 46: 744–67.

Morris, Aldon D. 1984. *The Origins of the Civil Rights Movement: Black Communities Organizing for Change.* New York: Free Press.

———. 1992. "Political Consciousness and Collective Action." Pp. 351–73 in *Frontiers in Social Movement Theory,* edited by Aldon D. Morris and Carol McClurg Mueller. New Haven, Conn.: Yale University Press.

Morris, Aldon D. 1993. "Birmingham Confrontation Reconsidered: An Analysis of the Dynamics and Tactics of Mobilization." *American Sociological Review* 58: 621–36.

———. 1999. "A Retrospective on the Civil Rights Movement." *Annual Review of Sociology* 25: 517–39.

———. 2000. "Reflections on Social Movement Theory: Criticisms and Proposals." *Contemporary Sociology* 29: 445–54.

Morris, Aldon D. and Cedric Herring. 1988. "Theory and Research in Social Movements: A Critical Review." Pp. 137–98 in *Annual Review of Political Behavior,* vol. 2, edited by S. Long. Boulder, CO: Westview Press.

Morris, Aldon D., and Carol M. Mueller, eds. 1992. *Frontiers in Social Movement Theory.* New Haven: Yale University Press.

Morris, Aldon and Suzanne Staggenborg. 2004. "Leadership in Social Movements." Pp. 171–96 in *The Blackwell Companion to Social Movements,* edited by D. Snow, S. Soule, and H. Kriesi. Malden, MA: Blackwell Publishing.

Morris, George. 1967. *The CIA, the AFL-CIO, and American Foreign Policy.* New York: International Publishers.

Mosley, Donald C. and D. C. Williams. 1967. *An Analysis and Evaluation of a Community Action Anti-Poverty Program in the Mississippi Delta.* State College, MS: College of Business and Industry, Mississippi State University.

Mottl, Tahi L. 1980. "The Analysis of Countermovements." *Social Problems* 27: 620–35.

Mueller, Carol. 1987. "Collective Consciousness, Identity Transformation, and the Rise of the Women in

Public Office in the United States." Pp. 89–108 in *The Women's Movements of the United States and Western Europe,* edited by M. Katzenstein and C. Mueller. Philadelphia, PA: Temple University Press.

———. 1987b. "The Life Cycle of Equal Rights Feminism: Resource Mobilization, Political Process, and Dramaturgical Explanations." Paper presented at the 1987 Annual Meetings of the American Sociological Association, Chicago.

Mueller, Carol McClurg. 1992. "Building social movement theory." Pp. 3–25 in *Frontiers of Social Movement Theory* edited by Aldon Morris and Carol McChurg Mueller.. New Haven: Yale.

Mueller, Carolyn McClurg. 1994. "Conflict Networks and the Origins of Women's Liberation." Pp. 234–63 in *New Social Movements: From Ideology to Identity,* edited by E. Larana, H. Johnston, and J. R. Gusfield. Philadelphia, PA: Temple University Press.

Mueller, Carol. 1997. "Media Measurement Models." *Mobilization* 2: 165–84.

Mueller, Carol. 1999. "Claim 'Radicalization?' The 1989 Protest Cycle in the GDR." *Social Problems* 46 (4): 528–47.

Muller, E.N. 1980. "The psychology of political protest and violence." Pp. 69–100 in *Handbook of Political Conflict Theory and Research,* edited by Ted Robert Gurr. New York: Free Press.

Muller, Edward. 1985a. "Income Inequality, Regime Repressiveness, and Political Violence." *American Sociological Review* 50 (1): 47–61.

———. 1985b. "New Social Movements and Smaller Parties: A Comparative Perspective." *West European Politics* 8: 41–54.

Muller, Edward, and Mitchell Seligson. 1987. "Inequality and Insurgency." *American Political Science Review* 81 (2): 425–51.

Muller, Edward, and Erich Weede. 1994. "Theories of Rebellion—Relative Deprivation and Power Contention." *Rationality and Society* 6 (1): 40–57.

Mueller, John E. 1973. *War, Presidents, and Public Opinion.* New York: Wiley.

Müller-Rommel, F. (ed.). 1989. *New Politics in Western Europe: The Rise and Success of Green Parties and Alternative Lists.* London: Westview Press.

Münz, Rainer, Wolfgang Seifert, and Ralf Ulrich. 1997. *Zuwanderung nach Deutschland: Strukturen, Wirkungen, Perspektiven.* Frankfurt: Campus.

Murphy, Gillian Hughs. 2002. "A Double-Edged Sword: Coalitions and the Development of the Global Environmental Movement." M.A. thesis, Department of Sociology, University of Washington, Seattle.

Murphy, Seamus. 2002. "The Sullen Majority." *New York Times Magazine* September 1: 42–47.

Murray, Stephen O. 1996. *American Gay.* Chicago: University of Chicago Press.

Mushaben, Joyce, Sara Lennox, and Geoffrey Giles. 1997. "Women, Men and Unification: Gender Politics and the Abortion Struggle since 1989." Pp. 137–72 in *After Unity,* edited by Konrad Jarausch. Providence, R.I.: Berghahn.

Myers, Daniel J. 1997a. "An Event History Analysis of Racial Rioting in the 1960s." *American Sociological Review* 62: 94–112.

Myers, Daniel J. 1997b. "Racial Rioting in the 1960s: An Event-History Analysis of Local Conditions." *American Sociological Review* 62 (1): 94–112.

Myers, Daniel J. 2000. "The Diffusion of Collective Violence: Infectiousness, Susceptibility, and Mass Media Networks." *American Journal of Sociology* 106: 173–208.

NAACP (National Association for the Advancement of Colored People). 1947–82. *NAACP Annual Report.* New York: NAACP.

Nagel, Joane. 1996. *American Indian Ethnic Renewal: Red Power and the Resurgence of Identity.* New York: Oxford University Press.

Nall, J. O. *The Tobacco Night Riders of Kentucky and Tennessee. 1905–09.* Louisville, KY: Standard Press, 1942.

Naples, Nancy A. 1997. "The 'New Consensus' on the Gendered 'Social Contract': The 1987–1988 U.S. Congressional Hearings on Welfare Reform." *Signs: Journal of Women in Culture and Society* 22: 907–45.

———. 2002. "Materialist Feminist Discourse Analysis and Social Movement Research: Mapping the Changing Cultural Context for Community Control." Pp. 226–46 in *Social Movements: Identity, Culture, and the State,* edited by David S. Meyer, Nancy Whittier, and Belinda Robnett. New York: Oxford University Press.

NARAL of Illinois papers. Manuscripts Department, University of Illinois, Chicago, library.

Nasr, Vali. 2006. *The Shia Revival: How Conflicts within Islam Will Shape the Future.* New York: W. W. Norton & Company.

Neal, Arthur G., and Melvin Seeman. 1964. "Organizations and Powerlessness: A Test of the Mediation Hypothesis." *American Sociological Review* 29: 216–26.

Neidhardt, Friedhelm. 1994. "Öffentlichkeit, öffentliche Meinung, soziale Bewegungen." Special issue no. 34 of *Kölner Zeitschrift für Soziologie und Sozialpsychologie* 46: S7–S41.

Neiwert, David A. 1999. *In God's Country—The Patriot Movement and the Pacific Northwest.* Pullman: Washington State University Press.

Nepstad, Sharon Erickson and Christian Smith. 1999. "Rethinking Recruitment to High-Risk/Cost Activism: The Case of Nicaragua Exchange." *Mobilization* 4: 25–40.

Nepstad, Sharon Erickson, and Christian Smith. 2001. "The Social Structure of Moral Outrage in Recruitment to the U.S. Central America Peace Movement" Pp. 158–74 in *Passionate Politics: Emotions and Social Movements,* edited by Jeff Goodwin, James Jasper, and Francesca Polletta. Chicago: University of Chicago Press.

Nestle, Joan. 1987. *A Restricted Country.* Ithaca, N.Y.: Firebrand.

Neuhouser, Kevin. 1998. "'If I Had Abandoned My Children': Community Mobilization and Commitment to the Identity of Mother in Northeast Brazil." *Social Forces* 77: 331–58.

Neuman, Johanna. 2003. "Lesson of 'Hanoi Jane' Leads Antiwar Forces to Shift Strategy." *Los Angeles Times.* March 19.

New York Times. 1902. "Chorus Girls as Jurors." August 30, p. 1.

———. 1912. "Women Jurors Defy Court." December 6, p. 1.

———. 1930. "Lehman and Ward Urge Women Jurors." February 28, p. 3.

New York Times. 1948–97. *New York Times Index.* New York: New York Times.

New York Times. 1955–71. *The New York Times Index.* New York: . New York Times.

New York Times. 1965a. "Bans on Job Bias Effective Today." July 2.

———. 1965b. "Help Wanted: Picking the Sex for the Job." International ed., September 28.

Newcomb, Theodore M. 1943. *Personality and Social Change: Attitude Formation in a Student Community.* New York: Dryden Press.

Newcomb, Theodore M. 1961. *Acquaintance Process.* New York: Holt, Rinehart & Winston.

Newcomb, Theodore M., Kathryn E. Koenig, Richard Flacks, and Donald P. Warwick. 1967. *Persistence and Change: Bennington College and Its Students after Twenty-Five Years.* New York: Wiley.

Newman, Oscar. 1973. *Defensible Space.* New York: Macmillian.

Newton, Esther. 1993. *Cherry Grove, Fire Island: Sixty Years in America's First Gay and Lesbian Town.* Boston: Beacon Press.

Nickerson, Colin. 2002. "U.S. Gets Little Sympathy from Arab Muslims in Middle East." *Orange County Register.* September 12: 5.

Niederhoffer, Arthur. 1969. *Behind the Shield: The Police in Urban Society.* New York: Doubleday.

Nielsen, Laura Beth. 2000. "Situating Legal Consciousness: Experiences and Attitudes of Ordinary Citizens about Law and Street Harassment" *Law and Society Review* 34: 1055–90.

Nisbett, Richard E., and Dov Cohen. 1996. *Culture of Honor. The Psychology of Violence in the South.* Boulder, Colo.: Westview.

Nishikawa, S. 1986. "Grain Consumption: The Case of Choshu." Pp. 421–466 in *Japan in Transition: From Tokugawa to Meiji,* edited by M.B. Jansen and G. Rozman. Princeton: Princeton University Press.

NOW (National Organization for Women). 1966. "Petition to the Equal Employment Opportunity Commission." Box 6, folder "EEOC petition, Phineas Indritz, December 1966." Attached to letter from Phineas Indritz to officers and directors. December 6. Schlesinger Library, Cambridge, Mass.

———. 1967. Statement by Marguerite Rawalt to EEOC at public hearings. Box 44, folder 1549. May 2. Schlesinger Library, Cambridge, Mass.

———. 1968. *NOW Acts.* Vol. 1 (fall). Schlesinger Library, Cambridge, Mass.

———. 1969. *NOW Acts.* Vol. 2, no. I (winter/spring). Schlesinger Library, Cambridge, Mass.

———. N.d. *NOW: The First Five Years, 1966–71.* Schlesinger Library, Cambridge, Mass.

NOW Papers. N.d. "Task Force on Compliance and Enforcement." Box 18, folder "Employment Goals, 1966–71." Schlesinger Library, Cambridge, Mass.

O'Connor, Julia, Ann Shola Orloff, and Sheila Shaver. 1999. *States, Markets, Families: Gender, Liberalism, and Social Policy in Australia, Canada, Great Britain, and the United States.* New York: Cambridge University Press.

O'Reilly, Kenneth. 1989. *Racial Matters: The FBI's Secret File on Black America, 1960-1972*. New York: The Free Press.

Obear, Frederick W. 1970. "Student Activism in the Sixties." Pp. 11–26 in *Protest: Student Activism in America 1970*, edited by Julian Foster and Durward Long. New York: William Morrow.

Oberschall, Anthony. 1973. *Social Conflict and Social Movements*. Englewood Cliffs, N.J.: Prentice-Hall.

Oberschall, Anthony R. 1978b. "Theories of Social Conflict." Pp. 291–315 in *Annual Review of Sociology*, edited by Ralph Turner, James Coleman, and Renee C. Fox. Palo Alto, CA: Annual Review.

———. 1980. "Loosely Structured Collective Conflicts: A Theory and an Application." Pp. 45–68 in *Research in Social Movements, Conflict, and Change*, vol. 3. Edited by L. Kriesberg. Greenwich, Conn.: JAI Press.

Oberschall, Anthony. 1989. "The 1960 sit-ins: Protest diffusion and movement take-off." *Research in Social Movements, Conflict and Change* 11: 31–53.

———. 1993. *Social Movements: Ideologies, Interests, and Identities*. New Brunswick, N.J.: Transaction.

———. 1994. "Rational Choice in Collective Protests." *Rationality and Society* 6: 79–100.

Offen, Karen. 1988. "Defining Feminism: A Comparative Historical Approach." *Signs* 14 (1): 119–57.

Ogden, Frederic D. 1958. *The Poll Tax in the South*. Tuscaloosa, AL: University of Alabama Press.

Ohlemacher, Thomas. 1994. "Xenophobia in the Reunited Germany: Public Opinion and Violence against Foreigners in the Reunified Germany." *Zeitschrift für Soziologie* 23: 222–36.

Okamoto, Dina, and Paula England. 1999. "Is There a Supply Side to Occupational Sex Segregation?" *Sociological Perspectives* 42: 557–82.

Oleson, Thomas. 2005. *International Zapatismo: The Construction of Solidarity in the Age of Globalization*. London: ZED Books.

Oliver, Pamela. 1983. "The Mobilization of Paid and Volunteer Activists in the Neighborhood Movement." *Research in Social Movements, Conflicts and Change* 5: 133–70.

Oliver, Pamela. 1984. "'If You Don't Do It, Nobody Else Will': Active and Token Contributors to Local Collective Action." *American Sociological Review* 49: 601–10.

Oliver, Pamela and Mark Furman. 1989. "Contradictions between National and Local Organizational Strength: The Case of the John Birch Society." Pp. 155–78 in *International Social Movement Research*, vol.2, *Organizing for Change*, edited by B. Klandermans. Greenwich, CT: JAI Press.

Oliver, Pamela, and Hank Johnston. 2000. "What a Good Ideal! Ideology and Frames in Social Movement Research." *Mobilization* 5: 37–54.

Oliver, Pamela E., and Gregory Maney. 2000. "Political Processes and Local Newspaper Coverage of Protest Events: From Selection Bias to Triadic Interactions." *American Journal of Sociology* 106: 463–505.

Oliver, Pamela E. and Gerald Marwell. 1988. "The Paradox of Group Size in Collective Action: A Theory of the Critical Mass. II." *American Sociological Review* 53: 1–8.

Oliver, Pamela E. and Gerald Marwell. 1992. "Mobilizing Technologies for Collective Action." Pp. 251–72 in *Frontiers in Social Movement Theory*, edited by A. D. Morris and C. M. Mueller. New Haven, CT: Yale University Press.

Oliver, Pamela, Gerald Marwell, and Ruy Teixeira 1985. "A Theory of the Critical Mass: I. Group Heterogeneity, Interdependence, and the Production of Collective Goods." *American Journal of Sociology* 91: 522–56.

Oliver, Pamela E., and Daniel J. Myers. 1999. "How Events Enter the Public Sphere: Conflict, Location, and Sponsorship in Local Newspaper Coverage of Public Events." *American Journal of Sociology*. 105: 38–87.

Olivier, Johan. 1991. "State Repression and Collective Action in South Africa, 1970-84." *South African Journal of Sociology* 22: 109–17.

Olson, Mancur. 1965. *The Logic of Collective Action: Public Goods and the Theory of Groups*. Cambridge, Mass.: Harvard University Press.

Olson, Mancur. 1979. Published letter. Pp. 149–50 in *Research in Social Movements, Conflicts and Change*, edited by Louis Kriesberg. Vol. 2. Greenwich, CT: JAI Press.

Olson, Mancur. 1990. "The Logic of Collective Action in Soviet-Type Societies." *Journal of Soviet Nationalities* 1: 8–27.

Olzak, Susan. 1989. "Analysis of Events in the Study of Collective Action." *Annual Review of Sociology* 15: 119–141.

Olzak, Susan. 1992. *The Dynamics of Ethnic Competition and Conflict*. Stanford, CA: Stanford University Press.

Olzak, Susan, Maya Beasley, and Johan Olivier. 2003. "The Impact of State Reforms on Protest against Apartheid in South Africa." *Mobilization* 8 (1): 27–50.

Olzak, Susan, and Suzanne Shanahan. 1996. "Deprivation and Race Riots, 1960–1993." *Social Forces* 74: 931–61.

Olzak, Susan, and Suzanne Shanahan. 2003. "Racial Policy and Racial Conflict in the Urban United States, 1869–1924." *Social Forces* 82: 481–517.

Olzak, Susan, and S. C. Noah Uhrig. 2001. "The Ecology of Tactical Overlap." *American Sociological Review* 66: 1–25.

Ong, Aihwa. 1987. *Spirits of Resistance and Capitalist Discipline: Factory Women in Malaysia.* Albany: State University of New York Press.

Opp, Karl Dieter. 1988. "Grievances and Participation in Social Movements." *American Sociological Review* 53: 853–64.

Opp, Karl-Dieter. 1989. *The Rationality of Political Protest: A Comparative Analysis of Rational Choice Theory.* Boulder, Colo.: Westview.

Opp, Karl-Dieter, and Christiane Gern. 1993. "Dissident Groups, Personal Networks, and Spontaneous Cooperation: The East Germany Revolution of 1989." *American Sociological Review* 58: 659–80.

Oppeln, S. von. 1989. *Die Links im Kernenergie Konflikt: Deutschland und Franeicht im Vergleich.* Frankfurt: Campus.

Oppenheimer, Martin. 1963. "The Genesis of the Southern Negro Student Movement (Sit-In Movement): A Study in Contemporary Negro Protest." Unpublished. Ph.D. dissertation, University of Pennsylvania.

Oppenheimer, Martin. 1964. "The southern student movement: year 1." Journal of Negro Education 33: 396–403.

Oppenheimer, Martin. 1989. *The Sit-in Movement of 1960.* Brooklyn, N.Y.: Carlson.

Orbell, John M. 1972. "Protest participation among Southern Negro college students." In *The Seeds of Politics,* edited by Anthony M. Orum, 232–46. Englewood Cliffs: Prentice-Hall.

Ornstein, Norman J., Thomas E. Mann, and Michael J. Malbin. 1982–2002. *Vital Statistics on Congress* (1982–2001). Washington, D.C.: Congressional Quarterly Press.

Orum, Anthony M. 1972. *Black Students in Protest.* Washington, D.C.: American Sociological Association.

Osa, Maryjane. 2001. "Mobilizing Structures and Cycles of Protest: Post-Stalinist Contention in Poland, 1954–1959." *Mobilization* 6 (2): 211–31.

Oskamp, S. J. Bordin, and T. Edwards. 1992. "Background Experiences and Attitudes of Peace Activists." *Journal of Psychology* 126: 49–61.

Osmond, Humphry. 1957. "The Relationship between Architect and Psychiatrist." Pp. 16–20 in *Psychiatric Architecture,* edited by Charles E. Goshen. Washington, D.C.: American Psychiatric Association.

Ost, David. 1990. *Solidarity and the Politics of Anti-Politics.* Philadelphia: Temple University Press.

Ostner, Ilona. 2002. "A New Role for Fathers? The German Case." Pp. 150–67 in *Making Men into Fathers,* edited by Barbara Hobson. New York: Oxford University Press.

Out in the Mountains. 1986. "VT Demos Support ERA/G/L Rights." 1 (9): 3.

Overbeck, J. 1974. *History of Population Theories.* Rotterdam: Rotterdam University Press.

Padgett, John F., and Christopher K. Ansell. 1993. "Robust Action and the Rise of the Medici, 1400–1434." *American Journal of Sociology* 98 (6): 1259–1319.

Paige, Jeffery M. 1975. *Agrarian Revolution,* New York: Free Press.

Paige, Jeffrey. 1996. "Land Reform and Agrarian Revolution in El Salvador: Comment on Seligson and Diskin." *Latin American Research Review* 31 (2): 127–39.

———. 1997. *Coffee and Power: Revolution and the Rise of Democracy in Central America.* Cambridge, Mass.: Harvard University Press.

Pajetta, Giovanna. 1994. *Il Grande Camaleonte* (The Big Chameleon). Milan, Italy: Feltrinelli.

Panebianco, Angelo. 1988. *Political Parties: Organization and Power.* Cambridge, England: Cambridge University Press.

Pape, Robert A. 2003. "The Strategic Logic of Suicide Terrorism." *American Political Science Review* 97: 343–61.

Pape, Robert A. 2005. *Dying to Win: The Strategic Logic of Suicide Terrorism.* New York: Random House.

Parenti, Michael. 1993. *Inventing Reality: The Politics of the News Media.* New York: St. Martin's.

Park, Robert E. 1915. "The City: Suggestions for the Investigation of Human Behavior in the City Environment" *American Journal of Sociology* 20: 557–612.

———. 1936. "Human Ecology." *American Journal of Sociology* 42: 1–15.

Parker, Frank. 1990. *Black Votes Count.* Chapel Hill, NC: University of North Carolina Press.

Parkman, Patricia. 1988. *Nonviolent Insurrection in El Salvador: The Fall of Maximiliano Hernandez Martinez.* Tucson: University of Arizona Press.

Parks, Rosa, 1977. Interview with Rosa Parks. Pp. 31–33 in *My Soul is Rested,* edited by Howell Raines. New York: Bantam.

Parkum, Kurt H. and Virginia Cohn Parkum. 1980. "Citizen participation in community planning and decision making." Pp. 153–67 in *Participation in Social and Political Activities,* edited by David Horton Smith, Jecqueline Macaulay and Associates. San Francisco: Jossey-Bass.

Parsons, Talcott, 1947. "Introduction." Pp. 3–86 in *Max Weber: The Theory of Social and Economic Organization,* edited by T. Parsons. New York: Oxford University Press.

Pastor, Paul. 1978. "Mobilization in Public Drunkenness Control: A Comparison of Legal and Medical Approaches." *Social Problems* 25: 373–84.

Patterson, James. 1994. *America's Struggle against Poverty.* 2d ed. Cambridge, MA: Harvard University Press.

Paul, William. 1982. "Minority Status for Gay People: Majority Reaction and Social Context." Pp. 351–70 in *Homosexuality: Social, Psychological, and Biological Issues,* edited by William Paul, James D. Weinrich, John C. Gonsiorek, and Mary E. Hotvedt, Beverly Hills, Calif.: Sage.

Paulsen, Ronnelle D. 1990. *Class and Collective Action: Variation in the Participation of Young Adults in Non-Institutionalized Politics.* Ph.D. dissertation. University of Arizona, Department of Sociology.

———. 1991. "Education, Social Class, and Participation in Collective Action." *Sociology of Education* 64 (2): 96–110.

Paulson, Justin. 2000. "Peasant Struggles and International Solidarity: The Case of Chiapas." In *Socialist Register, 2001,* edited by Leo Panitch and Colin Leys. London: Merlin Press.

Payne, Charles. 1995. *I've Got the Light of Freedom: The Organizing Tradition and the Mississippi Freedom Struggle.* Berkeley, CA: University of California Press.

Pearce, Jenny. 1986. *Promised Land: Peasant Rebellion in Chalatenango, El Salvador.* London: Latin America Bureau.

Pedriana, Nicholas. 2004a. "The Strength of a Weak Agency: Title VII of the 1964 Civil Rights Act and Expansion of State Capacity, 1965–1971." *American Journal of Sociology* 110: 709–60.

Pedriana, Nicholas. 2004b. "Help Wanted NOW: Legal Resources, the Women's Movement and the Battle over Sex-Segregated Job Advertisements." *Social Problems* 51: 182–201.

———. 2005. "Rational Choice, Structural Context, and Increasing Returns: A Strategy for Analytic Narrative in Historical Sociology." *Sociological Methods and Research* 33: 349–82.

Pedriana, Nicholas, and Robin Stryker. 1997. "Political Culture Wars 1960s Style: Equal Employment Opportunity–Affirmative Action Law and the Philadelphia Plan." *American Journal of Sociology* 103: 633–91.

Peoples' Global Action. 2000. "Worldwide Resistance Roundup: Newsletter 'Inspired by' Peoples' Global Action." London.

Pérez Brignoli, Héctor. 1995. "Indians, Communists, and Peasants: The 1932 Rebellion in El Salvador." Pp. 232–61 in *Coffee, Society, and Power in Latin America,* edited by W. Roseberry, L. Gudmunson, and M. Samper Kutschbach. Baltimore: Johns Hopkins University Press.

Perrow, Charles. 1979. "The Sixties Observed." Pp. 192–211 in *The Dynamics of Social Movements: Resource Mobilization, Social Control, and Tactics,* edited by Mayer N. Zald and John McCarthy. Cambridge, Mass.: Winthrop.

Perry, Elisabeth Israels. 2001. "Rhetoric, Strategy, and Politics in the New York Campaign for Women's Jury Service, 1917–1975." *New York History* 82: 53–78.

Perry, Ronald, David F. Gillespie, and Howard A. Parker. 1976. *Social Movements and the Local Community.* Beverly Hills, Calif.: Sage.

Petchesky, Rosalind Pollack. 1984. *Abortion and Woman's Choice: The State, Sexuality, and Reproductive Freedom.* New York: Longman.

Petersen, Roger. 2001. *Resistance and Rebellion: Lessons from Eastern Europe.* Cambridge: Cambridge University Press.

Peterson, Anna. 1997. *Martyrdom and the Politics of Religion: Progressive Catholicism in El Salvador's Civil War.* Albany: State University of New York Press.

Peterson, David. 1971. "Informal Norms and Police Practice: The Traffic Ticket Quota System." *Sociology and Social Research* 55: 354–62.

Peterson, Paul and David Greenstone. 1977. "Racial Change and Citizen Participation." Pp. 241–78 in

A Decade of Federal Antipoverty Programs, edited by R. H. Haveman. New York: Academic.

Petras, James and Maurice Zeitlin. 1967. "Miners and Agriculture Radicalism." *American Sociological Review* 32: 578–586.

Pettigrew, Thomas E. 1964. *A Profile of the Negro American.* New York.: Van Nostrand.

Pettigrew, Thomas F. 1998. "Reactions toward the New Minorities of Western Europe." *Annual Review of Sociology* 24: 77–103.

———. 2002. "Summing Up: Relative Deprivation as a Key Social Psychological Concept." Pp. 351–74 in *Relative Deprivation,* edited by Iain Walker and Heather J. Smith. New York: Cambridge University Press.

Petty, R. E., and J. T. Cacioppo. 1981. *Attitudes and Attitude Change: The Social Judgement-Involvement Approach.* Dubuque, Iowa: W. C. Brown.

Pfeffer, Jeffrey and Gerald R. Salancik. 1978. *The External Control of Organizations: A Resource-Dependence Perspective.* New York: Harper and Row.

Pfetsch, Barbara. 1999. *"In Russia We Were Germans, and Now We Are Russians": Dilemmas of Identity Formation and Communication among German-Russian Aussiedler.* Discussion Paper FS III 99–103. Berlin: Wissenschaftszentrum (WZB).

Pichardo, Nelson A. 1988. "Resource Mobilization: An Analysis of Conflicting Theoretical Variations." *Sociological Quarterly* 29: 97–110.

Pichardo, Nelson A. 1997. "New Social Movements: A Critical Review." *Annual Review of Sociology* 23: 411–30.

Pierson, Paul. 2000a. "Not Just What, But When: Timing and Sequence in Political Processes." *Studies in American Political Development* 14 (Spring): 72–92.

Pinard, Maurice. 1971. *The Rise of a Third Party: A Study in Crisis Politics.* Englewood Cliffs, N.J.: Prentice-Hall.

Pinard, Maurice and Richard Hamilton. 1988. "Intellectuals and the Leadership of Social Movements: Some Comparative Perspectives." *McGill Working Papers on Social Behavior.*

Piven, Frances Fox and Richard Cloward. 1977. *Poor People's Movements: Why They Succeed. How They Fail.* New York: Pantheon Books.

———. 1984. "Disruption and Organization: A Reply to Gamson and Schmeidler." *Theory and Society* 13: 587–99.

Piven, Frances F. and Richard Cloward. 1992. "Normalizing Collective Protest." Pp. 301–25 in *Frontiers in Social Movement Theory,* edited by A. Morris and C. McClurg Mueller. New Haven, CT: Yale University Press.

Pizzorno, Alessandro. 1978. "Political Exchange and Collective Identity in Industrial Conflict." Pp. 277–98 in *The Resurgence of Class Conflict in Western Europe Since 1968.* edited by C. Crouch and A. Pizzomo. London: Macmillan.

———. 1986. "Decision or Interactions? Microanalysis of Social Change." *Rassegna Italiana di Sociologia* 37: 107–32.

Ploski, Harry A. and Warren Marr II (eds.). 1976. *The Afro American.* New York: Bellwether.

Plummer, Brenda Gayle. 1996. *Rising Wind: Black Americans and U.S. Foreign Affairs, 1935–1960.* Chapel Hill: University of North Carolina Press.

Poche, Bernard. 1994. "Scomposizione e Ricomposizione dei Territori Europei" (Decomposition and Recomposition of European Territories). Pp. 239–77 in *Figli di un Benessere Minore. La Lega 1979–1993* (Children of a Minor Wealth: The League 1979–1993), edited by G. De Luna. Florence, Italy: La Nuova Italia.

Poe, Steven C., C. Neal Tate, Linda Camp Keith, and Drew Lanier. 2000. "Domestic Threats: The Abuse of Personal Integrity." Pp. 27–70 in *Paths to State Repression,* edited by C. Davenport. Lanham, MD: Rowman and Littlefield.

Poggio, Pier Paolo. 1994. "Il Naturalismo Sociale e l'Ideologia delta Lega" (Social Darwinism and the League's Ideology). Pp. 138–96 in *Figli di un Benessere Minore. La Lega 1979–1993* (Children of a Minor Wealth: The League 1979–1993), edited by G. De Luna. Florence, Italy: La Nuova Italia.

Polkinghome, Donald E. 1988. *Narrative Knowing and the Human Sciences.* Albany: StateUniversity of New York.

Polletta, Francesca. 1994. "Strategy and Identity in 1960s Black Protest." *Research in Social Movements, Conflicts and Change* 17: 85–114.

———. 1999. "'Free Spaces' in Collective Action." *Theory and Society* 28: 1–38.

———. 1999. "Snarls, Quacks, and Quarrels: Culture and Structure in Political Process Theory." *Sociological Forum* 14: 63–70.

———. 2002. *Freedom Is an Endless Meeting: Democracy in American Social Movements.* Chicago: University of Chicago Press.

———. 2004. "Culture Is Not Just in Your Head," pp. 97–110 in Jeff Goodwin and James M. Jasper (eds.) *Rethinking Social Movements.* Lanham, MD: Rowman and Littlefield.

Polletta, Francesca, and M. Kai Ho. 2006. "Frames and Their Consequences." Pp. 187–209 in *The Oxford Handbook of Contextual Political Analysis,* edited by Robert E. Goodin and Charles Tilly. Oxford: Oxford University Press.

Polletta, Francesca and James Jasper. 2001. "Collective Identity and Social Movements." *Annual Review of Sociology* 27: 283–305.

Polner, Murray and Jim O'Grady. 1997. *Disarmed and Dangerous: The Radical Lives and Times of Daniel and Philip Berrigan.* New York: Basic Books.

Powell, Walter W. 1990. "Neither Market nor Hierarchy: Network Forms of Organization." *Research in Organizational Behavior* 12: 295–336.

Powell, Walter W. 1991. "Expanding the Scope of Institutional Analysis." Pp. 183–203 in *The New Institutionalism in Organizational Analysis,* edited by Walter Powell and Paul DiMaggio. Chicago: University of Chicago Press.

Powell, Walter W., and Paul J. DiMaggio, eds. 1991. *The New Institutionalism in Organizational Analysis.* Chicago: University of Chicago Press.

Powledge, Fred. 1991. *Free At Last? The Civil Rights Movement and the People Who Made It.* New York: Harper Collins.

Poznanski, Kazimerg. 1992. *Constructing Capitalism: The Reemergence of Civil Society and Liberal Economy in the Post-Communist World.* Boulder, Colo.: Westview.

President's Commission on the Status of Women (PCSW). 1961. Box 12, folder "Committee on Private Employment." Reprint of Executive Order 10928, December 16. John F. Kennedy Library, Boston.

———. 1962. "The Role of Protective Labor Legislation." Box 12, folder "Committee on Protective Labor Legislation." June 6. John F. Kennedy Library, Boston.

———. 1963*a. American Women.* Washington, D.C.: Government Printing Office.

———. 1963*b. Report of the Committee on Protective Legislation.* Box 12, folder "Committee on Protec-

tive Labor Legislation." October. John F. Kennedy Library, Boston.

Press, Andrea, and Elizabeth R. Cole. 1999. *Speaking of Abortion: Television and Authority in the Lives of Women.* Chicago: University of Chicago Press.

Pruett, Holly, and Julie Davis. 1995. "Oregon's No on 13 Campaign: A Case Study in Movement Building through Electoral Organizing." Basic Rights Oregon, Portland (courtesy of Julie Davis).

Przeworski, Adam. 1991. *Democracy and the Market.* Cambridge: Cambridge University Press.

PTC (Portland Town Council). 1976. "A Legislative Guide to Gay Rights." Collection 7301 (National Gay and Lesbian Task Force), box 54, folder "Portland Town Council." Cornell University Library.

Putnam, Robert D., with Robert Leonardi and Raffaella Y. Nanetti. 1993. *Making Democracy Work.* Princeton, NJ: Princeton University Press.

Pye, Lucian, 1968. *The Spirit of Chinese Politics.* Cambridge, MA: MIT Press.

Quadagno, Jill S. 1988. "From Old-Age Assistance to Supplemental Security Income: The Political Economy of Relief in the South, 1935–1972." Pp. 235–64 in *The Politics of Social Policy in the United States,* edited by Margaret Weir, Ann Shola Orloff, and Theda Skocpol. Princeton, NJ: Princeton University Press.

Quadagno, Jill. 1992. "Social Movements and State Transformation: Labor Unions and Racial Conflict in the War on Poverty." *American Sociological Review* 57: 616–34.

———. 1994. *The Color of Welfare.* New York: Oxford University Press.

Quattrone, George A., and Amos Tversky. 1988. "Contrasting Rational and Psychological Analysis of Political Choice." *American Political Science Review* 82: 719–36.

Quindlen, Anna. 1992. "Putting Hatred to a Vote in Oregon." *Chicago Tribune,* November 3, C17.

Qureshi, I. A. 1978. "Islam and the West—Past, Present and Future." In *Challenge of Islam,* edited by A. Ganhar. London: Islamic Council of Europe.

Ragin, Charles C. 1987. *The Comparative Method: Moving Beyond Qualitative and Quantitative Strategies.* Berkeley, CA: University of California Press.

Ragin, Charles. 1989. "The Logic of Comparative Method and the Algebra of Logic." *Journal of Quantitative Anthropology* 1: 373–98.

Ragin, Charles C. 1991. "Introduction: The Problems of Balancing Discourse on Cases and Variables in Comparative Research." Pp. 1–8 in *Issues and Alternatives in Comparative Social Research*, edited by Charles C. Ragin. Leiden: E. J. Brill.

———. 2000. *Fuzzy-Set Social Science*. Chicago, IL: University of Chicago Press.

Ragin, Charles C., and Howard S. Becker. 1992. *What Is a Case? Exploring the Foundations of Social Inquiry*. New York: Cambridge University Press.

Randolph, Homer. 1981. *Interview*. East St. Louis, Illinois.

Rao, Hayagreeva. 1998. "Caveat Emptor: The Construction of Nonprofit Watch-dog Organizations." *American Journal of Sociology* 103: 912–61.

Rapoport, David C. 1990. "Sacred Terror: A Contemporary Example from Islam." Pp. 103–130 in *Origins of Terrorism: Psychologies, Theologies, States of Mind*, edited by Walter Reich. Cambridge: Cambridge University Press.

Raric, Ethan. 1990. "Abortion Opponent to Run for Governor." United Press International, April 18.

———. 1991. "Oregon Governor Backs Gay Rights Bill." United Press International, April 16.

Rashid, Ahmed. 2000. *Taliban: Militant Islam, Oil and Fundamentalism in Central Asia*. New Haven, CT: Yale University Press.

———. 2002. *Jihad: The Rise of Militant Islam in Central Asia*. New Hayen, CT: Yale University Press.

Rasler, Karen. 1996. "Concessions, Repression and Political Protest in the Iranian Revolution." *American Sociological Review* 61: 132–52.

Rauber, Paul. 1986. "With Friends Like These…" *Mother Jones* 11: 35–37, 47–49.

Ray, Raka. 1999. *Fields of Protest: Women's Movements in India*. Minneapolis: University of Minnesota Press.

Ray, Raka, and A. C. Korteweg. 1999. "Women's Movements in the Third World: Identity, Mobilization, and Autonomy." *Annual Review of Sociology* 25: 47–71.

Reese, Ellen. 1996. "Maternalism and Political Mobilization: How California's Postwar Child Care Campaign was Won." *Gender & Society* 10: 566–89.

Reger, Jo. 2002. "Organizational Dynamics and Construction of Multiple Feminist Identities in the National Organization for Women." *Gender & Society* 16: 710–27.

Reich, Walter (ed.). 1990. *Origins of Terrorism: Psychologies, Ideologies, Theologies, States of Mind*. Cambridge: Cambridge University Press.

Reichertz, J. 2002. "Objective Hermeneutics and Hermeneutic Sociology of Knowledge." In *Qualitative Research: A Handbook*, edited by U. Flick, E. v. Kardorff, and L Steinke. London: Sage.

Reinarman, Craig. 1985. "Social Movements and Social Problems: 'Mothers Against Drunk Drivers,' Restrictive Alcohol Laws and Social Control in the 1980s." Paper presented at the Annual Meeting of the Society for the Study of Social Problems, Washington, DC, Aug. 23–26.

Reissman, Catherine Kohler. 2000. "Stigma and Everyday Resistance Practices: Childless Women in South India." *Gender and Society* 14: 111–32.

Ren, Yanshen. 1990. "Shoudu wusuo gaoxiao xuesheng zhengzhi sixiang zhuangkuang de diaocha baogao" (A report on the investigation of students' political attitude in five Beijing universities). Pp. 112–27 in *Dui bashi niandai shoudu daxuesheng zongxian yanjiu* (Longitudinal studies on university students in Beijing during the eighties), edited by Lixin Cang (for internal circulation only). Beijing: Beijing Shifan Xueyuan Chubanshe.

Rheingold, Howard. 2002. *Smart Mobs: The Next Social Revolution*. Cambridge, MA: Perseus Publishing.

Richardson, Valerie. 1992. "Oregon to Vote on Gay-Rights Curbs." *Washington Times*, November 2, A7.

Richter, Ernesto. 1980. "Social Classes, Accumulation, and the Crisis of 'Overpopulation' in El Salvador." *Latin American Perspectives* 7: 114–39.

Ricoeur, Paul. 1984. *Time and Narrative*. Trans. Kathleen McLaughlin and David Pellauer. Illinois: University of Chicago Press.

Rinehart, James. 1997. *Revolution and the Millennium: China, Mexico, and Iran*. Westport, CT: Praeger.

Ritter, Gretchen. 2002. "Jury Service and Women's Citizenship Before and After the Nineteenth Amendment." *Law and History Review* 20: 479–515.

Rivera Damas, Arturo. 1977. "Labor pastoral de la Arquidiocesis de San Salvador especialmente de las comunidades eclesiales de base en su proyección a la justicia." *Estudios Centroamericanos* 32 (348–49): 805–14.

Robbins. Thomas and Dick Anthony. 1979. "The sociology of contemporary religious movements." Pp. 75–89 in *Annual Review of Sociology*, edited by Alex Inkeles. Vol. 5. Palo Alto, CA: Annual Reviews.

Roberts, Dorothy. 1997. *Killing the Black Body: Race, Reproduction, and the Meaning of Liberty.* New York: Pantheon Books.

Roberts, Ron E., and Robert Marsh Kloss. 1979. *Social Movements: Between the Balcony and the Barricade.* Second Edition. St. Louis: C. V. Mosby and Company.

Robinson, Ian. 2002. "The International Dimension of Labor Federation Economic Strategy in Canada and the United States, 1947-2000." In *Global Unions? Theory and Strategies of Organized Labour in the Global Political Economy,* edited by Jeffrey Harrod and Robert O'Brien. London: Routledge.

Robinson, William. 1996. *Promoting Polyarchy.* New York: Cambridge University Press.

Robnett, Belinda. 1996. "African-American Women in the Civil Rights Movement, 1954-1965: Gender, Leadership, and Micromobilization." *American Journal of Sociology* 101: 1661-93.

Robnett, Belinda. 1997. *How Long? How Long? African-American Women in the Struggle for Civil Rights.* New York: Oxford University Press.

Roche, John P. and Stephen Sachs. 1965. "The Bureaucrat and the Enthusiast: An Exploration of the Leadership of Social Movements." *Western Political Quarterly* 8: 248-61.

Rochford, E. Burke. 1985. *Hare Krishna in America.* New Brunswick, N.J.: Rutgers University Press.

Rochford, E.B., Jr. 1987a. "Shifting Public Definitions of Hare Krishna." Pp. 258-60 in*Collective Behavior,* 3rd ed. edited by R. Turner and L. Killian. Englewood Cliffs, NJ: Prentice-Hall.

———. 1987b. "Dialectical processes in the development of Hare Krishna: Tension, public definition, and strategy." Pp. 109-22 in *The Future of New Religious Movements,* edited by D. Bromley and P. Hammond. Macon, GA: Mercer University Press.

Rochon, Thomas and Daniel Mazmanian. 1993. "Social Movements and the Policy Process." *Annals of the American Academy of Political and Social Sciences* 528: 75-156.

Rochon, Thomas R. and David S. Meyer, eds. 1997. *Coalitions and Political Movements: The Lessons of the Nuclear Freeze.* Boulder, Colorado: Lynne-Rienner.

Rodríguez, David. 1976. "Situación de un sacerdote trabajando directamente en comunidades cristianas de base, afronta la tensión entre el laico y la jerarquía." Pp. 27-48 in *El laico en el compromiso social,* edited by P. Vega, E. Ortiz, and D. Rodríguez. San Salvador: Secretario Regional de Justicia y Paz.

Roefs, Marlene, Bert Klandermans, and Johan Olivier. 1998. "Protest Intentions on the Eve of South Africa's First Non-Racial Elections: Optimists Look Beyond Injustice." *Mobilization* 3: 51-68.

Roeser, Thomas F. 1983. "The Pro-life Movement's Holy Terror." *Chicago Reader* 12(44): 1, 14-24.

Rogers, Everett M. 1983. *Diffusion of Innovations.* New York: Free Press.

Rogers, Mary F. 1974. "Instrumental and Infra-Resources: The Bases of Power." *American Journal of Sociology* 79: 1418-33.

Rohlinger, Deana. 2002. "Framing the Abortion Debate: Organizational Resources, Media Strategies, and Movement-Countermovement Dynamics." *The Sociological Quarterly* 43 (4): 479-507.

Rohlinger, Deana and David A. Snow. 2003. "Social Psychological Perspectives on Crowds and Social Movements." Pp. 503-527 in *Handbook of Social Psychology,* edited by John Delamater. New York: Kluwer Academic/Plenum Publishers.

Rojecki, Andrew. 1999. *Silencing the Opposition: Antinuclear Movements and the Media in the Cold War.* Urbana and Chicago: University of Illinois Press.

Rokeach, Milton. 1973. *The Nature of Human Values.* New York: Free Press.

Roscigno, Vincent J., and Cynthia D. Anderson. 1995. "Subordination and Struggle: Social Movement Dynamics and Processes of Inequality." *Perspectives on Social Problems* 7: 249-74.

Roscigno, Vincent J., and William Danaher. 2001. "Media and Mobilization: The Case of Radio and Southern Textile Worker Insurgency, 1929-1934." *American Sociological Review* 66: 21-48.

Roscigno, Vincent J., and M. Keith Kimble. 1995. "Elite Power, Race, and the Persistence of Low Unionization in the South." *Work and Occupations* 22: 271-300.

Roscigno, Vincent and Donald Tomaskovic-Devey. 1994. "Racial Politics in the Contemporary South." *Social Problems* 41: 585-607.

Rose, Gregory. 1983. "Velayat-e Faqih and the Recovery of Islamic Identity in the Thought of Ayatollah Khomeini." In *Religion and Politics in Iran: Shi'ism from Quietism to Revolution,* edited by N. R. Keddie. New Haven, CT: Yale University Press.

Rosen, Ruth. 2000. *The World Split Open: How the Modern Women's Movement Changed America*. New York: Viking.

Rosen, Stanley. 1982. *Red Guard Factionalism and the Cultural Revolution in Guangzhou (Canton)*. Boulder, CO: Westview Press.

Rosen, Steven A. 1980/81. "Police Harassment of Homosexual Women and Men in New York City, 1960–1980." *Columbia Human Rights Law Review* 12: 159–90.

Rosenbaum, Alan S., ed. 2001. *Is The Holocaust Unique?* (2nd edition). Boulder, CO: Westview Press.

Rosenberg, Morris. 1979. *Conceiving the Self*. New York: Basic.

Rosenfeld, Michael J. 2005. *The Age of Independence: Interracial Unions, Same-Sex Unions, and the Changing American Family*. Cambridge, MA: Harvard University Press.

Rosenfeld, Rachel A. and Kathryn B. Ward. 1996. "Evolution of the Contemporary U.S. Women's Movement." *Research in Social Movements, Conflict, and Change* 19: 51–73.

Rosenthal, Howard L. and Keith T. Poole. 2000. "United States Congressional Roll Call Voting Records, 1789–1990: Reformatted Data." Carnegie Mellon University, Graduate School of Industrial Administration; Ann Arbor, MI: Inter-university Consortium for Political and Social Research.

Rosenthal, Naomi, M. Fingrutd, M. Ethier, R. Karant, and D. McDonald. 1985. "Social Movements and Network Analysis: A Case of Nineteenth Century Women's Reform in New York State." *American Journal of Sociology* 90: 1022–54.

Rosenthal, Naomi, and Michael Schwartz. 1989. "Spontaneity and democracy in social movements." *International Social Movement Research* 2: 33–59.

Rosenthal, Rob. 1994. *Homeless in Paradise: A Map of the Terrain*. Philadelphia, PA: Temple University Press.

Rossi, Alice, 1967. "Equality Between the Sexes: An Immodest Proposal." Pp. 98–143 in *The Woman in America*, edited by Robert Lay Lifton. Boston: Beacon Press.

Rossi, Peter H. 1989. *Down and Out in America: The Origins of Homelessness*. Chicago, IL: University of Chicago Press.

Rotem, Simha. 1994. *Memoirs of a Warsaw Gherto Fighter: The Past within Me*. New Haven: Yale University Press.

Roth, Dieter. 1994. "Was bewegt den Wähler?" *Aus Politik und Zeitgeschichte*, no. 11, pp. 3–13.

Roth, Rachel. 2000. *Making Women Pay: The Hidden Costs of Fetal Rights*. Ithaca, N.Y.: Cornell University Press.

Rothman, Franklin Daniel, and Pamela E. Oliver. 2002. "From Local to Global: The Anti-Dam Movement in Southern Brazil, 1979–1992." Pp. 115–31 in *Globalization and Resistance: Transnational Dimensions of Social Movements*, edited by J. Smith and H. Johnston. Lanham, MD: Rowman and Littlefield.

Rothschild-Whitt, Joyce. 1979. "The Collectivist Organization: An Alternative to Rational-Bureaucratic Models." *American Sociological Review* 44: 509–27.

Rowan, Richard W. *Secret Agents against America*. New York: Doubleday, Doran, 1939.

Rubin, Beth A. 1986. "Class Struggle American Style: Unions, Strikes and Wages." *American Sociological Review* 51: 618–31.

Rubin, Beth, Larry Griffin, and Michael Wallace. 1983. "Provided That Their Voice Was Strong." *Work and Occupations* 10: 325–47.

Rubin, Lilian B. 1972. *Busing and Backlash: White Against White in a California School District*. Berkeley: University of California Press.

Rucht, Dieter. 1996. "The Impact of National Contexts on Social Movement Structure: A Cross-Movement and Cross-National Comparison." Pp. 185–204 in *Comparative Perspectives on Social Movements*, edited by Doug McAdam, John D. McCarthy, and Mayer N. Zald. Cambridge: Cambridge University Press.

Rucht, Dieter. 1998. "The Structure and Culture of Collective Protest in Germany since 1950." Pp. 29–57 in *The Social Movement Society: Contentious Politics for a New Century*, edited by David S. Meyer and Sidney G. Tarrow. Lanham, MD: Tarrow, Rowan and Littlefield.

Rucht, Dieter, 1999. "Linking Organization and Mobilization: Michels' 'Iron Law of Oligarchy' Reconsidered." *Mobilization* 4: 151–70.

Rucht, Dieter. 2004. "Movement Allies, Adversaries, and Third Parties." Pp. 197–216 in *The Blackwell Companion to Social Movements*, edited by D. A. Snow, S. A. Soule, and H. Kriesi. Oxford, UK: Blackwell Publishing.

Rucht, Dieter, Ruud Koopmans, and Friedhelm Neidhardt. eds. 1999. *Acts of Dissent: New*

Developments in the Study of Protest. Lanham: Rowman & Littlefield.

Rucht, Dieter and Friedhelm Neidhardt. 1998. "Methodological Issues in Collecting Protest Event Data." Pp. 65–89 in *Acts of Dissent,* edited by D. Rucht, R. Koopmans, and F. Neidhardt. Berlin, Germany: Edition Sigma.

Rucht, Dieter, and Thomas Ohlemacher. 1992. "Protest Event Data: Collection, Uses and Perspectives." Pp. 76–106 in *Studying Collective Action,* edited by R. Eyerman and M. Diani Newbury Park, Calif.: Sage.

Rudé, George. 1964. *The Croud in History, 1730–1848.* New York: John Wiley & Sons.

Rüdig, Wolfgang. 1990. *Antinuclear Movements.* London, England: Longman.

Ruggie, John. 1993. "Multilateralism: The Anatomy of an Institution." In *Multilateralism Matters: The Theory and Praxis of an Institutional Form,* edited by John Ruggie. New York: Columbia University Press.

Ruiz Abarca, Antonio Eli. 1967. "I.M.P.R.E.S.S.: Unidad Magisterial." *El Periodista* (Department of Journalism newspaper, University of El Salvador). September 12.

Runciman, W.G. 1966. *Relative Deprivation and Social Justice.* London: Routledge and Kegan Paul.

Rupp, Leila J. 1982. "The Survival of American Feminism." Pp. 33–65 in *Reshaping America.* edited by R.H. Bremner and G.W. Reichard. Columbus: Ohio State University Press.

———. 1985. "The Women's Community in the National Woman's Party, 1945 to the 1960's." *Signs* 10: 715–40.

Rupp, Leila J. 1997. *Worlds of Women: The Making of an International Women's Movement.* Princeton: Princeton University Press.

Rupp, Leila and Verta Taylor. 1987. *Survival in the Doldrums: the American Women's Rights Movement.* New York: Oxford University Press.

Rural Organizing Cultural Center. 1991. *Minds Stayed on Freedom.* Boulder, CO: Westview.

Rutland Daily Herald, 1939. "Vermont Women Fight Senate Bill Designed to Let Them Be Jurors," February 15, p. 2.

Ruzza, Carlo and Oliver Schmidtke. 1993. "Roots of Success of the Northern League." *West European Politics* 16: 1–23.

Ryan, Barbara. 1992. *Feminism and the Women's Movement: Dynamics of Change in Social Movement Ideology and Activism.* New York: Routledge.

Ryan, Charlotte. 1991. *Prime Time Activism.* Boston: South End Press.

Sabatier, Paul. 1975. "Social Movements and Regulatory Agencies." *Policy Sciences* 6: 301–42.

Saegert, Susan, and Gary H. Winkel. 1990. "Environmental Psychology." *Annual Review of Psychology* 41: 441–77.

Sageman, Marc. 2004. *Understanding Terror Networks.* Philadelphia: University of Pennsylvania Press.

Sahlins, Marshall. 1981. *Historical Metaphors and Mythical Realities.* Ann Arbor: University of Michigan Press.

Sahlins, Marshall. 1985. *Islands of History.* Chicago: University of Chicago Press.

Salamon, Lester. 1971. "Protest, Politics, and Modernization in the American South: Mississippi as a 'Developing Society.'" Ph.D. dissertation, Department of Government, Harvard University, Cambridge, MA.

Sale, Kirkpatrick. 1973. SDS. New York: Vintage.

Salehi, M. M. 1996. "Radical Islamic Insurgency in the Iranian Revolution of 1978–1979." Pp. 47–63 in *Disruptive Religion,* edited by Christian Smith. New York: Routledge.

Saletan, William. 1998. "Electoral Politics and Abortion: Narrowing the Message." Pp. 111–23 in *Abortion Wars: A Half-Century of Struggle,* edited by Rickie Solinger. Berkeley and Los Angeles: University of California Press.

Samaniego, Carlos. 1980. "?Movimiento campesino o lucha del proletariado rural en El Salvador?" *Revista Mexicana de Sociología* 62 (2): 652–67.

Santoro, Wayne. 2002. "The Civil Rights Movement's Struggle for Equal Employment Rights." *Social Forces* 81: 177–206.

Sarat, Austin, and Thomas R. Kearns. 1993. *Law in Everyday Life.* Ann Arbor: University of Michigan Press.

Sarbin, Theodore, ed. 1986. "Narrative Psychology: The Storied Nature of Human Conduct". New York: Praeger.

Sartori, Giovanni. 1976. *Parties and Party Systems: A Framework for Analysis.* Cambridge, England and New York: Cambridge University Press.

———. 1982. *Teoria dei Partiti e Caso Italiano* (Theories of Political Parties and the Italian Case). Milan, Italy: Sugarco.

Sauer, Birgit. 1995. "'Doing Gender': Das Parlament als Ort der Geschlechter konstruktion."

Pp. 172–99 in *Sprache des Parlaments und Semiotik der Demokratie,* edited by Andreas Dörner and Ludgera Vogt. Berlin: Walter de Gruyter.

Sawyers, Traci M. and David S. Meyer. 1999. "Missed Opportunities." *Social Problems* 46 (2): 187–206.

Sayre, Cynthia Woolever. 1980. "The Impact of Voluntary Association Involvement on Social-Psychological Attitudes." Paper presented at the annual meetings of the American Sociological Association, New York City, August.

Schapiro, Leonard and John Lewis. 1969. "The Roles of the Monolithic Party under the Totalitarian Leader." *The China Quarterly* 40: 39–64.

Scharpf, F.W. 1984. "Economic and institutional constraints of full employment strategies: Sweden, Austria and West-Germany, 1973–82." Pp. 257–90 in *Order and Conflict in Contemporary Capitalism: Studies in the Political Economy of West European Nations,* edited by J. H. Goldthorpe. New York: Oxford University Press.

Scheepers, Peer, Merove Gijsberts, and Marcel Coenders. 2002. "Ethnic Exclusionism in European Countries." *European Sociological Review* 18: 17–34.

Scheer, Robert. 1970. "Editor's note to 'The Biography of Huey P. Newton' by Bobby Seale in *Ramparts.*" Pp. 202–6 in *The Movement toward a New America: The Beginnings of a Long Revolution,* edited by Mitchell Goodman. New York: United Church Press and Alfred A. Knopf.

Scheingold, Stuart. 1974. *The Politics of Rights: Lawyers, Public Policy, and Political Change.* New Haven, Conn.: Yale University Press.

Schell, Jonathan. 2003. *The Uncomquerable World: Power, Nonviolence, and the Will of the People.* New York: Metropolitan Books.

Schenk, Herrad. 1980. *Die feministische Herausforderung: 150 Jahre Frauenbewegung in Deutschland.* München: Beck.

Schiltz, Michael A. 1971. *Public Attitudes toward Social Security, 1935–1965.* Washington, DC: U.S. Government Printing Office.

Schlozman, Kay Lehman and John Tiemey. 1986. *Organized Interests and American Democracy.* New York: Little, Brown.

Schneider, Beth E. 1984. "Peril and promise: Lesbians' Workplace Participation." Pp. 211–230 in *Women-Identified Women,* edited by Trudy Darty

and Sandee Potter. Palo Alto, CA: Mayfield Publishing Company.

Schneider, Beth E. 1988. "Invisible and Independent: Lesbians' Experiences in the Workplace." Pp. 273–96 in *Women Working,* edited by A. Stromsburg and S. Hankess.. Palo, Alto, CA: Mayfield Publishing Company.

Schneider, Cathy Lisa. 1995. *Shantytown Protest in Pinochet's Chile.* Philadelphia: Temple University Press.

Schock, Kurt. 1999. "People Power and Political Opportunities: Social Movement Mobilization and Outcomes in the Philippines and Burma." *Social Problems* 46 (3): 355–75.

Schoggen, Phil. 1989. *Behavior Settings.* Stanford, Calif.: Stanford University Press.

Schram, Sanford F. and J. Patrick Turbett. 1983. "Civil disorder and the welfare explosion." *American Sociological Review* 48: 408–414.

Schroer, Todd. 2003. "Tertiary Deviance and New Media: White Racialist 'Love Groups' and 'White Civil Rights' Organizations." Paper presented at the annual meetings of the Midwest Sociological Society, Chicago II.

Schudson, Michael. 1995. *The Power of the News.* Cambridge, Mass.: Harvard University Press.

Schulz, Winfried. 1997. *Politische Kommunikation: Theoretische Artsätze und Ergebnisse empirischer Forschung zur Rolle der Massenmedien in der Politik.* Opladen: Westdeutscher Verlag.

Schumaker, Paul. 1975. "Policy Responsiveness to Protest Group Demands." *Journal of Politics* 37: 488–521.

Schurmann, Franz. 1968. *Ideology and Organization in Communist China.* Berkeley: University of California Press.

Schurmann, Franz. 1968. *Ideology and Organization in Communist China,* 2d ed. Berkeley, CA: University of California Press.

Schutz, Alfred. 1962. *Collected Papers I. The Problem of Social Reality.* The Hague: Martinus Nijhoff.

———. 1964. *Collected Papers II. Studies in Social Theory.* The Hague: Martinus Nijhoff.

Schwartz, Michael. 1976. *Radical Protest and Social Structure.* New York: Academic.

Schwartz, Michael and Shuva Paul. 1992. "Resource Mobilization versus the Mobilization of People." Pp. 205–23 in *Frontiers in Social Movement Theory,* edited by A. Morris and C. Mueller. New Haven, CT: Yale University Press.

Schwartz. Benjamin. 1968. "The Reign of Virtue: Some Broad Perspectives on Leader and Party in the Cultural Revolution." *The China Quarterly* 35: 1–17.

Schweber, Claudine A. 1979. "But Some Were Less Equal…The Fight for Women Jurors." Pp. 329–44 in *Women Organizing: An Anthology,* edited by B. Cummings and V. Schuck, Metuchen, NJ: Scarecrow Press.

Schweitzer, Arthur, 1984. *The Age of Charisma,* Chicago, IL: University of Chicago Press.

Scott, Anne Firor. 1970. *The Southern Lady: From Pedestal to Politics. 1830–30,* Chicago, IL: University of Chicago Press.

Scott, James C. 1976. *The Moral Economy of the Peasant: Rebellions and Subsistence in Southeast Asia.* New Haven: Yale University Press.

Scott, James C. 1986. *Weapons of the Weak: Everyday Forms of Peasant Resistance.* New Haven, Conn.: Yale University Press.

Scott, James. 1990. *Domination and the Arts of Resistance: Hidden Transcripts.* New Haven, CT: Yale University Press.

Scott, Robert A. 2003. *The Gothic Enterprise: A Guide to Understanding the Medieval Cathedral.* Berkeley: University of California Press.

Scott, Robert, et al. 2001. "NAFTA at Seven: Its Impact on Workers in All Three Nations." Economic Policy Institute briefing paper, Washington, D.C.

Scott, W. Richard. 1994a. "Conceptualizing Organizational Fields: Linking Organizations and Societal Systems." Pp. 203–21 in *Systemrationalitat und Partialinteresse,* edited by Hans-Ulrich Derlien, Uta Gerhardt, and Fritz W. Scharpf. Baden-Baden: Nomos.

Scott, W. Richard. 1995. *Institutions and Organizations.* Beverly Hills, Calif.: Sage.

Seeman, Melvin. 1972. "Alienation and Engagement." Pp. 467–527 in *The Human Meaning of Social Change.* Agnus Campbell and Philip Converse, eds. New York: Russell Sage.

Segatti, Paolo. 1992. "L'offerta politica e i candidati della Lega alle amministrative del 1990" (Political Offer and the League Candidates at the 1992 Local Elections). *Polis* 6: 257–80.

Seidman, Steven. 1993. "Identity and Politics in a 'Postmodern' Gay Culture: Some Historical and Conceptual Notes." Pp. 105–42 in *Fear of a Queer Planet: Queer Politics and Social Theory,* edited by Michael Warner. Minneapolis: University of Minnesota Press.

Seliger, M. 1976. *Ideology and Politics.* New York: Free Press.

Sewell William Jr. 1992a. "Introduction: Narratives and Social Identities." *Social Science History* 16: 479–88.

Sewell, William H., Jr. 1992b. "A Theory of Structure: Duality, Agency, and Transformation." *American Journal of Sociology* 98: 1–29.

Sewell, William H., Jr. 1996a. "Historical Events as Transformations of Structures: Inventing Revolution at the Bastille." *Theory and Society* 25: 841–81.

Sewell, William H., Jr. 1996b. "Three Temporalities: Toward an Eventful Sociology." Pp. 245–80 in *The Historic Turn in the Human Sciences,* edited by Terrance J. McDonald. Ann Arbor: University of Michigan Press.

Sewell, William H., Jr. 2001. "Space in Contentious Politics." In *Silence and Voice in the Study of Contentious Politics,* edited by Ronald R. Aminzade, Jack A. Goldstone, Doug McAdam, Elizabeth J. Perry, William H. Sewell, Sidney Tarrow, and Charles Tilly. Cambridge: Cambridge University Press.

Sharp, Gene. 1973. *The Politics of Nonviolent Action.* Boston: Porter Sargent Publishers.

Sheahan, John. 1990. *Modelos de desarrollo en América Latina.* Mexico City: Alianza Editorial Mexicana.

Shen, Ruhuai. 2004. *Qinghua Daxue wenge jisht: Yige hongwelbing de zishu* (Tsinghua University Cultural Revolution Chronicle: A Red Guard's Memoir). Hong Kong: Shidai Yishu Publishing House.

Sherkat, Darren E., and John Wilson. 1995. "Preferences, Constraints, and Choices in Religious Markets: An Examination of Religious Switching and Apostasy." *Social Forces* 73 (3): 993–1026.

Shibutani, Tamotsu. 1973. "On the Personification of Adversaries." Pp. 223–33 in *Human Nature and Collective Behavior: Papers in Honor of Herbert Blumer,* edited by T. Shibutani. New Brunswick, NJ: Transaction Books.

Shinn, L. 1987b. "The Future of an Old Man's Vision: ISKCON in the twenty-first century." Pp. 123–40 in *The Future of New Religious Movements,* edited by D. Bromley and P. Hammond. Macon, GA: Mercer University Press.

Shinn, Marybeth and Colleen Gillespie. 1994. "The Roles of Housing and Poverty in the Origins of

Homelessness." *American Behavioral Scientist* 37: 505–21.

Shirk, Susan. 1982. *Competitive Comrades: Career Incentives and Student Strategies in China.* Berkeley, CA: University of California Press.

Shneidman, N. N. 2002. *The Three Tragic Heroes of the Vilnius Ghetto.* Oakville, Ontario: Mosaic Press.

Shook, Somer, Wesley Delano, and Robert W. Batch 1999. "Elohim City: A Participant-Observer Study of a Christian Identity Community." *Nova Religio* 2: 245–65.

Shorter, Edward, and Charles Tilly. 1974. *Strikes in France, 1830–1968.* New York: Cambridge University Press.

Shriver, Thomas E. 2000 "Risk and Recruitment: Patterns of Social Movement Mobilization in a Government Town." *Sociological Focus* 33: 321–37.

Shupe, Anson D., Roger Spielmann, and Sam Stigall. 1978. "Deprogramming: The new exorcism." Pp. 145–60 in *Conversion Careers,* edited by J. Richardson. Beverly Hills, CA: Sage.

Shuttlesworth, Rev. Fred. 1977. Interview with Fred Shuttlesworth. Pp. 166–76 in *My Soul is Rested,* edited by Howell Raines. New York: Bantam.

Shuttlesworth, Rev. Fred. 1978. *Interview.* Cincinnati, Ohio. September 12.

Siegel, Diane Joyce. 1981. "Justitia Mounts the Jury Bench: The Campaign for Women's Jury Service in Massachusetts." Department of History, Harvard University, Boston, MA. Unpublished honors thesis.

Sigmund, Paul E. 1984. "Chile: Free-market authoritarianism." Pp. 1–13 in *Politics, Policies, and Economic Development in Latin America,* edited by Robert Wesson. Stanford, CA: Hoover Institution Press.

Sikkink, Kathryn. 1993. "Human Rights, Principled Issue-Networks, and Sovereignty in Latin America." *International Organization* 47: 411–41.

Sikkink, Kathryn, and Jackie Smith. 2002. "Infrastructures for Change: Transnational Organizations, 1953–1993." Pp. 24–44 in *Restructuring World Politics: The Power of Transnational Agency and Norms,* edited by S. Khagram, J. Riker, and Kathryn Sikkink. Minneapolis: University of Minnesota Press.

Silveira, Ellen, and Peter Allebeck. 2001. "Migration, Ageing and Mental Health: An Ethnographic Study on Perceptions of Life Satisfaction, Anxiety and Depression in Older Somali Men in East London." *International Journal of Social Welfare* 10 (4): 309–20.

Simmel, Georg. 1971. *On Individuality and Social Forms,* edited by Donald N. Levine. Chicago: University of Chicago Press.

Simpson, Richard L. and David R. Norsworthy. 1965. "The Changing Occupational Structure of the South." in *The South in Continuity and Change,* edited by John C. McKinney and Edgar T. Thompson. Durham, NC: Duke University Press, 198–224.

Simpson, William Gayley. 1991. "The everlasting truth about race." *Christian Patriot Crusader* 7(4): 19–20.

Simpson, William. 1982. "The Birth of the Mississippi 'Loyalist Democrats' (1965–1968)." *Journal of Mississippi History* 44: 27–45.

Sisk, D. Timothy. 1995. *Democratization in South Africa: The Elusive Contract.* Princeton: Princeton University Press.

Sklair, Leslie. 2001. *The Transnational Capitalist Class.* Cambridge: Blackwell.

Skocpol, Theda. 1979. *States and Social Revolutions: A Comparative Analysis of France, Russia, and China.* Cambridge: Cambridge University Press.

Skocpol, Theda. 1992. *Protecting Soldiers and Mothers: The Political Origins of Social Policy in the United States.* Cambridge, MA: Belknap Press of Harvard University Press.

———. 2003. *Diminished Democracy: From Membership to Management in American Civic Life.* Norman, OK: University of Oklahoma Press.

Skocpol, Theda, and Edwin Amenta. 1986. "States and Social Policies." *Annual Review of Sociology* 12: 131–57.

Skolnick, Jerome H. 1969. *The Politics of Protest.* New York: Simon & Schuster.

Skonovd, L. N. 1981. *Apostasy: The Process of Defection from Religious Totalism.* Ph.D. dissertation, Ann Arbor, MI: University Microfilms International.

Skonovd, L. N. 1983. "Leaving the cultic religious milieu." Pp. 91–103 in *The Brainwashing IDe programming Controversy: Sociological, Psychological, Legal and Historical Perspectives,* edited by D. Bromley and J. Richardson. New York: Edwin Mellen.

Skrentny, John David. 1996. *The Ironies of Affirmative Action: Politics, Culture, and Justice in America.* Chicago: University of Chicago Press.

Skrentny, John David. 1998. "The Effect of the Cold War on African-American Civil Rights: America and the

World Audience, 1945–1968." *Theory and Society* 27: 237–85.

Skrentny, John D. 2002. *The Minority Rights Revolution.* Cambridge, MA: Harvard University Press.

Smelser, Neil. 1962. *Theory of Collective Behavior.* New York: Free Press of Glencoe.

Smilde, David A. 1997. "The Fundamental Unity of the Conservative and Revolutionary Tendencies in Venezuelan Evangelicalism: The Case of Conjugal Relations." *Religion* 27 (4): 343–59.

———. 1998. "Letting God Govern: Supernatural Agency in the Venezuelan Pentecostal Approach to Social Change." *Sociology of Religion* 59 (3): 287–303.

———. 2003. "Skirting the Instrumental Paradox: Intentional Belief through Narrative in Latin American Pentecostalism." *Qualitative Sociology* 26 (3): 313–29.

———. 2004. "Popular Publics: Street Protest and Plaza Preachers in Caracas." *International Review of Social History* 49 (suppl.): 179–95.

Smith, Bryan. 1998. *Religious Politics in Latin America: Pentecostal vs. Catholic.* Notre Dame, Ind.: University of Notre Dame Press.

Smith, Charles V. and Lewis M. Killian. 1958. *The Tallahassee Bus Protest.* New York: Anti-Defamation League of B'nai B'rith.

Smith, Christian. 1991. *The Emergence of Liberation Theology.* Chicago: University of Chicago Press.

———. 1996. *Resisting Reagan.* Chicago: University of Chicago Press.

Smith, Dorothy E. 1999. *Writing the Social: Critique, Theory, and Investigations.* Toronto: University of Toronto Press.

Smith, Heather J., and Daniel Ortiz. 2002. "Is It Just Me? The Different Consequences of Personal and Group Relative Deprivation." Pp. 91–118 in *Relative Deprivation,* edited by Iain Walker and Heather J. Smith. New York: Cambridge University Press.

Smith, Jackie. 1997. "Characteristics of the Modern Transnational Social Movement Sector." Pp. 42–58 in *Transnational Social Movements and World Politics: Solidarity Beyond the State,* edited by Jackie Smith, Charles Chatfield, and Ron Pagnucco. Syracuse, NY: Syracuse University Press.

Smith, Jackie. 2002. "Bridging Global Divides? Strategic Framing and Solidarity in Transnational Social Movement Organizations." *International Sociology* 17(4): 505–28.

Smith, Jackie. 2004. "Exploring Connections Between Global Integration and Political Mobilization." *Journal of World Systems Research* 2004: 255–85.

Smith, Jackie, Ron Pagnucco, and George Lopez. 1998. "Globalizing Human Rights: Report on a Survey of Transnational Human Rights NGOs." *Human Rights Quarterly* 20: 379–412.

Smith, Jackie, Ron Pagnucco, and Winnie Romeril. 1994. "Transnational Social Movement Organizations in the Global Political Arena." *Voluntas* 5: 121–54.

Smith, Marie. 1964. "Sex Amendment in Rights Bill Stirs Reaction." *Washington Post,* February 10.

Smith, Rev. Kelly Miller. 1978. *Interview.* Nashville, Tennessee. October 13.

Snow, David A. 1976. "The Nichiren Shoshu Buddhist Movement in America: A Sociological Examination of Its Value Orientation, Recruitment Efforts, and Spread." Ann Arbor, Mich.: University Microfilms.

Snow, David A. 2001. "Collective Identity and Expressive Forms." Pp. 2212–19 in *International Encyclopedia of the Social and Behavioral Sciences,* edited by N. J. Smelser and P. B. Baltes. Oxford, UK: Pergamon Press.

Snow, David A. 2004a. "Framing Processes, Ideology, and Discursive Fields." Pp. 380–412 in *The Blackwell Companion to Social Movements,* edited by David A. Snow, Sarah A. Soule, and Hanspeter Kriesi. Malden, Mass.: Blackwell.

Snow, David A. 2004b. "Social Movements as Challenges to Authority: Resistance to an Emerging Conceptual Hegemony." Pp. 3–25 in *Authority in Contention: Research in Social Movements, Conflict, and Change,* Vol. 25, edited by Daniel J. Meyers and Daniel M. Cress. London/New York: Elsevier.

Snow, David A. and Leon Anderson. 1987. "Identity Work among the Homeless: The Verbal Construction and Avowal of Personal identities." *American Journal of Sociology* 92: 1336–71.

Snow, David A. and Leon Anderson. 1993. *Down on Their Luck: A Study of Homeless Street People.* Berkeley, CA: University of California Press.

Snow, David A. and Robert D. Benford. 1988. "Ideology, Frame Resonance, and Participant Mobilization," Pp. 197–218 in *International Social Movement Research,* vol.1, *From Structure to Action,* edited by B. Klandermans, H. Kriesi, and S. Tarrow. Greenwich, CT: JAI Press.

Snow, David A. and Robert D. Benford. 1992. "Master Frames and Cycles of Protest." Pp. 133–55 in *Frontiers of Social Movement Theory,* edited by A. Morris and C. McClurg Mueller. New Haven, CT Yale University Press.

Snow, Benford. 2000. "Comment on Oliver and Johnston: Clarifying the Relationship between Framing and Ideology." *Mobilization* 5: 55–60.

Snow, David A., Robert D. Benford, and Leon Anderson. 1986. "Fieldwork Roles and Informational Yield: A Comparison of Alternative Settings and Roles." *Urban Life* 15: 377–408.

Snow David A., Daniel M. Cress, Liam Downey, and Andrew Jones. 1998. Disrupting the 'Quotidian': Reconceptualizing the Relationship between Breakdown and the Emergence of Collective Action. *Mobilization* 3: 1–22.

Snow, David and Richard Machalek. 1984. "The sociology of conversion." Pp. 167–90 in *Annual Review of Sociology,* edited by R. Turner and J. Short. Palo Alto, CA: Annual Reviews Inc.

Snow, David. A., and Susan E. Marshall. 1984. "Cultural Imperialism, Social Movements, and the Islamic Revival." *Research in Social Movements, Conflict and Change* 7: 131–152.

Snow, David A., and Doug McAdam. 2000. "Identity Work Processes in the Context of Social Movements: Clarifying the Identity/Movement Nexus. Pp. 41–67 in *Self, Identity, and Social Movements,* edited by Sheldon Stryker, Timothy J. Owens, and Robert W. White. Minneapolis: University of Minnesota Press.

Snow, David A. and Pamela Oliver. 1995. "Social Movements and Collective Behavior: Social Psychological Dimensions and Considerations." Pp. 571–599 in *Sociological Perspectives on Social Psychology,* edited by K. Cook, G. Fine, and J. House. Boston: Allyn and Bacon.

Snow, David A., and Cynthia L. Phillips. 1980. "The Lofland-Stark Conversion Model: A Critical Reassessment." *Social Problems* 27 (4): 430–47.

Snow, David A., and E. Burke Rochford, Jr. 1983. "Structural Availability, the Alignment Process and Movement Recruitment" Paper presented at the annual meetings of the American Sociological Association, Detroit, August.

Snow, David A., E. Burke Rochford Jr., Steven K. Worden, and Robert D. Benford. 1986. "Frame Alignment Processes, Micromobilization, and Movement Participation." *American Sociological Review* 51: 464–81.

Snow, David A., Sarah A. Soule, and Daniel M. Cress. 2001. "Homeless Protest across 17 U.S. Cities, 1980–1991: Assessment of the Explanatory Utility of Strain, Resource Mobilization, and Political Opportunity Theories." Paper presented at the annual meeting of the American Sociological Association, August 21, Anaheim, CA.

Snow, David E., Sarah A. Soule, and Hanspeter Kriesi, eds. 2004. *The Blackwell Companion to Social Movements.* Malden, Mass.: Blackwell.

Snow, David A., Lewis A. Zurcher, and Sheldon Eckland-Olson. 1980. "Social Networks and Social Movements: A Microstructural Approach to Differential Recruitment." *American Sociological Review* 45: 787–801.

Snow, Edgar. 1971. *The Long Revolution.* New York: Vintage.

Snow, Robert L. 1999. *The Militia Threat: Terrorists among Us.* New York: Plenum Trade.

Snyder, David and William Kelly. 1979. "Strategies for Investigating Violence and Social Change." Pp. 212–37 in *The Dynamics of Social Movements,* edited by M. Zald and J. McCarthy. Cambridge, MA: Winthrop.

Snyder, David, and Charles Tilly. 1972. "Hardship and Collective Violence in France, 1830 to 1960." *American Sociological Review* 37: 520–32.

Sociological Forum. 1999. Special issue: "Mini-Symposium on Social Movements." 14 (1).

Socorro Jurídico Cristiano. 1981. *El Salvador, La situación de los derechos humanos: Octubre 1979–Julio 1981.* Mexico City: Consejo Mundial de Iglesias.

———. 1984. *Informe No. 11, Año IX.* San Salvador: Arzobispado de San Salvador. Stanley, William. 1996. *The Protection Racket State: Elite Politics, Military Extortion, and Civil War in El Salvador.* Philadelphia: Temple University Press.

Solinger, Rickie, ed. 1998. *Abortion Wars: A Half-Century of Struggle.* Berkeley and Los Angeles: University of California Press.

———, 2001. *Beggars and Choosers: How the Politics of Choice Shapes Adoption, Abortion, and Welfare in the United States.* New York: Hill & Wang.

Solo, Pam. 1988. *From Protest to Policy: Beyond the Freeze to Common Security.* Cambridge, MA: Ballinger.

Solomon, Richard. 1971. *Mao's Revolution and the Chinese Political Culture.* Berkeley, CA: University of California Press.

Somers, Margaret R. 1992. "Narrativity, narrative Identity, and social action: Rethinking English working-class formation." *Social Science History* 16: 591–630.

Somers, Margaret R. 1994. "The narrative constitution of identity: A relational and network approach." *Theory and Society* 23: 605–49.

Sommer, Robert. 1967. "Small Group Ecology." *Sociometry* 28: 337–48.

———. 1969. *Personal Space: The Behavioral Basis of Design.* Englewood Cliffs, N.J.: Prentice-Hall.

Song, Yongyi and Dajin Sun. 1996. *Wenhua da geming he ta de yiduan sichao* (Heterodox Thinking During the Cultural Revolution). Hong Kong: Tianyuan Bookhouse.

Sorin, Gerald. 1972. *Abolitionism: A New Perspective.* New York: Praeger.

Soule, Sarah A. 1992. "Populism and black lynching in Georgia, 1890–1900." *Social Forces* 71: 431–449.

———. 1995. "The Student Anti-Apartheid Movement in the United States: Diffusion of Protest Tactics and Policy Reform." Ph.D. dissertation, Department of Sociology, Cornell University, Ithaca, NY.

———. 1997. "The Student Divestment Movement in the United States and Tactical Diffusion: The Shantytown Protest." *Social Forces* 75: 855–83.

Soule, Sarah A. 2004. "Diffusion Processes within and across Social Movements." Pp. 294–310 in *The Blackwell Companion to Social Movements,* edited by David A. Snow, Sarah A. Soule, and Hanspeter Kriesi. Malden, Mass.: Blackwell.

Soule, Sarah A., and Jennifer Earl. 2001. "The enactment of state-level hate crime law in the United States: Intrastate and interstate factors." *Sociological Perspectives* 44(3): 281–305.

Soule, Sarah A., Doug McAdam, John McCarthy, and Yang Su. 1999. "Protest Events: Cause or Consequence of State Action? The U.S. Women's Movement and Federal Congressional Activities, 1956–1979." *Mobilization* 4: 239–56.

Soule, Sarah A. and Susan Olzak. 2004. "When Do Movements Matter? The Politics of Contingency and the Equal Rights Amendment." *American Sociological Review* 69: 473–97.

Soule, Sarah A., and Nella Van Dyke. 1999. "Black church arson in the United States, 1989–1996." *Ethnic and Racial Studies* 22(4): 724–42.

Soule, Sarah A., and Yvonne Zylan. 1997. "Runaway train? The diffusion of state-level reforms in ADC/AFDC eligibility requirements, 1950–67." *American Journal of Sociology* 3: 733–62.

South Africa Survey 1996/97. 1997. Johannesburg: South African Institute of Race Relations.

Southern Poverty Law Center. 1996. "False patriots." *Intelligence Report* 83: 58–68.

Southern Poverty Law Center. 1997. "Compound Troubles: Separatist Communities Worry Law Enforcement." *Intelligence Report* 87: 6–9.

———. 1999. "The world of patriots." *Intelligence Report* 94: 10–11.

———. 1999. "The Year in Hate: Hate Group Counts Top 500." Retrieved January 30, 2001 (http: // www. splcenter.org/intelligenceproject/ip-index.html).

———. 2000. "Aryans Without a Nation." Retrieved November 30, 2001 (http: //www.splcenter.org/cgi-bin/goframe.pl?dimame=/.&pagename=site map).

———. 2000. "Patriot' free fall." *Intelligence Report* 106, http: //www.splcenter.org/intelligenceproject/ip-4v6.html.

———. 2001a. "Present at the Creation." Retrieved March 30, 2002 (http: //www.splcenter.org/ intelligenceproject/ip-index.html).

———. 2001b. "Reevaluating the Net." *Intelligence Report* 102. Retrieved November 30, 2001 (http: //www. splcenter.org/intelligenceproject/ip-index.html).

———. 2001c. "From America, with Hate." *Intelligence Report* 103. Retrieved August 29, 2001 (http: //splcenter.org/cgi-bin/goframe.pl?refname=? intelligenceproject/ip-index.html).

———. 2002. "Year in Hate." Retrieved December 1, 2002 (http: //www.splcenter.org/intelligenceproject/ip-index.html).

Southern Regional Council. 1960. "The student protest movement, winter 1960." SRC-13. April 1.

Southern Regional Council. 1961. *The Student Protest Movement: A Recapitulation.* Atlanta: Southern Regional Council.

Spalding, Hobart. 1992. "The Two Latin American Foreign Policies of the U.S. Labor Movement," *Science and Society* 56 (4): 421–439.

Spender, Dale. 1981. "The gatekeepers: A feminist critique of academic publishing." Pp. 186–202 in *Doing Feminist Research,* edited by Helen Roberts. London: Routledge & Kegan Paul.

Spengler, Joseph J. 1963. "Demographic and Economic Change in the South." In*Change in the Contemporary South,* edited by Allan P. Sindler. Durham, NC: Duke University Press, 26–63.

Spilerman, Seymour. 1976. "Structural Characteristics of Cities and the Severity of Racial Disorders." *American Sociological Review* 41: 771–93.

Spira, Henry. 1985. "Fighting to win." Pp. 194–208 in *In Defense of Animals,* edited by Peter Singer. New York: Harper & Row.

Sprinzak, Ehud. 2000. "Rational Fanatics." *Foreign Policy,* 120 (September–October): 66–73.

Spykman, Nicholas J. 1964. *The Social Theory of Georg Simmel.* New York: Atherton.

Staggenborg, Suzanne. 1985. *Patterns of Collective Action in the Abortion Conflict: An Organizational Analysis of the Pro-Choice Movement.* Ph.D. diss., Northwestern University.

———. 1986. "Coalition Work in the Pro-Choice Movement: Organizational and Environmental Opportunities and Obstacles." *Social Problems* 33: 374–90.

Staggenborg, Suzanne. 1988. "Consequences of Professionalization and Formalization in the Pro-Choice Movement." *American Sociological Review* 53: 585–606.

———. 1989. "Stability and Innovation in the Women's Movement: A Comparison of Two Movement Organizations." *Social Problems* 36: 75–92.

Staggenborg, Suzanne. 1991. *The Pro-choice Movement: Organization and Activism in the Abortion Conflict.* New York: Oxford University Press.

———. 1995. "Can Feminist Organizations Be Effective?" Pp. 339–55 in *Feminist Organizations: Harvest of the New Women's Movement,* edited by Myra Marx Ferree and Patricia Yancey Martin. Philadelphia: Temple University Press.

Stam, Jerome M., Steven R. Koenig, Susan E. Bentley, and H. Frederick Gale, Jr. 1991. *Farm Financial Stress, Farm Exits, and Public Sector Assistance to the Farm Sector in the 1980s.* Agricultural Economic Report Number 645. Washington, DC: U.S. Department of Agriculture, Economic Research Service.

Stark, Rodney. 1972. *Police Riots: Collective Violence and Law Enforcement.* Belmont, CA: Wadsworth.

———. 1987a. *A Theory of Religion.* New York: Peter Lang.

———. 1987b. "How new religions succeed: A theoretical model." Pp. 11–29 in *The Future of New Religious Movements,* edited by D. Bromley and P. Hammond. Macon, GA: Mercer University Press.

Stark, Rodney. 1996. *The Rise of Christianity: How the Obscure, Marginal Jesus Movement Became the Dominant Religious Forces in the Western World in a Few Centuries.* Princeton, N.J.: Princeton University Press.

Stark, Rodney, and William Sims Bainbridge. 1980. "Networks of Faith: Interpersonal Bonds and Recruitment to Cults and Sects." *American Journal of Sociology* 85 (6): 1376–95.

Stark, Rodney, and Roger Finke. 2000. *Acts of Faith: Explaining the Human Side of Religion.* Berkeley and Los Angeles: University of California Press.

Stark, Rodney, and Laurence R. Iannaccone. 1997. "Why the Jehovah's Witnesses Grow So Rapidly: A Theoretical Application." *Journal of Contemporary Religion* 12 (2): 133–57.

Starr, Paul M. 1982. *The Social Transformation of American Medicine.* New York: Basic Books.

Steams, Linda Brewster and Paul D. Almeida. 2004. "The Formation of State Actor-Social Movement Coalitions and Favorable Policy Outcomes." *Social Problems* 51: 478–504.

Stegner, Wallace. 1949. "The Radio Priest and His Flock." In *The Aspirin Age, 1919–41,* edited by Isabell Leighton. New York: Simon & Schuster.

Steigenga, Timothy J. 2001. *The Politics of the Spirit: The Political Implications of Pentecostalized Religion in Costa Rica and Guatemala.* Lanham, Md.: Lexington.

Stein, Marc. 2000. *City of Sisterly and Brotherly Loves: Lesbian and Gay Philadelphia, 1945-1972.* Chicago: University of Chicago Press.

Steinberg, Marc W. 1993. "Rethinking Ideology: A Dialogue with Fine and Sandstrom from a Dialogic Perspective." *Sociological Theory* 11: 314–20.

———. 1994. "The Dialogue of Struggle: The Contest over Ideological Boundaries in the Case of London Silk Weavers in the Early Nineteenth Century." *Social Science History* 18: 505–41.

Steinberg, Marc W. 1995. "The Roar of the Crowd: Repertoires of Discourse and Collective Action among the Spitalfields Silk Weavers in Nineteenth-Century

London." Pp. 57–87 in *Repertoires and Cycles of Collective Action.* Durham, N.C.: Duke University Press.

Steinberg, Mare W. 1996. "The labour of the country is the wealth of the country": Class identity, consciousness, and the role of discourse in the making of the English working class." *International Labor and Working-Class History* 49: 1–25.

Steinberg, Marc W. 1999. "The Talk and Back Talk of Collective Action: A Dialogic Analysis of Repertoires of Discourse among Nineteenth-Century English Cotton Spinners." *American Journal of Sociology* 105: 736–80.

———. 2002. "Toward a More Dialogic Analysis of Social Movement Culture." Pp. 208–25 in *Social Movements: Identity, Culture, and the State,* edited by David S. Meyer, Nancy Whittier, and Belinda Robnett New York: Oxford University Press.

Steinmetz, George, ed. 1999. *State/Culture: State-Formation after the Cultural Turn.* Ithaca, N.Y.: Cornell University Press.

Stems, Jessica. 2003. *Terror in the Name of God: Why Religious Militants Kill.* New York: Harper Collins.

Stepan, Alfred. 1985. "State Power and the Strength of Civil Society in the Southern Cone of Latin America." Pp. 317–343 in *Bringing the State Back In,* edited by Peter Evans, Dietrich Rueschemeyer, and Theda Skocpol. Cambridge: Cambridge University Press.

Stepan-Norris, Judith and Maurice Zeitlin. 1995. "Union Democracy, Radical Leadership, and the Hegemony of Capital." *American Sociological Review* 60: 829–50.

Stern, Kenneth S. 1996. *A Force Upon the Plain: The American Militia Movement and the Politics of Hate.* New York: Simon and Schuster.

Stevis, Dimitris. 1998. "International Labor Organizations, 1864–1997: The Weight of History and the Challenges of the Present." *Journal of World-Systems Research* 4: 52–75.

Stillerman, Joel. 2003. "Transnational Activist Networks and the Emergence of Labor Internationalism in the NAFTA Countries." *Social Science History* 27 (4): 577–601.

Stinchcombe, Arthur L. 1965. "Social Structure and Organizations." Pp. 142–93 in *Handbook of Organizations,* edited by J. G. March. Chicago: Rand McNally.

Stinchcombe, Arthur L. 1999. "Ending Revolutions and Building New Governments." *Annual Review of Political Science* 2: 49–73.

Stockdill, Brett C. 1996. "Multiple Oppressions and Their Influence on Collective Action: The Case of the AIDS Movement." Ph.D. dissertation, Department of Sociology, Northwestern University, Evanston, IL.

Stone, L. 1972. *The Causes of the English Revolution, 1529–42.* New York: Harper & Row.

Stoper, Emily. 1989. "The Student Nonviolent Coordinating Committee: The Growth of Radicalism in a Civil Rights Organization". Brooklyn, New York: Carlson.

Stormfront.org. No date. "Mothers in the Movement Home-schooling Archive." Retrieved January 3, 2002 (http: //www.stormfront.org).

Stouffer, Samuel A., Edward A. Suchman, Leland C. DeVinney, Shirley A. Star, and Robin M. Williams. 1949. *The American Soldier: Adjustment During Army Life.* Princeton: Princeton University Press.

Strand, David. 1993. "Civil Society and Public Sphere in Modern Chinese History." Pp. 53–86 in *Chinese Democracy and the Crisis of 1989,* edited by Roger V. Des Forges, Luo Ning, and Wu Yen-bo. Albany: State University of New York Press.

Strang, David, and John Meyer. 1993. "Institutional Conditions for Diffusion." *Theory and Society* 22: 487–511.

Strang, David, and Sarah A. Soule. 1998. "Diffusion in Organizations and Social Movements: From Hybrid Corn to Poison Pills." *Annual Review of Sociology* 24: 265–90.

Straus, R. 1976. "Changing oneself: Seekers and the creative transformation of life experience." Pp. 252–72 in *Doing Social Life,* edited by J. Lofland. New York: John Wiley.

Stryker, Robin. 1994. "Rules, Resources, and Legitimacy Processes: Some Implications for Social Order, Conflict, and Change." *American Journal of Sociology* 99: 847–910.

———. 1996. "Beyond History vs. Theory: Strategic Narrative and Sociological Explanation." *Sociological Methods and Research* 24: 304–52.

———. 2003. "Mind the Gap: Law, Institutional Analysis, and Socioeconomics." *Socio-Economic Review* 1: 335–67.

Stryker, Sheldon. 1968. "Identity Salience and Role Performance: The Relevance of Symbolic Interaction Theory for Family Research." *Journal of Marriage and the Family* 30: 558–64.

———. 1981. "Symbolic Interactionism: Themes and Variations." Pp. 3–29 in *Social Psychology:*

Sociological Perspectives, edited by Morris Rosenberg and Ralph H. Turner. New York: Basic.

Stryker, Sheldon, Timothy J. Owens, and Robert W. White, eds. 2000. *Self, Identity, and Social Movements.* Minneapolis: University of Minnesota Press.

Stryker, Susan, and Jim Van Buskirk. 1996. *Gay by the Bay: A History of Queer Culture in the San Francisco Bay Area.* San Francisco: Chronicle Books.

Student Nonviolent Coordinating Committee. 1960. *The Student Voice.* August.

Suchman, Mark. 1995. "Managing Legitimacy: Strategic and Institutional Approaches." *Academy of Management Review* 20: 571–610.

Sullivan, Lawrence R. 1990. "The Emergence of Civil Society in China, Spring 1989." Pp. 126–44 in *The Chinese People's Movement, Perspectives on Spring 1989,* edited by Tony Saich. Armonk, N.Y.: Sharpe.

Sutherland, S. L. 1981. *Patterns in Belief and Action: Measurement of Student Political Activism.* Toronto: University of Toronto Press.

Suttles, Gerald D. 1968. *The Social Order of the Slum.* Chicago: University of Chicago Press.

———. 1972. *Social Construction of Communities.* Chicago: University of Chicago Press.

Swafford, Michael. 1980. "Three parametric techniques for contingency table analysis: a nontechnical commentary." *American Sociological Review* 45: 664–90.

Swank, Eric. 1997. "The Ebbs and Flows of Gulf War Protests." *Journal of Political and Military Sociology* 25: 211–31.

Swank, Eric. 2000. "In Newspapers We Trust? Assessing the Credibility of News Sources that Cover Protest Campaigns." *Research in Social Movements. Conflict, and Change* 22: 27–52.

Swidler, Ann. 1986. "Culture in Action: Symbols and Strategies." *American Sociological Review* 51: 273–86.

Swidler, Ann. 2001. *Talk of Love: How Culture Matters.* Chicago: University of Chicago Press.

Swomley, John M. 1999. "The militia movement presents a serious threat." Pp. 112–124 in *Hate Groups: Opposing Viewpoints,* edited by Tamara L. Roleff, Brenda Stalcup, and Mary E. Williams. San Diego, CA: Greenhave Press, Inc.

Szwajger, Adina Blady. 1990. *I Remember Nothing More: The Warsow Children's Hospital and the Jewish Resistance.* New York: Pantheon Books

Tang, Shaojie. 1996. "Qinghua Jinggangshan bingtuan de xingshuai" (The Rise and Fall of the Tsinghua Jinggangshan Regiment). Pp. 49–63 in *Wenhua da geming: shishi yu yanjiu* (Cultural Revolution: Facts and Analysis), edited by Q. Liu. Hong Kong: Chinese University Press.

———. 2003. *Yi ye zhiqiu: Qinghua Daxue 1968 nian "bairi da wudou"* (An Episode of the Cultural Revolution: The 1968 "Hundred Day War" at Tsinghua University). Hong Kong: Chinese University Press.

Tarrow, Sidney. 1983. *Struggling to Reform: Social Movements and Policy Change during Cycles of Protest.* Center for International Studies, Western Societies Occasional Paper no. 15. Ithaca, NY: Cornell University.

Tarrow, Sidney. 1988. "National Politics and Collective Action: Recent Theory and Research in Western Europe and the United States." *Annual Review of Sociology* 14: 421–40.

Tarrow, Sidney. 1989a. "Struggle, Politics and Reform: Collective Action, Social Movements and Cycles of Protest." Ithaca, NY: Western Societies Occasional Paper no. 21.

———. 1989b. *Democracy and Disorder: Protest and Politics in Italy 1965–75.* Oxford, England: Clarendon Press.

———. 1989c. "Mutamenti nella Cultura di Opposizione in Italia 1965–1975" (Changes in Oppositional Culture in Italy 1965–1975). *Polis* 3: 41–63.

Tarrow, Sidney. 1993. "Social Protest and Policy Reform: May 1968 and the *Loi d'Orientation* in France." *Comparative Political Studies* 25: 579–607.

———. 1994. *Power in Movement.* Cambridge, England and New York: Cambridge University Press.

———. 1996a. "Social Movements in Contentious Politics: A Review Article." *American Political Science Review* 90: 873–83.

———. 1996. "States and Opportunities: The Political Structuring of Social Movements." Pp. 41–61 in *Comparative Perspectives on Social Movements: Political Opportunities, Mobilizing Structures, and Cultural Framings,* edited by Doug McAdam, John D. McCarthy, and Mayer N. Zald. Cambridge: Cambridge University Press.

———. 1998a. "Fishnets, Internets, and Carnets: Globalization and Transnational Collective Action." Chap. 15 in *Challenging Authority: The Historical Study of Contentious Politics,* edited by Michael Hanagan,

Leslie Page Moch, and Wayne Ph. Te Brake. Minneapolis: University of Minnesota Press.

———. 1998*b*. *Power in Movement: Social Movements and Contentious Politics,* 2d ed. New York: Cambridge University Press.

———. 1999. "Paradigm Warriors: Regress and Progress in the Study of Contentious Politics." *Sociological Forum* 14 (1): 71–77.

———. 2001. "Silence and Voice in the Study of Contentious Politics." Pp. 1–13 in *Silence and Voice in the Study of Contentious Politics,* edited by R. Aminzade et al. Cambridge: Cambridge University Press.

Tarrow, Sidney. 2001a. "Transnational Politics: Contention and Institutions in International Politics." *Annual Review of Political Science* 4: 1–20.

Tarrow, Sidney. 2001b. "Rooted Cosmopolitans: Transnational Activists in a World of States." Working Paper 2001-3, Cornell University Workshop on Transnational Contention, Ithaca, NY.

———. 2005. *The New Transnational Activism.* Cambridge: Cambridge University Press.

Tarrow, Sidney, and Doug McAdam. 2005. "Scale Shift in Transnational Contention." In *Transnational Protest and Global Activism,* edited by Donatella della Porta and Sidney Tarrow. Lanham, MD: Rowman and Littlefield.

Taylor, Ralph B. 1987. "Toward an Environmental Psychology of Disorder: Delinquency, Crime, and Fear." Pp. 951–86 in *Handbook of Environment Psychology,* vol. 2. Edited by Daniel Stokols and Irwin Altman. New York: Wiley.

Taylor, Verta. 1989a. "Social Movement Continuity: The Women's Movement in Abeyance." *American Sociological Review* 54: 761–75.

———. 1989b. "The Future of Feminism: A Social Movement Analysis." Pp. 473–90 in *Feminist Frontiers II.* edited by Laurel Richardson and Verta Taylor. New York: Random House.

———. 1993. "The New Feminist Movement." In *Feminist Frontiers III,* edited by Verta Taylor and Laurel Richardson. New York: McGraw-Hill.

Taylor, Verta. 1996. *Rock-a-by Baby: Feminism, Self-Help, and Postpartum Depression.* New York: Routledge.

———. 1999. "Gender and Social Movements: Gender Processes in Women's Self-Help Movements." *Gender & Society* 13: 8–33.

———. 2000. "Emotions and Identity in Women's Self-help Movements." Pp. 271–99 in *Self,. Identity, and Social Movements,* edited by S. Stryker, T. J. Owens, and R. W. White. Minneapolis: University of Minnesota Press.

Taylor, Verta and Nicole C. Raeburn. 1995. "Identity Politics as High-Risk Activism: Career Consequences for Lesbian, Gay, and Bisexual Sociologists." *Social Problems* 42: 252–73.

Taylor, Verta, and Nancy E. Whittier, 1992. "Collective Identity in Social Movement Communities: Lesbian Feminist Mobilization." Pp. 104–29 in *Frontiers in Social Movement Theory,* edited by Aldon Morris and Carol McClurg. New Haven, Conn.: Yale University Press.

Taylor, Verta, and Nancy Whittier. 1994. "Cultures in conflict: Conceptualizing the cultural dimensions of political protest." In *Culture and Social Movements,* edited by Hank Johnston and Bert Klandermans.

Teal, Donn. 1971. *The Gay Militants.* New York: Stein & Day.

Teal, Donn. 1995. *The Gay Militants: How Gay Liberation Began in America, 1969–1971.* New York: St. Martin's Press.

Tec, Nechama, 1993. *Defiance: The Bielski Partisans.* New York: Oxford University Press.

Tetreault, Mary Ann. 1993. "Civil Society in Kuwait: Protected Spaces and Women's Rights." *Middle East Journal* 47: 275–91.

Texas League of Women Voters Records. 1954, November 2. "Jury Service for Women: A Kit for Community Action." Box 74, Folder 8. Texas Tech University.

The Hezbollah Program. 1985. "An Open Letter to the Downtrodden in Lebanon and the World." Arlington, VA: Institute for Counterterrorism. Retrieved on August 24, 2006. (http://www.ict.org.il/Articles/Hiz_letter.htm).

The Intelligent Voter. 1925. "Jury Service for Women." 2: 11.

Thelen, Kathleen. 2000a. "Timing and Temporality in the Analysis of Institutional Evolution and Change." *Studies in American Political Development* 14 (Spring): 101–8.

Thibault, J. and L. Walker. 1975. *Procedural Justice: A Psychological Analysis.* Hillsdale, NJ: Erlbaum.

Thom, Mary. 2000. "Promises to Keep: Beijing and Beyond." *Ford Foundation Report* 31: 30–3.

Thomas, Alice, 2000. "OSU Says Class Comes First: School Trying To Ease Disruptions of Strike." *Columbus Dispatch,* May 9, p. 1B.

Thompson, E. P. 1971. "The Moral Economy of the English Crowd in the Eighteenth Century." *Past and Present* 50: 76–136.

Thompson, James B. 1984. *Studies in the Theory of Ideology.* Cambridge: Polity Press.

Thompson, Lorin A. 1971. "Urbanization, Occupational Shift and Economic Progress." In *The Urban South,* edited by Rupert B. Vance and Nicholas J. Demerath. Freeport, NY: Books for Libraries Press, 38–53.

Thomton, Thomas Perry. 1964. "Terror as a Weapon of Political Agitation." Pp. 71–99 in *Internal War: Problems and Approaches,* edited by Harry Eckstein. New York: Free Press of Glencoe.

Thornton, Russell. 1981. "Demographic Antecedents of a Revitalization Movement: Population Change, Population Size, and the 1890 Ghost Dance." *American Sociological Review* 46: 88–96.

Thorup, Cathryn. 1993. "Redefining Governance in North America: Citizen Diplomacy and Cross-Border Coalitions." *Enfoque.* La Jolla: University of California, San Diego, Center for U.S.-Mexican Studies.

Tillock, H. and Denton E. Morrison. 1979. "Group size and contributions to collective action: an examination of Mancur Olson's theory using data from Zero Population Growth, Inc." Pp. 131–158 in *Research in Social Movements, Conflict and Change,* edited by Louis Kriesberg. Vol. 4. Greenwich, CT: JAI Press.

Tilly, Charles. 1964. *The Vendée.* Cambridge, MA: Harvard Univeristy Press.

Tilly, Charles. 1975a. "Food Supply and Public Order in Modern Europe." Pp. 380–455 In *The Formation of National States in Western Europe.* Charles Tilly, ed. Princeton: Princeton University Press.

Tilly, Charles. 1975b. "Revolutions and Collective Violence." Pp. 483–555 in *Handbook of Political Science,* edited by F. I. Greenstein and N. W. Polsby. Reading, Mass.: Addison Wesley.

Tilly, Charles. 1978. *From Mobilization to Revolution.* Reading, MA: Addison-Wesley.

———, 1979a. "Did the Cake of Custom Break?" Pp. 17–44 in *Consciousness and Class: Experience in Nineteenth Century Europe.* John M. Merriman. ed. New York: Holmes and Meler.

Tilly, Charles. 1979b. "Repertoires of Contention in America and Britain, 1750–1830." Pp. 126–55 in *The Dynamics of Social Movements,* edited by M. Zald and J. McCarthy, Cambridge, MA: Winthrop.

———. 1981. "Useless Durkheim." Pp. 95–108 in *As Sociology Meets History.* Charles Tilly, ed. New York: Academic Press.

Tilly, Charles. 1984. "Social Movements and National Politics." Pp. 297–317 in *Statemaking and Social Movements: Essays in History and Theory,* edited by C. Bright and S. Harding. Ann Arbor: University of Michigan Press.

———. 1986. *The Contentious French.* Cambridge, MA: Harvard University Press, Bellknap Press.

———. 1993. *European Revolutions, 1492–1992.* Oxford, UK: Blackwell Publishers.

———. 1995a. "To Explain Political Processes." *American Journal of Sociology* 100: 1594–1610.

———. 1995b. *Popular Contention in Great Britain, 1758–1834.* Cambridge, MA: Harvard University Press.

Tilly, Charles. 1998a. "The trouble with stories." In *Teaching for the 21st Century: The Handbook for Understanding and Rebuilding the Social World of Higher Education,* edited by Ronald Aminzade and Bernice Pescosolido. Thousand Oaks, California: Pine Forge Press.

Tilly, Charles. 1998b. *Durable Inequalities.* Berkeley: University of California Press.

Tilly, Charles. 1999a. "Regimes and Contention." Columbia International Affairs Online Working Paper. Manuscript.

———. 1999b. "Conclusion: From Interactions to Outcomes in Social Movements." Pp. 253–70 in *How Movements Matter: Theoretical and Comparative Studies on the Consequences of Social Movements,* edited by Marco Giugni, Doug McAdam, and Charles Tilly. Minneapolis, MN: University of Minnesota Press.

———. 2002. "Historical Analysis of Political Processes." Pp. 567–88 in *Handbook of Sociological Theory,* edited by J. H. Turner. New York: Plenum.

———. 2004b. *Social Movements, 1768–2004.* Boulder: Paradigm Publishers.

Tilly, Charles, Louise Tilly, and Richard Tilly. 1975. *The Rebellious Century.* Cambridge, Mass.: Harvard University Press.

Tismaneanu, Vladimir. 1990. *In Search of Civil Society: Independent Peace Movements in the Soviet Bloc.* New York: Routledge.

Titarenko. Larissa. John D. McCarthy, Clark McPhail, and Boguslaw Augustyn. 2001. "The Interaction of State Repression. Protest Form and Protest Sponsor Strength during the Transition from Communism in Minsk, Belarus, 1990–1995." *Mobilization* 6: 129–50.

Todesco, Fabio. 1992. "Marketing Elettorale e Comunicazione Politica. Il Caso Lega Nord" (Electoral Marketing and Political Communication. The Case of the Northern League). Undergraduate Dissertation. Department of Economics, Università Bocconi, Milan, Italy.

Tolbert, Charles M., II. 1989. "Labor market areas in stratification research: Concepts, definitions and issues." *Research in Rural Sociology and Development* 4: 81–97.

Tolbert, Charles M., II, and Molly Sizer. 1996. *U.S. commuting zones and labor market areas: A 1990 update.* Rural Economy Division, U.S. Department of Agriculture. Staff Paper No: AGES-9614.

Tolnay, Stewart E., and E. M. Beck. 1995. *A Festival of Violence: An Analysis of Southern Lynchings, 1882–1930.* Urbana: University of Illinois Press.

Tomaskovic-Devey, Donald. 1993. *Gender and Racial Inequality at Work; The Sources and Consequences of Job Segregation.* Ithaca, N.Y.: ILR Press.

Tong, Rosemarie. 1989. *Feminist Thought: A Comprehensive Introduction.* Boulder, Colo.: Westview.

Toqueville, Alexis de. 2000. *Democracy in America.* Translated and edited by Harvey C. Mansfield and Delba Winthrop. Chicago: University of Chicago Press.

Touraine, Alain. 1971. *The Post-Industrial Society.* New York: Random House.

Touraine, Alain. 1981. *The Voice and the Eye: An Analysis of Social Movements.* Cambridge: Cambridge University Press.

Townsend National Weekly. 1938–1950. Townsend National Weekly, Chicago, IL.

Towslee, Tom. 1987. "Goldschmidt Signs Gay Rights Order." United Press International. October 15.

———. 1988a. "Commentary: Election Winners and Losers Not Always Candidates, Issues." United Press International, November 11.

———. 1988b. "Goldschmidt Signs Gay Rights Order." United Press International. February 22.

Travers, Eva. F. 1982. "Ideology and Political Participation among High School Students: Changes from 1970 to 1979." *Youth and Society* 13 (3): 327–52.

Travisano, Richard V. 1970. "Alternation and conversion as qualitatively different transformations." Pp. 594–606 in *Social Psychology Through Symbolic Interaction,* edited by G. P. Stone and H. A. Farberman. Waltham, MA: Ginn H-Blaisdell.

Tricontinental Society. 1980. *El Salvador: The Development of the People's Struggle.* London: Tricontinental Society.

Trouillot, Michel-Roph. 1995. *Silencing the Past: Power and the Production of History.* Boston: Beacon Press.

Tsou, Tang. 1969. "The Cultural Revolution and the Chinese Political System." *The China Quarterly* 38: 63–91.

Tucker, Robert. 1961. "Towards a Comparative Politics of Movement-Regimes." *American Political Science Review* 55: 281–9.

———. 1968. "The Theory of Charismatic Leadership." *Daedalus* 97: 731–56.

Tull, Charles J. 1965. *Father Coughlin and the New Deal.* Syracuse, NY: Syracuse University Press.

Turcios, Roberto. 1993. "¿Una oportunidad para la modernización democrática?" Pp. 40–53 in *Tradición y Modernidad en El Salvador,* edited by S. Roggenbuck. San Salvador: Editorial Epoca.

———. 1970. "Determinants of social movement strategies." Pp. 145–64 in *Human Nature and Collective Behavior: Essays in Honor of Herbert Blumer,* edited by Tamotsu Stributani. Englewood Cliffs, NJ: Prentice-Hall.

Turner, Ralph H. 1981. "Collective behavior and resource mobilization as approaches to social movements: Issues and continuities." Pp. 1–24 in *Research in Social Movements, Conflict and Change,* edited by Louis Kriesberg. Vol. 4. Greenwich, CT: JAI Press.

Turner, Ralph and Lewis Killian. 1957. *Collective Behavior.* Englewood Cliffs, N.J.: Prentice-Hall.

Turner, Ralph, and L. Killian. 1972. *Collective Behavior.* Englewood Cliffs, N.J.: Prentice-Hall.

Turner, Ralph H., and Lewis M. Killian. 1987. *Collective Behavior, 3rd edition.* Englewood Cliffs, NJ: Prentice-Hall Inc.

Tversky, Amos, and Daniel Kahneman. 1981. "The Framing of Decisions and the Psychology of Choice." *Science* 211: 453–58.

Tyler, Tom R., Robert J. Boeckmaun, Heather Smith, and Yuen J. Huo. 1997. *Social Justice in a Diverse Society.* Boulder: Westview.

Tyler, Tom R. and E. Allan Lind. 1992. "A Relational Model of Authority in Groups." *Advances in Experimental Social Psychology* 25: 115–191.

Tyler, Tom R. and Heather Smith. 1998. "Social Justice and Social Movements." Pp. 595–626 in *Handbook of Social Psychology,* 4th ed., edited by D. Gilbert, S.T. Fiske, and G. Lindzey. New York: McGraw-Hill.

U.S. AID (Agency for International Development). 1973. *Statistics for the Analysis of the Education Sector, El Salvador.* Washington, D.C.: U.S. Bureau of the Census.

U.S. Bureau of Economic Analysis. 2001. "State Personal Income 1929–2000" [Computer File]. Washington, DC: U.S. Department of Commerce, Economics and Statistics Administration.

U.S. Bureau of the Census. 1914, 1923, 1933, 1943, 1953, 1963, 1973. *Thirteenth through Nineteenth Census of the United States Population.* Washington, DC: Government Printing Office.

U.S. Bureau of the Census. 1963. *Census of the Population: 1960.* Vol. 1, *Characteristics of the Population.* Washington, DC: Government Printing Office.

———. 1967. *County and City Data Book, 1967.* Washington, DC: Government Printing Office.

———. 1969. *Census of Agriculture, Mississippi.* Part 33, sect. 1, vol. 1. Washington, DC: Government Printing Office.

U.S. Bureau of the Census. 1983. *1980 Census of the Population: General Social and Economic Characteristics.* Washington, DC: U.S. Dept. of Commerce, Economics and Statistics Administration, Bureau of the Census.

———. 1985. *Statistical Abstract of the United States.* Washington, DC: Government Publishing Office.

———. 1991. *Statistical Abstract of the United States.* Washington, DC: Government Publishing Office.

———. 1992. *Statistical Abstract of the United States.* Washington, DC: Government Publishing Office.

———. 1993. *1990 Census of the Population: General Social and Economic Characteristics.* Washington, DC: U.S. Dept. of Commerce, Economics and Statistics Administration, Bureau of the Census.

———. 1994. *Statistical Abstract of the United States.* Washington, DC: Government Publishing Office.

U.S. Bureau of the Census. *Historical Statistics of the United States, Colonial Times to 1970.* Bicentennial ed. U.S. Department of Commerce Bureau of the

Census. Washington, DC: U.S. Government Printing Office.

U.S. Commission on Civil Rights. 1977. *Reviewing a Decade of School Desegregation 1966–1975.* Washington, D.C.: U.S. Government Printing Office.

U.S. Committee on the Judiciary. 1997a. *Terrorism in the United States: The Nature and Extent of the Threat and Possible Legislative Responses.* Hearings before the Committee on the Judiciary, United States Senate. April 27 and May 24, 1995. Washington, DC: U.S. Government Printing Office.

U.S. Committee on the Judiciary. 1997b *The Militia Movement in the United States.* Hearing before the Subcommittee on Terrorism, Technology, and Government Information of the Committee on the Judiciary, United States Senate. June 15, 1995. Washington, DC: U.S. Government Printing Office.

U.S. Congress. House. 1964. *Congressional Record.* 88th Congress, vol. 110. Washington, D.C.: Government Printing Office.

———. 1966. *Congressional Record.* 89th Congress, vol. 112. Washington, D.C.: Government Printing Office.

U.S. House of Representatives, Committee on Un-American Activities. 1965. *Activities of the Ku Klux Klan Organizations in the U.S.* Washington, DC: Government Printing Office.

U.S. Senate, Committee on Labor and Public Welfare, Subcommittee on Employment, Manpower, and Poverty. 1967. "Examination of the War on Poverty." 90th Cong., 1st sess.

U.S. Social Security Board. 1945. *Social Security Yearbook.* Washington, DC: U.S. Government Printing Office.

U.S. Social Security Board/Administration. 1935–1950. *Annual Report of the Federal Security Agency.* Washington, DC: U.S. Government Printing Office.

Ueltzen, Stefan, ed. 1994. *Conversatorio con los hijos del siglo.* San Salvador: Algier's Impresores.

Ullrich, Kerstin. 1998. *Soziale Bewegung und kollektive Identität: Der Diskurs über Abtreibung und Reproduktionstechnologien als Beispiel feministischer Identitätskonstruktion.* Ph.D. dissertation. European University Institute, Department of Political Science.

UNDP. 1999. *Human Development Report.* New York: Oxford University Press.

UPI (United Press International). 1987. Regional news section, November 8.

——. 1988a. Regional news section, July 8.

——. 1988b. Regional news section, October 2.

USDOC (U.S. Department of Commerce, Bureau of the Census). 1948–99. *Statistical Abstract of the United States*. Washington, D.C.: Government Printing Office.

——. 1999. *Current Population Survey…Annual Demographic File*. Washington, D.C.: U.S. Bureau of the Census.

Useem, Bert. 1980. "Solidarity Model, Breakdown Model and the Boston Anti-Busing Movement." *American Sociological Review* 45: 357–69.

Useem, Bert. 1985. "Disorganization and the New Mexico Prison Riot of 1980." *American Sociological Review* 50 (5): 677–88.

Useem, Bert. 1998. "Breakdown Theories of Collective Action." *Annual Review of Sociology* 24: 215–238.

Useem, Bert, and Peter Kimball, 1989. *States of Siege: U.S. Prison Riots 1971–1986*. New York: Oxford University Press.

Useem, Bert and Mayer N. Zald. 1982. "From Pressure Group to Social Movement: Organizational Dilemmas of the Effort to Promote Nuclear Power." *Social Problems* 30: 144–56.

Utah State Courts. 2006. *The Changing Face of Jurors in Utah*. Retrieved February 24, 2006 (http: //www. utcourts.gov/specproj/changingface.pdf).

Vaid, Urvashi. 1995. *Virtual Equality: The Mainstreaming of Gay and Lesbian Liberation*. New York: Anchor Books.

Valelly, Richard M. 1993. "Party, Coercion and Inclusion: The Two Reconstructions of the South's Electoral Politics." *Politics and Society* 21: 37–68.

Vallas, Steven Peter. 1987. "The Labor Process as a Source of Class Consciousness: A Critical Examination" *Sociological Forum* 2: 237–56.

Valle, Victor. 1993. *Siembra de vienlos: El Salvador 1960–69*. San Salvador: CINAS.

Valocchi, Steve. 1996. "The Emergence of the Integrationist Ideology in the Civil Rights Movement." *Social Problems* 43: 116–30.

Van Dijk, Teun A. 1992. "Discourse and the Denial of Racism." *Discourse and Society* 3: 87–118.

van Dijk, Teun A. 1993. *Elite Discourse and Racism*. Newbury Park, Calif.: Sage.

Van Dyke, Nella. 2003a. "Crossing Movement Boundaries: Factors That Facilitate Coalition Protest by American College Students, 1930–1990." *Social Problems* 49: 497–520.

Van Dyke, Nella. 2003b. "Protest Cycles and Party Politics." Pp. 226–45 in *States, Parties and Social Movements*, edited by Jack Goldstone. New York: Cambridge University Press.

Van Dyke, Nella, and Sarah Soule. 2002. "Structural Social Change and the Mobilizing Effect of Threat: Explaining Levels of Patriot and Militia Organizing in the United States." *Social Problems* 49 (4): 497–520.

Van Dyke, Nella, Sarah A. Soule, and Verts A. Taylor. 2004. "The Targets of Social Movements: Beyond a Focus on the State." *Research in Social Movements, Conflicts and Change* 25: 27–51.

Vector. 1971. Untitled article, 4.

Vega, Juan Ramon. 1994. *Las comunidades cristianas de base en América Central: Estudio sociológico*. San Salvador: Publicaciones del Arzobispado.

——. 1997. *Las 54 Cartas pastorales de Monseñor Chávez*. San Salvador: Ediciones del Arzobispado.

Vejvoda, Ivan. 1997. "Cogito ergo ambulo; First Steps in Belgrade." *Bulletin of the East and Central Europe Program*: 1–2. New School for Social Research, New York.

Viorst, Milton. 1979. *Fire in the Streets: America in the 1960s*. New York: Simon and Schuster.

Von Eschen, Donald, Jerome Kirk and Maurice Pinard. 1969. "The disintegration of the Negro nonviolent movement." *Journal of Peace Research* 3: 216–34.

Von Eschen, Donald, Jerome Kirk, and Maurice Pinard. 1971. "The Organizational Substructure of Disorderly Politics." *Social Forces* 49: 529–44.

Von Hippel, Paul T. 2003. "Normalization." In *Encyclopedia of Social Science Research Methods*, edited by M. Lewis-Beck, A. Bryman, and T. F. Liao. Thousand Oaks, Calif.: Sage.

Voss, Kim. 1996a. "Defeat 'frames' and solidarity: Researching the impact of social movement culture." *Paper presented at the American Sociological Association Annual Meeting*. (August)

Voss, Kim. 1996b. "The Collapse of a Social Movement: The Interplay of Mobilizing Structures, Framing, and Political Opportunities in the Knights of Labor." Pp. 227–58 in *Comparative Perspectives on Social Movements*, edited by D. McAdam, J. D. McCarthy, and M. N. Zald, Cambridge, U.K.: Cambridge University Press.

Voss, Kim. 1998. "Claim Making and the Framing of Defeats: The Interpretation of Losses by American and British Labor Activists, 1886–1895." Pp. 136–48 in *Challenging Authority: The Historical Study of Contentious Politics,* edited by M. P. Hanagan, L. P. Moch, and W. te Brake. Minneapolis: University of Minnesota Press.

Voss, Kim, and Rachel Sherman. 2000. "Breaking the Iron Law of Oligarchy: Union Revitalization in the American Labor Movement." *American Journal of Sociology* 106: 303–49.

Waddington, P. A. J. 1994. *Liberty and Order: Public Order Policing in a Capital City.* London, England: University College London Press.

———. 1998. "Controlling Protest in Contemporary Historical and Comparative Perspective." Pp. 117–40 in *Policing Protest: The Control of Mass Demonstrations in Western Democracies,* edited by D. della Porta and H. Reiter. Minneapolis, MN: University of Minnesota Press.

Wade, Wyn Craig. 1987. *The Fiery Cross: The Ku Klux Klan in America.* New York: Simon & Schuster.

Wagner, David. 1993. *Checkerboard Square: Culture and Resistance in a Homeless Community.* Boulder, CO: Westview Press.

Wakefield. Dan. 1960. "Eye of the storm." *The Nation* (May)190: 396–405.

Walder, Andrew, 1986. *Communist Neo-Traditionalism: Work and Authority in Chinese Industry.* Berkeley, CA: University of California Press.

Walder, Andrew G. 1994. "Implications of Loss Avoidance for Theories of Social Movements." Paper presented at the 13th World Congress of Sociology, Bielefeld, Germany.

———. 2002. "Beijing Red Guard Factionalism: Social Interpretations Reconsidered." *Journal of Asian Studies* 61: 437–71.

Walder, Andrew. 2009. *Fractured Rebellion: The Beijing Red Guard Movement.* Cambridge, MA: Harvard University Press.

Waldinger, Roger, Chris Erikson, Ruth Milkman, Daniel J. B. Mitchell, Abel Valenzuela, Kent Wong, and Maurice Zeitlin. 1998. "Helots No More: A Case Study of the Justice for Janitors Campaign in Los Angeles." Pp. 102–20 in *Organizing to Win: New Strategies on Union Research,* edited by Kate Bronfenbrenner, Shel-

don Friedman, Richard W. Hurd, Rudolph A. Oswald, and Ronald L. Seeber. Ithaca, N.Y.: ILR Press.

Walker, Daniel. 1968. *Rights in Conflict: Chicago's 7 Brutal Days.* New York: Grosser and Dunlap.

Walker, Jack L. 1983. "The Origins and Maintenance of Interest Groups in America." *American Political Science Review* 77: 390–406.

Walker, Jack L. 1991. *Mobilizing Interest Groups in America: Patrons, Professions and Social Movements.* Ann Arbor: University of Michigan Press.

Walker, Michael E., Stanley Wasserman, and Barry Wellman. 1994. "Statistical Models for Social Support Networks." Pp. 71–98 in *Advances in Social Network Analysis: Research in the Social and Behavioral Sciences,* edited by Stanley Wasserman and Joseph Galaskiewicz. Thousand Oaks, Calif.: Sage.

Walker, Rev. Waytt Tee. 1978. *Interview.* New York City, New York. September 29.

Wall Street Journal. 1965. "New Guidelines on Job Sex Discrimination Recognize Some Exceptions, but Limit Them." November 23.

———. 1966. "Help Wanted Rule Eased on Sex as a Basis for Bias." April 29.

Wallace, Anthony. 1956. "Revitalization Movements: Some Theoretical Considerations for Their Comparative Study." *American Anthropologist* 58: 264–81.

Wallach, Lori, and Michelle Sforza. 1999. *Whose Trade Organization? Corporate Globalization and the Erosion of Democracy.* Washington, DC: Public Citizen.

Wallis, Roy. 1984. *The Elementary Forms of the New Religious Life.* London: Routledge & Kegan Paul.

Walsh, Edward J. 1978. "Mobilization Theory vis-a-vis a Mobilization Process: The Case of the United Farm Workers' Movement." Pp. 155–77 in *Research in Social Movements; Conflicts and Change,* edited by Louis Kriesberg. Vol. 1. Greenwich, CT: JAI Press.

Walsh, Edward J. 1981. "Resource Mobilization and Citizen Protest in Communities around Three Mile Island." *Social Problems* 29: 1–21.

———. 1988. *Democracy in the Shadows: Citizen Mobilization in the Wake of the Accident of Three Mile Island.* New York: Greenwood Press.

Walsh, Edward J., and Rex H. Warland. 1983. "Social Movement Involvement in the Wake of a Nuclear Accident: Activists and Free Riders in the Three Mile Island Area." *American Sociological Review* 48: 764–81.

Walton, John. 1992. *Western Water Wars.* Berkeley and Los Angeles: University of California Press.

Walton, John, and Charles Ragin. 1990. "Global and National Sources of Political Protest: Third World Responses to the Debt Crisis." *American Sociological Review* 55 (6): 876–91.

Walton, John, and David Seddon. 1994. "Food Riots Past and Present." Pp. 23–54 in *Free Markets and Food Riots: The Politics of Global Adjustment,* edited by J. Walton and D. Seddon. Oxford: Blackwell.

Walton, John, and Robert Shefner. 1994. "Latin America: Popular Protest and the State." Pp. 97–134 in *Free Markets and Food Riots: The Politics of Global Adjustment,* edited by J. Walton and D. Seddon. Oxford: Blackwell.

Walton, Norman W. 1956. "The walking city, a history of the Montgomery boycott." *The Negro History Bulletin* 20 (October, November): 17–20.

Walzer, Michael. 1960a. "A cup of coffee and a seat." *Dissent* (Spring)7: 111–20.

Walzer, Michael. 1960b. "The politics of the new Negro." *Dissent* 8: 235–43.

Walzer, Michael. 1971. *Revolution of the Saints: A Study in the Origins of Radical Politics.* New York: Atheneum.

Walzer, Michael. 2003. "The Right Way." *The New York Review of Books.* March 13.

Wang, Shaoguang, 1995. *Failure of Charisma: The Cultural Revolution in Wuhan.* Oxford, England: Oxford University Press.

Warkentin, Craig. 2001. *Reshaping World Politics: NGOs, the Internet, and Global Civil Society.* New York: Rowman and Littlefield.

Warner, W. Lloyd. 1963. *Yankee City.* New Haven, Conn.: Yale University Press.

Warren, Mark R., J. Phillip Thompson, and Susan Saegert. 2001. "The Role of Social Capital in Combatting Poverty." Pp. 1–28 in *Social Capital and Poor Communities,* edited by Susan Saegert, J. Phillip Thompson, and Mark R. Warren. New York: Russell Sage.

Washington Post. 1937. "How States Vote on Question of Jury Service for Women." February 21, p. B2.

———. 1947. "Maryland News." February 5, p. 3. Wuthnow, Robert. 1987. *Meaning and Moral Order: Explorations in Cultural Analysis.* Berkeley, CA: University of California Press.

Wasserman, Stanley, and Katherine Faust 1997. *Social Network Analysis: Methods and Applications.* Cambridge: Cambridge University Press.

Wasserstrom, Jeffrey N. 1991. *Student Protests in Twentieth-Century China: The View from Shanghai.* Stanford, Calif.: Stanford University Press.

Waterman, Peter. 1991. "Understanding Socialist and Proletarian Internationalism." Working Paper no. 97. Hague: Institute of Social Studies.

———. 1998. *Globalization, Social Movements, and the New Internationalisms.* London: Mansell.

Watters. Pat. 1971. *Down to Now: Reflections on the Southern Civil Rights Movement.* New York: Pantheon.

Weakliem, David L. 2003. "Public Opinion Research and Political Sociology." *Research in Political Sociology* 12: 49–80.

Weber, Max. 1958. *The Protestant Ethic and the Spirit of Capitalism.* New York: Charles Scribner's Sons.

Weber, Max. 1963. *The Sociology of Religion.* Boston: Beacon Press.

Weber, Max. 1968. *Economy and Society.* Berkeley: University of California Press.

Weber, Max. 1978. *Economy and Society: An Outline of Interpretive Sociology.* Translated and edited by Guenther Roth. Berkeley, Calif.: University of California Press.

Webre, Stephen. 1979. *Jose Napoleon Duarte and the Christian Democratic Party.* Baton Rouge: Louisiana State University Press.

Wechsler, James A. 1935. *Revolt on the Campus.* New York: Covici, Friede.

Weeks, Jeffrey. 1989. *Sexuality and Its Discontents: Meanings, Myths and Modern Sexualities.* London: Routledge.

Wehr, Paul. 1960. "The sit-down protests." M.A. Thesis, Department of Sociology and Anthropology, University of North Carolina.

Wehr, Paul. 1986. "Nuclear Pacifism as Collective Action." *Journal of Peace Research* 22: 103–13.

Wellman, Barry. 1982. "Studying Personal Communities." Pp. 61–80 in *Social Structure and Network Analysis,* edited by Peter V. Marsden and Nan Lin. Beverly Hills, Calif.: Sage.

———. 1988. "Structural Analysis: From Method and Metaphor to Theory and Substance." Pp. 19–61 in *Social Structures: A Network Approach,* edited by B. Wellman and S. D. Berkowitz. Cambridge: Cambridge University Press.

Wellman, David T. 1993. *Portraits of White Racism.* Second Edition. Cambridge, UK: Cambridge University Press.

Werlen, Benno. 1993. *Society, Action and Space: An Alterative Human Geography.* London: Routledge.

West, Cornel. 1993. *Race Matters.* Boston: Beacon.

West, Guida, and Rhoda Lois Blumberg, eds. 1990. *Women and Social Protest.* New York: Oxford University Press.

Westby, David L. 1976. *The Clouded Vision: The Student Movement in the United States in the 1960s.* London: Associated University Press.

Westby, David L. 2002. "Strategic Imperative, Ideology, and Frame." *Mobilization* 7: 287–304.

Western, Bruce and Katherine Beckett. 1999. "How Unregulated Is the U.S. Labor Market? The Penal System as a Labor Market Institution." *American Journal of Sociology* 104: 1030–60.

Whalen, Jack, and Richard Flacks. 1980. "The Isla Vista 'Bank Burners' Ten Years Later: Notes on the Fate of Student Activists." *Sociological Focus* 13: 215–36.

White, Hayden. 1980. "The value of narrativity in the representation of reality." *Critical Inquiry* 7: 5–27.

White, Robert W. 1999. "Comparing State Repression of Pro-State Vigilantes and Anti-State Insurgents: Northern Ireland, 1972–1975." *Mobilization* 4: 189–202.

White, Robert. 1988. "Commitment, Efficacy, and Personal Sacrifice Among Irish Republicans." *Journal of Political and Military Sociology* 16: 77–90.

White, Robert. 1989. "From Peaceful Protest to Guerrilla War: Micromobilization of the Provisional Irish Republican Army." *American Journal of Sociology* 94 (6): 1277–1302.

White, Robert W. and Michael R. Fraser. 2000. "Personal and Collective Identities and Long-Term Social Movement Activism: Republican Sinn Féin." Pp. 324–46 in *Self, Identity, and Social Movements,* edited by S. Stryker, T. J. Owens, and R. W. White, Minneapolis: University of Minnesota Press.

Whitfield, Teresa. 1994. *Paying the Price.* Philadelphia: Temple University Press.

Whitter, Nancy E. 1991. *Feminists in the post-feminist age: Collective identity and the persistence of the women's movement.* Ph.D. dissertation. Ohio State University.

Whittier, Nancy. 1995. *Feminist Generations: The Persistence of the Radical Women's Movement.* Philadelphia: Temple University Press.

———. 2001. "Emotional Strategies: The Collective Reconstruction and Display of Oppositional Emotions in the Movement against Child Sexual Abuse." Pp. 233–50 in *Passionate Politics,* edited by J. Goodwin, J. M. Jasper, and F. Polletta. Chicago: University of Chicago Press.

Whyte, Martin, 1974. "Iron Law Versus Mass Democracy: Weber, Michels, and the Maoist Vision." Pp. 37–61 in *The Logic of "Maoism": Critiques and Explication,* edited by J. Hsiung. New York: Praeger Publishers.

Whyte, William H. 1956. *Organization Man.* New York: Doubleday.

Wicker, Allan. 1969. "Attitudes vs. Action: The Relationship of Verbal and Overt Behavioral Responses to Attitude Objects." *Journal of Social Issues* 25: 41–78.

Wicker, Tom. [1975] 1994. *A Time to Die: The Attica Prison Revolt.* Reprint, Lincoln, NE: University of Nebraska Press.

Wickham, Carrie Rosefsky. 2002. *Mobilizing Islam: Religion, Activism, and Political Change in Egypt.* New York: Columbia University Press.

Wickham-Crowley, Timothy. 1989. "Winners, Losers, and Also-Rans: Toward a Comparative Sociology of Latin American Guerrilla Movements." Pp. 132–81 in *Power and Popular Protest: Latin American Social Movements,* edited by S. Eckstein. Berkeley and Los Angeles: University of California Press.

———. 1992. *Guerrillas and Revolution in Latin America: A Comparative Study of Insurgents and Regimes since 1956.* Princeton: University of Princeton Press.

Wiktorowicz, Quintan. 2001. *The Management of Islamic Activism: Salafis, the Muslim Brotherhood, and State Power in Jordan.* Albany: State University of New York Press.

Wiktorowitz, Quintan. 2004. "Framing Jihad: Intramovement Framing Contests and al-Qaeda's Struggle for Sacred Authority." *International Review of Social History* 49 (supplement): 159–177.

Wilcox, Laird. 1995. *Guide to the American Right.* Olathe, KS: Laird Wilcox.

Wilde, Melissa J. 2004. "How Culture Mattered at Vatican II: Collegiality Trumps Authority in the Council's Social Movement Organizations." *American Sociological Review* 69: 576–602.

Wilensky, Harold L. 1975. *Welfare State and Equality: Structural and Ideological Roots of Public Expenditures.* Berkeley, CA: University of California Press.

Wiles, Peter. 1969. "A Syndrome, Not a Doctrine: Some Elementary Theses on Populism." Pp. 166–79 in *Populism,* edited by G. Ionescu and E. Gellner. London, England: Weidenfeld and Nicolson.

Wilkie, James W., ed. 2001. *Statistical Abstract of Latin America* 37. Los Angeles: UCLA Latin American Center.

Wilkinson, Tracy. 2002. "In Growing Numbers, Palestinian Boys Are Choosing the Brief Life of a 'Martyr.'" *Los Angeles Times* June 10: A1 & A11.

Willems, Helmut, Roland Eckert, Stefanie Würtz, and Linda Steinmetz. 1993. *Fremdenfeindliche Gewalt. Einstellungen, Täter, Konflikteskalation.* Opladen: Leske und Budrich.

Willetts, Peter. 1999. "The Rules of the Game: The United Nations and Civil Society." Pp. 274–83 in *Whose World Is It Anyway? Civil Society, the United Nations, and the Multilateral Future,* edited by J. W. Foster and A. Anand. Ottawa: United Nations Association of Canada.

Williams, Gareth. 1997. "The genesis of chronic illness: Narrative reconstruction." In *Memory. Identity, Community: The Idea of Narrative in the Human Sciences,* edited by Lewis P. Hinchman and Sandra K. Hinchman. 185–212. Albany: State University of New York.

Williams, Hosea. 1978. *Interview.* Atlanta, Georgia. September 22.

Williams, Raymood. 1973. "Base and Superstructure in Marxist Cultural Theory." *New Left Review* 82: 3–16.

Williams, Rhys H. 1995. "Constructing the Public Good: Social Movements and Cultural Resources." *Social Problems* 42 (1): 124–44.

Williams, Rhys H. 2004. "The Cultural Contexts of Collective Action: Constraints, Opportunities, and the Symbolic Life of Social Movements." Pp. 91–115 in *The Blackwell Companion to Social Movements,* edited by David A. Snow, Sarah A. Soule, and Hanspeter Kriesi. Malden, Mass.: Blackwell.

Williams, Robert. 1986. *Export Agriculture and the Crisis in Central America.* Chapel Hill: University of North Carolina Press.

Williams, Robin M. 1970. *American Society: A Sociological Interpretation.* 3rd ed. New York: Alfred A. Knopf.

Willner, Ann Ruth. 1984. *The Spellbinders: Charismatic Political Leadership.* New Haven, CT: Yale University Press.

Wilson, F.L. 1987. *Interest-Group Politics in France.* Cambridge University Press.

Wilson, James Q. 1961. "The strategy of protest: problems of Negro civil action." *Journal of Conflict Resolution* 5: 291–303.

Wilson, James Q. 1968. *Varieties of Police Behavior.* Cambridge, MA: Harvard University Press.

Wilson, James Q. 1995. *Political Organizations.* 2nd ed. Princeton, NJ: Princeton University Press.

Wilson, Jim. 2002. "From 'Solidarity' to Convergence: International Trade Union Cooperation in the Media Sector." In *Transnational Cooperation among Labor Unions,* edited by Michael E. Gordon and Lowell Turner. Ithaca, N.Y.: Cornell University Press.

Wilson, John. 1973. *Introduction to Social Movements.* New York: Basic Books.

Wilson. Kenneth L. and Anthony M. Orum. 1976. "Mobilizing people for collective political action." *Journal of Political and Military Sociology* 4: 187–202.

Wiltfang, Greg and Doug McAdam. 1991. "Distinguishing Cost and Risk in Sanctuary Activism." *Social Forces* 69: 987–1010.

Wimmer, Andreas. 1997. "A Critical Review of Current Research Approaches." *Ethnic and Racial Studies* 20: 17–41.

Winerup, Michael. 1996. "An American place: The paramilitary movement. Ohio case typifies the tensions between militia groups and the law." *The New York Times,* June 23, Al.

Wirth, David. 1998. "Partnership Advocacy in World Bank Environmental Reform." Pp. 51–79 in *The Struggle for Accountability: The World Bank, NGOs, and Grassroots Movements,* edited by J. A. Fox and L. D. Brown. Cambridge: MIT Press.

Wirtz, Willard. 1965a. Papers of Secretary of Labor Willard Wirtz. RG 174, box 237, folder "1965 Commission-EEO (August)." Wirtz to FDR, Jr. August 9. National Archives, College Park, Md.

———. 1965b. Papers of Secretary of Labor Willard Wirtz. RG 174, box 349, folder "1966, Committee—ICSW, June–July." CACSW memorandum "Equal Employment Opportunities for Women under Title VII of the Civil Rights Act of 1964," October 1. Attached to letter from Wirtz to Jacob Potofsky, general president of Amalgamated Clothing Workers of America, July 2, 1966. National Archives, College Park, Md.

Wirtz, Willard. 1966a. Papers of Secretary of Labor Willard Wirtz. RG 174, box 349, folder "1966, Committee—ICSW, November–December." Letter from NOW to President Johnson, November 11. Attached to letter from Wirtz to Friedan, November 25. National Archives, College Park, Md.

———. 1966b. Papers of Secretary of Labor Willard Wirtz. RG 174, box 349, folder "1966, Committee—ICSW, November–December." Letter from NOW to EEOC, November 11. Attached to letter from Wirtz to Friedan, November 25. National Archives, College Park, Md.

Wisler, Dominique and Marco Giugni. 1999. "Under the Spotlight: The Impact of Media Attention on Protest Policing." *Mobilization* 4: 171–87.

Wittman, Carl. 1972. "A Gay Manifesto." Pp. 330–41 in *Out of the Closets,* edited by Karla Jay and Allen Young. New York: New York University Press.

Wittner, Lawrence. 1997. *Resisting the Bomb: A History of the World Nuclear Disarmament Movement,* vol. II of *The Struggle against the Bomb.* Stanford: Stanford University Press.

———. 2003. *Toward Nuclear Abolition: A History of the World Nuclear Disarmament Movement 1971-the Present,* vol. III of *The Struggle Against the Bomb.* Stanford: Stanford University Press.

Wolf, Eric R. 1969. *Peasant Wars in the Twentieth Century.* New York: Harper.

Wolff, Miles. 1970. Lunch at the Five and Ten. New York: Stien and Day.

Woliver, Laura R. 1998. "Social Movements and Abortion Law." Pp. 233–47 in *Social Movements and American Political Institutions* edited by Anne N. Costain and Andrew S. McFarland. New York: Rowman & Littlefield Publishers.

Women's Bureau. 1964. "Problems Raised by Title VII of the Federal Civil Rights Act." RG 86, box 29, folder "Legislation." Attached to letter from Dorothy Pendergast to Alice Morrison, November 13.

Wood, Elisabeth Jean. 2000. *Forging Democracy from Below: Insurgent Transitions in South Africa and El Salvador.* Cambridge: Cambridge University Press.

———. 2003. *Insurgent Collective Action and Civil War in El Salvador.* Cambridge: Cambridge University Press.

Woods, Dwayne. 1991. "Il Fenomeno delle Leghe" (The League Phenomenon). Pp. 171–95 in *Politica in Italia: 1991,* editedIby S. Hellman and G. Pasquino. Bologna, Italy: il Mulino. (English translation in *Italian Politics Yearbook: 1991.* London, England: Pinter.)

Wooldridge, Jeffrey. 2002. *Econometric Analysis of Cross Section and Panel Data.* Cambridge, MA: MIT Press.

Worsley, Peter. 1974. *The Trumpet Shall Sound: A Study of Cargo Cults in Melanesia.* Rev. 2d ed. New York: Schocken Books.

Wright, Erik Olin. 1978. *Class, Crisis and the State.* London: New Left Books.

———. 1985. *Classes.* London: Verso.

Wright, Gerald C., Robert S. Erickson, and John P. Mclver. 1985. "Measuring state partisanship and ideology with survey data." *The Journal of Politics* 47(2): 469–89.

Wright, James D. 1989. *Address Unknown: The Homeless in America.* New York: Aldine de Gruyter.

Wright, Lawrence. 2006. "The Master Plan: For the New Theorists of Jihad, Al Qaeda is Just the Beginning." *The New Yorker,* September 11: 48.

———. 1983b. *A Sociological Study of Defection from Controversial: New Religious Movements.* Ph.D. dissertation, Ann Arbor, MI: University Microfilms International.

Wright, S. 1988. "Leaving new religious movements: Issues, theory, and research." Pp. 143–65 in *Falling from the Faith, Causes and Consequences of Religious Apostasy,* edited by D. Bromley. Newbury Park, CA: Sage.

———. 1993a. "Defection from New Religious Movements: A Test of Some Theoretical Propositions." Pp. 106–21 in *The Brainwashing/Deprogramming Controversy: Sociological, Psychological, Legal and Historical Perspectives,* edited by D. Bromley and J. Richardson (Eds.). New York: Edwin Mellen.

Wright, Talmadge. 1995. "Tranquility City: Self-Organization, Protest, and Collective Gains within a Chicago Homeless Encampment." Pp. 37–68 in *Marginal Spaces,* edited by M. P. Smith. New Brunswick, NJ: Transaction Publishers.

Wu, Ren. 1990. "Wuyue fengbo de qiyin yu fazhan. Dierbufen: 'Fengbo' de quanguocheng (yanjiu ziliao)" (The causes and development of the May disturbance. Part 2, The whole process of "the disturbance" [research materials]). *Qingnian yanjiu* (Youth research), no. 11/12, pp. 29–93.

Wuerth, Andrea. 1999. "National Politics/Local Identities: Abortion Rights Activism in Post-Wall Berlin." *Feminist Studies* 25 (3): 601–31.

Xaviere, Jean-Marie. 1980. *Sayings of the Ayatollah Khomeini.* English edition translation, J. J. Salemson and Tony Hendra. New York: Bantam.

Yashar, Deborah. 2005. *Contesting Citizenship in Latin America: The Rise of Indigenous Movements and the Postliberal Challenge.* Cambridge: Cambridge University Press.

Yngvesson, Barbara. 1988. "Making Law at the Doorway: The Clerk, The Court, and the Construction of Community in a New England Town." *Law and Society Review* 22: 409–48.

Young, Allen. 1992 [1972]. "Out of the Closets, Into the Streets." Pp. 6–30 in *Out of the Clasets: Voices of Gay Liberation,* edited by Karla Jay and Allen Young. New York: New York University Press.

Young, Andrew. 1977. Interview with Andrew Young. Pp. 472–80 in *My Soul is Rested,* edited by Howell Raines. New York: Bantam.

Young, Brigitte. 1991. "The Dairy Industry: From Yeomanry to the Institutionalization of Multilateral Governance." Pp. 236–58 in *Governance of the American Economy,* edited by John L. Campbell, J. Rogers Hollingsworth, and Leon N. Lindberg. New York: Cambridge University Press.

Young, Brigitte. 1999. *Triumph of the Fatherland: German Unification and the Marginalization of Women.* Ann Arbor: University of Michigan Press.

Young, Elizabeth. 1996. "Confederate Counterfeit: The Case of the Cross-Dressed Civil War Soldier." Pp. 181–217 in *Passing and the Fictions of Identity,* edited by E. K. Ginsberg. Durham, NC: Duke University Press.

Zald, Mayer N. 1978b. "Introduction, the infrastructure of movements." Pp. 45–7 in *Social Movements in an Organizational Society,* edited by M. Zald and J. McCarthy. New Brunswick, NJ: Transaction Books.

———. 1987c. "Social movement industries: Conflict and cooperation among SMOs." Pp. 161–180 in *Social Movements in an Organizational Society,* edited by Mayer N. Zald and John D. McCarthy. New Brunswick, NJ: Transaction.

———. 1992. "Looking Backward and Forward: Reflections on the Past and Future of the Resource Mobi-

lization Program." Pp. 326–48 in *Frontiers in Social Movement Theory,* edited by A. D. Morris and C. M. Mueller. New Haven, CT: Yale University Press.

———. 1996. "Culture, Ideology, and Strategic Framing." Pp. 261–74 in *Comparative Perspectives on Social Movements,* edited by Doug McAdam, John D. McCarthy, and Mayer N. Zald. Cambridge: Cambridge University Press.

———. 2000. "Ideologically Structured Action: An Enlarged Agenda for Social Movement Research." *Mobilization* 5: 1–16.

———. and Roberta Ash. 1966. "Social Movement Organizations: Growth, Decay and Change." *Social Forces* 44: 327–41.

Zald, Mayer, N., and Michael A. Berger. 1987a. "Religious groups as crucibles of Social Movements." Pp. 67–95 in *Social Movements in an Organizational Society,* edited by M. Zald and McCarthy. New Brunswick, NJ: Transaction Books.

Zald, Mayer and John McCarthy. 1987a. *Social Movements in an Organizational Society.* New Brunswick, NJ: Transaction.

Zald, Mayer N., and John D. McCarthy. 1987b. "Social Movement Industries: Competition and Conflict among SMOs." Pp. 161–180 in *Social Movements in an Organizational Society.* Edited by Mayer Zald and John McCarthy. New Brunswick, NJ: Transaction.

Zald, Mayer N. and Bert Useem. 1982. "Movement and countermovement; loosely coupled interaction." Paper presented at Annual Meetings of the American Sociological Association, San Francisco, CA, September 8, 1982.

Zald, Mayer N. and Bert Useem. 1987. "Movement and countermovement interaction: Mobilization, tactics, and state involvement." Pp. 247–272 in *Social Movements in an Organizational Society,* edited by Mayer N. Zald and John D. McCarthy. New Brunswick, NJ: Transaction Books.

Zamora, Rubén. 1998. *El Salvador, heridas que no cierran: Los partidos políticos en la post-guerra.* San Salvador. FLACSO.

Zamosc, Leon. 1989. "Class Conflict in an Export Economy: The Social Roots of the Salvadoran Insurrection of 1932." Pp. 56–75 in *Sociology of "Developing Societies": Central America,* edited by J. Flores and E. Torres-Rivas. New York: Monthly Review Press.

Zelman, Patricia. 1980. *Women, Work and National Policy: The Kennedy-Johnson Years.* Ann Arbor, Mich.: UMI Research Press.

Zemike, Kate and Dean E. Murphy. 2003. "Protesters Across the Nation Try to 'Stop Business as Usual.'" *New York Times.* March 20.

Zernike, Kate. 2003. "Antiwar Movement Divided by Thoughts on Civil Disobedience." *Los Angeles Times.* March 19.

Zetka, James R., Jr. 1992. "Work Organization and Wildcat Strikes in the U.S. Automobile Industry, 1946–1963." *American Sociological Review* 57: 214–26.

———. 1995. "Union Homogenization and the Organizational Foundations of Plantwide Militancy in the U.S. Automobile Industry, 1959–1979." *Social Forces* 73: 789–910.

Zhang, Boli, and Meng Bai. 1993. *Huigu yu fansi* (Retrospection and introspection). Germany: Rhine Forum.

Zhang, Jian, and Yuliang Zhou. 1989. *China Education Yearbook: 1948–1984.* Changsha: Hunan Jiaoyu Chubanshe (Hunan Education Publishing House).

Zhao, Dingxin. 1997. "Decline of Political Control in Chinese Universities and the Rise of the 1989 Chinese Student Movement." *Sociological Perspectives* 40: 159–82.

Zhao, Dingxin. 1998. "Ecologies of Social Movements: Student Mobilization during the 1989 Prodemocracy Movement in Beijing." *American Journal of Sociology* 103 (6): 1493–1529.

Zhao, Dingxin. 1998. "Ecologies of Social Movements: Student Mobilization during the 1989 Prodemocracy Movement in Beijing." *American Journal of Sociology* 103: 1493–1529.

Zhao, Dingxin. 2001. *The Power of Tiananmen: State-Society Relations and the 1989 Beijing Student Movement.* Chicago: University of Chicago Press.

Zheng, Xiaowei. 2006. "Passion, Reflection, and Survival: Political Choices of Red Guards at Qinghua University, June 1966–July 1968." *The Chinese Cultural Revolution as History,* edited by J. Esherick, P. Pickowicz, and A. Walder, Stanford, CA: Stanford University Press.

Zhongguo gaodeng jaoyu daquan (Encyclopedia of Chinese universities). 1989. Beijing: Gaodeng Jaoyu Chubanshe (Higher Education Publishing House).

Zhou, Yuan, ed. 1999. *A New Collection of Red Guard Publications, Part 1: Newspapers.* Oakton, VA: Center for Chinese Research Materials.

Zincone, Giovanna. 1992. *Da Sudditi a Cittadini* (From Subjects to Citizens). Bologna, Italy: il Mulino.

Zingraff, Rhonda, and Michael D. Schulman. 1984. "Social Bases of Class Consciousness: A Study of Southern Textile Workers with a Comparison by Race." *Social Forces* 63: 98–116.

Zinn, Howard. 1962. *Albany, a study in national responsibility.* Atlanta: Southern Regional Council.

Zinn, Howard. 1964. SNCC: The New Abolitionists. Boston: Beacon.

———. 1965. *SNCC, The New Abolitionists.* Boston: Beacon Press.

Zinn, Kenneth, 2002. "Solidarity across Borders: The UMWA's Corporate Campaign against Peabody and Hanson PLC." In *Transnational Cooperation among Labor Unions,* edited by Michael E. Gordon and Lowell Turner. Ithaca, N.Y.: Cornell University Press.

Zuckerman, Yitzhak. 1993. *A Surplus of Memory: Chronicle of the Warsaw Ghetto Uprising.* Berkeley: University of California Press.

Zuo, Jiping and Robert D. Benford. 1994. "Mobilization Processes and the 1989 Chinese Democracy Movement." *Sociological Quarterly* 36: 801–28.

Zurcher, Louis A., Jr., and R. George Kirkpatrick. 1976. *Citizens for Decency: Antipornography Crusades as Status Defense.* Austin: University of Texas Press.

Zurcher, Louis A., Jr., and David A. Snow. 1981. "Collective Behavior: Social Movements." Pp. 447–82 in *Social Psychology: Sociological Perspectives,* edited by Morris Rosenberg and Ralph H. Turner. New York: Basic Books.

Zylan, Yvonne, and Sarah A. Soule. 2000. "Ending welfare as we know it (again): Welfare state retrenchment, 1989–1995." *Social Forces* 79(2): 623–52.

Zysman, J. 1983. *Governments, Markets, and Growth.* Ithaca, NY: Cornell University Press.

Zysman, John. 1994. "How Institutions Create Historically Rooted Trajectories of Growth." *Industrial and Corporate Change* 3: 243–83.

ARCHIVAL SOURCES

Library of Congress. NAACP Papers, Box 75. 1963. File: Mississippi State Conference, 1956–1972. Report on Memberships and Freedom Fund Contributions from Mississippi Branches.

Mississippi Department of Archives and History. Mississippi Freedom Democratic Party Records, Reel 2. n.d. List of Candidates.

———. Mississippi Freedom Democratic Party Records, Reel 3. n.d. Item 6, "Black Politics in the South," David Emmons.

———. Record Group 381, Box 108. July 5, 1965. File: CDGM 1965. Head Start—Mississippi. Letter from Scott to Haddad.

———. Record Group 381, Box 108: July 30, 1966. File: Mississippi. Inspection Report, CDGM Area B.

———. Record Group 381, Box 110. July 17, 1966. File: Mid-State Opportunity, Inc. Inspector's Field Report, Jenneman.

———. Record Group 381, Box 14. n.d. File: Multiple files by organization name, Region IV, Mississippi, Grant Profiles 1965–1972, Policy Research Division, Office of Operations, OEO.

———. Record Group 381, Box 2. December 30, 1966. File: Southeast Region, 1966; Regional Organizational Subject Files, 1966–1969; CAP Office, Records of the Director. Memo from Sloan to Shriver and Harding.

———. Record Group 381, Box 2. November 8, 1966. File: Regional Organizational Subject Files, 1966–1969, CAP Office, Records of the Director. Letter from Sloan to Shriver.

———. Record Group 381, Box 2. October 14, 1966. File: Southeast Region, 1966, Regional Organizational Subject Files, 1966–1969; CAP Office, Records of the Director. Letter from Sloan to Bozman.

———. Record Group 381, Box 40. 1965. File: Mississippi OEO Program (Compilation), July–September 1965. Memo from Redwine to Director, CAP.

———. Record Group 381, Box 40. March 17, 1966. File: Mississippi—OEO Program (Compilation), January–March 1966. Memo from Seward to May.

———. Record Group 381, Box 40. March 3, 1966. File: Mississippi—OEO Program (Compilation), January–March 1966. Preliminary Report—Bolivar County, Mississippi.

———. Record Group 381, Box 40. March 31, 1966. File: Mississippi—OEO Program (Compilation), January–March 1966. Memo from Berry to May.

———. Record Group 381, Box 5. December 11, 1965. File: Administrative, Mississippi; State Files, 1965–1968, CAP Office, Records of the Director. Memo from Westgate to Gonzales.

———. Record Group 381, Box 5. January 13, 1967. File: Administrative, Mississippi; State File. 1965–1968; CAP Office, Records of the Director. Memo from Dean to Berry.

National Archives (NA). Record Group 381. Box 2. February 24, 1966. File: Southeast Region, 1966; Regional Organizational Subject Files, 1966–1969; CAP Office. Records of the Director. Memo from Dean to Shriver.

———. Amzie Moore Papers, Box 2. March 22, 1966. File: 8. A Report of the Meeting Held with CAP.

State Historical Society of Wisconsin (SHSW). Alvin Oderman Papers. August 27, 1966. News Sheet on the Lorenzi's—Holmes, County, MS, Sue Lorenzi.

———. Amzie Moore Papers, Box 2. N.d.a. File: 6. Resident Participation, Bolivar County CAP, Inc.

———. Amzie Moore Papers, Box 2. N.d.b. File: 8. An Outline of Important Events.

———. Amzie Moore Papers, Box 2. N.d.c. File: 10. Petition from ACBC to Sargent Shriver.

———. Amzie Moore Papers, Box 2. 1966. File: 8. Telegram from Associated Communities of Bolivar County to Shriver and Sloan.

———. Amzie Moore Papers, Box 2. Jaunary 19, 1966. Minutes of the Proceedings, St. Peter's Rock M. B. Church.

———. Amzie Moore Papers, Box 2. March 13, 1966. File: 8. Letter from Velma Bartley.

———. Amzie Moore Papers, Box 3. N.d. File: 1. Chronological History.

———. Amzie Moore Papers. Box 3. April 14, 1966. File: 1. Letter from Berry to Long, Smith, and Moore.

———. Ed King Papers, Box 11. 1966. File: 607. Holmes County Community Newsletter.

Tougaloo College. Ed King Papers, Box 11. August 23, 1965. File: 579. FDP Projects by County and Contacts.

———. Rims Barber Papers, Box 1. August 4, 1967. File: Black Candidates, F.I.S. Newsletter.

———. Tom Dent Collection, July 2. 1979. Interview of Ed Brown by Tom Dent.